Henry O. Bourke,
Barrister.

A CASEBOOK ON EQUITY AND TRUSTS IN IRELAND

March '87

Also by the author:
IRISH LAND LAW (1975); SUPP. 1975-80 (1981)
IRISH CONVEYANCING LAW (1978)
A CASEBOOK ON IRISH LAND LAW (1984)

A CASEBOOK ON EQUITY AND TRUSTS IN IRELAND

by
J.C.W. WYLIE
LL.M. (Harvard), LL.D. (Belfast)
Professor of Law,
University College, Cardiff

PROFESSIONAL BOOKS LIMITED
1985

Published in 1985 by
Professional Books Limited,
Milton Trading Estate, Abingdon, Oxon.
Typeset by Adset Limited, Glasgow
and printed in Great Britain by
Redwood Burn Limited Trowbridge, Wiltshire

ISBN: Hardback: 0 86205 112 6
Paperback: 0 86205 114 2

PREFACE

This is the second of two casebooks designed to be companion volumes to my textbook, *Irish Land Law* (1975; Supp. 1975-80, 1981). The first casebook, *A Casebook on Irish Land Law,* published last year, contained material relating to what by tradition in the universities and other educational institutions comprises land law. This casebook deals largely with equity and trusts and thus covers the remaining ground encompassed by the textbook.

The objects of the casebook were spelt out in the Preface to the land law one and need not be repeated here. Like the earlier casebook, the present one concentrates on the law in the Republic of Ireland, though much of this, particularly the principles of equity, is equally applicable to the North.

J.C.W. WYLIE
Cardiff, 15th April, 1985

ACKNOWLEDGMENTS

The publishers and the author gratefully acknowledge permission from the following to reproduce materials from the sources indicated:

The Controller of the Stationary Office, Dublin: excerpts from Irish statutes.

Department of Justice: unreported judgments.

The Incorporated Council of Law Reporting for Ireland: *Irish Reports*.

The Round Hall Press: *Irish Law Times Reports, Irish Law Reports Monthly*.

The Incorporated Council of Law Reporting for Northern Ireland: *Northern Ireland Law Reports*.

CONTENTS

PART IV: TRUSTS

PART V: ADMINISTRATION OF TRUSTS

PART VI: POWERS OF APPOINTMENT

TABLE OF STATUTES

[*N.B.* Page reference in **bold** type indicate statutory provisions reproduced in full in the text.]

1. STATUTES OF THE PARLIAMENT OF IRELAND

2. STATUTES OF THE PARLIAMENTS OF ENGLAND, GREAT BRITAIN AND THE UNITED KINGDOM

3. STATUTES OF SAORSṪAṪ ÉIREANN AND OF THE OIREACHTAS

TABLE OF CASES

[*N.B.* Page references in **bold** type indicate cases whose judgments are reproduced in full in the text.]

Chapter 1

FUNDAMENTAL PRINCIPLES

This chapter contains material which highlights some of the fundamental principles of equity, such as the distinction between equitable jurisdiction and the common law, see *Irish Land Law,* ch. 3. Many of these principles have been enshrined in the so-called "maxims", but extreme caution must be exercised with these maxims, for they often mislead the unwary, *ibid.,* para. 3.043 *et seq.*

Space clearly cannot be afforded to illustrate every principle of equity, and, of course, arguably it would be foolish to attempt to do so given the nature of equitable jurisdiction, but it must be appreciated that in a sense the material in the ensuing chapters provides a comprehensive picture of the wide-ranging nature of equitable principles and their application by the courts.

I. EQUITY AND COMMON LAW

JUDICATURE (IRELAND) ACT, 1877

28. – . . .

(11) In all matters not hereinbefore mentioned, in which there is any conflict or variance between the rules of equity and the rules of common law, with reference to that matter, the rules of equity shall prevail.

BARBOUR V. HOUSTON

(1884) 14 L.R. Ir. 273 (Exchequer Division); (1885) 18 L.R. Ir. 475 (Court of Appeal)

In an action to recover damages for fraudulent representation of the quality of certain lands, whereby the Plaintiff was induced to take leases thereof, the Defendants pleaded the Statute of Limitations. The Plaintiff replied that the cause of action relied on was the fraud and fraudulent misrepresentation of the Defendants, and the injuries occasioned to the Plaintiff thereby; and the Plaintiff said that he did not and could not, by the exercise of reasonable diligence, have discovered the said fraud, or that the said representation was untrue and fraudulent, until within six years before the commencement of this action.

The Defendents argued on demurrer, that the reply was no answer to the plea relying on the statute.

Palles, C.B.:

Were we to decide this demurrer exclusively upon grounds which before the Judicature Act were cognizable in Courts of Common Law, we should be coerced by authority to hold the reply bad. *The Imperial Gas Light and Coke Company* v. *The London Gas Light Company* 10 Exch. 39, although it appears to have been doubted by the majority of the Court of Appeal in England in *Gibbs* v. *Guild* 9 Q. B. D. 59, has not been expressly overruled, and is still binding upon us.

However, since the Judicature Act, our consideration of the case cannot be confined within these narrow limits. The same system of jurisprudence now prevails in all Divisions of the High Court; and if, upon the facts pleaded, the Plaintiff could, before the Judicature Act, have had in Equity the relief which he seeks in this action, he is now entitled to it in this Court. That Act changed forms of procedure, but did not alter rights or remedies.

What relief then would the Plaintiff have been entitled to before the Judicature Act, upon the facts stated in the pleadings here? I think it clear that in a case like the present where, by the fraudulent representation of the lessor and another, a lessee has been induced to take a lease, under circumstances in which, as here, an estate vested in him, such lessee had either of two alternative rights— (1) to have the lease set aside, and to recover back what he had paid thereunder, accounting for the sums received out of the lands; or, (2) to retain the lease and recover damages for the loss sustained by the false representation. It was, and is, for him to elect upon which of these rights he will rely; and the Courts of Law and Equity, before the Act, provided, and the High Court now provides, appropriate relief applicable to the particular right sought to be enforced; relief, however, necessarily different in the one case from that which would be afforded in the other. Before the Act, relief of the first class, viz., to set aside the lease, could have been obtained in a Court of Equity only; whilst on the other hand, if the lessee elected to retain the lease and relied upon his right to recover damages on that basis, he might have sued at Law and in many cases in Equity also. The Judicature Act has abolished the distinction as to the Court in which the particular relief may be obtained; but the essential difference between the two rights, and the relief applicable to each, still exists.

The allegation in the present case is that the Plaintiff was induced by fraud to execute a lease reserving rent, and to enter into possession of the lands demised. The fraud did not render the lease void. It may have made it impeachable in a Court of Equity at the election of the Plaintiff; but this election the Plaintiff has not exercised, and even had he done so (as the Defendant Rooper does not appear to have had any estate in the lands, or to have received anything by reason of the fraud), the only relief which could have been obtained *against him,* if such election had been made, and if a suit had been instituted to set aside the lease, would have been the payment of costs.

Not then having elected to set aside the lease, the Plaintiff's only other right was to seek damages for the fraud. This is the right sought to be asserted in this action, and the question is whether the assertion of *this* right is barred by the Statute of Limitations. The action is one which (to use the words of the 20th section of our Common Law Procedure Act, 1853), was "for a cause which would theretofore have been brought in the form of action called trespass on the case." *Prima facie,* therefore, the period of limitation would be six years, and would run from the time of the "cause of such action." To this the Plaintiff presents two answers:— 1st. That in a suit for a cause such as the present in a Court of Equity, before the Judicature Act, the period of limitation would have been calculated from the discovery, and not from the commission, of the fraud; and, 2ndly. That the allegations in the reply involve a statement of fraudulent concealment of the original fraud till within six years.

In my opinion, the argument that in a suit *for a cause such as the present* in a Court of Equity, before the Judicature Act, the period of six years would be calculated from the discovery and not from the committal of the fraud cannot be sustained.

The Statute of Limitations prescribed a period of limitation for some, but only for some, forms of action, and such forms of action were exclusively forms of proceedings in Courts of Common Law. Those statutes were, however, always held, and in my opinion rightly held, to be applicable to the *causes* of action for which those *forms* of action were the appropriate remedies, although for some collateral reasons such causes of action were sought to be made available in Courts of Equity. In the leading case of *Hovenden* v. *Lord Annesley* 2 Sch. & Lef. 630-1 Lord Redesdale says: "But it is said that Courts of Equity are not within the Statutes of Limitations. This is true in one respect: they are not within the words of the statutes, because the words apply to particular legal remedies; but they are within the spirit and meaning of the statutes, and have been always so considered. I think it is a mistake in point of language to say that Courts of Equity act merely *by analogy* to the statute; they act in *obedience* to it . . . I think, therefore, Courts of Equity are bound to yield obedience to the Statute of Limitations upon all legal titles and legal demands, and cannot act contrary to the spirit of its provisions. I think the statute must be taken virtually to include Courts of Equity, for when the legislature by statute limited the proceedings at Law in certain cases and provided no express limitation for proceedings in Equity, it must be taken to have contemplated that Equity followed the law, and, therefore, it must be taken to have virtually enacted, *in the same cases,* a limitation for Courts of Equity also."

The remedies or forms of action mentioned in these statutes did not include a proceeding to set aside or cancel for fraud an instrument under which an estate had passed. I use these limited words advisedly, instead of the more general ones, "to avoid a contract for fraud," in order to exclude the simple cases not material here, but to which I shall have to refer in distinguishing some of the cases cited, in which the parties could be reinstated in their former position, and in which, therefore, an action for money had and received, or an action of trover (both of which were within the terms of the Statute of Limitations), would lie to recover back money or goods which had been obtained under a contract avoided for fraud. It follows, therefore, that whenever the cause of action was to avoid a contract under which an estate passed, the Statute of Limitations was inapplicable; but it was so inapplicable, not because the *cause* of action was before the statute cognisable in a Court of Equity, but because it was one which was not within the Statute of Limitations. So also, since the Judicature Act, if such a suit be depending in a Common Law Division, as, notwithstanding section 36 of the Judicature Act, it may be (when, for instance, it is the subject of a counterclaim), the Statute of Limitations will not afford a defence. On the other hand, in actions or suits before the Judicature Act, in which damages were sought to be recovered for the fraud upon the basis of non-avoidance, the statute applied, whether the proceeding in which the question arose was one at Law or in Equity; and such statute equally applies, since the Judicature Act, in a suit for the same purpose, irrespective of the Division in which such suit may appear to have been commenced or be pending.

None of the cases cited are at variance with this view. In none of them, whether the forum was a Common Law or an Equitable one, was it attempted to apply a period of limitation commensurate with that fixed by the Statute of Limitations, but commencing not from the accrual of the cause of action, but from the discovery of the fraud, to an action based upon the non-avoidance of the transaction alleged to be impeachable for fraud.

Upon the contrary, in *Peek* v. *Gurney* L.R. 6 H. L. 377, which was a proceeding of this nature in a Court of Equity, upon the correlative question whether a lapse of time less than that prescribed by the Statute of Limitations could be relied on as disentitling the plaintiff to relief, the House of Lords is very specific in defining the time which in such a case (a case which *ad hoc* is identical with the present) precludes a plaintiff from suing, as being that and that only which is mentioned in the statute. There Lord Chelmsford says L.R. 6 H. L. 384:— "The suit in the present case is not for the rescission of the contract, but is founded upon the loss the appellant has sustained and may sustain in consequence of his being bound by the contract he has entered into. It is a proceeding similar to an action at Law for deceit; and the only amount of delay which could be a bar to relief is fixed by the Statute of Limitations, by analogy to which Equity generally proceeds in questions of *laches*." So also, Lord Cairns says *Ib.* 402:— "The suit is in the nature of an action for damages for misrepresentation; it is in the nature of an action or proceeding *ex delicto*; and it appears to me that to such an action or proceeding there is no bar arising from delay, unless the delay be such as would bring the Statute of Limitations applicable to the case into operation."

In all the cases cited for the Plaintiff, in which the period was computed from the discovery of the fraud, save one, *Ecclesiastical Commissioners* v. *The North Eastern Railway Company* 4 Ch. Div. 845, it will be found that the cause of suit was of such a nature that the Statute of Limitations did not apply, and that the Court acted not in obedience to, but by analogy to, such statute.

In cases within the Statute of Limitations, Courts of Equity were bound by its terms as conclusively as Courts of Law, and they were powerless to alter its provisions; but in framing a rule of their own (from, or by analogy to, that statute) which was to be applicable to cases within neither its letter nor spirit, Courts of Equity were not bound to follow in all respects the statute, but were entitled to apply it, subject to such modification as they thought consonant with justice. They accordingly laid down the rule that in suits to rescind or set aside transactions for fraud (to which no statutable period of limitation was applicable), they would deem the title to avoid the transaction as not having completely arisen until the discovery of the fraud, and that the period, the lapse of which would amount to a bar to relief, should therefore be calculated not from the commission, but from the discovery, of the fraud, provided it could not with due diligence have been previously known.

In no case, however, that I am aware of (save *The Ecclesiastical Commissioners for England* v. *The North Eastern Railway Company* 4 Ch. Div. 845) can it be contended that the rule applied to a cause of action which was within the Statute of Limitations. In that case, which is a decision of the Court upon the hearing of the cause, and not upon demurrer, the pleadings are not given in the report, and they may have contained an allegation of concealment which (if proved) might, upon a ground I shall afterwards mention, have supported the decision. If the decision be not susceptible of this explanation, I can only say that I do not agree in it, and must decline to follow it.

The Plaintiff, however, denies that the equitable rule is restricted to cases outside the Statute of Limitations, where the court acts by analogy and not in obedience to it; and in support of their denial they rely on *Booth* v. *Lord Warrington* 4 Br. P.C. 163, and the numerous cases in Equity to recover money procured by fraud which have followed that decision. As our judgment mainly depends upon this question, I must explain at some little length my view of that decision.

There was in Equity a general jurisdiction to set aside contracts procured through fraud. Some of these contracts, however, were of such a nature that if the defrauded party returned the property (or, in the case of money, an equivalent amount) which he had received under the fraudulent contract, such contract might at Law be avoided by him for the fraud. It was, however, clearly settled that the jurisdiction of Courts of Equity to set aside transactions as fraudulent was not confined to cases in which the transaction could not be avoided at Law, Story's Eq. Jur. 184. There were, therefore, cases in which there was concurrent jurisdiction in Courts of Law and Equity to recover back money paid under a contract avoided for fraud; and, in my opinion, there was a difference in the application of the Statute of Limitations, according to the Court in which the proceeding was instituted. When it was taken in a Common Law Court, it was held that, as the avoidance of the contract related back, and such contract when avoided was so avoided *ab initio*, the money paid under it continued, notwithstanding its payment under the fraudulent contract, the property of the defrauded party. The right to recover it, therefore, arose upon the moment of its payment under the contract; and as the only form of action known to the common law in which it could be recovered back was an action for money had and received, which was within the Statute of Limitations, the period of six years ran from the time of the payment, and not from the discovery of the fraud. In truth, this form of action rested on what, if the case were dealt with according to the intention of the parties, would have been a fiction, viz. that the money was all through the money of the payer, although both parties (from the time of the payment to the discovery of the fraud) treated it as that of the payee.

In *Booth* v. *Lord Warrington* 4 Br. P.C. 163 the question was raised whether the same result ensued when, under such circumstances, the defrauded party sued in Equity instead of at Law. In such a proceeding he did not rely upon the fiction of the money procured by the fraud always having continued to be his. He asked the same doctrine to be applied in reference to a suit to recover back money procured by fraud as would have applied had that which had been so procured been an estate in land, or any other property; and it was there held that, although the plaintiff there at one time had a remedy at Law, and that remedy had been barred by the Statute of Limitations, he also had a remedy in Equity which was not within the statute. That remedy, however, was, in my opinion, based upon the avoidance or rescission of the transaction for fraud; or, in other words, one which was not within the Statute of Limitations, and in which the Court acted not in obedience, but by analogy, to that statute.

For these reasons, it appears to me to be clear that the Statute of Limitations applies; and that if a suit for a cause of action such as the present had before the Judicature Act been determined by a Court of Equity, the period of limitation would have been held to run from the accrual of the cause of action, and not from the discovery of the fraud.

This brings me to the second question. A state of facts may exist which would show that it is against conscience to rely upon any particular defence; and this doctrine applies as well to a defence founded upon the Statute of Limitations as to any other. If, then, such a state of facts be shown by the reply, it is a good answer to the defence – as this Court, applying the principles of equity, cannot allow effect to be given to that which is against good conscience to rely on. This is the effect of the decision of Lord Redesdale in *Bond* v. *Hopkins* 1 Sch. & Lef. 431; and Brett, L.J., in *Gibbs* v. *Guild* 9 Q.B. Div. 68, lays down the same principle as having been the ground of the decisions of Courts of Equity. "But assuming," he says, "that the Statute of Limitations would be binding, the Courts of Equity, on doctrines of their own, sometimes applied, if other circumstances arose, a particular kind of equity. They did not construe the statute so as to give equity; they adopted an equity which was quite independent of the statute, but which, no doubt, had an effect on the transaction notwithstanding the statute – that is to say, they said if the existence of the cause of action given by the defendant was fraudulently concealed by the defendant from the plaintiff until a period beyond six years, then they would not allow the defendant to prevent the plaintiff from supporting his right to his remedy on the ground that the statute was a bar. It seems to me that there is some little confusion in the expressions used in some cases as to the origin of the cause of action being a fraud. That is not the fraud which raised the equity; but if there was a cause of action, and if its existence was fraudulently concealed from the plaintiff by the defendant who had given that cause of action, it was then that the plaintiff's equity arose, notwithstanding that his cause of action had arisen more than six years before."

Now, does this reply show a state of facts which renders it against conscience in the Defendant to rely upon the Statute of Limitations? The equity to prevent him relying upon it is, as I have shown, rested by Brett, L.J., upon the fraudulent concealment by the defendant from the plaintiff of the existence of the cause of action. That concealment was, in *Gibbs* v. *Guild,* stated as a fact in the replication 9 Q.B. Div. 59. The distinction between that case and the present is, that here the allegation of concealment, which is the entire foundation of the equity, is absent. To hold therefore, the present reply good, we should hold as a matter of law that every fraudulent representation involves a continuous fraudulent and intentional concealment of that fraud until the injured party might or ought to have discovered it. To say that, however, would be as effectually to alter the Statute of Limitations as to substitute the words "after discovery of the fraud" for "after the cause of such action;" for, if fraudulent representation necessarily involves subsequent fraudulent concealment, by suing upon the concealment which was involved, instead of on the representation which involved it, the statute would run, not from the accrual of the cause of action upon the representation, but from the discovery of the fraud.

I do not decide, nor do I think, that active or aggressive concealment is in all cases essential to afford an equitable answer to the Statute of Limitations. In many cases there may be a duty to disclose the truth, and in such a case non-disclosure may have the same effect as active concealment would have in other cases. Again, I think it clear that a fraudulent misrepresentation may be made under such circumstances that an inference of fact may rightly be drawn of a subsequent active and intentional concealment of the fraud. But, in my opinion, whether the concealment sufficient to amount to this equitable answer must be active, or may in some instances be mere non-disclosure – whether such concealment may or may not in any particular case be inferred from the original fraud, the question whether there was or was not concealment is in every case one of fact; and in the present case, there being no allegation of such fact, the entire basis of the equity to be relieved against the Statute of Limitations is absent.

Upon the whole, my opinion is, that the reply is bad, and that the demurrer thereto ought to be allowed.

DOWSE, B., and **ANDREWS, J.,** concurred.

Notes and Questions

1. This decision was affirmed by the Court of Appeal (18 L.R. Ir. 475).
2. Do you agree with Palles C.B.'s views on the effect of the Judicature Act? *Cf.* the recent views of the Irish Supreme Court in *Hynes Ltd* v. *Independent Newspapers Ltd.,infra,* and the House of Lords in *United Scientific Holdings* v. *Burnley Borough Council* [1978] A.C. 904.

HYNES LTD. V. INDEPENDENT NEWSPAPERS LTD.
[1980] I.R. 204 (Supreme Court)

The facts are set out in the judgments.

O' Higgins C.J.:
This is an appeal by the plaintiffs against the judgment and order of Mr. Justice McWilliam in the High Court dismissing their claim for a declaration that a rent review notice served by the defendants was ineffective as being out of ime. The action was heard by Mr. Justice McWilliam, without oral evidence, but having regard to the provisions of a lease dated the 29th March, 1972, and made between Sisk Properties Ltd. of the one part and the plaintiffs of the other part under which the plaintiffs hold certain premises in Galway from the defendants (the successors of Sisk Properties Ltd.), and having regard to certain facts which were urged in the pleadings and were admitted. These facts can be set out shortly and succinctly but the issue which arises thereon cannot be disposed of so easily.

On the 29th March, 1972, Sisk Properties Ltd. demised to the plaintiffs certain premises in St. Augustine Street and Merchant's Road, Galway, for a term of 99 years commencing on the 1st January, 1972. The rent reserved was the yearly rent of £42,000 but provision was made for a rent review in the seventh year and at seven-year intervals thereafter. The lease went on to provide that, if the lessee wished to dispute the amount of the proposed new rent, he should within six weeks of the service upon him of the revised rent notice serve upon the lessor a notice of dispute and that, thereupon, the amount of the new rent would be determined by arbitration in the manner provided.

It was further provided as follows:— "But if no such Notice of Dispute is so served by the Lessee then the sums specified by the Lessor in such Revised Rent Notice shall become and be the yearly rent payable hereunder as from the seventh anniversary of the commencement of the term hereby created and for the residue then unexpired of the term hereby granted until varied by virtue of any further Revised Rent Notice that may be served by the Lessor pursuant to the provisions hereinbefore contained." The reddendum in the lease had earlier provided in the following terms:— "Yielding and Paying therefor during the said term unto the Lessor the yearly rent of £42,000 and such increased rent as may from time to time be payable hereunder as herinafter provided . . ."

On the 17th November, 1978, the defendants (as lessors) served on the plaintiffs a revised rent notice claiming an increased or new rent of £160,000 p.a. While this notice was served in the seventh year of the term created by the lease, it was so served some six weeks later than the date specified in paragraph D.3. of the lease, namely, the 1st October. By letter dated the 14th December, 1978, the plaintiffs' solicitors indicated on behalf of the plaintiffs that the notice was out of time and ineffective and also, as a precaution, they gave notice of dispute. The plaintiffs then commenced these proceedings in which they claim a declaration that the defendants' notice was ineffective to require a rent review. Having lost in the High Court, the plaintiffs have brought this appeal to this Court.

The plaintiffs' claim raises the question whether, in relation to the effectiveness of the rent review notice, observance by the defendants of the time limited for such service was or was not essential. In holding in the High Court that such observance was not essential, Mr. Justice McWilliam was guided by his view that, since there was no express stipulation making time of the essence, neither the nature of the subject matter of the contract nor the surrounding circumstances showed that time should be of the essence. In applying this test he followed the recent decision of the House of Lords in *United Scientific Holdings* v. *Burnley Borough Council* [1978] A.C. 904 and *Cheapside Land Development Co.* v. *Messels Service Co.* [1978] A.C. 904 (together referred to as the *Burnley Case).* The burden of the plaintiffs' appeal to this Court is that Mr. Justice McWilliam was wrong in so doing and that the decision of the House of Lords in the *Burnley Case* ought not to be followed in our courts.

As this matter is of considerable importance both to practitioners and to those involved in the property market, it is necessary to make a few general observations about rent review clauses. Having done so, I propose to examine the manner in which the observance of time in such clauses was regarded, certainly in the English courts, prior to the decision in the *Burnley Case*. Then I propose to consider the reasoning behind the *Burnley Case* and whether it is appropriate that that decision be followed in our courts.

Over the past two decades, in both the United Kingdom and Ireland, the prevalence of inflation in the property market has led to the introduction of some provision for rent review if the term being negotiated is for any significant number of years. Lessors, faced with constantly changing money and property values, have not been prepared to lease their property for a long period without providing for a periodic revision or adjustment of rent. Such rent review clauses vary in form and content. In some cases the rent review may be initiated only by the lessor, in others it may be initiated by either the lessor or the lessee. In some cases a rent review clause may be associated with a "break clause" which entitles a lessee to surrender the demised premises if he is unwilling or unable to pay the increased rent. In other cases the lease clearly contemplates periodic revisions of the rent and the lessee undertakes to pay the original rent and also any revised rent coming into operation during the term. Whatever form such clauses take, in general they specify a procedure for the determination of the revised rent and a time-table for the taking of the necessary steps in that procedure which, when followed, leads to the declaration of the new rent not later than the review date.

The question which has arisen in this case is whether the failure to observe the stipulated time-table has deprived the defendants of the review they seek; that question has not previously arisen in our courts. However, as indicated, it has arisen in a number of reported cases in England, the latest of these is the decision of the House of Lords in the *Burnley Case*. In order to consider whether that decision ought to be followed, I find it necessary not only to examine the reasoning which led to it but also the basis upon which the earlier decisions (many of which it expressly overruled) were decided. Therefore, it seems convenient to consider the earlier decisions first.

In *Samuel Properties Ltd.* v. *Hayek* [1972] 1 W.L.R. 1296 the Court of Appeal in England held that, where the words of the rent review clause import an option or privilege for the lessor to increase the rent which would otherwise be payable, any conditions as to time must be strictly observed and that, accordingly, the time specified for the exercise of the option must be treated as inflexible and mandatory. In that case particular attention was paid to the reddendum in the lease and in the course of his judgment Russell L.J. said at p. 1301 of the report:- "The language of the reddendum indicates that the basic rent is to remain unchanged throughout the term unless it be increased by compliance with those provisions. Clause 1 of the fourth schedule in terms confers an option on the lessor to require rent review in the manner thereafter provided. The process thereafter laid down in clause 2 uses the language of a condition precedent in requiring a notice in writing with an express time requirement." Having considered *Eaton* v. *Lyon* (1798) 3 Ves. 690, *Harries* v. *Bryant* (1827) 4 Russ. 89, *Reid* v. *Blagrave* (1831) 9 L.J.O.S. (Ch) 245 and *Barrow* v. *Isaacs & Son* [1891] 1 Q.B. 417, (and particular passages from the judgments therein) on the question of equitable relief where the time requirement for the exercise of the option was not observed, Russell L.J. said at p.1305 of the report:- "I am not prepared to extend those comments to a case such as the present. They are relevant to a case where a failure to comply with a covenanted obligation has exposed a person to the danger of forfeiture of a lease or other estate. I decline to extend them to a case such as the present, in which the party is given an option to improve his financial position if he chooses to take particular steps laid down."

Edmund Davies L.J. in his judgment in *Samuel Properties Ltd.* v. *Hayek* drew a similar distinction about equitable relief against forfeiture; at p.1307 of the report he said:- "The circumstances in which relief against forfeiture is granted are widely different from those under present consideration. In the former, a right of forfeiture is expressly reserved or implied by law in order to ensure the performance by the lessee of his obligations, and the court will grant relief if terms can be imposed which will ensure due protection for the lessor. But the power of a lessor on due notice to increase rent involves, in effect, the making of a new contract between the parties, subject in the present case to compliance by the lessor with a condition precedent. It resembles options and these are undoubtedly required to be exercised in strict conformity with the terms by which they were created: see *Hinds* v. *Randall* (1961) 177 E.G. 733 and *Peeling* v. *Guidice* (1963) 186 E.G. 113. If this is not done, relief will in general be granted only where, by unconscionable conduct by the proposed recipient of the notice to exercise the option, the other party has been led to believe that strict adherence to its terms will not be insisted upon."

A similar conclusion had been reached earlier by Goulding J. in *C. Richards & Son Ltd.* v. *Karenita Ltd* (1972) 221 E.G. 25. In both those cases the significant feature was that there was a fixed rent throughout the whole term with a provision granting an option or saying that the rent should be subject to increase or should be increased if the landlord took certain steps in accordance with the time-table laid down. However, where the terms of the lease were such as to express or imply on the part of the lessee an obligation to pay not only the original rent but also a revised rent, and the actual review provisions were merely machinery provisions for implementing the agreement, failure on the part of the lessor to act in time was not regarded as fatal to a review sought by him. This distinction was established in *Kenilworth Sites Ltd.* v. *Little & Co.* [1975] 1 W.L.R. 143 and *Accuba Ltd.* v. *Allied Shoe Repairs* [1975] 1 W.L.R. 1559. The result was that until the *Burnley Case* the courts in England, deciding in relation to such review clauses whether time was or was not of the essence, looked to see whether what the lessor sought to do was in purported exercise of an "option" or "privilege" or whether it was being done pursuant to an obligation already accepted by the lessee and as part of the machinery for implementing what was already agreed. In the former case time was presumed to be of the essence, while in the latter the presumption was to the contrary. This dichotomy between "option" on the one hand and "obligation" or "machinery" on the other continued until the leases involved in the *Burnley Case* became the subject of litigation.

In the *Burnley Case* proper a Court of Appeal (Buckley, Roskill and Browne L.JJ.) discarded the distinction between "option" clauses and "obligation" or "machinery" clauses. A different and new test was applied. The court held that the commercial character of the contract contained in a lease incorporating a rent review clause raised the presumption that the parties intended time to be of the essence of the contract in respect of each step to be taken by the lessor in order to obtain a determination of any increased rent under a rent review clause. In *Cheapside Land Development Co.* v. *Messels Service Co.* another Court of Appeal (Stamp, Scarman and Goff L.JJ.) also discarded the "option" or "machinery" test. The court concluded that time was of the essence, prima facie, in all rent review clauses. Its view was not based on the presumed intentions of the parties arising from the suggested commercial nature of the transaction, but upon the ground that in its legal nature a rent review clause is a grant of a unilateral right to the lessor and that equity would not have granted relief to the grantee of such a right for failure to perform any of the conditions of the grant timeously.

Appeals were taken against both decisions and the appeals were heard together by the House of Lords. As already indicated, I have referred to both decisions as the *Burnley Case*. The issue which arose for decision was stated thus by Lord Diplock in his speech at pp. 923-4 of the report:-

> "What the Court of Appeal have decided is that the commercial nature of the contract and/or the legal nature of the right granted to the landlord by a rent review clause raises a presumption that time specified in such a clause for anything that needs to be done by him is of the essence; and that this presumption will prevail unless there are strong contra-indications in the actual wording of the clause . . . My Lords, the reason why these two appeals have been heard together

in the House, although the two rent review clauses that are in question differ widely in their wording, is to obtain a ruling whether the presumption as to the construction and effect of rent review clauses is as the Court of Appeal held it to be, or whether it is the contrary presumption, viz. that time is not of the essence."

In considering this issue the Law Lords were concerned with the application of equitable principles. This arose initially because of the provisions of s. 25(7) of the Supreme Court of Judicature Act, 1873, to the effect that stipulations in contracts as to time which would not before the passing of that Act have been deemed to be, or to have become, of the essence in a court of equity should receive in all courts the same construction as they would have theretofore received in equity. There was also the general provision in that Act that in case of conflict between the rules of equity and the rules of common law, the rules of equity should prevail.

I think it is clear from the report that, in considering the application of equitable principles or rules, the general view of the House of Lords was that neither the Act of 1873 nor the later and similar provisions of s.41 of the Law of Property Act, 1925, placed any ban upon further development of equitable rules by judicial decisions: see per Lord Diplock at p.926 and Lord Fraser at p.957 of the report.

It is not necessary to examine in any detail the careful, long and detailed speeches of the Law Lords who participated in the *Burnley Case*. It is sufficient to say that, with one reservation, they were prepared to regard the inclusion in a lease of a rent review clause as an acceptance by the tenant of an obligation to pay the landlord a rent so determined and, further, that this acceptance was an inseverable part of the whole consideration for the landlord's grant of the terms of years for the length agreed. The majority view was to this effect even when the right to initiate or to "trigger" the rent review was exclusively that of the landlord. It was recognised that there could be exceptions as where a break-clause was included in the lease entitling the tenant to surrender if the rent were increased.

Viewed in this light, the time-table for the review or determination of the new rent was regarded by the court as subsidiary to an obligation already accepted by the tenant and as mere machinery for carrying into effect the real intention of the parties that periodic increases of rent should take place. In particular, the majority view was that the unilateral right of the landlord to initiate or to commence a rent review was not a right to create a new relationship or contract between landlord and tenant but was merely a power or right to determine the amount of a new rent already agreed to. It merely altered a term in a continuing contract. In this respect it differed from an option under which one party was empowered to create a new and binding contract with the other. Accordingly, the House of Lords adopted and applied to such rent review clauses, when considered in relation to the observance of time limits, the following rule which appears in Halsbury's Laws of England (4th ed., vol. 9, para.481):-

> "Time will not be considered to be of the essence unless: (1) the parties expressly stipulate that conditions as to time must be strictly complied with; or (2) the nature of the subject matter of the contract or the surrounding circumstances show that time should be considered to be of the essence . . ."

The result was that, in the absence of any contra indication in the lease itself, the House of Lords in the *Burnley Case* ruled that there is a presumption (stemming from the application of equitable principles) that in all rent review clauses time should not be regarded as essential to the initiation or operation of the rent review, even if the right to review is unilateral.

I have considered very carefully the reasoning which led to the decision in the *Burnley Case*. It is based on the assertion that such leases for long terms would not be granted or concluded without acceptance by the tenant of rent reviews and that, as a consequence, it would be unfair and inequitable that such a tenant should be allowed to repudiate an obligation he had accepted merely because, in carrying out what was agreed, a time clause was not observed. I find this reasoning compelling. I accept that there may be circumstances in which delay has been extreme or where, because of it, other factors have arisen which alter the equities. However, in the ordinary case where the payment of an increased rent is expressly envisaged and accepted, and where the failure to observe the requirements of a time clause is due to mere inadvertence and is not prolonged and in no way alters obligations already undertaken, I see no reason for saying that the equitable rule as to time in contracts should not apply. This is not to say that failure by the landlord to act in time may not be a breach of contract for which he may be liable in damages, if damage is caused. However, his failure in this respect should not be regarded as such a breach as would entitle the tenant to repudiate obligations which under the contract he has already accepted.

In Ireland the fusion of common-law and equitable rules was initiated by the Supreme Court of Judicature Act (Ireland), 1877, which contains similar provisions in s.28(7) to those already noted in the English Acts, and was completed by the Courts of Justice Act, 1924, and the Courts (Establishment and Constitution) Act, 1961.

In the circumstances existing in this appeal, it seems to me that the reasoning in the *Burnley Case* applies. The wording of the reddendum indicates that the plaintiffs accepted an obligation to pay not only the initial rent but also "such increased rent as may from time to time be payable hereunder." The lease contains no break clause or anything which would distinguish it from a lease under which the lessee accepts the normal obligation of periodic reviews of rent. It appears to me that the rent review clause amounts to machinery for the implementation of what was accepted from the commencement of the lease, that is to say, a review of the rent at the stipulated periods. In these circumstances, I am of the view that observance by the defendants of the time prescribed for the implementation of the agreed rent review was not of the essence and that, accordingly, the decision of the High Court judge to this effect was correct. Therefore, I would dismiss this appeal.

Kenny J.:

This is an important case to the parties. If the plaintiffs' argument is correct, they will hold property in Galway from the defendants until the 1st January, 1985, at an annual rent of £42,000 while, if the defendants' contention is right, the rent payable until the same date may be £160,000. It is important also because the plaintiffs' counsel has submitted that we should not follow the decision of the House of Lords in *United Scientific Holdings* v. *Burnley Borough Council* [1978] A.C. 904 as, he says, it is not a correct statement of the law in this State in relation to rent review clauses in leases.

By a lease dated the 29th March, 1972, Sisk Properties Ltd. (whose estate as lessors has been assigned to the defendants) let property in Galway to the plaintiffs for a term of 99 years from the 1st January, 1972, "yielding and paying therefor during the said term unto the Lessor the yearly rent of £42,000 and such increased rent as may from time to time be payable hereunder as hereinafter provided." The rent is payable by equal quarterly payments in advance on the 1st January and the 1st April, July and October in every year.

[*The judge here referred to the terms of clause D.3 of the lease, and continued*] On the 17th November, 1978, the defendants gave notice to the plaintiffs "pursuant to the provisions of the lease . . . that we intend to review the rent payable under the said lease in accordance with the terms thereof with effect that as from the first day of January, 1979, the annual rent payable will be £160,000 and we hereby call upon you to agree this amount with us." The plaintiffs' solicitors replied to this notice pointing out that the revised rent notice should have been served before 1st October, 1978, and that the notice sent by the defendants was out of time and ineffective. This contention was not accepted and the plaintiffs brought this action on the 22nd February, 1979, in which they claimed declarations that the notice of 17th November, 1978, was ineffective to require a review of the rent payable under the lease and that the rent payable under it remained unchanged at £42,000. The action was dismissed by Mr. Justice McWilliam, who followed the decision in *United Scientific Holdings* v. *Burnley Borough Council,* and the plaintiffs have appealed.

There are some features about the lease to which I wish to refer. The first is that the premises were demised for a term of 99 years and there was no provision under which the lessees could surrender or determine the lease, even if they were dissatisfied with the rent fixed by the arbitrator or even considered it exorbitant. The second is that the lease was made subject to a number of sub-leases which were made for business purposes for, although this is not stated, the sub-tenants included Radio Telefís Éireann and the Minister for Posts and Telegraphs. The lease was obviously made to the plaintiffs for business purposes; the demised premises are in the commercial centre of Galway. In 1972, leases of commercial properties for lengthy terms of years invariably contained rent review clauses as a protection for the lessors' interest in a period in which an annual, recurring and high inflation rate was then, as it is now, a feature of our life.

Section 28 of the Supreme Court of Judicature Act (Ireland), 1877, provides;-

> "And whereas it is expedient to take occasion of the union of the several Courts whose jurisdiction is hereby transferred to the said High Court of Justice to amend and declare the law to be hereafter administered in Ireland as to the matters next hereinafter mentioned: Be it enacted as follows . . .
>
> (7) Stipulations in contracts, as to time or otherwise, which would not before the commencement of this Act have been deemed to be or to have become of the essence of such contracts in a Court of Equity, shall receive in all Courts the same construction and effect as they would have heretofore received in equity."

Equity was a gloss on or an improvement and reform of the common law and different constructions were placed in the common-law and chancery courts on stipulations in contracts as to time. So it is necessary to deal with the rules applied in the common-law courts as to such stipulations. In the common-law courts, when a contract provided that certain things were to be done within a certain time or on a specified date, the party who sought to sue on the contract had to plead and prove that he had complied with the stipulation as to time and was ready and willing to perform any other parts of the contract which remained unperformed (see the notes to *Cutter* v. *Powell* (1795) 6 Term Rep. 320 in Smith's Leading Cases). This rule resulted in such injustice that the common-law judges worked out a number of exceptions to it. The history of these is dealt with in the judgment of Diplock L.J. (as he then was) in *Hong Kong Fir Shipping Co.* v. *Kawasaki Kisen Kaisha* [1962] 2 Q.B. 26. In the courts of equity (where the ideas summarised in the maxim "Equity looks to the intent, not to the form" were applied and developed) relief would be given against failure to comply with a stipulation as to time in a contract, unless time was of the essence of the contract. A plaintiff or defendant who had not complied with a stipulation as to time in a contract could succeed on his claim or defence unless it was established that time was of the essence of the contract.

There is a happy summary of the position in Ireland in the judgment of Lord Redesdale, the Lord Chancellor, in *Lennon* v. *Napper* (1802) 2 Sch. & Lef. 682; the decision is also helpful in that it shows that this doctrine had become established in Ireland in 1802, while the decision in *Dyas* v. *Rooney* (1980) 27 L.R. Ir. 4 indicates that it continued to be applied. At p.684 of the report of *Lennon* v. *Napper* to Lord Redesdale said:-

> "Courts of equity have therefore enforced contracts specifically, where no action for damages could be maintained; for at law, the party plaintiff must have strictly performed his part, and the inconvenience of insisting upon that in all cases, was sufficient to require the interference of courts of equity. They dispense with that which would make compliance with what the law requires oppressive: and in various cases of such contracts, they are in the constant habit of relieving the man who has acted fairly, though negligently. Thus in the case of an estate sold by auction, there is a condition to forfeit the deposit, if the purchase be not completed within a certain time; yet the court is in the constant habit of relieving against the lapse of time: and so in the case of mortgages, and, in many instances,

relief is given against mere lapse of time, where lapse of time is not essential to the substance of the contract."

When is time of the essence of the contract? There have been such a number of cases (both Irish and English) on this matter that I do not intend to review them because the law is, I believe, correctly stated in a text-book of high authority in a passage which has been judicially approved on a number of occasions. The passage appears at p.502 of the 6th edition of Fry on Specific Performance:-

> "Time is originally of the essence of the contract, in the view of a Court of Equity, whenever it appears to have been part of the real intention of the parties that it should be so, and not to have been inserted as a merely formal part of the contract. As this intention may either be separately expressed, or may be implied from the nature or structure of the contract, it follows that time may be originally of the essence of a contract, as to any one or more of its terms, either by virtue of an express condition in the contract itself making it so, or by reason of its being implied."

The provisions in the lease as to the service of a revised rent notice do not state that time is to be of the essence of the contract and, indeed, there is no reference to time being of the essence of the contract anywhere in the lease.

On many occasions counsel for the plaintiffs referred to the lessors' option to serve a revised rent notice. In my opinion, the use of the word "option" to describe the lessors' right to serve such a notice is both incorrect and apt to mislead. In most cases the specified dates within which an option may be exercised are of the essence. An option gives a right to acquire property – usually at a specified price and within a named time. Its exercise creates the relationship of vendor and purchaser or of landlord and tenant. In the instant case neither the plaintiffs nor the defendants acquire any property by the service of a revised rent notice. When it is served, the plaintiffs continue to hold for the term created by the lease and on its terms: the only change is that a term of the lease (which is a contract) is altered.

Then it was said that the nature of the lease showed that time was of the essence in relation to the date for the service of the revised rent notice. The argument was that the provision for service of the notice before the 1st October was inserted so that the plaintiffs would know before the 1st January of the following year the amount of the higher rent, and so that they could dispose of their interest as lessees if the new rent were so high that it would be uneconomic to retain the premises. If that were the purpose of the insertion of the 1st October as the material date, one would expect a provision requiring the arbitrator to give his award within a specified period, but there is no such provision. Moreover, an assignment of the premises by the plaintiffs would require considerable time to complete and the new rent would be fixed (even if the revised rent notice was late) long before a sale of the premises by the plaintiffs could be negotiated and completed.

I think that the nature of the clause in the lease shows that time is not of the essence for the purpose of the service of the revised rent notice. If the new rent is fixed after the 1st January, the plaintiffs will have the use of the money which represents the rent until the rent is determined – though when it is fixed they will have to pay it from the 1st January. They suffer no disadvantage if the rent is fixed after the 1st January and they get some advantage. However, if we hold that time is of the essence, the defendants will have to continue until 1985 to receive a rent which was fixed in 1972. During the last three years there has been an inflation of between 15% and 20% in each year and it is clear that one of the main purposes of the relevant clause in the lease was to prevent the rent remaining constant at the 1972 amount if the high rate of inflation continued.

Then it was said that service of the revised rent notice before the 1st October, 1978, was a condition precedent to any revision of the rent for the second seven years of the term and that it had not been complied with. Service of the notice before 1st October would have been a condition precedent in the common-law courts before 1877 but its service before that date was a stipulation as to time in a contract and the Court of Chancery would, before 1877, have relieved the lessor from his failure to serve the notice in time. The result of the Act of 1877 is that the law which was applied in the Court of Chancery before 1877 now prevails.

Counsel for the plaintiffs gave us, very diffidently, a reference to an article in the Law Quarterly Review which is relevant to the issues in this case: P.V. Baker, The Future of Equity (1977) 93 L.Q.R. 529. Counsel said that he knew that he should not cite the article in this Court. I disagree as strongly as I can with the view of counsel that articles in reputable legal periodicals should not be cited in this Court. Speaking for myself, I am always glad when such articles are referred to as they are of considerable assistance to me when I am making up my mind what my final judgment should be. Mr. Baker was a joint author (with the Vice-Chancellor, Mr. Justice Megarry) of the latest editions of that legal classic, Snell's Principles of Equity, which is frequently cited in this Court. I do not understand why his views in an article should not be cited while a text-book for which he is responsible is frequently referred to in this Court without any objection from any of its members. I may add that last year I attended as an auditor (giving that word its original meaning of one who listens) at a sitting of the Judicial Committee of the House of Lords and counsel arguing the case referred to many articles in reputable legal periodicals without any objection from any of the five Law Lords who sat.

In that article Mr. Baker wrote that the decision in *United Scientific Holdings* v. *Burnley Borough Council* was "new doctrine." I do not agree with this. It is new in the sense that the Judicial Committee overruled the decision of the English Court of Appeal in *Samuel Properties Ltd.* v. *Hayek* and many other decisions of the Court of Appeal and of the High Court; but those decisions had ignored or overlooked the principles developed in the Court of Chancery two hundred years ago. I regard the decision in the *Burnley Case* as a restoration of a fundamental equitable principle which, unfortunately, has tended to be ignored in many recent decisions.

After the argument in this case had concluded, I became aware (through the medium of a note in the Law Quarterly Review) that the *Burnley Case* had been discussed by the House of Lords in *Raineri* v. *Miles* [1980] 2 W.L.R. 847. In that case a third party agreed to sell his house in Guildford to the defendant and contracted to deliver possession of the property to the defendant on the 12th July, 1977. The defendant had agreed to sell his house in Ealing to the plaintiff and had agreed to deliver possession to the plaintiff on the 12th July, 1977. The third party failed to complete the sale of his house (for reasons other than matters of title) on the date specified but did complete it on the 11th August, 1977, and delivered possession to the defendant on that date. The plaintiff, being unable to obtain possession of the defendant's house on the 12th July, was compelled to find alternative accommodation for himself and his family until the 11th August when he obtained possession of the defendant's house. The plaintiff recovered damages against the defendant and the latter sought to recover the amount of such damages from the third party. The third party contended, on the authority of the *Burnley Case*, that his obligation under his contract with the defendant was to complete his sale on the 12th July or within a reasonable time thereafter. This contention was rejected. I mention the case to show that I have not overlooked it, and so that I may state that I do not agree with the explanation by Lord Edmund Davies of the principle on which the *Burnley Case* was decided. In my opinion the decision of the House of Lords in the *Burnley Case* was correct and so we should follow it. I think that the judgment of the High Court in the instant case was correct and should be affirmed. It follows that, in my opinion, this appeal should be dismissed.

Parke J.:

I agree with the judgments which have been delivered.

Notes and Questions

1. Do you agree with Kenny J.'s interpretation of the *Burnley Case* and his disagreement with P.V. Baker's views?
2. See further on time clauses, *Irish Conveyancing Law*, paras. 12. 09-24.
3. How significant do you think are Kenny J.'s views on the citation of periodical literature?

II. EQUITY ACTS IN PERSONAM

LETT V. LETT

[1906] 1 I.R. 618 (Court of Appeal)

The facts are set out in the judgments.

Sir Samuel Walker, C.:

In this case the Master of the Rolls has granted an injunction restraining the defendant, who is the wife of the plaintiff, from instituting or continuing any proceedings in the Court of the Argentine Republic, or elsewhere, against the plaintiff, or his property, for the purposes of claiming alimony, or separation of goods, or any payment, from the plaintiff, or out of his property, for her support, maintenance, debts, or otherwise.

The plaintiff and defendant were married on the 3rd April, 1874, in the Anglican Church, Buenos Ayres, in the Argentine Republic. The plaintiff had an Irish domicil. They lived at Buenos Ayres for some time, and the plaintiff had a school there. He appears to have formed an adulterous intercourse with a woman in his service, and in 1888 they were both in Ireland. He had become the owner of a farm and residence called Woodville, in Wexford. The adultery naturally led to unpleasantness, and on the 22nd September, 1888, the defendant presented a petition in the Irish Court for divorce *a mensa et thoro* on account of his adultery, which he answered. The Irish domicil of each was admitted in that suit, and a decree was pronounced in it by Judge Warren on the 17th December, 1888. In such a suit alimony *pendente lite,* and permanent alimony, subsequent to the decree are, of course, obtainable, and the obtaining of them was part of the object of that suit.

According to the Argentine law a woman becomes entitled to certain rights in her husband's property in the nature of a partnership, and it appears that all property acquired by them during the marriage belongs to both – everything except legacies or inheritances. The partnership is called "Sociedad conjugale." This is the statement given by the plaintiff, and is the only evidence given here of Argentine law. The husband is the administrator of it, and managing partner, and that partnership remains until it is dissolved by the decree of a competent Court on divorce, or by death; and on a divorce the wife can claim a separation of goods.

There was a petition for alimony *pendente lite,* in which the defendant set forth, according to her estimate, all the property to which her husband was entitled, both in Ireland and the Argentine Republic, and she included Woodville, and an estate or cattle-run in the Argentine Republic, and other property. The husband filed his answer on the 22nd November, 1888, in which he dealt with the various items in the petition; and as regards the Argentine property, alleged it had been realized, and that all from this source was represented by a sum of £2000 in cash. No alimony was in fact awarded. The suit came on for hearing; the adultery was admitted, and a decree was made for divorce on the 17th December, 1888, and on the same day a consent was entered into and made a rule of Court to settle the suit, and all relief under it, and all claims for alimony, whether *pendente lite* or permanent.

This consent provided that the plaintiff should pay her a sum of £480 net, and should also pay her solicitor's costs, and execute a deed assigning to her the premises of Woodville, and furniture and chattels therein, and that she should execute a deed releasing him from all claims in respect of relief in the suit and costs, and alimony, *pendente lite* and permanent, and all debts to be incurred by her, and all claims whatsoever, by or on account of the said Charlotte Lett, and indemnifying the said Richard Lett against the same. Two deeds were accordingly executed, each bearing date the 3rd January, 1889, by one of which he assigned to her the premises of Woodville, and the furniture and chattels therein. The lands have since had a judicial rent fixed in respect of them, and it appears to be a valuable interest, and the moneys stipulated for were paid; and, by the other deed of the same date, she released the plaintiff from all claims for alimony, *pendente lite* and permanent, in the terms of the consent, "and from all claims whatsoever by or on account of the said Charlotte Lett against the said Richard Lett, or his estate or property, real or personal, movable or immovable, now in possession, or hereafter to be acquired by him, and from all rights and interests, claims, and demands which the said Charlotte Lett has, or may have, in, to or upon the same, or any part thereof."

Such were the contracts contained in the consent and deeds. Was she competent to enter into them? I consider it to be settled law that a married woman suing her husband in the Matrimonial Court is at arm's length: and, in the absence of fraud, free to enter into a contract with him for the settlement of the litigation. *Besant* v. *Wood* 12 Ch. D. 605 is one of many cases establishing this. The compromise of litigation would itself furnish an ample consideration; but she also obtained the assignment of Woodville and furniture, of which she went into possession.

Next, what is the construction of the contract? Was she left free to assert a claim in the Argentine Republic against the property he might acquire there, seeking a division of property under the Argentine law? This is a question of construction, for I do not think it is open to serious argument that she could not bind herself not to enforce a claim in any Court – domestic or foreign – or a claim of any nature, whether under Argentine law or English law, against his property, whether it be in the nature of alimony, or of any other kind: and the claim for division of property is of the character of alimony, which she had specifically contracted not to claim. In 1895 she went over to Buenos Ayres, and preferred a claim on account of her poverty, by reason of which he agreed by deed to give her an allowance of £100 per annum in addition to what she got under the deed of 1889. As this deed of 1895 is not relied on in the pleadings, or at the bar, I do not rest anything upon it.

Well, in 1903, she commenced proceedings in the Argentine Court, in which she claimed a divorce (though it had been already granted), and it is stated the divorce in that republic can only have the same efficacy as a divorce in Ireland, and as consequential to this divorce she claimed a separation of goods – in other words, claimed to be maintained out of the property he had acquired in the Republic, subsequent to the divorce and deeds in Ireland. He has defended that suit, and relies upon the contracts and transactions and deeds of 1889 as a defence, and also on the deed of 1895; and these proceedings are still pending, and the Argentine Court is, I assume, competent to pronounce on them.

It is not disputed that in the interval since the Irish proceedings he had acquired very considerable property, and was comparatively a wealthy man, and, therefore, she was interested in trying to get out of her contract of 1889, and get further maintenance; but whether she can do so or not depends, I think, on the contract she made. It is not suggested that it was obtained by, or can be avoided for, fraud, and the suggestion in the defence that it could be reformed was not argued.

Does it make any difference that the proceeding sought to be restrained is a proceeding in a foreign Court? I think not, because the equity against her is founded not upon the tribunal to which she has resorted, but upon the personal contract binding her conscience. The jurisdiction asserted is not against the foreign tribunal, but against the person within the jurisdiction, who has made a contract not to resort to proceedings; and whether such proceedings are in a foreign Court or not, is immaterial for the purpose of the equity on which the jurisdiction rests – an equity *in personam*.

The rule is clearly laid down in *The Carron Iron Co. Case* 5 H.L. Cas. 416, and numerous other cases. I was for a time inclined to think that ascertainment of the Argentine law as to this division of property, and its limitations, and the circumstances under which it would arise, was material to the relief, and should be before the Court before we interfered; but, on further consideration, I do not think this is so. It is a claim against the husband's property covered by her contract; and if that be so, she is bound not to put it forward in any Court – just as she would be restrained according to the decision in *Gandy* v. *Gandy* 7 P.D. 168 from prosecuting a claim for further alimony in the Irish Court. The plaintiff has, no doubt, allowed three years to go by before instituting this suit on the 3rd March, 1906. He never could get an interlocutory injunction; but if he has the right under the covenant, the delay does not deprive him of the only remedy he has for its assertion.

I am of opinion that the decison of the Master of the Rolls should be affirmed, and the appeal dismissed; but having regard to the delay which has taken place, and the time he allowed the Argentine proceedings to continue before he resorted to his rights under the contract of 1889, and also to the relations between the parties, I think there should be no costs awarded against the defendant in the Court below or here.

Fitzgibbon, L.J.:

It appears to me that the rights of the parties in this case can be best determined by considering two questions.

(1) What were the rights, if any, which the plaintiff had in the way of restraining proceedings against his person or property by his wife, on the completion of the arrangement which was carried out by the two deeds of January 3, 1889, on which the action is based?

(2) If the plaintiff could have restrained the action, which his wife commenced against him in the Argentine Republic on August 26, 1903, has anything happened since to justify the Court, in its judicial discretion, in now refusing to give him relief?

I think it clear that the answer to the first question can in no way depend upon any question of foreign law. The law of the Argentine Republic may regulate the rights of the parties with respect to property there; but it cannot possibly affect the jurisdiction or duty of the Irish Courts, as to the enforcement of a contract made in this country when both parties were domiciled here, and which contract arose out of proceedings in the Irish Matrimonial Court, to whose jurisdiction both of them had submitted.

It seems equally clear that no conflict of laws, or question of the comity of Courts, can arise with respect to an Argentine tribunal, which would not have arisen with respect to an English or Scotch Court, or between Irish Courts of law and equity, while those departments of our judicature were assigned to different tribunals.

The transactions of 1888-9 comprise two stages – one judicial, and the other contractual; they began with an action by the wife against the husband for divorce *a mensa et thoro* and for judicial separation, based on the husband's misconduct, and enabling her to obtain, by prosecuting her suit, an enforceable provision by way of alimony – first *pendente lite,* and afterwards permanent – to be measured in just proportion to her husband's means.

The judicial proceedings in the main suit had gone to petition, answer, and decree for separation, and an interlocutory proceeding for alimony had gone to petition and answer, when the litigation was settled upon the terms that the separation decree should stand, and that the provision for the wife should be determined by contract, and should be carried out by the execution of mutual deeds of conveyance and release, on terms judicially sanctioned. The ruling instrument is the consent, which was made a rule of Court on December 17, 1888.

I am satisfied that the subsequent deed of release of January 3, 1889, must be construed by reference to this consent, and I assume that the deed cannot, by general words, deprive the wife in equity of any property or right which she had not by the consent agreed to surrender. But I can find no real difference between the terms of the two documents, and the wife's counterclaim that the deed should be reformed if it releases her husband's property in Argentina, would, in my opinion, be maintainable if the deed, as distinguished from the consent, had released that property. But, on the other hand, if she bound herself by the consent to surrender any claim she had to that property, the deed must have the effect of binding her not to claim it, either here or in Argentina.

I, therefore, consider the question upon the nature and terms of the consent itself. It provided for the settlement of all proceedings in the cause in reference to alimony, whether *pendente lite* or permanent, and of all claims and proceedings in respect of the costs of the cause and proceedings for alimony therein. If the cause had not been settled, an order for permanent alimony was the proceeding by which the wife from time to time could enforce a provision during her life proportionate to his means here or elsewhere, and either party would have had the right, from time to time, to vary the amount of that provision, if his means had increased or diminished. The provision would also have been inalienable by her.

The interlocutory petition and answer show that his property in Argentina, at that date, was the subject of discussion ; she alleging that it was very large, and he, on the contrary, alleging that he had converted the whole of it into money, had left Argentina, had invested the larger part of the proceeds of his property there in buying and stocking a house and farm in Ireland, intended as a home and means of subsistence for himself and his wife, which intention was frustrated by the "unhappy differences" which arose between them, and culminated in the suit and in their separation.

He alleged that his only remaining property was the balance of the proceeds of the Argentine property over and above what he had spent in costs of travelling and litigation, and in the purchase of the Irish property, which balance he alleged to amount to only about £1,000. If the suit had not been settled, alimony would have been the judicial form in which the wife's claim for subsistence must have been satisfied so long as she lived, and it is utterly inconsistent with the terms of the deeds, and with the proceedings which led up to the settlement, to suggest that the Argentine property, whatever it was, was not taken into consideration, as being the husband's.

The substance of the consent was that he should pay her £500, and assign to her all his property in Ireland, house, land, furniture, stock, and chattels; and that she, in consideration of that provision, should release him from all claims, present or future, in respect of the relief sought by her in the suit, or in respect of alimony, whether *pendente lite,* or permanent, and in respect of her debts, present or future, and of all claims whatever on her account, and should indemnify him against the same.

I can give this arrangement no less effect than that of a final determination by and between a husband and wife, when at arm's length, contracting with each other as distinct parties each *sui juris,* that for better or worse, for richer or poorer, he should give and she should take the consideration fixed by agreement, in lieu and satisfaction of all claims which, then or at any future time, she could otherwise have made as his wife against him or his property, wherever situate, during their joint lives.

If there were no other answer to the wife's demand of liberty to prosecute her pending suit in Argentina, it would seem to me to be enough to say that equity can not permit her to do so, so long as she retains and enjoys the agreed consideration for the contract not to sue which the deed of 1889 imports – except upon the terms of accounting, against her present claim, for what she has received, and is receiving, under the contract which she now seeks to "reprobate." An injunction which can be enforced, if necessary, by sequestration of the Irish property is the appropriate – if not the only – remedy for such a breach of contract, and it is not argument, but caricature, to describe this suit as one "brought by the plaintiff to put his wife into gaol."

The arrangement of 1888-9 necessarily imported on each side that no subsequent change in their circumstances could alter the rights of the parties: neither could the husband, if he became poorer, get back any of the property he gave; nor could the wife, if he became richer, make any demand for further provision for her maintenance.

I do not understand the possibility of contending that the judicial provision for a separated wife in the form of alimony is not to be measured in proportion to the husband's means *wherever situated,* and in the particular case it is proved that the amount of the Argentine property was actually in controversy when the contractual substitute for permanent alimony was accepted; and this controversy was one of the claims which was settled for the consideration fixed by the deeds.

Gandy v. *Gandy* 7 P.D. 168 is an authority of the Court of Appeal that a separated wife, by covenanting not to take proceedings against her husband, on his covenanting to allow her a sum fixed by a separation deed, for the maintenance of herself and her children, even in the case of his subsequent misconduct, and of his becoming subsequently wealthy, debars the Court from giving her any increased provision by way of alimony, because she is bound by deed to accept the sum fixed by the contract in satisfaction of all her claims for support.

It can make no distinction in law between that case and this, that the deed there preceded the suit, for here the final settlement of the suit itself was part of the consideration for the fixed provision which was made and accepted.

The validity and binding effect of separation deeds have varied under our law, but it was never contended that their operation *in personam* was in any way affected by the situation of property, or governed by any other law than the *lex loci contractus.*

Lord Justice Fry says, Sp. Perf. (4th ed.), p.52, sects. 126, 127:-

> "A contract made abroad may be enforced against a defendant within the jurisdiction of this country, and, as the remedies for breach of a contract are clearly governed by the *lex fori,* it follows that it is no objection to the specific performance in England of a foreign contract that the foreign law might have given no such remedy.
>
> "This jurisdiction extends to cases of contracts relative to real or immovable property where the defendant is within the jurisdiction of the Court. The maxim is *Æquitas agit in personam,* and any operation of the judgment of the immovable estate abroad is not direct but indirect, and only through the medium of the person affected by the judgment."

He notices a case, *Hart* v. *Herwig* L.R. 8 Ch. 860, in which the Court of Chancery granted relief with a view to specific performance against a defendant not within the jurisdiction, and he says "the decision is remarkable, but it has the authority of three unanimous judges."

These statements of the law follow the statement that—

> "Although the Court has no jurisdiction in matrimonial causes, yet, where there has been a contract or covenant, it may interfere to enforce the execution of a proper separation deed, or to restrain the breach of a covenant contained in it."

The personal covenant of a separated wife not to molest or sue a husband is, from its very nature, an obligation for the breach of which there is no practical remedy except a decree, in the nature of specific performance, for an injunction to restrain a suit threatened or commenced; therefore, if the covenant is lawful and proper, the decree for specific performance by injunction, being the only remedy, is *ex debito justitiæ* and not discretionary.

If a suit was not maintainable, it could be defeated on the merits; it is only where there *is* a legal claim, that the interference of a Court of Equity becomes necessary; therefore, proof that the suit which it is sought to restrain will, if it proceeds, result in the establishment of a claim against the defendant therein, only shows the necessity for the suit *in personam,* by which its prosecution is to be restrained.

That the situation of the Court in which the suit is instituted, and the extent of its jurisdiction, are immaterial to the question whether the suit is to be restrained or not, is plain on principle. A striking instance is to be found in *Booth* v. *Leycester* 3 M. & C. 459 where Lord Cottenham restrained the prosecution of a suit in Ireland to recover annuities which had already been the subject of a suit in England, notwithstanding that the Irish suit had been prosecuted for a considerable time.

In his judgment he says:-

> "This Court will not permit him to retain, for the purpose of suing elsewhere, securities upon which, according to the judgment of the Court, nothing remains due." Whether he would or would not have got more if he had at first proceeded in Ireland is immaterial."

This principle must apply to a case where the person suing abroad is here in conscience bound not to sue.

The Carron Case 5 H.L. Cas. 416 lays down the principle in even more general terms—

> "If the circumstances are such as would make it the duty of one Court in this country to restrain a party from instituting proceedings in another Court here, they will also warrant it in imposing on him a similar restraint with regard to proceedings in a foreign Court.
>
> "Where there is a plain equity in favour of an injunction, and those who seek it are in this country, the Court will grant it, and restrain the proceedings in the Courts of a foreign country."

For these reasons, and on the facts of this case, including the construction and effect of the release, I have no doubt that the Master of the Rolls was right in holding that the injunction against the Argentine proceeding should go, provided this suit had been brought with sufficient promptitude.

It is a further important circumstance in favour of the plaintiff that, by the second deed of January 3rd, 1889, he completed the consideration for the release by absolutely assigning to his wife the house and land, and paid her the money, and gave her the chattels, which she agreed to accept as the consideration for her covenant not to molest or sue him either personally or in respect of his property. The Irish property assigned to her was valuable, and it has increased in value since she got it, through a purchase under the Land Acts. It comprised what had been intended as the home and means of subsistence of both husband and wife, if they had not separated; and there is nothing to suggest that, as matters stood in 1889, it was not a reasonable provision for the wife alone. Therefore, after-acquired property of the husband, and nothing else, is now at stake.

The transaction of 1895 is not put in issue, and the deed of that year, though proved by the exemplification of it from the Argentine Registry, is not relied upon in pleading, and, therefore, cannot be made a ground of relief. But it is evidence, by way of admission, of the validity of the release of 1889, and it may also be referred to upon the second question – namely, whether anything has occurred since 1889 which could justify the Court, in the exercise of its discretion, in refusing relief now. We have the defendant's own representation of that transaction in the recitals contained in the "protocol" filed in the Argentine Court. Neither in the deed itself, nor in the protocol, is it suggested that the additional provision of £100 a year, which the husband then covenanted to give her, out of his increased means, was given otherwise than as a voluntary act of bounty. She set out and confirmed the release of 1889, and she described the occasion of the additional grant of £100 a year as being "her having arrived at a state of poverty, and solicited from him some means with which to meet her requirements," and she stated that, "having with that object come to Buenos Ayres, she and her husband had entered into the private arrangement" expressed in the deed, for which they both solicited, and obtained, the approbation of the Argentine Court in the form of "protocolization" of the instrument, which appears to be an Argentine form of registration.

No injunction is sought, nor do I think could it have been given, upon the present proofs, against any proceeding on that instrument. It is not now before us in any way except as evidence of ratification of the release of 1889, which is the only foundation of this suit. The husband alleges that he regularly paid the money up to the time when she sued him in 1903, and even afterwards, and he admits his liability to pay it still, subject only to her abiding by her contract not to sue for more. If he had failed to do so, and she had sued him in Argentina *upon that deed,* such a suit could not be restrained under the release of seven years before.

The only remaining suggested ground of defence is that the plaintiff has pleaded in the Argentine suit, and has allowed it to proceed for three years. He could not help pleading, and he was free to defend himself. If the bringing of the suit was a breach of the contract of 1889, allowing it to go on could not disentitle him to stop it at any stage, unless his doing so amounted to laches or acquiescence, or changed the wife's position for the worse. He has proved that he was in Argentina when the suit began; that an embargo was put upon his property there, and that he could not conveniently come to this country for relief until the tedious and expensive proceedings had reached their present stage. It seems to me to be only an aggravation of the injury inflicted upon him by the breach of the contract not to molest or sue him, that he was not able to have recourse to this Court until the oppressiveness of the Argentine litigation had become intolerable.

I, therefore, concur in all respects with the judgment of the Master of the Rolls, and hold that his appeal ought to be dismissed. But, having regard to the delay, and to the relations of the parties, and to all the circumstances, including the fact that the husband's misconduct began the trouble, I think it just that he should bear all his own costs, including the costs of the appeal.

Holmes, L.J.:

The plaintiff and defendant, both British by birth, were married in 1874 in Buenos

Ayres, where the plaintiff had been residing for some years. They lived there together, except for six or seven months during which the wife was on a visit to England, until 1880, when she discovered that her husband was having an adulterous intercourse with one of their female servants. She thereupon left Argentina, and came to London to live with her mother. The plaintiff, having remained in Buenos Ayres until 1885, came in that year to Ireland for a short time; and before he returned to Argentina there was a reconciliation between him and his wife. It was then arranged that he should come home after he had sold his property in South America, and that they were to live together in this country. The plaintiff carried out this arrangement by realizing the greater part of his Argentine property, by coming back to his wife, and by residing with her first in London, then at Rosslare, and afterwards at Woodville, County Wexford, of which he obtained a lease, and on which he expended a considerable sum of money. If he had continued to live in Ireland, there might have been no litigation; but, unfortunately, after some time he went back to Argentina to sell some stock that remained undisposed of. I gather from what afterwards took place in the Probate and Matrimonial Division that during his absence the old temptation was too strong for him, for when he returned to Ireland his wife presented a petition to Judge Warren praying for a divorce *a mensa et thoro* on the ground of adultery, and she succeeded in obtaining the decree sought for. There had been previously a petition for alimony *pendente lite*, but an agreement was then entered into providing that all proceedings in the cause on reference to alimony, whether *pendente lite* or permanent, claimed by the wife, and also all claims in respect of the costs of the proceedings, should be settled on the terms of plaintiff paying the defendant the sum of £500, and assigning to her the lands of Woodville, and the chattels thereon. This consent also provided that in consideration thereof the wife should execute a deed releasing the plaintiff from all claims present and future by the defendant in respect of the relief sought against her in the action before Judge Warren and the costs thereof, and in respect of alimony, and in respect of any debts or liability incurred, by her, and from all claims whatever by or on account of her, and indemnifying the plaintiff against the same.

Immediately after this litigation the plaintiff returned to Argentina, where he has since lived and prospered. He has become very wealthy; and, in 1895, his wife, finding it hard to subsist on what was provided for her by the consent, visited Buenos Ayres for the purpose of obtaining, if possible, some further provision; and, without litigation, the plaintiff agreed to give her £100 a year, which has been since regularly paid. His prosperity has apparently gone on increasing; and the defendant, in April, 1903, instituted proceedings in the Court of the Argentine Republic, which, according to the statement of claim, seek for divorce, division of property, and alimony, against the plaintiff.

The present action is brought – (1) for a declaration that the final decree of Judge Warren, in 1888, was a binding sentence of divorce *a mensa et thoro* between the plaintiff and defendant; and (2) for an injunction to restrain the defendant from instituting or continuing any proceedings for divorce, or separation of goods, in the Court of the Argentine Republic against the plaintiff. The Master of the Rolls, I need hardly say, refused to give the declaration asked for, which is too fantastic to call for comment; but he granted the injunction on terms which do not substantially differ from what was claimed by the plaintiff. From this the defendant has appealed; and I am of opinion that she is entitled to succeed.

The plaintiff's claim for the injunction is based upon the consent entered into in the Probate and Matrimonial Division, and the indenture executed in pursuance thereof on the 3rd January, 1889. A document, said to be registered in 1895 in some office in Argentina, relating to the payment of the annuity of £100 already mentioned, was produced during the trial in the Rolls Court, but it is not relied on in the pleadings or in the arguments in this Court; and I do not propose to refer to it. I deal with the case upon the only ground put forward by the plaintiff – the contents of the consent and indenture.

Now, I have no doubt that the High Court in this country has jurisdiction to restrain the defendant from commencing or continuing a suit before a foreign tribunal, the object of which is to enforce against her husband a right from which she has released him by these documents. But whether this jurisdiction will be exercised, depends upon all the circumstances of the case. The injunction, although it only binds the defendant, has the effect of preventing a foreign Court from entering on or proceeding with litigation within its jurisdiction; and this is a step which British Courts are, and ought to be, slow to take. Justice may require it to be taken in some cases; but is the present one of them? Argentina has been the home of the plaintiff for almost forty years; and all his property is in that State. It is, therefore, the natural place in which a person, who claims a legal right against him, would take steps to enforce it. The defendant's suit was begun in April, 1903; and had been proceeding for two years and eleven months before the writ in this action was issued. During this period the parties were not idle, as the plaintiff says that the record of the proceedings has attained to great dimensions; and I gather from his evidence that he has himself contributed considerably to its bulk. All the documents are in Argentina, and the defendant was examined there in November last. We are told that the case would have been ripe for trial next month; but the plaintiff, having been defeated in an interlocutory appeal, came to Ireland, and brought this action. A plaintiff seeking an injunction, which will have the effect of putting a stop to a suit long pending, and soon to be tried, in a foreign country, ought at least to give some evidence of the nature of such suit, and the steps that have been taken in it, and also offer some reasonable explanation of why, after much expense and trouble have been incurred, he seeks to transfer the litigation to a country thousands of miles from his own residence, and from where all his property is situated. He has not done this. The only document produced by him from the Argentine Court is what is called the petition of the defendant, but which seems to me to be more like a speech of counsel. He proves that he has pleaded as a defence the deed of 1889; and it is not suggested by his counsel that this would not be a good answer to the action in the foreign Court, if it has the effect of releasing him from what his wife now claims. If the circumstances of this case were reversed, if the parties were natives of Argentina, and the judicial separation followed by the consent and deed had been obtained and executed there, an English or Irish Court would allow the husband to show, if he could do so, that an action therein brought against him by his wife was a violation of what was then agreed to. I do not know the law of Argentina; but I presume it to be a scientific system, and that it does not differ from our own in recognizing an elementary principle of jurisprudence.

For all these reasons, I should be prepared to hold, even if there was no other ground for doing so, that the injunction ought not to be granted. The Court is entitled, in a case like this, to consider whether the plaintiff is to put a summary stop to legal proceedings which he has allowed to go on for so long without objection, and whether, having failed to change the venue of the action from one province of Argentina to another, he should now be permitted to bring it to Ireland. I can find no precedent resembling even remotely in its circumstances the present case; and I think one ought not now to be made.

There is, however, another ground for dismissing this action. It appears from the statement of claim therein that one of the objects of the foreign suit is to obtain division of property. We have no expert evidence as to what this means in Argentine law; but the plaintiff himself gave some answers, which can be used for the purpose of showing what it is. He said: "All the property that was gained during the marriage, *gamancia,* belongs to both, and the partnership is called 'Sociedad conjugale,' . . . everything except legacies or inheritance. The husband is the administrator of the property, and he is the managing partner." He afterwards said that the partnership remains until it is dissolved by a competent Court, and added that the "Sociedad" is dissolved by a decree for divorce; but after stating that there is no absolute divorce as in England, he went on to say – "I think the divorce only affects the personal separation of the couple. The 'Sociedad,' I believe, ends with it. I cannot remember that I have taken the opinion of a lawyer on the point." He says a little later that his wife claimed in the pending action a separation of goods, and the ascertainment of her share in the property. Now it is to be noted that the witness stated without doubt or hesitation that all the property gained during the marriage, except by legacies or inheritance, belongs to both husband and wife, the husband being the managing partner. In this case all the property of which the plaintiff is now in possession in Argentina was gained during the marriage, and after the deed of 1889. Therefore, unless the judicial separation makes a difference, this property belongs to the husband and wife jointly; but the plaintiff was in doubt as to the effect of the divorce. He cannot say whether it puts an end to the wife's rights or not – nor, in the absence of all other evidence of Argentine law on the subject, can this Court say. But suppose that in the words of the plaintiff the divorce only affects the personal separation of the couple, the wife is entitled to an undivided share of the property, which is as much her own as if the property had been conveyed to her and her husband as joint tenants.

Now, turning to the consent of 1888, I think that it is clear that it only relates to alimony, the costs of suit, and the claims arising in, or connected with, the action. I agree that it substitutes for alimony the benefits conferred on the wife by its terms, and the wife could not afterwards claim from her husband alimony, or anything in the nature of alimony – in other words, money for her subsistence. As the deed purports in its recitals to be the deed stipulated for in the consent, I am disposed to think that it goes no farther; but, even if I were to accept Mr. Samuels' construction that it releases all her rights in her husband's property, including the rights she would have therein if he were to die intestate, it certainly does not give him anything that is her own. But if I am to accept the plaintiff's evidence, the property acquired during coverture belongs to the two jointly. Her share thereof belongs to her just as his share belongs to him; and what she seeks for in her suit is a separation of goods, and an ascertainment of her share of the acquired property. I am satisfied that this right, if it exists under the law of Argentina, has not been affected by the consent or deed; and if, in ignorance of that law, I were to prevent the matter from being decided by a Court that is acquainted with it, I might be doing serious injustice to a lady who, as far as I can see, has done nothing calculated in law or morals to forfeit her rights, whatever they may be.

Notes and Questions

1. What difference would it have made if the "contract" between the parties had been made outside Ireland? Or there was no property owned by the parties in Ireland?
2. Why was the doctrine of laches not applied in this case? See further, p.27, *post*.
3. See further on the maxim "Equity acts *in personam*," *Irish Land Law*, para. 3.044 *et seq*. See also *C. & A. Modes* v. *C. & A. (Waterford) Ltd.*, p.153, *post*.

III. EQUITABLE REMEDIES ARE DISCRETIONARY

CONLON V. MURRAY

[1958] N.I. 17 (Court of Appeal)

The facts are set out in Black L.J.'s judgment.

Lord Macdermott L.C.J.: I have read the judgment which Black L.J. is about to deliver and I am in agreement with him.

Black L.J.: This is an appeal by the plaintiff Patrick Conlon from the dismissal by Curran J. on July 30, 1956, of an action in which the plaintiff claimed specific performance of an agreement in writing dated May 26, 1954, by which one Mary Sheridan agreed to sell to the plaintiff for the sum of £2,000 the farm on which she lived situated at Ballinarea in the southern part of Co. Armagh. Mary Sheridan died on September 22, 1955, and the action was continued against James Murray and Peter Murray her executors.

At the time of signing the agreement Mary Sheridan was about 69 years of age. According to the evidence of her medical attendant, Dr O'Reilly, which was not challenged, her eyesight had been troubling her. She had had an operation on her left eye which necessitated the use of glasses and in her right eye she had no sight at all owing to glaucoma which is associated with increasing pressure of fluid in the eye. This condition was acute and according to Dr. O'Reilly was probably quite painful. Dr. O'Reilly saw her on May 24, 1954. She then also complained of bleeding from the womb. That suggested to Dr. O'Reilly the probability of something malignant and he arranged for her to be treated by a specialist gynaecologist. She was seen by the specialist at Newry Hospital on June 1, she was admitted to the hospital on June 7, and her womb was removed on June 18. She was discharged from hospital on July 14, and readmitted on July 18, with an acute urinary infection. She was allowed home on the 1 or 2 August, but entered a nursing home on August 6, where she remained until her death on September 22, 1955. Dr. O'Reilly says that in May 1954 her uterus trouble was fairly advanced and that it would be distressing with constant bleeding and general weakness due to carcinoma. She was ill and was generally weak but was mentally alert at any time he saw her apart from the effect of drugs given to relieve her pain.

Mrs. Sheridan had a brother called Patrick Toner who had sold his own farm in 1953 and had come to live with her in the house on her farm. He was a man somewhat addicted to drink and had become rather a trial to Mrs. Sheridan. It appears that on May 24, 1954, the same day as she had been seen by Dr. O'Reilly, Mrs. Sheridan arrived sometime between 4.30 p.m. and 6 p.m. at the house of a Mr. Michael Sheridan. She had had a row that day with her brother and according to Michael Sheridan's daughter Miss Mary Sheridan, a trained nurse, she was not terribly distressed, but when she arrived she was slightly distressed but settled down. Mrs. Sheridan asked Miss Mary Sheridan would she go when it got dark to Cullyhannna and get her brother's car and take Mrs. Sheridan to the house of her sister Mrs. Murray. Miss Mary Sheridan cycled over to Cullyhanna but was unable to get her brother's car as he had the engine down cleaning it. She then went to Mrs. Murray's house and they both came over to Mr. Michael Sheridan's house on their bicycles. When they arrived there about 10.30 p.m. Mrs. Sheridan was missing and Mrs. Murray went out to look for her. Mrs. Murray found Mrs. Sheridan in one of her own fields going in the direction of her own home with no coat or hat. They came up to the road where they met a man called Bernard Collins who plays a not unimportant part in the case and had a conversation with him. Eventually Mrs. Sheridan agreed to go back home to Mrs. Murray's house – a distance of 3 miles away – where they arrived about 1.30 a.m. Collins agreed that Mrs. Sheridan was worried that night and that although it was late she had no coat on.

The details of the conversation with Collins on the road on the night of Monday, May 24, are in dispute. According to Collins' own story Mrs. Sheridan said that she had had a dispute with her brother Paddy and that he had thrown a bucket of water round her. Collins then, according to his story, advised her to go and live with Mrs. Murray and to put up the farm for sale and asked her if she would be willing to take £2,000 for the farm, and if so, he would try to get her a customer. Mrs. Sheridan, according to Collins, said that she would indeed be willing to take £2,000 and would give Collins a good shakehand and the purchaser a good luckpenny. Collins said that he himself meant to be the customer for the farm but when he saw his wife he decided not to buy and then thought of the plaintiff Patrick Conlon as a possible purchaser. Accordingly, Collins sought to get in touch with the plaintiff next day (Tuesday, May 25). The plaintiff, however, was at Ardee Fair but Collins left a message for him and the plaintiff went over to the Collins' house about 7 p.m. As a result they went over to Mrs. Murray's house to interview Mrs. Sheridan. This was quite late at night. Collins says about 11 p.m. Collins apparently got there first and went up to see Mrs. Sheridan who was in bed. According to his account Mrs. Sheridan was at first averse to selling to Conlon on personal grounds but ultimately said that Conlon's money was as good as any other man's, that she was getting a good price and it was no odds who got it. Conlon was then brought up to the bedroom and according to him Mrs. Sheridan and he agreed to the sale of the farm for £2,000. There was then some discussion about getting a solicitor to draw up the agreement. Mrs. Sheridan stipulated that she wanted her own solicitor Mr. O'Connor of Crossmaglen. It is agreed that on the night of May 25 there was no talk of Conlon getting vacant possession of the lands or what was to be done about Mrs. Sheridan's brother being in the house.

No time was wasted about getting the agreement reduced to writing. On the morning of Wednesday, May 26, Gerard Conlon a brother of the plaintiff, went into Crossmaglen for Mr. O'Connor. Unfortunately Mr. O'Connor was in Dublin that day but his managing clerk Mr. Carahar was in the office and was apprised that his services were required for the purpose of drawing an agreement for the sale of a farm. Apparently there was no question of waiting until Mr. O'Connor himself should be available. Gerard Conlon got a taxi and drove out with Mr. Carahar to Mrs. Murray's at Cullyhanna, stopping by arrangement about 20 yards past the house. The plaintiff was already there in the kitchen of Mrs. Murray's house. Mr. Carahar was shown up to Mrs. Sheridan's bedroom. Up till then Mr. Cararhar had not seen the plaintiff although apparently even up to the trial he was under the impression that the man who had called for him and had taken him out in the taxi was not a brother of the plaintiff but the plaintiff himself. At Mrs. Sheridan's bedside Mr. Carahar proceeded to draft the agreement upon the information given to him by Mrs. Sheridan who was sitting up in bed propped up by pillows. Carahar says that he pointed out to Mrs. Sheridan what was to happen to her when she had disposed of her home and she replied that she could live anywhere. Mr. Carahar did not appear clear for whom he was supposed to be acting when he was drafting the agreement. He had been brought out to Mrs. Murray's house by an emissary of the plaintiff's and although Mrs. Sheridan in the past had been a client of Mr. O'Connor's Mr. Carahar had not been informed that he was to be regarded as acting on her behalf. There would seem little doubt, however, but that Mrs. Sheridan regarded Mr. O'Connor as her solicitor and had asked for him for that reason and accordingly would consider Carahar as looking after her interests in the matter. Mr. Carahar says that Mrs. Sheridan did not ask for any advice, that he pointed out she was disposing of her home, that she told him she had got a good price for it and that he did not suggest that an auction might bring a better price. Mr. Carahar says his state of mind was that he might be acting for both parties and thought it his duty to look after both Conlon's and Mrs. Sheridan's interests. Conlon conveyed to Mr. Carahar that he wanted the contract signed there and then. And Conlon paid for the taxi.

The real difficulty in drafting the agreement was in regard to giving possession of the farm. What was to be done about Toner? Mr. Carahar says that he told Mrs. Sheridan that she should get her brother to leave as it was her duty to give clear possession and that she did not dispute that but said that she had rather not take proceedings against him. Mr. Carahar says she meant that she would rather the purchaser did it and that she said there would be no trouble with her brother. She believed he would leave when asked and she instructed Mr. Carahar to write him immediately informing him of the sale and asking him to leave. Mr. Carahar then apparently added Clause 9 of the agreement which reads: "The said Mary Sheridan agrees to take all steps necessary to evict said Patrick Toner if he refuses to leave said dwellinghouse and to pay costs of same." Mr. Carahar says that he did not speak to Conlon before he put in this clause and that he put it in to protect Conlon. In so doing Mr. Carahar was, of course, acting in Conlon's interest though it is tolerably clear that Mrs. Sheridan was looking upon him as acting on her behalf. In view of the circumstances and of what were obviously Mrs. Sheridan's strong feelings in the matter I think that if an independent solicitor had been acting upon behalf of Mrs. Sheridan he would have struggled hard to negotiate a modification of this clause. Mr. O'Connor himself frankly says that he would agree that in this aspect of the matter she would require independent legal advice and says that he would have taken proper instructions and advised her and such advice would be independent of any obligation to the purchaser.

Mr. Carahar says that he read the agreement to Mrs. Sheridan and she approved it. He then brought Conlon into the room and read it over again in his presence and he approved and said he was paying £500 deposit which he paid then and there in cash.

Conlon's account of the transaction is substantially different. He says that Mr. Carahar called him up to Mrs. Sheridan's bedroom after he had part of an agreement drawn up, that the clause about possession had not yet been inserted, that next they talked about possession of the house and Carahar asked him would he take it on him to put Toner out of the house. Conlon says he said "No" as he earned the first shilling he ever earned with Paddy Toner and he would not be the man to put him out, that Mr. Carahar then said to Mrs. Sheridan "You see the situation now?" and that he, Conlon, then said he wasn't putting him out and the deal was off. Conlon says that Mrs. Sheridan then said: "Seeing you won't put him out Paddy, I'll have to put him out," and she proposed that if Conlon put him out she would bear the expenses. Conlon says he would not agree, so she agreed she would put him out in her own name.

Whether Carahar's account of this matter or the plaintiff's is the true one I have no means of knowing. Both were called as witnesses for the plaintiff. On another point, where the plaintiff's evidence differed from Carahar's, Curran J., who had the advantage of seeing the witnesses, roundly held that he was satisfied that the plaintiff was not telling the truth. But he did not find it necessary in his judgment to assess where the truth lies on any other particular point.

It is obvious from Mr. O'Connor's evidence as regards his visit to Mrs. Sheridan on May 31 that Mrs. Sheridan fully appreciated that she had entered into an agreement to sell the farm to Conlon and that she was to put her brother out. This was apparently the term of the agreement that she particularly objected to and the term which on May 31 she felt to impose particular hardship on her.

The remedy of specific performance still retains the character of an equitable remedy. It is not granted as of right but is a discretionary remedy which may be withheld in cases of a type where the court, having regard to the conduct of the parties and all the circumstances of the case, considers in its discretion that the remedy ought not to be granted. This discretion is not, of course, the arbitrary discretion of the individual judge but is a discretion to be exercised on the principles which have been worked out in a multitude of decided cases. And it is well established that there is a class of cases in which a contract may be such and entered into in such conditions that the court will not order it to be rescinded but, at the same time, looking to the substantial justice of the case, will not order it to be specifically performed. It follows naturally, as observed in Kerr on Fraud and Mistake, 7th ed. (1952) p. 568, that when the aid of a court is sought by way of specific performance of a contract the principles of ethics have a more extensive sway than when a contract is sought to be rescinded.

In the present case Mrs. Sheridan was 69 years of age and, although admitted to be mentally alert and vigorous, was suffering from two painful and weakening ailments. It is not surprising that after the trouble with her brother she should have an impulse to get rid of the responsibility of the house and the farm and express a readiness to sell it. This might prove a mere transitory mood or it might not. But the idea of selling the farm raised questions requiring deliberation and reflection. If the treatment which she might have to undergo was successful (and for all that she then knew it might have been) where was she to go to live when she came out of hospital? And what was to happen to her brother? Where was he to go to live if the farm was sold? Both of these were matters which required thoughtful and anxious consideration. But neither seems to have been mentioned or considered when the bargain was made in Mrs. Sheridan's bedroom on the night of May 25 and, whether one accepts Carahar's evidence or Conlon's, the question of what was to happen to the brother was not even raised until the agreement was actually being drafted by Carahar on the morning of May 26. The truth of the matter seems to be that in her plight on the night of May 24 the plaintiff impulsively accepted Collins' suggestion that she should sell her farm and that Collins and Conlon both recognised that this mood might well prove to be a transitory one and that if Conlon was to get the farm it behoved them to obtain Mrs. Sheridan's signature to a document without delay. Conlon seems to have first heard of the opportunity from Collins about 7 o'clock on the evening of May 25, and at 11 p.m. on the same evening – a peculiar hour for legitimate business – they visit Mrs. Sheridan in her bedroom and the bargain is made for the sale of the farm to Conlon at £2,000 – the figure mentioned by Collins the previous night – without any higgling or negotiation and without any mention of when possession would be given or that it would be necessary to put Toner out. Then on the next morning Mr. Carahar is brought out in a taxi paid for by Mr. Conlon to draft the necessary agreement. The reason why Mr. Carahar is brought is because Mrs. Sheridan regards Mr. O'Connor as her solicitor. But conceiving himself as being there as much in the interests of Mr. Conlon as of Mrs. Sheridan he inserts on his own volition (if his evidence on this point is to be accepted) a special clause in the agreement for the benefit of Conlon. I quite appreciate that specific performance of a contract will not be refused on the sole ground that one of the parties had not legal advice. A man can enter into a binding contract without having his solicitor at his elbow. But as Mr. O'Connor observed in his evidence, Mrs. Sheridan should have had independent legal advice in a transaction of this kind. And quite apart from any other consideration the way in which Mrs. Sheridan's expression of her willingness to sell the farm was jumped at by Collins and Conlon and the extraordinary and unexplained haste with which the transaction was rushed through raise of themselves such a degree of suspicion as would lead a court of Equity to be hesitant about granting specific performance of a contract concluded in such circumstances.

It was argued on behalf of the plaintiff that cases in which equity refuses the remedy of specific performance fall within one or other of certain defined categories. I cannot accept this view. Certainly equity acts on certain broad and ascertained principles but it has always refused to be forced into rigid categories. This is, I think, well stated in Story's Equity Jurisprudence 10th ed. (1870), vol. 1, p. 739: "In truth the exercise of this whole branch of equity jurisprudence respecting the rescission and specific performance of contracts is not a matter of right in either party; but it is a matter in the discretion of the Court, not indeed of arbitrary or capricious discretion, dependent upon the mere pleasure of the judge, but of that sound and reasonable discretion which governs itself so far as it may by general principles; but at the same time which withholds or grants relief according to the circumstances of each particular case, when these rules and principles will not furnish any exact measure of justice between the parties. On this account it is not possible to lay down any rules and principles which are of absolute obligation and authority in all cases; and, therefore, it would be a waste of time to attempt to limit the principles, or the exceptions, which the complicated transactions of the parties and the everchanging habits of society may at different times and under different circumstances require the Court to recognise or consider." A good instance of a case which it would be found difficult to fit into any of the suggested categories in which specific performance will be refused is the case *Twining* v. *Morrice* (1788) 2 Bro. C.C. 326 referred to in the course of the hearing.

I am accordingly of opinion that Curran J's judgment refusing the plaintiff's claim for specific performance should be affirmed.

Sheil J.: I have found this case a very difficult one, one which is very near the border line, but after full consideration I am not prepared to differ from the conclusions at which my Lords have arrived.

Notes and Questions

1. Upon what ground did the Court refuse specific performance? Was it one of the well-known defences to such a suit? See further ch. 6, *post.*

2. See further on the discretionary nature of equitable remedies, *Irish Land Law,* paras. 3.050-51. See also *Smelter Corporation of Ireland Ltd.* v. *O'Driscoll,* p.157, *post.*

IV. DELAY DEFEATS EQUITY

McCAUSLAND V. YOUNG
[1949] N.I. 49 (Court of Appeal)

The facts are set out in the judgments.

Andrews L.C.J.: The facts of this case and the circumstances under which proceedings were instituted have been so fully dealt with in the exhaustive judgment of Black J., from whose order the appeal has been brought to this court, that I propose to dispense with any general recital of facts, and shall confine my introductory words to a brief reference to the terms of that order and of the notice of appeal and cross-notice which are before us.

That order, dated the 8th March, 1948, declared that in the events which have happened the plaintiff, Connolly Robert McCausland (to whom, for the sake of brevity, I shall hereinafter refer as "Connolly McCausland") is precluded from contending that the provisions of clause 15 contained in the indenture of re-settlement of the 4th August, 1927, do not apply to or affect his life estate in the properties comprised in that settlement, and that in so far as the said provisions purport to affect his life estate in the said properties, they are to be regarded as valid and effective. By the said order it is further declared that as from the 3rd May, 1940, the hereditaments and premises and capital monies comprised in the said re-settlement are to be treated during the remainder of the life of Connolly McCausland as being held to the uses and upon the trusts and subject to the powers and provisions to and upon and subject to which the same would have stood limited and settled by virtue of the said re-settlement if Connolly McCausland were dead without issue. A further declaration provided that the said clause 15 is not binding on the plaintiff Marcus Edgcumbe McCausland (the eldest son of Connolly McCausland) or any person entitled in remainder to him under the limitations contained in the said re-settlement. The order also provided that the re-settlement be rectified in accordance with the foregoing declarations; and further declared that the provisions of clause 15 do not apply to the jointure rent-charge appointed to the plaintiff Margaret Louisa McCausland (in the event of her surviving her husband Connolly McCausland) by the marriage settlement of the 6th June, 1932.

The first notice of appeal from this order, bearing date the 8th June, 1948, was served on behalf of the defendant, Charles Norman Stronge (surviving trustee of the said indenture of re-settlement) for an order that the judgment and declarations be varied in so far as they fail to adjudge and declare that Connolly McCausland was and is in all events bound by clause 15, and that the foregoing declaration as to how the hereditaments, premises and moneys should be treated during the remainder of the life of Connolly McCausland be varied by expunging therefrom the words limiting such declaration to such period; that the declaration that clause 15 is not binding on the plaintiff Marcus Edgcumbe McCausland or any person entitled in remainder to him be reversed, and that in lieu thereof it be declared that the said plaintiff and any such persons so entitled in remainder are bound by the said clause 15; that the order that the said re-settlement be rectified be set aside; that the declaration in reference to the jointure rent-charge be reversed and set aside; that it be declared that clause 15 is valid, effective and binding upon the plaintiffs and each of them; and that the learned judge's direction as to costs be varied as in said notice mentioned. The grounds of appeal expressed briefly were that the declarations were against evidence and the weight of evidence, and were wrong in law.

A fortnight later than the said notice of appeal, a cross-notice of appeal, dated the 23rd June, 1948, was served, in which Connolly McCausland sought a variation of the learned judge's order:–

(1) by striking out the declarations –
  (a) as to Connolly McCausland being precluded from contending that the provisions of clause 15 did not apply to or affect his life estate; and
  (b) that in so far as the said provisions purport to affect his life estate they are to

be regarded as valid; and

(c) as to how the hereditaments, premises and moneys were to be treated during the remainder of Connolly McCausland's life; and

(2) by deleting the order that the re-settlement be rectified in accordance with such declarations.

The said notice of appeal further asked that it might be declared that notwithstanding clause 15 Connolly McCausland is now and has always been entitled to the estate for his life limited to him, and that said clause 15 is not binding on him; and for an order that the said re-settlement be rectified accordingly. The said notice of appeal also contained an intimation on behalf of Connolly McCausland and his said son Marcus that they would contend that clause 15 is – (a) void for uncertainty; (b) void as contrary to public policy; and (c) not binding on them or either of them or on any person entitled in remainder. There followed in this notice of appeal an alternative prayer in the following terms: "That, otherwise as aforesaid, the respondents will contend that the order appealed from is correct and should stand affirmed, including the rectification ordered in accordance with the declaration that the said clause 15 is not binding on the respondent Marcus Edgcumbe McCausland or any person entitled in remainder to him under the limitations contained in the said re-settlement." Though nothing was heard of this alternative prayer in the notice of appeal during the course of the arguments which occupied eleven days in our court, its presence in the notice was not without significance. In this connection I would add that all the other parties served with the notices of appeal, with the exception of the trustee, expressed through their counsel, at the opening of the appeal, their willingness to abide by the order of Black J., and took no part in the hearing in this court.

The first submission which was pressed upon us by Connolly McCausland's counsel was that the so-called religion or forfeiture clause (No. 15) of the re-settlement of the 4th August, 1927, is void for uncertainty; and, secondly, it was contended that it is void as being contrary to public policy. Whilst these are separate and distinct issues, yet are they somewhat analogous; and for that reason it appears to me that they may be conveniently grouped, and to a certain limited extent considered together.

The material words of the forfeiture clause are as follows:– "If any person hereby made tenant for life or tenant in tail by purchase of the settled freeholds shall become a Roman Catholic or profess that he or she is of the Roman Catholic religion then and so often as the same shall happen the settled freeholds shall go and remain to the uses upon the trusts and subject to the powers and provisions upon and subject to which the same would have stood limited and settled by virtue of these presents if such person were dead without issue."

It was upon the words "shall become a Roman Catholic or profess that he or she is of the Roman Catholic religion" that the attack on this branch of the case was directed. It was argued that the meaning of these words is so uncertain that it cannot be ascertained with the requisite degree of definiteness. Some standard, it was said, must be available and applied in order to determine if any person has become a Roman Catholic. To be legally binding, it was argued, the clause which defeats on a contingency a vested estate must be such that the court may be able to appreciate from the beginning its meaning and significance: see the speech of Lord Cranworth in *Clavering* v. *Ellison* (1859) 7 H.L.C. 707, 725. Reliance was also placed on the words to the like effect of Parker J. in *In re Sandbrook* [1912] 2 Ch. 471, 477, that conditions subsequent, in order to defeat vested estates, or cause a forfeiture, must be such that from the moment of their creation the court can say with reasonable certainty in what events the forfeiture will occur. In other words, the court must be able to say with certainty when and in what circumstances the clause will become operative and the forfeiture will be worked. The test, it was submitted, is not what Connolly McCausland or his father thought was the meaning of "Roman Catholic." Is it to be the meaning which would be assigned to it by a member of the general public or by a canonist? The settlor has failed to provide the test. Again, it was asked, may a beneficiary under the trust "become a Roman Catholic" by gradual process, or can he only become such by a ceremony of reception into the Church? Further, what is meant by the word "profess" – a word which, it was contended, is most ambiguous. No limits of "profession" it was argued are prescribed by the settlor. What must its degree be? Must it be by words, or may it be by conduct? And, if by words, to whom must the profession or affirmation of adherence to the Roman Catholic religion be made?

Such are the doubts and difficulties which, it was contended in argument, render clause 15 of the deed uncertain and unenforceable; and in support of these contentions the plaintiffs produced as witnesses two eminent Doctors of Divinity and authorities on the canon law, Dr. William Conway, of Maynooth, and Dr. Arthur Ryan, of The Queen's University of Belfast, the submission being that the issues of fact raised in the forfeiture clause could only be determined by the law and practice of the Roman Catholic Church. They were, indeed, able exponents of the case which they were presenting; but, having given it my most careful consideration, I am forced to the conclusion that their evidence is not of any real assistance to the plaintiffs' case. In expressing this opinion I am not unmindful of the admission made by Dr. Ryan to the learned Attorney-General in cross-examination that "when you find in a document a phrase 'Roman Catholic' or 'Roman Catholic religion' it is not a phrase taken from the canon law of the Church; and in searching for a meaning you will not get any assistance from the canon law." If this be so, one naturally asks why have recourse to them or seek their aid? Why not interpret the words as, what Black J. calls, "an ordinary English phrase"? Why should they not bear the meaning in which they would naturally be used by the settlor – the meaning assigned to them in ordinary every-day speech? It is evidence such as that given by Dr. Conway and Dr. Ryan which, if accepted, would be calculated, as was doubtless intended, to create doubts where in my opinion there were really none. It is the words of the settlor, not of the canonist, which we are called upon to construe ; and in my opinion it would be entirely wrong of us if we were to interpret the words of the settlor by reference to criteria of the canon law with which he was in all probability quite unfamiliar. In this connection I may say that I am impressed by the words of Gavan Duffy P. in *In re McKenna* [1947] I.R. 277, that a Protestant farmer testator knew what he meant, and practically every citizen in every walk of life, be he Catholic or Protestant, knew the meaning conveyed, by the words "marry a Roman Catholic"; and the learned President added that he had only to construe the plain words used by a plain man in a sense plain to all of us. This, in my view, is common sense, which I am not prepared to hold in the present case to be in conflict with any settled principles of law.

The clause, when examined, is found to contain two alternatives, in either of which event the forfeiture operates. I entirely agree with Black J. when he says that the first of these "shall become a Roman Catholic" must be taken as referring to a person who had previously not been a Roman Catholic, but had come to embrace that religion; and that the second "profess that he or she is of the Roman Catholic religion" was intended to cover a case where a person had always been a Roman Catholic, or where there was a doubt whether the person so professing had been formally accepted into the Roman Catholic Church. Greater width of meaning must be given to the words of this composite clause, with its two limbs thus disjunctively expressed, than would be possible had they been, as in *Clayton* v. *Ramsden* [1943] A.C. 320, expressed in conjunctive form. The clause was in my opinion designedly drafted in this wide form so as to embrace within its scope everyone of the character mentioned in it, who, whether by formal or ceremonial admission to the Roman Catholic Church or otherwise, accepted the authority of the Roman Catholic Church.

Black J. has referred to several cases in which it does not appear to have been even suggested that conditions working a forfeiture in the event of a legatee becoming a Roman Catholic were void. I need not repeat them here. Suffice it to say that it is only recently, as it appears to me, that such an argument could be advanced with any hope of success. One might also refer to statutory enactments such as the Act of Settlement, 1701 (12 & 13 W. 3, c.2), in which similar, if not in all cases, identical, language has been employed by Parliament, and is thus part of the accepted public law of our country. How, I ask, can it be said that such words have no defined meaning?

In these circumstances the plaintiffs mainly based their case on the issue in its legal aspect upon two recent authoritative decisions. The first is *Sifton* v. *Sifton* [1938] A.C. 656, in which the provision that payments were to be made only so long as the testator's daughter should continue to reside in Canada was held to be a condition subsequent which was void for uncertainty upon Lord Cranworth's principle in *Clavering* v. *Ellison* (1859) 7 H.L.C. 707, the words "to reside in Canada" being regarded as uncertain and ambiguous in meaning owing to the elasticity of the word "residence," and the fact that the testator had clearly intended that his daughter should be at liberty to leave Canada for some purposes and periods undefined. To attempt to define precisely or distinctly the events that would constitute a ceasing "to reside in Canada" would necessarily end in failure. This case, so different in its facts from the present, is, as it appears to me, only of importance in the present case because of its approval and application of Lord Cranworth's principle, with the addition that the events referred to in the condition should be apparent not only to the court but also to the parties concerned: (see the opinion of Lord Romer) [1938] A.C. at 675.

The second case, so strongly relied upon by the plaintiffs, is *Clayton* v. *Ramsden* [1943] A.C. 320, which bears a closer resemblance on its facts to the present, yet in my opinion there are important and vital differences. In it a condition of forfeiture applied if the testator's daughter should at any time after his death marry a person "not of Jewish parentage and of the Jewish faith." The House of Lords held that this was one composite clause, and accordingly, that there was only one condition of forfeiture and not two alternative conditions, so that the condition would be void as a whole if one limb of it were void. They further held that the first limb of the condition (as to Jewish parentage) was void for uncertainty, doubts clearly existing as to whether the words referred to race or religion or to both; and, if they referred to race, as the House thought more probable, as to what proportion of Jewish blood in the husband would satisfy the requirement that he should be of Jewish parentage. The House further considered that the second limb (as to Jewish faith) was also void for want of sufficient indication by the testator as to the requisite degree of attachment or adherence to the faith which he required on the part of his daughter's husband.

I do not regard these cases as authorities which govern the present case. The clause which we are considering is not composite in the sense of constituting only one single condition of defeasance. Forfeiture arises if the party concerned either becomes a Roman Catholic *or* professes that he or she is of the Roman Catholic religion. I do not regard the first limb of this condition as in any way more uncertain than was the condition in *In re Evans* [1940] Ch. 629, in which the relevant words were "become a convert to the Roman Catholic religion," where it was held that the baptism into the Roman Catholic Church of a person becoming a convert to the Roman Catholic religion was an act which the court could ascertain with certainty and which would, in a proper case, create a forfeiture. In this connection, I may say, it was not surprising to find that the plaintiff Connolly McCausland admitted in cross-examination that he thought both he and his father knew in 1927 what was meant by the words "Roman Catholic."

But, even if I am wrong in the view which I have expressed, I am quite unable to appreciate the existence of any element of doubt or uncertainty in whether a person "professes" that he or she is of the Roman Catholic religion. It is a question of fact – a purely subjective act or pronouncement – as to which, I may say again, it is admitted that no doubt exists in the mind of the plaintiff Connolly McCausland. I fully appreciate that the test as to the validity and binding character of the clause does not rest on the knowledge and appreciation of its meaning by the individual; but, when the individual is one so vitally interested as Connolly McCausland, I cannot think that such considerations are wholly irrelevant. However this may be, I am clearly of opinion that the forfeiture clause in the re-settlement of the 4th August, 1927, satisfies the most exacting requirements of Fry J. in *In re Viscount Exmouth* (1883) 23 Ch.D. 158, 164, as to clarity and certainty of expression in the creation of the limitation, and also in its operation; and that it is also consonant with judicial dicta in the later cases to which I have referred. The argument contra is that the term "profess" may have many degrees; and that it may not always be possible to state with accuracy and certainty what words or deeds would clearly amount to a "profession." In my clear opinion, any one who openly accepts the authority of the Roman Catholic Church in religious matters may reasonably and properly be said to "profess that he is of the Roman Catholic religion." The possibility of a difficulty of proof arising in an individual case will not render a condition void if it is clear, distinct and certain in itself. This second limb of the clause is of greater width and scope than the first, and so embraces a larger class, to which, in my opinion, the tests, conditions and requirements imposed by the canon law have no application.

I pass now to the contention that clause 15 is void as being against public policy. I hope I am doing the plaintiffs' counsel no injustice when I say that I did not understand this submission to be strongly pressed in our court. Thus, whilst *In re Borwick* [1933] Ch. 657 was cited, *In re Tegg* [1936] 2 All E R. 878, which was apparently relied upon before Black J., was not opened. I am in full agreement with Black J. in all that he says on this issue. The principle underlying these decisions was that the condition which was held to be void operated to interfere with the free exercise of the parent's duty in regard to the religious instruction or upbringing of his children, or that it was a fetter upon the beneficiary's free discretion as to what was best for the welfare and education of the beneficiary's children. This principle was referred to by Parker J. in *In re Sandbrook* [1912] 2 Ch. 471, 476, 477, in which he cited a passage from Sheppard's "Touchstone" at p. 132, that a condition is bad which operates to restrain or forbid a man from doing his duty. In *Borwick's case* [1933] Ch. 657 the condition against any of the settlor's grandchildren becoming a Roman Catholic was intended to operate during minority, i.e., before the attainment of a vested interest at twenty-one. In *In re Tegg* [1936] 2 All E.R. 878 the condition was to operate during the infancy of the children of the testator's daughter. The present case is entirely different in this respect; for, as Black J. points out, the condition is only to operate if the individual does a certain positive act, namely, becomes a Roman Catholic or professes the Roman Catholic religion; and such cases as *In re May* [1917] 2 Ch. 126, *In re May* [1932] 1 Ch. 99, and *Patton* v. *Toronto General Trusts Corporation* [1930] A.C. 629 clearly establish that in such circumstances the court, unless compelled by the express terms of the clause, will not hold the doing of the act by the beneficiary to work a forfeiture until he has reached an age, namely twenty-one years, when he can exercise a free and a real choice of his own. It is not unimportant to note that in the second of the two reported cases of *In re May* [1932] 1 Ch. 99 above cited, the contention that the condition was contrary to public policy was abandoned in the Court of Appeal; and, further, that in neither of the cases was the argument advanced that the words "shall not be a Roman Catholic" or "shall cease to be a Roman Catholic" were so uncertain or indefinite in meaning as in themselves to render the condition void. For the reasons above stated I hold that clause 15 in the re-settlement of the 4th August, 1927, cannot be declared void on the ground that it is contrary to public policy.

My next enquiry in this difficult case passes to a consideration of the submission made on behalf of the plaintiffs, which is collected from several paragraphs of the statement of claim, that clause 15 was inserted in the re-settlement without the knowledge or approval of Connolly McCausland, and without his having independent advice; and that the deed was executed by him under a misrepresentation as to its contents. This submission of fact is followed by the further submission of law that in such circumstances the deed of re-settlement must be rectified by the striking out or omission of the clause from the deed.

I shall first consider the question of fact, though not in every relevant detail, for that would be impracticable if this judgment is to be confined to reasonable limits. But certain facts of paramount importance appear to me to stand out as either admitted or as clearly established in evidence. To these I must refer.

The plaintiff, Connolly McCausland, came of age on the 11th July, 1927. Educated at Eton, he went to Sandhurst in the autumn of 1925, and from there obtained a commission in the Irish Guards on the 29th January, 1927. Joining his regiment a fortnight later, he was not at home until some months after his twenty-first birthday. He states in his evidence that his father had not discussed the family property with him, and that he did not know how it was held; that his father was a Low-Churchman, but a strong and convinced supporter of the Church of Ireland; and that he, Connolly, was gradually becoming a "Higher and Higher Churchman," and his father knew it. He sums up the position in the words "we were never in agreement on these matters."

The proposal for a re-settlement of the family property (which was at the time held under a deed of re-settlement of the 9th August, 1897, by which Connolly McCausland's father, Maurice Marcus McCausland, was tenant for life and Connolly McCausland was tenant in tail male in remainder) was first made in a letter written by the father to the son about the month of March or April, 1927. Unfortunately, the letter is not forthcoming, and we know nothing of its contents save as stated by Connolly McCausland, in his evidence – that it would be necessary to re-settle the property when he, Connolly McCausland, came of age; and that he, the father, would go over to England and talk about it which he, in fact, did in July, 1927. Connolly McCausland fixes the date of the visit by saying that his father was in London on his twenty-first birthday, i.e., the 11th July, 1927; and this is fully confirmed by Mr. Ingram's letter to Mr. Longfield of the 5th July, from which it appears that he left on the 4th July and would not return till after the 12th. Connolly McCausland's account of the interview (and unfortunately owing to his father's death on the 14th January, 1938, we have no other account of it) is that his father told him of the necessity for a deed of re-settlement and for a disentailing deed, and that Mr. Ingram, the family solicitor, and a cousin by marriage of the father, would send the necessary deeds and instructions. Connolly McCausland further states that his father said that he had settled with his father in the same way; and, accordingly, he, Connolly McCausland, gathered it was a thing which was done between most fathers and sons when a son came of age. He declares that he did not know what his rights were under the previous settlement, and that his father did not convey to him what the effect would be. He adds that his father emphasised the importance of signing the deed when it was sent across without delay, because, as he puts it, "of some stamp duty which would expire fairly soon."

Such is Connolly McCausland's recollection of this all-important interview as detailed in his evidence. Its accuracy and sufficiency are, of course, challenged by the learned Attorney-General on behalf of Sir Norman Stronge, the sole surviving trustee of the re-settlement of the 4th August 1927. The Attorney-General rests his contention on this point in a large measure upon the fact that when Mr. Ingram stated in his letter of 3rd October, 1940, to Connolly McCausland that he had at the time "concurred" with his father's intentions and wishes, Connolly McCausland left this letter unanswered. To me it is a complete answer to this omission that on receipt of the letter he immediately got leave and went to Londonderry to see Mr. Ingram, with whom he had an interview on the 9th October, when he asserted, as appears in Mr. Ingram's office entry, that he had never heard of the religion clause in the re-settlement of 1927 till the terms of his own marriage settlement were being discussed in 1932, and that he did not realise then that a forfeiture would affect his family.

The Attorney-General's argument, however, necessitates a closer examination of the contemporaneous entries in Mr. Ingram's records as the only evidence, other than Connolly McCausland's, which is available; for unfortunately Mr. Ingram died in May, 1943. These records show that on the 15th June, 1927, Mr. Ingram had an attendance on the father, Maurice Marcus McCausland, and had discussed with him the terms of the proposed re-settlement, a copy of which he sent to him later on the same day, together with a covering letter in which he called attention to the fact that certain matters, including "the proposed condition as to religion," were not dealt with in the draft, as he proposed instructing counsel to draw the additional clauses which would be necessary to give effect to his, Maurice Marcus McCausland's intentions. There was a further attendance by Mr. Ingram on Maurice Marcus McCausland on the following day, going through the draft re-settlement and advising; and on the same day instructions were sent by Mr. Ingram to the well-known conveyancing counsel, Mr. Longfield – then in semi-retirement – to settle draft disentailing deeds and re-settlement. These instructions purported to have been sent on behalf of both the father, Maurice Marcus, and the plaintiff Connolly McCausland, though there is not a particle of evidence to show that at the time Connolly McCausland had ever been consulted about or informed as to the contents of the draft deeds. The instructions contained an intimation that it was desired that certain clauses should be drafted by counsel and inserted in the re-settlement. One of these (No.3) was expressed in the following terms:- "It is suggested that a clause might be inserted in the re-settlement providing that if any person benefiting under the limitations in the re-settlement shall become a Roman Catholic such benefit shall cease and the property go over to the next in remainder. Counsel will please draft such a clause for the consideration of querists."

It was the 21st July before Mr. Ingram received back the draft deed from Mr. Longfield, with a covering letter of the 19th July, in a postscript to which he said that "a clause shifting the investments if one of the takers changes his or her religion, etc., is very difficult to draw, but I will attempt it of course while you are having the drafts copied." This was followed by a further letter from Mr. Longfield of the 26th July, in the course of which he wrote: "I have settled as you requested a draft of a shifting clause, designed to prevent a person who is or becomes a Roman Catholic from enjoying the settled property. These provisions are unusual, and I am rather against their insertion as they often lead to costly litigation." The next day, on receipt of the draft, Mr. Ingram wrote to Mr. Maurice Marcus McCausland asking for a call on the following day, and requesting him, if unable to do so, to let him know whether he approved of the clause of which he sent a copy, and if he wished to have it inserted in the deed. It does not appear that Mr. Ingram ever conveyed to Mr. McCausland counsel's opinion against the insertion of the clause in the deed, or his prophetic words as to these clauses often leading to costly litigation.

On the same day Mr. McCausland replied directing the insertion of clause 15 (1). He was obviously troubled with the meaning of clauses 15 (2) and 15 (3), but said he concluded that all these three clauses, having been drawn up by Mr. Longfield, were, "necessary and correct to carry out the instructions which he, Mr. McCausland, had given; for this view is confirmed by the further paragraph in Mr. McCausland's letter: "If you approve of them (i.e., te clauses) I am satisfied, as what I desire is that a R.C. cannot succeed to the lands or to the Trust money." Here I would observe that, if Mr. McCausland ever intended that the Protestant issue of a Roman Catholic father or grandfather should be deprived of his right of succession to the property under the re-settlement, he certainly never so expressed himself. In my opinion his instructions on the matter to counsel clearly indicated otherwise.

And so these three clauses 15 (1), 15 (2) and 15 (3) were inserted in the deed apparently without Mr. McCausland ever being informed of counsel's opinion in regard to them, and, further, and of still greater importance, without it being appreciated apparently by any one that by the inclusion of the last two words in sub-clause (1) – "without issue" – a tenant for life or in tail who brought himself within its provisions by becoming a Roman Catholic, or by professing that he or she was of that religion, not merely defeated his own interest, but also that of his issue, though such issue might themselves be Protestants. It was a much wider and more far-reaching clause than counsel had been instructed to draft, or, indeed, than counsel had himself indicated its effect to be in his letter of the 26th July; yet this, I repeat, was apparently not appreciated by either Mr. McCausland or Mr. Ingram at the time. The correspondence and office entries to which I have referred are, in my opinion, conclusive as to this.

If such be the position of the matter so far as Mr. Maurice Marcus McCausland is concerned, how much stronger is the position of the plaintiff, Connolly McCausland? Wholly apart from this last point to which I have refered, namely, the defeasance of the interests of the issue of a Roman Catholic – Connolly McCausland's evidence is to the effect that he neither heard nor knew anything about this religious clause in 1927, and that he would not have signed the deed if he had known what he knew after Mr. Ingram had explained it to him in August, 1940. The Attorney-General has asked us not to accept Connolly McCausland's evidence as to his ignorance of the clause, submitting that, as Black J. rejected his evidence in so far as it was in conflict with that of his brother-in-law Lucius Thompson, it should not be accepted on the important issue which I am now considering. I am unable to accept the Attorney-General's submission, as all the probabilities of the case appear to me to support Connolly McCausland's evidence as to his ignorance of the existence of the clause. It was not, as I have already mentioned, until the 27th July that the draft of the clause reached Mr. Ingram, and that it was decided by Mr. McCausland that it should be inserted in the deed. Prior to that the instructions to counsel, the correspondence with counsel, and the office entries had merely contained such expressions as "it is *suggested* that a clause might be inserted in the re-settlement" etc., or "the *proposed* condition as to religion." Nothing definite was decided upon until the 27th July. How then could Connolly McCausland have been informed when his father visited him in London two or three weeks earlier that the re-settlement would contain such a clause? Yet this was the only personal contact which he, Connolly McCausland, had at this time with his father about the deed. Admittedly, he never saw Mr. Ingram; and in my opinion the strongest evidence in Connolly McCausland's favour on this point is the latter's letter to him of the 4th August, addressed to him at the camp at Woking, Surrey, where he was stationed with his regiment. This letter was written at a later hour on the day upon which his father had already signed the re-settlement and the other necessary documents. This letter is referred to in Mr. Ingram's office entry as "a very long letter to Mr. C. R. McCausland informing him and explaining effect of re-settlement." It well merits the reference in the entry to its length, but I cannot say the same of the rest of the entry. It commences with words which were definitely misleading (I have no doubt unintentionally so), in which Mr. Ingram states that the re-settlement had been prepared following the general lines of the re-settlement which was executed in 1897 after his father attained age. The rest of the letter contains reference to the £400 annuity which Connolly McCausland was to receive during his father's lifetime, and to the life estate which he would receive after his father's death with remainders over. So also is mentioned the power to charge a jointure for his wife and sums for his younger children. The lands comprised in the re-settlement are referred to specifically, including those mentioned as having been purchased by his father out of his private means; and, as against this, reference is also made to the withdrawal of substantial settlement moneys. The names of the trustees are stated; the disentailing deeds and memorials are mentioned; the name of London solicitors is given at whose office the deeds could be signed; and an urgent request is made that there should be no delay as the time for stamping the documents was limited. All this is detailed and explicit. On the other hand, from beginning to end of this long letter there is not a single word about the religion clause, though such a clause was a clear departure, in a way that Connolly McCausland's father considered most material, from "the general lines" of the re-settlement of 1897. Further, there is no reference to Mr. Longfield's opinion against the insertion of such a clause. One wonders why this silence. Connolly McCausland's father was obviously concerned about the religious outlook of his son. For this very reason it was doubly important that both the existence and the legal effect of this clause should be mentioned and explained; but this was not done. With no more legal instruction in reference to the terms of the re-settlement deed than is contained in Mr. Ingram's letter, Connolly McCausland complied with the request that he should attend at the office of the London solicitors, who had still less information than Connolly McCausland had in regard to the contents of the re-settlement, the two disentailing deeds and the four memorials, which, according to Mr. Ingram's letter of the 29th July, were being sent to them in order that they might be "duly witnessed and verified." With such limited authority and instructions I am not surprised that, as Connolly McCausland stated in his evidence, no explantions were given to him by the solicitor, though he was asked if wanted to read the several documents. He tells us that he endeavoured to do so, "trying to understand them" but he "couldn't make very much of it." After two pages or so he abandoned the task and signed the deed, not knowing that such a clause was in the deed. Black J., who heard the witness give his evidence, says that he has no reason to disbelieve his account of what happened.

Whilst the instructions to counsel purported to have been sent on behalf of both Mr. Maurice Marcus McCausland and Connolly McCausland it is obvious, as Black J. has held, that they were given to Mr. Ingram by the father alone. Connolly McCausland, as I have stated, was never informed as to counsel's opinion, nor of course of the fact that the clause was so much more drastic than that which counsel had been instructed to draft. Connolly McCausland was never sent a draft of the deed, or, in particular, of the religion clause for his consideration or approval. He was not even afforded an opportunity – much less was he advised – to obtain the services of an independent solicitor. The London solicitors were named by Mr. Ingram, apparently because a partner in the firm – a Mr. Borrer – was a personal friend of his own; and the letter and subsequent wire to Connolly McCausland emphasised the urgency of the matter, and the importance of there being no delay. It is quite clear that the necessity for expedition in the matter at the outset was due to the desire on the part of Mr. Maurice Marcus McCausland to have the documents completed and executed by him before he left for Evian-les-Bains in France, and at a later stage to the limited time available for stamping them without penalty.

Is it the law that in such circumstances as I have mentioned a young man, who had just been emancipated from the legal disability of minority, who had no knowledge or prior experience of legal matters and no independent advice, who had just embarked upon his military career and undertaken the responsibilities of a commissioned officer, must be held bound by all the terms of a lengthy and complicated deed of re-settlement solely because of his having appended his signature to the deed, though it contained a clause, admittedly of an unusual or unreasonable character, of which he was never informed, and to which his attention was never directed, notwithstanding the adverse opinion of counsel as to the wisdom and propriety of including it in the deed? If this were the law I should, indeed, deplore it; but in my opinion it is not. I consider that Black J. has stated the law on this branch of the case with complete accuracy. It is to be found in the judgment of Sir John Romilly M.R., in *Hoghton* v. *Hoghton* (1852) 15 Beav. 278, and has been re-affirmed or adopted by Lord Campbell L.C. in *Jenner* v. *Jenner* (1860) 2 De G.F. & J. 359, by Lord Hatherley L.C. in *Turner* v. *Collins* (1871) L.R. 7 Ch. 329, 339, and by Kekewich J. in *Hoblyn* v. *Hoblyn* (1889) 41 Ch. D. 200, 207.

It must be admitted that the principles which are applied to family arrangements, such as a deed of re-settlement, are different to those applicable to transactions between strangers. The court takes a wider view of the matter and considers the interests of the family generally, the reasonable and natural desire for the preservation in the family of the family property, the upholding of the family honour, and the maintenance of family peace and security. These it will, when possible, endeavour to uphold. Thus, the exercise of parental influence, if not undue or improper, or the mere absence of independent advice, where there is nothing unusual in the transaction, or where proper precautions are taken to explain it with adequate clearness and fullness to the son as tenant in tail, will not justify the court in making an order for the rescission or rectification of the deed. From the very nature of the transaction a re-settlement is, as Kekewich J. says "generally the father's work," and his is necessarily "the guiding hand." Such parental influence is both natural and good – that species of influence which springs from kindness and affection, not from terror, coercion or fear.

At the same time, the court, in exercising this salutary and beneficent jursidiction, acts within well-defined limits. Thus one circumstance which the court has always recognised as warranting, though not necessarily compelling, a departure from the law or practice as stated above, is the acquisition of a benefit by the father to the detriment or prejudice of the son, for this changes the character of the re-settlement. The court will inquire jealously in such cases in order to ascertain if the bargain involving this benefit resulted from the exercise of undue influence by the father, without due regard to the necessity for the provision of adequate protection for the son. Lord Romilly expressed the opinion in *Chambers* v. *Crabbe* (1865) 34 Beav. 457 that the slightest personal advantage to the parent who induced the transaction is sufficient unless it can be proved that the child knew the nature and effect of the transaction, and was not influenced by the relations in which they stood to one another. In the case of a direct benefit of this character the law properly imposes upon the father the burden of proving that the bargain was a fair one and was fairly made. There is no difference between the confidential relationship of solicitor and client on the one hand, and of parent and child on the other. See judgment of Lord Selborne L.C. in *Mitchell* v. *Homfray* (1881) 8 Q.B.D. 587, 592.

The same principle, in my opinion, clearly applies where a clause of substance and importance is inserted in the re-settlement of which the son was not informed and of which he had no knowledge. *Hoblyn* v. *Hoblyn* (1889) 41 Ch. D. 200 in one of its issues was a case of this character. It does not appear to me to be really material whether the defect be styled ignorance, non-disclosure, suppression or misrepresentation, if the responsibility for it lay with the father and the son is misled. The binding character of family arrangements, such as re-settlements, is dependent upon parties being on an equal footing as regards all material information, and this involves full disclosure and, where necessary, full explanation. The absence of such precautions involves risk. This is so even though there be no dishonest motive or intention. If parties are not on equal terms, and one of them stands in a fiduciary relationship to the other, the court requires a fuller and more explicit account of the matter than would otherwise be necessary.

Wright v. *Vanderplank* (1856) 8 De G. M. & G. 133 is the only other case to which I propose to refer in this connection – a case of high authority in which the judgments of Knight-Bruce and Turner L.JJ. contain many well accepted principles. It was the case of a daughter executing a deed of gift of a life estate to her father soon after she attained twenty-one. Knight-Bruce L.J. conveniently sets out various grounds upon which such transactions might be impeached – that it was immoderate or irrational, that the solicitor had failed in his duty to the lady, that the deed was induced by suppression, misrepresentation, coercion, fraud or deceit, or that the lady executed it under mistake, misapprehension or ignorance. Ibid, 136, 137. None of these he held, on the evidence before him, to be established; but had it not been for acquiescence, to which I shall refer later, the learned judge would have held the plaintiff, who was the husband of the daughter and the person to whom her rights had devolved, entitled to relief on the ground of "the close attention, the strictness, and the jealousy with which, upon principles of natural justice, and upon considerations important to the interests of society, the law of this country examines, scrutinizes, and if I may borrow and old expression, weighs in golden scales every transaction between a guardian and his ward, or between a parent and his child, which, including or consisting of a gift from the younger to the elder, takes place so soon after the termination of the legal authority, as that the ward or child may, in consequence, probably be – not, in the largest and amplest sense of the term – not, in mind as well as person – an entirely free agent." Turner L.J., after expressing the opinion that such questions depend more on fact than law, stated his view of the law to be that "a child may make a gift to a parent, and such a gift is good if it is not tainted by parental influence. A child is presumed to be under the exercise of parental influence as long as the dominion of the parent lasts. Whilst that dominion lasts, it lies on the parent maintaining the gift to disprove the exercise of parental influence, by showing that the child had independent advice, or in some other way. When the parental influence is disproved, or that influence has ceased, a gift from a child stands on the same footing as any other gift; and the question to be determined is, whether there was a deliberate, unbiassed intention on the part of the child to give to the parent." Ibid. 146. Whilst the present case is not one of a "gift" by a son to his parent in the strict sense of that term, yet the principles above enunciated would appear to me to be equally applicable to the present case in which the father obtained from his son an advantage or benefit in the nature of this forfeiture clause which he obviously regarded as of the utmost importance, but which he never brought to the notice of the son.

In the present case the failure, as I hold on the part of both the father, Mr. Maurice Marcus McCausland, and the solicitor, Mr. Ingram, to furnish any information to the son Connolly in regard to the inclusion of the "religion clause" in the deed would, even if there were nothing more, have been a grave omission; it was doubly so when one remembers Mr. Longfield's obvious reluctance to prepare a draft of the clause which, when he did forward it, he advised was "unusual" and often "led to costly litigation." Mr. Maurice Marcus McCausland's relationship to his son had not wholly ceased to be of a fiduciary character on the day that the son attained the age of twenty-one years. Parental influence, so inseparable from most cases of family arrangement, was still present. In any event, from the dates of his visit to London, it is most probable that such conversation as he had with his son about the re-settlement was prior to the 11th July, 1927 – the day upon which he came of age. In the matter of age, knowledge of legal matters, experience of the world and family relationship these parties did not stand to one another on equal terms; and this in itself made it incumbent on the father to make a full disclosure. The knowledge which should be imparted must be "exact and complete," 23 Hailsham 84. Relief in such a case is not, in my opinion, dependent on the existence of intentional fraud.

But, it is argued, Connolly McCausland had a full opportunity of reading the re-settlement as well as the disentailing deeds for himself, if he so desired, in the office of the London solicitors before he executed them, and that he ought therefore to be bound by them. Here again the judgment of Romilly M.R., in *Hoghton* v. *Hoghton* (1852) 15 Beav. 278, 311, comes to our aid in a passage cited by Black J., but which I must here repeat: – "The mere reading over of a deed would not be sufficient to satisfy me that the person hearing it read understood it. To an unprofessional person, however intelligent, and exerting the closest attention, the long and involved sentences and technical language of a deed render it frequently unintelligible; and even the Court not infrequently misapprehends the limitations and effect of the provisions of a deed read in open Court, where the greatest pains are exerted to read it clearly and intelligibly. In my opinion, unless it is accompanied with an explanation of the contents of a deed, the reading over to an unprofessional person is more likely to confuse than to enlighten him." In my opinion it is almost an *a fortiori* case when a young man with no legal training or experience was left entirely to his own resources to endeavour to fathom what must have been to him the gloomy and confused depths of legal phraseology. It is not surprising that he soon tired in the struggle, and signed the deeds without any explanation, and without knowing that this "religion clause" was contained in the re-settlement. In a word the general nature of this re-settlement deed, with its many and complicated provisions including, in particular, clause 15, was such as to demand the most careful explanation by a duly qualified legal adviser; and this, in my opinion upon the evidence, Connolly McCausland never received.

In my opinion, therefore, apart from any question of acquiescence, laches or subsequent ratification of the deed, Connolly McCausland was entitled to relief from a forfeiture clause, so unusual in its character, and so drastic in both its conception and its form, that its full effect – the disentitling of the issue of a Roman Catholic – was never understood or appreciated by *either* the father or his son.

The next question – and the one which, perhaps, presents the greatest difficulty in the case – is whether the plaintiff, Connolly McCausland, has been deprived of his right to relief by his subsequent conduct. Did he, with knowledge of the existence of the forfeiture clause and of his rights, so acquiesce in it, or so accept its terms, that he must be taken to have confirmed or ratified it, and to have abandoned any legal or equitable claim which he may have been possessed of in respect thereof?

For a proper appreciation of this issue it is necessary in the first place to consider the material facts, and, in particular, the somewhat lengthy correspondence which is in evidence; and, subsequently, to apply the law as it appears in settled authority.

The first date upon which we have any evidence of Connolly McCausland having been brought into contact with the re-settlement of 1927 subsequent to its execution is 1932, when, shortly before his marriage, the terms of his marriage settlement were under consideration. Nothing of importance arises in any discussions which took place prior to March of that year when, according to Mr. Ingram's office entry, he, Mr. Ingram, attended both Connolly McCausland and his father, and the former read and approved of the proposals for the settlement, and was given a copy of same. Connolly McCausland admits that he received this document, took it away with him, and kept it for quite a long time. He admits that he read it later, in the summer after his marriage, but he denies that he read it at the meeting. The materiality of this part of the evidence is that the first paragraph of these proposals, in a brief reference to the terms of the re-settlement of 1927, ends with the words, "All such limitations being subject to certain clauses as to bearing the name and arms of McCausland and change of religion which are contained in the deed." On his direct examination Connolly McCausland admitted that the words "change of religion" brought to his mind Roman Catholic, and he felt that it might be his change of religion, or that he was not to marry a Roman Catholic. He added: "I felt that as long as my father was alive, and I changed my religion, and he disapproved of the change, he could cut me off from all things in which I hoped to follow him. I didn't think it had anything to do with my wife and children, certainly not my children."

I shall not, however, examine this evidence further; for I agree entirely with Black J. that there is nothing in it which, taken alone, would justify a finding that Connolly McCausland understood or had explained to him at the time of this marriage settlement the precise terms or the effect of the religion clause; and, if it be said that he had at least sufficient notice to make it reasonable that he should have enquired further into the matter, it may fairly be urged in reply not only that he was under no legal compulsion to make such enquiry, but also that the clause had no direct relevance to the matter which he then had in hand – his marriage settlement – more especially as he tells us that at the time of his marriage he had no intention of joining the Roman Catholic Church. The matter would, therefore, at that time have had for him at most an academic interest; and, whilst this evidence relating to the year 1932 cannot be wholly ignored, one would not in my opinion be justified in holding that Connolly McCausland had acquiesced in or confirmed the re-settlement merely because, with insufficient knowledge of the facts, he did not consider it desirable to prosecute any further enquiry into a matter which, as we now know it, might have brought him into serious conflict with his father.

Next in point of time comes the interview which took place at the Bank of England in November, 1939, between Connolly McCausland and his brother-in-law, Lucius Thompson. There is some discrepancy in the evidence of these two parties as to what precisely passed between them on that occasion. This is not altogether to be wondered at when one remembers that several years had passed before they were called upon to state their recollections in court. Black J. prefers the evidence of Lucius Thompson where, as here, it is in conflict with that of Connolly McCausland. He had the advantage of seeing and hearing the witnesses, and I have no hesitation in accepting his conclusion upon that point. Indeed, from a very careful perusal of the evidence and correspondence, I have not the slightest doubt that, had I been the trial judge, I should have formed the same opinion. Never was I more impressed with correspondence in any case that has come before me than I have been with the tone and Christian spirit of Lucius Thompson's letters. They are, indeed, the letters of a high-minded, honourable English gentleman, who evidently preferred the happiness of his family home to all the McCausland property, with the material advantages, but also with the serious responsibilities which its possession would necessarily entail.

Strangely enough, however, it is this very friendly, responsive spirit which adds to our difficulty in the present case; for it seemed to be wholly foreign to his nature to turn a deaf ear to any proposal that was made to him or his wife by Connolly McCausland. The issue which I am at the moment considering would have been much simplified had the parties been at arm's length.

However, to revert to the interview of November, 1939, which, it is said, lasted about two hours, Connolly McCausland "unburdened himself" to Lucius Thompson on the religious matter; and, as the latter said in his evidence, he had always recollected the mention in the conversation of the religion clause in the settlement. This clause had been read out to him when his own marriage settlement was signed about April, 1930; and he, accordingly, advised Connolly McCausland to look into it before he took any action. Lucius Thompson was, however, himself labouring under a misapprhension at that time. He thought that if Connolly McCausland was dispossessed of the property by the clause it would pass to his (Connolly McCausland's) son. It never occurred to him that it would "go his way." i.e., to his wife or family. For this reason I am clearly of opinion that it is impossible from that interview alone to fix Connolly McCausland with full knowledge of the meaning and scope of the religion clause. It might certainly, as Black J. says, have put him on enquiry as to its contents and provisions; but, further than that, it is only material as undoubtedly fixing Connolly McCausland for the second time at least with knowledge of the existence of *a* "religion" clause. For this reason it is a circumstance which cannot be ignored.

It was in these circumstances, and to this extent alive to the danger from the material standpoint of the step which he was taking, that Connolly McCausland was admitted to the Roman Catholic Church six months later, namely, on the 3rd May, 1940. It is not irrelevant to note that for some reason or other he kept the news of the important step which he had taken to himself, possibly because he thought it would not meet with family favour, possibly because he was apprehensive of the consequences which might ensue to his interest under the settlement in the family estates. However this may be, it appears clear from an attendance which Mr. Ingram had upon Connolly McCausland's mother on the 19th July following that even she was unaware at that time of his admission to the Roman Catholic Church; she merely "feared that he might be induced to join it." When she had read to her by Mr. Ingram the religion clause in the re-settlement, and appreciated that, if her son came within its provisions, not only he but his children would forfeit their claim to Drenagh and the settled property, she said that she would write to him; but she had not done so when, on the following day, Mr. Ingram further informed her that, if any such change of religion occurred, it would be the duty of the trustees to hold the property in trust for his sister, Mrs. Helen Thompson, and her sons; and that, even if Connolly McCausland should later revert to his original religion, the lost property could not be recovered. She said she would write to him to that effect. Connolly McCausland admits that she did write to him and he fixes the date of the receipt of her letter as the 24th or 25th July; but, unfortunately, this letter, which would have been most important as to the knowledge which it imparted, is not forthcoming. It is for this reason that I have referred, with some particularity, to the office entries of Mr. Ingram's attendances upon Mrs. McCausland (who, not unnaturally, was not called as a witness) as affording the best evidence available of the probable contents of the letter. In passing I may say that, in view of the matters to which I have referred above, I have difficulty in accepting without considerable qualification Connolly McCausland's testimony that he first knew that there was something in the deed which affected him in regard to religion when he received this letter from his mother.

However, all doubt as to Connolly McCausland's knowledge of the nature and scope of this "religion" clause appears to me to be set at rest by an office entry of Mr. Ingram's of the 18th August, 1940, when he attended Connolly McCausland and advised him fully as to the results which would follow under the provisions of the re-settlement in the event of his becoming or professing to be a Roman Catholic, and when Connolly McCausland read some sentences from an opinion which he had obtained from Mr. Arthur Cole, a member of the English Bar. At a further attendance on the following day Mr. Ingram again advised caution against taking any action without further serious and careful consideration of the religious question, and, if necessary, obtaining further legal advice, as Mr. Ingram thought that *Hoblyn* v. *Hoblyn* (1889) 41 ChD. 200 which had been referred to by Mr. Cole, did not support the view that the re-settlement would be altered by the court. The accuracy of these entries is not challenged in any material respect by Connolly McCausland. Immediately after that interview Connolly McCausland consulted Mr. Currie who has since remained his solicitor in Northern Ireland, and who appears for him in this action.

It will have been observed that at neither of these important interviews, which followed and were doubtless consequent upon his mother's letter, did Connolly McCausland disclose to Mr. Ingram that he had been actually received into the Roman Catholic Church some three and a half months previously. This was a strange omission; and it certainly displayed a very remarkable want of candour on the part of one who came to the family solicitor seeking information, and receiving from him legal advice. One naturally asks oneself, even at this stage, what was the reason for this reticence. It is suggestive of a greater, and, perhaps, an earlier knowledge of his legal position than he would wish us to accept, and of the consequences which might naturally result from full and candid disclosure.

In the circumstances it was left for Mr. Ingram to write to Connolly McCausland on the 19th September, 1940, stating that, in view of the persistent rumours that he had already changed his religion, he (Mr. Ingram) thought it his duty, as a trustee of the settlement of 1927, to ask whether he had in fact become a Roman Catholic. To this letter Connolly McCausland replied on the 27th September that he was a Roman Catholic, having been received into the Church on May 3rd last; adding to this admission the very pregnant words; "I had always hoped that you would not ask me this question, but I realise that you have acted as your own conscience dictated." In a subsequent paragraph in his letter Connolly McCausland wrote: "You will realise that more is at stake than the disinheriting of one individual, for there are other people involved who have no more thoughts of embracing Catholicism than you have, and these would be made to suffer, and will in fact suffer now, unless this forfeiture clause can be set aside." He added that he had decided to take the advice of a London counsel, and that he had already seen Mr. Currie.

Mr. Ingram acted promptly in his reply of the 3rd October, 1940, expressing his distress at the news; and stating that he had written to Mrs. Helen Thompson, to whose credit all dividends and rents would be placed, an apportionment being made up to the 3rd May. Mr. Ingram also decided on the same day to get the opinion of an eminent counsel, Mr. Hewitt Poole, as to the duties and responsibilities of the trustees. Connolly McCausland was, not unnaturally, so concerned with the contents of Mr. Ingram's letter, that he immediately came across, and had an interview with Mr. Ingram on the 9th October, to discuss the possibility of a compromise; but Mr. Ingram held out no hope of the trustees having power to enter into any negotiations for a settlement. Connolly McCausland then stated, according to Mr. Ingram's entry – and this is a very important matter as showing his then attitude of mind – that he would be willing to forgo any personal claim if the succession of his son Marcus could be assured. He added that he had never heard of the religion clause till the terms of his own marriage settlement were being discussed in 1932, and that he did not realise (i.e., that he did not realise at that time) that a forfeiture would affect his family. If the accuracy of this entry be accepted – and there is no reason to doubt it – it would be a reasonable inference that as long ago as 1932 he did know that the religion clause woud affect himself if he became a Roman Catholic.

In January, 1941, Connolly McCausland also sought the legal advice of the well-known firm of solicitors, Messrs. Charles Russell & Co., of London, who wrote to Mr. Ingram for certain documents which their counsel wished to see, and which were immediately forwarded. Months passed without any definite decision; and, accordingly, on the 3rd May, 1941, Mr. Ingram wrote to Messrs. Charles Russell &

Co. that his firm presumed that the contemplated application for alteration of the re-settlement had been abandoned. He asked, accordingly, for the return of the documents. To this letter Mr. Ingram received a reply that the matter was still under consideration. A further letter of the 8th August, 1941, from Mr. Ingram, requesting the return of the documents, was answered by Messrs. Russell on the 11th August in a letter which stated that they were writing to their client to obtain his instruction as to whether he desired to take any further steps in the matter; if not, the documents would be immediately returned. The importance of this letter lies in the fact that on the 5th September, 1941, the documents were returned. The legitimate inference from this action would naturally be that all thought of court proceedings by Connolly McCausland had been abandoned. However, when Mr. Ingram so expressed himself in his letter of the 8th September, 1941, Messrs. Russell replied on the 18th September that they were afraid they could not give an answer to that; but that they did not think that Connolly McCausland had come to a final decision in the matter.

On the 9th September, 1941, Lucius Thompson wrote to Connolly McCausland a very long letter in the course of which he pointed out his wife's inability to do anything which disregarded the interests of her sons, who were minors, in the succession, and also her own personal limitation of action by reason of the proviso against anticipation. There was, he continued, no middle way between accepting the settlement of 1927 and going to the court to have it set aside; that if he (Connolly) decided to go the the court his (Lucius Thompson's) wife and he would do nothing to defend the settlement beyond the minimum which they were apparently compelled to do as guardian of their children's interest under it; and that Mr. Ingram had said that if he did decide to go to the court he should do it soon; *otherwise he might prejudice his case by apparent acquiescence.* Connolly McCausland's reply of the 14th September shows a distinct reluctance to proceed, apart at any rate from "a quiet family arrangement." Life in the altered circumstances would not be easy for him at Drenagh. There would be a lot of difficulties and misunderstandings to contend with. "As to bringing a case," he wrote, "I am not keen to do so since I have taken the best legal opinion which I could get on the subject, and this opinion is, on the whole, against it . . . If I brought a case I might so easily lose it and have heavy costs to pay as well. So you see the law apparently upholds the settlement *as we all realise now.*" These words, followed, by an acceptence of Lucius Thompson's attitude that there was "no middle way" between accepting the settlement and fighting to get it set aside, fairly represent the general tenor of the whole letter, with the exception of portion of one paragraph near its close in which he wrote: "You must never think that I hold anything against you, either of you, over Drenagh whatever may happen in the future; but I would be a hypocrite and worse if I did let (*sic*) you understand that, if ever the law changes or the administration of it in that part of our country ceases to lie in the hands of those who now control such matters, I would appeal the case supposing it to go against me (a foregone conclusion) in the present issue." Let me say at once that I attach no importance whatever to this unmeaning reservation, if it be intended as such – an attempt, if it means anything, to keep the matter open indefinitely, or as he says, for "ever" until there might be a change in the law or its administration.

Connolly McCausland left the witness-box without assigning any meaning to these qualifying words in his letter; and in his argument before us Mr. Nicholson could only explain them by attributing them to the presence of those "midges in his hair" to which he had referred in an earlier part of his letter. Whatever the words meant, or were intended to mean, and whatever the event may have been which Connolly McCausland had in mind when he wrote them, it is not argued that that event has ever occurred.

On the 17th November, 1941, Lucius Thompson, in the course of a further friendly letter to Connolly McCausland, said: "So would you write as soon as you can to Ingrams (if you still think fit) and say that you are not going to bring an action, but accept the settlement." This was, in my opinion, a reasonable request. A year and a half had elapsed since Connolly McCausland had become a Roman Catholic, and yet, by the introduction of those ambiguous – I might say unmeaning – words in Connolly McCausland's letter of the 14th September, Lucius Thompson felt there was, perhaps, some room, however small, for uncertainty which must be removed, not only for his own and his wife's peace of mind, but also in the interests of the estates. In reply to Lucius Thompson's request Mr. Ingram received from Connolly McCausland a letter, dated the 18th November, 1941, which in my opinion, properly understood, is the most important letter in the case upon this issue.

The material part of the letter is contained in the first two paragraphs, and reads as follows: "I am writing to tell you that I no longer feel myself in a position to bring an action in the courts against the re-settlement of 1927."

I do wish, however, to make it perfectly clear that by 'accepting' the settlement I hope to make things easier for you and the other trustees; and I do not wish to prejudice any re-opening of the case by me or my descendants at some future and more favourable time."

This letter, read in conjunction with the earlier correspondence and with the statement in Lucius Thompson's evidence that on the 1st November, 1941, Connolly McCausland had told him that he was not going to take proceedings, leaves no doubt in my mind that Connolly McCausland, acting on the advice which he had received both in England and in Northern Ireland that legal opinion was against him, had definitely, to quote his own words, "*accepted* the settlement," and abandoned any idea of instituting contentious proceedings, or, as he expressed it, "an action . . . *against* the re-settlement" – to have the re-settlement set aside in whole or in part; but that he still harboured the hope that, although the settlement stood, and must stand, yet at some future indefinite date, possibly, as Lucius Thompson had himself indicated, when his (Lucius's) son Mark had come of age and could act for himself, it might be possible, wholly apart from legal rights, to effect an amicable arrangement, by re-settlement or otherwise, under which he or his descendants might be restored to the inheritance. In this way, and in this way only, as it seems to me, can the two paragraphs in the letter be reconciled with one another, and the letter be made into one consistent whole. Any other interpretation would involve a claim on the part of Connolly McCausland to an indefinite postponement of decision – a claim which the law would not recognise. Further, any other interpretation would not "make things easier," as Connolly McCausland had expressed the hope that he could do, for Lucius Thompson and the trustees; he would only make them more difficult. In my opinion, accordingly, Mr. Ingram was perfectly justified in replying to Connolly McCausland on the 25th November, 1941, to the effect that he was glad that Connolly would not proceed with the suggested application to the courts for the alteration of the settlement, which he had always felt sure could not be successful. A few days later – the 1st December, 1941 – Mr. Ingram, in writing to Helen Thompson again clearly showed the interpretation he had put upon Connolly's letter when he used the words: "Now that you are in undisputed possession."

If Mr. Ingram was wrong in placing this – to my mind the obvious – meaning on Connolly McCausland's words the latter should at once have so informed him. However, he did not do so; and then there follows a series of acts either on his part, or, to his knowledge, on the part of the trustees, which in my opinion are consistent, and consistent only, with Connolly McCausland's complete acquiescence in and acceptance of the settlement. I shall only briefly summarize them:–

(1) The payment as from the 1st November, 1940, of rents and profits by the trustees to his sister Helen Thompson, who had succeeded to the estates. Strictly speaking, there should have been an apportionment of these rents and profits as of the 3rd May, 1940; but by the direction of Lucius and Helen Thompson the later date was substituted in Connolly's case.

(2) The sum of £6,000, payable under clause 13 of the re-settlement to Eileen McCausland (Eila) in the event of her sister Helen becoming entitled in actual possession, was raised by the trustees by an indenture of sub-demise of the 25th June, 1942, as Connolly was informed and well knew they were proceeding to do.

(3) Succession Duty in the sums of £131 16*s*. 4*d*. and £333 11*s*. 9*d*. was paid by

Helen Thompson on her succession to the property real and personal respectively.

(4) Repayment of the greater part of the Succession Duty paid by Connolly McCausland on his succession after his father's death was applied for and obtained, to the amount fo £454 5*s*. 9*d*. on the basis of his interest having determined after two years and four months from the date of his entry into possession, instead of after the number of years when it had been estimated that his death would occur. The claim for repayment of this duty was grounded on an affidavit by Connolly McCausland to the effect that he had forfeited his estate, and that his succession had extended only to the 3rd May, 1940. "Please do all that you can," he wrote to Mr. Ingram, "to recover what you consider a fair and just amount." Here is an unambiguous affirmative act, and a statement on oath by Connolly McCausland in unqualified terms, which admit of no meaning or explanation save one – his estate had been determined by reason of the forfeiture effected by the religion clause contained in the re-settlement.

(5) An agreement was entered into for the sale by Connolly McCausland to his sister of stock, crop, agricultural implements and certain pictures and furniture, etc., for the sum of upwards of £9,000. Connolly's own suggestion contained in his letter to Mr. Ingram of the 24th January, 1942 – a letter, which I may say parenthetically, is consistent only with finality in regard to legal rights – was that these goods and chattels should be leased to his sister for ten years from the 17th February, 1942, at the end of which time, as he stated, Mark, his sister's eldest son, would be "of age" and the mother and son would "presumably have to re-settle." This was a proposal absolutely inconsistent with the institution of proceedings to rescind or to rectify the settlement. It was an express recognition of his sister's and her son's rights, but the visualising at the same time of the possibility of him or his son being restored to the inheritance as the result of a new re-settlement which would omit the religion clause. I regard the proposal also as strongly corroborative of my interpretation of Connolly McCausland's letter of the 18th November as to what might be effected by friendly negotiation after Mark came of age. The proposal that there should be a re-sale at the same valuation (or, if less, at the market value) in the event of Connolly McCausland becoming life tenant, does not affect my conclusion as to legal finality. It only illustrates what might result from friendly negotiation at some indefinite date in the future. Ultimately a sale was agreed to, Connolly McCausland writing to Lucius Thompson on the 25th March, 1942; "I think it is better for all concerned, you, us, the Lowdens (Land Agent) and Drenagh itself, if we do sell out and *depart (in peace).*"

(6) Next there was a proposal for the granting to Connolly McCausland by his sister of an agricultural lease for a period of ten years, subject to the right of either side to break on one year's previous notice at the end of five years in case the arrangement did not prove to be a success. Such proposal was obviously based upon a transfer of interest consequent upon the forfeiture of Connolly McCausland's estate.

(7) The sale by Connolly McCausland to the trustees in October and November, 1942, of his own unsettled lands for the sum of £2,688, when it appeared that the proposed "dual control" of the lands might lead to trouble and difficulty, and that all the lands could be worked more conveniently together.

On a somewhat different basis, but not irrelevant to the issue into which we are enquiring, rests the assumption by Thompson of the name of Thompson-McCausland, in reference to which Lucius wrote to Connolly McCausland on the 14th June, 1942: "I am only one of those concerned. Helen, *who has now succeeded to the McCausland Estates,* is a McCausland."

All these several acts are, in my opinion, properly relied upon by the trustees as either indicating Connolly McCausland's state of mind in regard to his acceptance of the re-settlement and abandonment of any claim, or as involving a loss or detriment to his sister directly resulting from the change in her position. Taken collectively they unequivocally treat the religion clause as a subsisting part of the re-settlement which had already worked a forfeiture. They are deeds which speak stronger than words, and deeds which are in my opinion not only inconsistent with a mere temporary arrangement, but are strongly confirmatory of the interpretation which I have placed on Connolly McCausland's letters in the foregoing pages.

What, then, is the law of acquiescence and laches? Acquiescence may arise whilst an infringement of legal rights is actually taking place, or it may result from the failure to seek redress or remedy when a violation of his rights, unknown to a party at the time, is brought to his notice. It is acquiescence in this second sense which is relied upon in the present case – an element in laches operating by way of estoppel. The principle underlying the doctrine of laches, as I understand it, is that in a court of equity, assuming there to be no statutory bar, a person is bound to prosecute his claim with reasonable diligence and without undue delay. The mere assertion of a claim will not suffice. The special circumstances of each case must, of course, be considered, especially the plaintiff's acquiescence as a free agent after he has acquired knowledge of the facts and of his rights. A change in the position of the party alleging acquiescence as a consequence of the other party's conduct is also always a most material and relevant circumstance. "Acquiescence." said Turner L.J. in *Life Association of Scotland* v. *Siddal* (1861) 3 De G.F. & J. 58, 74, "imports knowledge, for I do not see how a man can be said to have acquiesced in what he did not know, and in cases of this sort I think that acquiescence imports full knowledge, for I take the rule to be quite settled that a *cestui que trust* cannot be bound by acquiescence unless he has been fully informed of his rights and of all the material facts and circumstances of the case."

But when one speaks of "knowledge of rights" it is not in my opinion to be understood that a party must know the full and precise relief to which he is entitled. That is something which, in a difficult and intricate case such as the present, would only be known with certainty after the termination of proceedings in the highest court. He must, however, have "sufficient knowledge of the facts which constitute his title to relief": see the judgment of Sir Barnes Peacock in *Lindsay Petroleum Co.* v. *Hurd* (1874) L.R. 5 P.C. 221, 241; and, generally speaking, when the facts are known from which a right arises, the right is presumed to be known: *Stafford* v. *Stafford* (1857) 1 De G. & J. 193, 202. No doubt it has been held that, if mistaken as to his rights, a person is not guilty of laches until he has discovered the mistake, or had reasonable means of doing so. In this respect the law as to laches in courts of equity differs from that at law where a claim is barred by the Statute of Limitations: see the judgments of Alderson B. in *Brooksbank* v. *Smith* (1836) 2 Y. & C. Ex. 58, and of Hamilton J. in *Baker* v. *Courage & Co* [1910] 1 K.B. 56, 63. In my opinion in the present case Connolly McCausland, with all papers furnished to his legal advisers which they required, and with such competent lawyers both in London and in Northern Ireland to advise him, had not only "reasonable means," but the most ample opportunity of inquiring into and of ascertaining his rights.

Wright v. *Vanderplank* (1856) 8 De G. M. & G. 133 to which I have already referred for another purpose, is also an illuminating authority on this branch of the case. The court there held acquiescence to be established on facts not, of course, identical with the present, but which, taken in their entirety, do not appear to me to be appreciably, if indeed, at all stronger than those with which we have to deal. It, accordingly, refused to set aside a transaction in the nature of a deed of gift by a daughter, who had recently attained the age of twenty-one years, to her father, which otherwise would have been impeachable. What the court looked at was the acts and conduct of the parties, including the intention to treat and deal with the property as bound by the life estate which the deed conferred on the defendant. Turner L.J. expressed the clear opinion that a positive act (such as, in my opinion, we have in the present case) was not necessary to render the transaction unimpeachable by acquiescence; and that all that was required was proof of "a fixed deliberate and unbiassed determination that the transaction should not be impeached." I fully appreciate, as was pressed upon us by plaintiff's counsel, that the words of the learned Lord Justice are strong; but in my opinion the present case is brought within them not only by Connolly McCausland's letters and conduct immediately subsequent to his admission that he had become a Roman Catholic, but also by his consenting to his sister Helen entering into receipt of the rents and profits, and by his several other acts and submissions to which I have referred. In my opinion such conduct on Connolly McCausland's part constitutes not merely an unequivocal act, but a series of unequivocal acts, which are consistent only with a fixed and final determination on his part to abandon any claim *as of right* to the property comprised in the re-settlement.

The statements of the law in regard to acquiescence and laches which I have made have not only a general application, but they appear to have a special application to a case of this nature in which rescission or rectification is sought, and which is one of a well recognised class of cases in which the law required special promptitude in the advancement of a claim to relief because of the probability of the other party to the contract altering his position on the faith of the contract standing. *Turner* v. *Collins* (1871) L.R. 7 Ch. 329, 338, 341 affords a good illustration of the danger of delay in such a case. Lord Hatherley L.C. there speaks of the importance of the court watching over and protecting those who are placed in a situation to require protection as against the acts of those who have influence over them, by which acts the person having such influence obtains any benefit to himself; but he adds that *Wright* v. *Vanderplank* (1856) 8 De G. M. & G. 133 goes a long way to show that, if the intention to set aside such a deed exists, it should at once be put into execution. When the facts are known and the influence has ceased, the court, in fairness to other parties affected, expects promptness in the assertion of rights and in proceedings for their enforcement. To the like effect are the words of Lord Blackburn in *Erlanger* v. *New Sombrero Phosphate Co.* (1878) 3 App. Cas. 1218, 1279: "A Court of Equity requires that those who come to it to ask its active interposition to give them relief, should use due diligence, after there has been such notice or knowledge as to make it inequitable to lie by. And any change which occurs in the position of the parties or the state of the property after such notice or knowledge should tell much more against the party *in mora* than a similar change before he was *in mora* should do."

Delay has, to my mind, a special significance in the present case, in which Connolly McCausland had been informed that there was "no middle way" between accepting the re-settlement and going to the court to have it set aside, and in which he had been told of Mr. Ingram's view that if he did not go to the court soon he might prejudice his case by apparent acquiescence. With such a warning Connolly McCausland had, in my opinion, no right to assume that the indulgent attitude of his sister and brother-in-law would continue indefinitely, wholly irrespective of any trouble and expense which they might incur. It would be monstrously unjust to them in the circumstances to say that their actions were consequent upon a mere temporary arrangement, yet one of indefinite duration, of which there is no evidence. When it is urged that the institution of the present proceedings is evidence that Connolly McCausland at least understood any arrangement to be of a merely temporary character, I can only say that this argument is, to me, quite unconvincing. There was, in fact, no such arrangement; and in my own mind I much more directly connect the issue of the writ in June, 1944, when the war, be it remembered, was still at its height, with the report in the Appeal Cases of 1943, of the case of *Clayton* v. *Ramsden* [1943] A.C. 320, which was so strongly relied upon by Connolly McCausland's counsel in the earlier branch of the case.

For the reasons stated I am of opinion that acquiescence in the deed on Connolly McCausland's part is fully established; and that it would be a grave injustice to permit him now to change his whole attitude in the matter; and in an action, instituted a year after Mr. Ingram's death, to assert rights "against the re-settlement" which, on my interpretation of the facts, he had definitely abandoned both by his own word and deed, and by acquiescence, without protest, in the word and deed of others.

The next matter which remains to be considered is the extent, if at all, to which Connolly McCausland's son and co-plaintiff is affected by his father's acquiescence. No conclusive authority was cited on either side during the argument, and accordingly the question must be determined on principle. The learned Attorney-General contended strenuously on behalf of the trustee that the issue does not properly arise on the pleadings, and that it was merely as an afterthought that Mr. Nicholson, towards the close of his argument in reply before Black J., sought to differentiate between the positions of Connolly McCausland and his son on the question of acquiescence, with the result that it did not receive, as he submitted, sufficient argument and consideration. I am not prepared to say that the issue is not open on paragraphs 29, 38, 39 and 40 of the trusteee's defence, in which I regard the varied use of the words "plaintiff" and "plaintiffs" as not accidental, but as the deliberate act of the pleaders amply justifying a submission of differentiation of rights. The provisions of Order xix, rule 14, excepting admissions as against infants, and of Order xix, rule 26, rendering it unnecessary for a party to allege matters which the law presumes in his favour, or as to which the burden lies on the other side, also support the minor plaintiff's right to have the matter determined; and, fully argued, as it had been in this court, its determination cannot be evaded by any member of the court who holds the view, as I do, that Connolly McCausland's rights were barred by his acquiescence and laches.

My view on this issue may be briefly stated. Connolly McCausland's right to a rectification of the deed, apart from his acquiescence, I have held to be established. Such rectification would have enured for the benefit of his eldest son and others having interests in remainder. Such eldest son, who was and is an infant, had, in my opinion, his own independent right of action which he could have maintained either alone or, as in the present case, jointly with his father. No doubt such eldest son must be regarded as only a volunteer, and authority is lacking in regard to a volunteer's right of action for rectification in a case of this nature; but Black J. has referred to several cases, which I need not occupy time in examining closely here, in which the volunteer's right to institute proceedings has been recognised. It is said that they are all cases of breaches of trust, but I know of no reason why the appropriate remedy should not be applied to a case of this character. Black J. has illustrated the injustice which might result, were the law otherwise, to a remainder man, if a settlor in the position of Connolly McCausland dies shortly after a settlement, containing an unauthorised or otherwise unwarranted provision, had been executed, and before it could be rectified. Another illustration of a like injustice would be provided if such a settlor, to the prejudice of a remainder man who was a pure volunteer, accepted a personal benefit or advantage financial or otherwise, as a consideration for his not seeking the rectification to which he was entitled.

Now, on the assumption that Connolly McCausland's son possessed such a right it could not be lost or prejudiced in any way by his personal acquiescence, both because, presumably, he had no knowledge of the facts or of his rights, and also because, as a matter of law, there can be no acquiescence by an infant, and laches will not be imputed to a party whilst under such disability: *March* v. *Russell* (1837) 3 My. & Cr. 31 and *Young* v. *Harris* (1891) 65 L.T. 45. If this be so, it would, indeed, seem to me to be incomprehensible that such infant should be so adversely affected, as to be deprived of his rights by the acquiescence of another, namely, his father. Acquiescence operates by way of estoppel. It is a personal bar to relief. In *Butler* v. *Carter* (1868) L.R. 5 Eq. 276, acquiescence in a breach of trust by a tenant for life, who had brought the funds into settlement, did not bind a remainder man. Acquiescence is dependent in each case on knowledge, capacity and freedom; and, as these vary from one individual to another, it would in my opinion be impossible in law to impute the acquiescence of one party to another, especially when that other was under legal disability. The importance of this view is well illustrated in the facts of the present case, in which the infant son might well be regarded on the merits of the case as having even a stronger case of rectification than his father by reason of the introduction into clause 15 of those two concluding words – "without issue" – which so directly affected his legal rights. I think it must have been the view of Mr. Poole that Connolly McCausland's son had a right to maintain suit when, before any question of acquiescence had arisen, he expressed the opinion that Connolly McCausland *and his infant son* might make a strong case for modification of the re-settlement.

One last question remains – the issue raised in argument as to whether the plaintiffs' remedy, if any, lies in rescission or rectification of the re-settlement. I do not propose at the end of this already too lengthy judgment to refer to all the cases cited. Suffice it to say, that I find in the case of *Hoblyn* v. *Hoblyn* (1889) 41 Ch. D. 200 ample authority for remedy by rectification: see the judgment of Kekewich J. at pp. 207 and 213. *Lovesy* v. *Smith* (1880) 15 Ch. D. 655, 659 – a marriage settlement case – would afford an earlier illustration, if such were needed, of the court's power to rectify a deed, where the plaintiff did not rely on any mutual mistake, but rather on a violation by her husband of the agreement or understanding which had been come to between her and him prior to the execution of the deed: see the interlocutory observation of Denman J.

In the present case to set aside the deed *in toto* would be as in *Bentley* v. *Mackay* (1862) 4 De. G. F. & J. 279, 286, 287, "to undo what had been acted upon for many years." The allegation of mistake, misrepresentation or equitable fraud, by whatever name it be called, has been entirely directed to the forfeiture clause. This was a clause super-imposed, as it were, on the contract by Connolly McCausland's father, without, as I have held, Connolly's knowledge or consent; and, from its very character, and from the manner in which it was introduced into the re-settlement, it is, in my opinion, severable from the real contract contained in the rest of the deed. This is in my opinion the complete answer to the argument that this forfeiture clause was only part of the bargain, and that, if that part went, the whole should go. To rescind the whole deed after it had been in operation for twenty years, would produce a state little short of chaos, and an injustice far greater than that which exists with the deed as it stands; for it must be borne in mind that the disentailing deeds were part of the same transaction with the re-settlement, and that the principal settlor, Connolly McCausland's father, is long since dead. The judgment of Turner L.J., in *Bentley* v. *Mackay* (1862) 4 De G. F. & J. 279, 286, 287, in my opinion fully supports the view which I have expressed – a conclusion which is, indeed, irresistible as providing the only possible solution of our difficulties, if I am right in holding that Connolly McCausland has lost or waived his rights by acquiescence, and that he is, accordingly, himself bound by the terms of the deed.

For the reasons stated I am of opinion that clause 15 is not binding on the plaintiff, Marcus Edgcumbe McCausland, or on any person entitled in remainder to him under the limitations contained in the re-settlement, and that the said re-settlement should be rectified accordingly.

In my opinion the order of Black J. should be affirmed in all respects, including the declaration that the provisions of clause 15 do not apply to the jointure rent charge appointed to the plaintiff, Margaret Louisa McCausland (in the event of her surviving her husband Connolly McCausland) by the marriage settlement of the 6th June, 1932. The appeal against this declaration was unsustainable, and was expressly abandoned in this court.

Babington L.J. [dealt with the facts of the case and continued]: It was contended that the forfeiture clause (numbered 15 in the deed of re-settlement) was void for uncertainty, but Black J. rejected this argument and I agree with his decision. He admitted the evidence of two Roman Catholic canonists who were called to prove the various ways in which a person can become a Roman Catholic according to the law of the Church, and the difficulty of averring with certainty that a person either is a Roman Catholic or that he professes the Roman Catholic religion. This evidence was objected to and I have considerable doubt as to whether it was properly admitted.

Most of it deals with matters with which the court is not concerned and should have been rejected, but as the trial judge has held that neither the words "professing the Roman Catholic religion" nor the words "shall become a Roman Catholic" are void for uncertainty, and that the forfeiture clause as a whole is not void on this ground it is unnecessary to go into their evidence to see whether some of it may have been relevant to the issue of uncertainty. This evidence was produced to establish that the event prescribed in the forfeiture clause which might determine the vested interest is uncertain within the rule laid down by the House of Lords in *Clavering* v. *Ellison* (1859) 7 H.L.C. 707.

We were pressed with the opinion of Lord Cranworth where he said: "And I consider that, from the earliest times one of the cardinal rules on the subject has been this: that where a vested estate is to be defeated by a condition on a contingency that is to happen afterwards, that condition must be such that the Court can see from the beginning, precisely and distinctly upon the happening of what event it was that the preceding vested estate was to determine" Ibid. 725. Lord Campbell L.C. states the rule from the point of view of the parties and not of the court. He says: "Even as conditions subsequent, to defeat vested estates they must be construed strictly, and to work a forfeiture there must be shown a breach of a defined line of conduct which the parties concerned must reasonably have known would work a forfeiture" Ibid. 721.

In *In re Sandbrook* [1912] 2 Ch. 471, 477 Parker J. accepts but qualifies the passage from Lord Cranworth's judgment and says: "Conditions subsequent, in order to defeat vested estates, or cause a forfeiture, must be such that from the moment of their creation the Court can say with reasonable certainty in what events the forfeiture will occur." The test must be the same for the court as for the parties and the court has to be satisfied in this case that the parties concerned must reasonably have known what acts of theirs would amount to a breach of the defined line of conduct so as to work a forfeiture under clause 15.

As the parties concerned cannot be members of the Roman Catholic church when they elect to join it they must decide whether their action in becoming members of or professing the Roman Catholic religion will be a breach of the line of conduct prescribed for them by the clause, according to the accepted meaning of the words used, as reasonably understood by persons who are not Roman Catholics. Interpreted in this way I agree with the learned judge that there is no uncertainty as to the acts which will work a forfeiture though there may be a failure of proof as to whether or not these acts have taken place.

In the present case, however, the plaintiff, Connolly Robert McCausland, wrote to Mr. Ingram, one of the trustees, on the 27th September, 1940, saying: "I am a Roman Catholic having been received into the Church on May 3rd last at Ascot Priory, Berks.", so that the breach is here admitted, and assuming that he is bound by the clause his estate has been forfeited.

In *In re Evans* [1940] Ch. 629 Farwell J. held that the question whether a person has "become a convert to the Roman Catholic religion" can be ascertained with certainty, but he appears to have had some doubt as to whether the fact that a person professes the Roman Catholic religion can be similarly ascertained. Viewing the matter as one depending on evidence I think the court is as competent to ascertain whether a person professes that he or she is of the Roman Catholic religion as to ascertain whether he or she has become a Roman Catholic, and to use Lord Cranworth's words, "can see from the beginning precisely or distinctly upon the happening of what event it was that the preceding vested estate was to determine." But even if this be not so the two contingencies are disjunctive and the decision of the House of Lords in *Clayton* v. *Ramsden* [1943] A.C. 320, 325 does not apply, so that if either event can be ascertained the forfeiture will operate.

Black J. has pointed out that the word "profess" has been used in connection with the Roman Catholic religion in many statutes. The Bill of Rights (1 W. & M. sess. 2, c. 2) enacts that every person who shall "*profess* the Popish Religion" shall be excluded from the Crown and this is re-enacted by section 2 of the Act of Settlement (12 & 13 W. 3, c. 2). The legislature must, therefore, have considered that the fact as to whether a person does or does not "profess the popish religion" is an event capable of being understood with certainty and of being ascertained by evidence. The clause in this case appears to have been adopted from the precedent in Key and Elphinstone's "Conveyancing" and it is probable that the learned editors had regard to these statutory enactments when they drafted it.

It was further urged that this forfeiture clause is void as being against public policy.

This was not advanced with any great confidence and is not borne out by the authorities cited.

These authorities have been fully considered by Black J and I will not deal with them again but be content to say that I agree in the conclusion he arrived at that this clause is not void as being contrary to public policy. If it were I cannot see how any condition subsequent which provides for forfeiture on the ground of a change of religion or adherence to any creed or sect or to any body professing ideas or principles, however objectionable in the opinion of the settlors, could be supported even though it be worded with the greatest precision and distinctness and the event which creates the forfeiture be clear and certain. Such provisions have, however, been severely criticised from time to time and in *Clayton* v. *Ramsden* [1943] A.C. 320, 325 Lord Atkin said: "I view with disfavour the power of testators to control from their grave the choice in marriage of their beneficiaries, and should not be dismayed if the power were to disappear," but he did not suggest that the condition then being considered was void on the grounds of public policy and no authority for this proposition was cited to us.

[The Lord Justice then examined the evidence relating to the circumstances in which the re-settlement was drafted and executed, and concluded that neither the father nor the family solicitor, Mr. Ingram, disclosed to the son the presence of the forfeiture clause; and that the son did not at any time before execution receive separate or, indeed, any advice on the matter. His Lordship then continued]:

The most charitable view of this fatality is that the father left all explanations to Mr. Ingram and Mr. Ingram assumed that they had been given by the father. Mr. Ingram knew that when Maurice M. McCausland went over to see his son in July, 1927, the forfeiture clause was not in draft and could not, therefore, have been explained to him by his father, at any rate in its final form, so that Mr. Ingram's duty to communicate it to the son was clear, more especially since the clause which disinherits the issue of any person in possession of the settled estates who becomes a Roman Catholic as well as the offending person, does not follow the original instructions, which only suggest that on the happening of the event the property should go over to the next in remainder who might be his issue, nor does it carry out the expressed wishes of Maurice M. McCausland who says in his letter of the 27th July, 1927, approving of the clause, that what he desired was that a Roman Catholic cannot succeed to the lands or to the trust money.

Moreover, it is apparent from Mr. Longfield's letter of the 26th July, 1927, returning the re-settlement, as approved by him, together with the draft clause, that he did not appreciate the fact that the clause as drawn by him, which he says is designed to prevent a person who may become a Roman Catholic from enjoying the settled property, operates to exclude not only such offending person but also his possibly unoffending issue. This shows that Maurice M. McCausland did not himself realize how the clause would operate and that he probably executed the re-settlement under a misapprehension as to its effect. There may, therefore, have been mutual error, the father having executed a deed which would cut out the offending person's issue, which was not his intention, and the son having executed it without knowledge or advice as to its contents. Apart, however, from this consideration which by itself may be sufficient to render clause 15 invalid, the other facts bring the case within the decision of Lord Romilly in *Hoghton* v. *Hoghton* (1852) 15 Beav. 278. The circumstances of the two cases are very similar in their general outline, except that in *Hoghton* v. *Hoghton* (1852) 15 Beav. 278 the father obtained a benefit for himself in the resettlement. There Maurice McCausland obtained no direct benefit for himself, but he procured this forfeiture clause to be inserted in the re-settlement. This was his own wish, the instructions for it came from him and he approved of the clause, and it must be treated as a benefit to him requiring the same care to ensure that his son was consulted about it and advised either independently or by the family solicitor, as was required in *Hoghton* v. *Hoghton* (1852) 15 Beav. 278. In the words of Lord Romilly: "In addition also to its being a case of a re-settlement containing some material provisions which are of an unreasonable"– in this case *unusual* – character, it is, in my opinion, proved that the contents of it were not properly made known to the son and that he was left without the assistance and information which are indispensable to enable this Court to sustain such a transaction" Ibid. 314.

In that case, as here, the property was disentailed prior to re-settlement. Father and son were then free agents and the re-settlement was read over to the son before he signed it, but Lord Romilly held that transactions between parent and child, prior to the complete emancipation of the latter, must be watched with great jealousy, and that the mere reading over of a deed is not sufficient to satisfy the court that the person hearing it read understood it. He says: "In my opinion, unless it is accompanied with an explanation of the contents of a deed, the reading over to an unprofessional person is more likely to confuse than to enlighten him" Ibid. 311.

In the present case the documents were sent to the London solicitors without any instructions beyond securing their due execution. The re-settlement was not read over to Connolly McCausland, but he was asked if he wanted to read it himself. He says he started to do so but could not make very much of it and eventually turned to the schedules to see how much money there was, and he signed it without seeing the forfeiture clause and in ignorance of the fact that it was in the deed.

A great number of authorities were cited to us but I do not find it necessary to go through them all. Independent advice is not always necessary in cases of family settlements and re-settlements but when one of the parties is a young man who has just come of age, the court will treat him as being still subject to the influence of his father whose fiduciary relationship imposes on him the obligation of showing that the son knew and understood the contents of the re-settlement and more especially of such provisions in the deed as are unusual and which the court would not sanction if it had to decide the matter. In *Turner* v. *Collins* (1871) L.R. 7 Ch. 329, 339 Lord Hatherley L.C. approved of the observations of Lord Romilly in *Hoghton* v. *Hoghton* (1852) 15 Beav. 278, and Kekewich J. in *Hoblyn* v. *Hoblyn* (1889) 41 Ch. D. 200 considered them again and came to the conclusion that they apply to re-settlements generally and not exclusively to those in which the father gains a benefit. In my opinion they apply to cases where some unusual clause is introduced into the settlement which has not got the sanction of long usage and which, therefore, requires explanation to ensure that it is the conscious and voluntary act of the son and not one of those well settled provisions which he may fairly be allowed to take on trust. In my experience solicitors are usually well acquainted with the steps which the law requires to be taken in such cases. It was well put by Kekewich J. in *Hoblyn* v. *Hoblyn* (1889) 41 Ch.D. 200, 205: "On what does this presumption in favour of the propriety and reasonableness of a re-settlement rest? Take the frequent case illustrated here of such a settlement made by father tenant for life in possession and son tenant in tail in remainder shortly after the latter attains his majority. Does the Court presume that the son has had independent advice or insist that he ought to have had it? I think not. *Where proper precautions are taken the position of the son as tenant in tail is fully explained to him, as are also the proposed limitations and burdens on property which would otherwise in the ordinary course of nature become absolutely his own.* And if this duty is often, and in simple cases sufficiently, discharged by the father's solicitor, it is sometimes with advantage handed over to another solicitor called in for the particular purpose, or, according to a commendable practice familiar to me through an eminent conveyancer referred to counsel instructed to advise the young man independently. To omit all these precautions is to incur risk."

The italics are mine. No precautions were taken in this case. The proposed limitation was not explained to the son or brought to his notice by the father's solicitor, and the warning signs given by counsel both before and after he had drawn the clause, were disregarded.

And there can be no doubt as to what precautions should have been taken in this case. In *Tucker* v. *Bennet* (1887) 38 Ch. D. 1, 17, Lopes L.J. says: "A father living on affectionate terms with his daughter is the proper person to recommend and advise her, and her natural agent in matters relating to the preparation of her marriage settlement, and in my opinion there is no occasion for any independent legal advice beyond that of the family solicitor."

This is good sense as well as good law. If independent advice is not sought the family solicitor should in a case like the present satisfy himself that the father has recommended and advised the son, he should form an independent judgment as to the propriety of such advice, and if he does not approve of it should give the son such other advice as he considers necessary, and he must see to it that the son knows his rights and understands what he is doing and finally he should keep a record of these matters to provide against such contingencies as those that have arisen in this case.

I think Mr. Ingram must have considered that the father was in a position to force this clause on his son because he was bringing in free property without realizing that this would have been equally fatal, for the decision to adopt the clause was one requiring the assent of both, irrespective of whether there was anything in the scales to balance it or not.

The Attorney-General said that it is to be assumed that the clause was discussed by Maurice M. McCausland with his son and that he therefore executed the re-settlement with full knowledge, but when the facts relating to the preparation of this clause and to its insertion in the re-settlement, together with the evidence of Connolly McCausland that when he executed the deed he was unaware that the clause was in it, placed the onus on the parties upholding the re-settlement to show that this was untrue and that he was fully informed and instructed prior to execution. The burden of proof was, therefore, on the parties trying to uphold the forfeiture clause, as Denman J. held it to be in *Lovesy* v. *Smith* (1880) 15 Ch. D. 655, and they have failed to discharge it.

The Attorney-General further claimed that the long period of time which was allowed to elapse before clause 15 was definitely challenged had greatly prejudiced the trustees, since both Maurice M. McCausland and Mr. Ingram had died before action and their evidence was lost. Unless the delay can be relied on as a defence to the action under the circumstances of the case this complaint has no substance, nor can it be charged against Connolly McCausland as something unfair for which he is responsible because if he was informed about clause 15 by any one, a record of the source and nature of such information should have been kept by Mr. Ingram for the protection of himself and his client Mr. Maurice M. McCausland, and no such record is forthcoming.

On all the foregoing evidence and arguments I am satisfied that the recital in the re-settlement to the effect that father and son had agreed to make the settlement therein contained is erroneous and untrue and that clause 15 was improperly inserted in the re-settlement. It follows that if it had been challenged before Connolly McCausland committed himself to the acts which are now relied on as acquiescence by him in the re-settlement and the consequent forfeiture it would have been struck out or the settlement would have been set aside, and I think it is necessary to point out in this connection that the case of *Turner* v. *Collins* (1871) L.R. 7 Ch. 329 where it was held that a minor who had made a voluntary gift to his father must challenge it within a reasonable time after attaining full age belongs to a different line of authorities which have no application here.

The only difficulty which presented itself to me during the arguments on this branch of the case was whether Connolly McCausland, being of full age when he executed this re-settlement, should not be treated as knowing its contents, as Lord Macnaghten said in *Edwards* v. *Carter* [1893] A.C. 360, 367. In that case a minor after coming of age repudiated a settlement executed by him on his marriage. This settlement contained a covenant to settle after-acquired property. He could have avoided it within a reasonable time after coming of age but did not do so until nearly five years later, which the House of Lords held was too late, the settlement being merely voidable and not void. But no question arose as to the clause being unusual or as to the matters in issue in *Hoghton* v. *Hoghton* (1852) 15 Beav. 278 or in this case, it being assumed or admitted that the deed must stand unless it could be repudiated on the ground that the settlor was a minor when he executed it.

Edwards v. *Carter* [1893] A.C. 360, 367 is an entirely different class of case from *Hoghton* v. *Hoghton* (1852) 15 Beav. 278 and other cases like the present in which settlements have been executed by persons of full age and afterwards set aside or rectified on equitable grounds as Kay L.J. points out in *Carter* v. *Silber* [1892] 2 Ch. 278, 288.

Connolly McCausland having therefore substantiated his plea that clause 15 was introduced into the re-settlement of 1927 under such circumstances as not to be binding on him, the further questions then arise as to whether his subsequent acts are a confirmation of, or acquiescence in the settlement, or are of such a nature as to make it impossible for the court to grant him relief. These matters are in issue on the facts and it is upon the facts that they must primarily be determined.

[The Lord Justice then examined the evidence relating to the events between the execution of the re-settlement of 1927 and 1940, and concluded that though Connolly McCausland knew, or ought to have known, as a result of his interview with Lucius Thompson in 1939 that there was some provision in the re-settlement relating to change of religion, it was not until his interviews with Mr. Ingram on the 18th and 19th August, 1940, that he was for the first time acquainted with the full and precise terms and effect of the forfeiture clause. His Lordship continued]:

Black J. has held that Connolly McCausland, by his acts subsequent to the interview with Mr. Ingram on the 18th and 19th August, 1940, when he was informed of the provisions of the re-settlement, has acquiesced in the forfeiture of his estates. These acts must, therefore, be carefully scrutinised to see whether this conclusion is a just and proper one.

The principles governing acquiescence are not in doubt. In *Wright* v. *Vanderplank* (1856) 8 De G. M. & G. 133 a daughter conferred a life estate in property belonging to her on her father which would have been set aside if she had not subsequently confirmed the gift by a post nuptial settlement. Turner L.J. says: "The question to be determined is, whether there was a deliberate, unbiassed intention on the part of the child to give to the parent" Ibid. 146, and again: "I am not of opinion that a positive act is necessary to render the transaction unimpeachable. All that is required is proof of a fixed, deliberate and unbiassed determination that the act should not be impeached" Ibid. 147. The case was treated in the head-note as one of acquiescence and it illustrated the final and irrevocable nature of the acts required by law to defeat prior legal rights, but when Turner L.J. refers to a "deliberate intention not to impeach the gift" he is saying in effect that the daughter confirmed or acknowledged the gift and thereby set it up. This was not therefore a case of acquiescence but of confirmation and in *De Busche* v. *Alt* (1878) 8 Ch. D. 286, 314 Thesiger L.J. (1878) 8 Ch. D. 286, 314 says: "The term 'acquiescence ' . . . is one which was said by Lord Cottenham in *Duke of Leeds* v. *Earl Amherst* (1846) 2 PH. 117, 123 ought not to be used; in other words, it does not accurately express any known legal defence"; and he goes on to point out the difference between acquiescence which occurs while the act acquiesced in is in progress and acquiescence after it has been completed.

In the former case a person who stands by while another infringes his rights and thereby induces such other person to believe that he assents to the infringement cannot be heard to complain. This is no more than an instance of the law of estoppel by words or conduct and may reasonably be called acquiescence. "But," says Thesiger L.J., "when once the act is completed without any knowledge or assent upon the part of the person whose right is infringed" – which is the present case – "the matter is to be determined on very different legal considerations. A right of action has then vested in him which, at all events as a general rule, cannot be divested without accord and satisfaction or release under seal. Mere submission to the injury for any time short of the period limited by statute for the enforcement of the right of action cannot take away such right, although under the name of laches it may afford a ground for refusing relief under some particular circumstances; and it is clear that even an express promise by the person injured that he would not take any legal proceedings to redress the injury done to him could not by itself constitute a bar to such proceedings, for the promise would be without consideration, and therefore not binding" (1878) 8 Ch. D. 286, 314.

Having regard to the authorities the delay in this case is not, in my opinion, of such a duration and nature as to compel the court to refuse the relief sought. This delay is explained by the way in which the forfeiture was dealt with by all the parties interested, and the answer to Connolly McCausland's claim to avoid the forfeiture must be either that he has by his acts shown a "fixed deliberate and unbiassed determination" to abide by it, or that he has so dealt with the property as to make it impossible for the court to grant him relief. An intention to confirm the re-settlement or an intention to abandon the claim to impeach it must be proved. This is established by the authorities and is well settled. The reality of the act of confirmation or abandonment depends on the intention of the party against whom it is alleged, whether it be the confirmation of a substantive gift as in *Wright* v. *Vanderplank* (1856) 8 De. G. M. & G. 133 or the abandonment of a right of action as in this case, and when the facts are complicated and the inferences to be drawn from them are in doubt, the determination "must largely depend on the turn of mind of those who have to decide and most therefore be subject to uncertainty": see Lord Blackburn in *Erlanger* v. *New Sombrero Phosphate Co.* (1878) 3 App, Cas. 1218, 1279. I, therefore, approach this issue of confirmation in an endeavour to ascertain from the facts whether Connolly McCausland has shown an intention to confirm the re-settlement or has estopped himself from challenging it.

Connolly McCausland obtained knowledge of the clause to which he had committed himself in August, 1940, but he could have had no knowledge of the circumstances under which it came to be in the re-settlement until he got discovery of the contemporaneous documents. Messrs. Charles Russell wrote to Mr. Ingram for the original instructions and draft deed of re-settlement on the 30th January, 1941, and these were sent to them along with the entries in his firm's books and copies of all letters relating to clause 15 under cover of the letter of the 6th February, 1941; and on May 3rd, 1941, Mr. Ingram's firm wrote to Messrs. Charles Russell saying: "As we have not heard further from you we presume that the contemplated application for alteration of the re-settlement has been abandoned and we shall therefore be obliged if you will return the original documents."

There was some further correspondence and Mr. Ingram's firm wrote again on the 8th September, 1941, thanking Messrs. Russell for returning the documents and saying: "May we assume that Major McCausland has decided not to institute the proceedings that he was at one time contemplating." To which they replied that they did not think that Major McCausland had come to a final decision on the matter.

A parallel correspondence was proceeding at this time between Connolly McCausland and his brother-in-law, who says in a long letter of the 9th September, 1941: "So far as the settlement is concerned therefore we conclude that there is no way between accepting it and going to the court to have it set aside. If you decide to got to the court Helen and I will do nothing to defend the settlement beyond the minimum which we are apparently compelled to do as guardian of our children's interests under it." And later in the same letter: "I think we should get the main point settled one way or the other as soon as may be. Ingram says that if you do decide to go to the court you should do it soon, otherwise you might prejudice your case by apparent acquiescence. I do not know how far that would apply to a serving officer but on all counts an early settlement is desirable."

Connolly McCausland answered this on the 14th September, 1941, and after referring to his hopes of a family arrangement says: "But Drenagh is morally mine and my children's after I am dead, no matter what the law as it now stands may say to the contrary. You agree with this I know and so we need not discuss it. As to bringing a case I am not keen to do so since I have taken the best legal opinion I could get on the subject and this opinion is on the whole against it. If I brought a case I might easily lose it and have heavy costs to pay as well. It 'kills' me without issue, deprives Peggy of her jointure and my children of their portions. The same law prevents Helen from doing anything to help though she wants to do so – the whole having been conceived in a brain which has now no interest in the affairs of men."

There was some further correspondence between the solicitors and between Connolly McCausland and his brother-in-law who was trying to force him to come to a decision whether to prosecute his claim in the courts or accept some settlement that the parties were trying to arrive at among themselves.

Finally, Connolly McCausland wrote to Mr. Ingram on the 18th November, 1941, as follows: "Dear Cousin Alex., I am writing to tell you that I no longer feel myself in a position to bring an action in the courts against the re-settlement of 1927. I do wish, however, to make it perfectly clear that by *accepting* the settlement I hope to make things easier for you and the other trustees and I do not wish to prejudice any re-opening of the case by me or by my descendants at some future or more favourable time. Yours affectionately, Connolly McCausland."

Mr. Ingram accepted this so-called abandonment by a letter written to Connolly McCausland on the 25th November, 1941, saying: "I am glad you will not proceed with the suggested application to the courts for the alteration of the settlement which I always felt sure could not be successful and would necessarily have led to the expenditure of very large sums in legal costs." Mr. Ingram wrote to his partner and co-trustee, Mr. Young, on the same day quoting Connolly McCausland's letter and saying: "It would seem *sufficiently clear* from this that he has abandoned the proceedings which he contemplated taking to have the settlement amended and I should like to know whether you agree in this view."

The war was then at its most critical stage. Connolly McCausland had been overseas in action in May, 1940, first in Holland and then in France, where he was awarded the Military Cross; and when his regiment came back from France they were preparing to resist invasion. He said that towards the end of 1941 he was very busy tank training and was very busily engaged with other things. It does not, therefore, require a great deal of imagination to realize that there must have been considerable foundation for the statement in his letter of the 14th September, 1941, to his brother-in-law; "The whole thing could not have boiled up again at a worse time for me when I have to concentrate with every atom of my will on the intricacies of epicylic gears and the behaviour of electrons under varying conditions. The whole thing is like a bee buzzing to distract me or like midges in the hair when one's hands are occupied. I condemn it to the bottomist pit very frequently which is the mentality of the weak minded and the slow witted." In my view of the evidence these were compelling considerations inducing him to write the letter of the 18th November, 1941, saying that he no longer felt himself in a position to bring an action and that the abandonment was largely dictated by his military commitments and was in his view temporary only, submitted to without any deliberate intention to give up his rights and the rights of his issue once and for all.

In this letter of 18th November, 1941, he "accepts" the settlement to make things easier for the trustees, but without prejudice to any reopening of the case by him or his descendants at some more favourable time.

This is not an irrevocable acceptance of the forfeiture clause or an abandonment of his right to impeach it. It is not a lawyer's letter and its terms are inconsistent, but Connolly McCausland denied, on cross-examination, that he had come to a final conclusion not to take proceedings, and I cannot read this letter in the light of all the other facts in the case as being a "fixed deliberate and unbiassed determination" that the settlement should not be impeached.

Black J. says that after Mr. Ingram's reply it appears to have been assumed by all parties that after having been fully advised by his own solicitors and counsel as to his chance of success in proceedings to have the re-settlement set aside or rectified, Colonel McCausland had abandoned the idea of instituting such proceedings. I find myself in disagreement with this finding, as I believe that the true inference to be drawn from this letter, and from the subsequent correspondence between Connolly McCausland and Lucius Thompson, is that both of them looked on the matter as being open at least down to 8th April, 1944, when Lucius Thompson wrote the letter of that date dealing with a proposed application to the court to have the forfeiture clause cancelled and setting out the terms on which he thought this could be done.

This letter was written less than two months from the service of the writ and I cannot reconcile it with the trial judge's finding that all parties thought that Connolly McCausland had abandoned the idea of instituting proceedings, and I am satisfied that so far as the parties, other than the trustees, were concerned they all took the view that proceedings might be instituted.

Black J. seems to have attached some importance to the fact that Connolly McCausland did not answer Mr. Ingram's letter of the 25th November, 1941, in which he assumed that Connolly's letter of the 18th November was a final abandonment of his right of action, but I do not attach any importance to this having regard to the relationship between them – the failure of Mr. Ingram to follow up his doubts as to the meaning of the letter with Connolly himself and the general circumstances in which the latter was then placed, more especially his military commitments to which he refers in his letter to Lucius Thompson of the 14th September, 1941.

The letter of the 18th November was relied on as a clear abandonment, but Mr. Ingram was himself dubious as to its meaning and asked for his partner's views. It does not appear what reply he got from Mr. Young, if any, but it may well be asked why did he not express the doubts he communicated to his partner and co-trustee in the letter of the 25th November, 1941, to Connolly McCausland himself and ask him to say definitely whether he was on or off. He still owed this young man a duty. As trustee of the settlement and as the solicitor in charge of the trust he should not have accepted this conditional abandonment as final and absolute, and his failure to clear the matter up with Connolly McCausland directly contributed to the subsequent difficulties.

He further conveyed his construction of this letter to Helen Thompson in a letter of the 1st December, 1941, in which he says: "I have heard from Connolly that he will not proceed with his contemplated application to the court for modification of the settlement of 1927." This misrepresents the import of the letter which on its face is without prejudice and conditional, and Mr. Ingram's acceptance of it as a final and unconditional abandonment of Connolly McCausland's right is open to very grave exception, especially in the light of his letter to Mr. Young and the doubts therein expressed which are not repeated in this letter to Helen Thompson. He assumed that Connolly McCausland had closed the matter and left himself no loophole, but the loophole was there in the letter of the 18th November, 1941, and, though Mr. Ingram turned a blind eye towards it, the Thompsons, notwithstanding Mr. Ingram's letter of the 1st December, in my opinion fully understood that the abandonment was not final.

Connolly McCausland was cross-examined with reference to his letter of the 25th March, 1942, to Lucius Thompson, in which he wrote: "However I think it is better for all concerned, you, us, the Lowdens and Drengagh itself, if we do sell out and depart (in peace)"; and he said: "I was still referring to a temporary leaving of Drenagh. The paragraph would not deceive anyone who knew what was in my mind and my sister's and her husband's. It was subject always to a case being brought. I intended to come back if I possibly could." Lucius Thompson apparently appreciated this when he said: "It was always clearly understood between us that my brother-in-law was free to go to the courts if there were a change in the law or a change in the government and also that when the minors had ceased to be minors a new situation would come into existence." What the brother-in-law understood is by no means clear beyond this, that the understanding expressed by Lucius Thompson was one which recognized that Connolly McCausland's failure to challenge the entry of the Thompsons under the forfeiture was not based on a fixed determination not to impeach the forfeiture clause, but that it was, as he said in his letter of the 18th November, 1941, without prejudice to his reopening the case at some future and more favourable time. And the subsequent correspondence between the brothers-in-law dealing with the business aspect of handing over the demesne and settled property to the Thompsons recognizes this.

In a long letter of 22nd February, 1942, Lucius Thompson dealing with the sale of furniture in Drenagh says: "I would suggest agreeing on a price based on a mean between the valuations for Probate and for insurance subject to an understanding that we would re-sell any or all to you at the same value in the event of your becoming life tenant." As Connolly could only become life tenant if the forfeiture clause was successfully challenged, this recognises that the Thompson's entry was not necessarily final and that proceedings might be taken by Connolly to challenge clause 15.

Again in a letter of 13th March, 1942, Lucius Thompson says with reference to a farm at Drenagh: "It has occurred to me that a possible arrangement would be that we should agree that *if the place should revert to you* we would re-sell to you the stock and implements at the same valuation as we paid or at the market value, whichever was the less"; and again in the same letter he says: "I needn't set out the reasons why we think a clear cut settlement best since they all amount to this that barring an annulment of the settlement (which my suggestion above tries to provide for) Helen has no choice but to become a life tenant"; and the "*depart in peace*" letter of the 25th March, 1942, which was put to Connolly McCausland as an irrevocable decision by him never to challenge the settlement, appears to have had reference, as he said in evidence, to a suggestion in the letter of the 18th March that he should continue in Drenagh as a farming tenant. On this evidence I am satisfied that the letter of the 18th November, 1941, was based on the idea that in some way he could effect a settlement or compromise with his sister and her husband without reference to the courts.

On the 12th February he wrote to Lucius Thompson saying: "I need not say that I have always hoped for an amicable settlement of the whole of this tragic business and that it would take the form of an understanding or 'gentleman's agreement" by which the property would be made over to Marcus at the next re-settlement in 1952. This suggestion was, of course, impracticable while the re-settlement stood and Lucius Thompson rejected it. Connolly wrote again on the 14th March, 1944, and suggested a friendly application to the courts to restore the status quo by striking the clause out of the re-settlement on terms that all parties would agree to.

In answer to this proposal Lucius wrote on the 8th April, 1944, and said: "I am wondering whether the trustees will feel obliged to oppose a plea whether joint or otherwise for the cancellation of the forfeiture clause. If so I imagine it will be a thing that you will want to take into consideration as we shall too. I have asked Brown" (the solicitor then acting for the trustees, Mr. Ingram having died on 3rd May, 1943) "to let me know the trustees' attitude as soon as he can. It may interest you to know the suggestion I made to Brown though it cannot be considered as any final or formal decision that I am communicating to you. I suggested that *we should join you in an appeal to have the R.C. forfeiture clause deleted as being a proven cause of bitterness and strife*. If the court agreed to that and you wished to proceed with a plea that the deletion should be made retrospective Helen would not join formally in the plea but would offer no opposition to it provided that –

(*a*) If the court were to accept your plea—

- (i) no compensation should be paid to Helen from any source;
- (ii) no compensation should be paid to the minors out of or be a charge on the settled estate and investments;
- (iii) a subscription of £10 per annum should be paid to the general parochial funds of Drumachose and of £5 per annum to the general parochial funds of Balteagh;
- (iv) a title of undoubted soundness be conferred on you and your heirs;

or (*b*) If the court were to refuse your plea and your heirs and representatives *should regard the question as finally settled*."

This is a very strange correspondence if the Thompsons held the view that Connolly McCausland had irrevocably abandoned his intention to challenge clause 15 in 1941. Both parties treated the matter as being still open, and though Connolly McCausland's mind fluctuated from time to time and was not at any time clear, I cannot find any satisfactory evidence that he ever abandoned his rights. Indeed the evidence is all the other way and I am satisfied that he never acquiesced in the forfeiture, and that though often at his wits end to know what he should do he still held on to the life-line which alone could save him, namely, his right to appeal to the courts.

He was eventually driven to take this course and Messrs. Currie wrote to the trustees' solicitors on 30th May, 1944, while Connolly McCausland and his brother-in-law were discussing what they were going to do saying: "As you are aware Major McCausland has been on active service since 1939 and had determined to allow the matter to be shelved until a more favourable time. It has recently been brought home to him, which of course he does not admit, it may be necessary to go into evidence and that his evidence would die with him in the event of his being killed in action. For this reason it is essential that the action to determine his rights should be launched at once."

Messrs. Martin King French & Ingram replied on the 5th June, 1944, saying that they would oppose any application to alter the terms of the re-settlement on the grounds that it would be contrary to the intention of the deed and that it prejudices persons whose interests the trustees consider they are bound to protect.

The writ was accordingly issued on the 19th June, 1944.

When considering this plea of acquiescence it is impossible to dismiss from one's mind the fact that the forfeiture clause must be held not to be binding on Connolly McCausland which, as I said earlier in this judgment, colours all the subsequent evidence for if acquiescence or non-acquiescence have to be judged upon the balance of justice or injustice, (see *Lindsay Petroleum Company* v. *Hurd*(1874 L.R.5 P.C. 221, 239 adopted by Lawrence L.J. in *Weld* v. *Petre* [1929] 1 Ch. 33, 52), I cannot help feeling that it would be unjust to bind Connolly McCausland to submit to the forfeiture upon the ground of acquiescence except on the very clearest evidence not only that he did acquiesce but also that he was in possession of the facts necessary to inform him of the strength or weakness of his claim to be relieved from it. This raises the question as to what knowledge Connolly McCausland had of his rights.

In *Life Association of Scotland* v. *Liddal* (1861) 3 De G. F. & J. 58, 74, Turner L.J. says: "Acquiescence, as I conceive, imports knowledge, for I do not see how a man can be said to have acquiesced in what he did not know, and in cases of this sort I think that acquiescence imports full knowledge, for I take the rule to be quite settled that a *cestui que trust* cannot be bound by acquiescence unless he has been fully informed of his rights and of all the material facts and circumstances of the case."

Messrs. Charles Russell received certain documents on his behalf early in 1941. What exactly these documents were is not in evidence and we do not know what information they had before them or upon what question their advice was taken. I am not satisfied that they were fully informed. If they had known or appreciated the discrepancy between the intentions of Maurice M. McCausland and the final form in which clause 15 emerged, I think they would have advised immediate proceedings, but this is mere speculation, and I do not attach the importance which Black J. appears to have done to the fact that Connolly McCausland consulted them before writing the letter of the 18th November, 1941.

This was put forward to show that he acquiesced with full knowledge of his right, but I am satisfied that he never had such knowledge and that the forfeiture clause, which has now been held not to be binding on him, had a coercive effect on his mind which cannot be lost sight of when examining his acts and correspondence.

In my view, though he submitted under pressure to the surrender of his estate, he never adopted the forfeiture or confirmed it or expressed a fixed deliberate and unbiassed determination not to challenge it in the courts, and he was, in fact, in a somewhat similar position to the plaintiff in *De Busche* v. *Alt* (1878) 8 Ch. D. 286, of whom Thesiger L.J. says that he grumblingly submitted to the transaction as something he could not help.

He was never a free agent. He was in the toils of this clause which had been forced on him, and this must be borne in mind when considering this issue of acquiescence. The onus of establishing Connolly's intention to abandon his rights was on the defendants, and as the war was in a critical stage in the autumn of 1941 and Connolly McCausland was on active service and had compelling reasons for getting rid of this dispute, temporarily at any rate, I do not think the court should draw inferences against him or spell out an intention on his part to abandon his claim to his estates and property unless it is compelled to do so by evidence which is conclusive.

Helen and Lucius Thompson were under no misapprehension as to his intentions. They were doing their best to assist him in getting rid of the forfeiture. They went into possession under directions from the trustees protesting that they did not want to do so. They consulted with him as to possible ways of escaping from the forfeiture and alternatively as to how the property might be managed as a joint concern or whether Connolly could be made a tenant of Drenagh, and when they took over possession the letters written by Lucius Thompson to Connolly McCausland on the 22nd February, 1942, and 13th March, 1942, show that even then they thought the matter might be re-opened, which is further borne out by the fact that neither they nor any other persons who take in the remainder have appeared on this appeal to uphold the plea of acquiescence.

The Thompsons were in a very individous and distasteful position and agreed to take over the property and estates with obvious reluctance. Neither side knew whether the settlement could be successfully challenged and until this was done the forfeiture had to be accepted.

After the trustees had put the forfeiture in operation in October, 1940, a number of acts were done which are pleaded in paragraphs 30 to 37 of the defence filed by the trustees as a confirmation and acceptance of the re-settlement, including the forfeiture clause.

The first, of course, is that Connolly McCausland gave up possession of his estates and property to his sister. This is obviously the most significant of the acts done by him and is alleged to be evidence of his intention not to challenge the forfeiture, but though he submitted to it the act was not his, for the forfeiture was put in operation by the trustees against his will and in spite of his protests. This yielding up of possession, however, is not such a bar as to raise a counter equity in favour of Helen Thompson, and it is not of itself evidence of an intention not to challenge the forfeiture clause under which his property was taken from him.

The next is that Mr. Ingram recovered £454 5*s* 9*d.* succession duty on behalf of Connolly McCausland, being a refund due to him on the cesser of his life estates. This was, no doubt, in law a confirmation of the re-settlement and of the forfeiture clause but in equity it should, I think, be treated as conditional if the act on which it was based was itself conditional and as being consequential on that act and as capable of re-adjustment if it turns out that the surrender of the property cannot be supported.

Then Connolly McCausland agreed to transfer the stock, crops and farming implements in Drenagh to the Thompsons and conveyed to the trustees certain lands of which he was owner. It is only necessary to say with reference to this that Lucius Thompson's letters of the 22nd February, 1942, and 13th March, 1942, show that it was an arrangement which might only be a temporary one and liable to be reversed.

The trustees raised a sum of £6,000 by a mortgage of the settled estates for Eileen Mary McCausland, Connolly McCausland's sister, which became due to her as a result of the forfeiture and the succession of her sister Helen Thompson. Here again the act was the act of the trustee and not of Connolly McCausland and it should in equity be regarded as consequential only and subject to confirmation by him or to revision by the court if the basis on which the money was raised turns out to be erroneous.

Lastly, the Thompsons adopted the McCausland name and arms in 1942 and this was put forward as an act by Connolly McCausland confirming the re-settlement – but not only was this not his act but he actively dissented from it and said in a letter to Lucius Thompson that he found it "the only distasteful action in the whole affair," possibly to challenge its appearance of finality.

In my opinion all these acts were consequential on the handing over of the property and estates and were understood to be so by the parties other than the trustees, and to be always subject to Connolly McCausland's right to re-open the question of forfeiture in the courts. Under other circumstances these acts might be regarded as corroborative of an intention by Connolly McCausland to abandon his right to challenge the forfeiture or as being themselves evidence of such intention, but the evidence displaces this inference and establishes that when he "accepted" the re-settlement he did so conditionally and without prejudice, and that no one thought or assumed that he had done so irrevocably except the trustees, until at the earliest the spring of 1944, when the impossibility of reaching finality otherwise than through the courts became apparent to everyone.

If this issue of acquiescence is examined as one arising between Connolly McCausland and the trustees alone I cannot understand what equity the latter can have to insist that Connolly McCausland has acquiesced in the forfeiture of his estate. The right of action vested in him could not be divested at their suit without accord and satisfaction or release under seal and if the letter of the 18th November, 1941, be regarded as an express promise that he would not take any proceedings it was without consideration and not binding as Thesiger L.J. points out in *De Busche* v. *Alt* (1878) 8 Ch. D. 286, 314.

As between Connolly McCausland and his sister and brother-in-law on the other hand the equitable question remains. Has he within the decision of the Privy Council in *Lindsay Petroleum Co.* v. *Hurd* (1874) L.R. 5 P.C. 221 placed them in a situation in which it would be unreasonable to place them if the remedy is to be asserted?

The answer to this question is decisive, and in determining on which side the balance of justice or injustice falls I am stongly influenced by the fact that this forfeiture clause was not his own disposition as in *Allcard* v. *Skinner* (1887) 36 Ch. D. 145 and is not binding on him, and by the further consideration that those on whose behalf the plea of acquiescence is advanced objected to the forfeiture almost as strongly as Connolly McCausland himself and throughout the whole transaction were aiding and assisting him in his endeavours to escape from its results.

These parties have not appeared to substantiate their equitable claim to hold Connolly McCausland to the forfeiture, and I am satisfied that by granting him the relief he claims this court will not be placing them in any unreasonable situation or in any situation which they have not already assented to in principle; and that the forfeiture clause being out of the way their minor son can have no interest in the settled estates except through the alleged estoppel with respect to which he can be in no stronger position than his parents.

The only question remaining arises in connection with these consequential acts and dealings with the settled property, namely, whether other people have so altered their position as a result of Connolly McCausland's action as to make it impossible to restore the parties to their original positions, and therefore inequitable for the court to grant the relief of Connolly McCausland's action as to make it impossible to restore the parties to their original positions, and therefore inequitable for the court to grant the relief he asks. This is a question of estoppel properly so called.

On the correspondence and the evidence it cannot be maintained that Helen and Lucius Thompson-McCausland have been losers by what has happened or that their position has been altered to their detriment. On the contrary, they have received benefits, and unless their adoption of the name and arms of McCausland must be held to be a bar, there can be little difficulty in restoring them to the position they occupied prior to November, 1941. There is a long argument as to the change of name in a letter from Lucius Thompson-McCausland to Connolly McCausland justifying the change. He treats it as an open question and not as a provision with which they were bound to comply, and though the result of a decision in Connolly McCausland's favour may be embarrassing to the Thompson-McCauslands, I do not feel that this is a matter that should be allowed to weigh very heavily in the balance against Connolly McCausland's right to challenge the forfeiture.

I therefore hold that none of the foregoing acts were final or conclusive and that they can be readjusted either by agreement between the parties or by the court. More difficult questions are dealt with satisfactorily almost every day in the Chancery

Court; and Lucius Thompson-McCausland's letter of the 8th April, 1944, does not suggest that any insuperable barrier exists in the case.

The solution of this intricate and protracted argument, therefore, is that Connolly McCausland is not bound by the forfeiture clause in the re-settlement, that he did not at any time before action either confirm it or abandon his claim to challenge it or acknowledge it to be binding on him. He is, therefore, entitled to such relief as the court can grant him under the circumstances.

The Attorney-General maintained that even if Connolly McCausland has succeeded in establishing that the forefeiture clause is not binding on him and that he has not acquiesced in it, nevertheless this is not a case of mutual mistake and the court cannot, therefore, reform the instrument but must either allow it to stand or set it aside altogether. I will not deal with this argument at length. Black J. has rightly rejected it and I agree with him that the power of the court to rectify a settlement is not limited to cases where there has been mutual mistake.

As I have said, I am not sure that there was a mutual mistake in the present case, and though it is unnecessary to decide whether there was or not, but the way in which the final forms of the forfeiture clause came about and its adoption by Maurice McCausland are facts which we are bound to have regard to when deciding whether rectification should be ordered.

This is an unusual clause. It was included in the re-settlement without the knowledge of Connolly McCausland, who was not advised independently or at all, and appears in a form which is not in conformity with the expressed wishes of his father so far as they can be gathered from the evidence. It stands completely alone, as was said in *Hoblyn* v. *Hoblyn* (1889) 41 Ch. D. 200, 213, and can be expunged without upsetting any of the other provisions of the deed.

But above all, the case is one which is coloured throughout by the fiduciary relationship which the father owned to his son and which the family solicitors should have made certain was adequately discharged, and as this was not done the authorities cited by Black J. and especially the cases of *Bentley* v. *Mackay* (1882) 4 De G. F. & J. 279, *Clark* v. *Girdwood* (1877) 7 Ch. D. 9, *Lovesy* v. *Smith* (1880) 15 Ch. D. 655 and *James* v. *Couchman* (1885) 29 Ch. D. 212 show that a settlement can be rectified under the circumstances here established, even though there was no mutual mistake.

The conclusion at which I have arrived makes it unnecessary to consider whether, if Connolly McCausland were to be held bound by acquiescence or any form of estoppel, his son could challenge the forfeiture clause.

If a forfeiture clause in this form is included in a re-settlement with the knowledge and approval of a settlor it binds him and his issue. If such knowledge and approval is disputed by a settlor who subsequently acknowledges the re-settlement with the forfeiture clause in it or confirms it or does acts which estop him from challenging it, I have some difficulty in understanding how a volunteer taking under him can be in any better position. If it were so it would lead to endless confusion and uncertainty with no limit of time within which the claim must be made. No authority was cited for this proposition and I will only say that as at present advised, the deed must stand or fall by the acts of the settlors. If Connolly McCausland had bound himself by acquiescence this would have set up the deed with the forfeiture clause included and would have been binding on his issue, because being one of the settlors the alleged estoppel would operate through him as a confirmation of the settlement.

The case is one of very great importance and it is a calamity for the parties that this Court is not fully constituted.

They are thereby deprived of a clear decision and this is a result which I need hardly say the Court as constituted has tried to avoid. But for my own part having arrived at a conclusion satisfactory to myself I feel bound to express it though I do so with great embarrassment, since my opinion differs from that of the trial judge and the Lord Chief Justice and this difference of finding makes the appeal abortive.

In my view the appeal of the trustees should be dismissed and Connolly McCausland's cross-appeal allowed, but as the judgment of Black J. must stand in the circumstances it is unnecessary for me to discuss the form of order which I think should be made.

Notes and Questions

1. What is the distinction between *laches* and acquiescence? See further, *Irish Land Law*, para 3.066. On the facts, do you agree with the conclusion of Andrews L.C.J. or Babington L.J.?
2. As regards family settlements and re-settlements, see *Irish Land Law*, para 8.004 *et seq*.
3. As regards forfeiture clauses, see *ibid.*, para. 4.052 *et seq*.
4. As regards rectification, see ch. 8, *post*.

V. EQUITY LOOKS TO THE INTENT, NOT THE FORM

LOMBANK LTD. V. KENNEDY
[1961] N.I. 192 (Court of Appeal)

In each of two actions a hire-purchase company issued a specially endorsed writ claiming a sum for "agreed depreciation" of a motor car, which was the subject of a hire-purchase agreement. The relevant clauses of the agreements were identical in each case, and provided for the calculation of the "agreed depreciation" being made by reference to a percentage of the total hire-purchase price. The percentage, not less than 45 per cent, and not more than 75 per cent, depended on the length of time the contract subsisted. In the first action the contract had been terminated by the company after the hirer's failure to pay the monthly hire rentals. In the second case the contract had been voluntarily terminated by the hirer. In each case the company applied to mark judgment in default of appearance but the applications were refused on the ground that the sum claimed on each writ was not a liquidated demand in respect of which judgment could be signed on default of appearance. An ex-parte application to the court for a direction that judgment should be entered was similarly refused, and the company appealed to the Court of Appeal.

Lord MacDermott L.C.J. stated the facts, set out the relevant clauses of the hire-purchase agreement, and continued: We have no memorandum from the officer who dealt with the application, but it is clear that the decision not to enter judgment was taken after a scrutiny of the special endorsements and of the contracts to which they referred, and was based on two conclusions – (1) that the stipulation in clause 6 for the payment of "agreed depreciation" was subject to the rule of law which distinguishes between penalties and liquidated damages; and (2) that, so regarded, this stipulation was in the nature of a penalty and could not therefore be considered as founding a liquidated demand which would make Order 13, rule 3 applicable.

Before going further it will be appropriate to say something about the scope and purpose of the rule of law to which I have just referred and which I shall speak of, for brevity, as the "penalty rule". Its precise origins are difficult to trace. It was a rule of equity and was regarded by Lord Thurlow, when Lord Chancellor, as well settled in 1783. That was in *Sloman* v. *Walter* (1783) 1 Bro. C.C. 418, a case concerned with the penalty stated in a bond, in which Lord Thurlow said: ". . . the only question was, whether this was to be considered as a penalty, or as assessed damages. The rule, that where a penalty is inserted merely to secure the enjoyment of a collateral object, the enjoyment of the object is considered as the principal intent of the deed, and the penalty only as accessional, and, therefore, only to secure the damage really incurred, is too strongly established in equity to be shaken."

In Story's Equity Jurisprudence, 10th ed. (1870) the learned author, in s. 1314, states the rule in terms which closely follow the language used by Lord Thurlow in *Sloman* v. *Walter* (1783) 1 Bro, C.C. 418. Then, in s. 1316 he says: "The true foundation of the relief in equity in all these cases is, that, as the penalty is designed as a mere security, if the party obtains his money, or his damages, he gets all that he expected, and all that, in justice, he is entitled to." And later, in s. 1318, we find this passage: "But we are careful to distinguish between cases of penalties strictly so called, and cases of liquidated damages. The latter properly occur, when the parties have agreed that, in case one party shall do a stipulated act, or omit to do it, the other party shall receive a certain sum, as the just, appropriate and conventional amount of the damages sustained by such act or omission. In cases of this sort, courts of equity will not interfere to grant relief; but will deem the parties entitled to fix their own measure of damages; provided always that the damages do not assume the character of gross extravagance, or of wanton and unreasonable disproportion to the nature or extent of the injury. But, on the other hand, courts of equity will not suffer their jurisdiction to be evaded merely by the fact, that the parties have called a sum damages, which is, in fact and in intent, a penalty; or because they have designedly used language and inserted provisions, which are in their nature penal, and yet have endeavoured to cover up their objects under other disguises."

A recent statement of the rule will be found in Cheshire and Fifoot on Contract, 5th ed. (1960) at pp. 512-3. In describing the distinction between liquidated damages and penalties, the learned authors say this of the latter class: "Secondly, it may be in the nature of a threat held over the other party *in terrorem* – a security to the promisee that the contract will be performed. A sum of this nature is called a penalty, and it has long been subject to equitable jurisdiction. Courts of Equity have taken the view that, since a penalty is designed as mere security for the performance of the contract, the promisee is sufficiently compensated by being indemnified for his actual loss, and that he acts unconscionably if he demands a sum which, though certainly fixed by agreement, may well be disproportionate to the injury".

That I would respectfully adopt as a correct statement of the law in so far as it goes. But text-writers and the courts have had more to say on how to distinguish between penalties and liquidated damages than on the scope or ambit of the penalty rule itself, and it is the latter question – which for ease of reference I shall refer to as the preliminary question – that seems to me to present the main problem in these appeals. The final conclusion on this problem calls for a consideration of the authorities, but the broad purpose of the rule is, I think, sufficiently clear to depict, in general terms, the nature of the field to which it relates, even if it does not fix the bounds thereof with precision. Thus, it may be said that to attract the rule – (a) there must have been a failure on the part of the promisor the perform some one or more of his contractual obligations; (b) the relevant stipulation, that is to say, the stipulation for payment of the sum alleged to be a penalty, must be referable to such non-performance, and (c) the relevant stipulation must also be of a nature capable of acting *in terrorem,* that is to say, of deterring the promisor from the relevant non-performance. A stipulation, for instance, that operated only on the occurrence of some event quite outside the control of the promisor would seem, at any rate at first blush, to lie beyond the scope of the penalty rule.

But this general description of the scope of the rule leaves a number of difficulties unnoticed. For example – must the promisor's non-performance be such as of itself to constitute an actionable breach of contract? And can the rule apply if the relevant stipulation purports to fix the sum which is to be paid, not only in the case of non-performance, but also on the happening of other events which do not amount to non-performance? As will appear, these and other aspects of the matter have been the subject of decision, though the difficulties involved are, unfortunately, reflected in the conflicting state of the authorities. Before coming to these, however, it will be convenient to say a little more about the facts in the cases before us.

In Kennedy's case the contract was made on March 10, 1959, in respect of the hire-purchase of a second-hand Hillman Minx Saloon which was valued or priced at the sum of £560. Kennedy made an initial payment of £119, leaving a balance of £441 due. The hire charges were agreed at £112 13s 0d and this sum, together with a purchase fee of £1, when added to the balance price, produced a figure of £554 13s. 0d. as the balance which Kennedy agreed to pay off in monthly hire rentals. The first rental payment was due on April 10, 1959. It and the thirty-four succeeding monthly rentals were fixed at £15 7s. 7d. and the final rental payment was to be £16 7s. 7d. Kennedy paid none of the instalments and the hiring was terminated by the owners on August 22, 1959, under clause 4 of the contract which became applicable on the hirer's default. The writ was issued on April 22, 1960, claiming £340 3s. 0d. under the contract. The particulars state that the "agreed depreciation" under clause 6 is £505 4s. 9d. being 75 per cent of the total hire-purchase price which is given as £673 13s. 0d. This latter figure is made up of the price of £560, plus the hire charges of £112 13s. 0d. plus the purchase fee of £1. Whether the purchase fee should be in this total I am not quite clear, but clause 6 (c) makes it plain that the expression "total hire-purchase price", of which a percentage is to be taken, includes the initial payment and the hire charges. Then, from the 75 per cent figure of £505 4s. 9d. is deducted the amount of the initial payment or deposit of £119. This leaves a balance of £386 4s. 9d. and the owners abandon £46 1s. 9d. of this (for reasons which are not explained in the statement of claim) and so arrive at the sum sued for. Kennedy's case is therefore one in which the hirer failed to perform his obligations to pay the hire rentals, as promised under clause 2, and in which the non-performance was a breach of contract directly connected with the termination of the contract and the demand for "agreed depreciation" under clause 6 (c).

Crossan's case is different and Mr. Brown, for the owners, submits that the difference is material. There, the hirer, one Arthur Jukes, was a serving soldier when the contract was made on March 24, 1959. He was posted away from this jurisdiction after this date and did not pay any of the monthly hire rentals. But in the month of July 1959, the owners say that he voluntarily determined the hiring in exercise of the powers conferred by clause 3 (a). In these circumstances, the owners, having regained possession of the vehicle, issued their writ on April 28, 1960, claiming, as already mentioned, four months' hire rental and £181 1s. 4d. for "agreed depreciation" under clause 6 (c), which clause, it will be remembered, applies in the event of the determination of the hiring by the hirer as well as by the owners, and also in the other events already listed. The contract in this case related to a second-hand Vauxhall Saloon, the price or value of which was given as £385. An initial payment of £85 was made, leaving a balance price of £300. This, plus a hire charge of £90 and a purchaser fee of £1, produces the sum of £391 as the amount to be paid off by monthly instalments. The first of these was due on April 28, 1959, and amounted to £10 16s. 8d. Thirty-four other monthly payments of the like amount were the payable, followed by a last monthly payment of £11 16s. 8d. The particulars in the statement of claim relating to the item of £181 1s. 4d. are based on a retention of the vehicle for a period of four months, the gross amount of "agreed depreciation" being shown as £309 8s. 0d. or 65 per cent of the total hire-purchase price of £476 which, as in the last case, is made up by adding to the price or value of £385 the hire charges and purchase fee of £90 and £1 respectively. From the 65 per cent sum of £309 8s. 0d. is deducted the amount of the deposit, £85, and the four months' arrears of hire rentals as provided for by clause 6 (c), leaving £181 1s. 4d., the sum claimed under this head. While, as in Kennedy's case, the hirer failed to perform his obligations to pay the hire rentals as promised under clause 2, it was he, and not the owners, who terminated the contract. For this reason it was said, on behalf of the owners, that there had been no breach by the hirer in respect of which a claim for damages would lie.

The next step must be to consider what I have called the preliminary question – to inquire whether either of these cases falls within the scope of the penalty rule. That takes me to the authorities, but before examining them I must observe that the further issue, namely, whether cluse 6 (c) provides for liquidated damages or for a penal sum, is relevant to this preliminary question. It will be convenient to discuss this further issue later in this judgment, but because of its present relevance I will now state my conclusion thereon which is that clause 6 (c) provides for a penal sum and not for liquidated damages.

The first of the authorities to which I would refer on the preliminary question is the case of *Elsey & Co. Ltd* v. *Hyde* (1926) (Unreported) (see Jones and Proudfoot's Notes on Hire Purchase Law, 2nd ed., at p. 107) decided by a Divisional Court, consisting of Salter and Fraser JJ. There, the claim was to recover money under certain hire-purchase contracts in respect of tricycles. These contracts were in many ways similar to those now before us. The hirer having got into arrears with the instalments due, the owners terminated the hiring and then sued to recover, in addition to certain other amounts, the sum of £25 by way of compensation for depreciation. Despite the contention that the penalty rule applied and that this was a penalty and not liquidated damages, the court held that the sum sued for was recoverable. The leading judgment was that of Salter J., Fraser J. agreeing in general terms and also holding that the sum was not a penalty but a genuine pre-estimate of damage. The importance of the case, however, lies in the fact that Salter J. went further than this, and held, in effect, that the case was not within the scope of the penalty rule. Salter J. seems to base his conclusion on three grounds. He takes first the case of a hirer exercising the right (such as he has in these contracts) to terminate the hiring and says: "Supposing the hirer exercises his right to terminate this hiring, how can it be said that this sum of money, which it is agreed shall be paid, is a penalty or that it is a case in which either the agreed sum or liquidated damages must be paid? If the hirer terminates this agreement, what right does that give the owner to recover any damages against him? He has done him no wrong, he has broken no contract, and I am quite unable to see that this sum would or could give a penalty if it were claimable in those circumstances", Salter J. then applies this view to the cases he had to decide, saying: "I think, therefore, as it is to my mind not a penalty where it is payable on the return of the article by the hirer, it ought not to be regarded as a penalty where it was payable on the retaking of the article by the owner". Secondly, he takes the case where there is a determination by the owner, not because the hirer has made default, but because of the happening of an event which is not a breach of contract, the example given being the levying of execution against the hirer, an event, which in that case, as in the present contracts, would justify, according to the terms of the documents, the same demand against the hirer as the termination of the hiring by either hirer or owners. Of such an event Salter J. says: "There is no wrong done by the hirer to the owner, and it is no breach of any contract which the hirer has made with the owner. How could that event give to the owner of the goods any right to recover damages against the hirer, liquidated or unliquidated?" And applying that to the instance before him, the learned judge then adds: "It appears to me that no question of penalty could arise in such a case, and if this sum is not a penalty where it is payable on the determination of the hiring by the owner, by reason of the levy of execution, it seems to me it would be a strange result if it were to be held a penalty where it is payable on the termination of the hiring by the owner on the ground of non-payment of rent by the hirer".

The third ground is related directly to the case with which Salter J. was dealing, where the hiring was determined by the owner because the hirer was in arrear with his payments. Salter J. says of this: "It is proved that this is a breach of contract, and it is proved that that breach, apart from any termination of the hirer, would give the owner a right to damages against the hirer. But what would those damages be? They would be interest on the amount unpaid and nothing more. The fact that the hirer is in arrear with his payment will not entitle the owner to any damages for depreciation of these things. The reason that they have suffered is that they have second-hand goods put on their hands before they have received very much money in respect of them. That is not the result of the hirer's breach of contract, in being late in his payments, it is the result of their own election to determine the hiring, and it appears to me, even in this case, there is no question of penalty at all, and there is no question whether the sum paid shall be regarded as liquidated damages or a penalty".

That was in 1926. Three years later, in 1929, in *Chester & Cole, Ltd.* v. *Avon* op. cit. 124, Hawke J. followed the case which I have just cited. Then, in 1930, a Divisional Court (Lord Hanworth M.R. and Greer L.J.) in *Chester & Cole, Ltd.* v. *Wright* op. cit.115 had to consider a claim under a hire-purchase contract, relating to a motor car, which had been brought against the administratix of a deceased hirer. Both members of the court appear to have reached a decision by finding that the sum sued for was not a penalty but liquidated damages, having regard to the tests laid down by Lord Dunedin in *Dunlop Pneumatic Tyre Co. Ltd.* v. *New Garage and Motor Co. Ltd.* [1915] A.C. 79. To that extent the decision does not involve the preliminary question now under consideration, but while this is so, the views of Salter J. in *Elsey's* case (1926) op. cit. 107 are certainly not questioned, and Greer L.J. says ibid. 130: ". . . and it may very well be that the view which is, I think, the view of Mr. Justice Salter in *Elsey's* case (1926) op. cit. 107, which was cited before us, is the right way to look at this clause, namely, that it is not either liquidated damages or a penalty, but it is a sum payable in respect of one event, namely, the determination and end of the hiring agreement, whether that end of the hiring agreement arises from the hirer delivering the car back again, or whether it arises from the owner taking it out of the possession of the hirer in the events in which he is entitled to take it out".

In *Associated Distributors Ltd* v. *Hall* [1938] 2 K.B. 83 the Court of Appeal (Slesser, Scott and Clauson L.JJ.) had to deal with a claim arising out of a hire-purchase contract relating to a tandem bicycle. By the terms of the contract the hirer was given the option of terminating the hiring at any time by returning the bicycle, but in the event of his doing so it was further agreed that the hirer should pay a certain sum by way of compensation for depreciation. The hirer having exercised this option after paying only one instalment, the owners claimed under the contract for arrears of rental and for depreciation. The county court judge held that this latter amount was a penalty. The Court of Appeal reversed this decision holding that no question as to liquidated damages or a penalty arose – in other words, that the case did not fall within the ambit of what I have called the penalty rule. Slesser L.J. stressed the option given to the hirer to terminate the hiring and said [1938] 2 K.B. at 88 that it followed that "no question of penalty or liquidated damage arises at all". His reasoning did not go further, and the other members of the court concurred. This decision, it should be noted, did not deal with the position arising where the contract is terminated, not by the hirer, but by the owners. That, as I read the judgments, was meant to be left open.

The next case to which I would refer is *In re Apex Supply Co., Ltd.* [1942] Ch. 108, a decision of Simonds J., as he then was. There, the contract was for the hire-purchase of certain articles of second-hand machinery. The hiring company agreed that if it should go into liquidation and the owner company should retake possession of the goods before the expiration of nine months from the date of the contract, the hiring company would pay a further sum which, together with the payments already made, should equal a stated figure "by way of compensation for the depreciation of the said goods". The hiring company went into liquidation and the owner company retook possession of the goods within the nine month period. The owner company then claimed under the contract for the sum fixed for depreciation. In the circumstances Simonds J. held that the question whether the sum in dispute was a penalty or liquidated damages did not arise since it was a sum to become payable in a certain event, namely, the termination of the contract as thereby provided, and not by way of damages for breach. In the course of his judgment the learned judge referred to the judgment of Salter J. in *Elsey's* case (1926) op. cit. 107 at considerable length, and he also quoted extensively from the judgment of Greer L.J. in *Chester & Cole, Ltd.* v. *Wright* ibid. 124. He then came to the conclusion that he was bound to follow the reasoning of Salter J. in *Elsey's* case (1926) op. cit. 107 and reached his conclusion accordingly. While he refrained from stating his own view on the point I cannot but think it would have been to the same effect. He had certainly no criticism to offer of the decision of the Divisional Court in *Elsey's* case (1926) op. cit. 107.

Then, on this important preliminary question, we come to the decision of the court of Appeal (Somervell, Jenkins and Hodson L.JJ.) in *Cooden Engineering Co. Ltd* v. *Stanford* [1953] 1 Q.B. 86. That case related to a contract of hire-purchase in respect of a motor car whereby the defendant agreed to hire the said motor car and to pay a hiring rental over a period of thirty months. The hirer could at any time return the car and determine the contract on payment of the instalments in arrear and a sum fixed in lieu of compensation for agreed depreciation. By another clause, clause 11, the owners were entitled to determine the hiring and retake possession should the hirer have made any incorrect statement, or suppressed any information in the proposal, or have failed to make the payments due under the contract, or have died. The hirer fell into arrears and the owners thereupon terminated the contract, retook possession and sued the hirer, as provided by clause 11, for the unpaid balance of the hiring instalments. The hirer contended that clause 11 constituted a penalty and that the sum was not recoverable. The court was unanimously of opinion that if the sum sued for could be regarded as a penalty that is, if the preliminary question were to be decided in favour of the hirer – it was a penalty rather than liquidated damages. Jenkins L.J. took the view that the penalty rule did not apply, but the majority held otherwise and, accordingly, ruled that the sum claimed was a penalty and not recoverable.

This decision, in effect, reverses *Elsey's* case (1926) op. cit. 107 and it will be helpful to note what was said on the main point of divergence. The opinion of Somervell L.J., on the reasoning which underlies the first two of the grounds that Salter J. relied upon, is thus expressed [1953] 1 Q.B. at 96: "But it cannot, I think, follow as a matter of law that a sum exigible for a breach or breaches cannot in law be a penalty because it is made payable in the happening of some other event which is not a breach". Hodson L.J. deals with the same matter, and after stating the argument, says ibid. 116: "I am unable to accept this contention, which seems to involve that a draftsman of a written contract can always draw his document in such a way as to defeat the common law by incorporating in the same clause provisions dealing with the right to determine the contract on the occurrence of an infinite number of events only one of which is a breach of contract".

On the other hand Jenkins L.J. founds his dissent on the view expressed in the following passage of his judgment ibid. 110. "Supposing the sum prescribed by clause 11 became payable upon a determination by notice founded on the death of the hirer, or on an automatic determination due to the presentation of a winding-up petition against the hirer (being a company), no question, so far as I can see, of the sum being a penalty in the relevant sense could arise, and that being so its seems to me impossible to invest the same sum with the character of a penalty where the determination by reason of which it becomes payable happens to be brought about by notice founded on or automatically by some breach of contract on the part of the hirer".

Opinions may well differ on various aspects of the law of hire-purchase, but on this point I would respectfully adhere to the view of the majority in the Court of Appeal. I see no sound answer to the reasoning of Somervell and Hodson L.JJ. and I think it should prevail.

Somervell L.J. then deals with a further line of argument which is really that adopted by Salter J. in what I have described as his third ground. Somervell L.J. states this argument and answers it in the following passage of his judgment [1953] 1 Q.B. at 96: "It is that the law as to penalties is inapplicable if the owner under the agreement is entitled to 'determine' the agreement as the result of any breach. If in a contract of this kind, without the special provisions of clause 11, the hirer committed a breach going to the root of the contract, the owner would be entitled to treat this as a repudiation, to retake possession of the car, to be free from all further obligations to let the hirer have possession of the car and to sue for damages: in other words, to determine the contract and claim damages. The effect of the words we are considering is, I think, to give the same rights in the event of any failure to make punctual payment. The effect of this clause is first to make punctual payment a condition of the contract, and then to provide for the financial consequences to the hirer if the owner treats that breach as a repudiation giving him the right to free himself from all further obligations and claim money. No objection can be taken to the former, but as it seems to me the law as laid down in *Dunlop Pneumatic Tyre Co. Ltd* v. *New Garage and Motor Co. Ltd.* [1915] A.C. 79 is applicable to the financial consequences, which are plainly a sum to be paid in consequence of the breach".

On this point Hodson L.J. observes [1953] 1. Q.B. at 116 :"My difficulty is to see the validity of the distinction between a claim to receive payment of a sum of money because of a right to determine arising from breach of contract and a claim to receive payment of the same sum by reason of breach of contract giving a right to determine. The latter situation arises in cases of breach of condition amounting to a repudiation of the contract giving the opposite party the right to accept the repudiation and sue for damages. In so acting he determines the contract. Clause 11 purports to produce exactly this situation in respect of any breach referred to therein, and it seems to me unreal to speak of a remedy arising from the right to determine as opposed to a remedy arising from the breach". These views have my respectful concurrence. To hold otherwise would be to divorce the rule of equity from the realities of the situation and place it at the mercy of the form in which the contract is expressed.

I cannot distinguish, as respects the preliminary question, between the *Cooden* case [1953] 1 Q.B. 86 and Kennedy's case. On this issue the relevant considerations are similar and clause 6 (c) is certainly of a nature capable of acting *in terrorem* as respects non-performance. I would therefore hold that Kennedy's case comes within the ambit of the rule.

In Crossan's case the material distinction has already been noted. The hirer terminated the contract under clause 3 (a) after breach of his promise to pay the rental instalments punctually. This would appear to bring the case within the decision of the Court of Appeal in *Associated Distributors Ltd.* v. *Hall* [1938] 2 K.B. 83, but, if so, it can only be distinguished from the *Cooden* case [1953] 1 Q.B.86 on the merest technicality, for the only material difference is that in Crossan's case the hirer gave the terminating notice when the owners might equally well have done so. It is clear that the penalty rule, as a rule of equity, is not to be circumvented by drafting devices and it would be strange to the point of absurdity if, other considerations being the same, the rule protected the hirer when the owners terminated the contract by notice, but not when he did so himself. In the *Cooden* case [1953] 1 Q.B. 86 the majority looked beyond the formal termination by notice to the antecedent breach and I do not see why this should not also be done where it is a defaulting hirer who gives the notice. In either case there is the same non-performance and the same stipulation for payment of compensation. In my opinion, therefore, Crossan's case is also within the scope of the penalty rule.

The same conclusion may, I think, be supported by another related, but rather broader, line of reasoning. The penalty rule has often been spoken of as applying where there has been a breach of contract. See, for a recent example, *Tool Metal Co.* v. *Tungsten Electric Co.* [1955] 2 All E.R. 657, 622, where Lord Simonds says : "No case was cited where the doctrine was invoked otherwise than for a penalty payable on the breach of a contractual obligation". The typical instance may be of such a breach when actionable per se ; but, in my view, the nature and purpose of the rule do not necessarily call for more than a breach by way of non-performance by the promisor, be that non-performance actionable in itself or otherwise. The kind of stipulation struck at by the rule is one which seeks to enforce performance by a sanction out of proportion to the loss suffered by the promisee through non-performance. If the contract is so drawn as to make the non-performance not in itself an actionable breach the mischief which the rule seeks to control may not be any less. Take, for example, an instance that could arise under the form of contract with which we are dealing. The initial payment has been made and delivery of the vehicle has been taken by the hirer who then changes his mind about the hiring before the date on which the first instalment is due. Without waiting for that date the hirer terminates the contract under clause 3 (a) by giving notice and returning the vehicle. So far he has committed no actionable breach for, though he has turned his back on his promise to pay the instalments as provided by clause 2 (b), he has lawfully ended the hiring before any default in payment has occurred. If clause 6 (c), the relevant stipulation, is to be taken at its face value he is, nevertheless, liable – it may be within a few days of the contract – to pay 45 per cent of the vehicle's price plus 45 per cent of the hire charges, less the initial payment which the owners already have. It would be strange if this were so when he could have the protection of the rule (as I would hold) by making default in his payments before the contract was terminated. I do not, however, rest merely on the anomalous character of this situation. A provision which is aimed at keeping the hiring alive throughout the stipulated hire period seems to me as capable of coming within the purpose and spirit of the penalty rule when non-performance is not actionable in itself as when it is. In either case the essential question is surely the same – is the relevant stipulation calculated to *secure the performance* of the hiring? If it is, I do not see why another provision, such as we have here, which allows the hirer to end the hiring prematurely and brings the relevant stipulation into operation if he does so, should have the effect of ousting the rule or of abating the mischief it is designed to meet. To hold otherwise would be to entertain a device for keeping the rule at bay while purporting to confer a privilege on the promisor. The facts in the *Tool Metal Co.* case [1955] 2 All E.R. 657 were not concerned with any kind of non-performance; they have nothing in common with the position under discussion, and the decision of the House of Lords does not, in my opinion, run contrary to the view I have just expressed. Lord Simonds, it is true, associates the penalty rule clearly with a breach of contractual obligation, but the question whether such breach must always be actionable per se did not arise and was not decided. In the case of an actionable breach, the promisee may recover his actual loss as damages even though the penalty rule prevents his recovery of the sum agreed upon as the amount of compensation payable. It has been suggeted that if the rule were applied to a case of non-actionable breach – as, for example, where a hirer, having promised to pay the hire instalments throughout the hire period, exercises a right to terminate the hiring prematurely – the promisee could recover neither his actual loss nor the agreed amount, and that this would be at variance with equitable principles. I do not see why such a distinction should have to be made in the application of an equitable doctrine. In the case of the breach or non-performance which is actionable what equity says to the parties is, in effect this – "You have agreed that a measured sum for compensation will be payable. That is really a penalty to secure performance and will not be enforced. But notwithstanding what you have agreed, the loss actually suffered will, as a matter of fairness, be recoverable instead". There seems to be no good reason why equity should not speak in the same terms where the non-performance is not actionable, and all the more so where the difference between what is actionable and what is not depends on a provision which does not really affect the equities of the situation. To judge from the reports, the courts do not seem to have been called upon to apply the penalty rule to non-actionable breaches. But, while that may be so, equitable principles which aim at the promotion of fair dealing have a way of outlasting the particular forms of conduct that begot them, and the question here, as I see it, is not one of extending the principles of the rule but of applying them to a modern form of contract dealing with a modern form of transaction. There is certainly no ground for thinking that the march of events has outmoded the rule, particularly in these days when the desires and needs of the individual so often put him at the mercy of documents devised to suit the interests of some powerful corporation.

For the reasons stated I would hold that the rule is not ousted by these contracts and that both Kennedy's case and Crossan's are within its scope. Like Somervell L.J. in the *Cooden* case [1953] 1 Q.B. 86. 98, I express no opinion as to the applicability of the rule, or some analogous equity, to cases within clause 6 (c) which, like death or liquidation, are outside the control of the hirer.

The next question is whether clause 6 (c) provides for liquidated damages or a penal sum. Depreciation is a difficult form of loss to measure in advance and I see no reason why it should not be the subject of a genuine pre-estimate of loss which would be liquidated damages and recoverable on a liquidated demand. On this branch of the case, however, Sheil J., following the decision of Denning L.J. in *Landom Trust, Ltd.* v. *Hurrell* [1955] 1 All E.R. 839, held that this was a penalty clause and refused the application accordingly. Applying the tests laid down by Lord Dunedin in *Dunlop Pneumatic Tyre Co., Ltd.* v. *New Garage and Motor Co. Ltd.* [1915] A.C. 79, I am of opinion that this conclusion was right. I do not think it can be said that clause 6 (c) operates with anything like uniform severity, for it would seem that its capacity to act *in terrorem* gets less as the hiring continues and more instalments are paid. But it is clear from the *Dunlop* case [1915] A.C. 79 that the crucial date in this connection is the date of the contract and not a later date. So regarded, the provison for depreciation at the rate of 45 per cent "of the total hire-purchase price", if the hiring is determined within a month, seems to me like anything but a genuine pre-estimate of loss under this head in the event of the vehicle being returned within that period. Whether the goods were second-hand or new, this percentage is in marked contrast with the subsequent monthly increase of 5 per cent and seems far more than might reasonably be expected as the loss in value in such a short ime. This view becomes all the stronger when it is observed – (i) that the 45 per cent is taken not only on the agreed value at the date of the contract but on a figure which includes that and the hire charges as well, and (ii) that the hirer is also chargeable with the cost of all necessary repairs and replacements. To my mind this "agreed depreciation" for the first month is plainly *in terrorem* and a penal sum. If that is so the whole of clause 6 (c) is penal and it is unnecessary to go further.

For these reasons I conclude that the demand was not a liquidated demand in either of the cases before us, and I would, therefore, dismiss the appeals.

The sum of £43 6s. 8d. claimed in Crossan's case as arrears of hire rental, is a liquidated demand and there is no suggestion that the penalty rule applies to it. I have not dealt with it, however, as the owners sought to have judgment entered for the entire sum claimed and we have not been asked for any special direction as respects this particular item.

Black L.J. stated the facts and continued : It appears that in the first of the cases before us (the case relating to the Hillman car) the defendant Kennedy fell behind in his payments and the plaintiffs retook possession of the car in exercise of their rights under clause 4 of the agreement whereas in the second of the cases (the case relating to the Vauxhall car) the hirer Jukes, though in arrear in his payment of the hire rentals, exercised his right under clause 3 of the agreement and voluntarily terminated the hiring.

The problem for the court in these cases seems to fall naturally under two heads : first, whether the plaintiffs are entitled as of right to have the payments agreed to be made for "agreed depreciation" under clause 6 (c) treated as liquidated damages or whether on the other hand they are of the type which equity will scrutinize and relieve against as not being liquidated damages but penalties ; and second, if the payments are held to be of this type, whether they are so excesssive in the present case that they should be regarded as penal.

It may be convenient to consider the second of these questions first.

As stated in the third of Lord Dunedin's propositions in *Dunlop Pneumatic Tyre Co., Ltd* v. *New Garage and Motor Co., Ltd.* [1915] A.C. 79, 86-87, the question whether a sum stipulated is a penalty or liquidated damages is a question of construction to be decided upon the terms and inherent circumstances of each particular contract, judged of as at the time of the making of the contract, not as at the time of the breach.

I would emphasize the words "the terms and inherent circumstances of each particular contract". What will be a reasonable pre-estimate of the depreciation of a motor car, kept and maintained in good order, repair and condition in accordance with the provisions of clause 2 of the plaintiff's printed form of agreement will in any individual case depend on a number of factors : the make of the car ; the type of the car, whether it is new or second-hand ; if second-hand, its age and the mileage it has done ; and for aught I know, various other considerations which a dealer in motor cars would take into account. In order to make a genuine pre-estimate of probable depreciation the circumstances of the particular vehicle must be taken into consideration. I appreciate that in contracts of this nature hire-purchase companies may desire to have a clause providing for a pre-estimate of depreciation if the motor car or other chattel is thrown back on their hands. But it seems to me ex facie a weakness of clause 6 (c) is that the agreement is obviously designed to apply to motor cars of all makes and types and whether new or old (and indeed from the wording of clause 6 (c) to other goods as well) and that exactly the same rigid calculation is applied to determine the depreciation of every individual car whatever its age, condition or quality.

I do not propose to encumber this judgment with figures and calculations, but if we address ourselves to the particular cases of the two agreements which are sued upon in these actions and judge clause 6 (c) as at the time of the making of the contracts in accordance with the principle enunciated by Lord Dunedin, it will readily appear that in certain circumstances at any rate it would be impossible to regard the amount calculated under clause 6 (c) as a genuine pre-estimate of damage. This will appear to be especially the case if the plaintiffs retake the car by reason of a breach of contract in the early days of the hiring. In such an event clause 6 (c) would provide for the payment by the hirer on foot of depreciation of an amount which, save perhaps in some very exceptional cases, would be totaly disproportionate to the actual depreciation and much in excess of what could possibly be recovered by the plaintiffs in the absence of clause 6 (c) in an action for damages for breach of contract. Accordingly, I would hold that in each of the two cases before the court the amounts provided for by clause 6 (c) are penal sums and are such that in actions at the suit of the plaintiffs claiming to recover them as liquidated damages for breach of contract, the court should hold that they were not genuine liquidated but arbitrary amounts fixed *in terrorem* with the object of deterring the hirers from breaking their contracts, and were in fact penalties against which the courts in actions claiming to recover them on foot of breaches of contract would grant relief.

Having come to the conclusion that the sums calculated in accordance with clause 6 (c) are penal sums I turn to consider the effect of this finding in the present cases.

In Kennedy's case, the case of the Hillman car, the hirer by falling behind in his payments was guilty of a breach of contract and the plaintiffs retook the car in reliance on clause 4 of the agreement. If the plaintiffs can establish that they sustained damages arising from the hirer's breach of contract, e.g. by having thrown back on their hands a car depreciated in value, they can sue the hirer and his guarantor for these damages, but it has now been decided by the English Court of Appeal in *Cooden Engineering Co., Ltd* v. *Stanford* [1953] 1 Q.B. 86, a decision followed and welcomed by Denning L.J. in *Landom Trust Ltd.* v. *Hurrell* [1955] 1 All E.R. 839, that the rule of equity regarding relief against penalties applies to clauses in hire-purchase agreements such as clause 6 (c) in the agreements now before us. I would express my respectful agreement with the judgments of Somervell L.J. and Hodson L.J. in the former case and with that of Denning L.J. in the latter case, and I would accordingly hold that in the case of the Hillman car the plaintiffs were not entitled to recover under clause 6 (c) a liquidated sum by way of depreciation of the car against the hirer or his guarantor and accordingly were not entitled to mark judgment on foot of the specially indorsed writ which they issued.

I have dealt with the position in this first case on the point of principle, but I think it is right to notice that in any event the endorsement on the writ must be wrong. According to the indorsement the basis of the calculation of the "agreed depreciation" under clause 6 is 75 per cent of the total hire-purchase price. This 75 per cent could not be arrived at under clause 6 (c) until six months had elapsed since the commencement of the hiring : and according to the terms of the clause at least six months' hire rentals (whether paid or unpaid) amounting at least to over £92 would then fall to be deducted from this 75 per cent. No such deduction is made in computing the amount alleged to be due in the indorsement of the writ.

Crossan's case, the case relating to the Vauxhall car, appears to me to stand on a different footing from the first. Though the hirer in this second case was in arrear in payment of the rentals it appears that the plaintiffs did not exercise their right to retake the car under the provisions of clause 4 of the agreement, but that the defendant voluntarily terminated the hiring as he was entitled to do under clause 3 (a) of the agreement. If this is so, the plaintiffs could not claim to be compensated on foot of breach of contract for the depreciation of the car so thrown back on their hands, for the car did not come back to them by reason of any breach of contract on the part of the hirer, but by reason of the exercise by the hirer of the option to terminate the hiring conferred on him by clause 3 (a) of the agreement. Accordingly in such case the plaintiffs could not recover compensation for the depreciation of the car in an action for breach of contract : they could only recover such compensation if it was provided for by some specific provision in the hiring agreement. Such a provision in the present case is clause 6 (c) of the agreement. Where the hirer voluntarily terminates the hiring in exercise of the right conferred on him by clause 3 (a) of the agreement and the car is returned to the plaintiffs, the amount expressed to be payable to the plaintiffs under clause 6 (c) does not represent damages for the breach of any contract. It is not an amount payable on foot of any default on the part of a hirer. It is an amount agreed to be paid by the hirer upon the exercise by him of the privilege of termination of the hiring conferred by clause 3 (a).

There is high authority for the proposition that the only cases in which the doctrine that equity relieves against penalties applies are cases where the penalty is imposed for breach of a contractual obligation. In *Tool Metal Manufacturing Co., Ltd.* v. *Tungsten Electric Co., Ltd.* [1955] 2 All E.R. 657 the appellant company entered into an agreement with the respondent company licensing the latter in consideration of a royalty of 10 per cent to deal in certain hard metal alloys (called "contract material") produced under patents owned by the appellant company. By clause 5 of the agreement it was provided that if in any month during the continuance of the licence the aggregate quantity of contract material sold or used by the respondent company should exceed a quota of fifty kilograms, it should pay to the appellant company compensation equal to 30 per cent of the net value of the excess contract material. This compensation provision turned out to be a very burdensome one for the respondent company, especially after the outbreak of the war when production of the contract material greatly increased. Somewhat complicated litigation ensued between the parties which was ultimately carried to the House of Lords. One of the contentions raised by the respondent company was that the compensation provision contained in clause 5 was a penalty provision against which equity would grant relief. This contention was rejected successively by Pearson J, the Court of Appeal in a judgment of Romer L.J. [1955] 2 All E.R. at 686, (with whom Somervell L.J. and Birkett L.J. concurred) and by the House of Lords, all on the ground that the penalties against which the relief will be granted according to the equitable doctrine are penalties designed as a punishment or a deterrent against a breach of contract, and that a production in excess of the fifty kilogram quota was not a breach of contract. In delivering his opinion in the House of Lords, Viscount Simonds says: "The plea that the provisions of the deed are unenforceable because they impose a penalty clearly cannot be maintained. It is, perhaps, enough to say that they do not impose, or purport to impose, a penalty. No doubt the consequences of certain actions by TECO may be detrimental to them, but that does not involve that a penalty is imposed in the sense in which that word is used in the equitable doctrine that equity relieves against penalties. No case was cited where the doctrine was invoked otherwise than for a penalty payable on the breach of a contractual obligation".

The case to which I have just referred was not, of course, a case arising out of a hire-purchase agreement, nevertheless what was said by Pearson J., Romer L.J. and Viscount Simonds was expressed sufficiently widely to cover the present case relating to the Vauxhall car. Moreover, the precise point arose for decision upon a hire-purchase agreement in the English Court of Appeal in *Associated Distributors, Ltd* v. *Hall* [1938] 2 K.B. 83. In that case the agreement was for the hire-purchase of a bicycle. Under clause 5 of the agreement the hirer could at any time terminate the hiring by returning the bicycle to the plaintiffs, and clause 6 entitled the plaintiffs to determine the hiring and resume possession of the bicycle if the hirer committed any breach of any terms or conditions of the agreement. Clause 7 provided that in the event of the hiring being determined for any cause whatsoever the hirer would pay the plaintiffs by way of compensation for depreciation such sums as with the amount previously paid for rent would make up a sum equivalent to not less than one-half of the total amount payable under the agreement. The hirer terminated the hiring under clause 5 and the plaintiffs sued for arrears of rent plus the sum due under clause 7. The county court judge held that the sum claimed under clause 7 was a penalty and therefore irrecoverable. The Court of Appeal, reversing the county court judge's decision, held that as it was the hirer who had terminated the hiring no question as to the plaintiff's claim under clause 7 being liquidated damages or in the nature of a penalty arose, and that the hirer was bound to pay the sum for which he had made himself liable under clause 7. Slesser L.J., after referring to certain previous decisions only reported in a text-book, continues ibid. 87 ". . . .it is not necessary in the present instance for us to express any opinion upon those decisions, because they have nothing to do with the particular case which we are here to determine, for here the hirer, not the owner, terminated the hiring. He has exercised an option and the terms on which he may exercise the option are those set out in clause 7. The question therefore whether these payments constitute liquidated damages or a penalty in the instances mentioned does not arise in the present case". Scott L.J. and Clauson L.J. agreed.

Even if we had not had the assistance of what was said in the *Tool Metal Manufacturing Company's* case [1955] 2 All E.R. 657, I would be of opinion that even if we thought the matter doubtful we ought to follow the decision of the English Court of Appeal in this case of *Associated Distributors, Ltd.* v. *Hall* [1938] 2 K.B. 83 on the ground stated by Holmes L.J. in a passage in *McCartan* v. *Belfast Harbour Commissioners* [1910] 2 I.R. 470, 494, which has been quoted with approval more than once in this court, that uniformity of decision is so desirable that it is better to accept the authority of the English Court and leave error, if there be error, to be corrected by the tribunal whose judgment is the same on both sides of the Channel.

In the result, I would hold in Kennedy's case (the case of the Hillman car) that the officials were justified in refusing to enter judgment, but that in Crossan's case (the case of the Vauxhall) the plaintiffs were entitled to have judgment upon filing the necessary affidavits.

I fully appreciate that it may appear to the ordinary layman not only anomalous but unjust if, while on the one hand the law will relieve a defaulting hirer against the payment of the penal sum stipulated for by clause 6 (c) when the finance company retake the car, yet on the other hand it will not give any such relief to a hirer who, without being guilty of any breach whatever of his agreement, decides to determine the hiring and return the car under the provisions of clause 3 (a), but will in this case leave the finance company to extract from such a man the full toll of the sum fixed by clause 6 (c). This, however, is the legal position as I understand it. And if this view is correct, the anomaly and any injustice which may involve can, I fear, only be corrected – if it is thought that they ought to be corrected – by the Legislature.

Curran L.J. : Each of these two actions was brought about by the plaintiffs on a specially indorsed writ. Neither defendant entered an appearance and thereupon the plaintiffs applied to the proper officer to enter final judgment in each case by reason of such default. The officer refused to enter final judgment, on the ground that the claim, in each case, was for a penalty and not for a liquidated demand. The question for determination is whether the officer was right.

The terms of the hire-purchase agreements, so far as they are relevant to the issue, are identical. In each case the amount in question is described as a sum "by way of agreed depreciation of the goods". It is a well known fact that motor cars do depreciate in value, and it is reasonable to assume that when a car which is the subject of a hire-purchase agreement is returned to, or is repossessed by, the owners its value will be less than its true value at the time the hire-purchase agreement was made. The rate of depreciation, or its extent at any particular time, would be difficult to pre-estimate. At the time, however, when the car is returned to or repossessed by the owners its then value can be assessed with reasonable accuracy and the resultant loss to the owners ascertained. Of course there is nothing to prevent the parties agreeing upon a pre-estimate of depreciation. But the fact that a reasonably accurate assessment can be made when the car comes back into the possession of the owners is, in my view, a factor to be taken into account when considering whether the purported pre-estimate of depreciaion is genuine or whether it is in reality a penalty.

In each of the present cases the purported pre-estimate of depreciation is 45 per cent plus 5 per cent per month of the total hire-purchase price, (including initial payment and hire charges) with a limit of 75 per cent and a reduction in respect of the total paid by the hirer and the monies due to the owners for hire rentals up to the time the cars are returned to or repossessed by the owners. If the price of the cars as stated in the agreements is to be taken as their true value the hire charge appears to be a strange element to introduce in pre-estimating depreciation. It would be otherwise if the true value of each car is the total amount the hirer has to pay, but this cannot be so. Each car is being purchased at the price stipulated (including the final nominal purchase fee) and the facilities provided by the owners are paid for by the hire charge. There is, therefore, an element introduced which has nothing to do with depreciation and which tends to point to the purported pre-estimate of depreciation being a penalty rather than liquidated damages. The purported pre-estimate of 75 per cent provides for such total depreciation taking place in six months from the date of the contract. That is only one-sixth of the total period of the hiring. This rapid rate of depreciation is heavily weighted at the outset by the figure of 45 per cent, plus 5 per cent immediately on the hirer signing the agreement. I cannot believe that the owners were pre-estimating such a sudden depreciation, and when I find that the hirer is, in addition, liable to maintain the car in good condition. I am satisfied that the purported pre-estimate of depreciation is nothing of the sort, but that it is *in terrorem,* that it is, in other words, a penalty, and not liquidated damages.

I accordingly agree that in the case of Lombank Ltd v. Kennedy and Whitelaw the officer was right in refusing to enter final judgment for the plaintiffs on the ground that the claim is not a liquidated demand.

As to the case of Lombank Ltd. v. Crossan, if the contract was duly terminated by the hirer under clause 3 (a) of the agreement and if the hirer duly returned the car to the owners, the owners in my opinion, cannot claim in respect of the purported agreed amount for depreciaion on any other basis. They could only claim such amount in respect of the hirer's default in paying hire rentals if they retook possession of the car under clause 4 (i) of the agreement. I find paragraphs 3 and 4 of the statement of claim somewhat vague. They are as follows: "3. The Hirer defaulted in the payment of the hire rentals and voluntarily terminated the hiring on the 28th July 1959, and the vehicle came into possession of the Plaintiff on the 20th August, 1959. 4. Under clause 6 of the aforesaid agreement, it was provided that in this event then the plaintiff would be entitled to the following....". Paragraph 4 then goes on to quote clause 6 (a) which refers to arrears of rent and 6 (c) which refers to the depreciation of the vehicle.

When the words "in this event" are used in paragraph 4 of the statement of claim it is not clear what the event is to which it refers. It must I think refer to some event recited in paragraph 3, but in that paragraph there appear to be three events – the hirer's default in paying hire rentals, the voluntary termination of the hiring by the hirer on July 28, 1959, and, thirdly, the vehicle coming into possession of the plaintiff on August 20, 1959. As possession can only be retaken by the owners after they have terminated the hiring, and as paragraph 3 of the statement of claim does not allege a termination of the hiring by the owners, I am of opinion that the paragraph must be read as meaning that the hirer voluntarily terminated the hiring and returned the car to the owners.

In these circumstances the plaintiffs, in my opinion, can only claim for depreciation on the basis that the hirer has duly terminated the hiring and duly returned the car.

This raises the point that, inasmuch as the claim in respect of depreciation arises from the due termination of the hiring, and the due return of the car by the hirer, it does not arise from any breach of contract by the hirer. Accordingly, it is contended, the question of penalty does not arise.

There is strong support for this contention in *Tool Metal Manufacturing Co., Ltd.* v. *Tungsten Electric Co., Ltd.* [1955] 2 All E.R. 657, 662 where Lord Simonds says : ".... but that does not involve that a penalty is imposed in the sense in which that word is used in the equitable doctrine that equity relieves against penalties. No case was cited where the doctrine was invoked otherwise than for a penalty payable on the breach of a contractual obligation". Lord Cohen ibid. 686 agrees with what Romer L.J. had said in the Court of Appeal. The relevant portion of the judgment of Romer L.J. is appended to the report of the case in the House of Lords. In that judgment he says ibid. 688 : "For my part, I cannot see any remote resemblance between these sums, which became payable in pursuance of TECO'S contractual obligations, and sums which are only payable on a breach of contractual obligations".

In my opinion it is important to observe that, in applying the doctrine, equity has never intervened to deprive the plaintiff of a remedy; he could always recover what he was justly entitled to by way of damages for breach of contract. In the present case, if my foregoing opinion is right, if it be declared that the amount in question is irrecoverable on the ground that it is a penalty, the plaintiff would have no remedy for any loss due to depreciation, although it was clearly the intention of the parties to the hiring that the hirer should be liable therefor.

If the defendant who is sued as the hirer's guarantor, has to pay an unreasonable sum for depreciation, he has the hirer to blame and, no doubt, has a remedy against him.

I would hold that the officer was wrong in refusing to enter final judgment in the action Lombank Ltd. v. Crossan.

Notes and Questions

1. Upon what principles of equity did the majority of the Court hold as they did? What was wrong with Lord MacDermott's reasoning? *Cf.* the divergent views of members of the House of Lords in *Bridge* v. *Campbell Discount Co.* [1962] A.C. 600. See also *Irish Land Law*, para. 3.060 *et seq.*
2. *Cf.* the courts' attitude to "penalties" in mortgage transactions, see *ibid.* para. 13.094.

VI. HE WHO COMES INTO EQUITY MUST COME WITH CLEAN HANDS

PARKES V. PARKES

Unreported (High Court) (1978 No. 641 P) (Judgment delivered 1st July 1980)

The facts are set out in the judgment.

Costello J. :

Mr. and Mrs. Parkes were married on the 28th June 1957. Mr. Parkes is a British subject; Mrs. Parkes is an Irish citizen. They were husband and wife in the year 1965 when 222 acres of land situated behind the strand at Tramore in the County of Waterford were purchased with money provided by Mr. Parkes. The land was registered land and the transfer was taken in Mrs. Parkes' name and she was duly registered as full owner. The consideration for the sale was £2,500. Some four years later Mr. and Mrs. Parkes were divorced by a decree of an English Court which was made absolute on the 24th September 1969. No reference to the Tramore land was made by either party on an application for maintenance made in the divorce proceedings and both would appear to have largely ignored its existence until the year 1977. In that year Mr. Parkes caused an Inhibition to be registered on the Folio which reads "no registration under a disposition by a transmission from the registered owner is to be made without prior notice to David Parkes" and in the affidavit grounding his application for registration of the Inhibition he swore that the lands were purchased by Mrs. Parkes in trust for him. Mrs. Parkes instituted these proceedings early in the year 1978 claiming a declaration that the Inhibition was wrongly registered and an order directing its removal from the Folio. Her reasons for doing so became apparent in the course of her evidence – she had received an offer to purchase the lands for the sum of £130,000 in the previous year. Although the sale did not in fact go through it is clear that the lands have now become extremely valuable and, not surprisingly, Mr. Parkes has counterclaimed a declaration that he is entitled to the entire beneficial ownership in the lands and that the plaintiff holds them in trust for him. The resolution of the conflict between the parties would involve no legal issues if I could have decided that Mrs. Parkes was expressly given the lands as a gift by her husband as she claimed in her evidence. But for reasons which I will develop later I cannot accept that this is what happened. This does not mean, however, that her claim fails and that of her husband succeeds because the transfer to her contained a certificate as follows :

> "It is hereby certified by Roberta O.P. Parkes being the person becoming entitled to the entire beneficial interest in the property conveyed or assigned that she is an Irish citizen".

This certificate was a false one. It was included in the instrument of transfer at Mr. Parkes' direction. The evidence (which I will consider in greater detail later) was to the effect that at the suggestion of his solicitor he directed that the transfer be taken in his wife's name in order to avoid the necessity of applying to the Land Commission for its consent to the transfer – an application which would have been necessary by virtue of section 45 of the Land Act 1965 had he taken the property in his own name as he was not an Irish citizen. And so the effect on the transaction of that false certificate falls for consideration and indeed is the crucial issue in this case. Before turning to it and to the findings of facts which I must make I think it would be helpful if I first outlined the relevant provisions of the Finance Acts and the Land Act 1965 which it is clear had a decisive influence on Mr. Parkes' actions in this case.

When Mr. Parkes first became interested in the lands at Tramore the stamp duty provisions relating to the sale of land to non-Irish nationals contained in the Finance (No. 2) Act 1947 were still in force. Section 13 (1) of that Act provided:

> "The stamp duties chargeable on conveyance or transfers of lands tenements and hereditaments under the heading 'Conveyance or transfer on sale of any property' in the First Schedule to the Stamp Act 1891, as amended by subsequent enactments shall, on and after the 1st day of December, 1947, be at the rate of £2/10s for every £50 or fractional part of £50 of the amount or value of the consideration in lieu of the rates immediately theretofore chargeable".

The rate of £2/10/0 for every £50 of the consideration was amended by section 17 of the Finance Act, 1951, to £1/10/0 for every £50 of the consideration.

But this rate of duty did not apply in every case. The exception to it with which this case is concerned is that which arises from the operation of sub-sections (4) and (5). Sub-section (4) of the section provided:

> "The foregoing provisions of this section shall have effect if, but only if, the instrument contains a statement by the party to whom the property is being conveyed or transferred certifying that the person who becomes entitled to the entire beneficial in the property . . . is some specified one of the following:
> (a) An Irish citizen"

If the instrument of transfer did not contain a certificate as required by sub-section (4) then a much higher rate of duty became payable by virtue of sub-section (5) which provided:

> "In any case in which by virtue of sub-section (4) of this section the provisions of sub-section (1), (2) and (3) of the section have no effect the stamp duties chargeable on conveyances or transfers of lands tenements and hereditaments under the heading 'Conveyance or transfer on sale of any property' in the First Schedule to the Stamp Act, 1891 as amended by subsequent enactments shall, on and after the 1st day of December 1947 be at the rate (in this section referred to as the higher rate) of £25 per cent of the amount or value of the consideration in lieu of the rates immediately theretofore chargeable."

As will later appear Mr. Parkes' solicitor was well aware of these provisions and advised him on them. However, in the year 1965 the Oireachtas enacted two measures which considerably altered the rates of duty payable on transfers of land to non-Irish citizens and the law relating to the transfer of such land. By virtue of section 66 (6) of the Finance Act 1965 (enacted on the 30th July 1965) sub-sections (4) and (5) of section 13 of the Finance Act 1947 were repealed. This meant that the certifying provisions of the 1947 Act no longer applied and that non-Irish citizens were no longer required to pay stamp duties at the rate of 25% of the amount of the consideration on a purchase of land. But prior to these repeals the Oireachtas had enacted on the 9th March 1965 the Land Act of 1965 which by section 45 had placed restrictions on the vesting of interests in agricultural land in non-Irish nationals. As the effect of this section is of considerable importance on the issues that arise in this case I must refer to it in some detail.

The section commences with definition provisions which provide that the term "qualified person" when used in the section means, inter alia, an Irish citizen and that the phrase "land to which this section applies" means land not situated in a county borough, borough, urban district or town. Sub-section 2 (a) of the section provides as follows:

> "Notwithstanding any other enactment or any rule of law but subject to sub-paragraph (b) of this sub-section and to sub-section (3) of this section, no interest in land to which this section applies shall become vested in a person who is not a qualified person except with the written consent (whether general or written) of the Land Commission and subject to any conditions having been complied with . . ."

The provisions of paragraph (b) of the sub-section are not of relevance in this case but those of sub-section (3) are. These read as follows:

> "Subject to paragraph (b) of this sub-section, an instrument by which an interest to which this section applies purports to become vested (being an instrument which, apart from this section, would affect such vesting) shall effect such vesting provided that it contains a certificate by the person in whom the interest is purported to be vested –
> (2) That the person who becomes entitled to the entire beneficial interest ... is a qualified person by reference to the special category of definition of 'qualified person' contained in sub-section (1) of this section".

The section goes on to make it a criminal offence to make a false statement in a certificate given for the purpose of sub-section (3) by providing in sub-section (6) as follows :

> "Where a person –
> (a) makes any statement which to his knowledge is false or misleading –
> (iii) in a certificate under sub-section (3) of this section he shall be guilty of an offence triable at the election of the prosecution either summarily or on indictment ..."

The legal effects of these provisions have been subject to some debate in this case but their meaning and effect on the facts as now established seem to me to be perfectly clear. Firstly Mrs. Parkes, being an Irish citizen, was a "qualified person" within the meaning of the section. There was nothing in section 45 which prevented the vesting of the land in her and as the transfer to her contained the certificate referred to in sub-section (3) of the section the legal estate in the land vested in her. What has to be determined in this case is whether the Court will permit Mr. Parkes to claim an equitable interest to the lands and give effect to such a claim. In this connection it is relevant to underline the fact that it is illegal for a person to make a statement in the certificate referred to in sub-section (3) which to his knowledge is false.

I come now to my findings of fact. It would seem that the defendant first became interested in the purchase of the lands at Tramore in the year 1964. These lands had formerly been used as a racecourse and golf links but the encroaching tides had long ago caused them to be abandoned and at the time of their purchase they were regularly flooded at high tide. The defendant, however, had since the year 1960 been actively associated with a large public company engaged in the business of land development and his experience and knowledge of this business caused him to consider that the lands behind the strand at Tramore – which to others might appear a picturesque but valueless wasteland – might have a development potential. He set about acquiring them and in addition two other parcels of adjoining land. At this time he and his wife were living in London and he employed a solicitor (who has since died) in Waterford as well as a local auctioneer to negotiate the purchases on his behalf. He failed to acquire any adjoining land but his solicitor was successful in agreeing a price with the owner of the land behind the strand which is contained in Folio No. 1405 of the County of Waterford. Having obtained acceptance of Mr. Parkes' offer of £2,500 for the land his solicitor wrote to him explaining certain aspects of the purchase and added a significant postscript to his letter as follows:

"As you recollect for stamp duty reasons you cannot be named as the purchser, but Roberta, being an Irish citizen, can be so named."

Mr. Parkes replied to this letter on the 5th July and stated:

"As you state in your P.S. the property should be put in Roberta's name".

The contract for sale was signed in trust by Mr. Parkes' solicitor on the 6th July 1965 and a deposit paid and a draft transfer sent on the 20th July for the approval of the vendor's solicitor. On the 28th July the vendor's solicitor wrote asking for Roberta's full name for insertion in the transfer deed and on the 6th September Mr. Parkes' solicitor wrote to Mr. Parkes a letter in which he stated :–

"I am now sending you for Roberta's signature the transfer deed of the above property".

What may well illustrate a somewhat casual approach to this transaction on the part of the solicitor is to be seen from the fact that he asked that Mrs. Parkes, signature on the deed should not be witnessed and added :–

"I can do that when you send back the transfer deed to me, as it saves complications if a solicitor is the witness".

The instrument of transfer is dated the 21st October 1965 and was sent to the Land Registry on the 26th October 1965. The exact date on which Mrs. Parkes executed it cannot now be established with precision – but it would appear that it was sometime not long before the 21st October.

It can clearly be inferred from the postscript to the letter of the 29th June 1965 which I have just quoted that sometime prior to that time Mr. Parkes had been informed by his solicitor of the fact that a higher rate of stamp duty would be payable if the purchase was taken in his name than would be paid if the transfer was taken in his wife's name. In the course of his evidence Mr. Parkes accepted that he may have obtained this advice but he stated that the reason why the land was put in his wife's name was not to avoid a high rate of stamp duty but to avoid having to apply to the Land Commission for its consent to the sale. He stated that he had been told by his solicitor that if he took the land in his own name such an application would be necessary because he was not an Irish citizen and he was informed that the application would take a long time to be processed and that it was very likely that it would become public knowledge that he was trying to buy land in the area. As he was still negotiating the purchase of adjoining land Mr. Parkes said that he did not want it known that he was the purchaser of the old racecourse. He was quite positive that he had no intention of giving the land to his wife as a gift and he claimed that the land was put in her name merely for the purpose of avoiding having to apply to the Land Commission for its consent to a sale to him.

Mrs. Parkes' evidence was to a different effect. She could not remember actually signing the transfer but she claimed that she was given the land as a present by her husband. She knew the land was of little value and she regarded the whole thing as a bit of a joke. She agreed that she did not disclose this asset in her maintenance application in the English divorce proceedings and that she did not swear in an affidavit filed in the Land Registry and sworn on the 12th August 1977 that the lands had been given to her as a gift.

I have little difficulty in preferring Mr. Parkes' recollection of the transaction to that of his wife's. Not only is his memorty of the matter clearer than his wife's but I am satisfied that he had decided to purchase the land with a view to its possible future development with other land in the area and that in such circumstances it is extremely improbable that he would have parted with the beneficial ownership in the old racecourse in favour of his wife. Whilst the contemporary correspondence makes no reference to the matter, I am satisfied that his solicitor was aware in the summer of

1965 (as most solicitors in the country were) of the changes effected by the Finance Act 1965 and the Land Act, 1965 and that Mr. Parkes was told some time before the transaction was completed that if the transfer was taken in his name he would have to apply to the Land Commission for its consent to the transfer. To avoid such an application he decided that the transfer should be taken in his wife's name. I am also satisfied that he must have read the Deed of Transfer sent by his solicitor to him and that he must have been aware that the certificate which was contained in it and which he requested his wife to sign was a false one. It is likely, however, that Mrs. Parkes did not bother to read it and that even had she done so I think it is unlikely that she appreciated that she was knowingly giving a false or misleading certificate. In the light of these findings of fact how should the Court determine the issue between the parties?

There are, it seems to me, four general principles of law which are relevant to the facts which I have just outlined. The first is that where a person buys property and pays the purchase money but takes the purchase in the name of another, who is neither his child, adopted child or his wife, there is prima facie no gift, but a resulting trust in favour of the person paying the money. The second principle is that where a person in whose name a purchase is taken is the wife, child, or adopted child of the person paying the purchase money there is a presumption that a gift was intended. Thirdly, however, the presumption in favour of a wife, child or adopted child may be rebutted by evidence which establishes that a gift was not intended. The Defendant relies on these principles and claims that as his intention was that no gift was to be effected the Plaintiff holds the land as trustee for him. But the Plaintiff's counsel ripostes with a fourth principle which it is claimed a court applying equitable principles should apply in this case. Put shortly, it is that a purchaser will not obtain relief in equity by setting up his own illegality or fraud. This is the crucial point of law in this dispute, and I will now consider the cases which it is claimed illustrate it and justify its application to the facts I am now considering.

The first case to which I was referred by the plaintiff's counsel was that of *Gascoigne* v. *Gascoigne* [1918] 1 K.B. 223. This was a case in which a husband took a lease of land in his wife's name and built a house on it with his own money. He used his wife's name with her knowledge and connivance because he was in debt and wished to protect the property from his creditors. He brought proceedings against his wife in which he sought a declaration that she held the property as trustee for him. His claim failed. In the course of the Court's judgment reference was made to the findings of fact in the lower Court and then went on (p.226) –

> "These findings of fact must be taken to mean that the plaintiff, with his wife's knowledge and connivance concocted the scheme of putting his property in her name, while retaining the beneficial interest, for the purpose of misleading, defeating and delaying present or future creditors. This was the whole basis of the plaintiff's case and it could not be put in any other way consistently with his claim to the ownership of the property. It was the reason he himself gave for his conduct. Now, assuming that there was evidence to support the finding that the defendant was a party to the scheme which the plaintiff admitted, but without deciding it, what the learned Judge has done is this : he has permitted the plaintiff to rebut the presumption which the law raises by setting up his own illegality and fraud, and to obtain relief in equity because he has succeeded in proving it. The plaintiff cannot do this : and whether the point was taken or not in the county Court this Court cannot allow a judgment to stand which has given relief under such circumstances as that."

The principle in *Gascoigne* was applied in somewhat different circumstances *In re Emery's Investment Trusts* [1959] 1 Ch. 410. In that case the plaintiff (who was a British subject) was married to an American citizen. American savings bonds were purchased with the plantiff's money (the defendant's husband) and were registered in the name of the wife with the husband expressly named as a beneficiary with her. Later the bonds were changed for common stock in American securities. These were registered in the name of the wife but with the intention that the beneficial interest in the securities should be as to one half in the wife and one half in the husband. But in order to avoid the payment of American withholding tax to which as an alien the plaintiff was liable under American Federal Law, no mention was made of his beneficial interest. After the wife had sold the securities the husband applied to the Courts in England for a declaration that at the date of the removal and sale of the securities his wife held them as to one half for him. His claim failed. Wynn-Parry, J. pointed out that had the tax involved in the case been United Kingdom tax the case would have been covered by *Gascoigne's Case* and would have been concluded against the plaintiff. Having considered the facts of *Gascoigne's Case* and the decision in it he went on as follows (p.419) :

> "In the analysis it will be found that there were two relevant intentions in *Gascoigne* v. *Gascoigne.* The first was the intention of the husband that the house and land should, so far as the beneficial interest was concerned, be and remain his. The second intention was that he put the land and house into his wife's name with a view to protecting it from his creditors in case he should get into financial difficulties. In this case the first intention, corresponding to that in *Gascoigne* v. *Gascoigne,* is the intention that the husband had throughout that the beneficial interest in the security should be shared between himself and his wife. The second intention, which corresponds with the second intention in *Gascoigne* v. *Gascoigne* is the intention which the husband had in putting the securities in his wife's name, without any reference being made to the retention by him of any beneficial interest, namely to avoid payment of withholding tax on his beneficial interest."

The Court held that it should apply the principle in *Gascoigne's Case* even though the tax involved in the transaction was an American tax. The judge pointed out that there was a clear breach of the federal law in the way the transactions were carried out by the husband's non-disclosure of his beneficial interest in the security and he concluded that the plaintiff could not seek the aid of equity in such circumstances.

More recently the principle to which I have referred was considered in the Court of Appeal in England in *Tinker* v. *Tinker* [1970] P.136. This was a case in which a husband intended to buy a house in his own name but was advised by his solicitors that if the new business venture he was then undertaking failed the house could be taken by his creditors as part of his business assets and his solicitors recommended that it should be put in his wife's name. This was done and the house was conveyed to her. The marriage broke down and the wife claimed the house as her own. It was held that on the evidence the husband had an honest intention at the time of the conveyance that the house would belong to his wife and accordingly the wife's claim to the property succeeded. In the course of his judgment Salmon L.J. said :

> "It is trite law that anyone coming to equity to be relieved against his own act must come with clean hands. If, in a case such as the present, he were to put forward, as a reason for being relieved against his own act, a dishonest plot on his part, for example, to defraud his creditors, the Court would refuse him relief and would say : let the estate lie where it falls. But, of course, that is not this case. . ." (p.143)

Finally, I was referred to a decision of the Court of Appeal in Northern Ireland [*i.e. McEvoy* v. *Belfast Banking Co.* [1934] N.I. 67, on appeal to House of Lords, [1935] A.C. 24, see *Irish Land Law,* para. 9.044 – Ed.] in which the principle in *Gascoigne's Case* was applied in relation to a deposit of £10,000 made by a father in the joint names of himself and his son. It was established that the object of the deposit was to avoid death duties. Although there was no intention on the father's part to benefit his son the Court took the view that it could not have regard to the evidence which established this fact "because of its illegal taint" (see: p.99).

In my opinion the fourth principle to which I have referred and which is illustrated in the cases quoted above should be applied in this case. Just as the Courts will not grant relief to a person who has allowed property to be placed in a wife's or son's name for the fraudulent purpose of defeating creditors *(Gascoigne)* or for the illegal purpose of evading liability to tax *(Emery* and *McEvoy)* so it seems to me the Court should not grant relief to a purchaser who has placed property in his wife's name dishonestly and by means of an illegal act performed for the purpose of evading the law relating to the transfer of land. This is what the defendant has done in this case. The Defendant claimed that he acted on his solicitor's advice – but I am sure that his solicitor did not advise him to commit a criminal offence and by suggesting that the property could be taken in his wife's name he did not advise him to procure a false certificate in the deed of transfer. The Defendant said that he thought the certificate was a mere formality – but he is an experienced man of affairs and no neophyte in the business of buying and selling land and he knew he was asking his wife to execute a transfer which contained a certificate which was false. I am not obliged to reach a conclusion as to whether or not Mr. Parkes committed a criminal offence under the section. It suffices in this case that he knowingly authorised the commission of an act which was prohibited by the section for the purpose of evading the statute. As a result the whole transaction is tainted with illegality. Mr. Parkes is in the same inescapable dilemma in which the Plaintiff in *Tinker's Case* found himself : if he acted honestly, and the certificate was a true one, then the property belongs to his wife ; if he acted dishonestly, and the certificate was a false one, the Court will not allow him to take advantage of his own dishonesty. What the Defendant asks is that the Court should apply its equitable principles and hold that a resulting trust exists and that the Plaintiff holds the land in trust for him. But the very equitable principles which the defendant calls in aid prevents the Court making a declaration in his favour. The estate must lie where it falls; the Plaintiff's claim succeeds; the Defendant's counterclaim fails.

In conclusion, I should add that my decision has been based on the equitable principles applicable when a husband purchases land and transfers it into his wife's name. The result would have been the same had I applied another well known principle which seems to me to be relevant to the facts of this case, ex dolo malo non oritur actio, and which was applied in a case where it was established that a purchaser had practised a deceit on the public administration (see: *Chettiar* v. *Chettiar* [1962] 2 W.L.R. 548).

Notes and Questions

1. See further on resulting trusts, ch. 12. *post.*
2. As regards s.45 of the Land Act, 1965, see *Irish Conveyancing Law,* ch. 8
3. If the element of illegality had not been present in this case, what would the result have been?

VII. EQUITABLE ESTOPPEL

SMITH V. IRELAND

Unreported (High Court) (1982 No. 1113 P) (Judgment delivered 11th February 1983)

The facts are set out in the judgment.

Finlay P.:

This is a claim brought by the Plaintiff by way of summary summons against the Defendants for the sum of £16,320 together with interest. The claim is in respect of a deduction suffered by the Plaintiff from what he alleges should have been the minimum statutory price payable to him by various Bacon Factories in the year 1972 in respect of pigs sold and delivered by him to those factories. Deduction was made pursuant to certain statutory instruments made by the Defendants, the Pigs and Bacon Commission, with the concurrence of the Minister for Agriculture pursuant to a power vested in the Commission by the provisions of the Pigs and Bacon Acts 1935 to 1961. Those instruments are Statutory Instruments Nos. 94; 109 and 293 respectively of 1972 which are in identical terms with varying minimum prices fixed. In the course of each of those Instruments the Pigs and Bacon Commission purported to provide in the Schedule an exclusion from the minimum prices fixed, of the price for pigs in respect of which the Minister for Agriculture and Fisheries was not satisfied that the pigs were produced in the State. The Plaintiff's claim is based on the fact that those orders and in particular that provision in the Schedule was invalid and ultra vires, constituted a breach of duty on the part of the Defendants to him the Plaintiff and was the cause of the loss claimed by him.

The summons herein was issued on the 19th February 1982 and the Plaintiff by Notice of Motion dated the 11th March 1982 applied to the Master of the High Court for liberty to enter final judgment. The matter came before Mr. Justice Barrington on the 12th July 1982 and he then made an Order that the action should stand adjourned for plenary hearing without pleadings.

In the affidavits filed on behalf of the Defendants, each of them indicated a defence to the Plaintiff's claim on the basis that the action was statute barred and in addition the first and second named Defendants put the Plaintiff on proof of the quantities of pigs alleged to have been delivered to the bacon factories during 1972 and also denied negligence.

When the matter came for hearing before me Counsel on behalf of the first two Defendants indicated that in the event of the court holding that the Plaintiff's claim was not statute barred, that those Defendants would accept liability for the sum claimed by the Plaintiff and that judgment by consent could be entered against them for that amount. Counsel on behalf of the Plaintiff also indicated to me at the outset of the proceedings before me that the Plaintiff was not pursuing the claim in negligence against any of the Defendants.

The sole issue therefore which arose for detemination by me was as to whether the claim of the Plaintiff against these Defendants was barred by virtue of the provisions of the Statute of Limitations 1957. By consent of the parties I tried that issue on the affidavits and the exhibits therein referred to and on the oral evidence of one witness, Mr. Fitzsimons, with regard to the admissibility of one letter.

Facts

The facts on which this matter falls to be determined having regard to the affidavits, the exhibits therein referred to and the concessions made by the parties before me may thus be summarised. The Plaintiff is a Pig Dealer who in the year 1972 was engaged in the activity of purchasing pigs and selling them to licensed bacon curing factories. In the year 1972, he sold and delivered to five separate licensed bacon curing factories a total of 2,720 pigs in respect of each of which he received a price which was £6.00 less than the minimum statutory price on the ground that the Minister for Agriculture was not satisfied as to the origin of each of the said pigs. The loss thus incurred by him was £16,320.

In the ordinary way, payment for pigs delivered to a licensed bacon curing factory became due upon delivery and was usually made within approximately 14 days of delivery. The 2,720 pigs in respect of which this claim arose were delivered between the 12th of April 1972 and 21st November 1972.

On the 2nd May 1972, solicitors acting on behalf of the Plaintiff wrote to the Secretary of the Department of Agriculture and Fisheries in the following terms –

> "We act for Mr. Alfred Smith of Virginia, Co. Cavan, our Client instructs us that he is involved in the buying and selling of pigs and that in recent times he has sold a number of pigs to the following factories :–
>
> Claremorris Bacon Co. Ltd.
> James Hanley & Sons, Rooskey
> McCarren & Co., Cavan
> Buttles of Enniscorthy.
>
> It has now transpired that as a result of information or an Order from your Department to these Companies, a sum of £6.00 per pig has been stopped on foot of the sale of a substantial number of the pigs to these factories, and as a result our Client is at a considerable loss of revenue. He is, therefore, unable to purchase or acquire his usual stock of animals. In addition, the information given to these factories has caused serious damage to our Client's reputation and trustworthiness and are a serious reflection on him.
>
> Accordingly, we are instructed that our Client's business is suffering serious damage, his reputation as a Pig Dealer has been jeopardised and we are instructed

> to state that unless you instruct the Bacon Factories concerned to pay the full amount of the retention money forthwith to him, proceedings will be issued for recovery of same.
>
> Unless we hear satisfactorily from you within seven days from this date our Client will take proceedings to recover all his loss and damage."

This letter was simply acknowledged on the 5th of May 1972 and received a full reply on the 6th June 1972 in the following terms:

> "With reference to your letter of 2 May about pigs sold to certain bacon factories by Mr. Alfred Smith, Virginia, Co. Cavan, I am directed by the Minister for Agriculture and Fisheries to state that as part of measures to counter serious damage caused by cross-Border smuggling of pigs from the Six Counties this Department has required bacon curers to keep detailed daily records of data from their suppliers as to the sources of all pigs delivered to them. In cases in which the Department is not satisfied as to the reliability of the data furnished regarding the origin of pigs, an appropriate deduction of subsidy at the rate of £6.00 per pig is made by the Pigs and Bacon Commission in respect of the curers' pigmeat exports. In this connection, the bacon curers, as announced publicly by the Irish Bacon Curers' Society some time ago, made it clear to all suppliers that it would be an express condition of purchase of all pigs by them that any export subsidy disallowed to them by the Commission will be passed on by them for the account of the pig suppliers concerned, all pigs supplied to them being deemed to be sold by the suppliers subject to that condition. Any deductions made in respect of pigs supplied to curers by Mr. Smith were made on the foregoing basis where this Department was not satisfied as to the reliability of the data furnished regarding the origin of the pigs."

On the 16th October 1972, the Plaintiff himself wrote to the Department of Agriculture and Fisheries referring to a recent telephone conversation in which he stated he was asked to write with details concerning his pigs and set out much detail concerning the pigs which had been sold by him and in particular stated where they had been purchased by him and from whom. The letter concluded with the following paragraphs:–

> "You will note from this letter Mr. Brennan that I am asking you to pay me the sum of £6,402.00 which is owed to me and which your Department has been the means of with-holding. I cannot afford to be at this loss and unless some attempt is made to settle this matter I am passing the matter along to someone more competent to deal with it on my behalf. You have also stopped other subsidies you had not any reason for with-holding, and I shall be writing to you shortly about these. I trust you will give this letter your most urgent attention as I need the money that is owed to me to continue my business."

That letter was replied to by the Department on the 19th October 1972 in the following terms :–

> "I am directed by the Minister for Agricultrue and Fisheries to acknowledge the receipt of your letter of the 16th October about pigs supplied to factories. You will appreciate that in view of the number of separate deliveries involved it will take some time to examine the position fully. A further letter will issue as soon as possible."

It would appear that no further letter did at that time or for some years issue from the Department of Agriculture and Fisheries but in 1972 one John McCrumlish instituted proceedings against the Pigs and Bacon Commission and the Minister for Agriculture and Fisheries claiming inter alia a declaration that the statutory instruments already referred to in this judgment fixing the minimum price for pigs in 1972 were invalid and ultra vires insofar as they purported to exclude from those minimum prices pigs the origin of which had not been established to the satisfaction of the Minister. Those proceedings came on for hearing before Mr. Justice Gannon and by agreement of the parties, he heard as a separate preliminary issue that question as to the validity of the statutory instruments concerned. By judgment delivered on the 28th May 1975 Mr. Justice Gannon held that portion of those

Instruments to be invalid and ultra vires but otherwise and with the exclusion of that portion upheld the validity of the minimum price orders. Against that judgment, no appeal was brought by either of the Defendants.

The next correspondence between the parties in this case appears to have been a letter written by the Plaintiff himself on the 30th December 1975 to the Department of Agriculture and Fisheries in the following terms :

> "I am writing you to know what is holding my cheque for money stopped on pigs in 1972 and 1973 at £6 per pig. May 28th, 1975 Justice Gannon in reserved judgment said that the order to stop this money by your Department was invalid. Since then I rang Mr. Coyle and Brennan three or four times to know when I was getting my money and they seem not to know the full position as they say it is your legal advisors that is holding the payment up. In my opinion they have no grounds to hold other peoples money and it is unjust in the eyes of God and Man. As time is passing on and you have this money held for so long you give me no other option only to take your Departments back into Court for my money and interest and damages to my whole business for the period involved. I give seven days notice from the date you receive this letter that I will take you back into Court unless I receive your cheque."

To that letter a reply was written by the Department on the 5th January 1976 in the following terms :

> "I am directed by the Minister for Agriculture and Fisheries to acknowledge receipt of your letter of the 30th December 1975 which was received in this Division on the 2nd January 1976 about the disallowance of pigmeat export subsidy on pigs supplied to various bacon factories by you in 1972 and 1973.
> The matter is receiving attention and a further reply will issue to you as soon as possible."

No further reply did in fact issue and there was no further correspondence between the parties. In 1978 however on the evidence I am satisfied that the Plaintiff sought the assistance of Mr. Jim Fitzsimons, T.D. who was a member of Dáil Éireann in his area. Mr. Fitzsimons gave evidence before me and whilst he felt that it was possible he wrote to the then Minister for Agriculture concerning Mr. Smith's complaint and the complaint of other persons in a like position it seems to me more probable though the matter is not very material that he made a verbal representation to the Minister for Agriculture. In any event the Minister for Agriculture who was then Deputy Gibbons replied to Deputy Fitzsimmons on the 29th August 1978 in the following terms :

> "I wish to refer further to your recent representations on behalf of pig merchants from whom export subsidies have been withheld under measures taken by my Department in 1972 to counter cross-border smuggling of pigs from the Six Counties.
> The position is that the High Court gave judgment on a point of law arising in a particular case in which pigmeat export subsidies were disallowed but, as yet, the Court has not heard evidence or made a determination on the matters of fact in connection with the withholding of the subsidies. In the circumstances the question of releasing any disallowed subsidies cannot be considered at the present time."

The Plaintiff himself wrote a further letter to the Department of Agriculture on the 24th June 1980 reiterating his claim for money stopped on pigs at £6 each in the years 1972 to 1973 though not quantifying that claim and seeking payment of the monies due to him. To that letter there does not appear to have been any reply.

On the 8th September 1980 solicitors on behalf of the Plaintiff wrote to the Department of Agriculture referring to previous correspondence, reiterating a claim for the return of the monies with interest without quantifying them and threatening to institute proceedings within seven days from the date of that letter. By letter of the 12th September 1980 the Department of Agriculture replied to the solicitors concerned noting the contents of their letter and informing them that the correspondence had been referred to the Pigs and Bacon Commission for their attention. To that letter a further reply was sent by the solicitors on behalf of the Plaintiff strongly protesting against this action, but nothing I am satisfied turns on the precise terms of that letter. A reply was received reiterating that it was a matter for the Pigs and Bacon Commission.

A letter was then written by solicitors on behalf of the Pigs and Bacon Commission on the 5th November 1980 in the following terms :

> "I act for the Pigs and Bacon Commission and I understand that you act for a Mr. Alfred Smith, Dean Ard, Virginia, Co. Cavan and a copy of your letter of the 13th ult. addressed to the Department of Agriculture has been forwarded to me.
>
> It would appear that your client indicated to the Department that he had a claim arising out of alleged disallowance of a pigmeat export subsidy. It would appear that any such claim by your client would have long since been statute barred under the Statute of Limitations."

Further correspondence ensued between the solicitor for the Plaintiff and the solicitor for the Pigs and Bacon Commission on which nothing turns in the issue before me and these proceedings were then instituted as I have already indicated by a summons issued on the 19th February 1982. The only other fact which may be material is that I was informed by Counsel, though the matter was not strictly proved before me, that the claim for money damages by Mr. McCrumlish in his proceedings was eventually settled by a consent order before Mr. Justice Gannon in the year 1980.

The Law

The Plaintiff's claim in effect consists of a series of causes of action, the first of which arose I am satisfied as a matter of law in the month of April or at the latest May of 1972 and the last of which arose at the latest in the month of December 1972. Prima facie, therefore, I am satisfied that by virtue of the provisions of Section 11 of the Statutes of Limitations 1957 no part of the claim could be brought after December 1978. By virtue of Section 3 (1) of the 1957 Act that period of limitation applied to proceedings by or against a State authority and therefore applied to the proceedings before me against these three Defendants in like manner as if these three Defendants were private individuals.

The Plaintiff seeking to avoid this apparent limitation of his claim relied through his Counsel upon the following submissions :

1. That the letter written by the Department of Agriculture and Fisheries of the 5th January 1976 which I have already quoted constituted an acknowledgment on behalf of these Defendants in writing of this claim within the meaning of the Act of 1957 and that the letter written by the Minister for Agriculture on the 29th August 1978 constituted a further acknowledgment of a claim which was still alive and that therefore the statute does not apply.
2. In the alternative it was submitted that the entire of the correspondence constituted representations on behalf of these Defendants that they would not raise against the Plaintiff any defence of a time limit and that they would eventually deal with and accept liability for the amount of his claim which induced the Plaintiff to abstain from the institution of proceedings to his disadvantage and that they are therefore estopped from now pleading the Statute of Limitations.
3. Thirdly, it was submitted that over and above the equitable doctrine of estoppel that certain principles enshrined in European Community law and in particular the prohibition therein contained against the defeating of legitimate expectation and against discrimination or inequality in the treatment of the producers and traders in agricultural products which form part of our domestic law by reason of our membership of the European Economic Community make it unlawful for the Defendants who are State authorites now to plead the Statute of Limitations.

Plea of Acknowledgment

By virtue of Section 56 (1) of the Statute of Limitations 1957 it is provided as follows :

"Where (a) any right of action has accrued to recover any debt and (b) the person liable therefor acknowledges the debt, the right of action shall be deemed to have accrued on and not before the date of the acknowledgment."

It is submitted that the letter written on behalf of the Department of Agriculture and Fisheries on the 5th January 1976 constituted an acknowledgment of this debt. I must reject this submission on two grounds. Firstly, it was contended that the reference in the first paragraph of that letter to a disallowance of pigmeat export subsidy read in conjunction with a letter from the Department of the 6th June 1972 which justified that disallowance solely on the basis of the provisions contained in the Statutory Instruments which by the decision of Mr. Justice Gannon were held to be invalid must be taken as being properly construed as an acceptance or acknowledgment that the disallowance was not only without statutory authority but that it created a liability which was being accepted by or on behalf of the Minister for the repayment of the sums disallowed. I cannot so construe this letter. The first paragraph of it appears to me patently to be no more than a paragraph indicating the letter to which it is a reply and identifying the subject matter of the claim or assertion contained in that letter. The only assurance contained in the letter is of a further communication and it would appear to me to be quite impossible to construe the letter as the acceptance of a liability or the acknowledgment of a debt. Secondly, I am satisfied that the views expressed by Lord Denning M.R. in *Good* v. *Parry* [1963] 2 All E.R. 59, are correct and are applicable to Section 56 of the Act of 1957, where at page 61 of the report he states :–

"in order to be an acknowledgment, however the debt must be quantified in figures or at all events it must be liquidated in this sense that it is capable of ascertainment by calculation or by extrinsic evidence without further agreement of the parties."

The Plaintiff did not and could not submit that the correspondence to which I have referred constituted an acknowledgment of an identified debt which had been quantified. There had not been at the time that letter was written any quantification made by the Plaintiff of the entire of the claim which is now before me. It was submitted, however, that by reason of the fact that the Plaintiff's claim can be quantified by multiplying the number of pigs in respect of which the deduction was made by the amount of the deduction namely, £6 per pig, that it was capable of being quantified by extrinsic evidence without further agreement. Reliance in this context was also placed on the fact that the Defendants do not seek in the event of the plea of the statute being unsuccessful to dispute the amount of the claim. I am satisfied that this submission must fail. The fact that there is a method of proving a Plaintiff's claim and of calculating from that method the amount of the claim is not the extrinsic evidence without further agreement referred to in the judgment which I have quoted. What must exist is that extrinsic evidence at the time of acknowledgment and I cannot infer from the conduct of these Defendants at this stage in relying only on one defence any acknowledgment made in 1976 as to the amount of the debt.

I am therefore satisfied that the plea of avoidance of the statute by acknowledgment must fail.

With regard to the plea of estoppel, particular reliance was placed upon the decision in *Crabb* v. *Arun District Council* [1975] 3 All E.R. 865. That is a decision of the Court of Appeal consisting of Lord Denning M.R., Lawton and Scarman L.JJ. in which the Court was unanimous. In the course of his judgment Lord Denning M.R. outlining the circumstances under which an equitable estoppel might arise stated at page 871 as follows :

"Short of an actual promise, if he, by his words or conduct, so behaves as to lead another to believe that he will not insist on his strict legal rights knowing or intending that the other will act on that behalf – and he does so act, that again will raise an equity in favour of the other, and it is for a court of equity to say in what way the equity may be satisfied."

In the course of his judgment Scarman L.J. at page 876 quoted with approval from the judgment of Fry J. in *Willmott* v. *Barber* (1880) 15 Ch. Div. 96 as follows –

> "It has been said that the acquiescence which will deprive a man of his legal rights must amount to fraud, and in my view that is an abbreviated statement of a very true proposition. A man is not to be deprived of his legal rights unless he has acted in such a way as would make it fraudulent for him to set up those rights. What, then, are the elements or requisites necessary to constitute fraud of that description? In the first place the plaintiff must have made a mistake as to his legal rights. Secondly, the plaintiff must have expended some money or must have done some act (not necessarily upon the defendant's land) on the faith of his mistaken belief. Thirdly, the defendant, the possessor of the legal right, must know of the existence of his own right which is inconsistent with the right claimed by the plaintiff. If he does not know of it he is in the same position as the plaintiff, and the doctrine of acquiescence is founded upon conduct with a knowledge of your legal rights. Fourthly, the defendant, the possessor of the legal right, must know of the plaintiff's mistaken belief of his rights. If he does not, there is nothing which calls upon him to assert his own rights. Lastly, (if I may digress, this is the important element as far as the appeal is concerned) the defendant, the possessor of the legal right, must have encouraged the plaintiff in his expenditure of money or in the other acts which he has done, either directly or by abstaining from asserting his legal right."

Although these two portions of the judgments in *Crabb* v. *Arun D.C.* do not deal with any case involving the plea of the Statute of Limitations, I am satisfied that they are a correct statement of the general law of equitable estoppel upon which the Plaintiff relies in this case and that they are consistent one with the other.

Accepting them as I do on the facts of this case I am satisfied that the Plaintiff has failed to establish that the Defendant is debarred by any form of equitable estoppel from now pleading the Statute of Limitations.

I cannot read the entire of this correspondence, and in particular the two letters of 1976 and 1978 upon which special reliance is placed on behalf of the Plaintiff, as either being calculated or intended to lead the Plaintiff to believe that the Defendants would not insist on their strict legal rights or as constituting an encouragement of the Plaintiff to act on that belief. The terms of the letter of January 1976 seem to me no more than the most common form of a postponing letter to be found either in the equipment of bureaucracy or in the common usage of solicitors for defendants. Equally the letter from the Minister for Agriculture of 1978 seems clearly to me to indicate not only a postponement of any decision as to whether to accept liability for any payment to the Plaintiff but to specifically mention that the matter remained in doubt having regard to the state of the action brought by Mr. McCrumlish. No evidence was given by the Plaintiff before me in this action and I have no evidence to suggest either that he was aware of the existence of a time limit on the claim which he had nor have I any positive evidence that he was induced to refrain from the institution of proceedings by reason of the correspondence which had taken place though I am asked to infer this latter conclusion from the terms of the correspondence itself.

I am therefore satisfied that the claim to avoid the provisions of the Statute of Limitations by reason of equitable estoppel must fail.

With regard to the third submission made on behalf of the Plaintiff, I am satisfied that the following is the position.

By virtue of the provisions of Section 2 of the European Communities Act, 1972 it was provided as follows –

> "From the first day of January 1973 the Treaties governing the European Communities and the existing and future Acts adopted by the institutions of those Communities shall be binding on the State and shall be part of the domestic law thereof under the conditions laid down in those Treaties."

The deductions made by the Pigs and Bacon Commission at the request or under the direction of the Minister for Agriculture and Fisheries from the payments to the Plaintiff in respect of which he now claims all occurred prior to the 1st January 1973. The Plaintiff's reliance on the provisions of the Treaties governing the European

Communities and the jurisprudence developed from them must therefore be not in regard to the original deductions but specifically and solely in regard to the decision of these Defendants to plead in answer to the Plaintiff's claim the Statute of Limitations. It was urged upon me that in particular the general provisions of the Treaties and the law thereunder prohibiting the defeat by a government agency of the legitimate expectation of a producer or trader in agricultural goods and the prohibition against discrimination or inequality in the treatment by a government agency of producers or traders in agricultural goods prohibits these Defendants from now pleading the statute. It is suggested that the legitimate expectation which was in the Plaintiff was that he would not be dealt with differently from Mr. McCrumlish and that the inequality or discrimination which has arisen is that he was.

Even if I were satisfied that the prohibitions and provisions contained in the European Community Law to which I have referred applied to the right of government or a government agency to rely upon a statutory time limit which was expressly applicable to them and I would reserve my decision on this point, I am not satisfied that there has been established in this case a legitimate expectation or an inequality or discrimination. Mr. McCrumlish instituted proceedings promptly upon suffering a deduction similar to that suffered by the Plaintiff. He instituted such proceedings taking upon himself the burden and risks of establishing the invalidity of the statutory instruments concerned. He pursued those proceedings to their ultimate conclusion with success. That he should have been dealt with by the Defendants by discharging their liability even on a consent or agreed basis was in a sense inevitable and was not a concession on their part.

I do not consider that there are any grounds for reaching a conclusion that the Plaintiff who instituted no proceedings within the time limited by law, had any legitimate expectation that he would be dealt with in a manner identical or similar to that of Mr. McCrumlish. Furthermore, I see no inequality in treatment between the case of a person instituting the appropriate proceedings within the time limited and the necessary and inevitable liability thus established against the Defendants in such a case and the case of a person who fails to institute proceedings within the time limited. For these reasons, I am satisfied that this further submission on behalf of the Plaintiff must fail in this case.

I am accordingly satisfied that the Plaintiff's claim herein is barred by virtue of the provisions of the Statute of Limitations of 1957 and must be dismissed.

Notes

1. See further on the application of the principle of equitable estoppel in Ireland, *Cullen* v. *Cullen* [1962] I.R. 268 (reproduced at p.657 of *A Casebook on Irish Land Law)* ; *Revenue Commissioners* v. *Moroney* [1972] I.R. 372.
2. On the Statute of Limitations, 1957, see *Irish Land Law*, ch. 23 ; Brady and Kerr, *Limitation of Actions in Ireland* (1984).

Chapter 2

CONVERSION AND RECONVERSION

The doctrine of conversion is an illustration of the well-known maxim of equity – "Equity regards as done what ought to be done." Its significance in the area of succession has been lessened by the assimilation of realty with personalty for the purposes of intestate succession, see *Irish Land Law,* para. 3.095 and ch. 15. The doctrine is still invoked where testators use general expressions like "realty" and "personalty" in wills and has been used, somewhat controversially, in other contexts by the courts, e.g., to determine the position of parties to conveyancing contracts, see *Irish Conveyancing Law,* para 11.07.

STEELE V. STEELE

[1913] 1 I. R. 292 (Court of Appeal)

The facts are set out in the judgments.

Palles, C.B.:

The question upon this appeal is whether a devise contained in the will of Robert Ball Steele, and confirmed by his codicil, of his estates in the counties of Kildare and Dublin, was adeemed by certain agreements made by the testator for sale of portions of those lands to tenants under the Land Purchase Act of 1903, to the extent of the portions of the lands comprised in those agreements.

The will bears date the 25th November, 1899. At that time the testator was seised in fee of the estates in Kildare and Dublin, and appears to have had four children living, viz., Major Robert Ball Steele the younger, the respondent in this appeal, who was his eldest son; John Treacy Steele, the appellant; and two daughters, Anne Treacy Steele, who was unmarried ; and Catherine, who was married to Arthur McCormick.

The will commences with a recital that the testator is absolute owner of certain estates in the counties of Kildare and Dublin; and then proceeds to charge those estates with life annuities for his younger son, John Treacy Steele, and for each of his two daughters; and subject to those annuities he devises his said estates to the use of his elder son, Robert Ball Steele, for life, with remainder to his first and other sons in tail male, with remainder to his younger son, John Treacy Steele, for life, remainder to his first and other sons in tail male, with an ultimate remainder to the testator's own right heirs.

He then bequeaths to his unmarried daughter, Anne Treacy Steele, his household goods, furniture, and effects, save his pictures and plate, which he bequeaths to his elder son, Robert Ball Steele; and finally, he appoints his son, John Treacy Steele, his residuary devisee and legatee; and his son-in-law, Arthur McCormick, executor of his will.

On the 1st January, 1906, being within two months of the execution of the codicil to his will, he signed separate agreements with each of thirty-one of his thirty-six tenants in the county Kildare. Each of these agreements is in the same form, and thereby he agreed that in case an estate of which the tenant's holding formed a part should be sold under the provisions of the Irish Land Act, 1903, he should sell, and the tenant should purchase, the fee-simple of the holding for a specified sum, upon which it was provided that interest should be payable to the Irish Land Commission from the date of the agreement, and that the sale should be carried out by means of a vesting order. In the same month he swore an affidavit verifying an original application to the Irish Land Commission to have all his Kildare estates declared fit to be regarded as separate estates for the purposes of sale under the Act of 1903.

On the 1st of February, 1906, the testator signed five similar agreements with tenants of portions of his Dublin estate.

On the 7th February, 1906, he made a codicil to his will, whereby he revoked the appointment of Arthur McCormick as executor of his will, and appointed his son,

Major Robert Ball Steele, sole executor; stating that he would have appointed him sole executor "had he known that he would be residing in Ireland, and retired from the army"; and he confirmed his will in other respects.

On the 17th February, 1906, the testator made an originating application to the Irish Land Commission in respect of his Dublin estate; and in March, 1906, he signed agreements with three others of the tenants of his Kildare estate similar to those which I have already stated.

The testator died on the 23rd May, 1906. The conditions contained in the agreements of an estate of which the tenants' holdings formed part being sold under the Act of 1903, were performed not, however, during his life, but after his death.

Under these circumstances, Barton, J., was of opinion that if it had not been for the codicil, once the conditions contained in the agreements had been performed, and the agreements had thus become absolute, the result of the application of the rule laid down by Lord Kenyon in *Lawes* v. *Bennett* 1 Cox, C. C. 167 would have been to effect a conversion of the devised estates into personalty, and that the residuary legatee, the present appellant, would have been entitled to the purchase-moneys.

He, however, also held that the codicil indicated a contrary intention; and consequently that the purchase-moneys were bound by the limitations contained in the will.

It is not absolutely necessary for us to decide the first question upon which Barton, J., has thus expressed an opinion. I shall hereafter say something in reference to it; but I prefer to consider, in the first instance, the effective *ratio decidendi* of Barton, J., that is the effect of the codicil, upon the assumption that the agreements did operate to adeem the devise of the lands agreed to be sold.

In the opinion of Barton, J., upon this second question, I entirely concur, and for the reasons he has expressed. We have here the three circumstances which occurred in *Emuss* v. *Smith* 2 De G. & S. 722, and in *Pyle* v. *Pyle,* [1895] 1 Ch. 724. viz., the specific devise, the conditional nature of the contracts for sale, and the republication after the contract of the the will by a codicil which did not refer to those contracts. If the rule laid down in *Lawes* v. *Bennett* 1 Cox, C. C. 167 be, as I think it is, quite too firmly established to be questioned in this, or indeed in any, Court, so, too, I hold to be firmly established the exception to the rule where there is the concurrence of these three circumstances. In *Drant* v. *Vanuse* 1 Y. & C. Ch. C. 580, decided in 1842, the will was made after the contract for sale, and therefore there was no necessity for republication, and the sole matter to distinguish it from *Lawes* v. *Bennett* 1 Cox, C. C. 167 was the specific nature of the devise. The report of the judgment of Lord Justice Knight-Bruce, then Vice-Chancellor, after referring to the general terms in which the will in *Lawes* v. *Bennett* 1 Cox, C. C. 167 was expressed, "to which," he says, "Lord Kenyon, at the commencement of his judgment, had adverted," proceeds: "Here the will was in very special terms. Without, therefore, meaning to suggest the slightest doubt as to the soundness of the decision in *Lawes* v. *Bennett* 1 Cox, C. C. 167, His Honour was of opinion that, the testator having made specific mention in his will of the estate which had been *previously* the subject of the lease," which gave the option to the lessee to purchase, "the general rule established by the authorities did not apply."

Emuss v. *Smith* 2 De G. & S. 772 was decided six years later by the same Vice-Chancellor. In it the devise was specific, and although made before the contract, the will in which it was contained was republished after the contract. The Vice-Chancellor, after stating that it was unnecessary to decide how the case would have stood had there not been a republication of the will, or had the contract been an absolute one not resting in option, nor exercised during the life of the testator, decided the case as it stood, taking together the language of the will and the language and nature of the contract, and upon the fact that no option was expressed during the life of the testator, coupled with the republication of the codicil.

These cases were next under consideration in 1861, when they came before Lord Hatherley, then Vice-Chancellor Sir W. Page-Wood, in *Weeding* v. *Weeding* 1 J. & H. 424, and from them that great Judge deduced the following principle, which as far as I can find, has ever since been followed:-

"When you find that in a will, made *after* a contract giving an option of purchase, the testator, knowing of the existence of the contract, devises the specific property which is the subject of the contract without referring in any way to the contract . . . then it is considered that there is sufficient indication of an intention to pass that property, to give to the devisee all the interest, whatever it may be, that the testator had in it." And he adds: "This was the nature of both the authorities relied on" – i.e., *Drant* v. *Vause* 1 Y. & C. Ch. C. 580 and *Emuss* v. *Smith* 2 De G. & S. 722 – "for, in one, the contract was before the will, and, in the other the same effect was produced by the subsequent republication of the will."

Lord Hatherley then distinguishes the case before him from *Drant* v. *Vause* 1 Y. & C. Ch. C. 580 and *Emuss* v. *Smith* 2 De G. & S. 722, upon the ground that the will was before the contract of sale, and was not republished after the contract.

In re Pyle, Pyle v. *Pyle* [1895] 1 Ch. 724, was a decision of Lord Justice Stirling when he was a Judge of first instance. In that case the will was, as here, before the contract ; but on the day on which the latter was executed, the testator made a codicil which expressly confirmed the will. Mr Justice Stirling, after referring to *Weeding* v. *Weeding* 1 J. & H. 424, held – following *Emuss* v. *Smith* 2 De G. & S. 722 – that the sale moneys were bound by the limitations of the will. There there was an uncertainty whether the codicil or the contract, which were both executed on the same day, was executed first ; but this circumstance was held by the learned Judge to be immaterial, as in either case the contract must have been present to the mind of the testator when he executed his will. This case is important here, not only as to the general question, but especially in reference to the lands the subject of the agreements executed after the codicil, which, in my opinion, the testator, at the time of the codicil, comtemplated executing.

The appellant's counsel strongly relied upon cases of the class of *Powys* v. *Mansfield* 3 My. & Cr. 359, and *Hopwood* v. *Hopwood* 7 H. L. C. 728, in which it is stated that a codicil republishing a will does not revive a legacy revoked, adeemed, or satisfied. That doctrine, in my opinion, applies to legacies either expressly revoked or adeemed by subsequent gifts or covenants to which the presumption against double portions applies ; and not to a case such as the present, in which the question depends upon the intention expressed in the subsequent testamentary instrument. *Powys* v. *Mansfield* 3 My. & Cr. 359. was, as Barton, J., rightly observed, cited in *Drant* v. *Vause* 1 Y. & C. Ch C. 580 and in *In re Pyle* [1895] 1 Ch. 724 ; and in the judgments in these two latter cases it was not thought necessary to distinguish or even to refer to it.

If, then, it had not been that Barton, J., held that, but for the republication of the will, the appellant would have been entitled to the purchase-money, I should have said nothing more than that the appeal should be dismissed with costs. As, however, Barton, J., has thought it right to express an opinion on this latter question, I fear that a simple affirmance of his judgment might be deemed an affirmance of his opinion upon this last question also; and, as I am not prepared to agree in that opinion, I must, to guard myself against being supposed to do so, add something to indicate the reasons why I entertain a serious doubt on the question. At the same time, my present opinion must be taken, not as a concluded one, but as provisional only, and subject to further consideration, if the question shall hereafter arise before me; as, strangely enough, the question, in the view in which it presents itself to my mind, has not been argued here; and as we agree with Barton, J., on the other question, we did not think it right to put the parties to the expense of a second argument.

The question, however, is one which must necessarily occur whenever agreements for sale to tenants intervene between a testamentary disposition of a landlord and his death; and two decisions of Courts of first instance have found their way into the reports, which, if the opinion I at present entertain be correct, are likely to mislead.

Mr Justice Barton's decision on this point is apparently based on the judgment of Holmes, L.J., in *In re Sherlock's Estate* [1899] 2 I. R. 561 in which the Lord Justice lucidly expounds the principle of the relation back of the conversion effected by conditional contracts to the date of the contract – a principle in which I entirely concur, but which does not support Barton J.'s, decision – and on the decision of Wylie, J., in *Doyle's Estate* [1907] 1 I. R. 204 and of Barton, J., himself in *Jones* v. *Bailey* [1910] 1 I. R. 110, neither of which latter decisions binds this Court.

In *In re Sherlock's Estate* [1899] 2 I. R. 561 the question arose under the Act of 1885, and to it the statutory provisions of the Act of 1903 did not apply; whilst, although the latter two cases arose on the latter Act, in neither did it appear to have occurred, either to the learned counsel or to the Judge, that it was material to contrast the relevant provisions of that latter Act with those of the previous legislation. I think that this question cannot be decided without such a contrast, as there is such a difference between them that I should find great difficulty in holding that the judgment of my brother Holmes in relation to ademption can apply to a purchase under the Act of 1903, under such conditional agreements as we have here, in cases where the testator dies before the performance of the condition.

I premise that the effect, in working a conversion, of a binding agreement to convey, as distinguished from an actual conveyance, is undoubtedly the equitable doctrine that that which ought to have been done is to be deemed to have been done; and that it is for that reason that a binding agreement to transfer property is, for that purpose, treated as having the same effect as the actual transfer of the property in pursuance of the agreement. It follows that where property is transferred by the operation of a statute in pursuance of an agreement, the agreement cannot work an ademption, if the statute provide that the actual transfer itself shall not have that effect.

Now, the Act of 1903 contains a provision (section 16) that the effect of the vesting order, when the Land Commission agree to purchase property, is to vest in the Commission the fee-simple of the land, subject to certain rights and interests defined by the section, but not material to be stated here, but, save as regards those rights and interest, and to the provisions of the Act, discharged from "the *claims* of all persons who are interested in the land, whether in respect of superior or intervening interests or incumbrances or otherwise; and *all such claims* shall, as from the date of the vesting order, cease as regards the land"; and then follows a provision not identical with any previous enactment of the code :- "and all such claims shall *attach to the purchase-money, in like manner* as immediately before the date of the order they attached to the land."

The sales here were not *to* the Land Commission; and consequently the section, *proprio vigore,* would not apply; but section 24 enacts that, in the case of a sale to a person other than the Land Commission, which is the present case, as soon as the land is vested in the purchaser, the Land Commission shall make an order attaching claims to the purchase-money; and that order is declared to be "as effectual *for that purpose*" – *i.e.* for the purpose of attaching claims to the purchase-money – "as a vesting order made by the Land Commission vesting land in them." Orders attaching claims were made in the matter of the sales in question here. Thus the provision I have read from section 16 applies here.

As to the effect of this provision of section 16, had it stood alone, I should have thought that there would be no doubt that the "claims" attached by it to the purchase-money included the claims of the vendors and those claiming through them, as well as those of owners of superior or intervening interests or incumbrances; but all possible question as to this is removed by section 25, sub-sect. 2, which describes the persons whose claims have been attached to the purchase-money by the words "whether as *vendor* or incumbrancer or owner of a superior or intervening interest."

Now, in the present case, as the condition of the estate of which the respective holdings formed parts being sold under the provisions of the Act of 1903 was not performed during the life of the testator, the lands upon his death passed under the devise (subject to the annuities) to the respondent here for life, with remainder to his first and other sons in tail male; and were so vested in them respectively, in the words of the statute, "immediately before the date of the vesting order"; and the respondent and his eldest son had at that time valid "claims" within the meaning of section 16, as tenant for life and tenant in tail male in remainder respectively, to the lands sold; and I am unable to see why those claims did not under the express words of that section attach "to the purchase-money in the like manner as immediately before the order they attached to the land"; that is, the previous limitations of the land attached to, and bound, the purchase-money. If so, there could be no ademption. In the ordinary case of ademption the effect of the conversion is that nothing remains to answer the description of the property devised. The thing devised is land; the property of the testator in the land has ceased to exist. A new subject-matter, the purchase-money, has become vested in the testator; but the doctrine of law is that the mere intention to give the land does not, without more, include an intention to give the purchase-money, and, therefore, that the purchase-money has not been given to the devisee.

But in the present case, assuming for the moment that the codicil had not been executed, although the construction which the law would have put on the words of the will would have been that *they* did not indicate an intention to give the purchase-money to the devisees, the Act of Parliament would step in; and that statute gives to a sale under the Act a more limited effect than an ordinary sale would have had – such a limited effect as precludes it working an ademption.

So much for the Act of 1903, upon the effect of which the decision of this case must rest. I have now to contrast the enactment I have referred to (section 16) with any similar provisions contained in the previous statutes of the code. This is neccessary only to show that the conclusion I am inclined to arrive at on this question is not contrary to any decision binding on this Court. The only enactments I can find which are at all analogous are in section 9 (5) of the Act of 1885, and section 14 of the Act of 1887. The sub-section in the Act of 1885 provides that in the case of a sale by a landlord to a tenant, where it is agreed that the sale shall be carried into efect by a vesting order of the Land Commission, such vesting order may be made though the landlord is only tenant for life, or has the powers of a tenant for life, and whether or not the holding, either solely or in common with other lands, is subject to an incumbrance or annual charge, and whether such incumbrance or annual charge affects only a partial interest in the estate sold; and then proceeds, "but the purchase-money shall, in all cases *where the Court shall think fit,* be paid into court to abide the further order of the Court, and shall, for all purposes as regards the rights or claims of any person to or against the estate sold, represent such estate, and unless and so far as the vesting order shall otherwise declare, the rights and claims of all persons in respect of the estate sold, or any incumbrance or annual charge thereon, shall from the date of such vesting order be transferred to the purchase-money, and the purchaser shall be wholly freed from any liability or claim in respect thereof."

Section 14(1) of the Act of 1887 is to substantially the same effect, but with more extended operation; but it need not be referred to, as there is no decision of this Court that a sale under that Act works an ademption.

The radical difference between the provision in section 9 (5) of the Act of 1885, and that which is contained in section 16 of the Act of 1903, is that the latter portion of section 9 (5) of the Act of 1885 appears to be limited to cases in which the Court has thought fit to exercise the power of directing the purchase-money to be paid into Court; and if that be its true construction, the provision is discretionary, and certainly could not apply unless that discretion were exercised; and the statute does not contain any indication of an intention that the rights of the parties (as distinguished from the mode of enforcing them) should so far depend upon the exercise of this discretion that the sale should operate as an ademption if, but only if, the money was paid into Court. As contrasted with this, the application of section 16 of the Act of 1903 is not only clear and free from doubt, but it does not depend upon discretion. It is absolute; and peremptorily governs the devolution of the purchase-money and the rights of the parties to it.

I by no means say that this provision in the Act of 1885 had any bearing on the question discussed in *Sherlock's Estate* [1899] 2 I. R. 561. I rather think it had not; but, at any rate, the matter was not there discussed, and decisions on it can have no bearing on the wholly different provision in section 16 of the Act of 1903.

So, too, under section 14 (1) of the Act of 1887, the provision that the claims shall attach to the purchase-money is plainly dependent on the exercise by the Land Commission of a discretionary power. In the cases of *Doyle's Estate* [1907] 1 I. R. 204 and *Jones* v. *Bailey* [1910] 1 I. R. 110, in which the decisions upon the Act of 1885 were applied to cases under the Act of 1903, the distinction between the two Acts is not adverted to; but, be this as it may, they are not binding upon this Court.

There is a recent case, *Latham* v. *Travers* [1912] 1 I. R. 306, which first came before the Master of the Rolls, and subsequently before this Court, in which a question arose as to the operation of a sale under the Act of 1903, as a conversion of the property of one of the vendors, who was a lunatic, upon which a consideration of section 16 of the Act of 1903 might have been material. It, however, was not referred to; and the *decision* has no bearing on the present case, as it turned upon a section of our Lunacy Act of 1871, which was held to prevent the sale being a conversion.

Upon the whole case I am clearly of opinion that the appeal should be dismissed with costs.

Holmes, L.J.:

The question for decision in this appeal, although difficult and important, can be briefly stated.

Robert Ball Steele being seised in fee-simple of estates in counties Kildare and Dublin, executed his will on the 25th November, 1899, and thereby charged the said estates with three life annuities, one of £60 in favour of his younger son, another of £60 in favour of his daughter Anne, and a third of £25 in favour of his daughter Catherine. Subject thereto he devised the said estates to his eldest son for life, with remainder to his first and other sons in tail male, with remainder to his younger son for life, with remainder to his first and other sons in tail male, with remainder to his own right heirs. He then bequeathed to his daughter Anne his household effects, except his pictures and plate, which he left to his eldest son. He appointed his younger son his residuary devisee and legatee, and his son-in-law, Arthur McCormick, executor.

Some time after the passing of the Irish Land Purchase Act of 1903, he took steps to sell to his tenants on the Dublin and Kildare estates their holdings, with the result that before his death on the 23rd May, 1906, he had entered into agreements with all his tenants in both counties except two. Thirty-one of the Kildare agreements were signed on the 1st January, 1906, two on the 1st March, and one on the 2nd March, while all the Dublin agreements were signed on the 1st February. Another document of importance is the originating application to the Irish Land Commission to have all his estates in county Kildare fit to be regarded as a separate estate for the purpose of a sale under the Land Purchase Acts; and I find that this application was verified by affidavit on the 31st January, 1906, and lodged in the offices of the Commission on the 28th February following. It will be noted that agreements relating to two of the Kildare holdings were not signed in the owner's lifetime. They were, however, entered into by his eldest son in the November following his father's death.

The agreements were in the form then prescribed by the Land Commission, and were conditional on the holdings in each county being declared an estate by the Estates Commissioners, which was done on the 6th June, 1912. The only other matter relevant to this appeal is the execution by Mr. Steele of a codicil to his will, dated the 7th February, 1906, by which he revoked the appointment of his son-in-law, Arthur McCormick, as the executor of his will, and appointed his eldest son as his sole executor, adding he would have so appointed him by his will had he known that he would be residing in Ireland and retired from the army. He also thereby confirmed his will in other respects.

A lawyer would probably hazard a guess that litigation arising from the aforesaid facts would relate to questions of ademption or equitable conversion, and he would be right.

The younger son, the plaintiff, seeks for a declaration that the effect of his father's agreements with the tenants was, on the fulfilment of the condition to which they were subject, to convert into personal estate the lands devised to his brother as from the dates of the agreements, and to give him, as residuary legatee, the proceeds of the sales. The defendants, the eldest son of the testator and his eldest son, reply that the conversion into personalty dates only from the fulfilment of the condition, and that, as up to that period the property sold continued to be real estate, the proceeds of the sale now belong to the first-named for life, with remainder to the other absolutely. It is also argued on their behalf that even if the legal effect of the will if it had stood alone would have been as contended by the plaintiff, the codicil made on the 7th February, 1906, after the agreements had been executed, gave the testator's then existing interest in the premises to the elest son for life, with remainder to his eldest son. A question of ademption and equitable conversion not unlike that arising in the present appeal was argued in this Court in the year 1899 in *In re Sherlock's Estate* [1899] 2 I. R. 561.

In one view of the facts in that case – the view which I accepted – certain documents were signed in the form prescribed under the Land Purchase Act of 1885, by the agent of the landlord and by certain of his tenants, and these documents might be construed as agreements for the sale and purchase of the latters' holdings subject to certain conditions as to advances by the Land Commission. I was of opinion that these documents constituted complete contracts subject to the fulfilment of the conditions. Soon afterwards the landlord died, having by will, made some years previous to the execution of the documents, devised the lands to his wife with remainder to his two sons, and appointed one of his sons residuary legatee. After the landlord's death, the Land Commission sanctioned the advances, thus fulfilling the conditions. The litigation, as in this case, arose after the sales were completed between the devisees and residuary legatee; and, assuming that my view of the facts and of the construction of the documents was correct, the case is precisely similar to the present, except in so far as the execution of Mr. Steele's codicil makes a difference. In these circumstances I held that as between the real and personal representatives of the landlord, who died before the sanction was given by the Land Commission, there was a conversion of the lands into personal estate as from the dates of the agreements.

This was not, however, the judgment of the Court. The Lord Chancellor and FitzGibbon L.J., while offering no opinion as to whether, if there had been conditional agreements for the sale and purchase of the holdings, the conversion into personalty upon fulfilment of the conditions related back to the date of the agreements, held that it was unnecessary to decide this question, inasmuch as, quite apart therefrom, the devisees were entitled to succeed on wholly different grounds, which I was then unable to accept, and which do not exist in the present case. The judgment I then delivered is now no more binding on me than on my colleagues, and I have thought it my duty to reconsider it. I have always felt that the doctrine of equitable conversion has been unduly extended, and I should have been glad to follow any authority enabling me to hold that in the agreements before us the lands remained the real estate of the vendor until the conditions were fulfilled. But, apart from some subsequent legislation, to which I shall presently refer, I have failed to find any reason for coming to a different conclusion, and in dealing with this branch of the case I can add nothing to what I said in *In re Sherlock's Estate* [1899] 2 I. R. 561.

There remains the question arising from the codicil which was executed after thirty-one of the Kildare agreements and all the Dublin agreements had been signed. The words relied on by the defendants are – "I confirm my said will in other respects"; and it is argued that the result thereof is the same as if there had been repeated in the codicil the gifts in the will. Let me assume that this were actually the case, that the testator had copied in the codicil all the language of the will, except the appointment of the executor, or, to put the same assumption in another form, that the testator's will had been executed on the 7th February, 1906, instead of some years earlier, what would have been the construction? Could it be argued that when, years after the testator's death, during which the devisee named in the will or codicil had been in enjoyment of the profits of the lands, the conditional agreements had, by the fulfilment of the conditions, become absolute and complete, the testamentary instrument executed after the agreements had been entered into must be read as if it contained no devise or specific gift of the lands? Mr. Walker would say, "Yes, because the effect in law of what happened was to cause the lands to disappear, so as to leave no subject-matter for the gift to operate on." I prefer to apply to conditional contracts the view taken by Lord Hatherley in *Weeding* v. *Weeding* 1 J. & H. 424 of the principle on which *Drant* v. *Vause* 1 Y. & C. Ch. C. 580 and *Emuss* v. *Smith* 2 De G. & S. 722 were decided. He says that "when you find that in a will made after a contract giving an option of purchase the testator, knowing of the existence of the contract, devises the specific property which is the subject of the contract without referring in any way to the contract he has entered into, then it is considered that there is sufficient indication of an intention to pass that property to give the devisee all the interest, whatever it may be, that the testator had in it. This was the nature of both the authorities relied on, for in one the contract was before the will, and in the other the same effect was produced by the subsequent republication of the will." I quite agree with Mr. Walker that the confirmation in other respects of the will does not, in all cases, make the contents of the will, except those altered by the codicil, speak as of the date of the latter. A legacy revoked by a previous codicil will not be restored. The testator may have so completely disposed of property given by the will that there would no longer be any subject to which the gift, even if repeated in the codicil, could apply. Mr. Walker has argued that this is what has happened in the present case.

He has pressed on the Court the proposition that the effect of the fulfilment of the conditions was to leave no subject-matter for the gift when the codicil confirmed the will. This is, I think, the fallacy of his argument. Mr. Steele had then a distinct and valuable interest in the two estates, which the confirmation of the will gave to the devisees, and which became their absolute property on the testator's death. This is, I think, in accordance with the law as stated in different authorities, to three of which I have referred. It is put most clearly in *In re Pyle* [1895] 1 Ch. 724. I am satisfied that the principle laid down therein is applicable to the present case, and I am not aware that any doubt has been thrown on that principle since it was decided by Stirling, J., in 1895. It rules not only the agreements that were signed previous to the execution of the codicil, but also the three which were signed on the 1st and 2nd March following.

The lease and the codicil in *In re Pyle* [1895] 1 Ch. 724 were executed on the same day, but it was uncertain which of the two preceded the other. Stirling, J., held that this was immaterial, inasmuch as the lease, if not actually executed, must have been present to the mind of the testator when he confirmed his will. In the present case the originating application to the Land Commission, verifed by Mr. Steele's affidavit of the 31st January, shows that he was then intending to sell all his Kildare estate, and that this was present in his mind when he confirmed his will a few days later.

Having thus come to the same conclusion as Barton, J., on the questions argued in this Court, it is unnecessary for me to consider a most important matter to which my attention has since been called by the Lord Chief Baron – the effect of section 16 (1), 24 (1), and 25 (1) of the Land Purchase Act of 1903. These provisions were not referred to by counsel on either side, and, in any circumstances, I avoid, as far as possible, dealing with questions that have not been discussed. Especially I feel it my duty to take this course at present. On the one hand, my opinion would be of little value without re-argument. On the other hand, it would be unfair to ask successful respondents to argue a question in which they are not now interested. I, therefore, confine myself to saying that if this matter comes before me hereafter I shall approach it with an open mind.

Cherry, L.J.:

I agree with the judgment of Barton, J., both in his statement of the law and in his application of it to the facts of this particular case.

The question really turns, as he says, upon the construction to be placed upon the codicil to the will; for the principles of the conversion of property in Equity in the case of contracts for sale are, apart from any consideration of the effect of the Irish Land Act, 1903, to which the Lord Chief Baron has referred, too well settled to admit of much discussion; but the effect of the confirmation of a will by a codicil at a date subsequent to a contract for sale of lands specifically devised by the will may be, on the authorities, a matter of some doubt.

Of the numerous cases cited to us in the course of the arguments, the one which most nearly resembles that now before us is the decision of Stirling, J., in *Pyle* v. *Pyle* [1895] 1 Ch. 724 ; and it is also, I think, the latest in point of date. There the testator had by his will specifically devised certain freehold lands, and had bequeathed his residuary real and personal estate to other persons. He afterwards made a codicil, which did not in terms refer to the specifically devised property, but expressly confirmed his will. On the same day that he executed the codicil he granted a lease of the lands with an option to purchase, which option was accepted by the lessee, after the testator's death. Under these circumstances it was held that, whether the codicil was executed before or after the lease giving the option to purchase, the testator at the time he executed the codicil must have had the circumstances present to his mind; and that by confirming his will he had indicated a sufficient intention to pass whatever estate he had in the property to his devisee so as to take the case out of the general rule established by *Lawes* v. *Bennett* 1 Cox, Ch. C. 167.

This decision of Stirling, J., was expressly based on a somewhat stronger decision of Vice-Chancellor Knight-Bruce, in *Emuss* v. *Smith* 2 De G. & S. 722. There the testator made his will, by which he specifically devised a farm called "Nash's Own Farm," and he gave his residuary real and personal estate to trustees upon certain trusts. Eight years afterwards he entered into a contract by which he granted in favour of a certain person the option to purchase the farm in question, together with another farm called "Williams' Farm" which he had purchased recently, or was then about to purchase. Next year he executed a codicil to his will whereby he devised "Williams' Farm," to certain uses, but did not in any way refer to "Nash's Own Farm," and did not otherwise refer to his will. The option to purchase was, after the testator's death, accepted in respect of both the properties. Under these circumstances it was held that the purchase-money of "Nash's Own Farm" belonged to those who would have enjoyed it if the option to purchase had not been accepted.

This decision was based upon three circumstances, all of them present in the case with which we are now dealing – the specific devise in the will, the conditional nature of the contract, and the republication of the will by the codicil. "How this case would have stood," says Knight-Bruce, V.-C. De G. & Sm., at p. 735, "if the codicil of 1839 had not amounted to a republication of the will, it is not necessary that I should say ; for I am of opinion that the codicil of 1839 did effect a republication of the will."

The authority of this decision was expressly recognized by the Vice-Chancellor Page-Wood (as he then was) in the leading case of *Weeding* v. *Weeding* 1 J. & H. 424, and he has laid down a principle based upon it and a similar case of *Drant* v. *Vause* 1 Y. & C. Ch. C. 580, which is quoted by Barton, J., in his judgment, and applied by him in the decision of this case.

Now, assuming that the principles of equitable conversion apply to contracts for sale under the Land Purchase Acts in the same way as to optional contracts of a private nature, we have it clearly established by the highest authority that the effect of a codicil, even though it does not in express terms confirm the will, amounts to a republication of the will. Surely the same principle must apply with greater force where, as in the present case, the testator in express terms confirms the will. I think, therefore, that the decision of Barton, J., is clearly right, that the effect of the confirmation of the will by the codicil is to make the specific devise of the lands apply to the only interest in the lands which the testator retained at the date of the codicil, namely, the right to receive the purchase-money. There is no doubt that the proceeds of the sale of lands may pass under a devise of the lands themselves : *In re Lowman ; Devenish* v. *Pester* [1895] 2 Ch. 348.

But, it is argued, although this may be true as regards the lands which the testator had contracted to sell before the execution of the codicil, the lands in respect of which contracts for sale were not entered into until after that date are in a different position, and, consequently, the three farms on the Kildare estate, where the agreements were only signed in March, 1906, must be excluded from the devise, applying the principle of *Lawes* v. *Bennett* 1 Cox, 167.

I do not think that this is so, for though it is true that the agreements in the latter cases were not signed by the testator until after the execution of the codicil, the originating application for the sale of the entire estate, including these holdings, had been verified before that date, and was lodged shortly afterwards. In that statement he had distinctly stated his intention of selling the entire estate, so that this circumstance must have been present to his mind when he executed the codicil. I think, therefore, that Barton, J., was quite right in applying the same rule in the case of these holdings as he did in dealing with the bulk of the estates. All cases of this kind depend upon questions of presumed intention, and it would be absurd to suppose that a testator, making his will, while proceedings for the sale of his entire estates were actually pending, should make any distinction as regards the devolution of the property depending upon the purely accidental circumstance that some of the agreements had actually been executed at the date he signed his will, while others had not reached that stage.

Mr. Walker, in his able argument for the appellant, relied upon a number of authorities which he said established the proposition that the republication of a will by a codicil does not operate so as to revive a legacy revoked, adeemed, or satisfied. The leading cases cited in support of this proposition were *Powys* v. *Mansfield* 3 My. & Cr. 359 and *Hopwood* v. *Hopwood* 7 H. L. C. 728. Both these cases dealt with the presumption of law against double portions, where a sum of money is given by the will of a parent, or of one standing *in loco parentis* to a child, and the like sum is afterwards secured by a settlement on the marriage of that child. Very different considerations arise in cases of this kind from those which exist where there is between the date of the will and the codicil merely a change in the circumstances of the property dealt with by the will and codicil. I think, therefore, that these cases are clearly distinguishable from *In re Pyle* [1895] 1 Ch. 724 and *Emuss* v. *Smith* 2 De G. & S. 722, and, whether they are so or not, I prefer to follow the two later decisions, which I consider conclusive authorities in favour of the decision of Barton, J.

Notes

1. See further on the principle of *Lawes* v. *Bennett*, *Irish Land Law*, para. 3.097.
2. On the relevance of the doctrine of conversion to the Land Purchase Acts, see *Re Desmond*, *infra*.

RE DESMOND

[1943] I.R. 534 ; 78 I.L.T.R. 145 (High Court)

The facts are set out in the judgment.

Overend J.:

This is an interesting case, raising, as it does, questions as to the devolution of lands compulsorily registrable under the provisions of s. 51 of the Land Act of 1927.

By an indenture of lease, dated the 8th day of December, 1874, made betweeen Nathaniel Webb Ware of the one part and William Murphy of the other part, part of the lands of Sleaveen East, containing one rood and 17¾ perches, were demised to William Murphy, his heirs, executors, administrators and assigns, from the 1st day of November, 1874, for and during the lives of the three persons therein named and the life of the survivor, or for the term of 31 years whichever should last the longer. There was no covenant for renewal.

The lessees' interest subsequently became vested in Michael Desmond, the father of the deceased in this matter, who by his will, dated the 5th day of August, 1901, devised and bequeathed (*inter alia*) the said lands to his wife, Margaret Desmond, in trust for herself for life and after her decease in trust for his daughter, Margaret Desmond, the deceased in this matter, and appointed his wife, Margaret Desmond, sole executrix.

The testator died on the 17th day of August, 1901, and on the 31st day of January, 1902, probate of the said will was granted to his widow, Margaret Desmond.

The estate of Nathaniel Webb Ware was subsequently sold by the Land Judge, as vendor, under the provisions of the Land Purchase Acts, and the widow purchased the holding for cash, £135. At this date some of the lives in the lease were still living and the tenancy continued to be freehold.

By a Vesting Order made by the Irish Land Commission, dated the 28th day of January, 1904, it was ordered that the said lands "do vest and the same are hereby vested in the said tenant [Margaret Desmond, widow] in fee simple freed from all charges."

Margaret Desmond, the testator's executrix, died intestate on the 5th January, 1905, leaving her daughter, Margaret, the deceased in this matter, her heiress-at-law and sole next-of-kin, her surviving.

At the expiration of the concurrent term of years on the 1st day of November, 1905, at least one of the *cestuis que vie,* King George V, was alive, and the tenancy (if not already merged) remained freehold.

The deceased herein, Margaret Desmond, was declared to be a person of unsound mind by order of the Court, dated 29th day of October, 1936, and she died a spinster and intestate on the 12th day of March, 1942.

On the 8th day of December, 1942, letters of administration of her personal estate and effects were granted to the plaintiff, and by an order of the President, dated the 12th day of February, 1943, made in the Lunacy Matter, the plaintiff was given liberty to issue the present summons against the defendants, who are first cousins and next-of-kin of the deceased. The defendant, William Donoghue, claims also to be her heir-at-law, and the defendant, Thomas Kearney, claims to be heir-at-law of the testator's widow, Margaret Desmond and alleges that she was the last purchaser.

The title to the property has never been registered under the provisions of the Local Registration of Title (Ireland) Act, 1891.

The first question I have to decide is whether on the death of Margaret Desmond Junior these lands devolved to and became vested in the plaintiff as her personal representative.

Now, s. 51 of the Land Act, 1927, provides :-

> "Registration under the Local Registration of Title (Ir.) Act., 1891, of the ownership of freehold land shall be compulsory in the following cases, that is to say:-
>
> ...
>
> (b) Where the land has been or is vested by the Irish Land Commission in a purchaser for cash;...
>
> ...
>
> and the provisions of the Local Registration of Title (Ir.) Act, 1891, relating to freehold lands, the registration of the ownership of which is by that Act declared to be compulsory, shall apply to such cases when registered."

The lands in question in this case are clearly within the section.

Counsel for the plaintiff have argued that, although the section only makes the provisions of the Act of 1891 applicable to such lands "*when registered,*" nevertheless the personal representative is entitled, for s. 84 of the Act of 1891 provides for the devolution of "freehold registered land," *i.e.* land which has been registered, and the Court of Appeal have held that where registration is compulsory and a tenant purchaser dies, after he has entered into a binding agreement for sale, but before registration, or even before vesting, the personal represe tative is the person entitled to the property, since equity regards as done that which ought to be done. They rely on the decisions in *McDonnell* v. *Stenson* [1921] 1 I. R. 80 and *Collins* v. *Collins* [1924] 1 I. R. 72, and say that these decisions are binding on the Court.

There is much force in this argument. Counsel for the defendants, on the other hand, point out that in those cases ss. 22 and 23 of the Act of 1891 applied at the date of the vesting order, which Ronan L.J. says effected a conversion, and they rely on the judgment of the Master of the Rolls in *Collins* v. *Collins* [1924] 1 I. R. 72 and also on the express words "when registered" in s. 51 of the Act of 1927.

This case is one which may be of far-reaching importance, for in all probability many holdings come within the scope of s.51 of the Land Act, 1927, and its decision has given me much ground for anxious consideration.

It is necessary to bear in mind that the property at all times was freehold and the heir would have been entitled as special occupant on any intestacy occurring prior to the purchase and thereafter would have been entitled to the fee simple (in the absence of registration under s. 83 of the Act of 1891) and is still so entitled on intestacy unless his rights have been taken away in the manner contended for by the plaintiff.

The first point is the true construction of s. 51 of the Land Act of 1927; its wording, giving it its plain and ordinary meaning, leaves no doubt in my mind that the particular provisions of the Act of 1891 were to become applicable to lands within the section when, and not until, those lands were registered under the Act of 1891. If the Legislature had the intention contended for by the plaintiff the section might have concluded with the words "shall apply," instead of "shall apply to such cases when registered." Am I, then, bound, notwithstanding the view I have expressed, to hold that the lands devolve to the plaintiff by reason of the decisions cited, and do not descend to the heir ?

I have considered the cases cited again and again and I find myself coerced to come to the same conclusion as the late Master of the Rolls. The inexorable, and, in my opinion, unanswerable reasoning contained in his judgment in *Collins' Case* [1924] 1 I. R. 72 establishes that he, too, was of opinion that the decision in *McDonnell* v. *Stenson* [1921] 1 I. R. 80 was clearly and demonstrably wrong, nevertheless he felt bound to follow it in *Collins Case* [1924] 1 I. R. 72 and the Court of Appeal apparently affirmed his decision without delivering any judgment.

I am of opinion I am not bound to accept or to follow those decisions: – first, because I hold that the Legislature had previously recognised the law to be otherwise, and I think no Court has power to overrule the Legislature; and, secondly, because in my opinion they conflict with an earlier decision of the Court of Appeal and the principle there laid down in 1897: *In re Mary Smith* 33 I. L. T. R. 69.

In *In re Mary Smith* 33 I. L. T. R. 69 the tenant, who held from year to year, agreed to purchase her holding under the Land Purchase Acts and the sale to her was completed in 1887. Unfortunately the records have been destroyed but the Registrar of Titles informed me in response to my enquiry that there could be no doubt that the case was one of compulsory registration under s. 22 of the Act of 1891, for which many thousands of applications were lodged after the Act of 1891 came into force. In January, 1892, she applied to have her title registered under the then new Local Registration of Title Act, 1891, but she died on 16th November, 1893, before the registration was completed. On the 29th March, 1895, a certificate of registration was issued in the name of Mary Smith, a supplemental application was then lodged by the personal representative and the death having come to the knowledge of the Registrar, Mr. Brougham Leech, he noted the fact on the certificate which had been lodged with the supplemental application for registration and added "the registration is consequently void. 14th Oct., 1895." On an application by the personal representative of Mary Smith to have the registration completed in her name Mr. Brougham Leech ruled :–"The registration of Mary Smith as owner having been effected after her death, the lands have not come within operation of the Act; accordingly the heir-at-law is entitled. 22nd Jan., 1896." Later, upon ascertaining that the applicant was not the heir-at-law the Registrar, on the 27th January, 1896, dismissed the application. An appeal was instituted before Madden J. who reversed the Registrar and held that the land was to be regarded as registered land, and the personal representative was to be regarded as registered owner.

The heir-at-law appealed to the Court of Appeal and Lord Ashbourne in the course of his judgment – in which FitzGibbon and Holmes L.JJ. concurred – says :– "To my mind it is plain that there was no completed registration in the lifetime of

Mary Smith, or anything that can be regarded as effective on the 29th March, 1895, and that there was nothing to interfere with the rights of William Smith, the heir-at-law; that he was the person who would be entitled to take up and make his claim; and, once the lands were registered, the other provisions will apply . . . This is an Act creating a great change in the status of lands, and it is not to be spelled out by uncertain and doubtful indications; if you change the status of lands, and divest the succession of them from the heir-at-law to the personal representative, you must have something clear and definite, and precise and practical . . . " The court accordingly discharged the order made by Madden J. and dismissed the application for registration made by the personal representative, leaving the heir-at-law to apply to be registered as owner.

It is to be noted that in that case (*a*) the tenant prior to the purchase had only a chattel interest; (*b*) this she had converted into a freehold by purchasing the fee simple which had been vested in her; (*c*) the registration of the ownership was compulsory, the lands being subject to some annuity or rent charge (s. 22, sub-s 1 of the Act of 1891) and could have been enforced (s. 23, sub-s 1 (*a*), Act of 1891) had the tenant not already made the application; (*d*) the tenant-purchaser had done all that lay in her power towards effecting registration and changing the status of the lands in her lifetime.

Madden J. evidently thought he could regard as done that which ought to have been done, and directed the registration of the personal representative, but was reversed by a unanimous decision of the Court of Appeal, who held that, until registration was complete, there could be nothing to interfere with the rights of the heir-at-law.

Meantime it had been realised that so soon as a tenant holding a chattel interest had obtained a binding contract for the sale to him of the reversion in fee simple he became equitable owner in fee of the holding and therefore, if he died intestate at any subsequent time before the title was registered, his equitable estate, or if the holding had vested, his legal estate, in fee simple, would pass to his heir-at-law.

The Legislature decided to alter the law in this respect, and by s. 32, sub-s. 4 of the Land Law (Ireland) Act, 1896, it was provided :– "An agreement for purchase, a vesting order, or fiat, shall not operate to convert the interest of the purchaser *into real estate."* This provision could not apply to tenancies which were already freehold, nor could it apply after registration to registered freeholds which after registration are clearly freehold but devolve to the personal representative (s. 84, Act. 1891), as was pointed out by the Master of the Rolls in *Collins' Case* [1924] 1 I. R. 72. The section has been held by R. E. Meredith M. R. only to apply to the period intervening between the date of the contract for sale and the date of actual registration of the ownership; *Longworth* v. *Campbell* [1910] 1 I. R. 23, at p. 30; and see *Naughten* v. *Naughten* ibid, p. 363; *Taylor* v. *Blake* [1912] 1 I. R. 1.

In my opinion the Legislature by so enacting recognised that under the law as it existed prior to this provision the interest of a tenant-purchaser must pass on intestacy to his heir-at-law, but altered the law only in cases in which the devolution would otherwise be changed because the tenant had had a chattel interest. Further, it is plain that the Legislature considered that Part IV of the Act of 1891 had no operation prior to registration, and interpreted the law in precisely the same way as the Court of Appeal subsequently did in *Smith's Case* 33 I. L. T. R. 69.

In these circumstances I hold that I am free to consider the decisions in *McDonnell* v. *Stenson* [1912] 1 I. R. 80 and in *Collins* v. *Collins* [1921] 1 I. R. 72, the latter case merely following the former.

It is important to note the facts in *McDonnell* v. *Stenson* [1921] 1 I. R. 80 some of which do not appear to have been present to the minds of the Court of Appeal.

Barbara McDonnell, the tenant, held the lands under two leases made in 1832 and 1855, respectively, each being for 3 lives with a concurrent term of 99 years. Each lease contained a limited covenant for renewal during the term and in each the *habendum* was unto the lessee, his heirs, executors, administrators and assigns.

The lessee's interest having become vested in Barbara McDonnell, she on the 1st of November, 1915, signed an agreement to purchase – apparently under the Land Act of 1903. On the 2nd of January, 1918, the advance was sanctioned and the agreement, hitherto conditional, became binding, at this date all the lives in both leases had dropped and no new life had been nominated, and accordingly the tenant's interest was but a chattel interest, unless the right to renew still subsisted : *In re O'Brien* 27 L. R. Ir. 372. Powell J. held that it did, and that the tenant-purchaser had acquired an equitable freehold estate prior to her death intestate on the 11th February, 1918. On the 29th May, 1919, a fiat was made purporting to vest the holding in the intestate, who had died fifteen months before. This Powell J. held to be void [1920] 1 I. R. 85, at p. 88. It does not appear that the point on which the Court of Appeal decided was argued in either Court.

The Lord Chancellor (Sir James Campbell) refused to decide the question whether the right to renew subsisted and then asks what was the effect of the agreement to purchase? and proceeds :– "It clearly had the effect of vesting the lands in this lady for an estate in fee simple. Of course she had her own original interest, but in addition she acquired the reversion, and became to all intents and purposes the owner in fee simple; but it is provided by the Local Registration of Title Act that the devolution in such a case is to be as if the property were personal estate, and therefore upon her death all her estate and interest passed" to the personal representative of the intestate.

I may point out that every one of these statements is erroneous. Barbara McDonnell never acquired the fee simple, but only an equitable estate in fee in reversion, the legal fee simple was never vested, and the Act of 1891 contains no such provision as that stated. Ronan L.J. says :– "We are all of opinion that it (the agreement for purchase) effected a conversion . . . If the vesting order had been made in the lifetime of the lady, there would have been no doubt at all in regard to the case. The principle of conversion stated by Palles C.B. in *Steele's Estate* [1913] 1 I. R. 292 depends on the principle that equity regards as done that which ought to be done . . . We have here an absolute contract at the date of the death of the deceased ; a contract capable of specific performance, and therefore a more complete case of conversion it is difficult to conceive. The conversion is not of real estate into money, but of a chattel interest into fee simple, and there is an absolute statutory duty on the Land Commission to register the land. For these reasons I agree with the Lord Chancellor and O'Conner L.J. on this question."

Again, in my opinion error has crept into the judgments. If the learned Lord Justice had been right in thinking that the tenant's interest was a chattel interest and it had been converted, then he would have been bound by the previous decision in *In re Mary Smith* 33 I. L. T. R. 69 (which was not cited), but he evidently overlooked the provision made by s. 32, sub-s. 4, of the Land Act of 1896 that an agreement for purchase should not operate to convert the interest of the purchaser into real estate. Nor does it appear to have occurred to the learned Judge that the statutory duty to register the ownership could not arise until it was ascertained who "had become owner of the land" (s. 23, sub-s. 2, Act, 1891) and until the land had been vested by conveyance, vesting order, or fiat. (*Cf.* form of application for registration.) O'Conner L.J. decided the case mainly on the ground that the right to renew still existed, and at the end of his judgment he says :– "On the plain ground that equity considers that as done which ought to be done, I consider that Barbara McDonnell, at the time of her death, held these lands as equitable owner in fee, the fee being, by statute, descendible as personalty."

The statute does not so provide, the devolution is not affected until actual registration is complete (s. 84 of the Act of 1891). This was decided in *Smith's Case* 33 I. L. T. R. 69 where the deceased was legal owner in fee and where the registration ought to have been completed, but was not. It is difficult to imagine a stronger case than *Smith's Case* 33 I. L. T. R. 69 for the application of the equitable principle mentioned if there was room for its application, yet the Court of Appeal held against the view taken by Madden J. I have always understood that equity follows the law, and in my opinion the decision in *McDonnell* v. *Stenson* [1921] 1 I. R. 80, so far from following the law, amounted to an attempt to forestall a statute.

I respectfully adopt the reasons given by the Master of the Rolls for his "personal opinion" in *Collins* v. *Collins* [1924] 1 I. R. 72, a case which bears a very close analogy to the present one, and I agree with that opinion. [Reads the judgment of the Master of the Rolls from the last paragraph on p. 73 of the report to the end of that paragraph on p. 74, and then reads from the words "If a tenant who had agreed to purchase his holding died before registration" on p. 74 to the end of the paragraph which concludes on p. 76.] The Master of the Rolls then referred to *McDonnell* v. *Stenson* [1921] 1 I. R. 80 and held that he was bound by that decision, although in his opinion it was not a satisfactory decision.

For the reasons I have indicated I do not yield to the plaintiff's contention that I am bound by the decision in *McDonnell* v. *Stenson* [1921] 1 I. R. 80, and I hold the law applicable to be as stated in *Smith's Case* [1924] 1 I. R. 72, and impliedly recognised by the Land Act of 1896, and I hold that under s.51 of the Land Act of 1927 (as under s. 84 of the Act of 1891) the devolution of these lands remains unaffected by Part IV of the Act of 1891 until the registration of the ownership has been completed. The lands in question do not devolve to the personal representative but to the heir-at-law of the last purchaser.

This brings me to the further question which arises between the two defendants, viz. :– whether Margaret Desmond, the mother, can be regarded as the last purchaser.

Mrs. Margaret Desmond, when she purchased the holding, was sole executrix of her husband's will and a trustee of the lands for herself for life and after her decease for her daughter, and there can be no doubt that she held the fee simple, which was a graft upon the previous interest, upon these trusts, even apart from the provisions of s. 8 of the Land Purchase Act, 1885, and s. 14, sub-s. 3, of the Land Law Act, 1887. The deceased herein, Margaret Desmond, the daughter, took these lands under the express trusts of her father's will and is clearly the last purchaser, and her heir-at-law is the person now entitled.

Notes and Questions

1. Do you agree with Overend J.'s interpretation of the previous case-law? Was his decision consistent with what may be taken to be the policy of the legislative provisions? See *Irish Land Law,* para. 3.099.
2. On the operation of the Land Acts generally, see *Irish Land Law,* para. 1.51 *et seq.*

McDONAGH v. NOLAN

(1881) 9L. R. Ir. 262 (Chancery Division)

The facts are set out in the judgment.

Chatterton V.-C.:

The principal question to be now decided is, whether a sum of £3000 Irish, portion of the fund in Court to the credit of the cause, is to be dealt with as real or as personal estate of the deceased. There is no doubt that this sum, which by the settlement of the 15th of June, 1813, was vested in the trustees of the deed upon trust to invest in the purchase of real estate, was thus made the subject of an imperative trust for conversion into real estate. The fund in fact was not so applied, but was invested upon mortgage by the trustees, and so held by them until it was brought into Court, as I shall presently mention. The lunatic was the only surviving issue of the marriage of 1813, and on the death of his father, in the year 1822, he became under the limitations of the settlement seised in possession of an estate in tail in this fund, with remainder to himself in fee. He never married, and was found a lunatic by the inquisition in the year 1851, and so continued until his death. The usual order having been made in lunacy, referring it to the Master to inquire into and report upon the nature and amount of the property of the lunatic, Master Henn, by his report of the 21st of November, 1853, found that the lunatic was entitled to the sum of £3000 Irish currency, secured by mortgage as therein set forth, and that it would be for his benefit that an account should be taken of the sum due on foot of the mortgage, and for that purpose that proceedings should be taken or instituted by cause petition against the representatives of the mortgagor. That report was duly confirmed by order in lunacy, dated the 26th of January, 1854, upon petition of Master Litton, the committee of the fortune of the lunatic, and it was thereby ordered that the committee should be at liberty to institute the proceedings recommended by Master Henn's report. A cause petition was accordingly filed by the lunatic, by his committee, against Sir Edward McDonnell and L. Mooney, the personal representatives of the mortgagor, who was also the surviving trustee of the settlement of 1813, stating, amongst other things, the settlement of 1813 and the mortgage to the trustees, and the finding in the report of Master Henn that the petitioner was entitled to the said sum of £3000 Irish, and that the said mortgage was then vested in the Respondents as personal representatives of the surviving trustee of the settlement, who were also the personàl representatives of the mortgagor, and praying an account on foot of the mortgage, and the Respondents might be ordered to pay to the credit of the lunacy matter the sum which should be found due on such account. By order of the Lord Chancellor made in this cause petition matter, dated the 12th of May, 1855, it was referred to the Master to take an account of the sum due by the respondents *to the petitioner,* that is the lunatic, on foot of the principal sum of £3000 Irish, being the trust fund in the petition mentioned, and secured by the mortgage in the petition mentioned, and of the interest thereof. It appears that the accounts directed by said order were taken, and the full amount of principal with a considerable arrear of interest was found due, and large sums were brought in to the credit of the cause petition matter of *Nolan* v. *McDonnell* which satisfied the sum due for principal and interest on foot of the mortgage, and also certain other demands of the lunatic against the Respondents on foot of other property comprised in the settlement. It further appears that some other proceedings took place in both the lunacy and cause petition matters which have not been stated, and I presume, therefore, are immaterial; but on the 6th of March, 1866, a petition was presented by Mister Litton, as committee, entitled both in the lunacy and cause petition matters, stating that there was then to the credit of the cause petition matter a sum of over £7500 Stock and a sum of £835 cash, *the whole of which fund was the property of the lunatic,* and praying that the whole of these funds should be carried over to the credit of *The Matter of Thomas Nolan a lunatic.* An order was made by the Lord Chancellor on that petition, dated the 20th of March, 1866, that these funds should be transferred to the credit of the lunacy matter as prayed. The funds were accordingly so transferred; the £3000 Irish was never separated from the rest of the fund, which, without any question, was the personal estate of the lunatic, and remained up to his death undistinguished in any way from it. Under these circumstances the question now arises whether the heir-at-law of the lunatic is entitled to the £3000 Irish as being impressed by the settlement with the character of real estate, or whether it is to go to the next-of-kin as personal estate.

There are, I think, two rules established in reference to the property of lunatics which apply to this question; one is, that the Lord Chancellor, or other person intrusted with the care of lunatics, will not unnecessarily direct or permit the property of a lunatic to be dealt with so as to change its nature and devolution; the other is, that he will look only to what is for the benefit of the lunatic, and will direct any dealing with his property which appears to him for the benefit of the lunatic, regardless of what effect this may have upon the expectant rights of others; and that those who, on the death of the lunatic, became entitled to his property, must take it as they find it. Looking at the proceedings to which I have referred, it is manifest the Lord Chancellor considered that it was for the benefit of the lunatic that the principal money due upon the mortgage on which this trust fund had been invested should be called in, and directed this to be done; and it was done. He not only did this, but he directed it to be taken out of the hands of the trustees of the settlement, who were also the mortgagees, and brought in to the credit of the lunacy matter, as part of the absolute property of the lunatic. It would have been better, of course, to have appointed new trustees of the settlement, and transferred the fund to them, or to have it carried to a separate credit in the lunacy matter of the trust fund of that settlement, if there had been any intention of still preserving the trusts affecting it; but it was plainly dealt with as the absolute property of the lunatic, for it was found by the report of Master Henn, of 1853, which was confirmed by the order of the 26th January, 1854, that the lunatic was entitled to that sum of £3000; it was prayed by the cause petition, presented by Master Litton by order of the Lord Chancellor, as committee of the lunatic, that the fund should be paid into the general credit of the lunacy matter; it was by the Lord Chancellor, in the cause petition of the 12th May, 1855, referred to the Master to take an account of the sum due to the lunatic on foot of the same fund; it was dealt with by petition of Master Litton, as committee, in 1866, as part of a larger fund, the whole of which, he stated, was the property of the lunatic; and, finally, on that petition it was, by order of the Lord Chancellor, of the 20th March, 1866, carried over as part of the general fund of the lunatic to the general credit of the lunacy matter. It seems to me, therefore, beyond question that there was no intention on the part of the Lord Chancellor, acting for the lunatic, to keep this fund still subject to the trust for conversion, and that if any intention on the subject was present to his mind it was to emancipate it from that trust.

In the case of *Batteste* v. *Maunsell* Ir. R. 10 Eq. 97 I decided that the surplus of the proceeds of a sale of part of the lunatic's real estate in the Landed Estates Court was converted, under the circumstances stated to me, namely, that by an order of that court the surplus had been paid in to the credit of the lunacy matter, and received by order of the Lord Chancellor in lunacy. My decision on that and other questions being appealed from, it appeared on the hearing of the appeal *ibid* 314, 318, 325 that the facts were not as supposed, but, on the contrary, that the order of the Landed Estates Court was, that the balance being in settlement, the residue was to be paid to trustees under the 64th section of the Act. If that order had been before me, I should have, of course, decided that the fund had not been converted, and on the true state of facts my decree on that point was rightly reversed. But there are other important differences between that case and the present. First, in that case the lunatic was only tenant in tail, with remainder in fee, to Madame Batteste, as devisee of the ultimate remainder in fee of the settlor; secondly, this fund was the surplus proceeds of real estate sold under the Landed Estates Act, and could not have been converted into personal estate without some act being done with that intention; but here the lunatic was tenant in tail, with immediate remainder to himself in fee, and the fund had in fact never been anything but money. On his death without issue, therefore, all possibility ceased of the right of any person arising which would require the actual conversion of the money into land, and the contention became one solely between the heir-at-law and the personal representative.

The case must be considered, first, in reference to the effect of the proceedings which I have stated; and, secondly, in reference to the established equities affecting the fund, under the circumstances, independent of those proceedings. As to the first, I think it is well settled by numerous authorities that when proceedings in lunacy are taken by the direction, or with the sanction, of the Lord Chancellor, or other person entrusted with the care of lunatics, which have the effect of changing the nature of the property in respect of conversion, even though taken without any intention of effecting such a change, still the relative rights of the heir and the personal representatives must be decided according to the actual state of the property at the death of the lunatic. This, of course, only applies to cases where there are no outstanding prior rights in other persons, as was the case here. It appears to me that the effect of the proceedings which I have stated was to free the fund from the trust for conversion, and to deprive the heir-at-law of the equity to call for payment of it to him. But if this be not so, those proceedings had at least the effect of placing the fund in the same position as if it had been paid over to the owner, if sane. If Thomas Nolan were *compos mentis,* and had instituted a suit to foreclose the mortgage, claiming the mortgage money as due to himself, and obtained a decree under which the amount was realized by sale or by the appointment of a Receiver, and brought in to the general credit of the suit, I cannot see any answer to an application by him to have it paid over to him; but it would be an *a fortiori* case if he had obtained a decree to take it out of the hands of the trustees of the settlement, and have it placed to his own separate credit. If this be so, then the fund was "at home." The principle established by *Chichester* v. *Bickerstaff* 2 Vern. 295, *Pulteney* v. *Darlington* 1 Bro. C. C. 223, and a long series of cases following the authority of those decisions, is that when money, subject to an imperative trust for conversion, is at the time of the death of the owner his absolute and exclusive property, and there is no outstanding right in any other person, the trust for conversion is extinguished, and the heir has no right to call for payment of it to him by the personal representatives. There is no right in anyone, then, to insist upon the actual conversion, nor any purpose remaining for which the money ought to be invested in the purchase of land. This rule is independent of election or intention, and arises from the position of the owner in reference to the fund. It applies, in my opinion, to the present case and I shall therefore declare that this sum of £3000, late Irish currency, forms part of the personal estate of the intestate. This renders it unnecessary to consider the other question.

Notes

1. The defendant appealed, but, while the appeal was at hearing, the case was settled by arrangement between the parties.
2. On the subject of "reconversion" generally, see *Irish Land Law*, para. 3.108 *et seq.*
3. As regards administration of a "lunatics" property, see *ibid,* para. 25. 17 *et seq.*

Chapter 3

ELECTION

This doctrine of equity is based upon the maxim – "Equity leans against double portions." It operates when what may appear to be rather unlikely circumstances occur, yet the law reports are scattered with cases where it has been invoked and applied, see *Irish Land Law,* para. 3.112 *et seq.*

RE SULLIVAN

[1917] 1 I. R. 38 (Court of Appeal)

A testator whose property at his death (exclusive of certain stocks and shares standing in the joint names of the testator and his wife, which at his death became, by survivorship, the absolute property of his wife) amounted in value to £1858, by his will gave his wife a legacy of £3000, "same to be paid to her either in cash or in such of my shares (including shares standing in her name jointly with mine) as she may select," and directed his executors to hold the residue of his property upon trust to pay the income to his wife during her life, and after her death to apply two-thirds in favour of a brother's children, and to hold one-third on a certain educational trust.

At first instance Barton J. held (see [1916] 1 I. R. 248) that the wife was bound to make her election between the benefits conferred by the will and her claim to any of the stocks and shares invested in the joint names of the testator and his wife.

Sir Ignatius J. O'Brien L.C.:

I do not get much assistance in this case from the authorities which have been cited. The question first to be determined is, what benefits on the construction of the whole will Michael Sullivan intended to give his wife? Taking the will as a whole, and avoiding any straining of its language, the answer appears to me to be clear. In the first place, the testator intended to give his wife £3000, and, when that was paid, apart from certain specific bequests, she was to get a life estate in the residue of his property. I refuse to dissociate the portion of the will which purports to give her £3000 with that portion which purports to put in a kind of settlement what the testator calls "the residue of" his property. He deals, in language that, to my mind, admits of no doubt, with all the shares which, in fact, were hers, as well as with the property, not shares, which was his own; and she is to get £3000, and no more, out of his property so defined, be it cash or shares. By so limiting the amount of this legacy, which she is to get absolutely, there is created a residue in which she is to get a life estate only. It was not seriously contended that if the words "including shares standing in her name jointly with mine" were to be found again in the clause dealing with the residue there would be much doubt in the case. My difficulty is to *avoid* taking the two clauses together, and, read together, they appear to me to bear the clear meaning I have put on them. Accordingly, for the plaintiff to claim to keep the shares which, as we now know, were all hers, and to take all the cash and property which were his, appears to me to be a clear attempt to approbate and reprobate at the same time. I think, accordingly, that it is a clear case in which the widow is put to her election, and I think the judgment of Mr. Justice Barton was right.

Ronan L.J.:

"Evidence of the circumstances surrounding the testator at the date of the will, the state of his family, and his property, is admissible in aid of construction. But evidence to show what were the *actual testamentary intentions* of the testator (as the instruction for a will . . .) is admissible only" for purposes not applicable in this case : Hawkins, p. 14, 2nd edition.

At the date of the will in this case, apart from the two sets of shares standing jointly in his name and that of his wife, the testator's property amounted to about £2000, consisting mainly of shares standing in his own name. At the date of his death this was reduced to in or about £1200 or £1300, mainly owing to reduction in value of these shares.

As to the shares valued at £1748 there was a presumption of law that the testator put them in the joint names with the intention that the wife should take them if she survived him. As to those valued at £4891 the presumption was that he put them in the joint names upon trust for himself. The Act 7 Edw. 7, c. 47, does not affect this presumption : sect. 52 of the Act and *Re Whitfield* [1911] 1 Ch. 310. In the present case it was affirmatively decided that the deceased had transferred these shares into the joint names with the actual intention that they should be her property if she survived him.

By the judgment in the case both sets of shares were declared to be the property of the wife.

The general principle applicable to election is thus stated by Lord Hatherley in *Cooper* v. *Cooper* L. R. 7 H. & L. 53, at p. 70 : "There is an obligation on him who takes a benefit under a will or other instrument to give full effect to that instrument under which he takes a benefit; and if it be found that that instrument purports to deal with something which it was beyond the power of the donor or settlor to dispose of, but to which effect can be given by the concurrence of him who receives a benefit under the same instrument, the law will impose on him who takes the benefit the obligation of carrying the instrument into full and complete force and effect." That is, of course, if he asserts his right to take the benefit under the instrument. It is for him to elect whether he will take it or not.

In the same case, at p. 67, Lord Cairns says : "The rule does not proceed either upon an expressed intention or upon a conjecture of a presumed intention, but it proceeds on a rule of equity, founded upon the highest principles of equity, and as to which the Court does not occupy itself in finding out whether the rule was present or was not present to the mind of the party making the will."

At pp. 70, 71 Lord Hatherley says : "The law inquires, on the death of the testator, when the will comes into operation, what is his intention, as expressed in the whole will, with reference to the disposition of that which he considers to be his property ; and it being found clearly and distinctly (for it must be clearly and distinctly found) that he has expressed his intention of disposing of what belongs to another – when once that is ascertained completely, there is nothing else which the law implies with regard to his intention, beyond the ordinary intent implied in every man who affects by a legal instrument to dispose of property, that he intends all that he has expressed, and, among other things, that he intends to dispose of property as to which he has so expressed an intention, though it really does not belong to him."

Lord Hatherley, of course, does not mean to exclude from consideration the matters referred to in the rule I have cited from Hawkins.

Lord Parker (then Parker J.) says in *Re Harris* [1909] 2 Ch. 206, at p. 209: "To raise a case of election under a will it must be, I think, reasonably clear from the will itself, having regard only to the circumstances under which it was made, and excluding evidence of intention, that the testator intended to dispose of property which in fact was not his own. Whether or not he knew it was not his own is, it seems to me, immaterial."

In the present case the testator, neither at the date of his will nor at any time afterwards, had any shares of *his own* standing in the names of himself and his wife.

It follows, therefore, that when he mentions "shares standing in her name jointly with mine," he must have meant either (*a*) these shares, or (*b*) shares which might afterwards be placed in their joint names upon trust for himself.

The strongest way the case can be put for the appellant is this :– Assume that after the date of the will the testator had done this, and that at the date of his death he had shares of his own in the joint names, then it is argued these shares alone would answer the entire description – "my shares standing in the joint names," and there would be no election ; that the fact that this did not happen cannot affect the construction of the will.

This is, I think, a fallacy ; in construing the will, we are bound to have regard to the state of the testator's property at the *date of the will.*

Having regard to the facts I have stated, I really have no doubt, reading the will by the light of these facts, as to the state of the testator's property and the position of these shares, that there is a clear and distinct expression of intention to treat these shares as part of his property, and to dispose of them as such under his will.

No case has been cited to us which goes quite to the point. But this is really a specific, not a general, description, as in *Dummer* v. *Pitcher* 2 M. & K. 262, where the words were "all my funded property or estate."

On the other hand, in *Coates* v. *Stevens* 1 Y. & C. Ex. 66, and *Grosvenor* v. *Durstin* 25 B. 97, there were words confining the bequests to the state of things at the date of the will, thought the descriptions were very general. In the latter case the words used were "my present funded stock."

It seems to me that the fallacy in the argument for the appellant lies in this. It assumes that no matter how specific the description may be, if it *is possible* for the testator, after the date of the will, to acquire property which will answer the description, there can be no claim of election.

For instance, if a testator gave to his son "my house in Merrion Square," and he was then living in a house in that square, the property of his wife, and had no other house there, could it be contended that because it was *possible* that he might afterwards purchase another house in the square, the wife would not be put to the election if she claimed benefits under the will? The question really is, as put in substance by Lord Parker in *Harris's Case* [1909] 2 Ch. 209, Is it reasonably clear that the testator intended to dispose of property not his own, or is it fairly open to the view that he meant property which he might afterwards acquire which would answer the description? He considered the case of the gold plate (see p. 212 of Report) "perhaps a more difficult one than the other." Comparing the description of the property in that instance with that in the present case, I think he certainly would have held the description in the present case sufficient to raise a case of election.

In my opinion, the notion that this testator in this will when speaking of the "shares in the joint names," ever thought of shares to be therefter put in the joint names, is fanciful and extravagant, and ought not to be entertained by the Court.

I form this opinion on the will itself read in connexion with the facts already referred to. If this is so, it follows that he meant these shares by the will.

If so, there can be no doubt that he intended to dispose of them by his will in precisely the same way as his own shares standing in his own name.

I agree that the Appeal ought to be dismissed.

Molony L.J.:

The testator bequeathed to his widow, the plaintiff, the sum of £3000 for her absolute use, "same to be paid to her either in cash, or in such of my shares (including shares standing in her name jointly with mine) as she may select." After providing some small legacies, he directed the executors to hold the residue of his property, both real and personal, upon trust to pay the income thereof to his wife during her life, and after her death for the children of his brother, John, and upon an educational trust. The plaintiff is a sister of the first wife of the deceased, and at the date of the Deceased Wife's Sister's Marriage Act, 1907, he had invested in the joint names £4891, and, subsequently, he invested in the joint names £1748. He had these investments at the date of the will, and no change took place in his lifetime. Apart from these his personal property was sworn at £1858, and he had no real estate. The shares in the joint names are admittedly the sole property of the plaintiff, and the question is whether she is put to her election to take under the will or against it. There is no difficulty about the law. As Lord Parker (then Parker J.) said in *Leacroft* v. *Harris* [1909] 2 Ch. 206, 209 : "To raise a case of election under a will, it must, I think, be reasonably clear from the will itself, having regard only to the circumstances under which it was made, and excluding evidence of intention, that the testator intended to dispose of property which in fact was not his own. Whether or not he knew it was not his own is, it seems to me, immaterial." The testator meant his wife to get £3000, but he realized it would be difficult for her to get it without having recourse to the shares standing in the joint names, and he, accordingly, gave her the right to be paid either in cash or in shares (including shares standing in the joint names). Did he show an intention to dispose of all the shares by his will, whether standing in the joint names or not? I think he was clearly referring to the shares which then were in fact standing in the joint names, rather than to shares which he might afterwards acquire and put into the joint names. If "the shares" are not required to meet the legacy of £3000, and so far as not required, they would clearly pass under the residuary gift, and although the residuary gift standing by itself would not be sufficient to raise a question of election, yet, taking in conjunction with the terms of the gift of £3000, it seems to me impossible to resist the conclusion that the testator was dealing with property not his own, and sufficiently identified as being his wife's, and that, consequently, she is put to her election.

Note
The doctrine of election has been incorporated into modern legislation, see *e.g.*, s. 115 of the Succession Act, 1965 (spouse's legal right), on which see *Re Urquhart* [1974] I. R. 197 (reproduced in *A Casebook on Irish Land Law*, p. 516). See also *Irish Land Law*, paras. 14. 57-8.

SWEETMAN V. SWEETMAN

(1868) I. R. 2 Eq. 141 ; 2 I. L. T. 136 (Vice-Chancellor's Court)

The facts are set out in the judgment.

Chatterton V.-C. :

This case comes before me upon exceptions to the report of Master Litton, signed the 4th of November, 1867, and made in pursuance of a decree of Lord Chancellor Brady, who has concluded by his decision the question, whether this was a case for election, and has left open merely the question of fact; as to which an inquiry was sent to the Master whether an election was made by William Sweetman (the second) during his life, or after his death, by his son and successor, William Andrew Sweetman, to take under the will, or against the will of the testator. The Master has arrived at the conclusion, and so reported, that William Sweetman, called the second, in his lifetime elected to take under the will and that his son William Andrew Sweetman also elected, and after his father's death adopted the election made by him. An exception has been taken to each of these three findings, and as, for the sake of convenience, the whole case has been argued upon the three exceptions together, I shall deal with it in like manner.

The facts of this case, so far as it is necessary to consider them with reference to the question before me, are these : In the year 1804, William Sweetman concluded an agreement with the Wide Street Commissioners, for the sale by him to them of certain property at the price of £10,579 12*s.* 7*d.* , on the terms that they were to remain his debtors for this sum till the time should arrive when they could convey to him fee simple estate of an annual value equal to interest at the rate of £5 per cent. per annum thereon, and that in the meantime they should pay him interest at that rate; and they bound themselves by covenant to convey to him lands producing the annual sum of £528 19*s.*, being the amount of such interest. William Sweetman accordingly, when he came to execute the deed of marriage settlement of 1805, was entitled to the sum of £10,579 12*s.* 7*d.*, as a debt due to him by the Commissioners, and also entitled to the benefit of, and was in a condition to enforce the contract with them for a grant of lands of the annual value of £528 19*s.* 6*d.* In 1805, he married a second time, and on that occassion executed a deed of settlement, in which he recited fully the dealings with the Wide Street Commissioners, and then assigned to the trustees this sum of £10,579 12*s.* 7*d.*, and in the *habendum,* though not in the parcels, he includes not only that sum, but also "all such grounds so to be demised by virtue of the said deed of the 20th of July, 1804, and all rents and reversions incident thereto, and all the estate, right, title, and interest of him, the said William Sweetman, in and to the same and every part thereof," and purports to carry same to the trustees of the settlement, and their heirs upon trusts, one of the trusts being to secure to his intended wife an annuity of £400, to be paid out of and charged on, "the said annual sum of £528 19s., being the interest of the said sum of £10,579 12*s.* 7*d.,*" until the Commissioners should settle and assure to the trustees "ground rents in the City of Dublin, equivalent and equal to said sums in manner hereinbefore particularly mentioned," and thenceforward to be paid out of and charged on "such grounds so to be settled and assured, and the rents and reversions incident thereto."

Nothing further was done until the year 1818, when William Sweetman made his will, the language of which is important in considering the questions to be disposed of in this case. It commences with a recital of the deed of 1804, whereby certain ground rents were agreed and covenanted to be conveyed by the Wide Street Commissioners to him, "which said ground rents were by the said deed specified and ascertained to be of the yearly value of £528 19*s.* sterling." The will then recites the deed of settlement of 1805, and that thereby the jointure of £400 a year "was, and still remains, charged on the before-mentioned sum, or on the ground rents so convenanted to be conveyed to me as aforesaid;" and then the testator desires that his wife shall receive over and above the annuity of £400, an additional sum of £200 a year, "£128 19*s.* thereof to be paid out of the aforesaid ground rents, and the remaining £71 1*s.* to be paid to her" by his executors, out of such funds as they should think proper to appropriate for that purpose.

The testator then proceeds in his will to make several specific bequests, and leaves all the rest, residue, and remainder of his property, real, freehold, and personal, which he should die seised, possessed of, or entitled to, to his two sons, William and John Sweetman, their heirs, &c., in equal shares.

On the 17th of October, 1823, the Wide Street Commissioners, in pursuance of their contract of 1804, executed to the testator a conveyance of several sets of premises in fee, producing an aggregate rental of £528 19*s.*

In the year 1824 the testator executed to the surviving trustees of the settlement of 1805 a conveyance of all these premises upon the trusts of that deed, and he died in the year 1826, seised of an estate in fee-simple therein, subject to the jointure of £400 a year. Before his death he executed a codicil, which however, since it was not attested, had no operation on his freehold estates.

In the year 1827 the testator's sons came to an arrangement, with respect to the property, which they carried into effect by a series of deeds, six in number, which is the main appear to have amounted to a selling by William Sweetman (the second), the testator's eldest son, of all his moiety of the premises comprised in them, to his brother John Sweetman, for a money consideration; but it is admitted, and this fact is relied upon by both parties in this case, that none of these deeds dealt in any way with the property now in dispute.

John Sweetman went into possession under these deeds of all the freehold and chattel real property comprised therein, and William Sweetman (the second), the eldest son of the testator, received, I presume, the money agreed on as the price. At all events, they divided the property between them, and the share of each amounted to about £35,000, at the least. Until 1834 no other act took place, except this, that during the entire period from the death of the testator, Mrs. Sweetman, his widow, received out of the premises in dispute, with the assent of both sons, not only the jointure of £400 a year, but also the entire residue of the income, neither brother interfering with her receipt of it, and thus dealing with it as if the property had passed under the will.

In 1834 a renewal was executed by both the brothers to an under-tenant, Smyth, and that conveyance contains this statement, simply that the reversion was vested in the two brothers by mesne assignment or otherwise. In 1845 William Sweetman (the second), the eldest son of the testator, died; and, upon his death, the present Respondent, William Andrew Sweetman, became entitled to all his interest in all the remaining freehold property, while the personalty went in a manner not necessary to be considered at present. In 1852 John Andrew Sweetman conveyed a moiety of the property in dispute, with other premises, to the present Petitioner, John Stanislaus Sweetman, by a voluntary deed; but nothing turns upon the fact of this conveyance. The deed itself, however, has a very important bearing upon the real question in this case, as I shall presently observe. In 1865 the widow of the testator died, having till then continued in the undisturbed possession of the whole of the rents of this property, taking the jointure of £400 a year under the settlement of 1805, and taking the difference, so far as the rental extended, in part payment of the additional annuity, the deficiency being made up in equal shares by the two brothers out of their shares of the property received by them under the will of their father.

These are the facts, with the exception of two others, which were strongly relied upon by the counsel for the Petitioner here, namely, that in 1854 William Andrew Sweetman executed a mortgage, and in 1856 a settlement of one moiety of this property, and thus dealt with it as if that was the amount of the interest to which he was entitled therein.

I shall now consider the rules of equity applicable to the case, and then deal with the evidence at each side.

The requisites for holding a party bound by an election as concluded are, I think, these :– first, he must have a knowledge of his rights, that is to say, he must know that the property, which the testator attempted to give to another person, was not the testator's property, and that it would, upon the testator's decease, become, independently of the testator's will, the property of the party called upon to elect. It must be known by him, as a matter of fact, that the testator had not the power to give the property which he purported to devise, and that it belongs, not by the will, but by an earlier title, to the person who is called upon to elect. Next, he must know the relative values of the properties between which he is called upon to elect; and further, he must know, as a matter of fact, and not as a presumption of law, that the rule of equity exists, that he cannot, under such circumstances, take both estates, but must make an election between the two. And, further, the Court must be satisfied that he made a deliberate choice with the intention of making it. That is perfectly ascertained law; and I need not go beyond the case of *Spread* v. *Morgan* 11 H. L. Cas. 588 for authority, as every one of these propositions was there laid down by the House of Lords.

But when I say that these propositions must be established to the satisfaction of the Court, I do not mean to say that there must be in every case actual, direct evidence of the existence of them. From a long course of dealing, from a series of acts, the court is at liberty, as an inference of fact, to conclude that the party called upon to elect knew his rights, knew the value of both estates, and knew the rule of equity, that he was bound to elect, and had, with full knowledge, made his choice, with the intention of making it, and of electing between the two estates. To justify the Court, however, in arriving at that conclusion, there must be a series of acts or dealings, consistent only with the knowledge which I have already mentioned, and with the deliberate intention to elect; or, at least, a series of acts or dealings that preponderates so strongly in the mind of the Court, that no person could come reasonably to another conclusion; and the *onus* of proof must rest always upon the party who alleges that the knowledge existed, and that the deliberate choice was made.

I shall next weigh the evidence relied on at each side. In the first place, as to the making of a deliberate choice, I can have no doubt whatever that, if the knowledge, if necessary for the purpose of having an intention to elect, could have been shown to have existed in the present case, there were such acts done by both the brothers as would warrant the Court in concluding that the election and choice had been made by William Sweetman, for he, from the time of his father's death, permitted the widow of the testator to receive, not merely the £400 a year, but to receive an additional sum out of that which was his own estate as heir-at-law of the testator, and which sum must otherwise have been provided out of the general estate of the testator, which passed under his will; and, therefore, if it was shown that he had so permitted the receipt of those moneys, with full knowledge of his rights and obligations, that permission and receipt would, in itself, amount to an evidence of an election made. Besides, there are some other dealings having a tendency in this direction, and perhaps the most clear of them is the deed of renewal in 1834, reciting that the property was vested in both brothers as tenants in common, when, independently of the will, the entire of it was vested in the eldest son as heir-at-law. There are two suppositions, upon either of which the parties may be deemed to have proceeded: one, that the property did, as a matter of fact, pass by the will. This is relied upon by the counsel for William Andrew Sweetman; and the other, which is relied upon the counsel for John Sweetman, that this property, though it did not pass actually by the will, was, however, operated upon virtually by it, by reason of the doctrine of election. With which of these two suppositions are the facts of this case most consistent? With sincere respect for the opinion of the Master, to whose report these exceptions have been taken, I, early in this case, formed the opinion that these dealings proceeded upon the mistaken assumption that this property did actually pass by the will; and that, therefore, there was an absence of that knowledge of rights, and of the rule of the Court, that is necessary to form an election. The will itself is quite enough to mislead parties not familiar with legal matters and documents, for it, on its face, deals with the property as if it was ground rents of premises to be conveyed by the Wide Street Commissioners, and dedicates the surplus rents to this lady. The settlement of 1805 recited the contract with the Commissioners, and gave powers of distress and entry for the recovery of the jointure. But, further, in 1827 I find that every other property, that had belonged to the testator, was dealt with by the two brothers, and divided between them, and that this property was omitted altogether from that arrangement. Why was it so omitted? Was it because the parties knew that a case of election arose, and that William Sweetman was bound to elect? or was it because they really believed that the property passed by the will, but that it effectually dedicated the entire of the rents to the widow, and that until her death nothing could come to them? If the matter rested there I should be strongly of opinion that they believed that the property actually, in point of fact, passed by the will, a belief which might have been strengthened by the fact that the testator had become the legal owner of it between the making of his will and his death. But I find next that a conveyance was executed in 1852 by John Andrew Sweetman to the Petitioner, which contains a recital that "under and by virtue of the settlement of 1805, and under and by virtue of the will of the said William Sweetman, bearing date the 11th of September, 1818, or under some other good and sufficient title; he, the said John Andrew Sweetman, was entitled to an estate in fee-simple in one undivided moiety of the premises, expectant upon the death of the said Charlotte Maria Dalton, otherwise Sweetman, the widow of the said William Sweetman, deceased, and which said several premises were granted and conveyed by the Commissioners of Wide Street of the City of Dublin unto the said William Sweetman, deceased, by indenture bearing date the 17th of October, 1823." That recital shows that what was passing through the mind of that side of the family then was that, under the settlement of 1805, and under the will, a property in one moiety of the fee had been acquired by John Andrew Sweetman. The same supposition would readily account for the renewal of 1834; for if the two brothers believed that the property had, in point of fact, passed by the will, they would have framed the recital in that deed just as it is.

Then come the deeds relied upon by counsel for the Petitioner as showing an election. One of those deeds was a deed of mortgage, of the 24th of November, 1854, by William Andrew Sweetman to some parties who were lending him money. The description of the lands conveyed by that mortgage is contained, not in the parcels, but in a schedule showing what he thought he was dealing with; and the words of the fifth schedule are remarkable. They run thus:– "Fifthly, all that and those the undivided moiety or half part, and other part or share, parts or shares of the said William Andrew Sweetman, whether in possession, reversion, remainder, or expectancy, or whether legal or equitable, or otherwise, of and in all and every the messages, tenements, ground, and hereditaments whatsoever, situate and being in the city of Dublin aforesaid, which the Commissioners of Wide Street in the said city, in or about or subsequently to the year 1804, granted or assigned, or are reputed to have granted or assured, or to have agreed to grant or assure, with certain ground rents incident thereto, amounting in the whole to the annual sum of £528 19*s*. sterling, unto William Sweetman, &c., and which the said William Sweetman, by his will, dated on or about the 11th day of September, 1818, devised, subject as therin mentioned, or incident thereto, unto his, the testator's, two sons, namely, William

Sweetman and John Andrew Sweetman, their heirs and assigns, as tenants in common, &c., and particularly subject to certain annual charges of £400 and £200, to or in favour of his then wife, and now widow," and to the trusts and provisions for securing the same.

In my opinion this language tends strongly to show that the impression on the mind of William Andrew Sweetman at that time was that the property had actually passed by the will. It certainly shows nothing to the contrary. I therefore think that on both sides there existed this mistaken belief, and this would account for the dealings with the rents of the estate. I therefore am of opinion that there is no proof of that knowledge and deliberate choice on the part of the Respondent and his father necessary to establish a concluded election.

But I was also pressed very strongly with the argument that this case was to be dealt with as one of a family arrangement, which, therefore, cannot be disturbed, it being in the nature of a family settlement. Without considering the grounds upon which an arrangement of that kind will be supported in many cases, it must be remembered that in order to make a family arrangement binding upon this Court, the Court must be satisfied that such an arrangement was actually come to. Such an arrangement may be presumed from a long course of dealings, but the course of dealings must be consistent reasonably only with the fact of such an arrangement having been come to. Here the supposition is based upon the fact that, in 1827, the two brothers executed a deed selling, the one to the other, his moiety of the property. But I think that that furnishes a very strong argument against the hypothesis that such an arrangement was intended with respect to these premises, for if it existed, why should they alone be excluded from these deeds? If it was matter of family arrangement, surely some one of these six deeds of 1827 would have contained some reference to this particular property, which really was the only one requiring anything in the nature of a family arrangement to be made.

It was said with some appearance of reason that the possession of John Andrew Sweetman and the Petitioner was adverse to the rights of William Andrew Sweetman, the Respondent, since the death of his grandfather in 1826; and Mr. Palles very ingeniously sought to bring in aid the Statue of Limitations as affording an argument in the Petitioner's favour in this case. But that is met at once by the frame of this suit, which is based solely on the doctrine of election. If such a case were to be made the parties should have brought their ejectment to recover this moiety. But this long possession affords neither a substantive case nor an arrangement to the Petitioner, founded on that Statute, as the possession was in fact that of Mrs. Sweetman, the widow; and it is really begging the first question, that of election, to convert this into a constructive possession by John Sweetman. If there was an election, this argument was unnecessary; if there was not, then it was not a possession by John, and the argument fails. No possession on which the Respondent could rely began till 1865, upon the death of Mrs. Sweetman, during whose life the two brothers had not any reason to complain of the application of the rents; and, therefore, I do not find any element here of a long possession which I should disturb, and which would influence my mind in coming to the conclusion that an arrangement in the nature of a family settlement would be interfered with.

These are all the topics with which I have to deal; and, with great respect for any decision arrived at by the very able Equity lawyer who made this report, I am clearly of opinion that there is not any evidence in this case, upon which I can act, showing that the parties made a concluded election. I shall, therefore, allow these three exceptions, and declare that the Respondent is to make his election. I shall permit the case to stand over for a few days, to give him time to do so. I shall reserve all question as to the costs until then.

Chapter 4

SATISFACTION, ADEMPTION AND PERFORMANCE

These doctrines are based upon the maxims – "Equity imputs an intention to fulfil an obligation" and "Equity leans against double portions." The various situations where they may be invoked were discussed in *Irish Land Law*, para. 3.115 *et seq*.

I. SATISFACTION OF DEBTS BY LEGACIES

COATES V. COATES

[1898] 1 I. R. 258 ; 32 I. L. T. R. 7 (Chancery Division)

By a separation deed S. covenanted that he, his executors and administrators would pay his wife an annuity during the term of her natural life of the weekly sum of 15s. By his will S. bequeathed to his wife a weekly sum of 12s. and the life use of a house and furniture. An originating summons was taken out to determine whether the annuity under the separation deed had determined with the husband's death and, if not, whether the bequest under the will, including use of the house and furniture, operated as a satisfaction of the obligation to pay the annuity.

Chatterton V.-C.:

The first question is whether the provision made for the plaintiff by the deed of separation of the 8th of September, 1884, terminated on the death of her husband? I am of opinion that on the true construction of the deed it did not. The deed states the occasion for its execution, namely, the separation of the husband and wife in consequence of unhappy variances existing between them, and, in consideration of the regular payment by the husband to the wife *during the term of her natural life* of the weekly sum of 15s., by way of separate allowance and maintenance, the wife bound herself not to cohabit thenceforth with her husband, or to annoy or molest him, and it was agreed that the weekly allowance should commence, accrue, and be payable to her from the 30th August, 1884. And the husband thereby for himself, his executors, administrators, and assigns covenanted with the wife, her executors, administrators, and assigns that he, *his executors, administrators,* and assigns should punctually pay to the wife, her executors, administrators, and assigns *the said* weekly separate maintenance as thereby provided. The allowance is therefore expressly payable to the wife for her life, and is payable not only by the husband but by his executors and administrators. No doubt this latter clause might be construed as applying only to any arrears due at the husband's death, but it is certainly wide enough to cover payments accruing after his death. As a matter of construction, I hold that the provision was made for the wife for her life, even in case she should survive her husband.

But it was contended that this, being a deed of separation, is to be dealt with in a different way from deeds for other purposes, and must be held to be incapable of subsisting after the death of the husband. There is no authority that I am aware of for this contention, and assuming the construction of the deed to be such as I hold it, I cannot so deal with it. That a deed of separation may be good after the death of the husband I find decided by the Vice-Chancellor of England in *Clough* v. *Lambert* 10 Sim. 174. The question is whether it is to be construed as restricted to the joint lives of the husband and wife, and this must depend on the language of the instrument. An analogy was contended for between the case of the death of the husband and the return to cohabitation; but the latter case depends entirely on considerations which have no application to the former.

The second question then arises, whether the bequests to the wife in the will of the husband are to be deemed a satisfaction of the liability of the husband's assets to the payment of the allowance secured by his covenant. The rule of this Court as to the satisfaction of a debt by a legacy is simple in its terms, but it has been so restricted by fine distinctions that it is often hard to know what cases are or are not within it. The debt or obligation here is the personal covenant of the husband and nothing more;

the amount is the weekly sum of 15s. The gifts by the will are, first, a weekly sum of 12s. and the life use of a house and its furniture. The objection that a legacy cannot operate in satisfaction of a debt of greater amount, even *pro tanto*, is sought to be got over by the proof that the use of the house and furniture exceeded the deficiency of 3s. a-week. But this introduces another objection, namely, that the nature of the gift must correspond with the nature of the obligation which was held in *Bartlett* v. *Gillard* 3 Russ. 149, following earlier cases, to be conclusive against satisfaction. If, then, recourse must be had to the house and furniture to get over the prior objection, it must be admitted that the whole of the obligation is not met by a gift of the same nature of the full amount; and, as satisfaction cannot operate *pro tanto*, this latter objection would seem to be equally conclusive. It was sought also to object on the ground that the allowance given by the will was not to arise till a week after the death of the testator. But even if such a trivial matter as the delay of one week were to be deemed sufficient evidence of an intention of the testator to take the case out of the general rule, it is conclusively met by the consideration that here there was no interval in the provision for the wife, as it ran from the death of the testator, although the first payment of it was not to be made till the end of a week from the death.

I am of opinion that on the other grounds I have mentioned I am precluded by the authorities referred to in argument from holding that the provision by the will was in satisfaction of the provision by the deed of separation, and I decide that the widow is entitled to both these provisions.

Notes and Questions

1. Do you agree with Chatterton V.-C.'s remarks about fine distinctions in this context? Why cannot satisfaction operate *pro tanto* in such cases? Why must the obligation be met by a gift of the same nature?
2. See further on this subject, *Irish Land Law*, paras. 3.115-6

II. SATISFACTION OF PORTIONS BY LEGACIES

RE BATTERSBY'S ESTATE

(1887) 19 L. R. Ir. 359 ; 27 I. L. T. R. 34 (Chancery Division)

The facts are set out in the judgment.

Monroe,J.:

The question arising in this case is, whether the provisions made by settlement for the children of an intended marriage are satisfied by the bequests to those children made by the settlor's will.

By a deed of settlement, made on the 23rd August, 1807, in contemplation of a marriage between John Battersby and Frances R. Wade, the lands of Lakefield, the property of John Battersby, were granted to trustees, in trust to raise the sum of £3000 for the children of the marriage, in such shares as the settlor should appoint, and, in default of appointment, equally among them. There were three sons and six daughters issue of the marriage. The power of appointment was never exercised. Two of the sons and all the six daughters were alive when John Battersby made his will, bearing the date the 24th April, 1839. By this will he devised to trustees the lands of Lakefield and several other denominations, in trust to raise the sum of £500 out of Herbertstown, and subject to this and some other charges, to hold these lands for his son Thomas Edward Battersby; and on further trust to raise the sum of £2000 out of the other lands, and, subject thereto, and to some other charges, to hold these other lands in trust for his son Robert Henry Battersby. These two sums of £500 and £2000 were to form part of his residuary estate. The residue of his real and personal estate he directed to be sold and invested. Portion of his wife's jointure was to be paid out of the interest. The residue of the interest he directed to be paid to his wife, during her life, for the maintenance of his six daughters. After his wife's death, the interest of this fund was to be paid to such of his daughters as should remain unmarried; on marriage, with the consent provided by the will, each daughter was to receive her share of one-sixth of the funds, and in the event of the death of any of the daughters, the others were to be entitled by survivorship. The residue of the testator's property, as directed to be realized, together with the sum of £2500, directed to be raised out of the real estates devised to his son, amounted to £6000. The widow of the testator is dead; Robert Henry Battersby, the owner, is the only surviving son. The daughters are still alive, except one.

By deed of the 18th December, 1880, the surviving daughters of John Battersby assigned to Joseph Kilbee whatever interest they had under the deed of settlement, if any, or under the will of their father, to secure advances made to the owner. The owner now contends that the provisions made by the will operated as a satisfaction of the portions given by the settlement. The assignees of Joseph Kilbee, who is a bankrupt, contend that they are entitled to both.

The question whether a portion given by a settlement is satisfied by a legacy in a subsequent will is entirely one of intention to be gathered in the absence of other evidence, from the terms of the two instruments, subject to this consideration, that the presumption of law is against double portions. If the provision made by the later instrument is equal to or greater than that made by the earlier one, and the limitations are substantially the same, double portions will not be allowed; the parties entitled will be put to their election. If the limitations are widely different, the presumption is that the provisions were to be cumulative.

It will be observed in this case that, under the terms of the settlement, John Battersby had the power of appointing the sum of £3000 among his children as he thought proper. Up to the date of making his will he had never done so, and by its terms he purports to dispose of all that he was possessed of. The sum set apart by the will for his daughters was more than twice as large as that given by the settlement, though there are some differences as regards the limitations. Under the settlement, in default of appointment, the daughters took their shares on their father's death; under the will, they do not become entitled to anything till after the mother's death: but the mother is entitled to the interest of the fund for her life, to be applied in the maintenance of her daughters. I consider this provision substantially the same.

Again, by the settlement in default of appointment, the daughters become absolutely entitled to equal shares in the fund. By the will each is entitled to her share of the interest in the fund, so long as she continues unmarried. If she dies unmarried she has no power of disposition; her share goes to the survivors. If she marries with consent, she is absolutely entitled to her share. Is this difference in the limitations sufficent to rebut the presumption that the testator did not intend to make a double provision for his daughters; or are the provisions substantially of the same nature? If the provisions are substantially the same, small differences will not operate to rebut the presumption of law: *Thynne* v. *Lord Glengall* 2 H. L. Cas 155; *Weal* v. *Rice* 2 Russ. & Myle, 251; *Chichester* v. *Coventry* L. R. 2 H. L. 87. The testator, purporting to make a just and fair distribution of all his property, and knowing that he had a power of appointment, sets apart a fund greater than that to which his daughters were entitled under the settlement. He enables each daughter, so long as she continues unmarried, to get her share of the interest, and when she marries to get her share absolutely. The only difference between the provisions of the two instruments is this – that in the event of her dying unmarried, she is precluded from making a disposition of her share, which, if she did make it, would, in ninety-nine cases out of a hundred, be the same as that contained in the father's will, viz. an equal distribution among the surviving members of the family.

In my opinion, there is not enough in this case to rebut the presumption against double portions, and I allow the owner's objection; but I give assignees their costs.

Notes and Questions

1. Is Monroe J.'s statement of the principles applicable complete? See *Irish Land Law*, para. 3.118.
2. The doctrine is confined to fathers and does not include advancement by a mother unless she stands *in loco parentis*. Why not? For criticism of this view by the Courts of Equity of the obligations of respective parents, see *Preston* v. *Greene* [1909] 1 I. R. 172 ; *Irish Land Law*, para. 3.117.

III. ADEMPTION OF LEGACIES BY PORTIONS

CURTIN V. EVANS

(1872) I.R. 9 Eq. 553 (Rolls Court)

The facts are set out in the judgment.

SULLIVAN, M.R.:

In this suit, which is one to administer the assets of the late Mr. William Johnston (a gentleman of very large property), a claim has been filed by Mr. and Mrs. Biggs, claiming a legacy of £5000 given by Mr. Johnston to Mrs. Biggs, by her maiden name of Elizabeth Geraldine Goodwin. She was his step-daughter, being daughter of his wife Mrs. Aveina Johnston by a former marriage.

The testator, who with the exception of Mrs. Biggs and her brother and his wife their mother, had no near connexion or relation, made his will on the 22nd of March, 1870, and bequeathed "To my step-daughter Elizabeth Geraldine Goodwin (in addition to the forty-five shares in the National Bank, which I have made her a present of some time since), I give, devise, and bequeath to her the sum of £5000."

It appears that the Bank shares mentioned in his will had been actually by his bounty made a present to Miss Goodwin (now Mrs. Biggs); and she being about to get married, he asked her to give them up, and with her consent he actually had them transferred to her brother as a free gift, about the 20th of May, 1870, a date which has been admitted before me. Reasons for this transaction are assigned in the evidence I shall afterwards read. They are in substance that Mr. Johnston did not wish Mr. Biggs to incur danger by reasons of the shares being in his wife's name; and Mr. Biggs being accepted as the husband of Miss Goodwin, Mr. Johnston agreed to give £5000 as a marriage portion, and accordingly a settlement was executed. The settlement bears date the 1st of June, 1870, and it recites that Samuel Dickson Biggs, the intended husband, was seised of certain estates in Tipperary and Limerick and that they were "subject to the charges in the schedule hereto annexed; and whereas a marriage is intended shortly to be had and solemnized between the said Samuel Dickson Biggs and Elizabeth Geraldine Goodwin, and upon the treaty for said intended marriage it was agreed that the said lands, hereditaments and premises should be limited as hereinafter mentioned, and that the marriage portion of said Elizabeth Geraldine Goodwin should be applied in payment and satisfaction of said charges." The settlement witnesses that in consideration of the marriage and of the sum of £5000, the marriage portion of said Elizabeth Geraldine Goodwin, the said Samuel D. Biggs grants to trustees the said several estates to hold to the use of the said Samuel D. Biggs for life, and after his decease "to the use and intent that if the said Elizabeth Geraldine Goodwin shall survive the said Samuel Dickson Biggs, she and her assigns may thenceforth receive during her life the yearly rent-charge of £300, to be increased to the yearly sum of £400 in the event of there being no children of said marriage, or, being such, that all the said children shall die before they or any of them shall attain the age of twenty-one years, or marry." The settlement then proceeds to limit the estates in the usual manner, and contains the following clause :– "And it is hereby agreed that the said sum of £5000, so paid to the (trustees), shall be applied by them in the payment of the sums of £5000 and £4084 12s. 3d., mentioned in the schedule hereto, and that until such payment the said trustees or trustee shall invest the said sum of £5000 in the public stocks," and hold the same "upon the trusts hereinbefore declared respecting the said lands and hereditaments, or as near thereto as circumstances will admit."

Under these circustances the claim of Mr. and Mrs. Biggs is resisted, on the ground that the advancement of the £5000 adeemed the legacy. It is fairly enough admitted by the counsel for Mr. and Mrs. Biggs that the case is to be looked on as if Mr. Johnston was *in loco parentis,* and that the £5000 is to be taken as advanced to Mrs. Biggs, notwithstanding the destination of it in the settlement. This admission seems to me perfectly right, as being in accordance with the law, and has my approval.

Owing to some arguments addressed to me on behalf of those who resist this claim, I think it is right that I should state my view as to the principles of law applicable to this case. They are, I conceive, very well settled, and they rest on a long line of decisions, many of them in the House of Lords. Those principles are as follow – viz., that there is a presumption raised by the law against double portions; and accordingly, when a parent, or one standing *in loco parentis,* gives by will a sum of money to a child, and afterwards a like or greater sum is secured by a settlement on the marriage of that child, the law presumes the legacy to be adeemed. But this is only a presumption, and therefore it may be rebutted by evidence of intention to the contrary. The burden of proof of intention to countervail the presumption rests on the person claiming the double portion. Parol evidence is admissible, even though the advancement is made under a marriage settlement as here, not (as explained by Vice-Chancellor Wigram, in *Kirk* v. *Eddowes* 3 Hare, 509) to show with what intent the written instrument was made, for the law has actually determined that intent; but for the purpose of ascertaining whether the presumption which the law has raised be well or ill founded. If the evidence rest in parol, the Court ought to view and examine it with scrupulous care and great discrimination, and ought not, I think, to act on it so as to rebut the legal presumption, unless it is free from suspicion, and it is clear to show the real intention of the party in reference to the very advancement he is making, which *primâ facie* has adeemed the legacy.

In *Lord Chichester* v. *Coventry* L. R. 2 H. L. 71, Lord Cranworth makes the following pointed observations; at p.87 he says:– "When, after the date of the will, he makes a settlement for the benefit of the person provided for by the will, the only question is, whether he intends the latter to supersede the former provision:" and at p.88, "It has been truly said that no positive rule has been or can be laid down as to what is sufficient to rebut the *primâ facie* presumption against double portions. That is a matter which, from the nature of things, must be left, in each particular case, to the judgment of the tribunal which has to decide it."

Accordingly particular cases which have been ruled, no matter what be their number, do not afford much assistance in determining on the special circumstances of future cases that arise, further than as elucidating or confirming the general principles which I have stated. In cases of this description the circumstances are constantly varying, from the shadowy line of demarcation which runs between two plainly distinguishable colours to that making the most decided contrast. The present seems to me a very peculiar case, having features quite its own.

The testator had presented his step-daughter with shares which have been proved to have been of the value of about £2600. He had confirmed that gift by his will, and left her in addition £5000. Within a few months she is about to be married, and he gets her to hand over the shares to her brother, and he pays down £5000 on her marriage, to be applied in paying off charges on the intended husband's estate, which was settled on her children, subject to a substantial annuity for herself. A good deal of evidence has been gone into to show what was Mr. Johnston's intention in relation to this transaction, with a view of showing that he did not mean the £5000 to adeem the legacy given by the will, and it is right that I should fully go through it.

Mr. and Mrs. Biggs have made a joint affidavit, the material facts of which are as follows:–

"I, the said Elizabeth Geraldine Biggs, for myself say that the said William Johnston, the testator, was my godfather and stepfather, and (although not related to me by blood) was greatly attached to me; and I say that in or about and during the years 1867 and 1868, he purchased for, and gave me, forty-five shares in the National Bank, and retained the documents relating thereto for me for safe keeping; and I understood from him that same were intended as a gift from him to me, and he frequently stated to me, then and afterwards, that he so gave them to me, so that if he died suddenly they were and would be mine, or words to that effect, he being then and for some years previous in a very delicate and precarious state of health. I, the said Elizabeth Geraldine Biggs, also say that, in or about the middle or end of the month of April, 1870, being then aged twenty-two years or thereabouts, I became engaged to my husband, with the complete approval and full sanction of the said William Johnston, and I say that some short time after I became so engaged to my said husband, I transferred said forty-five National Bank shares, at the request of the said William Johnston, to my brother Joseph A. Goodwin; and I did so because I was requested so to do, and without giving any thought or consideration to the transaction, or thinking that the said William Johnston was in any way affecting or lessening his bounty to me. And I say that, two days before my marriage, the said William Johnston said to me, 'I am taking the National Bank shares from you; but you will feel no disappointment hereafter, as I have left you in lieu of them much more than their value, but my motive for doing so is for fear your husband might suffer if the Bank failed.' And I say that when he said so, said sum of £5000 was paid, or about to be paid over."

Joseph A. Goodwin, the brother of Mrs. Biggs, has made an affidavit, and he states that–

"In the month of May, 1870, my late stepfather Mr. William Johnston said to me, while in the National Bank, College-green, Dublin, and on the occasion of my accepting the transfer of the forty-five National Bank shares transferred to me by my sister, Mrs. Elizabeth Geraldine Biggs, then Goodwin, 'I am taking the National Bank shares from Lizzie to make a present to you; but she need not be disappointed, as I am leaving her more than the value of them; and immediately after, and before leaving the Bank, he also stated that another reason why he took them from her was, lest the Bank might fail, and that her husband (meaning her then intended husband Samuel Dickson Biggs) might suffer if the Bank did fail, or words to that or the like effect, as I now best recollect. And I say this took place, as I believe, a short time before the marriage of my said sister Mrs. Biggs."

Another witness, Charlotte Montgomery, states that she knew the testator, and–

"I say that, in the latter end of the month of July, 1869, the said Mr. William Johnston stated to me in a private conversation, when walking in his own grounds at Somerset House aforesaid, that he would give his step-daughter as a portion £10,000, and he from time to time also in private conversation led me to believe that she, the said Elizabeth Geraldine Biggs, his said stepdaughter, was as dear to him as if she were his own daughter."

Another witness, Charles E. Young states:–

"That I knew and was acquainted with the late William Johnston, and I knew Mrs. Elizabeth Geraldine Biggs, otherwise Goodwin, his, the said William Johnston's step-daughter. I say that shortly prior to the marriage of said Elizabeth Geraldine Biggs, then Goodwin, with Mr. Samuel D. Biggs, he, the said William Johnston, stated to me that he would give his step-daughter, said Elizabeth Geraldine Goodwin, £5000 on her marriage, and that he would leave her more after, as he would not put her off with that, meaning said sum of £5000, but would give or leave her more after. And I also say that said William Johnston also stated to me, then or previous thereto, that few girls at Monkstown would have as good a fortune as his said step-daughter; and I say he made these or similar statements to me on several occasions. And I say that I have not the slightest doubt that he, the said William Johnston, intended to give his said step-daughter £10,000, and that the £5000 which he gave her on her marriage was only a part of said sum of £10,000, and of the sum which he so intended to give her, and that said bequest or legacy of £5000 was fully intended to be given her, said Elizabeth Geraldine Biggs, by him, said William Johnston, in addition to and over said sum of £5000 so given her on her marriage."

Mrs. Johnston, the testator's widow, thus deposes :–

"I, Aveina Johnston, widow of the late William Johnston, the testator in this cause, make oath and say, that from my own knowledge of the intentions of my late husband, the said testator, Mr. William Johnston, to my daughter his step-daughter and god-child, Elizabeth Geraldine Biggs, otherwise Goodwin, and from the great affection and attachment which he bore and had for her, and from the various statements he made to me prior to and after the marriage of the said Elizabeth Geraldine Biggs, that he, the said William Johnston, had not the slightest intention of substituting the £5000 given by him to her, said Elizabeth Geraldine Biggs, on the occasion of her marriage with my son-in-law Mr. Samuel D. Biggs, for the legacy of £5000 bequeathed by the said will of my said late husband to her, said Elizabeth Goodwin, otherwise Biggs. And I say that I have no doubt whatever, from my said late husband William Johnston's statements to me in his lifetime, that if he had not died so suddenly, and so soon after the marriage of said Mrs. Elizabeth Geraldine Biggs, his intentions were to have given her more than the said sum or legacy of £5000, in addition to and over said sum of £5000 so given on her said marriage; and I also say that I verily believe, from a statement made to me by the said William Johnston shortly prior to his sudden decease, that if he had lived to see a son of the said Mrs. Elizabeth Geraldine Biggs, he would have made it the object of his bounty, and over and above the said legacy of £5000 so bequeathed to said Elizabeth Geraldine Goodwin, otherwise Biggs; and I say it was with the complete and full sanction and approval of the said William Johnston that she, the said Elizabeth Geraldine Biggs, was married to her husband, the said Samuel D. Biggs; and I say that shortly prior to the engagement or marriage of said Elizabeth Geraldine Biggs, said William Johnston asked a friend of said Samuel D. Biggs what fortune he expected to get with his the said William Johnston's step-daughter; and it being stated a sum of £5000 or £6000 would be about the sum so expected, he, the said William Johnston, answered: 'Well, let it be £5000.' And I say that immediately after, on said friend of said Samuel D. Biggs leaving the room of said William Johnston's house, where said conversation took place, he, the said Willam Johnston, said to me that if he said Mr. Biggs' friend had stated that the sum of £8000 would have been expected, he would have given her that sum then as her marriage portion; but that it was as well to only give her £5000 then, and he could give it to her afterwards, when he saw how they would get on after their marriage. And I say that I was present when he, said William Johnston, said to said Elizabeth Geraldine Biggs, then Goodwin, 'I am taking the National Bank shares from you; but you will feel no disappointment hereafter, as I have left you in lieu of them much more than their value, but my motive for doing so is for fear your husband (meaning said Samuel D. Biggs) might suffer if the Bank failed.' And I say that immediately after the said Elizabeth Geraldine Biggs leaving the room, he, the said William Johnston, said to me that she need not feel disappointed at his taking the shares from her, as he had left her much more than their value, and which was in addition to said sum of £5000 so then given, or about to be given, her on her marriage. And I say that I have not the slightest doubt, as I always understood from the statements made to me by the said William Johnston after the marriage of the said Elizabeth Geraldine Biggs, that he, the said William Johnston, intended to give her £10,000; that the said sum of £5000 given her on her marriage was only part of said sum of £10,000, and of the sum which he so intended to give her, and that said bequest or legacy of £5000 was fully intended to be given her, said Elizabeth Geraldine Biggs, by him, said William Johnston, in addition to and over said sum of £5000 so given her on her marriage; and I have not the slightest doubt that he, the said

William Johnston, from such statements so made to me by him after the marriage of said Elizabeth Geraldine Biggs, fully believed that said bequest or legacy of £5000 was legal and valid, and that she would receive same under said will, in addition to said sum of £5000 so given her on her said marriage."

In another affidavit, Mrs. Johnston states :–

"I was present along with the said William Johnston and his step-daughter Mrs. Elizabeth Geraldine Biggs, then Godwin, when he, said William Johnston, said to said Elizabeth Geraldine Goodwin, now Biggs, 'I am taking the National Bank shares from you; but you will feel no disappointment hereafter, as I have left you in lieu of them much more than their value; but my motive for doing so is for fear your husband (meaning her intended husband, Samuel Dickson Biggs) might suffer if the Bank failed;' and I say that immediately after the said Elizabeth Geraldine Goodwin leaving the room he, the said William Johnston, said to me, that she need not feel disappointed at his taking the shares from her, as he had left her much more than their value, and which was (as he stated) in addition to the sum of £5000 then given her on her marriage; and I say that this occurred about two days prior to the marriage of my daughter, the said Elizabeth Geraldine Goodwin; and as I best recollect and believe, the sum of £5000, the marriage portion so given his said step-daughter, was actually paid over on that very day by him."

The only other affidavit is that of Mr. William D'Alton, who states :–

"I acted for many years as solicitor for the late William Johnston, in the pleadings in this matter mentioned, and as such solicitor prepared his will, and also the settlement executed on the marriage of his step-daughter, Elizabeth G. Goodwin, now Elizabeth G. Biggs. During the preparation of the said settlement, or shortly after said marriage, the said William Johnston mentioned to me that it would be necessary for him either to alter his will or to make a new one, in consequence of the provision he had made or was then making for his said step-daughter, or something to the same effect; and I say that I understood him to mean that as he had then given £5000 to his step-daughter, he would have to rescind the grant of the legacy given to her by his will. . . . . . . The said William Johnston did not afterwards give me any instructions so to alter said will or to prepare a new one for him, nor did he ever afterwards say anything to me from which I could infer that he had altered his intentions."

I regard Mrs. Johnston's evidence as conclusive; she was no stranger, and she has no interest in this matter; it was most natural that Mr. Johnston should state to her what his intentions were, and the declarations he made seem to me not the less weighty because they were not addressed to the intended husband; he perhaps, though intending future benefit to the young lady, did not wish to enter into any obligation on the subject.

Having gone through the evidence, my duty is, as observed in the judgment in *Trimmer* v. *Bayne,* to determine whether the parol evidence in this case has sufficient weight and power to weaken the presumption which it is admitted must *primâ facie* be applied.

Upon the most careful review and consideration of this evidence my opinion is, that it has the weight and power of rebutting this presumption.

There is nothing to impeach the testimony of Mrs. Johnston. The second affidavit, supplementing the first, has been strongly pressed as an element of suspicion. I have given every opportunity to the parties resisting the claim to have this witness cross-examined. I actually fixed two successive days in Chamber for the purpose, and the parties resisting the claim deliberately withdrew from the cross-examination. Taking this witness to be unimpeached, as I must, I think that her evidence is sufficient to show that, at the moment of the advancement and settlement of the £5000, he was declaring that he was not putting off his step-daughter with the £5000 advanced; and that, having regard to her giving up the shares, he meant the provision in the will giving her £5000 to take effect as it has done. I have not failed to give due consideration to Mr. D'Alton's affidavit; but I am bound to observe in reference to it that its frame is open to the gravest objection, inasmuch as it states Mr. William D'Alton's own conclusions as to the supposed meaning of Mr. Johnston's observations, which it ought not to have done. The meaning of the language is not for the witness, but for the Court. The witness should strictly confine himself to narrating the words used, or the substance of them, and should never put his own interpretation on them. I am perfectly astonished to find, nowithstanding the repeated injunctions given on this subject, that this system of making affidavits is persisted in. The conversation on the part of Mr. Johnston, as deposed to by Mr. D'Alton, strikes me as of the most vague and uncertain character, and by no means approaching what would be sufficient to meet the evidence of Mrs. Johnston. And it is further to be observed that, having regard to the transaction as to the shares, a very natural thing for Mr. Johnston to have said would have been, that he wished to alter his will. No doubt different minds will view parol evidence very differently, but mine is clear on the evidence that it was not Mr. Johnson's intention, in making the advance of the £5000, to adeem the legacy which he had given to Mrs. Biggs in his will.

Now, *Trimmer* v. *Bayne* 7 Ves. 508 has been much relied on by those resisting the claim of Mr. and Mrs. Biggs. It has been pressed to the length of being (as is asserted) an authority that the Court ought not to act on parol evidence (though it be admissible) in a case of this description; and again, that when a settlement such as here is executed, describing the advance as a marriage portion, it *i.e.* the settlement, must be taken as the final intention of the settlor. The case establishes neither of these positions, which in their very statement are inconsistent with each other; but it does, in the most unequivocal manner, recognise the rule which rested on high authority before it was decided, and which, even in cases like this, has never been controverted – that parol evidence is admissible, and ought to be acted on when it is addressed to and connected with advancement and settlement and the very time of the making of them. The closing observations of the judgment, at p. 521, make this plain to demonstration.

Lord Eldon says: "Upon the whole this evidence is not so connected with the act in December, 1794, as to destroy the effect of that act operating to an ademption of this legacy; and it would be extremely dangerous, however the evidence must be allowed as admissible, to say such evidence is sufficient to prevent the operation of a clear settled rule of law; if it is not clear and satisfactory to that point, to which it must be, to rebut the presumption, according to the clear settled rule, arising out of the effect of the settlement." Indeed the whole judgment seems to me at right angles with the propositions which have been inferred from it during the argument before me. *Debeze* v. *Mann* 2 Br. C. C. 165, before Lord Thurlow, is expressly recognized as well decided; and observe what is said at p. 514 :–"It is also clearly established that parol evidence is admissible to rebut the presumption." And again at p. 517., "I fear there is no possibility of saying parol declarations both previous and subsequent are not admissible, though Lord Coke would hardly have been brought to let them in, as well as declarations at the time. But there is a very great difference, as also upon these marriage treaties, upon the point whether they are all alike weighty and efficacious. A declaration at the time of making the will is of more consequence than one afterwards; and a declaration after the will as to what he had done (I am speaking as to the time merely) is entitled to more credit to one before the will as to what he intended to do: for that intention may very well be altered; but he knows what he has done; and is much more likely to speak correctly as to that, than as to what he proposes to do; though these parol declarations are all alike admissible; whether consisting of conversation with people who have nothing to do with it, people making impertinent inquiries and drawing from him angry answers, or in whatever form, they are all evidence. But they are entitled to very different credit and weight according to the time and circumstances. In *Debeze* v. *Mann,* the conversation between the two fathers upon the subject of the very contract, between two persons under a parental obligation to provide rationally for the interests of their children, upon every ground is entitled to much more weight than some others. So in *Ellison* v. *Cookson,* where old Ellison took the trouble to send a brother-in-law to the country to talk upon the subject; an authorized agent in the treaty; speaking of declarations between him and the principal; to settle the terms of the contract of marriage. That evidence has a character that does not belong to such as occurred in this case."

The case of *Debeze* v. *Mann* 2 Br. C. C. 165, which, as I have said, *Trimmer* v. *Bayne* recognises, seems to me far less strong than the case now before me, while *Shuddall* v. *Jekyll* 2 Atk. 516 seems almost in point. In that case Lord Hardwicke says, "I am of opinion that the evidence does import quite the contrary, and parol declarations have been constantly admitted in all these cases." *Dawson* v. *Dawson* L. R. 4 Eq. 504, and *The Earl of Durham* v. *Wharton* 3 Cl. & Fin. 146, have been much pressed upon me as authorities against the claimants. It is sufficient to say of *Dawson* v. *Dawson* that there existed the mere fact of an advance or liability entered into on the marriage, subsequent to the will; there was no parol evidence at all; while *The*

Earl of Durham v. *Wharton* stands on its own peculiar grounds, not touching the present state of facts, as will appear by examining the grounds of that decision, as clearly explained in *Lord Chichester* v. *Coventry* L. R. 2 H. L. 71.

I shall declare the claim of Mr. and Mrs. Biggs sustained, and that they, in her right, are entitled to the legacy of £5000, as given by the will.

The cause came on this day for further consideration, and on the Chief Clerk's certificate, when a decree was made, of which the following is the part relating to the claim of Mr. and Mrs. Biggs :–

"It is ordered that the Accountant-General do, out of the sum of £62,257 2*s.* 2*d.* Government New Three per Cent. Stock, now standing to the credit of this cause, transfer to the following so much thereof as, at the price of the day, will be equivalent to the sums set after their names respectively, in discharge of the principal and interest up to the 1st of June, 1875, on foot of their legacies, that is to say, &c. – to Samuel Gibson Biggs, &c., the sum of £4174 12*s.* 7*d.* cash, and to Elizabeth Geraldine Biggs, wife of the said Samuel Gibson Biggs, on her own receipt as her separate estate, &c., the sum of £1000; the said Mrs. Geraldine Biggs having been examined in Court separately and apart from her said husband, and having waived her equity to, and settlement of, the sum of £5174 12*s.* 7*d.*, payable in respect of her legacy, and having desired that the said sum of £4174 12*s.* 7*d.*, portion thereof, should be paid to her husband, and the remaining £1000 to herself in manner aforesaid."

Note

See further, *Irish Land Law,* para. 3.119, and *Griffith* v. *Burke, infra.*

GRIFFITH V. BOURKE

(1887) 21 L. R. Ir. 92 (Chancery Division)

The facts are set out in the judgment.

Porter M.R. :

This case is an interesting one, in point of fact and in point of law.

Two actions – *Griffith* v. *Bourke* in this Court, and *Bourke* v. *Griffith* in the Vice-Chancellor's Court, which was transferred to this Court – have been consolidated. The first suit was instituted by James Griffith, as executor and residuary legatee of Mathew Higgins, deceased, to administer his personal estate; and the suit in the Vice-Chancellor's Court was commenced by the Very Rev. Canon Bourke, P.P., of Kilcolman, who sues as legatee for £1000 in the will of the said Mathew Higgins. The statement of claim in each suit stands as a statement of defence in the other ; so that there is only one action in fact for the administration of the personal estate of Mathew Higgins.

There is but one question now ripe for decision, that is as to the legacy of £1000 claimed by the Very Rev. Canon Bourke. That legacy is given by the will, in these terms:– "To the parish priest, for the time being, of the parish of Kilcolman, the sum of £1000 Government New 3 per cent. Stock, free of legacy duty, to be laid out by him in the erection of a new Roman Catholic Chapel in the town of Claremorris." That is a clear gift of a legacy, payable to Canon Bourke, he being alive. If he had been dead, it would have been payable to the parish priest, for the time being, of the parish of Claremorris.

The testator died possessed of Government Stock, and the legacy was a demonstrative one – Government Stock, not of the Stock itself, nor of cash. The gift relied on as an ademption was not of Stock, but cash – part of a sum secured by a deposit receipt. But The MacDermot met the case fairly on its merits, and made no point upon this. The legacy ought to be paid at once, if it was not adeemed by the subsequent gift of £1000 to the Roman Catholic Archbishop of Tuam, of a like sum for the same purpose.

If a man leaves to another a specific legacy, as, for instance, of a horse, and the horse dies, or the testator disposes of it in his lifetime, the legacy fails. There is no subject on which the gift can take effect, and the legacy is adeemed. But that is not the only kind of ademption. Lord Manners, in *Monck* v. *Monck* 1 Ball. & B. 303, gives an illustration of the doctrine of ademption. He says:– "It is an established principle, laid down in several cases, particularly in *Debeze* v. *Mann* 2 Br. C. C. 165, 519, and denied in none, that where a legacy is given for a particular purpose, and that is anticipated by an advancement by the testator subsequent to the will, and for the same purpose, the legacy is presumed to be adeemed: that presumption is capable, however, of being rebutted by evidence. Here there is no evidence. I would put it thus. Suppose that the testator had, by his will, left £5000 to his brother to buy a house in Merrion-square, and afterwards he himself buys one, which he gives to his brother; are there to be two houses bought?" In the case of a parent, or one standing in *loco parentis,* the presumption is that the legacy is adeemed by the advancement. But where the legacy is to a stranger, and not to a child, or a child by adoption, the presumption is that, no matter what the testator does in his lifetime, it is not adeemed. The stranger may take both. But there is another exception in the case of a stranger. Where there is a gift in a will, of money or property, for an expressed object to which it is devoted by the testator, and there is afterwards a donation by the testator in his lifetime for the *same* object, the law presumes that he did not intend that both should take effect, but that the latter should be in substitution for the former gift. The object, however, must be clearly expressed, and it must clearly appear that what he did in his lifetime was done for the same object as that intended in his will – for the same identical object.

In this case Griffith, the plaintiff, and the principal person interested, is not only the devisee in remainder of all the lands, but he is also residuary legatee of the personalty; therefore he has a valid interest to cut down the legacy. The will was made in 1882, and made in duplicate. He was cognisant of the fact that the will was made, for he retained the duplicate. I asked to see it, but it was not produced. However, not much turns on the non-production of it. He was on confidential terms with the testator, and was as near to him in blood as any other person. I should judge, from the evidence, that the testator was a talkative person, fond of discussing his own affairs; and it appears that he made no secret of his having made his will, leaving £1000 towards building the church at Claremorris.

In September, 1885, the Roman Catholic Archbishop of Tuam, Dr. McEvilly, went to Claremorris. He knew the testator Mathew Higgins, who went to see him. The visit was a hurried one. The archbishop was going to a visitation in another part of his archdiocese, and the carriage was waiting at the door to convey him there. James Griffith was not present. But another person was there, the Rev. Father Curran. He is alive, and it is to be regretted that he has made no affidavit. The account which the archbishop gives of the interview, is as follows :– "I had an interview with the said Mathew Higgins, deceased, with whom I had been previously well acquainted, on the 15th September, 1885. It took place at the residence of the Rev. Michael Curran, where he called upon me, and was the only occasion on which the gift hereinafter mentioned was referred to between us. The conversation which took place was a short one, and I only remember the substance of it. Mr. Higgins said he had £1000 for me, for the building of the new Catholic church in Claremorris. I thanked him, and said, 'Give it to Father Curran; I am going to Tagheen for a visitation.' My carriage was then waiting for me at the door, and I made little further delay. Father Curran did join in the conversation. I do not recollect what he said; but Mr. Higgins did not then, or at any time, state to me, or in my hearing, that he intended leaving £1000 by his will for the building of the said church, not did he ever, in any way, convey to me that the £1000 spoken of in this interview, was to represent a like sum, which he intended leaving by his will. He did not, at any time, mention his will to me, and I was unaware of its existence at the time of the said conversation. 2. I never authorized anyone to apply to Mr. Higgins for this or any other sum of money. I knew nothing, at the time I received it, of the bequest in his will, and never caused any communication to be made to him on the subject, nor am I aware that any such communication was made. 3. I arranged with the said Mathew Higgins, at the before-mentioned interview, that I should pay him interest on the £1000 during his life, dividends to be paid in April and October in each year. On the 29th September, 1885, I paid by cheque to Mr. Higgins the sum of £17 18*s*. 2*d*. for interest, which had accrued up to that date, on the deposit receipt in the Bank of Ireland, Ballinrobe, for £1200 which I received on the 16th September, through Father Curran. No further interest was ever paid to or demanded by the said Mathew Higgins. 4. The £1000 was paid to me in the manner in the last paragraph mentioned. The balance I did not draw out at all, but left in the Bank to credit of Mr. Higgins." The deposit receipt is for £1267, it is endorsed by Mr. Higgins, and was cashed by Mr. Curran, who re-lodged the difference between its amount and £1000.

The transaction thus deposed to is perfect, complete, and distinct. What is the substance of it? It was a gift of £1000, the identical amount of the legacy (though the amount of the deposit receipt was different), and the dividends were to be paid to the testator during his life. What was the purpose to which the money was to be applied? It was the very identical purpose mentioned in the will – the building of the new Catholic church at Claremorris. It was not given to the same trustee; but I observed during the argument, the testator did not mind who was to be the trustee, provided the trust was carried out. We have, therefore, a gift of a sum of money for the identical purpose for which the legacy was given: not to the same person, but for the same purpose, which could and would be enforced in this Court, if the trustee was dead. Again, there is this peculiarity in the transaction, that the testator reserved for himself the interest of the £1000 during his life, which makes the gift correspond very closely in effect with a legacy. "I arranged with the said Mathew Higgins," says the archbishop, "at the before-mentioned interview, that I should pay him interest on the £1000, during his life, dividends to be paid in April and October of each year." There can be no doubt, therefore, that, if the matter stood there, the legal presumption would arise, that this transaction of 1885 was an ademption and satisfaction of the legacy given by the will of 1882. The affidavit of the archbishop is the only direct evidence we have of the interview. But we have also indirect evidence in the affidavit of James Griffith, the plaintiff. He is also, as I have said, residuary legatee, and therefore he has a direct pecuniary interest in the case – he has come to support his own case. But he was cross-examined before me, and I saw nothing in his demeanour in the witness-box, and I heard nothing, which induces me to believe that he is not a trustworthy witness, and I entirely believe his evidence. He is said to be a religious man, and one who stands well with his own Church. The transaction took place on the 15th of September, 1885. He states in his affidavit (p.5) that, "Early in the month of October, 1885, I called upon the testator, who informed me that he had given the £1000 that he had intended to have given by his will for the building of the church, to the archbishop, to be applied by the archbishop to such purposes, as he stated that they, meaning the priests, had the place of the chapel bought, and wanted the money to begin the work. He informed me that the archbishop had promised to give him the highest rate of interest for it during his life." Now that affidavit was sworn in July, 1886. He could not have got the statement about payment of interest from the archbishop's affidavit, which was not sworn until the 14th December, 1886. There is the statement that the archbishop promised to give the highest interest for the £1000. The plaintiff was cross-examined, and not a question was put to him as to this interview with the testator. The cross-examination was entirely directed to other topics, and elicited from him a statement that another witness, Mr. Waters, had stated in his affidavit what was not a fact.

There was another witness at the interview between the archbishop and Mathew Higgins when the £1000 was given – Father Curran, one of the curates of the parish. It was at his house that the interview took place, and it was by him that the money was received for the benefit of the church. Why did the defendant not bring him here to be examined? Mr. White may be right in his conjecture – founded, no doubt, upon instructions – that he did make an affidavit. If he did, I have not been permitted to see it. It would appear that the evidence of the defendant's witnesses to the transaction was procured by Father Curran himself; and two of his brothers, Martin Curran and James Curran, have made affidavits for the defendant. Why, then, was he not produced? Or if he made an affidavit, why was it not used? He is a clergy-man, and acquainted with the whole transaction – a disinterested witness – apart from any zeal or anxiety he may feel for the benefit of his church. I am forced to the conclusion that, at any rate, he could not have given evidence more favourable to the case of Canon Bourke than that given by the archbishop. I am thus left to the archbishop's evidence, and the second-hand evidence given by the plaintiff James Griffith, upon that which, in point of law, is the vital question in the case.

The affidavit of James Griffith states :– "Early in the month of October, 1885, I called on the testator, who informed me that he had given the £1000 that he had intended to give by his will for the building of the church to the archbishop to be applied by the archbishop for such purposes, as he stated that they, meaning the priests, had the place of the chapel bought, and they wanted the money to begin the work. He informed me that the archbishop had promised to give him the highest rate of interest for it during his life. He further added that he had given such sum by a deposit receipt for over £1200, which he stated he gave to the Rev. Father Curran, to hand to the archbishop, as he at the time was in Claremorris, for such purpose, and that he got back a deposit receipt for the balance and a cheque for the amount of interest due on it. The testator asked me if I had heard of this, and I replied to him that I had heard of it, but did not believe it; the priests and the archbishop had not acknowledged it through the local papers, as I thought them bound to do. The testator then replied to me, that both the priests and the archbishop had acknowledged it from the altars, and I replied that I thought it was not sufficient. He added that he did not wish Father Bourke to have any dealings with his money after his death. The Rev. Michael Curran then came by, and the testator stated to him that I said the money (meaning the £1000 so given) should be acknowledged in the local papers; and the Rev. Michael Curran replied that it would be easy to get an acknowledgment from the archbishop, and that he would get it for him from his Lordship. Testator then stated I should come in some day that he would afterwards name, and bring in the will to have it regulated, which I understood to mean that the testator was to add a codicil to it revoking the bequest of the £1000. Testator did not name a day, and I did not bring in the will which I retained as I received it, until the Rev. Michael Curran opened it."

The earlier and important part of this affidavit is not contradicted – I mean that part which relates to the circumstances of the gift, and corroborates the statement of the archbishop. The presumption is overwhelming, that the gift was intended to be an ademption of the legacy.

I come now to the evidence on the part of the defendants, chiefly consisting of statements alleged to have been made by the testator. That evidence is admissible, to show the character of the act, which is relied on as the ademption; and parol declarations, whether contemporaneous or subsequent, are admissible for that purpose. Sir James Wigram, in *Kirk* v. *Eddowes* 3 Hare. 522, would seem to have confined it to contemporaneous declarations; but that is explained in *Pollock* v. *Worrall* 28 Ch. Div. 552. And Lord Eldon, in *Trimmer* v. *Bayne* 7 Ves. 513, says:– "I fear there is no possibility of saying parol declarations, both previous and subsequent, are not admissible; though Lord Coke would hardly have been brought to let them in as well as declarations at the time." In *Powys* v. *Mansfield* 3 M. & Cr. 376, Lord Cottenham held that an adeemed legacy was not set up by a subsequent codicil, confirming the will, on the ground that an adeemed legacy is gone, and must be treated as if erased from the will. Thus parol evidence, where admitted, must be directed to the very transaction relied on as an ademption. If it were to be used with the view merely of showing that, after a distinct act of ademption, complete in itself, the testator entertained or even expressed, the desire that nevertheless the legacy should be paid in addition, there would be a virtual repeal of the Wills Act, should such evidence be regarded; and a legacy might be inserted and removed, and inserted again by word of mouth, according as the testator may have changed his mind from day to day. The evidence is not to be rejected, but is to be regarded solely so far as it throws light on the circumstances, under which, and the object for which, the £1000 was paid.

The first witness is John F. Noone. He is a shopkeeper in Claremorris. After stating that he knew Mathew Higgins, and was related to him, he says (p.3):– "I had previously heard that he had made a will, and left £1000 for the purpose of erecting a church. It was a matter of common gossip in Claremorris. I was present on many occasions after April, 1882, the date of the will, when I had conversations with the said Mathew Higgins, and he frequently stated no one could tell what he intended to give for the purpose of erecting a church; but that the clergymen would not be trusting to £1000 to build the church, and that he would give more. He often made use of such remarks, even after the date the £1000 had been given to the archbishop, which I knew of immediately after it was given."

The next witness is Miss Ellen Egan. She says (p.3):– "In the latter part of October, or beginning of November, 1885, the late Mr. Mathew Higgins came into my house, and in the presence of my sister, Mrs. Carey, said, after a few remarks: 'I have handed £1000 to the archbishop, free of law costs; and, if I don't change my mind soon, there is not a stone from the foundation to the roof, as far as my means go, but I will try to build.' He often expressed a wish that Ballinsmalla Chapel, or old church, would be repaired, and stated that he would be most willing to give every asisstance." Of course, by "law costs" the testator meant legacy duty. As to the intention expressed to build the chapel "from the foundation to the roof," it must be taken to be an expression of his anxiety in the matter. If taken literally, it points to an intention to devote not only £1000, but the whole of his assets, which amounted to about £4000, to the building of the chapel at Claremorris.

The next witness for the defendant is the Rev. Anthony Waters. There is a direct conflict between his evidence and that of the plaintiff James Griffith. He says :– "I saw James Griffith in the end of March of the beginning of April, 1886, as he was going to the post-office, Ballindine. He there told me that six or seven days before Mathew Higgin's death, he (James Griffith) asked Mr. Higgins to change his will in reference to the intended new church of Claremorris. Mr. Griffith told me that he brought Mr. Higgin's will to him (Mr. Higgins) for a change in this matter, and that Mr. Higgins would not, and did not, change it, but said he would consider it. I asked James Griffith if testator (Higgins) was competent to change it, to which Griffith replied he was competent to do so. I remember the date from the fact that I asked, 'Any news?' 'Yes,' said Griffith; 'did you not hear I am going to law with Canon Bourke?' 'No,' said I. I then asked, 'What for?' Griffith said, 'About that £1000.' 'But why,' said I; 'did you not try to get Higgins to omit it in the will? 'I did,' said he; 'but I failed to do that – he would not.' " Now, Griffith denies any such conversation ever took place. He denies it both in his affidavit and his cross-examination before the Court. I wish to say that I am satisfied that Mr. Waters swore nothing but what he believed to be strictly and literally true. It is to be observed that this conversation is put in evidence to prove that the plaintiff admitted that he had no case against Canon Bourke. A very slight alteration in the language would give an entirely different complexion to it. When I turn back to Griffith's affidavit, I find that he states that the testator told him he should come in some day and "bring in the will to have it regulated, which I understood to mean that the testator was to add a codicil to it, revoking the bequest of the £1000." I do not think Mr. Waters' recollection of the conversation can be accurate. It is most unlikely that Griffith admitted, in April or March, 1886, after he had commenced his action, that he had no case against Canon Bourke. The writ had been issued at the time, and the statement of claim was delivered in May, 1886. In my opinion, therefore, the affidavit of Mr. Waters does not touch the point of the case, and is not sufficient to induce me to discredit the plaintiff.

Mary Anne Sheridan states that she was intimately acquainted with the testator. He was the landlord of her shop, and was in the habit of coming in and telling her his private affairs. "Early in the month of October, 1885 (I remember the time from the fact that it was shortly after the sum of £1000 was given to the archbishop), the said Mathew Higgins came into my house, as was his custom, and I had a conversation with him. I knew well at that time that he had, in the month of September previously, given to the Archbishop of Tuam the sum of £1000 for a Roman Catholic church at Kilcolman, and he again informed me that he had so given the money. I then said to him, 'What about the £1000 in the will?' to which he replied 'Oh, never mind that – it is all right.'" And she says :– "I remember distinctly the 23rd of November, 1885, when the conversation took place at which Father McHugh was present, and when the said Mathew Higgins stated that he had that day done a good job by making a codicil. He said a man who, like himself, had no family had on that day promised to give something for the purpose of erecting the church. 'I know whom you mean,' said I – 'Mr King.' 'Yes,' said he. I replied, 'Sure he does not reside in the parish,' and he said, 'No, but that he would give something nevertheless.' I replied, 'If everyone had done as much as you have done – – ' Mathew Higgins, interrupting, jumped up, and, striking the counter, stated, in presence of Father McHugh and Miss McHale, 'I am glad of what I have done' (referring to the £1000 given to the archbishop) – 'I will do more.'" "I will do more." That does not seem to refer to the legacy of £1000 given by the will, which, so far as he was concerned, was already given.

Martin Curran, a farmer, deposes to a conversation which took place on the 28th September, 1885 :– "We spoke about the depressed times and the state of the country, and he said, 'All the money has not left the country. I gave £1000 the other day to the bishop for the purpose of erecting a church, and I am to give another £1000.' I replied that was very good, and that it was a pity there was not more of his class in the country. The conversation referred to took place in the public street, opposite the house of P. McVahy, merchant, Claremorris, and in the presence of testator and three of my brothers, James, Peter, and Thomas Curran, the latter remarking that I, Martin Curran, should have applauded him for his generous intention of a second thousand for the new church. The statement made by me is similar to that of my brother James, for he was present during the whole time of the conversation. There were five persons present at the time – namely, Mathew Higgins (testator), James Curran, Peter Curran, Thomas F. Curran (my brothers), and myself."

James Curran, the brother of Martin Curran, gives in his affidavit an account of the conversation and of what led to it, in identically the same words, with the result that, as the statement is in each made in the first person, the two affidavits are contradictory, each stating the conversation as with *himself.* Instead of each giving his own version of the conversation, they seem to have put their heads together and have adopted the same exact forms of expression. There is great difficulty in acting on such evidence. Of the five persons, including the testator, Peter Curran, and Thomas F. Curran, who, as I understand, are gentlemen of intelligence, have made no affidavits. Under these circumstances, I cannot act on the statement referred to.

Michael Noone has made an affidavit. He states:– "I knew Mathew Higgins very intimately . . . I had frequent conversations with Mathew Higgins as to the manner in which he proposed to dispose of his means, and he always spoke of giving £1000, and more, for the purpose of building a church. I knew well that he had left £1000 by his will in 1882. It was a matter of common gossip in Claremorris; and I remember distinctly, in September, 1885, the day following that on which he gave £1000 to the archbishop, when he informed me what he had done on the previous day, and that he would do more." This, however, does not show that the £1000 given to the archbishop was not intended to be the £1000 left by the will.

Patrick King says :– "I knew Mathew Higgins . . . and on or about the 15th November, 1885, I had a conversation with him. Said Mathew Higgins informed me that he would give as much more as he had already given for the building of the chapel in Claremorris. 'What do you think?' said he. 'Was I not right in doing so? Is it not far better than leaving it to people who may not thank me?' I replied, 'You are perfectly right; you could not do a better thing than leave it in charity. It is the proper thing to do.'" This conversation took place in P. McVahy's shop in Claremorris. Mr.

Bell of Claremorris was present at the conversation.

With regard to the general intention which this witness would seem to attribute to the testator of leaving the most of his property in charity, I may observe that it is not borne out by his will. His assets amount to £4000. All he left in charity was £1000, the legacy in dispute; £200 to buy blankets for the poor of Claremorris; and £20, each, to the three curates of the parish to say Masses for his soul – in all £1260. The evidence of all these witnesses is vague and unreliable, and, in my opinion, not sufficient to rebut the clear presumption of ademption which arises from the gift to the archbishop. I shall decree accordingly.

IV. SATISFACTION OF LEGACIES BY LEGACIES

QUIN V. ARMSTRONG
(1876) I. R. 11 Eq. 161 (Rolls Court)

The facts are set out in the judgment.

Sullivan M.R.:

The bill in this cause was filed for the purpose of raising out of the lands of Tinnerranny two annuities of £40 and £60 a-year, charged, as the Plaintiff alleges, on those lands by the joint operation of a deed of the 17th of July, 1866, and the will of Joseph Jeffares. In order to explain how the matter stands, it is necessary to go back and ascertain how the testator was circumstanced as to his property when he made his will. He was owner in fee of the lands of Tinneranny in 1856; and on the marriage of his daughter in that year he charged the whole lands of Tinneranny with an annuity of £100, the trusts of which he declared by deed. I had a suit before me recently in which I had to declare the construction of that deed, and some others executed by Mr. Jeffares. I held that that lady was entitled to the annuity for her life. That being so, it appears that on the 16th of July, 1866, by two deeds executed on that day he charged, not all the lands, but a portion of them, with an annuity of £50 by one deed, and by the other the same portion of the said lands with an additional annuity of £100 for the daughter to whom he had originally given the annuity of £100 above mentioned. The deed by which he charged this particular portion of the lands of Tinneranny with the £50 annuity contains a power to the grantor of revocation of the uses of the annuity. The deed granting the annuity of £50 contains a power to the grantor of revocation in the following terms :– "Provided always, and it is hereby agreed and declared, that the said Joseph Jeffares may at any time or times, by deed to be registered at the Office for Registering Deeds in Ireland, within six months from the execution thereof, or by will or codicil, either alter or absolutely revoke all or any of the uses, trusts, and estates hereinbefore limited and declared; and by the same or any other deed, or by will or codicil, limit and declare new uses, trusts, and estates of and concerning all or any of the said premises hereinbefore expressed to be hereby granted and assigned respectively, as he shall think fit." A question has been incidentally raised as to whether this power extends to a total revocation of the grant of the annuity, or merely to a revocation of the uses thereof. The strong inclination of my opinion is, that it is a power to revoke the annuity entirely. The deed of the 16th of July, 1866, which charged the additional £100 a-year for the daughter, also contains provisions the details of which I need not go into. The effect of them was that as, in the interval between the deed of 1856 and the 16th of July, 1866, the grantor had parted with a certain portion of the lands of Tinneranny, he gives the additional £100 a-year as a sort of amends to his daughter and her second husband, Mr. Wilson, and he purports to release the portion of the lands which he had parted with from the annuity of £100 which he had given in 1856, and the daughter and her husband are made parties to the deed of the 16th of July, 1866. They did not execute that deed – probably on account of the power of revocation; but in the suit I referred to, I proceeded on the basis that they had taken with this second deed. Now, on the morning of the 17th of July, 1866, Joseph Jeffares was master of the Tinneranny estate – save to the extent of the portion of it which he had parted with – subject to those three annuities, two of them of £100 each, the other of £50, which were to commence from the day of his death. I do not think it of moment whether he had a legal fee or an equitable fee in the lands. On the 17th of July, 1866, he executed a voluntary deed of a very peculiar character, by which he gives certain annuities to relatives and persons in his employment, and, subject to those annuities, he limits the estate, after a life interest to himself, substantially away from himself. He reserves a reversion after an estate tail, but of such a character that it is more than questionable whether he could ever enjoy the reversion. He recites the deeds which I have adverted to, and then proceeds :– "In consideration of the love and affection which the said Joseph Jeffares bears to his son Isaac Jeffares, he the said Joseph Jeffares doth by these presents grant, &c.," the part of the lands of Tinneranny on which he had charged the annuity of £50, and the additional annuity of £100 by the deed of the 16th of July, 1866, to the following uses : "To the use that Frances Jeffares, widow of Richard Jeffares deceased, son of the said Joseph Jeffares, and her assigns, shall during her natural life receive an annual sum of £40, to be charged upon the premises hereinbefore expressed to be hereby granted, &c.," payable half yearly on the 25th of March and 29th of September, the first payment to be made on the gale day next succeeding the death of the said Joseph Jeffares; and to the further use that Mathias Quin of New Ross, his clerk, "shall and may during his natural life receive an annual sum" of £40, payable in the same manner on the same gale days as the former annuity, "and to the further use and intent" that three other persons – Darby Doyle, Michael Murphy, and James Jeffares – should receive annuities of £20, £10 and £10 respectively, payable in the same manner; "and subject and charged as aforesaid to the use of the said Joseph Crawley and his heirs, upon the trusts, intents and purposes after declared and contained; that is to say, upon trust that the said Joseph Crawley, his heirs and assigns, do and shall pay the said annual sum or yearly rent of £100 granted by said in part recited indenture of the 1st day of February, 1856, so as to exonerate the part of the lands granted by the said in part recited indenture of the 28th of March, 1864, and 4th day of September, 1865, from the payment of the same, and subject thereto, that the trustees "do and shall pay and apply the rents, issues and profits which shall remain after payment of the said annual sums so charged thereon as aforesaid, including said annual sum of £100 granted by said in part recited deed of the 1st of February, 1856, unto or permit or suffer the same to be received by the said Isaac Jeffares" during his life, "or until he shall charge the same or any part thereof, or until any writ of execution shall issue against the said Isaac Jeffares, by virtue whereof his life interest in the rents, &c., shall be liable to be seized, &c., or that the said Isaac Jeffares shall be declared a bankrupt or insolvent debtor, or shall accept the benefit of any Act for the Relief of Insolvent Debtors, or become insolvent, or the interest of the said Isaac Jeffares shall otherwise become vested in any other person," &c. – in either of which cases the said last-mentioned trust for the said Isaac Jeffares shall determine; and then upon trust during the remainder of the life of the said Isaac Jeffares "to apply the rents of said lands for the maintenance of the present or any future wife of the said Isaac Jeffares, and for the maintenance, support and education of the child and children of any deceased child, &c.;" and after the death of Isaac Jeffares to the use of his children or remoter issue, or to the use of any other person or persons in trust for any such child or children or remoter issue as Isaac Jeffares should by deed, &c., appoint; and in default of appointment to the use of the child or children as tenants in common in tail, and in default of such issue to the use of the said Joseph Jeffares, his heirs and assigns.

This deed of the 17th of July, 1866, contains a power to Joseph Jeffares by deed or will to alter or absolutely revoke all or any of the uses or trusts thereby declared, and by the same or any other deed or will to limit or declare new uses and trusts of and concerning all or any of the lands thereby granted. Mr. Jeffares then came to make his will. He appears to have considerable property, but he had the great misfortune to have had it complicated by a set of badly drawn instruments, which it is difficult even to see one's way through. The will itself which he made, and which I am now going to mention, if it had not been preceded by those deeds, is plain and simple enough; but, having regard to the fact that he had executed those deeds, it was a task of no ordinary difficulty to make a will such as would steer clear of litigation – nay, it was impossible for any man, unless he had prior deeds before him, to draw a will which would not land the property into the very difficulties which have finally surrounded it. It has been proved, and it is a conceded fact, that the net rental of the lands, as conveyed and limited by the deed of 1866, is, and was when Mr. Jeffares died, about £460 a-year. The total of the annuities which the deed of the 17th of July, 1866, granted is £120; adding that sum to the tot of the three former annuities (£250) he makes £370. He made his will on the 16th of November, 1871, nearly five years and a half after the deed of the 17th of July, 1866. The will commences by devising various properties forming the bulk of the testator's estates, and then the testator devises "all my estate and interest of and in the town and lands of Tinneranny," to the trustees of his will, "upon the trusts herinafter declared of and concerning the same, that is to say, that my daughter-in-law, Mrs. Frances Jeffares, widow of my late son Richard Jeffares, may receive and take thereout during her natural life the yearly sum of £40 sterling; that my clerk, Mathias Quin, of New Ross may receive and take thereout for the term of his natural life the yearly sum of £20 sterling; that Micheal Murphy, of New Ross, at present in my service, may receive and take thereout for the term of his natural life the yearly sum of £10 sterling; and that James Jeffares, of new Ross, at present in my service, may receive and take thereout for the term of his natural life the yearly sum of £10 sterling; the said several and respective annuities to be paid and payable at or upon the two following days, that is, on the 25th day of March and 29th September." The will then gives the annuitants a power of distress, and proceeds : "And subject to the annuity already charged upon said town and lands, and to the several and respective annuities hereby charged on said town and lands, and to the remedy given for securing and recovering the same, to the use of my said daughter-in-law Isabella Jeffares, for and during the term of her natural life, to and for her own sole and separate use and benefit, or to such person or persons as she, by any writing, signed with her proper hand, shall from time to time, notwithstanding her coverture, appoint, &c.; and from and immediately after the decease of my said daughter-in-law Isabella Jeffares, to the use of her children by my said son, Joseph Jeffares, with the power of appointment and limitation over as hereinafter mentioned; but as the annual rents and profits of said town and lands of Tinneranny may not be sufficient to pay the annual charges affecting the said lands and said several annuities hereinbefore devised, now in the event of there being a deficiency in any year, after paying the charges affecting said lands of Tinneranny, to pay each and every of said annuities, I hereby will and direct that in each and every year there shall be any such deficiency, said deficiency shall be made up and paid to said annuity by my said daughter-in-law, Isabella Jeffares out of the rents and profits of the other estates and properties given, devised, and bequeathed to her for the term of her natural life." Then, after disposing of other propety, the will proceeds : "And, as to, for and concerning all the said several lands, tenements, and hereditaments before left and devised for the benefit of my said son William Jeffares, and of my daughter-in-law Isabella Jeffares, respectively, for their respective lives, my will is, that the same are hereby left upon trust for each, my said son William Jeffares, and my daughter-in-law Isabella Jeffares, to whom a life interest is given, remain and be to the use and for the benefit of all and every such one or more, exclusively of the other or others, of the children or remoter issue of my said son William Jeffares, and of my daughter-in-law Isabella Jeffares by my said son Isaac Jeffares, to whom any interest has been limited for life, at such ages, days or times, for such estate or estates" as his said son and daughter-in-law should appoint, and in default of appointment equally, as tenants in common in tail.

The important question now arises, whether that will revoked the deed of the 17th of July, 1866; in other words, whether the plaintiff Mathias Quin is entitled to the annuity of £40 under the deed and to the annuity of £60 bequeathed to him by the will or only to the latter.

The principles of law affecting this case are clear, and no controversy has been raised on either side in respect of them. It is not necessary for a man who has executed a voluntary deed with a general power of revocation to make an express revocation of it. It is a sufficient revocation within the power if he makes a disposition of the estate inconsistent and which cannot stand with the voluntary deed. A revocation may be implied from the manner in which he has given the estate and the extent to which he has given it. There is also a rule of law which has been established by the many cases which were relied on at the Bar, that where a testator by his will gives a benefit to a person, and by a codicil to his will gives a benefit to the same person, the presumption of law is that he means to give twice; and it lies on the party who disputes it, to show why that construction of them should not be adopted. That is a very sensible and a very wise rule of law. I doubt very much whether that rule of law, which is so clearly applicable to a will, and codicil, applies precisely to the case of a voluntary deed capable of being revoked by will, and to a will subsequently executed. However that may be in the abstract, in the case before me the question seems to me one of pure construction – namely, whether the disposition made by the will is of such a character as to compel the Court to hold that by it the voluntary deed is entirely revoked, or is left standing wholly or in part.

When the testator Joseph Jeffares came to devise these lands of Tinneranny, he had at the determination of his own life, when of course the will became operative, that shadowy reversion which I have described. It is plain that he was not merely dealing with that reversion; he plainly meant that his devise should have operation at the moment of his death. The Plaintiff's counsel are compelled to concede this. The testator was therefore to some extent exercising his power of revocation. No doubt this extent is not to be carried further than the dispositions in the will enforce it. If the new dispositions can to any extent fairly stand with the old ones, the rule is to preserve the old dispositions so far as the new dispositions do not interfere with them, and merely to hold the rest revoked.

Relying upon the rule of law as to cumulative gifts by will and codicil as applicable here, it was argued with great ability on the part of the Plaintiff, and rightly argued, that the Court ought not, from the similarity of the gifts being all annuities and from their being made to the same persons and apparently for the same reasons, to come to the conclusion that the testator meant to revoke the annuities given by the deed. So far I go entirely with the Plaintiff's argument before me. But there is a rule of law which is, in my opinion, of equal weight and importance as those which I have already mentioned – and that is, that you are to construe the language of a testator's will according to its plain well understood meaning, and if he tells you that he is disposing of his whole estate you are not to take upon yourself to say that he is disposing of part only. Well, but the Plaintiff's counsel say if you give the wide interpretation to the language of the devise, you must hold that the additional annuity of £100 granted by the deed of the 16th of July, 1866, to his daughter was revoked thereby. Now I may as well say that I think it clear he did not revoke that annuity, and that, without invading that annuity, the will may well operate to revoke all those granted by the deed of the 17th of July. *Pomfret* v. *Perring* 18 Beav. 618; 5 D. M. & Gor. 775 goes a long way to support the view that the annuity given by the deed of the 16th of July, 1866, was not revoked. It has been argued strongly that if the will did not revoke that additional annuity which was granted by the deed of the 16th of July, 1866, it could not have revoked the annuities granted by the deed of the 17th of July, 1866. I have not been able to appreciate the force of that argument. The two matters are essentially distinct, and stand on entirely different grounds.

Indeed I think that no two matters could be more distinct than the effect in law of the will on the state of things as it existed anterior to the deed of the 17th of July, 1866, and its effect after that deed, when he had nothing to dispose of but a shadowy reversion. If the testator was not by this will disposing of the estate under his power of revocation, what was the estate in Tinneranny which he was disposing of? The Plaintiff says that he was disposing of the estate subject to the annuities given by the deed of the 17th of July, 1866. In my opinion, the testator does not say anything of the sort; he tells me that he is disposing of all his estate and interest in the town and lands of Tinneranny. Now he had an estate and a present one under the deed of the 16th July, 1866; he had none such under the deed of the 17th of July, 1866; and in my opinion the true construction of the words of devise is that they include all that he could dispose of under the power of revocation in the deed of the 17th of July, 1866. If that construction is put on those words, the whole is at once intelligible. But if any other construction is put upon them, inextricable difficulties arise as to how much of the limitations of the deed of the 17th of July, 1866, is cut away, and how much is left unaffected by the will. The better construction, and the more reasonable and consistent one, is to give the words "estate and interest" their ordinary and full meaning. In coming to that conclusion, I do not bring in aid the limitations in the will itself, which would go a long way to sustain that meaning; for the whole estate and interest in the lands is given, and trusts are fastened on it which are commensurate with the entire estate, showing an intention to revoke the deed of the 17th of July, 1866, by giving estates inconsistent with its preservation.

The case of *Beckett* v. *Harden* 4 M. & Sel. 1, relied on by Mr. O'Hagan, was a very clear case. But cases on the construction of the words of one will are seldom of use when applied to the construction of another will. In my opinion, *Becket* v. *Harden* is not an authority for the Plaintiff in this case. That was a case sent to the Court of law by the Court of Chancery, and was disposed of according to the then existing practice by the certificate of the Judges, and the reasons for the decision are not given. But from the arguments in the report I am satisfied in my own mind what the reasons were; they are very readily to be gathered from the statement of the case.

It was suggested that in the clause "and subject to the annuity already charged upon said town and lands, and to the several and respective annuities newly charged," the word "annuity" should be read "annuities." I must leave the word "annuity" as I find it. I cannot change it into "annuities" for the purpose of controlling a very clear devise. It seems to me there is a clause in the will which much strengthens the view I have taken, namely, the testator's declaration "but as the annual rents and profits of said town and lands of Tinneranny may not be sufficient to pay the annual charges affecting the said lands and said several annuities hereinbefore devised, now in the event of there being a deficiency in any year after paying the charges affecting said lands of Tinneranny to pay each and every of said annuities, I hereby will and direct that in each and every year there shall be any such deficiency, said deficiency shall be made up and paid to said annuitants by my daughter-in-law Isabella Jeffares out of the rents and profits of the other estates and properties given and bequeathed to her for the term of her natural life." That clause has been relied on by both sides – by the Plaintiff as showing that no revocation was intended – by the Defendant as showing that it was not intended that the annuities should be cumulative. If the testator did not mean to revoke the deed of the 17th of July, 1866, the annuities charged on the property would amount to £510, and the rental which was to meet those annuities was only £460. If, on the other hand, the will operated as a revocation of the deed of the 17th of July, 1866, the charges amounted to £390 a-year, and they stood against a rental of £460. In my opinion, it appears to be a more reasonable construction to hold that the testator contemplated a charge of £390 against a rental of £460, than a charge of £510 against £460, which was £50 short of meeting it. The only answer which Mr. O'Hagan gave to that was that the testator may have contemplated the deaths of the annuitants, or of some of them. He does not say that; £390 is close of £460, and it might happen that in some years the rental of £460 might not be sufficient to meet it – and so the testator puts it. He treats the deficiency as an event which may happen, not as a thing which must happen, which it would be if there was a charge of £510 against a rental of £460.

Various other passages of the will have been relied upon, on the part of the Plaintiff, as inconsistent with the idea of revocation. I must say that, looking at the whole will – nay more, criticising its language as you may – I see nothing to take from the effect of the first devise of all his "estate and interest" in the lands of Tinneranny, but much to sustain it. The ground of my decision is that, by the devise of all his estate and interest in the lands of Tinneranny, the whole estate which he had power, by reason of the clause of revocation in the deed of the 17th of July, 1866, to devise, passed by the will, and that the annuities thereby given, and the limitations thereby made, entirely supersede those given and made by the deed of the 17th of July, 1866.

I shall therefore declare that the Plaintiff is entitled to the annuity of £60 given by the will, but that he is not entitled to the annuity of £40 given by the deed.

Note
See further, *Irish Land Law*, para. 3.121 *et seq*.

V. PERFORMANCE

CREED V. CAREY
(1857) 7 Ir. Ch. R. 295 (Chancery Appeal)

E., by antenuptial articles under seal, covenanted to purchase lands and to charge them with a jointure for his wife; he also professed to charge all property, of which he should during the coverture be seised, with the jointure. Those articles were registered. He afterwards purchased the lands of U., but did not execute any conveyance for the purpose of charging them with the jointure; and he subsequently mortgaged those lands to J., who had no notice of the articles, by deposit of title deeds, no conveyance having been executed to J.

At first instance it was held that the jointure was to be paid in priority to the equitable mortgage.

Brady L.C. :

In this case, which was argued yesterday, I have taken a view which makes it not at all necessary to go into the question of the validity or the invalidity of the registry, or the question of the binding effect of the decision in *Gubbins* v. *Gubbins*, if there were any such decision, upon which much doubt has been thrown by observations alleged to have been made by Baron Richards. Whatever that decision may have been, whether it was made in the Master's office or in the Court, it is not necessary now to consider it; and I shall therefore pass it by, without binding myself to any opinion respecting it, if an occasion for reviewing it should occur; which is not very probable, considering the present position of the Registry Acts.

Passing that question, therefore, I must consider the position of this lady, who, in consideration of a sum of money paid to her husband, and of marriage, which is also a valuable consideration, became the absolute purchaser of this annuity; that is to say, that for those considerations a contract was executed, purporting to affect property afterwards to be acquired. This case, however, goes much further than *Deacon* v. *Smith* 3 Atk. 323, and the other cases quoted; in this respect, that in addition to the contract to secure the jointure, that is, by deed to grant an annuity, and a term of years to secure it, it goes on actually to charge all the lands of which Eugene Carey was then seised, or might be seised during the coverture, independently of any deed which might afterwards be executed. Under these circumstances, the case does not involve that question of intention which was so much discussed during the argument; I mean the question whether, in purchasing these lands, the husband intended to satisfy the covenant to settle? Here, the moment Eugene Carey made any purchase, the property was bound by the trust creating the jointure. He could no more disaffirm the trust which attached upon the purchaser of these lands, than he could a direct and express trust.

The case is totally different from the decisions which were mentioned in the argument in that respect. The only ground upon which this equity was alleged to stand in a different position from any other in those cases was the want of evidence *quo animo* the purchase was made. In this case, however, no evidence of intention to satisfy the contract is necessary; for the charge of the annuity fastens upon any land purchased by the husband, from the moment of the purchase.

The case of *Manningford* v. *Toleman* 1 Coll. 670 is as clear an authority for Mr. Carey's right as can be required, when we remember that the evidence of intention to satisfy the covenant is not necessary in this case. In it the contract was between a person relying on a covenant of this sort, for the purchase by the husband of a proper house for himself and his wife, and a person who, after the house was bought, became an equitable mortgagee of it. That case was, therefore, almost the same as the present. In it there existed this further circumstance, at least it was assumed and presumed by the Judge, that the money with which the property was purchased was a part of the money provided by the settlement. I do not apprehend, however, that the fact went further than identifying the house as being bought for the purposes of the trust. There was no direction for the purchase of any particular house – the trust was only to procure a fit and proper house for himself and his wife, and there was no other evidence of his intention to satisfy the trust, beyond the house being proper for them. When, however, it was proved that the fund out of which it had been bought was the money which was to be applied in the purchase of a house, and it appeared that the house was proper for the purposes of the trust, it was at once identified as the particular house which was directed to be bought; and when that was once established, the mortgagee was treated as a person getting possession of trust property, and applying it for his own benefit.

In this case, the husband declares that all after-acquired lands should be bound by this annuity. So soon as they were acquired, he became a trustee for the purpose of carrying the articles into effect; and no expression of his intention could displace that right, or transfer it to other property, without the assent of the parties entitled. As to the possession of the title-deeds, that is completely beside the question; the equity founded upon it is met by the case of *Harper* v. *Faulder* 4 Mad. 129, where a subsequent legal mortgagee, who had obtained possession of the title-deeds, sought to obtain priority over an annuity granted before the mortgage, of which he had not any notice. The Court held that he was not entitled to displace the annuity; that the possession of the title-deeds was quite immaterial; and that even supposing the possession of the title-deeds involved any equitable considerations, beyond the greater of less degree of negligence which it showed in the earlier claimant, it had no effect at all where he had no right to the possession of them.

Wiseman v. *Westland* 1 Y. & Jer. 117 was a case in which the Court refused at the instance of the mortgagee of a term, to take the deeds out of the hands of a subsequent mortgagee; but the only relief given in that suit to the second mortgagee was permission to redeem the prior mortgage: the Court merely refusing to take the deeds from the second mortgagee, but not giving any further validity to his claim.

Here, however, we have an equitable contract, which attached the moment of the husband making his purchase, and which made him immediately a trustee for the purposes of the settlement. With those purposes there is nothing in conflict, except this equitable mortgage by deposit, and I think the earlier title must prevail.

In a case before Lord Eldon, *Mackreth* v. *Symmons* 15 Ves. 329, he considers the rights of a mortgagee in Equity and a vendor's lien, and he gives the preference to the vendor's lien, expressly on the ground of his priority of time. The case of a vendor's lien was brought before the Court in *Rice* v. *Rice* 2 Drew. 73; from which it would seem that, if nothing else intervened, the lien for purchase-money would prevail over an equitable mortgage; and a passage there shows that a contract of this sort is still stronger, on the ground that it is created by the contract, while the other is only established by the decree; the Vice-Chancellor saying :– "Each of the two equitable interests arises out of the forbearance by the party of the money due to him. There is, however, this difference between them, that the vendor's lien for unpaid purchase-money is a right created by a rule of Equity, without any special contract; the right of the equitable mortgagee is created by the special contract of the parties. I cannot say that, in my opinion, this constitutes any sufficient ground of preference; though, if it makes any difference at all, I should say it is rather in favour of the equitable mortgagee, inasmuch as there is no *constat* of the right of the vendor to his lien for purchase-money, until it has been declared by a decree of a Court of Equity; whereas there is a clear *consat* of the equitable mortgagee's title immediately on the contract being made. But I do not see in this any sufficient ground for holding that the equitable mortgagee has the better equity." *A fortiori* here, where there is an earlier contract, which, without any decree of the Court, charges the land, I think that it must have precedence of the equitable mortgage.

On all these grounds, I am of opinion that this lady's claim must not be disturbed. With reference to the observations of the Master of the Rolls, as to *Gubbins* v. *Gubbins,* it is proper to say that that is decided quite independently of that case.

Blackburne L.J. :

I concur in the opinion of the Lord Chancellor, and think that the rights of Mrs. Mary Anne Carey, as they are presented for our decision, should be disposed of without reference to the question on the effect of the Registry Act. This lady is entitled to a jointure under the articles executed on her marriage in 1827, and has established her right to it, and obtained a receiver under the decree of this Court. It is true that the petititioner is not bound by the proceedings in her suit, but he has not in any manner impeached them, nor made her a respondent in this matter. She has come in under the order obtained by him for the usual account of incumbrances, and her position is that of a defendant in possession, with a prior equity to the plaintiff, and claiming for valuable consideration. She asks for no relief, and is simply defending her possession, as the purchaser of a right, to which that of the plaintiff is *puisne.* How then has she forfeited her right to the ordinary protection of this Court? When that right attached, by her husband's acquisition of these lands, she was under coverture, and was so when he contracted the debt for which the petitioner sues, and for which he gave the equitable mortgage by the deposit of the title-deeds of the estate. It will not be said that to her any laches or fraud can be imputed; if at all, it must be to her trustee, and the case as to him must be that he was guilty of a breach of his duty, in not demanding the execution of the trust immediately after the purchase of the estate by the husband; and that by his neglect he enabled the husband to impose on his creditor.

Now as to this, I may remark that even if it were true that the trustee had a right to the possession of the title-deeds, there is no evidence that he had any notice of the purchase before the deposit of the deeds, and it is obvious that, until he had, no laches could be imputed even to him. There is therefore no fraud or breach of duty attributable to him, upon the evidence before us. But it is not, in my opinion, to be assumed that he could have insisted on the possession of the title-deeds; the marriage articles were a contract for the grant of a rentcharge; and some authority would be required to show that a jointress or her trustee has a right to the title-deeds of the estate. Thus divesting the case of fraud or gross neglect on the part of the trustees of the jointress, how can a Court of Equity be called into activity to deprive her of her prior and better equity? Her position is widely different from that in which she would have stood if she came here for the aid of the Court; but all she asks is that the Court shall not be put in activity against her, a purchaser for valuable consideration, at the instance and for the benefit of a *puisne* incumbrancer, with an inferior right, and without a legal title.

A case, *Harper* v. *Faulder* 4 Mad. 129, was mentioned by *Mr. Barry* at the close of the argument; I am obliged to him for his reference to it, for it contains sound positions, and refers to authorities that bear directly on the case before us; one of those is a passage from the judgment in *Evans* v. *Bicknell* 6 Ves. 174, in which the Lord Chancellor said, "The mere circumstance of parting with the title-deeds, unless there is fraud, concealment or some such purpose, or some concurrence in such purpose, or gross negligence that amounts to evidence of a fraudulent intention, is not of itself a sufficient ground to postpone the first mortgagee." It also states a proposition of Lord Eldon's, peculiarly applicable to this case, where he says, "There is no case in which it has ever been decided that the mere circumstance of a first mortgagee not taking the title-deeds will entitle the second mortgagee, who has got the deeds, to file a bill in Equity to obtain a preference." *Harper* v. *Faulder* 4 Mad. 129 is in itself also an important authority bearing on the case before us; for there the question arose between the grantee of an annuity, who had left the title-deeds in the hands of the grantors, and a subsequent mortgagee. The Vice-Chancellor there said,

"If a prior incumbrancer is to be postponed simply for leaving the title-deeds in the hands of the mortgagor, which is a proposition very difficult to be maintained at this day, either upon authority or principle, such a doctrine could only be applied in cases where the possession of the title-deeds was legally incident to the estate of the first incumbrancer, and where it might be said that he had failed to use reasonable diligence for his own protection."

I therefore am of opinion that we cannot act against the jointress, or postpone her demand to that of a confessedly *puisne* incumbrancer.

Notes and Questions

1. The equitable doctrine of performance was not in fact applied in this case, why not? See *Irish Land Law,* para. 3.125.
2. The case also raised some interesting questions as to priorities, see *ibid,* para. 3.069 *et seq.* and *A Casebook on Irish Land Law,* p. 84 *et seq.*

Chapter 5

INJUNCTIONS

This is equity's most wide-ranging remedy and one which the courts on both sides of the Irish Sea have been prepared to develop in recent times, see *Irish Land Law,* para. 3.127 *et seq.*, Supp. (1975-80), pp. 10-12. The material in this chapter concentrates on recent developments such as the intense judicial discussion of the principles governing the grant of interlocutory relief and special relief like the "Mareva" injunction. See also *Cullen v. Cullen* [1962] I.R. 268 (reproduced at p. 657 of *A Casebook on Irish Land Law).*

I. INTERLOCUTORY RELIEF

IRISH SHELL LTD V. ELM MOTORS LTD.

Unreported (Supreme Court) (128-82) (Judgments delivered 17th June 1983)

In 1965, the plaintiff motor fuel distributors purchased a plot of ground near Limerick for the purpose of developing the site as a retail petrol filling station. The site had a valid planning permission for such a development. In 1969, the defendants purchased a 6 acre plot adjoining the plaintiff's land and applied for planning permission for a large development to include a garage. This application was refused. In February 1970, the defendant requested the plaintiff to grant a lease of their land to them and to allow them to incorporate the land in their own proposed development. The plaintiffs agreed and on the strength of this agreement the defendants obtained a new planning permission in respect of a development which comprised a filling station covering both the plaintiff's and the defendant's land. The lease as finally engrossed included covenants by the defendant to, *inter alia,* erect a garage, sell only the petroleum products marketed by the plaintiffs, exhibit the plaintiff's advertising and identification signs, and decorate the garage in the plaintiff's colours. In January 1982, the defendants informed the plaintiffs that they had been advised that the covenant obliging them to purchase the plaintiff's products exclusively was unlawful as being an unreasonable restraint of trade, and warned the plaintiffs that they intended to determine their obligation to the plaintiffs due to, *inter alia,* the lack of interest shown by the plaintiffs in their business. The plaintiffs contended that the common law doctrine of restraint of trade did not apply to the covenants in their lease and that it was irrelevant whether the restraint was reasonable or not. The defendant subsequently ceased to purchase from the plaintiff, removed the plaintiff's insignia from their garage, and commenced to trade with one of the plaintiff's rivals. The plaintiffs commenced proceeding seeking various injunctions to enforce compliance by the defendants with the covenants in the lease and applied for interlocutory relief, which Costello J. granted, see [1982] I.L.R.M. 519. The defendants appealed to the Supreme Court.

McCarthy J.:

This is an appeal from a judgment and order of Costello J. made the 19th April 1982 whereby he granted "until further order" the relief sought in paragraphs 1 to 5 of the general endorsement of claim of the plenary summons herein, in effect directing the Defendant to comply in detail with the relevant provisions of a lease dated the 30th October 1973 and made between the Plaintiff and the Defendant, whereby inter alia the Defendant agreed to sell the Plaintiff's products. Somewhat unusually for an interlocutory application, the learned Judge further ordered that the Defendant pay the Plaintiff's costs of the motion. The order does not recite the standard form of undertaking given by a moving party in applications of this kind, nor is there any reference to such in the very comprehensive judgment of Costello J.. Counsel for the Plaintiff, in this Court, has freely offered such an undertaking. The Court has been further informed by counsel for both sides that the terms of the interlocutory order have been complied with and that, in effect, the Defendant since shortly after on 19th April 1982 has been retailing the Plaintiff's products and advertising them for sale. In his judgment, Costello J. set out, by way of introduction, the facts of the case as they were demonstrated by affidavits and exhibits, and drew the inference that "without the planning permission attached to the Plaintiff's land, it was extremely unlikely that they (the Defendant) would have obtained the planning permission to erect a petrol filling station"; this situation was so in 1970 and, indeed, at the time of the execution of the lease in 1973, but would not, necessarily, remain so. A variety of factors might well bring about major changes in policy such as would have affected the possibility of getting planning permission, one way or the other. The learned trial Judge, further, referring to the covenants in the lease, does not refer to the fact that, although the covenant by the Defendant was to build on the demised premises and its own premises a modern and fully equipped petrol filling and service sation and motor garage at a cost of not less than £50,000, in fact, according to the uncontradicted evidence of the managing director of the Defendant, as set out in paragraph 9 of his affidavit, "all of the development works have taken place on the lands of the Defendant and there are no constructions or buildings or developments situate on the Plaintiff's parcel of land". It may be that Costello J. did not consider this to be a relevant consideration although, at first sight, it would seem to me to be material to the complex questions of law that arise in this case.

The learned trial Judge, in a most careful analysis of law and fact, concluded that the principles of law governing the doctrine of restraint of trade did not apply to the relationship between the Plaintiff and the Defendant created by the lease; in the circumstances, he was not concerned to see whether the restraint contained in the lease was reasonable or not, nor, as he expressly held, was he concerned, at the interlocutory stage in the proceedings, with the balance of convenience. Whatever legal rights there may have been such as might affect the relationship or give rights to deny the validity of the lease or any part of it, it is clear that, apart from the period commencing on the week of the 10th March 1982 and ending in the week or so after the 19th April 1982, a total period of approximately six weeks, for the balance of time stretching from approximately October 1970 up to date, something over twelve years, the Defendant has been advertising and selling the Plaintiff's product. During the course of the argument the question arose as to what was the status quo in the case - in effect to what date does one look. The Plaintiff argued for the date immediately prior to the temporary change over in early March; the Defendant for the date of hearing of the motion before Costello J. Indeed, this issue became part of the Defendant's argument on the balance of convenience. Whilst, as I shall explain later, I accept, at least in part, the Defendant's argument on the question of balance of convenience, it will not afford the Defendant any immediate relief, since I have no hesitation in holding that, as of today, the balance of convenience lies heavily in favour of maintaining the property as an outlet for the sale of the Plaintiff's products; it is in prima facie enforcement of the restrictive covenant; it accords with the actual events of virtually the entire period of contractual relationship between the parties; the complaints of the Defendant as to deficiencies in the service from the Plaintiff, with the publicity consequent upon these proceedings, will be a major incentive to the Plaintiff, if such be needed, to remedy any such deficiencies, if such exist at all: on the other hand, since the Defendant has reverted to the advertising and sale of the Plaintiff's products, it is difficult to identify any particular hardship on the part of the Defendant, save having to honour a contract which it finds distasteful. For these reasons, in my view, the relevant date for the determination by this Court of the balance of convenience and, if necessary, the status quo which should be maintained, is today; I have no difficulty in resolving the balance of convenience in favour of the Plaintiff – happily, it is unneccessary to enquire into any conclusion on that topic by the learned trial Judge since, for the reasons that appear in his judgment, he came to no conclusion – and I would accordingly affirm the order of the High Court restraining the Defendant as set out in paragraph (a) of the order, and I would discharge the balance of the curial part of the order as being no longer necessary; I would allow the Defendant's appeal against the order for costs made on the interlocutory hearing and order that these costs should be reserved for the trial Judge.

Interlocutory Injunctions

In *The Educational Company of Ireland Ltd. & Others* v. *Fitzpatrick & Others* [1961] I.R. 323, the former Supreme Court laid down certain principles applicable on applications for interlocutory injunctions. The exact nature of the decision must be determined by an examination of the judgments of the majority, but, at first sight, it appears to me that the headnote of the report is incorrect in so far as it states that the issue of the balance of convenience was determined as follows:- "As it was not agreed between the parties that all the facts necessary to decide the issue in the case were properly established or admitted before the Court." Teevan J. in the High Court, had expressed the opinion that there were certain matters that could be made the basis of contentious issues in the case (325). Maguire C.J., who dissented from the majority of the Supreme Court on a different issue, concluded that "all the facts which the Plaintiffs think necessary to secure the interlocutory injunction are to be found in the affidavits and in my view a vague hope that other facts essential to a decision may emerge at the trial is not sufficient to bring this case within the judgment relied upon." (333) Lavery J., to whose judgment I shall revert, expressed the view (338) that "in this case there may well be further facts elicited at the trial, *but there can be no doubt that a serious question of law arises."*(emphasis added) Kingsmill Moore J. (342) says:-

> "Mr. Fitzgerald counters by saying that, even if this is so, the facts are not in dispute and the Court should decide that question of law here and now. I am not convinced that all relevant facts are established or admitted, though it seems to me likely that they are. Mr. Costello for the Plaintiffs does not accept that all relevant facts have been established and says that there are further facts which he hopes to establish if the case goes to a full hearing, and if he can avail himself of discovery, interrogatories, and cross-examination to elicit them. I am of opinion that a plaintiff is entitled to have his case fully investigated in the ordinary course of legal procedure and that it would be undesirable in the absence of consent to decide a legal question of this magnitude merely on the affidavits filed for the purpose of the interlocutory motion. In *Smyth and Anor.*v.*Beirne & Anor.* (supra) the Defendants (who were the picketers) resisted the motion for an interlocutory injunction on the grounds that they did not agree that all facts necessary to decide the issue were established or admitted, and the Court, while granting an interlocutory injunction, did not make any attempt then and there to decide the question of law. I think similar weight must be given to the refusal of the Plaintiff to agree that all necessary facts are established or admitted. Mr. Costello seeks to raise a question of bona fides on the part of the Union. He is entitled to a full investigation of the facts."

This quotation might appear to lend support to that part of the headnote of the report that I have cited but it is taken out of context in a case where Kingsmill Moore J. held that "a very important and difficult question of law is involved and one which requires the most careful consideration." Ó Dálaigh J., as he then was, makes no reference to there being any issue as to facts or any need to refer to the facts in any detail (342). Martin Maguire J. fully endorsed the judgment of Lavery J. and also agreed with those of Kingsmill Moore and O Dálaigh JJ. In *Esso Petroleum Company (Ireland) Limited* v.*Fogarty* [1965] I.R. 531, Ó Dàlaigh C.J. and Lavery J. (Walsh J. not expressly citing the case) affirmed the principles of law to be applied by this Court on the hearing of an appeal to justify an order granting an interlocutory injunction as set out in the judgment of Lavery J. in the case of *The Educational Company of Ireland Limited.* With great respect to the last Chief Justice, it appears to be that the principles of law set out by Lavery J. were not confined to the hearing of an appeal to set aside an order granting an interlocutory injunction, but were and are to be applied by the High Court or, on appeal, this Court, to any case concerning an interlocutory injunction, unless it is clear these principles of law cannot be applied. Ó Dálaigh C.J. (538) cited two passages from the judgment of Lavery J. quoting from *Kerr on Injunctions* and the first Hailsham ed. of the *Laws of England.*The quotation from *Kerr on Injunctions* is as follows:-

> "The office of the Court to interfere being founded on the existence of the legal right, a man who seeks the aid of the Court must be able to show a fair prima facie case in support of the title which he asserts. He is not required to make out a clear legal title, but he must satisfy the Court that he has a fair question to raise as to the

existence of the legal right which he sets up, and that there are substantial grounds for doubting the existence of the alleged legal right, the exercise of which he seeks to prevent. The Court must, before disturbing any man's legal right, of stripping him of any of the rights with which the law has clothed him, be satisfied that the probability is in favour of his case ultimately succeeding in the final issue of the suit. The mere existence of the doubt as to the Plaintiff's right to the property, interference with which he seeks to restrain, does not of itself constitute a sufficient ground for refusing an injunction, though it is always a circumstance which calls for the attention of the Court."

The probability test

He further quoted, as Lavery J. did, from the first Hailsham ed. of the *Laws of England* the observations of the learned author which are repeated in the second Hailsham ed. – 4 *Halsbury's Laws of England,* Vol. 24 at para. 956:-

"Where any doubt exists as to the Plaintiff's right, or if his right is not disputed, but its violation is denied, the Court, in determining whether an interlocutory injunction should be granted, takes into consideration the balance of convenience to the parties and the nature of the injury which the Defendant, on the one hand, would suffer if the injunction was granted and he should ultimately turn out to be right and that which the Plaintiff, on the other hand, might sustain if the injunction was refused and he should ultimately turn out to be right. The burden of proof that the inconvenience which the Plaintiff will suffer by the refusal of the injunction is greater than that which the Defendant will suffer, if it is granted, lies on the Plaintiff. Where there is a clear breach the question of balance of convenience does not arise."

I would respectfully adopt this statement of the law and add to it the observations of Lord Diplock in *American Cyanamid Company* v. *Ethicon Limited* [1975] 1 All E.R. 504 at 510:-

"It is no part of the Court's function at this stage of the litigation to try to resolve conflicts of evidence on affidavit as to facts on which the claims of either party may ultimately depend nor to decide difficult questions of law which call for detailed argument and mature considerations. *These are matters to be dealt with at the trial.* (emphasis added). One of the reasons for the introduction of the practice of requiring an undertaking as to damages on the grounds of an interlocutory injunction was that 'it aided the Court in doing that which was its great object, viz. abstaining from expressing any opinion upon the merits of the case until the hearing' (*Wakefield* v. *Duke of Buccleuch* (1865) 12 L.T. 628 at 629). So unless the material available to the Court at the hearing of the application for an interlocutory injunction fails to disclose that the Plaintiff has any real prospect of succeeding in his claim for a permanent injunction at the trial, the Court should go on to consider whether the balance of convenience lies in favour of granting or refusing the interlocutory relief that is sought."

The converse must also be true. Unless the material available to the Court at the hearing of the application for an interlocutory injunction fails to disclose that the Defendant has any real prospect of succeeding in his defence to a claim for a permanent injunction at the trial, the Court should go on to consider the balance of convenience. If it were otherwise, it appears to me that an interlocutory injunction, however detailed the argument and mature the consideration, in effect, determines the issue and a trial becomes superfluous. In the instant appeal, the learned trial Judge, clearly, took a very decided view on the complex legal issues raised and, indeed, it was after mature consideration, that the very positive nature of his decision and consequent finality is marked by the absence of any undertaking as to damages in the order and the awarding of costs to the Plaintiff at the interlocutory stage. In my judgment, whilst reserving the question as to whether or not there are cases in which it is proper for the Court to express a concluded view as to factual or legal issues arising at the interlocutory stage, ordinarily the determination of whether or not to grant an interlocutory injunction lies and lies only in answers to the two material questions as to there being a fair case to be made and where the balance of convenience lies. Since writing this judgment I have had the opportunity of reading the judgments of O'Higgins C.J. and Griffin J. in *Campus Oil Ltd. & Ors.* v. *Minister for Energy & Ors.* – 17.5.'83 – they appear to confirm the views I have expressed. In referring to the observations cited from *Kerr on Injunctions, Halsbury's Laws of England* and the *Amercian Cyanamid* case, I pause to draw attention to the observations of the learned trial Judge in his relatively lengthy judgment after his analysis of the English case law in *Esso Petroleum Company Limited* v. *Harper's Garage (Stourport) Ltd.* [1968] A.C. 269, *Cleveland Petroleum Co. Ltd.* v. *Dartstone Ltd.* [1969] 1 W.L.R. 116, and *Amoco Australia Pty Ltd.* v. *Rocca Bros. Motor Engineering Co. Pty Ltd.* [1975] A.C. 562, the latter being a decision of the Judicial Committee of the Privy Council. I do not necessarily agree or disagree with the analysis made by the learned trial Judge but I deem it proper to comment on his observation that – "the High Court in this country is not, of course, bound to follow the decisions and judgments to which I have referred if there are compelling reasons for rejecting them." I do not believe that the true inference from this observation is that, in the absence of compelling reasons for rejection, the High Court in this country is bound to follow decisions and judgments of the House of Lords, the Court of Appeal in England, or the Judicial Committee of the British Privy Council, but lest any such view should be entertained I would unequivocally deny the existence of any such principle or the propriety of any such practice. Of the decisions of these courts decided prior to 1922, it is proper to say that they are part of the corpus of jurisprudence and law that was taken over on the foundation of Saorstát Éireann being the laws in force in Saorstát Éireann at the date of the coming into operation of the Constitution of the Irish Free State (Saorstát Éireann), subject to that Constitution and to the extent to which they were not inconsistent therewith. Similarly Art. 50 of the Constitution provides:-

"1. Subject to this Constitution and to the extent to which they are not inconsistent therewith, the laws in force in Saorstát Éireann immediately prior to the date of the coming into operation of this Constitution shall continue to be of full force and effect until the same or any of them shall have been repealed or amended by enactment of the Oireachtas.

2. Laws enacted before, but expressed to come into force after, the coming into operation of this Constitution, shall, unless otherwise enacted by the Oireachtas come into force in accordance with the terms thereof."

Art. 50 was stated by Kingsmill Moore J. in *The Educational Company of Ireland Ltd.* v. *Fitzpatrick (No.2)*[1961] I.R. 345 as "carrying forward statutes or law into our corpus juris" but this view has been questioned by Walsh J. (with whom O'Higgins C.J. agreed) in *Gaffney* v. *Gaffney* [1975] I.R. 133 where he said:- "Contrary to what appears to have been the view of Kingsmill Moore J. I do not think that Art. 50 refers to any law other than statute law, and in my view the text of Art. 50 makes that clear." Walsh J. may well have been echoing the observations of Gavan Duffy J. in *Exham* v. *Beamish* [1939] I.R. 336 where he stated:-

"As a matter of practice, we constantly refer to judgments in the English Courts and such judgments, as every lawyer will recognise, have often proved to be of great service to us; but let us be clear. In my opinion when Saorstát Éireann, and afterwards Éire, continued the laws in force, they did not make binding on their courts anything short of law. In my opinion, judicial decisions in Ireland before the Treaty, and English decisions which were followed here, are binding upon this Court only when they represent a law so well settled or pronounced by so weighty a juristic authority that they may fairly be regarded, in a system built up upon the principle of stare decisis, as having become established as part of the law of the land before the Treaty; and to bind, they must, of course, not be inconsistent with the Constitution. In my opinion, this Court cannot be fettered in the exercise of the judicial power by opinions of very different courts under the old regime, unless those opinions must reasonably be considered to have had the force of law in Ireland, so that they formed part of the code expressly retained. If, before the Treaty, a particular law was administered in a way so repugnant to the common sense of our citizens as to make the law look ridiculous, it is not in the public interest that we should repeat the mistake. Our new High Court must mould its own cursus curiae; in so doing I hold that it is free, indeed bound, to decline to treat any such absurdity in the machinery of administration as having been imposed on it as part of the law of the land; nothing is law here which is inconsistent with derivation from the People." Whilst observations of Judges of the former Supreme Court in *Boylan* v. *Dublin Corporation* [1949] I.R. 60 and *Minister for Finance* v. *O'Brien* [1949] I.R. 91, appeared to support the view that decisions of the House of Lords upon law common to England and Ireland given before the coming into operation of the Constitution of 1922 are a binding force in our courts, in my view the decision of this Court in *Attorney General* v. *Ryan's Car Hire Limited* [1965] I.R. 70, wherein the rigidity of the principle of stare decisis was denied, must now call into question the binding force of any such pre-1922 decision. Since July 26th 1966, the House of Lords has recognised that too rigid adherence to precedent may lead to injustice in a particular case and also unduly restrict the proper development of the law. It stated its right, while treating former decisions of the House as normally binding, to depart from a previous decision when it appears right to do so. Practice Note in [1966] 3 All E.R. 77. Such a statement of principle by the House of Lords inevitably makes even weaker any case for following the decisions of that House whether they are in cases before or after 1922. There are many other jurisdictions likened to our own where the corpus juris includes the common law – the United States, Canada, Australia, New Zealand and so on. There are nations where, in addition, there are written and, consequently, rigid Constitutions, unlike that of the United Kingdom. Whilst the judgments in cases decided in the English Courts at all levels, will on a great many occasions prove convenient and, indeed, convincing statements of principle and attractive arguments in favour of such principles, they are no more than that and must be examined and questioned in the light of a jurisprudence whose fundamental law is radically different in its denial of a supremacy of parliament and its upholding of three co-equal organs of government, the Legislature, the Executive, and the Judiciary. In no sense are our courts a continuation of or successors to the British Courts. They derive their powers from a Constitution enacted by the people and would, in my view, find more appropriate guidance in the decisions of courts in other countries based upon a similar constitutional framework than in what at times appears to be an uncritical adherence to English precedent, which, itself, appears difficult to reconcile from time to time; see *Pirelli General Cable Works* v. *Oscar Faber & Partners* [1983] 1 All E.R. 65. Within the relatively narrow confines of the instant appeal, it is to be noted that the *American Cyanamid* case appears to have departed from an existing requirement of "probable success" and to substitute for it that of there being a serious issue to be tried.

The instant appeal

In my view, it is unnecessary to enter upon an examination of the conclusions to which the learned trial Judge came on the hearing of the interlocutory application, and the reasons for them. I am satisfied that it was unnecessary and, in an interlocutory application, undesirable, that he should have come to the firm conclusion as set out in his judgment. It may well be that his conclusion was correct – I express no view upon it save to state that an examination of the judgment itself demonstrates the complexity of the legal issue that arose and the certain need that all the facts, including the exact nature and location of the development that took place, should be established before any view of the legal position should be formed. The difficult legal issues raised by this undisputed fact, for instance, that the covenants are in form affirmatory rather than negative indicate the wide range of the problem; indeed the learned trial Judge's own analysis of the alleged anomalies originally suggested as arising out of the *Esso* case in an article in Vol. 85 of *The Law Quarterly Review* at p. 229 add force to this view. If the covenants are, in fact, negative, it is contended that the balance of convenience need not be taken into consideration upon the principle allegedly founding the decision in *Doherty* v. *Allman* 3 A.C. 709. This case was the subject of comment by Ó Dálaigh C.J. in *Dublin Port and Docks Board* v. *Brittania Dredging Company Ltd.* [1968] I.R. 136, which decision, itself, was considered by Keane J. In *TMG Group Limited* v. *Al-Babtain Trading and Contracting Company & Another* [1982] I.L.R.M. 349 at 353; there, referring to the *Brittania* case, he said:-

> "The defendants in that case were proposing to repudiate the contract in its entirety in circumstances where the Court was satisfied that they were not entitled so to do. The circumstances of the present case are wholly different: the defendants strenuously contend that neither of the transactions which the company proposes to enter into will constitute a breach of their contractual obligations under the share-holders' agreement. I do not think that Ó Dàlaigh C.J. in the passage to which I have referred, was laying down any general principle but, in all cases where the plaintiff establishes a prima facie case of a breach of a negative stipulation in a contract, the Court could disregard any question of the balance of convenience as between the parties. His observations were clearly confined to a case where one party to a contract was proposing to act in breach of a negative contract (and indeed to repudiate the whole contract) in circumstances where the Court was not satisfied on the evidence that they were entitled so to do. I do not think that the passage lends any support to the proposition that even where the violation of the plaintiff's right is denied, as it unquestionably is in the present case, the Court can disregard the balance of convenience to the parties."

It is right to point out that it does not appear the learned Judge in the High Court was referred to the decision of Keane J. in the *TMG* case which case, itself, was appealed to this Court but this point was not canvassed. I would endorse the views expressed by Keane J. as cited above and repeat my firm view that, save in the most exceptional circumstances, which it would be invidious to attempt to detail or delimit, the determination of whether or not to grant an interlocutory injunction lies and lies only in answers to the two material questions as to there being a fair case to be made and where the balance of convenience lies.

In the result, whilst, due to the passage of time, and the events that have taken place in the interval, it is clear that the balance of convenience lies in the continuance of the injunction, and, save as already indicated, the order of the High Court should stand, in principle, I would allow this appeal.

Griffin J.:

I agree with the judgment delivered by Mr Justice McCarthy save and except in respect of that portion of the judgment which deals with the effect of decisions of the House of Lords, the English Court of Appeal, or the Judicial Committee of the Privy Council, and of the effect of Article 50 of the Constitution. In respect of these matters I neither agree nor disagree – as they were not argued or discussed on the hearing of this appeal. I would express no opinion on them, and would reserve any such opinion until such questions arise and are argued in an appropriate case.

O'Higgins C.J. agreed with the judgment of McCarthy J. but also with the reservation expressed by Griffin J.

Notes and Questions

1. Do you agree with McCarthy J.'s interpretation of the earlier authorities, especially the *Educational Company of Ireland* case? *Cf.* the views expressed by the Supreme Court in *Campus Oil Ltd.* v. *Minister for Energy, infra.*
2. Do you agree with McCarthy J.'s views on the effect of pre-1922 English decisions and Article 50 of the Constitution?

CAMPUS OIL LTD V. MINISTER FOR ENERGY

Unreported (Supreme Court) (123-83) (Judgments delivered 17th May 1983)

The facts are set out in the Chief Justice's judgment.

O'Higgins C.J.:

The Plaintiffs in these proceedings, five of whom are the Appellants on this appeal, are companies engaged in the importation and sale of fuel oils who together constitute an association known as the "Irish Independent Petroleum Association". The main Defendants are the Minister for Industry and Energy (hereinafter referred to as "the Minister") and the Irish National Petroleum Corporation (hereinafter referred to as "the Corporation") established by the State in 1979 for the purpose of the purchase and importation of oil products and which now owns and operates, on behalf of the State, the oil refinery at Whitegate, Co. Cork (hereinafter referred to as "Whitegate"). Ireland and the Attorney General have also been joined as Defendants for procedural reasons. Before dealing with the issue which arises on this appeal it is necessary to refer to the legal steps which have already been taken in this litigation so that this issue can be considered in its proper background.

In these proceedings the Plaintiffs challenge the validity of a statutory instrument entitled Fuels (Control of Supplies) Order 1982 (hereinafter referred to as "the Order") made by the Minister on the 25th August 1982 pursuant to the provisions of the Fuels (Control of Supplies) Acts 1971 to 1982. Under the powers contained in the Order the Minister has required all traders in imported fuel oils to purchase 35 per cent of their requirements from Whitegate and to do so at prices and subject to terms fixed by the Corporation. This scheme or directive is known as the "mandatory regime". Its operation has been strongly resisted and opposed by the Plaintiffs who, in September 1982, commenced these proceedings, challenging the validity of the Order, when the directive was first sought to be imposed by the Minister. The challenge is based on the claim that the mandatory regime is contrary to the provisions of the Treaty Establishing the European Economic Community (the EEC Treaty) and in particular to Articles 30 and 31 thereof. Having commenced these proceedings the Plaintiffs applied in the High Court for an interlocutory injunction restraining the Defendants, pending the trial of the action, from implementing the mandatory regime. This application was heard by Mr. Justice Murphy and was refused by him for reasons which he outlined in a reserved judgment delivered on the 22nd September 1982. The Statement of Claim in the action was then delivered by the Plaintiffs as was the Defendants' Defence and the Plaintiffs' Reply. The proceedings were then re-listed before Mr. Justice Murphy for the purpose of considering an application by the Plaintiffs, which was opposed by the Defendants, that the Court should seek a preliminary ruling from the Court of Justice of the European Communities as to whether Articles 30 and 31 of the Treaty are to be interpreted as applying to the system or regime established by the Order. The Defendants, while opposing the application, suggested that if such a preliminary question were asked a further question should also go as to the application of Article 36 of the Treaty to the system or regime in the event of the first question being answered in the affirmative. Mr. Justice Murphy having considered the matter decided to seek a preliminary ruling on both questions, if necessary, from the Court of Justice. In so doing he was availing himself of the procedure laid down in Article 177 of the EEC Treaty which is in the following terms:

> "Articles 177. The Court of Justice shall have jurisdiction to give preliminary rulings concerning
> (a) the interpretation of this Treaty
> (b) the validity and interpretation of Acts of the institutions of the Community
> (c) the interpretation of the statutes of bodies established by an Act of the Council, where those statutes so provide.
>
> Where such a question is raised before any court or tribunal of a member state, that court or tribunal may, if it considers that decision on the question is necessary to enable it to give judgment, request the Court of Justice to give a ruling thereon.
>
> Where any such question is raised in a case pending before a court or tribunal of a member state, against whose decision there is no judicial remedy under national law, the court or tribunal shall bring the matter before the Court of Justice."

It is apparent from this Article that Mr. Justice Murphy had a discretion as to whether or not to make the reference sought. However, he concluded that he ought to seek a preliminary ruling and in so doing adjudged that the preliminary decision on the question was necessary to enable him to give judgment in the action between the parties. The Defendants appealed against this decision to the Supreme Court but their appeal was dismissed. Consequent on the decision to seek the preliminary ruling the further hearing and trial of the action has been adjourned.

In so far as the Defendants were concerned, when these steps had concluded they decided to seek full observance of the mandatory regime. This they concluded to be necessary in order to maintain Whitegate. Their decision was complied with by the large multi-national oil companies who were trading in this country (known as "the Majors") but was resisted by five of the Plaintiff companies. The fifth-named Plaintiff complied with the Defendants' decision, with the result that it is not involved in the Order made in the High Court, nor is it involved on this appeal. The other five Plaintiff companies continued to import their requirements without taking any percentage from Whitegate. The Minister and the Corporation were concerned that a continuance of this situation might lead to the Majors also pulling out of the mandatory regime. If this occurred it would result in the immediate closing of Whitegate with considerable disorganisation and damage to the Corporation's plans for the maintenance of Whitegate as a viable refinery. For this reason, having sought leave to amend the Defence by adding a counter-claim, the Defendants applied to the High Court for interlocutory injunctions against the five Plaintiffs who were so refusing to comply with the Order. This application was heard by Mr. Justice Keane in the High Court. Having considered the issue very carefully, he decided to grant the injunction sought on the grounds stated in his reserved judgment dated 24th March 1983. Against his decision this appeal has been brought.

The basic contention of the Appellants has been that Mr. Justice Keane in granting interlocutory relief on the application for the Defendants failed to have regard to the correct criteria to be applied in considering an application for an interlocutory injunction and in particular in considering an application for an injunction which was of a mandatory nature. In particular they submit that he was in error in failing to require of the Defendants that they should establish a substantial question to be tried and a probability that the Plaintiffs would fail at the trial in relation to such a question. It seems to me that these contentions raise a question of some importance as to the manner in which a court should act in considering interlocutory relief.

Interlocutory relief is granted where what is complained of is continuing and is causing harm or injury which may be irreparable in the sense that it may not fairly or properly be compensated for in damages. It is given because a period must necessarily elapse before the action can come for trial and for the purpose of keeping matters in *statu quo* until the hearing. The application is made on motion supported by affidavit. It frequently happens that neither the plaintiff's right nor the fact of its violation is disputed by the person whose acts are sought to be restrained. In such case an injunction may be given almost as of course. Often also, the application for the interlocutory injunction is, by consent, treated as the trial of the action. When this happens the rights of the parties are finally determined on the interlocutory motion. In cases, however, where rights are disputed and challenged and where a significant period must elapse before the trial, the Court must exercise its discretion whether to grant interlocutory relief with due regard to certain well-established principles. Not only will it have regard to what is complained of and whether damages would be an appropriate remedy, but it will also consider what inconvenience, loss and damage might be caused to the other party, and ask whether he who seeks relief has shown that the balance of convenience is in his favour. None of these matters, however, are directly in issue on this appeal. Here, interlocutory relief was granted to the Defendants in pursuance of their counter-claim seeking a permanent injunction at the trial. The Plaintiffs, against whom it was granted contend that the learned trial Judge should have required the Defendants to establish a probability that the counter-claim would succeed at the trial and that the Defendants' claim would be dismissed. Mr. Fitzsimons on their behalf argued that the existence of such a probability test as a guide to the granting of interlocutory relief was recognised by the former Supreme Court in *Educational Company of Ireland Limited* v. *Fitzpatrick and Ors.* [1961] I.R. 323. In particular he relied on the judgment of Lavery J. in that case. I must say at once that I do not agree. In my opinion, the judgments in that case do not support this argument. It is true that there is one reference to "probability" contained in an extract from *Kerr on Injunctions* (6th Edition) which was quoted by Lavery J. This reference, however, in its context, is of doubtful significance. Lavery J., however, in his judgment, at p.337 clearly laid down what he regarded as the proper test when he said:

> "The Plaintiffs have to establish that there is a fair question raised to be decided at the trial. The arguments, lasting three days in this Court, show, I think, that there is such a question to be determined."

In any event I would regard the application of such a test as contrary to principle. As I have already mentioned, interlocutory relief is intended to keep matters in *statu quo* until the trial and to do no more. No rights are determined nor are issues decided. I think the principle is stated correctly in the following passage from *Kerr on Injunctions* (6th Edition p.2) which was noted by Lavery J. in *The Educational Company of Ireland Limited* v. *Fitzpatrick*.

> "In interfering by interlocutory injunction, the Court does not, in general, profess to anticipate the determination of the right, but merely gives it as its opinion that there is a substantial question to be tried, and that till the question is ripe for trial, a case has been made out for the preservation of the property in the meantime in *statu quo*."

The application of the criterion suggested by the Appellants in this case would involve the Court in a determination on an application for interlocutory relief of an issue which properly arises for determination at the trial of the action. In my view, the test to be applied is whether a fair *bona fide* question has been raised by the person seeking relief. If such a question has been raised it is not for the Court on an interlocutory application to determine that question: that remains to be decided at the trial. Once a fair question has been raised, in the manner in which I have indicated, then the Court should consider the other matters appropriate to the exercise of its discretion as to whether to grant interlocutory relief. I note in this regard the views expressed by Lord Diplock, with the concurrence of the other members of the House of Lords, at p.407 of the Report of the English case of *American Cyanamid* v. *Ethicon* [1975] A.C. 396. I merely say that I entirely agree with what he said.

In my view, therefore, the learned trial Judge, in considering whether the Applicants had raised a fair question as to whether their rights had been violated, applied the correct test. I must add that, in my view, such a question had been raised and that he was correct in this respect in approaching the exercise of discretion on that basis.

The Appellants also argue that in so far as the relief which was granted was mandatory in nature, such should not have been given by way of interlocutory relief. It is correct that a mandatory injunction does not usually issue prior to the trial of an action. There are, however, exceptions and, in my view, this case is one of these. The Order which is challenged was made under the provisions of an Act of the Oireachtas. It is, therefore, on its face, valid and is to be regarded as a part of the law of the land, unless and until its invalidity is established. It is and has been implemented amongst traders in fuel, but the Appellants have stood aside and have openly defied its implementation. Their action clearly, on the evidence, threatens the continued operation of the regime established by the Order in question. This is so because the other oil companies, particularly the Majors, have threatened to pull out of the regime unless it is observed by all traders. It seems to me that in such circumstances it was proper to direct, by way of mandatory injunction, compliance with the Order. If this were not done the existing position, in so far as the operation of the Order is concerned, could not be preserved, and on the evidence before the learned trial Judge, there was a grave danger of very great and extensive damage being caused to Whitegate. Therefore, although one of the injunctions granted was mandatory in its nature, I think it was proper in the circumstances of this case that it should have been granted by way of interlocutory relief. For these reasons, in my view, this appeal should be dismissed.

Griffin J.:

I agree with the judgment of the Chief Justice. I would however like to add some observations of my own.

Mr. Fitzsimons on behalf of the plaintiffs submitted that, as the provisions of the Treaty Establishing the European Community (the E.E.C. Treaty) forms part of the domestic law of the State, before determining whether or not the interlocutory injunction sought by the defendants should be granted, this Court should first interpret Articles 30, 31 and 36 of that Treaty. This should be done, they say, for the purpose of determining whether Articles 30 and 31 apply to a system such as that established by the Fuels (Control of Supplies) Order 1982, and, if they did, whether such a system is exempt by the provisions of Article 36. These are the precise matters which, at the instance of the plaintiffs, Murphy J., pursuant to Article 177 of the E.E.C. Treaty, referred to the Court of Justice of the European Communities at Luxembourg ("the E.E.C. Court") for the preliminary rulings of that Court. Before doing so, he had to determine that the ruling of the E.E.C. Court *is necessary* to enable him to give judgment on the issues in dispute between the parties in this action. The plaintiffs stood over and successfully defended his order of referral on the defendants' appeal to this Court against the making of that order.

In my opinion, it would be highly undesirable, to put it at its lowest, for this Court to interpret those Articles in anticipation of the rulings of the E.E.C. Court and the plaintiffs should not be allowed to blow hot and cold in the course of the same proceedings between the same parties. It is for the E.E.C. Court to *interpret* the provisions of the E.E.C. Treaty, and it is for our courts to *apply* it. Mr. Fennelly was in my opinion correct in pointing out that the primary object of Article 177 is to ensure uniform interpretation of Community law within all member states, as otherwise the application of Community law by the national courts of the member states could lead to divergent application in different member states, or even to application which would be contrary to the principles of Community law. It is for this reason that although national courts, other than the court of last instance, have a discretion to seek preliminary rulings under Article 177, the courts of last instance, whose cases set the important precedents, are obliged to refer to the E.E.C. Court any questions of Community law raised.

On the question of the principles to be applied in the granting or refusing of an interlocutory injunction, Mr. Fitzsimons sought to rely on the judgment of Lavery J. in the *Educational Company of Ireland Limited* v. *Fitzpatrick and Others* [1961] I.R. 323 as establishing that the plaintiffs seeking the injunction must satisfy the Court that the probability is in favour of the defendants' case ultimately failing in the final issue of the suit. An analysis of the judgments in that case is of interest. Lavery J. cited with approval two passages in *Kerr on Injunctions*, (6th Edn., p. 2 and pp. 15/16 respectively) as settling the principles on which an interlocutory injunction will be granted. These passages are fully set out in the judgment of Keane J. and I do not propose to repeat them. In the first passage, reference is made to the necessity of there being "a substantial question to be tried", and "a fair question to raise" as to the existence of the right alleged. In the second passage the requirement of there being a fair question to raise as to the existence of the right which the party seeking the injunction sets up is repeated, and then reference is made to the requirement that the Court must, before disturbing any man's legal right or stripping him of any of the rights with which the law has clothed him, be satisfied that the *probability* is in favour of his case ultimately failing in the final issue of the suit.

Having cited the two passages referred to, Lavery J. dealt with the issues that arose in the case. He referred to the requirement that the plaintiffs have to establish "that there is a fair question raised to be decided at the trial", and gave as his opinion "that the issues raised a question and a difficult one." And at p. 338 he said that "In this case there may well be further facts elicited at the trial, but there can be no doubt that a serious question of law arises", but he did not deal with the question of whether or not the "probability" test had been satisfied.

Maguire C.J., who dissented, cited with approval the passage at p. 15 in *Kerr* of which Lavery J. approved, but he omitted that portion of it which dealt with the probability of success at the trial. Although he based his decision on the ground that the plaintiffs had not shown that there were substantial grounds for doubting the existence of a trade dispute, he did, however, say that "on the other point argued" he was not satisfied from what had been said on that point that it was probable that the plaintiffs would establish it.

Kingsmill Moore J. at p. 342 said that it appeared to him that a very important and difficult question of law was involved and one which required the most careful consideration. He cited *Smyth and Another* v. *Beirne and Another* (unreported) in which the Court unanimously held that on the facts as accepted by the Judge of first instance a serious question of law arose as to whether a trade dispute existed and that this warranted the granting of an interlocutory injunction, where the balance of convenience was in favour of granting it. He said:-

> "Mr. Costello for the plaintiffs does not accept that all relevant facts have been established and says that there are further facts which he hopes to establish if the case goes to a full hearing, and if he can avail himself of discovery, interrogatories, and cross-examination to elicit them. I am of opinion that a plaintiff is entitled to have his case fully investigated in the ordinary course of legal procedure and that it would be undesirable in the absence of consent to decide a legal question of this magnitude merely on the affidavits filed for the purpose of the interlocutory motion."

Ó Dálaigh J. said that he inclined to the view that the constitutional issue raised by the plaintiffs is prima facie sufficient to turn the scales in their favour, and that accordingly the only remaining matter was the balance of convenience. Maguire J. agreed with Lavery J., and also with Kingsmill Moore and Ó Dálaigh JJ.

It would appear therefore that the Chief Justice, who dissented, impliedly accepted the probability test, that Lavery J. stated but does not seem to have applied it, and that Kingsmill Moore J. and Ó Dálaigh J. were satisfied that there was a serious question to be tried.

Subsequently, in *Esso Petroleum Company (Ireland) Limited* v. *Fogarty* [1965] I.R. 531, Ó Dálaigh C.J., with whom Lavery J. agreed, accepted that the principles to be applied are well summarised in the passages from Kerr cited in the judgment of Lavery J. in the *Educational Company of Ireland Limited* case. Having stated that the plaintiffs were required to show that in the language of *Kerr* there are substantial grounds for doubting the existence of the alleged legal right of the defendant, the exercise of which they seek to prevent, he said at p. 539:-

> "The Court before stripping him of this right must be satisfied that the probability is in favour of the defendant's case ultimately failing in the final issue of this suit."

On the other hand, Walsh J., at p. 541, stated the principle applicable as follows:-

> "The principles upon which interlocutory injunctions are granted are well established and a Court will grant one when a case has been made out for the preservation of the property *in statu quo* pending the trial of the action if it is of opinion that there is a substantial question to be tried."

This is a clear and concise statement of the principles to be applied in such cases.

The question was also considered by the House of Lords some ten years later in *American Cyanamid* v. *Ethicon Ltd.*[1975] A.C. 396. It was there laid down that the Court in exercising its discretion as to granting or refusing an interlocutory injunction, ought not to weigh up the relative strengths of the parties' cases on the evidence available at the interlocutory stage, that evidence being then necessarily imcomplete. Lord Diplock, with whose speech the other members of the House agreed, referred at p. 407 to what he called "the supposed rule that the Court is not entitled to take any account of the balance of convenience unless it has first been satisfied that if the case went to trial on no other evidence than is before the Court at the hearing of the application the plaintiff would be entitled to judgment for a

permanent injunction in the same terms as the interlocutory injunction sought."
He then continued:-

"Your Lordships should in my view take this opportunity of declaring that there is no such rule. The use of such expressions as 'a probability', 'a prima facie case', or 'a strong prima facie case' in the context of the exercise of a discretionary power to grant an interlocutory injunction leads to confusion as to the object sought to be achieved by this form of temporary relief. The Court no doubt must be satisfied that the claim is not frivolous or vexatious; in other words, that there is a serious question to be tried.

It is no part of the court's function at this stage of the litigation to try to resolve conflicts of evidence on affidavit as to facts on which the claims of either party may ultimately depend nor to decide difficult questions of law which call for detailed argument and mature considerations. These are matters to be dealt with at the trial. One of the reasons for the introduction of the practice of requiring an undertaking as to damages on the grant of an interlocutory injunction was that 'it aided the court in doing that which was its great object, viz. abstaining from expressing any opinion upon the merits of the case until the hearing' *(Wakefield* v. *Duke of Buccleuch)*. So unless the material available to the court at the hearing of the application for an interlocutory injunction fails to disclose that the plaintiff has any real prospect of succeeding in his claim for a permanent injunction at the trial, the court should go on to consider whether the balance of convenience lies in favour of granting or refusing the interlocutory relief that he sought."

It was submitted on behalf of the plaintiffs that there are differences between the test applied in the *American Cyanamid* case and those applied in the *Educational Company of Ireland Limited* and the *Esso Petroleum Company (Ireland) Limited* cases but, as Murphy J. said in his judgment in the application for an interlocutory judgment by the plaintiffs in this case, any such differences are more apparent than real. The tests applied by Lavery J. ("that there is a fair question raised to be decided at the trial"); by Kingsmill Moore J. ("that a serious question of law arose"); by Walsh J. ("that there is a substantial question to be tried") and by Lord Diplock ("that there is a serious question to be tried") are essentially the same. A similar view was taken by Finlay P. in *Rex Pet Foods Limited and Another* v. *Lamb Brothers (Dublin) Limited and Others*,(unreported, 26th August 1982), where he stated that the statement of principles contained in these decisions do not differ but to some extent each complements the other in certain aspects of the questions raised.

It seems to me that the passage from the speech of Lord Diplock to which I have referred has much to recommend it in logic, common sense and principle and I would respectfully adopt it as being a correct statement of the law to be applied in cases of this kind. In a number of cases in recent years this Court has applied, as the true test, whether a fair or serious question has been raised to be decided at the trial, and, if so, whether the balance of convenience was in favour of granting or refusing the interlocutory injunction sought. The latest of these cases was *T.M.G. Group Ltd.* v. *Al-Babtain Trading and Contracting Company and Another,* (28th March 1980), but in none of them was judgment reserved by reason of their extremely urgent nature.

Keane J. held that there is a fair question to be tried on the hearing of this action, and there undoubtedly is. He also held that in terms of the balance of convenience between the parties and the preservation of the status quo, he should exercise his discretion in favour of granting the interlocutory injunction sought. There was evidence before him on which he was in my opinion justified in coming to that conclusion.

I would dismiss this appeal.

Hederman J. agreed with both judgments.

II. MAREVA INJUNCTION

FLEMING V. RANKS (IRELAND) LTD

Unreported (High Court) (1983 No 1347P) (Judgment delivered 16th March 1983)

The facts are set out in the judgment.

McWilliam J.:

This application has been brought for an interlocutory injunction to restrain the Defendants from disposing of or dealing with the assets of the first-named Defendant, hereinafter described as Ranks, so as to reduce the value thereof below the sum of £83,724.92, and for an Order giving the Plaintiffs liberty to inspect the books and records of Ranks so as to ascertain what funds are available to satisfy the Plaintiffs' claim in this action.

There are five Plaintiffs and they are claiming the sum above-mentioned which they allege is due to them for breach of contract or for misrepresentation, either innocent or fraudulent.

The agreement on which the Plaintiffs base their claim was entered into between Ranks and the Irish Transport and General Workers' Union (hereinafter called the Union). The Union was expressed to be acting on behalf of its members attached to Ranks' Dublin North City Mill and the agreement was headed Ranks (Ireland) Limited – Dublin North City Mills Re-organisation 1978 – Productivity. Schedule B to this agreement set out details of compensation for various categories of employees made redundant.

The Plaintiff, Harry Fleming, filed two affidavits but did not state to which category of employees he belongs or any facts necessary to make the calculation of the alleged entitlement of the Plaintiffs in accordance with Schedule B. This aspect of the case was not considered at the hearing before me although there is a formal denial in an affidavit filed on behalf of the Defendants that the 1978 agreement does relate to Mr. Fleming's case. On the other hand, it is accepted on behalf of Ranks that, if the agreement does apply, Mr. Fleming would be entitled to approximately £24,000.

The 1978 agreement was followed by an undated letter to an officer of the Union written by the second-named Defendant on behalf of Ranks which stated as follows:- "The Company in the event of 'redundancy' following future plant investment or organisational alteration causing job reductions, would not discontinue the 1978/79 Company Redundancy Scheme unless it could be shown to the mutual satisfaction of the parties that such payments were financially unsustainable." Although an affidavit by an officer of the Union was filed on behalf of the Plaintiffs, neither party has suggested that there was any reply to this letter.

On 13th October, 1982, Ranks sent a letter to all employees stating that the company was sustaining huge and insupportable losses and that, to survive, up to two hundred jobs would be lost but that it was hoped that total site closures could be avoided. References in the letter to survival clearly indicated that the total closure mentioned was a possibility. This led to meetings between representatives from Ranks and from the Union and, at a meeting on 25th November 1982, Ranks offered redundancy payments at the rates set out in the Redundancy Payments Acts plus sixty per cent. of such payments. This offer was rejected by the Union and the matter was referred to the Labour Court which, by determination made on 7th January, 1983, recommended that redundancy payments should be made on the basis of paying one half of the payments set out in the 1978 agreement immediately and the balance one year later. Ranks then stated that it was unable to make such a substantial payment and the Union issued strike notice for 19th January, 1982. This was followed by an announcement by Ranks that the mills in Dublin and Limerick would have to close on 4th February, 1983. Further meetings took place which resulted in proposals which were accepted by a majority of members of the Union, but this decision was not accepted by the Plaintiffs who commenced to picket the Dublin mill.

Whatever terms were agreed by the members who accepted the proposals, Ranks now claim that the Plaintiffs are only entitled to the statutory redundancy payments.

The agreement accepted by the majority appears to have been reached on the basis that it involved Ranks in no legal liability and that the Union's acceptance was without prejudice to its position in relation to the decision of the Labour Court. Fortunately, on this application, I am not required to consider the effect of this unusual provision.

Accounts have been furnished by Ranks purporting to show that the terms of the 1978 agreement are now financially unsustainable but these accounts are not accepted by the Plaintiffs as establishing this.

There are unusual features in the case. The Plaintiffs refused to accept the closure of the mill and went into occupation of it. They were committed to Mountjoy prison for this activity but, on their release, returned to their occupation of it and are still denying Ranks access to it.

The Plaintiffs, Harry Fleming and Dermot O'Donnell, have stated on affidavit that they are members of the Union, but they wrote to Ranks in May and June, 1982, respectively, to say that they were no longer members of the Union and asking that their subscriptions should be discontinued. The affidavit by the officer of the Union does not refer to the membership or non-membership of the Plaintiffs in the Union.

In the affidavit of the Plaintiff, Harry Fleming, he alleges that a substantial asset of Ranks consists of wheat and flour at the Dublin mill and that this asset is perishable, but, by their occupation of the mill, the Plaintiffs have prevented necessary steps being taken to preserve it.

There are clearly difficult questions to be decided. Amongst these are:- 1. The period of the duration of the 1978 agreement: 2. Whether it enured for the benefit of persons who remained in the employment of Ranks: 3. The effect of the decision of the Labour Court when considered in conjunction with the admission by Ranks that the Union's acceptance of the new terms was without prejudice to the position in relation to the decision of the Labour Court: 4. The extent to which members are bound by the agreements of the Union of which they claim to be members and which they allege was negotiating on their behalf: 5. The extent to which Ranks are bound to employees by an agreement with the Union of which the Plaintiffs notified Ranks that they were not members: 6. The financial position of Ranks having regard to the controlling interest of the parent company or companies..

These are not matters to be decided at this stage of the proceedings, but they indicate that there are serious questions to be decided in the proceedings and that there is definitely a case to be made on behalf of the Plaintiffs.

The case made for granting the injunction is that the association of Ranks with its subsidiary companies and its parent company is likely to enable Ranks to dispose of its assets so that any judgment obtained by the Plaintiffs will be of no value

The case made on behalf of the Defendants is that there is no actual evidence that Ranks are trying to get rid of their property or are likely to do so, that the company is an Irish company with no record of defaulting on its commitments, that an injunction in the terms sought by the Plaintiffs will not make the Plaintiffs secured creditors and that the balance of convenience is all in favour of refusing to grant an injunction, particularly having regard to the admitted perishable nature of the wheat and flour which must be disposed of, and that the Court should take account of the behaviour of the Plaintiffs in refusing to permit these commodities to be properly preserved.

I have been referred to a number of cases on behalf of the parties.

Barclay-Johnson v. *Yuill* [1980] 1 W.L.R. 1259.

Rahman v. *Abu-Taha* [1980] 1 W.L.R. 1268.

Rasu Maritima S.A. v. *Perusahaan Pertambangan Minyakdangas Bumi Negara* [1978] Q.B. 644; [1977] 3 W.L.R. 518.

Z Ltd. v. *A-Z and AA-LL* [1982] 2 W.L.R. 288.

Searose Ltd. v. *Seatrain U.K. Ltd.* [1981] Q.B. 923; [1981] 2 W.L.R. 601.

Goulding Chemicals Ltd v. *Bolger* [1977] I.R. 211.

American Cyanamid Co. v. *Ethicon Ltd.* [1975] A.C. 396; [1975] 2 W.L.R. 316.

The injunction sought by the Plaintiffs is of a type which has become known as a Mareva injunction because it was first considered in England and there granted in the case of *Mareva Compania S.A.* v. *International Bulk Carriers S.A.* [1975] Lloyd's Reports 509 and now also reported in [1980] 1 All E.R. 213n. Prior to that case the principle generally applicable was that "you cannot get an injunction to restrain a man who is alleged to be a debtor from parting with his property." See *Lister* v. *Stubbs* [1980] 45 Ch. D.1. In the *Mareva* case an injunction was granted to restrain a defendant out of the jurisdiction from removing property within the jurisdiction so as to prevent a plaintiff with a good arguable case for damages against the defendant which can properly be brought within the jurisdiction from recovering the amount of any award he may obtain.

This principle has been extended in England by a long line of cases ending in the *Rahman* case in which Lord Denning said, at page 1237: "So I would hold that a Mareva injunction can be granted against a man even though he is based in this country if the circumstances are such that there is a danger of his absconding, or a danger of the assets being removed out of the jurisdiction or disposed of within the jurisdiction, or otherwise dealt with so that there is a danger that the Plaintiff, if he gets judgment, will not be able to get it satisfied."

This principle has now been given statutory force in England by section 37 (3) of the Supreme Court Act, 1981.

I have not been referred to any Irish case dealing with a Mareva injunction although the jurisdiction to grant such an injunction was raised before me in the *Matter of Brendan Molloy Limited* but I was of opinion that the injunction there sought was not a Mareva type injunction. I note also that an article at page 114 of the *Dublin University Law Journal* for 1982 considers the application of such injunctions in family law matters.

The jurisdiction to grant such injunctions in England was, prior to 1981, based on provisions similar to those contained in subsection (8) of section 28 of the Judicature (Ireland) Act, 1877. The relevant part of this subsection is as follows:- "an injunction may be granted by an interlocutory order of the Court in all cases in which it shall appear to the Court to be just or convenient that such order shall be made."

I am satisfied that there is jurisdiction to grant such an injunction and that the cases in which it may be granted are not confined to cases in which a defendant is resident outside the State. From the cases cited I would accept that there must be a real risk of the removal or disposal of the defendant's assets, that there must be a danger of default by the defendant, that the plaintiff must show that he has a good arguable case, and, weighing the considerations for and against the grant of an injunction, the balance of convenience must be in favour of granting it. See *Barclay-Johnson* v. *Yuill* at page 1265.

As I have already stated, it appears to me that there is a good arguable case to be made on behalf of the Plaintiffs. The affidavits filed on behalf of the Defendants indicate fairly clearly that Ranks is insolvent and it is not alleged that the company does not propose to dispose of its assets although it is averred that there is no intention of disposing of assets to evade any obligation to the Plaintiffs.

Inter-company debts between parent companies, associated companies and subsidiary companies should, in my opinion, be scrutinised by a court where the assets available by companies for the payment of their debts are involved even though there is no legal distinction between such debts and the debts owed by a company to its ordinary creditors. On this basis it might be argued in some cases that an order for liberty to inspect the books of a company might be granted but no arguments were advanced on behalf of the Plaintiffs on this basis and there was no discussion of the accounts which were exhibited.

Although a special account has been opened by Ranks for the sums to which the Plaintiffs are entitled under the Redundancy Acts, it appears to me that, if damages are awarded to the Plaintiffs on the basis of their claims, there is a danger of default by Ranks through inability to pay the amounts of the awards.

But I am of opinion that, to justify such an injunction, the anticipated disposal of a defendant's assets must be for the purpose of preventing a plaintiff from recovering damages and not merely for the purpose of carrying on a business or discharging lawful debts.

On the question of the balance of convenience, on the evidence before me, there can be very little question about the advantage of disposing of the stocks of wheat and flour which is stated by both parties to be perishable. It is also clear that, if the Defendants were to be successful in the action, no undertaking as to damages given by the Plaintiffs would be of any value.

I would accept as correct the statement of Sir Robert Megarry, V.C., at page 1266 of the *Barclay-Johnson* case, where he said "I would regard the Lister principle as remaining the rule, and the Mareva doctrine as constituting a limited exception to it." "The Lister Rule" refers to the case of *Lister & Co.* v. *Stubbs* mentioned above, and is that the Court will not grant an injunction to restrain a defendant from parting with his assets so that they may be preserved in case the plaintiff's claim succeeds.

Under all the circumstances of this case I am of opinion that I should not grant the application made on behalf of the Plaintiffs.

Note

See also the judgment of McWilliam J. in *Powerscourt Estates* v. *Gallagher*[1984] I.L.R.M. 123.

III. QUIA TIMET INJUNCTION

C. & A. MODES V. C. & A. (WATERFORD) LTD

[1976] I.R. 198 (Supreme Court)

The facts are set out in Henchy J.'s judgment.

O'Higgins C.J.:

I agree with the judgment which is about to be delivered and have nothing to add to it.

Henchy J.:

In the High Court the following matters were held to have been established as facts:

1. C. & A. Modes (the first plaintiffs) carry on a retail clothing business in a chain of 65 shops throughout the United Kingdom, including one in Belfast, and use as a symbol or hallmark of that business the combination "C. & A." For a number of reasons, particularly because of the number of people from this State who frequent the C. & A. shop in Belfast and because of the widespread advertising of C. & A. in English newspapers circulating in this State and on television, the business of C. & A. is well known in this State.

2. Michael Vincent O'Toole and Samuel McClure (the individual defendants) adopted "C. & A." as a component of the names of C. & A. (Waterford) Ltd. and C. & A. (Finance) Ltd. (the defendant companies) and used the symbol "C. & A" on a van operated by one of the defendant companies with the intention that people in this State would associate their business with that of C. & A.

3. If the defendants continue to use the name and symbol "C. & A." in that way, there will be a confusion in the public mind between their business activities and those of the first plaintiffs.

4. If C. & A. Ireland (the second plaintiffs and a subsidiary company of the first plaintiffs) proceed, as had apparently been intended, to open a C. & A. shop in Dublin, there will be substantial confusion between the trading activities of that shop and those of the defendant companies.

5. It is the intention of the individual defendants to deceive by associating the goods or business activities of the defendant companies in the minds of people with the goods or business of the first plaintiffs.

As the note of the evidence and the careful and comprehensive judgment of the President of the High Court show, those findings of fact were fully substantiated. In this appeal by the defendants against the injunction granted to the plaintiffs restraining the defendants from passing off or attempting to pass off in that manner, the only challenge to those findings was a submission that the evidence did not support the finding that the conduct of the defendants was likely to lead to confusion in the public mind between the goods or business of C. & A. Modes and the goods or business of the defendant companies. I must reject that submission.

The name and symbol "C & A" were not chosen through any bona fide coincidence or mischance. They were plainly chosen with the intention that members of the public would be confused into thinking that the goods or business of the defendant companies emanated from the C & A ambience. When the individual defendants were sent a letter of complaint, they, as the sole directors and shareholders of the defendant companies, had an opportunity of asserting an innocent or harmless purpose in the conduct complained of. They did not do so. Instead, they claimed a right to do what was complained of because neither of the plantiff companies was trading in this State. They allowed to go by default the complaint that their conduct was calculated to deceive members of the public. In those circumstances the judge was fully justified in finding an intention to deceive. While that mental element is not of the essence of the cause of action, it shows that the conduct complained of was in fact likely to deceive – which goes to the gist of the action for passing off.

It is, of course, correct to say, as counsel for the defendants say, that even where conduct likely to deceive is proved the plaintiffs cannot succeed unless they show that their goodwill is at least imperilled by that conduct. Here it is contended that there was no breach of the plaintiffs' goodwill which could be affected by the defendants' conduct. The plaintiffs have no shop or place of trading within the State, and it is urged that the evidence fell short of showing that the orbit of their trading activities outside the State was capable of carrying with it a public awareness within the State of the import of "C. & A." as a business name or symbol, and that, consequently, the defendants' conduct was incapable of invading their goodwill.

Consider this submission in the light of the evidence. Sixty-five shops throughout the United Kingdom, including the one in Belfast, purvey the distinctive C. & A. wearing apparel. It would be remarkable, considering the movement of people between this State and the United Kingdom, if there were not a significant number of at least intermittent C. & A. customers in this State. The evidence also showed that there has been massive advertising of C. & A. goods on television and in some of the most widely read British newspapers and magazines circulating in the Republic of Ireland, as well as in Northern Ireland newspapers. The Belfast shop draws a not inconsiderable number of its customers from the Republic. The C. & A. organization recruits staff from the Republic. In 1975, one factory in Cork manufactured 850,000 items which were sold in the C. & A. shops.

Can it be said in these circumstances that, because the plaintiffs have no direct retailing outlet in the Republic, they have no protectable goodwill in the Republic? In my opinion, the answer is "No." Goodwill does not necessarily stop at a frontier. Whether in a particular area a plaintiff has a goodwill which is liable to be damaged by the unlawful competition resulting from passing off is a question of fact and of degree. What has to be established for the success of a plaintiff's claim in an action such as this is that by his business activities–be they by direct selling within the State or otherwise–he has generated within the State a property right in a goodwill which will be violated by the passing-off. It is true that there is authority for the proposition that a plaintiff's reputation which owes nothing to user in this State is not sufficient to support a passing-off action (*Alan Bernardin et Cie* v. *Pavilion Properties Ltd.* [1967] R.P.C. 581) but, as is stated in *Kerry's Law of Trade Marks and Trade Names* (10th ed., p. 386), it is difficult to see any rational basis for this distinction. If there are in this State sufficient customers of a plaintiff's business to justify his claim to have a vested right to retain and expand that custom, then there is ample authority in principle and in the decided cases for the conclusion that, no matter where the plaintiff's business is based, he is entitled to be protected against its being taken away or dissipated by someone whose deceptive conduct is calculated to create a confusion of identity in the minds of existing or potential customers.

I consider that the evidence in this case amply satisfies the test. The nature and spread of the C & A trade throughout the United Kingsom, the extent to which the shop in Belfast draws its custom from this State, the advertising campaign in papers and magazines circulating here, the distinctive nature of C & A goods in their labelling and packaging and in the C & A symbol, all these in combination point to a goodwill in this State. If there were any doubt that the first plaintiffs enjoy in this State "the attractive force which brings in custom" (*per* Lord Macnaghten in *Commissioners of Inland Revenue* **v.** *Muller & Co.'s Margarine Ltd.* [1904] 1 I.R.

161, 171), one might ask why did the individual defendants purloin the name and symbol of C & A? The answer is that they did so to gain commercial advantage from the resulting confusion in the public mind between their trading activities and those of the first plaintiffs. Their passing-off was calculated to operate to the detriment of the goodwill in this State of the first plaintiffs. It is to prevent unfair competition of that kind that the action for passing-off lies.

Finally, it was submitted on behalf of the defendants that as this is in reality an action for a *quia timet* injunction, the plaintiffs should be held to have failed to prove "a well-founded apprehension of injury-proof of actual and real danger-a strong probability, almost amounting to moral certainty," which is the degree of proof laid down by FitzGibbon L.J. in *The Attorney General* v. *Rathmines & Pembroke Joint Hospital Board* [1904] 1 I.R. 161, 171 as necessary before such an injunction should be granted. The trial judge held that, if that was the degree of proof necessary in this action, the onus of proof had been discharged. Having regard to the whole of the evidence, I think there was more than sufficient ground for that conclusion.

However, while so holding, the trial judge did not decide that what the plaintiffs claimed in this action was a *quia timet* injunction. I think it was not. A *quia timet* injunction restrains a feared or threatened infringement of a right. That is not the situation that the plaintiffs sought to have redressed in this action. A passing-off was not threatened: it had actually taken place. The "C & A" name and symbol had been taken and put to use by the defendants in an impermissible manner. In such circumstances, the plaintiffs, in order to succeed in their claim for an injunction, were not required to prove by further evidence that they had suffered or would suffer damage. Their right to their goodwill had been violated by the passing-off, and in those circumstances the law assumes a resulting damage: see the remarks of Sir Wilfred Greene M.R. at p. 518 and of Goddard L.J. at p. 526 of the report of *Draper* v. *Trist* [1939] 3 All E.R. 513. The facts proved would have justified as award of at least nominal damages and, as there was a continuing completed tort, the plaintiffs were entitled to the injunction restraining the commission of that tort. I would dismiss these appeals.

Kenny J.:

The facts in this case have been so fully stated by the President of the High Court that I need not repeat them. There was ample evidence to support his findings of fact and I agree with his conclusions.

The legal wrong known as passing-off includes the incorporation in the Republic of Ireland of a company with a name likely to give the impression to the public that it is a subsidiary or branch of or is associated or connected with another company which has an established goodwill, whether the latter company is incorporated in the Republic or outside it. The incorporation with the name selected may have been with the intention of creating that impression (*Lloyds & Dawson Bros.* v. *Lloyds (Southampton) Ltd* [1912] 29 R.P.C. 433; *Harrods Ltd.* v.*R. Harrod Ltd* [1924] 41 R.P.C. 74) or innocently without knowledge of the existence of the well-known company: *Ewing* v. *Buttercup Margarine Co. Ltd* [1917] 2 Ch. 1. In either event, the wrong of passing-off may be restrained by the company with the established goodwill.

The defendants urged that this principle should be limited to cases where the well-known company has acquired some of its goodwill in the Republic by user or trading in this country. I do not see any reason why this limitation on the general principle should be imposed to-day when extensive advertising can be carried out by television, radio and newspapers-all of which go into almost every home in this State. Programmes broadcast by B.B.C.1, B.B.C.2 and U.T.V. are regularly looked at on television sets in this State. I suspect that the idea that some of the goodwill must be acquired by user or trading in the country where it is sought to protect it comes from the days when television and radio were unknown and when international trade in domestic goods was not as extensive as it is to-day. It is not an appropriate rule for this age and as no authority binds me to accept it, I refuse to do so.

The defendants relied on two cases to support the limitation which they suggested should be imposed on the general principle. The first of these of *Oertli A.G.* v. *Bowman (London) Ltd* [1957] R.P.C. 388; [1959] R.P.C. 1, in which the decision of the English Court of Appeal was confirmed in the House of Lords; it related to the passing off of goods of a Swiss company. It was not established in the case that the plaintiffs were associated in the public mind with the goods: their name did not appear on them or in the advertisements in connection with them. The plaintiffs were unknown so far as the public in Britain was concerned. In the case which we are considering, the name "C & A" is well known in this country although the company does not carry on any trading activities here because they have a large store in Belfast and many others in Britain and because they have carried out extensive advertising on television and radio and in the newspapers. The second case on which the defendants rely is *Alain Bernardin* v. *Pavilion Properties Ltd.* [1967] R.P.C. 581 and, in my opinion, it is incorrect and should not be followed. I think that the judge who decided it erred in thinking that *Oertli's Case* [1957] R.P.C. 388; [1959] R.P.C. 1 required him to decide that a company with a goodwill in France and which had carried out an extensive advertising campaign in Britain could not protect its well-known name ("The Crazy Horse Saloon") in England because it could not establish that it had carried on any activities (other than advertising) in that country. This decision is rightly criticised in *Kerly's Law of Trade Marks and Trade Names* (10th ed.p.386).

The passage so strongly relied on by the defendants in the judgment of Jenkins L.J. in the Court of Appeal in the *Oertli Case* [1957] R.P.C. 388; [1959] R.P.C. 1 reads at p.397 of the report:–"It is of course essential to the success of any claim in respect of passing-off based on the use of a given mark or get-up that the plaintiff should be able to show that the disputed mark or get-up has become by user in this country distinctive of the plaintiff's goods so that the use in relation to any goods of the kind dealt in by the plaintiff of that mark or get-up will be understood by the trade and the public in this country as meaning that the goods are the plaintiff's goods. The gist of the action is that the plaintiff, by using and making known the mark or get-up in relation to his goods, and thus causing it to be associated or identified with those goods, has acquired a quasi-proprietary right to the exclusive use of the mark or get-up in relation to goods of that kind, which right is invaded by any person who, by using the same or some deceptively similar mark or get-up in relation to goods not of the plaintiff's manufacture, induces customers to buy from him goods not of the plaintiff's manufacture as goods of the plaintiff's manufacture, thereby diverting to himself orders intended for and rightfully belonging to the plaintiff." This passage relates to passing off by the use of a trade mark or get-up of goods (as the judge emphasises) and has no application to passing off by the use of a well-known name. This is, I think, the distinction which the judge who decided the *Bernardin Case* [1967] R.P.C. 581 did not make. I think that an injunction should have been granted in that case.

The plaintiffs in the cases before us have a goodwill in the Republic of Ireland although they do not carry on any trading activities here. No explanation has been given by the defendants as to why they adopted the symbol "C & A" in the names of the two companies which they formed. I have no doubt that their sole motive in forming the two defendant companies with the name which they used was to create the false impression that these two companies were, in some way, associated with or connected with the plaintiffs. I think that these two appeals should be dismissed.

Chapter 6

SPECIFIC PERFORMANCE

This is the second major remedy developed by equity which is of special relevance to conveyancing contracts, see *Irish Conveyancing Law,* para. 12.36 *et seq, ;* also *Irish Land Law,* para. 3.142 *et seq.* It is, however, a more limited remedy than an injunction being confined to certain contracts only and being subject to a wide range of "defences".

I. GENERAL PRINCIPLES

BAGNELL V. EDWARDS
(1876) I.R. 10 Eq. 215 (Vice-Chancellor's Court)

Specific performance was sought of a partnership agreement under which the defendant agreed, *inter alia* , to pay one-half of the capital sum of £2000 in respect of a joint operation with the plaintiff to build a branch line of a railway for the Midland Great Western Railway Co.

Chatterton V.-C. :

I am of opinion that this suit cannot be maintained. It does not pray a dissolution of the partnership, but asks for a decree for the specific performance of the partnership contract in general terms. The only breach of that contract proved against the Defendant is that he has not paid up his one-half of the presented capital, in which respect, I may observe the Plaintiff is admittedly in the same position, not having paid his half of the £2000 into the Bank. The Plaintiff has, in consequence of this default, been obliged to advance sums out of his own monies to pay the current expenses of the concerns, while the Defendant has not paid anything. Such an event is contemplated by the partnership agreement, which by its 9th clause provides that a partner providing a larger share of the capital than his own moiety shall be repaid his advances by the defaulter with interest at 10 per cent per annum. The relief actually sought is nothing but the payment of money, for which an action at law can be maintained by one partner against the other, and the 9th clause measures the damages so to be recovered. The principle of this Court is not to decree specific performance in such a case. The allegations made about the refusal of the Defendant to sign cheques show that these were only temporary objections yielded by the Defendant soon after they were made, and no such default existed when the bill was filed.

I must, therefore, dismiss the bill, but as the Defendant is by his own admissions in default, I shall do so without costs.

Note

Cf. Gorringe v. *The Land Improvement Society,* p.*161* , *infra.*

SMELTER CORPORATION OF IRELAND LTD. V. O'DRISCOLL
[1977] I.R. 305 (Supreme Court)

The facts are set out in the Chief Justice's judgment.

O'Higgins C.J.:

This is an appeal brought by the plaintiffs from the decision and judgment of Mr. Justice Butler refusing their claim for specific performance of an agreement entered into by the defendant for the sale to them of 55 acres 0 roods and 36 perches of land situate at Carrigrenan in the county of Cork.

The plaintiffs are a limited liability company formed for the purpose of establishing in Ireland a smelter or base-metal reduction plant. At the time of the agreement sought to be enforced, the plaintiffs were engaged in the acquisition of land as a suitable site for such a plant in the Little Island area of Cork. The defendant is the owner of the land which is the subject of the agreement, but the negotiations in relation to the agreement were conducted on her behalf by her husband, Michael O'Driscoll, and later by her solicitor who has since died. The agreement necessarily took the form of an option to purchase, and was dated the 25th November, 1969.

Under the agreement the plaintiffs, in consideration of the payment of £7,000, were given for 12 months an option to purchase at a price to be determined by Mr. Owen MacCarthy (the well-known arbitrator to the Land Values Reference Committee) on an arbitration specially held for that purpose. Provision was made for the extension of the option for a further period of six months on the payment of a further sum of £3,250 and there were other clauses which are not relevant to the issues raised in this appeal. In the event of the option being exercised, it was provided that the option payments should be credited against the purchase money and, if the option was not exercised for any of the three grounds set out in clause 9, it was provided that one-half of such sums should be returned to the plaintiffs and that, in the meantime, such one-half should be secured on deposit. On the 10th January, 1970, Mr. Owen MacCarthy determined in his arbitration award that the purchase price of the land should be at the rate of £1,500 per acre, which resulted in a purchase price of £82,837.50.

By letter dated the 23rd November, 1970, the plaintiffs took a second option for six months for the sum of £3,250 which was thereupon paid to the defendant's solicitor. A third option for six months was then purchased by the plaintiffs as a result of negotiations between the auctioneer acting for the plaintiffs, Mr. Ahern, and the defendant's solicitor. The consideration for this option was also £3,250, but this sum was not to be credited against the purchase money should the plaintiffs exercise the option. At the expiration of the third option, a fourth was negotiated as is evidenced by a letter dated the 24th November, 1971, from the defendant's solicitor to the plaintiffs. This option was for a further six months for a nominal consideration but on the terms that the option monies paid under the original option should now be freed to the defendant and should not be credited against the purchase money in the event of the option being exercised. In effect, this arrangement constituted the ground of a fresh option to purchase for a fixed price of £93,087.50 being £82,837.50 as fixed by Mr. MacCarthy, plus the £10,250 paid in respect of the options under the agreement of 25th November, 1969. By letter dated 15th May, 1972, the plaintiffs purported to exercise this final option. The defendant was unwilling and refused to complete and these proceedings were commenced by the plaintiffs seeking specific performance of the agreement to sell, and associated relief.

The defence to the plaintiffs' claim is based on two main grounds. In the first place it is contended at paragraph 3 of the defence that the option or options to purchase were given by the defendant "subject to a condition precedent that a smelter plant otherwise a base metal reduction plant would be built on the said lands and that the said lands would be used for no other purpose but the plaintiffs do not propose to build or utilise a smelter plant or base metal reduction plant on the said lands and the said condition precedent to the exercise of the said option has not been fulfilled and will not be fulfilled and the plaintiff is thereby debarred from exercising the said or any option."

At paragraph 4 of the defence it is also contended with regard to the option that "the same was obtained from the defendant under duress and coercion whereby the plaintiffs caused or permitted a local authority to clearly give her to understand that if she did not sell the said lands or give an option over the same to the plaintiffs for the purpose of a smelter plant or base metal reduction plant, then the said lands would be acquired by compulsory acquisition by the said local authority and given to the plaintiffs for the stated purpose, and the defendant believed that this threat would be carried out to her damage and it was further represented to the defendant that she had a national and patriotic duty to permit employment on a large scale to be afforded by the plaintiffs at the said smelter plant or base metal reduction plant and it was in those circumstances and only on the understanding and pre-condition, express or implied, as hereinbefore indicated, that the defendant afforded such option to the plaintiffs."

To assess the validity of these two grounds of defence or of either of them, regard must be had to the evidence adduced at the trial before the learned High Court judge. Apart from the documents already referred to which relate to evidence of the option arrangements entered into between the parties, it appears that much happened before these arrangements became possible. The plaintiffs had engaged Mr. Ahern (the principle of Marsh & Co., auctioneers) to conduct negotiations on their behalf with local land owners including the defendant.

On behalf of the plaintiffs Mr. Ahern interviewed the defendant's husband and offered £800 per acre for the land which was subsequently the subject of the options. Believing that the Cork County Council as the planning authority had power under s. 77 of the Local Government (Planning and Development) Act, 1963, to acquire these lands compulsorily for the development contemplated by the plaintiffs, and further believing that, as a matter of probability, this power would be exercised, Mr Ahern so informed the defendant's husband. He did this in good faith, as the learned trial judge has found, believing his statement to represent the reality of the situation facing the defendant. Mr. Ahern followed up this verbal statement with a letter dated the 11th August, 1969, which was written to the solicitor acting for the defendant. In this letter he again made an offer of £800 per acre but added :– "We are suggesting that, since the probability of a compulsory purchase order being made is admitted, the necessity of having the order made be dispensed with and that the value of the land be submitted to an independant arbitrator acceptable to both parties, and that both parties be bound by his decision." This letter was a clear indication of Mr. Ahern's view, as the negotiator on behalf of the plaintiffs, that if the £800 per acre was not acceptable the defendant ought to agree to the price being determined by an independent arbitrator in order to avoid a compulsory purchase order.

It seems clear that the defendant's solicitor did not doubt for a moment the soundness of the view expressed by Mr. Ahern, and that subsequent negotiations were conducted on the basis that, if agreement was not possible, compulsory purchase would be the next step.

It appears that Mr. Filer, the managing director of the plaintiffs, was made aware of the manner in which Mr. Ahern was negotiating with the defendant, and of the arguments and representations he used and made. This appears from the fact that at the end of August, 1969, Mr. Filer was given Mr. Ahern's complete file of correspondence which included the letter of the 11th August.

Despite the efforts of Mr. Ahern, the defendant, through her husband, could not be persuaded to sell although the offer made on behalf of the plaintiffs was substantially increased.

By the 9th October, 1969, all negotiations had come to an end and the possibility of the plaintiffs securing the defendant's lands by agreement seemed remote in the extreme. On that date a number of people, representing the plaintiffs, called to the County Hall in Cork which is the headquarters of the Cork County Council. These included Mr. Filer, the managing director and Mr. Ahern, the auctioneer. They there met the county manager, Mr. Conlon, the chairman of the County Council, Mr. Michael Pat Murphy, the vice-chairman, Mr. Denis O'Sullivan, and the development officer, Mr. David Murphy. There appears to have been some slight conflict in the evidence at the trial as to the immediate purpose of this meeting. However, it is clear that following this meeting the county manager, the chairman, the vice-chairman, Mr. Ahern and the development officer went in a body to see the defendant's husband for the purpose of urging him to resume negotiations with the plaintiffs for the sale of the land. There was again a conflict in the evidence at the trial as to what was said at this interview with the defendant's husband. The defendant's husband maintained that it was made clear to him by the gentlemen who called to see him that, if he was not willing to sell, the lands would be acquired compulsorily by the County Council. This was disputed by the County Council witnesses. However, the learned trial judge was satisfied that at this interview there had been a reference to the compulsory purchase of the lands and that this, coupled with what had previously been said and written by Mr. Ahern, operated on the mind of the defendant's husband. This, of course, is a finding of fact by the learned trial judge which is binding on this Court.

On the following day the defendant's husband telephoned the development officer to say that he was prepared to negotiate with the plaintiffs, and the agreement was executed on the 25th November, 1969.

At the trial it was made clear by the county manager when he gave evidence that the belief held and expressed by Mr. Ahern was incorrect. The county manager made it perfectly clear in his evidence that there was no question of the County Council acquiring these lands for the plaintiffs. Whatever views he may have had as to the Council's powers in this respect, he said that such an exercise of compulsory acquisition had never been attempted and certainly was neither planned nor contemplated in this case. From this it follows that all suggestions made to the defendant's husband, to the effect that if the lands were not sold voluntarily they would be acquired compulsorily, were ill-founded.

I now turn to the grounds relied on by the defendant for resisting the order for specific performance claimed in this case. I wish to say at once that I find no substance in the first ground of objection. In my view, the purpose for which the plaintiffs sought to purchase lands or the use to which they intended to put them in no way affected the transaction. I can see no basis for suggesting that the proposed acquisition of the defendant's lands depended on the smelter project proceeding.

However, the second objection must be viewed in a different light. Specific performance is a discretionary remedy. The discretion to grant or refuse the relief must be exercised in a manner which is neither arbitrary nor capricious but which has regard to the essential fairness of the transaction involved. In effect, it is here suggested that the defendant was coerced or forced into granting the option or options to the plaintiffs by the threat of compulsory purchase. It does not seem to me on the evidence that a threat, as such, was ever used. At the same time it seems perfectly clear that the defendant was at a serious disadvantage.

The defendant's husband, who acted for her throughout the negotiations, believed that if there was not a voluntary sale there would be a compulsory acquisition of the lands. He so believed because he was told this by the plaintiffs' agent, Mr. Ahern. It is quite clear that this view was repeated to him by the defendant's solicitor, and on the 9th October, 1969, further corroboration was provided by those who came to see him and who represented Cork County Council. Believing this to be the situation, there was no real purpose in refusing to sell or to give an option once, as was suggested, the price was to be determined by an agreed arbitrator. To refuse in these circumstances meant acquisition anyway, and the determination of the price by an arbitrator in whose appointment the defendant might have no say. It now transpires that the situation was not as was intimated to the defendant's husband. It is now clear that, at the time that these negotiations were proceeding, the County Council had no plans whatsoever to interfere by way of the compulsory acquisition of the defendant's lands.

It is well established that the discretion to grant specific performance should not be exercised if the contract is not equal and fair. In this instance the defendant was under a fundamental misapprehension as to the true facts. This misapprehension was brought about by the plaintiffs' agent, Mr Ahern. While Mr. Ahern acted bona fide, this does not alter the situation which he created. He led the defendant's husband and her solicitor to believe that, if the defendant did not agree to sell, the lands would be acquired. It appears clear also that the plaintiffs' managing director was aware of the true position so far as the compulsory acquisition was concerned. It is to be noted that he had Mr Ahern's file of correspondence and, therefore, should have been aware of the incorrect picture which Mr. Ahern had painted. Nevertheless, the plaintiffs' managing director allowed the negotiations to proceed.

In these circumstance it appears to me that there was a fundamental unfairness in the transaction. The defendant agreed to sell believing that she had no real option, and the plaintiffs accepted her agreement to sell knowing that this was not so. In my view it would create a hardship and would be unjust to decree specific performance in this case. I agree with the decision of the learned trial judge. I would refuse specific performance but would order that all monies paid to the defendant by the plaintiffs be returned to the plaintiffs by the defendant.

Kenny J.:
I agree.:

Parke J.
I agree.

Notes
1. As to the discretionary nature of the remedy *cf.* the views of Black L.J. in *Conlon* v. *Murray*, p.000, *ante*.
2. As regards unfairness, see p.193, *post*.

II. CONTRACTS

GORRINGE V. THE LAND IMPROVEMENT SOCIETY
[1899] 1 I.R. 142 (Chancery Division)

The facts are set out in the judgment.

Porter M.R. :
The plaintiff, a gentleman residing in England, is the owner in fee of the estate of Fintra, in county Donegal, on which he was desirous of effecting improvements at an outlay not exceeding £4000. In 1895 he conceived the idea of charging the money upon the lands under the provisions of the Improvement of Land Act, 1864 (27 & 28 Vict., c. 114). By that Act, sect. 25 it is provided that "If the Commissioners (the Board of Works) shall find that the proposed improvements or any part thereof, whether with or without any alterations by them required or sanctioned, would effect a permanent increase of the yearly value of the lands proposed to be improved, or of any part thereof, exceeding the yearly amount proposed to be charged thereon, they shall sanction such improvements, or such part thereof as they shall think expedient, if under the preceding sections it shall be lawful for them so to do, by an Order under their hands and seal; and they shall by the same Order fix the rate of interest to be allowed on the cost of the sanctioned improvements, having regard to the market value of money at the time, but such interest shall never exceed five *per cent. per annum.*" The Order here referred to is the Provisional Order. Then section 26 provides – "The Commissioners shall from time to time prepare forms of Orders for sanctioning improvements, and shall also, whenever required by the landowner so to do, frame and entitle their said Orders under this Act in such manner that they may also be and operate as provisional, sanctioning, or other corresponding Orders under the respective Acts applying to any Company with which he may have contracted relating to the loan or improvements in question: Provided that every Order operating under this Act to sanction any improvements shall name the landowner to whom it is issued; shall express the greatest sum to be charged in addition to any cost, charges, and expenses under the fiftieth section hereof, and the rate of interest and term of years for the repayment thereof, the former not exceeding five *per cent. per annum,* and the latter not exceeding twenty-five years; shall specify the lands on which such repayment is to be charged; and shall either express or refer to some contract or other document expressing the general scheme of the improvements to be executed." And sect. 27 provides "Every Order operating under this Act alone to sanction any improvement may be in the form set forth in Schedule (A) hereto, and shall be called a Provisional Order, and shall, subject to the following section hereof, create in favour of the landowner named therein the title to an absolute charge on the completion of the sanctioned improvements, which title such landowner may assign, either absolutely or by way of security, to any person; and such assignment may be made by endorsement on the Provisional Order." The 49th, 50th and 51st sections provide for an absolute Order executing a charge on the completion of the works, or some part therof, and the expenses of application and certain contracts may be

included in the charge, the charges to be by way of rentcharge created by the absolute Order. Why Mr. Gorringe, who was, as I have said, owner in fee and not a limited owner, preferred to have recourse to the machinery of this Act, instead of raising the money by an ordinary mortgage, does not appear. The defendants' counsel say he is a rich man. I do not know how that is, not does it affect the case.

The statutory rentcharge does not take effect (save provisionally) till the money is expended. Accordingly, as he wanted the money in the first instance, he applied to the defendant company, which is incorporated amongst other things for the purpose of making such advances, for an advance, to be repaid by means of rentcharge under Provisional Orders, and after some letter-writing (of which there is no lack in the case) the defendants agreed to advance not exceeding in all £4000, in sums of not less than £400 at a time, receiving 5 per cent. commission, and being entitled to an assignment of the Provisional Order. I do not mean to read the letters, because, owing to the course which the trial took, the existence of the contract was expressly admitted. A Provisional Order was, after great delay, obtained, dated 1st June, 1896. It is as follows:– "The Commissioners of Public Works in Ireland, in pursuance of 'The Improvement of Land Act, 1864, and the Settled Land Acts, 1882, to 1890,' do by this Order under their seal sanction the proposed improvements expressed in an application made by said Thomas James Hamilton Gorringe, upon the terms and conditions that such improvements be executed in the manner mentioned or specified in the second schedule hereto, and which schedule expresses the general scheme of the improvements to be executed, and at an expense not exceeding the sum of £4000, and do hereby declare and provisionally order that it is right and proper, and for the benefit of the parties interested in the lands mentioned in the first schedule hereto, that the inheritance or fee of such lands should be charged with the said sum of £4000, together with the costs, charges, and expenses, preparatory or in relation to and consequent on the said application, and that the same should, to the whole amount of such respective moneys, be charged in the manner following, that is to say, by way of annuity, after the rate of £6 14*s* 11*d.* per centum, per annum, payable by equal half-yearly payments for the period of twenty-five years."

By instrument under seal, and bearing the same date (1st June, 1896), Mr. Gorringe assigned this Provisional Order to the defendants. It was part of the agreement for the advance that both Mr. Gorringe and Mr. Guy, his agent, should enter into a bond with the defendants for the due expenditure of the money, and they did so. Money to the extent of £1500 was actually advanced from time to time by the defendants, and there is no question but that the whole of it, and a good deal more, was duly expended by the plaintiff in exact conformity with his obligation; and so matters continued till 10th February, 1897, when the defendants insisted upon having an absolute Order from the Board of Works before making further advances (letter of February 10th, 1897). The effect of this would be, of course, that the plaintiff would have to provide the money himself in the first instance, instead of the defendants. It is admitted that they had no right to this, and that their requirement was inconsistent with their contract. Thus the contract is admitted, and its breach is admitted, and the only question is, what is the plaintiff's remedy? The plaintiff claims specific performance by the defendants of their agreement. The defendants say, No; the remedy is damages merely, and the £50 paid into Court is more than sufficient legally to compensate the plaintiff for his loss. They say that he could have had no difficulty in raising the money elsewhere, and he ought to have done so. Had he taken this course he need not have been put to any loss at all, and in short all that he can claim is nominal damages merely.

If I thought that the plaintiff's remedy was confined to damages there would have to be an inquiry, for I am clearly of opinion that the case is not one for nominal damages. See *Larios* v. *Antonio Bonany y Gurety* L.R. 5 P.C. 346 on the question of damages.

The plaintiff has incurred much trouble, inconvenience, and delay, besides some costs, in consequence of the defendants' unjustifiable conduct. He had a number of workmen engaged at Fintra whom he had to dismiss, and whom it might not be easy to replace. He lost a whole season. If he had raised the money, as was suggested, from a bank, he would have raised it as a personal loan, and upon terms quite different from those on which the defendants bargained to provide it. If he desired, as he was entitled, to raise it on the same terms and in the same way as the defendants contracted to advance it, it is not shown who would have given it on those terms, nor at what outlay nor how soon. The defendants deliberately decided to break their agreement; and whatever amount the plaintiff could lawfully recover, I am quite clear it is idle to speak of it as a case for nominal damages. All the circumstances were within the defendants' knowledge.

But the real question is, is it a case for damages only, or is the plaintiff entitled, if he chooses, to specific performance of the contract ?

The defendants say no. The contract is one for the loan of money, and that only, and this Court never specifically performs such a contract. As a general proposition it is correct to say that a mere agreement to lend money, even upon security, will not be specifically performed. If money is lent, the lender may call it in again, and therefore specific performance would be futile. Money compensation in such a case affords an adequate, and, indeed, the best remedy, and goes nearer to a complete *restitutio in integrum* than the enforcement of a loan which the lender might straightway proceed to require back, leaving the borrower in no better position after the interference of the Court. The very recent case of *South African Territories (Limited)* v. *Wallington* [1895] App. Cas. 309 was relied on as decisive of the case on this point. That was an action by a joint-stock company against a person who had agreed to take sixteen debentures, if allotted to him, and had paid a deposit of part of the amount, but after allotment refused to pay up the remaining instalments. The company claimed specific performance, and the House of Lords decided against the claim. Some of the points mainly argued in the case do not arise here, but the views of their Lordships' House on the question of specific performance, have to be noted and regarded. At page 312 Lord Halsbury, C. says: "The applicant for debentures on the face of the instrument contracts to pay something, but the real nature of the whole transaction is an agreement by the applicant to lend money at certain interest, and the action in this case was in truth mainly, if not altogether, directed to compel the intending lender to perform his contract to lend, which undoubtedly he had refused and neglected to do. With respect to the claim for specific performance, a long and uniform course of decision has prevented the application of any such remedy, and I do not understand that any Court or any member of any Court has entertained a doubt but that the refusal of the learned Judge below to grant a decree for specific performance was perfectly right." To the same effect is the opinion of Lord Watson, stated at p. 314, and that of Lord Herschell (p.315). And Lord MacNaghten says (p. 318) : "It is quite plain that the contract made by the offer of these debentures, and the acceptance of that offer is nothing more or less than a contract to borrow and a contract to lend so much money payable by instalments. The essential character of the transaction is not altered either by the circumstance that the creditor in a certain event is to have the option of exchanging his position for that of a shareholder, or by the complicated nature of the arrangements made for the lender's security. That specific performance of a contract to lend money cannot be enforced is so well establshied, and obviously so wholesome a rule, that it would be idle to say a word about it." And Lord Morris states his concurrence at page 320.

These *dicta* do no more than state what the undoubted rule of law is. It must be a question in each case whether there are facts to which the rule can be applied. In Fry on Specific Performance the law is stated thus :– "Again, the Court will specifically enforce a contract to execute a mortgage, and that even with an immediate power of sale where the money has been actually advanced either before or at the time of the contract; though it will not so enforce a mere agreement to lend, advance, or pay money (though the loan be one to be secured by mortgage), while it rests entirely unperformed either by the intended lender or by the intended borrower." And again: – "The Statute of Frauds does not apply to such a case. Therefore, if the Court has jurisdiction in such a case, any conversation may be made the subject of a suit for specific performance: thus if two friends are walking together and one says, 'will you lend me £100 at £5 per cent. for a year on good security?' and the other says, 'I will,' that conversation might be made the subject of a suit for specific performance in this Court if on the next day one friend should say, 'I do not want the money,' or the other should say, 'I will not lend it.' Nothing would be more difficult and more dangerous than the task which this Court would have to perform if it were to investigate cases of that description."

It will be observed that this is a guarded statement, and it will be found to be borne out by the cases cited. Take for instance *Rogers* v. *Challis* 27 Beav. 175, in which the law is stated with great clearness by the Master of the Rolls. He says : "The case cannot be put higher than this :–that the defendant applies to the plaintiff for the loan of £1000 upon a security which he specifies, and the plaintiff assents to the proposal, but on the next day the defendant says, 'I have changed my mind, I do not require your £1000. I can get it upon better terms elsewhere.' Is that a case in which a person can come to this Court for a specific performance, and say 'you, the defendant, are bound to let me advance the £1000 to you – it is true your circumstances may be altered, but you are bound to let me advance the money to you'?" He then puts the case quoted by Fry, L.J. in his book. He continues:– "This is not an agreement to purchase or sell anything, it is not the case of a contract to buy a particular debt upon certain terms, or a contract for the purchase of a certain quantity of goods, to be paid for by instalments and in a particular manner, in which case the Court has held, that these were circumstances which took the transaction out of the rule of this Court, that an ordinary contract for the sale or purchase of goods is not the proper subject of a suit for specific performance in this Court. It is nothing more than this:– a proposal to borrow a certain sum of money, upon certain terms, for a certain time, which is accepted, and the borrower says two or three days afterwards, I do not want the money, and I have got it elsewhere, upon better terms. It certainly is new to me that this Court has ever entertained jurisdiction in a case where the only personal obligation created is, that one person says, if you will lend me the money I will repay it and give you good security, and the terms are settled between them. The Court has said, that the reason for compelling a specific performance of a contract is because the remedy at law is inadequate or defective. But by what possibility can it be said that the remedy here is inadequate or defective ?"

Hermann v. *Hodges* L.R. 16 Eq. 18 is no exception to the general rule: for there the plaintiff had advanced his money on a contract to have a mortgage, and a common law judgment instead might have been a very different remedy for its recovery.

I do not know of any case in which when there has been a substantial part performance so that the parties cannot be restored to their original position, the aid of the Court has been withheld.

But is the present case one of a mere contract to lend money ? No doubt it is spoken of in the correspondence, and indeed for that matter in the plaintiff's pleading, as a loan; but that cannot shut out the consideration of what the real transaction was. The defendants were bound to advance money, which, when received by the plaintiff, was to be by him laid out in a specified manner in effecting certain defined and sanctioned improvements upon the lands. When completed these improvements must add to the value of the lands, and so provide part of the security for the advances which were to be repaid by a rentcharge, created by the Board of Works, and calculated so that principal and interest at 5 per cent. would be wiped off in 25 years. The defendants were to become owners of the rentcharge. There was no covenant by the plaintiff, and no personal liability, to pay off the advances; and if there were any personal liability on the part of the plaintiff, it would at most be only in aid of or as security for the payment of the rentcharge. *Thomas* v. *Sylvester* L.R. 8 Q.B. 368 does not apply to this case. If there is anything plain it is that there was no loan in the ordinary sense. The defendants having advanced their £4000, and got their absolute order and rentcharge, would plainly have no right to go to the plaintiff and say, "Now pay back our £4000." The answer would be, "Your £4000 has been spent, as you contracted it should be spent, on land. I cannot, therefore, repay it. But it adds £4000 to the value of the estate; and you are entitled to get payment, not now, but spread over 25 years; not from me, but out of the land." It is an abuse of language to call that a loan. The rentcharge was not to be a security to the defendants for an advance. It was to be their own sole and absolute property. This is in substance a purchase of a rentcharge to be created in part by means of the purchase money to be paid for it.

Now, will a common law action for damages afford an adequate remedy for the breach of this agreement? The Provisional Order sanctions expenditure to the extent of £4000. That Order has been transferred to and is at this moment vested in the defendants. No doubt it might be made part of a decree in this Court, that the defendants should retransfer this Provisional Order or so much of it as would enable the plaintiff to try to get the rest of the money elsewhere. But what would be the position then? He would have to find another purchaser of a second rentcharge, *puisne* to the first. Could he get that on the same terms ? I think it is impossible to suppose that a *puisne* rentcharge would bring as good a price as a prior one, even if a purchaser could be found for it at all. And besides this, the plaintiff would lose the benefit of his advantageous contract whereby the defendants were to take his bond in lieu of inspections of the works, and to waive all investigation of his title. No one else might be very easily and promptly found to make that arrangement; and inspections are very costly things, as the facts of this very case show.

I think that the defendants having proceeded so far with this bargain are bound to complete it. They cannot be permitted to say, we will stop short in the middle, having got the best part of the transaction: we will treat it as a contract to give us a rentcharge representing £1500; and you may go and look for someone to advance the £2500 remaining, on equally favourable terms, if you can find him. Had the plaintiff chosen to take a decree for damages, he would have been entitled to substantial and probably large damages. As he desires to have the contract carried out and completed, I think he is entitled to a decree on the ground that it would be inequitable to allow the defendants, under the circumstances proved, deliberately to violate their engagement by repudiating it in part while holding on to it so far as they considered it beneficial for themselves to do so, at the expense of plaintiff and his estate.

Notes and Questions

1. What took this case out of the general rule that specific performance will not be granted of a contract to lend money ? See *Irish Conveyancing Law*, para. 12.39.
2. *Cf. Duggan* v. *Allied Irish Building Society* Unrep. (High Court) (1974 No. 230P), *Irish Land Law*, Supp. (1975-880), p.13.

RUSHBROOKE V. O'SULLIVAN
[1908] 1 I.R. 232 (Chancery Division)

The defendant agreed to take a lease of certain premises from the plaintiff, and within twelve months from the date of the agreement to expend the sum of £600 in such substantial repairs and improvements as were mentioned in the schedule to the agreement, viz. to take down, rebuild, and repair such portion of the premises as the plaintiff's architect should direct, under his direction and to his satisfaction. The defendant did not execute the repairs and improvements mentioned in the schedule. The plaintiff brought an action against the defendant, claiming specific performance of the agreement to rebuild and repair the premises in accordance with the terms of the agreement, and damages by reason of the defendant's failure to carry out the agreement. There was no appearance for the defendant.

Meredith M.R.:

I do not see my way to make an order for specific performance in this case. The views of Courts of Equity as to enforcing covenants to build and covenants to repair have not always been consistent. In earlier days the Courts of Equity appear to have specifically enforced such covenants. Sir Edward Fry, in his book on Specific Performance, section 98 (4th ed.), p.41 states that "in some old cases, the Court of Chancery entertained suits in respect of building contracts: and what has been considered one of the earliest traces of the jurisdiction in specific performance is a dictum of Genney, J., in the 8 Edward 4, that a promise to build a house would be specifically enforced. Lord Hardwicke also maintained this view of the jurisdiction of the Court. But it is now clearly settled that, subject to certain exceptions, the Court will not specifically enforce contracts to build or repair, both because specific performance is 'decreed only where the party wants the thing in specie, and cannot have it any other way,' and because such contracts are for the most part so uncertain that the Court would be unable to enforce its own judgment." The case of *Wolverhampton Corporation* v. *Emmons* [1901] 1 K.B. 515 gives judicial sanction to the statment of the eminent text writer, and, while recognizing the general rule, affords a notable illustration and example of the class of cases in which the Courts have recognized exceptions from the general rule.

What were the facts of that case? [The Master of the Rolls referred to the report and continued.] It is plain that the determining factor in the decision of that case was the "subsequent agreement," the "supplemental agreement," by which, as Cotton L.J., says (at page 524), "the buildings to be erected were specifically defined in the particulars." This is plain from the judgments of the Master of the Rolls and and the Lords Justices.

The Master of the Rolls says (at page 522):–

> "The authorities to which reference has been made appear to me to show that, where there is a definite contract, by which a person, who has acquired land in consideration thereof, has agreed to erect on the land so acquired a building, of which the particulars are clearly specified, and the erection of which is of an importance to the other party which cannot adequately be measured by pecuniary damages, that is a case in which, according to the doctrine acted upon by Courts of Equity in relation to such matters, specific performance ought to be ordered."

Collins L.J., says (at page 524):–

> "Whatever the exact prinicple of equity on the subject may be, I think it is clear on the authorities that the elements exist in this case which in previous cases of the kind have been held to justify the Court in making a decree for specific performance. In this case land was conveyed to the defendant by the plaintiffs, part of the consideration being the covenant by him to erect buildings on it: by the subsequent agreement the buildings to be erected were specifically defined in all particulars; and, having regard to the circumstances and the position of the plaintiffs, it appear to me that damages would not be an adequate compensation to the plaintiffs for the breach by the defendant of his contract. I think, therefore, that this is a case in which the Court has power to make an order for specific performance, and in which such an order ought to be made."

Romer, L.J. says (at page 524):–

> "There is no doubt as a general rule the Court will not enforce specific performance of a building contract, but an exception from the rule has been recognized. It has, I think, for some time been held that, in order to bring himself within that exception, a plaintiff must establish three things. The first is that the building work, of which he seeks to enforce the performance, is defined by the contract; that is to say, that the particulars of the work are so far definitely ascertained that the Court can sufficiently see what is the exact nature of the work of which it is asked to order the performance. The second is that the plaintiff has a substantial interest in having the contract performed, which is of such a nature that he cannot be adequately compensated for the breach of contract by damages."

The present case does not fall within the class of exceptional cases. It fails because there are no plans, particulars, or specifications. The contract is "within twelve months from the date of the agreement to expend the sum of £600 at the least in such substantial repairs and improvements as are mentioned in the second schedule hereto of and in the said messuage, hereditaments, and premises described in the first schedule hereto, and in such manner as the landlord or his architect or surveyor shall approve or direct, and shall prove such expenditure as aforesaid to the satisfaction of the landlord or his architect or surveyor." The repairs and improvements mentioned in the second schedule are these: "To take down, rebuild, and repair such portion or portions of said premises as said architect shall direct under his directions and to his satisfaction." Where is there anything definite in that? Where is there any plan showing the particulars of the work to be done, such as was held to have been arranged and agreed upon in *Wolverhampton Corporation* v. *Emmons* [1901] 1 K.B. 515? Could anything be less definite than this schedule? If the plaintiff's architect had before action brought made out his plans and specifications, and had said: "There is what you must do: you must take down here; you must rebuild and repair there," then *Wolverhamption Corporation* v. *Emmons* [1901] 1

K.B. 515 would apply; but personally I am not disposed to extend the class of exceptions further than it has been extended. I agree that the question is a most difficult one; it must often be a matter of the utmost delicacy for the Court to determine how far it will go in granting specific performance of a covenant to build or repair; but in the present case I am clear that the exact nature of the work to be done has not been so specifically defined or ascertained as to justify a decree for specific performance.

The plaintiff is entitled to judgment on the pleadings for the breach by the defendant of his covenant; but the remedy lies in damages and in damages only. There will be judgement for the plaintiff with costs, and an inquiry as to damages. I hope that the judgment of the Court will not be misinterpreted by the defendant; he is mistaken if he thinks he will escape his liability.

Note
See further *Irish Conveyancing Law,* para. 12.40.

III. DEFENCES

1. *Lack of Formalities – Part Performance*

MULHALL V. HAREN
[1981] I.R. 364 (High Court)

The facts are set out in the judgment.

Keane J.:
The plaintiffs who live at No. 89 Patrician Villa, Stillorgan in the county of Dublin were thinking of moving house in the summer of 1978. They eventually saw a house with which they were happy, *i.e.,* No. 131 Upper Kilmacud Road, Stillorgan. This house was owned jointly by the defendants. It was on the books of a firm of estate agents called Hibernian Auctioneers Ltd. The plaintiffs made an offer of £24,000 to Mr. O'Reilly of that firm; he communicated the offer to his clients, who wanted £25,000. Ultimately, the defendants agreed to accept £24,500 and the plaintiffs informed Mr. O'Reilly on the 10th July, 1978, that this was acceptable to them. They agreed to a deposit of 25% of which £750 was to be paid immediately. On the 28th August the plaintiffs signed a contract for the sale of their own house and, as that contract provided for a closing date of the 29th September, the plaintiffs suggested that the 22nd September should be the closing date for the purchase of the defendants' house. Both parties envisaged that the transaction would be completed in the normal way by solicitors acting on their behalf, and they each instructed firms of solicitors.

On the 20th July Mr. McCarroll, on behalf of the plaintiffs, wrote to Hibernian Auctioneers as follows:–

> "*Re: 131 Upper Kilmacud Road.*
>
> Dear Sirs,
> We are acting for Mrs. Mulhall in the proposed purchase of the above property for the sum of £24,500 and we have received a bank draft in your favour for £750 and as the sale is subject to contract perhaps your would send us the contract."

On the same day Mr. McCarroll wrote to Mrs. Mulhall as follows:–

> "Dear Mrs. Mulhall,
> We duly received yours of the 19th instant and by the same post we received a letter from the Bank of Ireland sending us bank draft for £750 in favour of Hibernian Auctioneers, 20 Main Street, Clondalkin, County Dublin, but needless to remark we will not part with this bank draft until we get the contract

for sale and as soon as we do we will contact you as it will be necessary for you to sign the Contract."

On the 21st July Mr. McCarroll wrote again to Hibernian Auctioneers as follows:–

"Re: 131 Upper Kilmacud Road, re : Mrs Valerie Mulhall

Dear Sirs,
With further reference to the above, we now enclose herewith bank draft for £750, which of course, is subject to contract, and we would be obliged if you would let us have the contract immediately."

On the 26th July Mr. O'Reilly wrote to Mr. McCarroll as follows:–

"Re:Your client Mrs. Valerie Mulhall. Premises: 131 Upper Kilmacud Road, Stillorgan, County Dublin.

Dear Sirs,
We acknowledge yours of 21st instant with bank draft enclosed in the sum of £750 as deposit on the above on behalf of your client Mrs. Valerie Mulhall. We enclose receipt for same. We have written to the vendor's solicitors and no doubt you shall be hearing from them shortly. Thanking you."

The enclosed receipt was as follows:–

"Received from Mrs. Valerie Mulhall the sum of £750 deposit on property at 131 Upper Kilmacud Road, Stillorgan, Co. Dublin. Full purchase price £24,500. It is agreed that deposit would be refunded in full in event of cancellation due to inability to obtain loan or non-completion of sale due to any defect in lease on said premises."

On the 26th July Mr. O'Reilly wrote to Messrs. M.B. O'Cleirigh & Co. the solicitors for the defendants, as follows:–

"Re: Your clients, Mr. and Mrs. John Haren Sale: 131 Upper Kilmacud Road, Stillorgan, County Dublin.

Dear Sirs,
On the instructions of Mr Haren, we would confirm having sold the above property for a sum of £24,500. This sum includes floor coverings, window coverings and light fittings excepting dining-room light fittings. The purchasers are Mr. and Mrs. Mulhall, 89, Patrician Villas, Stillorgan, who are represented by J.H. McCarroll and Company, solicitors, 4 Church Street, Wicklow who await contract. We would also confirm having received a booking deposit of £750 from Mrs. Mulhall through her solicitor. Our fees agreed with Mr. Haren are £490. We trust you will now be able to proceed in this matter."

That letter was acknowledged by Messrs. O'Cleirigh & Co. on the 3rd August and they wrote to Messrs. McCarroll & Co. on the 15th August as follows:–

"Haren and Another to Mulhall and Another, 131 Upper Kilmacud Road, Stillorgan, County Dublin.

Dear Sirs,
We understand that you are acting for the purchasers of the above premises and we enclose herewith contract in duplicate together with vouching documents for completion by your clients. A holding deposit of £750 has already been paid to

Hibernian Auctioneers Limited and the balance of the deposit is £5,375. As you will see from the contract, we have inserted the 22nd September as a completion date. However, the final date for handing over possession is to be agreed between our respective clients. Please let us hear from you at your early convenience."

The contract was in the standard form of the Incorporated Law Society of Ireland and presented no unusual features. It was not returned by Mr. McCarroll and on the 6th September O'Cleirigh & Co. wrote him a reminder. The reason it was not returned was that, while Mr McCaroll was satisfied that the necessary loan finance would be available to his clients to complete the purchase, they were not actually in funds. In order to save time, Mr. McCarroll sent requisitions on title together with a draft assignment to O'Cleirigh & Co. on the 6th September, 1978. His clients having been put in funds, he wrote again on the 20th September enclosing the contract executed by the plaintiffs together with a bank draft in favour of O'Cleirigh & Co. for £5,375 (the balance of the deposit).

On the 27th September O'Cleirigh & Co. wrote to McCarroll & Co. stating that they had written to their clients regarding the signing of the contract. They wrote in those terms because Mrs. Haren had informed them that certain marital problems, which she was having with her husband, had come to a head and she was now unhappy about proceeding with the sale. Mr McCarroll, having heard nothing further, became naturally concerned with the lack of progress and, having been unable to make contact with Mr. Lane (who was the solicitor in O'Cleirigh & Co. dealing with the matter), advised his client to call directly on Mrs. Haren to find out what was holding up matters. Mrs. Mulhall did so, and was told by Mrs. Haren that she thought the deal was off. Mr McCarroll wrote on the 5th October to O'Cleirigh & Co. expressing his anxiety. There being no reply to his letter, he wrote again on the 11th October pointing out that the purchaer of Mrs. Mulhall's premises was now threatening proceedings unless possession was given.

On the 13th October O'Cleirigh & Co. wrote to McCarroll & Co. informing them that Mrs. Haren had instructed a separate solicitor and was not at present prepared to sign the contract. They suggested that Mr. McCarroll should get in touch with her solicitors, Messrs. Gerard A. Walsh, Harte & Co. McCarroll & Co. replied on the 16th October pointing out the difficulties that this created and stating their intention, if necessary, of seeking compensation from Mrs. Haren. On the same day they wrote to Gerard A. Walsh, Harte & Co. informing them of the position. There being no reply to that letter, they wrote again on the 20th October and threatened to institute proceedings. They wrote in similar terms on the 27th October, but that letter appears to have crossed a letter from Gerard A. Walsh, Harte & Co. in which they indicated that they were awaiting details of the transaction from O'Cleirigh & Co. in order to enable them to advise their client as to whether she was under any liability in contract to the plaintiffs. Gerard A. Walsh, Harte & Co. wrote again on the 2nd November stating that they had not received any further instructions and were not in a position to accept notice of any proceedings. They suggested that McCarroll & Co. should get in touch again with Mr. Lane of O'Cleirigh & Co., which they did on the 6th November. On the 13th November, 1978, O'Cleirigh & Co. wrote confirming that, as far as Mrs Haren was concerned, their instructions were withdrawn. They made it clear that, as far as Mr. Haren was concerned, he was still prepared to proceed with the transaction.

The matter did not proceed any further in correspondence; but at some time early in 1979, the plaintiffs met Mr. Haren in a licensed premises in Killorgan. When they enquired what the difficulty was, he said that, as it happened, his solicitor (Mr. Lane) was also on the premises. He brought Mr. Lane over and introduced him to Mr. and Mrs. Mulhall. There was some dispute as to the conversation that followed. Mr. and Mrs. Mulhall are under the impression that Mr. Lane told them that Mrs. Haren had signed the contract and that it had been posted to their solicitor. Mr. Lane says that he told them that he had been informed by Mrs. Haren that she was now prepared to sign the contract and was sending it to him for transmission to Mr. McCarroll. I do not attach any significance to this difference in memory: I have no doubt that all concerned were honestly trying to give their recollection of the conversation to the best of their ability, but it does not touch on any issue which has to be resolved in these proceedings. The present proceedings for specific performance had already been commenced by the issue of a plenary summons on the 20th December, 1978.

The only other matter of importance, as far as the facts are concerned, is that, although a completion date of the 22nd September had originally been typed on the contract, this was altered in ink to the 29th September. Both Mr. McCarroll and Mrs. Mulhall said that they had no recollection of making any such alteration, although Mr. Lane was satisfied that the contract, as returned to him, contained the alteration.

The plaintiffs, in these circumstances, claim specific performance of an oral agreement which, they say, was entered into for the sale to them of the property. They say that the agreement is evidenced in writing by a memorandum or note contained in the letters dated the 20th July, 21st July, 26th July, 15th August, 20th September and 27th September, 1978, and in the receipt dated the 27th July, 1978, and the draft contract executed by Mrs. Mulhall. The defendants resist the claim on the grounds, first, that there was no concluded oral agreement for the sale of the land; secondly, that if there was such an agreement, there was no memorandum or note thereof sufficent to satisfy the requirements of s. 2 of the Statute of Frauds, 1695; and, thirdly, that if there was such a memorandum or note, the agreement is, nevertheless, void by virtue of the provisions of the Family Home Protection Act, 1976.

In my opinion, there was a concluded oral agreement for the sale of the property. It is not disputed that Mr. O'Reilly was authorised by the defendants to accept an offer of £24,500 from the plaintiffs for the house. If an offer is made to an estate agent and if he communicates it to the owner and is authorised to accept it, or if the owner states that he will accept it, the agent has authority to make an open contract with the purchaser: see *Law* v. *Robert Roberts & Co.* [1964] I.R. 292 at p. 302. There is no evidence that the words "subject to contract" were used by the parties at any stage in the course of the negotiations which led to this agreement. Nor is there any evidence that the agreement was conditional upon the plaintiffs obtaining the necessary loan finance or upon no defect being ascertained in the title, as stated in the receipt furnished by Mr. O'Reilly.

The second ground of defence relied upon, *i.e.* that there was no memorandum or note of the oral agreement sufficient to satisfy the Statute of Frauds, presents considerably more difficulty and I will return to it at a later stage in this judgment.

The third gound of defence is based upon s. 3 sub-s. 1, of the Act of 1976, which provides that:– "Where a spouse, without the prior consent in writing of the other spouse, purports to convey any interest in the family home to any person except the other spouse, then, subject to subsections (2) and (3) and section 4, the purported conveyance shall be void." Section 1 sub-s. 1, defines a "conveyance" as including "... an enforceable agreement (whether conditional or unconditional) to make any such conveyance" and states that the word "convey" shall be construed accordingly. Counsel for the second defendant submitted that, assuming there was an otherwise enforceable agreement for the sale of the house to which both defendants were parties, it was nonetheless void because the second defendant had not given her prior consent in writing to that agreement. In my opinion, the ground of defence is conclusively disposed of by the recent decision of the Supreme Court in *Nestor* v. *Murphy* [1979] I.R. 326 to which I was referred. In that case, both the defendants (who were husband and wife) had signed a binding and enforceable contract for the sale of a house, which was a family home within the meaning of the Act of 1976. It was argued that the contract was void, since there had been no prior consent in writing by the wife, but that argument was unanimously rejected by the Supreme Court. In the course of his judgment, Mr. Justice Henchy said at pp. 328-9 of the report:–

> "The provisions of s. 3, sub-s. 1, are directed against unilateral alienation by one spouse. When both spouses join in the 'conveyance', the evil at which the

sub-section is directed does not exist. To construe the sub-section in the way proposed on behalf of the defendants would lead to a pointless absurdity. As is conceded by counsel for the defendants, if their construction of s. 3, sub-s. 1 is correct then either the husband or the wife could have the contract declared void because the other did not give a prior consent in writing. Such an avoidance of an otherwise enforceable obligation would be required for the protection of the family home when both spouses have entered into a contract to sell it. Therefore, it would be outside the spirit and purpose of the Act."

In my opinion, the reasoning in this passage is wholly applicable to the circumstances of the present case. I do not regard it as material that, on the assumptions I have made, the wife in the present case did not sign the contract, although she was party to it. The judgment of the Supreme Court is plainly based on the principle that a transaction to which both spouses are parties is not captured at all by the Act of 1976. In this context it is manifestly immaterial whether the spouse on whose behalf protection is claimed signs the contract herself or authorises someone to sign it on her behalf. If, for example, the evidence in *Nestor* v. *Murphy* had established that the wife's solicitor had signed the contract as agent on her behalf with her full authority because she was away at the time, I do not believe that the decision would have been any different. It follows that this ground of defence fails.

There remains the defence under s. 2 of the Statute of Frauds, 1695, which provides:–

"No action shall be brought whereby to charge any executor or administrator upon any special promise, to answer damages out of his own estate, or whereby to charge the defendant upon any special promise to answer for the debt, default, or miscarriage of another person, or to charge any person upon any agreement made upon consideration of marriage, *or upon any contract of sale of lands, tenements, or hereditaments, or any interest in or concerning them, or upon any* agreement that is not to be performed within the space of one year from the making thereof, unless the agreement upon which such action shall be brought, or some memorandum or note thereof, shall be in writing, and signed by the party to be charged therewith or some other person thereunto by him lawfully authorized."

The section is in identical terms to s. 4 of the (English) Statute of Frauds 1677. With regard to the Act of 1677, the italicised words were repealed in England and replaced by s. 40 of the Law of Property Act, 1925, which provides:–

"No action may be brought upon any contract for the sale, or other disposition of land or any interest in land, unless the agreement upon which such action is brought, or some memorandum or note thereof, is in writing, and signed by the party to be charged or by some other person thereunto by him lawfully authorised."

It has been held in England that s. 40, sub-s. 1, of the Act of 1925 is to be construed in the same manner as was applied to s. 4 of the Statute of 1677 prior to 1926: see *Tiverton Ltd.* v. *Wearwell Ltd.* [1975] Ch. 146.

It was submitted on behalf of the plaintiffs that the letters to which reference has already been made, the receipt and the draft contract together constituted a memorandum or note sufficient to satisfy the Statute of 1695. It was submitted on behalf of the defendants that the use of the expression "subject to contract" in the letters which initiated the correspondence prevented that correspondence, and the documents incorporated therewith, from constituting a sufficient memorandum or note. As I understand this submission, it is based on the proposition that the memorandum or note to which the section refers must be a memorandum or note of the agreement sued upon and, accordingly, it must recognise, either expressly or by implication, the existence of that contract. Since the use of the words "subject to contract" is inconsistent with the existence of a concluded agreement (the argument runs), the use of that expression in the memorandum or note relied upon prevents it from being a sufficient memorandum or note for the purpose of the statute.

Had the question arisen prior to the decision of the English Court of Appeal in *Law* v. *Jones* [1974] Ch. 12, it would have been possible to resolve it with comparative ease. Indeed, I venture to think that, prior to that decision, very few members of either branch of the legal profession in England or Ireland would have thought that a writing which expressly stated that a sale of property was "subject to contract" could constitute a memorandum or note sufficient to satisfy the Statute of Frauds. I believe that the same view would have been taken of a letter from a solicitor which formed part of a chain of correspondence commencing with a letter containing the "subject to contract" stipulation. A series of authorities in both jurisdictions commencing with *Winn* v. *Bull* (1877) 7 Ch.D. 29 had established beyond serious doubt the principle that an oral agreement for the sale of land which was stated to be subject to contract was not enforceable. As a result, it had become a common practice for solicitors, who were acting for parties who had entered into such oral agreements, to commence the correspondence with a letter stating that the sale was "subject to contract." Their reasons for doing so were twofold. In the first place, they were conscious of the danger of committing their clients to an open contract for the sale of land by writing a letter which provided the necessary writing to satisfy the statute, a danger which was of particular significance having regard to the complexity of the law of real property. In the second place, they were alive to the possibility that disputes might arise as to the actual terms of the concluded bargain which could only result in expensive litigation.

But while this practice was common, it was by no means universal. Occasions arose, perhaps particularly in the sale of registered land, when the title was so abundantly clear as greatly to reduce the dangers to either party of an open title. There were also occasions on which solicitors, mindful of the fact that their clients had secured good bargains, avoided the use of the phrase "subject to contract." In such cases, however, the solicitors frequently used language which indicated that the parties contemplated the execution of a formal agreement. Thus, a solicitor initiating the correspondence, while not stating that the sale was "subject to contract," might use some expression such as "please let us have draft contract for approval." In cases where a dispute arose as to whether, in such circumstances, an enforceable contract existed, the court had to undertake an enquiry as to what was the intention of the parties and, in particlar, what was the significance of the fact that they comtemplated the execution of a formal agreement. These cases must be carefully distinguished from the cases in which the documents stated that the sale was "subject to contract." They are fully reviewed in the judgment of Mr. Justice Kenny in *Law* v. *Robert Roberts & Co.* [1964] I.R. 292, which was unanimously upheld by the Supreme Court on appeal. They are also reviewed in detail in the judgment delivered by Mr. Justice Costello on the 28th July, 1977, in *Arnold* v. *Veale* (No. 3242P) [1979] I.R. 342n where the judge was at pains to draw the distinction between the two lines of authority.

One of the earliest statements of the principle that the use of the phrase "subject to contract" normally indicates that neither party to an arrangement intends to be bound by the terms of the arrangement until they are embodied in a form of contract is to be found in *Winn* v. *Bull* (1877) 7 Ch. D. 29. In that case, the defendant agreed with the plaintiff to take a lease of a house for a certain term at a certain rent "subject to the preparation and approval of a formal contract." No other contract was ever entered into between the parties. At p. 30 of the report Jessel M.R. said:– "Now with regard to the construction of letters which are relied upon as constituting a contract, I have always thought that the authorities are too favourable to specific performance. When a man agrees to buy an estate, there are a great many more stipulations wanted than a mere agreement to buy the estate and the amount of purchase-money that is to be paid. What is called an open contract was formerly a more perilous thing, and even now, notwithstanding the provisions of a recent Act of Parliament – the Vendor and Purchaser Act, 1874 – no prudent man who has an estate to sell would sign a contract of that kind, but would stipulate that certain conditions should be inserted for his protection. When, therefore, you see a stipulation as to a formal agreement put into a contract, you may say it was not put in for nothing, but to protect the vendor against that very thing. Indeed, notwithstanding protective conditions, the vendor has not infrequently to allow a deduction from the purchase-money to induce the purchaser not to press requisitions which the law allows him to make. All this shews that contracts for purchase of lands should contain something more than can be found in the short and meagre form of an ordinary letter."

At p. 32 Jessel M.R. said:– "It comes, therefore, to this, that where you have a proposal or agreement made in writing expressed to be subject to a formal contract being prepared, it means what is says; it is subject to and is dependent upon a formal contract being prepared. When it is not expressly stated to be subject to a formal contract it becomes a question of construction, whether the parties intended that the terms agreed on should merely be put into form, or whether they should be subject to a new agreement the terms of which are not expressed in detail. The result is, that I must hold that there is no binding contract in this case, and there must therefore be judgment for the Defendant."

The latter passage was cited by Molony C.J. in the leading Irish case: *Thompson* v. *The King* [1920] 2 I.R. 365. In that case, the words used were "subject contract" and it was held that the agreement came within what might be called the "subject to contract" line of authorities as distinct from the line of authorities applied in *Law* v. *Robert Roberts & Co.* [1964] I.R. 292. Accordingly, the agreement was held to be unforceable. Gibson J. put the matter thus at p. 390 of the report:– "2. Did this expression 'subject contract' defer contractual obligation till a formal contract was settled, accepted, and executed; or does it mean that the purchase terms having been fully and finally settled, a further contract was only contemplated for the purpose of putting the bargain into legal shape, without substantial additions or alterations? I adopt the former constuction."

In *Lowis* v. *Wilson* [1949] I.R. 347 an attempt was made to distinguish *Winn* v. *Bull* (1877) 7 Ch. D. 29 on the ground that the agreement signed by Lowis, the plaintiff purchaser, stated that it was "subject to the preparation of a formal contract to be prepared by W.O. Armstrong, Solicitor for the vendor . . . " Dixon J. rejected the submissions that this rendered the case distinguishable from *Winn* v. *Bull.* Recently in *In re Hibernian Transport Co. Ltd* [1972] I.R. 190 Mr. Justice Walsh said at p. 202 of the report:– ". . . in the ordinary course of events an agreement for the sale or purchase of land subject to contract means nothing more than an agreement to enter into a contract for the sale of land and, as such, it is not enforceable as if it were a contract." It is right to say that this observation of the learned judge was probably *obiter,* but it is nonetheless noteworthy that no other member of the full Supreme Court who agreed with his judgment on the principal issue expressed any dissent from his view on this matter.

The same principle was applied in England in a number of cases subsequent to *Winn* v. *Bull* (1877) 7 Ch. D. 29: see *Sante Fé Land Co. Ltd.* v. *Forestal Land Co. Ltd.* (1910) 26 T.L.R. 534, *Coope* v. *Rideout* [1921] 1 Ch. 291; *Chillingworth* v. *Esche* [1924] 1 Ch. 97; *Locket* v. *Norman-Wright* [1925] Ch. 56; *Keppel* v. *Wheeler* [1927] 1 K.B. 577; *Raingold* v. *Bromley* [1931] 2 Ch. 307; *George Trollope & Sons* v. *Martyn Bros.* [1934] 2 K.B. 436 – that case was disapproved of by the House of Lords in *Luxor (Eastbourne) Ltd.* v. *Cooper* [1941] A.C. 108, but not on this "subject to contract" point – *Spottiswoode, Ballantyne & Co.* v. *Doreen Appliances Ltd.* [1942] 2 K.B. 32 (*per* Lord Greene M.R. at p. 35) and *D'Silva* v. *Lister House Ltd.* [1971] Ch. 17. It was also the view of a particularly strong Court of Appeal (consisting of Lord Greene M.R., Cohen and Asquith L.JJ.) in *Eccles* v. *Bryant & Pollock* [1948] Ch. 93. In this latter case, indeed, it was made clear that, in England at all events, where parties enter into an agreement for the sale of real property "subject to contract," the contract is not complete until the parties have exchanged their copies in accordance with ordinary conveyancing practice in that country. Accordingly, in that case, even though the vendor's solicitors had signed the contract, it was held that the fact that no exchange of contracts had taken place was sufficient to prevent an enforceable contract from coming into being. In this country, however, the practice of exchanging contracts is not so universally followed as in England, at all events outside Dublin, as is borne out by the evidence of Mr. McCarroll, the very experienced solicitor for the plaintiffs. Subject to that qualification, however, the law in both jurisdictions on this topic was the same and, until recent years, was settled, in my view, by this massive body of authority beyond any serious doubt.

But while the law on this topic had the advantages of reasonable certainty, it was also capable of producing results which appeared harsh and unjust. The extraordinary volatile market in land which developed in England and Ireland during the 1970's also led to a practice as unattractive as its name which is "gazumping." A vendor of land who had shaken hands on a deal frequently found himself with a substantially more attractive offer for the property within days, or even hours. There were many vendors who, whatever the temptations, refused to resile from bargains freely entered into, whether they were legally enforceable or not. But there were also some who either accepted the higher offer or went back to their original purchaser and attempted to squeeze more money out of him. Where no shadow of a memorandum in writing existed, even the most resourceful of lawyers or courts were powerless to redress such inequities unless, indeed, the doctrine of part performance could be successfully invoked. But where anything which could conceivably be regarded as a memorandum existed considerable ingenuity was naturally expended upon bringing about the downfall of the "gazumper." It was perhaps to be expected that, in that context, some attempt would be made to dislodge the well-entrenched "subject to contract" rule.

The first bridgehead was effected in *Griffiths* v. *Young* [1970] Ch. 675. The plaintiff in that case wished to buy a plot of land from the defendant, who was not anxious to complete the contract of sale immediately. In April, 1963, the defendant asked the plaintiff to guarantee his bank overdraft and the plaintiff said that he was prepared to consider doing so if the defendant would agree to sell the land in question. The parties discussed all the terms of the contract of sale and subsequently visited their solicitors. On the 2nd May the plaintiff's solicitor wrote to the defendant's solicitor setting out all the terms of the agreement for the sale of the land, but the price was expresssed to be "subject to contract." On the 3rd May the defendants began pressing the plaintiff to provide the bank guarantee. The plaintiff got in touch with his solicitor, who telephoned the defendant's solicitor and informed him that if the defendant was to have the plaintiff's guarantee at once there must be a binding contract of sale at once, and that the reference to the arrangements being treated as "subject to contract" must be regarded as having been amended. Later on the same day, the defendant's solicitor replied to the letter of the 2nd May as follows:– "With reference to your letter of the 2nd instant, we confirm that we have received instructions from Mr. Young (*the defendant*) to sell the property mentioned in your letter . . . for £3,500 with completion at Michaelmas 12 month . . . " He signed the letter as agent for the defendant. On the 7th May the plaintiff gave the guarantee. In an action for specific performance of the agreement, the trial judge held that the letter of 2nd May amounted to an unconditional offer and the letter of 3rd May was an acceptance of this offer, and he granted a decree of specific performance. The defendant appealed on the ground that there was no sufficient memorandum or note of the agreement to satisfy s. 40, sub-s. 1, of the Act of 1925.

It was argued on behalf of the defendant that, while the two letters taken together constituted a memorandum, they could not constitute a memorandum of the agreement mentioned in s. 40, since the first letter contained on its face an assertion (in the words "subject to contract") that no agreement had been concluded. It was argued on behalf of the plaintiff that the phrase "subject to contract" was not a term of the contract but merely referrred to a "suspensive condition" which had been subsequently waived and could, accordingly, be ignored for the purpose of determining whether there was a sufficient memorandum or not of the agreement actually concluded. Widgery L.J., as he then was, thought the point a difficult one; but he appears to have accepted the general principle that a memorandum which, on its face, asserted that agreement had not been reached, could not be a memorandum for the purpose of section 40. He accepted the submission made on behalf of the plaintiff that this principle had no application where the only defect in the memorandum was a reference to a "suspensive provision" which had subsequently been waived. The other members of the Court (Russell and Cross L.JJ.) came to the same conclusion, but neither of them appear to have experienced the same difficulty which troubled Widgery L.J. They were both satisfied that the subsequent oral waiver of the "suspensive condition" cured any defect in the memorandum.

The far-reaching implications of the decision in *Griffiths* v. *Young* [1970] Ch. 675 soon became apparent when *Law* v. *Jones* [1974] Ch. 112 came before the same court – this time composed of Russell, Buckley and Orr L.JJ. In that case there was an oral agreement on the 17th February, 1972, for the sale by the defendant to the plaintiff of a certain property for £6,500. On the 18th February, the defendant's solicitors wrote to the plaintiff's solicitors referring to the plaintiff's "proposed purchase of the above property for £6,500 subject to contract" and stating that they would obtain the title deeds and submit a draft contract as soon as possible. On the 25th February, they wrote again referring to the earlier letter and enclosing the draft contract which contained all the essential terms of the agreement. On the 7th March the plaintiff's solicitors acknowledged receipt of both letters and draft contract. The defendant then sought a further £1,000 and on the 13th March the parties agreed orally to increase the price to £7,000. The trial judge accepted the plaintiff's evidence that on that occasion the defendant said to the plaintiff:– "I shall not go back on my word. My word is my bond. It is yours now: carry on and make all your arrangements." The defendant's solicitors wrote on the 17th March confirming that an increase in the purchase price to £7,000 had been agreed. A completion date of the 21st April, 1972, was agreed. But on the 13th April the defendant wrote to the plaintiff informing him that, because of the upsurge in house prices, he had decided to put the property up for auction. It was as blatant and indefensible a piece of "gazumping" as could be imagined.

On this occasion, Russell L.J. found himself in the minority. He said at p. 119 of the report that the language of the writings prior to the letter dated the 17th March could not constitute a sufficient memorandum of the oral contract of the 17th February at the price of £6,500 because of the language of the first letter in the chain dated the 18th February, *i.e.* the reference to a "proposed purchase . . . subject to contract." The letter of 17th March was, accordingly, no more than a written record of an agreed variation of a term in a contract which was still in the course of negotiation. He thought it unnecessary to decide whether the written memorandum had to point positively to an existing contract; it was clear, in his view, that at the very least, the language used must not negative the existence of a contract. He distinguished *Griffiths* v. *Young* [1970] Ch. 675 on the basis that in that case "subject to contract" was merely a suspensive condition which had been later orally agreed to be waived and was, therefore, to be treated as not incorporated in the letter of the 3rd May.

Buckley L.J. considered that little turned on the use of the expression "his proposed purchase" in the letter of the 18th February, 1972. Much of his judgment is devoted to considering the effect of the words "subject to contract" in the same letter. He accepted that a writing which denied the existence of a contract could note constitute a written memorandum or note for the purposes of the section: but he did not consider it necessary that the writing should positively acknowledge the existence of a contract. There was only one qualification, in his view, to the latter proposition. The qualification was that, where the writing denied liability under the contract, it was essential that the writing should also acknowledge the existence of the contract since, otherwise, it could only reasonably be read as a denial of its existence. In the instant case, an entirely new contract had been entered into on the 13th March, the terms of which had admittedly to be ascertained by reference to the earlier contract of the 17th February and the correspondence arising out of it, but in his view this did not mean that the letter of the 17th March acknowledging the new contract should be read as being qualified by the words "subject to contract" contained in the letter of the 18th February.

So far as the applicable law is concerned, the crucial passage from the judgment of

Buckley L.J. appears at p. 124 of the report:– "But it is not, in my judgment, necessary that the note or memorandum should acknowledge the existence of a contract. It is not the fact of agreement but the terms agreed upon that must be found recorded in writing." In support of this far-reaching proposition, Buckley L.J. cited a passage from the judgment of Lord Westbury L.C. in *Chinnock* v. *Ely* (1865) 4 De G.J. & Sm. 638 which had also been cited with approval by Lord Cairns in *Rossiter* v. *Miller* (1878) 3 App. Cas. 1124. He also referred to what he described as the "well established law" that an offer in writing, signed by or on behalf of the offeror, may serve as an effective memorandum or note in writing although accepted only orally; he said that in such a case the writing clearly could not record or acknowledge a contract existing at the time of writing. One other feature of Buckley L.J.'s judgment must be noted. He said at p. 124 of the report:– "It is clear that where a principal has entered into a binding contract, neither he nor his solicitor can thereafter deprive it of its binding effect by unilaterally treating the transaction as 'subject to contract' ..." He also appears to have taken the view that the solicitor in that case when using the phrase "subject to contract" had acted without authority.

Orr L.J. agreed with Buckley L.J. and, accordingly, the appeal in *Law* v. *Jones* was dismissed.

In the words of Lord Denning M.R. at p. 159 of the report of *Tiverton Ltd* v. *Wearwell Ltd* [1975] Ch. 146, the decision in *Law* v. *Jones* [1974] Ch. 112 "sounded an alarm bell" in the offices of every solicitor in England. I recall the decision being greeted with equal consternation in Ireland. In England, it prompted a leading article in the Solicitor's Journal (117 So. Jo. 293) and a lengthy correspondence from solicitors in the same periodical. The earliest possible opportunity was taken of questioning the correctness of the decision. The appeal from the order of Goulding J. in *Tiverton Ltd* v. *Wearwell Ltd.* [1975] Ch. 146 was heard by the Court of Appeal (Lord Denning M.R., Stamp and Scarman L.JJ.) as a matter of urgency within a few months.

In the *Tiverton Case* the plaintiffs orally agreed on the 4th July, 1973, on a sale of property in Stepney to the defendants for £190,000. All the terms of the contract were agreed. Each side agreed to instruct their solicitors to confirm the sale. The purchasers' solicitors wrote on the same day to the vendors' solicitors as follows :–

> *"Empire House*
> We understand that you act for the vendor in respect of the proposed sale of the above-mentioned property to our clients Wearwell Ltd. at £190,000 leasehold subject to contract. We look forward to receiving the draft contract for approval together with copy of the lease at an early date."

On the next day the vendors wrote to the purchasers as follows :–

> "This is to confirm my telephone conversation with you this morning when you agreed that the completion of the purchase of the property can take place as soon as possible."

On the 9th July the vendors' solicitors wrote to the purchasers' solicitors :–

"We refer to your letter dated July 4, upon which we have taken our client's instructions. We now send you draft contract for approval, together with a spare copy for your use, together with a copy of the lease dated October 30, 1934, and photocopy entries on our client's land certificate. We await hearing from you."

On the 19th July the vendors' solicitors wrote to the purchasers' solicitors saying that they understood that the matter was not proceeding any further. The purchasers' solicitors thereupon registered a caution at the Land Registry to prevent any dealings with the property by the vendors. The vendors thereupon issued proceedings claiming a declaration that there was no valid and enforceable contract, and asking for an order that the registration of the caution be vacated. Goulding J. ordered that the caution be cancelled and the purchasers appealed to the Court of Appeal. The appeal was specially expedited because of the importance of the point.

Lord Denning, after a detailed review of the authorities, summed up his view of the law as follows at p. 160 of the report :– "I cannot myself see any difference between a writing which –(i) denies there was any contract; (ii) does not admit there was any contract; (iii) says that the parties are in negotiation; or (iv) says that there was an agreement 'subject to contract,' for that comes to the same thing. The reason why none of those writings satisfies the statute is because none of them contains any recognition or admission of the existence of a contract." He thought that *Griffiths* v. *Young* [1970] Ch. 675 could be distinguished. In his view, however, *Law* v. *Jones* [1974] Ch. 112 was not capable of being distinguished; it was wrongly decided and should be overruled. In the course of his judgment, Lord Denning expressed his disagreement with the view of Buckley L.J. that authority for the proposition that the writing need not recognise the existence of a contract was to be found in a series of decisions dealing with offers in writing which were accepted by the other party by word of mouth or by conduct. He pointed out at p. 158 of the report that these were decisions of common-law courts which did not recognise the doctrine of part performance and were, accordingly, necessary to meet the justice of the individual cases. It was accordingly held that a proposal made in writing but accepted verbally was capable of constituting a sufficient memorandum or note : see *Reuss* v. *Picksley* (1866) L.R. 1 Exch. 342. But Denning M.R. also cited a passage from the judgment of Bowen L.J. in *In re New Eberhardt Co.* (1889) 43 Ch. D. 118, in which he said that *Reuss* v. *Picksley* had pushed the literal construction of the Statute of Frauds "to a limited beyond which it would perhaps be not easy to go."

At p. 162 of the report of the *Tiverton Case* [1975] Ch. 146 Stamp L.J. posed the question for decision as being ". . .whether it is the law of England that a note or memorandum can satisfy the statute if, when read alone or with other documents which can properly be read with it, he who has signed it does not thereby recognise the existence of the contract upon which the other party seeks to make him liable." He went on to say that the letter of 9th July, 1973, whether read in isolation or together with the letter to which it was a reply, did not recognise the existence of a contract made orally on the 4th July or any contract. While he does not say so in so many words, I think it is an inescapable inference that it was the use of the phrase "proposed sale . . . subject to contract" in the letter of the 4th July which rendered that letter incapable of being read as recognising the existence of a contract. Having gone on to consider the authorities in detail, at p. 168 of the report he summarised his view as follows:– "I consider that prior to the year 1970 it had been recognised by authorities binding upon this court (viz. *Buxton* v. *Rust* (1872) L.R. 7 Exch. 279 and *Thirkell* v. *Cambi* [1919] 2 K.B. 590) that to satisfy the requirements of the statute there must be in the note or memorandum of the contract upon which the action is brought something to indicate that the party signing it thereby acknowledges or recognises the existence of the contract." He also dealt with the "offer" cases and said that they did not assist the defendants since those cases proceeded on the basis that a proposal in writing, though prior in time, could be a memorandum or note of a contract brought into being by the oral acceptance. He said that in such cases the court, in so holding, was accepting that the memorandum must recognise the contract on which the party charged is sued.

At p. 165 of the report of the *Tiverton Case* Stamp L.J. quoted the succinct observation of Bowen L.J. in *In re Hoyle ; Hoyle* v. *Hoyle* [1893] 1 Ch. 84 that the court, in determining whether a document is a sufficient memorandum, is not "in quest of the intention of the parties, but only of evidence under the hand of one of the parties to the contract that he has entered into it." At p. 167 he also pointed out that in *Buxton* v. *Rust* (which was not cited to the court in *Law* v. *Jones)* Willes J. and Lush J. both clearly indicated that, in their view, it was necessary that the letter relied on should constitute a recognition of the contract sued upon. At p. 170 he closely analysed the passage from *Chinnock* v. *Ely* (1865) 4 De G.J. & Sm. 638, on which

Buckley L.J. had placed reliance, and concluded that it did not support the inferences drawn from it by Buckley L.J. He went on to express his view that *Griffiths* v. *Young,* in so far as it decides the contrary, was in conflict with the earlier decisions to which he had referred in his judgment. Although accepting that *Law* v. *Jones* was plainly in conflict with the view of the law which he considered had been established by earlier authorities, he did not consider that the court had jurisdiction to overrule it and simply preferred to follow earlier authorities.

Scarman L.J. agreed with Stamp L.J. In the result, the appeal in the *Tiverton Case* was dismissed. Leave to appeal to the House of Lords was granted but the appeal, so far as I can ascertain, was never pursued.

There are two features of the *Tiverton Case* which are of cardinal importance. In the first place, it proceeded on the assumption that the evidence would establish, if the issue had to be resolved, that there was a concluded oral agreement for the sale of the property. In the second place, the letter containing the words "subject to contract" was written by the solicitors for the purchasers, *i.e.* the party who was seeking to enforce the oral agreement. The letter which was relied on as a memorandum did not contain those words, but it formed part of the same chain of correspondence. In its major features, accordingly, that case is indistinguishable from the present case.

Since the other members of the court did not share the view of Lord Denning that the Court of Appeal in England had jurisdiction to overrule its earlier decisions, the position in theory in England is that there are at least two conflicting decisions of the Court of Appeal and that the law in that jurisdiction cannot be regarded as certain beyond doubt. However, I think that it is more sensible to regard the forceful judgments of Lord Denning and Stamp L.J. as representing the view of the law generally now held in England.

Buckley L.J. in *Daulia Ltd.* v. *Four Millbank* [1978] Ch. 231 had this to say about the two cases at p. 250 of the report:– "*Law* v. *Jones* did not decide that a letter written 'subject to contract' or forming part of a correspondence conducted subject to a 'subject to contract' stipulation can constitute a note or memorandum of an oral agreement to which it relates sufficient to satisfy the Statute of Frauds, at any rate so long as the 'subject to contract' stipulation remains operative. What it did decide was that, if the parties subsequently enter into a new and distinct oral agreement, the facts may be such that the earlier letter may form part of a sufficient note or memorandum of the later oral agreement notwithstanding that it was 'subject to contract' in relation to the earlier bargain. It also, of course, decided the quite different point that a written note or memorandum to satisfy the statute need not acknowledge the existence of the contract, although it must record all its essential terms. In that respect *Law* v. *Jones* and *Tiverton Estates Ltd.* v. *Wearwell Ltd.* are undoubtedly in conflict."

The reconciliation by the court in the *Tiverton Case* of the offer cases was sharply criticised by Buckley L.J. in the *Daulia Case.* But it also seems clear that the authority of *Law* v. *Jones* must be significantly weakened by the fact that *Buxton* v. *Rust,* a decision strongly in favour of the defendant, was not cited to the court.

The *Tiverton Case* was referred to in two subsequent English decisions. In *Michael Richards Properties* v. *St. Saviour's Parish* [1973] 3 All E.R. 416 Goff, J., (as he then was) treated the words "subject to contract" as meaningless where they appeared in a tender document which set out all the conditions which would normally appear in a standard contract of sale. He made it clear that his decision was not intended to cast any doubt on the meaning, effect and protection of the words "subject to contract" as used in the normal conveyancing practice of everyday life. In *Munton* v. *Greater London Council* [1976] 1 W.L.R. 649 the Court of Appeal (Lord Denning, Scarman and Goff L.JJ.) treated the earlier case as distinguishable. Lord Denning, in particular, treated it as a very special case which had been decided on its own facts. I may finally note that the opinion of academic commentators upon *Law* v. *Jones* and the *Tiverton Case* appears to favour strongly the view taken in the latter case: see (1974) 90 L.Q.R. 1 and (1974) 37 M.L.R. 695. I have come to the conclusion that I should follow the latter case unless, of course, it has been disapproved of in this country.

It appears to me that the wording of s. 2 of the Statute of 1695 plainly envisages a writing which is evidence of a contract entered into by the party sought to be charged, and that this is not met by a writing which uses language inconsistent with the existence of a concluded contract. It also appears to mean that a long line of authorities has clearly established that the use of the words "subject to contract" is inconsistent with the existence of a concluded agreement, save in the most exceptional cases.

The post-1970 Irish decisions commence with *Arnold* v. *Veale* [1979] I.R. 342 n. That, as I have already indicated, was not a "subject to contract" case when it was heard and decided by Mr. Justice Costello. However, prior to the hearing of the defendant's appeal, a letter came to light written by the plaintiff to the defendant's auctioneer; in the course of that letter it was stated that certain matters remained to be agreed and that the sale was "subject to contract". The Supreme Court (the Chief Justice, Mr. Justice Kenny and Mr. Justice Parke) allowed the appeal. The main judgment of the Supreme Court was delivered ex tempore by Mr. Justice Kenny and there is no written judgment available. However, it is clear from the judgment of Mr. Justice Costello in the High Court that he found that there was a concluded oral agreement for the sale of the property. I appeared as counsel on the hearing of the appeal in the Supreme Court and my recollection is that it was not sought to disturb any finding of fact made by Mr. Justice Costello and that the argument advanced on behalf of the defendant was that, in view of the plaintiff's letter to which I have referred, the correspondence could not constitute a sufficient memorandum to satisfy the requirements of the Statute of 1695. Accordingly, I take that decision as accepting, at least by implication, the principle that the writing relied on must acknowledge the existence of a concluded contract.

The next decision to which reference must be made is *Kelly* v. *Park Hall School* [1979] I.R. 340. In that case the trial judge (Mr. Justice Hamilton) found that there was a concluded oral contract for the sale of the land. Two documents were relied upon as constituting a sufficient memorandum. The first was a letter dated the 19th December, 1977, from the auctioneers acting on behalf of the defendant vendors to the vendors' property adviser in the following terms:–

> *"Hall School – Lands at Rere"*
>
> Dear Michael,
>
> Further to our telephone conversation this morning, I confirm that we have agreed terms, subject to contract, for the sale of these lands to Mr. Paddy Kelly of Berkeley Homes Ltd, who were purchasers of the front lands. The principal terms to be included in the contract for sale are as follows:–
>
> Proposed purchaser:– Hickey, Beauchamp, Kirwan & O'Reilly (in trust).
>
> Proposed price:– £175,000.
>
> A non-refundable deposit of £35,000 to be paid on exchange of contracts, the balance to be paid not later than 6 months thereafter with interest at 12% from the contract date until the closing date. I am sending a copy of this letter to Mr. Haugh of A. & L. Goodbody and perhaps you could kindly confirm instructions to him on behalf of the Committee."

The second writing relied on was a letter from the defendants' solicitors to the plaintiffs' solicitors dated the 13th January, 1978, which enclosed a draft contract and concluded with the following sentence:– "On the instructions of our clients, this offer remains open for acceptance by your clients for a period of seven days only from the date of this letter and we are instructed that, if the contract is not back with us within the said period of time, duly executed, the offer is deemed to be withdrawn." In the High Court Mr. Justice Hamilton held that this latter document was a sufficient memorandum, since it enclosed a draft contract containing all the material terms. On appeal to the Supreme Court (Mr. Justice Henchy, Mr. Justice Kenny and Mr.

Justice Parke) it was held that the letter from the auctioneers dated the 19th December, 1977, was a sufficient memorandum, and the appeal was dismissed. Mr. Justice Henchy said at p. 352 of the report:–

> "The case hangs on whether the letter of the 19th December, 1977, which I have quoted, constitutes a sufficient memorandum for the purpose of the Statute of Frauds. In my opinion it does. *It contains not only all the essential terms of the contract but also recognition that a contract had been made.* It says:– '. . . we have agreed terms, subject to contract. . .' Since the judge, having heard oral evidence, held that the oral agreement recorded in the letter was a completed agreement in the sense that nothing further was left to be negotiated, the words 'we have agreed terms subject to contract' must be taken to mean that a contract had been made, subject to its being formalised in writing. Therefore, it constitutes a sufficient memorandum."

The words which I have reproduced in italics appear to indicate an acceptance by Mr. Justice Henchy of the proposition that the memorandum must recognise the existence of a concluded contract. Moreover, if the situation were otherwise, I consider it inevitable that the Supreme Court in that case would have expressed their disapproval of the decision in the *Tiverton Case.* It is noteworthy that Mr. Justice Henchy appears not to have shared the view of the High Court judge that the letter of 13th January, 1978, was a sufficient memorandum – presumably because he did not consider that that letter recognised the existence of a concluded contract. I am fortified in arriving at this conclusion on the effect of the decision in the *Park Hall Case* by the fact that a similar view of its effect was taken by Mr. Justice Hamilton in *McInerney Properties Ltd.* v. *Roper* (High Court – 31st July 1979).

While the decision in the *Park Hall Case* seems to have proceeded on the basis that the memorandum must contain a recognition that a contract has been made, it might on first reading appear to lend support to the proposition that the words "subject to contract" are not inconsistent with the existence of a concluded contract. If that were the effect of the decision, it would mean that the Supreme Court, by necessary implication, was disapproving of the decision in the *Tiverton Case* and, also by implication, was overrruling or disapproving of the long line of authority on the "subject to contract" topic to which I have already referred. I doubt very much whether the Supreme Court intended to disapprove of the decision in the *Tiverton Case* or to disturb the authorities in question. Had that been their intention, I think it would have been made clear in the judgment of Mr. Justice Henchy. It may be significant that the plaintiff in the *Park Hall Case* had already purchased the adjoining lands of the defendant and that, therefore, the title to the propety being sold had been fully investigated by the plaintiff, so that the necessity for a formal contract had been significantly reduced. The actual wording used ("we have agreed terms, subject to contract") was also treated as being of importance. I think that the *Park Hall Case* should properly be regarded as a special one decided on particular facts which do not arise in the present case and, as such, to be more akin to the *St. Saviour's Case* [1975] 3 All E.R. 416 to which I have already referred.

The next case is *Casey v. Irish Intercontinental Bank* [1979] I.R. 364. In that case also the High Court found that there had been a concluded oral contract for the sale of the lands and that, as in the *Tiverton Case,* the oral agreement had not been made expressly "subject to contract." However, the writing relied on as a memorandum, so far as material, was in the following terms:– "I, Patrick Casey, Gurrane House, Donoughmore, agree to purchase Park House and lands for £110,000 subject to contract and title. I agree to pay £25,250 as deposti." Mr. Justice Costello found in favour of the plaintiff. I believe that he did so in a written judgment but, as the text is not available in the Central Office, I cannot say what his reasons were for arriving at this conclusion. On appeal his decision was upheld by the Supreme Court (Mr. Justice Henchy, Mr. Justice Kenny and Mr. Justice Parke). The main judgment in the Supreme Court (with which the other two judges agreed) was delivered by Mr. Justice Kenny. The greater part of that judgment is taken up with a point which does not arise in the present case. The only reference to the fact that the writing relied on had used the phrase "subject to contract and title" is in the following passage from the judgment of Mr. Justice Kenny at p. 368 of the report:–

> "The words subject to contract and title were not introduced into the transaction until the 2nd February when an oral contract for sale had already been made. Even if the reference to the contract and title is regarded as being incorporated in the contract, it does not make the execution of a contract a term of the agreement or a condition precedent to any contractual liability arising. I have already discussed this matter in the judgment which I gave, when I was a judge of the High Court, in *Law* v. *Robert Roberts & co.* That decision was affirmed by the Supreme Court and I do not intend to repeat what I said there."

Before preparing this judgment I read with the utmost care the judgment delivered by Mr. Justice Kenny in *Law* v. *Robert Roberts & Co.* In none of the letters to which reference is made in the statement of facts taken from that judgment (and appearing at pp. 293-6 of the report) does the phrase "subject to contract" or "subject to contract and title" appear. Not merely are the letters in that case perfectly consistent with the existence of a concluded contract, but they go further. In his letter of the 7th November, 1960, Mr. Hamilton, who was the auctioneer acting on behalf of the defendant vendors, said:– "We confirm herewith that acting on the instructions of our clients, Messrs. Robert Roberts, we have accepted your offer of £4,750 and fees at 2½ per cent for the above property . . ." *Law* v. *Robert Roberts & Co.* is in no sense a decision on the meaning of the words "subject to contract." Nor is it an authority on the question as to whether a writing which does not acknowledge the existence of a concluded contract can be a sufficient memorandum. As the letter of the 7th November, 1960 (and the other letters referred to in the judgment) recognised in the plainest terms the existence of a concluded contract, that question did not arise. In these circumstances, I confess to finding some difficulty in understanding the reference to the *Roberts Case* in the above passage from the judgment of Mr. Justice Kenny in *Casey's Case.*

In the course of argument counsel suggested that Mr. Justice Kenny, in delivering judgment in *Casey's Case* must have overlooked the fact that the *Roberts Case* was not an authority on the "subject to contract" issue. Whether that be so or not, I must apply the law as stated by the Supreme Court. If this passage has the effect contended for by counsel for the plaintiffs then, however that conclusion may have been arrived at, I am bound to apply the principle of law laid down. But it is stretching credibility too far for me to suppose that in this brief passge Mr. Justice Kenny intended to overrule *Winn* v. *Bull* and the other pre-1921 decisions on the "subject to contract" point, *Thompson* v. *The King* and *Lowis* v. *Wilson* ; and to express his disapproval of the numerous English authorities since 1921 on the same topic culminating in the *Tiverton Case.* Since *Casey's Case* has not yet been reported, I do not know what arguments may have been advanced or what concessions made in the course of argument on either side. In these circumstances, I have come to the conclusion that I should not treat the decision as laying down any general principle of the nature contended for by counsel for the plaintiffs.

The last Irish case is *McInerney Properties Ltd.* v. *Roper.* In this case again the High Court (Mr. Justice Hamilton) found as a fact that there was a concluded oral contract for the sale of the land. The writings relied on by the plaintiff as constituting a sufficient memorandum were two letters (each being headed "subject to contract") dated the 23rd March and the 17th April, 1978, from the defendant's solicitors, and a draft contract which, it was claimed, was incorporated therewith. Mr. Justice Hamilton, having considered the authorities and, in particular, *Law* v. *Jones* , the *Tiverton Case* and the *Park Hall Case,* came to the conclusion that the letters were a sufficient memorandum. He summarised his conclusion as to the effect of the *Tiverton Case* as follows:– "Consequently, it appears to me that the decision in *Tiverton Estates Ltd.* v. *Wearwell Ltd.* was based not on the fact that the words 'subject to contract' were used but that the writings sought to be relied upon as a sufficient note or memorandum did not contain an admission or a recognition that a contract had in fact been entered into." That is a view which, with respect, I do not share. On the contrary, it seems to met that Lord Denning was at pains to emphasise that it was precisely the use of the words "subject to contract" which prevented the writings from constituting an acknowledgment of the existence of a contract.

From this analysis of the authorities, I think that the following conclusions emerge:–

1. A memorandum or note cannot satisfy the Statute of Frauds if, when it is read alone or with other documents which can properly be read with it, it does not contain a recognition, express or implied, of the existence of the oral contract sought to be enforced.
2. A letter, which expressly states that a transaction is "subject to contract" cannot be sufficient note or memorandum, since the use of those words is normally inconsistent with the existence of a concluded contract. It is only in certain rare and exceptional circumstances such as arose in *Kelly* v. *Park Hall School* and *Michael Richards Properties* v. *St. Saviour's Parish* that the words "subject to contract" can be treated as being of no effect.
3. In applying the two foregoing principles, it is immaterial whether the writing relied on itself contains the words "subject to contract" or is part of a chain of correspondence initiated by a letter which makes it clear that any oral agreement already arrived at is "subject to contract."

It seems to me that the application of those principles to the present case is sufficient to dispose of the contention that the letters referred to can be treated as a sufficient note or memorandum.

It was urged on behalf of the plaintiffs that the words "subject to contract" had been inserted by Mr. McCarroll when he was acting on his own initiative and without any authority from his clients and that, accordingly, they should be disregarded. If words which are clearly destructive of any recognition of a concluded contract appear in the memorandum, then it appears to me not to be a material consideration that they may have been inserted without authority. But altogether apart from that consideration, I cannot agree with the suggestion that these words were inserted by Mr. McCarroll without his clients' authority. There was no question of his clients' having expressly authorised him to use that expression; but I have not the smallest doubt that it was within his implied authority to do so. Any other view of the law would lead to the absurd consequences mentioned by Russell L.J. in his dissenting judgment in *Law* v. *Jones.* A solicitor who is instructed by a party who has entered into an oral agreement for the sale of land is perfectly entitled, in my view, to write a letter which expressly prevents his client from being committed to an open contract and ensures that his client will have the full protection of a formal contract of sale. I think that this view of the law is consistent with the leading Irish authorities, *i.e. Cloncurry* v. *Laffan; Kerns* v. *Manning; Godley* v. *Power* and *Black* v. *Kavanagh.* All of these cases emphasise that it is not part of a solicitor's function to alter the terms of an oral contract already entered into by his client. They also make it clear that a letter written by a solicitor for the purpose of carrying into effect an oral agreement already made *may* constitute a sufficient memorandum to satisfy the Statute of Frauds. But it would seem strange and illogical that a solicitor, whose function is not to alter the terms of the bargain or to indulge in further negotiations, but to embody the bargain already concluded in a formal contract which gives his client the maximum protection consistent with that bargain – as contrasted with an open contract – should be regarded as exceeding his authority when he seeks to ensure that his client has the protection of a formal contract.

I indicated at an earlier stage of this judgment that there may indeed be cases in which a solicitor may feel that it is positively advantageous to his client to commit him to an open contract. I am far from saying that in such cases the solicitor is in any sense acting in dereliction of his duty to his client. But in the everyday case of a sale of property, where the parties have shaken hands on price but trust their respective solicitors to do everything that is necessary to protect them against all the traps and pitfalls that still beset the completion of sales of real property, a solicitor, in my view, is acting fully within the scope of his authority by making it clear in his initial letter that any oral agreement already concluded must be treated as "subject to contract." In so doing, he protects his client from the consequences of entering into an open contract. In the words of Lord Denning in the *Tiverton Case* at pp. 159-160 of the report, he does it "in the confidence that it protects his client. It means that the client is not bound by what has taken place in conversation. The reason is that, for over a hundred years, the courts have held that the effect of the words 'subject to contract' is that the matter remains in negotiation until a formal contract is executed. . ."

That seems to me to be both good law and good sense. Its practical application is indeed well illustrated by the present case. I have already said that the oral agreement in this case was plainly unconditional. The parties did not expressly say that their oral agreement was "subject to contract." Nor did they say that it was subject to the plaintiffs obtaining the loan finance that they needed in order to complete the transaction; but Mr. McCarroll refrained from sending the formal contract back to the defendants' solicitors signed by his clients until such time as he was satisfied that they were in funds to complete the transaction. I have not the slightest doubt that the plaintiffs would have been appalled if, as a result of an unguarded letter written by Mr. McCarroll in the early stages of the transaction they found themselves faced with serious financial consequences because, for some unforeseen reason, the offer of loan finance was suddenly withdrawn. If the plaintiffs' case is well founded, it would mean that, in those circumstances, they would have had no answer to a decree for specific performance in circumstances where they would not have had the finance to complete the transaction. The reason why the plaintiffs did not expressly say to Mr. O'Reilly, or the defendants, that they regarded their oral agreement as subject to the obtaining of the necessary finance is obvious; they relied, as generations of house purchasers have relied, on the good sense and experience of their solicitor to protect them. If the submission made on behalf of the plaintiffs is well founded, it means that persons entering into property transactions of this nature have been deprived of a very important protection. For the reasons I have already given, I do not think that the *Park Hall Case* and *Casey's Case* would support so far-reaching a proposition. In so far as the proposition is supported by *Law* v. *Jones* and *McInerney Properties Ltd.* v. *Roper,* I must respectfully decline to follow those decisions.

I should add that solicitors in search of guidance on this topic could not do better, in my view, than to follow the advice given in Wylie's *Irish Conveyancing Law,* the authority of which is, of course, substantially enhanced by the fact that the consultant editor for the Republic of Ireland is Mr. Justice Kenny. At para. 9.047 on p. 364 Mr. Wylie has this to say:– "Thirdly, if explicit instructions have not been obtained, the greatest care should be taken in dealing with all correspondence relating to the transaction. If it is intended that the matter should be regarded as still subject to negotiation, *i.e.* in the pre-contract stage, this should be stated expressly in the correspondence, perhaps *all* correspondence, *e.g.,* by entering a note that the matter is still 'subject to contract'." And he adds in a foot-note:– "This will probably be enough to prevent the correspondence from being regarded as sufficient memorandum, *i.e.,* by denying the existence of an agreement . . ." In this case, I think that Mr. McCarroll achieved precisely that result by his prudence in making it clear in the initial letters that he wrote that the matter was still "subject to contract." I am satisfied that the use of those words was sufficient to prevent any subsequent letter in that correspondence from being a valid memorandum or note for the purpose of the Statute of Frauds.

There is another feature of the writing relied upon which is also fatal, in my view, to its validity as a memorandum or note for the purpose of the statute. It is clear that the writing must contain *all* the material terms of the oral agreement: *Hawkins* v. *Price* [1947] Ch. 645 and *per* Lord Denning at p. 161 of the *Tiverton Case.* In this case the letter from the defendants' solicitors dated the 15th August, 1978, expressly stated that the date for handing over possession remained to be agreed between the parties. In other words, one of the material terms was still in negotiation. Whether that statement correctly reflected the terms of the oral agreemetn is *nihil ad rem;* the fact remains that the writing relied upon expressly states that the closing date – a material item – remained to be agreed. There was, of course, no reference to the closing date in the other letters.

One cannot help feeling considerable sympathy for the plaintiffs in this case; but sympathy cannot determine the legal rights of the parties. I must apply the law as it appears to me to have been stated by courts of the highest authority in this country and in England. It follows that I must dismiss the plaintiffs' claim for specific performance.

Notes and Questions

1. Do you agree with Keane J.'s survey of the authorities and his conclusions? *Cf.* Clark, "Subject to Contract" [1984] Conv. 173 and 251.
2. See further, *Irish Conveyancing Law,* para. 9.072 *et seq.*

LOWRY V. REID

[1927] N.I. 142 (Court of Appeal)

The facts are set out in the judgments.

Moore L.C.J.: This was an action by William Lowry, upon a contract made between his deceased mother, Mary Lowry, and himself on or about April 28th, 1916, under which the plaintiff, at the request of his mother, transferred his farm of forty-eight acres to his brother Andrew, and in return Mary Lowry undertook to plaintiff that she would by will devise and bequeath to him at her death her own farm of seventy-four acres and twenty-six perches.

Two years before her death, on 1st May, 1923, Mary Lowry revoked the previous will which she had made in pursuance of the contract above stated, and left the plaintiff a life interest merely in said farm, and (after limitations not now material) the ultimate interest to her grandson, Thomas Carlisle Reid, Junior, one of the defendants.

Wilson J. at the trial held, as appears both from his spoken judgment and the order, that the contract alleged by the plaintiff was in fact made, but that it could not be enforced as against the representatives of Mary Lowry, inasmuch as it was a contract relating to land, and there was no sufficient note or memorandum in writing signed by Mary Lowry as required by the Statute of Frauds, and that there had not been any sufficient part performance of the contract by Mary Lowry to take the contract out of the provisions of that statute. On these grounds he dismissed the action so far as it related to the lands, and from this judgment William Lowry has appealed.

Counsel for the defendant, however, have admitted that they cannot sustain the order of the learned judge on this ground, and it is admitted before us that if there is part performance by the party seeking to enforce a contract that is sufficient to bind both, and acts by the person to be charged are not in themselves evidence of acts of part performance. See *Caton* v. *Caton* L.R. 1 Ch. 137.

But counsel for the respondents have attempted to put the case on a different ground based on certain dicta in the judgment of Lord Selborne in *Maddison* v. *Alderson* 8 A.C. 457. They say that evidence of the parol contract cannot be admitted unless it is first established that the alleged acts of part performance unequivocally established the existence of some such contract. If I have correctly stated this proposition, I can only say that I do not accept it. I think it is an inversion of the principle which should obtain. In my opinion, we must at some stage consider the contract and its effect, before we are in a position to judge, whether or not the acts relied on to take the case out of the statute are acts of part performance of the contract.

If such acts are not unequivocally referable to the performance of the contract, in whole or part, then the evidence as to them is irrelevant and the necessary proof of part performance fails. Lord Selborne's speech in *Maddison* v. *Alderson* 8 A.C. 457 lays it down that "the doctrine of part performance is applicable to any case in which a court of equity would before the statute have decreed specific performance." These are the words of Palles C.B., in *Crowley* v. *Sullivan* [1900] 2 I.R. 478, at p. 492. In this case, therefore, I take the parol contract and I find it proved as set out in paragraph 5 of the statement of claim. What facts do we find as proving acts of part performance unequivocally referable to this contract? First of all as to the status ante quo – (a) That on 16th August, 1902, Mary Lowry was possessed of two farms one of which was subsequently divided into two. (b) That on 21st August, 1902, she made a will whereby she left the 74 acres at Drumhirk to Andrew (I omit the charges for legacies) and the 115 acre farm at Ballykeigle to William and Hugh jointly. (c) That the Ballykeigle farm, at Mary Lowry's wish, in 1905 was divided between Hugh and William, and William became registered owner of 48 acres of it, and Hugh of the balance leaving Mary Lowry in possession of the Drumhirk farm of 74 acres. This was the position except for one further factor immediately prior to the parol contract of April, 1916, of which specific performance is sought in the present action. That further factor was that William was about to get married, and, as he had no house on his farm at Ballykeigle, he was about to sell it and buy another elsewhere.

At this stage then the mother, being anxious to keep William at home and also to provide for her son Andrew, who had been invalided from the Great War, makes a new arrangement in the nature of a re-settlement. (I purposely omit all references to legacies, chattels, etc.) She said to William, in effect, "if you will now give up possession of your 48 acres of land to Andrew, and come and live with your wife with me and help me to work my 74 acres, I will leave you the 74 acres at my death." Now has there been such part performance of that contract as would entitle William to succeed in equity in a suit for specific performance? Would it be a fraud on the part of Mary Lowry to take advantage of the fact that there was no contract in writing pursuant to the statute?

With this in mind, let us see what occurred. William, immediately after the contract, puts Andrew in possession of his 48 acres, and with his wife retires to live with his mother on her farm. Mary Lowry on her part makes a will leaving her farm to William pursuant to the arrangement. This is not relied on as an act of part performance but as an act corroborating the making of the parol contract. William, having transferred his own farm, lives on with his mother who ultimately dies, leaving him only a limited interest; the learned judge says he has been defrauded and that for him there is no relief. In my judgment there is relief for him, because on the facts of the case, having given up his own property to his own detriment, on the faith of his mother's representations, this is a parol contract for the specific performance of which he is entitled in equity to a decree to carry those representations into execution, and if he is entitled to such a decree, he is equally entitled to rely on the doctrine of part performance to take the case out of the statute, *Crowley* v. *O'Sullivan* [1900] 2 Ir. R. 492.

In my opinion, the plaintiff, William Lowry, is entitled to judgment in the terms of his notice of appeal, and in that respect the judgment of Wilson J. should be reversed and altered accordingly. The plaintiff, who should have succeeded in the court below, is entitled to his costs of the action there as well as the costs of this appeal, to be paid by the executor and his co-defendant.

Andrews L.J.: I entirely agree with Wilson J. in the conclusion of fact at which he arrived in this case, namely, that in the year 1916 a valid verbal contract was entered into between Mary Lowry and her sons, Andrew and William, by which Mary Lowry agreed that she would leave to William at her death her two farms of land in Drumhirk, subject to certain legacies, and also her furniture and household effects, and that the residue, including all stock, crop and outside effects, should be divided between William and Andrew in equal shares. In return for and as the consideration for this undertaking William Lowry agreed to convey his farm of 48 acres in Ballykeigle to Andrew Lowry and to pay him the sum of £200.

We are not concerned on this appeal with the variation in terms of this agreement which found expression in the codicil of 10th January, 1920, as it only affected that portion of the contract which related to the stock, crop and outside effects. The appeal relates to the rights of the rival claimants to the lands in Drumhirk; and the only assistance which we derive from further reference to that portion of the contract which contained the proposed disposition of the stock, crop and outside effects, is that the defendants have not challenged Wilson J.'s decision of that part of the action in the plaintiff's favour, and must, therefore, be taken to have acquiesced in his view as to the existence of a valid contract affecting such stock, crop, and outside effects. The attitude of the defendants concerning this part of the agreement confirms the opinion at which I have independently arrived, that the agreement between the mother and her sons extended to the lands of Drumhirk. The only question, therefore, to be determined is whether it is an agreement which is capable of being legally enforced at the plaintiff's suit.

I further agree with Wilson J. that there is no sufficient note or memorandum of this parol agreement to satisfy the provisions of the Statute of Frauds; and, accordingly, the plaintiff must fail unless there has been a sufficient part performance of the contract to take the case out of the statute. Wilson J. held that the performance by William Lowry is complete. I agree. William conveyed all his estate and interest in the 48 acre Ballykeigle Farm to Andrew, who forthwith entered into and remained in possession until he sold it to his brother Hugh in 1920. William also paid Andrew the £200 agreed upon. But Wilson J. held that it was necessary that there should also be a part performance of the contract by Mary Lowry, and that the making of the will of 19th April, 1916, and her allowing William to bring his wife to live at Drumhirk did not amount to such part performance.

When one considers the principle upon which the doctrine of part performance is based, it becomes, in my opinion, clear that no such performance on her part is required. In *Bond* v. *Hopkins* 1 Sch. & L., 413 at 433 Lord Redesdale said :–"The Statute of Frauds says that no action or suit shall be maintained on an agreement relating to lands which is not in writing, signed by the party to be charged with it; and yet the court is in the daily habit of relieving, where the party seeking relief has been put into a situation which makes it against conscience in the other party to insist on the want of writing so signed, as a bar to his relief." Thus the doctrine is a purely equitable one. Its underlying principle is, that the Court will not allow a statute which was passed to prevent fraud to be made itself an instrument of fraud. In other words, the court disregards the absence of that formality which the statute requires when insistence upon it would render it a means of effecting, instead of a means of averting, fraud. The question in each case is, whether the plaintiff has an equity arising from part performance which is so affixed upon the conscience of the defendant that it would amount to a fraud on his part to take advantage of the fact that the contract is not in writing. The right to relief rests not so much on the contract as on what has been done in pursuance or in execution of it. Under the statute the note or memorandum of the contract must be signed by the party to be charged. Under the doctrine of part performance the equity must be possessed, not by the party to be charged, but by the plaintiff – the person who seeks relief; and this equity arises from his part performance of the contract. This view is not only recognized by all the leading text book writers on the subject, but it has also been enunciated in the clearest terms by Lord Cranworth, C., in the English Court of Appeal in the case of *Caton* v. *Caton* L.R. 1 Ch. 137 at 147-8, in terms which were approved of by the House of Lords in the same case L.R. 2 H. L., 127. "the preparing and executing of the will," said Lord Cranworth C., at p. 148, "caused no alteration in the position of the lady (i.e., the plaintiff), and I presume it will not be argued that any consequence can be attached to acts of part performance by the party sought to be charged." In the House of Lords the plaintiff's counsel did not challenge this view of the law; and, abandoning any argument based on alleged part performance, they sought, unsuccessfully as it proved, to establish that a certain paper constituted a contract within the statute. In his speech Lord Chelmsford, however, left no room for doubt that he entirely concurred in Lord Cranworth's judgment. "If," he says at p. 136, "the same questions had been raised on the argument upon this appeal I should have had no difficulty in agreeing with the judgment of my noble and learned friend (Lord Cranworth)"; and at p.145 Lord Westbury expresses the same opinion when he says- "My Lords, I would only add that I entirely concur with my noble and learned friend, the Lord Chancellor, in overruling the grounds on which the Vice-Chancellor's judgment appears to have proceeded. . . . I agree entirely in the ground upon which my noble and learned friend rested his judgment in the court below."

It is clear from both the written judgment of Wilson J. and also from two consecutive recitals in the formal judgment of the court, that the grounds on which he dismissed the plaintiff's action were the absence of a sufficient note or memorandum of the contract, and the absence of sufficient part performance by Mary Lowry. For the reasons I have given this latter ground is, in my opinion, unsustainable; and it was virtually abandoned by the defendants' counsel on the arguments in this court.

Mr. McGonigal endeavoured, however, to support Wilson J.'s judgment on the ground that the acts of part performance of the contract by the plaintiff which have been relied upon are insufficient to take the case out of the statute, not being, he contends, unequivocally referable to the contract. The acts of part performance by the plaintiff which were relied upon consist mainly of the conveyance of the farm of 48 acres in Ballykeigle to Andrew Lowry followed by the giving up of possession to him; and he submits that the equity can only arise from acts of part performance relating to the lands which form the subject matter of the suit. In support of this argument he contends that the terms of the parol agreement can only be looked at after unequivocal acts of part performance have been proved; and that in the present case without the parol agreement there is no connexion between the lands of Drumhirk and those of Ballykeigle. He, therefore, concludes that acts to Ballykeigle cannot be regarded as part performance of a contract relating to Drumhirk. The argument, though plausible, is in my opinion unsustainable. The fallacy which underlies it is that, though the subject matter of the action is the farm in Drumhirk, the subject matter of the contract is the farms both in Drumhirk and Ballykeigle.. I see no reason in principle, nor has any authority been cited to us to show, why a party who seeks contractual relief in regard to certain lands cannot rely as acts of part performance upon his own acts to other lands in furtherance of the same contract. Let me give two illustrations. A. agrees verbally to sell Whiteacre and Blackacre to B. for, say, £1,000. Delay arises in completing the conveyance; and B., being anxious to get immediate possession of Whiteacre for building purposes, pays the £1,000 to A., is allowed into possession of Whiteacre and proceeds to erect buildings thereon. A. subsequently refuses to convey Blackacre, and, when sued, pleads the Statute of Frauds. In my opinion B.'s acts in relation to Whiteacre constitutes a valid part performance which takes the case out of the statute, for both lands form the subject matter of the contract, and B.'s acts to Whiteacre are, therefore, a part performance of the contract. The other illustration I put during the argument to Mr. McGonigal:– A., the owner of Whiteacre agrees verbally to exchange it for Blackacre, which belongs to B. If the latter executes a conveyance of Blackacre to A., how can it be contended that this is not such an act of part performance by B. as may be relied upon by him in an action to compel A. to perform his part of the contract by conveying Whiteacre to him? Unless the doctrine of part performance finds no place in the law relating to a contract for the exchange of lands, B.'s conveyance must be a sufficient act of part performance; and, in my opinion, there could be no foundation for the suggestion that the doctrine does not apply to contracts for the exchange of lands, as in my judgment the doctrine applies to all contracts which, before the Judicature Act, a Court of Equity would have granted specific performance if the alleged contract had been in writing; and these are not confined to contracts for the sale of land, (See *Maddison* v. *Alderson* 8 A.C., 467, 474 and *McManus* v. *Cooke* 35 Ch. D. 681, at 697 (approved of by Palles C.B., in *Crowley* v. *O'Sullivan* [1900] 2 I.R. 478, at 490 & 492)) but include contracts for the exchange of lands. Seton 7th Edit. 1228.

I would add that I can find no authority to support Mr. McGonigal's contention that it is not permissible even to consider the terms of the parol agreement until it is clearly established that the acts of part performance refer unequivocally to the contract relied upon, and to that alone. Indeed, it would be, in my opinion, impossible to apply the proposition as so stated in practice; for how, I ask, could it be said that the acts of part performance referred unequivocally to an agreement of the terms of which were ex hypothesi not known, unless, indeed, they were acts of such a clear, cogent, and conclusive character that they embodied and themselves proved the actual terms of the agreement, in which case it would be wholly unnecessary for the plaintiff to make any reference to or to rely in any way upon the parol agreement. In support of his contention Mr. McGonigal referred us to a passage in Lord O'Hagan's judgment in *Maddison* v. *Alderson* 8 A.C. 467, at 483, where he said:– "Next, assuming that the action must be considered maintainable, if at all, for the purpose of enforcing a parol contract, partly performed, the course of the argument appears to me to have been further erroneous in this, that, instead of seeking to establish primarily such a performance as must necessarily imply the existence of the contract, and then proceeding to ascertain its terms, it reversed the order of the contention. The Court was asked, from the findings of the jury and the testimony supporting them, to say there was a contract; and then to discover in the conduct of the parties acts of peformance sufficient to validate the bargain so previously ascertained." If these words are to be taken literally, and to be construed as deciding that the acts of performance must in themselves necessarily imply the existence of *the* contract, that is, the precise contract pleaded, I am not prepared to accept them as containing a correct statement of the law, being, as they are, at variance with the terms of the classical judgment of the Earl of Selborne, C., in the same case, and, indeed, as it seems to me, with other passages of Lord O'Hagan's own judgment. Thus in the central paragraph on page 485, he says:–" It (i.e., the act which shall amount to a part performance) must be sufficient of itself, and without any other information or evidence, to satisfy a court, from the circumstances it has created and the relations it has formed, that they are only consistent with the assumption of the existence of *a* contract, the terms of which equity requires, if possible, to be ascertained and enforced" (The italics are my own).

It may be said that in the next paragraph of his judgment Lord O'Hagan again reverts to the principle that the acts must, of necessity, imply the existence of *the* agreement pleaded; but this portion of his judgment follows and is inconsistent with the passage from the judgment of Sir William Grant in *Frame* v. *Dawson* 14 Ves. 387, which he cited with approval on p. 484:– "The principle of the cases is, that the act must be of such a nature, that if stated, it would of itself infer the existence of *some* agreement," (again the italics are my own); "and then parol evidence is admitted to show what the agreement is."

I have referred to the Earl of Selborne's judgment, from which I shall only make two extracts – the first, the passage at p. 476, to which Mr. Murphy referred us in his very forcible reply:– "It is not arbitrary or unreasonable to hold that when the statute says that no action is to be brought to charge any person upon a contract concerning land, it has in view the simple case in which he is charged upon the contract only, and not that in which there are equities resulting from res gestae subsequent to and arising out of the contract. So long as the connexion of those res gestae with the alleged contract does not depend upon mere parol testimony, but is reasonably to be inferred from the res gestae themselves, justice seems to require some such limitation of the scope of the statute." The second passage is taken from page 479, where the learned Lord Chancellor summarizes the effect of the cases in the following terms:– "All the authorities show that the acts relied upon as part performance must be unequivocally and in their own nature referable to some such agreement as that alleged." These words "some such agreement" are also adopted as his own by Lord Fitzgerald in his judgment in the same case at p. 491.

I would like to refer to one other case of recognized authority, *Morphett* v. *Jones* 1 Swanston, 181, where Sir T. Plumer, referring to the equitable doctrine, says that "Admission into possession, having unequivocal reference to the contract, has always been considered an act of part performance. The acknowledged possession of a stranger in the land of another is not explicable except on the supposition of an agreement, and has, therefore, constantly been received as evidence of an antecedent contract, and as sufficient to authorize an inquiry into the terms." In the opinion, therefore, of this eminent authority the sole requisite preliminary to inquiry into and proof of the terms of the parol agreement is the establishment of an act which is only explicable on the basis of the existence of some contract.

I make no apology for citing, in conclusion, as a correct summary of the law a passage from Fry on Specific Performance, 5th Edit. 292, where the editor states that the true principle of the operation of acts of part performance seems only to require that the acts in question be such as must be referred to some contract, and may be referred to the alleged one; that they prove the existence of some contract, and are consistent with the contract alleged. As Mr. Murphy pointed out, this paragraph gains special weight from the fact that it appeared in precisely the same form in the 2nd Edition of the book, for which the learned author was himself responsible, published in 1881. The decision in *Maddison* v. *Alderson* 8 A.C. 467 necessitated no alteration in the test.

When I apply these principles to the facts of the present case, I have no difficulty in holding that such facts have been proved as take it entirely outside the statute. The transfer by William to Andrew, followed by the latter's taking over possession, must be referred to some contract, and may be referred to the alleged contract; for though it would appear from the folio that this transfer was stated to be made in consideration of the sum of two hundred and fifty pounds, it is well settled that a receipt for money, even though contained in an instrument under seal, is not conclusive that the money was in fact paid, and parol evidence may be given to prove that the whole or part of it was not paid. Mr. McKee's evidence as to the non-payment of the money is supported by the evidence of the other witnesses; and this part of their evidence remains, even if it be admitted, as it must be, that there is difficulty in justifying the admission of that other portion of their evidence which appears directly to contradict the transfer.

As I look at the res gestae and other proved circumstances of the case, and, particularly, at the comtemporaneous will of Mary Lowry of 29th April, 1916, in which she left to William her farms in Drumhirk, which she had by previous wills devised to Andrew; as I bear in mind the fact that William was then about to get married, and consider the evident natural desire of the mother that the home farms at Drumhirk should remain in possession of the Lowry family; as I consider the subsequent residence of William and his wife on the farms with his mother; his work upon the farms; the handing over of the surplus profits to him by his mother; the disposition by the same will of 1916 of the stock, crop, and outside effects to Andrew and William in equal shares; the subsequent parol agreement of January, 1920, whereby the mother agreed with William that in consideration of his paying Andrew £250 she would leave him the entire of the stock, crop and outside effects; as I bear in mind that that agreement, though clearly indicated in the letter of instruction for codicil of 10th January, 1920, and given effect to by that instrument, was similarly ignored by the will of 1st May, 1923, but enforced by the order of Wilson J. unappealed from this action – as I think of all these matters, I feel I have not merely ample corroboration of the agreement deposed to in evidence by the plaintiff, his brother, James and Hugh, and the family solicitor, Mr. McKee, but I have also in certain of them such evidence of part performance as enables this court, whilst acting within the principles of established authority, to do justice, and to prevent the perpetration on the plaintiff of what I, like Wilson J., would consider a great fraud. The appeal must be allowed with costs.

Best L.J.: I have had an opportunity of perusing the judgments of the Lord Chief Justice and Lord Justice Andrews. I agree with the conclusions arrived at, for the reasons stated.

Notes and Questions

1. From this case what is the basis of the doctrine of part performance? *Cf.* the discussion by the House of Lords in *Steadman* v. *Steadman* [1976] A.C. 536. See also *Haire-Foster* v. *McIntee*, p.203, *post*.
2. See further, *Irish Conveyancing Law*, para. 9.048 *et seq*.

2. *Lack of Mutuality*

FENNELLY V. ANDERSON

(1851) 1 Ir. Ch. R. 706; 4 Ir. Jur (o.s.) 33 (Chancery Court)

Specific performance was sought of a contract concerning leasehold interests held by three married women. The contract was entered into by them and their husbands, but the other party argued that it could not be enforced against him.

Brady L.C.:

This case comes before me under circumstances raising a question of importance, which in the present state of authorities I cannot say that I am prepared to decide so as to preclude the further maintenance of the suit.

The contract, being one for the sale of real estate of married women has been entered into by them and their husbands, and is specific in its terms, and not alleged to be in any respect unreasonable or improper. The objection raised on behalf of the respondent is that this contract cannot be enforced against him, inasmuch as he could not enforce it against the married women. It is conceded that there is not any case deciding that such an agreement could not be enforced at the suit of the husband and wife. Formerly it was the doctrine of Courts of Equity that such a contract might be enforced against the husband. Decrees have more than once required the husband to procure the wife to levy a fine, or that he should stand by the consequences if she refused. So long as that was the rule of the Court, I apprehend that such an objection as the present would have been unsustainable, because it rests upon the absence of mutuality of remedies for enforcement of the contract, viz., that as the petitioners could not have been compelled to perform it, the respondent cannot be so compelled.

But it is said that according to the modern authorities, the rule appears to have been changed, and that the Court will not compel the husband to procure the concurrence of his wife if she refuse to join him. And that I apprehend is now well settled notwithstanding any fluctuation of opinion which may have taken place on the point. But still the question remains, whether the change of the doctrine of the Court in that particular involves a change in another; whether although the Court will not enforce the contract against the husband, it will do so against the other party to the agreement, he being competent to perform it, and being aware of the position of the vendors. The only case which by analogy bears upon the point is *Flight* v. *Bolland* 4 Russ. 298, where Sir John Leach, M.R., held that an infant cannot sustain a suit for the specific performance of a contract, because the remedy is not mutual. Such undoubtedly was the decision; but it is worthy of note, that Counsel for the plaintiff there said:– "If a husband seised *jure uxoris* were to contract for the sale of his wife's estate, the husband and wife could enforce the contract against the purchaser; yet if the purchaser were to file a bill against the husband and wife for specific performance, and the husband were to swear in his answer that the wife would not consent, a Court of Equtiy would not now interfere; it would neither decree the wife to join in the conveyance, nor would it order the husband to procure her concurrence, and send him to prison until that concurrence was obtained." This tends to show that the opinion of the Profession is, that the contract might be enforced by the husband and wife, notwithstanding the want of mutuality. The only answer attempted there by Counsel for the defendant was:– "No case has occurred, or at least none has occurred since the time when it was settled that the Court will not decree a husband, who has contracted for the sale of his wife's estate, to procure her to join in making a good conveyance, in which such a contract has been enforced against the purchaser." The question does not appear to have been adverted to in the judgment of the Court.

The next case in which this point appears to have been alluded to is *Salisbury* v. *Hatcher* 2 Y. & C., C. C. 54, where Knight Bruce, V.C., in the progress of the argument, puts this question:– "Suppose husband and wife, seised in fee in the wife's right, to contract to sell; is there any case which decides that they cannot by bill enforce the contract?" Counsel for the defendant did not venture to say that there was such a decision, but assuming the position to be inconvertible, replies:– "In that case the purchaser buys the estate subject to the chance of the wife repudiating the contract. But if the contract of sale states the property to be the husband's and, in the course of the negotiation it turns out to be the wife's, the vendors cannot compel a sale." The Vice-Chancellor did not again mention the point, but he decreed specific performance of the contract, which was one for the sale of an estate in fee-simple, in favour of a vendor who at the time of entering into the contract was tenant for life only, the purchaser not having rejected the purchase as soon as he had ascertained the real interested of the vendor, and the latter being able, by the consent of parties interested, in remainder, to make a good *prima facie* title to the fee-simple at the hearing. So far, therefore, as regards the modern authorities, since the change in the rule as to enforcing the contract against the husband, no decision has occurred; but to the extent to which the opinion of the Profession at Westminster Hall has been expressed in reference to it, when casually mentioned, that opinion would appear to be in support of the suit in such a case as the present.

Returning to the earlier authorities, I find that in *Daniel* v. *Adams* Ambler, 495, 497, which was a suit by a purchaser for the specific performance of an agreement for the sale of real estate by a husband and wife, Counsel for the plaintiff, of whom Mr. Ambler, the reporter, was one, *arguendo,* said, that if a bill had been brought by the husband and wife for performance of the agreement, the purchaser could not have made the objection, and therefore the husband and wife ought not to be permitted to do it on the bill brought by the purchaser. Sir Thomas Sewell, M.R. dismissed the bill, but said that "the argument that both or neither should be bound does not hold in all cases." At all events Mr. Ambler's position was not denied by the Court.

That the objection of want of mutuality of remedy to enforce the contract does not in all cases prevail, is manifested by cases decided under the Statute of Frauds, where it has been held that the plaintiff may obtain a decree for specific performance of a contract signed by the defendant but not signed by the plaintiff. The reason of this doctrine is, that the plaintiff by filing his bill submits to perform his part of the contract; and of the plaintiff's non-signature the other party is not allowed to avail himself, because although he could not have compelled the plaintiff to complete the contract, yet he (the defendant) has, by signing, thought proper to run the chance of the plaintiff performing his part, which, if he do not rely upon the Statute of Frauds, the Court will decree him to perform. True it may be, however, that these decisions rest upon the particular language of that statute.

But in the present case the married women are willing to join in the conveyance, and I am not aware of any precedent for holding that the Court will not enforce a contract against a husband and wife where it appears that the wife is willing to concur in performing her part of the contract, if the Court be of opinion that it is a proper contract and one to the benefit of which the plaintiff would irrespectively of the question of the wife's competency be entitled. Nor will the Court, as I am yet aware, on the other hand decline to entertain a suit by the husband and wife, merely on the ground of the wife's incompetency to contract. Pending the negotiation these married women might have validated the contract by acknowledging it under the statute 4 & 5 *W.* 4, c.92. The success of every suit for specific performance of contracts with regard to real estate is contingent upon the ability of the plaintiffs to make out title (unless the contract be a qualified one), and upon this question I must deem that this suit is so contingent; therefore if the petitioners cannot or will not convey, there cannot be any relief: but in this respect the case of the parties here is not in my opinion in any greater infirmity than any other case. I can easily imagine instances in which it would be very beneficial to married women that the contracts entered into by them and their husbands should be carried out. On the whole, there are difficulties in coming to the conclusion that they cannot; and I should not feel justified in introducing a restriction which may not be a wise one, and which I no where find already established. I therefore shall not, upon the ground of non-mutuality, dismiss this petition.

The next question is one depending on the particular terms of the contract, viz., what is the extent to which the petitioners are bound to make out title to the property? They insist that the contract is a qualified one, and excludes accordingly the ordinary rule that the vendors must show their lessor's title. The contract does not contain any reservation in direct terms as to the extent of title to be made out. The lease is recited to be one for three lives with a covenant for perpetual renewal, and in the conclusion of the contract there is an agreement on the part of the vendors to allow the vendee out of the purchase money the sum of £15 for the costs to be by him incurred in obtaining from the owner of the fee-simple in the lands a grant thereof in fee-farm under the statute 12 & 13 *Vic.* c. 105; so that it is virtually a contract for the sale of lands in fee-farm. It recites an agreement by the petitioners with the respondent "to covey to him all their interest in the said lands for the sum of £1000." What is their interest? It is a lease for lives renewable for ever, and having regard to the Renewable Leasehold Conversion Act, it is an estate in fee-farm. The petitioners then covenant that they will at their own expense make out and deliver within a given time "an abstract of their title to the lessee's interest in said recited lease of the 20th day of December 1813 of said lands and premises." The words "their title to the lessee's interest" have been relied on as showing that the compact was merely for the sale of such title as they have to the interest of the lessee, whatever that may have been. Perhaps that passage may only refer to the title deducible from the lessee to the petitioners. But I do not think that it excludes the necessity of proving the title fully. I do not think that it protects them from showing that the lease is one conveying a valid interest. Then comes a covenant by the petitioners that, on payment of the purchase money they will "well and sufficiently grant, release, convey or otherwise assure," not the lease or their interest in it, but "all and singular the said lands and premises with the timber," &c., to the use of the respondent, his heirs and assigns, free from all incumbrances, except the rent, renewal fines and covenants contained in the original lease. There is not a phrase from the beginning to the end of this instrument which imports that the sale was one of a limited interest only. To hold that such a limitation exists here would, it seems to me, almost be rescinding altogether the salutary rule which requires the vendor to prove his title to the property which he affects to sell.

I cannot distinguish this case from *Anderson* v. *Higgins* 1 Jo. & Lat. 718, where, by an agreement reciting that the vendor was then seised and possessed of certain premises in as full, ample and beneficial a manner as the same were held by him under a lease thereof made to him by the Earl of Lucan, for lives renewable for ever; and that the vendee had agreed with the vendor "for the actual purchase of his right, title and interest in and to said lease, and the premises thereby demised, upon clear title being made out to him, for the sum of £1250;" and that it appeared that several judgments had been confessed and remained unsatisfied by the vendor, in consequence whereof and until same were satisfied or paid off, a clear title could not be made to the vendee: it was witnessed that the vendee should cause the judgments, and any other incumbrances that might affect the premises, to be satisfied "so as that the vendee should have a clear and marketable title thereto." And in a subsequent part of the agreement the vendor covenanted with the vendee, "to make out a clear title to the premises, free and discharged from all incumbrances whatsoever." Sir Edward Sugden there said:– "Upon the part of the vendor it is contended that the contract was for a sale of the interest in the lease in question, whatever it might be, and that the parties, when speaking in their contract of a good title being made out, only meant that it should be free from incumbrances. But whatever ambiguity there may be in the first part of the contract there is none in the latter part; for there is an express agreement that the seller shall make out a good and marketable title, free from incumbrances, no doubt; but these words were emphatically introduced, because it was anticipated that delay in completing the sale would arise from paying off the incumbrances. Therefore the contract was not only that a good title should be made out, but also that it should be free from incumbrances. I think it clear upon this contract that the seller was bound to make out a good title." Now I do not think that was even so strong a case against the vendor as the present, because here the contract is to convey, not the title to the lease, but the lands and premises, and contemplates the conversion of the vendor's interest into a fee-farm grant procurable under the statute.

Undoubtedly there are cases which show that if the party mean to sell such interest only as he may happen to have, the contract may be so limited. It is unnecessary that I should now go through those authorities, as I have recently stated my opinion upon them in the case of *Leathem* v. *Allen,* to which I still adhere. By merely using the words "all their interest in the said lands," I do not think the vendors have guarded themselves against the production of their lessor's title.–[His Lordship here referred to the broad manner in which the general rule that the vendor of a leasehold must show his title, as laid down by Richards, C.B., in *Purvis* v. *Rayer* 9 Price, 488, 525, and to the observations of Rolfe, B., in *Sellick* v. *Trevor* 11 M. & W. 722,729.]–I have no hesitation in holding that the petitioners have not, by the terms of their contract, protected themselves from the operation of the general rule; and that they must show that the original lease is a valid instrument, conveying a good title to an estate for lives renewable for ever. I cannot make any declaration limiting the title, which they are bound to make out.

There is nothing in the case warranting me in saying that there was a waiver of the production of title. The very first question put by Counsel for the respondent was, whether and when the lease was registered? – a very pertinent question; if registered at one time the lease might be good, and *vice versâ.*

Notes

1. *Cf. Price* v. *Strange* [1978] Ch. 337, *Irish Land Law,* Supp. (1975-80), p.13.
2. See further, *Irish Conveyancing Law,* para. 12.46

3. *Hardship or Lack of Fairness*

ROBERTS V. O'NEILL

Unreported (Supreme Court) (221-1981) (Judgments delivered 8th December 1982)

The facts are set out in McCarthy J.'s judgment.

McCarthy J.

This is an action for specific performance of a contract dated the 17th January 1978 made between the Plaintiff (in trust) and the Defendants for the sale by the Defendants to the Plaintiff of "The Silver Tassie", a licensed premises at Loughlinstown, Co. Dublin. In the High Court McWilliam J. granted the order sought for specific performance and awarded damages measured at bank interest on the sum of £30,000 paid as deposit on the signing of the contract, up to the date of judgment. The first-named Defendant, who is the husband of the second-named Defendant, has appealed against the order for specific performance seeking, in effect, an order that the Plaintiff be compensated in damages only, so that he, that Defendant and his wife may retain the licensed premises. For the reasons that I shall state, in my judgment, the appeal fails.

The Facts

It is desirable to set out, in some detail, the sequence of events.

In 1973, the Defendants bought the Silver Tassie, for an undisclosed sum, and, thereafter, remained joint owners. In November 1977, their daughter was "coshed" in a burglary at their home which is a bungalow adjoining the Silver Tassie. Because of this, Mr. O'Neill became increasingly worried and thought it might be better to sell the premises, a view not shared by his wife who wanted their son, then aged 13, to continue in the business. What one might call the O'Neill experience in the public house business only began in 1973. During the weekend before the 16th January 1978, discussions took place between Corry Buckley, acting on behalf of one Gerard Carthy, the O'Neills, and Gerard Black who was their solicitor, arising from which discussions it was subsequently maintained by Carthy that there was an enforceable contract for the purchase by him of the premises for £190,000. On the 16th January the Plaintiff, who is, in effect, a nominee for the Madigan Group, owners of a chain of public houses, learnt of the possibility that the premises might be on the market and called there on that night. His son-in-law, Mr. Madigan, contacted Mr. Moore, the agent for the O'Neills. The next day, a formal contract in the printed form authorised and issued by the Incorporated Law Society of Ireland, suitably completed as to amount, closing date, deposit and details of title was executed by the Plaintiff personally, and by Mr. Black, solicitor as agent for the O'Neills. The closing date was fixed for the 17th February upon which date, in fact, the Plaintiff's solicitors sent a draft conveyance to the O'Neill's solicitors. On the 21st February, in a letter to the Plaintiff's solicitors, Mr. Black stated –

> "6. Since formally replying to your requisitions on title herein we have been notified by another firm of solicitors that a client of theirs may institute proceedings against the vendor. Such proceedings were in fact issued against the wrong party (not our client) about three weeks ago but we returned same to the said solicitors indicating that the proceedings were not in order. To-date neither we nor our clients have received any amended or new summonses.
> On the 28th February, Mr. Black wrote to the Plaintiff's solicitors enclosing 'herewith memorandum and Index relating this matter'."

On the 6th March, the Plaintiff's solicitors wrote to Mr. Black –

> "In order to protect our clients' interest, we have registered the contract for sale dated the 17th January 1978 and in order to protect our clients' interests further, we feel that a Lis Pendens must be registered. This means that proceedings must be commenced and we will be issuing plenary summons in this regard tomorrow. Please let us know what steps your clients intend to take to have the Lis Pendens in the Carthy action removed as obviously while this is still on the record we cannot advise our client to complete."

On the 7th March 1978, a plenary summons was issued by the Plaintiff but no reply to the observation about the Lis Pendens appears to have been received at any time.

On the 7th June a statement of claim was delivered claiming an order for specific performance of the agreement and damages.

On the 19th July a joint defence and counterclaim delivered on behalf of the Defendants pleading, essentially, that because of Carthy's action, the Defendants were unable to complete and pleading, in particular –

> "4. If, contrary to the Defendant's (sic) contention, the contract for sale was not conditional upon the said Gerard Carthy not succeeding in claiming that he had entered into a binding contract for the sale of the said premises to him, the contract is in any event impossible of performance until the determination of the said proceedings, *and, in the event of the said proceedings being determined in favour of the Defendants, they are ready and willing to complete the sale to the Plaintiff.*" (emphasis added)

The action by Carthy against O'Neill was heard on the 4th and 5th July 1979 by Gannon J. and judgment was delivered in October, when the learned Judge held that the Carthy contract was legally enforceable, and joined Mrs. O'Neill as a defendant to that action. The O'Neills appealed and in its judgment of the 30th January 1981, the Supreme Court allowed the appeal and dismissed Carthy's action.

On the 2nd March 1981, the Plaintiff's solicitors called upon the Defendants, through their solicitors, forthwith to complete the sale and indicated a claim for damages for delay.

On the 19th March, Mr. Black informed the Plaintiff's solicitors that "we will be applying on behalf of the first named Defendant to amend the defence as it is the first named Defendant's contention that this is not a proper case for specific performance." Mr. Black had ceased to act on behalf of Eileen O'Neill, the second Defendant. The terms of the amended defence were sent sometime towards the end of March 1981 to the Plaintiff's solicitors, and an amended defence by Eileen O'Neill, in which she denied Mr. Black's authority, was filed on the 5th of May 1981. This contention of Mrs. O'Neill was rejected by the trial Judge, and no appeal has been brought against that finding.

On the 6th May 1981, an amended defence and counterclaim was filed on behalf of Michael O'Neill, the first Defendant, and the material portion of this was to strike out the words to which I have added emphasis in the original defence and counterclaim at paragraph 4 and add a plea to this effect:–

> "In the period between the making of the contract for sale to the plaintiff in these proceedings and the delivery of the judgment (of the Supreme Court in *Carthy* v. *O'Neill*) the value of the said premises had greatly increased as has the value of licensed premises generally. The first named Defendant is a publican and it would be grossly unjust if the Defendants were obliged to sell said premises to the Plaintiff at the contract price, which would now be a gross undervalue and whereby the Plaintiff would be unjustly enriched. Accordingly, the Court in its discretion should refuse to grant an order of specific performance."

Up to that date, from the delivery of the original defence and counterclaim on the 19th July 1978, the attitude expressly maintained on behalf of both Defendants insofar as an examination of the Court record would disclose was that the sole bar to the closing of the sale to the Plaintiff was the existence of the *Carthy* v. *O'Neill* proceedings.

The adjourned hearing of the action took place before McWilliam J. on the 4th and 5th June, and on the 3rd July 1981, he delivered judgment in which he rejected the Defendants' contention that specific performance should not be granted and that damages in lieu thereof was the appropirate remedy.

The Appeal

The first Defendant, the husband, has appealed, by a notice of appeal dated the 5th August, 1981 against the order for specific performance, without stating in the notice of appeal what it is suggested is the alternative order, but, on the hearing of this appeal, counsel for the first Defendant has limited the appeal to seeking a finding that the order of specific performance would cause excessive hardship to the Defendants and should, therefore, be refused, and that, in lieu thereof, damages, to be assessed in the High Court, should be awarded to the Plaintiff in accordance with Lord Cairns' Act. It is fair to say that ground 6 of the grounds of Appeal contains this essential matter and that no argument was advanced on any other of the grounds of appeal. During the course of the argument, Hederman J. drew attention to the absence of any appeal by the second Defendant and postulated the question as to what the situation would be if the Court were to allow the first Defendant's appeal whilst an order for specific performance remained in existence against the second Defendant. It was indicated that the second Defendant was prepared to join in the appeal if necessary; having regard, however, as to my view on the substantial matter raised in the appeal, it is unnecessary to consider this aspect of the case further. There would appear to be adequate powers under 0. 58 r. 8 to deal with such a situation.

The Argument

As I understand the argument advanced on behalf of the first Defendant, and which I accept as being appropriate to be considered as if advanced on behalf of the second Defendant the case may be stated as follows:–

1. An order of specific performance is an equitable remedy and, accordingly, discretionary in all cases.
2. There may be cases of real hardship caused by the grant of an order for specific performance.
3. The time to test or measure the degree of hardship is not as of the date of the contract sought to be specifically performed, but rather at the date of the trial.
4. In the instant case, a circumstance over which neither Plaintiff nor Defendant had control – the Carthy action – prevented the closing of the sale until after the judgment of this Court in *Carthy* v. *O'Neill and Anor.* on the 30th January, 1981, by which time the original purchase price was but half of the then current value because of the huge increase in the value of licensed premises, national in character and, in part at least, related to the high inflationary trends at the time.
5. This is a circumstance over which none of the parties had any control; it effects a great hardship on the Defendants because they cannot now afford to buy an alternative public house such as would cater for their plans to have their son continue in that business; the only hardship on the Plaintiff, and it is, perhaps, a nominal one only, since he appears to have been buying in trust, is the very fact of not obtaining specific performance and having to settle for damages.

The Plaintiff's answer is a short one – any hardship that has arisen is subsequent to the date of the contract and/or the date for completion; the Plaintiff has, in no way, caused or added to that hardship – he is wholly innocent; in addition, it might be added that the Defendants had been in receipt of all the profits of the business since the original intended date for closing and are still in receipt of these profits. A further comment is made that, initially, at least the first named Defendant wanted to get out of the public house business because of the unhappy burglary incident. Neither the High Court nor this Court has any information as to the purchase price paid by the Defendants in 1973 and, consequently, cannot assess the degree of hardship necessitated by having to pay Capital Gains Tax.

The Law

Mr. Fennelly has argued that the correct approach is to measure the hardship as of the date of the hearing; this argument is unsupported by authority and is, indeed, contradicted by *Lavan* v. *Walsh* [1964] I.R. 87 in which Budd J. at p. 102 said:-

> "The Defendant in this case also relies on the plea that enforcement of the contract in this case would cause grave hardship on her. It is pointed out that the order is a discretionary one and it is strongly urged that the Court in the exercise of a proper judicial discretion should not grant the relief of specific performance because of the special facts of the case which I will deal with later. Again, however, I must refer to a matter of law. The Court, it is well established, will not enforce the specific performance of the contract the result of which would be to impose great hardship on either of the parties to it. It is conceded, however, that the question of the hardship of a contract is generally to be judged at the time it is entered into. Change of circumstances taking place later, making the contract less beneficial to one party, are immaterial as a rule unless it is brought about by the action of the other party. It is stated, however, in Fry on Specific Performance (6th ed., at p. 200):– 'It cannot, however, be denied that there are cases in which the Court has refused its interference by reason of events subsequent to the contract.' From an examination of the cases of *The City of London* v. *Nash* and *Costigan* v. *Hastler* it appears that this is so, but exceptions to the general rule appear very rare .... I must, however, approach the consideration of these matters dispassionately and exercise what I conceive to be the proper judicial discretion. In the first place, as I have pointed out, it is undoubtedly the position in law save in exceptional cases only a matter of hardship existing at the time of the contract can be taken into consideration. Hardship existing at the time of the contract is out of the case. It thus requires a strong case to be made out before one should accede to a plea for the exercise of judicial discretion in a quite unusual way, that is, by reason of hardship arising subsequently to the contract, and the

onus being on the Defendant to satisfy me of the existence and genuineness of the hardship on her, that proof of it should be strong and above suspicion."

Whilst, as Budd J. says, the relevant time issue appears to have been conceded, I do not overlook the quite exceptional standing as a lawyer in which the late Mr. Roger O'Hanrahan S.C. (counsel who made the concession) was held by Bench and Bar alike. Further, although Budd J. refers to the matter as being conceded, without reference to such concession he expresses his own view in the most positive terms. Mr. Fennelly has suggested that there is an illogicality in taking the date of the contract as the relevant one, since it was unlikely that there would be any contract if the hardship were then known. This very argument perhaps answers the problem – hardship is permitted to defeat specific performance where an existing hardship was not known at the relevant time – the date of the contract. While recognising that there may be cases in which hardship occuring later is such that to decree specific performance would result in great injury, such cases must be few and far between and, in my view, would not, ordinarily, include cases of hardship resulting from inflation alone. To permit, as an ordinary rule, a defence of subsequent hardship, would be adding a further hazard to the already trouble strewn area of the law of contracts for the sale of land.

The Application of the law

An examination of the evidence, including the summary at the commencement of this judgment, throws doubt upon the reality of the alleged claim for hardship. At all material times the Defendants knew that they would have to complete a sale of the premises to somebody – either Carthy or Roberts. The original motivation to leave the particular type of business was because of personal hazards; at no time from February 1978 to March, 1981 was it ever suggested to the Plaintiff or his advisers, who showed meticulous care to make the Plaintiff's position clear and, indeed, readily accepted that they could not press for completion until the Carthy case was resolved, that there was any doubt about the eventual completion, assuming a satisfactory result to the first action; at no time did the Defendants embark on any inquiry as to a substitute public house in order that their son might pursue what was alleged to be their wish for his career; Mrs. O'Neill, having dispensed with the service of her original solicitor, embarked upon a spurious defence of the absence of authority and now seeks to join her husband in criticising the Plaintiff, a 76 year old vehicle builder, without any other connection with the licensed trade save that his daughter is married to one of the Madigans, because he assented, in evidence, to an extract from a letter dated 29th July, 1979, written by his solicitors to Mr. Black in which 4 items of alleged damages were specified including, at item 4 "the difference in value between the premises as they are valued at the date of the hearing and their value at which we purchased them." It is to be noted that this letter, to which, incidentally, there appears to have been no reply, was written after the hearing before Gannon J. and before judgment was delivered. I know little of what transpired at that hearing save for some extracts from the transcript of it which were used in evidence in the trial of this case but it does not appear that Mrs. O'Neill did not give evidence at that hearing, apparently because she would have supported Mr. Carthy's claim.

The Result

It may be that there are other circumstances surrounding the alleged hardship but I think I have cited the salient ones. In my judgment, they fall far short of establishing the type of case in which the Court should intervene to deny the ordinary remedy to one of the contracting parties in what was, at the time, a perfectly fair and proper transaction. There may be cases in which the Court should intervene or, to put it more crudely, interfere with the express wording of a contract – the duty to do justice may override strictly legal principles and the well recognised procedures of the courts of equity. Such is not the case here – indeed, justice here demands that the contract be specifically performed.

I have not overlooked the observations of the learned trial Judge in respect of the balancing of the hardship to the Defendants themselves whether or not the specific performance is granted; in no way, do I dissent from his views as so expressed, but I prefer to rest my judgment as I have endeavoured to explain.

O'Higgins C.J. and **Hederman J.** agreed with this judgment.

Notes and Questions

1. Do you agree with McCarthy J.'s reasoning concerning the time when the question of hardships must be judged? See *Irish Conveyancing Law,* para. 12.48.
2. See also *Conlon* v. *Murray,* p.22, *ante.*
3. As regards damages under Lord Cairns' Act, see p.205, *post.*

4. *Lack of Title*

UNITED YEAST CO. LTD. V. CAMEO INVESTMENTS LTD
(1977) 111 I.L.T.R. 13 (High Court)

The facts are set out in the judgment.

Butler J.:

This is an action for specific performance of a contract in writing dated the 5th of November, 1973, for the sale of a certain premises at Fleming Place in the City of Dublin. The plaintiffs were the vendors in the contract which was signed in trust on behalf of the purchasers by Messrs. J.G. O'Connor & Co. a firm of solicitors of which Messrs. Thomas H. Bacon, John M. O'Connor, J. Philip O'Connor, Daire Walsh, Berchmans Gannon and Michael P. Farrell are the principals. These solicitors were the original defendants in this action and I shall hereinafter refer to them as such. The vendors at all material times knew that the original defendants were acting as agents and that their principals were Cameo Investments Limited and associated interests. These associates transpired to be Mr. Patrick P. O'Neill and Buns Limited. The three principals were subsequently added as defendants to the action and I shall hereafter refer to them as the purchasers.

The property agreed to be sold comprised three parcels, all leasehold: Number 18 Fleming Place, Number 17e Fleming Place and portion of the rear of the premises 9 and 11 Upper Baggot Street. The purchase price of the entire was £134,840 and a deposit of £23,000 was paid on the signing of the contract.

The purchasers had entered into two other contracts of even date with the contract with which we are concerned with the Manchester Chemical Company Limited and the Manchester Chemical Company (Ireland) Limited who I gather are subsidiaries of the plaintiff company and it was provided as a condition of all three contracts that they should be completed at one and the same time and that no party should be entitled to compel the completion of any one of the contracts without completing all three.

The closing date was expressed to be the 30th October, 1974, and one of the special conditions of sale expressly made time of the essence of the contract in this regard in the following terms:

> "It is hereby agreed that time is of the essence of this contract and that if this sale is not completed on the closing date that the vendor shall be entitled without giving any notice whatsoever to the purchaser to rescind this sale in which even the purchasers' deposit shall be absolutely forfeited to the vendor."

The purchasers' intention in purchasing all the properties was to use the site for an office development. It appears that the cost to them of the entire scheme would have been many hundreds of thousands of pounds. The property was expressed to be sold with vacant possession (subject to an existing right of way from Number 11 Baggot Street to Fleming Place). The purchasers were not over-concerned with the right of way as they also intended to purchase Number 9 and 11 Baggot Street as part of their development plans. The vendor replies to the purchasers' requisitions on title confirmed that vacant possession would be given and correspondence between the solicitors clearly proceeded on the basis that this would be done.

The part of the property sold comprising portions of the rear of Numbers 9 and 11 Upper Baggot Street had been purchased by the vendors' associate company Manchester Chemical Company Limited (hereinafter referred to as the Manchester Company) in 1955 from a Mr. Robert Pryce. This property consisted of the coach houses and approximately two-thirds of what originally were the gardens of the houses. Mrs. Pryce was the owner of the houses at Baggot Street and they were occupied by him and various tenants. The portions sold were never fenced off or even marked off. The vendors never used this property and it appears that Mr. Pryce and his tenants continued to use them informally even after they were sold. Among these tenants was a Mr. Thomas McLaughlin who lived in a rear flat of Number 9 and carried on a light machinery business in the rear of Number 11. The right of way subject to which the premises were purchased was a passage eight feet wide extending from the rear of Number 11 to the laneway at Fleming Place. In the year 1972 the Manchester Company noticed that someone had covered part of the property including part of the right of way with a rough shed and that a boat was being built under this shed. It seems that Mr. McLaughlin and Mr. Richard Pryce a son of Mr. Pryce were concerned in building the boat. As a result of this Mr. Pryce's son was informed that the rear portion of the gardens and laneway were no longer his father's, he was shown the assignment of the property to the Manchester Company and was warned that unless he acknowledged that the Pryces had no claim thereto proceedings would be instituted. A letter which in the view of earlier correspondence is to be construed as such an acknowledgment was written by Richard Pryce on the 10th of September, 1972. I am satisfied that from then on all the Pryces and through them Mr. McLaughlin knew that the property was owned by the Manchester Company and that their use of the yards was tolerated on the basis that it would cease at any time on demand.

By the summer of 1974 the proposed transaction had become less attractive from the point of view of the purchasers. They had difficulty in securing the necessary finances for their plans, and because of the general economic climate, escalating building costs and the fall off in the projected demand for office space, the project had become a doubtful investment. All these factors rendered the market value of the site considerably less than they had agreed to pay. On the 29th of August, 1974, Mr. Dermot O'Rourke who had acted as Estate Agents for the purchasers from the beginning called on the vendors' solicitor. He explained that his clients were having some difficulty in obtaining finance which they had arranged and canvassed the desirability and possibility of the vendors in their own interests agreeing to re-negotiate the contract in one of several ways (a) by agreeing to accept a lower price or (b) to extend the closing date with his clients possibly agreeing to a higher price or (c) by his clients agreeing to pay interest or some other form of penalty in return for an extension of the closing date. The vendors' solicitors immediate reaction was that it was extremely unlikely that his client would co-operate in any way to meet the purchasers' difficulties. The solicitors contacted the vendors' solicitors and, referring to Mr. O' Rouke's call, reminded them that the time of closing had been made of the essence of the contract for sale, asked for confirmation that the purchaser would be in a position to close on the agreed date. In response to this the purchasers' solicitors wrote on the 12th of September, 1974, to state that their clients had confirmed that they were in a position to close at the end of October. On the 13th of September the vendors' solicitors wrote about some ancillary matters relating to the sale in the course of which they stated "The closing date is the 30th October, 1974, and time is of the essence of the contract" and again "our clients are most anxious to complete on the closing date". They wrote again to the purchasers' solicitors on the 19th of September welcoming the confirmation of the purchasers' ability to close and continued "Our clients would of course have a substantial claim for damages against your good selves if completion does not take place by the 30th of October and we shall be glad therefore if you will take all steps necessary to have the sale closed by the 30th of October". They wrote again on the 26th of September agreeing to the nomination of Buns Limited as Assignees "on the basis that our clients' rights against Messrs. O'Connor & Co. in trust remain in full force and can be exercised against them should the purchase not be completed on the 30th of October as provided by the contracts".

Apart from this rather unusual pressure by one firm of solicitors on another preparations for the sale proceeded normally. Draft assignments were prepared, approved, engrossed and I think in part executed subject to the preparation and attachments of maps which I do not regard as of much importance. The member of the vendors' solicitors firm who was handling the transaction was going on holidays and accordingly a trial closing took place on the 25th of October which left nothing to be done on the 30th except the exchange of the completed assurances and a cheque for the amount shown due on the apportionment account.

During all this to the knowledge of all the vendors, Mr. McLaughlin continued to use the right of way and the rear portion of Number 11 Baggot Street for the purpose of his business. Photographs taken on the 27th of November, 1974, and which it is agreed fairly represent the position as it existed on the 30th of October, show an extension of a shed covering portion of the right of way and a considerable amount of material and equipment that belonged to McLaughlin stored or dumped over the vendors' portion of the rear of Number 11. The photographs also show that the vendors' portion of the rear of Number 9 as used in conjunction with the occupation of that house apparently by Mr. McLaughlin and his family who, as I have indicated, were tenants of a flat in that house.

The vendors through their factory manager Mr. Sidney Hill and other employees were aware of this use of the rear of both premises. Although there is a conflict of evidence on this point I am satisfied that in September of 1974 Mr. Hill in the course of an interview when he introduced Mr. McLaughlin to a representative of the purchasers asked him to ensure that he would have everything removed from the vendors' property by the 30th of October and that Mr. McLaughlin clearly acknowledged the extent of the vendors' property when he said something to the effect that he understood that he could continue to use a distance of twenty five feet from the back of Number 11 which is approximately the portion retained by Mr. Pryce when he sold the premises to the Manchester Company.

I am further satisfied, although again the evidence conflicts, that early in October Mr. McLaughlin again acknowledged the position to Mr. Hill and another employee of the vendors, Mr. Jack Reid, when he was cooperative in agreeing to clear the vendors' portion of the rear of the Baggot Street premises by the 30th of October.

Although these conversations did take place, I am satisfied that the vendors did not take any active steps to ensure that the premises would be vacated by Mr. McLaughlin for the possible reasons that they knew that the purchasers would not actually enter on the premises until their building operations started and that they were satisfied that Mr. McLaughlin would vacate the premises on demand and secondly, they knew that in any event the purchasers intended to buy and use the Baggot Street houses as part of the development and that they would then automatically have the whole site vacant.

The sale was to have been closed at noon on the 30th of October. That morning Mr. Reid had a final look over the premises, locked up the Fleming Place factory and said goodbye to Mr. McLaughlin. At that time Mr. McLaughlin had not removed himself from the rear of the Baggot Street premises and this was obvious. Nothing was said by either as regards this. Some time later that morning the purchasers' agent Mr. Michael Smyth visited the premises to see that everything was in order and that the premises were vacant. He found Mr. McLaughlin there and with no intention of moving. Here I may digress somewhat to explain that at this stage the purchasers were also anxious to have the sale closed. They had secured the necessary finances and were concerned, once they had acquired the property, to conclude negotiations to purchase Numbers 9 and 11 Baggot Street before the vendors of those premises became aware of how essential it was for the purchasers to acquire them.

When he learned that Mr. McLaughlin was claiming a right to remain on the premises Mr. Smyth got in touch with the purchasers' solicitors who in turn contacted Mr. Kirwan. All three went to the premises where they were met by Mr. McLaughlin who claimed that he had a right to be there and ordered them off. On the grounds that the premises were not vacant the purchasers refused to close the sale and on the following day the 31st October their solicitors wrote rescinding the contract and asking for a return of the deposit. They did so on the ground that the vendors were in breach of the terms of the contract in failing to yield up vacant possession and referred to the represenatations that had been made verbally and in reply to requisitions that this would be done. The vendors' attitude was and is that Mr. McLaughlin was a trespasser. However, when subsequently they took proceedings against him for possession they compromised the action by the payment to Mr. McLaughlin of a sum of £2,500 in return for possession.

I am satisfied that Mr. McLaughlin was a trespasser and that he knew it. However it is clear from authority cited to me and not dissented from by the plaintiffs in this action, that the presence of a trespasser is a breach of a stipulation by a vendor to hand over vacant possession. The plaintiffs, however, contend that although time was of the essence of the contract to bind the purchasers to complete on the date fixed it did not similarly bind them and that they should have been given an equitable extension of time to enable them to eject Mr. McLaughlin; that they had got rid of him and were in a position to close when their action was compromised on the 19th of December, 1974, and that in all circumstances this was reasonable time. Accordingly they contend the purchasers had no right to rescind the contract.

In these circumstances they brought this suit for specific performance first against the purchasers' solicitors who had signed the contract in trust and secondly against the other defendants as purchasers. I have already dismissed the claim against the solicitors. Where an agent, acting for an un-disclosed principal, is clearly shown to have contracted merely as agent then the true position and intention of the parties is recognised and the agent drops out of the transaction. I am satisfied that by common usage a solicitor who signs a contract to purchase in trust is clearly recognised as acting merely as agent and, in the absence of a clear stipulation to the contrary, incurs no personal liability.

The real question to be decided in this case is whether the provision as to time was mutually binding or bound only the purchasers. If the vendors were not bound by the provision making time the essence of the contract they were entitled to a reasonable extension of such time and an extension until after the 19th of December would have been reasonable. This is the rule of equity as to time which by section 28 (7) of the Judicature (Ireland) Act, 1877, was applied to all contracts, but it is clear that even in equity, stipulations as to time may not always be disregarded and one case in which such a stipulation cannot be disregarded is where the parties themselves have provided that it should be essential. In this case it is agreed that the provision in the contract as to closing was inserted at the instance of and for the benefit of the vendors. Does that render it unilateral so as to bind only the purchasers leaving the vendors the benefit of the equitable rule? I think not. *Finkielkraut* v. *Monohan* [1949] 2 All E.R. 234 was a case where, subsequent to a contract for sale, the vendor sent to the purchaser a notice to complete within fourteen days. On the date fixed for completion the purchaser was ready and willing to complete but the vendor was not although she was in a position to complete some two weeks later. In an action by the purchaser for rescission and a counterclaim by the vendor claiming specific performance it was held that as the vendor was unable to complete on the day fixed she was not entitled to an order for specific performance. Dealing with the matter at page 237 of the report Danckwerts J. says

> "The question to be decided is whether owing to the circumstances and history of the case the vendor in her cross action is entitled to ask for specific performance. In my opinion she is not. It is true that this was a contract in which originally the time for completion would not have been regarded by equity as of

the essence but by her notice of March 31, 1948, sent by her solicitor the vendor made completion by April 14, 1948, an essential term at any rate on the purchaser's part. Notwithstanding the fact that he or his solicitor was told the completion would not take place the purchaser was I think within his rights in appearing on April 14 to complete the purchase by paying the balance of the purchase money and it is claimed that he was in a position to do so. In my view the vendor can't be heard to say that time was not essential on April the 14th, 1948. A number of cases were cited but none of them really touches the point although they do not indicate that where a party gives a notice requiring completion by a certain date and the date is a reasonable one the rule of equity that the time fixed for completion is not the essence of the contract no longer operates: see *per* Lord Parker of Waddington in *Stickney* v. *Keeble* [1915] A.C. 416; and the notice does at any rate bind the person to whom it is given. If it binds the person to whom it was given I cannot see why the person who has elected to give such a notice is not also bound."

More recently in *Quadrangle Development and Construction Company Limited* v. *Jenner* [1974] 1 All E.R. 729 the same principles were reiterated by the Judges of the Court of Appeal. The case concerned a notice to complete served in accordance with the provisions of the English National Conditions of Sale which empowered the vendor to serve a notice requiring the purchaser to complete within twenty-eight days. In the course of his judgment Russell L.J. says at page 732 of the report:–

"It is pointed out that it is only that party who appears to be the subject of the terms in respect of which time shall be of the essence; if it had been intended that both parties the giver and the recipient of the notice shall be the subject of that term then instead of the words 'that the party to whom notice is given shall complete the contract" surely it was argued one would have found it much more simply expressed with the words 'that completion shall take place'. I see myself the semantic force of that argument but it seems to me that exactly the same considerations apply to this clause as apply in what has been referred to as the common law notice case. It is as Templeman J. said – I borrow his word – really ludicrous to think of an obligation on the one party to complete the contract time being of the essence without there being necessarily on the other side of the coin a similar obligation on the party giving the notice. Under the language of the clause the party giving the notice must be ready and willing at the time of giving the notice to fulfil his own outstanding obligations under the contract. I should have thought it not really difficult to infer that the same party must continue to be ready and willing at any time during the period to fulfil his part of the contract.

Counsel for the vendor in this connection drew our attention to the passage in *Mackay* v. *Dick* where Lord Blackburn used this phrase of general application which Counsel particularly applied – I think rightly – to the present case:'I think I may safely say as a general rule that where in a written contract it appears that both parties have agreed that something shall be done which cannot effectually be done unless both concur in doing it, the construction of the contract is that each agrees to do all that is necesary to be done on his part for carrying out of that thing though there may be no express words to that effect'. It seems to me that if by the notice the giver of the notice brings into existence a term in respect of which time shall be of the essence that the recipient of the notice shall complete it is implicit in that the term equally binds the giver of the notice because completion despite strenuous argument to the contrary by Counsel for the purchasers is in my judgment an activity in which two parties necessarily co-operate. Completion by one cannot be effected without the co-operation of the other."

And dealing with the decision in *Finkielkraut* v. *Monohan* he says at page 733:–

"Counsel for the purchasers has advanced vigorously every argument that really could be put forward I think but I am by no means persuaded that the learned judge was anything but perfectly correct in the conclusion at which he arrived and perfectly correct therefore in declining to order specific performance and in giving leave to defend."

And Buckley L.J. says also at page 733:–

"I am of the opinion that when notice is given to complete in this form it has the effect of making time of the essence of the contract as a whole and in respect of both parties of the contract and on that ground in my judgment the learned judge reached the right conclusion and this appeal fails."

The present case is I think even stronger in that the stipulation as to time does not depend on a notice unilaterally given but on what was an original term of the contract mutually entered into by the parties. Accordingly, in my view, the plaintiffs are not entitled to rescind the contract and are entitled to a return of their deposit.

Note
See further *Irish Conveyancing Law*, para. 12.12.

5. *Laches*

HAIRE-FOSTER V. McINTEE
(1889) 23 L.R. Ir. 529; 24 I.L.T.R. 44 (Chancery Division)

The facts are set out in the judgment.

Monroe, J.:

The plaintiff in this equity civil bill alleges that in the month of December, 1882, the defendant, who was his tenant from year to year of a farm of land, at a rent of £24 6*s*. 8*d*., entered into an agreement to fix a fair rent on the holding under the Land Act of 1881, at the sum fo £20 per annum, and that the plaintiff was to prepare and send him the usual form for his signature. The plaintiff alleges that he filled up the form and left it at the defendant's residence; that in pursuance of the agreement the rent was taken at the reduced rent of £20; that the plaintiff was always ready and willing to execute the agreement and have same filed, pursuant to the rules of the Land Commission, but that the defendant refused to execute it. The plaintiff therefore seeks to have specific performance of the agreement.

The defendant by his answer denies the agreement. He denies that any form was ever left at his house. He alleges that the rent was reduced, not in pursuance of the alleged agreement, but as a mere temporary abatement, owing to agricultrual depression. He relies on the Statute of Frauds, and the absence of any acts of part performance, and he alleges that the plaintiff has been guilty of such delay in these proceedings as to disentitle him to relief.

On the question of fact, as to whether the alleged agreement was entered into, I believe, as the County Court Judge who heard the evidence believed, that the plaintiff's version is correct. The defendant admits he had a conversation with the plaintiff in November, 1882, about the Land Act of 1881, at a time when nearly all tenants in his townland had served originating notices. He does not say what that conversation was. He alleges that the plaintiff spoke to him about requiring a judicial agreement, though he states this conversation to have taken place in the month of June, 1883, when he refused to comply with the landlord's suggestion. The plaintiff, on the other hand, gives particulars of the interview: how the extent of the proposed reduction was discussed and agreed upon, and how the tenant mentioned the names of the persons before whom he would get the execution of the agreement by him witnessed, as required by the rules which were then in existence. The County Court Judge heard the evidence of both, given before him in Court, and had no difficulty in believing the plaintiff. I concur in his opinion. I am also of opinion that the form of agreement was left at the tenant's house. The plaintiff alleges that he filled up the form (No. 33) in duplicate, adding thereto a clause reserving his right to the game; that he kept one, which he produced in Court, signed by himself, but undated; that he left one at the defendant's house with a woman whom he did not identify or appear to know. The defendant, while he produced his wife and only daughter to prove that no document was ever given to either of them by the plaintiff, did not himself deny that he had received it, or that it had come to his hands. The County Court Judge believed the statement of the plaintiff, and I am of the same opinion. I must, therefore, take it that the defendant, whose rent up to that time was £24 6*s*. 8*d*., verbally agreed, in December, 1882, to sign an agreement for a judicial rent, as contained in the form sent to him, the rent in future to be £20 per annum. No rent appears to have been paid after the date of the agreement until the 2nd April, 1884. The tenant produced a receipt of that date for the sum of £20, "being one year's rent," due the 1st November, 1882. Another half-year's rent of £10, up to the 1st May, 1883, was paid on the 1st August, 1884. Further rent was paid at the same rate, and in proceedings by ejectment, taken by the landlord in March, 1886, the rent was treated in the civil bill as a rent of £20.

Under these circumstances several objections were raised on the part of the defendant to the decree for specific performance pronounced by the County Court Judge. The jurisdiction of the Court to grant such a decree upon proper evidence was not seriously questioned, having regard to the two cases decided by the Vice-Chancellor, of *Kelly* v. *Enright* 11 L.R. Ir. 379, and *Beauclerk* v. *Hanna* 23 L.R. Ir. 144. It was, however, urged that a decree could not be given, inasmuch as neither in the parol agreement, nor in the form which was left with the defendant, was there any date for the commencement of the lease. In my opinion this argument cannot prevail. Once the agreement sought to be enforced has been executed and filed in the prescribed manner, it is by the 8th section, sub-sect. 6, Land Law (Ireland) Act, 1881, to have the same effect and consequence in all respects as if the rent so agreed on were a judicial rent fixed by the Court under the provisions of the Act. The rent so fixed (sub-sect. 2) is to be deemed to be the rent payable by the tenant as from the period commencing at the rent-day next succeeding the decision of the Court. The gale-days of the defendant were May and November, so that in the case of a judicial agreement filed in the month of December, 1882, or at any time between that date and the 1st May following, the new rent, and the judicial term, would commence from the 1st May, 1883. The Act of Parliament specifies the date, in reference to which the contract was silent.

It was further contended that there was no act of part performance to get rid of the Statute of Frauds. Mere decrease in the rent paid was not, it was said, an act of part performance which could be relied on. It was not shown to be referable to the agreement, and there was no proof to corroborate the plaintiff's statement, which was entirely denied by the defendant. The authorities are quite clear to the effect that the payment of an increased rent satisfactorily proved to be referable to a parol agreement is an act of part performance: *Nunn* v. *Fabian* L.R. 1 Ch. 35; *Archbold* v. *Lord Howth* Ir. R. 1 C. L. 621; *Conner* v. *Fitzgerald* 11 L.R. Ir. 106. So also payment of a decreased rent, proved to be referable to a parol agreement, had been held to be an act of part performance: *Beauclerk* v. *Hanna* 23 L.R. Ir. 144. But clear and specific proof should be given to satisfy the Court that the increased or decreased rent was referable to an alleged parol agreement, and that it could not reasonably be attributed to anything else. I confess I should have had great difficulty in saying the evidence on this point was satisfactory if the tenant had told one consistent story and the landlord another, and that there was nothing in the circumstances of the case to corroborate either. This would be, in fact, to accept doubtful and unsatisfactory parol evidence of an act of part performance, the very class of evidence which the Statute of Frauds was intended to get rid of. Here, however, the case of the tenant is most unsatisfactory. He pleads one thing and swears another. In his defence he alleged that the rent was reduced merely temporarily, owing to agricultural depression. In his evidence he contradicts this statement altogether, and alleges that the landlord of a holding containing 20 A. 3 R. 20 P., at a rent of £24 6*s*. 8*d*., reduced the rent to £20, merely because the tenant alleged that he had less land, by an acre and fifteen perches, than he was paying rent for. The case sworn to was palpably false; and I have no hesitation, on the particular facts of this case, in arriving at the conclusion that the reduced rent taken by the plaintiff, and sued for by civil bill, corresponding as it did with that set out in the form of agreement left for the tenant's signature, was a rent reduced by reason of, and in accordance with, the terms of the parol agreement.

There is but one other matter which was also strongly urged by the defendant, viz. that the plaintiff has been guilty of such laches in this case as to deprive him of the relief which he seeks. The facts relied on are these:– The alleged agreement was made in December, 1882; the form was never signed by the tenant. He was sued for rent in April, 1885; he was then asked would he sign the agreement; he positively refused, and repudiated the agreement altogether. Still the landlord took no step to enforce it. In the month of October, 1887, the tenant served the landlord with an originating notice, stating his then rent to be £24 6*s*. 8*d*. The landlord even then took no step, until he filed the equity civil bill for specific performance on the 16th May, 1889.

I know of no case in which a plaintiff has ever succeeded in getting a decree for the specific performance of an agreement six years and a-half after it is alleged to have been entered into, four years after it had been repudiated in open Court, and nearly two years after the defendant had himself instituted proceedings entirely inconsistent with the existence of such a contract. If the plaintiff had instituted proceedings within a reasonable time after the contract was made – if he had shown himself, in the language of the cases, ready, prompt, and eager to carry out the contract for the execution of a statutory agreement – I think he would have been entitled to a decree. The County Court Judge was stated at the bar to have held that the tenant was not at liberty to rely on the landlord's laches so long as he enjoyed the benefit of the alleged contract. I cannot go to this length at all. The continuance by the tenant in possession at the lower rent referable to the agreement may, to a certain extent, explain why the landlord did not at once insist on the execution of the agreement. But there is no excuse for the delay after the tenant had repudiated its existence, though he paid only the reduced rent which the landlord demanded. I must therefore reverse the decree of the County Court Judge, and dismiss the equity civil bill.

Note

1. See further *Irish Conveyancing Law*, para. 12.49.
2. See also on laches *McCausland* v. *Young*, p.27, *ante*.

IV. DAMAGES

O'CONNOR V. McCARTHY
[1982] I.L.R.M. 201 (High Court)

The facts are set out in the judgment.

Costello J. delivered his judgment on 15 October 1981 saying: In September 1980 I gave judgment in a dispute that had arisen about the sale of premises in Skibbereen owned by a company, Fuller and Co Ltd, which is now in liquidation. I decided that the company throught its agent had entered into two separate binding contracts to sell this property. For the reasons which I set out in my judgment I granted an order for specific performance in favour of a Mr Walsh and a Mr O'Connor and I declared that another purchaser, Mr John Field, was not entitled to an order for specific performance but to damages in lieu thereof. The matter was relisted before me on 8 October 1981 to consider the evidence and the issues of law which have been raised in these proceedings.

The claim for damages is brought under three separate Heads.

Under Head (1) it is said that the purchase price provided for in the contract of sale was £31,000; that the value of the property on the date of my judgment had increased to £80,000; that Mr Field was thereof entitled to £49,000 under this heading.

Under Head (2) a claim for loss of profits was made. The claim is for £33,384 to the date of judgment and a sum of £55,640 for future loss of profits.

Under Head (3) it is said that the cost of purchasing and renovating the premises of

Fuller would have been £40,276; that the present cost of acquiring a site and constructing a premises suitable for Mr Phelan's needs is £106,558, and it is said that the claimant is entitled to the difference between these two sums, namely £66,282.

In the course of the case Mr Blayney on behalf of Mr Field accepted that the claimant was not entitled to damages based on loss of future profits as well as damages under Head (3) and reduced the claim to loss of profits to £33,384, that is to say the loss of profits to date of judgment. Even so, the claim is still for a startlingly substantial sum; namely, the sum of £148,666 lost, it is said, under a contract whose consideration was £31,000.

Turning firstly to Head (1), it is to be borne in mind that I refused the claimant relief by way of specific performance and that I am now awarding him damages in lieu of such an order. In *Malhotra* v. *Choudhury* [1980] 1 Ch. 52 the Court of Appeal had to consider, *inter alia,* whether damages which are awarded in substitution for a decree of specific performance are to be assessed by reference to the value of the premises at the date of the judgment or at the date of the defendant's breach of contract and (2) whether the damages were to include such loss of profits as the plaintiff could prove as flowing from the failure of the defendant to deliver to him the premises the subject matter of the sale. As to (1), following the approach suggested in *Wroth* v. *Tyler* [1974] Ch. 33 the court held that

> equity is following the law if in relation to an award of damages in substitution for an award for specific performance of a contract of sale of real property, it awards damages assessing the value of the realty at date of judgment and not at the date of breach.

In the instant case the date of my judgment was 8 September 1980 and counsel agree that I should assess damages in this case on the value of the property on that date and deduct from that figure the contract price. There agreement ends. There is wide disagreement as to the property's market value in September 1980 and in addition Mr Butler on behalf of the liquidator of Fuller claims that there should be a discount on this sum by reason of the fact that the purchaser never in fact paid the purchase money to the vendor and has had the benefit of it since.

I have had widely divergent evidence as to the market value of the property in September 1980. Mr McCarthy who is an auctioneer practising in Skibbereen says it would have fetched £80,000 on the open market at that time. Mr Ryan, on the other hand, who practises as an auctioneer in Cork city, puts its value at £31,000 in September 1980 and was in no way nonplussed by the fact that this was the price at which it was sold three and a half years previously. Evidence of sales of other premises in the town which has been given was only of limited value. I agree with Mr McCarthy that it would be unrealistic to calculate the price per square foot of such sales and to use the result as a basis for valuing the Fuller property. I also feel that the price paid for other premises is subject to the disability that the evidence related to retail shops and to premises which are not really comparable to that with which we are concerned in this case. I think I should approach this case by considering the nature and condition of the property, the subject matter of this application. Although there is a small shop premises attached to it the premises were basically used for storage purposes, but they comprise a large area which, if planning approval could be obtained, make them suitable for re-development. They were situated off the main thoroughfare and some distance from the roadway with an access by means of what was little more than a lane. The principal stone buildings were in good repair. So I have to decide what increase, if any, there would have been in the market between April 1977 and September 1980 for this particular premises. Mr McCarthy says that property values more than doubled in that period in the town and as Mr Field purchased the property at an undervalue he valued the market price in September 1980 at £80,000. Mr Ryan, however, makes the point that the number of potential purchasers for this type of property is limited and that it would not have increased in value at anything like the rate of other types of commercial property. I think there is something in this argument but I cannot accept the view that no increase in its value would have occurred in the relevant period. I am satisfied that property prices generally rose very considerably in the three and a half year period with which I am concerned and I conclude that the market price at the relevant date of this property would have been approximately 75% above the price which Mr Phelan paid for the property, that is to say approximately £55,000 and so Mr Phelan is entitled to £24,000 damages under Head (1), subject to a possible deduction to which I will now refer.

Mr Butler on behalf of the liquidator submits that damages under this Head should be reduced because the purchaser had not in fact paid the purchase price and has had the benefit of the sum of £31,000 during the relevant period. Mr Blayney disagrees and points out that the liquidator can cite no authority to justify the deduction claimed. I conclude that the deduction should not be allowed. The fundamental rule in contract cases is that the plaintiff is entitled to be placed, so far as money can do it, in the same position as he would have been in had the contract been performed. In the present case had the contract been performed Mr Phelan would have paid over his purchase money on the date provided for in the contract but would from that date have been entitled to the rents and profits. In the absence of evidence I cannot assume that the purchaser has received any financial advantage from the vendor's wrongful repudiation of the contract and so it is unnecessary for me to make any finding on the point had such evidence been adduced.

I come then to the damages claimed under Head (2), namely damages for loss of profit. As a preliminary point Mr Butler urges that in principle claims under Head (1) and Head (2) are mutually exclusive as a purchaser cannot claim both for the loss of the enhanced value of the property and the loss of the profits he would have made had he acquired the property as such claims would result in double compensation. I must confess that I found it difficult to follow the argument advanced in support of this submission and I note that in fact in *Malhotra* v. *Choudhury* the Court of Appeal allowed damages under both these Heads. I am not convinced therefore that as a matter of principle the claim for loss of profits should be disallowed.

The claim is advanced on the basis of the second rule relating to damages for breach of contract enunciated by Anderson B. in the well known case of *Hadley* v. *Baxendale* (1854) 9 Exch. 341. In the course of that judgment it was pointed out that damages payable by a contractbreaker should be such as 'may fairly and reasonably be considered either arising naturally, i.e. according to the usual course of things from such breach of contract itself, or such as may reasonably be supposed to have been in the contemplation of both parties at the time they made the contract as the probable result of the breach of it'. Mr Blayney does not suggest that the loss of profits which it is said Mr Field suffered arose natrually in the ordinary course of things, but he says there were special circumstances which were communicated to the vendors and that the loss of profits would ordinarily follow from the breach of contract under these special circumstances. He says that the special circumstances in this case were that Fuller's premises were requried for the expansion of the supermarket and bakery business which Mr Field carried on in Skibbereen and that it was in the contemplation of the parties to this contract that if that expansion was stopped by breach of a contract on the seller's part that Mr Field would suffer loss of profits.

Firstly, I will give my findings of fact on this claim. I am satisfied that in the month of April 1977 Mr Field wished to expand his business and that he bought Fullers premises for this purpose. He intended to reconstruct them so that they could be used for the bakery part of his business. He had two ovens in his existing premises and he intended to move them and purchase a third oven and use all three in the new premises. Thus he hoped to expand his bakery outlet by one third and expand the turnover of the supermarket business by utilising the space made available by the removal of the ovens. But did the company, that is to say, Fuller and company, know about these plans?

Fuller and company at the date of the sale was being managed by Mr O'Connor with its director's consent. He is an accountant practising in the city of Dublin and was then the liquidator of Fuller's parent company. The sale was negotiated by Mr

Phelan, an apprentice in Mr O'Connor's office and by Mr Field personally. They spent some hours on a Friday afternoon in negotiation and then orally concluded a deal. Having done so they spent a social evening together with Mr Nathan, Mr Field's accountant. On the following Monday a memorandum of the agreement prepared by Mr McCarthy the auctioneer who negotiated the sale was signed by Mr McCarthy and Mr Field and Mr Phelan. I am satisfied that Mr Phelan must have known before the oral agreement was concluded that Mr Field was buying the property for the purpose of expanding his business. I am also satisfied that Mr Field did not at any time communicate to Mr Phelan any details about how he would utilise the property if he got it and in particular he did not specifically inform him at any time as to what his plans were relating to the purchase of the new oven and the removal of the old ones to the new premises.

In the light of these findings of fact I must now consider whether a claim for loss of profits is sustainable.

There are not many authorities on the point I am now considering. *Diamone* v. *Campbell-Jones* [1961] 1 Ch. 22 was a case in which the purchaser claimed damages arising from the wrongful repudiation of a contract of sale by the vendor. He contended that the proper measure of damage was the profit which it was reasonable to suppose he would have made had he converted the property into maisonettes and offices. His claim failed. It was held that the purchaser had not made known to the vendor the work of conversion which he proposed and that there were no special circumstances from which that knowledge could be imputed to the vendor. Accordingly damages were assessed on the basis of the difference between the contract price and the market value of the premises as unconverted at the date of the breach. A different result occurred in *Cottril* v. *Steyning and Lettlehampton Building Society* [1966] 1 WLR 753. In that case the purchaser had purchased property with a view to converting it into flats and building six dwelling houses. His plans were known to the vendors and the Court held that the market value of the property as converted was to be ascertained and damages assessed at that figure less expenses attributable to the building work and matters ancillary thereto. In *Malhotra* v. *Choudhury* [1980] 1 Ch. 52 it was held that the parties had contemplated that if there was a failure to sell the house the subject matter of the proceedings the plaintiff would suffer damage for loss to his medical practice and directed damages to be assessed accordingly.

Mr Blayney accepts as correct the statement in *Anson on Contract* (24th Ed. at 535) to the effect that liability under the second branch of the rule depends on a purchaser establishing that there were special circumstances under which the contract was made and that these were known to the vendor. To my mind the mere fact that the purchaser in this case intended using the property he was buying for the expansion of an existing business did not constitute 'special circumstances' within the meaning of the rule. Had he drawn up detailed plans for their reconstruction and told Mr Phelan of the new way it was proposed to use the property so that special damaging consequences of a breach of contract would have been brought to his attention then the second branch of the rule might well fall to be applied. But this did not happen in the present case. I am satisfied that beyond a general statment that the property was to be used to expand an existing supermarket and bakery business Mr Phelan was not aware of any other or special use to which the property would be put. Thus it seems to me that the vendors were not aware of any special circumstances in this case which would render them liable to recoup the claimant for any loss of profit he may have sustained. It becomes unnecessary for me therefore to make any finding on the evidence relating to the quantum of the alleged loss, or to consider the submission made on the vendors' behalf that any knowledge which Mr Phelan may have had could not be imputed to Fuller and company.

The claim under Head (3) arises in this way. It is said that the cost of acquiring the Fuller premises and the cost of reconstructing them to make them suitable for Mr Field's purposes in 1977 would have been £40,276, £7,776.40 of which being the reconversion costs at 1977 prices. Mr Field now proposes to buy a site outside the town (at a cost of £20,000) and build on it a premises suitable for his bakery business, at a cost of £81,588 at current prices. The total cost of acquiring the site and building on it will be £106,558 and the difference between the 1977 costs and the total of the current costs namely the sum of £66,282 is claimed under Head (3). It seems to me that if any damages can be claimed by reason of the increase in building costs which occurred in the relevant period, it cannot be based on the construction costs of an entirely new building as has been suggested in this case. Apart from this, however, it seems to me that the purchaser has not shown that there were any special circumstances in relation to the contract of sale which were brought to the attention of the vendors so as to justify the claim as now formulated. It was a fact known to Mr Phelan that the property was to be used for the expansion of Mr Field's business and Mr Phelan would have appreciated that it was probable that some work of reconstruction on them would be undertaken by the new owner. But if Mr Field had any details finalised at the time of the sale as to how the property was to be reconstructed these were not conveyed to Mr Phelan. So, it seems to me that as Mr Phelan was not informed of any detailed plans of reconstruction or how exactly the property was to be used by the purchaser he was not in the possession of knowledge of any special circumstances within the meaning of the rule so as to render Fuller liable under Head (3) of the claim.

In the result, the claim under Head (1) only succeeds and I will declare that Mr Field is entitled to £24,000 damages.

Notes

1. See also *Roberts* v. *O'Neill*, p.193, *ante*.
2. See further on Lord Cairns' Act, *Irish Conveyancing Law*, para. 12.53; *Irish Land Law*, Supp. (1975-80), pp. 12-13.

Chapter 7

RESCISSION

"Rescission" has come to mean many things and the greatest care should be exercised over the use of the word, see *Irish Conveyancing Law,* para. 12.56 *et seq.* In this context we are concerned with rescission, *i.e.,* avoiding, of transactions by an action in court upon principles developed in equity, see *ibid.* and *Irish Land Law,* para 3.157 *et seq.* Central to this remedy is the notion of *restitutio in integrum,* a subject which has been reviewed by the Supreme Court in recent times.

I. RESTITUTIO IN INTEGRUM

NORTHERN BANK FINANCE CORPORATION LTD. V. CHARLTON
[1979] I.R. 149 (Supreme Court)

The facts are set out in the judgments.

O'Higgins C.J.:

This is an appeal brought by the plaintiffs, who are a merchant bank against the judgment and order of the President of the High Court dismissing their claim against the defendants and allowing to the defendants the relief which they sought in a counterclaim against the plaintiffs. The plaintiffs claim was for the sum of £38,581.90, with interest thereon, which was alleged to be monies due on a loan. The defendants are a solicitor and two businessmen respectively; the first and second defendants are brothers. The defendants resisted the plaintiffs' claim on the grounds that the loan relied on by the plaintiffs arose out of a larger transaction or series of transactions into which the defendants were induced to enter by the fraudulent misrepresentations of the plaintiffs' servants and agents. They further counter-claimed against the plaintiffs for damages and other relief because of the alleged fraud. As the amount due on foot of the loan, if valid, was not a dispute, the real question which was tried by the learned President was whether the defendants' claim in fraud was well-founded or not. In this respect the trial proceeded as if the defendants were the plaintiffs.

The transactions which gave rise to the defendants' allegations related to a take-over of a public company called J.G. Mooney and Co. Ltd. This took place in 1972. The take-over was promoted by the three defendants together with two others, Patrick Quinn and Vincent Duignan. It was assisted by the plaintiffs, both by way of a loan and by the plaintiffs agreeing to act as the promoters' agents in relation to the carrying out of the payments. The defendants claimed that they were induced to enter into this transaction by a number of fraudulent misrepresentations made by the servants of the plaintiffs. These representations, it was alleged, related to the amount and the continued existence, during the currency of the take-over bid, of a cash deposit made by Patrick Quinn as his contribution towards the total contribution in cash to be put forward by the promoters. The defendants further alleged that they were later induced to purchase the shares of Patrick Quinn in the enterprise by the continuance of these fraudulent representations and by a further representation, which was also fraudulent that at that time Patrick Quinn was not indebted to the plaintiffs.

The trial before the learned President occupied 16 days during which he heard the evidence of each of the defendants and that of Mr. Tierney, the plaintiffs' manager, and also two assistant managers, Mr. Tuomey and Mr. Byrne. In addition, the President was referred to a large number of documents which related to the transactions and which were duly proved in evidence. Having considered all this evidence, both oral and documentary, the President came to the conclusion that the defendants' allegations that the defendants had been induced by fraudulent misrepresentations to enter into the transactions in question were well-founded.

Accordingly, he dismissed the plaintiffs' claim and granted the defendants a series of orders and declarations which were designed to set aside all the acts and transactions they had done and entered into with the plaintiffs and to restore to the defendants, in so far as was possible, all property or rights transferred by them to the plaintiffs. In addition, the learned President held that the defendants were entitled to a sum for damages, measured in terms of interest on the sums repayable to them by the plaintiffs; this interest was to run from the date upon which each sum was deposited or paid.

In this appeal the plaintiffs call into question each and every finding of disputed facts ma le by the learned President which led him to make the orders and declarations mentioned. In a long and detailed notice of appeal these findings are questioned as being either unjustifiably inferred from the evidence, or as being unsupported by and inconsistent with the evidence, or as arising from misdirections in fact and in law. In this notice of appeal it was also alleged that the learned President was wrong in law in permitting evidence to be adduced by the defendants as to misrepresentations which had not been previously alleged or pleaded, and in basing on such evidence his holding that the plaintiffs had been guilty of fraudulent misrepresentations. The appeal also calls into question, as a separate issue, the various orders and declarations made by the learned President; it was submitted that, even if the allegations of fraud were well-founded, these various orders and declarations were not justified and ought not to have been made.

Findings of Fraud

The general background and circumstances under which the five promoters came together are fully set out in the judgments of the learned President. This judgment also contains details of the various steps that were taken, either by or on behalf of the promoters, to pursue with the assistance of the plaintiff bank the intended take-over of Mooney and Company. I do not propose in this judgment to repeat all these details. It is, I think, sufficient if I refer to the representations which the learned President found to have been made and to have been fraudulent. These representations are four in number.

The first of these was made by Mr. Tierney, the plaintiffs' manager, in September, 1972. The President found that Mr. Tierney then represented to the defendant Gerard Charlton, as the spokesman or representative of the three defendants, that Patrick Quinn had duly deposited £200,000 with the plaintiffs in accordance with the arrangement made between the promoters and the plaintiffs. The fact was that Patrick Quinn had deposited only the sum of £150,000 and, on the evidence which the President accepted, the knowledge of this shortfall in Patrick Quinn's contribution would have caused the defendants not to proceed in a joint enterprise with him. The President found this representation to have been made and to have been fraudulent.

The second representation which the President found to have been fraudulent was one of non-disclosure or silence. This related to Mr. Tierney the plaintiffs' manager, and Mr. Tuomey, the plaintiffs' assistant manager, and concerned a meeting attended by the plaintiff's officials and the promoters on the 26th November, 1972. At this meeting it was agreed to commence the purchase of Mooney shares on the stock exchange market and, in particular, to try to purchase a block of 10% of these shares in London. This decision involved the promoters' contributions being committed unconditionally to the purchase of such shares and the making of a further deposit by Hugh Charlton of £100,000. At that stage Patrick Quinn's deposit had been reduced by withdrawals to a mere £25,000. The learned President held that in these circumstances the failure of Mr. Tierney and Mr. Tuomey to disclose to the defendants the true position with regard to Patrick Quinn's cash account constituted a representation (which was false) that the condition of this account was in accordance with the arrangement that had been made between the promoters *inter se* and the plaintiff bank.

The next representation related to a meeting held in the office of Mr. Michael

Dickson, who is a member of the firm of solicitors acting for the plaintiffs. An enquiry was made by the defendant Gerard Charlton as to whether all the agreed contributions were in; he had come, both as a promoter and a solicitor, to finalise matters with the legal representatives of the plaintiffs. The President held that, having made that enquiry, Gerard Charlton was informed by Mr. Tuomey, in a three-way telephone conversation, that all the money was in. The President held that the representation was false and fraudulent in that, at that stage, Patrick Quinn's contribution was represented not by £100,000 cash provided by himself, as the defendants believed, but by £47,000 worth of Mooney shares and a £53,000 loan from the plaintiffs.

Finally, the President held that a further fraudulent misrepresentation took place in relation to the purchase by the defendants of Patrick Quinn's shares in the holding company which was effecting the take-over of J.G. Mooney & Co. Ltd. This purchase was suggested by the plaintiffs' manager, Mr. Tierney. Prior to agreeing to this the defendants enquired, as the President found, whether Patrick Quinn was then indebted to the plaintiffs to any extent. The President held that the plaintiffs' manager thereupon gave an assurance to the defendants that Patrick Quinn was in no way so indebted. This assurance the President held was false and fraudulent.

These then are the representations which the learned President found to have been made by the plaintiffs' agents, and to have been made fraudulently and in such a manner as to induce the defendants to enter into the original transaction concerned with the promotion of the take-over and, later, to purchase the shares of Patrick Quinn in the venture. The learned President held that other representations which were relied on by the defendants had not been proved or established to the degree necessary to sustain an allegation of fraud. In coming to his findings of fraud, the learned President chose between the affirmative evidence adduced by the defendants in support of the allegations they made and the directly contradictory evidence adduced by the plaintiffs in denial that the representations were made. The President's findings were clearly based on the view he formed as to the credibility of each witness whom he heard.

Appeals to the Supreme Court

Appeals to the Supreme Court are governed by Order 58 of the Rules of the Superior Courts, 1962. While these Rules provide that the appeal shall be by way of re-hearing, this does not mean that the proceedings in the court below are completely re-heard or re-enacted in the Supreme Court. Under Order 58, r. 14, where any question of fact is involved in an appeal, this Court hears and considers the evidence which was before the trial court. Under the rule this evidence is brought before the court:– "(a) as to any evidence taken by affidavit, by the production of printed copies of such of the affidavits as have been printed, and copies of such of them as have not been printed; (b) as to any evidence given orally, by the production of a copy of the Judge's notes, or such other materials as the Supreme Court may deem expedient." It follows that in the normal case, while the evidence given at the trial may be heard again on the appeal in the form of the judge's notes or the transcript, the witness who gave it will not be heard again. In such cases, therefore, where findings of fact are challenged on appeal, it is the existence or sufficiency of evidence to support such findings which is considered by this Court and not whether what was accepted or regarded as credible at the trial ought to have been so accepted or regarded – unless, of course, something manifestly wrong has taken place.

The appeal provisions contained in Order 58 cover both appeals from decisions and orders of judges and, with some necessary modification appeals in relation to jury trial: see Order 76, r. 92. These latter appeals take the form of new-trial motions or motions to set aside a jury's verdict or finding. These motions relating to jury trials have always been dealt with separately because of the accepted finality of a jury's finding of fact. Such a finding, if supported by evidence and if the trial was otherwise unassailable, could not be interfered with.

In relation to trials by a judge sitting without a jury, a different view has always been taken with regard to findings of fact once an issue is raised on appeal. This difference was expressed towards the end of the last century by Holmes L.J. in the Irish Court of Appeal; in *The S.S. Gairloch* [1899] 2 I.R.1, at p. 18 of the report, he said:-

"When a Judge after trying a case upon *viva voce* evidence comes to a conclusion regarding a specific and definite matter of fact, his finding ought not to be reversed by a Court that has not the same opportunity of seeing and hearing the witnesses unless it is as clearly against the weight of the testimony as to amount to a manifest defeat of justice. The same rule does not apply, at least to the same degree, where the conclusion is an inference of fact. It often happens, as in the present instance, that the decisive finding is a deduction of facts hardly disputed or easily ascertained. In such a case the appellate tribunal is in as good a position for arriving at a correct conclusion as the Judge appealed from, and it would be an undue restriction of the functions of the former if it were to hold itself bound by what has been found by the latter. Of course the view of the Judge who tried the case is of the greatest weight, and for my own part I would only depart from it with much hesitation when as here, we have not been furnished with a report or note of the judgment appealed from."

At about the same time Lindley M.R., in the course of delivering the judgment of the Court of Appeal in *Coghlan* v. *Cumberland* [1898] 1 Ch. 704, said at pp. 704 705 of the report:-

"The case was not tried with a jury, and the appeal from the judge is not governed by the rules applicable to new trials after a trial and verdict by a jury. Even where, as in this case, the appeal turns on a question of fact, the Court of Appeal has to bear in mind that its duty is to rehear the case, and the Court must reconsider the materials before the judge with such other materials as it may have decided to admit. The Court must then make up its own mind, not disregarding the judgment appealed from, but carefully weighing and considering it; and not shrinking from overruling it if on full consideration the Court come to the conclusion that the judgment is wrong. When, as often happens, much turns on the relative credibility of witnesses who have been examined and cross-examined before the judge, the Court is sensible of the great advantage he has had in seeing and hearing them. It is often very difficult to estimate correctly the relative credibility of witnesses from written depositions; and when the question arises which witness is to be believed rather than another, and the question turns on manner and demeanour, the Court of Appeal always is, and must be, guided by the impression made on the judge who saw the witness."

It was thus recognised as long as the end of the last century that a judge's findings of fact was not necessarily sacrosanct in the way of a jury's finding might be regarded. Such a finding was open to review and reconsideration in the Court of Appeal.

However, a definite limit or barrier to such reconsideration or review was always recognised. This was on the question of credibility which depends on the assessment of witnesses by a judge who sees and hears them. This is recognised in both the passages which I have quoted from the decisions in *The S.S. Gairloch* and *Coghlan* v. *Cumberland.* It was recognised also in *Montgomerie and Co. Ltd* v. *Wallace-James* [1904] A. C. 73 where the Earl of Halsbury L.C. said at p. 75 of the report:-

"It is simply a question of fact, and doubtless, where a question of fact has been decided by a tribunal which has seen and heard the witnesses, the greatest weight ought to be attached to the finding of such a tribunal. It has had the opportunity of observing the demeanour of the witnesses and judging of their veracity and accuracy in a way that no appellate tribunal can have. But where no question arises as to truthfulness, and where the question is as to the proper inferences to be drawn from truthful evidence, then the original tribunal is in no better position to decide than the judges of an Appellate Court."

It was again recognised in *Mersey Docks and Harbour Board* v. *Procter* [1923] A.C. 253 where Viscount Cave L.C. said at p. 258 of the report:-

"The procedure on an appeal from a judge sitting without a jury is not governed by the rules applicable to a motion for a new trial after a verdict of a jury. In such a case it is the duty of the Court of Appeal to make up its own mind, not disregarding the judgment appealed from and giving special weight to that judgment in cases where the credibility of witnesses comes into question, but with full liberty to draw its own inference from the facts proved or admitted and to decide accordingly. In the present case there is no question of the credibility of witnesses."

In my view these cases show a consistent line of thinking. A judge's findings on fact can and will be reviewed on appeal. Such findings will be subjected to the normal tests as to whether they are supported by the evidence given at the trial. If such findings are firmly based on the sworn testimony of witnesses seen and heard and accepted by the judge, then the court of appeal, recognising this to be the area of credibility, will not interfere. However, if the finding in question depends on the judge's view of the evidence or on inferences he draws from such evidence, then the court of appeal, while respecting this view, will nevertheless disagree if another view or a different inference be the proper one. This distinction was recognised in a different form by Viscount Simonds in *Benmax* v. *Austin Motor Co. Ltd.* [1955] A.C. 370 when he adopted the terms "perception" and "evaluation" as used by Professor Goodhart in writing on Appeals on Questions of Fact: (1955) 71 L.Q.R. 402. At p. 373 of the report, having referred to the relevant rules which are similar to our rules, he said:-

"This does not mean that an appellate court should lightly differ from the finding of a trial judge on a question of fact, and I would say that it would be difficult for it to do so where the finding turned solely on the credibility of a witness. But I cannot help thinking that some confusion may have arisen from failure to distinguish between the finding of a specific fact and a finding of fact which is really an inference from facts specifically found, or, as it has sometimes been said, between the perception and evaluation of facts."

In my view, these observations correctly describe the proper role of the Court of appeal in relation to appeals from a judge on a question or finding of fact. In my view it would be not only contrary to accepted practice but also manifest injustice if a court, which neither saw nor heard the witness, pronounced on his credibility. There may be circumstances in which the acceptance or rejection of particular evidence by a judge was so obviously and clearly wrong as to be unreasonable and unjust. Such instances have been extremely infrequent and one can say hopefully that they will continue to be so. In the normal case, however, in so far as the judge's finding of fact are based directly on evidence which he heard and believed, it being open to him to accept such evidence or to reject it, such findings cannot be interfered with by this court in my view.

It follows from what I have said that I cannot accept the submissions made on this aspect of the case by Mr. Liston. The task of this Court is not to look at and consider all the evidence for the purpose of deciding whether a judge ought to have accepted the particular evidence which he did accept: rather it is to consider whether such evidence is credible and supports fairly and properly the judge's findings, and whether such inferences as he drew were fairly and properly drawn. Further than this, in my view, this Court ought not and cannot go in reviewing questions of fact.

Findings of the trial judge

As already indicated, the judge's findings with which this appeal is concerned were based on positive evidence given by witnesses whom he saw and heard. From the very outset this was a case in which the real issue was one of credibility. This was not only appreciated by the parties but was fully understood and accepted by the learned trial judge. The assessment of witnesses and findings of fact made by the trial judge were made, as is apparent from his judgment, on a careful weighing and judging of each witness in the light of his view as to that witness's reliability and credibility. In my view, for the reasons which I have already given, these findings cannot be disturbed.

In so far as the notice of appeal contains grounds in which complaint is made as to unjustifiable inferences being drawn or misdirections in fact being made by the learned trial judge, I am equally of the opinion that such findings cannot be disturbed. In short, it seems to me that in so far as the judge's findings of fact consisted of inferences they were reasonable and properly drawn, and in so far as such findings were based on affirmative positive evidence they were based on evidence which the judge was fully entitled to accept. In addition, in my view, the judge correctly applied the law and correctly considered the onus to be discharged where fraud is alleged.

Appeal of Liability

In my view this disposes of the plaintiffs' appeal on liability, except for the complaint that the trial judge was wrong in law in permitting evidence to be adduced as to misrepresentations which had not been previously alleged or pleaded. The Courts have always insisted that a person who alleges fraud must not only give full particulars of his allegation but must confine the evidence he adduces to what he has pleaded. However, in this case it is apparent that much that was not pleaded appeared in the affidavits used at stages in the proceedings, and that allegations outside the pleadings were contained in the opening address made by counsel to the judge. No objection was taken or raised on behalf of the plaintiffs and, in effect, the judge was invited to consider these allegations and to hear evidence with regard to them. The first objection raised to this course is raised on this appeal. I cannot accept that there is merit in this ground of appeal. In my view the plaintiffs are bound by the run of the case in the High Court and cannot expect this Court to review on appeal matters and issues which were not raised before the trial judge.

Appeal as to Reliefs

I turn now to consider the consequences. Having come to the conclusion that fraud had been established, the President decided in the first place that the plaintiffs' claim could not be sustained as it arose from a transaction which had been induced by a fraudulent misrepresentation. I have no difficulty in saying that in this he was correct. He then decided, in so far as it was possible to do so, to rescind the transactions entered into between the parties. The plaintiffs contend that he was wrong. They say that this is not a case in which rescission can be ordered because the transactions were so far performed and were of such a nature as to make *restitutio in integrum* possible. They further submitted that neither is it a case for damages because there was no loss due to the fraud. They submit that the defendants got full value for their investment when it was made, and that any losses subsequently suffered were due to mistakes made, or lack of prudence displayed, by the defendants themselves. These submissions must be considered in the light of the legal principles which apply in cases of fraud.

Where a fraudulent misrepresentation has induced a transaction, the rule is that the person deceived has the right to rescind the entire transaction; but the right must be exercised *in toto* so that every part of the transaction, and everything given or obtained under it, is cancelled or restored. The representee is not permitted to affirm part and rescind another part of the same transaction. The fact that the contract has been executed or the transaction completed is no bar to rescission unless by reason thereof *restitutio in integrum* has become impossible. Whether such *restitutio* has become impossible or not is a matter for consideration and decision in relation to the facts of each particular case.

As is pointed out in Kerr on Fraud and Mistake (7th ed.) at p. 513:- "The phrase is somewhat vague and must be applied with care. It must be considered with regard to the facts of each case. Deterioration of the subject-matter does not destroy the right to rescind nor prevent *restitutio in integrum*. Indeed, it is only in cases where the plaintiff has sustained loss by deterioration of the subject-matter that he will desire to exert his power of rescission. The Court has full power to make all just allowances, and in practice it always grants such relief when it can do what is practically just, although it may not be able to restore the parties precisely to the state in which they were before they entered into the contract." And in Spencer Bower's Law of Actionable Misrepresentation (3rd ed.) it is stated (p. 310) in relation to such a possible defence to a claim for rescission:- "But it is of no avail to show a mere depreciation or deterioration of the property arising in the ordinary course of events, or from natural decay or inherent defects, and in no wise imputable to the positive acts and conduct of the representee . . . Further even when the defence is otherwise good, it is open to the representee to defeat it by proof that the representor has deliberately stood by and silently encouraged the acts of the representee which are alleged to have produced the alteration or extinction of the property . . . Further, the court will not refuse relief where, though not precise or punctilious, such a substantial restitution can be made as to render rescission 'practically just'." These two quotations are supported amply by the decided cases to which the learned authors refer (many of which have been cited in argument on this appeal) and in my view they correctly state the law. Do these principles apply in this case and, if so, to what extent? In the first place it seems to me that, although rescission is not expressly claimed in the defendants' counterclaim to the plaintiffs' claim in these proceedings, the reality of the defendants' claim for the various repayments sought is the rescission of the transactions under which these payments were made. It follows, in my view, that the President correctly regarded the counterclaim as a claim for rescission. Therefore, the question is whether such a claim is maintainable on the facts and in the circumstances of this case.

Rescission

There were two transactions which the President held to have been affected by fraudulent representations for which the plaintiffs are responsible. The first of these was the agreement between the plaintiffs and the five promoters for the financing of the take-over of Mooney. This involved the subscription by the promoters from their own resources of £500,000 in agreed shares and the granting of a loan by the plaintiffs; the actual operation was to be carried out by the plaintiffs through a holding company, called Pat Quinn Holdings Ltd., to which subscriptions and loans were to be credited. The agreement required that the plaintiffs' loan be secured by the share capital and assets of the holding company with, as collateral, joint and several guarantees from the five promoters, the pledging of the personal assets of the defendants and of the entire assets of I.T.G. Ltd. a company owned by the second and third defendants. Having been induced to enter into this transaction by the fraudulent misrepresentation of the plaintiffs' agents, the defendants did not become aware of the fraud until some years had elapsed. When the defendants discovered the true facts, not only had the take-over of Mooney been completed and the purchase by them of Patrick Quinn's share taken place but, in addition, the apparent or market value of the original investment had evaporated and it had become worthless.

The second transaction into which the defendants were induced to enter by the fraudulent misrepresentation of the plaintiffs' agents was the purchase by them of Patrick Quinn's shares in the holding company. These two transactions involved the first defendant in a total expenditure of £72,378.11 and they involved the second and third defendants in an expenditure of £344,757.10.

Can these transactions be rescinded? The plaintiffs say that they cannot be rescinded because, in the events which have happened, "an egg has been scrambled which cannot be unscrambled." They say that *restitutio in integrum* is an essential requirement for rescission and that it is now impossible. They point to the fact that, in pursuance of the original project, Mooney shares have changed hands and, through the agency of the plaintiffs, have become the property of Pat Quinn Holdings. To endeavour to rescind in such circumstances would be impossible because it would result in a situation in which the plaintiffs would end up owning shares which they never previously owned in a business which had nothing to do with banking.

It is also said that rescission is not now possible because the shares are now valueless and that this was caused and brought about by the actions and decisions of the promoters, including the defendants, after the take-over had succeeded. In this respect reliance was placed on the decision taken by the new board of Mooney that the company would purchase the property holding of I.T.G. Ltd. The decision was also to the effect that out of the proceeds of that sale I.T.G. Ltd. would invest £300,000 in Pat Quinn Holdings. This decision was said to be the cause of Mooney shares not obtaining a re-quotation on the stock exchange and thus led to the financial collapse of the enterprise. Whether the decision had this effect or not is not relevant because it is not the subject of these proceedings. What is relevant, however, is that after the take-over and as a result of this decision the second and third defendants invested, through I.T.G. Ltd., another £300,000 in the holding company. That entire investment, with other monies so invested, is now valueless.

I have considered very carefully whether in the circumstances of this case the legal principles which I have mentioned can be applied and whether, accordingly, relief in the nature of rescission can be given. In my view, such principles do apply and such relief can be given. It seems to me that it is the bounden duty of the Court to do what is practically just – this being a case of fraud – even though the precise restoration of the parties to their previous position is not now possible.

The transactions involved, in the first instance, the plaintiffs financing and purchasing, as agents for the promoters, whatever Mooney shares were obtainable. Were it not for the fraudulent misrepresentations which were established, the defendants would not have been involved in this transaction at all. It cost them, initially, their investment; this they should get back. That form of rescission is at least possible. The plaintiffs, having dealt with shares on a representation with regard to a particular stake and particular stakeholders which was untrue and fraudulent, cannot complain if they are now left holding these shares. Nor can they complain that the shares are now valueless. In my view, in this respect, this case is similar to *Armstrong* v. *Jackson* [1917] 2 K.B. 822.

Again, the plaintiffs having instigated the purchase by the defendants of Patrick Quinn's shares and having induced the defendants to proceed with such purchase by further fraudulent representations, ought to be ordered to repay what they received or caused to be paid by the defendants as a result of such transaction.

There remains the purchase of the property holding of I.T.G. Ltd. by Mooney and the consequent further investment in Pat Quinn Holdings of £300,000 by the second and third defendants. This investment, unlike the others, was not triggered off by any of the respresentations complained of. It was, however, made in the full knowledge of the plaintiffs' officers and with their agreement on behalf of the plaintiffs. For this reason the plaintiffs can scarcely be heard to suggest that this additional investment was a non sequitur so far as the misrepresentation was concerned. It was made by two people whom they had induced to enter into the transaction and was made with their knowledge and approval at a time when these two people were still the victims of deception as to what the real participation and stakeholding was in the transaction in which they were involved. It would seem to me to be in accordance with what is practically just to order that the plaintiffs, who knew of and encouraged this investment in a holding company, the assets of which were already pledged to them, should be ordered to repay such sums to those who were so encouraged to invest.

It follows also that the form of appropriate rescission which seems to be both possible and just in this case requires also the cancelling of all guarantees and pledges given by the defendants and their indemnity by the plaintiffs in respect of promissory notes executed by the defendants at the behest of the plaintiffs. In short, it seems to me that the various orders and declarations made by the President represent as effective a means as can be found to undo the wrong done to the defendants by the fraudulent misrepresentations which induced the transactions. These orders and declarations also represent as effective a means as possible to bring about such form of rescission as can be obtained in the circumstances of this case. I would, therefore, affirm the order made by the learned President.

As I am aware that the views which I have expressed on the availability of rescission as a relief in this case are not shared by a majority of my colleagues, I think it proper to add something on the subject of damages. If rescission be not the appropriate remedy, then the question must be what damages have been suffered as a result of the wrong or tort of deceit. By reason of the view taken by the President as to the appropriateness of rescission as a remedy, this aspect was not considered by him. If it is to be considered and examined at a further stage in these proceedings then, in my view, the enquiry should be as general as the law permits. The measure of damages for the tort of deceit is the actual loss flowing directly from the fraud. I adopt in this respect the views of Lord Atkin in *Clark* v. *Urquhart* [1930] A.C. 28 at p. 68 of the report. Such damages can cover consequential loss. This is a matter of proof. Clearly in this case this may be a matter of some complexity. The damage flowing from the original inducement to engage in the take-over may well be different in kind and degree from that flowing from the inducement to purchase Patrick Quinn's shares. Whether or not it is different will depend on the evidence that may be adduced. Since no evidence has been adduced and since there are no findings on this aspect of the casȩ, in my view it would not be proper for this Court to say in what way the damages in either case ought to be limited. If the case is to be remitted to the High Court to have damages assessed, I will express no opinion other than to say that the measure of damages should be the loss flowing directly from the tort.

Henchy J.:

In dismissing the claim of the plaintiff bank and holding with the defendants in their counterclaim, Mr. Justice Finlay held that the bank had been guilty of fraudulent misrepresentation. In the course of coming to that conclusion he found that the bank, knowing it to be false, represented to the defendants that, for the purpose of the take-over of J.G. Mooney & Co. Ltd. by Pat Quinn Holdings Ltd., Patrick Quinn had lodged in the bank the amount of the contribution which it had been agreed he would make towards the cost of the take-over; that that representation was material to the defendants' participation in the take-over; and that the defendants were induced, as was intended, by that representation to proceed with the take-over.

Those findings of fact were necessary for the judge's determination that the bank was guilty of fraud. In this appeal, which has been taken by the bank against the order made in the High Court, it has been contended on behalf of the bank that the evidence was such that it was not open to the judge to make those findings. Counsel for the bank therefore strongly contest the finding of fraud. Much of the argument on the hearing of the appeal has been occupied with a forceful and meticulous investigation of the evidence, by counsel on both sides, aimed at rebutting or supporting the judge's findings of fact on which fraud on the part of the bank was held to have taken place.

Overriding that scrutiny of the evidence, there has been presented the question, which has been fully and ably argued on both sides, whether regardless of any contrary conclusions which might seem open on a review of the evidence, it is competent for this Court to set aside any of those findings of fact. It is the submission of counsel for the defendants that those findings derive primarily and essentially from the judge's assessment of the credibility of the oral testimony of certain witnesses, and that this Court, deprived as it is of the opportunity of seeing and hearing those witnesses, is thereby debarred from casting aside the judge's findings.

Order 58, r.1, of the Rules of the Superior Courts, 1962, specifies that all appeals to this Court shall be "by way of re-hearing." However, the expression "re-hearing" in that context is necessarily a term of art in an application to cases such as this. As follows from the other requirements of Order 58, the Court will normally be precluded from hearing or seeing the witnesses whose oral testimony was the core of the hearing in the High Court. So the appeal will be "by way of re-hearing" only to the extent that that will be possible by examining documentary material, particularly a written version or report of the evidence, save for those exceptional cases when fresh or re-presented evidence is received, usually in the form of oral testimony or by way of visual consideration of a person or object (e.g. the cosmetics consequences of facial injury by scarring).

It is sometimes stated that this Court's appellate jurisdiction is confined to questions of law. That, however, is not quite accurate. Save for exceptional cases where a statutory provision may limit the Court's jurisdiction to questions of law, in civil cases this Court may exercise an appellate jursidiction from decisions of the High Court on both questions of law and questions of fact. But the exercise of that jurisdiction in regard to questions of fact is necessarily limited in practice as a result of the requirements of the Rules of the Superior Courts, 1962 – just as the jurisdiction of the Court of Appeal established by the Supreme Court of Judicature Act (Ireland), 1877, and that of the Supreme Court of Justice established by the Courts of Justice Act, 1924, were similarly restricted by the rules of court relevant to those courts. The restricting factor which produces that implied limitation is the requirement that the oral hearing in the High Court is to be transposed into written form for the purpose of the appeal. The relevant provision is to be found in Order 58, r.14, of the Rules of 1962.

In fact, in the present case the record of the oral hearing in the High court available for the purpose of the appeal is a verbatim transcript not only of the oral testimony but also of counsels' submissions to the trial judge. Considering that the hearing in the High Court took 16 days, that transcript (together with the pleadings, interlocutory orders, affidavits and the many documents adduced by way of discovery or otherwise) constitutes a formidably voluminous record of what took place in the High court. Nevertheless, comprehensive as it is, it is necessarily an imperfect record of the oral hearing because what was adduced *viva voce* in the sight and hearing of the trial judge has had to be converted into a written transcript. It cannot recapture the mood of the trial, the demeanour of witnesses, the essential nuances of particular responses, and many other features of the trial which, although they may have been crucially determinative in the judicial ascertainment of the facts, may have become blurred or lost when the oral evidence was reduced to writing. Herein lies the source of this Court's restricted jurisdication in regard to matters of fact. It cannot put itself in the position of the trial judge. He has had opportunities of judicial assessment that are denied to this Court.

To what extent, therefore, is it open to this Court to differ from the trial judge in his conclusions of fact? The judicial statement most commonly invoked in Ireland as laying down the range of an appellate court's jurisdiction to review findings of fact made by a trial judge is that enunciated by Holmes L.J. sitting in the Irish Court of Appeal in *The S.S. Gairloch* [1899] 2 J.R.1. *[The judge here quoted the passage from the judgment of Holmes L.J. which appears at p.000 supra].*

Support for the approach expressed in that passage is to be found in a number of cases. For example, in *Benmax* v. *Austin Motor Co. Ltd* [1955] A.C. 370 Viscount Simonds refers (at p. 373) to the distinction that requires to be drawn for appellate purposes "between the finding of a specific fact and a finding of fact which is really an inference from facts specifically found, or, as it has sometimes been said, between the perception and evaluation of facts." In the same case Lord Reid marks out the boundaries of an appeal court's jursidication to differ from findings of fact made in the court of trial; at pp. 375-6 of the report he said:- "Apart from cases where appeal is expressly limited to questions of law, an appellant is entitled to appeal against any finding of the trial judge, whether it be a finding of law, a finding of fact or a finding involving both law and fact. But the trial judge has seen and heard the witnesses, whereas the appeal court is denied that advantage and only has before it a written transcript of their evidence. No one would seek to minimize the advantage enjoyed by the trial judge in determining any question whether a witness is or is not trying to tell what he believes to be the truth, and it is only in rare cases that an appeal court could be satisfied that the trial judge has reached a wrong decision about the credibility of a witness. But the advantage of seeing and hearing a witness goes beyond that; the trial judge may be led to a conslusion about the reliability of a witness's memory or his powers of observation by material not available to an appeal court. Evidence may read well in print but may be rightly discounted by the trial judge or, on the other hand, he may rightly attach importance to evidence which reads badly in print. Of course, the weight of the other evidence may be such as to show that the judge must have formed a wrong impression, but an appeal court is and should be slow to reverse any finding which appears to be based on any such considerations . . . But in cases where there is no question of the credibility or reliability of any witness, and in cases where the point in dispute is the proper inference to be drawn from proved facts, an appeal court is generally in as good a position to evaluate the evidence as the trial judge, and ought not to shrink from that task, though it ought, of course, to give weight to his opinion."

The approach enunciated in the passages I have cited requires to be clarified in certain respects. First, it has to be borne in mind that the limitations of function of an appeal court that arise for consideration in this context are confined to civil cases. In criminal cases, where guilt has to be proved beyond reasonable doubt, if findings of fact, expressly or impliedly made, arise for consideration on appeal, the court of appeal will not feel bound to defer to the judge or jury by whom those findings were made, even when they are supported by a version of the evidence, if the resulting verdict of guilty seems unsafe or unsatisfactory. Secondly, the limitations we are dealing with are confined to questions of fact as distinct from questions of law. A question of fact in this context may be taken to mean a question which properly requires, if the trial is (or were to be) at *nisi prius,* to be answered by the jury; whereas all other questions requiring to be determined at the trial are said to be questions of law. In dealing with the latter, a court of appeal, unless restricted by statute, has an unfettered capacity to review the answers given by the trial judge. Thirdly, for appeal purposes, questions of fact fall into two categories: those the answers to which give a factual resolution of conflicting oral testimony and those the answers to which do not resolve conflicts of oral testimony but are in the nature of an evaluation of facts found or admitted. The answers to the former are usually matters of pure fact (e.g. whether a defendant driver applied his brakes before the collision), whereas the answers to the latter are in the nature of an opinion or a value judgment (e,g, whether, if the defendant did not apply his brakes before the collision, he was negligent). In regard to the former, a court of appeal is bound to recognize the unique advantages which the court of trial had in giving its answers, whereas such considerations do not buttress the answers given to the latter type of question. Fourthly, for appeal purposes there is no essential difference between the answer given by a jury to a question of specific fact and such an answer when given by a judge; save that the judge usually gives reasons in support of his answer, whereas the jury's reasoning is usually left unarticulated. An error in the judge's answer may therefore be disclosed by the reasons he gives in support of it, while the jury's answer, usually given in the form of a laconic "Yes" or "No" or expressed in figures, is normally susceptible of correction in a court of appeal only if it could not have been reached in the circumstances by a reasonable jury.

In a civil case such as this where a tribunal of fact, be it a judge or a jury, has decided a question of specific fact and the resolution of the question depended wholly or in substantial measure on the choice of one version of controverted oral testimony as against another, a court of appeal which is dependent on a written record of the oral evidence given at the trial will not normally reject that finding merely because an alternative version of the oral testimony seems more acceptable. The court of appeal will only set aside a finding of fact based on one version of the evidence when, on taking a conspectus of the evidence as a whole, oral and otherwise, it appears to the court that, notwithstanding the advantages which the tribunal of fact had in seeing and hearing the witnesses, the version of the evidence which was acted on could not reasonably be correct. For example, if the question of fact was whether a defendant was driving on his correct side of the road at the time of a collision and, out of a welter of conflicting oral testimony on the point, the judge (or the jury, as the case may be) expressly or by implication accepted the defendant's version to the effect that his vehicle was on its correct side of the road at the time of the collision, then in that event a court of appeal will normally hold itself to be debarred from rejecting that finding of fact on the ground that its fact-finding capacity in relation to conflicting oral testimony cannot be equated with that of the trial judge (or jury) who heard and saw the witnesses. If, however, on a review of all the evidence, it appears from uncontroverted evidence as to tyre marks or glass or mud on the road that the defendant's evidence (that his vehicle was on its correct side of the road) could not be correct, the court of appeal will feel free to reject the finding of fact to that effect.

On the other hand, if the question of fact that was answered in the court of trial does not depend on a choice of alternatives arising out of divergent oral testimony, but amounts to a conclusion in the nature of an evaluation of proved or admitted facts, the court of appeal will consider itself free to rely on its own judgment as to whether the evaluation made by the tribunal of fact is correct or not, on the ground that its competence to evaluate the fact in question is no less than that of the tribunal of fact, notwithstanding that it has not heard or seen the witnesses; for the evidential data for the answer to the question will be essentially the same in both courts. Thus, if the question of fact to be answered was whether the defendant, having been found to have been driving on his incorrect side of the road at the time of the collision (and the other relevant facts not being in controversy) was negligent, the court of appeal will be free to differ, if necessary, from the answer given to that question in the court of trial; in that event the court of appeal would do so on the ground that the judge (or jury) was in no better position to answer that question. This is not to say that inferences of fact may always be drawn equally reliably in a court of appeal as in the court of trial. On the contrary, if an inference of fact depends to any substantial extent on a choice of alternatives presented by a conflict of oral testimony, the court of appeal will normally defer to the inference drawn in the court of trial and will reject that inference only when a review of all the evidence shows that it could not reasonably be correct. Thus, if in the court of trial it was inferred from one version of conflicting medical evidence as to the plaintiff's injuries that he will have a loss of earnings in the future, the court of appeal will not feel free to reject that inference merely because other medical evidence which was given at the trial and which would support a contrary inference seems more credible. To do so would be to ignore the fact that where witnesses have given conflicting oral testimony, the version which commended itself to the judge (or jury) who had the benefit of hearing and seeing them cannot be safely rejected by a court of appeal which is deprived of that benefit, unless as appraisal of the whole record of the trial shows that the conclusion of fact drawn at the trial is erroneous.

On the other hand, if the issue in the court of appeal is whether a particular inference of fact is correct, and the question can be resolved in the court of appeal without usurping the trial court's function of choosing between conflicting altenatives arising out of the oral testimony, the court of appeal will not be debarred from differing from the trial court as to the proper inference to be drawn. For instance, if the question under appeal is whether the damages awarded to the plaintiff are excessive, the court of appeal will, in an appropriate case, be prepared to assume in favour of the plaintiff the version of the conflicting evidence which favours the plaintiff and then draw its own reference as to damages for the purpose of testing the correctness of the award. The statement in Order 58, r. 8, that when hearing an appeal this Court "shall have power to draw inferences of fact" must be read subject to the necessarily implied limitation that conflicts of oral testimony are usually more likely to be correctly resolved in the forensic atmosphere of the trial than on appeal in this Court, where subleties, inflexions and countless matters of direct personal impression tend to be distorted or blurred or even totally lost in the transmutation of the live trial into a written record.

With the foregoing considerations in mind, I now focus attention on the particular matters raised by this ground of appeal. The contention is that the judge's finding of fraud on the part of the plaintiff bank was unsupported by the evidence and should be set aside. As appears from the transcript of the evidence and from the judgment, it is clear that in the process of finding fraud on the part of the bank the judge addressed himself to the following questions:-

1. Was it part of the agreed arrangement for the take-over by Pat Quinn Holdings Ltd. of J.G. Mooney & Co. Ltd. that Patrick Quinn would deposit with the bank the sum of £200,000?

2. If so, did the bank falsely represent to the defendants that Patrick Quinn had made that deposit?

3. If so, was that false representation made with the intention of inducing the defendants to proceed with the take-over?

4. If so, did that false representation materially induce the defendants to proceed with the take-over?

To each of those four questions the judge gave an affirmative answer. While there was documentary evidence touching on each of those questions, it is clear from the judgment under review that the determinant in regard to the answer to each of them derived from the oral testimony. It could not have been otherwise. A persual of the evidence given at the trial shows that the central controversy on this aspect of the case was whether the bank's representatives (Mr. Tierney and Mr. Tuomey) had made certain statements or concealments on particular occasions. The judge held that they had. He carefully compared and contrasted the conflicting versions of events, correctly pitched the degree of proof at the high level required for fraud, distinguished one occasion from another, and eventually held certain versions of conversations propounded on behalf of the defendants to be credible and to support the answers he proceeded to give to those questions.

This case, therefore, as to this ground of appeal, falls into the category of cases where the issue under appeal has been resolved in the Court of trial by a choice of alternatives presented by conflicting oral testimony. The trial judge's choice of versions cannot be disturbed in this court unless the evidence, viewed in all its aspects, points to the invalidity of that choice. Therefore, counsel for the bank have grounded their argument on various matters arising out of the evidence, both documentary and oral, which they rely on as showing unlikelihoods, contradictions, uncertainties and other kinds of implausiblities in the versions of events which the judge found credible. Making due allowance for all such matters, and bearing in mind that no less cogent objections have been taken by counsel for the defendants against the contrary versions of events, I find no fixity of facts in the non-oral testimony or the other testimony generally, which would make the judge's conclusions untenable. This Court cannot assimilate its fact-finding competence to that of a trial judge when it comes to appraising the truthfulness or reliability of oral witnesses; it can but reject his conclusions when they are shown to be incorrect by reference to the totality of the evidence. This is not such a case. So, in my view, the finding on the issue of fraud should stand.

In reaching this conclusion I am not to be taken as implying that, if I had been the trial judge, I would necessarily have found that Mr. Tierney and Mr. Tuomey made fraudulent representations on the occasions in question. Not having heard or seen the witnesses, I cannot say whether I would or not. Therefore, my opinion does not amount to a positive affirmation of the correctness of the trial judge's conclusions. It is simply a recognition of the fact that his conclusions, having been reached after a due appraisal of the relevant controversies in the oral testimony, and not being discernibly untenable in the context of the evidence as a whole, must be held to withstand appeal in this Court.

I am satisfied that there was evidence to support the finding that the bank's representation that Patrick Quinn had made a cash deposit of £200,000 induced the defendants to proceed with the take-over, and also to support the further finding that the continuing representation together with the representation that Patrick Quinn was not indebted to the bank induced the defendants to purchase his shares in Pat Quinn Holdings. I do not consider that there is any real substance in the submission of counsel for the bank that the judge's findings in that respect are vitiated because evidence was allowed to be given as to matters which had not been previously alleged or pleaded. This was a lengthy trial, and while unpleaded matters were raised, and dealt with, in the course of the hearing, I consider that the bank had a reasonable opportunity of meeting all allegations made against it. I therefore, would reject the submission that the finding of fraud against the bank should be set aside.

Rescission

Having found that the defendants were induced to proceed with the take-over and with the purchase of Patrick Quinn's shares in Pat Quinn Holdings, the judge dealt with the resultant legal position as follows:-

> "On these findings of fraudulent misrepresentation inducing the defendants to enter into both the original transaction and the purchase of Patrick Quinn's shares, the general legal principle applicable is that the defendants are entitled to have all the consequent transactions between them and the bank declared invalid and set aside. Insofar as it does not prejudice rights or interests acquired by innocent third parties, they are entitled to the return of any property or rights purporting to have been transferred to or vested in the bank. In addition, they are entitled to a sum of damages which, reasonably and fairly assessed between the parties, will restore them, having regard to the other relief obtained, to the position in which they would have been if the fraud had not been committed and they had not engaged in the transactions induced by it."

That is the only passage in the judgment under review which deals with the law governing the relief that should be granted when a person has been induced by a fraudulent inducement to enter into a detrimental transaction of this kind. In the passage I have quoted, the judge deduced that there was a general legal principle entitling the defendants to rescission and *restitutio in integrum.* He thus rejected the submission, which was forcefully made both at the trial and in this Court, that the only relief that could be granted was an award of damages and that no damages resulting from fraudulent inducement had been proved. For the purpose of deciding whether rescission or damages is the relief to which the defendants are entitled, it is necessary to consider both the relevant factual situation and the applicable legal principles.

First, as to the role played by the bank, it is a merchant bank and a wholly-owned subsidiary of the Northern Bank Ltd; in regard to the venture in which the three defendants (in conjuction with Patrick Quinn and Vincent Duignan) proposed to purchase the Mooney share capital, the bank acted as the defendants' agent. This is a function which is nowadays regularly committed to a merchant bank by the company or group who propose to effect the take-over of a public company which has a stock exchange quotation for its shares. The financial, corporate and stock-exchange complexities of that situation are such that it is usually necessary to call on the services of a merchant bank, which will assist in arranging the financing of the offer, advise on the size and form of the offer, prepare and circulate the offer documents, ensure that stock-exchange requirements are complied with, and generally make its expertise available to its principals to the end that not only will the take-over be successful but that it will result in the principals having acquired ownership or control at an economic cost. The services of the bank for those purposes were particularly required by these defendants and their two associates, for they were five individuals who were not incorporated as a company. It was necessary to arrange for the formation of a company (Pat Quinn Holdings) to act as the take-over vehicle. The promoters of the take-over were dependent on the bank for part of the finance required for the operation, for the preparation and issue of the offer documents, for technical advice as to the various steps to be taken and, finally, for the purchase on their behalf of the Mooney shares.

However, important as it was in its various activities in connection with the take-over, the bank at all times continued to act as the agent of the promoters in its dealings with third parties. At no stage in the course of the take-over did the bank shed that agency and became a principal. The importance of that relationship in this case is that, when two of the bank's officials made faudulent inducements to the defendants in the course of the take-over and when, by the operation of *respondeat superior,* it became liable for those inducements, the bank's liability was the liability of an agent to a principal for whom it was advising and acting.

When an agent-adviser (such as a solicitor, banker, stockbroker, architect, auctioneer or estate agent) induces a client or customer, by means of a fraudulent misrepresentation, to purchase property from a third party, and when the purchaser, having completed the purchase and acquired ownership of the property, discovers the fraud, then I understand the law to be that the remedy of the purchaser lies in damages and not in rescission. The reason is that, in such circumstances, as betwen the agent-adviser and the purchaser there is no form of rescission and restitution which could restore, even substantially, the *status quo ante* – being the respective positions of the parties before the fraudulent misrepresentation was acted on to the purchaser's detriment. An order such as was made in this case (binding the misrepresentor to acquire the property which was bought on foot of the misrepresentation and to pay the purchase price to the misrepresentee) so far from restoring the *status quo ante* results in a situation which never before existed. In this case the return of the purchase money might be said to restore the purchasers' former position, but the compulsory subrogation whereby the misrepresentor would be required to step into the purchaser's shoes and take over the ownership of the property bought, which the misrepresentor had never owned, would have the effect of thrusting on the misrepresentor a wholly new factual and legal situation which would be incompatible with the mutuality and fairness inherent in the concept of restoring the *status quo ante.* Counsel for the defendants are unable to point to any judicial precedent for such an order.

Where a person has been induced by a fraudulent misrepresentation made collaterally by the other party to a contract to alter his position to his disadvantage, there are two alternative courses open to him: he may claim damages in tort for the deceit or he may sue for rescission of the contract which was induced by the misrepresentation. The latter relief, which is an equitable one, will be granted when the court considers that it would be just and equitable to do so in order to restore the parties, at least substantially, to their respective positions before the fraudulent misrepresentation was acted on. That is the relief which the defendants have chosen primarily in their counterclaim, and it is the relief which the order of the High Court purported to give them. But, be it noted, the *restitutio in integrum* by restoring the *status quo ante* (which is the object of this form of relief) can be granted only as an adjunct to the rescission of the contract between the parties. In this case the defendants sought and were granted rescission of the contract between the defendants and the bank but, in an effort to restore the *status quo ante,* the court went further. By requiring the bank to take the place of the defendants in each of the many instances of the purchase of shares, the court purported to rescind and amend executed contracts which had been made between the defendants and third-party vendors of shares who were not before the court. In my opinion, that is something which the court had no jurisdiction to do.

Since the purpose of the rescission of a contract on the ground of misrepresentation is the restoration of the *status quo ante* on the ground that the voidable contract is to be deemed wholly void *ab initio,* each side must divest itself in favour of the other of what it has received under the contract. As Bowen L.J. put it in *Newbigging* v. *Adam* (1886) 34 Ch. D. 582 at p. 595 of the report, there ought to be "a giving back and a taking back on both sides." Now, in the present case, the order of rescission made in the High Court cannot operate in that way. The moneys which it requires the bank to repay to the defendants are not moneys which it received, in any permanent or beneficial sense, under the contract with the defendants. Those moneys only passed through the bank's hands on their way to the vendors of the shares in question. It was those vendors who really received those moneys under the contract. So the bank cannot, by way of rescission, be compelled to repay them to the defendants. But, even more radically, the order of rescission, in requiring the bank to take up all the shares purchased by them for the defendants, runs counter to the object of the restoration of the *status quo ante.* The compulsory acquisition by the bank of those shares could not be said to be a "taking back" since the bank had never owned those shares. If effect were to be given to the order of rescission made in the High Court, the bank (which, as far as one can gather from the evidence, was never the beneficial owner of a single Mooney share) would become the unwilling owners of over 900,000 shares in that company. Clearly an order of rescission with that result could not be said to restore the *status quo ante.*

Counsel for the defendants, in arguing in support of the order of rescission made in the High Court, have been unable to refer to any case in which such a result was produced. The authority they rely on most is *Armstrong* v. *Jackson* [1917] 2 K.B. 822 but, in my view, that decision defeats the argument for the defendants. In that case, the plaintiff had engaged the defendant stockbroker to buy 600 shares in a company. In purported execution of that order, the defendant sent to the plaintiff a contract note showing that the shares had been purchased for him at a specified price. The plaintiff allowed some time to elapse before taking up the shares and, during that time, the value of the shares dropped. Nevertheless, the defendant advised the plaintiff to complete the purchase and he did so. Some four years later, the plaintiff obtained information which caused him to issue proceedings seeking rescission of the transaction or, in the alternatives, damages. In the course of the hearing it was shown that, at the time of the purchase, the defendant was the *owner* of the shares – a fact which he had fraudulently concealed from the plaintiff. In granting an order of rescission, under which the defendant was required to repay all sums received by him from the plaintiff (less a credit for the amount of a dividend paid to the plaintiff) and the plaintiff to transfer the 600 shares to the defendant, McCardie J. said at p. 823 of the report:- "From first to last the defendant made no disclosure whatever to the plaintiff as to the true facts. He purported to act as a broker, whereas he was really acting as a principal." Therein lies the basis of the rescission granted in that case: the fact that the stockbroker, being the owner of the shares, was really acting as principal. It is inherent in the decision that, if the defendant had not been the owner of the shares and had been merely an agent (which was the position of the bank in the present case), rescission would not have been granted since the mutual repayment of money and re-transfer of shares would not have accorded with the *status quo ante.* Instead, there would have been a decree for damages.

In my opinion, the order of rescission made in the High Court, and the orders consequential and ancillary thereto, should be set aside.

Damages

In their counterclaim the defendants have pitched their claim for damages in comprehensively wide terms but, in view of the judge's specific finding that they were induced by the enumerated misrepresentations, in their separate and cumulative effect, to buy the Mooney shares and Patrick Quinn's shares in Pat Quinn Holdings, they are confined in this action to a claim for damages for the tort of fraud or deceit in that respect. While it is said that the measure of damages for breach of contract is the amount of money necessary to put the damnified person in the position in which he would have been if the contract had not been broken, the claimant in tort is entitled, by an award of damages, to be notionally restored to the position in which he would have been in the tort had not been committed. As far as the tort of fraud or deceit is concerned, it is well settled that the measure of damages is based on the actual damage directly flowing from the fraudulent inducement, and that the award may include, in an appropriate case (of which this may not be an example), consequential damages representing what was reasonably and necessarily expended as a result of acting on the inducement: *Doyle* v. *Olby Ltd.* [1969] 2 Q.B. 158.

In this case the defendants were induced by the deceit to purchase shares, of which the plaintiff bank was not the owner. It is well established by judicial authority that the correct measure of damages in such a case is the cost of acquiring the shares, less their actual value at the time of acquisition, see *Twycross* v. *Grant* (1877) 2 C.P.D. 469; *Peek* v. *Derry* (1877) 37 Ch. P. 541; *Broome* v. *Speak* [1903] 1 Ch. 586; and the cases referred to in McGregor on Damages (13th edn.) at paragraphs 1363-4. The price paid for the shares is to be regarded only as evidence of their value and not as proof of it (*per* Lord Coleridge C. J. in *Twycross* v. *Grant*), so it will be for the court to make a true and fair valuation of the shares as they stood when they were transferred to the defendants or their nominees; that is the crucial time for the assessment of their value. Subsequent fluctuations in their value, from whatever cause, may be taken into reckoning for that purpose only to the extent that such movements in value may throw light on their real value at the time they were transferred to the defendants. As Cotton L.J. put it in *Peek* v. *Derry* at p. 592 of the report:– "Nor do I think he *[the plaintiff]* ought to be precluded from taking into account the subsequent events. Although the value of the shares is not to be ascertained at the subsequent period so as to take into account for the benefit of the Plaintiff events subsequent which depreciated their value, yet those events, if they shew that the company was originally, with the capital which it had got, a company which was worthless, may, in my opinion, be taken into account as evidence of what was the value of the shares immediately after they were allotted to the Plaintiff."

Because the trial judge considered that the defendants' remedy lay in rescission, there was no adjudication in the High Court of the question of the measure of damages and of their assessment. Therefore, there is no judicial determination of the correct amount which each of the defendants may be said to have laid out in the purchase of the shares which were transferred to him or his nominee, nor is there any judicial finding as to the true value of those shares at the time of such transfer. Because the measure of damages will be the difference between those two figures, and because the defendants failed to adduce at the trial the evidential data which would enable those figures to be computed, it is not possible for this Court to assess the damages.

Therefore, I would remit the case to the High Court to have the defendants' damages assessed on the basis I have indicated.

The bank's claim

The bank's claim is for the sum of £46,161.20, of which portion consists of instalments of principal and portion consists of arrears of interest due under a loan of £50,000 made by the bank to the defendants of the 8th January, 1974. The purpose of this loan was expressed in writing by the bank to be "towards the purchase of the shareholding in Pat Quinn Holdings Limited, presently owned by Mr. Pat Quinn." One of the findings of fact made by the judge was that the defendants were induced to enter into that purcahse by the bank's fraudulent misrepresentations that Patrick Quinn had made the financial contribution to the take-over which it had been agreed that he would make, and that at the time of the loan Patrick Quinn was not indebted to the bank. It necessarily follows that the defendants were induced by the same fraudulent misrepresentations to enter into this loan. Since the bank's claim is for the direct enforcement of the contract of loan by the recovery of instalments of prinicpal and certain instalments of interest, the defendants are entitled to set up those fraudulent misrepresentations as a good defence on the ground that they make the contract of loan void and unenforceable. Since the only claim by the bank before the Court is one that seeks to give direct effect to the contract of loan, it is sufficient to say that the pleas raised in the defence must be held to defeat that claim on the basis that the contract must be held to stand rescinded. But that ruling should not be taken as necessarily affecting the bank's rights if it raises a claim in respect of the £50,000 which does not involve the enforcement of the contract of loan.

The result

To sum up, I would dispose of this appeal by discharging the orders of the High Court dated the 8th August, 1977, and the 7th September, 1977, and would substitute therefor an order:-

1. Directing (in affirmation of the decision of the High Court) that the bank's claim for the recovery of £46,161.20 do stand dismissed.

2. Declaring (in affirmation of the decision of the High Court) that the defendants' purchases of shares in J.G. Mooney & Co. Ltd. and Pat Quinn's shares in Pat Quinn Holdings Ltd. were induced by the bank's fraudulent misrepresentations as found in the High Court.

3. Declaring that the defendants' remedy for the said fraudulent misrepresentations lies in damages for the tort of deceit, and not in rescission of the purchases of shares thus induced.

4. Remitting the case to the High Court for the assessment of those damages.

5. Giving liberty to each party to apply in the High Court in respect of any matter arising in these proceedings (including costs and the disposition of moneys lodged in court) and not specifically dealt with by this order.

Griffin J.:

The facts are set forth in the judgment of the learned President and I do not find it necessary to repeat them or to repeat all the findings made by the President. The servants of the plaintiff bank were found by the President to have made a number of fraudulent representations to the defendants. These were:-

1. The representations made by Mr. Gerard Tierney, (the managing director of the bank) to Mr. Gerard Charlton on either the 27th or 28th September, 1972, that Mr. Patrick Quinn had deposited £200,000 with the bank in pursuance of the arrangements made between the defendants, Patrick Quinn and Vincent Duignan who were the promoters.

2. That on the 26th November, 1972, at a vitally important meeting held between the promoters and the bank, Gerard Tierney and Laurence Tuomey (an assistant manager of the bank) failed to disclose that Patrick Quinn's deposit with the bank had been by then reduced to some £25,000.

3. That on the 13th December, 1972, Mr. Tuomey made a representation on the telephone to Mr. Michael Dickson, a member of the firm of solicitors acting for the bank, that "all the promoters money was in," in reply to a question asked for the benefit of Gerard Charlton who was at the time present with Mr. Dickson.

4. That, in relation to the sale to the defendants of the shares of Patrick Quinn in Pat Quinn Holdings Ltd. (the company formed to be the vehicle of the take-over of J.G. Mooney and Co. Ltd.), Mr. Tierney represented to the defendants that Patrick Quinn was in no way indebted to the bank, although this was false and fraudulent.

The first and third representations were made to the defendant Gerard Charlton alone, and he was one of the persons present when the second and fourth representations were made.

Therefore, for all practical purposes the defendants' case depended in the main on the credibility of Gerard Chartlon as a witness. Having heard all the evidence, the President found Gerard Charlton to be a credible witness. As his version of the matters in dispute was accepted by the President, it became necessary for counsel for the bank to impugn Gerard Charlton's credibility if they were to succeed in this appeal. Therefore, Mr. Liston (for the bank) over a period of several days examined this evidence minutely, contrasted it with the witnesses called on behalf of the bank and the contemporaneous documents, and undertook the task of demonstrating that the recollection of Gerard Chartlon was faulty and that his accuracy was highly questionable. Although it was necessary for the defendants to prove that the representations alleged by them were false to the knowledge of the bank, he submitted that it was not necessary for him to question the *veracity* of Gerard Charlton, and that he was only concerned to submit that the various factors to which he referred demonstrated that Gerard Charlton was not reliable as to *credibility*.

Mr. Liston submitted that the President, before making his findings on the credibility of Gerard Charlton, did not fully or correctly evaluate (inter alia) the following important matters which, it was alleged, seriously affected his credibility.

First, the take-over of the Mooney company took place between September and December, 1972 – almost five years before the trial – and at the trial Gerard Charlton was relying exclusively on his memory and recollection. He did not have what Mr. Liston called "a single scrap of paper" to produce, notwithstanding the fact that his entire training and practice as a solicitor over a number of years required it; he did not keep a diary, or make a single memorandum, note or attendance in respect of any of the meetings, discussions or matters involved in this take-over; he did not open a file despite the facts that, with £2.3 million at stake, this was probably by far the largest transaction in which he was ever involved, and that he was also very heavily committed in the venture financially. This he contrasted with Mr. Dickson, who had entries in his desk diaries, attendances, and the usual documents to be expected of a solicitor in respect of the matters of which he gave evidence.

Secondly, he submitted that during the trial Gerard Charlton's recollection was demonstrated to be suspect, and he instanced several examples of which the following were the most important:-

(a) Gerard Charlton's failure to recollect an important meeting which, it was alleged, took place in the board room of Quinnsworth in Stillorgan on the 25th September, 1972, in relation to the take-over bid. The President made no reference to or finding in respect of this meeting in his judgment, but it seems likely from the evidence and surrounding circumstances that such a meeting did take place.

(b) His evidence in relation to a meeting which, according to him, took place on either the 5th or 11th November, 1972. This was a crucial meeting because it had been discovered that Moore Holdings (the promoters' competitors in the take-over bid) intended raising their bid to 208.75p, and a decision had to be made by the promoters as to whether they should make an increased bid or retire from the contest. At that time Patrick Quinn was disinclined to proceed further, but he ultimately agreed to reduce his stake in the take-over bid to £100,000. In evidence, having described what transpired at the meeting, which he said was called and chaired by Mr. Tierney, and having described the discussions which led to the reduction by Patrick Quinn of his stake to £100,000, Gerard Charlton stated that Gerard Tierney then said:- "We will give Pat back £100,000 of his £200,000" – thus falsely representing that Patrick Quinn had at the time a deposit of £200,000. Although it was put to him in cross-examination that Gerard Tierney was not at that meeting but was in fact in America at the time, Gerard Charlton was quite dogmatic that this was in fact said by Gerard Tierney and he was corroborated by Hugh Charlton. The subsequent evidence was conclusive that Gerard Tierney was not at that meeting and had in fact been in America at that time, and the President so held.

(c) As to the meeting between Gerard Charlton and Michael Dickson on the 13th December, 1972, the purpose of which was to deal with the legal formalities in relation to the guarantees for the loan of £1.6 million to be advanced by the bank, Gerard Charlton placed this meeting at between the 15th and 18th December. Gerard Charlton said that the first thing that happened was that Mr. Dickson said it was his understanding that the bank had collected the £500,000, and said that he would telephone the bank; that he did so; that he spoke to Mr. Tuomey, who could be heard by Gerard Charlton by means of a table speaker, and that Mr. Tuomey confirmed that they had the £500,000, that during the meeting Mr. Dickson handed to him document No. 16 (the bank's requirements in connection with the title) which he said had already been prepared, and that he wrote "agreed" opposite the various items agreed upon as they went through the document. On the other hand, Mr. Dickson, who had the benefit of his desk diaries, files, and the usual solicitor's attendances and memoranda, and who was accepted by the President as "an entirely truthful and a most careful witness," said that in the course of the meeting there were quite a number of areas where difficulties arose. He said that the bank had earlier agreed to accept a certificate of good marketable title from Mr. Charlton's firm instead of investigating the title and that, after some differences between them on the nature of the certificate, he *then* telephoned Mr. Tuomey and got instructions to accept the certificate in the form in which Gerard Charlton was willing to give it. He said that after Gerard Chartlon had left his office, he *then* wrote out document No. 16 by hand, made a copy of it and put it in Mr. Charlton's letter box on the way home.

He said that he had no recollection of the conversation in relation to the £500,000 but he added, with the utmost candour, that neither could he deny that it was said. Having regard to the President's acceptance of Mr. Dickson as an entirely truthful and a most careful witness, inferentially all the matters in controversy between Gerard Charlton and him, except the conversation with Mr. Tuomey in relation to the £500,000, were resolved in Mr. Dickson's favour although, as Mr. Liston argued, it was surprising that Mr. Dickson had so attendance in relation to the £500,000 conversation, if it took place.

Mr. Liston submitted that the Court, having read and considered all the evidene in the transcript, must itself make an evaluation of the evidence of Gerard Charlton and that this would lead inevitably to the conclusion that his recollection was faulty and suspect; he submitted that this evaluation would thus seriously affect the credibility of this witness and show that the evidence fell far short of the degree of proof requisite to sustain an allegation of fraud.

I have set out these submissions at some length because they formed a very substantial part of the bank's case on the hearing of this appeal and in view of the finding of fraud against the bank. The nett question on this branch of the appeal is whether, on the evidence as a whole (and, in particular, in view of the matters which, as alleged, cast doubt on the credibility of Gerard Chartlon), it was open to the trial judge to find for the defendants on the issue of fraud. This necessarily involves a consideration of the circumstances in which this Court can review the findings of a trial judge on question of fact. I have had the advantage of reading the judgment delivered by Mr. Justice Henchy in which he has considered this question; I agree with his reasoning and his conclusions.

The President found as a matter of probability that the conversations deposed to by Gerard Charlton, which formed the basis of the allegations of fraud, did occur. He had the advantage (not possessed by this Court) of seeing and hearing the witnesses. He heard the conflicting versions of the conversations, discussions and meetings which took place over a period of some three months at the end of the year 1972 and in the months leading up to the 8th January, 1974, when the defendants purchased the shares of Patrick Quinn in Pat Quinn Holdings. He was able to make and did make a choice between these versions. Having heard and evaluated all the evidence, he reached his conclusions of fact. This Court has only the written transcript of evidence and it cannot evaluate the evidence in such a way as to equate its ability to assess the credibility of a witness with the ability of the trial judge. In my judgment it is not competent for this Court, on the evidence given at the trial, to set aside any of the facts found by the President. He was entitled to find the facts as he did, and his findings on the issue of the fraudulent representations made by the servants of the bank must be upheld. However, I should like to add that, like Mr. Justice Henchy, this does not necessarily mean that, had I been the trial judge, I would have found that the fraudulent representations were made by Mr. Tierney and Mr. Tuomey, or either of them. I did not have the President's advantage of seeing and hearing the witnesses and of making a judicial evaluation of their credibility, and so I am unable to say what findings of fact I would have made had I tried the case.

The next question argued in the appeal was the form of the relief to which the defendants are entitled. Although in their defence and counterclaim the defendants did not expressly claim rescission, the order of the President effectively granted rescission and this was in line with the run of the case and the arguments advanced on behalf of the defendants. Although we have no copy of the transcript of the hearing when the matter came back to the President on the 17th September, 1977, pursuant to his order of the 8th August, 1977, we were informed by counsel that the President held that the defendants sought rescission; and this appeal proceeded on that basis.

An action or counterclaim for rescission is the usual form of proceeding for obtaining a judicial annulment of a contract induced by misrepresentation. As stated in Spencer Bower and Turner's Law of Actionable Misrepresentation (3rd ed., para 249) the primary purpose of all proceedings for rescission, as contrasted with that of actions for damages, is to restore the "status quo" and bring back the original position by undoing all that has intervened between it and the present. "The purpose of the relief is not punishment, but compensation" – *per* Lord Wright in *Spence* v. *Crawford* [1937] 3 All E.R. 271 at p. 289 of the report. Therefore, the rule is that rescission cannot be enforced if events, which have occurred since the contract and in which the representee has participated, make it impossible to restore the parties substantially to their original position. If a contract cannot be rescinded *in toto* it cannot be rescinded at all – see Cheshire and Fifoot's Law of Contract (9th ed. p. 269).

The object to be achieved by rescission is the restoration of *both parties* as nearly as may be to the position which each occupied before the transaction. The representee must be not only willing but also able to make *restitutio in integrum.* A large number of cases were cited both in the High Court and on this appeal, and what is recognised as the classical statement on this topic is that of Lord Blackburn in *Erlanger* v. *New Sombrero Phosphate Co* (1878) 3 App. Cas. 1218 where he says at pp. 1278-9 of the report:- "It is, I think, clear on principles of general justice, that as a condition to a rescission there must be a *restitutio in integrum.* The parties must be put *in status quo* . . . It is a doctrine which has often been acted upon both at law and in equity. But there is a considerable difference in the mode in which it is applied in Courts of Law and Equity, owing, as I think, to the difference of the machinery which the Courts have at command." Having dealt with the common-law remedy of damages, he went on to say:- "But a Court of Equity could not give damages, and, unless it can rescind the contract, can give no relief. And, on the other hand, it can take accounts of profits, and make allowance for deterioration. And I think the practice has always been for a Court of Equity to give this relief whenever, by the exercise of its powers, it can do what is practically just, though it cannot restore the parties precisely to the state they were in before the contract."

At law, if precise restitution was impossible, the defrauded party had to fall back on his action for damages for deceit. The distinction between the remedies at law and equity to which Lord Blackburn referred is no longer of importance as the High Court has full original jurisdiction and power to determine all matters and questions. As stated by the High Court of Australia (Dixon C.J., Webb, Kitto and Taylor JJ.) in *Alati* v. *Kruger* (1955) 94 C.L.R. 216 at p. 223-4 of the report, even though precise *restitutio in integrum* is not possible it is now sufficient "if the situation is such that, by the exercise of its powers, including the power to take accounts of profits and to direct inquiries as to allowances proper to be made for deterioration, it can do what is practically just between the parties, and by so doing restore them substantially to the *status quo.*"

Although these principles are quite clear and there was no real dispute in argument concerning them, they are not easy to apply in practice. The type of contract in respect of which rescission is claimed is commonly that in which there is what might be called a vendor and purchaser relationship – for example, contracts relating to sales of land, goods, or of shares; the sale of a business or of an interest in a professional practice; and such like, where property has passed *from* the representor *to* the representee, or vice versa under the contract. Many cases are to be found in the law reports in which an order for rescission was made on the application of the defrauded representee, whether he be vendor or purchaser. In such cases, there will be a decree for rescission because mutual restoration *in specie* of all benefits received by either party under the contract can take place and, even though precise *resitutio in integrum* is not possible, the parties can be restored substantially to the *status quo.*

Both parties to a transaction can "as nearly as may be" be put back to the position they occupied before the transaction was entered into, even though the property which was the subject matter of the contract may have deteriorated in value in the meantime. For example, in *Armstrong* v. *Jackson* [1917] 2 K.B. 822 a contract for the sale of shares by the defendant, a stockbroker, to the plaintiff was induced by the fraudulent misrepresentation of the defendant who represented that he was purchasing shares for the plaintiff on the market whereas he was selling his own shares. The contract was rescinded although the shares had fallen considerably on the stock exchange in the meantime. The shares were the same shares and the defendant was getting back the shares he would have had if he had not sold them fraudulently to the plaintiff.

However, counsel for the plaintiff bank submitted that, in the circumstances of this case, there cannot be *restitutio in integrum* because the parties to the transactions cannot be restored to their original positions either substantially or at all. The defendants claimed that they were induced by the fraudulent misrepresentations of the bank's servants, to embark on and continue in their attempt to take over Mooney and, in 1972, to enter into the commitments referred to in the judgment of the President, which included the payment by them of £350,000 and the raising of a loan from the bank of approximately £1.6 million. The defendants also claimed that subsequently they were induced, by a continuance of those fraudulent representations and by further fraudulent representations made by the servants of the bank, to purchase the shares of Patrick Quinn in Pat Quinn Holdings for a total sum of £225,000. When the take-over was successful, approximately 83% of the issued shares in Mooney were acquired by Pat Quinn Holdings in which the defendants had a controlling interest. These shares were acquired by Pat Quinn Holdings as purchasers from the several shareholders who owned the shares and who sold their shares on the terms offered in the take-over. The principals in each transaction were the acquiring company, as purchasers and the several shareholders, as vendors. The price of the shares was paid from (inter alia) the £350,000 contributed by the defendants and the loan raised from the bank. Shortly after the take-over, the board of Mooney acquired 32 premises formerly owned by Tara Electric Co. and so counsel on behalf of the bank say that Mooney (the sole asset of Pat Quinn Holdings) has been altered radically in nature since it was acquired and that it is now essentially a property company rather than a company carrying on the business of licensed premises. Again, in respect of the sale to the defendants of the shares of Patrick Quinn in Pat Quinn Holdings, counsel for the bank submit that this sale, although induced by the fraud of the bank, was a sale by Patrick Quinn, as vendor, to the defendants, as purchasers; they contend that there cannot be an order for rescission of that transaction, especially when Patrick Quinn is not a party to the proceedings.

At the trial, and again on this appeal, the defendants sought rescission of the entire of the transactions entered into between them and the bank; they submitted to the High Court and to this Court that, in the words of Lord Wright in *Spence* v. *Crawford* [1939] 3 All E.R. 271, the Court should do its best to unravel the complexities of the case and that, to do this, it would be necessary to rescind the transactions between the bank and them. Accepting the submissions of counsel for the defendants, the President made orders (inter alia) for the repayment to the defendants of the sum of £350,000 deposited by them in the bank for the purposes of the take-over, and of the £300,000 paid by the defendants Hugh Charlton and Gerard Sheehy in respect of the issue and allotment to them and their nominees of shares in Pat Quinn Holdings. He also ordered the payment by the bank to the defendants of the sums paid by them in part to Patrick Quinn and in part to the bank in respect of the purported purchase of the shares of Patrick Quinn in Pat Quinn Holdings in January, 1974.

Even if the order made in the High Court were capable of restoring the defendants substantially to the position they occupied before entering into these transactions – and this would be doubtful having regard to the events that have occurred since I.T.G. was backed into Mooney – in my view it is not possible to restore the bank substantially to its pre-contractual situation. As stated earlier, there cannot be partial rescission; it has to be *in toto* or not at all.

The order of the President, inter alia, requires Hugh Charlton to transfer 19,440 stock units of 50p each to the plaintiff bank; it requires each of the defendants to transfer to the bank all the shares in Pat Quinn Holdings issued and allotted to them and to Charlton Holdings; and it requires each of the defendants to transfer to the bank all the shares in Pat Quinn Holdings purchased by them from Patrick Quinn. This order purports to rescind the contract between the defendants and Patrick

Quinn in respect of the sale of his shares to the defendants, but I find it difficult to understand the basis on which the transfer to the bank of the shares held by Patrick Quinn in Pat Quinn Holdings could be *restitutio in integrum,* or could be regarded as restoring the bank to the status quo, since the bank never had any interest in these shares which passed between Patrick Quinn as vendor and the defendants as purchasers. In the same way, it seems to me that the order requiring Hugh Charlton to transfer the 19,440 Mooney shares to the bank, or the order requiring the defendants to transfer to the bank the shares issued or allotted to them or to Charlton Holdings in Pat Quinn Holdings, cannot be regarded as substantially restoring the status quo since, again, the bank never had any interest whatever in these shares.

Therefore, in my view there cannot be *restitutio in integrum* in this case particularly and additionally where the nature of Mooney (the sole asset of Pat Quinn Holdings) has altered radically in the meantime from being a company carrying on the business of licensed premises to that substantially of a property company; the reason for the change may be in dispute but is not relevant on this topic. In my opinion, counsel for the bank are correct in their submission that, on the facts of this case, an order effectively rescinding the transactions between the bank and the defendant should not have been made.

However, that does not conclude this appeal. The defendants would be entitled to any damages suffered by them as a result of, and directly flowing from, the representations that induced them to enter into these transactions. Counsel for the bank contend the defendants sought rescission and not damages because, as they alleged, no damage was suffered by the defendants as a result of the aforesaid representations. At the trial, the defendants did not adduce any evidence on the damage suffered by them because they nailed their flag to the mast of rescission. Counsel for the bank, from the outset of the trial, took the precaution of endeavouring to show that no damage resulted or flowed directly from the representations which were subsequently held by the learned President to be fraudulent.

The first witness for the defendants was Gerard Charlton and it was put to him by Mr. Liston that the first major step taken by the board of Mooney was to purchase the premises of Tara Electric (some 32 premises in all, of which most, or all, were unlet) at a cost of £616,000, and that this was done even before backing I.T.G. into Mooney. The tender of Mooney for these premises was accepted on the 16th December, 1972, just 16 days after the defendants' offer for the Mooney shares became unconditional. This purchase apparently had the effect of turning the company into a property company in the eyes of the committee of the stock exchange and dealing in Mooney shares was suspended by the committee on the 19th December, 1972, pending the issue of further information in relation to the Tara properties. The re-quotation of the shares on the stock exchange, upon which the whole future of the company depended, could not be obtained when 90% of the premises were unlet. There was no re-examination of Gerard Charlton on this topic. The bank subsequently led evidence as to the requirements of the stock exchange and as to the policy of the new board of Mooney which was, according to them, inconsistent with the requirements of the stock exchange; and they alleged that Hugh Charlton, who was in charge of these operations of Mooney, bought further premises and was slow in letting.

This Court has been invited by counsel for the bank to hold that, on the evidence adduced, no damage was suffered by the defendants as a result of the aforesaid representations. They base their submission on the following:-

1. In exchange for the moneys paid by the defendants they got shares in Pat Quinn Holdings directly, and in Mooney indirectly.
2. The defendants obtained full value for what they paid.
3. Within a year of the take-over, the shares and the assets of Mooney were worth considerably more than had been paid for them in the take-over.
4. On the authorities, the relevant date for ascertaining the value of what the defendants obtained was the date on which they acquired the shares; and counsel

relied on *Peek* v. *Derry*. (1887) 37 Ch. D. 541

In *Peek* v. *Derry*, in what is accepted as the authoritative statement on this topic, Cotton L.J. said at pp. 591-2 of the report:-

> "The damage to be recovered by the plaintiff is the loss which he sustained by acting on the representations of the defendants. That action was taking the shares . . . The loss, therefore, must be the difference between his £4000 [*the cost of the shares*] and the then value of the shares. Now, it must not be taken that the value of the shares must be what they would have sold for on the market, because that might not shew the real value at all . . . But I think it is in accordance with the cases, and in accordance with principle, that the real value, and not the market value, has to be ascertained immediately after the day when the shares were allotted to the plaintiff."

The reversal of the decision of the Court of Appeal by the House of Lords (on other grounds) in no way detracts from the authority of the decision on the question of damages: see also *McConnell* v. *Wright*. [1903] 1Ch. 546

The President made no finding on the question of whether or not the defendants suffered any loss as a result of the representations, and this is understandable because he was effectively dealing with rescission. Therefore, this Court is being invited to find primary facts. It is not the function of this Court to find primary facts; they must be found by the court of trial. In my opinion, the case should be remitted to the High Court for the purpose of the ascertainment of what damages, if any, were suffered by the defendants as a result of the representations made by the bank's servants inducing the defendants to enter into the relevant transactions. In my judgment, the correct measure of damages is that laid down by Cotton L.J. in *Peek* v. *Derry* which is the difference between what the defendants paid for the shares in Mooney and the value of the shares on the date on which they were acquired. I agree with the order proposed by Mr. Justice Henchy.

Parke J.:

I agree with the views expressed by the other members of the court on the issues of fraud. I only wish to add that, when considering the distinction which has been drawn in many of the authorities between the findings of a jury and the findings of fact by a judge sitting without a jury, one must also consider the nature of the questions which have been put to the jury. In the case of general questions (for example, as to whether a defendant is guilty of negligence) the answer embodies not only a finding of fact but also conclusions drawn from facts. However, if the questions are so framed that each answer is confined to a specific question of fact, it would seem to me that an appellate court can treat such a finding in very much the same way as a finding of fact by a judge sitting without a jury – save in so far as the judge has not given reasons for his finding.

On the issue of rescission, I agree with the judgments delivered by Mr. Justice Henchy and by Mr. Justice Griffin. It is, of course, always the desire of a court to give relief to a victim of fraud by rescinding the fraudulent transaction and restoring the parties, as far as possible, to the position in which they were respectively before the transaction was embarked upon. It is clear that this is what the learned President sought to do in making the order which is the subject of this appeal but, with the greatest respect to him and to the other members of this Court who take a different view from me on the matter, I consider that the facts in this case are such as to preclude the granting of relief by rescission. It seems to be clear on the authorities that rescission will only be granted where a true restitution of the original position can be attained, or can be attained to such an extent that no injustice will be suffered. If I compare the situation which existed at the commencement of this transaction with that which would result on the implementation of the learned President's order, I regret that I cannot accept that this is the kind of restitution which can be reconciled with the authorities.

During the course of the hearing in the High Court the defendants offered no evidence of damage, flowing directly or indirectly from the fraud, because they presented their case as being one for rescission. As the learned President accepted this submission, he made no finding upon which this Court, as an appellate tribunal, can adjudicate on the issue of damages. Accordingly, I am of opinion that the matter should be remitted to the High Court to assess what damages, if any, can be recovered. I agree with the principles set out in the judgment of Mr. Justice Henchy as to the assessment of damages in cases of the tort of fraud.

In view of the findings as to fraud which, in my opinion, should not be disturbed, the bank's claim must be dismissed.

O'Higgins C.J.:

Mr. Justice Butler has authorised me to say that he agrees with the judgment which I have delivered, and that he has nothing to add.

Notes and Questions

1. Was there any disagreement between the majority and minority on the principles of equity to be applied? As to their application, do you think the majority were right? Does their decision reveal an unsatisfactory, and, perhaps, unnecessary, limit to equitable relief? To what extent was their decision influenced by the availability of a remedy in tort for deceit?
2. See further on *restitutio in integrum, Irish Conveyancing Law,* para. 12. 58 *et seq.*

II. GROUNDS OF RELIEF

1. *Fraud*

See *Northern Bank Finance Corporation Ltd* v. *Charlton, supra.*

2. *Undue Influence*

GREALISH V. MURPHY
[1946] I.R. 35; 80 I.L.T.R. 111 (High Court)

The facts are set out in the judgment.

Gavan Duffy J.:

The plaintiff sues (1) to have an indenture of settlement of October, 1942, set aside, either (a) as improvident, or (b) for his own mental infirmity and incapacity to understand the deed, coupled with undue influence by the defendant; (2) to assert his sole title to a sum fo £2,000 standing at the National Bank, Galway, in the joint names of plaintiff and defendant; (3) to recover two sums of £500 and £645, as moneys improperly obtained or retained by the defendant from the plaintiff; and (4) to have an account taken. The defendant justifies his action under each head.

Peter Grealish, the plaintiff, is by way of being a farmer; he is a bachelor in the sixties; he is a man of a generous turn, but obstinate; he can hardly read and he signs as a marksman; he is afflicted with a worse than Boeotian head-piece and a very poor memory; a long life has not taught him sense. At the opening of the year 1942 this poor old victim of his circumstances was living under rather dismal conditions; Peter, for as Peter he is known, had a couple of labouring men sleeping under his roof, but otherwise lived alone on a remote farm and ranch of some 180 acres at Carnmore in the Oranmore district of the County of Galway, neglected by his relatives and almost bereft of friends; he was loaded with possessions, far above his modest wants and far beyond his modest capacity for management; moneys exceeding £5,500 lay to his credit on deposit at a bank in Galway, though considerable portions of this fortune were destined to be dissipated in the course of the year 1942; he had some cattle and his land had for many years brought him into frequent conflict with certain of his smaller neighbours, who were in the habit of taking conacre from him; he felt, as I surmise, that he could not by himself hope to hold his own in any considerable purchases or sales of cattle; he also owned a little farm a few miles away from Carnmore; and he needed, and realised that he needed, a reliable factotum as manager and as protector.

Peter had tried hard, and failed, to solve his problem; he had sought to marry first a cousin of his, then a niece, and finally another niece, to one, Thomas Fox, who had promised to bring in a marriage portion, payable to the plaintiff, first of £400, then of £1,000 and lastly of £500, and to look after Peter and his affairs, in exchange for a settlement of the big farm, as from Peter's death, on Fox and his bride, and their maintenance on the farm during Peter's life; Fox had eventually refused the first two ladies; the third deed had been executed on December 3rd, 1941; but a few weeks later the third lady had positively said "No."

Peter was bitterly disappointed, but he was not defeated. His family had known a family of Murphys, who lived as far away as Headford, and he resolved to invite one of the sons to step into the breach. Accordingly Thomas Murphy, the defendant, whom Peter had never seen, presented himself at Carnmore on January 26th, 1942; Peter liked his looks and at once came to business; he admits that he promised to give Murphy the farm after his own (Peter's) death, if Murphy would in the meantime work the land for him. In view of that admission, borne out by Peter's later instructions to his own solicitor, I need not determine precisely how much further Peter's promises may have gone, though Murphy is much more explicit; his evidence is that Peter explained that he was boycotted and that his land had been forcibly seized and that he wished to put an end to the conacre holdings on his land and to have a man to manage and work the farm and live with him; he says that Peter went on to promise that, if Murphy would come, Peter would leave him the farm, buy him a new lorry and also, if he wished, a new car, settle on Murphy any sum of money he required and let him marry any girl he liked; Murphy says that Peter wanted to go to a solicitor the very next day to "sign me over the farm."

Murphy's reply, he says, was that he must see his own solicitor, Mr. McDonagh, at Tuam, and he saw him on January 27th, and discovered the Fox settlement of the previous month; he returned at once to Carnmore, when Peter assured him that he had already given instructions for a suit to set that deed aside; they agreed, Murphy continues, to call on Mr. Concannon, Peter's solicitor, at Galway on the following day; they did so, according to Murphy, and during that visit he and Peter agreed, in the presence of the solicitor and his clerk, Costello, that pending the setting aside of the Fox settlement, Murphy should manage for Peter Grealish, take him into town to buy and sell generally and do any business that Peter might ask him to do. This agreement of January 28th, 1942, is decisive upon the onus of proof for any transaction prior to the impugned indenture of October, 1942. This agreement is not corroborated; Peter is incapable of affirming or disputing it; Concannon denies it; Costello, called as a witness by Murphy, was asked nothing about it, and his answer, were it available, would have carried little weight; but, as against Murphy, I must accept his own evidence as proving at least that on some day at the outset of his dealings with Peter he undertook, in consideration of Peter's promises, to act for him in business matters generally, pending the action against Fox. And during the time that elapsed before October, 1942, when that action was heard, Murphy must have discovered beyond doubt, if he did not know from the first day, that Peter needed decidedly more protection than the ordinary western farmer and cattle dealer.

Mr. Fitzgerald pressed on me vigorously the view that Peter is merely a simple-minded and not a feeble-minded old man, but that is not the impression made on me by his performance as a witness; I must go with the medical evidence to the extent of classifying him among the mentally deficient, though I should not myself assimilate him to a child of twelve. I cannot measure his deficiency in scientific terms and I need say no more than this, that, as I appraise him, the brain, while it must have developed with time, has never since childhood attained the normal powers of an adult; and he is liable to be erratic, especially outside the daily routine of his life at home. The trial threw occasional side-lights on Peter's faculties; for instance, he can read the clock, but cannot tell the time; Murphy virtually admitted that Peter was unable to count £2,000 in £50, £10 and £5 notes; and, having made to Murphy in October, 1942, an astounding present of, as Murphy says, £700, Peter was unable, as I must necessarily infer from the pleadings, to give his advisers in this action any instructions whatever on the matter, which came to light only through a question in Murphy's cross-examination by Mr. Costello at the trial; I gather, moreover, that Peter had completely lost all trace of a further large sum of money, which he drew from the Bank at the same time.

Murphy, who comes of farming stock, had been a road worker and he was a haulier in a small way, with a car and a lorry of his own, when Peter's proposal burst upon him and a bright vista suddenly opened out before his eyes. True, he was being asked to give up his freedom, he had no idea what sort of principal Peter would prove to be and he could not tell what stings he would have to endure from waspish neighbours. But he was only 32 years of age and the possible difficulties may well have loomed dim in the dazzle of the glittering reward proffered by his glowing benefactor; the golden prospect was that he would be a rich man after a few years of not too arduous labour and surely he could well bear any little passing troubles that the venture might entail. Murphy accepted Peter's proposal, but did nothing at this time to rush the old man; I do not think he called on him again until the following March. Then he began to see him, as he says himself, about twice a week until June, and I see no reason to believe that his attentions slackened during the summer; he used to take Peter for shopping or business purposes to Galway by car; he drove him at different dates as far as Dublin and Limerick and to several fairs; he says he bought cattle for him to the value of £480 at Gort Fair in May, and early in October sold cattle for him at Tuam Fair, taking £530 net, and immediately afterwards bought cattle for him at Westport Fair. He was kind to Peter and that solicitude did not go unrewarded; Peter gave Murphy £450 towards a motor lorry in May, 1942, and (at about the same time, I think, or earlier) £250 for a Chrysler car. In June Peter actually placed a sum of £2,000 in the joint names of himself and Murphy at the National Bank, in Galway, though not necessarily out of munificence towards Murphy and primarily, I think, as a strategic diversion to defeat the apprehended machinations of a rapacious Estate Duty Office.

In June, 1942, the court adjourned the Fox action, and Peter, blaming Mr. Concannon and chafing at the delay, entrusted his case to another solicitor, Dr. Comyn of Loughrea. On October 10th, 1942, the Circuit Court in Galway annulled the Fox deed on Peter's evidence, Fox not appearing, and on October 13th Peter gave the instructions upon which Dr. Comyn drew the settlement that is the chief bone of contention in this action. The deed was executed on October 20th, and bears date October 24th, 1942, and Peter, theretofore full owner of the Carnmore land, was registered as limited owner by reference to this document. The stamp duty puts the net value of the farm at some £1,000. The deed, in pursuance of the January agreement, gave Murphy a position at Carnmore equivalent to, but really better than, that of an adopted son.

On October 30th, 1942, Peter drew out £1,900, standing on deposit in his own name at the Bank of Ireland in Galway, thus closing the account, which was distinct from the still subsisting joint account for £2,000 with the National Bank. There is some evidence that Peter, when taking the money out, alleged that he was buying a farm. Murphy avowed in cross-examination that Peter had given him £700 of this money and had lodged £1,000 out of the £1,900 in the National Bank (presumably at Galway). I understand that, until this admission by Murphy as to his £700, the whole sum drawn had vanished, and, unless the money has been discovered during the long vacation, the sum of £1,000 still has to be found. Murphy may be mistaken as to the precise bank, but his evidence of a bank lodgement is specific, and the mystery cannot be brushed aside as if a mere bagatelle were involved. I am not to be understood as throwing blame on Murphy for the loss of the money; I do not know who is to blame. This extraordinary disappearance of the money of an irresponsible old man calls, in my view, for close and persistent investigation, with the aid, if necessary, of the Gárda Síochána; but that matter is outside the preview of this action on the pleadings and the evidence.

Murphy says that he did not go to live at Carnmore in pursuance of the settlement until early in December, 1942, when he lodged, hard by Peter's own house, with a

Mrs. Fahy; a young Fahy lived with Peter and worked for him. Local hositility had declared itself against Murphy as early as October, but, after his arrival, a quite unforeseen and particularly unpleasant series of attacks came from one of Peter's sisters, a bedlam, living some three miles away, who would descend in wrath upon Carnmore at intervals, giving tongue to loud maledictions upon the grabber of her brother's land. Murphy, I think, actually went in fear of his life from some of the local roughs, a number of whom had stoned his car, and he found the onslaughts of the termagant almost equally hard to endure.

Early in January, 1943, I find (in a conflict of evidence) that Murphy, as Peter says, told Peter that he must have money or he would leave; I find that Peter offered him £500 and that Murphy refused this sum and went off to Galway; and that Peter at once sent him an urgent message with an offer, if he would come back. Murphy's evidence for which there is some corroboration, is that the messenger brought him an offer of £500 and of all Peter's cattle, and that Peter also promised to keep his sister away; so he returned and accepted the offer. I find that Murphy did return and come to terms with Peter, but, as his witness, the messenger, says – "I suppose he really meant to stay anyway"; my reading of the position is that Murphy knew that Peter was afraid of being beaten or killed, if deprived of Murphy's protection, and knew that Peter was sure to succumb to the demand for money, to prevent his desertion by Murphy. Murphy now says that he had not decided to abandon the undertaking, but he could not live there nor work the farm "on account of the trouble," he did not like the place "inside or outside," he was under police protection (in fact the Gárdaí had not yet come) and he wanted to go home to see his own people and to consult his solicitor. He admits having gone away, but denies having demanded money before he left. Peter (whose evidence here I do not accept) says that Murphy got the £500 before leaving and he denies having sent a messenger with an offer to bring him back. The fact that Murphy got the money is not in dispute. But I do not know where Peter got the £500; he says that he drew it from the Bank of Ireland, Murphy having driven him to Galway for the purpose; Murphy, as I follow him, says that Peter drew the money from the National Bank and paid him on January 15th, 1943. But neither bank account shows any such drawing and no witness has suggested that the justly timorous owner kept any large sum of money at home.

On the night of January 12th, 1943, a day or two after Murphy's return, shots were fired into Mrs. Fahy's house; the incident was described by the police as "an attempted murder on the house of Fahy"; young Fahy was afraid to work for Peter or live with him any more, though the other labourer stayed; Peter's house and Fahy's were kept under police protection for eighteen months thereafter, as was also Murphy's person on dark nights, while he remained at Carnmore.

On March 10th, Murphy sold on the land 39 head of cattle (Peter's alleged present to him), realising £643, for his own account. The deal was not carried out as openly as the circumstances required. I see no need to determine whether Peter had given Murphy the cattle or not; Peter vehemently denies the gift; but I think the probabilities are that Peter had regretted and repudiated his excessive liberality in a crisis and that Murphy felt uneasy about the whole discreditable affair. On May 3rd Murphy fell ill and went home; he and Peter parted on good terms. But Murphy's amazing statement that, when leaving, he was "under the impression" (*sic!*) that Peter knew that the cattle were gone, throws a nasty light on the rape of the cattle. On May 28th Murphy returned; Peter was angry and at once taxed him with having sold Peter's cattle surreptitiously. By this time Peter had another man, a relative, living in the house. Early in June Peter consulted Mr. Conway, his present solicitor, with a view to taking action against Murphy. By June 22nd Peter and Murphy were not on speaking terms and on that night Murphy was locked out by Peter and went five miles away for a bed, under police protection. At the end of June, Murphy, feeling that he was in effect supplanted by the new arrival, left Carnmore.

That is the story in outline. But the difficulty of ascertaining the facts has been prodigious. I could not depend much on Peter's memory, nor on the accuracy of either contestant; the other local witnesses did not impress me; and several witnesses who might have been called did not appear.

Let me now examine the making of the settlement which the plaintiff seeks to set aside. We have Peter's promise to Murphy at the very outset of their connection; that was a promise, according to Murphy, to "leave me the farm" and "settle any sum of money I wanted on me," and Peter had wished to go to a solicitor at once to "sign me over the farm." Then, according to Murphy, "he used to say every time I would meet him that he had decided to leave the place to me and that the marriage settlement would be set aside." And there is ample evidence (whatever the terms actually were in which Peter expressed himself to Murphy) that Peter was fuming with impatience to rid himself of his commitments to Fox, obviously in order to be free to conclude his arrangements with Murphy. There is evidence that Costello, Mr. Concannon's clerk, who claims to have been an old friend of Peter's and was called as a witness for Murphy, in March, 1942, definitely ascertained that Mr. Concannon would have nothing to do with any settlement of the land by Grealish upon Murphy, and I cannot doubt that Costello made this fact known to Murphy, if not to Peter, who changed his solicitor in June, 1942, as I have said. Costello lost his place in the Concannon office early in July. Peter paid several visits to Dr. Comyn during the summer, always accompanied, I think by Murphy and by Costello; Costello's presence on these occasions is unexplained, but Peter clearly trusted him and afterwards rewarded him liberally for his miscellaneous services. According to Dr. Comyn's recollection, Costello occasionally made some remarks on these occasions, but Peter did the talking, while Murphy "never uttered a word", a singularly modest attitude for the heir-presumptive during the long wait from June to October; if this persistent silence is an example of western caution, it suggests tactical caution carried rather too far.

On October 13th, 1942, three days after the Court had set aside the Fox deed, Peter, duly accompanied by Murphy and Costello, called on Dr. Comyn. In the outer office Peter intimated to the solicitor that he intended to "take in" a man and Dr. Comyn understood the man to be Murphy, whereupon Dr. Comyn took Peter by himself upstairs and wrote down his instructions; he had no coversation at all with Murphy. If Murphy is to be believed (and there are limits to my credulity), Peter (who may fairly be said to have been living for this day) did not tell Murphy when he came down, that he had actually given the instructions; but Murphy did admit in cross-examination that Peter had said he was going in (that is, to Dr. Comyn) in order to transfer the land to Murphy.

The effect of the detailed instructions, as taken down, was that, being old, delicate and unable to work his land without loss, Peter wished to take Murphy, who was not a relative, into his house as factotum and general worker and, while keeping a life interest, to transfer the big farm after his death to Murphy, who was to be supported and to live at Carnmore in the meantime; Peter meant to deal with the other farm and with his stock and moneys later. The instructions were read to Peter, who approved of them, and upon them Dr. Comyn instructed counsel, verbally, as I understand, to settle the deed.

On October 20th the engrossment was read to Peter, who executed the deed as a marksman. The solicitor was acting for Peter alone; he was not told that Murphy had a solicitor of his own; Murphy had no adviser at all and had not been consulted in any way during the preparation of the settlement. Dr. Comyn himself "knew about the boycotting thoroughly well"; "boycott" was counsel's term and it is right to say that the evidence, so far as it goes, suggests that the facts do not warrant so strong an expression to describe Peter's annoyances from his neighbours up to this time. Dr. Comyn says that he explained Murphy's covenants to him and that Murphy also then executed the deed. Finally he "told Peter, in the presence of Murphy, that, if Murphy did not comply with the covenants, he, Peter, knew where to find me." He did not give Murphy any copy or duplicate of the deed. It is not suggested that Murphy made any claim to a money settlement.

The settlement purports to make Peter Grealish, as beneficial owner, assign the farm absolutely as from Peter's death to Thomas Murphy, his heirs and assigns, subject to a life interest in Peter; the land is expressly charged with a right for Murphy to reside in Peter's house and to be supported and maintained out of the land during Peter's life; Murphy for his part covenants with Peter, during Peter's life, without reward to reside in the house and work and manage the land and sow and harvest the crops and attend to and take proper care of all farm stock and implements and the buying and selling of stock and generally to perform all the farm work and the duties of a labourer as required by Peter and (a very important covenant) duly and properly to account for all moneys expended or received by him on behalf of Peter; and Murphy covenants to pay Peter £1 a week for every week in which he fails to reside with Peter and to indemnify Peter for any loss and expense incurred on the maintenance or wages of any person employed by Peter to perform any work that Murphy may fail to do.

Thus Peter executed an improvident settlement, surrendering irrevocably his own absolute title for a life interest in consideration of personal covenants, backed by no adequate sanctions; the farm itself was hypothecated to secure the newcomer, beside whom Peter was a Croesus; and Peter was to be left for the remainder of his life very much at the mercy of a rather impecunious young man, who had no ties of blood and was still unproved as a friend. I think effective safeguards for Peter could have been devised, if there was to be a settlement, or alternatively Peter might have contracted to settle the property on Murphy by will, upon the lines suggested by *Coverdale* v. *Eastwood* 15 Eq. 121; whatever plan was adopted, I think that suitable conditions could and should have been determined in negotiation between the solicitors for the parties, each of whom ought to have been separately represented. But these reflections are otiose, if the conclusive answer to Peter's present claim is that he was separately advised by an independent solicitor.

That contention deserves careful examination and I have examined it with great care. I am satisfied that Peter received from an experienced solicitor advice that was absolutely independent and I am satisfied that the draft deed was settled by very able counsel, upon instructions reflecting, of course, the state of mind and knowledge of the solicitor. Nevertheless, the question of Peter's actual understanding of the solemn document that he executed on October 20th, 1942, is a question of first importance. Dr. Comyn, who avows that he looked upon the settlement as a transaction similar to the three attempts which, as Peter told him, had broken down, says that he was absolutely satisfied that Peter understood the instructions he gave for the deed. I have no doubt that Peter did know that the deed would secure the land to Murphy at Peter's death and that he knew generally the undertakings that Murphy was giving in return; Peter showed his own understanding of the young man's obligations, when he formulated his grievance in his own words: – "He (Murphy) did not do anything about the agreement; he failed . . . He was bound to look after me and buy and sell and give up the money – what he did not do." But the trouble is that the solicitor, whose advice was essential to Peter, did not advise *en connaissance de cause* and that Peter's actual knowledge of what he was doing fell very short of the knowledge that the settlor ought to have had. That is the result in my mind of candid evidence from Dr. Comyn himself and of inferences thereform. Consequently the principle of *Harrison* v. *Guest* De G., M. & G. 424; 8 H.L.C. 481 and *Coomber* v. *Coomber* [1911] 1 Ch. 723, that a competent assignor, who knows what he is doing, must be held to his deed, does not apply here.

The evidence proves that the solicitor did not know all the material facts, that he did not give Peter a complete explanation of the nature and effect of the deed, and that the duty of illuminating Peter's benighted mind was more imperative and more formidable, if the task was possible, than the solicitor supposed.

First. Dr. Comyn did not get the facts. He did not ascertain the total of Peter's property, nor the proportion between that total and the value of the farm at Carnmore; yet that was relevant and material information for an adviser. Still more important to be known was the fact that Peter had already placed £2,000 on deposit in the joint names of himself and Murphy, with Murphy's ready acquiescence, under the illusion, known to Murphy, that this device would ward off the imaginary terrors of Dublin Castle. Murphy, knowing Peter for what he was, could not assume that

Peter had mentioned the episode, still less that he had given an accurate account of it; Murphy ought to have told the solicitor all about it, but he persisted in his curious policy of silence. Perhaps Murphy did not know positively how silly Peter's ruse was as a measure of defence, but he is intelligent enough, in my estimate of him, to have felt the transaction to be one of questionable virtue and of very dubious value, and, both for this reason and because he stood to gain a large sum of money from his pitiable patron, he ought to have spoken out at this juncture. Here was cogent evidence, had the solicitor and counsel known it, that Peter was and would be incapable of taking care of his own interests and that Peter and Murphy combined were and would be unequal to the burden of taking care of his property. Instead of favouring the projected settlement, as he did, Dr. Comyn must have gone into the whole affair very much more warily, had he known. He did not know, because, by agreement or coincidence, each of the two men vitally concerned said nothing.

Secondly. Peter was not told and did not realise how gravely he was committing himself and jeopardising his own interests; he probably understood neither the immediate pledging of his favour to Murphy nor the effect of that charge; certainly the difference between this deed and a will was not explained to him, nor the fact that the settlement was to be irrevocable and his alienation irretrievable, no matter how badly Murphy might behave, no matter what untoward development might supervene; and he was certainly not a man to apprehend the risks, at least without the clearest and most insistent exposition of them. What precautions were taken in the deed against the vicissitudes of life? Murphy might have mismanaged the farm hopelessly, for all the solicitor could tell; or, for all he could tell, Murphy might have taken to drink or gone to the devil or married a shrew who would make Peter's life a torture; he might have become a bankrupt; he might have been sent to hospital for years, or been committed for some time to an asylum; he might even have been sentenced to imprisonment. Unlikely events, very unlikely? Perhaps, but why do I insure my house against fire, and how was the solicitor, a stranger to Murphy, to gauge the probabilities of an ensuing incapacity or incompetence? An act of God is always unlikely (before it happens) and the devil's action may often seem unlikely too. And if some such calamity had smitten Peter, the law might or might not have given him some costly redress. It was unlikely, perhaps very unlikely, that the young man would predecease the old; but how deplorable would Peter's position have been, if Murphy had died after a few months' work under the deed and perhaps twenty years before Peter himself! However, Peter's advisers had no more dark forebodings than their client. Clearly there were some important aspects of the deed far outside poor Peter's ken, when he scratched his rude mark upon the paper.

Thirdly. The solicitor quite erroneously considered and treated Peter as a normal member of the farming community; in fact I think he treated him as a man of high intelligence. Taking his client to be a competent judge of his own man, the solicitor, who just knew Murphy to be a farmer's son and no relative and Peter's dumb attendant, made no inquiries at all as to Murphy's antecedents, character, capacity or financial position; he assumed both the fitness of Murphy and the value of his covenants; he did not suspect how easily the young man might become master of the situation, nor how much he would be tempted to abuse his trust; and the deed reflects that kindly confidence; whether Dr. Comyn seriously expected Murphy to keep accounts, I do not know. No need was felt to appoint trustees; perhaps they would have been hard to find, but, had the solicitor realised the settlor's weakness, he would have seen that Peter required and must have the protection for which trusts were invented. Unless there be a legal presumption of undue influence against Murphy, making other questions quite subordinate. I regard it as a matter of high importance that Peter's advisers in this particular transaction should have been equipped to advise him with a just appreciation of his mental debility and his special need of protection. They were not so equipped and Peter did not get the circumspect advice and protection so necessary to him.

Now, how is Murphy affected by any critisism reflecting upon the advice under which Peter acted? I have shown that Murphy's own conduct in the matter was not beyond reproach, but any impartial person will see that it is quite impossible to say that the deed was procured through Murphy's undue influence, even if he did his part during nearly nine months, as he naturally would, to keep the old man's ardour alive. Nor is this the familiar case in which the Court, from the relation of the parties, must presume undue influence until disproved positively by the recipient of the bounty; Murphy had constituted himself Peter's interim confidential agent in January, 1942, and had thus placed himself in a very delicate position, an exceptionally delicate position in view of Peter's mentality; but the undoubted fact is that some such transaction as that eventuating in the actual settlement had been expressly envisaged by the parties from the outset, before Murphy can have acquired any influence whatsoever; therefore I cannot fairly impute to him Peter's decision to put the business on a legal basis as soon as the way was made clear by the final elimination of the Fox interest, the only obstacle. And Murphy in no way interfered with the drafting of the deed in the particular form which it took.

Peter had intended all through to leave the property to Murphy and to bind himself to that effect, in return for the precious services to be rendered by the vigorous young man to the rather helpless old one. As from January, 1942, Murphy had only to be kind to Peter, as he was, and to retain his goodwill, as he certainly did, in order to secure his reward from that eager benefactor.

Besides, the plan was not originated by Murphy, but by Peter, and by Peter alone. Murphy on his side had faced appreciable risks in accepting Peter's advances; and any picture of him as an adventurer, inveigling his witless victim into a trap in the October settlement, would be a caricature. Much as I blame Murphy for his reticence (partly perhaps through ignorance) as to the existence of his own solicitor and for his want of candour in suppressing the eccentric and disquieting £2,000 deposit in the joint names, I could not in common sense treat these faults as any evidence of undue influence in relation to the settlement on the facts; and, if Murphy throws doubt on the veracity of his own evidence concerning Peter's alleged original offer to settle money on him, by his failure to mention that important promise to Dr. Comyn and his failure to call upon the solicitor to make good that promise in the deed, here again my criticism of Murphy as a witness is foreign to the issue of undue influence in fact and remote from any evidence that would raise a legal presumption of undue influence against Murphy, so far as the settlement is concerned.

The result is that the plaintiff's attempt to set aside the deed on the ground of undue influence, whether actual or presumptive, by Murphy cannot succeed, and, if the deed had to stand or fall upon that issue, there would be nothing more to say. But the position in law as I see it, upon the pleadings, is not so simple as that; there is another crucial matter to be determined.

Peter cannot avoid the deed for undue influence; but his claim is further based on the improvidence of the transaction and also he directly alleges (though in connection with the charge of undue influence) his own mental incapacity; I think I can reasonably read these averments together without calling for an amendment of his pleadings.

The issue thus raised brings into play Lord Hatherley's cardinal principle (from which the exceptions are rare) that Equity comes to the rescue whenever the parties to a contract have not met upon equal terms, see Lord Hatherley's judgment (dissenting on facts) in *O'Rourke* v. *Bolingbroke* 2 A.C. 814 at p. 823; the corollary is that the Court must inquire whether a grantor, shown to be unequal to protecting himself, has had the protection which was his due by reason of his infirmity, and the infirmity may take various forms. The deed here was in law a transaction for value: *Colreavy* v. *Colreavy* [1940] I.R. 71; however tenuous the value may have proved to be in fact, and, of course, a Court must be very much slower to undo a transaction for value but the fundamental principle to justify radical interference by the court is the identical principle, whether value be shown or not, and the recorded examples run from gifts and voluntary settlements (including an abortive marriage settlement) to assignments for a money consideration. The principle has been applied to improvident grants, whether the particular disadvantage entailing the need for protection to the grantor were merely low station and surprise (though the grantor's rights were fully explained): *Evans* v. *Llewellin* 1 Cox, Eq. Cas. 333, or youth and inexperience: *Prideaux* v. *Lonsdale* 1 de G.J. & S. 433; *Everitt* v. *Everitt* 10 Eq. 405, or age and weak intellect, short of total incapacity, with no fiduciary relation and no "arts of inducement" to condemn the grantee: *Longmate* v. *Ledger* 2 Giff. 157; *Andersen* v. *Elsworth* 3 Giff. 154. Even the exuberant or ill-considered dispositions of feckless middle-aged women have had to yield to the same principle: *Phillipson* v. *Kerry* 32 Beav. 628; *Wollaston* v. *Tribe* 9 Eq. 44.

The principle prevailed, when the deed was "the most honest thing in the world" so far as the settlor and her solicitor were concerned: *Everitt* v. *Everitt* 10 Eq. 405, and though the evidence of the solicitor acting for the grantor was fully accepted: *Phillipson* v. *Kerry* 32 Beav. 628, and again where the deed had been prepared by the grantor's own solicitor, a man of honour, but the grantor, while fully understanding the benefit to accrue to the grantee, had not fully understood the effect of her deed as it affected her own interests: *Anderson* v. *Elsworth* 3 Giff. 154; in several other instances the inadequacy of the explanations given to the grantor has been a conspicuous, indeed a decisive, factor in the Court's action against an improvident deed, the Court either assuming: *Prideaux* v. *Lonsdale* 1 de G.J. & S. 433, or having direct evidence: *Phillipson* v. *Kerry* 32 Beav, 628; *Wollaston* v. *Tribe* 9 Eq. 44, to prove a serious lack of understanding. The least the Court can demand is that an infirm grantor shall have known what he was doing. In the much more frequent, but analogous, instances of deeds attacked for undue influence the Judicial Committee has insisted that the donor must have had a complete explanation of the nature and effect of the transaction, from an advisor who himself knew all the relevant circumstances: *Inch Noriah* v. *Shaik Allie bin Omar* [1929] A.C. 127, 135, even where the advisor was selected by the donor: *Williams* v. *Williams* [1937] 4 All E.R. 34, 83, and the same imperative requirement was stressed in a transaction for value by Isaacs J. upon a deed closely resembling the deed in this action in some aspects, but obtained by undue influence: *Watkins* v. *Combes* 30 C.L.R. 180, 196-7.

In my judgment, without any regard to any question of undue influence, upon Lord Hatherley's principle and the concurrent authorities the plaintiff by reason of his own weakness of mind, coupled with the deficiencies in the legal advice under which he acted and his unawareness, is entitled to have the improvident indenture of settlement, dated October 24th, 1942, set aside and the Register of Freeholders rectified.

I may add that the balancing of equities is not complicated here by any plea of estoppel, nor have I on the evidence any reason to suppose that the defendant has suffered any prejudice worth mentioning through executing the settlement.

I pass to the other heads of complaint and first to the £2,000 deposit. On June 19th, 1942, Peter, with Murphy at his elbow, first called at the Bank of Ireland in Galway, and removed in notes a sum of £2,000 standing on deposit there in his own sole name, and then went to the National Bank in Galway, and put the money on deposit there in a new account made out in the joint names of himself and Murphy. He had had some difficulty concerning another deposit account in the Bank of Ireland, standing in his own name and that of a deceased brother, because the Bank had demurred to paying Peter from that deposit without being satisfied that the duty payable to the State on his brother's death had been discharged; the brother had died some years before, and, as the beneficial owner of the money, fiercely resenting the suggestion of its depletion by fiscal claims and the delay, Peter was angry at the Bank's attitude. I cannot, on the evidence of a single witness, a partisan, hold as a fact that Murphy pressed Peter to make the change to another bank by frightening him with the Revenue bogey, even though Peter in part supports the story. But the following answers by Murphy himself show that the money was withdrawn under a delusion, in fear of the Revenue commissioners, and discover Murphy with varying explanations for the insertion of his own name in the second Bank's account:-

Q. 1570. (In chief) "Was he (Peter) going to assail the Bank of Ireland again?" (The reference is to a visit to the Bank on the previous day.)

"Yes. He said, when leaving the office (that is the Bank) the day before that he noticed a Customs and Excise man leaving the office. He said – 'If I don't take my money out of that Bank, they will rob me completely.'"

"Was the £2,000 eventually paid over on to the counter to him?" "Yes."

"Before he got to the National did he say anything about what he was going to do with the money?"

"I asked him first what he was going to do and he said 'I'm going to put it into the National.'"

"After that, did he tell you what he was going to do with the money?"

"He said, 'I will put your name with it.'"

"Was that the first time he ever said anything to you about putting your name on the deposit?" "Yes."

"What did you say?"

"I said nothing at all for the time being (*sic!*). Then a bit further down he said, 'I don't want my relatives to get any of the money.'"

(In cross-examination.) "And, according to your case, you had got a gift of £2,000?"

"I don't know about the £2,000. I left it at that."

"You are claiming it here in this action as a gift?"

"I am. Grealish told me he intended leaving it to me after his death."

"You are claiming that £2,000 as a gift; did I hear you say that Grealish told you he intended leaving that after his death?" "Yes."

"When did he say that?"

"He said, 'I intend leaving all my money to you'; he did not mention £2,000 or £3,000."

"When did he make that interesting announcement to you?"

"On the way down to the Bank."

"What day was that?"

"19th June."

"The day you went down to the Bank?" "Yes"

"He made that interesting announcement, which you forgot in your direct evidence, that he was going to leave you all his money, not mentioning this particular sum?" "Yes"

"He intended leaving you everything he had after his death?" "Yes."

Mr. Thunder, the Manager of the National Bank, who knew that the money belonged to Grealish, says that he saw the plaintiff privately, because he was a marksman; he told him that both signatures would be required to draw any money, and explained to him, and was satisfied that Grealish understood, that a lodgment in joint names meant that the survivor would be entitled to the money, if one of them died; Peter just replied that "*Murphy was managing his business and looking after him in general*": he said nothing about wanting to make a present to Murphy.

"Were you able to form any impression of his intention about the money, whether he intended making a present of it to Murphy?"

"No, I could not tell you that."

Mr. Thunder says that Peter was quite clear with him. The deposit receipt was given to Peter.

The unsatisfactory features of this episode are patent. The transaction was shocking and the two men did not stand on equal terms, so that I think I might, following Lord Hatherley's principle, or perhaps the even more emphatic language of Sullivan M.R. in *Slator* v. *Nolan* I.R. 11 Eq. 367, at p. 386, against any party taking undue advantage of another, uphold the plaintiff's claim, without any regard to the peculiar relations of the parties. But Murphy, on his own evidence had become Peter's interim manager and business agent, his confidential man, as early as January, 1942; their relations were such that the Court must on long settled principles assume undue influence, if not rebutted, and for this issue the burden of proof is definitely upon Murphy, who has wholly failed to discharge it. Murphy had put himself into such a position towards this old man as to be bound to protect his patron in money matters, even against the patron himself; and Murphy was bound to refuse any gross prodigality in his own favour, made in secret or without competent advice. Moreover, quite apart from any confidential relations, the presumption of a resulting trust stands unrebutted, for I must discount Murphy's own evidence here. I need not labour this matter. I disregard the fact that interest on the deposit was paid to the joint holders and shared between them. Peter's vagary in the matter of the £2,000 must be redressed. The transaction cannot stand.

I come to the present of Peter's cattle to Murphy after the deed of settlement and Murphy's realisation of the cattle for his own use. I need say nothing more of Murphy's method of acquisition, for his position under the deed puts him out of Court. Here was a flagrant abuse by Murphy and he must make good Peter's loss, which I measure, on Murphy's evidence, at the sum of £643.

Finally, the plaintiff is entitled to an account. He is entitled to an account of all dealings by the defendant with, or in relation to, cattle for, or on behalf of, the plaintiff during the calendar year 1942, and a further account of all moneys, the property of the plaintiff, come to the hands of the defendant.

The first account (which I hope the plaintiff will be advised to waive) relates in particular to the sale of cattle for some £530 by Murphy at the Tuam Fair in October, 1942; Murphy says that he bought cattle at Westport Fair immediately afterwards for the plaintiff to the value of £500, and he was at pains to give some account of the balance. But Murphy has in his power or procurement one or more banking documents in this connection, which he omitted from his affidavit of documents. That is why I have to order the first account, if it is sought, but I do not think that Peter has anything to gain from it. Murphy's purchase of cattle for Peter at Gort in May, 1942, to the value of £480 is not disputed and must be allowed in the account.

The second account is necessitated by Murphy's admission in cross-examination that he received on October 30th, 1942, from Peter a sum of £700, whereof (though he may be able to justify more) he has so far accounted to my satisfaction for only £115 paid by Peter's direction to Costello; for the moment I shall extend the charity of silence to the remainder of his evidence on this subject, including the reappearance of the fiscal vampire. This account will deal also with the £500 paid by Peter to Murphy in January, 1943. Murphy may object that the statement of claim does complain of this particular payment, and it does not; that is why I deal with the matter by way of an account instead of giving judgment for the amount; but I think the answer to the objection is that Peter's advisers probably did their best upon incoherent instructions; they did complain of a gift of £500 by Peter to Murphy and properly attributed it to undue influence upon Murphy's threat to abandon Peter, but they placed the gift in October, 1942, confusing it with the price (£530 on Murphy's evidence) realised at that time by the aforesaid sale of Peter's cattle at Tuam Fair. I think the mistake was understandable in lawyers who had Peter for a client, and Peter did in fact depose to this payment in his evidence. I see no need for the statement of claim to be amended, because the prayer for an account seems to me sufficiently to cover this claim and Murphy has not been misled.

I have said nothing about the two cars for Murphy, bought with Peter's moneys; I do not regard these gifts as tainted; I am satisfied that the private car was promised by Peter at his first interview with Murphy; probably he promised the lorry too, though here Murphy's evidence is not corroborated. The statement of claim makes no specific claim under this head and the moneys paid by Peter for the two cars may reasonably be treated as having been properly expended by Murphy. In all the circumstances the accounts will be directed without interest.

Notes

See further *Irish Land Law,* para. 9.075 and *Irish Conveyancing Law.* para. 19.35. See also *Smyth* v. *Smyth,* p. 410, *post.*

3. *Innocent Misrepresentation*

LECKY V. WALTER
[1914] 1 I.R. 378 (Chancery Division)

Bonds of a Dutch company, having property in America, were purchased on the faith of a representation that they were a charge on the property. They were not, in fact, a charge on the property, but the representation was made innocently.

O'Connor, M.R.:

[The Master of the Rolls, having stated the facts as above set out, proceeded as follows:–]

I do not consider that the failure of the plaintiff to prove the second misrepresentation is a material element in the case, because the first representation was one of a most important character, and such as would necessarily influence any person invited to purchase the bonds, and I am satisfied from the plaintiff's evidence that the statement that the bonds were charged on the oil-fields was, if not the only inducement, a material inducement to purchase them.

I need not pause to establish the proposition that it is not necessary to prove that a particular representation was the sole cause of the transaction, and that it is enough that it constituted a material inducement. I have now come to the point when I consider it established that the plaintiff purchased the bonds from the defendant, and that he was induced to make the purchase by misrepresentation by the defendant's agent, which is equivalent to misrepresentation by the defendant himself. The purely legal question then arises, Does this state of affairs give the plaintiff the right to set aside a transaction which has been in fact completed, and is not merely in the process of completion? It must be borne in mind that there is no allegation of fraudulent misrepresentation, and therefore the case is to be treated as one in which a *bona fide* mistake was made by the defendant.

Mr. Healy, counsel for the defendant, contended that in such circumstances the plaintiff had no cause of action, and he relied upon the judgment of Lord Campbell in the House of Lords in *Wilde* v. *Gibson* 1 H.L.C. 605, at pp. 632-3, where he says:- "My Lords, after the very attentive and anxious consideration which this case has received, I have come to the clear conclusion that the decree appealed against ought to be reversed; and I must say that in the Court below the distinction between a bill for carrying into execution an executory contract, and a bill to set aside a conveyance that has been executed, has not been very distinctly borne in mind. With regard to the first: if there be, in any way whatever, misrepresentation or concealment, which is material to the purchaser, a court of equity will not compel him to complete the purchase; but where the conveyance has been executed, I apprehend, my Lords, that a court of equity will set aside the conveyance only on the ground of actual fraud. And there would be no safety for the transactions of mankind, if, upon a discovery being made at any distance of time of a material fact not disclosed to the purchaser, of which the vendor had merely constructive notice, a conveyance which had been executed could be set aside."

In *Brownlie* v. *Campbell* 5 A.C. 925, at p. 937, Lord Selborne affirms the same principle. He says there: "Passing from the stages of correspondence and negotiation to the stage of written agreement, the purchaser takes upon himself the risk of errors. I assume them to be errors unconnected with fraud in the particulars, and when the conveyance takes place it is not, so far as I know, in either country the principle of equity that relief should afterwards be given against that conveyance, unless there be a case of fraud, or a case of misrepresentation amounting to fraud, by which the purchaser may have been deceived."

There appears to be no doubt that the law established by these cases is just as applicable to the sale of a chattel or a chose in action as to the sale of real property which is carried out by conveyance: *Seddon* v. *The North Eastern Salt Co. Limited*

[1905] 1 Ch. 326.

How are these authorities met by the plaintiff's counsel? Mr. Wilson in reply admitted, as of course he was obliged to admit, that the authorities referred to were binding on this Court, but argued that they only apply to cases in which the purchaser has got in substance what he contracted to buy, and have no application when he has got something substantially different; and he relies upon the judgment of Blackburn, J., in *Kennedy* v. *Panama, New Zealand, and Australian Mail Co.* L.R. 2 Q.B. 580, and particularly on the passage quoted by Joyce, J., in *Seddon* v. *The North Eastern Salt Co., Limited,* [1905] 1 Ch. 326. Lord Blackburn, then Blackburn, J., says at p. 587 – "There is, however, a very important difference between cases where a contract may be rescinded on the ground that there is a difference in substance between the thing bargained for and that obtained. It is enough to show that there was fraudulent representation as to *any part* of that which induced the party to enter into the contract which he seeks to rescind; but where there has been an innocent misrepresentation or misapprehension, it does not authorize a rescission unless it is such as to show that there is a complete difference in substance between what was supposed to be and what was taken, so as to constitute a failure of consideration. For example, where a horse is bought under the belief that it is sound, if the purchaser was induced to buy by a fraudulent representation as to the horse's soundness, the contract may be rescinded. If he was induced by an honest misrepresentation as to its soundness, though it may be clear that both vendor and purchaser thought they were dealing about a sound horse and were in error, yet the purchaser must pay the whole price, unless there was a warranty; and even if there was a warranty, he cannot return the horse and claim back the whole price, unless there was a condition to that effect in the contract."

Now, if I may so speak of such an eminent judge as Lord Blackburn, the proposition which he there lays down must commend itself, not only to all lawyers, but to all persons of sound judgment. If there is a complete difference in substance between the thing contracted for and the thing delivered, there is a complete failure of consideration, and the price may be recovered. But if the thing delivered is in substance what was contracted for, and the price is paid, the transaction stands, and the purchaser has no remedy unless there has been a warranty. I am speaking of course of cases in which there has been no fraud, and where any misrepresentation which has induced the contract was a wholly innocent misrepresentation. Lord Blackburn gives as an example the common case of a horse bought on the representation that it was sound. The purchaser has no remedy unless he has got a warranty; and why? Because he has got in substance what he contracted for, viz., a horse. The horse may be in fact unsound, but still it is a horse, even though a very inferior one; and there is not a complete failure of consideration.

There would, of course, be a complete difference in substance if some animal other than a horse had been delivered, if such a thing can be imagined. I will try to give an example nearer akin to the present case. If a man contracts to purchase mortgage debentures of a public company, and takes delivery of what he believes to be such, but what he afterwards discovers to be ordinary shares, he has not got in substance what he bargained for, but something quite different, one being a specifically secured liability of the company, the other being a share in the company's undertaking on which the liability is imposed. Here again there is a complete failure of consideration. In *Kennedy* v. *Panama, New Zealand, and Australian Mail Co.* L.R. 2 Q.B. 580, the plaintiff sought to set aside the contract for taking shares in the company on the ground that it was induced by an untrue statement in the company's prospectus that the company had a contract with the Government of New Zealand for an important monthly mail service. The statement was made quite innocently, and as the result of mistake. It was held that the plaintiff was not entitled to any relief, there having been no fraud, and he having got what he contracted for, viz., shares, although not so valuable as they would have been if the company had had the mail contract mentioned. Lord Blackburn, in his judgment, referred to two reported cases: *Gompertz* v. *Bartlett* 2 E. & B. 849 and *Gurney* v. *Wormersley* 4 E. & B. 133, in which the plaintiffs got relief on the ground that they did not get what they bargained for. In each case there was a sale of a bill of exchange: in one case the bill was a forgery; in the other the bill was void under the stamp laws. In neither case did the plaintiff get what he contracted for – a valid bill of exchange.

I think that these decisions make it easy to determine whether in the present case the plaintiff got in substance what he agreed to buy.

Let me refer to the statement of claim. In the second paragraph the contract is stated thus – "2. By a contract made in the month of May, 1910, the plaintiff agreed to purchase from the defendant, and the defendant agreed to sell to the plaintiff, eight 6 per cent. bonds of the face value of 1000 florins (Dutch), equivalent to £83 6*s*. 8*d*. of the Petroleum Maatschappij 'Henderson,' a limited liability company established in the Hague in Holland, at the price of £72 18*s*. 4*d*. per bond." Well, the plaintiff has got what he bought. He agreed to buy bonds and he has got bonds. They may be of little or no value, but they are bonds. It is not alleged that they are forgeries. Their validity is not in any way impeached. In substance, then, the plaintiff has got what he bargained for. Mr. Wilson's answer to this is that the bonds were represented to the plaintiff to be charged upon and fully secured on the oil-fields. But this is not alleged as a matter of contract. It is alleged as a matter of inducement leading up to the contract, which is wholly different. This is the way the case was presented both by the statement of claim, by the opening statement of counsel, and by the evidence. It was not until the defence was opened up by Mr. Healy that any attempt was made to represent the contract as anything other than that alleged in the second paragraph of the statement of claim. If the contract was as contended for by Mr. Wilson, that is, if the representation was part of the contract, there might have been a warranty which would give the plaintiff the right to relief. But a representation is not necessarily a warranty. It may be only an inducement, and such it appears to me to have been in the present case. I am, therefore, bound to hold that inasmuch as the contract was completed, and there was no fraud, the sale cannot be set aside, and the action must be dismissed with costs to be paid by the plaintiff to the defendant.

Notes

1. See further *Irish Conveyancing Law,* para. 6.68 *et seq.*
2. *Cf Peilow* v. *O'Carroll, infra.*

PEILOW V. O'CARROLL
(1972) 106 I.L.T.R. 29 (Supreme Court)

The facts are set out in the judgments.

Budd J.:

These proceedings arose out of the sale by public auction of certain premises known as No. 6 Manders Terrace on the 24th January, 1966. The premises are situate in Ranelagh in the City of Dublin. The purchase price was a sum of £3,300. The premises form part of the estate of one Frederick C. Ward who had been the occupier thereof and the plaintiff/respondent is his executor. He is a solicitor and sold as personal representative of Frederick C. Ward. The defendant/appellant was the purchaser of the premises. As well as being a medical doctor he is interested in the purchase of property for the purpose of development and conversion.

The premises in question are part of a terrace of houses. There is a roadway in front which leads down to the Ranelagh Road. No. 6 has a large garden at the back. There is a double gate at the bottom of the garden giving access to a laneway which runs at the end of the gardens of Nos. 1 to 8 of the houses in the terrace. The laneway is blocked at one end but in the other direction the laneway runs along the end of the gardens parallel with the terrace, turns sharply after passing the last garden, and runs out to the roadway in front of the terrace through an archway underneath the upper part of the first house in the terrace. Virtually the only means of access to the premises for the purpose of any major conversion including the extension of the premises into the garden would be via the laneway and through the garden door at the end of the garden. Where the laneway passes under the archway there is a large double gateway which was bolted and barred for some time before the auction.

While there were many subsidiary points at issue between the parties, what gave rise to these proceedings was a dispute as to whether or not a right of way over this laneway was included in the contract for the sale of the premises. The appellant claims that it was and he also alleges that he was induced to understand that it was included and to enter into the contract by fraudulent or alternatively innocent misrepresentations made by or on behalf of the respondent. The allegation that the representations were made fraudulently was relied on in the court below but was abandoned before this Court. The respondent says the right of way was not included in the sale and that any representations that may have been made to the contrary did not induce the contract.

The proceedings were launched on the 30th June, 1966, and sought the specific performance by the appellant of the agreement to purchase executed on the 24th January, 1966, at the close of the auction. As well as seeking specific performance of the contract the respondent also sought damages for breach of contract, the usual declaration of lien and alternatively a declaration that the deposit made on the sale had become forfeited.

The memorandum of agreement to purchase was contained at the end of the conditions of sale and was in the ususal form. It was duly signed by the appellant's solicitor, Mr. McCormack, who was purchasing in trust for the appellant. The closing date was the 28th February, 1966. The particulars and tenure of the property were stated in very brief form immediately before the conditions proper and read: "All that and those the dwellinghouse and premises known as No. 6 Manders Terrace, Ranelagh in the City of Dublin held in fee simple R.V. £21." There also appears on the same page as the particulars: "For further particulars apply to W.J. Shannon & Co., 19 Upper Ormond Quay, Dublin 7, solicitors having carriage, or to James Adams and Sons, 17 Merrion Row, Dublin 2, the auctioneers." The appellant sought further particulars from the auctioneers and was given a leaflet which described the house as containing *inter alia* a large walled rear garden with back entrance. The advertised description of the house was similar. The title offered was to commence with an indenture of conveyance of the premises dated the 6th day of March, 1908, Eileen C. Goulding to Richard Davis and then to pass to an indenture of conveyance dated the 8th day of April, 1927, made between the said Richard Davis of the one part and Frederick C. Ward of the other part. A right of way over the laneway to the public road in common with the owners and occupiers of the adjoining houses was conveyed to the respective grantees, their tenants, servants and workmen with or without horses and carts and carriages in both of these conveyances. The said conveyances also conveyed a right in common with the other occupiers of the houses on Manders Terrace to use the plot of ground in front of the houses.

The respondent's contention was that there was no mention of the right of way in the description of the premises in the particulars and tenure contained in the conditions of sale and, therefore, that the contract did not include it. He sought specific performance of the agreement to sell the premises simpliciter, that is to say, without any conveyance of the right of way.

The appellant in his pleadings admitted that he had entered into an agreement on the 24th January, 1966, to purchase the freehold together with the right of way. He claimed that it was an express or in the alternative an implied term of the contract that the sale included the use of the right of way which was described and conveyed by the said two conveyances of 1908 and 1927 constituting the title offered. He claimed that the respondent had refused to complete in accordance with the terms and conditions. The respondent, it was claimed, was well aware at all material times that the premises were useless to the appellant without the right of way. In his counterclaim the appellant claimed a declaration that the plaintiff was bound to put him into possession of the entire premises including user of the right of way. He also claimed rescission of the contract and repayment of the deposit and auctioneers' fees and also damages for breach of contract. Alternatively he claimed specific performance of the contract as pleaded by him, that is to say, including the right of way and he also claimed damages.

During the hearing of the case the appellant sought liberty to amend his defence and counterclaim, which was later granted, by pleading that he was induced to enter into the contract by representations by parol or in writing made by the respondent or his agents with the intention to induce him to enter into the contract which were not true to their knowledge. These representations were of a material nature as to the existence of the right of way. On discovering that the misrepresentations had been made the appellant refused to complete and claimed that he was entitled to rescind the contract. Alternatively he relied on innocent misrepresentations by the same parties with the intention to induce him to enter into the contract which they in fact did. The misrepresentations relied on as inducing the contract were stated to be contained in an advertisement in the press inserted by the auctioneers and also in a circular or hand-out describing the property also issued to the appellant by the respondent's agents, the auctioneers. The appellant also relied on a statement alleged to have been made by the auctioneer at the auction that the right of way was included in the sale. The appellant claimed that in breach of these representations the respondent refused to put him into possession of the premises with access to the right of way. The appellant also relied on mutual mistake as to the subject-matter of the contract and consequently there was no consensus of mind and no contract between the parties so that the respondent was not entitled to specific performance. The appellant claimed damages for misrepresentation. On this appeal the appellant relied only upon the alleged innocent misrepresentations of the respondent or his agents and did not seek to rely on any fraudulent misrepresentations.

Leave having been sought to amend the pleadings during the trial and granted in the judgment the respondent did not have the opportunity to put in a further reply. The respondent, however, submitted during the hearing that what was contained in the advertisement and leaflet did not amount to representations that a right of way existed and that if it did that the appellant did not rely upon the representations because of his knowledge gained by inspection of the physical state of the laneway which was overgrown and virtually impassable and closed by a barred gateway. This was supported, he contended, by the appellant's failure to raise the matter in the requisitions. It was also submitted that such representations, if made, did not mislead the appellant or induce him to contract. The respondent also submitted during the hearing that the appellant had made the property his own and had elected to affirm the contract for the sale of the property simpliciter, that is to say, without the right of way, by applying to the Dublin Corporation for planning permission after he knew that he was not going to get a conveyance of the right of way.

The contentions in the Court below were in the main confined to the issues as to whether misrepresentations had been made and, if so, what was their effect. The point as to the right of way being included in the contract was not as fully developed as on the hearing of this appeal.

The learned trial judge gave the respondent a decree for specific performance and he dismissed the appellant's counterclaim for specific performance or rescission or damages for misrepresentation. He took the view that the right of way was not included in the contract of sale because the inclusion of the right of way in the two deeds offered as part of the title did not have the effect of enlarging the subject matter of the contract and he also held that neither the advertisement nor the leaflet nor what was included therein formed any part of the contract. Dealing with the alleged misrepresentation the learned judge's view was that if the appellant had bought simply on the faith of the advertisement the latter contained a misrepresentation that the Court would have to take notice of, presumably as a ground for rescission. He did not determine this finally I assume because of his view that there were other factors in the case which prevented the purchaser from relying on the misrepresentation. He took the view that the appellant had inspected the laneway and could appreciate the significance of the obstacle staring him in the face and thus purchased with his eyes open. He also took the view that by his visiting the premises under which the gateway to the road ran he had notice of the interests of the occupier of the house under which the laneway ran through the archway. It is implied in what the learned judge said that the appellant should have seen from the take of the laneway that it had not been used for a long time and that all that he saw should have made clear to him that he should not rely on what was stated in either the advertisement or pamphlet. He accordingly gave no relief on the ground of misrepresentation. He held moreover that the appellant, by his action in lodging the application for planning permission, had elected to accept the respondent's contention as to the nature of the contract or had in any event elected to proceed with the contract on the basis that the right of way was not included therein.

It was contended on this appeal that the learned trial judge was wrong in law in holding that the right of way was not included in the sale and should have held that the agreement for sale included the right of way first because a contract for the sale of a house and land in law includes all rights appurtenant to the the land and this right of way was appurtenant at the time of the sale, secondly, because of the reference in the two deeds offered as the title to the right of way and, thirdly, because the conditions of sale invited any interested party to apply to the auctioneers for further particulars and the information given in writing in the leaflet implied the existence of the right of way. It was contended that the information so given in writing thus formed part of the written agreement so as to include the right of way in the sale.

It was also contended that the learned trial judge was wrong in law in holding that the appellant was not entitled to resist specific performance of the contract as relied on by the vendor, namely, an agreement to purchase without the right of way by reason of any representations that might have been made because he knew what the situation with regard to the right of way was from his visual inspection. It was submitted in reply to this contention that the judge should have found that the misrepresentations induced the contract because the evidence did not support his view that the appellant's knowledge of the physical state of the laneway should have had the effect of causing him not to rely on the representations. It was further contended that the learned trial judge was wrong in law in finding that the appellant had by his action in submitting plans to the Dublin Corporation made the property his own and elected to affirm the contract in the form contended for by the respondent.

I must now refer more fully to some of the salient facts of the case in so far as relevant to the matters in issue between the parties. The respondent decided to sell sometime early in January 1966 and advertised the premises in the press. The appellant saw the advertisement appearing in the Irish Times on the 13th January, 1966. The advertisement appeared under the name of James Adam and Sons, the auctioneers employed by the respondent, and offered 6 Manders Terrace for sale as a freehold with vacant possession. After describing the situation of the premises there appeared the words "ideal residence or for conversion." After stating the date of the sale these words appeared: "The house contains eight rooms, bathroom, W.C., fuel store, large walled rear garden with back entrance." This advertisement attracted the appellant and he went to the auctioneers' premises for further information where he was given the hand-out or leaflet about the proposed sale of the premises which also contained the material matters contained in the advertisement which I have already recited. The appellant drove out and saw the premises from the outside and later on the 20th January, 1966, he got the key of the premises from the auctioneer and inspected the house and garden. He also went out into the laneway through the double doors at the back and saw the condition of the laneway which was very much overgrown and was blocked to a great extent by deposits of rubbish. While departing in his car along the roadway in front of the terrace he had a look at the gate leading from the laneway to the roadway but did not make a close inspection of it. I may conveniently add here that sometime towards the end of February or beginning of March he made a detailed inspection of the gate and saw that it was barred up but this was after the auction.

Another event of importance took place before the auction. As a result of seeing the state of the laneway the appellant was put on the alert and wished to make sure that the right of way was included in the sale. He discussed the position with Mr. Walsh, an assistant solicitor in the offices of his solicitor Mr. McCormack, and as a result Mr. Walsh made an appointment with the respondent to examine the title deeds, with the object of seeing what was the position about the right of way and as to whether there were any restrictive covenants affecting the premises. He went to the respondent's office on the 21st January, 1966, and made an inspection of the title deeds. He found that both the deeds offered as the title to the premises conveyed the premises together with a right of way over the laneway and the right to use the plot in front in the form I have already stated. Mr. Walsh says that he asked a question about the location of the right of way. Mr. Peilow says he made it clear to Mr. Walsh that the right of way was not included in the sale. He says that he went on say: "The laneway is there and we may or may not have a right of way over it," giving as his reason for this view that the late owner lived alone and had not relatives in the country and that he, Mr. Peilow, could give no information about it. He says that he added that if there were any rights the purchaser was welcome to them. Mr. Walsh denied that Peilow had made any reservations with regard to the right of way and said that he did not tell him that it was not to be included in the sale. Mr. Walsh subsequently included the right of way in the draft conveyance of the premises. The learned trial judge was satisfied that Mr. Peilow did say that the right of way was not being included but his view was that Mr. Peilow did not make the matter as clear to Mr. Walsh as he, Mr. Peilow, thought he had and that what was said about the right of way not being included was not taken in by Mr. Walsh.

Another incident should also be referred to which took place, it is alleged, at the auction. The evidence adduced on behalf of the appellant as to this incident was to the effect that someone had asked at the auction as to whether or not the right of way was included in the sale and that the auctioner, Mr. Coyle, of Adam & Co., auctioneer, had stated after consultation with Mr. Peilow, who was beside him, that the right of way was included in the sale. Neither Mr. Peilow nor Mr. Coyle had any recollection of such an incident. The learned trial judge said that he did not have to make a hard and fast finding on the issue but I shall have to refer to this incident in more detail later.

After the sale the usual steps were taken for its completion. Requisitions were delivered on the 4th February, 1966, and replied to on the 7th February, 1966. No requisition bears directly on the issue as to whether or not the right of way was included in the sale. The respondent contended that the nature of the requisitions indicated that the appellant was not concerned about the right of way and was not affected in his decision to purchase by what was stated in the advertisement and leaflet. The appellant says that it was unnecessary to raise any point about its inclusion in the sale in the requisitions because the existence of the back gate leading from the garden to the laneway and the other gate on to the public road were physical indications that a right of way existed and this was confirmed by clear implication in the advertisement and leaflet and, as he says, also indicated at the auction. The respondent's attitude was that the appellant, on seeing the state of the laneway and that the gateway leading to the public highway was closed up, should, if he believed that the right of way was being included in the sale, have made requisitions as to who, if anybody, was under obligation to clean the laneway and as to how he was to obtain exit and entrance through the gateway. His failure to do so, it was submitted, indicated that he knew there was no right of way and was not relying on any representation that such a right of way existed.

Another event of importance occurred shortly afterwards on the 21st February, 1966, when Mr. Peilow himself approved on behalf of the vendor of the draft conveyance of the property to the purchaser which included in it a conveyance of the right of way. Mr. Peilow says that he did this inadvertently but the appellant naturally says that the approval of the conveyance including the right of way confirms his contention that its inclusion in the sale was intended by the vendor.

After the auction correspondence ensued between the parties. The appellant insisted throughout that he was entitled to have the right of way included in the conveyance while the respondent was unwilling to convey it.

While the correspondence was taking place between the solicitors the appellant lodged plans with the Dublin corporation showing a plan for a proposed conversion and addition to the premises and sought planning permission from the Corporation. It appears that the appellant was anxious to see if he could work out a plan providing for the off street parking of cars for the future residents of the converted premises in front of the premises rather than at the back. His difficulty was as to showing title to the plot in front of the premises of which occupants of No. 6 Manders Terrace only had the use along with the occupants of other houses in the terrace. The Corporation, by a letter dated 21st June, 1966, required title to be shown to the area proposed to be used for parking purposes and that a suitable layout plan should be lodged. Plans were accordingly submitted it would appear on the 11th July, 1966, but planning permission was refused on the 9th September, 1966, on the grounds of an excessive density in the number of flats proposed and because off street parking for the exclusive use of the occupants of the proposed flats had not been provided for.

With regard to the submission made on behalf of the appellant that the inclusion of the two conveyances conveying the right of way in the conditions of sale had the effect of enlarging the subject matter of the agreement for sale. Having perused the conditions of sale, I would agree with the learned judge that the mention of the right of way in the two conveyances in the deeds offered as the title to the premises could not enlarge the subject matter of the agreement. Section 6 of the conditions of sale and the first schedule thereto state the title offerred and do not define the subject matter. What was offered for sale was stated in the particulars.

It was also submitted on behalf of the appellant that the particulars contained in the conditions of sale were enlarged by the representations contained in the leaflet to include the sale of the right of way as part of the contract. The argument was that these particular conditions of sale had in them after the portion describing the premises the words "for further particulars apply to W. J. Shannon & Co., 19 Upper Ormond Quay, Dublin 7, solicitors having carriage of the sale, or James Adam and Sons, 17 Merrion Row, Dublin 2, the auctioneers." It was submitted that these words invited any would-be purchaser to apply for further particulars to either of these firms and that when further particulars were supplied in writing they formed part of or were an addition to the particulars contained in the conditions of sale and that since the leaflet on its true construction indicated the existence of a right of way to the premises the enlarged particulars had the effect of including the right of way in the contract. I am at present inclined to the view that what is contained in the leaflet cannot be said properly to enlarge the particulars in the conditions of sale. It would seem to me that what was intended by the invitation to apply for further particulars was that further particulars of that which was offered for sale in the conditions of sale, such as the accommodation in the house and the like, would be furnished on request. To hold that every particular furnished by an auctioneer with regard to the nature of a premises for sale becomes incorporated into the contract on his furnishing such particulars seems to me to be prima facie a somewhat untenable proposition in that it would involve the inclusion in the contract of puffing descriptions by an auctioneer. It is, however, not necessary to come to a final conclusion on this matter having regard to the views which I have formed as to the true construction of the contract and I therefore express no final view on the matter.

Mr. Conolly submitted that a contract for the sale of a house and land described in the particulars and conditions of sale comprises and includes in it such rights of way as exist as appurtenant to the premises even though they are not mentioned in the particulars in the conditions of sale. Such rights if not intended to be included must be excluded.

It may be remarked apart from any citation of authority for the proposition that it seems well founded in common sense having regard to the ideas usually held by those having to deal with the sale of land either for vendor or purchaser. The usual view of such persons is I venture to think that when a house is sold there goes with it such rights in the way of easements as are appurtenant to it. There readily occur to the mind such easements as rights of ancient lights and the right to have ones water supply and drainage system pass under a neighbour's lands. It would surprise most people engaged in the sale of houses to find that such rights would not pass on the sale of a house unless expressly mentioned.

Mr. Conolly, moreover, referred the Court to several passages in works by authors of authority supporting his proposition. In Dart on Vendor and Purchaser 8th edition it is stated at p. 109 that "An agreement to sell land is, in the absence of any restrictive expressions, an agreement to sell the whole of the vendor's interest." Further at p. 110 it is stated "The interest offered for sale (whether it be absolute or qualified), will be presumed to be accompanied by all these advantages which are legally incidental to it." Emmet on Title 11th edition at p. 647 says: "Rights strictly appurtenant need not be mentioned either in a contract or in a conveyance. They, being annexed to the land, are included in the sale of the land." Finally the Simonds edition of Halsbury vol. 34 at p. 218 has a paragraph as follows: "An agreement to sell land implies, in the absence of indication to the contrary, that the whole of the vendor's interest in the land is the subject of the agreement, and that that interest is an estate in fee simple free from encumbrances, unless the purchaser had notice, before entering into the contract, that the title which the vendor was able to give was subject to limitations or encumbrances which the vendor could not remove."

I should state here that Mr. Ellis submitted that the proposition in Dart was not supported by the case cited in support thereof, namely, *Skull* v. *Glenister* (1864) 16 C.B.N.S. 81. In that case the view of Erle C.J. was that if there be a right of way appurtenant to and the land is demised, the right of way will pass to the lessee and that is so even though nothing was said about it at the time of the demise, so that the statement in Dart would appear to be borne out.

Finally Mr. Ellis accepted the first part of the proposition saying: "I must accede to the proposition that although the right of way was not mentioned in the particulars in the conditions of sale, the conditions of sale itself involved such right of way as there was being comprised in the sale." This acceptance of the proposition being of course subject to a contention that the right of way had been excluded from the sale. I am satisfied that Mr. Conolly's proposition is a correct statement of the law and the right of way over this laneway was included in the sale provided that the evidence shows that it was appurtenant to the premises at the time of the sale and was not excluded in some fashion from the sale.

The next question to be considered is as to whether there was at the time of the sale such a right of way as the appellant claims appurtenant to the property. The evidence before the Court on this topic was, in my view, all the one way. While a right of way is an incorporeal hereditament the physical features of the ground over which the right of way is alleged to exist may afford valuable evidence as to its existence. In the present case there is the fact that there exists physically at the ends of the gardens of this terrace a laneway which gives access to the public highway and there are at the ends of the gardens of these houses doors or gates giving access to the lane. The houses were apparently in existence for some time before the conveyance of 1908. The laneway is a cul-de-sac at one end and appears to serve no other houses or land as a means of ingress and egress. The physical features, therefore, strongly suggest that the laneway came into existence for the purpose of giving access from the back of the houses to the public highway. That may fall short of showing existence of an easement in law but it goes a long way towards it. Next we have the fact that a right of way over this very laneway was conveyed to the grantee under the deed of 1908 as a then existing right of way. There was, therefore, a right of way in law appurtenant to the house, 6 Manders Terrace, prior to 1908. This right of way was further conveyed to the grantee in the conveyance of 1927. The grantee under that deed was Mr. Ward of whom the plaintiff is personal representative and he apparently resided in the house during the rest of his lifetime from 1927. In addition to the evidence afforded by the physical features of the case and the two title deeds in question there are also certain other factors which point to the existence and continuance to the present time of an easement appurtenant to the house. There is the fact that the draft conveyance submitted by the purchaser, incorporating a conveyance of this right of way, was approved by the vendor's solicitor on the 21st February, 1966. One is, therefore, driven to the conclusion that the fact that the right of way was allowed to be included in the conveyance by the vendor should be viewed as a factor going to the proof of its existence. There is then the matter of the advertisement and the leaflet. With regard to the meaning of the representations made in the advertisement and leaflet I would have little doubt as to what they meant and that they were subsisting up to the date of the sale. Both the advertisement and the leaflet described the house as having a back entrance. There was some controversy as to whether or not this would convey to a would-be purchaser that the house was being sold with a right of way at the back. The title offered included the assignments conveying the right of way. The back entrance to the laneway existed physically and the laneway led to the public highway. A back entrance is no use whatsoever unless you can pass through it and use it and, having regard to the physical nature of the surroundings, the only way that the back entrance could be used would be to go out on to the laneway and thence to the public road. In the circumstances existing the words to my mind clearly convey that a right of way was included in the sale. The representations in these two documents, coming as they do from the vendor, the person in the best position to know the facts or at least under a duty to find out about them, seem to me to afford at least some further evidence corroborative of the appellant's contention that a right of way existed and was appurtenant to the premises at the date of the sale and continued to the present time. As I shall show later in this judgment the appellant had no reason to doubt the truth of the representations.

The proper inference to be drawn from the facts narrated is that a right of way existed and was appurtenant to the premises sold and such inference could only be refuted if it was shown that the right of way was abandoned in such fashion as to extinguish it or that it was excluded from the sale. Kingsmill Moore J. in his judgment in *Cullen* v. *Dublic Corporation* (22 July, 1960, unreported) in dealing with the question of abandonment in that case of the right to use water to produce power on a presumption only of a grant of such rights as a riparian owner could acquire by prescription in an artificial stream, pointed out that disuse was not abandonment. He said that there could be no abandonment without an intention to abandon. Long disuse might raise a presumption of such intention but the circumstances must be considered to see if such an intention should be implied. In the case relied on by Mr. Conolly of *Dogherty* v. *Beasley* (1838) Jones Reports 123 Joy C.B. rejected the suggestion that the dominant owner had to go over a right of way continuously to preserve it and was not excluded *per se* from his right by twenty years non-user. Such non-user was only of evidential value as to abandonment. It is indeed admitted that mere non-user on the part of the owner of the dominant tenement is not sufficient to show an abandonment of a right of way nor does such a right of way become extinguished by mere lapse of time. There must be an intention to abandon and extinguish. There was, in my view, no evidence of intention to abandon before the Court. There was no evidence of long disuse. Such evidence of non-user as there is is confined to the fact that the laneway was overgrown and blocked with debris and had saplings growing on it so as to make it physically impassable and that it had a barred gate across it. Apart from the matter of the gate this evidence is quite consistent with the blocking of the laneway having taken place in recent times and is of no value as evidence of an intention to abandon. The existence of a gateway, bolted or not, over a right of way does not itself lead to the conclusion that the right of way had become abandoned or extinguished in the absence of evidence of acquiescence in a permanent closure of the right of way by such a gate by the owner of the dominant tenement. There is in fact no evidence of acquiescence on the part of the dominant owner to any such obstruction of the right of way as existed.

On the matter of the continuous existence of the right of way it seems to me to be established on the evidence as it stands that the right of way existed at the time of sale and was appurtenant to the premises.

It was, however, alleged that the right of way was in fact expressly excluded from the sale by the respondent. As to this I may in preliminary fashion observe that where in a sale of land a vendor has inadvertently described the property for sale in such fashion that the contract includes either expressly or by implication of law such rights of way as are appurtenant to the property it is the duty of the vendor to correct the conditions of sale so as to exclude that which he does not wish to sell or convey or which he cannot sell or convey. If he does not do this he must make it clear to any would-be purchaser either before or at the sale that such a right is not in fact included in the sale.

In this case there was no attempt to amend the conditions of sale which would as they stand include the right of way in the agreement for sale. It is said, however, that it was made clear before the sale to Mr. Walsh or at the sale by the auctioneer that the right of way was not included in the sale. In my view the learned trial judge's finding with regard to what happened at the interview between Mr. Peilow and Mr. Walsh amounted to a finding that the position was not corrected at that interview. The onus was on Mr. Peilow as vendor to correct the position arising on the contract, namely, that the right of way appurtenant to the premises was included in the sale and would be conveyed under the conditions of sale. Mr. Peilow says that he told Mr. Walsh that the right of way was not included in the sale but the learned judge's finding is that what was said was not taken in by Mr. Walsh. In the result the contract of sale stands, as far as this interview was concerned, with the position as to the right of way not being corrected.

In so far as what occurred at the auction is concerned it would appear clear from the evidence that there was no statement immediately before the bidding took place that the right of way was not being included in the sale. The evidence adduced on behalf of the appellant was to the effect that someone had asked at the auction as to whether or not the right of way was included in the sale and that the auctioneer Mr. Coyle of Adam & Co., had stated after consultation with Mr. Peilow, who was beside him, that the right of way was included in the sale. Neither Mr. Peilow nor Mr. Coyle had any recollection of such an incident. The learned Judge does, however, indicate that he thought that the most likely solution of the question was that some such question was asked but that Dr. ffrench O'Carroll and Mr. McCormack may have misconstrued whatever answer was given. He pointed out that the words "are" and "aren't" can be very easily confused so that "we aren't selling with the right of way" might very well be taken up as "we are selling with the right of way." This is tantamount to finding that any attempted correction of the form of the contract was not brought home to the appellant's mind. There was thus nothing to show that it had been brought home to the appellant at the time of the auction that the sale did not include the right of way and there is no finding that the information was conveyed otherwise either before or at the auction. The appellant is, therefore, entitled to succeed on this claim that the right of way was included in the sale.

The appellant also contended in the alternative to the pleas that I have already dealt with that he was also entitled to resist any order for the specific performance of the contract without the right of way, if it could be so construed, and further to rescind the contract, by reason of its having been obtained by misrepresentations that the right of way was included in the sale. The contest in the Court below was in fact mainly on the issue as to whether or not the appellant had induced to enter into a contract to purchase 6 Manders Terrace without the benefit of the right of way over the laneway by misrepresentations made by the respondent and as to whether these misrepresentations, if made, were material and induced the contract. As counsel on both sides argued this matter I feel that the parties are entitled to have their contentions dealt with notwithstanding the views I have expressed as to the proper construction of the contract.

The learned trial judge in dealing with the matter of misrepresentation proceeded on the assumption that he was concerned with a contract to sell without the benefit of a right of way. He took the view that having regard to his state of knowledge of the condition of the laneway the appellant should not have relied and was entitled to rely on any misstatements in the leaflet or advertisement. He also held that the appellant had elected to affirm the contract he had assumed he was dealing with, namely, to purchase without the right of way. Accordingly he gave no relief on the ground of misrepresentation.

The learned judge in the course of his judgment did state, however, that if it could be shown that the purchaser and his solicitor bought solely on the representations contained in the advertisement and leaflet a case might well be made for relieving the purchaser of his contract but that he did not think it would because another factor in the circumstances would have to be considered, presumably that of the alleged affirmance of the contract. He then went on to say that he would proceed on the basis of assuming that might be the case. Even so he thought that the defence would fail on the ground that Dr. ffrench O'Carroll had inspected the way and saw its condition and that is was obstructed by the bolted gate. In other words he bought with his eyes open. He also stated at a later stage in his judgment that Dr. ffrench O'Carroll had inspected the property and saw the situation for himself and that he was satisfied that Dr. ffrench O'Carroll was capable of appreciating the significance of the obstacle that stared him in the face and that he was put on sufficient notice before buying of the difficulty in the user of the laneway. I would regard the learned judge's observations as meaning that in his view the appellant knew, before entering into the contract, that there was no existing right of way to the premises in that it had been extinguished by abandonment and that accordingly he was entitled to rely on the alleged misrepresentations to enable him to resist an order for the specific performance of the contract without the right of way. The question is, was he entitled to arrive at such a conclusion on the evidence before him?

There is no doubt that representations were made in the advertisement and leaflet as to there being a back entrance to the garden and that these were made to the purchaser because of his having read the advertisement inserted by the respondent's agents and intended to be read by a possible purchaser and also because the leaflet containing them was also given to the appellant by the respondent's same agents. They were calculated to induce a person, wishing to convert the house into flats, to buy by reason of the suitable access which the laneway would give for the conveyance of the necessary materials. I have already stated my view that these representations contained in the leaflet and advertisement clearly represented that a right of way was included in the sale.

It would seem to me further that since both the advertisement and the leaflet carried the implication that a right of way existed it should have been made clear at, or prior to, the auction that the advertisement and leaflet were erroneous. The judge found that this had not been done. His view was that the position was not rectified during the interview between Mr. Peilow and Mr. Walsh, in that Mr. Peilow had not brought home to Mr. Walsh's mind that the right of way was not included in the sale. In effect he took the same view with regard to what was said at the auction. The position of the appellant at the date of the auction was that these representations implying that a right of way existed had been made made to him and that it had not been made clear to him that they were untrue or that he should not rely on them. He was entitled, therefore, to believe them and rely on them unless there was some further reason why he should not do so, such as his having knowledge that the representations were not correct.

It was however, then submitted that the judge's view that the appellant was in possession of such knowledge as should have indicated to him that the representations were untrue and not to be relied on was correct. It is important to consider what a purchaser's position is when a misrepresentation has been made. It is, of course, sufficient to prove that he knew the truth to take away his right to rely upon any misrepresentation made. But it must be shown that he had full and complete knowledge. It is not sufficient to show that he had partial or fragmentary knowledge or that he could have found out for himself. I have already pointed out that there was no evidence of intention to abandon or extinguish the right of way on the part of the owner of the dominant tenement. As I have said the appellant's inspection of the laneway prior to the auction merely disclosed that it was at that time too overgrown to be passable and that there was a closed gate at the end leading to the road-way. Such physical obstructions as he saw could be removed and the gate opened assuming, as he was entitled to assume, that the right of way existed. There was no reason to assume from what he saw that the right of way did not, despite the physical obstructions, continue to have a legal existence.

It was, however, submitted that the appellant's failure to raise the matter of the existence of the right of way in the requisitions indicated knowledge on his part that there was no right of way. It would seem to me that what was stated in the advertisement and leaflet implying the existence of a right of way together with the apparent physical existence of a right of way, supported by Mr. Walsh's understanding of what took place at the interview with Mr. Peilow (which the judge accepted as bona fide) was sufficient explanation as to why the matter of the existence of the right of way was not raised in the requisitions. The matter had been cleared up already. I cannot regard the failure of the appellant to raise the matter in the requisitions as providing any such grounds as would justify a finding that he had knowledge that the right of way did not exist or as disentitling the appellant to rely on the misrepresentations made in the leaflet and advertisement.

The learned judge was, it would appear to me, dealing solely with the physical circumstances relating to the laneway and not with considerations of a legal nature as to whether the right of way existed in law or not. It was these later considerations that were those relevant to consider on the point at issue. Dr. ffrench O'Carroll could scarcely be expected to have approached this consideration from a lawyer's point of view but even if he had it would seem to me that what he saw should only have conveyed to his mind that the laneway had not been used in recent times. There was no evidence of a nature sufficient to lead him to the conclusion that the right of way had been abandoned with the intention of extinguishing it. On the contrary the documents including the two conveyances and such other evidence as there was apart from the physical condition of the laneway all pointed the other way. The representations contained in the advertisement and leaflet pointed to the existence of the right of way. The auctioneer, Mr. Coyle, thought that a right of way existed by reason of what he saw on his inspection. The respondent himself never arrived at a definite conclusion to the effect that the right of way did not exist and as we know did not at the time when he was approving of the conveyance strike out the portion thereof containing the right of way. One may well ask why the appellant should come to the conclusion on his inspection of the laneway that the right of way did not exist in law when neither Mr. Coyle, the auctioneer, nor Mr. Peilow himself arrived at that conclusion although they had also seen the physical condition of the laneway. There was, in my view, no reason for the appellant to assume from what he saw that the right of way did not exist in law. Apart from such conclusions as the appellant might come to as a result of seeing the laneway there is in fact before this Court no evidence that the right of way was ever legally extinguished. There is, therefore, in my view no such evidence as would support a finding that the appellant knew or should have known at the time that he entered into the contract that the right of way over the laneway did not exist from the legal point of view. The appellant has, therefore, made out his contentions that the representations alleged were made and that they implied that a right of way existed. On the assumption which the learned judge was proceeding on this aspect of the case, namely, that the right of way was not included in the sale or did not exist, these representations were false.

I would have little doubt that the misrepresentations made in the advertisement and leaflet were of a material character. They indicated an advantage which the premises had and were one of the inducements held out to a purchaser. They were intended to induce the contract. The house was advertised as being suitable for conversion which could be reasonably understood by an intending developer of itself to mean that suitable access was available for conversion purposes. The appellant intended to buy for conversion into flats and extending into the back garden for that purpose. The leaflet and advertisement clearly indicated that suitable access was in fact available for this purpose. Further the garden would provide suitable space for off street parking of motor cars which would have to be provided to satisfy the town planning authorities. With regard to reliance on the representations and their inducing the contract the appellant said he would not have bought unless he got the right of way since he could not carry out his plans for conversion without the user of the right of way. His keen interest in the right of way is shown by his raising the point with Mr. Walsh with the result that Mr. Walsh went to see the documents at Mr. Peilow's office, to assure himself on the matter. Since the appellant was buying for conversion and sought through Mr. Walsh assurance on the point, it is also clear that the appellant was induced to enter into the contract by reason of the misrepresentations being made and that he also relied on these misrepresentations.

It was then submitted that even if the premises were misdescribed expressly or by implication as having a right of way thereto such misstatement would not annul the sale and that the alleged contract for the sale of the premises without the right of way could be specifically enforced.

It is provided in condition 12 of the conditions of sale that any error, misstatement or omission in the particulars or the conditions should not annul the sale or be a ground of any abatement or compensation on either side. It was submitted that by reason of this condition any such misstatement as there might have been in any particulars given as to the nature of the property to be sold should not annul this sale and that the respondent was entitled to enforce the contract notwithstanding such misstatements. Mr. Connolly submitted, however, that this condition does not apply where the misstatement goes to root of the contract. I need not, however, dwell on the point of law because Mr. Ellis for the respondent does not dispute the correctness of this proposition of law and I accept it as well established. In my view the misstatements made as to the existence of the right of way were, in the circumstances of this case where the premises were held out as being suitable for conversion, most material because of the necessity of obtaining a reasonable form of access and were thus such as to go to the root of the contract. This, in my view, prevents the respondent from relying upon this condition.

In my view, therefore, the misrepresentations which were made were such as would entitle the appellant to repudiate and rescind a contract for the purchase of the premises without the right of way and to successfully resist a claim to have it specifically enforced unless there was some other reason preventing him from doing so. It was in fact next suggested that there was such a reason, which I deal with next.

It was contended on behalf of the respondent on this aspect of the case that the appellant had by his actions indicated his intention to affirm the alleged contract without the right of way and to waive his right to rescind notwithstanding the misrepresentations made. It was submitted that the correspondence should have conveyed to the appellant that the right of way was not to be conveyed and that the appellant had manifested his intention to accept the property without the right of way by lodging plans with the planning authority of the Dublin Corporation first on the 28th April and secondly in a more completed form on the 11th July, 1966, plans which were based upon the provision of parking sites for the residents of the converted premises in front of No. 6 Manders Terrace and ignoring any space there might be for parking at the rear of the premises, thus indicating that he accepted the position that he was not getting the right of way and that there was no right of way thereto.

The learned judge found that the appellant, after discovery of the facts entitling him to rescind and with full appreciation that the right of way was not to be given by the vendor, proceeded to deal with the property as his own and had thus by his actions indicated that he had elected to affirm the contract for sale without the right of way.

Counsel for the appellant invited this Court to take the view that the proper approach to the question as to whether there had been an affirmance of the contract after discovery of facts entitling the purchaser to avoid the contract was to be found in Volume 23 of the Hailsham edition of Halsbury's Laws of England, volume 23, page

110, where it is stated: "The acts and conduct relied upon as evincing the representee's affirmance must be such as are more consistent, on reasonable view of them, with that than with any other theory. It is not sufficient to point to acts of a neutral character, or acts which are equally consistent with a possible ultimate intention to disaffirm or with a mere suspension of judgment." It was pointed out that in *Watson* v. *Burton* [1956] 3 All E.R. 129 Wynn Parry J. had accepted this statement as correctly stating the proper approach to be adopted in considering whether a party to a contract who had been induced to enter a contract by misrepresentation had by his acts and conduct affirmed it. I also accept the statement as stating the correct approach. It was submitted that the finding was, on any reasonable view of the facts, without evidence to support it.

There is not in the correspondence any letter in which it is stated that the appellant was waiving any claim to have the right of way conveyed with the premises. Not only is there no acceptance of the contention that the right of way was not included in the sale but a clear insistence that the appellant was entitled to have the right of way conveyed to him as part of his contract. This claim was made right up to May 18th, 1966, a date after the first lodgment of the plans with the Corporation. The appellant did not state or give any verbal indication that he was giving up such rights as he might have had with regard to the right of way or state that he was accepting the position that a right of way would not or could not be conveyed. The appellant on the other hand, makes it clear in his evidence that the premises would be of no avail to him unless he got the right of way. His attitude was that he wanted the right of way over the lane. I am unable to find that there is anything in his evidence to indicate that he changed his position. This Court was not shown that there was in the plans or documents lodged any statement which would indicate that he was abandoning his rights or that was inconsistent with an intention to insist upon the conveyance of a right of way. When the action was launched the appellant's pleadings in his defence and counterclaim delivered on the 7th November, 1966, indicates that he still claimed that the right of way should be conveyed to him. The first paragraph of the defence admits the agreement for the sale of the premises was entered into but pleads the agreement entered into as being for the sale of the house together with the right of way. Further, an examination of the appellant's evidence shows that throughout he was insisting that even if he got approval by the Corporation for the alternative plan for car parking he still could not have built in the garden unless he could get in by the back as the front entrance was entirely unsuitable for bringing in building materials which was inconsistent with an intention to abandon his claim to the right of way. These matters then would appear to be the background against which his acts in seeking planning permission should be judged. The only reasonable inference to be drawn from the circumstances narrated is that throughout the appellant was insisting on his right to have the right of way conveyed. An affirmance of a contract to buy without the right of way would be quite inconsistent with the attitude of the appellant. As against all this there is only the fact of the lodgment of the plans without showing the right of way to support the contention of an election to affirm a contract not including the right of way.

The mere act of lodging documents seeking planning permission for a layout not indicating a user of the right of way does not at all indicate an abandonment of a claim to the right of way. It is equally consistent with an attempt by the appellant to see if some other way out of his difficulties was feasible. At the best this action of the appellant was of an equivocal nature and an act of that nature is not sufficient in law to prove affirmance. When all the matters I have just mentioned are taken together they seem to me to be clearly more consistent with a view that the appellant had no intention of affirming any alleged contract to buy without the right of way than with any other theory. They seem to me to show that the appellant was up to the time of the commencement of proceedings and the filing of the pleadings insisting on the completion of the contract with the inclusion in the conveyance of the right of way. In my view the evidence, on any reasonable view of it, leads only to the conclusion that the appellant did not at any time waive his rights to enforce such remedies as he had arising on the misrepresentations made to him or elect to affirm the contract without the right of way. In my view the evidence does not support the finding of affirmation made by the learned judge, which cannot, therefore, stand.

A further argument advanced by the respondent was that the appellant had failed to repudiate or rescind the contract immediately on discovering that misrepresentations had been made to him as to the existence of the right of way and its inclusion in the sale and that he was not going to get the right of way. This, it was contended, he should have done if he desired to be relieved of the contract. Whether a contract such as this must be repudiated or rescinded immediately after a purchaser discovers that he is not getting what he bargained for appears to be a matter of some doubt and I express no view on the point as it is unnecessary to do so because the argument as far as this case is concerned is founded on a misconception of the position in the case. The position as has been shown is that the contract of sale included the right of way. That was the appellant's attitude. He was ready and willing to take a conveyance of the house which included the right of way. He was maintaining, not repudiating, the contract. No occasion to repudiate, therefore, arose. He sought a declaration that the respondent was bound by the terms of the contract to put him into possession of the entire premises including the right of way. It was in fact the respondent and not the appellant who repudiated the contract by refusing to complete the sale by his refusal to execute a conveyance of the house to the appellant including the right of way and in endeavouring to enforce the sale of the house without the right of way and it is only because of that that the appellant sought to rescind. The claim to rescind in fact only arose in the pleadings in reply to the respondent's claim for specific performance of the contract of sale without the right of way. Even then it was accompanied by a claim for specific performance in the alternative showing that the appellant maintains still that the contract includes the right of way. The appellant's claim to rescind by virtue of the misrepresentations made is a plea in the alternative and it would be quite illogical for him to repudiate on this basis when in fact his first and main point was that the contract in law included the right of way. In my view therefore the respondent's contention based on the appellant's alleged delay in repudiation fails.

The respondent's claim in this case is for specific performance or damages for breach of contract but the contract which he seeks to have specifically performed is a contract to sell without the right of way. He is not entitled to either relief because the right of way was included in the agreement for sale and he cannot, or will not, make title to the right of way. No defect in the title to the right of way was ever finally proved. The respondent's attitude, as taken up in the letters of the 7th March, 1966, and the 3rd May, 1966, was that the premises were sold in the condition in which they were and that if there was still an existing right of way that would be a matter for the purchaser to deal with which is tantamount to saying that he did not know if the right of way existed or not and that it was up to the purchaser to assert it if he saw fit. His counsel moreover stated that his attitude was that "you can have whatever right of way is there" and that he was only prepared to say "we will give you what we have." Finally the respondent insisted upon the exclusion of the right of way from the conveyance. This attitude and his refusal and failure to convey without qualification a right of way exercisable immediately was a clear breach of contract which disentitled the respondent to succeed in his claim for the specific performance of the contract or to recover damages for its breach. His proceedings must, therefore, fail and the order for specific performance of the alleged contract without the right of way will be set aside.

The appellant is, in my view, entitled to succeed on his counter-claim and there still remains to be considered what relief the appellant is entitled to on it. In it he claims inter alia specific performance of the contract, that is to say, the contract including the right of way and also damages for breach of contract. Having regard to the delay which has occurred and the uncertainty as to the title to the right of way which the respondent has created the appellant no longer seeks specific performance. He is, however, entitled to recover damages for breach of contract in lieu of specific performance and it remains to be considered what damages he is entitled to in the circumstances.

Condition 11 of the conditions of sale provides that if the purchaser shall make any objection or requisition which the vendor is unable to comply with vendor may annul the sale whereupon the purchaser shall be entitled to the return of his deposit and a sum equivalent to the auctioneers' fees. The parties, therefore, envisaged that the purchaser would be entitled to get back his deposit and a sum equivalent to the auctioneers' fees when the sale is rightfully called off. It must follow a fortiori that the parties must have envisaged that where the sale is not rightfully called off but instead the vendor commits a breach of contract in failing to convey that which he contracted to sell the purchaser would be entitled to the same rights.

The case of *McMahon* v. *Gaffney* 64 I.L.T.R. 233; [1930] IR. 576 is in point in that both Meredith J. and Johnston J. recognise that where there is a breach of contract for the sale of land on the part of the vendor the purchaser can recover the fees paid to the auctioneer from the vendor as damages for breach of contract.

In any event the purchaser cannot be in a worse position than when the contract is rescinded, an order for which the appellant would be entitled to in this case. On such an order being obtained the respondent would be bound to indemnify the appellant against the consequences and obligations of the contract. This would, in addition to the deposit and auctioneers' fees, include the costs of investigating the title.

In my view, therefore, the appellant is entitled to recover by way of damages the above amounts and also the costs of investigating title. The loss sustained by him is the amount of the deposit made, £825, the auctioneers' fee of £165 and the costs of investigating the title. There will be judgment for the first two amounts and also for the costs of investigating title, when taxed and ascertained, together with interest on the first two items from the dates on which the expenditures were respectively incurred at the rate of 6 per cent. The expenditure incurred in connection with the lodgment of the plans and seeking planning permission, including the architect's fees, was not, in my view, an expenditure which the appellant was obliged to make under the contract or by reason of his having been induced to enter into the contract. It was rather an expenditure made for his own purposes and in my view this expenditure is not recoverable against the respondent as being too remote.

Fitzgerald J.:

The plaintiff in this action is a solicitor, being the principal partner in the firm of Messrs. W.J. Shannon and Company, and is the executor of one Frederick Charles Ward, deceased, who died on the 18th December, 1965. The said deceased was the owner in fee simple of and resided in the dwellinghouse No. 6 Manders Terrace, Ranelagh, in the City of Dublin. The house is one of a terrace of nine houses, of which Nos. 1 to 8 inclusive, have large gardens at the rear abutting on a laneway to which each garden has a gate. The laneway originally gave access to the public road by way of a gateway at the side of the garden of No. 1, the passageway passing under a portion of that house. The laneway was the only means of access from the public road to the rear gardens of the houses Nos. 1 to 8 Manders Terrace. The house No. 6 Manders Terrace had been conveyed by indenture dated the 6th March, 1908, from Evelyn Goulding to Richard Davis in fee simple "with the right of way in common with the owners and occupiers of the adjoining houses through the laneway at the rear of the said houses and with the right of ingress, egress and regress for the said Richard Davis, his tenants, servants and workmen and all persons employed by him and them with or without horses and carts and carriages at all times over and through the said laneway to and from the public roadway." The said indenture also granted a right in common with the other occupiers of the houses on Manders Terrace to use the plot of ground in front of the houses.

By an indenture dated the 8th April, 1927, the said Richard Davis conveyed the said house to the said Frederick Charles Ward together with the right of way and the use of the plot in front of the houses in precisely the same manner as they had been conveyed to Davis in 1908. Incidentally Ward's address is stated in the deed of 1927 as being No. 6 Manders Terrace. Presumably he was already a tenant holding from Davis. The evidence established that Ward continued to reside in the house until his death on the 18th December, 1965. By the end of 1965 the laneway had fallen into a state of disuse. Rubbish had been dumped on it, presumably thrown over the boundary walls. It had been heavily overgrown with weeds and saplings and the gateway under portion of No. 1 Manders Terrace was secured by an iron bar. The physical state of the laneway would indicate that it had not been used as a passageway for a number of years.

Probate of Ward's will which was dated the 19th March, 1959, was granted to the plaintiff on the 27th January, 1966. The will directed the executor to sell the house as soon as convenient; it made provision for a number of pecuniary bequests and devised and bequeathed the residue of the testator's estate to his brother George Victor Ward who resided and still resides in Canada. Pursuant to the directions in the will the plaintiff proceeded to arrange for the sale of the house by public auction. For this purpose he prepared particulars and conditions of sale in which the premises were described as "all that the dwellinghouse and premises known as No. 6 Manders Terrace, Ranelagh, in the City of Dublin held in fee simple R.V. £21." There was no reference to any right of way or right to the use of the plot in front of the houses. It was stated that further particulars could be obtained from Messrs. W. J. Shannon & Co., Solicitors, or from Messrs. James Adam and Sons, Auctioneers. The plaintiff, Mr. Peilow, said that he decided to exclude the laneway from the conditions of sale because, from an inspection by him of the laneway, it appeared to be disused and derelict and blocked by the gate at No. 1. He in fact excluded it merely by making no reference to it.

He instructed Messrs. James Adam and Sons to offer the property for sale by public auction and for this purpose he furnished them with the particulars and conditions of sale. Messrs. Adam arranged to hold the auction on Monday the 24th January, 1966, and in relation thereto they inserted an advertisement in the Irish Times which appeared in the issue of that paper on the 6th January. The advertisement described the location and accommodation of the premises and stated, inter alia, that it was "double-fronted", ideal for residence or conversion and that it had "a large walled garden with back entrance". The "double fronted, ideal for residence or conversion and having a large walled garden with back entrance" was not given to the auctioneers by Mr. Peilow but was inserted in the advertisement as a result of a personal inspection of the premises by Mr. Coyle of Messrs. Adam and Sons. This advertisement was repeated in the Irish Times published on the 13th January.

The defendant is a medical doctor by profession and also for a number of years prior to 1966 engaged in the purchase and development of property. He read the advertisement in the Irish Times of the 13th January and called to Messrs. Adams to enquire about the property 6 Manders Terrace. Messrs. Adam supplied him with a hand-out which contained the same information as had appeared in the Irish Times advertisement. He then drove to Ranelagh and viewed the premises from the outside. He called back to Messrs. Adam on the 20th January and asked for the key of the house so that he might inspect it. He was provided with the key and proceeded to the premises accompanied by his wife. He inspected the house, the back garden and the laneway as far as the corner where it turned at right angles beyond No. 1 Manders Terrace. He observed the neglected condition of the laneway and estimated that it would cost £60 to £75 to have it cleared. He also observed that the gates from the gardens of the other houses were barricaded or bolted. When driving away from the house he observed that the doorway to the lane under No. 1 was bolted in some way.

Dr. ffrench O'Carroll's evidence was that his intention was, if successful in purchasing the property, to develop it by converting it into flats and that this work would include the extension of the existing house into the back garden. He regarded access through the laneway as essential to the development which he intended. His intention as to the type of development envisaged was not challenged although it was put to him that conversion of the property did not necessarily mean any development or reconstruction outside the walls of the existing house.

Following his inspection of the property on the 20th January Dr. ffrench O'Carroll got in touch with Mr. Walsh, an assistant in the office of his solicitor, Mr. McCormack, as a result of which Mr. Walsh called on Mr. Peilow on the following day, January 21st, to inspect the title deeds and to ascertain if there was any covenant restrictive of development in the deeds and to see whether the right of way was included in them. His inspection of the deeds of 1908 and 1927 disclosed that the right of way was included and that there were no covenants restrictive of development. There followed a discussion between Mr. Walsh and Mr. Peilow as to the right of way. There is a conflict between the evidence of Mr. Walsh and Mr. Peilow as to whether Mr. Peilow informed Mr. Walsh that the right of way was not being conveyed. It is clear that Mr. Peilow believed that he informed Mr. Walsh that the right of way was not being included in the sale, and equally clear that Mr Walsh left Mr. Peilow's office believing that the right of way was included and this is confirmed by the fact that he subsequently included the right of way in the draft convyance which he prepared.

The auction on the 24th January was attended by Dr. ffrench O'Carroll and his solicitor, Mr. McCormack. Mr. Peilow was also present at the auction which was conducted by Mr. Coyle of the firm of Messrs. Adam. There is a conflict between the evidence of Mr. Peilow and Mr. Coyle on the one hand and Dr. ffrench O'Carroll and Mr. McCormack on the other as to whether a question relating to the inclusion of the right of way was asked at the auction prior to the bidding. Dr. ffrench O'Carroll and Mr. McCormack say that the question was asked and that Mr. Coyle replied that they were selling the right of way. Mr. Peilow and Mr. Coyle had no recollection of any question being asked with reference to the right of way.

The auction proceeded and Mr. McCormack purchased the property at £3,300. He duly signed the contract and paid the deposit of £825 and auction fees amounting to £165. The date for completion was to be the 28th February. Mr. McCormack furnished his requisitions on title on the 4th February and these were replied to on February 7th. The requisitions did not raise any query as to the right of way. The draft conveyance prepared by Mr. Walsh and including the right of way was sent by Mr. McCormack to Messrs. Shannon on the 25th February and was approved by them on the same day. Subsequently the issue arose between the parties that gave rise to this litigation. Dr. ffrench O'Carroll maintained that he had purchased the property including the right of way and Mr. Peilow maintained that the right of way was not included in the sale. Both parties have maintained their respective stands on this issue throughout, save that the vendor, through his counsel, has maintained that while not being bound to convey the right of way, the purchaser would be entitled to it if the right of way still exists. The pleadings in the action brought by the plaintiff for specific performance and the defence and counterclaim seeking specific performance of the contract including the right of way and damage for breach of contract, were amended during the course of the trial to permit the defendant to rely on fraudulent or alternatively innocent misrepresentation and in the further alternative to be relieved of his contract on the ground of mutual mistake. The allegation that the alleged misrepresentations were fraudulent was relied upon at the trial but abandoned on the hearing of the appeal.

The advertisement in the Irish Times and the hand-out given to Dr. ffrench O'Carroll by Messrs. Adam when he called on the 20th January clearly stated that the property was suitable as a residence or for conversion, was inclusive of a large walled garden with a back entrance. Having regard to the physical existence of the laneway this latter statement could only mean that there was a right of way over the laneway to the public road. Mr. Justice Teevan, having heard Dr. ffrench O'Carroll, was satisfied that he instructed Mr. McCormack to bid for the property on the basis that the right of way existed.

A vital issue of fact to be decided is whether either at the interview between Mr. Peilow and Mr. Walsh on the 21st January or at the auction on the 24th January the statement in the newspaper advertisement and the hand-out that there was a rear entrance was corrected effectively, so that anyone who was relying on the statement in the advertisement or the hand-out would be informed that the statement was incorrect. Both Mr. Peilow and Mr. Coyle appear to accept the necessity for such a correction. Mr. Peilow said that he told Mr. Coyle to inform any prospective purchaser that the right of way was not being sold and Mr. Coyle said that he agreed that such a correction was necessary.

In relation to the interview between Mr. Peilow and Mr. Walsh, Mr. Justice Teevan was satisfied that both were truthful in their evidence as to their recollection of what was said. He finds that Mr. Peilow did say to Mr. Walsh that the right of way was not being included but that it cannot have been made quite as plain as Mr. Peilow thought it had, and he finds that this information was not taken in by Mr. Walsh. The learned judge also comments that Mr. Peilow's attitude throughout was rather carefree and casual and that what Mr. Peilow said may not have had its full impact on Mr. Walsh's mind and that there was ample opportunity for error or a failure of understanding. These findings by the trial judge do not amount to a finding that Mr. Walsh was clearly informed that the statement in the advertisement and hand-out was incorrect and that the right of way was not being sold. In effect the judge decided that Mr. Walsh was not clearly so informed.

In relation to the conduct of the auction Mr. Justice Teevan comments upon the evidence given by Mr. Peilow, Mr. Coyle, Dr. ffrench O'Carroll and Mr. McCormack as to whether any question was asked with reference to the right of way and whether any answer was given. Again he accepts that the witnesses had given evidence in accordance with their belief. He was satisfied that the question was asked, which is an acceptance of the evidence of Dr. ffrench O'Carroll and Mr. McCormack. He then finds that the answer given by Mr. Coyle may have been misunderstood by reason of a possible confusion from the words "we aren't selling the right of way" being taken up as "we are selling the right of way." In my opinion this also amounts to a finding that the necessary correction of the description of the property in the advertisement and hand-out was not made at the auction.

It was submitted by Mr. Connolly on behalf of the appellant that the appeal should be allowed on a number of grounds.

He contended, firstly, that the contract signed by Mr. McCormack following the auction was a contract to sell the premises with any appurtenances or rights, unless they were specifically excluded and that this was so, independently of any reference to the information contained in the newspaper advertisements or the hand-out which was given to Dr. ffrench O'Carroll. For this proposition he relied on a statement in Dart's Vendor and Purchaser 1929 Edition at page 110 and to a further statement in Halsbury's Laws of England Simonds 3rd edition, volume 34, page 218, paragraph 361, that "An agreement to sell land implies the whole of the interest of the vendor will be conveyed".

Mr Ellis submitted that the case cited in Dart's Vendor and Purchaser *Skull* v. *Gleniston* 16 C.B.N.S. H.E. 1, did not support the statements in the textbook. In that case an appeal was taken to the Court of Common Pleas in an action for trespass which had been tried before a judge and jury. On its particular facts a number of issues arose which are irrelevant to this issue in the present case. Earl C.J. does, however, state at page 188 that "this right of way was appurtenant to the lands demised by the Wheelers to the defendants." The lease which the defendants had obtained was apparently in general terms, no right of way being mentioned. The learned Chief Justice seemed to be satisfied that the right of way being appurtenant to the land, passed with it under the demise and in point of fact this issue does not appear to have been debated. Other cases cited included (a) *Stanton* v. *Tattersall* 1 Sm. & G. page 529. This was an action brought by a purchaser for a declaration that he was entitled to rescind a contract for the purchase of certain premises at Pall Mall, London, on the ground that the access to the premises was by means of a right of way which in fact passed through the ground floor of another building, portion of which was below the right of way in the basement and the rest of the building above it. It was held by the Vice-Chancellor that the plaintiff having contracted to buy certain property with a right of way to it, was now being offered an unusual right of way having regard to its situation and construction and that he was entitled to rescind the contract and his deposit was ordered to be returned to him. (b) *Denne* v. *Light* 8 De G.M. & G. This was a vendor's action for specific performance. On the trial the plaintiff had succeeded but on appeal before the Lord Justices it was held that in the absence of special circumstances a Court of Equity would not enforce specific performance of a contract for the purchase of land which was silent as to the means of acceess to it when it is reasonably uncertain whether any means of entering on the land at all times could be inferred. (e) *Curling* v. *Austin* 2 Drew & Sm. 129. This was a purchaser's action for specific performance. While the action succeeded, the circumstances were somewhat unusual. The purchaser required the vendor to make title to a right of way which was in fact a cul-de-sac serving a number of houses. It was held that the vendor under the contract was not bound to make title to the right of way but in addition following the primary decree on the trial of which this issue had not been raised, the vendor raised it for the first time when the matter was before the Examination and then came before the Court on further consideration.

It appears to me that the effect of these decisions establish that on a failure by a vendor to disclose to the purchaser any unusual feature of the property which is material, and a refusal by him to convey the property contracted to be sold without having inserted in the conveyance a limiting definition of the property, specific performance will not be granted in a suit brought by him and the purchaser is entitled to rescind.

Mr. Ellis conceded that under the contract Dr. ffrench O'Carroll became the equitable owner of the premises and of whatever right of way might be subsisting. He ultimately conceded that although the right of way was not mentioned in the particulars in the conditions of sale the sale itself involved such a right of way as was there, being comprised in the sale.

This appears to me to restrict the issue to a question as to whether the contract, quite apart from any representation by advertisement or hand-out or given verbally, included a full right of way in the terms of the deeds of 1908 and 1927, or alternatively only the possibility of such a right of way still existing having regard to the evidence of the apparent disuse of the laneway for a number of years.

It appears to me that when it is admitted that such a contract would carry the right of way, if it still subsisted, the onus of proving that in this case that the effect of the contract should be limited, rested upon the vendor to establish such a limitation. Such a limitation could be established by proving either an express communication to the purchaser that such was the position, or that the circumstances were such that he must have known it from observation of the property itself. There is no finding by the trial judge that such a limitation was ever communicated to the purchaser by the vendor prior to the contract being signed by his solicitor, Mr. McCormack.

Neither, in my opinion, was there sufficient evidence to support the trial judge's finding that in the absence of such a communication the condition of the laneway on his inspection prior to the auction should have conveyed to Dr. ffrench O'Carroll that the right of way might have been lost by abandonment. Mr. Coyle after his examination of the premises and having no specific instruction to do so, included in the description of the property its suitability for conversion and that it had a rere entrance, which statements were based on his own assessment of the position as he saw it. If Mr. Coyle, an experienced auctioneer, arrived at these conclusions I see no reason why it should be held that Dr. ffrench O'Carroll should have come to any different conclusion. Consequently, in my opinion, there is no basis upon which it could be held that Dr. ffrench O'Carroll should have realised that the property which he had agreed to buy would be conveyed to him without a full right of way. The vendor has refused to convey the property without any limitation.

Consequently, in my opinion, under the contract the vendor was bound to convey the premises No. 6 Manders Terrace with its appurtenances which included the right of way. His refusal to execute such a conveyance is, in my opinion, a breach of contract by him and consequently he is not entitled to succeed in his claim for specific performance. It appears to me that the defendant is entitled on his counterclaim to damages for breach of contract. Having regard to the view which I take on this issue it is possibly superfluous to deal with the other issues realised other than the question of damages.

I find myself unable to accept Mr. Conolly's second proposition that the particulars contained in the hand-out must be incorporated in the contract having regard to the fact that the conditions of sale referred the person reading them to Messrs. Adam for further particulars and that the hand-out furnished by them referred to the rere entrance and thus indicated that a right of way existed. Mr. Conolly agreed that the fact that the information about the right of way happened to be in a hand-out put him in no better position than if the enquirer at Messrs. Adam had been told verbally of the existence of the rere entrance. It appears to me to be going too far to suggest that any information given by the auctioneers over the counter should be taken as being incorporated in the contract. No authority to support Mr. Conolly's second proposition was cited and in my opinion such a decision in this case would amount to an unwarranted alteration in the law of contract.

Mr. Conolly abandoned his third ground which related to the admissability of evidence.

His fourth submission was that the exclusion of the right of way amounted to a breach of contract by the vendor in which, as I have stated above, I consider that his submission is correct.

His fifth proposition was that it was a condition of the contract that the right of way was included and that the purchaser was entitled to rescind and recover damages. Having regard to my conclusion that the vendor was guilty of a breach of contract it is unnecessary for the defendant to rescind the contract as he does not require to be relieved of it having regard to the vendor's breach.

Mr. Conolly submitted, ground 6, that on the evidence of Mr. Coyle and the plaintiff the further particulars furnished by Messrs. Adams and contained in the advertisements were misleading and that the plaintiff could not be granted specific performance, where the contract was not clear. For the reasons stated above I think Mr. Conolly's submission on this point is well founded.

Ground 7 – I think that for the reasons stated above Mr. Conolly's submission that the trial judge was wrong in law in holding that Dr. ffrench O'Carroll should have appreciated that the right of way had been abandoned is also well founded.

In my opinion Mr. Conolly was also correct in submitting that the advertisement and the hand-out amounted to representations that the right of way existed, that its existence was a material matter to the purchaser and that the misrepresentations entitled the purchaser to rescind.

A further issue was raised by the plaintiff at the trial that the purchaser had elected to treat the contract as subsisting and that he affirmed it after he had ascertained that the vendor refused to convey the right of way. This issue was not raised in the pleadings as the plaintiff was not aware of the relevant facts prior to the hearing. The facts relevant to this issue are that subsequent to his being informed that the vendor would not convey the right of way Dr. ffrench O'Carroll lodged plans with the Dublin Corporation seeking planning permission in relation to the property, which plans did not depend upon his having any title to the right of way. While his action in lodging the plans is consistent with an intention to complete the sale without the right of way being conveyed, it is equally consistent with his endeavouring to utilise the property if it were decided in litigation that he was bound to complete although the right of way was excluded. The evidence and the correspondence establish that Dr. ffrench O'Carroll always maintained his claim to have the right of way included and that he persisted in his refusal to complete if the right of way was not included. Mr. Justice Teevan came to the conclusion that the action of Dr. ffrench O'Carroll in submitting plans to the Corporation after he became aware that the vendor would not convey the right of way amounted to a recognition or affirmation of the contract, and that he was not entitled to repudiate it subsequently. I respectfully differ with the trial judge. A recognition or affirmation of a contract would normally arise where such was communicated to the other party and might possibly be inferred without any such communication where the purchaser's conduct was consistent only with an intention to complete. It appears to me, however, that recognition or confirmation are not to be inferred where the purchaser's conduct is equally consistent with a different intention and where no such communication is made to the vendor. In the present case, on the contrary, there is a persistent demand by the purchaser for completion of the contract in accordance with the purchaser's version of it.

Consequently, in my opinion, Dr. ffrench O'Carroll is entitled to damages for the loss sustained by him consequent upon the breach of contract committed by the vendor. The loss sustained was the deposit, the auction fees and the costs of investigating the title. It was submitted on behalf of the plaintiff that the auction fees were not recoverable as this was not money paid to the plaintiff. It appears to me, however, that the money paid by the defendant to the auctioneer was a loss sustained by him directly attributable to the breach by the plaintiff of the contract to sell and I see no reason why it should not be recoverable as part of the damages for breach of contract. As pointed out by Mr. Justice Budd in his judgment the liability of the vendor to refund the deposit would arise under the conditions of sale if the vendor lawfully rescinded the contract. Consequently this was a loss which was envisaged and there appears to me to be no good reason why the vendor should be liable to reimburse the purchaser if the contract was lawfully rescinded, but that he should not be liable where the contract goes off because of the vendor's breach of it.

The purchaser also claimed the expense of submitting the plans for planning permission to the Dublin Corporation. In my opinion these latter expenses are not recoverable. They would have been incurred in any event if he was forced to accept the conveyance without the right of way and somewhat similar expense would have been incurred even if he had obtained the conveyance with the right of way. I am consequently of the opinion that the order of the High Court should be set aside, that Dr. ffrench O'Carroll is entitled to damages for breach of contract as above set out and interest at 6 per cent.

McLoughlin J.:

I agree.

GAHAN V. BOLAND

Unreported (Supreme Court) (37-1983) (Judgments delivered 20th January, 1984)

The facts are set out in Henchy J.'s judgment.

Henchy J.:

The defendants Maurice and Wendy Boland are husband and wife. In February 1981 they had on offer for sale the property known as Glencarrig, situate at Bride's Glen, Loughlinstown, Co. Dublin. That property consists of a dwellinghouse and some 3¼ acres of land.

The plaintiff, who is a solicitor, entered into a written contract on Monday the 16 February 1981 for the purchase of the property for £135,000. In the present proceedings he has sought an order for the rescission of that contract. When his case came for hearing before Murphy J. in the High Court he succeeded in getting that order. The defendants now appeal.

The order for rescission was made as a result of certain events which are said to have taken place on Friday the 13 February 1981. On that day the plaintiff visited the defendants at Glencarrig. The purpose of the visit was to inspect the property and to make certain inquiries about it. The plaintiff says that amongst the inquiries he made was one as to whether a projected motorway connecting Dublin and Wicklow would affect the Glencarrig property. His evidence was that Mr. Boland assured him that the property would not be affected by the proposed motorway and that this assurance led him to enter into a written contract on the following Monday for the purchase of the property. It seems to be common case that the proposed motorway is in fact routed to pass through the Glencarrig property. That is something the plaintiff did not discover until after he had signed the contract.

There was a conflict of evidence as to what representation, if any, was made as to the motorway. The judge, however, having reviewed the evidence was of the clear opinion that an innocent but false representation was made by Mr. Boland to the effect that the property would not be affected by the motorway, if and when it came to be constructed; that this representation was a material one made with the intention of inducing the plaintiff to act on it; and that it was one of the factors that induced the plaintiff to enter into the written contract on the following Monday to purchase the property.

Having perused the transcript of the evidence, I am satisfied that there was ample evidence to support those findings as to the misrepresentation relied on by the plaintiff for rescission of the contract. Once there was evidence to support the judge's findings in that respect, the defendants' main ground of appeal, namely that the findings as to misrepresentation are unsustainable, must be held to fail. This Court cannot set aside primary facts of that nature found by the judge and supported by evidence.

The alternative or secondary ground of appeal argued was that, even if the defendants' argument as to the misrepresentation fails, the claim for rescission should have been rejected because the plaintiff should be held to have had constructive notice of the true position as to the route of the proposed motorway. It was suggested that the plaintiff, a solicitor and an intending purchaser, having made inquiries of the vendors as to whether the property would be affected by the motorway, was required, by the application of the doctrine of constructive notice, to pursue those inquiries in quarters where he would have been reliably informed as to the true position. For that reason, it is submitted, he should be held disentitled, for the purposes of rescission, to rely on the misrepresentation made and should be deemed to have constructive notice of the true position as to the route of the motorway.

I was unable to accept this argument. I consider it to be well-settled law that the only knowledge that will debar a purchaser from repudiating a contract he has been induced into by the vendor's misrepresentation is actual and complete knowledge of the true situation. It does not lie with a vendor, who has by his misrepresentation induced the purchaser to enter into a contract to purchase, to have his misrepresentation excused or overlooked and to have the purchaser deprived of a right to rescind because he did not ignore the misrepresentation and pursue matters further so as to establish the truth of what was misrepresented. That would be unconscionable and unfair. The doctrine of constructive notice, as it arises under s. 3 of the Conveyancing Act, 1882 and as it was applied by this Court in *Somers* v. *W.* [1979] I.R. 94, has no application to the facts of this case.

I would dismiss this appeal.

Walsh and **Hederman JJ.** agreed with this judgment.

Note

On the subject of constructive notice, see *Irish Land Law,* para. 3.072 *et seq.*, *Irish Conveyancing Law,* para. 6.38 and *A Casebook on Irish Land Law,* p. 84 *et seq.*

4. *Mistake*

GUN V. McCARTHY

(1883) 13 L.R. Ir. 304 (Chancery Division)

After negotiations for a lease of certain premises had been for some time pending, R., who was acting in the matter on behalf of G., the intended lessor, wrote a letter to M., the intended lessee, offering a lease at a rent of £33.10*s.* yearly, which was immediately accepted in writing by M., and a lease at that rent was afterwards prepared and executed by G. and M. G. afterwards brought an action in the County Court to have the agreement and lease rectified by inserting £53 10*s.* as the yearly rent; or, in the alternative, that the agreement and lease might be cancelled. The Country Court Judge made a decree for rectification, and the Defendant appealed.

Flanagan J.:

[His Lordship, having stated the facts as above, proceeded]:-

It was strongly argued by Mr. Jellett and Sergeant Hemphill that parol evidence is not admissible. Their argument comes to this, that where there is an agreement for a lease, and that lease is afterwards executed – in other words where an executory agreement becomes an executed one – parol evidence cannot be received to explain it, or to prove that the terms expressed in it are different from the real terms between the parties; that under the provisions of the Statute of Frauds the terms of the agreement are to be discovered from the agreement itself, where that agreement is in writing, and that you cannot resort to any parol evidence to explain it. In my opinion the determination of that question depends upon the character of the suit which is instituted, and of the relief which is sought. If the relief sought is to reform an instrument, it may, on the authorities as they exist, be doubtful whether, if there be a written agreement and subsequently an executed conveyance, parol evidence is admissible *dehors* the agreement; though where there is no written agreement, but simply an executed conveyance, parol evidence is clearly admissible to prove what the real agreement was. In *Davies* v. *Fitton* 2 Dr. & W. 225, Lord St. Leonards held that parol evidence was not admissible to prove that a lease executed in the expressed terms of a written agreement for the lease was contrary to the real agreement, and that there was something *dehors* the terms of the written contract omitted from the written agreement and the lease: *see* Lord St. Leonards' judgment, p. 232. The other case relied upon in support of this view is *The Attorney-General* v. *Sitwell* 1 Y. & C. Ex. 559, before Baron Alderson, in which he expressed a strong opinion that where the mistake is not admitted by *both sides* the Court would not on parol evidence reform an executory agreement and then enforce the agreement as reformed. On the other hand, these cases have not been received with universal or perhaps general assent. In Mr. Justice Fry's book he discusses these cases and expresses a strong opinion [Fry on Specific Performance (2nd ed.) §§ 789-790, p. 349] as to the absurd anomaly that if there is a written agreement for a lease, and afterwards a lease executed, parol evidence cannot be given; but if there is no written agreement, but only an executed conveyance or lease, you can give parol evidence. And he refers to numerous cases which would appear to show, as a universal proposition, that if there be an agreement, whether in writing or not, and you can prove there was a mistake in the conveyance as executed, common to both parties, parol evidence is admissible.

I have always understood the law to be that when you seek to reform a conveyance you must first establish – whether by parol evidence or otherwise – that there was a definite concluded agreement between the parties, but which, by mistake common to both parties to the agreement, had not been carried out in the conveyance executed pursuant to the real agreement. But when the mistake is not common, what can you reform by? To reform implies a previous *agreement;* but when the evidence shows that there was no agreement to which both parties assented, but only a mistake on one side, and not a common mistake, in my opinion it is impossible to support a suit to *reform,* whatever equity the party who has made the mistake may have in certain cases to rescind, the conveyance.

The only cases referred to which seem not to bear out that proposition are *Garrard* v. *Frankel* 30 Beav. 445 and *Harris* v. *Pepperell* L.R. 5 Eq. 1, in which Lord Romilly held that the Court could reform an agreement where there was a mistake on one side only. It will be observed, however, that he gave the other party the option of having the contract rescinded if he did not wish to have it reformed; and it appears to me that is the true ground on which those cases can be supported. Mr. Justice Fry, in his book on Specific Performance (2nd ed.), p.340, § 759, says:– "The mistake of one party can never be a ground for compulsory rectification. It may be a reason for setting the whole thing aside, but never for imposing on one party the erroneous conception of the other." So, in *Mortimer* v. *Shortall* 2 Dr. & W. 363, Lord St. Leonards lays it down that a mistake on one side may be a ground for rescinding a contract; but that, unless there was evidence of a mistake on both sides, the contract could not be rectified. And I find the same proposition laid down in *Fowler* v. *Fowler* 4 De G. & J. 250.

Whether, however, parol evidence be admissible or not where a written agreement exists, I am clearly of opinion that so far as the relief sought is to reform the lease, a mutual mistake must be proved; and this, in my opinion, the facts show did not exist. But, further, I am of opinion that so far as the relief sought is to rescind the contract, parol evidence is admissible, whether there was or was not a written agreement prior to the executed conveyance; and that, on such facts, it becomes a question whether they raise a sufficient equity to justify the court in making a decree for the rescission of the contract as executed.

[His Lordship, having reviewed the evidence as to the alleged mistake, stated that he had clearly come to the conclusion that the Defendant, on the 1st October, 1881, when he accepted the offer of Rahilly, knew perfectly well that Rahilly had inserted £33 10*s*. by mistake; and that the evidence clearly showed that £53 10*s*. was the rent which *the Plaintiff* intended to reserve; and proceeded:-]

In my opinion, where there being a clear undoubted mistake by one party in reference to a material term of the contract which he entered into with another, and the other party knowingly seeks to avail himself of that, and seeks to bind the other to the mistake, the law of this Court is, that it will not allow such a contract to be binding on the parties, but will give relief against it. I do not think the contract could be reformed; there is nothing to reform it by. If the Court comes to the conclusion that the parties have never entered into an agreement, it would be a contradiction in terms for it to say that it could reform the agreement. I say that with the greatest respect for the decisions in *Garrard* v. *Frankel* 30 Beav. 445, and *Harris* v. *Pepperall* L.R. 5 Eq. 1. I confess I think these decisions can only be supported in the way suggested by Mr. Justice Fry: that the contracts were reformed on the ground that the party, against whom the decision was, elected to take the contracts reformed. But where the party insists generally on his right to retain the contract in the terms of the conveyance as executed, my opinion is, that the contract ought to be rescinded: and the decision I have come to is, I shall reverse the decision of the County Court Judge, so far as he directs this lease and agreement to be reformed, but I shall direct the lease and agreement to be delivered up to be cancelled, as I think the contract cannot be retained by the Defendant, as I think his seeking to do so is uncandid and dishonest, and that if he had come in here to enforce the contract his action would have been dismissed; and on the authority of the case of *Tamplin* v. *James* 15 Ch. Div. 215, I have no hesitation in saying it would be dismissed with costs, on the ground that it was a dishonest attempt on his part to take advantage of a mistake. Lord Justice James, in his judgment in that case, says that the only fault he has to find with the case of *Webster* v. *Cecil* 30 Beav. 62 was that in his opinion the bill in that case ought to have been dismissed with costs. *Webster* v. *Cecil* was a case where the defendant proposed to sell to the plaintiff his premises for £1250, and the plaintiff by letter accepted the offer. As a matter of fact, his so fixing the sum for which the premises were offered was proved to be a mistake; the sum intended was £2250, and the error arose from a mistake in the tot of a calculation made by the defendant. Then the plaintiff filed a bill for specific performance. The mistake of the defendant was clearly proved, and that before bill filed it was communicated to the plaintiff, and the bill was dismissed without costs. James L.J., says, as I have observed, that it ought to have been dismissed with costs.

In the present case, having regard to all the facts, I shall direct the lease and agreement to be delivered up to be cancelled. I shall direct that the Plaintiff shall pay to the Defendant all moneys *bonâ fide* expended by him in improvement of the premises, and shall direct an account of those moneys. I shall direct that the National Bank, they so consenting, shall be paid the sum due to them on foot of their equitable mortgage by deposit. I shall direct that the Defendant be charged with an occupation rent with regard to these premises; and I shall let both parties abide their own costs of the appeal, and shall give the Plaintiff the costs of the hearing below. I rule the costs in this way for this reason – I quite accede to the argument of Mr. Jellett, that there was no fraud on the part of the Defendant in the inception of this agreement, but in my opinion he dishonestly availed himself of the Plaintiff's mistake, and his doing so was what led to this suit. He acted unconscientiously in reference to the original agreement, having been aware all through of the Plaintiff's mistake, and never called his attention to it.

Notes

1. See further as to rescission for mistake, *Irish Conveyancing Law,* paras. 12.65–5 and as to cancellation of a document, *Irish Land Law,* para. 3.161.
2. As to rectification, see Ch. 8, *post.*

Chapter 8

RECTIFICATION

This is a special remedy of particular use in conveyancing transactions. It is, however, important to note the basis upon which equity operates and to observe the limits to the remedy.

McCORMACK v. McCORMACK
(1877) 1 L.R. Ir. 119 (Chancery Appeal Court)

By a post-nuptial settlement of 1841–after reciting that in consideration of £352, a share of residue to which E. the wife had become entitled under a will taking effect a few days before the marriage, C., the husband, in order to provide for her after his death, and for their issue, had proposed to settle a freehold house and field, upon the trusts therein mentioned–the freehold premises were conveyed to T. upon trust for C. for life, or until he should become bankrupt, or assign, or charge "the rents, issues, and annual produce of the said trust estate *moneys,* etc.," then upon trust for E. for life; "it being the true intent and meaning of these presents, and the parties thereto, that the said tenements, hereditaments and premises," should in the event of any such charge, &c., be for the separate maintenance of E. for life, then, "as to the rents, issues and annual profits arising off the said house and premises," for children, in the usual form, with an ultimate "trust to pay the said rents, issues and annual produce," to C.'s next-of-kin. The settlement provided that on the appointment of any new trustee, "all the trust estate *moneys* and premises" should be assigned to him. T., who was also the trustee of the will, had paid part of the £352 to C. before the execution of the deed, and the rest immediately after. The solicitor who prepared the settlement, on T.'s verbal instructions, had died in 1848, and there were no papers to show what the instructions were; but C., E. and T. all deposed now that it had not been intended to settle any part of the £352, and their bill, filed in 1876, to reform the deed accordingly, was not opposed by the adult children. Chatterton V.C. dismissed the bill with costs (see I.R. 11 Eq. 130) and an appeal was lodged.

Ball C.:

The jurisdiction of a Court of Equity to reform a settlement, in which it is established by evidence that error or mistake has occurred, is undoubted. Parol evidence will suffice, but it is obvious that when the claim for relief rests upon testimony exclusively, and is not supported by any written record of the intention of the parties, especially should time have clapsed since the deed was executed, much vigilance and caution are required on the part of the tribunal which is called upon to exercise the jurisdiction. Still if, after due deliberation, it arrives at the conclusion that the actual contract which was made between the parties differs from that expressed in the intsrument, it is, in my judgment, as much bound to act as in any other case depending upon testimony.

The only question in this suit relates to a matter in its nature simple and easy to be understood by any person of ordinary intelligence–was it intended that a particular sum of £352 should have been included along with other property in a postnuptial settlement? We may well distrust the recollection of witnesses as to what is complicated or difficult, such as an elaborate train of limitations of an estate, or a portion of them, subjects in respect of which the intention may very easily not have been clear at the time, and naturally the memory not retentive, but here this ground of distrust does not exist. It is also to be kept in mind, that although the subject of controversy be simple, yet the language of the instrument in relation to it is not simple; on the contrary, it is by no means free from ambiguity, and its construction has been debated before the Master of the Rolls, and again before the Vice-Chancellor, both of whom have, upon inferences from a minute examination of particular words, and not from any plain declaration of intention, held that this sum of money, whether it was so designed or not, is affected by the trusts of the settlement. I am myself clearly of opinion that an unprofessional person might have heard read, or himself have read, the deed without perceiving that this money was settled. The matter in question is, therefore, one in its nature easy to be remembered, and we are not embarrassed by any plain declaration in the deed under the hands of the parties, in conflict with their present statements.

Then comes what must always be an important inquiry in a case of this character–have the parties acquiesced all this time–thirty six years, for the deed bears date in 1841? Has the provision complained of been acted upon? Nothing of the kind. The acts of the parties are inconsistent with the expressed contract, and consistent with that now asserted. Before the settlement was executed, and again, contemporaneously with its execution, portions of this sum of £352 were paid to the husband; and, afterwards, the balance not then paid was handed to him. The person who held the money for the wife was to be the trustee of the settlement, and seems himself to have negotiated, and given instructions for its terms; and unless what is alleged be true–that it was neither intended nor supposed that the £352 was settled–how can this conduct on his part be explained?

Let us now examine the evidence which, under such circumstances, comes before us. There never could have been more than four persons aware of the real nature of the agreement: viz, the husband, the wife, Mr. Tener, who was the trustee originally of the money and afterwards of the settlement, and Mr. Holmes, the solicitor. The last died in 1848; and the other three all coincide in saying this money was not to be a subject of settlement. Mr Tener must know all about it; he told the husband he ought to make a settlement; he personally communicated with the solicitor as to its preparation, and told him what was and what was not to be included; there never were any written directions or instructions; the whole rested in parol, and was conducted by him. Then his acts at the time–paying the husband, when by so doing he must, if the money were settled, have involved himself in liability to make good the money for the settlement–are in exact conformity with what he says was then intended, and as he supposed effected by the deed. I regard this as satisfactory confirmation of the testimony of the three surviving persons acquainted with the treaty; and having this confirmation, notwithstanding the interest which the husband, and for his sake the wife, have in the case they support, and being favourably impressed with the testimony itself, I feel bound to act upon it.

As for delay–I think the topic answered by the fact that, from the ambiguous nature of the language of the deed, the parties seem not to have perceived its effect until the argument before the Master of the Rolls in 1871.

The decree appealed from will be altered, by declaring this sum of £352 was by mistake introduced into the settlement; the husband must pay the costs of his minor children, who have properly been brought as Defendants before the Court, and whose rights have been with much ability protected by their counsel.

Christian L.J.:

I am quite of the same opinion; and I must add that it appears to me that unless the Court of Chancery were prepared to abdicate this head of its jurisdiction, it could not refuse to apply it in the present case; for we have here a convergence of almost every circumstance by which Courts of Equity have been induced to reform settlements – unreasonableness in their provisions, and the consequent improbability of their truly representing the intentions of the parties; their contemporaneous acts at variance with those provisions; incongruitites apparent on the face of the settlement itself; and, finally, a perfect concurrence of evidence from the parties themselves, all of whom fortunately happen to be still living in this instance, and who give unanimous consent and assent to the view to which the mind would naturally be led. In addition to that, no resistance is offered by the only persons competent to express an opinion upon the subject – I mean the adult children; and against all that evidence, which is all on one side, nothing on the other except the passive resistance, the *non possumus,* of the two minor children. Though I speak of their passive resistance, their counsel has argued this case with an energy and a zeal which became him, acting as he was on behalf of minors. This lady had no actual fortune at the time of her marriage. Her husband had a perpetual real estate, but he did not think proper to make any settlement. In process of time this sum of £352 became available, and was in the hands of Tener as trustee. The state of rights under these circumstances was, that the husband was entitled to reduce that *chose in action* into possession, and call for payment of the money; but the trustee could have said, "I insist on the wife's equity to a settlement, and that the whole sum, as it is so small, be settled." The husband could then say, "I would rather get the money and give you a settlement on my real estate." The two properties produced about the same sum yearly. Seeing that McCormack had already refused to make a settlement when he was married, it was plain that he did not intend to settle anything afterwards but what the trustee had a right to require him to settle. Therefore the probabilities of the case were, that the husband should get the money, and make a settlement out of his real estate. What else have we before we come to the deed itself? We have the fact that before the settlement was suggested, Tener had paid a large part of the money to the husband; and therefore the first thing Tener should have done, if it was to be put into settlement, in duty to himself as well as to the other members of the family, was to call upon McCormack to refund what he had got, so that the whole might be united as a subject of the settlement. Instead, however, of doing that, upon the execution of the deed he handed over the rest of the fund to McCormack. Whatever suggestion can be made as to Tener's being an interested witness, he is swearing upon this point from memory refreshed by entries from his books which were refused to be admitted in evidence; also, he is here in Court now, and might have been cross-examined. With these facts and probabilities then before us, we come now to the consideration of the settlement itself. [His Lordship having then red and analysed the provisions of the settlement *seriatim* down to the beginning of the clause as to the appointment of new trustees, with the view of showing that they pointed to the exclusion of the £352 from its operation, proceeded:] If there were no further indication of intention to deal with the money, I think I should say, as a mere matter of construction, that the lady's fortune was not included. What makes the difficulty is the proviso as to the appointment of new trustees. [His Lordship read the clause.] There unquestionably it is stated that the "moneys" were part of the trust fund; that alone gives rise, in my opinion, to the necessity of a suit for reformation, and the question is, whether any sufficient case for that has been made. I think that, even if all the parties were dead a *primâ facie* probability would be sufficient to show that the introduction of the word "moneys" was a mistake. In *Smith* v. *Iliffe* L.R. 20 Eq. 167 the Court went upon the inherent improbabilities of the settlement. [His Lordship stated the facts of that case.] There a great difficulty in the way was the existence of previous articles with which the settlement agreed. The parol evidence was worthless; there was only the lady's own affidavit, and she knew nothing of the terms of the contract which she admitted had been arranged by her mother and her advisers without reference to herself. Are not the improbabilities here quite as great? Is it not improbable that the husband agreed to settle anything more than he was obliged to settle? Is it not improbable that Tener would pay over the money to the husband and execute a deed which would fasten a breach of trust round his own neck? Even without the parol evidence here, I should be disposed to hold, following *Smith* v. *Iliffe,* that it was a mistake to introduce the word "moneys.

But what have we after that? Why it appears that though a very long time has elapsed, all the parties to the settlement are still living. A search, which I have no doubt was *bonâ fide,* has been made among Mr. Holmes' papers, and nothing has been found; and Mr. Tener, whom I called up, says that his instructions were verbal, that none were given to include the £352 in the settlement, and that the doing so was a mistake. I do not know what would be required if that be not sufficient. Of course the parties have an interest, but parties always have an interest in these cases; and if there be any of the parties on the other side who have an adverse interest and deny the statements of those opposed to them, the difficulty of reforming a settlement under such circumstances would probably be insuperable. But where we have all the parties agreeing, I do not know what the most fastidious of Courts could further require. This power of reforming deeds is one of the most useful features of our law, and I must repeat, what I have already said, that we might as well strike this head of our jurisdiction out of our books altogether, as refuse to apply it in this instance, and to make an order in favour of the Appellants. I agree with the Lord Chancellor as to the form which our decree should take; the declaration should be indorsed on the deed.

The material portion of the decree was as follows:-

"THEIR LORDSHIPS do order that the said decretal order of the Vice-Chancellor, bearing date the 16th day of November, 1876, be and the same is hereby reversed, and instead thereof the Court doth declare that the postnuptial settlement bearing date the 13th day of October, 1841, is not in all respects in conformity with the intention or agreement of the parties to the said deed, or any of them, to settle by the said deed any property except the tenements and premises in the town of Coal Island and county of Tyrone thereby assigned. And doth further declare that the word 'moneys' in line sixteen of the second page, and line twenty-six of the third page of the said deed, was inserted therein by mistake, and ought to be omitted. And it is hereby ordered that the said deed be construed and take effect as if the same had been framed accordingly, and that the foregoing declaration and order be indorsed on the said settlement, and that the same be certified by the Registrar of this Court to be a true copy thereof."

Notes and Questions
How far have the Irish courts abided by the principles laid down by Ball C.? *Cf. Monaghan C.C.* v. *Vaughan, infra, Fitzgerald* v. *Fitzgerald, infra* and *King* v. *King-Harman, infra.*

MONAGHAN COUNTY COUNCIL V. VAUGHAN
[1948] I.R. 306 (High Court)

The facts are set out in the judgment.

Dixon J.:
I have had an opportunity of considering fully the facts in this case and of considering the numerous authorities opened to me by counsel. The case has been so well presented to the Court by counsel for each party, that I feel that I can give judgment now while the facts are fresh in my mind.

My view of the facts in the case is this. At the close of the plaintiffs' case, I had no doubt (and still have none), that a mistake was made by them in the written form of the contract. The terms of the advertisement and of the form of tender, together with the prior offers made by Messrs. McEntee and Roche Brothers, show that the contract was regarded by the plaintiffs as a valuable concession. In addition, the circumstances themselves indicated that valuable material would be obtained from the demolition work – material for which there was a rising market price, as a result of which, no doubt, the offers already received had been refused as insufficient. These factors, of course, do not all necessarily affect the defendant.

The clear intention of the County Council was that they should be paid for granting the right to carry out the work of demolition, and, while the defendant's offer was ambiguous in form, leaving it doubtful as to whether it contemplated that he was to pay or to be paid the sum of £1,200, I have no doubt that the County Council construed it as meaning that they were to be paid that sum by the defendant, particularly as they had already received and refused an offer by Messrs. Roche Brothers to do the work and to pay a sum of £1,125 for the concession.

As to what the defendant's intention really was, I regard his evidence as being very unconvincing and, having regard to his demeanour in the witness box, I am unable to accept very much of what he said. Furthermore, most of his evidence conflicts sharply with the probabilities in the matter.

The plaintiffs have made a *prima facie* case of the language of the advertisement, that their offer was for a payment to them of whatever sum should be agreed upon in return for the right to carry out the demolition work. Clause 13 of the specification was called to the attention of the defendant, and both its terms and the fact that the material to be obtained by way of salvage on the demolition would have a substantial value, are consistent only with the intention of both parties having been that the County Council should be paid and not that they should have to pay. This conclusion appears to me to be strengthened rather than rebutted by the evidence of the defendant himself.

Accordingly, I must hold that the intention of the defendant as well as that of the plaintiffs was that the defendant should pay to the plaintiffs a sum of £1,200 for the right to carry out the demoliton work.

I am prepared to accept the evidence of the defendant that he saw his solicitor with respect to the matter, but here a difficulty arises as to the date of the interview. He says that it was after he had submitted the tender, although on re-examination he admitted that he did not definitely know when it was. Mr. O'Malley, his solicitor, states that the interview was some time before tender was made, and I accept that evidence, but it does not strengthen the defendant's case.

On the 26th September, the specification was sent by the County Council to the defendant, after which the defendant went and saw his solicitor. I feel that the probability is that he went and saw his solicitor before travelling to Clones on the 3rd October, and therefore that he did not then know exactly the nature of the work to be done, and probably consulted his solicitor mainly with a view to ascertaining the precise meaning of the contract and particularly clause 13. Mr. O'Malley very properly advised him that clause 13 was more consistent with the defendant paying the County Council, but if payment were to be the other way, it might be construed consistently with that by modifying the meaning of the word "credit" in it. Having made the inspection on October the 3rd, the defendant submitted his offer to the County Council on October the 5th, and he must then have known that the position was that he would have to pay, rather than be paid. He had then also an approximate idea of the value of the materials and had also the advantage of fifteen years' experience of demolition work, including several contracts in which he had paid for the right to carry out the work.

The only meaning which I can give to his offer, is that he intended to pay this sum of £1,200. He produced two pages of notes of calculations said to have been made by him on October the 3rd, but I view them with the gravest suspicion and feel that they were probably made after the event with a view to this litigation. They were produced by him when asked by his solicitor how he had arrived at the contract price, and were probably prepared at that stage. Even on their face value, however, they do not give much help. They show an estimated profit of £3 and an arbitrary figure of £1,200 as the amount to be asked for, representing an 80% profit on outlay. I find nothing helpful to the defendant's case in such calculations and figures.

Digressing for a moment, I view with equal suspicion the defendant's evidence as to the actual outlay and receipts. The figures show a lack of particularity and many items are open to doubt or suspicion. I may instance the payment of £10 per week to his nephew, the complete mystery as to the item of £72 10s., the absence of particulars of private sales, and the obscurity as to approximately 2,200 slates taken to Limerick. Even, however, accepting what the defendant said, if he were to be paid £1,200, his profit would have been £2,400, while if he were to pay £1,200 the transaction would work out about evenly.

I therefore hold that the offer meant, and that the defendant intended it to mean, that he would pay the sum of £1,200 to the County Council. As to the evidence of Mr. Griffin, it does not establish a state of mind of the defendant which would displace the conclusion at which I have arrived. Here again there is a difficulty about a date, namely, that upon which the amount of the bond was fixed. The proposal form is dated 23rd of November, and in my opinion the earliest date on which the defendant could have known of the amount of the bond would have been a date on which he also must have known the contents of the draft contract. Mr. Griffin's evidence does not satisfy me that the defendant genuinely thought he was to be paid a sum of £1,200. This constitutes no reflection whatever on Mr. Griffin's evidence, as it is quite natural that he is unable, after the lapse of time, to recollect with sufficient accuracy for my purposes what took place at the interview except so far as the documents disclose it.

For these reasons I am satisfied that it was the intention of both parties that the defendant should pay the sum of £1,200 to the County Council, and I am of opinion that the defendant saw the error into which the County Council had fallen when the contract was read over to him and decided to take advantage of it. I regard this as a case of mutual mistake. I think that it is immaterial that one party knows the document to be inaccurate for the purposes of the application of the principles of law applicable to mutual mistake. What is material is that both parties were agreed upon certain matters and that the completed contract did not correctly represent the substance of their agreement. A unilateral mistake arises where one of two or more parties is not *ad idem* with the other party or parties, and there is, therefore, no real agreement between them. In such a case, rescission may be appropriate, but the present is a different case. It is not a case of unilateral mistake in that sense, but to speak of it as a case of mutual mistake may obscure its true character of a common or mutual intention misrepresented by the record of that intention.

If the defendant had really intended that he should be paid the sum of £1,200 the position would be entirely different, but on the evidence I reject that view and hold that he attempted to take advantage of the error made by the County Council and that his conduct was dishonest and approximated to fraud.

The cases which were opened to me, turning on the law of conveyancing, are somewhat different from the present, for they are instances of mistake arising from the failure of the conveyance to conform with the prior written agreement (i.e. the contract of sale). Such mistake might be mutual or unilateral, these terms being used in the sense of the parties' knowledge of the conformance or otherwise of the conveyance in question with the prior contract, and the conveyance being a sequel to, rather than a record of, such contract. Here, however, when the document alleged to be erroneously framed does not record the agreed intention, it represents a case for rectification if the plaintiffs are in a position to overcome the legal difficulties they have to face.

I have been referred to some relevant passages in the sixth edition of Fry on Specific Performance. The first of these (par. 791), reads as follows:–"It follows from the nature of the jurisdiction that there can be no rectification where there is not a prior actual contract by which to rectify the written document: so that, for instance. a policy cannot be rectified by the slip, because the slip constituted no contract, and there was no contract till the policy was signed and the premium paid."

I think this only means that there must be some agreement between the parties. In the instance given, the "slip" was only a proposal and, until the policy had been signed and the first premium paid, there was no agreed intention. The paragraph is consistent with the statement that the Court will not rectify contracts in themselves, but merely the instruments in which the contracts are set out.

The next paragraph illustrates this:– "It equally follows that the mistake of one party to a contract can never be ground for compulsory rectification, so as to impose on the second party the erroneous conception of the first. The error of the plaintiff alone may, however, where (but, it is conceived, only where) there has been fraud or conduct equivalent to fraud on the part of the defendant, be a ground for putting the defendant to elect between having the transaction annulled altogether or submitting to the rectification of the deed in accordance with the plaintiff's intention."

In other words, an erroneous conception of the intended agreement by one of the parties is sufficient to prevent there being a mutual agreement.

Paragraph 793 of the same work is also of importance:–"Parol evidence is admitted to show the common mistake of both parties in reducing the contract into writing, and as the ground for rectifying it. 'I think it impossible,' said Lord Thurlow, 'to refuse, as incompetent, parol evidence which goes to prove that the words taken down in writing were contrary to the concurrent intention of all parties.'"

The "concurrent intention" referred to here by the author is shown in the present case by the documents and by the circumstances existing before the formal document was executed.

The essence of the present case is that this written document is inconsistent with the mutual agreement between the parties, and for that reason the decision at which I have arrived does not, in my opinion, conflict with the result of cases such as *Garrard* v. *Frankel* 30 Beav. 445. In that case an intended lessee signed an agreement to take a lease of premises at a yearly rent of £230 and on the terms of a lease on which the said agreement was written but which erroneously stated the yearly rent to be £130. A lease was subsequently executed in which the rent was erroneously stated to be £130 per annum. The error on the part of the lessor was proved, and the Court considered that the lessee must have perceived the discrepancy between the amount of rent previously stated by the lessor and specified in the agreement and that reserved by the lease, but held that the lessor was not entitled to have the lease reformed and that the proper relief was to give the lessee an option of agreeing to having the lease reformed or of rejecting it and paying a rental for past occupation and a mortagage on the lease created by the lessee.

It is clear that that was a case of unilateral mistake because of the possiblity that the lessor had changed his mind as to the amount of the rent. I find it impossible however, in the present case to hold that the County Council had changed its mind in the manner suggested by the defendant or that the defendant honestly believed such a change of mind to have taken place.

The case of *Paget* v. *Marshall* 28 Ch. D. 255 is also distinguishable from the present case for the reason that in that case the Judge felt that he had insufficient evidence before him of the existence of a mutual mistake.

In *Hartog* v. *Colin and Shields* [1939] 3 All E.R. 566 the claim of the plaintiffs was somewhat different from that in the present case and the mistake there may, upon my reading of the report, have been unilateral mistake.

Similarly, in *Nolan* v. *Graves and Hamilton* [1946] I.R. 376, Haugh J. held that the mistake was unilateral. Furthermore, the circumstances there were different from those in the present case and I think it is very questionable that his Lordship intended to lay down, as has been suggested, that the knowledge of one party of the true facts will always prevent a mistake being treated as a mutual mistake.

I think that the principle which is applciable here is most clearly set out in the decision in *Fowler* v. *Fowler* 4 De G. & J. 250 where, at page 265, the Lord Chancellor said:– "It is clear that a person who seeks to rectify a deed upon the ground of mistake must be required to establish, in the clearest and most satisfactory manner, that the alleged intention to which he desires it to be made conformable continued concurrently in the minds of all parties down to the time of its execution, and also must be able to show exactly and precisely the form to which the deed ought to be brought. For there is a material difference between setting aside an instrument and rectifying it on the ground of mistake. In the latter case you can only act upon the mutual and concurrent intention of all parties for whom the Court is virtually making a new written agreement." I am satisfied that in the present case the two requirements mentioned in this passage have been fulfilled by the plaintiffs.

Gun v. *McCarthy* 13 L.R. Ir. 304 was also a case of mutual mistake and there Flanagan J. said (at p. 309) that he had always understood the law to be that when you seek to reform a conveyance you must first establish that there was a definite concluded agreement between the parties, but which, by mistake common to both parties, had not been carried out in the conveyance executed pursuant to the real agreement. But when the mistake is not common, he asks, by what can it be reformed? "To reform," he continues, "implies a previous *agreement;* but when the evidence shows that there was no agreement to which both parties assented, but only a mistake on one side, and not a common mistake, in my opinion it is impossible to support a suit to *reform,* whatever equity the party who has made the mistake may have in certain cases to rescind, the conveyance." His Lordship here seems to be drawing a contrast between cases where the parties are *ad idem* in intention and cases where they are not.

As to the question of negligence, there may have been a degree of negligence on the part of the County Council and their officials and possibly also, although to a much lesser extent, on the part of their solicitor, but I am not satisfied (and there is authority to the contrary), that in the case of a claim for rectification of a contract on the ground of mutual mistake, negligence on the part of the plaintiffs can be raised as a defence.

Again as to estoppel, the contention of the defendant upon this plea is inapplicable to the circumstances before me. I am satisfied that the County Council did not change its mind between the date of receiving the tender and the date of the making of the contract, nor did it intend to make a fresh offer. I am satisfied that the defendant could not honestly have believed such a complete reversal of intention on the part of the plaintiffs to have been intended. He was not misled, he did not act on the basis of any misrepresentation and he is not entitled now, in my opinion, to rely upon estoppel.

Lastly, it has been argued on behalf of the defendant that s. 100 of the Local Government (Ir.) Act, 1898, has had the effect of removing an essential condition necessary to confer upon the Court, in a case such as the present, any jurisdiction to rectify a contract. This section deals mainly with a question of procedure rather than with matters of *ultra vires,* that is, with form rather than substance, and does not render the local authority incapable of making the particular contract. If construed in the manner suggested, the section would lead to absurd and harsh results, and I would be slow to accept such a construction as being correct, unless supported by well-settled or coercive authorities. So far from this being the case, an answer to the contention is to be found in the judgment of Lord Birkenhead in the case of *United States* v. *Motor Trucks, Ltd.* [1924] A.C. 196, where, at pages 200 and 201, he said:– "And indeed the power of the Court to rectify mutual mistake implies that this power may be exercised notwithstanding that the true agreement of the parties has not been expressed in writing. Nor does the rule make any inroad upon another principle, that the plaintiff must shew first that here was an actually concluded agreement antecedent to the instrument which is sought to be rectified; and secondly, that such agreement has been inaccurately represented in the instrument. When this is proved, either party may claim, in spite of the Statute of Frauds, that the instrument on which the other insists does not represent the real agreement. The statute, in fact, only provides that no agreement not in writing and not duly signed shall be sued on; but when the written instrument is rectified there is a writing which satisfies the statute, the jurisdiction of the Court to rectify being outside the prohibition of the statute." I find it impossible to see any difference in principle between the case of a contract which cannot be enforced because of the Statute of Frauds and one which is alleged to be unenforceable by reason of s. 100 of the Act of 1898.

Again, the precise point is dealt with in the case of *Shipley U.D.C.* v. *Bradford Corporation* [1936] Ch. 375 and I adopt the reasoning and conclusions of Mr. Justice Clauson at page 398 where he says:– "If the matter had rested there, it may be that the defendants' argument would never have been put forward, but there are two cases in which the exact point arose which is in issue here – namely, whether a document sealed by a corporation which can bind itself only by seal, can be rectified. In each case an actual decision was unnecessry, but in each case the learned judge (Younger J. in the one case and Romer J. in the other), expressed by way of *dictum* a provisional view which certainly supports the defendants' argument, but in neither case were the early authorities discussed. Those cases are *Faraday* v. *Tamworth Union* 86 L.J. Ch. 436 and *Higgins (W.) Ltd.* v. *Mayor of Northampton* [1927] 1 Ch. 128. In each case the Court found that there was no mutual mistake, but in each case the judge intimated that he would have felt a difficulty in rectifying the document, because that would amount to binding that corporate body to a document which requires a seal, but which the body have in fact never sealed. Not only were the earlier cases not cited, but attention was not in either case drawn to the decision of the Court of Appeal in *Hall-Dare* v. *Hall-Dare* 31 Ch. D. 251, which seems to show that a deed rectified by the Court so as to conform to the true intention of the executing party at the moment of execution must be taken to be his deed and to have been (at all events, for any purpose relevant to this case) his deed in the rectified form as from the date of execution: see also *Meeking* v. *Meeking* [1917] 1 Ch. 77.

"Had it been necessary for me to decide the point, I should have felt some difficulty in following the *dicta* in these two cases, and I should have felt bound to hold that the proof in the present case that the concurrent intention of the parties was, at the moment of execution, to contract on the footing of the £540 being a sum per annum and the 450,000 gallons a yield per diem would have made it necessary (but for my construing the instrument as I have construed it) to rectify the instrument so as to accord with that concurrent intention, notwithstanding that the parties can be bound only by their respective seals."

This is the latest of three cases (the earlier two of which are cited in the passage just read), in which the point is dealt with by way of *obiter dictum,* and I prefer the view expressed in it.

For all these reasons, I consider that the plaintiffs' case for rectification has been fully established and I grant the relief as claimed. The plaintiffs are entitled to their costs.

Notes and Questions

1. Why was this case not treated as more appropriate for rescission rather than rectification? *Cf. Gun* v. *McCarthy,* p.268, ante.
2. See *Irish Land Law,* para. 3.164.

FITZGERALD V. FITZGERALD

[1902] 1 I.R. 477 ; 36 I.L.T.R. 18 (Court of Appeal)

The facts are set out in the judgments.

Lord Ashbourne, C.:

The question in this appeal arises on the terms of a marriage settlement, executed in the year 1859, by which certain lands were settled, which are now represented by the funds in Court. The estates in the lands limited by the settlement are – first, a life estate to Miss Maria Fitzgerald, the settlor; then a life estate to her brother Stephen, on whose marriage the settlement was made, with remainder to the use of the children of the marriage for such estates as Stephen Fitzgerald should by deed or will appoint, and in default of such appointment, if there should be only one child of the marriage, "to the use of such only child *in tail.*" There was only one child born of the marriage, the plaintiff in this action. Miss Maria Fitzgerald has died, and Stephen Fitzgerald has died without exercising the power of appointment conferred on him by the settlement. On these facts the question is now raised – Is there evidence of an intention on the part of the settlor to confer an estate tail in the property on the plaintiff, and should the deed be rectified so as to carry out this intention? It is not a question of construction. It is admitted by the plaintiff that in construing the deed the words used are not sufficient to effectuate the intention of the parties, but she seeks to have the deed rectified by the substitution of appropriate words in order to carry out that intention. It has been argued on her behalf that there is on the face of the settlement itself abundant evidence of the settlor's intention to give an estate tail to the plaintiff in the events that have happened, and that this intention would be set at naught by the rules of construction if the deed is not rectified.

It was argued by the appellant that for the purpose of establishing a case for rectification you must gather the intention of the parties from evidence *dehors* the deed itself, and Mr. Ronan contended that the cases in which the Court gathered the intention from the recitals did not violate this supposed rule, because the recitals were evidence of antecedent agreements. Mr. Ronan further contended that no inference of the intention of the parties could be drawn from the words "in tail," because as those words occurred in the operative part of the deed they could afford no evidence of an inention to confer any larger estate than they actually gave by the rules of law.

The usual object of the parties to a marriage settlement is to provide that the settled property shall ultimately devolve upon the issue of the marriage. By the express terms of this settlement a power was given to the plaintiff's father by which –

if he had executed it – he could have bestowed on her the fee-simple of these lands. Because he did not execute this power, it is said that, as the settlement omits the usual words of inheritance and only uses the words "in tail," we are to shut our eyes to the obvious import of what those words imply. To my mind it would be painful to be driven by any technical rule to such a conclusion. In interpreting the language used for the purpose of ascertaining the intention of the parties, as distinct from the construction of the deed, I can see no supreme difference between the different parts of the document. The powers of leasing and of sale were rightly relied on by the respondent's counsel. No doubt they coincide with the view that it was intended that the plaintiff should take more than a life estate. But I put all these matters aside as insignificant beside the words "in tail." I find in them a plain indication of the intention of the parties, so strong that I do not feel at liberty to disregard it. The cases cited by the Master of the Rolls and in the course of the argument before us show that there is ample authority for the conclusion at which I have arrived. I regard this case as one in which I should do violence to the obvious meaning of the parties if I refused the relief asked for by the plaintiff.

In my opinion, the decision of the Master of the Rolls is right, and should be affirmed with costs.

FitzGibbon, L.J.:

I am duly deferential to the venerable authorities which have been cited. I absolutely accept, as a rule of law resting upon foundations which it would be sacrilegious to shake, that, apart from the Conveyancing Act, no deed can create an estate tail without the words "heirs of the body," or equivalent words of procreation. Further, I think that the language of the Conveyancing Act plainly shows that a deed previously executed, which contained words which the Act made sufficient to create an estate tail, had not the effect which the Act gave for the first time to those words. The restriction of the Act to deeds executed after its passing prohibits its application to any earlier instrument. This deed, therefore, as it stands, does not give an estate tail to the plaintiff, and the only open question is – Can it be rectified?

In my opinion it can – on clear and recognized rules of equity. The opposition to rectification rests upon an endeavour to restrict those rules in a manner not warranted by authority. The intention of the parties here may be gathered from – (1) the fact that this is a marriage settlement, the object of which is to provide for the issue of the marriage; (2) the use in the *habendum* of the words "in tail"; (3) other provisions in the settlement which indicate that, in the events which have happened, the plaintiff was intended to take more than a life estate. The use of the words "in tail" in the *habendum* proves the intention – in *fact* – of the parties that, in the events which have happened, the estate should pass to the only child of the marriage. The fact that the draftsman blundered by using popular language incapable of conferring the estate cannot obscure the evidence of the intention, though – if we cannot recitfy the deed – it may defeat the object of the instrument. It is admitted that if the intention had been declared in a recital, the omission of effective words of limitation from the operative part, or the use of wrong words therein, could be cured in the case of a marriage contract, or other contract for value.

The contention that words occurring in the *habendum* are not evidence of the same intention which they would evidence if they were in a recital, has no intelligible foundation, and would limit the jurisdiction of equity to rectify deeds to cases where the blunder took the form of a contradiction between a recital and the *habendum*. For this restriction there is no authority. But here we also have the additional evidence of intention supplied by the marriage consideration, and by the other provisions to which I have referred. This supplies a technical answer to the appellant's contention as satisfactory as the substantial one which the *habendum* establishes beyond doubt.

In rectifying this deed, the Master of the Rolls has, in my opinion, expressed a jurisdiction to rectify mistakes which Courts of Equity have possessed from the earliest times, and which was exercised, under circumstances peculiarly like the present, by Lord Sugden in *Averall* v. *Wade* Ll. & G. temp. Sug. 252.

It is conceded that an order in the form which he has adopted is now the recognised mode of rectification, and that it is equivalent to an actual alteration of the deed.

Walker, L.J.:

I concur. I think the Court might well feel ashamed if it could not grant the relief sought. The venerable authorities citied by Mr. Ronan establish beyond all doubt what is the legal construction of this deed. But these authorities are not what we have to consider. They supply the reason why the plaintiff's advisers resorted to this action, which is brought not to construe but to rectify the deed. The parties here have said that the only child of the marriage – the plaintiff – shall take "in tail," though the unhappy draftsman has failed to carry out their object by the terms he has used. Hence it is to the Court of Equity in which deeds are rectified that the plaintiff comes for help to remedy the draftsman's blunder.

In looking for the intention of the parties it is a powerful consideration that we are dealing with a marriage settlement, because the object of such a deed is to provide for the issue of the marriage, not to give merely a life estate to the children or an only child. Again, the estate which is given back to the settlor here is expressly limited to her "in default of issue" of the marriage. But powerful as these considerations are in gathering the intention of the parties to the deed, they fade to almost nothing beside the words in the *habendum*. If these words had occurred in a recital, it is not disputed that they would have been enough to correct a blunder in the operative part of the deed. I am unable to see why they should be less potent in the *habendum* than in a recital.

On these grounds I should be quite prepared, apart from authority, to rectify this deed by introducing words of limitation. But I find that a similar course was taken in *Bird's Trusts* 3 Ch. D. 214, a decision of which I entirely approve.

Holmes, L.J.:

The jurisdiction of the Court of Chancery to rectify a deed or other instrument, for the purpose of correcting a material mistake and making it conform to the intention or contract of the parties, has been applied in this case by the Master of the Rolls to what is, perhaps, a new state of circumstances; but I think that it has not been extended beyond its legal and logical limits. The principle of rectification is, I think, in its strict sense only applicable, except under exceptional circumstances, to cases where there is valuable consideration and mutual mistake. Where mistake is shown in a voluntary deed, the appropriate remedy at least in most cases is for the grantor or settlor to have it set aside; and the mistake of one of the parties to a contract for valuable consideration is a ground for rescission, although the other party may be offered rectification as an alternative. Where, however, it is shown that a deed executed in pursuance of and for the purpose of carrying out a contract for valuable consideration fails in any substantial particular to do so, a party to it or a person within its consideration is entitled to have it brought into conformity with the contract; provided that subsequent rights and interests acquired in good faith by outsiders would not be prejudiced thereby. Mere lapse of time is not in itself an answer to an action for rectification, although it may make it more difficult to prove mutual mistake. I take an illustration from the most common and usual kind of deed – a conveyance carrying out the purchase of lands. This is generally preceded by either a formal contract in writing, or the agreement can be ascertained from documentary evidence. Now, if by ignorance, or inadvertence, where the vendor has contracted to sell an estate in fee-simple, the lands are granted to the purchaser and his assigns, without any words of inheritance, the deed would be rectified upon proof of the true agreement and intention of the parties. Even if the mistake were discovered after the deaths of the grantor and grantee by the heir or devisee of the latter, it would not be too late for him to apply for relief. It may be, however, that there is no evidence of a written contract before the deed, and no account can be given of the transaction beyond a recital in the conveyance that the grantor has agreed in consideration of a certain sum then paid to grant the lands for an estate in fee-simple to the grantee. In this instance I should think that rectification would be as much a matter of course as in the other. But there may be yet a third case. By deed, executed before the Conveyancing Act, without a recital or any other evidence of the contract beyond the instrument itself, A B, in consideration of a large sum of money, grants lands to C D to hold for an estate in fee-simple. Would this be a case for rectification? Mr. Ronan would say no. The Master of the Rolls would, I think, be of opinion that it was, and I can see no good reason to the contrary. In this instance, just as clearly as in the two others, the contract and intention of the parties are shown. The only argument the other way is that by a rule of law a grant in the words suggested must be construed as giving a life estate only, and that the Court is not at liberty to infer from them any other intention. But to hold this would, I think, be to confuse two things that are distinct. By the rule of law the words "for an estate in fee-simple," are not sufficient to convey an estate of inheritance, but why can they not be referred to for the purpose of seeing what was intended ?

I admit that if I am wrong in what I have said, I should be obliged to allow this appeal. We are here dealing with a marriage settlement, without knowing anything of the negotiations that preceded it. The instrument is one by which estates tail are frequently created; and therefore it does not violate probability to find an intention to give such an estate. But this does not bring one very far, for estates for life and estates in fee-simple are often given by a marriage settlement. There is, however, no difficulty in ascertaining the intention; for it is declared in the clearest language in the deed itself. The words "in tail" as applied to an estate are not merely a legal term of art but are familiar to educated men. When a man says that he is granting lands to a grantee in tail, it must be assumed that he is not intending to convey an estate for life or an estate in fee-simple, but the estate usually described in those terms. If those words were not there, I should be unable to infer the intention from any other parts of the deed; but with them, I am left in no doubt as to what were the contract and intention of the parties, and that such intention was not carried out by mistake arising from ignorance or carelessness. I am of opinion that, under these circumstances, the deed ought to be rectified.

Notes

See further *Irish Land Law,* paras. 3.164 and 4.033.

KING V. KING-HARMAN

(1873) I.R. 7 Eq. 446 (Rolls Court)

The facts are set out in the judgment.

Sullivan M.R. :

The bill in this case was filed by Lady Blanche Sybil King by her mother and next friend, the Hon. Augusta Dowager Countess of Kingston, to have the settlement executed on the marriage of her father and mother, and dated the 15th of July, 1854, reformed. The facts of the case on which the bill is rested are as follow :– On the 15th of July, 1854, a marriage took place between the Hon. Robert Edward King, afterwards seventh Earl of Kingston, and the Hon. Augusta Chichester. It appears that at that time, Viscount Lorton and the Hon. Robert King, the father of the Hon. Robert Edward King, had power to limit a considerable portion of the Lorton estates to such uses as they should think proper; and accordingly a settlement was executed on the 15th of July, 1854, between Viscount Lorton of the first part, the Hon. Robert King, his eldest son, of the second part, the Hon. Robert Edward King, the eldest son of the said Robert King, of the third part, the Hon. Augusta Chichester, of the fourth part, and certain other persons named as trustees therein, by which settlement the Lorton estates were settled in the manner which I shall now describe. The settlement recited that upon the treaty for the marriage it was agreed, in order to make a suitable provision for the intended wife and the issue of the intended marriage, that the Lorton estates should be settled in the manner thereinafter mentioned, and it proceeds, in consideration of the intended marriage and of £5000 the fortune of the Hon. Augusta Chichester, to convey the estates to the use of trustees for a term of years to secure an annuity of £1000 to Robert Edward King during the joint lives of his father and grandfather; and in case of the death of either of them an increased anuity of £2250 during the joint lives of himself and the survivor of them; and, subject to that annuity, to trustees for a term of one hundred years; and, subject thereto, to the use of Lord Lorton for life, with remainder to his eldest son for life, with remainder to Robert Edward King for life, and after his death to the use that the said Augusta Chichester, in case she should survive him, should receive the jointure therein mentioned; and, subject thereto, to a third set of trustees for 500 years; and subject thereto, to the use of the first son of Robert Edward King and of the said Augusta Chichester, and the heirs male of the body of that son; with successive remainders to each of the sons of Robert E. King and Augusta Chichester in tail male; with remainder to the use of the sons of Robert Edward King by any after-taken wife in tail male in succession; and in default of such issue to the use of Laurence Harman King-Harman, second son of Viscount Lorton, for life; with remainder to Edward Robert King-Harman, his eldest son, for life, and after his death to the use of the first son of E.R. K.-Harman, and the heirs male of his body; with further remainders over, and an ultimate limitation to Lord Lorton in fee. The settlement then proceeds to declare the trusts of the third term of 500 years, by which it was intended that portions for the younger children of the marriage should be secured, as follows:– "in case there should be issue of the intended marriage an eldest or only son, and also one or more other child or children," then the trustees, &c., should, on the decease of the said Robert Edward King, but subject and without prejudice to the jointure thereinbefore provided for the said Augusta Chichester, by sale or mortgage, &c., raise such sum or sums of money for the portion or portions of the said younger child or children as thereinafter mentioned, that is to say, "in case there shall be but one younger child of said intended marriage, the sum of £5000 for the portion of such younger child, to be paid and payable to and to become a vested interest in such younger child, at such time and in such manner, after the death of the said Viscount Lorton and Robert King, as the said Robert Edward King shall by any deed or instrument under his hand direct or appoint; and in default of such direction or appointment to vest in such younger child, being a son, at twenty-one years, or being a daughter, at her age of twenty-one years or day of marriage, whichever shall first happen;" and in case there should be two children of the said intended marriage, and no more, other than and besides and eldest or only son, then the sum of £10,000 for the portions of such two younger children; and in case there should be three or more children of the said intended marriage, other than and besides an eldest or only son, then the sum of £15,000 for the portions of such three or more younger children. After giving directions in reference to those portions as to maintenance and other matters, the settlement proceeds to declare the trusts as to the fortune of the Hon. Augusta Chichester, which was to be applied by the trustees "either towards payment of any of the charges or incumbrances mentioned in the schedule thereto," which were charges affecting the Lorton estates, "or towards payment of the portions thereby provided for the younger children of the intended marriage;" with a provision that, until the principal was so disposed of, the dividends might be applied towards pin-money for the Hon. Augusta Chichester, and that the residue should go to the Hon. Robert Edward King for his life, and, after his death, that the whole of the dividends should be applied towards payment of the interest which should from time to time become due on the said incumbrances specified in the schedule. Then follows a provision that, in the event of Robert Edward King becoming entitled to the Mitchelstown estate, which then stood limited to him in remainder, he should do and execute all such acts and deeds as should be necessary for effectually charging all the lands and premises, to which he should become entitled, with an additional jointure for his wife and to increase the portions thereinbefore provided for the younger children of the intended marriage; that is to say, "in case there should be only one younger child of the said intended marriage, then to the sum of £10,000; and in case there should be two younger children and no more, then to the sum of £20,000; and in case there should be three or more younger children, then to the sum of £30,000, with all and such or the like powers as are hereinbefore limited with respect to the portions hereby provided."

The marriage took place, and on the 19th of November, 1854, the then Lord Lorton died, and was succeeded by the Hon. Robert King, who became Viscount Lorton. The bill then proceeds to state the effect of a deed of the 10th of August, 1869, by which a certain term of 500 years was created out of the Mitchelstown estate, in trust to raise the sum of £120,000 for the benefit of Robert Edward King. James, the 5th Earl of Kingston, died without issue, on the 9th of September, 1869, and he was succeeded by Robert Lord Lorton, who became 6th Earl of Kingston. That Robert died on the 16th of October, 1869, and Robert Edward King, who was married to Augusta Chichester, thereupon became 7th Earl of Kingston, and, under the limitations of the settlement which I have read, entitled to an estate for life in the Lorton estates. He was also, as I mentioned, the owner of the charge of £120,000 on the Mitchelstown estates. This Robert Edward King, the 7th Earl of Kingston, died on the 21st of June, 1871, leaving the Plaintiff the only surviving issue of his marriage with the Hon. Augusta Chichester; and, on his death without male issue, Laurence Harman King-Harman became entitled to the Lorton estates for life, with remainder to Robert Edward King-Harman, his eldest son, for life, with remainder to the first and other son of R.E.K.-Harman successively in tail male. Under the will of Robert Edward, 7th Earl of Kingston, dated the 14th of June, 1871, the Plaintiff Lady Blanche Sybil King will, at all events after her mother's death, be entitled to an apparently large fortune, the precise value of which is not before me, but is stated to amount to a very large sum. The result of the settlement which I have read, having regard to the contingencies that have happened, is quite apparent, viz., that the only daughter of the marriage of 1854 is unprovided for under the limitations of that deed; and the case of Lady Blanche Sybil King, is that the settlement has been the result of a common mistake made by the two contracting parties in 1854, in relation to the trusts of the term of 500 years, which only provides portions for the younger children of the marriage in case there shall be an eldest or only son. It is said, on behalf of Lady Blanche Sybil King, that the true contract, entered into between her father and mother, was that the portions should not be made dependent on the fact of there being an eldest or only son born, but that they should be raisable whether a son was born or not – in other words, that daughters, or a daughter, were intended to be the objects of the settlement and entitled to portions. Now, that is a very plausible and intelligible case, and undoubtedly it is very difficult to conceive how a marriage contract, dealing with estates of this description, and contemplating the birth of issue of the marriage then intended, should have excluded an only daughter, or more daughters than one, if there happened to be no son, more particularly when the ultimate limitation of the estates was not to the father, but was made to collaterals, and the daughters themselves were excluded from all the limitations of the estates.

The fact that Lady Blanche Sybil King will have property, either in her own right or through her father's will outside the settlement cannot, I think, affect the question raised here. The case must be disposed of independently of that circumstance, particularly as it does not appear that it was ever contemplated, when the marrige contract was entered into, that a daughter or daughters would have any provision outside the settlement then intended to be made. In aid of the case made by the Plaintiff, her counsel have called attention to this remarkable circumstance, that the settlement recites on the face of it that it was made in order to have a suitable provision made for the wife of the marriage then contemplated and also for the issue of the marriage; and in addition they rely on the ante-nuptial contract in writing for the settlement, the original of which has been produced and laid before me. That document is of the greatest moment to the case made by the bill, as constituting the undoubted contract of both parties at a period before the marriage and the execution of the settlement. It is called "Heads of settlement to be executed on the intended marrige of R.E. King, Esq., with the Hon. Augusta Chichester," and is as follows:–

"Estates to be settled subject to the life estate of Lord Lorton, and to all existing incumbrances, with like powers of sale for payment of the principal of such incumbrances, as are in last family settlement of 3rd January, 1850, and subject thereto the use of the Hon. Robert King for life; remainder to the first and other sons of the now intended marriage; remainder the the issue male of Mr. R.E. King by any after-taken wife, in the event of his surviving Miss Chichester; remainder to the Hon. King-Harman, and his first and other sons, with like remainders as are in the said settlement of the 3rd of January, 1850." Now so far as I have read, the settlement of 1854 is in strict conformity with those heads of settlement. After stating what was to be the present provision for Robert Edward King, which I have already mentioned as contained in the setttlement, and providing for the jointure of the intended wife, this document proceeds in these words:– "Portions for the younger children £5000 in the event of there being only one younger child; £10,000 in the event of there being two younger children, and £15,000 in the event of there being three or more." Then it provides for the disposition of the wife's fortune, and it contains a clause as to increasing the portions for younger children, if the Mitchelstown estates fell into possession, up to £10,000, £20,000 or £30,000 respectively.

It is contended on behalf of the Plaintiff that these heads of settlement, according to their legal construction, would have been carried out in such a way as to provide portions for an only daughter, or for two or three or more daughters; and I entirely agree with that view, and entertain no doubt that if these heads of settlement had been properly carried out according to their legal construction, the settlement should have provided for daughters, even though no son was ever born. Now there is no doubt that this settlement does not carry out that view, because it is clear and distinct in its operative part, that the only children who are to get portions under its provisions are children who should be in existence other than and besides an elder or only son; and the question now arises, have I sufficient materials before me to make the settlement conformable to the true meaning of the articles entered into before the marriage was solemnized and this settlement existed? In consequence of the death of many of the parties surrounding this contract the case is destitute of much evidence, but we have the benefit of the evidence of Lady Blanche Sybil King's mother, the effect of which is that the paper called "Heads of Settlement" was the marriage contract, and that, up to the time the settlement was executed, there was none other. I have before me the draft of the settlement, as revised by counsel, before it was engrossed, and the affidavit of the counsel who revised that draft. That affidavit throws little light as to what was the view that was taken by him of that portion of the document called "Heads of Settlement," which is conversant with the younger children's portions; and that fact impressed me much during the hearing of the cause, because there is not in that affidavit any assertion or statement that a mistake had been committed in carrying out these heads of settlement, or otherwise. But this, I think, is to be gathered from the affidavit – meagre as it is – that the attention of counsel was particularly directed only to that part of the settlement that secured the Lorton estates in the line that would make them go in accordance with, and in analogy to, the settlement of 1850, the last settlement of these estates. The present tenant in tail of Lorton estates, affected by the reformation of this settlment to the extent of £5000, is a minor. The present tenants for life of the Lorton estates are adult and do not dispute the Plaintiff's right to relief, they believing that the settlement has miscarried in the very point alleged by the Plaintiff. The counsel for the minor, the tenant in tail, have done their duty by him most properly, and they have argued with great ability that there are not sufficient materials before me for reforming the settlement by charging £5000 on the estates for the Plaintiff. The view presented on behalf of the minor, tenant in tail, is, that the settlement not reciting the marriage contract or not purporting to be made in pursuance of it, even though it departs from the ante-nuptial contract, may have resulted from some other arrangement made between the drawing up of the "Heads of Settlement" and the execution of the settlement itself; and it is argued that the operative part of this settlement is clear and unambiguous, and that it cannot be controlled by any recital.

The latter proposition in the abstract is true. If the operative part of a deed is clear and unambiguous, you cannot put a different construction on it by reason of a recital; and it is by no means necessary for the Plaintiff to contravene that proposition. It is also no doubt true that there is no express reference in the settlement to the ante-nuptial contract as an existing document. But it appears to me, after having given all these arguments due consideration, that it is impossible in this case to separate or disconnect the settlement which was executed, and which, on the face of it, purports to be made in order to have a provision for *the issue* of the marriage, from these "Heads of Settlement" which preceded it, and that there is in the settlement itself, coupled with the evidence, sufficient to show that the contract, which the heads of settlement import as to younger children's portions, continued, unaltered and in full force, down to the moment when the settlement was executed. Accordingly, I have come to the conclusion, aided by the authorities to which I shall refer, that the trust of this deed ought to be reformed, so as to entitle the only daughter of the marriage to her portion. Against the evidence of the then Augusta Chichester, who afterwards became Countess of Kingston, there really is none. This, therefore, is not a case of conflicting evidence. To reform a settlement, the evidence of one party against another resisting would be totally insufficient, as the mistake must be shown to have been a *mutual* mistake. The law as to the reformation of settlements is, I think, stated with great accuracy in the case of *Fowler* v. *Folwer* 4 De G. & J. 264, where the Lord Chancellor says:–

"The power which the Court possesses of reforming written agreements where there has been an omission or insertion of stipulations contrary to the intention of the parties and under a mutual mistake, is one which had been frequently and most usefully exercised. But it is also one which should be used with extreme care and caution. To substitute a new agreement for one to which the parties have deliberately subscribed ought only to be permitted upon evidence of a different intention of the clearest and most satisfactory description."

He then quotes the language of Lord Thurlow in *Lady Shelburne* v. *Lord Inchiquin* 1 Br. C.C. 341, and says (p.265):–

"It is clear that a person who seeks to rectify a deed, upon the ground of mistake, must be required to establish, in the clearest and most satisfactory manner, that the alleged intention to which he desires it to be made conformable continued concurrently in the minds of all parties down to the time of its execution, and also must be able to show exactly and precisely the form to which the deed ought to be brought. For there is a material difference between setting aside an instrument and rectifying it on the ground of mistake. In the latter case, you can only rely upon the mutual and concurrent intention of all parties for whom the Court is actually making a new written agreement."

My opinion in this case is, that I have satisfactory evidence that there was a mutual and concurrent intention, down to the execution of the settlement, that the issue of the marriage should be provided for. I have a document prepared with the consent of both contract parties, which, if it had been followed, would have provided for an only daughter – "younger child" having been frequently construed to mean a child not entitled to the settled estates. In this case there is every reason for putting that construction on the contract. The settlement itself recites that it was intended to provide for the issue of the marriage; the mother's fortune was taken away and applied to purposes of the estates from all limitations of which the female issues are excluded; and the affidavit of the Plaintiff's mother proves in substance that there was but the one agreement, viz., the "Heads of Settlement." I think that *Bold* v. *Hutchinson* 5 De G. M. & G. 568 is an authority expressly warranting me in holding that there are satisfactory grounds for reforming this settlement. *Bold* v. *Hutchinson* is a case of the highest authority. It is a decision of Lord Cranworth after taking time to examine all the authorities bearing upon the point before him. At p. 568 of the report, Lord Cranworth says:–

"The doctrine now is, that when a settlement purports to be in pursuance of articles entered into before marriage and there is any variance, there no evidence is necessary in order to have the settlement corrected; and although the settlement contains no reference to the articles, yet if it can be shown that the settlement was intended to be in conformity with the articles, yet if there is clear and satisfactory evidence showing that the discrepancy had arisen from a mistake, the Court will reform the settlement and make it conformable to the real intention of the parties."

And in p. 569:–

"In these and other cases referred to by Lord St. Leonards, the settlements were rectified and the later authorities have put the matter upon the true footing, i.e., that if it is perfectly palpable that there has been a mistake on which the settlement has been made, the Court will admit evidence to correct it. The question before me is, whether I am satisfied that the settlement here has been made in error. I think in this case it is put beyond all doubt. The agreement was written out by the son, in the shape of articles which were shown to Sir W. Hutchinson, his father, and approved by him. It was argued, that they were only Mr. Bold's instructions, but there was no attempt on the part of Sir W. Hutchinson to alter them after they were submitted to him. On the whole, I am clearly of opinion that the settlement was framed in error. I do not, however think that this is a legitimate deduction from the settlement itself; and if the Master of the Rolls was of that opinion, I disagree with him; but I am not satisfied that such was his opinion."

The case of *Murray* v. *Parker* 19 Beav. 305 proceeded before Sir John Romilly and was rested upon similar views.

In the case before me, I could not, from the settlement itself, as Lord Cranworth says, draw a legitimate deduction that it has been framed in error; but having regard to the written ante-nuptial contract and the evidence in the case, I can, I think, safely come to the conclusion that the settlement has been framed in error in respect of the matter contended for by the Plaintiff.

Note
See further *Irish Land Law,* para. 3.164.

NOLAN V. GRAVES
[1946] I.R. 376; 81 I.L.T.R. 9 (High Court)

The facts are set out in the judgment.

Haugh J.:
This is an action brought by the plaintiff, Mrs. Anne Nolan, against the defendants, Mr. Willoughby Hamilton, who carries on business as an auctioneer in this city, and Mr. Allen Percival Graves, of Kilcroney, Wicklow, who was the purported vendor in the series of transactions that took place at Mr. Hamilton's premises on 20th of January last.

It is a highly unusual action and one of a most surprising nature.

[His Lordship dealt with the pleadings and then proceeded as follows:–]

Now, the closing of these pleadings certainly raised a very net issue of fact, and only one issue of fact, and that issue is:– was the sum at which the premises were knocked down to the plaintiff as a result of her last offer £4,500, or £1,000 more – namely, £5,500?

In support of her claim, the plaintiff in evidence gave her account of the events preceding the 20th of January, when she first became interested in this auction – at least, in lot four of this auction. She gave evidence of some meetings she had with Mr. Hamilton, the auctioneer, and of her inspection of the premises offered for sale, and of her attendance at the auction. She gave a detailed account of her version of the events that led up to the signing of this memorandum, and her version of what happened in the office that evening after the signing, and of some other matters that arose on the next day. In particular, she produced this memorandum of agreement, subjoined to the conditions of sale in the ordinary way, and that was her case.

Now, at an early stage of the cross-examination of the plaintiff, counsel sought to put a question to her suggestive of the answer that she was either mistaken or deliberately stating something she knew not to be true when she said that the final bid was £4,550. Her counsel objected to that question, or any question of that nature, being put to her, on the grounds, shortly, that there was, between the parties to the action, a contract in writing which represented the true intention between the parties as to what took place at the auction, and that this contract having been produced by her, containing a recital that she was declared the purchaser at the price of £4,550, such questions were not admissible, because they tended to be at least the basis of an attempt to introduce parol evidence to vary substantially the terms of that memorandum.

At that stage, beyond stating the general nature of the objection, the lengthy arguments which I heard in the matter afterwards, were not gone into, as I disallowed the objection, but without prejudice to hearing the whole matter afresh in detail later.

Accordingly, these questions were allowed to be put, and the lady reasserted her account as regards the price of £4,550 and vigorously denied any suggestions to the contrary. On her evidence, there was no room for doubt; there was no ground for saying that there was a mistake as far as she was concerned; that is, a mistake through faulty hearing or faulty observation, or through any misstatements or through any want of clarity on the part of the auctioneer, or for any other reason. After that cross-examination alone, it was quite clear that no mistake had been made on her part, and that I could not entertain the view (on her evidence) that she was anything but crystal-clear and had a perfect and detailed recollection (I do not think I misstate it when I say perfect recollection) of the bidding and of the price that she bid for these premises at the auction on that day. There the case for the plaintiff closed, and there is not the slightest doubt that if the case had to stand there, and, that if she had asked for it, she would have been entitled to specific performance of this agreement at the sum of £4,550; and that she was clearly entitled to the return of the sum of £1,365 paid by her to the defendant, Mr. Hamilton, because the evidence was all the one way. Not only was the evidence all the one way, but she had possession of the memorandum signed on the auctioneers' premises, with their names set out as agents for the vendor, and signed by the vendor's solicitor-agent (Mr. Richardson), and signed by her, reciting in most unambiguous terms that she was the purchaser at the public auction at the price of £4,550.

Well, at that stage, the defendants went into evidence. I do not propose to deal in any detail with the evidence at this stage. The first witness was the vendor, Mr. Graves, and he narrated the circumstances leading up to the sale of these four lots (his property) at this auction. He referred to certain introductory matters that took place between himself, his solicitor, and his auctioneer on that morning and how he took up his position there through curiosity (and, I think, a perfectly understandable curiosity), outside the saleroom, with a telephone, if necessary, to hear the bidding. And he was about to give his version of what he heard at the auction as regards bidding and the final price, when, logically and consistently with the first objection to the plaintiff's cross-examination on the topic, her counsel objected to such evidence by him or by any other witness called on behalf of either of the defendants – any evidence whatsoever that purported to contradict the evidence-in-chief given by the plaintiff, that is, any evidence to show that the price was other than £4,550. Well, I, in the same way, allowed that evidence (Mr. Campbell was not here, I think at the time) by again making it clear that I took it *de bene esse,* and I took it without prejudice, believing that, if I could not entertain such evidence after it was given, it was quite clear the defendants must lose on every ground and that the plaintiff must succeed on all grounds. The objection at that stage (to put it generally) was made on the ground that it was only in certain exceptional cases that parol evidence can be admitted to vary the terms of a written contract, and that although mistake, or even conduct amounting to fraud, may have been imputed to the plaintiff, yet that as she was not endeavouring to force her price on the defendant-vendor (that is, that she was not making him suffer for any mistake that may have been made by his agent), such evidence was not admissible.

At a later stage counsel suggested that even on the pleadings in that case, fraud was not pleaded with that particularly that a plea of fraud, or a plea of conduct amounting to fraud, requires. He also relied on the fact that, as she was not seeking specific performance at the lower price against the defendant, and merely sought rescission and the return of the deposit and the auctioneer's fees, and, further, that as it was in the nature of what might be called an executory contract, and was only preliminary to the actual conveyance, no irreparable damage could be done to either party, as the premises had not passed from Mr. Graves to her. It was argued that on these grounds such evidence should not be admitted, and that accordingly I was entitled to look only at the written contract, and that, (as Dr. Baker put it), she in fact only gave her evidence in detail about bidding, in anticipation of contradictory evidence being called by the defendants and in anticipation that I should hear such evidence and then be called upon to weigh both sides.

Logically and consistently, her counsel say that, for any reason, it was not necessary for her to go into evidence of the sale with any particularity at all, beyond stating that she was the purchaser at that price and that there was an agreement apparently signed on behalf of both parties. They do admit that if she had sought to enforce the lower price on the defendants and that if she was a plaintiff for specific performance, by reason of the pleadings (even with a plea of mutual mistake and no allegation of conduct amounting to fraud against her), then, in such circumstances, the Court might hear such evidence on behalf of defendants resisting such a claim. But that was not this case. Counsel for both defendants urged me to hear this evidence. I heard many cases on the topic, and having listened to them. I look on this branch of the case shortly as follows:– The pleadings have raised, as I have said, one issue of fact only, and a very simple one in the sense that it is capable of very easy appreciation: what was the price. If the plaintiff is correct in what she says as regards the price, she must, of course, win. Accordingly, if she (through her counsel) is correct in saying that I cannot hear any evidence on the matter to contradict her, my hands are naturally tied, inasmuch as I cannot try the issues raised by the pleadings in this action, and again she must win.

I think it was Dr. Baker, who, in closing (again logically and consistently), admitted that on the view urged on her behalf, he was entitled to come to this Court on his case and on his facts, in a summary manner, on affidavit sworn by her (and a very bare affidavit at that) exhibiting the memorandum and ask for judgment, and that if, in answer to such summary application, the defendant vendor sought to put in an affidavit alleging matters that were later sworn to here, I would not be permitted to look at such affidavit for the same reasons, and that in law, in such summary way, she would be entitled to the relief she has claimed; or, if it had not been done by affidavit, but if a statement of claim and a defence were entered (as in this case), it would also have been within the rights of the plaintiff to come here by way of motion to short-circuit all these proceedings and save a lot of expense and to have both defences struck out on the ground that they disclosed no answer whatever in law to her claim. That would seem to me to be what follows logically from the stand that has been taken.

However, I have come to the conclusion – and I reached that conclusion at an early stage – that, on the issues that have been raised for me to try in this case, and because of the matters alleged against the plaintiff, in order to know what the contract was between the parties, I am entitled to hear parol evidence, in common with a great many other cases in which such evidence was heard; that the evidence was properly admissible, and that it was relevant, and solely relevant, to the one issue I have got to try, and that I am bound in fact to listen to it.

But having said that, I would like to say this with emphasis: the fact that the plaintiff has in her possession this written memorandum (which, on its face, purports to be an agreed record of the transaction that took place at the public auction, made within some minutes of the event, and properly ratified by the vendor's agents and by herself), almost goes the whole way with her in her case, and the defendants, having made the case they have made, have undertaken a very onerous burden. What I want to emphasise is this: after listening to the evidence, I do not think that on its conclusion I am entitled in the ordinary way to go in for what I might call weighing the probabilities, and saying, in the ordinary way, where the balance of probabilities lies. If the defendants only succeeded in proving that she was probably incorrect, mistaken, or lying in her evidence, in my view that would be far short of the onus upon them after she has produced this written and signed contract. I think the burden of proof on the defendants is so heavy that any such evidence must be oppressive in its weight against her – it must be utterly conclusive. I think the onus on the defendants is to prove that that written record is not a true record of what took place at the auction. They must satisfy me beyond all reasonable doubt that what they say is true on oral evidence, and until they have so satisfied me, on consideration of that evidence, I would reject such evidence and hold that they have not discharged the onus which they have elected to put upon themselves.

[His Lordship then examined the evidence in detail.]

Accordingly, the conclusion I have come to with regard to the contract – the offer and acceptance – was that there was a bidding that had begun around £3,500; that it proceeded, roughly, by increases of £250; that it reached £5,000; thereafter the bidding became slower; that it increased by hundreds and by fifties until it reached the sum of £5,500. That figure was repeated over and over again with monotonous repetition, as stated by some of the witnesses, by Mr. Hamilton, clearly and audibly, and Mrs. Nolan plainly intended to bid that as her offer, or as her acceptance, or at least as her offer to the auctioneers, which, at the fall of the hammer, Mr. Hamilton (for Mr. Graves) accepted. I am further satisfied that she well knew, and at all times knew, that she had offered the sum of £5,500 for these premises, and that she sat with Mr. Houlihan for some minutes, discussing with him her purchase, and that they both knew that the final bid was £5,500 when she and Mr. Houlihan were consulting as to what each individual house had cost her, having regard to the payment of the auctioneer's fees and to the legal costs; and I am abundantly satisifed that at the conclusion of the rapid calculation made by Mr. Houlihan (a solicitor and an experienced buyer) he said, "You have got a good bargain at £1,000 each house": and that (as she admits) he referred to his own purchase of a property in Sandymount, a similar class of houses, with similar rents, which he purchased at £1,150 each. She accepts that conversation, but I am satisifed that she knowingly mistates the figure stated by Mr. Houlihan to be £800. I accept him in his version of that conversation and I reject what she has sworn.

I have come to the conclusion very definitely that this lady went to the table with the intention of signing, particularly after her conversation with Mr. Houlihan – that she went to the table with the intention (begotten of experience) to sign a contract binding upon her and binding upon the auctioneers, for a sale for £5,500; that she saw this mistake; that she realised its importance to her should she ever succeed in upholding it, or making it permanent in its effect; that she, in my view, knowingly and immediately decided to take such advantage of it as, in her lay mind, she might think she was entitled to take.

For these reasons, I have viewed with some suspicion, and still do, the real intention that lay behind her acts when she asked Mr. Richardson to prepare this pink slip that contained more than the auctioneer's fees, because it contained the purchase price in detail and it also contained the amount of the deposit. Again to her lay mind (as against the mind of a person trained in law), it appeared that there would have been some advantage to her to have another permanent record, written by Mr. Richardson in reference to these important matters, which she could permanently have and which she certainly had in her possession up to the hearing of this action.

Now, normally I would be inclined to accept her account that she usually, or sometimes, hands her cheque-book to her creditors so that they may fill in the body of the cheque. That may happen. Perhaps there are some people who would do that. But I certainly view with some suspicion her immediate doing of that act in this case, because it seemed to me to be utterly unnecessary in the circumstances. My view is that the lady handed that cheque to Mr. Richardson because she had promptly realised the mistake made by Mr. Richardson in putting a figure of £1,000 too little, and that it seemed to her lay mind that some advantage would accrue to her by getting him to fill in the money; it was act three, to put it down a third time: on the memorandum, on the pink slip, and again on the cheque. In my view, on the facts of this case, an innocent and very careless mistake was made by the auctioneer's servants in the conduct of this sale. The plaintiff immediately realised that a mistake had been made and attempted to take an immediate advantage of it. She consistently followed it up on the next moring and she followed it up to some extent when she was in the hands of her solicitor until the time she asked for mere rescission instead of any other relief.

The jurisdiction of the Court as regards both rectification and specific performance is a delicate jurisdiction, and it is clear, from the mass of decisions cited before me, that it must be exercised with discretion and care. But before I embark upon it I feel I ought, in view of my findings of fact, to look upon the realities of the matters that I have now got to try in this counterclaim.

The view I take is that Mr. Graves lawfully and properly put up four lots of his properly for sale in Dublin that day. Mr Hamilton conducted himself properly as an auctioneer and conducted the bidding properly. The plaintiff, as a free agent, attended that auction. She had the opportunity of seeing these premises beforehand, and in fact did so that morning and discussed the matter with her Bank Manager, and she had funds to pay up to £5,550 and a considerable amount more – or at least she had a certain sum more at her disposal. She was in a position to talk to Mr. Houlihan, who seemed to be an expert on these matters, and she was in every sense a completely free agent to elect to do what she would like at that auction – not to bid at all or to bid as far as she wanted to. She had more experience than most people, men and women, in the buying and selling of houses. In my view she freely and voluntarily and willingly wanted pay £5,550 for these premises. I have no doubt that she heard the penultimate bid of £5,500 and made an extra bid of £50, which bid was accepted, and the property was knocked down to her at that price, and that she took advantage of this mistake deliberately for the purposes I have said. Incidentally, I might digress here for a moment and say that in considering this matter I ask myself, if this lady in fact wanted premises for £5,550, and they were what is called "a good buy" at that price, why would she not eventually agree to buy them at any price? I have answered that question at least to my own satisfaction. I believe that eventually when the controversy arose she said she never agreed to buy at the higher price, because, of course, if she did, it would be a most serious admission by herself against herself of her own misconduct and her own want of good faith; if, after the stand she had taken at the early stages through her solicitor, she eventually agreed to pay £5,550, of course it would be as good an admission as one could require of her dishonesty. My view is that she had to be consistent, although she was at the auction prepared to give £5,550 – she had to be consistent in the interest of her own reputation and in view of the charges impliedly made against her in the correspondence, and she could do nothing but adhere to the evidence she had given. However, as I have said, she took advantage of this error in this memorandum and the matter came to a head within a day or two. Mr. Graves had done everything, rightly and properly, as far as he was concerned and as far as he and the plaintiff were concerned. True it is that his agent, or one of his agents, acting for these parties made a careless mistake, and, of course, if that careless mistake in any way contributed to causing her to do anything to her prejudice, I, for one moment, would not let it weigh against her. Of course I do not take that view at all. My view is that the mistake contributed nothing to her misfortunes, because it immediately lay in her power, the moment she saw it, to say to Mr. Comyn, or whatever the name of the gentleman was: "You are mistaken there. That is wrong. It is down as £4,550; it should be £5,550. That is what I bid; ask Mr. Hamilton; ask any of the others." That was the remedy of a person dealing *bona fide* and honestly. I want to make that clear. I do not think this mistake was a cause over which she had no control in respect of the subsequent controversy or the present proceedings. She (and in fact at that time she alone) had that control, because, as I have said, she, of course knew what the right price was and, in a word, could have put Mr. Richardson right. Well, to that extent the mistake was caused by the vendor's agent, but it did not prejudice the lady in the slightest degree in that she could have had the whole thing straightened. What is the result of her refusal then to carry out her contract? The result is a completely abortive auction. Mr. Graves, who put up these premises for sale and who received a bid from her for the highest amount, still has his houses and has not got his money. He could have had the next bidder and would have had what was to him a satisfactory price – the reserve price of £5,500. That person is unidentified and may never be found, and, even if he could, he might change his mind. Mr Graves had the right, as soon as the contract was concluded, to sell at the price of £5,550 and if the plaintiff had refused to sign for £5,550, the auctioneer, as agent for both parties, could have signed, altogether against her will, a memorandum which would force her to buy from Mr. Graves at that price. His energies and the time and energies of the firm have all been wasted.

I do not know whether these premises will ever sell. They may. They may sell better. What I do know is that there was a perfectly concluded contract between the principals on that day and that one of them refused to perform it on grounds which, to my mind, are dishonest, unfounded, unreal and fabricated. So, in the light of these matters, as Mr. Graves said in the witness-box, he has always looked upon these premises as being properly sold, and he does not know what to do. He gets the rents into his hand, but does not regard himself as the owner and he wants the premises sold to her. I asked him what relief he seeks and he says he does not want rescission and simply wants her to be made conscientously to honour her bargain.

It was at this stage that certain important questions of law arose. At the close of the case, a long list of legal decisions, mostly English, were cited to me. I think I must at this stage, pay high tribute to the great zeal and learning of the junior counsel for the plaintiff, Dr. Baker, and I would like to recognise the industry and research he has shown in citing all these cases, in linking them together, and pointing out the conclusions that he submitted to me. He certainly earns the highest tribute from me for his great research and great reading. Well, I look upon this aspect of the case in this way: Mr. Graves is a man wronged and he ought at least to have the remedy to undo the wrong that has been done to him, i.e., the loss of the benefit of his auction. Secondly, even if he has not lost that; he has certainly lost the penultimate bid, through the misconduct of the plaintiff. That bid would have given him a satisfactory price, because it represented the reserve figure which had been previously fixed.

The question is, has Mr. Graves any remedy in law? The substance of the submissions made by the plaintiff is, No. Her counsel submits that even at the worst view of her evidence he has no redress other than rescission, by means of which the Court would undo the contract and leave all the parties in their former position. I cannot see that rescission in itself will afford Mr. Graves any remedy or redress for the wrong done to him. It is clear that he could have had that, on the plaintiff's submission, without ever coming into Court, or without ever making a counterclaim, by simply handing back her money and having another auction on some other day by Mr. Hamilton. I cannot and do not, from his point of view, regard rescission of the contract even at £4,550 without rectification, or by rectifying it to the higher figure and then rescinding it, as being a real remedy at all to the vendor, Mr. Graves, though plaintifff's counsel say that that is his only right.

A great number of cases have been cited, some of which conflict. The case of *Craddock Brothers* v. *Hunt* [1923] 2 Ch. 136 decided by the Court of Appeal in England and the case of the *United States of America* v. *Motor Trucks, Ltd.* [1924] A.C. 196 were cited by counsel for the defendants as establishing from their point of view, the principles upon which I should act. Now, these cases have been referred to over and over again; and Dr. Baker points out that in *Craddock's Case* [1923] 2 Ch. 136 the contract was an executed contract. It was a case in which the parties had gone into possession of the respective premises, portion of one of which was in dispute, and in which the persons who later became plaintiffs, actually received the rent of the yard in dispute for some years; and it was only when they sent out an architect for some building purpose who measured the yard and compared it with the parcels shown on the plaintiffs' deeds and plans and found that the plaintiffs, Craddock Brothers, had never, in fact, under their conveyance got this yard, that the defendant on his part for the first time realised that it was in the conveyance to him, and immediately and for the first time sought to take advantage of what he knew he never got at the sale. He took advantage of the actual conveveyance to him and refused any relief, by way of rectification or otherwise, to the plaintiffs who had paid for the yard in question. Dr. Baker, with some force, pointed out that that was a case in which, if the Court did not rectify the transaction the man who had bought and paid for the disputed plot could not get any other form of relief; and the defendant, who had got possession of the disputed plot, could have retained it, although he was dishonestly in possession of it, and dishonestly making claim to it, even though he knew at the auction that he never got it and only found he had got it when he examined his conveyance. The difference between that case and this case is that there is no similar conclusion between the parties. There has been no conveyance here; no parting by Mr. Graves with his houses to the plaintiff, Mrs. Nolan. At most there is only a contract made pursuant to the Statute of Frauds and in anticipation of the actual conveyance. For all one knows, this present contract might have broken down through some answers to the requisitions on title, as they sometimes do.

I see the difference between the altered position of the parties in *Craddock's Case* [1924] A.C. 196 against what I might call the unaltered position of the parties in this case. At p. 151 of the report, the Master of the Rolls said:– "I think I am at liberty, at any rate since the Judicature Act, 1873, to express my opinion that rectification can be granted of a written agreement on parol evidence of mutual mistake, although that agreement is complete in itself, and has been carried out by a more formal document based upon it." Well, in this case I have a written agreement complete in itself, the parties' names are there; it recites the auction, and contains all that it should. There is no ambiguity about the words; it recites clearly the purchase-price and the other figures based upon that purchase-price. The parol evidence is there, and Dr. Baker has pressed very strongly upon me to note that that case, and indeed most of the other cases, are decided on what is called mutual mistake or common mistake. It seems to me that, on his contention, the defendant, Mr. Graves, would be in a better position as regards the counter-claim if Mr. Nolan was only guilty of some mistake in common with Mr. Richardson leading to this incorrect memorandum being drawn – for instance, instead of seeing the figure £4,550, that she never looked at the figure at all, but signed her name to the memorandum and then sent up a cheque which was based on the wrong amount and went home. There you have a clear mistake on her part in signing the memorandum without reading it. Or at a later stage, if she sought to take advantage of what was a mistake on her part, it would seem to me, on the strict reading of the words "mutual mistake", Mr. Graves would be in a stronger position than in this case where I hold there was no mistake on her part, but a deliberate attempt to take advantage of a one-sided error. I cannot, in equity at least, see why he should be in any way weaker position by reason of the fact that her conduct is worse than that of making a mere mistake. Why should the principle stated by the Master of the Rolls in *Craddock's Case* [1923] 2 Ch. 136 which I have just quoted, not apply here? Lord Warrington, at p.159 of the report in *Craddock's Case* [1923] 2 Ch. 136 says, "The jurisdiction of Courts of Equity in this respect is to bring the written document executed in pursuance of an antecedent agreement into conformity with that agreement. Now, that is the jurisdiction – to bring a written document, executed in pursuance of an antecedent agreement into conformity with that agreement." Translate that passage in reference to this case: "The jurisdiction of Courts of Equity in this respect is to bring" the memorandum, "executed in pursuance of" the bidding, "into conformity with" the bidding. Lord Warrington goes on:–" The conditions to its exercise are that there must be an antecedent contract." Well, the condition to the exercise of that jurisdiction in this case is that there must have been an antecedent agreement – antecedent to the memorandum. There is an offer to pay £5,550 and the acceptance of that offer. That is the antecedent agreement here. "And the common intention of embodying or giving effect to the whole of that contract by the writing." I am satisfied, as I have said before, that the plaintiff's bid was one of £5,550; I am satisfied that her conversation with Mr. Houlihan was on the basis of such an offer. I am satisfied that it was the common intention of Mr. Richardson, representing the vendor, and of the plaintiff, "to bring the document into conformity with that agreement" (in the words of the learned Lord Justice in *Craddock's Case* [1923] 2 Ch. 136; they had "the common intention of embodying or giving effect to the whole of that contract by writing." To put it shortly, these two parties came together with the common intention of reducing to writing a sale at £5,550, "and," as Lord Warrington continued, "there must be clear evidence that the document, by common mistake, failed to embody such contract and either contained provisions not agreed upon or omitted something that was agreed upon, or otherwise departed from its terms." There is cogent, clear and preponderating evidence in this case that this document failed to embody the contract, because the price is different. It contains a provision that has a lower price which is not agreed upon and omits something agreed upon, that is the higher price, and in that respect it departs from its terms. I can only repeat that I do not see why this lady, who is in a worse position than that of making a mistake in common with the defendant, should be at least in the same position as if common mistake and common mistake only, was the cause of this incorrect document being executed.

The case of the *United States of America* v. *Motor Trucks Ltd.* [1924] A.C. 196, has been referred to already. "That was a case brought by the United States Government against Motor Trucks Ltd., who were a firm who, during the last war, agreed to make munitions for the American Government, subject to hostilities ceasing, when the contract could be terminated. Some time after the armistice the United States Government did serve notice of termination and certain accounts had to be taken as to what amount of money the United States Government owed to the defendant company. A sum of a million and a half dollars was agreed upon, which included the sum of 376,000 dollars, being the amount which the company claimed in respect of certain lands and buildings which had been erected by them following their activities as munition makers. After deducting large sums from the above total, which the Government had already advanced to the appellants, it was agreed that the sum of 637,812 dollars was due. Now, one has to bear in mind that the sum included the 376,000 dollars for the premises, and it was agreed that a contract should be drawn up.

It was drawn up between the parties and the schedule to the contract failed to include those buildings in the conveyance although the Government of the United States paid for them; and, when they realised this omission, they sued before the appropriate Court in Ontario for specific performance of the agreement. This was decreed by the trial Judge and the Truck Company appealed to the Supreme Court in Ontario and succeeded. The matter then came for decision before the Judicial Committee of the Privy Council, where the judgment of the Supreme Court of Ontario was reversed and the judgment of the trial Judge (decreeing specific performance), restored. Now, it is well to recollect the facts in that case because there, in a sense, there was a concluded contract; that is to say, the Truck Company had been paid for these buildings, and it would appear that they were in possession of them. Dr. Baker points out in regard to this case that it, too, deals with what is termed a mutual mistake or a "common mistake." He also points out that there was a concluded contract. Money had passed and he says that it was not (as in the case) a contract of an executory nature. It struck me that, if that were so, and if the Court in that case had no power to rectify or to order specific performance, all the Court should have done was to rescind (which plaintiff's counsel says is all that can be done in this case). In that case why not rescind the contract and simply order the Truck Company to send back the 376,000 dollars for the premises ? Why not order them to hand that money back to the United States Government and rescind merely? The trial Judge and the Privy Council later, in effect, ordered rectification and specific performance of the agreement. The learned Judge who delivered the judgment of the Privy Council, with clarity, put his views as to the position between the parties in passages which I do not intend to read fully but some of which I shall quote. He says (at p. 200 of the report): "And indeed the power of the Court to rectify mutual mistake implies that this power may be exercised notwithstanding that the true agreement of the parties has not been expressed in writing. Nor does the rule make any inroad upon another principle, that the plaintiff must show first, that there was an actually concluded agreement antecedent to the instrument which is sought to be rectified." (In this case the antecedent agreement is the bidding.) "And secondly, that such agreement has been inaccurately represented in the instrument." (I have found that it has been.) "When this is proved either party" (be it vendor or purchaser, in the capacity of plaintiff or defendant),"may claim", in spite of the Statute of Frauds, that the instrument on which the other insists does not represent the real agreement."

I am satisfied from my reading of these cases that I have jurisdiction to rectify, and ought to rectify, the memorandum in such a way that it will represent the actual contract, voluntarily entered into between the plaintiff and the defendants. The mistake was one over which the plaintiff had full power to remedy, every opportunity and chance of remedying, and it in no way prejudiced her; but she knowingly sought to take advantage of it for the reasons I have stated. I shall therefore decree rectification of this memorandum, not on the terms upon which the defendant in his counterclaim asks, because I cannot do so. I shall decree rectification of the figure of £4,550 to the figure of £5,550 and I will leave it at that, because that will make it right. Then I shall declare that Mrs. Annie Nolan, the plaintiff, was the highest bidder and was declared the purchaser at the price of £5,550 and has paid to Mr. Hamilton, a sum of £1,137 10s. by way of deposit and a sum of £227 10s. by way of auctioneer's fees. That is all she has paid; and if I altered these figures I would be simply making the document read and relate to something that has not in fact happened. The position is that all she has paid is a sum of £227 10s. being five per cent. on £4,550 and the balance £1,137 10s. by way of deposit on a similar sum. Now, that is what has happened, and it would be wrong of me to alter these figures when, in truth and in fact, she has paid no more. I shall decree rectification and order that the first figure to be changed to the higher sum of £5,550 and any consequential figures that may follow in respect of the deposit and auctioneer's fees. I shall also decree that the balance at the bottom shall be changed from £3,412 to the correct figure that follows from the purchase-price being £5,550.

After rectification, there arises the question of the specific performance of the agreement. I rather think that under the circumstances I cannot give specific performance of this agreement because it is my view that the document has been rectified as against the written memorandum. It is only now that it becomes effective as an instrument required by the Statute of Frauds. From now on, at least from the time my order is made up, it remains for the plaintiff to elect whether she will, or will not, perform the sale at the price that she has contracted to buy the premises for. However, I am satisfied on the document that I rectify that the vendor will have the ordinary rights that accrue to him under what I now call the contract that correctly represents the intention of the parties, and for the same reasons I will not decree forfeiture of the deposit. The only relief I give is rectification of the memorandum to the figure of £5,550, and rectification of the necessary balances now due by the plaintiff to the defendant, Mr. Graves.

As regards the defendant, Mr. Willoughby Hamilton, I do not want to criticise any more than is necessary and any more than it is my business to do, the way the sale was conducted. Anyway it is clear that the most elementary care should have been taken as regards the permanency of the bidding and the most elementary case as regards the information supplied to those who were about to fill up the conditions of sale, particularly as the person dealing with it was not present in the room. If such care had been taken, and if there was some form of check and counter-check, this thing would not have happened and this expensive and protracted litigation would not have occurred, and the animadversions I have had to make would not have been necessary. If Mr. Richardson had been properly informed, by simple methods, as to what in fact was the bid that had been made only some five or ten minutes before in respect to property running into thousands of pounds, this thing would not have happened.

I am giving the plaintiff no relief in her action. I am not decreeing the return of the sum of £227; I am not increasing that sum because the defendants have not counter-claimed for it. They say they do not want it and that figure has not been altered in any way in the memorandum; but I shall not allow them their costs as against the plaintiff; they must abide their own costs. I allow Mr. Graves his costs as against the plaintiff.

Note

See further, *Irish Land Law,* para. 3.165.

Chapter 9

ACCOUNTS

The equitable remedy of accounts may be invoked in a wide range of situations, e.g., as between trustee and beneficiary (see *Moore* v. *McGlynn*, p.000, *post* and *O'Flanagan* v. *Ray-ger Ltd.*, p.000, *post;* also *Grealish* v. *Murphy*, p.000, *ante*). Other common cases for accounts are as between co-owners and mortgagor and mortgagee.

MONTGOMERY V. SWAN

(1859) 9 Ir. Ch. R. 131; Dru. *temp.* Nap. 520; 4 Ir. Jur. (N.S.) 213 (Chancery)

A petition was filed by the holder of a one-third interest in land against the holder of the other two-thirds interest for an account of the rents received by the latter from the time he took possession of the land.

Brady L.C.:

The rule of the Common Law is familiar, that the mere relation of tenants in common to each other did not, of itself, constitute any one a bailiff of the common property, for the benefit of another. But even at Common Law, where one received what were the proceeds of the common property of both, and did not take the proceeds to his own use, he was held liable to his co-tenant. This is laid down in 1 *Rolle Abr.*, p. 117, cc. 25, 30, and it is adopted by Chief Baron *Comyns,* in his *Digest, Accompt, B,* where it is said that "A tenant in common may have account against his companion, who takes all the profits of the land". This, I think, he intended to be confined to the case where one takes the profits for the common benefit of both, and not for his own use; and this is in accordance with what is stated in *Bro. Abr., Account,* p.8, and in several recorded cases (see 1 *Vin. Abr.*, 140, pl. 7, in margin); and in *Leon.*, 219, referred to in *Co. Litt*, 172 a (8), it is said by Periam, and not denied by any:– "If one become my bailiff, of his own wrong, without any appointment, he is accountable to me". In *Bro. Abr., Accounts, pl.* 8, it is thus given:– "Where a man takes upon him, of his own head, to be my bailiff, action of account lies."

I think, therefore, on the facts of this case, there is enough to make the defendant liable at Common Law. Indeed there is more than enough; for having regard to the way in which this property has been so long managed, and the privity of the defendant before his purchase, it is a reasonable inference that it was originally arranged that the owner of two-thirds should manage the whole, and account to the owner of the one-third; and the defendant has acted on this arrangement.

As to the statute, the case is equally clear. I need not enter into the nice criticism between taking and receiving, on which the decision in *Henderson* v. *Eason* 17 Q.B. 710 seems to have proceeded. I certainly would have supposed that where one tenant in common takes the whole of the profits, he thereby receives more than his just share or proportion. And this is confirmed by the decision in *Walker* v. *Holyday* Com. Rep. 272, where the qualified liability as bailiff under the statute is so plainly put and explained; and the exposition in *Co. Lit.*, p. 172a, is that, "by 'bailiff' is understood a servant that hath administration and charge of lands, &c., to make the best benefit for the owner, against whom an action of account doth lie, for the profits which he hath raised or made, or might, by his industry or care, have reasonably raised or made, his reasonable charges and expenses deducted."

After this, and looking to the words of the statute, which makes the tenant in common who receives more than his just share or proportion chargeable *as bailiff,* and emphatically distinguishes the liability as bailiff from that of a receiver, I would certainly have supposed that the statute was not confined to the mere case of receiving more than his share of rents *in money*. But, in that case of *Henderson* v. *Eason,* there was not, according to the judgment, a finding, warranted by legal evidence, that the farm was in fact managed for the common profit of both. Be this as it may, there is no doubt of the present case being within the statute. But it is then said the statute is repealed in Ireland; it is so, only and so far as it gave the inconvenient remedy of account at Law; and another more convenient proceeding is now substituted.

In Equity, the case is clear. The cases before and since the statute, and the reasons on which they proceeded, are well given in the argument in *Putney* v. *Warren* 6 Ves. 78 and in the case of *Henderson* v. *Eason,* Parke, B., says:– "In Chancery, the tenant in common who received the rent would certainly be liable to account to the other."

Indeed in the present case there may be a further and special reason, which may be stated in the words of Lord Hardwicke, in *Benson* v. *Baldwyn* 1 Atk. 578.:–"Where a man is entitled to a rent out of lands, and through process of time the remedy at Law is lost, or become very difficult, this Court has interfered, and given relief, upon the foundation only of payment of the rent for a long time, which bills are called bills founded on the *solet.* Nay, the Court has gone so far as to give relief where the nature of the rent (as there are many kinds at Law) has not been known, so as to be set forth." Here the title, though admitted at the Bar, was not so admitted by the answer, but depends on the long course of payment and dealing, which in its result establishes everything necessary to give the plaintiffs a title to relief; and therefore I have no hesitation in granting the relief which is prayed.

Note

See further, *Irish Land Law,* para. 7.07

COMYNS V. COMYNS

(1871) I.R. 5 Eq. 583 (Rolls Court)

A mortgage deed contained a proviso for redemption on payment of the debt, which was a sum advanced to redeem the lands from eviction, and also contained a stipulation that the sum of £100 a year was to be allowed to the mortgagee, who had an immediate right to go into possession, for his trouble in managing the lands which he should be in possession of; the mortgagee went into possession on the execution of the mortgage. Subsequently a redemption suit was brought by the mortgagor seeking, *inter alia,* an account.

Sullivan M.R.:

There is nothing whatever in the answer to show that the Plaintiff, as mortgagor, is not entitled to an account; but it is insisted, on the part of the Defendant, that I should declare, on the face of my decree for that account, that the £100 a year provided by the mortgage is a just and fair allowance for the Defendant to claim, and that is the principal, if not the only question which I have now to decide. The Plaintiff contends that this stipulation for paying to the Defendant himself, a mortgagee in possession, for his trouble of management, is against the policy of the law, and cannot be maintained. Although there are many peculiarities in this transaction, and in the frame of the deed, it appears to me that there is nothing to take this transaction out of the ordinary rule, that a mortgagee cannot stipulate with the mortgagor for what is called a collateral advantage in relation to the possession of the mortaged land. The deed in question is, to all intents and purposes, a mortgage, and the stipulations in it are, I think, plainly made with the mortgagee, in consideration of his advancing the loan, and, as it seems to me, on condition of his forbearing the demand of his advance for a certain time. The provision for the allowance of £100 from the very beginning is part of the contract under which the mortgagee gets into possession, and appears to me equally invalid, as if it were merely to begin when the mortgage became absolute. The case of *Leith* v. *Irvine* 1 M & K. 277, before Lord Brougham, sums up all the cases on the subject, and lays down the precise rule applicable to these cases most correctly, and defines with accuracy the distinctions which separate and mark them. At p.288, Lord Brougham says:–"So long as he stood thus," that is, a creditor with a lien having a right to better his security by putting himself in his debtor's shoes, "there was nothing inconsistent in his being employed for a certain reward in the management of the estate; and *provided he did not make that employment a condition of forbearing the demand* of his debt, there was nothing to prevent him from taking that reward. But when once he takes possession, he assumes a different character; all he does is for himself, and he is not at liberty to charge the mortgagor, whom he has ousted, with the trouble which he takes on his own account."

The decision in *Parkinson* v. *Hanbury* L.R. 2 H.L.1, relied on by the Counsel for the Defendant, has, in my opinion, no application whatever here. In that case the

House of Lords merely held that mortgagees who entered into possession, not as mortgagees, but under the supposed character of purchasers, would not be held liable to account as mortgagees, they never having insisted on the possession or receipt of rents in that character: *Douglas* v. *Archbutt* 2 D. & J. 148 has, I think, still less application.

I shall, therefore, declare that in taking the accounts the Defendant is not entitled to the £100 a year provided for him by the deed. I shall make the ordinary decree, that the Defendant shall account for what he received, or might have received, without wilful default, out of the premises, with all fair and just allowances. I have been required by the Plaintiff to direct an occupation rent to be fixed for the Defendant to pay or account for. I do not think that on the facts before me, and having regard to the form of the deed of mortgage, I can do this; and, indeed, the account which I direct against the Defendant is a more onerous one. I reserve the costs till the accounts are taken.

Note

See further, *Irish Land Law,* paras. 13. 046-7; also *Cassidy* v. *Sullivan, infra.*

CASSIDY V. SULLIVAN

(1878) 1 L.R. Ir. 313 (Chancery Division)

The facts are set out in the judgment.

Chatterton V. C.:

It is quite true that a mortgagee by claiming a larger sum than is due, when the mortgagor comes to redeem, does not necessarily disentitle himself to the costs of the suit. Generally speaking, there are two classes of cases where the mortgagee is disentitled to, or occasionally has even to pay, costs. First, where at the time the bill is filed the mortgage debt has been paid off. Again, when an answer is filed claiming money to be due, and it is found that the mortgage has been paid off since bill filed, but before answer.

The Plaintiff in this case has not shown that the mortgage debt was fully paid when the bill was filed, or when the answer was put in. The account here shows that, on the 25th of March, 1874, there was a sum due of £1 10s. 8d. That sum must be increased by £15 allowed for repairs at foot of the account. It is not contended that this sum was due for repairs done after the commencement of the suit, and it seems plain on the dealings between these parties that it was for repairs executed before the bill was filed. At all events, I think the Plaintiff would have adduced evidence on this point if the fact were otherwise. Therefore, there was a sum of £16 10s. 8d. due at the time the bill was filed. Another half year is accounted for up to 29th September, 1874, during which £10 17s. 8d. was received by the mortgagee, which would have reduced the sum due at the date of the filing of the answer by that amount, leaving £5 13s. due. It is said by Mr. Trench that it must be presumed that this sum was paid off by the receipt of weekly rents during the further interval that elapsed before the filing of the answer. But there would be no half-yearly rent until the 25th of March, 1875. I do not, therefore, think that I ought to refuse the Defendant his costs on this ground.

The other question remaining is that of misconduct; and I must say I think there has been misconduct on the part of the Defendant. He was bound to have his accounts ready – to furnish them, and to vouch them. He was called on for an account by the letter of the 7th of April 1874, three months before the bill was filed, and was required to state within a limited period whether he would account or not; but, instead of rendering an account, he lay by until the bill was filed. I must say that is a course of conduct which I cannot approve of, especially when he was bound, not only by the rule of this Court, but by the stipulation in his deed, to account. Although I will not go the length of making him pay costs, I will let him abide his own costs. I may add to the reasons assigned already, that the Defendant failed in another part of his duty, in not having vouchers to vouch his expenditure, and it was only by the consent of the parties that this sum of £15 odd, which has turned the scale in his favour, was allowed.

Chapter 10

RECEIVERS

Appointment of a receiver is one of the oldest remedies developed by the Court of Chancery. Although commonly appointed by the Court, express power to appoint out of court may be conferred by deed or statute, see *Irish Land Law,* para. 3.166 *et seq*. Receivership may also be used as a method of equitable execution, *ibid.*

RE LORD ANNALY

(1891) 27 L.R. Jr. 523 (Chancery Division)

A was tenant for life of estates, the fee-simple of one of which had been mortgaged to B by his predecessor in title. A mortgaged his life-interest in the estates to an Insurance Company, effecting policies on his life with the Company as collateral security. At the instance of the Company and of B, who had obtained from the Land Judge an order for the sale of the estate comprised in his mortgage, A, by deed, appointed D receiver over all the estates for the purpose of keeping down interest on the incumbrances. Upon A's death an action was brought against his personal represetative to administer his estate, and D was appointed by the Land Judge receiver over the estate mortgaged to B. The Insurance Company proved in the action for the balance due to it after giving credit for the amounts of the policies, and also claimed a lien on the rents due and accruing due at A's death, which were returned in the Chief Clerk's certificate as part of A's personal estate. D as receiver of the Court had collected portion of the arrears of the rent due at the date of his appointment, and had, pursuant to an order of the Land Judge, paid thereout to B a sum in respect of interest. A's personal representative claimed the rents due and accruing due at A's death, as personal estate, to be administered in the action.

Porter, M.R.:

In the present case the claim of the Scottish Equitable Society comes first in point of time, and it will be more convenient to deal with it first. It is not disputed that this Society holds the first incumbrance, and their claim is to retain the rents received by them from the receiver to the amount of £1050. As regards the Rathcline Estate, as to which the present question is alone concerned, the Society claim in virtue of a mortgage from the owner in fee, and their incumbrance is therefore paramount to any interest which the first Lord Annaly could create under his will, and so prior to the tenancy for life of the late Lord Annaly.

A mortgagee having a charge upon lands need not intervene at all unless he choose. He may be content to look for payment otherwise; but if he so choose, he has the right to step in at any time, and take proceedings to obtain possession of the rents by ejectment or by a receiver. Here the Society applied for and obtained a receiver from Mr. Justice Monroe on the 5th October, 1888. It was said in argument that the tenant for life was not represented on the hearing of that motion, but I am clearly bound by the order made on that occasion, and do not for a moment suppose that there was any irregularity in the case. Under it a receiver was appointed, and he has since received rents from the Rathcline estate, some of which accrued due during the lifetime of Luke, second Lord Annaly.

It was contended by Mr. Oulton that, though the rents were received by the receiver by virtue of a paramount incumbrance, they must now be surrendered by the mortgagees because they accrued due during the lifetime of the tenant for life, and could only have been sued for by his personal representative. I cannot accede to that argument. I am bound by the proceedings before Mr. Justice Monroe, and in addition to that it is a principle of this Court, recognised in the case of *Hollier* v. *Hedges* 2 Ir. Ch. R. 370, that a receiver is entitled to collect and receive all arrears, subject of course to this limitation, that they are arrears of rent belonging to the estate over which he has been appointed. If a receiver over the estate of a remainderman collect rents which belonged to a prior tenant for life he must of course give them up. But here the incumbrance is over the fee, and the Society may retain sufficient of the rents to keep down interest upon their incumbrance, which it was the duty of the tenant for life to keep down; and if his personal representative had been allowed to get possession of these rents he would have been obliged to return them.

I have therefore no difficulty as to the claim of this Society. They have intervened in this case, and they are accordingly entitled to retain the rents received by them.

Now as to the question between the Standard Life Assurance Company and the personal representative and the creditors of the testator (for the two latter have a common interest to swell the assets), this Company's incumbrance extended only to the life-estate. I can quite understand the importance of this case to Life Insurance Companies, many of whom have large dealings with tenants for life, securing their advances by policies of insurance in addition to a mortgage of the life-estate of the borrower.

Lord Annaly the tenant for life appears to have allowed the interest upon this charge to get into arrears, enough apparently to enable the Company to apply to the Court for a receiver. It appears from the affidavit of their solicitor that they were preparing a notice for that purpose, but they did not proceed further, for at their instance and under pressure by them it appears that the deed of the 31st May, 1887, was executed by the tenant for life. To that deed Lord Annaly, the Trustees of the Standard Insurance Company, the Scottish Equitable Life Assurance Society, William Lane Joynt, the National Bank, Hugh Lindsay Antrobus, and Henry Dudley Ryder, and Mathew Weld O'Connor were parties. After reciting that the Standard Life Assurance Company had required that Lord Annaly should appoint a receiver, and that the other incumbrancers parties thereto had concurred with the Standard Company in so requiring, in order to procure punctual payment of the incumbrances mentioned in the second schedule, and that it was agreed that Mr. Mathew Weld O'Connor, the land agent of Lord Annaly, should be the first receiver, and that his first account as such receiver should date from the end of the account furnished by him as such land agent, namely up to and ending the 1st November, 1886, the deed witnessed that Lord Annaly, with the privity of the said incumbrancers, appointed Mr. O'Connor receiver, agent, and attorney, from time to time, in the name of Lord Annaly, or otherwise, to receive the rents and profits of the lands in the first schedule mentioned, and that he directed the tenants to pay their rents to the receiver; and it was declared that the receiver should out of the rents pay the costs and expenses therein mentioned, and pay and keep down the interest on all principal moneys and the yearly sums and the premiums of assurance and interest thereon for the time being charged upon and payable out of the said lands according to the priorities set forth in the second schedule; and in the next place should pay an annuity of £300 for Alice Viscountess Coke, as therein mentioned, and pay the surplus, if any, to Lord Annaly, his executors, administrators, or assigns. It was provided that the receiver should keep separate accounts of the rents of the several lands, and he covenanted with the trustees of the Standard Insurance Company and with the Scottish Equitable Society as well as with Lord Annaly to use his best endeavours to collect the rents and apply the same in manner aforesaid. The deed also contained a covenant by Lord Annaly not to revoke the appointment of the receiver without the consent of the Standard Insurance Company, nor to do anything to obstruct him in receiving the rents, and a covenant to appoint another receiver in the event of the death of Mr. O'Connor, or of his becoming incapable or unfit to discharge the duties of receiver.

It provided that the incumbrancers parties thereto should not by reason of the appointment of Mr. O'Connor be deemed to be mortgagees in possession or accountable for the rents and profits of the lands, nor answerable for any loss or misapplication thereof by reason of any default of Mr. O'Connor, and that nothing in the deed was to be taken as lessening or abridging the ordinary remedies of the incumbrancers.

This deed, in my opinion, operates as the deed of Lord Annaly, and as his authority to Mr. O'Connor to act as agent and attorney; but it does not operate so far as the collection of the rents is concerned as the deed of the Standard Company, or of the other mortgagees who were parties to it, none of whom were in possession. It contains, however, as I have already stated, provisions secured by the covenants of Lord Annaly, and of Mr. O'Connor, that the latter is to apply the rents received by him in keeping down the interest upon the incumbrances, and that Mr. O'Connor shall render an account to Lord Annaly and to the mortgagees of all rents received.

I do not see how this deed differs in effect from a deed which might have been made under the provisions of Lord Cranworth's Act, or of the Conveyancing Act, 1881, under which an incumbrancer might take steps to have a receiver appointed by writing under his hand, who would by the provisions of those Acts be the agent of the owner and not of the incumbrancers. The incumbrancer naturally does not wish to go into possession and incur the risk of being held responsible to account not only for rents which he has received, but also for rents which he might have received, and, accordingly, deeds of this nature are frequently preferred by mortgagees.

But when the rents are collected by the receiver under such a deed the object of the deed is that they are to be dedicated in the particular way therein prescribed for the benefit of the incumbrancers. Suppose that here Mr. O'Connor had collectd some of the rents, could the owner have interfered to prevent him from paying them over to the incumbrancers? This would be contrary to the language of the deed, and to the covenant of the owner. But it is argued that the rents due at the death of the tenant for life, and the apportioned part of the gale which fell due soon after his death, belong to the personal representative of the tenant for life, because they were still uncollected at his death, and because the receivership came to an end by the death of the tenant for life. That argument is based on the assumption that all that took place under the deed had no positive effect upon the status of the incumbrancers, and that they were in the same position as if they had done nothing, and had taken no steps to obtain a receiver deed in their favour. Any such argument is contrary to the terms of the deed, and no authority has been cited in support of it.

The principle upon which a mortgagee who allows the owner to receive the rents is debarred from seeking to make him afterwards account for them, is perfectly plain. The incumbrancer, as I have said, is not bound to take proceedings. The debt is the substance, and the security is the shadow. If he prefers to allow the owner to remain in possession, so much the worse for him if the rents are not applied to keep down his interest; but if he takes no steps, he does not lose anything–he retains his rights–he has only omitted to take advantage of his security. Serjeant Jellett mainly replied on the case of *Flight* v. *Camac* 25 L.J. Ch. 654; in that case the trustees of a settlement made in the year 1821 had pursuant to a power in the settlement mortgaged in the year 1831 the fee of the settled lands to secure the sum of £40,000 with interest at 4¼ per cent. Camac, who was entitled to the surplus rents for life, mortgaged in 1833 his interest to one Grant, to secure repayment of £1461, and interest at 5 per cent. In 1837 the mortgage for £40,000 was assigned to other parties discharged from the original proviso for redemption, but subject to a proviso for redemption on repayment of the £40,000 with interest at 5 per cent. By a deed of the same date, made between Camac, the trustees of the settlement, and the assignees of the mortgage deed of 1831, and one Bennett, reciting, *inter alia,* the mortgage to Grant, Camac appointed Bennett receiver of the rents and profits of the mortgaged property, with the usual provisions for keeping down the interest on the mortgage for £40,000, and payment of the surplus to Camac. Bennett was afterwards appointed receiver by an order made in the suit, which was brought by a puisne incumbrancer to administer the trusts of the settlement of 1821. Camac died during the course of the suit; and the master found that the balance of income at the death of Camac, in respect of his life interest in the estate, after payment of interest on the £40,000 at the original rate of 4½ per cent, was £727 13s. 3d., and that the same was due to the subsequent incumbrancers on such life-estate, the first of whom was Grant, whose claim would exhaust the whole amount. The Vice-Chancellor decided that the mortgagees for £40,000 were entitled as against Grant to retain the said sum of £727. 13s. 3d., in respect of their claim to interest at 5 per cent. Grant appealed.

The Lord Chancellor said that, before the appointment of the receiver, Camac had clearly a right to order the surplus rents to be paid in any way he liked. By the deed of 1837 he did order the receiver then appointed to keep down the interest on the £40,000, and pay the balance to himself. Therefore no possible claim could be made to so much of the £727 13s. 3d. as arose before the appointment of the receiver by the

Court, and the only question was, What was the difference made by that order? His Lordship then commented on the terms of the order, and considered that neither before or after the appointment thereby made was there anything to prevent him from treating Camac as mortgagor in possession as against the defendant Grant; and the latter having omitted to take the necessary steps for the satisfaction of his mortgage debt and interest during the life of Camac, the mortgagee could not then apply for a retrospective account of the rents, but that the above-mentioned sum, as representing such rents, must be considered as part of the mortgagor's personal estate; and in that view of the case the first mortgagees were entitled to retain the whole as against the appellant, and be affirmed the decision of the Vice-Chancellor.

In *Gresley* v. *Adderley* 1 Swanston, 573, the same principle was recognised. The Lord Chancellor there says:– "The order appointing a receiver is for the benefit of incumbrancers only so far as expressed to be for their benefit, and only so far as they choose to avail themselves of it. The Court would not deprive them of the advantage of their legal estate. They might, of course, be obliged to come here to be examined *pro interesse suo,* but this Court would not interfere against them. But I apprehend that when the Court interposed to receive the rents beyond what was required for keeping down the interest on incumbrances, all the surplus rent, after payment of interest, was received for the benefit of the heir."

In *Bertie* v. *Abingdon* 3 Merivale, 560, the principle is similarly stated:– "It is said that though the interest be in fact unpaid, the order of the Court directing the receiver to keep down the incumbrances had the effect of an appropriation of the rents and profits to that specific purpose, and that the rights of the parties are therefore now the same as if the rents and profits had been so applied. Now such a direction is given without the least view to the interests of the real and personal representatives. It is given partly in justice to the incumbrancers that they may not be injured by the act of the Court in taking possession of the rents and profits, to which they had a right to resort for payment of their interest, partly for the benefit of the estate itself, lest the incumbrancers, having their interest stopped, might be induced to resort to proceedings injurious to those who stood behind them. The incumbrancers may or may not avail themselves of the order by applying to the receiver. If they apply to him they will either be paid their interest, or if he refuses or neglects to pay them, they may complain to the Court of such neglect or refusal; but if they omit to apply for the interest, it is to be presumed that they are satisfied with the security they have, both for the interest and for the principal. The Court does not force payment upon them; nor does it set apart any portion of the rents and profits to answer unclaimed interest."

And so it was in the other cases cited; the persons whose incumbrances were sought to be affected had taken no steps; here the incumbrancers have taken very active steps; they threatened to get a receiver appointed by the Court, and they only abandoned that position when their demand to have a receiver was conceded, and the receiver-deed executed; this receiver, once he had received the rents, though in their collection he was agent for the mortgagor, became an agent for the mortgagees, and was bound to pay the same over to them.

The case that most resembles the present is *Ford* v. *Rackham* 17 Beav. 485. The deed there is practically undistinguishable from the deed in the present case. It was made between the tenant for life, incumbrancers, and receiver; it contained an agreement to appoint, and an appointment of, the defendant Rackham as receiver; and it was agreed that he should keep down the incumbrances according to their priorities, and pay the surplus to the tenant for life. The receiver covenanted with the tenant for life and with the incumbrancers so to apply the income, and the tenant for life covenanted not to revoke the power given to the receiver, and it was declared that the incumbrancers should not be declared incumbrancers in possession or charged with the misapplication of the rents. With an alteration of the names, the statement of the deed given in the report of that case would, if the dates, and amounts were altered, make a very good abstract of the deed before me. The plaintiff in that case, whose incumbrance was subsequent to the deed, desired an injunction to restrain the receiver from paying any of the rents to the tenant for life, and an order that he might pay into Court the clear residue, which under the deed would be payable to the tenant for life, and that an account might be taken of what was due to the plaintiff. Objection was taken that the prior incumbrancers had not been made parties to the suit. Lord Romilly there says:– "I entertain no doubt that the owner of an estate may enter into such an arrangement or contract with a steward or other person to receive the rents of his property, which will be binding not only on the owner but on any person to whom the owner may afterwards convey that property with notice of the contract. If Mr. Lane Fox had appointed Mr. Rackham the receiver under such a contract, and had directed him to make certain payments out of the income to various other persons, his receipt would then be a mere matter of account between him and Mr. Lane Fox, or the person to whom Mr. Lane Fox might afterwards convey the property. I am also of opinion that a fiduciary relation would exist between Mr. Rackham and the person to whom Mr. Lane Fox so conveyed the property, and who, in order to ascertain the surplus, would be entitled to an account of his management of the property; but the persons to whom Mr. Lane Fox had directed payments to be made, would have no right to such an account. The present, however, is a different case, because it appears that Mr. Rackham was appointed receiver by a contract made, not only between him and Mr. Lane Fox, but between him and various other persons, with whom, individually and severally, Mr. Rackham contracted to make certain payments. The question then is, whether Mr. Ford can question the manner in which Mr. Rackham has performed his duties, so far as relates to the interests of Mr. Lane Fox himself, and as claiming under him. I am of opinion that he cannot." Lord Romilly goes on to say:– "It therefore appears to me that Mr. Rackham stands in a fiduciary relation, not to Mr. Lane Fox alone; but that it is a contract between him and all those annuitants who were parties to the deed, and by which contract he is made a receiver of the property, and covenants to pay them." He then decided that the bill was defective by reason of the other parties to the deed not being parties to the suit. It is plain that upon a deed so framed the receiver, though, as Lord Romilly decided, he stood in a fiduciary position to the owner along, was bound by contract also to the incumbrancers who were parties to the deed, and that the position of the receiver there was analogous to that of Mr. O'Connor here.

In my opinion, the tenant for life having appointed an agent by this deed was bound by it until the appointment was revoked; and so was the agent. Therefore, except as to the apportioned part of the rents of the gale in the currency of which Lord Annaly died, there is no question. But as to that apportioned part it is contended the death of Lord Annaly operated as a revocation of the power conferred by the deed, and that therefore Mr. O'Connor ceased to be agent. As a legal proposition, that is so, no doubt; the death put an end to his authority as agent. But the question is not merely one between Mr. O'Connor and the Insurance Company; it is also one between Lord Annaly and his representative and the Company. In my opinion the whole effect of the deed was to make an equitable disposition of the rents in favour of the incumbrancers. It is a common case between Lord Annaly and the Company that the rents must be apportioned. The effect in equity of the deed was that until revocation the rents which belonged to Lord Annaly were dedicated to the trusts expressed in it; and that the apportioned part of the last gale, though belonging to Lord Annaly, and after his death to his personal representative, was by his act and disposition impressed with a trust in favour of the incumbrancers. It was contended that the power contained in the deed was revocable in Lord Annaly's lifetime. I doubt if this was so, so long as the agent discharged his duties properly; but even if it was revocable, and Lord Annaly had discharged the agent between two gale days, and had closed upon the rents against the rights of the incumbrancers, I am of opinion that though he might have recovered them at law, yet that in this Court the rents would be held to belong to the incumbrancers. Therefore, upon the question between the personal representative and the incumbrancers, I am of opinion that the portion of the rents now in dispute must be held to be bound by the trusts of the deed of the 31st May, 1887, and to belong to the Standard Life Assurance Company. As, however, the estate is an insolvent one, they must value their security.

Note

See further, *Irish Land Law*, para. 13. 048 *et seq.*; also *Re Marchesa Della Rocella's Estate, infra*

RE MARCHESA DELLA ROCELLA'S ESTATE

(1889) 29 L.R. Ir. 464 (Chancery Division)

In 1886 A, who was a mortgagee of the owner's life estate in lands, appointed a receiver (B) by deed under the Conveyancing Act, 1881, s. 19. The deed provided that B should apply all moneys received by him in manner directed by section 24 of the Act, save that, in priority to all other charges except rents, rates, and taxes, specified in section 24, sub-sect. 8 (i), he should pay any reasonable costs or charges incurred by A. An absolute order for sale was made in 1890; and on A's application a receiver was appointed by the Court. On settling the schedule of priorities on which prior and puisne incumbrances appeared, there being a dispute as to the amount due to A, it was referred to the examiner to take an account of what was due on A's mortgage, and A showed in detail by affidavit the amount which had accrued due for interest and premiums on policies, and the sums which he had received on account through B, or otherwise.

Monroe, J.:

(Having stated the facts as above given, continued–)

The question then is whether any obligation is thrown on Harrison and Ingram to show what have been Mr. Moore's receipts and disbursements before being allowed to prove their debt and receive payments on foot of their interest through the present Court receiver. They should of course be bound to bring in such an account if the moneys which have reached their receiver's hands are to be taken to have been received by them, or if they are responsible for all moneys which he may have received and wrongfully applied. Are they so responsible?

Mr. Moore was appointed receiver under the provisions of the Conveyancing Act, 1881, sect. 19. That Act enables a mortgagee to appoint a receiver in the same way as if such power were conferred by the mortgage deed. The receiver when so appointed is, by the terms of the 24th section, sub-sect. 2, to be deemed the agent of the mortgagor; and the mortgagor is to be solely responsible for the receiver's acts or defaults, unless the mortgage deed otherwise provides. If a receiver so appointed gets money into his hands and gives it to the owner, or otherwise than is provided by sect. 24, sub-sect. 8, or by the deed appointing him, the mortgagee who appointed him is not responsible for his defaults. The mortgagee is bound only to give credit for such sums as reach his hands. If the receiver in this case has at the present moment money for which he might be bound to account to the Court receiver, if he has collected money which he has contrary to his duty paid over to the owner (and it is not suggested that either is the case), yet if the mortgagee is not responsible for these alleged defaults, why should he be prevented from proving his debt until an account has been taken, the result of which can in no way affect his claim?

I must direct the reference to proceed without insisting on an affidavit showing the receipts and disbursements of Mr. Moore. If the amount verified by Mr.Harrison be considered incorrect or unreliable, if it is thought he has received money from Mr. Moore or from other sources for which he has not given credit, he may be made, on the proper steps being taken, to attend for cross-examination, or the attendance of Mr. Moore before the Examiner may be secured in the usual way.

I have no reason to think that Mr. Moore is not perfectly ready, if he has not done so already, to furnish his accounts to anyone who is entitled to ask for it.

Messrs. Harrison and Ingram are entitled to their costs with their demand.

KERNOHAN ESTATES LTD v. BOYD

[1967] N.I.27 (High Court)

The facts are set out in the judgment.

Lowry J.:

This is an application by two companies and their principal shareholder, who may be described as their alter ego, to restrain Mr. Boyd, the receiver, from dismissing employees, from taking steps to discontinue the business and from taking steps likely to injure the goodwill of the business carried on by these two companies. The receiver has been appointed receiver of the two companies under four debentures, two of which are held by the Bank of Ireland and two by Bowmaker (Ulster) Ltd. The debentures are in the customary wide terms and they give wide and full powers to the receiver who is also appointed manager of the companies. For the purpose of the motion the applicant admits the validity and regularity of the debentures and the appointment of the receiver, and also his prima facie power to do what he is seeking to do, namely, to cut down all but the maintenance staff and to sell the assets of the companies for what they would fetch. It is also agreed that the Bank of Ireland take priority on each debenture. I have said that the admissions are made for the purpose of the motion because Mr. Carswell indicated the possiblity of attacking at a later stage the debenture which is most relevant to the matter in hand, that is to say, the debenture of the Bank of Ireland in respect of Kernohan Estates Ltd. If I reject the motion, it may be too late to achieve by trial of the action the object which the applicants seek, namely, to prevent the receiver from dismissing the staff, discontinuing the business and thereby injuring such goodwill as the business may have. But I feel that I must leave this possibility out of consideration in deciding the present motion. This does not cause me undue anxiety because although, of course, counsel has not been in a position, and I dare say his solicitors have not been in a position, to make any more constructive move, the applicants, and in particular the applicant Mr. Kernohan, have had plenty of time in which to move. He could have joined the Bank of Ireland in this action and it would seem to me that he has had an opportunity, which is very much prior in time to the present crisis, of moving to rectify the situation in his own favour. Now the point that I have to deal with is this. The quarry is one of the assets, and one may say from the business point of view the principal asset, of Kernohan Estates Ltd. Mr. Kernohan wants to carry on that part of the business and to restore it or develop it, as the case may be; to a very profitable state, which will be to the possible benefit of all concerned, including himself. The Bank of Ireland, Bowmaker (Ulster) Ltd., preferential creditors, the unsecured creditors and the contributories, in descending order, have an interest in the success of such a venture, and I may point out that Mr. Boyd is the receiver for the debenture holders who are the second in priority, namely, Bowmakers (Ulster) Ltd., as well as for the Bank of Ireland. The receiver, on the other hand, by his affidavit and through his counsel, says that he has tried to sell the quarry as a going concern and has failed. Furthermore, he is not so optimistic about the profits of the quarry as is Mr. Kernohan. The receiver wishes to sell as best he can, and submits and is of the opinion that the most economical course is to close the business and to dismiss all but the maintenance staff. He sets out in his affidavit the efforts which he has made to sell the quarry as a going concern, which should if possible be done as being obviously the most advantageous way to dispose of it. Now these two points of view are set out on affidavit and there has been no cross-examination about them. Certain ancillary matters have also been set out in the affidavits as showing their different points of view and one may summarise them by saying that whereas Mr. Kernohan submits that assets could be realised for greater value, Mr. Boyd, relying to some extent on advice which he has received, considers that lower values could be realised for these assets. I was pressed with the proposition that prima facie a receiver and manager has no right to damage the goodwill of the business and must prove his case very clearly if he wishes to take a step which is likely to do so. One examines such a proposition sceptically, or at least with circumspection, since the power of sale over all or any of the assets of the company endows a receiver and manager with the prima facie ability to destroy the goodwill in whole or in part. If Mr. Boyd were simply a receiver, there is no doubt that, if he acted in good faith as those words are defined in *Kennedy* **v.** *De Trafford,* [1897] A.C. 180. a mortgage suit which reached the House of Lords, he could sell the assets of these companies, and it is really because he is the manager that it is submitted that his liberty of action is circumscribed. Now the appointment of a receiver to be a manager as well gives him additional powers and is very often considered to be beneficial to the debenture holder. It would be curious if the widening of his powers were to place the receiver or his debenture holder in a greater difficulty in realising the security. Of course, curious results can occur and the fact that something was parodoxical would not necessarily mean that it is not the law. The authority relied on principally by the applicants is *In re Newdigate Colliery Co* [1912] 1 Ch. 468, where a very strong Court of Appeal in an extempore judgment–the case lasted one day–refused to direct the receiver appointed by the court to sell coal at the ruling price of the day and thereby to disregard existing contracts to sell the output of the colliery at somewhat lower prices per ton. Now the first thing that one notices in the case is that the application was made by the debenture holders, and was required to be made if the receiver appointed by the court was to have power to disregard these contracts and to sell the coal at a higher price. Both in the course of the argument, which is very fully reported and contains many interjections from the bench, and in course of the judgments the emphasis appears to have been placed on three points. Firstly, the fact that the receiver had been appointed by the court and that it was his duty to safeguard the interests of all concerned; secondly, the fact that the mortgagor had an interest in the preservation of the goodwill for the future; and thirdly, the existence of the contracts and the requirement in honour on the part of the receiver not to disregard the company's obligations. The respondents, on the other hand relied on *In re B. Johnson & Co. (Builders) Ltd.* [1955] Ch. 634; [1955] 3 W.L.R. 269., a case whose direct concern was the interpretation of section 333 of the Companies Act, 1948, and, in order to give an impression of the points relied on by the respondent, I cannot improve on the actual words used by the learned judges who made up the Court of Appeal in that case, judges who in their generation compare in every way with the eminent and famous judges who decided the *Newdigate* case [1912] 1 Ch. 468. The judgments in *Johnson's* case [1955] Ch. 634. [1955] 3 W.L.R. 269. were also extempore, and I note that the case lasted for four days.

Lord Evershed M.R. said [1955] Ch. at 644., "The situation of someone appointed by a mortgagee or a debenture holder to be a receiver and manager–as it is said, 'out of court'–is familiar. It has long been recognised and established that receivers and managers so appointed are, by the effect of the statute law, or of the terms of the debenture, or both, treated, while in possession of the company's assets and exercising the various powers conferred upon them, as agents of the company, in order that they may be able to deal effectively with third parties. But, in such a case as the present at any rate, it is quite plain that a person appointed as receiver and manager is concerned, not for the benefit of the company but for the benefit of the mortgagee bank, to realize the security; that is the whole purpose of his appointment; and the powers which are conferred upon him, and which I have to some extent recited, are (as Sir Lynn observed, and I think fairly observed) really ancillary to the main purpose of the appointment, which is the realization by the mortgagee of the security (in this case, as commonly) by the sale of the assets.

All that is perhaps elementary; but it bears upon what I shall have to say as regards the charges made against the receiver; for it appears to me inevitably to negative the proposition that a person appointed, as Mr. Aizlewood was appointed, owes some duty to the company to carry on the business of the company and to preserve its goodwill." And further [1955] Ch. at 646.: "The distinction may at first sight seem fine between a receiver and manager of the property of a company, on the one hand, and a manager of the company, on the other, being the formula found in section 333: but the logic of it and the substance of it is that which is to be found in what I have already said–that a person appointed receiver and manager, so-called, is not managing on the company's behalf but is managing in order to facilitate the exercise by him, for the mortgagees, of the mortgagees' power to enforce the security. I think myself, also, that the point is further emphasized by the consideration that, so far as I can see, if [counsel for the applicant] were right, a receiver and manager appointed by the court would equally have to be held to be a 'manager' within section 333, although in that case the receiver would not for any purpose be the agent of the company at all: he would be an officer of the court. In short the word 'manager' in this section, to my mind, excludes one who is only a manager because he is, as receiver (which is his real capacity), endowed for the purposes of his receivership with certain powers of management.

Two further points seem to me to emphasize the sense that I seek to give to this word. They really are two riders or corollaries of the general principle that I have stated. The first is this: It may well be that a mortgagee, a debenture holder, who has, say, a fixed charge on the real property of the company and a floating charge on everything else, is not going to realize an amount by sales sufficient to discharge the indebtedness to him. I understand that in this case, by a small margin, that has been achieved. But it is elementary that a mortgagee seeking to realize his security has no duty of care to see that there is as much as possible left over for those who are interested in what is called the 'equity'. In other words, it may well be (as Jenkins L.J. pointed out in the course of the argument) that the company may have, in such a case as this, no equity whatever, in any real sense; and, if that is so, it would be indeed a strange use of language to describe one appointed as receiver and manager under the debenture as a manager of the company."

He also says [1955] Ch. at 651.: "In other words, the gist of the charge (expanded in the points of claim, which I will mention in a moment) is that the receiver had a duty to the company and its contributors to preserve the goodwill and business of the company. In my judgment, that allegation rests upon a fundamental misapprehension. There was not, in this case, and there is not in similar cases, any such duty on a mortgagee or a receiver appointed by a mortgagee for the purpose of realizing the mortgagee's security. I have no doubt that the plaintiff in this case is greatly disappointed. He has said that the transactions which the company entered into were the happy sort that you cannot lose upon them; but, unfortunately, the plaintiff and his company depended upon the goodwill of Barclay's Bank, which provided the whole of the money for the company's speculations. The bank, the plaintiff says, became altogether unduly alarmed at the effect of the Town and Country Planning Act, 1947. Whether they did or whether they did not, it is not necessary for me to determine; but the moral (as it seems to me) of the matter is this, that, if you depend exclusively on borrowed money for the business you propose to carry on, you must at all costs retain the confidence of your lender. In this case, further, in so far as the charges against the receiver involve the proposition that the receiver did not get the best price he could have got and should have got, equally those charges, in my judgment, rest upon a misapprehension of the elementary principle that a mortgagee, or a receiver exercising the mortgagee's powers of sale, is under no such duty to the mortgagor to obtain the best possible price for the property charged".

Jenkins L.J. (as he then was) says Ibid. 662: "The duties of a receiver and manager for debenture holders are widely different from those of a manager of the company. He is under no obligation to carry on the company's business at the expense of the debenture holders. Therefore he commits no breach of duty to the company by refusing to do so, even though his discontinuance of the business may be detrimental from the company's point of view. Again, his power of sale is, in effect, that of a mortgagee, and he therefore commits no breach of duty to the company by a bona fide sale, even though he might have obtained a higher price and even though, from the point of view of the company, as distinct from the debenture holders, the terms might be regarded as disadvantageous.

In a word, in the absence of fraud or mala fides (of which there is not a faintest suggestion here), the company cannot complain of any act or omission of the receiver and manager, provided that he does nothing that he is not empowered to do, and omits nothing that he is enjoined to do by the terms of his appointment."

I would not be minded, even if it became necessary to do so, to set up in opposition to each other these distinguished teams of judges. Neither decision is directly concerned with the point before me, but in each of them the judges made their views of the particular problem they are dealing with quite clear, even though many of the points were obiter dicta. I prefer to think that both courts were right in the cases with which they were dealing, instead of postulating that the judgments are at variance and that the trends of these judgments are inconsistent with each other. I think the key to the *Newdigate* case [1912] 1 Ch. 468 is that here was a receiver appointed who was seeking a special power which he could not exercise without leave, and who, in order to exercise the power, had to disregard existing obligations. I also consider that in the *Newdigate* case [1912] 1 Ch. 468, unlike the *Johnson* case [1955] Ch. 634, the court took the view (as noted) that the mortgagor had a very definite interest in the future and, I might say, immediate future of the company. On the other hand, it is obvious that the learned judges in the *Johnson* case [1955] Ch. 634 were quite clear and quite content about the analogy which they were drawing between a receiver and manager under a debenture and a mortgagee under a mortgage deed and therefore I am inclined to think that the guidance received from *Kennedy* v. *de Trafford* [1897] A.C. 180, which modifies certain observations made in earlier cases regarding the duty owed by a mortgagee to his mortgagor in respect of the sale, provides a good starting point for considering the present case. But lest I leave the matter in a state of controversy, I will deal with it from the strictly factual point of view. Accepting for the sake of argument the rather stringent test of the receiver's duty which has been put before me and applying that stringest test, and having read very carefully all the affidavits and exhibits and tried to weigh them with as much judgment as I can command, I take the view, that the interest of the companies here and of Mr. Kernohan himself is not sufficiently immediate or substantial to warrant my interfering with the receiver's proposed line of action. I agree that, merely because it is difficult to form a view, that would not be a reason for the court to set its face against interfering. But if one tries to consider the probable future course of these companies, and particularly of Kernohan Estates which owns the quarry, one is presented with a vista of applications by one party or another to permit or alternatively to prevent a sale of the assets, according to the commercial prospects from time to time. I do not consider that the course which the receiver is proposing to take could be described as wanton, reckless, negligent or even inconsiderate. There has been plenty of time for reflection and it seems obvious to me that the receiver has taken pains to extract the best results from his receivership that could be got. I am satisfied that he has acted and will continue to act in good faith in the interests of all concerned, and, from the most worldly standpoint, the size of the Bank of Ireland's debt and the fact that the receiver is also the receiver appointed by the second debenture holders should provide a sufficient guarantee for those interested in realising the assets in the best possible way. I have not forgotten that there is a large tax loss which under modern financial conditions may prove to be a considerable asset. One has even heard of people who buy a large interest in a company in order to acquire possession of something which the ordinary man would regard as a serious disadvantage, namely, tax loss. But even taking that into account, and trying to look at the next few months or even years, I am of opinion that the situation by no means warrants interference by the court, and that in fact a court would probably reach the conclusion, if the matter were considered afresh, that it would be better to sell the concern rather than to persevere with it. I agree that the companies and their shareholders may have been most unfortunate in their business dealings, but one always must have regard to the terms on which large sums of money are borrowed in order to finance a business, and to the power of the lender to realise his security. It seems to me that if one weakens the confidence of lenders one may end up by doing a great deal of harm commercially. Accordingly on the facts, no less than on my view of the law, I refuse this application. I would only add that so far as I can elucidate the facts, the desire of Kernohan Contractors to stay in business seems to depend largely on the fate of the quarry owned by Kernohan Estates Limited, since one of the objects of Kernoham Contractors would be to maintain the contracts in respect of which it is hoped that the retention moneys would be realised.

Accordingly the motion is refused and it remains only to hear applications on the question of costs.

GARRAHAN v. GARRAHAN

[1959] I.R. 168; Ir. Jur. Rep. 1 (High Court)

A judgment obtained in the High Court by the plaintiff against the defendant remained unsatisfied, and the defendant was in receipt of no income from any office or property within the jurisdiction other than a pension payable under s. 8 of the Gárda Siochána Act, 1924, in respect of past services as a Gárda officer. The Gárda Siochána Pensions Order, 1925, which regulated the conditions under which such pensions were to be payable, provided by Article 12 (1) that such pensions should be inalienable by the voluntary act of the pensioner otherwise than for the benefit of the pensioner's family.

Dixon J.:

I shall first decide the question of principle in this case, and see what the practical position then is.

The net question is whether the pension of a member of the Gárda Síochána who has retired from the Force is subject to involuntary alienation. No distinction arises in this case between a pension which is a reward for past services and one which is in the nature of continuing pay. There is no possibility of a retired member of the Gárda Síochána being called on again for service and the pension is, accordingly, one wholly payable for past services. Unless some restriction on alienability were imposed, this pension could always be made liable to answer for any debt of the pensioner's by process of execution such as the appointment of a receiver over the pension. A question arises by reason of Article 12 (1) of the Gárda Síochána Pensions Order, 1925, which does impose a restriction on the power to deal with the pension. The terms of that article, so far as relevant, are as follows:– "Every assignment of and charge on a grant, and every agreement to assign or charge a grant, shall, except so far as made for the benefit of the family of the pensioner, be void, and on the bankruptcy of the pensioner the grant shall not pass to any trustee or other person acting on behalf of the creditors."

On first impression it seems to me that the first portion of this article relates to a voluntary dealing with the pension, to an assignment or charge which the pensioner himself makes, or agrees or attempts to make, and leaves untouched the liability of the pension to involuntary alienation. The second portion, concerning the bankruptcy of the pensioner, is perhaps inserted as much as a protection to the Minister or party paying the pension as to the pensioner himself, so that the pension shall not be liable to be paid to the pensioner's assignee in bankruptcy, nor be commuted. I do not think that the fact that a provision for the bankruptcy of the pensioner is made in the second portion of the article affects the interpretation of the first which is, I think, limited to the pensioner's own acts and prohibits the pensioner himself from assigning or charging his pension. That distinction in interpretation must have been accepted by Mr. Justice Haugh in *Higgins* v. *Higgins* [1951] Ir. Jur. Rep. 29, where he made an order similar to that which I am asked to make here.

A difficulty is created by contrary views taken by the Court of Appeal in England concerning pensions of a different kind, but subject to somewhat similar provisions against alienation to those applicable here. The provisions considered by the Court of Appeal were statutory, while these are merely in an order made by the Minister for Justice under statutory authority, though I do not consider that that factor materially affects the issue. In *Lucas* v. *Harris* 18 Q. B. D. 127, it was held that the pension of a retired officer of the Indian Army was not capable of being taken in execution by means of the appointment of a receiver. In the relevant Indian Act, the Pensions Act, 1871, the material provisions are those of ss. 11 and 12. Sect. 11 expressly precluded the seizure, attachment or sequestration of a pension granted by the Government on account of past services by process of any Court in British India. Sect. 12 had a general provision that all assignments, agreements, orders, sales and securities of every kind made by the person entitled to any such pension, in respect of any money not payable at or before the making therof, on account of any such pension, or for giving or assigning any future interest therein, should be null and void.

The Court of Appeal in England took the view that, while those provisions did not apply to England, their effect was intended to be such that the taking of such a pension in execution should not be permitted in England. This decision was based to some extent on s. 141 of the Army Act, 1881, which was worded as follows:– "Every assignment of, and every charge on, and every agreement to assign or charge any . . . pension payable to any officer or soldier of any of Her Majesty's forces, or any pension payable to any such officer . . . or to any person in respect of any military service, shall, except so far as the same is made in pursuance of a royal warrant for the benefit of the family of the person entitled thereto, or as may be authorised by any Act, for the time being in force, be void". It will be seen that this section is very similar in its terms to the first portion of Article 12 (1) of the Gárda Síochána Pensions Order, 1925.

The view taken by Lindley L.J. (at p. 134) was that "These Indian enactments alone may not of themselves be sufficient to render these pensions incapable of being attached, sequestered or otherwise reached by legal process in this country. But the Indian Acts create the pensions and determine their nature, and the Courts of this country ought not, I think, to make an order which, if operative, will defeat the objects of the Indian legislature, unless the law of this country is such as to compel the Courts so to do." His Lordship, having considered the Army Act, 1881, took the view, somewhat as a matter of public policy, that execution should not be extended to pensions of this kind. Lopes L.J. took the different view that s. 141 of the Army Act, 1881, extended to prohibit involuntary alienation, saying (at p. 137):– "It is to be observed that the section does not speak only of an 'assignment,' but uses the expression 'charge on,' and I think by the latter term intended to cover judgment obtained against the party entitled to the pension, and the consequences of such judgment."

As a matter of interpretation, I should have difficulty in accepting Lord Justice Lopes' interpretation of s. 141, but should rather prefer the view of the section expressed by Denman J. in the Court below (at p. 131):– "Then again s. 141 of the Army Act, 1881, is upon the face of it, it seems to me, applicable to assignments made by the person who has the right to assign, or would have had a right to assign except for this enactment." Denman J. regarded the section, as I should have thought that its wording suggested, as applying only to a voluntary alienation, an assignment or charge of the pension made by the pensioner himself.

The question remains whether I am bound to follow the decision in *Lucas* v. *Harris* 18 Q.B.D. 127 as being a decision given by the Court of Appeal in England in 1886. I do not think that, in the circumstances of the present case, I am so bound. That decision is not exactly *in pari materia* with the present case; it relates to different enactments and is concerned with English public policy as to officers of a class or category different from the defendant.

So far as public policy is concerned, I am entitled to take into account that the Minister for Justice, when communicated with in this case, expressed no view as to any question of policy being involved so far as his Department was concerned. I must also take into account the circumstances that, although the case was not defended, a similar order to that sought by the plaintiff here was made by Mr. Justice Haugh in *Higgins* v. *Higgins* [1951] Ir. Jur. Rep. 29. Accordingly, I think myself free to express my own opinion as to the position, namely, that the Order of 1925 does not, either in terms or by implication, preclude any form of execution against this pension, and in particular, does not preclude the appointment of a receiver by way of equitable execution.

I can see that it may be a matter of public policy to ensure so far as possible that a retired member of the Gárda Síochána shall continue to receive his pension in the sense that he should be precluded from disposing of it by way of assignment or from charging it himself, unless such assignment or charge be made for the benefit of the pensioner's family. I do not see that public policy requires that his pension should be wholly incapable of being touched or attached if he incurs liabilities which cannot be met except by resort to the pension. If the Minister had taken the view that public policy did so require, I think that the article would have been phrased in wider terms.

I hold that the plaintiff is entitled to the appointment of a receiver by way of equitable execution over the defendant's pension. If he is so entitled, he would also be entitled, under the Enforcement of Court Orders Act, 1926, to an instalment order, when the District Justice would be bound to have regard to the means of the defendant and to his ability to pay. The question is not one of the plaintiff's right to attach the whole pension but of the amount of the pension that should be paid to the plaintiff having regard to the ability to pay and to the means of the defendant. It will be necessary to hear whatever evidence is available before deciding this question.

Chapter 11

CREATION OF EXPRESS TRUSTS

In this chapter we are concerned with the various rules governing the creation of express trusts. Implied, resulting and constructive trusts are dealt with in the next chapter.

I. THE THREE CERTAINTIES

CHAMBER V. FAHY
[1931] I.R. 17 (High Court)

The facts are set out in the judgments.

Sullivan P.:
The will of Patrick Fahy, father of the plaintiff, Margaret Chambers, reads as follows:-

"I leave and bequeath to my brother, Rev. J. Fahy, 8 George's Quay, Cork, my two farms, the insurance on my life, and the insurance on the joint lives of myself and my wife, with all the property which I shall die possessed of or entitled to. He is to pay all my just debts and funeral expenses. After my debts are paid, I leave absolutely all my property to my brother, Rev. J. Fahy, with full power to dispose of it as he thinks fit for the use and benefit of my wife and children."

The plaintiff claims that under that will Father Fahy took the property not beneficially, but as a trustee for the testator's wife and children, as joint tenants or as tenants in common, and that he had not any power of appointment. For the defendants, Mr. Ryan submitted that Father Fahy took the property beneficially; and Mr. Hungerford and Mr. Walker contended that he took as a trustee, with wide powers of appointment among the beneficiaries.

In the course of the argument our attention was directed to *McCabe* v. *Campbell* [1918] 1 I.R. 429, and to earlier cases, in which wills in somewhat similar terms to the present will were considered and construed. There is, however, no contest here as to the general principles applicable in such cases.

I am of opinion, notwithstanding the argument of Mr. Ryan, that the Rev. J. Fahy did not take for his own use. Mr. Ryan relies upon the words: "I leave absolutely all my property to my brother Rev. J. Fahy." I do not think we can stop at that point and disregard what follows, namely, the words: "with full power to dispose of it as he thinks for the use and benefit of my wife and children." We must read the will as a whole; and, so doing, I am satisfied that the testator did not intend that his brother should hold the property beneficially. Accordingly, in my opinion, the Rev. J. Fahy held the property as a trustee.

The next question is whether the trustee had any power of appointment among the beneficiaries. I was influenced at first by Mr. McCarthy's argument that "dispose" means to "realise," to "sell," but during the course of the argument I altered my opinion. I think that construction of the words "dispose . . . as he thinks fit," is unnecessarily narrow, and that the words confer a power to appoint among the wife and children in such shares as the trustee thinks proper. If that construction of the will be correct, there only remains for determination one question of fact. In the course of his administration of the trust Father Fahy did apportion the property in different shares among the children. Mrs. Chambers thinks she did not get a fair share, but that was a matter to be determined by the trustee. It was, however, suggested on her behalf that the trustee did not distribute among the *cestuis que trustent* the entire trust property, and that he disposed of a part of it for which he did not account. It lay upon the plaintiff to adduce some evidence to support that suggestion, and to show that part of the trust property remained unadministered by Father Fahy. She stated in the course of her evidence that part of her father's farm was given by Father Fahy to Denis Duggan, the executor of her father's will. That was denied by Denis Duggan, and there the matter rested. The Circuit Judge accepted Denis Duggan's evidence, and was satisfied that Father Fahy had fully administered the trust created by the will. On the evidence, as it appears in the transcript before us, it would be difficult for us to differ from the Circuit Judge, but we have had the advantage of seeing the schedule of assets and the deed of assignment by Father Fahy to Denis Duggan of the land which it was alleged formed part of the testator's assets. These documents were not in evidence in the Circuit Court, and it was suggested that if they were produced they would support the case made by the plaintiff. These documents do not assist the plaintiff; on the contrary, they go to show that the land assigned to Duggan formed no part of the testator's estate.

The decision of the Circuit Judge was right, and this appeal must be dismissed. Mr. Ryan's client must bear his own costs. The other defendants will get their costs out of the estate.

O'Byrne J.:

I agree with the decision of the President, and with the reasons expressed by him. I desire, however, to say a few words in regard to the construction of this will.

It is argued by Mr. Ryan that, on the true construction of the will, Rev. Father Fahy took the entire residuary estate beneficially, unencumbered by any trust. The other parties in this suit contend that he took as a trustee. A considerable number of authorities have been cited before us, and I do not intend to go through them, or attempt to reconcile them. These authorities establish certain general principles which must be applied in this as in every other case, for the purpose of gathering, as best one can, the intention of the testator in the particular case.

It has been established that, in order that a trust may be created, the subject-matter must be certain, the objects of the trust must be certain, and the words relied upon as creating the trust must have been used in an imperative sense, so as to show that the testator intended to create an obligation. Now, as far as the first two matters are concerned, there is no difficulty. The subject-matter is certain: it consists of the entire estate after the testator's debts and funeral expenses were paid. The objects of the trust are certain: they are stated in the will to be the testator's wife and children. It only remains to be considered whether the words used by the testator were used in an imperative sense, so as to create an obligation upon Rev. Father Fahy to apply the property for the purpose stated by the testator in the will. The words relied upon are:- "I leave absolutely all my property to my brother, Rev. J. Fahy, with full power to dispose of it as he thinks fit for the use and benefit of my wife and children." That clause, Mr. Ryan contends, was merely intended to express the reason for the testator's gift of the property to Father Fahy – to express, perhaps, a pious hope that he might possibly dispose of the property in favour of some of the children. If that were the object of the testator, I must say that the words used were singularly inapt and inappropriate for that purpose.

The will is a very short one. After the appointment of executor, it consists of three sentences. In construing the will, we are entitled to have regard to all the circumstances in which the will was made. This will was made five days before the testator's death. He had at that time a wife and five young children, the youngest being aged eleven years. He had a brother who was a clergyman: a clergyman, as we gather from the evidence, who was well provided for; a gentleman who, out of his own private means, was able to supply very considerable sums of money for the benefit of this family. I take it he was quite independent; and it strikes one as being very strange that a testator with a wife and five young children should pass them over, and dispose of his entire property in favour of a reverend gentleman, who was obviously in no need of it. But it was competent for him to do so, and such a bequest, if clearly expressed by the testator, must be upheld by this Court. Now, the first sentence relied upon is: "I leave and bequeath to my brother, Rev. J. Fahy, 8 George's Quay, Cork my two farms, the insurance on my life, and the insurance on the joint lives of myself and my wife, with all the property that I shall die possessed of or entitled to." This sentence is relied on by Mr. Ryan as showing that Father Fahy was not a trustee. He says that, in the first instance, the testator made a clear, absolute bequest to Father Fahy. In these circumstances, Mr. Ryan contends that the gift is not to be cut down or controlled by any trust unless such was clearly intended. I think Mr. Ryan is right in that contention; but I think the subsequent words do clearly show that the testator intended that the gift was to be cut down and controlled by the following provisions. The next sentence is to the following effect:– "He is to pay all my just debts and funeral expenses." It is fairly clear that the testator did not know that the executors are bound to pay the testator's debts and funeral expenses. That consideration is of no importance; the important consideration is what effect was intended by the testator to be given to these words. They seem to me in the clearest manner to have been intended to create a legal obligation upon Rev. Father Fahy; an obligation binding upon this property. In other words, Father Fahy took this property upon trust, in the first instance, to apply it for the purposes named, namely, to pay the debts and funeral expenses. I now come to the next and final sentence: "After my debts are paid I leave absolutely all my property to my brother, Rev. J. Fahy, with full power to dispose of it as he thinks fit for the use and benefit of my wife and children." The first sentence (with reference to the debts and funeral expenses) clearly controlled the disposal of the property: I am of opinion that the succeeding sentence has a similar object. I think I am entitled to approach the construction of this sentence in the same manner as Holmes L.J. approached the construction of a similar clause in the case of *Hickey* v. *Hickey* [1913] 1 I.R. 390. Approaching it in this way, I leave out the words "with full power to dispose of it as he thinks fit." The clause now reads: "After my debts are paid I leave absolutely all my property to my brother, Rev. J. Fahy, for the use and benefit of my wife and children." If the clause were in that form it seems to me unarguable that a trust was not intended. Can it be suggested that the insertion of the words, "with full power to dispose of it as he thinks fit," so alters that construction as to give Father Fahy a beneficial interest? I consider that it would be impossible to give such a construction to these words. They were inserted for a definite purpose; they were not intended to give Father Fahy a beneficial interest, or to cut down the clear meaning of the trust. It seems to me that the object of the words was to give Father Fahy wide descretionary powers in connection with the execution of the trust, and not to give him a beneficial interest in the property.

As to the alleged power of appointment, I am of opinion that Father Fahy had full power to appoint among the children; and I agree with the President that to give the words the meaning contended for by Mr. McCarthy would involve giving them an unnecessarily narrow construction.

It seems to me to be clear that the words, "with full power to dispose as he thinks fit for the use and benefit of my wife and children" were intended by the testator to confer upon Father Fahy rather wide discretionary powers. The words seem to me to confer a power to dispose of the property in favour of any of the persons named in the trust. I think he would be equally disposing of it for the benefit of the wife and children if he alienated it for their benefit, or distributed it amongst them. Accordingly, I am of opinion that Father Fahy was entitled to dispose of the property by appointing it amongst the objects of the trust.

I do not think it necessary to comment upon any of the questions of fact which have been dealt with by the President.

Notes

1. See further, *Irish Land Law,* para. 9.015 *et seq*.
2. On powers of appointment, see ch. 21, *post*.

RE HUMPHREY'S ESTATE

[1916] 1 I.R. 21 (Chancery Division)

A testator, having left all his property, real and personal of every kind, to his wife, added the words: "I express the wish that she should leave by her will, or transfer during her life, as she shall think fit, my house and demsne of K. to my son John . . . The remainder of my property I wish to be left, or transferred, to my daughters, Elinor Frances Beatrice and Margaret Lilian, in such way as" his wife should think fit.

Ross J.: [His lordship having stated the facts and read the will, proceeded as follows:-]

The earlier words in the will confer an absolute interest on the wife. The question is whether the later clauses cut down this interest to an estate for life. In the latter event the daughter who was born after the date of the will is altogether excluded from participation. To the ordinary man of intelligence, uninstructed in the doctrine of what are called precatory trusts, it would, no doubt, cause astonishment that there could be any doubt about the true meaning of this will.

The testator in clear words gives all his property to his wife, and appoints her executrix. He then expresses a wish that she should dispose of it for the benefit of his chidlren in a certain way. I am sure the testator himself would have been amazed if the mere expression of his wish for the guidance of his wife should have the effect of creating a legal obligation of the strictest character, tying up all the property and preventing her from providing for any children that might be born after the making of the will. After a devise and bequest in clear and explicit terms, if a trust is intended to be created one would expect that this would be done in terms equally clear and explicit. When we come to consider the innumerable decisions in which the Courts of equity have displayed their benevolent astuteness in imposing an obligatory meaning upon words merely expressive of desire, the mind is reduced to a condition of perplexity and confusion. Trusts have been held to be created by the following expressions:- "I desire him to give," "I advise him to settle," "It is my dying request," "It is my will and desire," "I recommend," "Well knowing," and such like. All these one would think impose at most a moral obligation. On the other hand, an expression of hope that the devisee would continue the estate in the family has been held to create no trust. I think it is quite impossible to reconcile the cases. However that may be, there is no doubt that the tide has turned and is running strong against precatory trusts.

In *Lambe* v. *Eames* L.R. 6 Ch. 597, at p. 599 Lord Justice James said:- "In hearing case after case cited, I could not help feeling that the officious kindness of the Court of Chancery, in interposing trusts where in many cases the father of the family never meant to create trusts, must have been a very cruel kindness indeed." These words are approved of by Lopes L.J. in *Hill* v. *Hill* [1897] 1 Q.B. 483, at p. 488, who further says: "It is inconceivable to me that a testator who really meant his hope, recommendation, confidence, or request to be imperative should not express his intention in a mandatory form. I agree with Mr. Farwell in his book on Powers, when he says at p. 480, 'It would not be a very strained inference to regard all such expressions as stating the motive that induced the absolute gift rather than as a fetter imposed upon it.' " He adds, "It is in every case a question of intention, and the whole document with the surrounding circumstances must be considered."

Lord Lindley says in *In re Hamilton* [1895] 2 Ch. 370, at p. 373:– "You must take the will which you have to construe and see what it means, and if you come to the conclusion that no trust was intended, you say so, although previous judges have said the contrary on some wills more or less similar to the one which you have to construe."

Lord St. Leonards, in his work on the Law of Property, published in 1849, wrote as follows (p. 375):– "The law as to the operation of words of recommendation, confidence, request, or the like, attached to an absolute gift, has in late times varied from the earlier authorities. In nearly every recent case the gift has been held to be uncontrolled by the request or recommendation made or confidence expressed. This undoubtedly simplifies the law, and it is not an unwholesome rule that, if a testator really mean his recommendation to be imperative, he should express his intention in a mandatory form; but this conclusion was not arrived at without a considerable struggle."

Lord Lindley approves of these words in *In re Williams* [1897] 2 Ch. 12, and calls it a sensible rule. In the same case he puts the matter thus (at p. 18):– "There can be no doubt that equitable obligations, whether trusts or conditions, can be imposed by any language which is clear enough to show an intention to impose an obligation, and is definite enough to enable the Court to ascertain what the precise obligation is, and in whose favour it is to be performed. There is also abundant authority for saying that, if property is left to a person in confidence that he will dispose of it in a particular way as to which there is no ambiguity, such words are amply sufficient to impose an obligation . . . Unless it appears from the whole will that an obligation was intended to be imposed, no obligation will be held to exist; yet, moreover, in some of the older cases obligations were inferred from language which in modern times would be thought insufficient to justify such an inference."

In *In re Hamilton* [1895] 2 Ch. 370, at p. 373 a testatrix left legacies to her two nieces, and added, "I wish them to bequeath the same equally between the families of O and P." The English Court of Appeal held that these words merely amounted to an expression of the wish of the testatrix, and created no trust in favour of the families indicated.

In *In re Diggles* 39 Ch. D. 253 the Court held that in considering whether on the whole will the testator's intention was to create a trust, regard may be had to any embarrassment and difficulty which would arise from a trust. Applying this to the case before me, surely the possibility that children might be born to the testator after making his will, for whom his wife could not provide, is such an embarrassment and difficulty.

In *Wright* v. *Atkyns*, Turn. & R. 143 which was much relied on in the contention in favour of a trust, it was laid down (at p. 157) that three things are required to create such a trust:- (1) the words must be imperative; (2) the subject must be certain; (3) the object must be certain. Assuming certainty in the subject and object indicated in this will, am I obliged to hold the words used imperative? I think not.

The outcome of the cases is simply this, that the words are to be interpreted in their ordinary sense, unless there is something in the terms of the will operating upon the property disposed of, from which a Court ought to infer that a trust is intended or a condition imposed. In this will there is not a trust, in language, from the beginning to the end of it, or anything in the will from which a trust can be legitimately inferred.

I therefore hold that Elinor Mary Augusta Longfield took the property absolutely uncontrolled by any legal obligation, and I make a declaration accordingly in respect of the £900 now in Court.

Notes and Questions

1. Do you agree with Ross J.'s comment about the tide running against precatory trusts? See *Irish Land Law*, para 9.016 *et seq*.
2. *Cf* The views of Kennedy C.J. in *Re McIntosh, infra*.

RE McINTOSH
[1933] I.R. 69 (High Court)

The facts are set out in the judgment.

Kennedy C.J.:

The father of the Minors, Peter Joseph McIntosh, died on the first of March, 1919, having made his last will on the same day. It is a short will which I should quote in full:–

"I leave devise and bequeath all my property of every nature kind and description including my business house and premises moneys cattle horses hay and the farms comprising about eleven Irish acres which I own in and about Garristown to my wife Mary Anne McIntosh until my son Richard Christopher reaches the age of twenty-five years when he is to become the absolute owner. In the meantime she may utilise it in any way she deems best for the improvement education and general welfare of my three daughters Alacoque, Esther, Marie Gertrude. Should my wife Mary Anne McIntosh re-marry instead of the above bequest she is to receive the sum of One Hundred Pounds sterling. I hereby appoint my wife sole Executrix of this my will."

The testator carried on a grocery business at Garristown, in County Wicklow, and he also worked the small farm referred to in the will. He left surviving his wife and four young children who are the Minors with whom this matter is concerned. The ages of the four children were respectively as follows:- Alacoque was ten years, Esther was eight years and Marie Gertrude was five years, and the boy who was the youngest was then aged two years. They were all living in the dwelling-house connected with the premises where the grocery business was carried on.

Probate of the will was granted on the 7th of May, 1919, to the testator's wife, Mary Anne McIntosh. She subsequently died in the year 1927 as the result of a tragic accident, when Letters of Administration *de bonis non* with the will annexed were granted to Mrs. Mary Ellen Killian, guardian of the children, for their use and benefit. The situation created by the death of Mrs. McIntosh, during the minority of all the children, was not expressly provided for by the testator when making his will. It is not surprising that in the peculiar circumstances, the business of grocer was not carried on successfully after the death of the minors' parents and had to be sold as also was the case with the small farm. The children were all taken into wardship of the Court after the mother's death, namely in the year 1927, and their education, maintenance and upbringing has been a matter of serious concern, particularly having regard to the terms of the will and to the fact that the youngest of them, the son, was to become absolute residuary legatee and devisee of the testator on attaining the age of twenty-five years.

A question has arisen as to whether, during the interval until the son reaches his age of twenty-five years, there is any power under the will to apply any part of the capital or income of the testator's property for the benefit of any of his three daughters, who, if there is no such power, are wholly unprovided for. One of them has now attained her full age and been discharged from wardship of the Court, but, though she has been trained for business, she is not yet earning sufficient income for her maintenance.

I have been requested by all the parties so as to avoid expense to entertain a summons in the Minor Matter for the construction of the will and the determination as between the Minors (including the late Minor) of this question which has been very fully argued before my by Mr. McCann for the three girls and Mr. Bacon for the boy Richard Christopher.

In all these construction cases, the tendency to read extensively from the now formidable mass of reported decisions upon the construction of an immense variety of wills affording an almost infinite choice from which to find support for any proposed interpretation of any given set of words, calls for frequent repetition of the reminder that we are seeking the intention of a particular testator in making a particular will and that we shall not find a ready-made solution in the construction put upon an apparently similar set of words in the will of another testator. The effort to fit the will of an Irish farmer into the mould of the will of some English landholding testator is, an extreme no doubt yet common, instance of a futile proceeding. Of the reported interpretation cases the only cases which help are those which lay down some canon of construction applicable to the particular problem to be solved or which explain or clarify such a canon. One group of cases cited in the present argument was concerned with a rule applicable to the determination of the nature of the interest given to the son Richard Christopher, viz., whether contingent on attaining the age of twenty-five years or immediately vested subject to the interest given to the testator's wife. I refer to *Boraston's Case* 3 Co. 19 (a), 21 (a) (b): *Mansfield* v. *Dugard* 1 Eq. Cas. Abr. 195, and the statement in Hawkins on Wills of the rule illustrated by these cases. See also *Lane* v. *Goudge* 9 Ves. 225. Of more direct bearing on the question immediately for decision are *Smith* v. *Havens* Cro. Eliz. 252; 1 Eq. Cas. Abr. 194 (G), Proposition No. 3; *Anon.* Pre. Ch. 598; *Lomax* v. *Holmeden* 3 P. Wms. 176; *Howorth . Dewell* 29 Beav. 18; *Lambe* v. *Eames* L.R. 10 Eq. 267; *Murtagh* v. *Murtagh* 36 I.L.T.R. 129; *Pickley* v. *Leahy* 34 I.L.T.R. 178, 180, though the cases of this last group are rather examples of the way in which analogous dispositions have been construed than declarations as to any rule or principle governing them.

Now in order to construe the will of Peter Jospeh McIntosh I must first look at his position, his property, and the state of his family, and then read his will as a whole. He was a grocer and very small farmer in a small country town. He was paying his way and able to support his family in the residence attached to the shop. His family consisted of his wife and four children, viz., three girls and one boy. The boy was very young and was some three years younger than the youngest girl. He contemplated the carrying on of his business so that it would ultimately come to the boy when he would reach the age of twenty-three years later. In the meantime the three girls would have to be reared and educated and the testator's wife would have to be supported and maintained. When the boy would reach the age of twenty-five years, the youngest girl would be some twenty-eight years of age, and it might be assumed that all the girls would be then settled in life or able to support themselves, if given a suitable education and training which he would have expected would be provided out of the income of the grocery business and farm carried on and managed by his wife.

Now, in my opinion, the short will made by the testator follows precisely along the line of thought I have just sketched. He put his wife in his own shoes for the twenty-three years until the boy should attain his age of twenty-five years when he was to become absolute owner of everything. In the meantime the wife would carry on the business as the testator would have done if living and would bring up and educate the family, subject only to this that if she re-married her beneficial interest was cut down to the sum of £100, an event which did not occur and the consequences whereof, therefore, we need not consider.

In my opinion the true construction of the will is that the testator gave to his wife his business as a going concern and all his property until his son Richard Christopher should reach the age of twenty-five years and that he gave Richard Christopher a vested interest in all his property subject to the estate and interest carved out of it and given to the wife. I am further of opinon that the interest given to the testator's wife was an absolute beneficial interest during the term of period of enjoyment (subject to being defeated by her marriage), and I am of opinion that it was not subject to any precatory or other trust. I do not think that it was affected in any way by the statement that she could utilise the property for the benefit of the daughters, a clause which I understand to indicate that he was not injuring them, in his view, by the disposition he was making in favour of his wife. I do not think that this clause gave power to apply capital for the benefit of the daughters.

In my opinion the interest which the testator gave to his wife devolved on her death, without having re-married, to her legal personal representatives and her four children as her next-of-kin then became equally entitled to the income of the property until the son shall reach the age of twenty-five years when he will become absolutely entitled to the whole. I do not consider, because it has not arisen, what would happen if the son should die before attaining his age of twenty-five years.

I will make a declaration according to the opinion I have stated.

II. STATUTORY REQUIREMENTS – SECRET TRUSTS

DONOHOE V. CONRAHY

(1845) 8 Ir. Eq. R. 679; 2 Jo & Lat. 668 (Chancery)

A, B and C were tenants of certain lands. A took a lease of the entire lands in the common form, describing them as in the possession of A, B and C. It was alleged that he took the lease upon trust for the benefit of B and C as to the portions in their possession. He sub-leased to B his portion, but subject to special covenants, and allowed C and his representatives to continue in possession, paying him the same acreable rent he was himself subject to, and they paid the tithe rentcharge. Parol acknowledgments were proved by A, that he would execute a lease to C when called on, and that the original lease was as good for the occupiers as for himself. In his will he devised the profits rents of the other parts, but did not notice the part in possession of C's representatives, and they were evicted by his heir.

Sugden L.C.:

I entirely agree with the regret which has been expressed on both sides, that so trifling a matter should be made the subject of an equity suit. The case, however, involves a serious question of law. The facts, I think, present to great difficulty. The parties were not in possession exactly in the way which was stated; but they had among them an unwise species of holding, under which no one man held one part in connection with any other. In the result, according to the defendant's evidence, the landlord being on the spot, refused to grant lease of the several portions, but ulimately he agreed to give a lease of the whole to one of the tenants, who had held what might be called an undivided portion. This lease contains no reference whatever to any trust or obligation on the part of the lessee to make a subdemise. Nothing of the sort is contained in it; but the lessee enters into all the obligations of a lessee, and is bound to perform them, whatever may be the liability to him of other people claiming under him.

It is said, in the first place, that in describing the property, it is mentioned to be in the possession of several tenants, and that that is unusual in this country. I am unable to say whether that representation is correct according to the custom, but there is certainly nothing extraordinary in stating the names of the persons in whose possession, at the time, the lands are described as being. Therefore, it appears to me, that that fact goes for nothing.

The claim is by two brothers, claiming under one of the previous tenants, to have leases granted to them upon a trust or agreement alleged to subsist between the actual tenant and the persons who were in possession at the time the lease was made. What are the statements in proof of that? There is no attempt to prove that any party desisted from bidding for the property in order to enable the tenant to obtain the lease of the whole as a benefit for all; such proof is generally the first step in a case of this nature. It is said to be an instance of what often takes place in the country, viz., that one of the parties should be allowed to obtain the lease, to share among all. If that had been proved, *Lamas* v. *Bayly* 2 Vern. 627, and *Atkins* v. *Rowe* More, 39 are both considerable authorities against the power of the Court to treat that as a binding agreement, even with a sufficient consideration, so as to take the case out of the Statute of Frauds. I am, therefore, not at all prepared to say, that if that had been proved, I should have been able to consider this case as out of the statute. But no such case is made, and it is an important circumstance that there is no general foundation for a claim of this kind.

Then the next step must be a promise, something amounting to what would absolutely bind the parties in this Court, or an agreement or declaration amounting to a contract to create a trust. Now, no promise is at all proved. The only attempt to prove one is, a statement which may amount to an admission or an intention that these persons should have a benefit; that goes for nothing, and no actual promise is proved, or indeed alleged. The cases referred to are all cases of actual promises, and cases in which the promise being made and not carried into execution, was a fraud on a third party and proved a delusion to the persons to whom the promise was made. Such was the case of *Thynn* v. *Thynn;* the case before Lord Eldon was of the same nature, and so were the other authorities. Here nothing of the sort is proved. The case, therefore, cannot stand on that ground.

There being thus not a shadow of evidence of a contract, the question is then, is there a trust? The only way in which the Statute of Frauds was attempted to be avoided was this:– The statute requires that every trust should be evidenced by writing, not that it should be declared in writing at the time, but that it should be evidenced by writing, therefore the writing may be subsequent to the creation of the trust; and the way in which the plaintiff here attempts to get out of the statute is, that from the *res gestæ,* taking the whole case from beginning to end, one must come more morally to the conclusion that the lease was taken on the trust. Supposing that to be so, the question still would be, whether that moral conviction amounts to a legal conclusion; whether, if I be morally convinced, I can act on that conviction and enforce that trust? But what are the facts, and do they justify the assertion that the trust is made out? The leading facts are these:– First, there is possession, and that possession is consistent with the previous holding. I think the plaintiff's evidence rather damaged the case in that respect, because it shows that the possession after the lease did not correspond with the possession before the lease; and therefore there was not a continuation of possession but a new holding. The leases granted to some of the parties afterwards are, however, stronger to show that the lessee considered himself bound to grant something like the previous holdings; but in answer to that, it is proved, not only that there was a consideration in the nature of a fine, but that the portion of the land which was previously held by these undertenants was delivered up before any underlease was granted. That is a very strong circumstance, and indeed entirely rebuts the case attempted to be founded on the grant of the underlease. But on the face of the lease itself there is a clause which puts an end to the case founded on it; for there is a right of preemption to the lessor in case the lessee should wish to let, sell or dispose of the property. That is a stipulation wholly unwarranted by this supposed trust. Therefore, when we find the lessor imposing conditions which he was not entitled to impose if he was a trustee, we must consider that the transaction proceeded on bounty or contract, and was not an execution of a trust.

Then it is said that there was imposition, and damage done by payment of the tithe rent-charge. That was satisfactorily answered by the Act of Parliament, because, although the lessee is not, as he was previously to the Act, responsible to the clergyman, yet he is responsible to the landlord, and therefore he paid. Then it is said, that the land was of more value, and from that an inference is attempted to be drawn, but I cannot enter into the question of value; the owner might let the property at what rent he chose; and even if that was to be considered, it is met by the circumstance that the parties were relatives, and therefore the one might choose to let the other hold at the same rent. Beside, the lease relied on does not refer to any preceding obligation or any trust; and that, after the lapse of so many years, is enough to show that it was not granted in execution of a contract or trust.

Then the will is referred to, in which the testator disposes only of the portion which he held himself, and not of the other portion, which was held by his former co-tenants; but I cannot deal thus with a landlord's not devising his property: a man is not forced to devise everything which he possesses; he may allow part to go to his heir-at-law; and beside, the answer probably is, that the testator nowhere devises the lands themselves in the will, but he goes on from clause to clause disposing of the profit rents only, and out of these parts he had none, as they were set at the same rent he held for; that does not impose any obligation or trust; it accounts for his not disposing of the land, because he did not dispose of a profit rent which did not, and might never, exist.

In this case there was no expenditure. There is a bare continuance of possession, which may have been as tenant from year to year. A parol contract for a lease, without any change of the relative rights of the parties, cannot be executed by this Court. Possession may be referred to other grounds, *ex gr.*, to a continuing tenancy. There must be some charge or damage to the party, or fraud, to enable the Court to interpose against the statute.

If I am to look to the parol evidence, that on the part of the plaintiff is most unsatisfactory; it goes many years back, consisting of evidence of what a man said, who is long since dead, from conversations with whom the plaintiff now endeavours to establish a trust. No such conversation is put in issue by the bill, and yet this is the very case in which it would be necessary to do so. If it was, there is not sufficient proof, and the evidence of it is altogether rebutted by the evidence on the part of the defendant. I think therefore that the case fails upon every ground of law.

Then another question arises, and a serious one, upon the right of the plaintiff, if a case was made to maintain the bill. When a party comes to a hearing, he must be prepared to show to the Court that he has the right which he claims as entitling him to sue. I see no such right here. If there was any contract or trust, this was an equitable freehold estate. These parties have proved no title to it either by devolution, or by transfer, or conveyance. Therefore they stand as mere strangers on this record, having not title to that by reason of which they sue. If the title had been proved as alleged, there is a misjoinder of plaintiffs. One would be entitled, and the other would have no right to sue. Though, morally speaking, I have some suspicion on my mind of the original intention, the case has broken down. It is a distressing case, and I have every disposition to save the plaintiffs from paying the costs, if I could; but I cannot. The case is one at which the parties should have looked with great caution before they incurred the risk of filing this bill, and putting all parties, who are in an humble situation in life, to so much expense. The bill therefore must be dismissed with costs.

Note
See further, *Irish Land Law*, para. 9.022.

RE BROWNE

[1944] I.R. 90; 77 I.L.T.R. 155 (High Court)

The facts are set out in the judgment.

Overend J.:-

This is a summary summons brought by the plaintiff, Mr. George Joseph Leo Ward, as sole executor of the will of the late Mr. Maurice Browne, of 21 Elgin Road, Dublin, for the determination of certain questions arising in the administration of the deceased's estate.

The major portion of the assets has already been realised and the plaintiff estimates that the entire proceeds will not exceed £2,000.

The defendants are Mrs. Madeline Lawler, who claims to be one of the next-of-kin of the deceased, and Miss Nora Josephine Cummings, who claims as a beneficiary.

The deceased made his will on the 17th October, 1935, some time after he had become acquainted with the plaintiff, with whom he had become intimate, and whom he had asked to act as executor to carry out his wishes, and the plaintiff had agreed. So far as appears, the testator had not at that time expressed his wishes with regard to any of his property except, perhaps, furniture.

The will is as follows:– [Reads the will.]

On the forenoon of the 25th February, 1942, the plaintiff received a message that the testator, who had been ailing for some months, was seriously ill, and he at once went out to see him. He found the testator sitting up in bed, he had been anointed that morning and knew that he was dying, but his mind was quite clear and his speech articulate. The testator asked the plaintiff to bring him a bundle of papers from a tin box in the front room. The plaintiff got the papers and handed them to the testator who himself untied the bundle, took out his will and handed it to the plaintiff saying, "This is my will." The testator then asked the plaintiff to get his fountain pen as he wanted to alter his "Instructions" with regard to the plaintiff. The document referred to as his "Instructions" is the document in the testator's writing headed:- "The wishes of Maurice Browne, of 21 Elgin Road, Dublin, which Mr. George J.L. Ward has kindly agreed to carry out." It bears in pencil at its head the date "Nov. 23rd. 1939."

The plaintiff got the pen for the testator who said he wished to give the plaintiff £100, and he struck out the word "fifty" and interlined the words "one hundred" in the Instructions. The testator appeared to read and consider them and finally handed them to the plaintiff and also handed back the other documents. He told the plaintiff that Miss Cummings was to have the income of £2,000 for life and that on her marrying or dying the £2,000 was to be divided equally between the Dominican Nuns at Cabra and the Committee of the Deaf and Dumb Institute, North Great George's Street, Dublin.

The plaintiff says the testator explained to him the essentials of the Instructions, but did not go into all the details. The plaintiff read the will after it was handed to him, but did not read the Instructions at that time and did not know exactly all they contained till after the testator's death, which took place that afternoon. The testator had said his house and shares ought to produce £2,000.

The plaintiff's interview with the testator lasted about an hour, during which the testator, amongst other things, discussed his share holdings in the Commonwealth Mining and Finance Ltd., and Great Boulder Mining and Finance Ltd., and their realisation.

When the testator handed back the other documents to the plaintiff the latter did not retain the will and instructions, but put all in the bundle and replaced it in the tin box. He took possession of the bundle later the same day some fifteen minutes or so after the testator's death had taken place.

The plaintiff says that on the 25th February, 1942, the testator clearly understood that he, the plaintiff, would act as executor and would carry out his wishes. He had first promised to do so in 1935, before the execution of the will. The Instructions are as follows:– [Reads the relevant portions of the Instructions.]

The plaintiff makes no claim beneficially to anything beyond the £100 and, I think, the roll-top desk, but he wants to have it decided whether he can lawfully carry out the testator's wishes as expressed to him verbally, or as contained in the "Instructions," or whether the next-of-kin are entitled.

Mrs. Lawler claims to be one of the next-of-kin, and as the class is apparently numerous and unascertained, I appointed her to represent the next-of-kin.

Counsel for Miss Cummings argued that an enforceable trust has been created, that plaintiff is bound to give effect to the testator's wishes (a) as expressed in the "Instructions", or (b) as verbally told to the plaintiff by the testator; while counsel for Mrs. Lawler contend that the entire transaction is in contravention of s. 9 of the Wills Act and that the testator's next-of-kin are entitled.

Now, the first matter to be considered is the will itself. It contains a clear bequest of the testator's property of every kind to the plaintiff in terms which would pass the absolute ownership. This is followed by the words "I relying on his carrying out the wishes that I have expressed to him and/or may do so hereafter.

For the next-of-kin it is contended that these words make it clear that the plaintiff took the property merely as a trustee, and that the testator was thereby reserving to himself the right to make future dispositions of his property.

I do not accept this view. We know from the plaintiff's testimony that prior to the date of the will he had consented to act as testator's executor and had agreed to carry out his wishes. There is nothing in the will to connect the wishes with the testator's property, the wish might be to have certain masses said, to upkeep a grave, to pay an annuity, or one hundred and one other things having no relation to the subject-matter of the gift to the plaintiff. The wishes might be of a kind, such as the rendering of some personal service, quite incapable of being enforced. So far as the will is concerned I find a universal gift to the plaintiff absolutely, and I see nothing to indicate that he is merely a trustee of the property so bequeathed, and nothing to subject him to any legal obligation or condition, though, of course, apart from the will he would be bound by the secret trust which has been established by the evidence in this case.

But assuming that the will in this case did indicate in some way the gift, though absolute in form, was not intended to be enjoyed by the legatee beneficially, in my opinion, this would make no difference. This view of the law was long since accepted in this country and in the year 1888 the law as to secret trusts was summarised in a most succinct and accurate manner by Mr. Justice Monroe, a well-known Common Law lawyer, in *Kings's Estate* 21 L.R. Ir. 273, at p. 277. [His Lordship quoted the passage from the judgment in which these rules are stated.]

In England all doubts have been finally disposed of by the House of Lords in *Blackwell* v. *Blackwell* [1929] A.C. 318.

It is also immaterial that the trusts were communicated after the execution of the will, so long as they were communicated to the legatee, and accepted by him, in the lifetime of the testator.

All the essentials are proved in the present case. On 25th February, 1942, the testator gave the plaintiff his will and the plaintiff read it. That made it clear that the testator was parting absolutely with his property and with all power of disposition over it and relying solely on the plaintiff's good faith, as legal owner, to give effect to his wishes. He then produced the so-called "Instructions," which are expressed to contain his wishes, and told the plaintiff all the essentials, though without going into every detail. The plaintiff made it clear to the testator that he accepted the trusts. I hold that this was sufficient communication of the trusts: *In re Keen* [1937] Ch. 236; *McCormack* v. *Grogan* L.R. 4 H.L. 82. This case is not affected by the Wills Act as is clear from the speeches in *Blackwell's Case* [1929] A.C. 318. I have so far refrained from quoting passages from the judgments in that case because every line is worthy of the closest consideration, but in this connection I may refer to Lord Warrington's speech at p. 342. He says:- "I think the solution is to be found by bearing in mind that what is enforced is not a trust imposed by the will, but one arising from the acceptance by the legatee of the trust, communicated by him to the testator, on the faith of which acceptance the will was made or left unrevoked, as the case might be. If the evidence had merely established who were the persons and what were the purposes indicated it would in my opinion have been inadmissible, as to admit it would be to allow the making of a will by parol. It is the fact of the acceptance of the personal obligation which is the essential feature, and the rest of the evidence which is merely for the purpose of ascertaining the nature of that obligation." Great Judges as far back as Lord Cairns and Lord Hatherley have had no difficulty in saying that Equity will circumvent the Wills Act in order to prevent a breach of undertaking given to a testator. In *Jones* v. *Badley* L.R. 3 Ch. 362, at p. 363 Lord Cairns says:– "Where a person knowing that a testator, in making a disposition in his favour, intends it to be applied for purposes other than for his own benefit, either expressly promises, or by silence implies, that he will carry the testator's intention into effect, and the property is left to him upon the faith of that promise or undertaking, it is in effect a case of trust, and in such case the Court will not allow the devisee to set up the Statute of Frauds, or, rather, the Statute of Wills, by which the Statute of Frauds is now in this respect superseded, and for this reason:– The devisee, by his conduct, has induced the testator to leave him the property, and, as the Lord Justice Turner says in *Russell* v. *Jackson* 10 Hare 204, no one can doubt that if the devisee had stated that he would not carry into effect the intentions of the testator, the disposition in his favour would not have been found in the will. But in this the Court does not violate the spirit of the statutes; but for the same end, namely, prevention of fraud, it engrafts the trusts on the devise by admitting evidence which the statute would in terms exclude, in order to prevent a devisee from applying property to a purpose foreign to that for which he undertook to hold it." In *McCormack* v. *Grogan* L.R. 4 H.L. 82, at p.89, Lord Hatherley says that this doctrine "is in itself a doctrine which involves a wide departure from the policy which induced the Legislature to pass the Statute of Frauds." In the same case Lord Westbury says:– "It is a jurdisdiction by which a Court of Equity, proceeding on the ground of fraud, converts the party who has committed it into a trustee for the party who is injured by that fraud . . . . The Court of Equity has, from a very early period, decided that even an Act of Parliament shall not be used as an instrument of fraud; and if in the machinery of perpetrating a fraud an Act of Parliament intervenes, the Court of Equity, it is true, does not set aside the Act of Parliament, but it fastens on the individual who gets a title under that Act, and imposes upon him a personal obligation, because he applies the Act as an instrument for accomplishing a fraud."

It is clear from Lord Warrington's judgment that there is an enforceable trust in this case. The plaintiff wishes to perform the trust, if he can lawfully do so. I am of opinion that he can, and accordingly, I shall answer question 1 (a) in the affirmative.

Note

See further *Irish Land Law*, para. 9.029 *et seq.*

GEDDIS V. SEMPLE

[1903] 1 I.R. 73 (Court of Appeal)

A testator devised certain houses, and also a legacy of £600 charged on the remainder of his property, which comprised landed property, to three persons absolutely, as tenants in common, coupled with a secret trust for charitable purposes. One of the legatees at the time the will was made was informed of the trust, the other two had no knowledge of it until after the death of the testator. The testator died within three months after making his will. It was held by Chatterton, V.-C. that the bequest of the three houses failed, and also the legacy of £600 so far as same was payable out of the real estate or chattels real of the testator. An appeal was made.

FitzGibbon L.J.:

We do not require a reply. The appeal was opened by Mr. Andrews in a manner that left nothing to be desired. He referred to all the authorities, and we have fully heard Mr. Matheson on the other side, and the question is a difficult case with much to be said on each side.

The disposition of the property in dispute is not one single gift to three people; there are three distinct gifts of different shares of property, one to each of three devisees, tenants in common, no doubt made with the purpose and in the expectation, on the part of the testator, that the property given to each and all shall and will be applied to the same charitable object. As regards one of the three, the Rev. Mr. Semple, it has been proved that he was party to an arrangement, or understanding, with the testator before the will was made, that the property should be so applied; and whether that arrangement or understanding was indicated by express language, or by silent acquiescence on Mr. Semple's part, makes no difference. His conscience was bound by a secret trust which, in the event which has happened, invalidates the devise to him. He knew beforehand that the gift to him was made in form absolute, but with the intention on his part, as well as on that of the testator, of evading the law, which would make it void, if given for the charitable purpose, if the testator should die within three months.

It is established law that a secret trust invalidates the gift when, if the property had been given upon an express trust to the same effect, the gift would have failed.

It is also established that, where property is given to several persons jointly on a secret trust which binds one of them, and fails, the infirmity affects the whole gift. But where property is given in separate shares to distinct people as devisees in common, one being bound by a secret trust, and the others not, the only gift which can be affected is that which is taken by the secret trustee. Whether the intended purpose is identical as to each of the shares, or whether, as in the case referred to by Lord Hatherley see *Tee* v. *Ferris,* 2 K. & J. 365, one piece of property is given to A for one purpose, another to B for another purpose, and a third to C for a third purpose, the result must be the same; if two of the devisees are not affected by any trust, though the third is bound, the devises to the two who are entitled to take absolutely cannot be avoided by the trust which affects the gift to the third.

A distinction was sought to be made between the case where the charitable purpose is indicated *before the will* to one of several devisees, and is accepted by him as a secret trust; and the case where the gift in terms absolute is first made in joint tenancy and a statement of the charitable purpose is afterwards made to one or more of the devisees. But I think the distinction must depend upon whether the gift is one single joint gift of the whole property, or there are several gifts; and a gift in common is, in my opinion, to be regarded as so many separate gifts of distinct things to different people. If the man who was the *dux facti,* in accepting the trust, took the property jointly with others, knowing it to be intended for a charitable purpose, none of it could be taken absolutely; but if it, or any part of it, was given absolutely to a person who, when it was given, knew nothing of the intention to devote it to charity, that devisee could not be deprived of it by the fact that some one else knew of the intention.

The "O'Hagan Clause" has been recognised in Ireland as a valid mode of disposition, and under it an express trust for a charitable purpose is followed by an absolute gift, very often to the same devisee, which is to take effect in the event of the charitable trust becoming or proving void.

The law is settled that an absolute gift by will cannot be defeated by proof that it was made in the expectation that the devisee will apply, or will even hold himself bound in honour to apply, the property to a charitable purpose which would otherwise fail, provided always that the gift is absolute, and that the property is intended by the testator to reach the destination for which it is intended, through the voluntary exercise by the devisee of his own right of ownership, and not through any obligation of conscience, or of contract, or in pursuance of any previous arrangement or understanding, binding the conscience of the devisee, and so making him a secret trustee for a purpose which is illegal.

The circumstances show that there never was a disposition of property which more clearly originated with the testator himself, or which was more clearly intended to be in law and fact an absolute gift, though expected to benefit a charity, than the present one. He first made a will expressing the charitable trust. He had some misgiving as to its validity; and he asked the solicitor's clerk, who was taking his instructions, whether it would be good if he died within three months. The clerk, who seems to have been a prudent and intelligent man, consulted his principals, and they advised that the property must be given absolutely, in order to make the devise good; but that it might be so given to persons upon whom the testator could rely to carry out his wishes, if he should die within three months. The first devisee was the clergyman of the church for the benefit of which the gift was intended. He knew all about it before the absolute gift was made; he and the testator mutually understood from the beginning that the property was to be devoted to the charity, and it is conceded that the gift to him is bound by a secret trust, and fails.

The second devisee was the doctor who was attending the testator, but he knew nothing about the trust. The third was Mr. Shean, who was first mentioned by the clergyman, and was made a devisee by the testator on the very shadowy statement that he would carry out anything that the testator wished. Mr. Shean knew nothing about the will until after the testator's death, and then he proclaimed that, so far as he was concerned, he would not take the property for himself, and that he would not have anything to do with it. That being so, we have three distinct gifts, each of one-third of the property, and two of them were made without any element of duty or trust, but simply in reliance on the willingness, or on the honour, of the devisees, to devote the property to the purpose to which the testator desired to devote it, in the event of his dying within three months.

The vast number of cases in which testators with children have given their property absolutely to their wives are really cases depending on the same principle. There is an intention, in every such case, that the property shall not be retained by the wife as exclusively her own, but that she shall devote it to the children; but the testator leaves it to her to apply it for their benefit, in the exercise of the absolute ownership which he confers upon her. It would be as impossible, as it would be inexpedient, to attempt to affect such gifts by trusts.

It was suggested that because, after the testator's death, Mr. Shean said that he was a trustee, and that he would only take the property as a trustee, he could not take or keep it. But in effect he said: "I will take the property only to do with it what the testator intended." That is not a declaration of trust, and it can not affect the right of the devisee to take the property. If he were a trustee he could not take it at all; but he has not disclaimed the devise, he has only stated that he will not apply it for his own benefit, and he, as absolute devisee, is at liberty to apply it to the object of the charity none the less because that object was in the testator's mind.

We must vary the order of the Vice-Chancellor by limiting the declaration of invalidity to the one-third of the property which was left to the Rev. Mr. Semple, and declare that the other two-thirds went absolutely to Dr. Steele and Mr. Shean as tenants in common. The plaintiff will be allowed her costs of suit up to and including the hearing before the Vice-Chancellor, to be paid out of the estate, as she represents all the legatees, and the case is one in which it was necessary to take the opinion of the Court of Chancery. The executors will have their costs in the same manner. Dr. Steele and Mr. Shean must be allowed their costs in the Court below, and of the appeal. These costs will be paid, in the first instance, so far as the amount will allow, out of the one-third portion of the property which was devised to the Rev. Mr. Semple. He must abide his own costs.

Walker L.J.:

Upon the facts in this case I do not think there was any inducement used by Mr. Semple, even as regards Mr. Shean, to attract the doctrine of *Huguenin* v. *Baseley* 14 Ves. 273 and *Russell* v. *Jackson* 10 Hare, 204 so far as it applies to that case.

The testator knew the law perfectly well, and knew that he must rely on the honour of the persons whom he would name as legatees, and accordingly by a will which has been proved in solemn form he gives the houses by separate gifts to those three gentlemen as independent gifts. Mr. Semple first suggested, in order to satisfy the object of the testator, the name of McMillan; the testator would not accept him, and then Mr. Semple mentioned the name of Shean, whom the testator accepted, being satisfied, with full knowledge of the law and the effect of the gift, that he might rely on his honour. The testator was as much the person who selected Shean as Mr. Semple was. Each legatee gets a separate interest, and I cannot see how any inducement of Semple as regards himself can be extended to Shean, much less to Dr. Steele, whom he did not name.

Then Mr. Matheson, on the hypothesis that Mr. Semple has induced the gifts in the will, argues as matter of law that the gifts not only to Semple, but to Dr. Steele and Mr. Shean, as tenants in common, fail though neither of them had any knowledge of the dispositions in the will, or the testator's wishes, till after the death of the testator. I suggested to him during the argument that this could have no application to the case of Dr. Steele, whom Mr. Semple did not name; but, apart from that, I do not agree that the authorities bear out Mr. Matheson's contention.

It is true that the cases have established that if a testator is induced by A, on the faith of a promise made by him, that he will carry out a trust communicated to him to make a gift in joint tenancy to him A and B, the trust binds both A and B; but if the gift having been made in joint tenancy without any knowledge or promise of A, he (A) after the will makes a similar promise by reason of which the will is left unrevoked, the trust binds A only. I share the difficulty felt by Farewell, J., in *Witham* v. *Andrew* [1900] 1 Ch. 237 of seeing the difference between the two cases, but it is not necessary in the present case to express any opinion on the point. In the case before us the gift is to Semple, Steele, and Shean as tenants in common – gifts quite as separate and independent as if a different house were left to each of them – and in such a case *Tee* v. *Ferris* 2 K. & J. 357 and *Witham* v. *Andrew* [1900] 1 Ch. 237 have established that a different rule applies from the case of a joint tenancy. Farwell, J., says– "If A induces B either to make or leave unrevoked a will leaving property to A and C as tenants in common by expressly promising or tacitly consenting that he and C will carry out the testator's wishes, and C knows nothing of the matter until after B's death, A is bound, but C is not bound." On the two grounds therefore that there was no inducement, even in the case of Mr. Shean, within the meaning of the authorities, and that the gift here was to the devisees as tenants in common, I am unable to concur in the argument for the respondents.

The last contention put forward, viz. that there was here a trust declared after the death, which the Court should carry out, seems to me quite untenable. It proceeds on the assumption that the legatees had an absolute interest unfettered by any trust, and what they, or one of them, said was attributable to that ownership – an expression of intention to do what they liked with their own – in other words that, quite irrespective of any trust, they would as a matter of honour, and by virtue of their ownership, do what they know now the testator would have wished. Mr. Shean's statement means – I will hold the property for the church, because I am owner, and by virtue of my absolute ownership.

I concur in the rule as to costs.

Holmes L.J.:

It often happens, when the doctrine of secret trust is sought to be applied, that there is a difficulty in ascertaining the facts. This does not exist in the present case, as the evidence shows clearly what happened. The testator desired to give three houses and £600 in trust for a charitable purpose, and he executed a will containing a gift of this property to his executors upon the trust intended. It then occurred to him that if he were to die (as he did) within three months, the trust, in so far as it related to real estate or chattels real, would fail; and, having consulted his lawyer, he was advised that the only way in which the suggested difficulty could be avoided would be to give the property to one or more persons absolutely, in the hope that when they would come to know the testator's wishes, he or they would carry them out. The testator accordingly had a new will prepared, by which he gave the houses and money to three persons, named Semple, Steele, and Shean, as tenants in common, without attaching any trust. It has been assumed by Mr. Matheson in his argument that there was some impropriety in this; and, on my asking him in what it consisted, he said that it was a fraud upon the statute. I have heard this expression before, but I do not understand it. There is no fraud in doing what the law permits; and an absolute devise of lands, unfettered by a trust, is valid, even if the testator were to die the next day, and if the devise were made on the chance and in the hope that the devisee would apply it to some charitable purpose. In this case there is no doubt that if the three legatees had heard nothing about the gift to them until after the testator's death, the property would have belonged to them in equal shares, each being entitled to do what he liked with his own share. This happened in the case of two of them, Dr. Steele and Mr. Shean. The first knowledge they had of the contents of the will, or of the fact that they were named in it, was when it was read on the day of the funeral. Mr. Semple was present when the matter was discussed between the testator and his lawyer, and he knew that the property was given to the devisees in the hope that it would be applied by them to the charitable purpose. Mr. Matheson has spoken of Mr. Semple inducing the testator to make the gift and of his being an agent in bringing about a fraud. There is nothing to justify either allegation. The plan of making an absolute gift came from the solicitor, and was adopted by the testator, Mr. Semple's only interference being that he suggested the name of Mr. Shean. The reference to fraud arises from a confusion of ideas. When we speak of fraud in connexion with secret trusts, what is referred to is the fraud of a man allowing a testator to bequeath him property in the expectation that he will hold it in trust, and afterwards claiming it as his own. To prevent such a fraud as this, the law attaches the trust to the property; and as Mr. Semple was informed by the testator of the object of the gift, he must be held to have taken his third share in trust, with all the consequences flowing therefrom. But why should any trust be attached to the other two-thirds?

It is, I think, settled that where a gift is given to two persons as joint tenants, a secret trust imparted to one of them will affect the whole gift; but that this arises from the peculiar nature of a joint estate is shown by repeated decisions that this rule does not apply to tenants in common. It is admitted that if, after he had made the will, the testator had informed Mr. Semple alone of what he had done and of his object, the shares of the others would not have been affected with the trust; but a distinction is sought to be drawn from the fact that the communication was made before the will. This would be a purely arbitrary and illogical distinction. There is no difference in principle between the gift of undivided shares to three persons in severalty and a gift of one of the houses and £200 to each of the legatees. I hold, therefore, that Steele and Shean became absolutely entitled to their shares; and although they may now say that they will hold them for the charitable purpose intended by the testator, this is their own act, and, not being a trust imposed by the testator, is legal and valid.

Notes and Questions

1.Do you agree with the reasoning of the Court of Appeal? Why should the rules for joint tenants be different? See *Irish Land Law,* para. 9.032.
2. As regards the "O'Hagan" clause, see *ibid.*, para. 9.094.

O'BRIEN V. CONDON

[1905] 1 I.R. 51; 5 N.I.J.R.9; 38 I.L.T.R. 252 (Chancery Division)

A testator bequeathed personalty to O., "to be distributed as he thinks right." He appointed no executor. O. was the person who prepared testator's will, and was verbally informed at the time of the execution thereof by testator that he wished him to do "as he thought fit with the money, to distribute it, after payment of debts, &c.," among five named persons, of whom B. (one of the next-of-kin) was one. O. accepted the trust:

PORTER M.R. (after stating the facts):

The facts, therefore, are simple, but they give rise to two points of some nicety.

First, what estate and interest did the Rev. Father O'Brien take under the will of 7th March, 1904, which is in these terms:– "I do hereby will and bequeath any money I shall die possessed of to the Rev. Walter O'Brien, C.C., Doneraile, to be distributed as he thinks right."

There is no executor named in the will. If the Rev. Walter O'Brien had been an executor, there could be no question but that a gift to him to distribute would deprive him of any beneficial interest in the property, because a devise to him in these terms would be primarily given to him in his capacity as executor; and if there were no trusts named in the will, the gift would enure for the benefit of the next-of-kin under the Statute of Distributions. But as the will does not designate any executor, the point to consider in the first instance is this, "Did Father O'Brien take on the face of the will a beneficial interest, or does he take merely as trustee by virtue of the word 'distribute'?"

It is very difficult to construe the language of such wills by merely parsing it. Testators use different language, sometimes one word, and sometimes another, and there is no decision that there is any necessary meaning of the word "distribute" standing alone; but there is nothing in the word itself to imply an absence of beneficial interest in property. *Fenton* v. *Nevin* 31 L.R. Ir. 478 is distinguishable on the ground mentioned, and which formed the basis of the judgment of FitzGibbon, L.J., in the Court of Appeal, viz. that there was an indication that the property was to be taken by the legatees in the character of executors *Ibid,* 485. But in this case the word "distribute" does not, in my opinion, show that it was intended that Father O'Brien should be merely a conduit-pipe or donee of a power to appoint among beneficiaries. "Distribute" does not imply an absence of beneficial interest in the property, nor can I see any solid distinction in law or fact between "distribute" and "dispose of." If the expression were "dispose of," it would be the very essence of the gift that the donee should be able to dispose of it as he wishes, and there is nothing etymologically in the word "distribute" making it different from "dispose of." Then is there any trust on the face of the will so that Father O'Brien must give away the property devised to him without retaining any beneficial interest in it himself? I think it is unarguable that there is any trust appearing on the face of the will; and if the transaction began and ended there, Father O' Brien would have got the property with an unconditional right to distribute it as he thought fit, in payment of his own debts, or by using it in any way he thought fit. But in order to get at the testator's meaning in this case, we must consider something outside the will. If there were no question of a secret trust, I have no doubt that the gift to the man of the property, to distribute as he thought right, made him complete *dominus* of it.

The case on that point is free from authority; but inasmuch as Father O'Brien does not claim that in fact there is an absolute gift to him of any beneficial interest in the property, the next question is whether, as it is given on a trust not disclosed by the will, it is a trust enforceable against him and binding on his conscience. This is a typical illustration of a secret trust. That phrase does not necessarily mean a trust of a clandestine nature, or one that is suppressed from the world. It only means a trust which is not disclosed on the face of the will itself. It is unnecessary to go through the authorities on the subject. It cannot be contended that if Father O'Brien were to put this money in his pocket, and refuse to give any of it to Bridget Condon or Ellen Roche, or any of the other persons named by the testator, he would not be guilty of personal fraud. He led the testator to infer that he would carry out his wishes; and if he were now to set them aside and close on the money, he would be guilty of gross personal fraud. That being so, it is a case of secret trust which, notwithstanding the Wills Act or the Statute of Frauds, will now be enforced, as binding on the conscience and honour of the legatee. A series of cases such as *Moss* v. *Cooper* 1 J. & H. 352, 366 and *Johnson* v. *Ball* 5 De G. & Sm. 85, and especially *In re Fleetwood* 15 Ch. D. 594, show that the law is fixed, and that it does not make any matter whether the trust is disclosed before the making of the will or at the time it was made, or even afterwards, if the legatee, knowing the testator's wishes, has given him to understand that he will carry out his intentions. The statement of the testator in the present case appears to have been a contemporaneous transaction with the will, and constitutes a secret trust within the meaning of the doctrine of the Court, and the legatee takes subject to this trust which is fastened on his conscience and will be enforced.

Another question has arisen for decision which has not evoked much sympathy from anyone. Bridget Condon is one of the next-of-kin of the testator, and is also one of the persons whom he declared his intention of benefiting, and who were the subject of the secret trust. She was one of the witnesses to the will, and it is said that she consequently loses all benefit under it *quâcunque viâ*, whether she takes by virtue of the will alone, as one of the next-of-kin, or by virtue of the will giving the property on trust for certain named persons of whom she is one; but the argument chiefly turned on the ground that she took a benefit under a declaration of secret trust. The 15th section of the Wills Act (1 Vict. c. 26) provides:– "And be it further enacted, that if any person shall attest the execution of any will to whom, or to whose wife or husband, any beneficial devise, legacy, estate, interest, gift, or appointment, of or affecting any real or personal estate," omitting the words in brackets, "shall be thereby given or made, such devise, legacy, estate, interest, gift, or appointment shall, so far only as concerns such person attesting the execution of such will, or the wife or husband of such person, or any person claiming under such person or wife or husband, be utterly null and void, and such person so attesting shall be admitted as a witness to prove the execution of such will or to prove the validity or invalidity thereof, notwithstanding such devise, legacy, estate, interest, gift or appointment mentioned in such will."

The question therefore is, whether Bridget Condon is a person to whom a "legacy, estate, interest, gift, or appointment" is "thereby" given or made, that is, by the will. She is not named in the will, and therefore she is not on the face of the will, at any rate, a legatee, and so far as her position is concerned under the will she would take nothing were it not for the secret trust.

Granting that on the face of the will she takes nothing and is not a legatee under it, it is said that by virtue of the will she takes an interest under the trust, because except for the will she could take nothing. If it were not for authority on the subject, I should have no difficulty in holding that the case is not within the mischief contemplated by the 15th section, and which it was intended to prevent; that is, to prevent a person taking any benefit under it because a person taking a benefit under the instrument ought not to be a witness to it. The witnesses ought to be independent. Here the person putting her signature to a document by which on the face of it she takes nothing, of whose contents she knew nothing, and as to the existence of any right under which she knew nothing, but which rather negatives the gift of any benefit to her, because there is an absolute gift to Father O'Brien, seems outside the mischief provided against by the statute; and if it were not for *In re Fleetwood* 15 Ch. D. 594, I should have no hesitation in deciding that Mrs. Condon did not take anything under the will of John O'Brien. What she takes under the trust is something not under the will, but solely by virtue of the secret trust not disclosed on the will; and if authority for that proposition be wanting, it is supplied by *Attorney-General for Ireland* v. *Cullen* 14 Ir. C.L.R. 137, in which case property subject to a secret trust for charity was devised by will to two individuals; and it was held that the interest under the trust was not a legacy for charitable purposes under the will so as to be exempted from duty. The gift to the charity was held not to be a legacy, but something coming from a source different from the will.

No doubt, Hall, V.-C., did decide this very point in *In re Fleetwood* 15 Ch. D. 594. He says, at the end of a long judgment on an entirely different subject, "Miss Mary Head, one of the attesting witnesses to the fourth codicil, being intended to be a beneficiary under the parol trust declared of the furniture, I think that the trust for her and her sister fails as to her beneficial interest, as it would have done had the trust been declared in the codicil, and that she and her sister being joint tenants of the beneficial interests of the furniture, the whole belongs to the sister."

No doubt that is a decision in point. It is open to the observation that the matter does not appear to have been argued; and I think the decision, so far as this point is concerned, is contrary to principle, and strains the language of the 15th section of the Wills Act. The benefit provided for Mrs. Condon is not, in my opinion, a legacy given by will; nor is it an interest or benefit given by will, but rather something claimed and obtained against the will. Under those circumstances what ought I to do? English Judges do not consider Irish decisions binding on them, though they always treat them with respect. Where there is no conflict with Irish cases, we are in the habit of treating English decisions as governing us here, though technically, perhaps, we may not be bound by them. If there is a conflict in principle between an English and an Irish case, we in Courts of first instance are bound to follow the Irish decision.

Having a strong and clear opinion, should I give effect to it, or should I follow a decision with which I do not agree, leaving it to the parties if they wish to go to the Court of Appeal?

On the whole, as the case was not argued before Hall, V.-C., and as this is a small estate, and I think it would be a hardship to put the parties to the perhaps unnecessary cost of an appeal, I think it better to give effect to my own opinon, which is in accordance with the governing principle in *Attorney-General* v. *Cullen*, 14 Ir.C.L.R. 137; affirmed – L.R.1 H.L.C. 190, and I decide that Bridget Condon does not lose her interest under the trust by reason of her being a witness to the will. I do not rest my judgment upon the fact (which seems to be immaterial) that she was a third witness – a complete attestation having preceded her signature, which was thus quite useless.

Note
See further, *Irish Land Law*, para. 9.037

III. EXECUTED AND EXECUTORY TRUSTS

BOSWELL V. DILLON
(1844) 6 Ir. Eq. R. 389; Dru. *temp.* Sug. 291 (Chancery)

A testator devised his property to trustees, and the will contained the following passages, among others: "The said sum I will shall be taken from my real, freehold and personal property;" the residue "to be divided between them by my said trustees share and share alike, at such time and in such manner as to my said trustees shall seem most expedient, subject to this limitation," &c; shares of sons, in certain events, were to go to survivors, "subject, however, to such jointure as my said sons, or any of them, may settle on any wife," &c.; premises were devised to the son carrying on the testator's business "at such reasonable rent as my trustees shall think proper;" "I further will my trustees shall lend out at interest" certain sums bequeathed, in the way prescribed; a small annuity was given to W.B., "to be paid to him by my said trustees out of the issues," &c. A codicil bequeathed other property "to be divided equally among, &c., agreeable to the real intention of my will."

Sugden L.C.:
Every trust is in a sense executory; when however there is a mere trust, giving just a legal estate to the trustee, who has a *certain* trust to perform, we are not in the habit of calling that an executory trust. In the proper sense, an executory trust is a trust in which something more is to be done. Executory trusts may thus be of two kinds, one in which something is to be done; yet where the testator has acted as his own conveyancer, as it is called, and the Court has nothing to do but to follow out and enforce the limitations. Such trusts do not differ from ordinary estates. They must be construed according to the clear intent of the settlor. The other species of executory trust is, when the testator, intending something beyond what is effected by the words creating the estate, has imperfectly stated what is to be done; and the Court is thus invested with a larger discretion, than if the words stood by themselves. The question in the present instance is, to which of these two classes the case before me now belongs? This is the only question now before me, and the only one argued, for I am not now going to decide the questions on the construction of the will fully.

I will assume – indeed it has been so argued, and I must assume – that the trustees take the legal fee. Then the question is, is there any such direction as will enable me to mould the limitations of the property according to the presumed intention of the testator, and not according to the strict legal construction of the words of the will? The only words that could empower me to do so, are the words which follow the gift to the daughters: "And as to all the rest and residue of my real, freehold, and personal property, I devise to my three sons, to be divided between them by my said trustees, share and share alike, at such time and in such manner as to my said trustees shall seem most expedient," subject to the limitations in case of death, and so on. But what is the meaning of these words? Do they, as it is contended, imply that the objects are to take estates limited under a direction given to the trustees, with other restrictions than those mentioned in the will? Or that they are to take the property precisely as the testator has given it, but that the conveyance is to be made at such time and in such manner as the trustees shall determine? The passage next following is, "Subject to this limitation, that, in case of the death of a son under age, or in case of any dying unmarried, or without issue, the property shall go the survivor." Does the will then say more than this, "You shall put my sons into possession subject to these directions as to their dying under age and soforth?" – the testator looking to the *time*, and not to the division, the proportions of which are expressly declared. It contains no power, nor any allusion to a power, or intention to give authority, to the trustees as to the limitations to be made. It is expressly said, "share and share alike." I am clearly of opinion the discretion given to the trustees is as to the time and manner only.

An argument has been founded on the passage relating to the jointures of the sons' wives. But I do not think this implies any such discretion as contended for. The testator had already given his sons such an estate as would allow them to jointure, and this is merely a declaration respecting any such jointure, in the event of the estate previously given being cut down. The will says afterwards expressly, my sons shall only have estates for life in certain events. This by no means implies that the trustees, in a settlement they are to make, shall have any power as to giving an estate for life or not, but that the sons shall in no event have more. The whole will is thus consistent. There is nothing therefore to give me jurisdiction. I must construe this will as it would be construed in a Court of Law.

Note
See further *Irish Land Law*, para. 9.038 and *Rochfort* v. *Fitzmaurice*, *infra*.

ROCHFORT V. FITZMAURICE

(1842) 4 Ir. Eq. R. 375; 2 Dr. & War. 1; 1 Con. & L. 158 (Chancery)

The facts are set out in the judgment.

Sugden L.C.:

I desired this case to stand over, not from any doubt which I entertained as to the conclusion to be come to upon the settlement, respecting the intention of the parties, nor from any doubt I entertained as to the rule of law in such cases, but in consequence of a statement made in the course of an argument, that what has fallen from a learned Judge in a recent case, coupled with one or two of the earlier cases, has given rise to difficulties respecting the law in such cases. That statement certainly surprised me not a little, because until then I thought that the law in such a case was perfectly well settled.

The question in the present case arises upon articles for a settlement entered into after marriage, by the grandfather of the present defendant. He was tenant in tail before those articles were entered into, and on his marriage he had settled an annuity on his wife, charged on the lands. He afterwards, it appears, sold part of the lands which were subject to the annuity, and he was desirous to obtain his wife's concurrence, in order to destroy her rights over the lands which he had sold. The deed recites the desire of the husband to complete the purchase, and that he had agreed, in consideration of the wife's concurrence, to settle an annuity on her and to settle the property upon the children of the marriage, and then he professes to convey the estate to the trustees upon the trusts thereinafter mentioned. Then he covenants with the trustees "with the advice and assistance of Counsel," to convey the estate to the uses therein mentioned; that is, to secure in the first place an annuity for his wife, and subject thereto upon trust to permit him to receive the rents for his life, in such a manner as would not only render him dispunishable of waste, but even authorise him to commit waste. Then there is an estate given to trustees for preserving contingent remainders, which is not confined to the life estate of the settlor. Then follows a limitation to the eldest son for life, with remainder at his decease to the heirs of his body; and in default of such issue, there is a limitation to the second son Thomas for his life, but neither the life estate of Thomas nor that of Harman is made dispunishable of waste. At the decease of Thomas the lands are limited to his issue male, and in default of such issue it is limited to the daughters, in words which, according to their grammatical import, would give to all the daughters except an only daughter, merely estates for life, but which in legal construction would give them estates in tail; because it is perfectly well settled by the case of *Doe* v. *Martin* 4 T.R. 39 that where there is a devise to a class, and words of limitation are used which expressly refer merely to a surviving or only member of that class, they shall be construed as equally applicable to every member of that class. The articles contain powers of several kinds, – a power to the father to raise £3000 for his own benefit, a power to him to jointure an after-taken wife, and a power to raise portions for his younger children. Then there is a general power of leasing, which is less than the statutable power, and a power to the sons to charge a jointure.

On this the question arises, whether this is such a trust as the Court can mould according to the intention of the parties, or whether it must adhere to the legal construction of the words which they have used. Before determining that question, however, it is necessary to consider what is the legal effect of the limitations as they stand now. If we take the limitations subsequent to the father's life estate, the first is the estate to trustees to preserve contingent remainders, which is not confined in terms to the life estate of the father. If we were to stop there, it might be held that the trustees took an estate only during the father's life, but the subsequent parts of the instrument render that construction impossible; because according to the cases of *Venables* v. *Morris* 7 T.R. 342, and *Doe* v. *Hicks* 7 T.R. 433, if there be a general limitation to trustees to preserve contingent remainders, although it may, in some cases, be cut down by construction to an estate during a life merely, yet that cannot be if there are subsequent limitations in the same instrument which require the protection of such an estate. Because if there be, the ground of intention upon which to cut down their estate by construction, is altogether taken away. Then would the true construction of this instrument be, that the estate of theee trustees should be cut down by implication to an estate during the father's life? That cannot be, because there are contingent remainders afttterwards, which would require the protection of such an estate. There is the remainder after Harman's life estate to the heirs of his body, and then there is the limitation to Thomas for life, and, at his death, to his issue. Now, the limitation to Harman for life, and at his death, to the heirs of his body, if it stood unaffected by anything else, would, undoubtedly, be an estate tail; and even if you interpose an estatee to trustees to preserve contingent remainders, as by construction you must, that would not alter the construction. That doctrine is now well settled, although it is rather singular, and if you look back to the history of it, you will find it was not established without much doubt and hesitation. It never was decided until the case of *Colson* v. *Colson* 2 Str. 1125, that it would give an estate tail, because it was thought that such a limitation was inconsistent with an estate tail. The decision was very much douted at the time, and it was doubted by Lord Hardwicke, who brought forward the well known proposition in *Bagshaw* v. *Spencer* 1 Ves. sen. 141, about trusts executed and trusts executory, in order to evade the application of the rule in *Colson* v. *Colson*, but it was held to be settled law in the case of *Hodgson* v. *Ambrose* 1 Doug. 337. There would, therefore, be an estate tail in Harman, and then by the subsequent limitation, Thomas would take an estate for life, with remainder to his issue as purchasers; because where there is a limitation to issue in a deed, that cannot unite with a preceding life estate given by the same deed, so as to make the issue take by descent; but, taking the limitation to be so, you cannot model it so as to make it correspond with the evident intention. As far as regards the intention (I am speaking in this part of the case altogether of the intention according to the mere legal construction of the words), the powers given by the articles are not adverse to an estate tail. They are important upon the other branch of the case, but I do not think they are important upon this; because as a power of leasing would enable the owner to make leases which would bind the remainder-man, and a power to jointure would enable him to provide for his wife without opening the entail, there is a reason for their being given. Suppose, however, in the present case, the limitations were to be governed entirely according to the legal construction, and that I were to execute a settlement accordingly, I should execute a settlement such as no one ever intended, and such as no practical conveyancer ever framed: because I should give to the eldest son an estate tail, and after the expiration of that estate, a remainder to the second son for life, with remainder to his issue, as purchasers. If, then, I turn them into legal limitations, and find that they are absurd and irrational, I must infer that something else was intended by the parties to these articles.

Then comes the question, what was the intention of the parties, as expressed upon the articles. Until the argument of this case I always considered the rule of law upon this subject to be perfectly settled, that when there is a settlement before marriage, the marriage of itself supplies a purpose which pervades the settlement, and amounts to a declaration of an intention that there should be a strict settlement. Because it would be a manifest absurdity, when a man agrees upon his marriage to settle his estate in such a way as to provide for his wife and children, to adopt such limitation as would leave it in his power to destroy that provision at any time. By giving such a construction to the settlement, it would not effect the objects for which it was intended. In such cases, the Courts say that the purpose of the deed shews that it was not intended to bear any such construction. There you have to find some other reason why the rule should not apply, as, for instance, where the estate is limited to the wife; there, as by the statute *ex provisione viri* 32 *Hen*. 8, c. 36, it would not be in her power to bar the entail without the assent of her husband, and that is considered an exception, because the parties might very well intend to leave it in the power of both the parents to defeat the provision made by the settlement. This case approaches as nearly as can be to the case of a settlement before marriage, because here it is expressly stated that one of the objects of the parties was to provide for the children, and it is difficult to say that the father meant to divest himself of an estate which might have travelled through the entire family, in order to give to his son an estate which would have enabled him to defeat the intended object. This is also a settlement for valuable consideration, because the wife not only released the lands which were sold from any rights of hers to dower, but she released them from an annuity of £300 provided as a jointure for her in case she survived her husband; and the consideration might or might not (for I give no opinion upon the point) he held to extend to all the limitations of the settlement.

If you take the cases of voluntary settlements and wills, both of which must be considered as standing on the same footing (a voluntary settlement, I may observe, cannot be inferior to a will because the act of settling his estate in his lifetime rather more strongly imports an intention in the settlor of making a strict settlement, than can be gathered from his inserting the same limitations in his will), the rule of law is plain enough in both cases, that a general intention cannot be collected from the act itself, but you must find something in the instrument manifesting such an intention. If a man states that he has made a settlement before his marriage, then you can say that it was his intention to make a strict settlement, but in either of the cases you must find something in the settlement or will to show that he did intend a strict settlement. Now, take this settlement for instance; here the father is tenant in tail, and he professes to cut down his own estate to an estate for life, in order to give his son an estate tail, which would enable him to defeat all the limitations over. That is not a probable intention for him to entertain, but still it is not irrational or absurd, and if it be the intention, I must, of course, act upon it. At the time the articles were executed some of the children were born, and life estates could be limited to them with remainders to their issue. Some were unborn, and that could not be done as to them; they could only be made tenants in tail. Now, when I find technical words in an instrument, I must suppose that they were used in their proper technical sense, unless something appears on the face of the instrument to shew that they were used in some other sense, and certainly that raises the only difficulty here. Because, where it was clearly the intention to give estates tail, as to the unborn children, strict and proper words for the purpose are used, shewing that the parties understood the use of technical language.

In considering, however, whether this is an estate tail or an estate for life, I must first ask whether it is an executory trust or not. If it is executory, then it is perfectly clear that a strict settlement was intended, because there is no difference between executory trusts raised by a settlement before marriage, and executory trusts raised by a voluntary settlement or a will. In voluntary settlements and wills there is greater difficulty in establishing that the trust is executory; but when once that is established, the construction is the same in the two latter as in a settlement before marriage. In the one case, the nature of the instrument amounts to a declaration that the trusts are executory; in the two other cases, you must infer an intention from the contents of the instrument that it should be executory. In the present case I entertain no doubt that the trusts are executory; the settlor covenants to convey to two trustees upon the trusts thereinafter declared. All trusts are, it is true, in one sense executory, but in some cases the settlor may be what is called his own conveyancer, that is, he may have declared the limitations in such a manner as to shew that he did not contemplate any further act being done, – and the Court would have to construe them according to their legal effect. That that could not have been intended in the present case I have already shewn, and that from the nature of the limitations themselves they must have been intended to be executory. Then, must I not sacrifice some part of the words which the settlor has used, in order to carry into effect the remainder? Can I make the eldest son tenant in tail with remainder to the second son for life, and at his decease remainder to his issue as purchasers? What then am I to sacrifice? There is no mode of effecting the intention as to Thomas, but by taking a greater liberty with the estate given to him by the words of the instrument, than by interfering with the limitation to Harman. It was with great difficulty that the Courts of Law decided, that such words as those used in the limitation to Harman, by legal construction gave an estate tail; and if such difficulty existed in the legal construction, must not I, when construing the intention of the parties, say that it was their intention not to use them in their ordinary legal meaning? It appears evidently from the language of this instrument, that the framer of it had no idea of the nature of the limitations, because when he is referring to the preceding limitations to which the estate had been subject, he does not recite them correctly. This shews his ignorance of the subject, and it shews that it was in consequence of that ignorance that the intentions of the parties were not properly carried into effect. Here the estate for life given to the father is made unimpeachable of waste, but those words are not repeated in the limitations of the life estates to the sons, and no power to charge portions is given to the sons; and it is argued, that, therefore, it must have been the intention to make the sons tenants in tail. However, as to the power to charge portions, that is not usually inserted in a case like this, and the omission of it accounts in some decree for the sons not being made impeachable of waste; because the father, who was thus cutting down his own estate to an estate for life, might very well intend to give himself a more ample dominion over the property than he chose to bestow upon his sons. Then I find Harman is made, in express words, tenant for life, and his life estate is by necessary construction, as I have shewn before, followed by a limitation to trustees to preserve contingent remainders, with remainder to the heirs male of his body. The words of the instrument are certainly as Mr Moore has remarked, very peculiar, because they are just the very words that would be used if there were an intervening limitation. If then, I find an estate to trustees to preserve contingent remainders following the life estates given to the sons, and that succeeded in one case by a limitation to the heirs male of the body, in the other by a limitation to the issues, can I interpret the limitation in the one case to mean first and other sons, so as that they should take by descent, in the other to confer an estate tail on the father?

In *Glenorchy* v. *Bosville* Forrester, cas. *temp*. Talbot, 3, which came on first before Lord King, and afterwards came before Lord Talbot, the estate was devised to trustees, upon trust, to convey to the use of testator's grand-daughter for life, without impeachment of waste; remainder to her husband for his life; remainder to the issue of her body: Lord King says, when it came before him Ib. 5, "I should, upon the first question, make no difficulty in determining it an estate tail, had this been an immediate devise; but when you apply to this Court for the carrying a trust estate into execution, the doubt is, whether we shall not vary from the rules of law, to follow the testator's intent; which will also bring on another question, What is the testator's intent in the present case?" It stood over, and the opinions of the Judges were taken upon it; and it came afterwards before Lord Talbot, and he held that it was an executory trust, and that the testator's grand-daughter (Lady Glenorchy) took only an estate for life, with remainder to her first and other sons.

Meure v. *Meure* 2 Atk. 265 is to the same effect. There, a testator devised to trustees, upon trust, to permit the plaintiff to receive the rents during his life, and after his decease, upon trust, for the issue of his body; and it was held that he took only an estate for life. The Master of the Rolls, in giving judgment in that case, says, "There is something in this will that denotes the intention of the testator, that the plaintiff should take only an estate for life, for there is a distinction between the wording and framing of the limitations. In the first place, the estate is, during the lives of the defendant and the plaintiff, to continue in the trustees; and when the testator limits it to the plaintiff for life, it is to permit and suffer the plaintiff to receive the rents and profits; and where the limitation is to the issue, it is to their use and behoof." This is very minute criticism; but it is the same here: because we find that the gift of the life estates to Harman is by a direction to the trustees to permit him to take the rents, and there is a direct gift to the heirs of his body. There is a recent case of *Stonor* v. *Curwen* 5 Sim, in which the same doctrine was acted on, and which it is only necessary to refer to.

Two cases have been referred to in the argument which appear to me to bear strongly upon this part of the subject. One is *White* v. *Carter* Anst. 670, where a testator gave money to trustees, upon trust, to lay out the same on land, to be settled as Counsel should advise, upon trust, and for the use of the plaintiff, and the heirs male of his body, to take in succession and priority of birth. The words there were considered as pointing to a strict settlement. That case was heard first before Lord Northington, and afterwards before Lord Camden; and the latter says Anst. 671, "Here the intention is very plain, he directs the settlement to be made by advice of Counsel, and in succession and priority. He meant something different from an estate tail, when he wanted the assistance of Counsel; and although the words 'in succession and priority' may have effect in case the plaintiff takes an estate tail, yet they were meant to give an interest to the sons after the death of the plaintiff."

The other case is *Bastard* v. *Proby* 2 Cox, 6, and is much stronger. The testator there devised his estate to trustees, upon trust, that they should, when his daughter attained twenty-one, "as Counsel should advise," convey and settle the same to the use of his daughter for life, and, after her death, on the heirs of her body; and it was held that the lands should be settled upon her for life, remainder to her first and other sons in tail, remainder to her daughters in tail.

That is the most marked case that can be conceived, because there was nothing there, except the words "as Counsel shall advise," to give the Court power to alter the limitations in the will. That case came before Lord Kenyon, who was perfectly acquainted with the doctrine upon the subject – and the Counsel engaged in it were Lord Eldon and Lord Redesdale, and they considered it so clear that an estate for life only was created by the limitation, that they gave it up without argument. It is difficult to persuade me that this is not a considerable authority: it amounts to this, that wherever a man directs a settlement to be made as Counsel shall direct, that that is to be done, not according as the words used by the testator import, but in such a manner as to effect what is considered to be his intention; and, by giving a life estate to the first taker, remainder to his issue, in strict settlement, to prevent the possibility of doubt that the lands shall devolve in the same manner exactly as if an estate tail had been given to the first taker.

It is said that those cases have been overruled by a recent decision, and that there are contrary doctrines laid down in some of the earlier cases. One of the cases referred to in support of that argument was *Leonard* v. *The Earl of Sussex* 2 Ver. 526. There, certainly, the intention of the testator was, that there should be a strict settlement, and the decree was accordingly for a strict settlement; but the Lord Keeper says, in giving judgment, "She has declared her mind to be, that her sons should not have it in their power to bar their children, which they would have if an estate tail was to be conveyed to them; and took it to be as strong, in the case of an executory devise for the benefit of the issue, as if the like provision had been contained in marriage articles; but had she, by her will, devised to her sons an estate tail, the law must have taken place and they have barred their issue, notwithstanding any subsequent clause or declaration in the will that they should not have power to dock the entail." Now, when he says, "It is as strong as an executory devise for the benefit of the issue, as if the same provision had been contained in marriage articles," he said what is quite clear, that there is no distinction in this respect between them; nor is there, because when once the intention appears in a will that the trusts created by it should be executory, you give the same construction to the words in the one case as in the other. That was all the Lord Keeper meant by the passage which has been relied on – and this is perfectly correct – and I altogether assent to what he said.

Another case relied on is *Legatt* v. *Sewell* 2 Ver. 551; and there the Lord Keeper says, "As to the principal point, whether William Legatt, by the will, was to be tenant in tail or only tenant for life – he claims by a voluntary devise, and although executory, it is to be taken in the very words of the will, as a devise, and is not to be supported or carried further in a Court of Equity, than what the same words would operate at Law in a voluntary conveyance." It is said that the latter passage is contradictory to the judgment in the former case, and so it is, if you put both passages in juxta-position, without more; but they are perfectly consistent, if you consider the cases with reference to which they were spoken. In the one case, the Court thought there was an executory trust, and, consequently, that the first taker took for life only; while in the other, the Court thought that there was no executory trust, and, consequently, that the legal construction of the limitations was to be adopted. In *Legatt* v. *Sewell* the opinions of the Judges were taken upon the question of construction, and the case is reported again in 1 *P. Wms.* 87, when it came on upon the Judge's certificate. It appeared that there was a difference of opinion among the Judges about the construction, and an ejectment was directed to be brought, but it is not clear whether it was ultimately decided.

The other case relied on was *Bale* v. *Coleman* 1 P. Wms. 142. Now, there, there was no pretence for saying that an executory trust was created; but there was a difference of opinion between the Judges before whom the case was heard. Lord Cowper, before whom the case came first, held that an estate for life only was given, while Lord Harcourt, his successor, before whom it was re-heard, held that an estate tail was created, and reversed Lord Cowper's decree. *Trevor* v. *Trevor* 1 P. Wms. 622 carries the doctine farther; that was a case which would not now admit of a doubt. It went, however, to the House of Lords, and there appeared to have been considerable difference of opinion about it: Lord Harcourt and Lord Trevor being inclined to reverse the decree of Lord Macclesfield, which declared that the first taker took only an estate for life, while Lord Nottingham and the Lord Chancellor were in favour of it, and the decree was ultimately affirmed. That case of *Trevor* v. *Trevor* left the doctrine beyond all possibility of doubt, and there is not the slightest difficulty as to the law upon the subject.

It is said, however, that *Blackburne* v. *Staples* 2 V. & Be. 369 has overruled *White* v. *Carter* and *White* v. *Proby*. The allegation certainly surprised me not a little; and I have since read over the case of *Blackburne* v. *Staples* again carefully, and I do not see in the entire of that case, a single expression shewing any such intention on the part of the learned Judge who decided it. The Master of the Rolls (Sir W. Grant) thought it an executory trust, but one to be executed according to the words. In his judgment he says:– "It seems clear that this is an executory trust, and I know of no difference between an executory trust in marriage articles and in a will, except that the object and purpose of the former furnish an indication of intention which must be wanting in the latter. When the object is to make a provision by the settlement of an estate for the issue of a marriage, it is not to be presumed that the parties meant to put it in the power of the father to defeat that purpose, and to appropriate the estate to himself. If, therefore, the agreement is to limit an estate for life, with remainder to the heirs of the body, the Court decrees a strict settlement in conformity to the presumable intention; but if a will directs a limitation for life, with remainder to the heirs of the body, the Court has no such ground for directing a strict settlement. A testator gives arbitrarily what estate he thinks fit. There is no presumption that he means one quantity of interest rather than another – an estate for life, rather than in tail or in fee. The subject being mere bounty, the intended extent of that bounty can be known only from the words in which it is given; but if it be clearly to be ascertained, from any thing in the will, that the testator did not mean to use the expressions which he has employed in their strict, proper technical sense, the Court, in decreeing such settlement as he has directed, will depart from his words in order to execute his intention; but the Court must necessarily follow his words, unless he has himself shewn that he did not mean to use them in their proper sense."

Now, I do not see one word in what I have read which points at overruling *White* v. *Carter* or *Carter* v. *Proby*. I accede to all that Sir W. Grant lays down, without saying whether he was right in that particular case or not. "The Court must necessarily follow his words, unless he has himself shewn that he did not mean to use them in their proper sense." I entirely concur in that; I admit that in wills or voluntary settlements I must find something in the instrument itself which shews an intention to create an executory trust. In *Jervois* v. *The Duke of Northumberland* 1 J. & Wal. 539 – where every argument that could be availed of, in order to shew that an estate tail was created, was made use of, Lord Eldon was much pressed with some general expressions said to have been used by him in the *Newcastle case* 12 Ves. 218; nom. *Countess of Lincoln* v. *Duke of Newcastle,* and which certainly required explanation; but no one ever thought of referring to *Blackburne* v. *Stables,* as establishing a new rule upon the subject. In that case, Lord Eldon takes particular pains to explain the expressions attributed to him (for, in point of fact, he never used them) – "If it is supposed that I said there was no difference between marriage articles and executory trusts, and that they stood precisely on the same grounds, I never meant to say so. In marriage articles, the object of such settlement, the issue to be provided for, the intention to provide for such issue, and in short all the considerations that belong particularly to them, afford *primâ facie* evidence of intent, that does not belong to executory trusts under wills. But I take it, according to all decisions, allowing for that an executory trust in a will is to be executed in the same way". That is, when you find an intention appearing on the face of the instrument that there should be an executory trust, there is no difficulty. Now, putting *Blackburne* v. *Stables* out of the way, as not impeaching the doctrine of the Court, nor intended to impeach it, we have Lord Eldon, in that case of *Jervois* v. *The Duke of Northumberland,* correcting the expressions which had been attributed to him, and putting the doctrine upon its acknowledged foundation.

I have taken considerable pains in looking at the law upon this subject, not from any doubt which I entertained myself, but in order to see whether it was really open to the difficulty suggested. As to the case at present before the Court, I have persuaded myself, not without some difficulty, that there is on these articles sufficient indication of an intention to create an executory trust; that, therefore, the settlor has used the words not according to their apparent meaning, and, consequently, that the conusor of the judgments took only a life estate.

As to the costs, the question certainly is one not free from difficulty, and one upon which it was necessary to have the opinion of the Court; but then the plaintiffs have had the opinion of the Master of the Rolls upon the case; and, although upon an application to appoint a receiver, the Court can scarcely be said to have judicial cognizance of the facts sufficient to enable it to pronounce a satisfactory decision, yet, as the plaintiffs have failed in overturning that decision, I think there is as reason for not applying the ordinary rule, and letting the costs abide the event. I must, therefore, dismiss the Bill, with costs.

IV. COMPLETELY AND INCOMPLETELY CONSTITUTED TRUSTS

MILLER V. HARRISON

(1871) I.R. 5 Eq. 324; 5 I.L.T.R.3 (Chancery Appeal)

A person died intestate in America, leaving real and personal estate in New York. At a meeting of his next of kin in Ireland, one of them, A., who was a naturalized American citizen, asserted that, as such, he was by the law of New York entitled to the whole of the produce of the real estate. This was disputed by the others; and an agreement was entered into by A., that if they would contribute to the expense of sending B. and C. to America to recover the property, he would relinquish his exclusive claim and allow it to be divided equally. The others did contribute, and B. and C. went to America, where a suit was pending in relation to the property. B., who was himself one of the next of kin wrote to A., saying that if he still entertained his notion as to his exclusive claim, he, B., would have the case tried; but asking him, if he still adhered to the orginal arrangement, to have a proper deed sent out to B. and C.

Thereupon A. executed a deed reciting the pendency of the American suit, and his being a naturalized American citizen, and declaring that, should the American Court declare him entitled in consequence to all or a larger portion of the property, he would not insist on his full claim, but thereby consented to accept an equal division with the other next of kin, and he thereby gave authority to B. and C. to give full effect to his declaration.

B. and C., on receipt of this instrument, and relying on it, suffered the American Court to make a decree in favour of A.

A. subsequently revoked the instrument.

Lord O'Hagan, after stating the pleadings, proceeded:-

The Plaintiff's case was rested in argument at the bar on three several grounds: First, that there was a family arrangement initiated in Castleblayney in 1863, and consummated by the instrument of the 18th of May, 1864, which this Court is bound to maintain on equitable principles; secondly, that the instrument of May, 1864, constituted in itself a declaration of trust, which, whether or not it was founded on an antecedent agreement, and whether it was with or without consideration, was complete and binding on the person making it, with full knowledge of facts, and full control over the property which it affected; and, finally, that the instrument of 1865, whether taken as confirmatory of the previous arrangement or operative in itself, conclusively established the Plaintiff's claim. On the third of these points we have heard no argument, and are not required to pronounce any decision, as we desired to have the first and second disposed of, so as to avoid a controversy of fact, which was referred by the learned Vice-Chancellor to the consideration of jury, and which, in the event, turns out to be immaterial for the purpose of our judgment here.

In the view which I take of the case, it would be sufficient for me to consider merely the effect of the instrument of May, 1864, as it seems to me in itself sufficient to establish the contention of the Plaintiff, and the safest and clearest ground on which a ruling in his favour can be based. But it is right to discuss briefly the antecedent facts, as well because they constituted in themselves a substantive and independent ground of that contention, as because they lead up to and naturally bear upon the transaction of May, which grew out of, completed, and is explained by, them.

There is a conflict of evidence as to the alleged meeting in Castleblaney in the year 1863. On the one side, the Plaintiff positively deposes to the truth of the statement in his bill to which I have adverted. His affidavit contains these allegations:- "At that meeting it was stated that Thomas Harrison had better rights to the property than the other members of the family, because he was a naturalized citizen of the States; but this proposition was not acceded to by the other members of the family present, who contended that each should receive an equal one-fifth share of all that should be recovered . . . Thomas Harrison stated at that meeting that he would relinquish any priority of claim or right which he might have as a naturalized citizen, and that he would allow the property to be divided equally between all the parties representing John Harrison, if each of the parties would join equally in the expense of sending out William Harrison and William Boyd. Each of the parties present at once agreed to contribute £20, in order to make up the required sum of £100. I also agreed to contribute my proportion of any further expenses and costs that might be incurred over and above the £100 . . . I paid my share, £20, of the said sum of £100, and William Mitchell paid his. I paid said sum of £20, relying on the agreement made at said meeting that the property would be equally divided."

These allegations are sustained by other witnesses – Agnes Mitchell and Catherine Cullen – and they are encountered by the denials of the Defendants, Thomas Harrison, William Harrison, and William Boyd; but I think they are substantially corroborated, not only by the persons to whom I have referred, but also by Mr. Persse, the solicitor who prepared the instrument of May, 1864, and still more persuasively by the letter of William Harrison, written from America to Thomas Harrison in 1864, which produced the execution of that instrument. These are the words of Mr. Persse, and they are wholly irreconcileable with the case of the Defendants:- "In the month of June, 1863, I received instructions from Plaintiff, and from William Harrison, Thomas Harrison, and William Boyd, to prepare powers of attorney for them in reference to the property of James Harrison, deceased. Thomas Harrison informed me that he understood the laws of the United States, and that it would be necessary that his wife should join him in his power of attorney to pass freehold estate. Two powers of attorney were prepared by me in pursuance of the instructions received by me as hereinbefore stated . . . The said parties to the said powers of attorney called frequently upon me with reference to them and to the preparation of them. I was informed by Thomas Harrison that he was a naturalized citizen of the United States of America, and that he believed he had greater rights than the others on account of being such naturalized citizen . . . I was informed by the parties in this suit, at one or other of said interviews, in presence of one another – and I have no doubt that, if Thomas Harrison was not the spokesman, he was present when it was told to me by some of the others – that it was agreed that all the parties should share equally all moneys to be recovered out of the estate of James Harrison, deceased; and, consequently, in preparing the two powers of attorney I used the same form of words, and made no difference, save *mutatis mutandis* for the different parties' names and addresses. I was also at the same time told by the said Thomas Harrison, or by some other of the said other parties in his presence that the said powers of attorney were to join equally in the expense of sending William Harrison and William Boyd to America. Either on the 17th or 18th of the month of May, 1864, Robert Miller and Thomas Harrison called upon me at my office. The latter produced a letter which he had shortly previous received from William Harrison from America. I have read the version of that letter in the Plaintiff's affidavit. I cannot pretend at this distance of time to give the exact wording of such a letter, but I believe the Plaintiff's version of said letter is correct. I can, however, distinctly recollect portions of said letter. I distinctly recollect that in referring to me my name was wrongly spelt, and I was not gratified with a 'Mister.' It simply said, 'Go up to Pierce, and get the letter of the attorney drawn out, adopting the original arrangement, and get it sworn before Mr. McMath;' and I also distinctly recollect that the object of getting the letter or power of attorney was to prevent expense, by taking the case to be tried in a higher Court. I asked Thomas Harrison if he wished me to prepare a letter of attorney carrying out that letter. He said that he did; that he had not any other intention, or words to that or the like effect. Thomas Harrison at that time said that Miller and the others might be thankful to him, and ought to make him a good present for giving them no trouble, and carrying out his original promise, or words to that effect."

And still more conclusive appear to me to be the terms of the letter of William

Harrison, imperfectly put in issue by the bill, and more fully stated in the Plaintiff's evidence, which is sustained by the recollection of Mr. Persse, and receives no contradiction from the other side. Now, it is impossible not to believe that there was an arrangement of some kind amongst the members of this family, and an arrangement of such great importance that the abandonment or sustainment of it was to determine the course to be taken with reference to a pending suit, affecting considerable interests in its result; and I think it also impossible to doubt that that arrangement was of the character theretofore freely and repeatedly communicated to Mr. Persse by his clients, and, in consequence of this very letter, reduced to effectual form by the instrument of May, 1864, which, in its substance, fully accords with that arrangement. Assuming, then, as a matter of fact, that the Plaintiff's case in this respect is true, and that the Defendant fails, we have a family meeting held for the purpose of arranging what should be done on the occurrence of the death of a wealthy relative, who died intestate, in whose estate all the members of that family had a material, but, at that time, unascertained interest. We find them discussing their respective rights – the Defendant, Thomas Harrison, asserting an exclusive claim to the property in question, on the ground of his naturalization in the United States; and, if the Plaintiff is to be believed, the other persons present disputing his proposition, and contending that "each should receive an equal share of all that should be recovered." We find that most material statement of the Plaintiff supported by William Harrison's demand of Thomas, long *ante litem motam,* threatening a trial at Albany, if the "original arrangement" should be abandoned, and so indicating forcibly that there was at least a controversy about the claim of Thomas, and a disposition to dispute it if that arrangement was not carried out; and, as I have said, the instrument of 1864, prepared at the instance of Thomas, and by his solicitor, signed by him, and preventing a contentious trial, goes far to demonstrate what the nature of it was. Then we have that arrangement acted upon, powers of attorney prepared, money advanced by the Plaintiff and the rest, agents sent abroad, proceedings taken for the benefit of all the parties, further advances by the Plaintiff to meet the needful expenditure, and a successful result in the realization of the estate of James Harrison. The question seems fairly raised whether, after all this, the Defendant, Thomas, is to be permitted by a Court of Equity, even if there were nothing more conclusive in the case, to possess himself exclusively of the share which he undertook to divide with his family. The prayer of the bill is not for the specific performance of an agreement; but it is said that the arrangement so made, from such motives, on such conditions, and with such results, ought not to be disturbed. There would be insuperable legal difficulties in the way of the suit, if instituted for specific performance; but the established principles as to family arrangements may enable the Plaintiff to escape from the embarrassment.

"The current of authorities has been uniform," says Lord St. Leonards; "and whatever doubts and disputes have arisen with regard to the different members of the same family . . . and fair compromises have been entered into to preserve the harmony and affection, or to save the honour of the family, those arrangements have been sustained by the Court, albeit, perhaps, resting upon grounds which would not have been considered satisfactory, if the transaction had occurred between strangers." Lord Eldon had said – *Stockley* v. *Stockley* 1 Ves. & B. 30: "It is true, in family arrangments, the Court has administerd an equity which is not applied to agreements generally." And again . . "In these family arrangements, the Court does not quite go to the length of denying relief upon the principle that prevails amongst strangers." And in *Neale* v. *Neale* 1 Ken, 679, Lord Langdale said: "I am of opinion that the arrangement, though parol, yet being in the nature of a family arrangement, and followed by the uninterrupted several enjoyment of the portions allotted to the two brothers respectively, is an agreement which this Court will enforce." So, the arrangement in *Stockley* v. *Stockley* 1 Ves. & B. 30 and *Thomas* v. *Gyles* 2 Vern. 232, was enforced. And here we have a stronger case, if I am right in holding, upon the evidence, that the instrument of 1864 gave merely an expression and completion in written words to the family agreement of 1863, which had been continuously acted on in the mean time. And, finally, in *Williams* v. *Williams* Law Rep. 2 Ch. App. 294, Lord Chelmsford held that, although there was in that case "no doubtful right to be compromised, no dispute which was to be set at rest, no honour of the family involved," still that there was "sufficient consideration to prevent its being a mere voluntary agreement; and that the Court will not scan with much nicety the amount of the consideration." And Lord Justice Turner adds, in words which are of weight, as bearing on the facts before us, "It was strongly argued for the Appellant that the case does not fall within the range of the authorities, that those cases extend no further than to arrangements for the settlement of doubtful or disputed questions, and that in this case there was not, and could not be, any doubtful or disputed right; but this, I think, is a very short-sighted view of the cases as to family arrangements. They extend, as I apprehend, much further than is contended for on behalf of the Appellant, and apply, as I conceive, not merely to cases in which arrangements are made between members of a family for the preservation of its peace, but to cases in which arrangements are made between them for the preservation of its property." And he declines to entertain a question on the Statute of Frauds, the arrangement having been acted on between the parties.

Now, applying these principles to the case before us here, there certainly seems much force in the contention that, even as a family arrangement, the parol agreement of 1863, so acted upon by all the parties, and issuing in the written declaration of 1864, ought to be maintained. It was made then, according to the Plaintiff's evidence, which I think, for the reasons I have given, more faithworthy than the Defendant's, persuasively corroborated by the letter of William Harrison, of May, 1864, there was dispute and controversy between the members of the family as to the claim of Thomas Harrison and the issue of the pending suit; it was made to put an end to that dispute and controversy, and it had its proposed effect, and prevented any of his relatives from appearing at the trial, or raising any question as to Thomas Harrison's legal rights, or putting forward their claims to equality with him, which they thought sufficiently guarded by the bargain at Castleblaney, the subsequent written declaration, and the power of attorney to carry it into effect. This appears to bring the case within the general principle; and then we have the payments made on the faith of the agreement, and in pursuance of an arrangement judiciously entered into by the family, in the language which I have quoted from Lord Justice Turner – "for the preservation of its property." These considerations appear to me to give more force to the Plaintiff's argument on this branch of the case than seems to have been attributed to it in the Court below; and this, whether the claim of Thomas Harrison was legally irresistible, or whether it was not. If the family thought it was not, as is sworn to have been the fact; and if the dispute which so arose was settled on terms involving change of position, and pecuniary loss to the Plaintiff, incurred by him on the faith of the Defendants' undertaking made in the interest of Thomas Harrison, and with the purpose and effect of having his claims effectively asserted and allowed, without troublesome and perhaps expensive controversy, the agreement appears to have been equally reasonable, and equally to invite enforcement in Equity, as if there had been real ground for balanced argument. Whether there was or not, we are not now in a very good position to determine either as to the law of America, or as to the facts which it was within the competence of Thomas Harrison to establish in proof, if he had been encountered adversely, instead of having purchased an uncontested success by the agreement which he has since sought to repudiate.

But, whatever be the strength or weakness of the Plaintiff's case on the first branch of it, it seems to me impregnable on the second; and I am clearly of opinion that the instrument of the 18th of May, 1864, whilst it evidenced and concluded a family arrangement, was binding and irrevocable as a declaration of trust, involving a valid gift to the members of the family.

There has been little controversy about the law of this matter, and the authorities do not afford room for any. The question is of their application to the document before us.

For the purpose of considering it, we may assume, what nobody denies, that Thomas Harrison, according to the principles of the law of America, had exclusively, as a naturalized citizen, a right to the property in question; and that, all opposition being withdrawn, there could be no reasonable doubt as to the establishment of that right by a legal tribunal. It was vested in him, and only needed recognition.

This being so, he signs the document of the 18th of May, 1864, a portion of which I have already read.

Before I go to consider, very briefly, the terms of this document, with a view to the application to them of clearly settled and established principles, I shall say a word as to those principles. A great number of cases were cited at the bar, but I think it wholly unnecessary to run through them all; for, in result, they really do not conflict; and there has been no substantial controversy as to the state of the law. "The rules and the distinction or distinctions between them," says Lord Justice Knight Bruce, "are, in theory, plain and simple enough, but are sometimes found to be difficult of application practically."

The doctrine of the cases is, that a man may make a free gift of his property if he please, and impress it with such a trust for another as will be irrevocable by himself. But the gift must be complete and perfect. Nothing must be left undone to carry it into effect in the very act of its creation. It must not be needful to invoke the aid of a Court to make it effectual; and, if it be, that aid will not be lent, and it will fail of operation. But, when the gift is complete, when the trust is declared in *præsenti,* so as to have effect at once, when there is no imperfection to be supplemented, and the whole beneficial interest is taken out of the donor, the transaction will be equitably enforceable, and cannot be undone.

The cases which establish these principles perhaps most authoritatively, although most briefly, are those of *Pulvertoft* v. *Pulvertoft* 18 Ves. 84 and *Ex parte Pye* 18 Ves. 140, 140, before Lord Eldon. In both, he distinguished between a mere voluntary settlement, with which this Court has nothing to do, and the creation of a trust, which it will enforce. His words in *Ex parte Pye* are especially applicable to the circumstances we have to consider:- "The other question involves," he says, "not only the construction of the French law, and the point whether that has been sufficiently investigated, but further whether the power of attorney amounts here to a declaration of trust? It is clear that the Court will not assist a volunteer; yet, if the act is completed, although voluntary, the Court will act upon it. It has been decided that, upon an agreement to transfer stock, the Court will not interpose; but if the party had declared himself to be the trustee of that stock, it becomes the property of the *cestui que trust* without more; and the Court will act upon it." And again he says:– "The distinction is settled that in the case of a contract merely voluntary, the Court will do nothing; but if it does not rest on voluntary agreement, but an actual trust is created, the Court does take jurisdiction." This is still a true exposition of the law, as it was in the time of Lord Eldon.

The whole of the cases from that time until his own were summarized in the judgment of Lord Justice Knight Bruce in *Kekewich* v. *Manning* De G. M. & G. 187; and the effect of them all was stated by him in striking words:– "Upon one hand it is, on legal and equitable principles, clear that a person, *sui juris*, acting freely, fairly, and with sufficient knowledge, ought to have, and has it in his power to make, in a binding and effectual manner, a voluntary gift of any part of his property, whether capable or incapable of manual delivery, whether in possession or reversionary, and howsoever circumstanced; so, on the other, it is as clear generally, if not universally, that a gratuitously expressed intention, a promise merely voluntary, or, to use a familiar phrase, *nudum pactum,* does not, the matter resting there, bind legally or equitably." And again, p. 189:– "But, whatever rule may be against 'volunteers,' it does not apply to the case of one who, in the language of this Court, is termed a *cestui que trust* claiming against his trustee; for that which is considered by this jurisdiction a trust, may certainly be created gratuitously; so that the absence of consideration for its creation is, in general, absolutely immaterial." And Lord Hatherley, in his judgment in *Richardson* v. *Richardson* Law Rep. 3 Eq. 691, continues the discussion of the cases until a very recent period, and thus pointedly puts the question to be asked in cases of this description:- "Reliance is often placed on the circumstance that the assignor has done all he can, and that there is nothing remaining for him to do; and it is contended that he must, in that case only, be taken to have made a complete and effectual assignment. But that is not the sound doctrine on which the case rests; for if there be an actual declaration of trust, although the assignor has not done all that he could do – for example although he has not given notice to the assignees, yet the interest is held to have passed effectually as between the donor and the donee. The difference must be rested simply on this – aye or no, has he constituted himself a trustee?" The answer to Lord Hatherley's question will be various in various circumstances, and the trusteeship may be evidenced by various forms of words, as in *Fortescue* v. *Barnett* 1 My. & K. 43; *Blakely* v. *Brady* 2 Dr. & Wal. 311, *Wilcocks* v. *Hannyngton* 5 Ir. Ch. R. 38, and in multitudes of other cases; but if the question can be answered affirmatively, the trust exists, and it is irrevocable.

Does it exist in this case? Did Thomas Harrison constitute himself a trustee?

We must remember two things in approaching this question. First, that the validity of the trust does not depend on the existence of any consideration; and, next, that the declaration of it "is not confined to any express form of words," but may be indicated by the character and general effect of the instrument creating it. The so-called power of attorney of May, 1864, must be judged of by itself; but we need not forget the position of the person who signed it, and the antecedent circumstances which induced its execution. And it seems to me that it does constitute a declaration of trust clear, complete, and final, which bound the maker of it, and bound him irrevocably.

He recites the pendency of proceedings, and the position of his family, and the appointment of William Harrison and William Boyd as his attorneys, to recover his share of the estate of his uncle; and contemplating the decision of the Court in favour of his claim to priority on the ground of his naturalization, he then and there, and by the instrument before him, declares, consents, and agrees that he will accept an equal division with his brothers and sisters, and declines to insist on his own superior legal right.

So far, this is no mere power of attorney, as the instrument has been improperly called at the Bar. It is an agreement, a consent, a declaration, as between him and his relatives, without the intervention of any third parties. It divests him of his exclusive property and vests proportions of it in those relatives, "in like manner as if they had been naturalized citizens of the States of America." But, inasmuch as the legal estate in the whole was his own, he, thereupon, at once made himself a trustee for them, as to all the shares of it, save that which he reserved to himself.

Now, there is here no imperfect assignment, requiring the aid of any individual, or any Court to carry it into full effect; the declaration is absolute and unconditional, and operates at once.

No future act is contemplated; no promise remains to be fulfilled; there is a gift, and not an engagement to give. The words of the donor denude him equitably of the shares which he bestows, save as a trustee for those so obtaining the beneficial interest, whilst the legal interest remains in himself; or, in the words of Lord Justice Knight Bruce, "this gift was a perfect act – a completed gift, resting neither in promise merely, nor merely in unfulfilled intention." And, therefore, it binds him, though it states no consideration, and uses no language expressly creating trusts, and would do so equally if we did not know that it was only the culmination of a series of transactions, in the course of which sufficient consideration, in my opinion, was supplied to sustain it, if consideration had been necessary, and if the facts had been, *eo intuitu,* spread upon the face of it.

The concluding portion of the instrument, constituting William Harrison and William Boyd, the attorneys under the power of 1863, attorneys, also, to give effect to this declaration and consent in the suit then pending, and to bind Thomas Harrison thereby in the events to happen, has been more or less relied on by the Appellant; but it seems to me strongly in favour of the Plaintiff's argument. It is, really, a power of attorney, superadded to the "declaration and consent," but distinct from them, for the purpose merely of carrying them into execution. They were sufficient and perfect in themselves, and only needed, for their practical application, the agency which this power of attorney supplied. The Appellant's counsel have ably contended, but, I think, unsuccessfully, that there was here no creation of any present effectual trust, but only a prospective arrangement on the contingency of a favourable issue of the pending cause, and that there are no words to make Thomas Harrison a trustee for his relatives. But it appears to me, as I have said, very clear taking the whole instrument together, that he declared the rights of those relatives to shares in the property, whatever it was, which was then actually his, as derived from his uncle, and that the future judicial recognition of his right, which was then vested in him, could not take from the force of that declaration; and further, that in consenting to accept "an equal division" of that, in the whole of which he continued to possess the legal estate, he, *ex necessitate*, made himself a trustee for those to whom he so disposed of a beneficial interest.

Many cases were relied on for the Appellant, but I think it necessary only to advert, in the briefest manner, to one of them, *Dipple* v. *Corles* 11 Hare, 183, which at first struck me as favouring his contention. But there no writing existed; there was "doubt and difficulty" on the words which had been used, and the precise character of which we do not know, as the report does not set them forth; and Lord Hatherley there relied on Lord Eldon's ascription of importance in *Ex parte Pye* to the fact that the declaration had been "committed to writing." "The question before me," Lord Hatherley says, "is whether the conversation which took place on the day of the funeral of the father amounts to a declaration by the Defendant of an intention to constitute himself a trustee of this estate, or of any specific part of it, for his brothers and sisters?" And he adds:– "It appears to me that a clear expression of intention should be found, before the Court, in a case like the present, can hold that a party intended to subject himself to all the consequences of the liability to account and inquiry, which is involved in the position of a trustee."Now, in the case before us, I think there was such an expression of clear and deliberate intention by a man, *sui juris*, understanding his position, and acting in pursuance of an honourable engagement with his family, by which he ought to have abided; and that expression was made, not in casual words spoken at a funeral, and difficult to be accurately remembered or reliably reported, but by a solemn instrument, prepared with care, and with the aid of professional persons, and leaving, in my mind, no reasonable doubt as to the purpose with which it was executed. I do not, therefore, think that *Dipple* v. *Corles* is an authority for the Appellant under the peculiar circumstances with which we have to deal.

Upon the whole I am of opinion that the decision of the Vice-Chancellor was right, and that his decree must be affirmed; and having reached this conclusion, which is founded in no degree on any reference to the agreement of February, 1865, the subject of such lengthened controversy in the Court below, it is, notwithstanding, satisfactory to me to know that, after the fullest inquiry, and a *vivâ voce* examination of witnesses before him, the learned Vice-Chancellor considered that agreement well sustained in evidence, and of great importance as corroborating and supporting the views on which he decided in favour of the Plaintiff.

The decree of the Vice-Chancellor must be affirmed, with costs.

Christian L.J.:

I am of opinion that the decree of the Vice-Chancellor should be affirmed.

This is a bill to have declared and performed a trust. The alleged trustees are the Defendants William Harrison and Thomas Boyd. The *cestui que trusts* are the children of John Harrison, of whom the Plaintiff Miller's wife (now deceased) was one, and the Defendants, Thomas Harrison, William Harrison, and the Defendant Thomas Boyd's wife, are others.

The bill presented three distinct cases, alternative or cumulative; but the decree of the Court below was based entirely upon one of them, upon the deed-poll, namely, of the 18th of May, 1864, which with such strange inappreciation of its import, strange especially on the part of the Plaintiff, who was relying on it, was called throughout the argument the power of attorney.

This instrument was presented by the Plaintiff's counsel in two several aspects; first, as a completed gift or fully constituted trust, to the obligation of which, consequently, consideration was immaterial; second, as, if not that, at least a promise or professed intention, second, as, if not that, at least a promise or professed intention, founded upon a consideration sufficient to induce the Court of Equity to enforce it. If the latter were the true construction, it was then insisted that the case, even in that aspect, ranged itself under the bill as framed; for that when the property, the subject of the promise or expressed intention, came to the hands of those who, by the terms of the document, were to be the depositaries of it, it became attached in their hands with a trust, similar to what it would have been subject to from the beginning, if the instrument had been penned *in verbis de præsenti.*

The decree can, in my opinion, be supported on either of those views; I mean, upon the one if not upon the other; and I think the bill, notwithstanding the objections that were taken to its form, is capable of adapting itself to either.

First, then, I am of opinion, upon the construction of the deed-poll of 18th May, 1864, that it contains a completed gift or fully constituted trust by Thomas Harrison, to or in favour of each of his brothers and sisters, of an equal share with himself of that real property in one of the States of the American Union, which it was assumed, and, as the result proved, correctly assumed, that he alone, as a naturalized American citizen, was entitled to.

The right which the deed professed to deal with was, in one sense, a right in possession, for it was possessory in interest; but in another it was a right in action, for it was the subject of a suit pending in one of the American Courts, in which its character and its subject were to be ascertained and realized. The deed in question, after reciting the pendency of the suit in America, proceeds thus (varying in a very slight and obviously allowable degree the collocation of its language):– "I do hereby declare, consent, and agree, that in the event of its being decided that I, being a naturalized subject, *am* entitled to a larger share than the others (and so on), I will not insist on my full right or claim, to the exclusion of the other children of my father, John Harrison, but *hereby consent to accept an equal division,* share, or proportion with my brother and sisters, in like manner as if they had been equally naturalized subjects of the United States." The deed then gives authority to William Harrison and William Boyd "to *give effect to this declaration* and consent in such manner as may by law be required in the pending suit, and on the conclusion thereof or otherwise, and to bind me thereby in the event that may happen as fully and effectually as if I myself were personally present."

In my opinion this instrument sounds in words of the present, and all there is of futurity or contingency in it lies in the anticipating the progress and result of a suit which it was expected would clothe with the sanction of a decision a right already existing. I think that, in intention and in equity, the property in a share passed immediately out of Thomas Harrison to each brother and sister, although it would, of course, be unfruitful of benefits until the subject would be realized. And I also think that the authority given to William Harrison and Boyd to give effect to that declaration was irrevocable, at all events in the sense of disabling him from recalling the so constituted equitable right. If this be so, consideration is immaterial; and when the proceeds of the property reached the hands of Harrison and Boyd, they held it on the trusts of the deed.

As to *Dipple* v. *Corles* 11 Hare, 183, so much relied on for the Defendant, it is enough to say that what the Court refused to act on there was a loose conversation on the day of the funeral, in which the son, who was sole legatee, said he would sell everything, and divide it equally. The Vice-Chancellor, among other reasons, rested strongly on the ground that the very fact of the promise not being committed to writing, was of itself evidence that it was not deliberate. Here we are dealing with a solemn deed, prepared by the donor's own solicitor, and given in compliance with a demand to make good a former parol promise to the same effect which had been found not to be binding.

I am, therefore, of opinion that, to borrow the words of Lord Justice Knight Bruce, in *Kekewich* v. *Manning*, this deed of 18th of May, 1864, was "a perfect act, a completed gift, resting neither in promise merely, nor merely in unfulfilled intention;" and that, consequenlty, even if it were purely voluntary, it would be binding in this Court.

Furthermore, I am of opinion that it contains sufficient consideration to validate it, even if, upon its construction, it were held to rest on promise merely or in unfulfilled intention.

The pendency in the American suit of the question, whether Thomas's American citizenship gave him larger rights than the others, is recited in the deed, and in terms which show it was regarded as matter more or less of uncertainty. "Should it be decided," "in such event," and so on. Now, reading this recital, as we have a perfect right to do, by the light of the preceding transactions, we will have no difficulty in understanding it. It appears that about a year before, that is, in June, 1863, when the news of the succession that had fallen to them in America first came over, a similar arrangement or understanding had been come to verbally. It was necessary that they, or some of them, should go over to America to look after the common interest. Thomas Harrison, or rather his wife, objected to his going, and it was settled that William Harrison and Thomas Boyd should be the persons to go, armed with powers of attorney from the others. I am satisfied by the weight of evidence, although there is some conflict about it, that it was at that time understood or arranged, certainly not agreed in such form as to be legally binding, that if Thomas Harrison's citizenship should be found to give him any larger rights, they should be deemed withdrawn, and all the letter of May, 1864, from William Harrison to Thomas Harrison, added to the Plaintiff's other proof, satisfy me of that. Well, William Harrison and Thomas Boyd, armed with ordinary powers of attorney from the others, did go to America in June 1863. In May 1864, the whole affair being then *sub lite* in the Supreme Court of New York, William Harrison and Boyd desired to ascertain, in a decisive and binding form, what Thomas's intentions were; and, accordingly, the former wrote over to the latter the letter which has been lost, but of the contents of which parol evidence has been given. I take it from the Plaintiff's affidavit, because that is substanially corroborated by Mr. Persee's, nor indeed does it differ substantially from the statement in the bill admitted by the Defendant in his answer, except that the "arrangement" is not mentioned in the bill. On receipt of the letter, the parties, Miller and Harrison, went at once to Mr. Persse, the deed-poll of 18th of May, 1864, was drawn by him, executed by Harrison, and sent off to America. Now, then, reading the recitals in that deed, with the knowledge of the foregoing transactions (which is the sole significance those transactions have in the case) it is obvious that the meaning of the parties was this, that in consideration of getting from Thomas Harrison this formal and legal confirmation of the original understanding, they would not bring up before the Court the question whether he really had the larger rights he asserted, but would allow his claim to those larger rights to go as it were by default. And that was the course which, in fact, was afterwards taken. It is clear that this imparts to the deed the element of valuable consideration, and there is quite enough of reference to it on the face of the deed to satisfy the Statute of Frauds, even if our Statute of Frauds could apply to such a case at all. To enter into an inquiry as to whether or not there were really any substantial grounds for contesting Thomas Harrison's claim to those asserted larger rights would be wholly irrelevant, and contrary to the familiar principles which regulate such arrangements of family controversies; and it is in that view only, that is, in its bearing on the question of consideration for the deed of 1864, that the doctrine of family arrangements has any value in the case whatever.

Therefore, in either view, whether the deed be regarded as a completed gift, even though it were but a voluntary one, or as a promise or unfulfilled intention, but clothed with valuable consideration, it is binding in this Court, and sustains the decree appealed from.

Note

See further, *Irish Land Law*, para. 9.040 *et seq.*

RE WILSON

[1933] I.R. 729; 67 I.L.T.R. 212 (High Court)

The facts are set out in the judgment.

Johnston J.:

The late Mr. W.H. Wilson of Carrickmines was very generous in his benefactions to his relatives, servants and friends. Most of his gifts were perfected by one or other of the methods by which a valid gift may be regularly and legally made – methods which are set out comprehensively by Turner L.J. in *Milroy* v. *Lord* 4 De F.G. & J. 264; but in the case of two of these alleged gifts a certain amount of doubt has been suggested as to whether the deceased had, in the words of Turner L.J., "done everything which, according to the nature of the property comprised in the settlement, was necessary to be done in order to transfer the property and render the settlement binding upon him." A gift is a gift, and, of course, if a donor, while expressing an intention to give something and taking certain steps in the direction of giving it, has not gone the whole way, the expectant donee has no equity to compel the completion of the gift. This is good sense and good law. As Grant M.R. put it in *Antrobus* v. *Smith* 12 Ves. 39, there is a *locus poenitentiae* as long as the gift is incomplete. Story London Edit., 1982, § 176 puts it in this way: "For, regularly, equity is remedial to those only who come in upon an actual consideration, and therefore there should be some consideration, equitable or otherwise, expressed or implied."

The first matter arises in regard to a transaction that took place in December, 1918, just after the termination of the late war. The deceased was at the time a member of the Dublin Stock Exchange in partnership with his nephew, Mr. Ion Grove-White, and he resided in Carrickmines. He had had three sons killed in the war and he was anxious (as I am informed through the affidavit of Mr. Gerald Grove-White, who, also, is a nephew of the deceased and one of the executors of his will) to provide a sum of £5,000 by way of gift for his only surviving son, Mr. John Hugh Wilson, who is one of the defendants. To effect this he is said to have credited his son's account in the clients' ledger of his firm with the sum fo £5,000 and to have debited his own account in the private ledger of the partners with the same sum. This sum was balanced on the other side of the account by £10,000 Manilla Railway Company preference shares and £3,000 United Havana Railway Company ordinary stock. These securities were in the name of the Hibernian Bank (with other securities) as collateral security for the testator's loan account. I am informed also by Mr. Grove-White that from time to time these investments were lodged as security with the bank, and "at the date of the testator's death the investments representing the original £5,000 were £500 Rhodesian Railway Company debentures (bonds), £3,500 Manilla Railway 5 per cent. debentures (bonds) and £5,000 Manilla Railway prefence shares which were in the name or custody of the said bank." Mr. Grove-White exhibits a letter, dated November 7th, 1924, in the handwriting of the testator, "which the said J. Hugh Wilson informs me was handed to him by the testator." This letter was in these terms: "To my Executors. The Manilla Railway securities (both bonds and shares) and £500 Rhodesian Railway 3 per cent. bonds deposited by me with the Hibernian Bank as part of the securities in my loan account, are the property of my son John Hugh Wilson and do not form part of my assets. W.H. Wilson, 7th November, 1924." The testator did not inform the bank then or subsequently that he had made over these securities to his son, but he addressed a letter to the bank on November 25th, 1925, in these terms: "Please accept release orders for shares held on my behalf when signed by my son, Mr. J. Hugh Wilson"; and all the dividends paid on the original and the substituted securities were credited by the late Mr. W.J H. Wilson's firm to the account of Mr. J.H. Wilson since December, 1919. Mr. Grove-White states further: "After the transaction referred to had been effected the testator informed me that as I was an executor of his will he thought I ought to know that he had made over the said bonds and preference shares to his son."

The testator died in London on February 10th, 1931, without having done anything further to perfect or complete the gift of these securities to his son, and there can scarcely be any doubt that if there was nothing more in the case, the gift, being incomplete, was not one that could have been enforced in equity. There was no assignment by deed or delivery to the donee, nor was there any transfer of the shares into his name. The case is not unlike that of *Lambert* v. *Overton* 11 L.T. Rep. 503, a case in which it appeared that shares had been deposited in a bank as security for a debt owing by the donor, and it was held that a gift of the shares by the donor to his son was incomplete and that the shares (when the debt to the bank had been satisfied) formed part of the estate of the deceased on the donor's death. In the present case, the shares, to the day of the death of the testator, remained in the Hibernian Bank as security for the deceased's liabilities, and under the circumstances the intended benefaction would have fallen to the ground had it not been for the fact that the testator, nominated Mr. J. H. Wilson as one of the executors of his will, and thereby gave validity to what would have been otherwise an imperfect and invalid gift, as decided in the case of *In re Stewart* [1908] 2 Ch. 251. I do not agree with Mr. Lavery's critical attitude towards that case. It was referred to with approval – or at any rate, without disapproval – by Kennedy L.J. in the Court of Appeal four years later in *Pink* v. *Pink* [1912] 2 Ch. 528, and has never been doubted in any case of which I am aware.

It was decided in *Hyslop* v. *Hyslop* [1894] 3 Ch. 522 that the mere appointment of a debtor of a deceased person as the executor of the will of the deceased was not in itself sufficient to enable a debt owing by the executor to be discharged. North J. said in that case that in order that the principle established in *Strong* v. *Bird* L.R. 18 Eq. 315 should be brought into operation there must be evidence of the creation of some equity in the debtor apart from his appointment as executor. Now, here there are, in the first place, the entries in the books of the firm of which the late Mr. Wilson was a partner. I must assume that these books were under his control, and although the entries are not in the handwriting of the alleged donor (as they were in the case of *Pink* v. *Pink* [1912] 2 Ch. 528 – a case which in all other respects resembles the present case) I am satisfied that they were made by Mr. Wilson's direction and that they undoubtedly represented his wishes. I think also that Mr. J.H. Wilson is entitled to rely upon the letter of directions "to my executors." A very similar document formed the subject-matter of a decision of North J. in *In re Hyslop, Hyslop* v. *Chamberlain* [1894] 3 Ch. 522. He held that, the document in question – "general instructions" to an executor – having been found amongst the papers of the deceased and never having been communicated to the alleged donee, must be regarded as testamentary in its character and, not having been executed as a will, could not be looked at. The document in this case, however, would appear to have been handed by the late Mr. Wilson to his son, and that fact raises the very distinguishing feature that is referred to by North J. in his judgment. The other matters that are set out in Mr. Grove-White's affidavit, in my opinion, place this question beyond controversy. I may say in conclusion that I have carefully considered the case of *In re Innes* [1910] 1 Ch. 188, which has been so strongly relied upon by Mr. Lavery, and in my opinion it has no application to this case. The answer to the question one, therefore, will be: "Yes, subject to the limitation that the excess, if any, in the value of the said securities when realised, over the sum of £5,000, belongs to the executors as assets of the deceased."

The second matter is more difficult and calls for rather more consideration. Mr. W.H. Wilson retired from the partnership in 1924, and, with the marked consideration that he had always shown for his son, he introduced Hugh as a partner in his place. Then in 1926 came the next benefit which the son was to receive from the father. On August 3rd in that year, Marcella Wilson, the testator's second wife, died, and he decided to make over the Carrickmines house and property to Hugh absolutely. This gift was properly and regularly effected by three deeds, executed on December 4th, 1926, and the property conveyed consisted of two parcels of land held by the testator in fee and registered in the Registry of Titles and another parcel of land held by the testator under two leases, made in 1861, and a third, made in 1862, for long terms, subject to three rents of £30, £10 and £24. These conveyances by the testator purported to be "for the natural love and affection for his son, the said John Hugh Wilson" and "for other good causes and considerations," none of which are set out. In the assignment of the leasehold premises there is a covenant by the son to pay the rent reserved by, and to observe the covenants contained in, the original leases. Mr. Grove-White in his affidavit says that in 1926 the testator decided to give up his Carrickmines House to his son, "he, the said John Hugh Wilson, agreeing to keep up Carrickmines House and grounds and to receive the testator as a guest whenever the testator wished to come there, and keep the testator's motor-car and chauffeur, the testator estimating the period during which he would probably desire to reside as four months in the year." It is strange that there is no reference to this agreement in any of the three deeds, or in any letter, note, or memorandum, supplemental to them. One would have thought that a donor who was giving up his home absolutely and forever to another, even though that other was his only surviving son, would, if he had intended to reserve to himself a right of residence therein as a legal and enforceable right, have seen to it that the agreement and its conditions and terms were dependent upon something more tangible than the recollection of the parties. But something more was left unexpressed. Mr. Grove-White adds that when the property was conveyed to Hugh in December, 1926, "the testator agreed to make up an allowance to the said John Hugh Wilson, with the said ground rents, of £600 per annum to help towards the maintenance and upkeep of the property." It was not until almost a year later – namely, on August 22nd, 1927 – when the testator was on the point of marrying the second defendant, who was then Miss Edna Gladys White, that the document upon which Hugh Wilson relies was drawn up, and as to it I wish to say generally that it differs very materially from the verbal agreement of December, 1926, which was made at the time when the property was legally transferred.

The document of August, 1927, is a most peculiar one. Instead of covenanting to pay to his son a certain sum per annum, or of charging specific property with the payment of that sum, or of assigning to him such stocks and shares or other property as would produce that sum, the late Mr. Wilson "agrees" "to give directions" to certain persons to pay certain moneys to Hugh Wilson, "which several sums together with certain rents reserved to the said John Hugh Wilson and out of the lands of Rampere would produce £600 per annum or thereabouts," a most unusual and most cautious way of securing an annuity. The persons who are to be given directions to pay these sums to the defendant are "the trustees of the will of C.H. Wilson, deceased; the trustees of the donor's own marriage settlement, and the Northern Nigeria (Bauchi) Tin Company (in which company the testator owned £1,000 preference shares). Down to this point the agreement was one to pay, or to secure the payment of the sum of £600 annually to Hugh, or rather to secure the payment of £600 yearly less the amount of the rents payable out of the property which had already been conveyed to Hugh. The agreement then proceeds in these terms:-

"For the purpose of securing said sum of £600 per annum after the death of the said William Henry Wilson, the said sum of £1,000 Preference Shares in the Northern Nigeria (Bauchi) Tin Company into the joint names of himself and the said John Hugh Wilson, also to tranfer three Policies of Insurance – 2 with the Scottish Amicable Co. and 1 with the Commercial Union Insurance Co. for £500 each on the life of Alfred T. Collins – to the said John Hugh Wilson, also to transfer to the said John Hugh Wilson the following Policy of Insurance on the life of the said William Henry Wilson with the Scottish Provident Institution, viz., Policy No. 72748, which last mentioned Policy is subject to a mortgage of £3,500 to the said Scottish Provident Institution, and also to convey the fee farm rent issuing out of the lands of Rampere or the Land Bonds representing the same. And the said William Henry Wilson agrees to execute formal transfers of the said several policies and property whenever called on so to do by the said John Hugh Wilson, or else to bequeath same to him by will."

Immediately after the making of this agreement – namely, on September 3rd, 1927 – the testator executed a marriage settlement on his marriage to Miss Edna White, by which a sum of £6,000 was to be provided, at the latest, six months after the death of Mr. Wilson, "to be a first charge on his estate after payment of his debts, funeral and testamentary expenses;" and the income of that sum is to be paid to Mrs. Wilson during her life. The marriage took place on September 16th, and the husband and wife went to the South of France where they lived for some time; and then a flat was taken in London. In the summer of 1928 they went to visit at Carrickmines where (as Mr. Wilson says in one of his letters) "Hugh was most courteous and kind"; but he adds that when they went back in the summer of 1929, "there was an air of hostility and a feeling that we weren't wanted there;" and they remained only three weeks. It is only fair to Mr. Hugh Wilson to say that he denies that there was any ground for his father's feeling in this matter. This unfortunate episode – it can scarcely be called a quarrel – left no bad effects, for we find the father making his will on September 16th, 1929, and making provision therein for the allowance that he had promised to his son. By this will the testator directed that the £6,000 that had been provided by the marriage settlement was to be "treated as a first charge on my estate, ranking equally with my debts, funeral and testamentary expenses." The wife was to get £200, "to be paid to her out of the first available moneys in my executor's hands," and she was given also the income for her life from a sum of £4,000. The testator then proceeded to carry out the promise he had made in the memorandum of agreement with Hugh in these terms:– "I leave to my son, John Hugh Wilson, certain policies on the life of A.T. Collins, also the balance of all moneys coming to me on foot of policy number 72748 on my own life with the Scottish Provident Institution. I also bequeath to him a holding in Land Bonds representing a fee-farm rent formerly paid out of the lands of Rampere (Raheen)"; and he appointed Hugh as his residuary devisee and legatee to the extent of one-third of any residue. There is no mention in the will of the Northern Nigeria (Bauchi) Tin Company preference shares (which had never been transferred out of the testator's own name), and that omission was not an accident. The testator had sold those shares on October 4th, 1929, retaining the proceeds of the sale for his own use. Further, the Policy of Insurance on his own life which is received in the memorandum of agreement to have been mortgaged to secure a sum of £3,500, was utilised by the testator to raise a further sum of £500. There was no difficulty in carrying out that transaction, as there had been no assignment or delivery of the Policy to Hugh and no notice of any right in Hugh had been given to the Insurance Company.

On that state of facts can it be held that the defendant, Mr. Hugh Wilson, has any legal or equitable right that can be enforced in this Court by virtue of the memorandum of agreement of August, 1927, or any subsequent agreement *inter vivos*, whether supplemental or substituted? I think that a good deal could be said for the view, though it was not relied upon very strongly by Mr. Lavery, that an entirely new arrangement was arrived at between the father and son in 1929, by which the former agreed to pay to the latter a sum fo £400 a year during the life of the father and that this arrangement was in substitution for the former one. The testator on October 21st, 1929, wrote to Mr. Grove-White:– "I won't allow him more than £400 a year, and if he doesn't accept it I will stop the whole £600, and let him do what he likes." On November 1st, he wrote:– "Don't worry me with any more letters until you have fixed up the £400 a year allowance." On November 18th Mr. Grove-White, writing on behalf of Hugh, says:– "Hugh does not wish to go further into the question of the Bauchi shares, Moore's wages, *or any other matters*. If you have decided to reduce his £600 to £400 a year, he accepts your decision." On the 28th the testator wrote:– "I send you the list with the dividends I propose to take over." And on December 20th, Mr. Grove-White writes to his uncle: "We went through your suggestions about making up the £400 a year," and a list of securities and properties is set out in this letter, the annual income from which is stated to be £413 10*s* 0*d*. I have analysed all this correspondence very closely and for myself I cannot see, in the face of the new terms that seem to have been arrived at, how the defendant can allege that any potency remained that in the document of August, 1927, or how any part of the arrangement of that date remained in force.

However, I am willing to consider the case from the point of view that is most favourable to Mr. Hugh Wilson, and, on the assumption that the new arrangement was merely supplemental to the old, how does the matter stand? The document provides for the payment of an allowance of £600 a year, reduced subsequently to £400, to Hugh Wilson during the lifetime of his father, and I assume that this payment was made and that there are no arrears. If there is some small amount of this allowance outstanding, I shall hear counsel later as to what ought to be done.

The second half of the document provides that "for the purpose of securing said sum of £600 per annum after the death of the said William Henry Wilson" the latter "hereby agrees to transfer" the Bauchi shares into the joint names of himself and his son and to transfer to the donee three policies of life insurance – one on his own life and two on the lives of another – and to convey to him a fee-farm rent issuing out of certain lands or land bonds (payable by the Land Commission) "representing the same." The operative part of this clause is contained in the last sentence: "And the said William Henry Wilson agrees to execute formal transfers of the said several policies and property whenever called on so to do by the said John Hugh Wilson or else to bequeath same to him by his will."

This document is alleged by the defendant to be an agreement for valuable consideration and enforceable as such. I do not think that it can possibly be so regarded. It is simply an agreement by a father, who, having made over certain property to his only surviving son "for natural love and affection," desired to make that son an allowance "to help towards the maintenance and upkeep of said property." The covenant entered into by Hugh, in one of the conveyances, to pay the rent and observe certain covenants cannot be regarded as valuable consideration for an agreement executed nearly nine months later for a collateral purpose that was not spoken of in the conveyance of the property; but even if the liability undertaken by Hugh in December, 1926, could by any process of implication be read into the memorandum executed in August, 1927, the rule established by the Court of Appeal in *Lee* v. *Mathews* 6 L.R. Ir. 530 would prevent it having the potency that Hugh Wilson wishes to give it. The principle of that decision is to be found very clearly set out in the judgment of FitzGibbon L.J. He decided that when leasehold premises are assigned subject to onerous burdens, the question "whether the transaction was a bargain involving mutual considerations, or was a gift involving merely bounty from one party to the other," was a question of fact to be decided upon the evidence and not a question of abstract law. The law on this question in England as laid down in *Price* v. *Jenkins* 5 Ch. D. 619 and some subsequent cases seems to be different; but I think that the decision of the Irish Court of Appeal, given three years later, is more in accordance with sound principle than that in the English case and I shall follow it. In *Price* v. *Jenkins* 5 Ch. D. 619, Hall V.C., a very distinguished equity Judge, was reversed by the court of Appeal; but that decision has not passed unscathed in England during the fifty years of its life. Applying, then, the test supplied by FitzGibbon L.J., it seems to me that, in view of the relationship of the parties and the circumstances under which the memorandum was drawn up, it would be impossible to do otherwise than find that it represented the conferring of bounty by a father upon a son and not the making of a bargain involving mutual considerations. Any other conclusion would be contrary both to common sense and sound judgment.

Then it is argued that there was an agreement between father and son in effect that the former should have a right of residence in Carrickmines House, and that this was part of the bargain. I can find no evidence of any such legal obligation. If such a right had been reserved by the deceased it would have been set out in the conveyance of the property to Hugh Wilson, but nothing of the kind is to be found in the deed; nor is there any reference to it in the subsequent memorandum. In the lengthy correspondence that took place in 1928 the deceased says: "There was an understanding that my wife and I were to be always welcome to Carrickmines House"; and later he said: "If he [Hugh] cannot keep Carrickmines House, let him sell it, or let it for four for five years." The complaint that runs through the whole of this correspondence is a complaint of inhospitable conduct on the part of the son; there is no definite suggestion of any breach of contract.

The memorandum of August, 1927, then, was a voluntary agreement and not one for valuable consideration, and it was an imperfect or incomplete contract at that. Indeed, there is on the face of the document a statement which amounts to an admission by the parties that the contract was incomplete. It was a mere promise on the part of the alleged donor to make a certain provision for his son after the death of the donor. If Hugh Wilson had taken proceedings in his father's lifetime to compel him to make the transfers referred to in the document, he would, I think, have failed, because he had no legal title to the property and equity would not have assisted him to enforce a voluntary statement which was incomplete. The rest of the promise was of a testamentary character and had all the defects of such, as decided in cases of the type of *Cross* v. *Cross* 1 L.R. Ir. 389 and *Towers* v. *Hogan* 23 L.R. Ir. 53. Nor can the alleged donee gain any assistance from the principle established in *Strong* v. *Bird* L.R. 18 Eq. 315 for the reason which is given by Neville J. in *In re Stewart* [1908] 2 Ch. 251. In the latter case the learned Judge decided that when a testator has expressed the intention of making a gift or personal estate to one who, upon his death, becomes his executor, the intention continuing unchanged, the executor is entitled to hold the property for his own benefit; but, adds Neville J., "the intention to give, however, must not be an intention of testamentary benefaction, although the intended donee is the executor; for, in that case, the rule cannot apply, the prescribed formalities for testamentary disposition not having been observed." The plain meaning of the document is that if the promise is not translated into an effective disposition by a legal transfer in the lifetime of the testator, then the donee must be satisfied with whatever testamentary provision the testator may make for him. The testator did make provision for his son by his will, and he must be satisfied with that provision.

Note
See further, *Irish Land Law*, para. 9.043.

RE MULROY
[1924] 1 I.R. 98; 58 I.L.T.R 113 (Court of Appeal)

Deceased lived in the house of his brother, the defendant, and shortly before his death told him to bring him a cash-box, which contained a deposit receipt and two "stale" cheques. The key of the cash-box was in the deceased's waistcoat pocket, and he opened the cash-box with it and took out the papers, saying, "Here is all belonging to me; I am sorry I have not more to give you. You were very good to me. You will do the same for me as you did for Kitty and Tom." The papers were then put back in the cash-box, which was locked by the deceased himself, who put the key back into his vest pocket. The deceased died intestate, and the defendant was granted administration of his estate. He included the deposit receipt and the two cheques in the schedule of assets of the deceased.

O'Connor M.R. held there was no valid *donatio mortis causa*. The defendant appealed.

Molony C.J.:

In this case the Master of the Rolls came to the conclusion that the evidence did not establish a good donatio mortis causa; and, after a careful examination of the evidence, I am not disposed to differ from him.

In order to establish an effective donatio mortis causa three things must combine, as was laid in *Cain* v. *Moon* [1896] 2 Q.B.D. 283, per Lord Russell C.J., p. 286: "First, the gift or donation must have been made in contemplation, though not necessarily in expectation, of death; secondly, there must have been delivery to the donee of the subject-matter of the gift; and thirdly, the gift must be made under such circumstances as show that the thing is to revert to the donor in case he should recover." As regards delivery, it was established in the *Union of London and Smith's Bank, Ltd.*, v. *Wasserberg* [1915] 1 Ch. 195, that an inchoate or imperfect delivery of chattels may be sufficient for effectuating a donatio mortis causa. In that case the testator, when about to undergo a serious operation, expressed in the clearest possible way a desire to give to his wife certain bonds to bearer, which he had in his locked box in the bank; and having discussed the matter with the assistant manager, he put his wife's name on the outside of the parcel containing the bonds, and locked it up in his locked box; and having done this in the presence of his wife, he left the locked box with the bank, and gave his wife a list of the bonds, telling her to keep it safely. After they had reached home, he gave his wife a bunch of keys containing the key of the locked box, and told her to lock them up with the list of the bonds which she accordingly did, in a drawer in her own room, of which she had always kept the key. The same day the testator went into a nursing home, where he shortly afterwards died; and it was held by Sargent J. that the delivery of the key transferring to the wife a partial dominion over or part of the means of getting at the box, though not a sufficient delivery to support a gift inter vivos, was under the circumstances a sufficient delivery to effectuate a donatio mortis causa. Sargent J. observed in the course of his judgment, p. 202: "With regard to the incident at the bank, the case of *Cochrane* v. *Moore* 25 Q.B.D. 57 shows that mere words of gift are not in themselves sufficient, but there must be delivery. If the testator had actually given the parcel to his wife, and she had handed it back to him for the purpose of safe custody, that would probably have been enough; but the facts are, I think, that the testator did not at any time during that incident part with the custody of the bonds."

The question of the effect of a redelivery of bank notes for the purpose of safe custody was discussed this year in the case of *In re Hawkins, Watts* v. *Nash* [1924] W.N. 131. In that case the testator, on his death-bed, handed over to his niece bank notes for £5,000, and to her husband bank notes for £2,000, and clearly indicated that the money was to be theirs respectively after his death. The niece, after having got possession of the notes, asked the testator if she should put the envelope in his deed-box for safety against fire, and upon the testator assenting, she took the key from a nail in the wall facing the testator's bed, unlocked the box, placed the envelope in the box, which she replaced under his bed, and she hung the key up again on its nail. It was contended on behalf of the niece and her husband that there was such a complete delivery of the notes as was sufficient to constitute a valid donatio mortis causa to each donee, and that the redelivery of the notes to the testator for safe custody on behalf of the donees did not affect the previous gift. P.O. Lawrence J. said in delivery judgment: "The only difficulty lay in the question whether the placing of the notes in the deed-box of the testator for safe custody destroyed the effect of the previous delivery by restoring to the donor possession of the notes."

Dealing with certain cases, including the case of *In re Wasserberg* [1915] 1 Ch. 195 and *Bunn* v. *Markham* 7 Taunton, 224, he said: "In the present case the previous effectual delivery was unaffected by the subsequent part of the transaction, namely, the placing of the envelope, with the donor's assent, in the deed-box by the donees for safe custody. The testator therefore was, until his death, merely the custodian of the notes for the donees. There was nothing in *Bunn* v. *Markham* 7 Taunton, 224 inconsistent with the proposition that when once the gifts (mortis causa) were complete, the subsequent agreement by the donor to take back the notes for safe custody did not affect the prior gifts."

In the case now before us the deceased man, who was a confirmed invalid, and died four days afterwards, on the 24th of March, asked his brother, the defendant, with whom he lived, to bring him down his cash-box; and it having been brought to him, he opened it with a key which was in his vest pocket, and the vest was at the foot of the bed, and having opened it and taken out the three documents – mainly, deposit receipt and two cheques – he called the defendant to his side, and said: "Here, Jamesie, is all belonging to me, all my property; and I am sorry I haven't more to give you; you were very good to me." And he added: "You will do for me the same as you did for Kitty and Tom," which was understood by the parties to mean to provide money for Masses and a monument. Nothing else was said; but it does appear that the documents were put into the hands of the defendant. Had the defendant thenceforward retained possession of the documents, there would have been strong evidence in favour of a donatio, but it appears that after the defendant had got possession of the documents he put them back into the box, and that the deceased himself locked the box, and having locked it, put the key back into his own waistcoat pocket, and then the defendant put away the box, and restored the vest containing the key to the place where it had previously been, at the foot of the bed. All this happened within the space of a couple of minutes, and the effect of the transaction is that, notwithstanding the gift, the deceased man had exactly the same dominion over the property that he had before. If the defendant had asked to be allowed to put the documents back into the box for safe custody, and the deceased had assented to this, *Watts* v. *Nash* [1924] W.N. 131 shows that this would not have destroyed the effect of the gift; but the unexplained replacing of the documents in the box immediately afterwards leads to the belief that the deceased never intended to part with the actual possession of the documents in such a way as to lose dominion and control over them during his life.

The case is one of some difficulty, and I hesitated in coming to a conclusion; but on the whole I cannot bring myself to differ from the Master of the Rolls in his conclusion, and consequently I think the appeal ought to be dimissed.

Ronan L.J.:

I have very great difficulty in this case. Donatio mortis causa depends on the intention with which certain acts are done, and the first matter we must try to ascertain is the intention with which the acts were done here. The testator was in bed; there was a box containing some documents belonging to the donee of the alleged donatio mortis causa.

The evidence of the defendant is that when he (the defendant) came into the kitchen, where Michael was in bed, he said to him, "Jamesie." I said, "What, Michael?" "He told me to bring him down the little cash-box." The deceased therefore started the transaction by asking James for the box. What did he want the box for? Was it to see if the things were in it or not, or was it to do something with them? The witness continues, in reply to the question, "Was it locked or open?": "It was locked." "Who opened it?" "Michael." "Where did he get the key?" "He asked me for his vest. I got the vest and gave it to him." "What did he do with it?" "I didn't see what he did. He called me again, 'Jamesie, come here.'" "Was the box open when you went there?" "It was," "What did he say after he said 'Come here'?" "He said, 'Here, Jamesie, here is all belonging to me, all of my property; and I am sorry I haven't more to give you; you were very good to me.'" He did not hand him the box with the documents in it. That is a very important distinction between this and other cases. He handed him the very documents themselves. Beyond all doubt, if the transaction ended there, there was on the evidence a good donatio mortis causa. But a donatio mortis causa can be revoked by the donor just as a legacy can; and the question in this case appears to me to be whether this complete donatio mortis causa was revoked. It could have been revoked by an act or statement of the donor showing that he intended to destroy the effect of what he had done, and to resume the entire control of the property himself. No further statement by him was proved. No further act by him was proved. Taking the evidence as a whole, I am not satisfied that there is anything proved sufficient to show that the donor said or did anything to revoke the gift he had already make. However, my view is immaterial, the majority of the Court holding the other way.

O'Connor L.J.:

I am of opinion that the appeal should be dismissed.

Counsel for the appellant asks us to split the transaction into two: the one a transfer of the possession of the documents to his client, and the other a retransfer of them from his client to Michael on the terms of Michael keeping them on trust for the appellant. If this were the effect of the transaction, the case would be within the authority of the case in the Weekly Notes, to which we have been referred. That, however, is not the view I take of the matter at all. The whole business took only a couple of minutes or so; when it was all over, the position of the documents and the indicium of the control over them were precisely where they always were; the documents were in the deceased's box, and the key of the box was in the deceased's pocket. The momentary tradition of the documents into the hands of James seems to me quite consistent with its being done for the purpose of showing to James the property the deceased intended to give him, and of enabling James afterwards to claim them. For, I think, there was an intention to benefit James; but that is a different thing from transferring the possession to James. The transfer of possession is the element necessary; it is, in my opinion, not alone not established by the evidence, but is negatived by the transaction, taken as a whole.

Note
See further, *Irish Land Law*, para. 9.043 *et seq*; also *Owens* v. *Greene, infra.*

OWENS V. GREENE
[1932] I.R. 225 (Supreme Court)

The facts are set out in the judgments.

Kennedy C.J.:
These two actions, which are concerned with the affairs of one, Austin Freeley, deceased, were tried together as one action, and the appeals, which have been taken by the defendant from the respective judgments, have also been heard together as one appeal. The defendant and appellant is the executor of the will of Austin Freeley, who died on the 29th day of December, 1930, having made his will on the preceding day. He had reached the age of 92 years. At the time of his death the old man, who had never married, was living in the residence on his farm at Ballyhaunis in the County Mayo. He had residing with him an aged sister, Mrs. Cunningham, a young cousin called Thomas Greene who had assisted in looking after him, and a nephew named Richard Owens (brother of the plaintiff – Father Michael J. Owens). He had at an earlier period of his life spent some time in the United States, and after a number of short visits he ultimately came home and settled down for the remainder of his life. Whatever may have been his occupation during his active years, as to which we have no information, he succeeded in building up a very substantial fortune before he returned to settle down at home. The largest part of his wealth consisted of cash, which for many years he kept on a number of deposit receipts in the Ballyhaunis Branch of the Ulster Bank. His active mind engaged itself in disputes with the Revenue authorities and it would appear that he cherished a grievance – like so many of his fellow-citizens – convinced that he had been compelled to contribute more than his share to the State.

This thought was constantly before his mind when dealing with his monies, which, as I have said, he had placed to a deposit account at the Ballyhaunis branch of the Ulster Bank and for which he had a number of receipts. These he kept in the Bank itself, in the custody of the Manager. He paid frequent, I think weekly, visits to inspect his receipts and to deal with them in various ways, but more particularly cashing the receipts for the purpose of drawing the interest and replacing the principal monies on fresh receipts. He seems to have had before his mind for many years a problem which has exercised many minds in the past and will, presumably, exercise many more in the future, namely, the problem of passing on his fortune to his intended beneficiaries in such a way as to defeat any claim by the State for a share by way of death duties, or otherwise. These actions are concerned with two sums which he had placed on deposit receipt, one a sum of £5,000, standing in his own name and that of the plaintiff, Patrick Freeley, and the other a sum of £10,826 6*s*. 3*d*., standing in the names of himself and of his nephew, the Revd. Michael J. Owens, C.C., plaintiff in the second action. The issue in each action is whether the monies were so placed by way of gift to the persons whose names are joined in the deposit account, and, if so, whether such gift has been effective.

The old man was very secretive, and practically the only evidence which is available to determine the matters in question is the evidence of Mr. Frank McNelis who had been the Manager of the Ballyhaunis Branch of the Ulster Bank for a number of years, and who was called as a witness in support of the claim of the two plaintiffs, that is to say, for the purpose of rebutting the resulting trust which would otherwise be presumed in favour of the deceased man and his personal representatives.

The evidence of the Bank Manager is not at all as full, and I think I may say, not at all as convincing as could be desired. Three dates emerge from his story as of importance. The first is the 2nd of March, 1927. Prior to that date Austin Freeley had kept large sums of money on deposit account with the Bank in his own name alone. On the date mentioned he began a new course of proceeding. He transferred large sums of money to a deposit account in the joint names of himself and Mr. Patrick Freeley – the plaintiff in one of these actions. Mr. Patrick Freeley carried on business in the town of Ballyhaunis and the old man used to visit him frequently. They were related in blood but not immediately. The relationship was somewhat indefinite – it was said to be that of cousins of the third or fourth degree. Now, on the 2nd of March, 1927, according to the Bank Manager's evidence Austin Freeley called to the Bank and asked for his receipts. He said that he wished to settle his money, and that he was not able to do so till he saw Father Owens, but that he thought Patrick Freeley was a decent man and he would like to do something for him, and he then gave the Manager a number of receipts which he asked him to put in the names of Patrick Freeley and himself. The Manager stated that the old man asked him to put the money in such a way that he could draw the interest without going to Mr. Freeley and the Manager added, "the only way he could do that was by putting it payable to them or either of them." This, it appears, is a peculiar form of deposit receipt familiar to Banks in Northern Ireland, but not familiar in other Banks. The total amount dealt with on this occasion was £16,917, represented by ten deposit receipts in the joint names of Austin Freeley and Patrick Freeley. Austin Freeley left the actual receipts in the custody of the Manager. Two days later he called again at the Bank and said that he wanted to take £700 out of the joint account and put it in his own name, which he accordingly did, leaving £16,217 standing in the joint names on nine receipts. (See questions and answers Nos. 30-40.)

The form of deposit receipts used for these transactions was the Bank's printed form which acknowledges the receipt of the sum deposited as from Austin Freeley and Patrick Freeley, and the printed form runs – "for which we promise to be accountable" – to which there was added, by a rubber stamp kept for the purpose in the Bank, the words: "To them or either of them." So that the receipt reads: "For which we promise to be accountable to them or either of them."

On the back of the receipt there is a printed endorsement to which is prefixed the word "Note" in which it is stated amongst other things that the receipt must be produced at the time of payment and that ten days' notice must be given when payment is required.

The money so placed remained on that account until the 8th of March, 1928, when Austin Freeley cashed all the deposit receipts with interest and, having taken the interest, relodged them to the same account where they remained until the 2nd of May, 1929, when he again cashed the receipts and re-lodged the principal.

On the 17th of October, 1929, he again cashed all the money standing to this deposit account in the joint names of Patrick Freeley and himself, but he only restored to that account the sum of £11,265, and placed the balance in his own name alone.

On the 29th of May, 1930, he again drew the money standing to the joint account and of this, only restored £6,000 to the joint account and put the balance in his own name alone.

Patrick Freeley, whose name he had joined in the account, was no party to any of these dealings, and appears to have known nothing whatever about the account or the dealings with it nor as to the fact of his name being associated in the account.

Now we come to the second date of importance, the crucial date, namely, the 8th of September, 1930, on which date there were standing in the names of Austin Freeley and Patrick Freeley the sum of £6,000, represented by one deposit receipt, and in the name of Austin Freeley alone, sums amounting in the whole to £13,450 17*s*. 5*d*., represented by nine deposit receipts. The first-mentioned receipt was in the form by which the Bank promised to be accountable for the £6,000 "to them (*i.e.* Austin Freeley and Patrick Freeley) or either of them." (Questions 64-68.)

The books of the Bank show the dealings with the deposit account on the 8th of September, 1930, as follows– Austin Freeley cashed the ten deposit receipts, receiving into his own hands the £6,000 which he had placed in his own name and that of Patrick Freeley, and the £13,450 17*s*. 5*d*. which then stood to the account of his own name alone, making £19,450 17*s*. 5*d*. in all. He disposed of this sum as follows: He put back to the account of himself and Patrick Freeley the sum of £5,000 only, taking a deposit receipt in the form by which the Bank promised to be "*accountable to them or either of them*." He put a sum of £3,506 to a deposit account in his own name alone. Finally he opened a new deposit account in the names of himself and the Rev. Michael J. Owens to which account he lodged the sum of £10,826 6*s*. 3*d*. for which he took four deposit receipts in unequal amounts, all in the form of which the Bank promised "to be accountable to them or either of them." (A small balance £118 11*s*. 2*d*. is not accounted for.) That is the naked money transaction of that date. I turn now to the evidence of Mr. McNelis, the Bank Manager, who, at questions Nos. 69 and following, gives us the only account we have of the circumstances of the transaction. He was asked to tell what occurred on the 8th of September, 1930, and answered as follows:–

"He called about 11.30 or 12 o'clock and asked for his receipts, and he said that he was going to settle the money finally. And he told me to put £5,000 in the names of Patrick Freeley and himself, and he gave me a number of receipts totalling £14,000 to put in the names of Father Owens and himself. He told me that he wished that no person would know anything of these monies, and that the monies were to be the property of Patrick Freeley and Father Owens if anything happened to him and that the receipts were to be handed to the survivors. And when the receipts came in done up. . . "

70. Q. "You filled in the requisitions as directed and the receipts came back?

A. "Yes. And when they came back, he said that he had made a mistake in Father Owens' receipt and he wanted to change it. He wanted £3,500 kept in his own name – he wanted it for a certain purpose. Which I did.

71. "Q. Was that what he said? A. Yes, those were his very words.

72. "Q. He did not tell you what the purpose was? A. No. So I got the receipts as he asked me and changed them as directed and handed them to him and he looked them over and handed them back again to me. And he told me that the joint receipts, if anything happened to him, were to be handed to the survivors, but that no one was to know anything of the money and the money was to be their property. So he told me to keep the receipts in my possession and I did so,

73. Q. "And the result then was that there were four receipts in the names of Austin Freeley and Father Owens totalling £10,846 8s. 3d. (*sic* in stenographer's transcript of evidence)? A. Yes."

Mr. McNelis then went on to tell of another deposit which Austin Freeley made on the same occasion of a sum of £200 in the joint names of the Rev. Michael Owens and one, Richard Owens, the receipt in this case was in favour of them (Richard Owens and Father Owens) "or the survivor of them." Richard Owens, a brother of Father Owens, had worked for Austin Freeley for a number of years. Austin Freeley instructed Mr. McNelis to get from Richard Owens a receipt acknowledging payment of all his claims up to date, and on getting such a release to deliver the deposit receipt to Richard Owens. The Manager carried out these instructions on the same day.

I come now to the third of the important dates, the 15th of December, 1930. If we look first at the record of the deposit accounts in the books of the Bank, we find the following entries. Austin Freeley cashed the deposit receipt for £3,506 standing in his own name alone and immediately relodged that sum on a new deposit receipt in his name alone. He likewise drew the sum of £5,000 standing on deposit account in his name and that of Patrick Freeley and immediately relodged the same sum on a new deposit receipt in the same names, and again to be accounted for "to them or other of them." He likewise drew the sums amounting to £10,826 6s. 3d. standing on deposit account in his own name with that of the Rev. M. J. Owens, represented by four deposit receipts of unequal amounts, and immediately relodged the same sums of money on four new deposit receipts of the same amounts in the same names and again to be accounted for "to them or either of them." The Bank Manager's story of these transactions is contained in his answer at question No. 87 as follows :–

87. Q. "Do you recollect any further dealing with the deposit receipts by Austin Freeley?

A. "Yes. On the 15th December he called and said that he had some bills to pay, and he would like to get the interest on those receipts. And I gave him the interest on the receipts, and he told me to keep the receipts as they were, which I did.

88. Q. "And that is what appears by the entries on the 15th? A. Yes."

From the 8th September, 1930, he never again operated on any of these deposit accounts except for the purpose of drawing interest on the one occasion just mentioned of the 15th of December, 1930. (Evidence of Mr. McNelis, questions Nos. 363 to 367.)

Austin Freeley died on the afternoon of Monday the 29th of December, 1930, after a very short illness. According to the evidence given by the Bank Manager at the trial, on the day of Austin Freeley's death, the son of Patrick Freeley called at the Bank and asked for the deposit receipt in the names of Austin Freeley and Patrick Freeley, and Mr. McNelis says that he handed it to him in an envelope to give to his father. Father Owens came to the Bank in the evening of the same day and Mr. McNelis handed him the four receipts in which he was named. (Evidence of Mr. McNelis at questions Nos. 102, 103, 184, 322.)

The prompt application of Father Owens and Patrick Freeley for delivery to them of the deposit receipts brings us to the very important questions as to when and by whom each of them had been informed of his name having been introduced into the deposit account by this very secretive old man, Austin Freeley. The Bank Manager's evidence on this point is certainly lacking in precision. The effect of it, as I understand it, as a whole (it is not free from contradictions and confusion) is this. Austin Freeley on the 8th of September, 1930, told him that no person was to know anything about this money except the people who were joined on the receipts with him and that if Mr. McNelis liked he could tell them any time about it. (He corrected a previous answer indicating that he might give any information necessary *to the survivors.*) (Questions Nos. 106 *a,* 103 *b,* to 105 *b.*) Patrick Freeley visited the Bank in the course of his business and told Mr. McNelis that Austin Freeley had told him that he had left him well off in the Bank and asked what the amount was, when Mr. McNelis informed him of the £5,000 in the joint names. He says that, some days later, Father Owens asked him the same question and he told him. (Question 105 *a.*) He placed the time of giving this information as after the 8th of September, 1930. (Question No. 156.) About six weeks after that date. (Question No. 182.)

Father Owen's evidence was very unhelpful. He used to see his uncle from time to time and discuss the old man's affairs with him. But Father Owens' health is poor, his memory is bad, and he had no notes or memoranda. On one occasion he advised the old man that when money is left on joint deposit receipts, the survivor takes the money without having to pay any duty whatever. Though he appears to have gleaned hints from his uncle of an intention to leave him something, the nearest to a definite statement which I can find in Father Owens' evidence is that about July, 1930 (*i.e.,* months before the joint deposit account), the old man gave him to understand that he had left him "a certain amount of money." (Questions Nos. 444-449, 452, 502-505, 509.) It was Mr. McNelis who, a couple of months before the death of Austin Freeley, informed Father Owens that there was money in his name, about £10,000. (Questions Nos. 538-546.) Father Owens according to his own evidence does not appear to have been told anything definite by Austin Freeley nor authorised by him to go to the Bank to inquire about it. On the contrary he says that he never discussed with his uncle the question whether he had left him any money nor tried to ascertain the fact from him. (Question No. 529.)

Patrick Freeley was also kept in the dark by the old man. He does say that in May or June, 1930, Austin Freeley told him he need not worry about business being bad because he (Austin Freeley) had money in the Bank in their two names. (Questions Nos. 749, 751.) But as we know, that joint account was brought to an end and was not intended to be a "final settlement." On cross-examination, Patrick Freeley stated quite definitely that Austin Freeley never told him that he was leaving money in the Bank for him. (Question No. 763.) He does not give any explanation of the circumstances in which the Bank Manager came to tell him of the deposit in joint names and the amount of it, but he admitted that that was his only definite information.

It is not necessary for the purpose of this judgment to refer to any other parts of the evidence, as for instance to a deposit receipt for £500 in the joint names of Austin Freeley and Thomas Greene "or survivor of them," which was a provision made for Thomas Greene in recognition of personal services. It was effected through a third person, and we have not Austin Freeley's instructions as to the form of receipt (if he gave any, which I doubt).

Before leaving the evidence, however, I should refer to the will of Austin Freeley made on his deathbed, the night before he died, but while still in possession of his faculties of mind. Amongst a number of pecunicary legacies he gave a legacy of £150 to Father Owens and a legacy of £150 to Patrick Freeley. He disposed of his house and farm and gave all the residue of his property to all his nephews and nieces, his sister Mrs. Cunningham, John and Thomas Greene in equal shares absolutely. He appointed John Greene and Patrick Freeley to be his executors. Probate was taken out by John Greene only.

The actions were tried by Mr. Justice Meredith who held that the plaintiffs had established their title to the respective sums in question and made declarations accordingly. The present appeals are taken by the defendant, the executor of Austin Freeley, against the judgment of Mr. Justice Meredith.

If, at the death of Austin Freeley, there were nothing more of information as to the several transactions than the records of the deposit accounts in the books of the Bank, a resulting trust would clearly arise by equitable presumption in favour of Austin Freeley and his legal personal representatives as to all the monies which were, on the 8th of September and the 15th of December, 1930, lodged to the deposit accounts in the names of Austin Freeley and Patrick Freeley and in the names of Austin Freeley and the Rev. M. J. Owens. There was no such relationship between Austin Freeley and Patrick Freeley or between Austin Freeley and the Rev. M. J. Owens as would raise a presumption of advancement to rebut the implication of a resulting trust. The onus of rebutting the implication of such a resulting trust by evidence rests upon the plaintiffs, Patrick Freeley and the Rev. M. J. Owens, who instituted these actions claiming to be beneficially entitled by survivorship to the monies standing to the accounts in which they were respectively named as joint creditors with Austin Freeley. They may discharge the onus which they have undertaken and rebut the presumption of a resulting trust by proving that it was the intention of Austin Freeley, when putting the monies to the deposit accounts in the Bank, to give to the plaintiffs respectively, then and there and by that act, a right, that is to say an immediate present right to take the monies with which he associated their respective names by survivorship (should they survive him), for their own respective use and benefit as surviving joint beneficial owners with him. It will not suffice to prove a merely testamentary intention on his part, for a testamentary disposition can be made only by will. It will not suffice to show an incomplete, or a conditional, or a postponed gift, nor can such an attempted gift be made good by means of a fictitious trust. But a gift completed by immediate transfer of legal ownership or by declaration of trust taking immediate effect will, if proved, support an intention to give a voluntary benefit and rebut the presumption of resulting trust. These principles (neatly summarised by FitzGibbon L.J. in *O'Flaherty* v. *Browne*

[1907] 2 I.R. at p. 434, are well established, and we have only to consider their application to the facts before us.

I should, however, say a word as to the form of the deposit receipts which is stated to be peculiar to Banks in Northern Ireland. The form of these receipts does not, in my opinion, determine the question under consideration. The intention of the depositor must still be ascertained. The use of the particular form may be part of a scheme of convenience in transacting the depositor's business, the other name in the receipt being that of an agent for the actual depositor, such an arrangement, for instance, as existed in the case of *Marshall* v. *Crutwell* L.R. 20 Eq. 328. Again, it may be an attempt to give whatever may remain undrawn to credit of the account at the depositor's death as Gibson J. appears to have held in the Circuit case of *Diver* v. *McCrea* 42 Ir. L.T.R. 249. In such a case, however, the intention is not to make a joint deposit operating as a present gift. It is an attempt to make an ambulatory and postponed gift of such (if any) monies as shall remain undrawn from the account at the depositor's death, which, in my opinion, is contrary to the established principles inasmuch as it is really testamentary in character and intention, and for that reason I am unable to accept the decision in *Diver* v. *McCrea* 42 Ir. L.T.R. 249 which is, I think, erroneous. It was a Circuit case and the report shows that some of the authorities were not cited to the learned Judge (who, however, gave judgment in Dublin after consideration). Again, this form of deposit receipt may be used for the purpose of creating a machinery of revocation of the trusts of a gift on trust, continuing until revoked, as the late Master of the Rolls held in the case of *McDowell* v. *McNeilly* [1917] 1 L.R. 117, which, however, could not, in the nature of things, apply to the case of a gift immediately complete and absolute, but only to the case of a gift on a continuing trust.

Now, in the present case, we have it on the evidence of Mr. McNelis that it was on his advice that the particular form of deposit receipt was adopted by Austin Freeley as a form which would allow him personally, without the concurrence of the other persons named in the account, to get the interest on the deposits paid to him from time to time while leaving the capital untouched. When Austin Freeley made the lodgments to the joint account in March, 1927, he had not yet formed an intention of making final settlement and there would have been a resulting trust in his favour. But if he had finally made up his mind, on the 8th of September, 1930, as to how he would dispose of his monies, it was, in my opinion, competent for him to have placed his monies on joint deposit accounts as he did, with the intention of making then and there immediate complete gifts in trust for himself and Patrick Freeley in one case and Father Owens in the other case, as joint tenants with right of survivorship as regards the capital sums only, the interest to be paid to him (Austin Freeley) during his life, such intention as regards the capital not to be capable of alteration. For effectuating such purpose, he might well have adopted the form of deposit receipt in question with the intention and for the purpose only of drawing the interest payable on the deposits and his use of the deposit receipts would be limited by that intention, notwithstanding their form ("accountable to them or either of them"), for it would follow from the complete gift of capital made that the other parties would have the right to intervene by proper proceedings to prevent him drawing, or at least appropriating to his own use, any part of the capital. Such, in my opinion, would be the only tenable basis upon which the plaintiffs could rest their claims in these actions. I suggested it to their counsel during the argument, but, probably because of the concealment of the transactions by the old man from the plaintiffs, his close retention of the deposit receipts under his own sole dominion, certain weaknesses and uncertainties in the evidence of the Bank Manager and of the plaintiffs themselves and no doubt for other good reasons in the case as they have it upon their instructions, the suggestion was not pursued, and the case of an immediate gift such as I have indicated as perhaps open to argument on the evidence was not put forward. On the contrary, counsel for the plaintiffs, who also definitely disclaimed any question of trust in the case, took their stand rather on the line of the judgment in *Diver* v. *McCrea* 42 IR. L.T.R. 249, and pressed the matter as one of a gift in each case of whatever, if anything, would remain to credit of the deposit accounts at the death of Austin Freeley, admitting that, in the meantime, by reason of the form of the deposit receipts, he might at any time withdraw all or any part of the capital monies for his own use or benefit. In my opinion, such a gift is an invalid gift as an attempt to make a testamentary disposition otherwise than by will.

Mr. Leonard relied on possession of the deposit receipts obtained after Austin Freeley's death, as making a complete legal title to the money. Even if the plaintiffs got the receipts properly (I question whether in the circumstances the receipts should not have been delivered to the executor of Austin Freeley at whose disposition they were held by the Bank Manager and whose voice directing that they be handed to the plaintiff was silenced by death), the legal title cannot defeat the resulting trust in equity.

I am, therefore, of opinion that the plaintiffs have failed to rebut the resulting trusts and that the appeals must be allowed with costs to be paid by the plaintiffs. The declarations and judgments of Meredith J. in favour of the plaintiffs respectively must be set aside, and the actions dismissed and the defendant must have judgment on his counterclaim in each case with a declaration and consequential relief as prayed.

The defendant will have his costs of action as executor's costs out of the assets of Austin Freeley deceased. No order as to the plaintiffs' costs of action.

FitzGibbon J.:

These two actions, though the plaintiffs are different, and though they relate to different sums of money, depend upon the same evidence and were heard together, and the considerations which apply to each are applicable to the other, and I shall therefore treat them, as they were treated in the Court below and in the argument here, as if they were one action. The common defendant is the personal representative of Austin Freeley, who died on the 29th of December, 1930, and the claim in each action is that certain monies placed by the deceased in his lifetime upon deposit receipt in the names of himself and the plaintiff are not assets of the deceased, and belong to the plaintiff as beneficial owner by right of survivorship. In each case the defendant has counterclaimed for a declaration that the plaintiff holds the deposit receipt as trustee for the defendant as personal representative of Austin Freeley, and that the sum deposited forms part of Austin Freeley's estate, and for consequential relief.

There is not much controvery about the facts, but the inferences to be drawn from the acts and declarations of the deceased as to his intention in his dealings with his property, and the legal effect to be given to that intention, require careful consideration, and are by no means free from doubt.

The deceased man, Austin Freeley, who is stated to have been over 92 when he died, had spent a large part of his life in America, whence he returned over twenty years ago to take up his residence at Carrowreagh, about a mile and a half from Ballyhaunis. He was possessed of considerable means, as, in addition to the sum of nearly £16,000 involved in these actions, he had £3,506 on deposit receipt in his own sole name in the Ulster Bank, fee simple property in Ballyhaunis valued at £1,000, the farm on which he resided, which was valued for probate purposes at £800, shares in Coats, English Sewing Cotton, and Guinness, and 5 per cent. War Loan and Free State National Loan, valued in all at £3,700, and real estate in America of unascertained value. Against that he kept an overdraft on his current account of £1,614.

The transactions with which these actions are concerned appear to have commenced in the year 1927, when, on March 2nd, he called at the Ballyhaunis Branch of the Ulster Bank, and asked for his deposit receipts, which, to the total amount of £16,601, were handed to him by the Manager. The account given by the latter of what then occurred is as follows:- "He said that he wished to settle his money, and that he was not able to do so till he saw Father Owens, but that Pat Freeley was a decent man and he would like to do something for him. And then he gave me a number of receipts, which he asked me to put in the names of Pat Freeley and himself. He asked me to put the money in such a way that he could draw the interest without going to Pat Freeley. And the only way I could do that was by putting it payable to them or either of them, which I did." The amount so lodged amounted to £16,917, £700 more than the sum withdrawn. The deceased came back two days later, withdrew this £700, and relodged it in his own name. Twelve months later, on March 8th, 1928, he called again at the Bank, withdrew the £16,217 from the account in the name of himself and Patrick Freeley and the £700 from his own account, and relodged £16,917 in the names of himself and Patrick Freeley, on the same form of deposit receipt as before. On May 2nd, 1929, he again withdrew the £16,917, and on the same day relodged it as before. On October 17th, in the same year, he withdrew the £16,917, lodged £5,652 in his own sole name, and replaced £11,265 in the names of himself and Patrick Freeley. On May 29th, 1930, he withdrew the £11,265, relodged £6,000, and transferred £5,265 to his own sole account, to which there was then standing £13,450 17*s*. 5. He operated on this account by additions and withdrawals in May, June and July, 1930.

It has not been contended on behalf of Patrick Freeley, and Meredith J. has expressly negatived the conclusion, that if Austin Freeley had died during the period between March 2nd, 1927, and September 8th, 1930, Patrick Freeley would have had, by survivorship or otherwise, any beneficial interest in any monies for the time being so standing on deposit in the names of the deceased and himself, but it is alleged that the transactions deposed to by the Bank Manager as having taken place upon September 8th, 1930, so altered the relationship between the deceased and Patrick Freeley in respect of the monies deposited in their names and payable to them or either of them, and created between the deceased and the plaintiff, Father Owens, a relationship in respect of the monies deposited by the deceased on that day in their names, and payable to them or either of them, as to entitle Patrick Freeley in the former case, and Father Owens in the latter, to succeed by survivorship upon the death of Austin Freeley.

The plaintiff's counsel have resolutely refused to state in any intelligible legal terms what this relationship is. They repudiate the suggestion that there was either a gift or a declaration by the deceased man of a trust affecting the monies on deposit in the two names. They admit, or at least they do not deny, that Austin Freeley could at any time during his life have withdrawn all monies standing in his own name and that of either of the plaintiffs, and have appropriated it to his own use, and that neither plaintiff would, in such an event, have had any claim upon Austin Freeley or his estate.

The Bank Manager's account of the transaction of September 8th is as follows:– "There was one deposit receipt for £6,000 in the joint names of Austin Freeley and Patrick Freeley and accountable to them or either of them, and there were nine in the sole name of Austin Freeley, and the aggregate of these nine was £13,450 17*s*. 5*d*." "He called in about 11.30 or 12 o'clock and asked for his receipts, and he said that he was going to settle the money finally. And he told me to put £5,000 in the names of Patrick Freeley and himself, and he gave me a number of receipts totalling £14,000 to put into the names of Father Owens and himself. He told me that he wished that no person would know anything of these monies, and that the monies were to be the property of Patrick Freeley and Father Owens if anything happened to him, and that the receipts were to be handed to the survivors. I filled in the requisitions as directed, and when they came back he said that he had made a mistake in Father Owens' receipt and he wanted to change it. He wanted £3,500 kept in his own name, he wanted it for a certain purpose, which I did. He did not tell me what the purpose was. So I got the receipts as he asked me, and changed them as directed, and handed them to him, and he looked them over and handed them back again to me. And he told me that the joint receipts, if anything happened to him, were to be handed to the survivors, but that no one was to know anything of the money, and the money was to be their property. So he told me to keep the receipts in my possession and I did so."

At a later stage in his evidence the Bank Manager, after a little judicious leading, says that "The deceased told me that I could give any information that was necessary *to the survivors* – at least to the joint depositors." As he had previously said "survivors" three times and had specifically stated "that the receipts if anything happened to him were to be handed *to the survivors,* but that no one was to know anything of the money," this belated correction is not very convincing. In any case, it would only be material if the question was one of the communication of a declaration of trust to the *cestui que trust,* and the plaintiffs have expressly disclaimed any suggestion that there was any declaration or creation of a trust in their favour.

Now, if Austin Freeley had been dangerously ill and in contemplation of death when this conversation took place, there is material to support a claim that there was a valid *donatio mortis causa* of these deposit receipts, the very expression, "if anything happened to him," reminds us of the condition in Justinian, Inst. 11. 7, § 1 "*si quid humanitus ei contigisset,*" but there is no suggestion that Austin Freeley was not in excellent health on the 8th of September, 1930, though he did in fact die on the following 29th of December. Anyhow, *donatio mortis causa* is out of the case.

Stress is laid by the plaintiffs upon the alleged statement by the deceased man "that he was going to settle the money finally." If he had insisted upon a change in the form of the deposit receipt, and had provided that the money deposited should really be placed in the joint names of himself and another, or that it should be payable "to them jointly," or "to them or the survivor of them," or should be so lodged as to be no longer under his own sole control, there would be ground for holding that he had an intention to alter the dominion over the deposited money, and to confer an immediate interest upon the co-depositor. Instead, he lodged the monies upon a receipt in the old form, under which the Bank acknowledged the receipt "from Austin Freeley, Esq., Carrowreagh, and Patrick Freeley, Esq., Ballyhaunis, of £——. For which we promise to be accountable to them or either of them," directed the Manager to keep the receipt for him, not to hand it to the co-depositor until after his death, and did in fact demand it back, endorse it and draw all the money deposited with interest, and redeposit the principal, on December 15th, 1930. The plaintiffs do not deny that if Austin Freeley had on December 15th lodged the money he had drawn upon a deposit receipt in his own sole name or appropriated part of all of it to his own use, he would have been within his rights in doing so, and neither of them would have had any claim. If that be, as I believe it is, the true state of affairs in relation to this money, I am unable to follow the contention that the monies became on relodgment any more the property of Patrick Freeley or Father Owens than they had been before they were withdrawn, or while they were in the actual possession of Austin Freeley.

In considering the question whether there was ever a gift to either of the individuals whose names appeared with that of the deceased upon the deposit receipts, the form of those documents appears to me to be of great importance. In the ordinary case of money invested or deposited in two names it cannot be withdrawn by either without the concurrence of the other. In the words of Lindley L.J. in *Standing* v. *Bowring* 31 Ch. D. 282, at p.290, "the donor has put the thing given out of his own power, and has placed it in such a position that he can only get the thing back with the concurrence of the donee." Even where there is such a transfer of the dominion, the law presumes, in the absence of additional evidence of intention, a resulting trust in favour of the donor, except where the joint owner is the wife or child of the donor, or a person to whom the donor stood *in loco parentis.* With the exception of *Diver* v. *McCrea* 42 Ir. L.T.R. 249, to which I shall refer later, I am not aware of any case in which the alleged donor retained throughout his life the complete power of disposition over the property in dispute, and it was held that there had been a complete gift by him in his life term. Austin Freeley was well acquainted with the various methods of depositing money in the names of two or more persons, and the effect which the form of the deposit had upon the powers of the depositors to deal with the sum deposited. It is expressly proved that he adopted the special form of deposit in the case of the sums in dispute here in order that he might have power to withdraw the principal money from time to time without the concurrence of any other person. It is also proved that he took the most careful precaution to prevent any person but himself from having any opportunity of dealing with the monies in any way; and it is proved that he did exercise his dominion over the money when he had occasion to do so.

Meredith J. appears to attribute some weight to the circumstance that there was only one dealing by Austin Freeley with the money after September 8th, 1930, viz., on December 15th. It is remarkable that he drew and relodged the sum which it is alleged he had given away, only three months after the date of the alleged gift, while his custom theretofore had been to leave it untouched for twelve months together. The money in the names of himself and Patrick Freeley remained untouched from March 2nd, 1927, to March 8th, 1928, and again from March 8th, 1928, to May 2nd, 1929, from May 2nd, 1929, to October 17th, 1929, from October 17th, 1929, to May 29th, 1930, and from May 29th, 1930, to September 8th, 1930, in each case a far longer period than that from September 8th to December 15th. When he did intend to make a gift, he knew well how to give effect to his intention. At the request of Father Crowe, the Prior of the Augustinian Abbey at Ballyhaunis, he decided to give £500 to a young man named Thomas Greene, and on the 13th of June, 1929, he deposited £500 in the joint names of himself and Thomas Greene, upon a deposit receipt which expressed that the money was to be payable "*to them or the survivor of them.*" thus putting it out of his own power to deal with the fund without the concurrence of his co-owner. And it appears that Austin Freeley knew that money deposited on a receipt in that form could not be withdrawn except upon the request of both depositors. Upon the 8th of September, 1930, the very day upon which he first deposited the sums in dispute here, he made a deposit of £200 in the joint names of Richard Owens and the Rev. Father Owens, expressed to be payable to them or the survivor of them. To my mind the inference is almost irresistible that when he made the other deposits in two names payable to himself and another *or either of them,* and kept absolute control of the receipt, without production of which the money could not be withdrawn, he had no present intention of parting with the property, but was endeavouring to make a disposition of it which would take effect upon his death on so much of the money as then remained upon deposit, but retaining all power of disposition over it during his life.

Mr. Leonard's statement of his contention is "that Austin Freeley did an act, the consequence of which was that on his death each of the co-depositors became legally entitled to the money. It was not a gift of £10,000, it was only a gift of what was left when he died." That statement appears to me to bring this case directly within such authorities as *Gason* v. *Rick* 19 L.R. Ir. 391, and *O'Flaherty* v. *Browne* [1907] 2 I.R. 416. In the former case a son held some bank shares in trust for his father, the trust being evidenced by a written acknowledgement. The father endorsed on the acknowledgement a transfer of the shares to his daughter, for her sole use and benefit. The father also held two I.O.U.'s, and upon each of these he wrote: "I transfer the debt of £—— to my daughter for her sole use and benefit." He handed the documents to his daughter. The Master of the Rolls, Sir Andrew Porter, after holding that there was nothing which could amount to a declaration of trust (which is admitted in the present case) went at on at p.395: "But beyond these considerations there is another, applying to them all, which I look upon as quite decisive against the claim of Miss Rich. From the sworn evidence, and the letters and other documents in the case . . . I am satisfied of two things:– First, that those attempted transfers were intended by Captain Rich to defeat *pro tanto* the covenants contained in the settlements of his several married daughters, which covenants would only become operative at his death; and, secondly, that notwithstanding the words of present transfer employed by him, he never meant to deprive himself of any property whatever by virtue of them during his lifetime. As a matter of fact, he continued for years after, and down to his death, in receipt of the dividends and interests, not a penny of which was paid to or intended to be the property of, or ever claimed by, Miss Rich. In fact those so-called transfers were meant in substance to be testamentary, while clothed with the appearance of gift *inter vivos*, designed only to mislead. The principle upon which Courts of Equity have sometimes aided imperfect transfers, is in order to give effect to the real intention of the parties. But to hold these transactions to have been in equity complete and binding according to their appearance, would be to do what the parties did not intend." "According to the appearance" of the deposit receipts in the present case, Father Owens and Patrick Freeley could on September 9th, the day after the deposit, have withdrawn every penny from the Bank, and appropriated it to their own uses. Anything more directly contrary to the intention of Austin Freeley, it is impossible to conceive. Sir Michael Morris L.C.J., speaking of the I.O.U.'s, says at p.398: "In my opinion, he never intended to deprive himself of the property in them during his lifetime, and trust (*sic*) reserved a *locus penitentiae*. Under such circumstances the property in them did not pass." Barry L.J. says at p. 402: "I am of opinion that the alleged donee here is defeated on the ground stated by the Master of the Rolls, namely, that the transaction was not intended at the time to be a complete and final divesting by the donor of all interest in the property purported to be assigned. I think the evidence shows that the transaction was intended to be revocable or ambulatory or testamentary in its nature, and that till the death of J.S. Rich the arrangement with his daughter was that he was to be master of the property." Austin Freeley took care that he did not even have to make "an arrangement," he ensured by his retention of the deposit receipt in the hands of his agent that he "was the master of the property." *O'Flaherty* v. *Browne* [1907] 2 I.R. 416 is even more closely analogous. In that case, the Rev. Maurice O'Flaherty, parish priest of Barraduff, having withdrawn some £880 which he had on deposit receipt, stated on June 15th, 1905, to the Bank Manager that he did not want to make a will, that he wished to leave all his money to his two nieces, and to leave *to his successor* as parish priest of Barraduff £60 for Masses and £50 for repair of Barraduff Chapel, but that he was in a difficulty, as he did not know who was to be his successor as parish priest. He then lodged on deposit receipt in the name of "the Parish Priest of Glenflesk and Barraduff the sum of £60 for Masses," and the sum of £50 "for repairs and building to church," and two sums of £385 each, one in the name of the Rev. Maurice O'Flaherty and Mary Griffin, and the other in the name of the Rev. Maurice O'Flaherty and Hannah Griffin. Shortly afterwards he withdrew the £50, and applied it to his own use. On September 20th he again called at the Bank with one, Father Costelloe, and Mary Griffin. He said he desired to leave £50 to his successor for the repair of Barraduff Chapel, but on the suggestion of Father Costelloe he decided to increase it to £100. He then withdrew £50 from each of the deposits in the names of himself and his two nieces, relodged £335 in place of £385 in the same names, and deposited £100 in favour of the Parish Priest of Barraduff for repairs and rebuilding of the church. He died on November 15th, having made a will. His successor as Parish Priest of Barraduff claimed the two sums of £100 and £60. The executor claimed that these two sums were assets of the testator. The King's Bench Divisional Court (O'Brien L.C.J., Johnson, Boyd and Wright JJ.) held that the deposits were good charitable gifts, and that Father Browne as successor of the Rev. M O'Flaherty as Parish Priest of Barraduff was entitled to the two sums claimed by him. This decision was reversed by the Court of Appeal (Walker L.C., FitzGibbon and Holmes LL.JJ.) upon the ground "that as the money on deposit receipt remained in the possession and under the control of the Rev. M. O'Flaherty during his life, the relationship of the bank and Father O'Flaherty was that of debtor and creditor, and that a valid trust had not been created." Walker L.C., after stating the facts, says at p. 43: "Under these circumstances what other conclusion can we draw from the facts than that this money remained the property of the Rev. M. O'Flaherty? First, on the form of the deposit receipts, these sums were lodged in his name, as Parish Priest of Barraduff, which he then was. At that date, on the face of the deposit receipt, the money belonged to him and no one else. He exercised proprietary rights over it, by taking up the money lodged on one of the deposit receipts, showing that he wished to retain control over it . . . In my opinion, the entire facts of the case show at most an intention on the part of the reverend gentleman to effect a disposition to become operative only at his death, and the principle laid down by the Court of Appeal in *Gason* v. *Rich* 19 L.R. Ir. 391 governs this case, that once there is a testamentary intention, and not an immediate gift, there is not a trust enforceable in equity." FitzGibbon L.J., after discussing the facts, which he decides to indicate an intention and understanding that "the depositor was the owner of the money, and retained in his own hands the power of dealing with it as long as he lived," says at p. 433: "The inevitable conclusion is that of the Lord Chancellor, viz., that this transaction was, in effect, an attempt to make a nuncupative testamentary disposition. Father O'Flaherty remained the owner during his life of money which, on his death, he wished to pass to his successor, just as he intended, in the case of his nieces, that the money which he intended for them should go by survivorship." "There are two principles applicable to the subject matter, of which one or other appears to be fatal to the respondent's contention. The first is that a testamentary disposition can only be made by will, and that any attempt to make it by parol *inter vivos* must fail. The other is exemplified in *Richards* v. *Delbridge* L.R. 18 Eq. 11. A voluntary trust may be created by a declaration of trust, or by a complete assignment of the legal ownership to a trustee; but it is impossible to turn an incomplete, *conditional or postponed gift* into a trust, where there is no intention to create the relationship of trustee and *cestui que trust.* It was not intended that this money should be left derelict, or that any trust should take effect upon it, during the life of Father O'Flaherty. So long as he lived he was owner and nothing less." (So was Austin Freeley.) "This is one of the many cases in which a man has tried to pass his property to another when he dies, but not until then, otherwise than as the law allows. In my opinion these dealings did not create a trust, and could not operate as a testamentary disposition." Holmes L.J., who agreed, says at p. 435: "The natural inference seems to me to be that he desired to substitute for a will some plan which, like a will, would give him full control over his property during his life."

The case of *McDowell* v. *McNeilly* [1917] 1 I.R. 117 decided by O'Connor M.R. was the same in result, though the Master of the Rolls put his decision upon a somewhat different ground. A husband deposited money in the names of himself and his wife – payable to either of them *or the survivor*. Shortly before his death he endorsed the receipt and handed it to a clergyman for charitable purposes, who cashed it. The wife brought an action for return of the money on the ground that there was a gift to her by way of advancement in the event of her surviving her husband, and that having made the gift he could not revoke it.

O'Connor M.R. held that there was a gift, with a power of revocation, which had been exercised. Neither *Gason* v. *Rich* 19 L.R. Ir. 391 or *O'Flaherty* v. *Browne* [1907] 2 I.R. 416 was cited. In view of those authorities I should have thought it more in accordance with the evidence to hold that there was no present gift at all, but that, in the words of Barry L.J., "the transaction was intended to be ambulatory or testamentary," having regard to the finding of the Master of the Rolls, "that the deceased was careful that he should have dominion over it, because the evidence is that he kept the custody of the deposit receipts, so that he alone during the joint lives should exercise the power of withdrawal." That case differs from the present in favour of the claimant in two respects. It was a case of husband and wife, where there is a presumption of advancement, and the deposit receipt was payable to husband or wife, *or the survivor*. The latter words are omitted from the receipts in the present case, yet the Master of the Rolls inferred an absence of intention to make a gift to the wife from the retention by the husband of a power of disposition during his own life, although "the survivor" was named in the receipt.

There is, however, one case which bears in its facts a close resemblance to the present one, and the plaintiffs have pressed it strongly upon us.

In *Diver* v. *McCrea* 42 Ir. L.T.R. 249 the deceased man had placed a sum of £65 upon deposit receipt in the names of himself and a nephew, with whom he resided until his death. The deposit was payable to either of the two parties named in the receipt, and it was proved that the deceased when depositing the money had expressed it to be his intention that any portion of the sum which might not be drawn during his lifetime should belong to his nephew. Gibson J. in a civil bill appeal from the County Court Judge of Donegal, held that there had been an effectual gift to the nephew, that there was no resulting trust, and that the sum of £65 did not form portion of the assets of the deceased. He based his decision upon the analogy of the cases of husband and wife, prior to the Married Women's Property Acts, where it had been held that the marital right of disposition possessed by a husband during his life over his wife's property did not rebut the presumption of advancement. No authority had been cited to him during argument upon the point of the retention by the deceased of the power of disposition, and Gibson J. refers to this, as leaving him to decide the point as best he could. The case, very much in point, of *O'Flaherty* v. *Browne* [1907] 2 1.R. 416 had only just been reported, and his attention was not called either to it or to *Gason* v. *Rich* 19 L.R. Ir. 391. It is remarkable that Gibson J. seems to treat the deceased man's disposition as in substance testamentary. "Kilpatrick's object was to avoid making a will, and he desired that the deposit receipt, *if uncashed, should, on his death,* belong to his nephew." "The substantial question argued was whether the circumstance that Kilpatrick was to possess power during his lifetime to draw the money defeated his intention that the deposit receipt should go to his nephew." Gibson J. had evidently much doubt about the case – in which there is a presumption of advancement – he would have felt much difficulty in deciding as he did. It does not appear from the report that the deceased kept absolute control over the receipt, which Gibson J. says was drawn in an unusual form, and was clearly not intended to divest Kilpatrick's ownership absolutely, but was for the purpose of enabling the nephew, as his uncle's agent, to draw the money for him should he require it.

In my opinion this decision is inconsistent with the reasoning of the Court of Appeal in *O'Flaherty* v. *Browne* [1907] 2 I.R. 416 and *Gason* v. *Rich* 19 L.R. Ir. 391, which were not cited to Gibson J. and which were binding on him. We are, of course, not bound by them, but I agree with them, and consider that *Diver* v. *McCrea* 42 Ir. L.T.R. 249 if, and in so far as, it is in conflict with them, is not good law. It appears to me to have been, and to have been upon the findings of Gibson J. himself, "an attempt to make a nuncupative testamentary disposition" [1907] 2 I.R. at p. 433, " a disposition to become operative only at his death" [1907] 2 I.R. at p. 431, and that accordingly the decree of the County Court should have been reversed, and the £65 should have been held to be part of the assets of the deceased.

In my opinion the plaintiffs have failed to establish any present intention on the part of Austin Freeley to part with his property in, and absolute dominion over, the deposited money during his lifetime, and a disposition, to take effect only upon his death, if he should not have previously disposed of the money, cannot be effected except by a declaration of trust, which is admitted not to have been made by him.

In my opinion the actions should be dismissed, and judgment should be given for the defendant upon his counterclaim for the declarations and consequential relief sought by him.

Murnaghan J:

I am also of opinion that the appeals in these two actions should be allowed.

We have been asked to take a view of the evidence given on behalf of the plaintiffs different from that taken by Mr. Justice Meredith, who tried the action. No sufficient ground has, however, been shown for departing from the general principle that the credibility and accuracy of the witnesses is particulary a matter for the Judge who heard the witnesses at the trial of the action. Accepting, then, the evidence given on behalf of the plaintiffs, the question remains as to what is the legal effect of that evidence and of the inferences which can properly be drawn from it.

The contention put forward on behalf of the plaintiffs depends upon refinement of legal subtlety rather than upon any broad view of the facts. They say that as Austin Freeley, on the 8th September, 1930, and again on the 15th December, 1930, placed the large sums of money in question on deposit receipt in his own name and in that of the respective plaintiffs, and as he died while the monies remained on deposit receipt the legal title remained in the survivor. And they further say that the beneficial interest in the monies, which would *prima facie* under equitable doctrines belong to

Austin Freeley as owner, does not form part of his estate, passing under his will, inasmuch as Austin Freeley desired that the beneficial interest should pass at his death to the plaintiffs.

When we seek to ascertain the intention of Austin Freeley on the critical dates, viz., the 8th September, 1930, and the 15th December, 1930, it is to my mind very material to know whether Austin Freeley intended to deprive himself of the power of dealing with the corpus during his lifetime. On this important matter the attitude which the plaintiffs take is extremely perplexing. They will not actually admit that Austin Freeley could have disposed of the corpus after the dates mentioned, but they do not argue that he was unable to do so. They state that they are willing to assume that he could have dealt with the money as he pleased, but, arguing the case on that basis, they say they are entitled to the money because he did not in fact remove it from the Bank and appropriate it to his own use.

My view of the evidence is that Austin Freeley never intended to part with his complete dominion over the corpus in his lifetime. He was familiar with another form of deposit in two names where it was necessary that both parties should concur to draw out the money. He chose a form of receipt under which he could draw out the money himself. He arranged that the deposit receipt would be available to himself at all times; he arranged that during his lifetime the receipts would not be available to the plaintiffs. Again, according to the practice of the Bank, interest on the deposit receipt can only be drawn by retiring the money lodged with accumulated interest, and the evidence is express that Austin Freeley required to be in a position to enable him to draw the interest.

If the plaintiffs could establish that on the 8th September, 1930, the deceased made a definite declaration of trust in relation to the money deposited, apart from its mode of investment on deposit receipt in the bank, effect might be given to such declaration of trust. For example, if the evidence supported a declaration of trust of the money under which Austin Freeley was to draw the interest during his lifetime and under which the principal sum should go to the survivor, there would be no impediment in the way of effecting the purpose so declared. Such a trust would put it out of the power of Austin Freeley to dispose of the corpus unless he survived the plaintiffs. But the plaintiffs will not state what precise trusts were declared in respect of the money: in fact they say that there was no declaration of trust at all. I agree that it is not possible to specify any precise trusts as having been declared on the 8th September, 1930, in respect of the money in question.

If, then, the money belonged beneficially to Austin Freeley during his lifetime, if he had not bound himself by any trust in reference to it, and if he retained full dominion over it, the contrivance to make the money pass on death was an attempt to make a nuncupative will which the law does not give effect to.

Quoting sect. 3 of the Wills Act, 1837, so far as material, it reads:- "It shall be lawful for every person to . . . bequeath or dispose of by his will executed in manner hereinafter required, . . . all personal estate which he shall be entitled to, either at law or in equity, at the time of his death, and which if not so . . . bequeathed or disposed of would devolve upon . . . his executor or administrator." Austin Freeley was during his life and at the time of his death entitled in equity to the money on deposit receipt in the bank, and his interest could only legally pass at his death by a will made in accordance with the Wills Act. The ingenious suggestion that on the death of Austin Freeley the property passed at law to the plaintiffs, and that this property, which was his up to the moment of his death, was not bound by a resulting trust, has to my mind neither principle nor established authority to support it. It would be a direct method of circumventing the Wills Act. I agree with the full statement of the law made by Mr. Justice FitzGibbon on this point, and am of opinion that the attempt of the deceased to circumvent the Wills Act must fail in law.

Note

See further as to resulting trusts, ch. 12, *post*.

Chapter 12

IMPLIED, RESULTING AND CONSTRUCTIVE TRUSTS

This chapter covers a wide range of non-express trusts, including both those designed to give effect to the supposed intention of the parties, *i.e.*, implied or resulting trust, and those which arise by operation of law independently of intention, see *Irish Land Law,* para. 9.045 *et seq.*

I. IMPLIED OR RESULTING TRUSTS

O'BRIEN V. SHEIL

(1873) I.R. 7 Eq. 255 (Rolls Court)

The facts are set out in the judgment.

O'Sullivan M.R.:

The question which remains undisposed of in this case is an important one. It is simply this:– Whether a sum of £2000 in Russian 5 per cent. bonds, and £200 in Victoria 6 per cent. bonds, having regard to the mode in which those securities were dealt with by Sir Justin Sheil, constituted any portion of his assets.

The facts with regard to these securities are as follows:– It appears that Sir Justin Sheil in his lifetime, as it appears by the books of the Bank of England Western Branch, Burlington Gardens, London, deposited the securities which I have mentioned in the name of his wife, Mary Leonora, Lady Sheil, and left them so deposited until her death. After that event, about the 5th of January, 1870, he transferred these securities into the joint names of himself, Sir Justin Shiel, and his daughter Miss Frances Sheil, one of the Defendants in this suit, and no alteration was made in this lodgment during the life of Sir Justin Sheil.

The question raised is, whether these securities have become the property of Miss Frances Sheil, she having survived her father, or whether they still remain assets of Sir Justin Sheil. The only evidence relating to the lodgment of the securities is what I have mentioned. There is no evidence of any contemporaneous writing under the hand of Sir Justin Sheil, or of any contemporaneous declaration by him as to the object he had in view in making the lodgment of these securities in the manner I have described. The securities, according to the evidence before me, are represented by bonds or certificates which pass from hand to hand like a bank note; and the lodgment of the securities at the Bank was made personally as if actual cash had been the subject-matter of it. After the death of Sir Justin Sheil there was found among his papers a memorandum in his handwriting, in the following words:–

"To Frances, Edward, Emily, Laura, Justin, Stephen, Richard, Honor, Denis, Grace. The money invested at the Bank of England, or branch, on a joint account (myself and Frances), amounting to £2000 in Russian 5 per cents., and £200 in Victoria 6 per cents., besides the balance in hands, was and is intended for the purchase of a trousseau, should any of the girls happen to be married. The expenses of my funeral should be paid out of this money; a portion of the expenses of probate and succession duties should be paid out of this money. Let the executors determine what portion.

"Justin Sheil.

"*April 7th, 1871.*

"Of course, I do not mean that the above sums are intended for the purchase of one trousseau. The trousseau is to be regulated by one's station in life.

"Justin Sheil.

"*April 7th, 1871.*"

The Frances mentioned in the above memorandum is the daughter of the late Sir Justin Sheil, and the other persons named therein are her brothers and sisters. The lodgment in the Bank of England Branch was on the 5th of January, 1870, a year and three months before the date of the memorandum. Frances, the daughter, claims these two sums under the ordinary doctrine of this Court, as being a gift by way of advancement, she having survived her father. She says she does not mean to keep the money herself, but to carry out the intention of her father; with that intention of hers I have nothing to do. She is at liberty to do what she likes with this money if she is entitled to it. But the course she has resolved upon is such as one would expect from a lady in her position, who has got a child's portion by her father's will.

It is contended on behalf of some of the children that this document is admissible in evidence, as indicating what the intention of Sir Justin Sheil was at the time he lodged these securities in the Branch of the Bank of England; and it is said that this is the document which regulates the trust which is to be attached to these two sums, and that the trust being vague and uncertain it must fail, and that the subject of it became the property of Sir Justin Sheil, and forms a portion of his personal estate. Now, the first point is, whether this document can be looked at at all – having regard to its date – as any evidence to control the lodgment of the securities made on the 5th of January, 1870.

Beyond a doubt, what took place on that day, unexplained by any contemporaneous evidence, would, on the authorities, amount to a plain and manifest advancement for Frances, she having survived her father. That is, I think, the clear result of the authorities. Whatever may at one time have been thought (see *Pole* v. *Pole,* 1 Ves. 76) of a lodgment in the name of a parent and child being a weaker case of advancement than a lodgment in the name of the child alone, it is now settled law that a lodgment by a father in the joint names of himself and his child is as powerful and strong an indication of advancement as a lodgment in the name of the child alone. Now, what is the effect of that doctrine of advancement attaching on a sum lodged in the joint names of father and child (the latter surviving), or in the name of a child alone, unexplained by any evidence? It is a gift of the property to the child in the one case immediately, and in the other if the child survives. It takes effect immediately in possession in the one case, the beneficial enjoyment being postponed in the other. Case after case establishes that proposition, and I need only refer to one of the most recent, *Hepworth* v. *Hepworth* L.R. 11 Eq. 10, where the consequence of advancement as being a direct gift, making the property pass, is explained and illustrated. That being so, it is difficult to see how a declaration by the father at a subsequent period can alter the property in the gift which he has made. In my opinion, the authorities are clear that the declarations of the father, subsequent to the advancement, if they are not so connected with it as to be reasonably regarded as contemporaneous, cannot be evidence to rebut the presumption of advancement. There is a case in this country of great importance, which was not referred to, *Fox* v. *Fox* 15 Ir. Ch. R. 89, heard before Lord Chancellor Brady, Lord Justice Blackburne, and Baron Deasy. That was the case of a lodgment of a sum of money by a father in the joint names of himself and his son, and having regard to the state of the family, an advancement operated very unequally. The hardship of the case influenced the Lord Chancellor's judgment when the case was heard before him, and he seems to have admitted subsequent declarations of the father, which affected his mind very much, and he held that there was no advancement. That decision undoubtedly interfered with the well-acknowledged rules of law respecting advancements. But on appeal he himself reversed his own decision, and there are some valuable observations in the judgments of the Lord Justice and Baron Deasy in relation to the entire want of value and weight to be attached to subsequent declarations. In my opinion, nothing is more dangerous than to allow the facts of a particular case to invade a rule of law which, when once settled, ought to be invariably applied.

Perhaps one of the most important cases on the subject is the decision of Lord Langdale in *Sidmouth* v. *Sidmouth* 2 Beav. 447, a well known case. It was stated in the argument before me, that Lord Langdale in that case weighed and considered the subsequent declarations made by Lord Stowell, as to his intention in making the lodgment which he had made. Lord Langdale did nothing of the sort. He had to deal with two sets of conversations, one set which was actually contemporaneous with the lodgment, and another set which was subsequent to the lodgment. He put aside altogether the latter, and entertained solely the conversations and declarations which were contemporaneous with the lodgment. And he has so expressed himself very plainly. He says, p. 455, "That contemporaneous acts, and even contemporaneous declarations of the parent, may amount to such evidence, has often been decided. Subsequent acts and declarations of the parent are not evidence to support the trust, although subsequent acts and declarations of the child may be so; but generally speaking we are to look to what was said and done at the time."

Sidmouth v. *Sidmouth* is accordingly one of the ruling authorities that subsequent declarations of the parent are not admissible to alter the presumption raised by the advancement; and if I were to name any one principle of law as better settled than another, I should say that it is the rule that no declaration of the father, at a period subsequent to the advancement, is admissible to control the gift which the law implies as against him. I should not have considered it necessary to comment on these principles of law but for the character and length of the arguments which were addressed to me.

But it is also contended that, whatever may have been the rule of law before, it has been altered by Vice-Chancellor Stuart's decision in *Devoy* v. *Devoy* 3 Sm. & G. 403, which it is said is an express authority to compel me to admit this document of April, 1871, in evidence, and the following passage in the judgment of Vice-Chancellor Stuart is referred to:– He says (3 Sm. & Gif. 406), "In support of that argument it has been said, that if the father had died before he gave evidence of the nature of the transaction, no record would have been preserved of the transaction, and the Court must then have given effect to it as an advancement to the child. The circumstance that if the father had died, the evidence would have been lost, cannot in the slightest degree affect the truth of the case, where the evidence is not lost." And then it is said, that the evidence here is not lost, and that we have it under the hand of the man himself that he made the lodgment for the purpose stated in the memorandum. It would appear to me, assuming *Devoy* v. *Devoy* to have been rightly decided, that there is a marked distinction between the evidence of a living man on his oath, and a scrap of paper written by him, and found among his papers after his death. In the former case you can probe his conscience, and examine him as to the truth and grounds of his statement. That case was followed in *Stone* v. *Stone* 3 Jur. N.S. 708; and it came again before the same Judge in *Forrest* v. *Forrest* 13 W.R. 380. Now the last case was a very peculiar case. Two points arose in it; first, whether certain transactions of the testator in relation to certain shares, he standing in *loco parentis* at the time, were to be considered as amounting to an advancement. These the Vice-Chancellor considered did not amount to an advancement, and it is unnecessary that I should go into the grounds on which he so decided. But I feel bound to say, that it appears to me that the report can scarcely be accurate as to the grounds on which he rested that decision. Because the Vice-Chancellor is made to state that, in order to support the advancement, it should be shown that the purchase of the shares, when it was made by the testator in the Defendant's name, was *intended* by him as an advancement. This view would throw the *onus* of proof on the party claiming the advancement, which is at right angles with all the authorities. But another question arose in that case, viz., whether there had been a subsequent gift *inter vivos*; and on this part of the case a document was produced in which the testator called the shares his own property: and the question was, whether that document was admissible in evidence. This case of *Forrest* v. *Forrest* has been relied on before me as an authority, that in a case of advancement, such a subsequent document was admissible. It decided no such thing. The document was offered in relation to the gift *inter vivos;* and Vice-Chancellor Stuart, apparently with great doubt, admitted the document, but at a stage of the case when he had entirely disposed of the question of advancement. He is reported to have said, that "he had great difficulty in making up his mind, whether the paper in the handwriting of the testator, giving an account of his property, was receivable in evidence or not." There was this entry in the paper, "South Wales Railway in C.B.T.'s (the Defendant's) hands belong to J.R.F." the testator. The Vice-Chancellor proceeds, "No doubt, if an advancement was once made, subsequent declarations by the person who made the advancement were immaterial, inasmuch as the property had already passed." It was another question, however, in a case of alleged gift, where the only evidence was that of the claimant. In the very valuable Treatise of Mr. Lewin on Trusts, p. 137 (4th Ed.), is this passage – "Of course the father cannot defeat the advancement by any subsequent declaration of intention. But his evidence is admissible for the purpose of showing what was the intention at the time." The only authority for that latter proposition was a case of *Devoy* v. *Devoy* 3 Sm. & Gif. 403; 5 W. R. 222. That was a very difficult case. There the father was living, and he had admitted his evidence as to the nature of the transaction. He still thought that he was justified in admitting the evidence of the father in that case; but he was not sure that the case went quite so far as to support the proposition of Mr. Lewin. After those observations I do not think that *Devoy* v. *Devoy* can be fairly cited as an authority that declarations of the father subsequently to the advancement are admissible. I say nothing about the actual decision in *Devoy* v. *Devoy*. I have no such case before me here; but I must say that it is no authority whatever for the admission in evidence of mere declarations of the father subsequent to the advancement. Vice-Chancellor Stuart himself, in *Forrest* v. *Forrest,* as will be observed in the passage I have quoted from his judgment, states the rule of law to be otherwise.

I think it right that I should call attention to the case of *Williams* v. *Williams* 32 Beav. 370, before Lord Romilly, who had to consider the admissibility of the father's evidence even in his lifetime. That was the case of a purchase of real estate made by the father in the name of the son, who afterwards had died. But the father was a living man, and the question was, whether that purchase was intended for the son, or whether the son was a trustee for the father. The father himself had given evidence, and Lord Romilly at page 372 says, "This is solely a question of intention; it depends on what the intention of the Plaintiff was when he made this purchase and these advances on mortgage, not what his intention now is." He then went through the evidence, and says, page 274, "I think myself therefore bound to reject from my consideration all that portion of the evidence of the father now, as to what his intention was before." That was the way Lord Romilly dealt with the evidence. "The decided cases show that his present declaration to that effect could not have been regarded after his decease to create a trust in the son, and I consider myself equally bound to disregard them now, although he is alive. On such occasions, the declaration to that effect by the father must be contemporaneous with the event itself." I am of opinion, therefore, that this document is not admissible in evidence.

It was also contended that this document was receivable in evidence, on the ground that it was an admission by Sir Justin Sheil against his pecuniary interest. I do not at all comprehend such a view of the memorandum. I have examined the cases relied on; they seem to me to have no application whatever, and that ground for the admission of the memorandum also fails.

The document being inadmissible, it is altogether unnecessary to consider the question whether the trust declared by it is too vague.

I shall, therefore, declare that the £2000 Russian 5 per cent. bonds, and £200 Victoria 6 per cent. bonds, form no part of the assets of Sir Justin Sheil.

Notes

1. *Cf.* the statement of the rules given by Costello J. in *Parkes* v. *Parkes*, p.74, *ante*. See further, *Irish Land Law,* para. 9.046 *et seq.*
2. See also *Heavey* v. *Heavey* (1977) 111 I.L.T.R. 1 (reproduced at p. 714 of *A Casebook on Irish Land Law),* and *Owens* v. *Greene,* p.356, *ante.*

II. CONSTRUCTIVE TRUSTS

MOORE V. McGLYNN

[1894] 1 I.R. 74 (Chancery Division)

A shopkeeper, who was also a local postmaster, by his will bequeathed all his property to his brother and son, to be held by them in trust, and to be managed by them for the benefit of his wife and children, and directed that the brother should have the right of maintenance and a salary for the management of the business, that the trustees should have power to arrange for the settlement of his children as they might determine, and that, in case they disagreed, the parish priest should have full and absolute power to determine both as to amount payable and times of payment. The testator left a widow and nine children. The trading was continued by the testator's brother, and some years after the testator's death the trustees made a valuation of the property available for distribution, and dividing the sum at which they valued it into ten equal shares, they decided that the sum representing one such share was the amount payable to one of the children. This she declined to accept.

In an action brought by her for administration of the estate, and accounts on the basis of wilful default and breach of trust.

Chatterton V.-C.:

It is necessary to consider in the first place the defence that the trustees and executors in exercise of the discretionary power given them by the will "to arrange for the settlement of the testator's children as they may determine," have decided that the plaintiff's share of the assets amounted to £60, in addition to £10 cash and £27 10*s.* worth of goods which she received, and that they tendered the sum of £60 accordingly which she refused to accept. The words of this clause are not clear, and do not with any precision express the extent of the power intended to be thereby conferred. "To arrange for the settlement of the children," if unexplained by the following clause, might fairly be construed as applying only to the settlement of ascertained shares. But the defendants contend, and I think rightly contend, that this uncertainty is sufficiently explained away by the following clause, which provides that in case of disagreement the parish priest should have full and absolute power to determine both as to the amounts payable and the times of payment. As it is improbable that the umpire was intended to possess larger powers than those between whom he was to decide, it seems to me that his powers may be resorted to to explain the meaning of the power to the trustees, and that consequently they must be taken to have power to determine the amounts and times of payment. The rule applicable to such cases of discretionary power is that the exercise of such power will not be interfered with or controlled if it be regularly and honestly used. What was done by the trustees was to make out a statement of the available assets for distribution, and to decide that this amount should be divided into ten equal shares, giving each child one-tenth. The division into equal shares is free from objection. But, in my opinion, in the circumstances of this case it is going too far to contend that the ascertainment of the assets so to be divided is not subject to investigation by this Court. The trustees may have had full and absolute authority to arrange and settle the shares to be given to each child of the sum to be divided; but it would be dangerous to hold that there is no control over their ascertainment of the total amount. They would in such case be judges in their own cause. They had from the death of the testator the entire administration of the assets entrusted to them, including the management of the trading carried on by them. The amount distributable among the children of course depended on the due discharge of those duties, so that if their decision on that amount was to be conclusive, it would be in their power to protect themselves against liability for any default. It is not necessary for the *cestuis que trust* to prove any breach of duty by the trustees for the purpose of having accounts taken of the trust property, as their right to this results from the mere relation between them. I therefore hold, without going for that purpose into the charges made by the plaintiff against them, that their defence on this ground cannot be sustained. There must, therefore, be the usual accounts of the real and personal estate.

The plaintiff claims to have accounts taken not only of the actual receipts of the defendants, but of what they without wilful default might have received. It has been sought to extend this liability in the present case far beyond its proper limits; for it was contended that it applies to possible loss of profits in trading, occasioned by the setting up of a rival business as complained of here. But the very words of the prayer here, which are in the form invariably used, seem sufficient to exclude this contention. Under this prayer, according to the settled practice, an executor or administrator, or a trustee can be charged with assets or trust funds actually in existence, which either came to his hands, or which, by his misfeasance or negligence as to getting them in, have been lost to the estate. I do not mean to say that trustees or executors cannot be held liable for losses sustained by such misconduct as here alleged, but I hold that it cannot be done under a mere direction as to wilful default. Another insuperable objection is that by the settled practice of the Court a plaintiff seeking relief against wilful default must allege in pleading some specific act of wilful default, or, at least, make a strong case for inquiry. Here there has not been any proof of wilful default, nor even any ground for inquiry as to it, in the view that I have expressed of its nature. I shall therefore dismiss the action so far as it seeks to have the accounts so taken.

The plaintiff is entitled to have an account of the profits of the business of the testator carried on by the defendants from his death in the testator's premises in Bridge-street, Clara.

The next relief prayed is an account of what portion of the trust property has been invested by the defendant Edward McGlynn in his own business, and a declaration that any trust funds or assets so invested were bound by the trusts of the will. The case put forward by the plaintiff as to this was that the defendant Edward McGlynn purchased the premises in Church-street, Clara, in which he set up business with money taken by him out of the testator's assets. This was positively denied by Edward McGlynn, and in the main, at least, he has completely disproved the charge. The sum paid by him for the purchase of the new premises was £500, which was paid in two sums of £175 and £325, into the Court of Bankruptcy, where the purchase was made. He has proved to my satisfaction that Edward McGlynn borrowed from Messrs. Baker, Wardell & Co., on his own personal security, the sum of £300 for the purpose of this purchase, and that they lent it to him as a mere act of kindness, and that he applied it towards payment of the £325. It appears that he passed the cheque he received for the £300 into his bank account, which contained also the cash transactions of the business of the testator, and immediately drew a cheque for the £325 and paid it into the Bankruptcy Court. Then as to the other £200 composed of the first payment of £175, and £25 of the second payment, his case is that both these sums, which were paid out of the same bank account, were his own private moneys. He has made out his own personal account with the business from the bank account, showing that he owned a sum of £100 arrears of his salary as manager of the business in the testator's lifetime (on which he has, probably without sufficient ground, charged interest amounting to £15), and also £200, being the salary of £60 a-year, to which he was entitled under the will, and on which he rightfully charged the interest given him by the will, amounting to £12, and against these sums he shows credits to which the business was entitled, and thus balances the account. No attempt was made to dispute any of these items except the £15 interest, which he seems to have claimed on the ground that the testator gave him by the will interest on any money he might have in the business, which he thought gave him a restrospective claim. Save as to this item he has, so far as the evidence before me goes, disproved the plaintiff's charge with which I am now dealing. But in order to have this question fully investigated, I shall direct an inquiry at Chambers, whether any, and if so what, portion of the personal estate of the testator was invested by the defendant Edward McGlynn in his own business.

The next relief prayed is the removal of the defendants from the trusteeship. No case has been proved which would call for the removal of the defendant Patrick J. McGlynn, whose conduct appears to me to be free from impropriety. When his father died he was living in Dublin in respectable commercial employment. He allowed his uncle and co-trustee to remain in the management of the testator's business, which he had managed for several years, in conjunction with his brother, the testator, and who by the will was directed to be continued in this management, and was thereby shown to have enjoyed the fullest confidence of the testator. There was, therefore, no default on the part of Patrick in leaving the management in his hands. Then, when Edward McGlynn contemplated setting up in business for himself, Patrick gave up his employment in Dublin, and in February, 1891, returned to live in the testator's house at Clara, and took charge of the business there. I do not find any evidence to bring the case within the rule of this Court, that one trustee standing by, and permitting his co-trustee to commit a breach of trust is liable for a breach of trust so committed. I therefore hold that no case has been made for his removal from the trusteeship, and shall dismiss the action with costs, so far as it prays for his removal.

Then as to the defendant Edward McGlynn. He has been accused of gross breaches of trust on several grounds. The chief complaint is for setting up in business in the same town, which, to a considerable extent, was of the same nature as that carried on in the testator's house of business. I have not been referred to, nor am I aware of, any case deciding that an executor or trustee of a will carrying on the business of his testator is disabled from setting up a similar business in the same locality on his own account. If he in any way represents to the public that his own business is the same concern as that of which he is trustee, as by using the name of the testator's concern in connexion with his own business, or otherwise seeking to draw away the customers to his own shop, there might be some ground for an application to restrain him from so doing. But I am not prepared to hold that a trustee is guilty of a breach of trust in setting up for himself in a similar line of business in the neighbourhood, provided that he does not resort to deception, or solicitation of custom from persons dealing at the old shop. I have no sufficient proof here of any such mal-practices by the defendant Edward McGlynn. It is admitted that he did, on first opening his shop, send out circulars in the town, stating his having done so. No copy of the circulars has been proved, and I must take them to be such as described by the defendant in his uncontradicted evidence, and as not containing any such misleading statements. It is plain that the setting up of a shop in a small town to a certain extent in rivalry with another must tend more or less to injure the business of any similar shop in the locality, and I think there would be an inconsistency between the duties of the defendant Edward, as trustee and manager of the testator's business, and the necessary personal interest which he must take in his own. I do not think I could, under such circumstances, grant an injunction to restrain him from carrying on his own business, or direct an inquiry whether any damages were occasioned by his doing so, but I am of opinion that his new position disqualifies him from remaining any longer a trustee, and it would have been better for him to have procured his removal from the trusteeship before setting up for himself. He should not be continued in a position where his duties and his self-interest may conflict. He has himself expressed by his counsel his willingness to retire from the trusts, and I shall remove him from being a trustee and manager, and appoint a new trustee in his place. I shall not appoint a receiver or manager of the business; the effect of my doing so would probably be ruinous to the business, and I have no reason to be dissatisfied with the management by the defendant Patrick J. McGlynn.

There was another matter which was made the subject of very strong charges against Edward McGlynn, namely, his having obtained, on the death of the testator, the office of local postmaster at Clara, which had been held for many years by the testator, who carried on the post office business in a part of his shop. He applied to the Postmaster-General for the appointment by a letter, stating his qualifications, and that the business could be still carried on in the same office, and that he was one of the trustees of his brother's will. He got the appointment, and the business was carried on as before, and he drew the salary and emoluments, and allowed them to go into the general trust fund. I cannot see any impropriety in his having done this.

There was nothing false in his representations, and it must be presumed that he was appointed upon his personal fitness to hold the office. The post was one in the gift of the Crown, and could not be made the subject of purchase, or of any dealing in the nature of purchase. He was absolutely entitled for his own personal benefit to the emoluments of the office, and any trafficking with them would have been illegal and void. I cannot give the slightest countenance to the proposition that there could be anything like a graft upon the former tenure of it for the benefit of the testator's assets, or any liability on the part of the officer to account for its profits. When he received his salary he was at liberty to do what he pleased with it, and it was his voluntary act to throw it into the fund for the benefit of his *cestuis que trust*. The utmost of his liability would be to payment of compensation for the use and occupation by him as postmaster of the office on the testator's premises. But when he set up his new shop he transferred to it the post office, which he must have got leave from the post office authorities to do, and thenceforth he performed the business there, and retained the emoluments for his own benefit. This I consider he had full right to do, as the office was a personal one, and he was the only person recognized by the Crown as the holder of it, liable to perform the duties, and entitled to receive the salary. Strictly speaking, he would have been entitled to the emoluments of the office, and during the period for which the business of that office was carried on by Edward McGlynn upon the premises of the testator, he would be chargeable with a reasonable sum for the use of the post office premises, the result of which would have been less beneficial to the testator's estate than what was done. I think it would be wrong to permit him now to go back of this course of dealing, nor does he seek to do so. I shall, therefore, not disturb the accounts in this respect; and, on the other hand, I shall not direct him to be charged for the use of the post office premises in the plaintiff's shop, thus allowing one to go against the other.

The writ of summons asks for an injunction against the defendants, but does not say what injunction is sought. In the prayer of the statement of claim no such relief is sought. The plaintiff, by her counsel, on the trial, appeared to expand this into an injunction against the defendant Edward McGlynn carrying on any business in the town of Clara, similar to that carried on by the testator, but, on grounds I have already stated, I decline to do so, and shall dismiss the action so far as it seeks an injunction against him. No case whatever has been made for an injunction against Patrick J. McGlynn, and this must be similarly dealt with, except that I must do so with costs.

It was also sought to have the new premises, purchased by Edward McGlynn in Church-street, Clara, and the business carried on by him there, affected with a trust for the benefit of the testator's estate, and to have an account of his trading there. I consider this to be without foundation, and shall dismiss so much of the action accordingly, and with costs.

The judgment in the case is as follows:- Declare that, notwithstanding the alleged exercise by the defendants of the power in the testator's will, given to the executors and trustees thereof for the settlement of the testator's children, by which the share of the plaintiff of the testator's assets was decided to be the sum of £87 10*s*., the plaintiff is entitled to have the accounts taken, which are hereinafter directed, and accordingly let the following accounts and inquiries be taken and made:–

1. Let the real and personal estate of testator be administered, and the usual accounts taken.
2. Dismiss the action with costs, so far as it seeks to have the accounts taken with wilful default.
3. Usual account of the trading of the testator carried on upon his premises in Bridge-street, Clara, by defendants, or either of them, since his death, and direct that, in taking such accounts, any sums received by defendant Edward McGlynn, for salary or emoluments of the office of postmaster, shall not be included, save so far as the same shall appear to have been actually brought into account by said Edward McGlynn, and that no sums shall be charged against him for the use or occupation of any portion of testator's said premises, for the carrying on the business of the said

office.

4. Inquiry whether any, and if so what, portion of the testator's assets was invested by said Edward McGlynn in his own business, or in the purchase of the premises in Church-street, in which such business was carried on by him.

5. Dismiss the action, with costs, so far as it seeks to remove defendant Patrick J. McGlynn from being a trustee of the testator's will. Discharge defendant Edward McGlynn from the further performance of the duties of trustee of the said will, and manager of the said testator's business under the same; and adjourn to Chambers to appoint a new trustee of said will in his place, jointly with defendant Patrick J. McGlynn. Make no order at present for the appointment of a receiver or a manager of said business. Dismiss the action (1) so far as it seeks an injunction against the defendants, and also so far as it seeks to affect the business carried on by Edward McGlynn in the premises at Church-street, with a trust for the benefit of the testator's estate.

Adjourn further consideration, and the costs, save those hereinbefore awarded.

Notes

1. See further, *Irish Land Law*, para. 9.063 *et seq*. and on the Irish doctrine of *graft*, *Gabett* v. *Lawder* and *Dempsey* v. *Ward*, *infra*.
2. See further on liability for breach of trust, ch. 20, *post*.

GABBETT V. LAWDER

(1883) 11 L.R. Ir. 295 (Chancery Division)

The facts are set out in the judgment.

Chatterton V.-C.:

The plaintiff, as administratrix *de bonis non* of William Lawder, claims to have it declared that the estate in fee-simple conveyed by the Commissioners of Church Temporalities to Matthew Nesbitt Lawder, the first administrator of William Lawder, in certain lands mentioned in the statement of claim, is personal estate of the intestate. The intestate held those lands under an ecclesiastical lease for twenty-one years customarily renewable, the last renewal to him being a lease of the 1st of February, 1870, from the Church Temporalities Commissioners, for twenty-one years. After his death Matthew Nesbitt Lawder, as his administrator, obtained a further renewal from the Commissioners for twenty-one years, dated the 14th of September, 1876. Under the 34th section of the Irish Church Act the Commissioners, in whom the reversion in fee became by that Act vested, were authorised to sell it by public auction or private contract; but were bound before selling to the public to offer the purchase to Matthew Nesbitt Lawder as their immediate tenant, at a price to be named by them. They did so offer it, and he declined to buy at the price named. The reversion in fee was thereupon set up by the Commissioners for sale by auction; and Matthew Nesbitt Lawder bought it for a less price, paid for it, and took the conveyance of it from the Commissioners, which the Plaintiff as administratrix contends he took as a constructive trustee for the persons entitled to the personal estate of William Lawder.

The fundamental principle upon which the doctrine of constructive trusts proceeds is, that no person in a fiduciary capacity shall be allowed to retain any advantage gained by him in his character as trustee. His *cestuis que trusts* are entitled to the benefit of any advantage so gained by him, to any addition or accretion to the trust estate which he may have acquired, and to all profit which he may have made by any dealing with it. It has long been settled by a current of authorities that a trustee of a leasehold interest who obtains a renewal of the lease, whether by covenant or custom, or by the voluntary act of the reversioner, comes within this principle, and that he cannot hold the interest he so acquired for his own benefit, but as a constructive trustee of it for his *cestuis que trusts*. In such cases this Court will not allow the trustee to say that he did not obtain the additional interest as trustee, or that he procured it from personal favour to himself, or from the refusal of the landlord to deal with the *cestuis que trusts,* or for any similar reason. If his position could have caused or even contributed to his obtaining the advantage, it is in my opinion enough; and the Court will not undertake the difficult and often impossible task of investigating the motives of the parties to the transaction. If it results in either gain to the trustee, or loss to the *cestuis que trusts,* the trustee is liable to hand over to them the one, or to make good the other. This principle of course applies to executors and administrators who stand in fiduciary relation to those entitled to the personal estate of their testator or intestate equal to that of any express trustees to their *cestuis que trusts,* and are subject to the same equities. It was therefore necessarily admitted that the renewal of the 14th September, 1876, to Matthew Nesbitt Lawder was a graft on the previous term, and that he held it as trustee for the persons entitled to the personal estate of the intestate. It was however contended by the Defendant James Ormsby Lawder that the purchase of the reversion in fee by Matthew from the Commissioners does not come within the principle, and that he took it for his own personal benefit. This contention was based on the cases of *Hardman* v. *Johnson* 3 Mer. 347, and *Randall* v. *Russell,* before Sir William Grant. These cases appear to have proceeded on the authority of the case of *Norris* v. *Le Neve* 3 Atk. 26, before Lord Hardwicke, which upon a careful examination will be found not to have been a decision on this question. In that case the owner of a reversion in fee, after several prior limitations by his will, made in pursuance of a power in the settlement by which the estate was limited, appointed the settled lands to Norris for a term of ten years, which took priority of the previously existing limitations, upon trust to raise money for payment of debts and legacies; and he did not, either by the settlement or his will, dispose of his reversion in the lands. Norris, who was only a trustee of the term so created, purchased from the heir-at-law this ultimate reversion, which afterwards fell into possession by the failure of the prior limitations. A protracted litigation took place which it is unnecessary to go into; and at a very late stage of it the question was directly raised, whether Norris was not to be held to be a trustee of the reversion so purchased. Lord Hardwicke pointed out the difficulty in that case of saying for whom he was to be deemed a trustee; and while he stated his opinion that the *Rumford Market Case* and other cases of leases were different from that, he refused, on the ground of the lapse of time and transactions between the parties, to allow the matter to be discussed, and dismissed the petition for rehearing.

The case of *Hardman* v. *Johnson* 3 Mer. 347 came before Sir William Grant before *Randall* v. *Russell,* Ibid, 190, though it appears later in the Reports. There a testator, seised and possessed of a leasehold for three lives and twenty-one years, devised it to one of his daughters, Betty, with a gift over to another daughter, Sarah, in case the former should die without issue living at her death, which event happened. Betty obtained a renewal of the lease and devised it to the defendant, who brought an ejectment and recovered possession, and while in possession purchased the reversion in fee. The plaintiff, the husband of Sarah and claiming in her right, brought his bill claiming to be entitled to the benefit of the purchase of the reversion, and insisting that Betty took the new lease obtained by her subject to the limitations in the will. Sir William Grant said that the question of the purchase of the reversion was a new one, but that he should hesitate a good deal before he refused to apply to it the principle which had been established as to the renewed of a lease, and that it would be dangerous to allow the trustee of a term to resort to the owner of the reversion to become a purchaser for his own benefit; for by that means he would debar his *cestuis que trust* of the fair chance of a renewal, getting into his own hands the power to grant a renewal or not at his option. He took time to consider, and held that the plaintiff was entitled to the benefit of the renewal lease, but not of the purchase of the reversion. It is to be observed that there was no fiduciary relation subsisting at the time of the purchase between the defendant who purchased the reversion and the plaintiff. The defendant insisted on his legal right as devisee of Betty Johnson to the new lease obtained by her, and claimed the interest for his own benefit adversely to the plaintiff. Sir William Grant gave no reason for not acting on the opinion he expressed at the hearing.

In *Randall* v. *Russell* 3 Mer. 190 the bill prayed that a tenant for life of lands held by a testator, under St. John's College, Oxford, as yearly tenant after the expiration of a lease, which appears to have been customarily renewable, should be declared a trustee of a new lease obtained by her from the college, and also of the reversion in fee, which she purchased from a third person, in whom, by a private Act of Parliament sanctioning an exchange, it had after the granting of the new lease become vested. It was held that the renewed lease was subject to the trusts of the will which created the tenancy for life, but that the reversion in fee was not, and that the tenant for life was entitled to hold it for her own benefit. Sir William Grant said that the ground commonly stated on which a renewed lease becomes subject to the trusts of a will disposing of the original lease is that the one is merely an extension or continuation of the other, but that the fee is a totally different subject which the testator had it not in his contemplation to acquire or dispose of. He suggested that it might be different if the purchase had been from the college; for, if so, it might be said that the tenant for life intercepted and cut off the chance of future renewals, and consequently made use of her situation to prejudice the interests of those who stood behind her, and that there might be a sort of equity in their claim to have the reversion considered as a substitution for those interests, though he was not aware of any decision to that effect. He distinguished the case before him from those as to the renewal of leases, on the ground that by the act of the landlord, without any intervention of the tenant for life, the situation of the parties was altered, and the tenant-right of renewal with a public body was gone, a lease at a rack-rent being all that was to be expected from a private proprietor. He held that it was not enough to say that the situation of the tenant for life gave her the opportunity of making the purchase, and that the persons interested in the lease must go on and show what right of theirs she acquired or defeated by making the purchase.

As this case constitutes the main support to the argument of the Defendant James Ormsby Lawder, and as at first sight it appears to countenance his contention, it is necessary to consider carefully whether it is substantially distinguishable from the present. If it be not, I should certainly consider myself bound by it, though I should not follow it in a case like this without hesitation; for I think that the rule supposed to be established by it would be a dangerous limitation of the application of the general principle. I first venture to say that Sir William Grant appears to me to have treated *Norris* v. *Le Neve* 3 Atk. 26 as a decision of Lord Hardwicke on the point, which for the reasons already stated I do not think it is. I also think that there is a material difference between that case and the present, in this, that there, as in *Hardman* v. *Johnson* 3 Mer. 347, the purchase of the reversion was made by a person who before and at the time of the purchase did not stand in any fiduciary relation to the persons who claimed to have the benefit of it. There is no such relation between successive remaindermen or person entitled under successive limitations of any kind. It is the fact of a renewal being obtained by the possessor of an interest earlier in the series that creates *de novo* the fiduciary relation in the nature of a constructive trust. The position of a trustee or personal representative, who fills the fiduciary relation altogether independently of and prior to such a purchase, and therefore has duties to his *cestuis que trusts* to discharge in respect of property of which he is already the legal owner, seems to me to impose on him the disability to hold for his personal benefit any advantage he may obtain which is attributable, or possibly attributable, to that position. This distinction would accord with the views expressed by Sir William Grant in *Randall* v. *Russell* Ibid, 190, which would otherwise appear opposed to the general rule. It would sustain his decision in the case of renewals by persons having limited interests, by placing such cases on what he states to be the common ground for holding them to be subject to a constructive trust, namely that the new lease is deemed a continuation of the former, and therefore within the possible contemplation of the author of the limitations; and not upon the ground of any supposed pre-existing fiduciary relation which would impose on such persons the disability which attaches to trustees, and it would probably support the distinction he takes between such renewals and purchases of the reversion in fee. It would explain the reason assigned by him for this distinction, namely, that the testator may have had the former in his contemplation, but not the latter; for this reason could well apply to cases between persons taking under successive limitations, whereas it would be altogether inapplicable to cases of pre-existing fiduciary relations, which may have been created without either will or deed or other written instrument, as in that before me, where the relation flows from the office of administrator; cases in which the existence of the relation creates the disability, no matter what may be the subject of the trust. I cannot think that he intended to apply to cases of ordinary fiduciary relation the proposition that it is not enough to say that the situation of the person making the purchase gave him the opportunity of making it, but that the persons interested must go on and show what right of theirs he acquired or defeated by making the purchase. His language on this is in express terms applied by him to the case of a purchase by a tenant for life, and the rights arising therefrom to the other persons interested in the lease; and I must understand him as confining his argument to such cases. I do not think that his decision can affect a case like the present, where a leasehold interest with a statutory right of renewal is vested in an administrator as such; where he takes the legal estate with all its incidental rights, not for his own benefit, but merely as a trustee for the creditors and next-of-kin of the intestate. The law casts upon him the duty of protecting the interests of those entitled to the personal estate; and he is in duty bound to realise for them every right incidental to it. Even in the case of persons respectively entitled in succession, the principle upon which Sir William Grant appears to have proceeded was not confined to renewals strictly so called, but extended to acquisitions of higher interests.

In *Giddings* v *Giddings* 3 Russ. 241 the leasehold interest which was held in trust was an underlease of premises called the Byde Mill, for eighteen years, carved out of a superior lease for twenty-one years of these and other premises, which was again carved out of a lease made by the Bishop of Salisbury. The tenant for life of the underlease purchased the interest in the superior lease, and obtained renewals of it from time to time from the immediate tenant to the See, the last of which bore date in the year 1819; and on his death the person entitled in remainder under the will which created the trusts of the underlease filed his bill against the representative of the tenant for life, to have it declared that the new lease of 1819, which it will be remembered was a renewal of the *superior* lease, was held upon the trusts of the will. The defendant claimed to hold the renewal in his own right, and not as trustee; and his counsel relied on *Randall* v. *Russell* 3 Mer. 190 and *Hardman* v. *Johnson* Ibid. 347, and contended that those cases proceeded not on any peculiarity in the nature of a reversion in fee, but on the ground that the purchase of the reversion was not an extension or continuation of the preceding lease, and did not defeat any right of the remainderman. Lord Lyndhurst, then Sir J. Copley, M.R., says:– "If an underlessee who has only a life estate in his lease, instead of taking a renewed lease, purchases the interest of an immediate lessor, and obtains from the superior lessor a renewal of the lease which he has so purchased, will he under such circumstances be entitled to the property absolutely? That state of things falls within the general rule; the mere circumstance of the lease being taken not from the immediate lessor but from a superior lessor cannot defeat the right of a remainderman; and the remainderman will still be entitled, on the principle that a lease obtained by a tenant for life enures for the benefit of all in remainder. What difference can it make in the application of that principle whether the lease be taken from the immediate lessor or from a superior lessor?" He stated that he did not think that the cases before Sir William Grant established a contrary principle, for they were cases where the reversion in fee was purchased, and there was no longer a leasehold interest existing. He deemed that the lease of 1819, so far as regards the Byde Mill and the premises held therewith, ought to be held upon the trusts of the will.

It will be observed that the Master of the Rolls did not declare that the original underlease was to be kept up out of the superior interest purchased by the tenant for life, but that the new lease of 1819, which was a renewal of the lease so purchased, was itself subject to the trusts of the will. Again, in *Buckley* v. *Lanauze* Ll. & G. t. Plunk. 327 a tenant for life of a lease for lives without any covenant for renewal obtained from the landlord a new lease for three lives (one of whom was the surviving *cestui que vie* in the former lease), with covenant for perpetual renewal at a largely increased rent. He sold his newly-acquired interest for valuable consideration; but, as it was held, with notice, and though a similar argument based on *Randall* v. *Russell* 3 Mer. 190, and also on *Norris* v. *Le Neve* 3 Atk. 26, was put forward for the defendant the purchaser, Lord Plunket held that the new lease was a graft on the old one, and decreed accordingly. He no doubt, as well as Sir J. Copley, distinguished the case from those cited to him for the defendant, as not being a purchase of a reversion in fee, and also on some special circumstances; but he expressed doubt as to the effect of the decision in *Randall* v. *Russell* 3 Mer. 190, and pointed out that in reality the question was not affected by *Norris* v. *Le Neve* 3 Atk. 26.

The case of *Postlethwaite* v. *Lewthwaite* 2 J. & H. 237, before Sir W.P. Wood, was cited in argument, but has not much application to this case. It was a purchase of a reversion in fee from the Ecclesiastical Commissioners of England by an immediate lessee, and an underlessee with a *toties quoties* covenant for renewal claimed a declaration that the interest so purchased was subject to his underlease. The Vice-Chancellor considered that the relation of a *purchasing* lessee was very much that of a fiduciary or partner with respect to his sublessee, and held that the equity of the latter was to call for a conveyance of the fee of the particular property comprised in his underlease, upon the terms of paying his share of the expenses of acquiring it. The question there was rather as to the terms on which the plaintiff was so entitled, and the construction was therefore different. In *Trumper* v. *Trumper* L.R. 14 Eq. 295 the plaintiff sought to charge certain sums, which were originally charged upon an estate for lives renewable for ever, upon the reversion in fee which had been purchased by a tenant for life of the leasehold interest subsequently to the creation of the charges. The defendant, who was the devisee of the reversion so purchased, disputed this claim. Bacon, V.C., held that the plaintiff was entitled to the relief he sought, and that the charges should be raised out of the entire estate in the lands. He held that, upon the general principles applicable in a Court of Equity to the circumstances, there ought to be no doubt, and that there could be no danger in holding, that a trustee or person in any degree in a fiduciary position who had acquired the legal possession of and dominion over an estate subject to a covenant for perpetual renewal, and who should so deal with the property as to make the renewal impossible by his own act, and for his benefit, would be bound to give full effect to the charges on the trust estate, and to satisfy these charges out of the acquired estate so far as might be necessary. He referred to the cases of *Evans* v. *Walshe* 2 Sch. & Lef. 519, and *Randall* v. *Russell* 3 Mer. 190, as confirming his view, and said that the dangers which would attend the exclusion of the principle were so numerous and so serious that they would go near to destroy the fixed rules by which the dealings of persons in a fiduciary position with respect to trust estates and interests are governed. This case is an important authority in favour of the plaintiff here; and I fully concur, not only in the decision, but in Sir J. Bacon's statement of the equitable principle on which he placed it. His decision was affirmed by the Court of Appeal in Chancery L.R. 8 Ch. App. 870. James, L.J., does not in terms apply to it the broad principle relied on by Sir J. Bacon, and in his judgment says that the right of the plaintiff would not be to claim the fee, but only a right to a leasehold interest subject to the life estate of the defendant, and with a right of renewal; and on that basis discuss the position of the tenant for life as paying off a charge on the entire leasehold interest – a question having no bearing on the case before me. His observations to which I refer would appear to be in accordance with those of Sir William Grant in *Randall* v. *Russell* 3 Mer. 190, as to the extent of the right of a *quasi* remainderman of a leasehold interest to the benefit of a purchase of the fee by a prior tenant for life. It was not necessary for him to go farther than to hold that the charges on the original interest must under the circumstances of that case be let in on the fee;

and he expressed no dissent from Sir James Bacon's statement and application of the general principle. The only relation between the parties in that case also was that of tenant for life and remainderman.

In none of the cases which have been cited in argument, or which I have found, is there any distinction taken as to the nature of the additional estate or interest acquired save in those between tenant for life and tenant *quasi* in remainder. I certainly am not disposed to extend this distinction to any other cases, and I am of opinion that it does not apply to cases like the present, where the relation is expressly fiduciary, and existed independently of the purchase. I think it would be impossible to hold that, if Matthew Lawder had accepted the offer of pre-emption given by the 34th section, he would be entitled to the reversion in fee so acquired for his own benefit. It would have clearly been an estate acquired by him by virtue of his fiduciary position, which alone entitled him to the tenancy in possession to which the Act accords that right. It is, no doubt, true that the 34th section enacts that any person purchasing the reversion shall hold it subject to all tenants' rights of renewal to which the same was subject in the hands of the Commissioners at the time of the sale. That would not, however, be the measure of the right of the creditors or next-of-kin, for their trustee, *quâ* trustee, would have gained an additional estate, presumably an advantageous one, but certainly one which they could claim as their own on recouping him what he had given for it. Surely the rule supposed to have been laid down by Sir William Grant could not have applied to such a case. I have no doubt that he never intended to express so wide a proposition.

I had occasion to apply this general rule to the acquisition by an administratrix of a new tenancy from year to year, in the case of *Kelly* v. *Kelly* I.R. 8 Eq. 403, where the old tenancy had been determined by notice to quit, and a new letting made to the widow of the former tenant, who was also his administratrix; and though there were circumstances relied on as showing that the new letting was to her as the widow, not as the administratrix, I refused to entertain that question, and held her to be a constructive trustee. Again, in *McCracken* v. *McClelland* I.R. 11 Eq. 172, I had to deal with a purchase by an executor of a farm subject to the Ulster tenant-right custom, which he paid for with his own money, and obtained a new letting of, according to the custom of the estate; and on the same principle I held him to be a trustee. In those cases I stated my views of the principle applicable to them; and I am of opinion that that principle applies with equal force to cases like the present.

It was urged here, as in those cases, that the circumstances of the purchase show that the administrator did not buy in his fiduciary capacity, but for his own personal benefit. It was contended that the statutory offer of pre-emption having been refused, he was at liberty to bid for the estate as any other member of the public could. If this were so, it would open a wide door to fraud, for a trustee, whose duty it is to secure for his *cestuis que trusts* every advantage incident to the trust property, would be at liberty for his own purposes to decline the offer of pre-emption, and thus secure the setting up of the estate by public auction, and then buy, as he did here, at a less price, and hold the property as his own. The fact of his being the possessor of the leasehold interest might, and probably would, be a reason for his getting it at a less price than a stranger. But into these probabilities this Court, in such cases, declines for wise reasons to enter, and holds that every advantage which may possibly arise from the fiduciary position shall enure to the benefit of the *cestuis que trusts*. If no statutory right of pre-emption had been conferred, and the reversion at once set up for public sale, a purchase by a trustee would, according to the opinion I have expressed, be held so to enure. It seems to me to make the case stronger against a trustee that he had previously been offered the purchase and declined it. I do not mean to say that Matthew N. Lawder declined the offer of the Commissioners fraudulently, with a view to a purchase by auction for his own use, and he possibly had no other reason for so doing, but that he thought the price too high. That consideration is, however, beside the question, for actual fraud is not necessary in cases between trustee and *cestui que trust*.

I am accordingly of opinion that Matthew N. Lawder became a constructive trustee of the reversion so purchased, for the persons entitled beneficially to the personal estate of Wm. Lawder, and that it forms part of such personal estate; the persons claiming the benefit of it, of course, paying the purchase-money and all expenses incurred by M. N. Lawder in the purchase.

Notes and Questions

1. What, if anything, does the doctrine of *graft* add to the notion of a constructive trust? See further *Irish Land Law*, para. 9.064 *et seq.*
2. See also *Dempsey* v. *Ward, infra.*

DEMPSEY V. WARD

[1899] 1 I.R. 463 (Court of Appeal)

The facts are set out in the judgments.

Lord Ashbourne C.:

This is an appeal from a judgment of the Master of the Rolls dismissing the action, and it presents some curious phases. Upon reading the statement of claim, one view is presented clearly, but anyone who heard the argument of the plaintiff's counsel in Court, and who afterwards read the statement of claim, would not consider there was much resemblance between the pleading and the case argued. The case put forward by the statement of claim states that a man named Dempsey, a farmer in the county of Meath, died in May, 1876, being possessed of certain lands called Killegland, containing 192 acres, which he held under lease for a term of years, which had expired, and for lives, of which he was the last survivor. He left a widow, Mary Anne Dempsey, and nine children. She continued in possession after his death, at the rent of £250, the former rent, and remained in possession till the month of July, 1887. It states that she was entitled to one-third of this tenancy for herself and the children were entitled to two-thirds as a graft upon the tenancy which had determined with her husband's life. The fifth paragraph states:– "In the month of December, 1886, the said Mary Anne Dempsey by an agreement in writing purported to sell the said tenancy in the said lands to one William Bobbett for the sum of £400," and the pleading states that there was fraud in the transaction, as the said Mary Anne Dempsey had not any independent advice and assistance on the occasion of the sale, that the solicitor for Bobbett acted for both parties on the occasion, that Mrs. Dempsey did not understand the full nature of the transaction into which she was induced to enter, and that the sale was at a gross undervalue, as the farm was worth a great deal more than £400. It then states that the plaintiff, one of the sons, went to America and only returned in 1896, that he obtained letters of administration to his father on the 23rd August, 1897, and that Bobbett died having left the holding to the defendant by his will. The relief prayed for is that the present tenancy subsisting in the lands may be declared to be a graft upon the interest of James Dempsey, in other words that the mother's tenancy was a graft on the father's expired tenancy, and that Bobbett's tenancy was a graft on the mother's.

The statement of defence states that Bobbett became tenant in 1887, that he died in January, 1888, having left his interest in this farm to his daughter, the defendant, and she sets out the facts and circumstances of the sale. She states that what occurred was this – Mrs. Dempsey being indebted to Charles P. Aungier, the landlord, in the sum of £625, two and a-half years' rent of the lands, a writ of possession, issued on foot of a judgment obtained in an action of ejectment for non-payment of rent at the suit of Charles P. Aungier, was duly executed by the sheriff of the county of Meath, and possession of the lands was given thereunder to Mr. Aungier, and Mrs.

Dempsey's interest determined. After the statutory period for redemption had expired Aungier demised the lands to Bobbett. The said Mary Anne Dempsey did not sell, or purport to sell the said tenancy in the said lands to William Bobbett; she had no interest in the lands to sell, and Bobbett did not purchase any estate or interest in the lands from her. The defendant further states that no such sum as £400 was paid by the said William Bobbett to Mrs. Dempsey, but the sum of £230 was given by Bobbett, who was apprehensive of being boycotted, to Mrs. Dempsey by way of gratuity, and in order to secure her good-will. It then states that subsequently to the ejectment Mrs. Dempsey remained for a period of about seven months as caretaker in care of the said lands, and in 1887 she was put out under a magistrate's order, and since then Bobbett has remained in possession.

There is a wide difference between the facts and circumstances as we now have them and the simple and innocent case put forward by the statement of claim. The first branch of the argument was the point presented to the Master of the Rolls – that there was a sale to Bobbett, that Mrs. Dempsey being in possession for her own interest sold to Bobbett, and that Bobbett must be regarded now as having the tenancy which is a graft upon hers. The Master of the Rolls seems also to have been pressed with the further point, although not in so much detail as it was pressed here, that the ejectment was void. The Master of the Rolls decided in favour of the respondent, and the case has been fully discussed before us on appeal. The counsel for the appellant have presented two broad branches of argument – (1), the question on the facts, that the tenancy was a graft on the old tenancy; and (2), the effect of the ejectment.

On the facts the argument addressed to us was this, that we ought to regard the substance of the transaction, that Bobbett had succeeded Mrs. Dempsey by virtue of the transaction with her, and that that transaction was handing over the interest or good-will, that it was a sale between Bobbett and Mrs. Dempsey, and that we were to ignore the fact that there was no evidence of a contract between Bobbett and Mrs. Dempsey. We were to pass that by because in Bobbett's will there is a statement that he purchased the farm from Mrs. Dempsey for £400, and because there is another statement in a letter written by Mr. Davoren to the Land Commission that Bobbett's rent was the same as the former tenant's, Mrs. Dempsey, whose good-will he purchased. That is, roughly speaking, the contention of the appellant as to how we should look at the case on the facts. I am not much impressed with the argument on the words of the will. The will is not well expressed, but the somewhat lax use of words by a testator cannot alter rights. As to the letter written by Mr. Davoren, that can scarcely affect the question. Bobbett was endeavouring to be a present tenant, but the idea semed to have existed that he could not do this unless he was in the shoes of Mrs. Dempsey. But Holmes, L.J., drew attention to the form of the order made by the Land Commission. The Land Commission struck out all reference to the former tenancy, and made the order simply certifying that the agreement was filed declaring the fair rent of the holding. Upon the facts, and the evidence, and the probabilities of the case, I hold that his was a new letting from the landlord to Bobbett, and it was not a sale or transfer from Mrs. Dempsey to Bobbett. In the position in which things stood, Bobbett would go to the landlord if he wanted a new tenancy clear of any complication, and he would only go to Mrs. Dempsey if he wished to have a transfer of the old tenancy with its obligations. On the evidence the arrangement made by Bobbett was with the landlord, and not with Mrs. Dempsey.

The question of graft plays a considerable part in the argument, but I am not going through all the cases on the doctrine of graft in detail. A man taking a new letting who is in a fiduciary position, that is one case; a man who is an executor taking a new letting, that is another; or a guardian of a minor, or a person who is a limited owner, and who gets the new letting by virtue of the position in which he stands in relation to the property; these are other instances in which the letting has been held a graft. The case of *O'Brien* v. *Egan* 5 L.R. Ir. 633 decided by the Vice-Chancellor is, without doubt, the strongest that can be found. But the facts of that case were quite different from those of the case now before the Court. There the person, to whom the new letting was made, was in possession of the holding, under the provisions of her husband's will, and on the expiration of the lease she obtained a new letting. That is very different from this case, where the term expired with the life of James Dempsey, and the landlord thought right to give the widow a new letting. But I do not rest my judgment on that. What did Mrs. Dempsey give Bobbett? If Mrs. Dempsey was there in possession of the old tenancy, and Bobbett purchased her interest, that would be another question, but that is not my reading of the facts. I hold that Bobbett came into possession by a contract with the landlord, that the £400 was paid under this arrangement to Mr. Charles Aungier, and it was quite legitimate to pay £230 to the widow not for her good-will, but for her good word.

Assuming the facts to be as I have stated, there is another question to be decided. Mr. Price and Mr. Matheson say you are leaning on a broken reed, the ejectment is void, because there were two joint tenants entitled to the reversion, and only one of them was joined as plaintiff in the ejectment. That is a strong way of putting the case, to suggest that there are several joint tenants entitled to the reversion, and the fact of one of them being omitted defeats the action, although the defendant did not raise the objection, or deny the plaintiff's right to recover. I can quite understand that in an ejectment for non-payment of rent, a defendant can say that a party ought to be added. But I am not aware of any case like this, where, after the lapse of twelve years, a person who was not a party to the ejectment comes forward to raise the point of non-joinder of a plaintiff. It is curious to consider what the result would be. What is the position and *status* of Bobbett, or of those who represent him? The contention would sweep away the tenant of the Aungiers, from whom they have been getting rent for eleven years, and affects their position without any notice to them, and without any representation to them in this action. Again it is sought to do this, though Mrs. Dempsey is not a party to the present action, while she was defendant in the ejectment. Then again, there is no notice to the landlord, although Mrs. Dempsey received £230 for her one-third interest in the holding. There is no case where such a thing was done after verdict and judgment, and after such a lapse of time. We have been familiar with Rules of pleading for ever so long, which have been passed for the purpose of preventing actions from being defeated from non-joinder of parties, and the matter was dealt with in the Rules of 1891 by Order XVI. R. 11, and yet we are asked to hold that this action of ejectment was void because one joint tenant was not added as a co-plaintiff. In my opinion, the question is one of title, rather than of jurisdiction. It is admitted that this single plaintiff could distrain, that he could give receipts for rent, and that he could serve a notice to quit. It is also admitted that he could bring an ejectment in his own name, if he acted for himself and others. In my opinion it would be indefensible for us to hold this ejectment to be void after such a lapse of time, and with some of the parties affected by it not before the Court, even if we held different views on the facts of the case.

Upon those facts I am entirely against the appellant, and in my judgment the decision of the Master of the Rolls is right, and should be affirmed, and the appeal should be dismissed with costs.

FitzGibbon, L.J.:

I concur. In my opinion, the plaintiff fails on the form in which the action has been framed, on the equitable question of graft, on the legal determination of the tenancy, and on the evidence. Though I shall express my opinion on each of these matters, any one of them would be a sufficient answer to the action.

What is the nature of the suit? The plaintiff sues as the personal representative of James Dempsey the former tenant. One of the defendants, Margaret Mary Ward, is a legatee under the will of William Bobbett, and the two other defendants are his personal representatives. To sustain the action the plaintiff must, therefore, show title to something which is personal estate of James Dempsey. The claim is independent of heirship, and independent of devolution. Accordingly, before the plaintiff can succeed, he must show that the existing tenancy in the farm in question is an accretion to the personal estate of the late James Dempsey.

Furthermore, the claim is for two-thirds of the land *in specie,* and without terms of any kind. No one is brought before the Court who might have any equity, claim, or interest in or against the two-thirds of the land. No terms can be imposed except what Bobbett, if living, could have given. The landlord is not a party; Mrs Dempsey is not a party, and unless a clear and unconditional title is established by the plaintiff, the suit, as framed, cannot succeed.

In my opinion there are four fatal objections to the case of the plaintiff. 1. There is no proof that the tenancy which Mrs. Dempsey originally got was a graft on her husband's interest. 2. The tenancy which Mrs. Dempsey got from the landlord after her husband's death was determined before Bobbett came in. I think that it was determined by the judgment in ejectment; but if not, it was determined by Mrs. Dempsey by act and operation of law. 3. I agree with the Master of the Rolls that the evidence proves that Bobbett became tenant and got possession, not by purchase from Mrs. Dempsey, but by direct contract with the landlord; and, 4. The new letting to Bobbett was not grafted on anything which had gone before, but became a new root of title. The only difficulty which I feel upon this part of the case arises on the language of Mr. Davoren's letter of January 27, 1887.

Not for the first time, I have to observe that I entertain grave doubts as to the extent to which the doctrine of graft has been pushed in this country. The use of the term "graft" is peculiar to Ireland. English Judges have found fault with our Irish use of the terms "graft" and "salvage" to designate separate heads of equity; they object to metaphor, and prefer to speak of "derivative equities." The terms have been used for a long time in Ireland; they happily express what is meant, but their use ought not to extend the doctrines of equity. To have a graft at all, there must still be life in the old stock. The vital principle of all the cases is to be found in *Keech* v. *Sandford* 1 Wh. & Tud. L.C. 48, where a trustee took a renewal of a lease for his own benefit, the lease being vested in him as guardian of an infant, and it was held that he could not hold the renewal against his ward.

In *Kelly* v. *Kelly* I.R. 8 Eq. 403 the personal representative took possession of a tenancy from year to year, and though an ejectment was brought, and possession was formally taken, the administratrix continued to occupy at the same rent, and was held to be in the same position as a trustee purchasing part of the trust property for his own benefit, and therefore incapable of acquiring beneficially for himself.

In *McCracken* v. *McClelland* I.R. 11 Eq. 172 the executor actually surrendered the holding to the landlord, while the old tenancy was in existence, and in compliance with the custom of the estate he was given the new tenancy because he was an old tenant. In other words, he gave up part of the assets as the consideration for the new tenancy. This was the same case as *Randall* v. *Russell* 3 Mer. 190.

Then came *O'Brien* v. *Egan* 5 L.R. Ir. 633. With all respect, I treat that as, at best, a frontier case: whether it goes beyond the true line, it is not necessary now to decide. But whenever it comes to this Court for decision, it will be open to serious question whether the argument of Serjeant O'Hagan was sufficiently answered. Where a specific piece of property, such as a tenancy for a fixed term, which is subject to certain rights, comes to its natural end, and ceases to exist, I shall require argument to satisfy me that a person who had an interest in what so came to an end, is under any disability, or is subject to any equity, which will affect him in an honest dealing for a new interest, in any way in which a stranger would not be affected. That does not seem to me to be the case of grafting on an old stock, but of acquiring or planting a new root. But, however that may be, all that it is now necessary to say of *O'Brien* v. *Egan* 5 L.R. Ir. 633 was well expressed by Holmes, L.J. in the course of the argument: "there is a chasm between that case and this." In *O'Brien* v. *Egan* 5 L.R. Ir. 633 there had been a continuing possession of the property which was surrendered. Here it is not even alleged, far less proved, that Mrs. Dempsey originally got into possession through her husband. The statement of claim alleges that James Dempsey was entitled to the lands of Killegland held under a lease for years and lives made prior to the year 1870. It then states– "The term of years had expired long prior to his death, and the surviving life was that of the said James

Dempsey. Immediately *after* the death of the said James Dempsey, the said Mary Ann Dempsey *entered into possession* of the said lands, and *was accepted* by the landlord thereof, one Mark Aungier, as, and *became tenant* of the said lands at the yearly rent of £250, and remained in possession thereof as such tenant *from the said 1st May,* 1876, down to the month of July, 1887."

It is not stated that Mrs. Dempsey was an over-holding tenant, or that she became tenant on the terms of the expired lease; or that she was accepted through any consideration of her relationship to James Dempsey, or that she took advantage of her relationship in any way. The statement of claim alleges no equity against her, and none has been proved.

In my opinion, where a tenancy has ended, and where it is in the power of the landlord to make a new letting to whomsoever he chooses to accept as tenant, there is no necessary disability attaching to the members of the family of the previous tenant, which, *per se*, and without more, prevents any one of them from taking and keeping a new tenancy, unencumbered by grafts or equities which would not affect other people. It is every day's experience. The tenant for his own life dies: if the landlord likes, he can turn the family out on the spot. The widow and sons go to the landlord's office, to see whether he will accept one or more of them, to succeed the old tenant. He may prefer the widow, because she is thrifty and industrious; or because the children are young. Or he may prefer the eldest son, because he is likely to work the farm well, or even because, if it was a freehold before, he wishes the son to succeed the father as a freeholder. Or he might prefer the second son, either because he was a better man than his eldest brother, or because the elder brother already had another farm. What equity is there, in such cases as those, in "grafting" liabilities, or disabilities, on new tenancies? The first effect of such a graft must be to make the grafted interest assets of the late tenant, and to bring in the creditors even before the beneficiaries. It appears to me that there is a "chasm" between such cases and the principle of *Keech* v. *Sandford* 1 Wh. & Tud. L.C. 48, and in the present case I find nothing to connect James Dempsey's tenancy with his widow's tenancy, except that she was his widow, and was living in his house when his tenancy ended by his death.

As to the second question – Whether the tenancy was determined? – I think the ejectment determined it. In *McSheffry* v. *Doherty* [1897] 2 I.R. 191 we were driven to hold that the ejectment was void. There was a mortgage of the interest supposed to be evicted, which was admittedly still existing. The pleading was wrong; it deliberately omitted part of the demised lands; and parties not bound by the ejectment were still interested in, and were in possession of, those lands. The existence of the mortgage, and the continuance of the demise in the outstanding lands, were alike incompatible with the validity of the eviction. No such difficulty arises here; the plaintiff who sued and recovered in the ejectment was in the position of bailiff for the co-owners, and it does not lie in the mouth of any party to the proceedings to say that possession was not recovered by him for himself and his co-owners. But, at all events, there was sufficient evidence to satisfy sect. 24 of the Landlord and Tenant Act of 1860, that the plaintiff in the ejectment was the landlord of the defendant, and in an ejectment brought by a landlord by estoppel against a tenant by estoppel, it cannot, in my opinion, be open after judgment to treat the eviction as void, merely on the ground of non-joinder of parties.

Besides, Mrs. Dempsey put an end to any tenancy with which she was capable of dealing, by act and operation of law.

The third question is one of fact. The whole dealing was between Bobbett and Mr. Aungier. The widow had become a permissive occupant; she could be put out by a magistrate's order; and Bobbett undertook to give her something, not for her tenancy, but for her "good-will." The suggestion that the tenancy was sold for less than it was worth is unfounded. The new letting to Bobbett was independent of the previous caretaker's occupation. It ought not to be lost sight of that the tenancy which Bobbett got was not one to which the advantages of a "present tenancy" attached. Care was taken to make it clear that what Bobbett purchased was an evicted farm, and not a subsisting tenancy, and therefore he got it cheap.

Lastly, an attempt to graft an equity on this new tenancy of Bobbett's would at once bring the parties seeking the equity under the obligation of doing equity by paying the mortgage that has been referred to, and discharging all the other liabilities of the deceased tenant. If the plaintiff here could succeed at all, he could do so only in a suit bringing the landlord, Bobbett's representative, and the mortgagee, all before the Court, and offering to pay the landlord his rent, the mortgagee his debt, and to take a fair account with Mrs. Dempsey of the rents and profits.

In my opinion, the action wholly fails, and the appeal must be dismissed with costs.

Holmes, L.J.:

It does not often happen that a case comes into this Court in which the plaintiff fails so completely in both law and merits as in the present instance. Objection has been taken to the action on the grounds that the proper parties are not before the Court, that the relief claimed has ben misconceived, and that there are other defects of a comparatively minor character. I do not stop to examine these defences, inasmuch as the plaintiff's cause of action depends upon his establishing two propositions neither of which can be sustained. The foundation of his alleged right is that the letting of Killegland to Mary Anne Dempsey on the death of her husband created a tenancy which became at once part of the husband's personal estate. I am clearly of opinion that it did not. James Dempsey the husband had a freehold lease of these lands which terminated with his life. His wife went to Liverpool to see the landlord and obtain from his a new letting. She asked for a freehold lease which the landlord declined to give, but he made her tenant from year to year. There was no intention on either side to increase the assets of the deceased. There was no trust declared. Neither the widow, nor any one else, except the landlord had any interest, legal or equitable, in the land; and when she applied to be made tenant, she had never occupied any fiduciary position in relation to it. The doctrine recognised in *Keech* v. *Sandford* 1 Wh. & Tud. 48 has been pushed in some instances very far, but it is impossible to apply it in the present case. The landlord was probably influenced in making the letting by a desire to benefit the widow of an old tenant; but, if so, it was a personal benefit he wished to confer on her, and not to create an interest that might be laid hold of by the creditors of the deceased.

On this ground alone the action must fail. But even if Mrs. Dempsey became a trustee for everyone interested in her husband's assets, the letting made to her has long since come to an end; and the tenancy to which the defendants are now entitled is a new and different interest. There has been a good deal of argument as to the nature and effect of the transactions which led to William Bobbett becoming the tenant; but the inference from the evidence is clear: *res ipsa loquitur*. Mrs. Dempsey fell behind in her rent; and in May, 1886, she owed on account of it £625. Her interest in the land was valuable; and the first idea of the landlord was to sell it under a judgment to be obtained by him for the amount due; but it was discovered that the sheriff would not have been able to seize the tenancy under a writ of *fieri facias* on account of a mortgage that affected it. A judgment in ejectment for non-payment of rent was then obtained; and when the writ of *habere* was executed, one of Mrs. Dempsey's sons was made temporary tenant pending the period of redemption. I have no doubt that she would have sold while there was yet time, if she could have got a purchaser willing to give a price that would cover the rent due and the mortgage debt; but none such was to be found, and as there would have been no advantage in a sale for a smaller sum, the period for redemption was allowed to expire, and the tenancy came to an end. When the landlord was proceeding to take possession, Bobbett turned up. He was willing to give £400; but I have no doubt that he would only give it to the landlord on getting the land from him. He is dead himself; but the landlord's solicitor, Mr. Davoren, tells us what happened when the arrangement was made. The £400 was paid to the landlord, and it was left to the latter to say what sum he would give as a matter of charity to the former tenant. The amount was fixed by him at £230; and this she got, not as the purchase-money of her tenancy which was gone, but for the purpose of obtaining the personal good-will of herself and her family.

It has been argued that the ejectment was a nullity because the reversion expectant on the tenancy was vested in two trustees jointly, and only one of them was named the plaintiff. He could, however, have given a good discharge for all the rent; and I doubt if the tenant could have taken advantage of the non-joinder of the other even before judgment. In any case, I am of opinion that it was too late to raise this objection years after judgment and execution. Besides, if the tenancy was not determined, the arrangement I have mentioned amounted to a surrender of it by Mrs. Dempsey.

It was part of the arrangement between the landlord and Bobbett that the latter should be given a statutory tenancy; and this is the only thing which affords some shadowy reason for saying that Bobbett had purchased the old tenancy. The usual form of agreement was altered by striking out all reference to an old rent or to a present tenancy; and nothing appears upon the face of the document to show that before its date any tenancy existed in the holding. It is, however, argued that inasmuch as such an agreement could only have been entered into when the tenancy had been in existence before 1881, it must be now assumed that this tenancy was of that duration. The cases, however, which decided, or are supposed to have decided, that a landlord and tenant could not create a present tenancy by agreement did not arise until long after this transaction; and at that time it was not unusual to have a fair rent fixed by consent on the creation of a future tenancy. I cannot hold that the subsequent judicial determination of a doubtful point of law can throw any light on the real nature of a previous transaction. Neither do I attach any importance to Mr. Davoren's letter to the Land Commission which, in my opinion, does not bear the construction sought to be placed upon it.

For these reasons I hold that the plaintiff has failed to establish either of the propositions which are necessary for his course of action.

ALLEYNE V. DARCY

(1854) 4 Ir. Ch. R. 199 (Chancery)

The facts are set out in the judgment.

Brady L.C.:

In this case, in which Robert Augustus Alleyne, by Hugh Massey, his next friend, is petitioner, and Nicholas Conyers Darcy and Elizabeth Alleyne are respondents, the prayer is, that the respondent Darcy may be declared a trustee for the petitioner of a sum of £400, which the petitioner charges to have been lost to him by the negligence or by the contrivance of Mr. Darcy. The petitioner claims this sum as a portion of the general assets of his father Richard Dunscombe Alleyne, to which the petitioner was entitled under the trusts of his father's will, in the events which have occurred. The charge here is, that the respondent Mrs. Alleyne, having possession of this fund as executrix of her husband, had, in that capacity, lent it on insufficient personal security; and that the respondent Darcy was so implicated in the transaction, as to entitle the petitioner to require payment from him of the amount, either in the capacity of a trustee, or as subject to the same liability as a trustee, under very peculiar circumstances:– I may assume that the petitioner was entitled to the beneficial interest in this money; that does not now seem to be seriously disputed, though it was said, on behalf of the respondent Darcy, that there had been no investigation or administration of Mr. Alleyne's affairs, so that the title of the petitioner was not clear. However, the executrix does not make that objection, and it now seems conceded that this fund is the property of the petitioner, as beneficially entitled to the assets of his father. In the consideration of the case, very many important topics were discussed, which, doubtless, involved questions of no small moment to the respondent personally, and to the general body of the profession. The respondent Mr. Nicholas C. Darcy was engaged, at any rate to some extent professionally, in lending this money; I limit the statement, for there is some doubt as to the extent to which he was retained; but at all events, he was engaged in this way, that he received a sum of money from Mrs. Alleyne, for the purpose of being handed over to the party to whom it was to be lent. To that extent, at least, it is admitted he was engaged in the lending; and it is contended that he has so involved himself in the transaction as to make himself liable to restore the fund. In the first place, that necessitates the consideration of the liability of an attorney under such circumstances; for it would be a serious proposition to lay down, that an attorney employed in negotiating a loan of trust-moneys, in no other way in privity with the transaction, should, from the mere fact of the fund being trust-moneys, in addition to his liability for negligence as an attorney, be held liable as a trustee of the fund. That is a startling proposition, and if I were to affirm it, it would make it almost impossible for any attorney to attempt to negotiate a loan of trust funds. Here, however, the question is, whether there are not circumstances added, which place Mr. Darcy in a more responsible position than that of an ordinary solicitor? The allegations in that respect are in substance these:– that knowing this fund to be trust-money in the hands of Mrs. Alleyne the executrix; and knowing, or being bound to know, that the loan on personal security was a breach of trust; and knowing that the person to whom the money was lent, and his security, were in circumstances which rendered it perilous to advance this fund to them, he, notwithstanding all this, advised the employment of the assets in thus making such a loan, and by means of such employment made them available for his own purposes: that, in fact, he was so much involved in this transaction, and received so much of this money, that he must be taken to have acted in concert with the borrower, and must be held to have been implicated in the breach of trust. The above is a short statement of the case on behalf of the petitioner. The facts clearly proved in the case are not many, but they are very important. That Mr. Darcy was well acquainted with the nature of the fund; that he knew it was the produce of a policy part of the assets of Dr. Alleyne, whose will, leaving it to the petitioner, he had prepared, is not in any way denied; that he knew, or as an attorney was bound to know, that a loan of trust funds on personal security was a breach of trust, are all allegations which cannot be questioned. That, therefore, he knew that this money was lent in violation of duty, and that it was so lent to persons with whom he had been engaged in pecuniary transactions, is plain; and it is further plain, that he well knew, that at least one of the borrowers was deeply distressed for present means, whatever might be the case as to the ultimate value of the property to which he was entitled. It is clearly proved that Mr. Darcy was employed to compel payment from him of a sum of money due by him to other persons, by threatening and even by commencing proceedings, and that he had in point of fact full knowledge of the circumstances of both borrower and security. It is also plain, that notwithstanding all this, the money was lent without investigation, inquiry or searches, merely upon the bond and judgment of the principal and surety; that out of the amount lent to them, Mr. Darcy retained more than a fourth, and that he has that sum, or equivalent advantages procured with it, still in his possession. The question then arises, whether those circumstances establish the claim of the petitioner against Mr. Darcy?

When the case came before me on a former occasion, it assumed the form of a criminal charge; the case was treated as one in which the conduct of Mr. Darcy, as a solicitor, rendered him amenable to the summary jurisdiction of this Court. It then seemed to me, however, that that extent of liability was not made out with sufficient clearness to warrant me in acting on it. Mrs. Alleyne, the executrix, at whose instance the charge was made, seemed to have involved herself so much in the negotiation of the loan, and the statements in the affidavits were so contradictory and conflicting, that the liability of Mr. Darcy seemed to me to belong to the ordinary, not to the summary jurisdiction of this Court, and I gave him the benefit of that better construction of his conduct which is due to all persons criminally charged. When that case was argued, it was much pressed on me that Mr. Darcy is chargeable in a Court of Law for negligence as an attorney, and that therefore this was not the proper forum for determining the questions raised in the suit; but in this case there exists the distinction, that the claim is not made by Mrs. Alleyne herself – that it is not made by the person who was actually Mr. Darcy's client in the loan transaction; but that, on the contrary, this suit is one to make both Mr. Darcy and Mrs. Alleyne responsible to the *cestui que trust*. Another objection was made in the present suit, that this belongs to a class of cases where the Court refuses to proceed against third persons, if there be no charge and no proof of collusion between the executor and such third persons. I perfectly understand the doctrine on which the respondent wishes to rely in making that objection; but I do no think it has any application to such a case as the present, which is impressed with a perfectly different character. If the petition had been filed against Mr. De Massey and Mr. Power, this rule would have been applicable, but here there is this distinction, that the petitioner seeks not to raise the fund from the persons to whom it was lent, but to convert Mr. Darcy into a trustee, and to treat him as a trustee, on the ground of his having so dealt with the assets as to assume the responsibilities of that character; I consider the case free from all objection upon that doctrine. Then it said, that the relief lies against Mrs. Alleyne in the first instance; but the case of *Wilson* v. *Moore* 1 M. & K. 126, 337 establishes that, at all events, there is no primary liability in cases of breach of trust, all being equally liable. I do not think that the doctrine of want of privity can be applied as against this case, which rests on considerations of a totally different character, and which, I think, discloses grounds sufficient to maintain the relief sought. The circumstances immediately in relation to this loan are substantially as follows:– Mr. Darcy appears to have been concerned for Mr. De Massey and Mr. Power in certain transactions, the precise character of which does not distinctly appear; but it is asserted that there were several money and bill-discounting transactions prior to and about the time of this loan of £400. That there were such dealings is expressly charged, and not denied; and it further appears that Darcy was concerned as solicitor for Mr. De Massey, and that he was at the same time engaged in pressing him on behalf of another client for the payment of some money. It is clear that Mr. De Massey was in fact exposed to considerable pressure. It further appears that Mr. De Massey was only tenant for life of his property, and that this property has since been sold, under the order of the Incumbered Estates Court, for a sum which proved insufficient to pay the incumbrances prior to the life estate; and further, it appears that Mr. Darcy, being aware of the precise position of his property, obtained the security of Mr. Power, step-father of Mr. De Massey. There has been much discussion on the subject of Power's circumstances. It appears that he was supposed to be an extensive farmer, in good circumstances: it turns out that within a year after the execution of this security he was arrested for debt, and discharged as an insolvent debtor, and that his property was sold and applied in payment of incumbrances and judgments prior to this. Then, to return to Darcy and the position in which he stood; it is certain that he was concerned in the lending, so far as to make him responsible in his professional character. His case is, that he was not Mrs. Alleyne's attorney; that he was employed to draw the bond – that he drew it, and then ceased to act as her attorney; that he entered the judgment, and then ceased to act; that he registered it, and then ceased to act; in short, that instead of being employed as attorney in the transaction in general, he was merely employed to accomplish several isolated matters, after each of which his functions ceased. However, there was no other attorney employed by either party, and it would be difficult to hold that the solicitor who had in point of fact performed all the professional business in the transaction was not to be considered the attorney of the person for whom he had accomplished the various professional acts. Whatever may have been the case as to the suggestion of adopting the security of Mr. Power's liability, there can be no doubt that the proposition of making the loan at all, as between Mrs. Alleyne and Mr. Darcy, emanated from Mr. Darcy. It is said that she wished to obtain the security of Mr. Power, that she was perfectly satisfied with his liability, and insisted on obtaining it; but she evidently did not know the real state of his circumstances. Perhaps Darcy entertained the belief that he was solvent; though it is singular that he seems never to have apprised her of one fact, with respect to Power, which would most probably have induced her to act cautiously. Darcy appears to have been engaged on behalf of Mr. Power in a most important matter, in which an investigation of his property took place when he was justifying as security for a receiver, and it seems that a portion of his property then proved to be subject to a very large amount of judgment debts. In answer to that, it is asserted that there was personalty which he was empowered to charge in exoneration of the rest of the property, and which was of sufficient value to discharge these debts; but it appears that in that investigation a statement had been made on his part, which was, to say the least, extremely uncandid, and that the personal property was not in point of fact his own at all, nor available for his purposes. All that may have occurred from negligence; but it seems strange that when Darcy shelters himself under the opinion of the Master, that Power was in the enjoyment of considerable property, he did not mention these circumstances to Mrs. Alleyne. It is said that he proposed another investment to Mrs. Alleyne. The question here, however, is not with respect to other suggestions which he may have made, but relates simply to the particular transaction which is now the subject of investigation. As I said, this transaction began in a proposal to hand this money to Mr. Massey; no other solicitor is employed on behalf of Mrs. Alleyne. Darcy conducted the whole affair from the beginning to the end, and retained out of the fund at least one-fourth; the borrower, as I feel bound to observe, being so much pressed, at least for ready money, being in point of fact in such distress as to pay £25 as commission for the procuration of a loan of £400. Under these circumstances, it seems to me impossible to consider Darcy as a mere agent of Mrs. Alleyne, and in no way personally involved in the improper investment. I do not say whether there may not be foundation for the exercise of the summary jurisdiction of the Court over solicitors in respect to transactions of this nature. As I have already said, when the case came before me in that form, I rested my decision chiefly on the ground that I was bound to give Mr. Darcy's conduct the most favourable construction, the proceeding being in the nature of a criminal charge; but when I am to decide on this as a mere legal question between party and party, it must be considered on the inferences to be drawn from plain facts proved in the cause. Now what is the summary of those facts, which, as I have stated, are clearly proved or admitted? – that Mr. Darcy obtained from Mrs. Alleyne a sum of money which she held as trustee, knowing that it was so held; that he obtained it from her for a purpose which was in itself a breach of trust; that he placed it in the hands of a person whom he knew to be deeply distressed, at least for ready money, and who had no title to his property beyond a life interest, which proved to be absolutely without value; that he obtained as security another person, without any investigation of his circumstances. It is not too much to say that he overlooked everything in his anxiety to get the money into his hands. I do not say that this was the motive, but it lay upon Darcy to remove the imputation, which he has not done.

The case of *Fyler* v. *Fyler* 3 Beav 550 is the nearest to the present which I have been able to find. It is true that in that case the attorney was exonerated, but it is a remarkable circumstance that all the facts, on the non-existence of which Lord Langdale relies in that case, as reasons for refusing to charge the attorney, are facts which do exist here. In that case the Court was of opinion that the solicitors did not induce their client to commit a breach of trust; that they did not apply to him, but were applied to by him to find an investment, and that the trustees did not rely on the solicitor's advice alone; but the contrary of all those circumstances has been proved in this suit.

I have therefore come to the conclusion that Mr. Darcy is not in the mere position of an attorney, but must be considered as having advised Mrs. Alleyne to lend this money to parties whose possession of any portion of the fund was in itself a breach of trust, and as having involved himself in the responsibility of the transaction. Upon these grounds I think Mr. Darcy must be held liable to make good the money, and pay the costs of the suit.

Note

See further, *Irish Land Law,* para. 9.068. See also *Carey* v. *Ryan Ltd., infra.*

CAREY V. RYAN LTD.

[1982] I.R. 179; I.L.R.M. 121 (Supreme Court)

The facts are set out in Henchy J.'s judgment.

Henchy J.:

The plaintiff was 19 years of age when he sustained a serious injury while working in June, 1977, for his employers, a company named W.H. Ryan Ltd. Suing by his father and next friend, the plaintiff instituted proceedings in the High Court against Ryans and claimed damages. Ryans Ltd. had arranged employer's liability insurance at Lloyds, under which they would be indemnified against liability for an accident of this kind. The indemnifiers were two syndicates of underwriters. They are represented in the present proceedings by the second and third defendants, whom I shall call "the underwriters."

Upon receipt of the plaintiff's statement of claim, and having investigated the circumstances of the accident, the underwriters instructed their Dublin solicitors to lodge in court with the defence the sum of £39,053 without admission of liability. This their solicitors did on the 25th April, 1978. This sum was apparently adequate to meet the plaintiff's claim. At least, there has been no suggestion that it was inadequate, and ever since the plaintiff became of full age in March, 1979, he has been anxious to be allowed to take the lodgment in full satisfaction of his claim.

However, certain difficulties intervened to prevent the plaintiff getting or being credited with the amount lodged in court. Under order 22, r.4, of the Rules of the Superior Courts, 1962, a plaintiff may serve, within 14 days of receipt of the notice of payment into court, a prescribed notice of acceptance; whereupon, in the words of the rule, he "shall be entitled to receive payment of the accepted sum." Such a notice of acceptance was not served in this case. This was, presumably, because the plaintiff was an infant and because r. 10 of order 22 provides that no compromise or payment or acceptance of money paid into court in the case of an infant plaintiff shall be valid without the approval of the court. Consequently, it was inescapable that, before the money lodged in court with the defence could operate to settle the plaintiff's claim, the matter would have to come before the court on a motion by the plaintiff's next friend seeking approval of acceptance of the amount lodged.

Meanwhile, a matter of considerable moment came to the notice of the underwriters. They discovered that the policy of insurance (under which they were expected to indemnify Ryan Ltd. against an action such as this) had been entered into by them as a result of fraudulent mis-statements made by Ryan Ltd as to the amounts of wages and salaries paid or payable by them to their employees, thus distorting the correct amount of the premium and, indeed, vitiating the whole policy. Understandably, when they became aware of this breach of the good faith which a would-be insured is bound in law to show, the underwriters repudiated the policy. They gave notice to Ryan Ltd. that the policy was a nullity and that they were not prepared to make any indemnity in respect of the liability of Ryan Ltd. for the accident to the plaintiff.

Ryan Ltd. refused to admit that they had nullified the relevant contract of insurance by their conduct. In those circumstances the underwriters were driven to bringing proceedings in the High Court seeking, inter alia, a declaration that the policy of insurance upon which Ryan Ltd. relied was void because of the fraudulent representations made by that company. In those proceedings the plaintiff in the present proceedings was joined as a defendant. The suit came before Mr. Justice McWilliam who, after a full oral hearing, made the declaration of nullity of contract sought by the underwriters. His order of the 20th December, 1978, has not been appealed.

It is therefore *res judicata,* and binding on both the plaintiff and Ryan Ltd., that at the time of the plaintiff's accident there was no liability on the underwriters to indemnify Ryan Ltd., either wholly or in part, for any liability incurred by that company to the plaintiff as a result of the plaintiff's accident. It follows that the sum of £39,053.00 which was paid into court by the underwriters was paid by them under a mistaken assumption of liability, which assumption was induced by the fraudulent misrepresentations of Ryan Ltd. This is unquestionably so and it does not lie in the mouth of the plaintiff to say otherwise. To be fair, his counsel has not attempted to contend otherwise in the present hearing. He merely says, quite correctly, that the plaintiff was not a party to the fraud, and he submits that, in the events that have happened, the plaintiff should be allowed, in satisfaction of his claim, to take the money lodged with the defence.

The present action between the plaintiff and Ryan Ltd. lay dormant until the action between the underwriters (as plaintiffs) and the plaintiff Ryan Ltd. (as defendants) was determined by Mr. Justice McWilliam on the 20th December, 1978.

On the 2nd January, 1979, a notice of motion was issued in the present action on behalf of the plaintiff (who was still an infant) seeking an order extending the time for accepting the money lodged in court with the defence. It has to be said that this notice of motion was misconceived and a nullity because the time fixed for accepting money which has been lodged in court with a defence (order 22, r. 4) does not apply to cases where the plaintiff is an infant: see order 22, r. 10. When a plaintiff is an infant, there can be no question of accepting a sum lodged by the defendant in satisfaction of a claim for damages – unless the court makes an order approving the acceptance and disposition of the sum. It is a misapplication of the time-extension rule to enlarge time for doing an act under a rule when that act could not have been legitimately done within the time limited by the rule. The rule in question here (order 22, r. 4) is a general rule which is qualified by the particular restraints of rr. 10 and 13 of order 22.

Following on that notice of motion, the underwriters caused a notice of motion to be served on the 11th January, 1979, seeking an order that the money lodged in court be paid out to them.

The two motions (which were brought in the present action) were heard together by Mr. Justice Hamilton on the 31st January, 1980. The plaintiff reached full age on the 3rd March, 1979. Having regard to the views expressed by Mr. Justice McWilliam in his judgment in the underwriters' action against the plaintiff and Ryan Ltd., Mr. Justice Hamilton made an order joining the underwriters as defendants in the present action. Having heard the two motions together, he delivered a reserved judgment on the 8th February, 1980. In that judgment he gave liberty to the plaintiff to proceed in his own name, extended the time fixed by the Rules for acceptance of the money lodged in court with the defence, and dismissed the underwriters' claim to have the money in court paid out to them. It is against that judgment that the underwriters have taken the appeal now before this Court.

The general rule is that where a person purports to pay money directly to another, or to pay it to his credit, and that other has notice that the payment has been induced by fraud, the payee or would-be payee does not get any title to the money: see *Nelson* v. *Larholt* [1948] 1 K.B. 339. If the money has reached the payee then, while it is in his hands, he is a constructive trustee of it for the rightful owner who has been defrauded into paying it and the payee can be compelled to repay it. If it has not been paid to the payee, but remains in the hands of an intermediary who becomes aware of the fraud, then the intermediary becomes a constructive trustee of the money for the defrauded payer and can be ordered to return it to him.

In the present case the money paid into court by the underwriters never reached the plaintiff and he never acquired title to it. It remained in court and stands (as the certificate of funds shows) not to the credit of the plaintiff or of Ryan Ltd. or of the underwriters but to the credit of the account specified by the title and serial number of the action. Its ultimate beneficial destination awaited an order of the court. As the plaintiff was an infant, he could not get any title to it without an order of the court: see order 22, r. 10(1). If Ryan Ltd. (or the underwriters after they became a party) wished to withdraw the money lodged or to vary it, they might be allowed to do so by the court if there were special circumstances justifying such a course of conduct: see *Goodman* v. *Whyte & Co.* (1949) 83 I.L.T.R. 159. As Goddard L.J. said in *Cumper* v. *Pothecary* [1941] 2 K.B. 58 at p. 70 of the report:-

> "Indeed, we think it is desirable to say that it must not be thought that a defendant who has paid a sum into court is entitled, as of right, to resile from that step. He must, in our opinion, show that there are good reasons for his application – for instance, the discovery of further evidence, which puts a wholly different complexion on the case, as in the two cases cited [*Frazer & Haws Ltd.* v. *Burns* (1934) 49 Ll.L. Rep. 216; *Williams* v. *Boag* [1941] 1 K.B. 1], or a change in the legal outlook brought about by a new judicial decision, as in the present case, and there may be others."

The present litigation is a classical example of a case where subsequent events rendered the lodgment nugatory. When it was made, it was made by the underwriters under a mistake of law. But, as Lord Denning said in *Kiriri Cotton Co. Ltd* v. *Dewani* [1960] A.C. 192 at p. 204 of the report:- "The true proposition is that money paid under a mistake of law, *by itself and without more*, cannot be recovered back." (Emphasis supplied). When the money was paid into court, both the underwriters and the plaintiff were ignorant of the fraud that had induced the underwriters to deposit the money in court. In the absence of a contract of insurance unvitiated by fraud, the underwriters were under no obligation to the plaintiff for the consequences of his accident and, therefore, they were under no obligation to lodge any money in court in satisfaction of his claim. When they did so, the plaintiff did not become entitled (because of the rules of court) to the money lodged: the finding to the contrary is a central flaw in the judgment under appeal. While he was an infant, the plaintiff could not become so entitled without getting a court order to that effect. No such order was made.

By the time an effort was made to establish the plaintiff's entitlement to the money lodged, the situation had radically changed. The underwriters had established by judicial order that it was the fraud of Ryan Ltd. that had hoodwinked them into making the lodgment in the first place. The same judicial finding of Mr. Justice McWilliam had brought that fact home beyond yea or nay to the plaintiff, who had been made a party to that action. From being an infant who was ignorant of the fraudulent misrepresentation that had led the underwriters to make the lodgment, the plaintiff had become a man of full age who was thoroughly aware of the fraud of Ryan Ltd. and of its implications to the underwriters and who, nevertheless, was trying to take advantage of that known fraud and of the equally known erroneous lodgment which that fraud had generated. If, while he was ignorant of the fraud, the plaintiff had been allowed to take the money and had spent it or used it irretrievably, the position might have been different. But the money remained with the accountant of the Courts of Justice in what was virtually a suspense account; it had to remain there until the court exercised its discretion as to who should be held entitled to it.

In coming to court and asking to have the money paid out to him, the plaintiff is asking the court to overlook the fraud, to ignore the fact that the underwriters would never have parted with a penny of this money if they had known of the fraud, to treat as irrelevant the fact that the plaintiff now fully knows that the money he is seeking is the fruit of a tree poisoned by fraud and, in short, to exercise its discretion by making an order which would have the effect of robbing Peter to pay Paul.

In such circumstances the Court's discretion can be exercised in only one way, which is by ordering that the money in court be paid back to the underwriters, who were plainly gulled into paying it into court by the fraud of Ryan Ltd. If the order sought by the plaintiff were to be made and the money paid out to him, the Court would thereby be wrongly exercising its discretion for, by such an order, it would give efficacy to a course of fraudulent conduct on the part of Ryan Ltd. It is, of course, unfortunate that the plaintiff should be left to pursue his claim against uninsured defendants, but the alternative of allowing him to take in settlement the sum of £39,053 which the underwriters were induced to lodge in Court by the fraud of Ryan Ltd., and which has lain there for almost four years awaiting the exercise of the High Court's discretion as to its disposition, would make the Court virtually an accessory to the consummation of a fraudulent scheme whereby the underwriters, because of a blameless error into which they were led by fraud, would be dishonestly deprived of £39,053.

I would allow the appeal to the extent of directing that the money in court be paid out to the underwriters and dismissing the plaintiff's claim to it.

Griffin J.:
I agree with the judgment which has been delivered by Mr. Justice Henchy.

Henchy J.:
Mr. Justice Kenny, who is unable to be present to-day, wishes me to say that he is in agreement with my judgment.

Chapter 13

VOID AND VOIDABLE TRUSTS

There are many grounds upon which a trust may be void, *i.e.,* declared to be invalid *ab initio,* or voidable, *i.e.,* subsequently set aside as a result of a court action to have it "avoided." See *Irish Land Law,* para. 9.069 *et seq.*

I. VOID TRUSTS

THOMPSON V. THOMAS
(1891) 27 L.R. Ir. 457 (Chancery Division)

The facts are set out in the judgment.

Porter M.R.:

I am of opinion that Joseph Thompson, if he is still living, as to which I have considerable doubts, is entitled to share in the proceeds of the mortgage money under the deed of October 27th, 1863.

As regards the deed of March 3rd, 1863, which deals with the distribution of the policy moneys, it provides that the trustees are to stand possessed of the said policy for £2000 and the moneys assured thereby "to the use of Henry B. H. Thompson, and Elizabeth Neville Thompson, being the two children now living of her the said Elizabeth Margaret Hargrave Thompson, and to all or every other child or children of the said Elizabeth Margaret Hargrave Thompson, hereafter to be born, and as may be living, at the time of her decease in equal shares and proportions."

From this it is plain that Joseph Thompson was not then born; and according to *Occleston* v. *Fullalove* L.R. 9 Ch. 147, and other similar cases, if the instrument in question had been a will, Joseph Thompson would have taken a share under it. It is , however, not a *will* but a deed and unless the principle laid down in *Occleston* v. *Fullalove* L.R. 9 Ch. 147 applies to the case of a deed it is impossible to hold that Joseph Thompson took under the terms of this instrument.

Since the case of *Blodwell* v. *Edwards* Cro. Eliz. 509 it has never been questioned that a provision by deed for future illegitimate children is void. I do not say that a deed containing such provision would be void for all intents and purposes, or in so far as it was not merely a provision for future illegitimate children. There is nothing in *Occleston* v. *Fullalove* L.R. 9 Ch. 147 contrary to this view, which has been adopted by the profession and by the textwriters, as well as being the considered opinion of the judges in *Blodwell* v. *Edwards* Cro. Eliz. 509. *Occleston* v. *Fullalove* L.R. 9 Ch. 147, when examined, appears to have been decided on two grounds: first, that as the will speaks from the death of the testator there was no uncertainty as to who would take under it; and secondly, that as a will was an ambulatory instrument capable of being revoked at any time, the provision in it did not tend to encourage immorality in the same way as if it had been in a deed. I need only refer to what Mellish, L.J., says in that case, in which he recognizes to the full extent the authority of the earlier cases as to such a provision in a deed. He says –"I agree that the earlier authorities, and in particular *Blodwell* v. *Edwards* Cro. Eliz. 509, as reported, do go a long way to establish that a settlement of property by deed on future reputed children, of bastards, is void, as being contrary to public policy. If a man, at the commencement of an illicit intercourse with a particular woman" (whether it is at the commencement or not to my mind makes no difference), "could make a valid settlement upon illegitimate children, this would, I think, manifestly encourage the immoral connexion, and discourage marriage, which the law favours. The present case, however, is the case of a will, and it is necessary to consider how far the same doctrine applies to wills."

A distinction is sought to be made in the present case, inasmuch as the provision in the instrument in question is made by the mother, and not by the father; but, in my opinion, that circumstance makes no real difference. Here the putative father was a party to the deed, was a trustee under it, and was aware of all the circumstances under which the deed was executed. A provision for the future issue of an improper intercourse must have the same tendency to encourage immorality, whether that provision be made by the father or by the mother. It is equally contrary to public policy whether the consideration proceeds from the man or from the woman. I am, therefore, clearly of opinion that the provision in this deed is good as regards the two children named in it, but bad as to Joseph Thompson.

Mr. Brady then expressly argued that the words would include a child *en ventre sa mère,* and that Joseph was *en ventre sa mère* at the time of the execution of the deed. That he was so is highly probable. He is mentioned by name in the deed of October 27th, 1863, while the deed of March contains no express reference to him, and only mentions the two other children, Henry and Elizabeth. If the deeds are accurate in their facts and dates, and the child was born within ordinary time, it would be a very strong circumstance in favour of this contention, but it is at best a matter of uncertainty, and the child might have been born prematurely. Certainly the mother, when she executed this deed, did not contemplate making a specific provision for this child as then being *en ventre.*

This point, therefore, in my opinion, is not open on the facts of the case; and I arrive at the conclusion that the provision is good as regards the two children named in the deed, but void as regards the other. Joseph Thompson therefore takes no part of the policy moneys, which are divisible in moieties; on the other hand, the mortgage moneys are divisible in thirds between Henry, Elizabeth, and Joseph.

Notes and Questions

Is the principle applied in this case still valid today? Note the recent legislative change in Northern Ireland, see *Irish Land Law,* Supp. (1975-80), p. 28.

RE BLAKE
[1955] I.R. 89 (High Court)

The facts are set out in the judgment.

Dixon J.:

The first question arising in this case is whether the conditions attached to the trusts in favour of the infant defendants (the children of the deceased's daughter, Mary Rosamund) in repect of the income and capital of the "trust legacy" of £6,000 bequeathed by the will are void for uncertainty or as being contrary to public policy or for any other reason. This legacy was given by the will in these terms:–"I bequeath a sum of £6,000 to my trustees upon the trusts and with and subject to the powers and provisions hereinafter expressed that is to say my trustees shall invest the said sum of £6,000 with power to vary the investment thereof and shall stand possessed thereof and of the investments representing the same (hereinafter called 'the trust legacy') in trust to apply the income thereof for or towards the maintenance and education of the children of my daughter Mary Rosamund provided they shall be brought up in the Roman Catholic faith and subject to the application of the said income in trust for all the children of my said daughter Mary Rosamund provided they shall have been brought up in the Roman Catholic faith who being sons attain the age of twenty-one years or being daughters attain that age or marry under that age in equal shares and if there shall be only one such child the whole to be for that one and if the said children shall not be brought up in the Roman Catholic faith and no one of them shall live to attain a vested interest in the trust legacy the same shall fall into my residuary estate."

At the date of the will, the testator's daughter had been already married to a member of the Church of Ireland and since her marriage has adhered to that Church. There are three infant children of the marriage, all of whom have been baptised as members of the Church of Ireland. All the children were born in the lifetime of the testator, two of them before the date of the will. The present position is that the daughter and her husband have brought up their children in the Church of Ireland and it is not their intention to make any change in that respect. The children are now aged ten, seven and three years respectively.

I do not think there is any uncertainty about the requirement that a child should be brought up or should have been brought up in the Roman Catholic faith. Analogous expressions have been considered in several cases and it was not held that there was insufficient certainty in ascertaining the meaning of such phrases as "be a Roman Catholic": *In re May. Eggar* v. *May* [1932] 1 Ch. 99; "become a convert to the Roman Catholic religion": *In re Evans. Hewitt* v. *Edwards* [1940] 1 Ch. 629; "marry a Roman Catholic": *In re McKenna; Higgins and Others* v. *Bank of Ireland and Others* [1947] I.R. 277 "become a Roman Catholic": *McCausland and Others* v. *Young and Others* [1949] N.I. 49. In the last-mentioned case, the Court of Appeal in Northern Ireland was considering the terms of a settlement but the words of Andrews L.C.J. (at p. 57) as to ascertaining the meaning of the expressions used by the settlor are fully as apt in the case of a will:– "Why should they not bear the meaning in which they would naturally be used by the settlor – the meaning assigned to them in ordinary every-day speech?"

The expressions used in the will in this case, and those used in the wills considered in the cases just cited, do not suffer from the ambiguity inherent in the use of phrases such as "be openly or avowedly Protestant": *In re Borwick. Borwick* v. *Borwick* [1933] 1 Ch. 657; "at all times conform to and be members of the Established Church of England": *Re Tegg, Public Trustee* v. *Bryent* [1936] 2 All E.R. 878; "cease to practise the Roman Catholic religion": *Burke and O'Reilly* v. *Burke and Quail* [1951] I.R. 216. There is a subjective element latent in such conditions which is, I think, absent in the requirement in the present case. Nothing active is required of the children and they do not have to hold or profess any particular beliefs. What is required is that they should be brought up in the Roman Catholic faith – a matter for those responsible for their religious education while under age. If the children are baptised and received into the Roman Catholic Church, receive the appropriate instruction and fulfil, so far as it can be secured, their appropriate religious duties, I do not think there could be any doubt, in the mind of any reasonable person, that that is what the testator contemplated by the words he used. I feel I may echo, and apply to the present case, the very cogent observations of Gavan Duffy P. in considering the expression "shall marry a Roman Catholic," in *In re McKenna; Higgins and Others* v. *Bank of Ireland and Others* [1947] I.R. 277, at p. 285:–"I have only to construe the plain words used by a plain man in a sense plain to all of us; and I shall not make the law justly ridiculous in the eyes of persons of common sense by declaring a current expression, which the People knows and understands, to be unintelligible in the High Court of Justice in Ireland."

It is true that it can be plausibly suggested that there might be uncertainty in particular circumstances, for example, while any child was too young to understand or profit by any form of religious instruction or where the instruction had only been intermittent or had not extended over the whole period of minority. Any such difficulties, however, seem to me to relate to the ascertainment of whether the intention of the testator had been fulfilled rather than to any uncertainty in that intention. It is significant that the parents of the children evidently felt that there was no difficulty or ambiguity in their stating to their solicitor that their children had been brought up in the Church of Ireland, although two of the children are now only aged seven and three respectively. A Court which had to consider the matter would probably take the view that, so far as the gift of the capital was concerned, the process of bringing up the children in the Roman Catholic faith was one which at least required to be in operation at the time of each child attaining his or her majority, but, subject to that, any difficulties in determining the question would be merely those created to some special or peculiar circumstances. Again, it has to be borne in mind that each requirement, so far as it is a condition, is in the nature of a condition precedent rather than a condition subsequent; and it was laid down in England by the

Court of Appeal in *In re Allen, Deceased, Faith* v. *Allen* [1953] 1 Ch. 810, that in the cae of a condition precedent or a qualification it was not necessary that its scope should be capable of exact definition. All that a claimant had to show was that he, at least, was within the requirement. This is a view which I respectfully adopt. Accordingly, in my view, neither requirement in the present case is void for uncertainty.

The testator's intention is manifest. He wished to secure, so far as the promise or gift of his bounty could do so, that his grandchildren should be brought up in the Roman Catholic faith and that only those grandchildren who were so brought up should benefit either during their minority or on coming of age. To take the last event first, there is only a gift of the capital to those who shall have been brought up in that faith. I am not at the moment concerned with the ambiguity that the gift is to "all the children" provided they shall have been so brought up, and that questions might arise as to the proper interpretation if only one or some of the children qualified for the gift, although I hardly think a Court would find these questions insoluble. A more fundamental difficulty arises from the nature of the condition itself. No child can take a vested interest in the capital unless the prescribed condition is fulfilled and this indicates the nature of it as being a condition precedent or a qualification antecedent to taking any benefit. No question of a voluntary choice or election on the part of the children arises, since the condition must be fulfilled at latest at the attainment of twenty-one years of age, that is, before any child would be legally capable of making a binding choice or election. This circumstance distinguishes the case from those in which an election was required of a minor and the requirement was held either not to be binding during minority or to be capable of being postponed until majority. Examples are *In re May* [1917] 2 Ch. 126; [1932] 1 Ch. 99; *McCausland and Others* v. *Young and Others* [1949] N.I. 49. What is involved in the present case is that the parents or other persons responsible for the upbringing of the children should have brought up the children in the Roman Catholic faith, irrespective of any independent volition on the part of the children and irrespective of the degree of success achieved in such upbringing. The testator was evidently sufficiently confident of the result of such upbringing not to impose any penalty, by way of defeasance or forfeiture – as was attempted to be done in many cases – if any child, after attaining the age of choice, changed his religion or ceased to practise or profess the religion in which he was brought up. As already pointed out, the testator was fully aware of the circumstances of his daughter's marriage and of the birth and baptism of two of his grandchildren, at the date of his will; and he must be taken to have made his will in the light of those circumstances.

Given the natural desire of parents to secure the welfare and material prosperity of their children, a provision such as the present could only operate, and be intended to operate, as an inducement to the parents and a form of indirect pressure on them to change the religion of their children from that which they themselves professed or had adopted and in which they had baptised the children. Similar provisions have been considered in a number of cases and have been held void as being contrary to public policy in tending to interfere with the parental right and duty of providing for and prescribing the manner of education, including the religious instruction, of children. This view was taken by Bennett J. in *In re Borwick. Borwick* v. *Borwick* [1933] 1 Ch, 657. An earlier case, which he followed, was *In re Sandbrook, Noel* v. *Sandbrook* [1912] 2 Ch. 471, a decision of Parker J. There, the condition was directed against the children living with their father and it was held void because it was inserted with the object of deterring the father from performing his parental duties. Another example of an analogous provision was *In re Boulter. Capital and Counties Bank* v. *Boulter* [1922] 1 Ch. 75, where Sargant J. held a condition against living abroad void as being against public policy in tending to the possible separation of the parents from their children. A more recent example was *Re Tegg, Public Trustee* v. *Bryant* [1936] 2 All E.R. 878, where Farwell J. held that a condition aimed at preventing the children being sent to any Roman Catholic school was void as being a fetter upon the right of the mother to do what she might think best for the welfare and education of her children. See also *Re Piper* [1946] 2 All E.R. 503, referred to later. While I accept and respectfully adopt the reasoning and conclusions in these cases, I have no need to have recourse to them, as the same result would follow from a recent decision of Gavan Duffy P. in our own Courts – the only case here to which I was referred – that seems to have touched on the point. This was *Burke and O'Reilly* v. *Burke and Quail* [1951] I.R. 216, where the learned President held that a direction in a will that the selection of a school should be in the absolute discretion of the trustees was inoperative and must be ignored since it tended to override the parental authority and right and duty of education declared by Article 42 of the Constitution.

This Article puts the matter on a different and higher plane in this country, as the parental right and duty is declared and guaranteed by our fundamental law. Under it, the State "guarantees to respect the inalienable right and duty of parents to provide, according to their means, for the religious and moral, intellectual, physical and social education of their children." It is clear that any attempt to restrict or fetter that right would be contrary to the solemnly declared policy and conceptions of the community as a whole and therefore such as the Courts established under that Constitution could not and would not lend their aid to. The provision in the will that the children to benefit should have been brought up in the Roman Catholic faith is, therefore, void as against public policy and cannot be given effect to. It is hardly necessary to add that this principle applies and must be applied irrespective of the particular religion involved.

It makes no difference, in my opinion, to this view whether the provision in the will as to the capital is called a condition precedent or a qualification. If it is regarded as a qualification, in the sense that the claimant to the capital must show at the prescribed age that he answers the particular description, this involves that, during all or some of the period when the matter was one for his parents and not for himself, he had been brought up in the Roman Catholic faith.

If the condition is void, is the gift void also or can it be allowed to take effect, whether the condition is fulfilled or not? Can the condition be simply disregarded, as could be done in the case of a void condition subsequent intended to operate by way of defeating or divesting, upon the happening of a given event, a previously vested interest ? As pointed out by Gavan Duffy P. In *Burke's Case* [1951] I.R. 216, at p. 224, a condition precedent is one which must be fulfilled before the gift can take effect at all and a gift made subject to a condition precedent fails altogether, as a rule, if the condition is found to be void. The use of the words, "as a rule," in this passage may have been intended to leave open the possibility of there being an exception to the rule – the point did not arise for decision in *Burke's Case* [1951] I.R. 216 – and it has been argued in the present case that the gift in question here belongs to an exceptional class which the law allows to take effect notwithstanding the general rule. Before dealing with this question, I think it preferable to consdier the provision in the will as to the application of the income of the property during the minority of the children.

The intention and effect of this provision seems to be that the income should be applied for the maintenance and education of the children so long as they are being brought up in the Roman Catholic faith and only so long as they are being so brought up. That seems to me to be the plain, ordinary meaning of the words used by the testator. It is implicit in them that before the income should be so applied it should be reasonably clear to the trustees that the children were being so brought up. It is, I think, also implicit that should it become equally clear to the trustees that there had been any fundamental or radical change in the religious upbringing of the children, the income should cease to be so applied. The provision would, thus, imply something in the nature of a series of intermittent or alternating conditions precedent and conditions subsequent, but such a series has never received legal recognition. The true view, I think, is that the provision constitutes a limitation of the income for the benefit of the children during a specified period or specific periods, that is, so long as the children are being brought up in the specified faith. Here, however, the element of an unlawful attempt to dictate the religious education of the children and to trammel the exclusive responsibility of the parents again obtrudes, and again it is an attempt which the Court will not aid. It was clearly not the intention of the testator that the income should be applied for the benefit of the children unless they were being brought up as he desired, and therefore they cannot have the income during the whole of their minority on the basis of disregarding his definition of the period of enjoyment except so far as it contemplated minority. This would not only disregard that definition and turn a limited gift into an unqualified one but would defeat his clear wishes. A similar question arose before and was decided by the Court of Appeal in England in *In re Moore. Trafford* v. *Maconochie* 39 Ch. D. 116. There the testator had made provision for a weekly payment to his sister during such time as she might live apart from her husband, and it was held that the payments were to be made during a period the commencement and duration of which were fixed in a way which the law does not allow and the gift was void. The principle and authority of this decision were not questioned by P.O. Lawrence J. in *In re Lovell, Sparks* v. *Southall* [1920] 1 Ch. 122, but he distinguished it on the ground that, in the case before him, the husband and wife were already separated at the date of the will and the bequest by the testator was intended to provide for the wife while so separated rather than to induce her to live apart from her husband, which would have conflicted with public policy.

I am of opinion, therefore, that the gift of the income fails by reason of the manner in which it is limited being contrary to public policy.

It is necessary now to return to the question whether the gift of the capital also fails, the condition upon which it depends being void. If it does not, the curious result would ensue that, by some over-refinement of the law, the children would become entitled to the capital, but not to the income, in circumstances in which it appears reasonably plain the testator never intended them to have either. I have no hesitation in saying that I should require to feel coerced by the weight and logic of an argument to this effect, before I would subscribe to such an absurd result, involving, as it would, disregarding or paying the merest lip-service to the consideration that the object of these proceedings, and the Court's function, is to endeavour to ascertain, and, so far as legally possible, to carry out the intentions of the testator as to the disposal of his property after his death.

The argument, for which some judicial sanction can be shown, is that there is an exception to the general rule of a gift dependent on a void condition precedent being also void where the condition contemplates or requires something which is *malum prohibitum* as opposed to something which is *malum in se*. This is a curious and somewhat pedantic distinction to introduce in ascertaining the wishes of testators who, in the vast majority of cases, would be quite unaware of the existence of the distinction and, even if they were aware of it, might be unable to obtain from lawyers any very precise idea of the nature and limits of the distinction. I feel I am entitled to say this because I have the authority of an eminent, contemporary English judge in a recent case on the topic. This is *Re Piper* [1946] 2 All E.R. 503, where Romer J. said (at p. 505):– "The difference between *malum prohibitum* and *malum in se* has never been very precisely defined or considered." Notwithstanding this uncertainty, he felt satisfied that the condition in question in the case before him – directed against children residing with their father – was *malum prohibitum* and not *malum in se* with the result that the gift took effect freed and discharged from the void condition. For the principle involved, he relied on a passage in Jarman on Wills (7th ed., vol. 2, at p. 1443), which was also relied on in other recent cases on the matter and which states the proposition in these terms:–" . . . the civil law, which in this respect has been adopted by courts of equity, differs in some respects from the common law in its treatment of conditions precedent; the rule of the civil law being that where a condition precedent is originally impossible, or is illegal as involving *malum prohibitum,* the bequest is absolute, just as if the condition had been subsequent. But where the performance of the condition is the sole motive of the bequest, or its impossibility was unknown to the testator, or the condition which was possible in its creation has since become impossible by the act of God, or where it is illegal as involving *malum in se,* in these cases the civil agrees with the common law in holding both gift and condition void."

Romer J. also derived assistance from a passage in Sheppard's Touchstone (vol. 1, at p. 132) which he quoted and which may be quoted here, before returning to the passage from Jarman. It is as follows:–"All conditions annexed to estates, being compulsory, to compel a man to do any thing that is in its nature good or indifferent; or being restrictive, to restrain or forbid the doing of anything, in its nature, is *malum in se,* as to kill a man, or the like; or *malum prohibitum,* being a thing prohibited by any statute, or the like; all such conditions are good, and may stand with the estates. But if the matter of the condition tend to provoke or further the doing of some unlawful act, or to restrain or forbid a man the doing of his duty; the condition for the most part is void."

I must confess I can derive no assistance whatever from this last passage on the question I am now concerned with, possibly because it does not seem to be concerned with that question. As I understand it, the author was distinguishing between conditions which were good from those which were "for the most part" void. In the former class he placed together those restraining or forbidding either *mala prohibita* or *mala in se,* thus treating the matter from the point of view of negative conditions. He was not considering at all the question of positive conditions directed to the procurement of either type of *malum,* nor was he considering the effect of a condition being void on the validity of the gift dependent on it. He says nothing as to this last matter and it is unlikely that he intended to convey any distinction in this respect, as the reference to "estates" suggests that he was dealing with devises of real property where the rule seems to be invariable that if the condition, being a condition precedent, is void, the devise is void. The passage is of some help as to the difference between the two types of *mala,* although, even here, the qualification imported in each case by the use of the words, "or the like," detracts from precision.

The passage from Jarman already quoted appears to depend in the main, as to some of the later cases, on the authority of *Reynish* v. *Martin* 3 Atk. 330, a decision of Lord Chancellor Hardwicke in reference to a legacy given to a daughter on condition of her marrying with the consent of trustees and in which he held that the legacy held good although she had married without consent. He first considered the matter as a personal legacy to be paid out of the personal estate only and said (at p. 331):–"I apprehend that taking this as a mere personal legacy, the plaintiff by the rules of the civil and ecclesiastical law, and which have been constantly adhered to in this court, will be intitled to the legacy; for it is an established rule in the civil law, and has long been the doctrine of this court, that where a personal legacy is given to a child on condition of marrying with consent, that this is not looked on as a condition annexed to the legacy, but as a declaration of the testator *in terrorem."*

This passage shows a sufficient ground for the decision and, to that extent, renders the subsequent passage, on the question in issue, *obiter.* This later passage, after referring to the difference in effect of a condition precedent being void and of a condition subsequent being void, continues:–"but this difference only holds where the legacy is a charge on the real assets, and therefore, if this had been merely a personal legacy, I should have been of opinion that as the marriage without consent would not have precluded Mary of her right to this legacy in the ecclesiastical court, no more would it have done so here; and to this purpose several cases were cited, which are taken notice of in the case of *Harvey* v. *Aston* 1 Atk. 361, and which I shall not repeat, but refer to that case for them."

This reference to *Harvey* v. *Aston* 1 Atk. 361 is significant as that case dealt only with conditions and limitations concerned with marriage with consent, and it shows, as the passage itself would suggest, that the Lord Chancellor was not dealing with any wider question. The remainder of his judgment dealt with the question whether, on the terms of the will, the legacy was a charge on the real estate, and having found that it was not, he concluded:–"this case must be considered as a mere personal legacy, and as such to be governed by the rules of the civil and ecclesiastical law."

Reynish v. *Martin* 3 Atk. 330, therefore, appears to be no more than authority for the proposition that, in the case of a personal legacy subject to a condition precedent as to marriage with consent, the legacy is not avoided by breach of the condition where there is no gift over. There is no reference anywhere in the case to *malum prohibitum* or *malum in se.*

Neither is there any such reference in the case of *Brown* v. *Peck* 1 Eden 140, which is cited as an authority in Roper on Legacies for the proposition which is relied on in support of the present argument. This is as follows (4th ed., at p. 757):–"When, however, the illegality of the condition does not concern anything *malum in se,* but is merely against a rule or the policy of law, the condition only is void, and the bequest single and good; for the condition not being lawful, it is held in the phrase of the Civil law *pro non adjecta.*"

As he had been speaking, in the preceding paragraph, of a condition precedent requiring the performance of an act *malum in se,* a cursory reading of the passage cited might suggest that he was there dealing with *mala prohibita,* as being the natural opposition to *mala in se.* Closer attention to it, however, makes it, I think, plain that this was not the meaning or intention of the passage. If this particular distinction had been intended, the learned author would probably have expressed it with his usual clarity. Instead he referred to things "merely against a rule or the policy of law." Such things are not necessarily *mala prohibita* (they are, in my view, entirely different) and it seems highly unlikely that the author intended to suggest that they were the same. By referring to the conditions as not being lawful, he may have meant no more than that they were unenforceable. This view of the passage is reinforced by turning to the case of *Brown* v. *Peck* 1 Eden 140 itself, where it will be found that the decision was that a condition as to a married woman living apart from her husband was *contra bonos mores* and void but the gift dependent on it was good. There is, quite understandably, no reference in it to *mala* either *prohibita* or *in se,* the condition belonging to neither category.

If Brown v. *Peck* 1 Eden 140 is an authority for anything, it is for the proposition that, if a condition precedent attached to a personal legacy is void as being against public policy, the gift may still be good. It is, however, a very doubtful authority. The report is short and not too easy to follow and it was subjected to some criticism by the Court of Appeal in *In re Moore. Trafford* v. *Maconochie* 39 Ch. D. 116, already referred to. Cotton L.J. (at p. 129) said that "the report is not clear either as regards the facts or the principle laid down"; and Bowen L.J. (at p. 132) said it "appears to have been compromised after an expression of opinion by the Court." In the Court of first instance in *In re Moore* 39 Ch. D. 116, Kay J. had said (at p. 124) of it and of *Wren* v. *Bradley* 2 De G & Sm. 49:–"I confess that I find it difficult to understand these two decisions"; and I respectfully echo his words. The latter case – *Wren* v. *Bradley* 2 De G & Sm. 49 – was interpreted by the Court of Appeal as having being a decision on the basis of the condition being a condition subsequent and therefore inapplicable in the case before them as it is also, for the same reason, inapplicable in the present case. *Brown* v. *Peck* 1 Eden 140 I regard as too obscure and doubtful a case to follow.

The proposition contended for has, as we have seen, been adopted in *Re Piper* [1946] 2 All E.R. 503, already referred to, and also in a later case of *In re Elliott, Deceased* [1952] 1 Ch. 217, decided by Harman J. Neither of these cases is, of course, binding on me although entitled to the greatest respect as persuasive authorities. In *In re Elliott, Deceased* [1952] 1 Ch. 217, Harman J. decided that a bequest of personalty subject to an illegal condition precedent is void if the condition be *malum in se,* but if the condition be only *malum prohibitum,* the bequest will be effective and unfettered by the condition; and this is a clear statement of the principle contended for in the present case. In that case, the condition offended against the rule against perpetuities and Harman J. held that this was *malum prohibitum.* He took the view that the principle he enunciated had been imported into equity from the civil law on the authority of *Reynish* v. *Martin* 3 Atk. 330, quoted and accepted by Bowen L.J. in *In re Moore* 39 Ch. D. 116 at p.131. I have already suggested that *Reynish* v. *Martin* 3 Atk. 330 is not an authority for this proposition; and the Court of Appeal decided *In re Moore* 39 Ch. D. 116 on the ground that they were concerned with a limitation and that, if any such principle applied in the case of a condition, it did not apply to a limitation: see Cotton L.J. at p. 129. What Bowen L.J. said, as to the matter, was (at p. 131):–"Accepting that as law with respect to legacies of personal estate on a condition, the question remains whether this is a legacy on a condition"; and he found that it was, instead a limitation. I do not think therefore that *In re Moore* 39 Ch. D. 116 could be rightly regarded as adopting or approving the supposed principle. It is difficult to see why, if a limitation which is contrary to public policy avoids a gift, a condition which is contrary to public policy should not do so also. It was however, sufficient for the decision in *In re Moore* 39 Ch. D. 116 that the provision was found to be a limitation. Harman J. in *In re Elliott, Deceased* [1952] 1 Ch. 217, may possibly have intended to convey some doubt on the matter in his own mind by saying (at p. 222):–". . . if this doctrine of the civil law has been imported into the English law, the condition can be disregarded," He then went on to say:–"Mr. Roper is of the opinion that this rule was imported into equity . . ."; and he referred to *Reynish* v. *Martin* 3 Atk. 330 and *In re Moore* 39 Ch. D. 116. As has been seen, the basis of Roper's assertion was *Brown* v. *Peck* 1 Eden 140.

I have devoted some time to this question because of the support to be apparently found for the proposition in textbooks and in high judicial decision; but there is a more fundamental consideration which would have disposed of the matter, in my view, more shortly, if it had not been for the decisions referred to. This is the question whether, assuming the proposition to be sound, the provision in question here is *malum in se* or *malum prohibitum* or neither. In my view it is neither. As already noted, the precise nature of the distinction is somewhat indefinite and elusive, but it seems reasonably certain that it is a distinction between different types of crime or offence according to the origin of their sanction. Thus, Holland, Jurisprudence (7th ed., p. 34), says:–"Acts prohibited by positive law, but not by the so-called natural law, are said to be '*mala prohibita,*' not '*mala in se.*' Thus a government may find it expedient to forbid certain acts, such as the planting of tobacco, which are not regarded as odious by the public sentiment." Byrne, Law Dictionary, says:–"*Mala in se* are acts which are wrong in themselves, such as murder, as opposed to *mala prohibita (mala quia prohibita),* that is to say, those acts (such as smuggling) which are only wrong because they are prohibited by law." *Cf.* the passage already quoted from Sheppard's Touchstone, where *malum prohibitum* is referred to as "a thing forbidden by any statute, or the like." This limitation in scope of the distinction is borne out by recalling the matters in which the distinction was or might be of any importance. These appear to be chiefly the question of ambassadorial exemption from criminal process and the question of the degree of *mens rea* requisite in the case of some offences.

An attempt to influence or fetter parents in their discretion as to the choice of religion and religious instruction for their children is not, so far as I am aware, a crime or offence of any kind. It is simply opposed to the policy of the law – now written into the fundamental law of this country. What this means was pointed out by Kekewich J. in *Re Hope Johnstone. Hope Johnstone* v. *Hope Johnstone* [1940] 1 Ch. 470, p.479 – and quoted by Romer J. in *Re Piper* [1946] 2 All E.R., at p. 503 at p. 505 – in these words:–"The phrase means no more than that and the provision is not enforceable by anyone or in any court."

So far, therefore, as the contention depends on the provision belonging to one branch rather than the other of this archaic distinction, I am of opinion that the contention fails for the reason that the provision belongs to neither branch. Could it, however, be said that the proposition has validity if it were put in a different way, namely, that, if a condition precedent is contrary to public policy, a gift of personalty dependent on the condition is nevertheless good? This might be the meaning of *Brown* v. *Peck* 1 Eden 140, in which the condition was stated to be *contra bonos mores,* and it seems to be the approach to the matter of Kay J. in *In re Moore* 39 Ch. D. 116, at p. 122, where he quoted from Swinburne on Wills and, later, refers to "the doctrine that conditions precedent as well as conditions subsequent which are against the policy of the law are treated as void in cases of legacies of personal estate, and that the legacy 'stands pure and simple.'" He quotes the second of Swinburne's four classses of impossible conditions, being those "which be contrary to law or good manners" and the two examples, respectively, given by Swinburne, i.e., "if he murder such a man or deflower such a woman"; but he does not quote the next part of the sentence, which is: "this condition is unlawful and unhonest, and consequently to be deemed unpossible" (Part IV, sect. 5, para. 8). Swinburne then states his rule that, with certain exceptions, when a condition is impossible the legacy may still be recovered; and proceeds to consider the exceptions. Amongst these occurs one set out in the following words (also quoted by Kay J.):– "When the condition is both impossible and unhonest, for then the disposition is thereby void; and that in disfavour of the testator, who added such a condition. Whereas if the condition had been only impossible or unlawful, the disposition had been good, and that in favour of the testament."

This last sentence is the only one that could possibly lend any support to the proposition now under consideration and such support would depend solely on the meaning to be given to the words "or unlawful" as used by the author. The disjunctive cannot have been intended to suggest an alternative to an impossible condition, as the whole section is only dealing with such conditions, and I confess I find it very hard to know what meaning could or should be given to the word, "unlawful." The sense of the passage, taken as a whole, would have led one to expect an opposition between "impossible and unhonest" conditions on the one hand and "impossible but not unlawful" conditions on the other hand; but it would be rather late in the day now to suggest a typographical error in a work of such antiquity. Whatever the meaning of the words, there is a clear and unambiguous statement that the disposition is void when the condition is "impossible and unhonest"; and the earlier passage made it equally clear that Swinburne included in this category of condition one "contrary to good manners," which is equivalent to one *contra bonos mores* or opposed to the policy of the law. The second example he gives also makes this clear, as it contemplates something which is not necessarily any crime or offence but merely disapproved by public morality. I cannot find, therefore, that Swinburne's statement of what the eclesiastical law was lends any support to the principle enunciated in *Brown* v. *Peck* 1 Eden 140, or the cases which have followed or applied its supposed principle. Swinburne seems to me to be authority for the directly contrary proposition.

To summarise:– the provisions in the will as to bringing up the children in the Roman Catholic faith are not too uncertain in their meaning not to be given effect to, if this were the only matter in issue. The phrase is one generally used and popularly understood, and an individual, or the Court if necessary, would not have too much difficulty in determining whether a particular child was being brought up or had been brought up in a particular faith. The provisions, however, constitute an attempt to interfere with or fetter the right and duty guaranteed to parents by the Constitution to provide for the education, including the religious education, of their children. As such, they are opposed to the policy of the law and cannot be enforced or given effect to in any Court in this country. Being, thus, void and unenforceable, the gifts, both of capital and income, dependent on their being carried out, are also void and enforceable. The gifts to the children therefore fail and the legacy falls into the residue of the estate.

In my view, the principle stated to have been imported from ecclesiastical law, that even though the condition upon which a legacy is given is contrary to public policy the legacy may still take effect, is not borne out by the authorities cited for it nor was it a rule of ecclesiastical law. If it had been part of ecclesiastical law, as applied to wills in the Church Courts in England, it might have been necessary to enquire as to when the principle was adopted, as those Courts retained a large part of their jurisdiction even after the Reformation and were not finally deprived of their temporal jurisdiction in testamentary and other matters until 1857. Rules adopted or laid down during the last two centuries of the functioning of those Courts could not be accepted without question as part of the law of this country. No Irish case was cited, nor do I know of one, which decided the point at issue.

On another ground, if necessary, I should have been inclined to hold that, the condition being contrary to public policy, the bequest failed. This is that the performance of the condition was the sole motive of the bequest. This is an admitted exception to the supposed principle that the bequest may hold good. Reading the will as a whole, it is impossible to escape the conclusion that the paramount object of the testator, so far as his grandchildren were concerned, was that they should be brought up in his own faith and that only on that basis should they benefit. There is no indication that he intended them to benefit even if his wishes could not be carried out and, therefore, as the law will not enforce the condition, it would be defeating his real intention to uphold the gift while allowing the condition to be disregarded or rejected.

For these reasons, the gift fails.

The next questions which arises is whether the pecuniary legacies are liable to pay the whole or any part of certain duties, in the nature of succession duty, payable to the dominion and a provincial government of Canada in respect of portion of the assets situate, at the death of the testator, in Canada. Some of these legacies were expressed to be left "free of legacy duty" but it was not disputed that, in the absence of any contrary indication in the will, this phrase must be taken to have been intended to refer only to the legacy duty payable in this country to our own Government. Accordingly, the use of these words does not affect the present question and all the pecuniary legacies are on the same footing as regards the foreign duties.

The general law as to the liability for such duties as between the different classes of beneficiaries under a will is stated by Jarman (8th ed., 1951, at p. 1842) in these words:– "In the absence of a contrary direction, local duties in respect of foreign property specifically devised or bequeathed are payable out of that property"; and again (at p. 1892):– "Testamentary expenses are expenses incident to the proper performance of the duty of an executor in connection with the personal estate, including the estate duty on personal property, the costs of proving the will, of obtaining legal advice as to the distribution of the estate, the expenses of ascertaining the person entitled to a legacy or specific fund, and the expenses of getting in property abroad." It would seem to follow from these two passages that, except in the case of a specific bequest, foreign duties payable in respect of personal estate situated abroad are part of the testamentary expenses and payable out of the general personal estate in exoneration (except so far as the estate may prove insufficient and the legacies may have to abate) of the pecuniary legacies. Another way of viewing the matter, as a question of principle, is that the pecuniary legacies are payable (subject to bearing their own local duty) out of the general personal estate before the existence or amount of any residue can be ascertained. To make them liable for even a proportionate part of the foreign duties would put the residue on at least an equal footing with the legacies.

The statement quoted from Jarman is supported by the cases there cited of *Peter* v. *Stirling* 10 Ch. D. 279 and *Re Maurice* 75 L.T. 415. The former case, which was not unlike the present, was considered and distinguished by Warrington J. in *In re Scott* [1914] 1 Ch. 847, at p. 854, where he said:– ". . . when that case comes to be looked at it seems to me that it is not an authority for the proposition contended for here, which is that the duty payable on a specific legacy is to be treated as an expense incurred by the executors." He held that, in the case of a specific legacy, the duty was not such an expense, and pointed out that Malins V.-C. had held in *Peter* v. *Stirling* 10 Ch. D. 279 that the duties he was concerned with were part of the expenses which had to be incurred by the executors in getting in and repatriating the foreign assets to complete the total of the estate which they had to administer. Similarly, here, no specific bequests are involved and the pecuniary legacies are not given out of the Canadian assets as such or in any way by specific reference to them. If there were no pecuniary legacies, the executors would still be under the duty of getting in the Canadian assets and, in order to do so, paying whatever local duties had to be paid in respect of them.

It is clearly different in the case of a specific bequest, unless there is a deficiency of other assets to meet debts and other liabilities.

The authority of *Peter* v. *Stirling* 10 Ch. D. 279 and *Re Maurice* 75 L. T. 415 was recognised in the latest case on the subject to which I was referred, a decision of the Court of Appeal in England in *In re Goetze* [1953] 1 Ch. 96. This was a case in which the principle of those cases could possibly have been applied, but the Court arrived at the same result – the exoneration of the legatees and annuitants – by reason of the existence of a provision for double taxation relief. The Court did not profess to question or overrule the earlier cases. Jenkins L.J. alone referred to the matter and he did so in these words (at p. 113):–". . . there is nothing in the judgment of Swinfen Eady J. in *In re Brewster* [1908] 2 Ch. 365 or of Warrington J. [1914] 1 Ch. 847 or the Court of Appeal in *In re Scott* [1915] 1 Ch. 592, to suggest that *Peter* v. *Stirling* 10 Ch. D. 279 and *In re Maurice* 75 L. T. 415 were wrongly decided. . . . As the point has not been argued in the present case, and if made good would lead to the same conclusion as I have reached on other grounds, I express no opinion about it one way or the other, but merely refer to it lest this judgment, which is framed in accordance with the arguments presented, should be regarded a simplicity concluding it if raised in any future case."

Two other cases only need be mentioned, as they were relied on in argument. *In re Norbury* [1939] 1 Ch. 528, a decision of Bennett J., did not deal with a foreign tax payable in respect of the foreign assets of the deceased but with a personal tax payable by the beneficiary, by reason of his nationality, on succession. The other case – *In re Cunliffe-Owen, Deceased* [1951] 1 Ch. 964, decided by Wynn-Parry J. – turned mainly on the special provision in the will in question there. There does not appear to be anything in it conflicting with the principle of the earlier cases but, if there is, I feel I should follow those cases. Accordingly, I hold that the pecuniary legacies are not liable to the foeign duties, these being an expense of administration.

The remaining question concerns an artificial category of "heirlooms" created by the testator in his will. These articles are not necessarily heirlooms in the accepted or established sense, the testator merely having indicated certain articles which he desired to be held and enjoyed as heirlooms, that is, with, and, so far as possible, on the same trusts as, the mansion house; and the only question is to what articles does this provision extend. The terms of the relevant provision are as follows:–"I bequeath my gold whip and all my plate jewels watches pictures glass books and furniture which shall at my death be in or about my said capital messuage or mansion house called Ballyglunin Park or belong or be appropriated thereto unto my trustees in trust to permit the same to be held and enjoyed as heirlooms by the person or persons for the time being entitled to the said capital messuage or mansion house under the limitations of my will as nearly as the rules of law and equity will permit." He has already devised this mansion house to his son for life and then in tail, and the intention was clearly that, so far as possible, the mansion house and its contents should be preserved and kept up as a family residence.

At first sight, a little difficulty is created by an earlier provision in the will, under which he bequeathed to his son "my wines liquors table and house linen and household effects other than those hereinafter bequeathed as heirlooms and all saleable stores and all livestock farming implements produce carts horses motor cars and all outdoor effects of every kind in or about or belonging to Ballyglunin Park, Brooklodge Demesne and Corbally North." As the only dwelling is at Ballyglunin Park, the intention to limit the class of "heirlooms" to indoor articles in the mansion house is emphasised. The only apparent conflict is created by the reference to household effects, but it is not a real conflict, as these household effects are defined by way of exception, that is, the bequest is not of all the household effects but only of such household effects as are not bequeathed as heirlooms. The governing description, is therefore, that of the "heirlooms" and this comprises several classes of articles, the widest of which is "furniture." Even if the latter word were interpreted in a wide sense there would still be a residue of articles which would be household effects rather than furniture. The scheme of the will, however, suggests "furniture" is not to be given too wide an interpretation. The scheme seems to be to make an absolute bequest of articles which, by reason of their nature or of the effect of constant use, will be consumed nor will deteriorate comparatively quickly, such as the wines, linen, saleable stores and farm stock and equipment. The gift of "heirlooms" is of more durable articles. This is clear as to the gold whip and plate, jewels, watches and pictures. It is reasonable to take the view that the same approach was intended as to the glass, books and furniture, that these articles were only intended to be considered as heirlooms so far as they were more durable and permanent in character or had some special value either intrinsically or by association. An inventory has been prepared which includes a number of articles as to which there is a difference of opinion, but I do not propose to deal with the inventory in detail. I apprehend that, in the light of what I have indicated as being, in my view, the proper approach, there should not be any great difficulty in the parties interested making their own segregation. If a solution cannot be found as to any particular item or items, application can be made to the Court. The order will reserve liberty to apply.

Notes and Questions

Do you agree with Dixon J.'s reasoning, particularly his conclusion as to the effect of holding the condition in question void? *Cf.* Kenny J. in *Re Doyle,* Unreported (1972 No. 143 Sp.). See *Irish Land Law,* para. 9.072.

II. VOIDABLE TRUSTS

1. *Undue Influence*

SMYTH V. SMYTH

Unreported (High Court) (1975 No. 4369 P) (Judgment delivered 22nd November 1978)

The facts are set out in the judgment.

Costello J.:

The Plaintiff had the good fortune to be given by the will of a wealthy uncle two valuable properties in the Finglas area of Dublin. 1 Beaupark Villas is a dwelling house with a dairy yard attached to it and the Plaintiff became absolutely entitled to this property. The position in relation to the other gift was different. His deceased uncle had been a farmer and part of his lands had consisted of a large field of a little over 11 acres on the Jamestown Road to the north-east of Finglas village. The deceased gave a life interest in this field to a brother of his (the Defendant herein) and the remainder interest to the Plaintiff absolutely. This action concerns the sale by the Plaintiff to the Defendant for the sum of £1500 of this remainder interest. The agreement for sale was made in 1968, when the Plaintiff was just 23 years of age. He now seeks to have the sale set aside. Firstly he relies on the equitable doctrine of undue influence. But as the Defendant was not only a life tenant of the field but also one of the trustees of the will the Plaintiff in addition claims that the sale infringed the equitable principles which apply to transactions between a cestui que trust and a trustee. Furthermore the Plaintiff says that the bargain was an unconscionable one and that it is vitiated by the equitable rules relating to such bargains.

There is a sharp conflict of evidence on a number of the important issues of fact which I have to determine in this case. In addition there is a quite remarkable difference between the valuations placed on the land by the expert valuers who gave evidence. I will examine the expert evidence later. As to the rest of the evidence, I will proceed now to give the conclusions which I have reached on it and then turn to the legal principles which are applicable to them. In doing so I should preface what I have to say by pointing out that it is not surprising that recollections should differ on events that occurred many years ago but that I am satisfied that all who have testified have done their best to tell the truth.

The Plaintiff was born on 4th November 1945. His father was a farmer, but his drinking habits became excessive and he was forced to sell his lands some years prior to his death. The Plaintiff's schooling finished at the age of 14. Thereafter he took up a number of casual jobs in England and in this country until at the age of 18 he was taken on by Messrs Morrissey and Sons (the well-known Auctioneers) as a trainee Auctioneer in the machinery-sales side of their business. He left this firm for a short while after his three years training period had expired, but returned to it again in the year 1968. He stayed with Messrs Morrisseys until 1969, in which year he went to London. On his return he was again employed by Messrs Morrisseys until the end of 1973. In the beginning of 1974 before he had reached his twenty-ninth birthday he was admitted to St. Patrick's Hospital, Dublin suffering from alcoholism and anxiety depression.

The Plaintiff's drinking habits and the effect which they had on his personality have prominently featured in this case and it will be convenient if I, at the outset, set out the conclusions which I have reached about them. The Plaintiff's local doctor, Dr. Moroney, was satisfied that the Plaintiff was suffering from alcoholism in 1972 and in the month of May of that year endeavoured, without success, to persuade the Plaintiff to consult a psychiatrist about his problems. Early in 1974 Dr. Cooney diagnosed the Plaintiff as an alcoholic and he was of the opinion that it was a condition from which the Plaintiff would have been suffering for two or three years prior to admission to St. Patrick's and that it was possible that it went back to an even earlier date. It will be recalled that the agreement which is now impugned was entered into in 1968 – to be precise, in the month of August of that year. I am quite satisfied that on the occasion it was entered into the Plaintiff had not been drinking. I am equally satisfied that although he had by that time started to drink more than was good for him he had not yet reached the stage when he could be regarded as an alcoholic.

The parties differ as to how the agreement for sale came about. Save for one detail, I prefer the evidence of the Defendant, his wife and Mr. Melvin to that of the Plaintiff. What happened was this. The Defendant (who is about thirty years older than the Plaintiff) got married in the month of May 1968. He was on very good terms with the Plaintiff and they agreed that the Defendant and his wife would come to live for a time with the Plaintiff in 1 Beaupark Villas (into which the Plaintiff had moved when he reached the age of twenty-one) and pay him £5 per week by way of rent. In addition the Defendant's wife kept house for the Plaintiff, cooking for him and doing his laundry. The Plaintiff at this time decided that he would like to sell his remainder interest and approached Mr. Melvin, who he knew was on friendly terms with the Defendant, and tried to enlist his help as a go-between. Mr. Melvin accepted the assignment but made no progress with the Defendant. The Defendant was himself a farmer but he had in 1967 sold his interest in 21 acres Finglas and had taken them back on a conacre letting from the Purchaser. In addition he had bought further land at St. Margaret's. So he told Mr. Melvin that he had enough land; and Mr. Melvin advised the Plaintiff of the Defendant's attitude and that he would have to approach the Defendant himself about the matter if he wanted to do a deal. This the Plaintiff did. In the middle of an August day in 1968 the Defendant was resting in bed. His wife was out at work (she was helping-out during the holidays in her former employer's shop in Finglas) and the Plaintiff and the Defendant were alone. The Plaintiff asked the Defendant would he buy out his interest in the field at Finglas; the Defendant replied that he was not very interested and that he had enough land; the Plaintiff then pointed out the advantage to him of a purchase drawing his attention to the fact that if he bought his interest that the Defendant could then do what he liked with the land. The Defendant then asked the Plaintiff: "What do you want for it?": "£3,000", was the reply. The Defendant said that this was too high, to which the Plaintiff replied, "What will you bid me for it?": The Defendant then offered him £1500. But this was refused and the Plaintiff left the house. He returned in an hour or so later and agreed to sell at the figure suggested by the Defendant, but asked for a deposit. The Defendant gave him a cheque for £300.

This then, was how the bargain came about. The Defendant's co-trustee was Mr. McGonagle, a principal of the firm of Messrs Kennedy and McGonagle Solicitors, then practising in O'Connell Street, and Mr. Mathews, a member of that firm, acted as the Defendant's solicitor. He was also at that time acting as the Plaintiff's solicitor, principally in relation to lettings which the Plaintiff made of the yard and outoffices attached to 1 Beaupark Villas. It was agreed that a formal contract would be drawn up and as it was natural for the parties to decide to allow Mr. Mathews to look after the legal arrangements the Defendant (not the Plaintiff) contacted Mr. Mathews and told him about the bargain. Mr. Mathews prepared a written agreement and the Defendant and the Plaintiff went into his office and signed it. The document is undated, but I am satisfied that it was executed in the month of August 1968.

Having heard all the evidence I am quite satisfied that the Defendant made no attempt to persuade the Plaintiff to sell him his interest in the field – he was in fact a rather unwilling Purchaser. He in no way influenced the Plaintiff's decision to sell – that decision was the Plaintiff's own. The Defendant has neither an aggressive or domineering personality. He struck me as being a quiet, straightforward, decent man who would not attempt to take unfair advantage of anyone.

The transaction took an inordinate length of time to complete. Again, controversy surrounds the execution of the deed of transfer. The Plaintiff says that he entered St. Patrick's in January 1974, and that he got special leave to go to his solicitor's office to execute the transfer, and that this was on the 14th March 1974. It is quite clear that the Plaintiff is mistaken about this – the contemporary records from Mr. Mathew's files and Mr. O'Shea's evidence establishes his error without doubt. The transfer was executed on 23rd August 1973. The papers had been prepared by Mr. Mathews prior to his going on holiday and the transfer was witnessed by his assistant, Mr. O'Shea. In relation to the execution of this document I find that at this time the Plaintiff was certainly suffering from alcoholism, but that he was not drunk when he signed it nor had he drink taken when he went to Mr. O'Shea's office. I also find that the Defendant in the years from 1968 onwards had not in any way brought pressure on the Plaintiff to have the transaction completed. The Plaintiff himself, not surprisingly, was anxious to obtain the balance of the purchase price (a further instalment of it had been paid in 1969 by the Defendant discharging some of the Plaintiff's debts leaving a balance due to him of £1,000) and he had on his own volition from time to time contacted Mr. O'Shea about the completion of the sale.

The issues of law which have to be considered in this case, require me to refer again to certain aspects of the Plaintiff's medical history and to his financial circumstances. The Plaintiff has had an unhappy life. He has, with great perseverence avoided alcohol since 1974 but unfortunately he has since then continued to suffer from anxiety depression for which he has had treatment both as an in-patient and as an out-patient. But on more than one occasion in the witness box the Plaintiff described himself as being "mad" in certain periods of his early life. I am sure that he had commenced to drink at any early age, but I do not think that his faculties had been impaired by drink when he originally entered into the bargain with his uncle; nor was he otherwise psychologically disturbed at that time. It is quite clear that he was in need of money, notwithstanding the fact that he had a steady job, and that he had an income from the yard at Beaupark Villas and had received nearly £2,000 from his uncle's estate. But it does not follow from this that the Plaintiff was in an impecunious state at the time or that he was driven to the agreement by pressing financial needs. It is equally clear that the Plaintiff in no way suggested to the Defendant that he was in urgent need of money; nor did he leave the Defendant with the impression that he was anything but a normal healthy young man. There is no question therefore in this case of a purchaser seeking to take advantage of a seller's infirmity or straitened financial circumstances.

I now come to one of the parts of this case which present considerable difficulties; namely the claim that the sale I am considering was at a gross undervalue. To arrive at the value of the Plaintiff's reversionary interest in the lands it is agreed that it is firstly necessary to ascertain their open market value with vacant possession in August 1968. An experienced member of the firm of Messrs Lisney and Son (Mr. Molloy) gave evidence on the Plaintiff's behalf and valued the lands at £30,000 (or about £2,727 per acre) on the relevant date. Mr. Ganly, one of the best known auctioneers in the country, valued them as of the same date, at £5,300 (or about £488 per acre). How can this extraordinary variation be explained? I think it is clear how it came about. In the year 1968 the area around Finglas village was developing at a fast rate. Mr. Molloy's evidence was that the Dublin Corporation had acquired by agreement in May 1968 90 acres of land in Finglas South for the sum of £230,000 which works out at about £2,555 per acre. He was also aware of land which was sold near the premises of Merville Dairies on the Finglas Road (opposite the Corporation's purchase) in March 1970 at a price which worked out at close to £9,000 per acre. I think Mr. Molloy was influenced in his valuation of the Plaintiff's land by these figures. But these prices were paid for land which (a) was close to main drainage and so was capable of being developed for housing and (b) was zoned under the Planning code so as to permit its use for building purposes. The Plaintiff's land was to the North of Finglas in a very different area to the lands referred to by Mr. Molloy. There was no main drainage near it and it was zoned for agricultural purposes only. Mr. Ganly approached the valuation of the land on the basis that it was good agricultural land, that it would be sold as such, but with an added factor, namely its "hope value" which would take into account the fact that some buyers might consider that there would be a chance that it might be rezoned under some future Planning Scheme which would allow its development for commmercial purposes. He supported his valuation with sales of non-residential holdings of agricultural land as follows: land near Ashbourne which produced £250 per acre in May 1968; further land near Ashbourne which sold at £642 per acre in August 1968; land near Castleknock which sold in May 1969 for £1,325 per acre; land at St. Margaret's which fetched £571 per acre in April 1969. I think that Mr. Ganly's approach is the correct one, and that the special features to which I have referred make comparison with lands south of Finglas almost meaningless.

There is a further piece of evidence of relevance to land values to which I should refer. The Defendant owned Herbuxton House which is a house with 21 acres of land on the opposite side of the road to the field now in dispute. He sold it to a firm of builders in 1967 for £55,000 but took back the land by means of conacre lettings for a number of years. In 1968 he purchased 70 acres of land at St. Margaret's for £23,000 or about £330 per acre. Having considered this evidence I do not think that it requires me to reject Mr. Ganly's opinion. The Defendant's sale was in respect of a residential holding, and there was a special feature in relation to it involved in the leasing-back provision. It is not therefore of assistance in ascertaining the open market value of the Plaintiff's field. I should also point out that Mr. Molloy did not base his opinion on the Herbuxton House sale. The Plaintiff was well aware of it and I think that if it was relevant Mr. Molloy would have used it to support his opinion. I conclude therefore that I can accept Mr. Ganly's valuation. Purchasers would have been well aware of the restrictions on its development which were then placed on the land. Whilst they might have been influenced by the fact that it was closer to the expanding city than, say, lands at St. Margaret's or Ashbourne, I do not think that this factor would have greatly affected its price. Its market price in 1968 would have been primarily based, as Mr. Ganly says, on its value as good agricultural land.

If its open market price with vacant possession was in the region of £5,300 in 1968 then the value of the Plaintiff's reversionary interest was not more than £1,200 approximately. This follows from the actuarial evidence called by the Plaintiff which values the reversionary interest at about 23% of the vacant possession market value. I conclude therefore that the Plaintiff did not sell at an undervalue. This conclusion gets some support from the fact that at no time after the bargain did the Plaintiff suggest that it was a bad one. I appreciate that from 1968 onwards his health was deteriorating, but he was in the auctioneering business (albeit on the machine-sales side of it) and would have had a good idea of land values in the Finglas area and I think that if the Plaintiff had believed that he had made a bad bargain notwithstanding his worsening condition he would have mentioned it to either his uncle or his aunt (with whom he had remained on very good terms) or to his solicitor with whom he had regular dealings. I should add that in reaching the conclusion which I have just stated I have not overlooked the fact that the sale was by a reversioner to the life tenant and that a vendor in such a position might expect to get an enhanced price from such a purchaser. But I do not consider that in the present case this is a factor which establishes that the sale was at an undervalue, as the life tenant was not a particularly eager purchaser: therefore when considering the price he paid I am satisfied to be guided by Mr. Ganly's figures.

I turn now from the facts of the case to the law. As I have already pointed out various equitable principles have been relied on to defeat the 1968 sale and 1973 transfer. For reasons which will become clear later, I will defer dealing with the undue influence claim until I have firstly considered the relevant principles applicable by reason of the fact that the transaction between the Plaintiff and the Defendant was a sale by a cestui que trust to a trustee.

I start by taking the following statement from *Lewin on Trusts* (16th ed. p. 697-698):

> "While a purchase by a trustee conducting the sale, either personally or by his agent, cannot stand, a purchase by a trustee from a cestui que trust of the interest of the latter in the trust may stand, if the trustee can show that the fullest information, and every advantage were given to the cestui que trust. However, a purchase by a trustee from his cestui que trust is at all times a transaction of great nicety, and one which the Courts will watch with the utmost jealousy and will set aside if the consideration was insufficient."

One of the authorities relied on to support the statement which I have just quoted is *Denton* v. *Donner* 23 Beav. 290. This was a case in which the Plaintiff sought to set aside a sale of his remainder interest to the Defendant, to whom he owed money on foot of a mortgage. The Court held that in the particular circumstances of the case the Defendant was in the position of a trustee and the Court had to consider what, as such Trustee his duties were. Romilly M.R. pointed out (p.290):

> "No doubt where a person is a trustee for sale, and he sells the estate to himself, the transaction is absolutely and ipso facto void, but if a trustee purchases from his cestui que trust his reversionary interest which he is liable to pay, I do not assert it is absolutely void, but certainly the burden of proof lies on the trustee to show that every possible security and advantage were given to the cestui que trust, and that as much as possible was gained for him in the transaction, as he could have gained under any other circumstances. There is in this respect, an absence which is strongly unfavourable to the defendant. It does not appear that any estimate was made of the value of this reversionary property for the purpose of the sale. If it was intended to be sold, the plaintiff ought to have been told what was the value, and the estimate that had been made of the value of the reversion of this property . . . . I think the burden of proof necessary falls upon the defendant to show the bona fides of the transaction throughout, and that everything was done for the plaintiff which could have been done if the property had been sold to a stranger, and that the utmost that could possibly have been produced was obtained."

In addition to these authorities I should refer to a recent decision of the Court of Appeal in England on which Mr. O'Hanlon relied. *Lloyds Bank* v. *Bundy* [1975] 1 Q.B. 326 concerned the validity of a guarantee and charge given by an elderly farmer in relation to a company owned by his son. The Court held that in the particular circumstances of the case a fiduciary relationship existed between the Bank and the Defendant (against whom proceedings for possession had been taken on foot of the charge); that the Defendant had reposed confidence in the Bank and as a result the Bank had a duty of care towards the Defendant; that in the particular circumstances of the case that duty imposed an obligation on the Bank to ensure that the Defendant had the benefit of independent legal advice; that it had been guilty of breach of that duty. The charge and guarantee were set aside, the Court holding that the absence of independent legal advice resulted in the transaction being voidable on the ground of undue influence. I am prepared to hold for the purposes of the present case that there may be circumstances in which a breach by a trustee-purchaser of a duty to ensure that the cestui que trust had obtained independent professional advice would justify the court in setting aside a sale by a cestui que trust apart from any question of undue influence that may arise in the case. I will now consider whether the present is such a case.

The authorities which I have quoted make it clear that the onus of proving the bona fides of the transaction I am considering is on the defendant, and that I am required to examine it with very great care for the purpose of ascertaining whether any unfair advantage was taken by the defendant in his dealings with the plaintiff. I am required to consider the particular duties which the Defendant owed to the Plaintiff in the circumstances of the fiduciary relationship which existed between the parties and to ascertain whether that duty was breached by the Defendant. The findings of fact which I have made (arrived at by bearing in mind where the onus of proof lay in this case) enable me to reach the following conclusions on this part of the case. The Defendant paid what he considered was a fair price for the land; and the price was in fact a fair one. The Defendant had no special knowledge about its value of which the Plaintiff was ignorant, and he made no effort either to take advantage of his special position as trustee of the Plaintiff's property or to influence the Plaintiff's decision to sell. What remains, however, to be considered (and this is perhaps the second most difficult aspect of the case) is whether the Defendant owed a duty to the Plaintiff to ensure that he obtained professional advice of some sort before he entered into the purchase agreement with him. The Plaintiff was a young man of only twenty-three; the bargain was struck in a very casual and informal way. But it is clear that the parties envisaged that a formal contract would be required and the Defendant was aware that the Plaintiff would have available to him the advice of a solicitor before the formal contract was executed. This case is, therefore, different from those cases (including *Bundy*) in which the impugned transaction was completed before any professional advice was available to the grantor of the advantage contained in it. In this case the Plaintiff had available to him the benefit of Mr. Mathews' advice before he signed the contract. Is the Defendant's duty affected by the fact that Mr. Mathews acted for both the Defendant and the Plaintiff? In other words, should the Defendant have ensured that the Plaintiff had independent legal advice? I do not think he was so obliged. It is of course clear that the Defendant gave no thought to the notion that he should advise his nephew to get separate advice, but if he had, I think he would have been entitled to conclude not only that Mr. Mathews was an experienced solicitor but that if he (Mr. Mathews) considered that separate advice was necessary he would have so advised the Plaintiff. That brings me to Mr. Mathews's duties and responsibilities. There is no doubt that Mr. Mathews's double role would have imposed on him a duty to inform the Plaintiff of the necessity to get independent advice if he thought that a conflict of interest existed. If he failed in this duty the Defendant would be liable for it. Naturally, Mr. Mathews cannot recall what precisely was in his mind ten years ago, but I think I am entitled to conclude that if he considered that a conflict had existed he would have advised the Plaintiff accordingly. Mr. Mathews had acted in the administration of the estate of which the lands formed part. He says that he would have been aware of its value sworn for probate purposes (£2,400) and that if he had considered the transaction an improvident one from the Plaintiff's point of view he believes he would have said so. I accept this evidence, and I conclude that in the particular circumstances of this case there was in fact no duty on the Defendant or his agent (Mr. Mathews) to advise the Plaintiff to obtain the advice of an independent solicitor. Nor were either under a duty to advise an independent valuation prior to execution of the formal contract. The Defendant and Mr. Mathews thought the price a fair one and in my view they were right.

The Deed of transfer was not executed until August 1973 at which time, of course, the value of the land had greatly increased. This fact would have been known to the Defendant but I do not think it affects in any way his duty to the Plaintiff. If a valid contract had been entered into in 1968 the Plaintiff was legally bound by it, and the delay in completion did not impose any new obligations on the Defendant.

I will now deal with the Plaintiff's claim that the transaction is vitiated by the undue influence exercised by the Defendant over him. This I can do shortly. The findings of fact which I made, make it clear that the Defendant did not in fact attempt to influence the Plaintiff's decision to sell, and that this decision was arrived at freely by the Plaintiff. But it has been urged in this case that the relationship of trustee and cestui que trust is one of those fiduciary relationships which give rise to a presumption of undue influence and that this presumption operates to defeat the sale I am considering. I am quite satisfied that the presumption of undue influence does arise in the present case. I am equally satisfied that it is one which *can* be rebutted (see for example decision of Black, J. *Provincial Bank* v. *McKeever* [1941] I.R. 471: and Gavan Duffy. J. *Grealish* v. *Murphy* [1946] I.R. 35) and that it *has* been rebutted in this case. The test applied by Mr. Justice Budd (In *Gregg* v. *Kidd* [1956] I.R. 183) was to ascertain whether the gift he was considering had resulted from the free exercise of the donor's will. Applying that test to the present case the evidence satisfies me that the Plaintiff freely and with an independent will entered into the bargain with the Defendant. It is, however, argued that even if this were so his judgment was not an "informed judgment", because of the failure of the Defendant to ensure that the Plaintiff had independent professional advice. It is submitted that I should apply the principles enunciated by the Court of Appeal in England in *Bundy* and hold that this failure rendered the transaction voidable by reason of the doctrine of undue influence. I have already decided that the Defendant was not required to ensure that the Plaintiff obtained independent professional advice. It is unnecessary for me to consider whether if he was so required, this would render the translation invalid for undue influence as well as by virtue of the equitable principles relating to purchases by trustees from cestui que trusts. I should add that when the presumption of undue influence arises the absence of independent professional advice does not necessarily render the transaction invalid and draw attention to a recent example of the application of this principle in England (see *In re Brocklehurst's Estate* [1977] 3 W.L.R. 696.). The claim of undue influence therefore fails.

Finally, I should refer to the submissions that the transaction in this case attracts the equitable principles relating to unconscionable bargains. This submission can be considered under two separate headings. As pointed out by Mr. Justice Gavan Duffy in *Grealish* v. *Murphy* [1946] I.R. at p. 49 Equity comes to the rescue whenever the parties to a contract have not met on equal terms and if it is shown that an infirm grantor could not adequately protect himself the Court will inquire whether he was given the protection which was his due by reason of his infirmity. I have, however, already recorded my conclusion that the Plaintiff was not suffering from any physical or mental infirmity when the agreement was entered into in 1968 such as would attract the equitable doctrine to which I have referred. It is true that in 1973 when the Transfer was executed the Plaintiff's health had seriously deteriorated – he was by then an alcoholic. But if the agreement he had earlier entered into was a legally valid one the subsequent deterioration in his health would not invalidate it, or entitle him to set aside the deed of transfer which it was his legal obligation to execute. Secondly, under the heading of unconscionable bargains, Equity will set aside sales by reversioners in certain circumstances. But the sale in this case was not at an undervalue, nor in the light of the findings of fact I have already made could it otherwise be regarded as unconscionable.

The result, therefore, is that the various attacks mounted on the transaction I have considered fail and I must dismiss this claim.

Notes

See the further remarks of Costello J. on the subject of undue influence in *Healy* v. *Lyons*, Unreported (1975 No. 4631 P) (judgment delivered 24th October 1978) and *O'Flanagan* v. *Ray-ger Ltd.* Unreported (1980 No. 2858((judgment delivered 28th April 1983). See also p.234, *ante* and *Irish Land Law*, para. 9.075.

2. Settlements Defrauding Creditors

BRYCE V. FLEMING

[1930] I.R. 376 (High Court)

The facts are set out in the judgment.

Meredith J.:

This is an appeal against the judgment of Circuit Court Judge Power, by which an assignment, dated the 9th March, 1928, whereby certain lands of Ballybroney and

Balladallagh, in the County of Mayo, were assigned by the defendant, Thomas Fleming, to the defendant, Mary Gilvarry, was declared void as against the plaintiff and all other the creditors of the defendant, Thomas Fleming, and was ordered to be delivered up to be cancelled.

The declaration and order purported to be made under the Irish statute, 10 Chas. 1, Sess. 2, c. 3, against covinous or fraudulent conveyances, which corresponds to the English statute, 13 Eliz. c. 5. The assigment was an out-and-out assignment. There was no reservation of any kind, express or secret, in favour of the vendor, Thomas Fleming, and the price was determined as the result of genuine bargaining, and reflected simply the estimate which the parties placed on the value of the lands. The assignment was, therefore, unquestionably for good consideration, and *bona fide*. But at the time it was made Patrick Bryce, the plaintiff, had obtained judgment against the defendant, Thomas Fleming, for necessaries supplied to his wife, and, as Fleming had unsuccessfully appealed against this judgment, the plaintiff was a creditor of Fleming to a considerable amount – apparently nearly half the value of the lands assigned. The learned Judge was satisfied that Fleming's intention in selling the lands was to divest himself of the only property on which the plaintiff, Bryce, could levy execution, and that, accordingly, the assignment came within sect. 10 of the statute. He further refused to believe the evidence of the defendant, Mary Gilvarry, that she had no notice of the fraudulent nature of the transaction. Accordingly, he held that the assignment to her was not protected by sect. 14, which contains a proviso in favour of *bona fide* conveyances for good consideration without notice, and so he declared the deed void as against the creditors of Thomas Fleming. The order further directed the assignment to be delivered up to be cancelled. That, of course, was a mistake; for it is quite clear that sect. 10 only makes an assignment which is fraudulent against creditors void as against them, and that in the present case Mary Gilvary is in any event entitled to the benefit of her purchase, subject to the claim of the plaintiff. The proper form of order is set out in *Bott* v. *Smith* 21 Beav. 511.

The circumstances under which a *bona fide* conveyance for valuable consideration might yet be fraudulent within sect. 10 are indicated in a passage in the judgment of Palles C.B. in *In re Moroney* 21 L.R. Ir. 27, at p. 63. Dealing with the case of a *bona fide* sale for value, he says that if "the intent were not only to sell the property, but forthwith to abscond with the proceeds, so as in effect to withdraw the property from the fund available for the creditors without providing an equivalent, I should entertain no doubt that in such a case there would be an intention to defraud creditors, which, if the purchaser had notice of, would avoid the sale." As a matter of fact, the point that a conveyance might be within sect. 10, or rather, the corresponding English section, though for valuable consideration, had been well settled as far back as the time of Lord Mansfield, who states the position with great clearness in his judgment in *Cadogan* v. *Kennell* 2 Cowp. 432 at p. 431: "But if the transaction be not *bona fide*, the circumstance of its being done for a *valuable consideration,* will not *alone* take it out of the statute. I have known several cases where persons have given a fair and *full price* for goods, and where the *possession* was *actually changed*; yet being done for the purpose of defeating creditors, the transaction has been held fraudulent, and therefore void. One case was, where there had been a decree in the Court of Chancery, and a sequestration. A person with knowledge of the decree, bought the house and goods belonging to the defendant, and gave a full price for them. The Court said the purchase, being with a manifest view to defeat the creditor, was fraudulent; and, therefore, notwithstanding a valuable consideration, void. So, if a man knows of a judgment and execution, and, with a view to defeat it, purchases the debtor's goods, it is void: because the *purpose* is iniquitous. It is assisting one man to cheat another, which the law will never allow." Later cases, where deeds for valuable consideration were held within the section, are referred to in *Bott* v. *Smith* 21 Beav. 511; see also the more modern case of *In re Johnson; Golden* v. *Gillam* 20 Ch. D. 389, at p. 393. The difficulties, however, in the way of a creditor who seeks to impugn a deed for valuable consideration are emphasised in *Harman* v. *Richards* 10 Hare 81, at p. 89. There Turner L.J. said: "A deed, though made for valuable consideration, may be affected by *mala fides*. But those who undertake to impeach for *mala fides* a deed which has been executed for valuable consideration, have, I think, a task of great difficulty to discharge.

These authorities indicate under what circumstances a creditor's claim under the statute will be good even against an assignee for valuable consideration. No such circumstances exist in the present case. If a man has lands, and can only pay his debts by selling his lands, the honest thing for him to do is to sell them. It is also the prudent thing to do; for if he sells them himself he will probably get a better price, and avoid unnecessary costs. Consequently, the mere fact that a man in such a position is selling his lands is no evidence whatever that his intention is to defeat his creditors rather than to obtain the wherewithal to pay his debts. Still more is it obvious that mere knowledge of such a simple fact is not a sufficient ground for imputing to a purchaser knowledge of a fraudulent intention on the part of his vendor. Voluntary assignments by a debtor stand on one footing. But once valuable consideration is given a new element enters into the case. As Fry J. says in *In re Johnson; Golden* v. *Gillam* 20 Ch. D. 389, at p.393, it is always "a material ingredient in considering the case, and for very obvious reasons: the fact that there is valuable consideration shows at once that there may be purposes in the transaction other than defeating or delaying creditors, and renders the case, therefore, of those who contest the deed more difficult."

Now, unquestionably the only knowledge bearing on the question of Fleming's intention that was brought home to the mind of Mary Gilvarry was the simple fact that Fleming probably could not satisfy the plaintiff's claim without a sale of the lands. Further, Mary Gilvarry's testimony was that she had no knowledge of or notice of any fraudulent intention on Fleming's part. The learned Judge, however, took the view that the *onus* of proving absence of knowledge lay on Mary Gilvarry, and, as he did not regard her as a creditable witness, he rejected her testimony, and so he considered that she had failed to discharge the *onus,* with the result that he avoided the deed. In this way the task which Turner L.J. described as so difficult to discharge was performed with such ease that Mary Gilvarry most probably left the Court in a state of utter bewilderment at the extreme simplicity of the proceeding by which, despite her uncontradicted testimony, she was deprived of all benefit of her £200.

Now, on this appeal, we are pressed with the point that the defendant's *onus* of proving that she had no notice cannot be discharged by her testimony if it is not to be believed, and that the question of the creditability of a witness if for the Judge of first instance. But, even assuming that the *onus* was on Mary Gilvarry of showing absence of notice, I am inclined to think that the *onus* was shifted once she swore that she had no notice, and that the learned Judge was not entitled to reject her testimony in the absence of any positive evidence whatever of anything from which knowledge should be imputed to her. This is not a case of conflict of testimony, and it is not like the case of the testimony of a claimant in support of a claim against the estate of a deceased. A number of authorities on the analogous case where absence of notice is averred to support the equitable plea of purchase for value without notice will be found correct in the note to *Jones* v. *Thomas* 3 P. Wms. 243; see also *Vane* v. *Vane* 8 Ch. App. 383, at p.398 where Sir Wm. James L.J. (having stated that the plaintiff alleged in so many words that he never did know or suspect at the time anything of the alleged fraud) said: "That we must take to be true, unless we are enabled judicially to conclude from other statments of his in the bill that that allegation is false." In general, "the defence of a purchase without notice is one which ought to be specifically alleged as well as proved by those who rely upon it": *Per* Thesiger L.J. in *Attorney-General* v. *Bishophated Guano Co.* 11 Ch. Div. 327, at p.337. The question, however, is one of some difficulty, as the learned Judge gave as his reason for disbelieving Mary Gilvarry that she denied having heard of the result of the unsuccessful appeal, heard in Dublin, in the action already referred to, taken by Bryce against Fleming, in respect of necessaries supplied to Mrs. Fleming. The learned Judge held that that was in itself an incredible statement, and so he said he would reject her evidence entirely.

If, however, the *onus* was on the plaintiff to prove that the defendant was aware of the intention of Thomas Fleming, then that *onus* could not be discharged by rejecting the evidence of the defendant that she had no knowledge. Hence, instead of examining the authorities as to the position if the defendant was to prove absence of notice, I prefer to turn to the question of whether, in the case of a purchase for valuable consideration, the *onus* is not on the creditor to prove that the purchaser was aware of his vendor's fraudulent intent. The answer to that question must depend upon whether an innocent purchaser is saved by reason of his conveyance not originally coming within sect. 10 at all, or only by reason of his being protected by the proviso contained in sect. 14. It may be anticipated that it will not prove an altogether easy matter to clear up this question by reference to the authorities, as a certain amount of confusion in the older authorities is recognised in the observation of Parker J. in *Glegg* v. *Bromley* [1912] 3 K.B. 474, at p. 492, that "There is, however, a proviso for the protection of a purchaser for good consideration without notice of the illegal intention. In the authorities which deal with the statute it is not always clear whether the Judges are dealing with the operative part of the Act or with the proviso." An example of one of the many passages which Parker J. must have had in view is the following, in *French* v. *French* 6 De G. M. & G. 95, at p.101:– "Mr. Gibbons had no knowledge of the state of Mr. French's affairs, therefore the transaction, as far as he is concerned, ought not to be impeached." Does Lord Cranworth mean that the transaction, as far as he is concerned, is not avoided under the operative section, or that his estate or interest is protected under the proviso? There is a similar difficulty in respect of the observation, already cited, of Palles C.B. in *In re Moroney* 21 L.R. Ir. 27, for it is implied that if the purchaser had no notice the sale would not be avoided. Are we entitled to press the implication, that it is the sale itself that would not be avoided, as against a suggestion that it is only the estate or interest of the purchaser that would be protected? Numerous other instances might be cited of passages in which an expectation of a clear statement on the point is disappointed. I must be admitted, however, that, from *Twyne's Case* 1 Smith's L.C. 1 down, there are several passages in the authorities which assume, but without considering any alternative view, that it is the proviso which protects a purchaser for value without notice. But these *obiter dicta* cannot have very much weight, since it was not until *Halifax Joint Stock Banking Co.* v. *Gledhill* [1891] 1 Ch. 31 that it was clearly decided that the proviso covered the case of a subsequent transfer; and, of course, if the proviso was not dealing with subsequent transactions it must have been dealing with the original transaction. Hence the assumption to which I have referred.

Turning to the wording of the operative section, it is obvious that the question whether or not it hits a *bona fide* purchaser for valuable consideration without notice must depend on whether the "intent" referred to in the section is solely the intent of the vendor in such a case or is the intent of the transaction as a whole, so as to make the intent of the purchaser material. Certainly, on the plain reading of the section itself, it is the latter view that would commend itself. But the authorities on which one most readily lights seem in favour of the former – as far as *dicta* go. Thus, in *Nunn* v. *Wilsmore* 8 T.R. 521, at p.530 Le Blane J. says: "Whether or not a deed is to be considered as fraudulent with respect to creditors must depend on the motives of the party making the deed." But it does not seem that deeds for valuable consideration were here in contemplation. The same may be said of the observations of Kindersley V.C. in *Thompson* v. *Webster* 4 Drew, 628, at p. 632: "The principle now established is this:– The language of the Act being, that any conveyance of property is void against creditors if it is made with *intent* to defeat, hinder, or delay creditors, the Court is to decide in each particular case whether, on all the circumstances, it can come to the conclusions that the *intention* of the settlor in making the settlement was to defeat, hinder, or delay his creditors." But I have not found any passage in which the case of a purchase for valuable consideration is expressly considered, and in which the intention of the purchaser is treated as immaterial. But there is authority to the contrary. In *Cadogan* v. *Kennett* 2 Cowp. 432 Lord Mansfield, in the passage already cited, stresses throughout the intention of the purchaser and of the purchaser. In the case where the creditor had obtained a decree, he says: "The Court said, the purchaser" – not the sale – "being with a manifest view to defeat the creditor, was fraudulent; and, therefore, notwithstanding a valuable consideration void." He uses similar language in the second instance which he gives:– "So, if a man knows of a judgment and execution, and, with a view to defeat it, purchases the debtor's goods, it is void: because the *purpose* is *iniquitous*. It is assisting one man to cheat another, which the law will never allow." *Cadogan* v. *Kennett* 2 Cowp. 432 does not appear to have been cited in *In re Johnson; Golden* v. *Gillam* 20 Ch. D. 389, but in that case Fry J. arrives independently at the same view as to the materiality of the purchaser's intention. He says: "I therefore proceed to inquire, look to all the circumstances of the case at the nature of the instrument itself, whether I can or ought to infer an intent ot defraud creditors in the parties to the deed. I say in the parties to the deed, because it appears to me to be plain that whatever fraudulent intent there may have been in the mind of Judith Johnson, it would not avoid the deed unless it was shown to have been concurred in by Alice, who became the purchaser under the deed. It has not been contended, and it could not be contended, that the mere fraudulent intent of the vendor could avoid the deed, if the purchaser were free from that fraud." Accordingly, the action was dismissed, and it is clear that the learned Judge was relying on his interpretation of the operative section, not on the proviso. The case is, therefore, an authority for the proposition that where there is a *bona fide* purchaser for valuable consideration the transaction cannot be impeached under the operative section unless the purchaser is shown to have been privy to the vendor's intention. Hence this appeal must be allowed, since the *onus* lay on the plaintiff, and he certainly made no attempt to dicharge it himself, and it certainly was not discharged by the learned trial Judge not accepting the defendant's denial.

Although it would be sufficient for me to rely on the clear decision of Fry J. in the case to which I have referred, I should like to add that to my mind that decision is in accord with the plain reading of the sections. Once it is seen that at all events the primary object of sect. 14 was to protect a certain class of tranferees under assignments subsequent to the original fraudulent conveyance, there is no incentive to construe sect. 10 in such a way that it will not already safeguard an original innocent purchaser. Similarly, if the purchase in such a case is not within sect. 10 there is no reason for not construing sect. 14 as dealing exclusively with subsequent transactions, and, in my opinion, sect. 14 does not deal with the original transaction at all, but only with subsequent transfers. First of all, it does not seem to me that sect. 14 is appropriately worded to meet the case of the original conveyance. For, if the original purchase is to be protected, then sect. 10 does not operate at all, and the provision should be that sect. 10 should not extend to, or be construed to, impeach the conveyance in such a case. The wording we should expect would be similar to that in sect. 4 of 27 Eliz. c. 4, viz.: "Provided also . . . that this Act . . . shall not extend or be construed to impeach, defeat, make void or frustrate any conveyance . . . made upon or for good consideration and *bona fide,"* &c. But sect. 14 does not exempt the fraudulent conveyance from the operation of sect. 10; in fact, it does not deal directly with any conveyance at all, but only with estates or interest conveyed in the manner stated. That is appropriate to a subsequent alienation, for what is alienated may only be a portion of the property originally conveyed or only a limited interest, and it is only such estate or interest that is protected in the case provided for, while, subject to the protection afforded to the estate or interest in question, sect. 10 operates on the original conveyance. Broadly, the effect of sect. 10 is only to charge the estate conveyed by the original conveyance, but the charge does not affect a subsequent *bona fide* purchaser for good consideration without notice. The case of *Halifax Joint Stock Banking Co.* v. *Gledhill* [1891] 1 Ch. 31 shows how appropriate sect. 14 is to a subsequent transfer, and sect. 4 of 27 Eliz. c. 4 shows how inappropriate it would be in the case of the original conveyance. Further, it may be said that the nature and circumstances of the original transaction and of a subsequent transfer generally stand on such a different footing that it seems unlikely that they would have been grouped together. Now that it has been definitely decided that the original purchaser is not hit by sect. 14, the way is clear, despite observations in the older authorities, to hold that sect. 14 only deals with subsequent transfers.

The appeal must, therefore, be allowed, and the action dismissed with costs.

Johnston J.:

I have considered very carefully the questions that were raised on this appeal, and I was prepared to set out at length the reasons which moved me to come to the conclusion that the appeal should be allowed, and the equity civil bill dismissed; but, having had the privilege of reading beforehand the judgment that has just been delivered, I feel that it would be a waste of public time to do more than state in a few words what my view is. I think that it is not necessary to go beyond the Act of Parliament to see that the slender case which the plaintiff has made is wholly unsustainable. The Act was designed to put a stop to all alienations of property "devised and contrived of malice, fraud, covin, collusion or guile, to the end, purpose and intent to delay, hinder or defraud creditors and others of their just and lawful" debts. Such alienations are deemed to be clearly and utterly void, but only "as against the person or persons, his or their heirs, successors, executors, administrators and assigns" whose debts shall thereby have been in any wise disturbed, hindered, delayed or defrauded. It seems to me that the provision is clear enought as it stands; but it is made even clearer by sect. 11 – a section which was not referred to in the course of the argument – which provides that "all and every, the parties" to such a fraudulent alienation who "shall wittingly put in ure, avow, maintain, defend or justify the same . . . as true, simple, and done, had or made *bona fide* and upon good consideration," shall suffer the penalty therein set out. Then sect. 14 provides that he legislation shall not extend to any estate or interest which had been lawfully conveyed *bona fide* and for good consideration to any person who had at the time of such conveyance no notice or knowledge of the fraud. "A conveyance, therefore," said Plumer V.C. in *Copis* v. *Middleton* 2 Madd. 410, "cannot be invalidated by this Act if there has been a *bona fide* purchaser."

A good many of the considerations that were addressed to us in this case were considerations that were relevant to the case of a voluntary conveyance rather than to one that admittedly was for valuable consideration.

I think, as Turner V.C. said in *Harman* v. *Richards* 10 Hare, 89, that "those who undertake to impeach for *mala fides* a deed which has been executed for valuable consideration have, I think, a task of great difficulty to discharge."

While accepting the view of Judge Power that the whole of Mrs. Gilvarry's evidence must be rejected as being untrue, and taking into account the fact that this was admittedly the case of a purchase for valuable consideration, I can find nothing in the evidence adduced on behalf of the plaintiff which even remotely suggests to my mind that she or her husband had any degree of knowledge of the fraud of which Fleming is alleged to have been guilty, or that the motive of her and her husband is purchasing this property was anything other than the desire to acquire the lands as a *bona fide* purchaser.

3. *Settlements Defrauding Purchasers*

RE MOORE

[1918] 1 I.R. 169 (Court of Appeal)

The facts are set out in the judgments.

Sir Ignatius J. O'Brien C.:

By indenture, made on the 11th October, 1888, between John Moore, of the first part; Joseph Kelly and Christopher Moore, of the second part; and Christoper

Moore, of the third part, Christopher Moore purported to convey to Joseph Kelly and Christopher Moore part of the lands of Finnea, to hold to them upon trust to pay the income to John Moore and his assigns during his life, and after his death for Christopher Moore absolutely; but, in the event of Christopher pre-deceasing John Moore without leaving issue him surviving at the decease of John Moore, it was provided that the lands should be held upon a series of trusts which it is not necessary to consider, as the events provided for did not happen. It was also provided that John Moore should grant to Rose Moore, his wife, if she survived him, a rent-charge of £40 per annum; and the lands were charged by him with the payment of the following sums of money:– £150 for his daughter Mary, £100 each for his daughters Kate and Anne, and £100 for each of his sons Peter, Thomas, John, Luke, and Owen – in all £750, to be payable on the death of John Moore. There was a provision for the maintenance, education, and advancement of his sons and daughters under the age of twenty-one, with power to pay to the daughters, on marriage, their portions.

Christopher Moore was married in September, 1901, to Julia White. She had a fortune of £300, and a settlement was made on the 14th September between John Moore, father, Rose Moore, his wife, Christopher Moore, son, and Julia White, the intended wife. It recited the indenture of the 11th October, 1888, and after the following recital:– "Whereas all the charges on the said lands of Finnea have been paid off and satisfied by the said John Moore," it was witnessed that in consideration of the marriage and of the sum of £300 to be secured to the said John Moore by the promisory note of Julia White and her brother, the lands were conveyed by John Moore to Christopher Moore and Julia White upon limitations which in effect conferred life estates upon them and the survivor of them with remainder to their children as appointed.

The recital that the charge created by the earlier deed had been paid off and was not true in fact. Mary, a daughter of John Moore, appears to have been paid a portion of the fortune of Julia White; but the other members of the family had not in fact received their portions; it may, however, have been thought that, although not paid, they had been, in fairness, settled with. Now, however, the father having died, the plaintiffs have brought the present action for a declaration that the sum of £750 provided by the settlement of 1888 – in so far, of course, as any claims may not have been paid or discharged – may be raised out of the lands.

One cannot help having very great sympathy with the defendant Christopher Moore; and, certainly, it is very hard that the fortune of his wife should have been parted with, and that the provision which was intended to be made for her may, to a great extent, if not altogether, fail. But one cannot decide a case having regard merely to sympathy. If, therefore, the claims of some of these children are good in law, and if the voluntary settlement made by their father must be regarded as an honest dealing with the property, they also have got rights which in justice ought not to be disturbed. It is to be regretted that the honest efforts which were made to effect an adjustment of the rights of all the parties, irrespective of strictly legal considerations, did not succeed. This cannot affect the decision.

The defence in substance is this: It is not admitted that the deed of 1888 was a voluntary settlement; but it is contended that the deed of the 14th September, 1901, placed the defendants in the position of purchasers for value, so that if the first deed was voluntary (and as everything had taken place prior to the statute 56 & 57 Vict. c. 21), the first deed should be treated as fraudulent and void as against those claiming under the second deed. I assume in my judgment that the first deed was voluntary. I have so clear an opinion of the legal question involved that I prefer to treat the case on the footing although it may be otherwise in fact. The Voluntary Conveyances Act, 1893, has, however, made a vital alteration in the law; and the contention on behalf of the respondents is that it operates as a complete answer to the defence.

Several questions of law have been argued before us on behalf of the appellants, the defendants in the action; and one question of pure fact has also been discussed. It was urged by the appellants that at the date of the execution of the deed of 1888, John Moore, the settlor, was indebted in a large sum of money to a man named Carson; that he was in embarrassed circumstances and financial difficulties; and that the deed was executed with the object of hindering and defeating this particular creditor, along with other creditors; that it was never intended to be acted upon, and was never acted upon; and that this arrangement was made with the consent of all the parties, and to aid in the carrying out of the fraudulent object in view.

Assuming the true view of the facts to be as suggested, and that the object of the deed was to hinder and defeat the creditors of John Moore, it was then argued as a matter of law that the deed was avoided by the second deed, even though none of the parties could be regarded as a creditor of John Moore; that, in order to bring the deed within the statute of 1893, it was necessary for the plaintiffs to negative the existence of any mala fides; and that if the object of the deed was to hinder, defeat, and delay creditors, a fraudulent intent was established, which would make it void in favour of a subsequent purchaser, even though there was no attempt to commit a fraud on a purchaser, as distinguished from a creditor, and although no creditor had elected to treat the deed as fraudulent as against him.

The Master of the Rolls held, as a fact, that there was no evidence from which he could infer any intention to defeat Carson or any other creditors, and I agree with him in that view. This, of course, is a complete answer to the appellants' case in so far as it is based on the argument that an intent to defeat creditors under the 13 Eliz. will enable a deed to be avoided as against a purchaser under the 27 Eliz. I do not, however, assent to the legal contention put forward, which I will deal with later on. There remains the other view, namely, that under the Act of 1893, the plaintiffs were bound, affirmatively, to prove that the deed as executed by John Moore, had been executed bona fide. I may say at once that I do not see any evidence from which to infer that this deed was not intended to be an operative instrument, or that there was in fact, and as distinguished from legal presumption, any intent to hinder or defeat any future purchasers.

It is true that the deed was not delivered to one of the trustees, and it certainly appears to have remainded in the house of the settlor; but when inquiries were made with regard to it, on the occasion of the marriage of Christopher Moore, it was treated as being a deed fully in operation, and the only question raised was whether the terms of it had been satisfied. Indeed the defendants are precluded, I think, from contending that the deed was a mere pocket instrument, inasmuch as it is treated in the deed under which they themselves take as having been a perfectly good instrument, although by an unhappy but innocent representation an error was made as to the beneficiaries under the first deed, in fact, having been satisfied. As for the contention which appears on the pleadings, that he beneficiaries had abandoned all claim under the deed, the evidence is all the other way. A case is sought to be made against one member of the family on the ground that she wrote letters which brought home to her mind the inaccuracy of the statement contained in the deed, but she was very young; moreover, she acted only as an amanuensis, and, in the circumstances, I can see no reason for binding her to any waiver of the trusts in her favour.

I do not think it is necessary to go into the details of the evidence which satisfies me as to the correctness of the inference which the master of the Rolls has drawn, and which I also draw. I propose now to deal with the questions of law which were raised, and which I have already indicated. It was decided by the Master of the Rolls in *National Bank* v. *Behan* [1913] 1 I.R. 512 that on the true construction of the Voluntary Conveyances Act, 1893, the onus of proving that a voluntary deed was made bona fide and without fraudulent intent lay upon the party seeking the protection of the Act. I need hardly say that the opinion and judgment of so experienced a lawyer as the Master of the Rolls would never be overruled by me unless I considered that I was absolutely bound to come to a different conclusion. The fact that a similar view of the law is stated in May on Fraudulent and Voluntary Conveyances 3rd ed., pp. 161 and 324-5 does not, of course, add any authoritative weight to the judgment of the Master of the Rolls; but it is, at the same time, a statement which I should not be disposed to treat in any other way than with respect.

Let us consider what was the position of affairs with regard to voluntary deeds under 27 Eliz. c. 4, apart from the Act of 1893. The purpose of that Act was to protect purchasers of lands against gifts and conveyances "meant and intended by the parties that so make the same to be fraudulent and convenous of purpose and intent to deceive such as have purchased or shall purchase the same"; and then for remedy it was enacted that every such conveyance had or made or to be had or made "for the intent and of purpose to defraud and deceive" such persons as had purchased or should purchase, should, as against such purchasers, be deemed to be utterly void. What, to many lawyers appeared to be a singular and unreasonable construction was put on an Act which, on the face of it, might be regarded as fairly clear. Although voluntary conveyances were not mentioned in the Act, it was ultimately determined judicially that the mere fact that a conveyance was voluntary and without consideration made it ipso facto void as against anyone who might afterwards become a purchaser of the lands dealt with by the voluntary conveyance. A fraudulent intent was presumed by the courts; and this presumption was conclusive and irrebuttable, so that, however honest, reasonable, fair, or just a voluntary conveyance was, it became mere waste paper on the production of a conveyance for value to a subsequent purchaser. A statute which was framed to prevent injustice was so read as to do grave and serious injustice. Against this construction of the statute the feeling both of the profession and the public became in the end so strong that in 1893 the statute at present under consideration was passed.

The Act 27 Eliz. c. 4, of course, is not repealed, and it remains in operation to prevent fraud of the character described in the statute; but a presumption of fraudulent intent, wholly the outcome of judicial decision, has been got rid of by the Act of 1893. By sect. 2 of the Voluntary Conveyances Act, 1893, the rule of law, which defeated, irrespective of fairness, a voluntary conveyance, was abrogated, and the statute 27 Eliz. c. 4 was allowed to speak for itself and to avoid deeds, the real object of which was proved to be to defeat a future purchaser; but the onus of proving fraud is always on the person alleging it, though in many cases its existence may be an almost certain inference. And it seems to me that it would defeat the very object of sect. 2 of the Act of 1893, which was intended to destroy the former rule of law, to hold that it was only intended to modify it to the extent that a party, supporting an honest deed, might be at liberty to show as a substantive case that the deed was made bona fide. How such an onus could be discharged it is difficult to see. It seems to me that practically it could only take the form of swearing to a negative – a perfectly futile proceeding. The words "if in fact made bona fide and without any fraudulent intent" appear to me to have been inserted lest the latter part of the section might be construed to have gone too far, and to have amounted to a repeal of 27 Eliz. c. 4, or of 10 Chas 1, s. 2, c.3 (Ir.), dealing with this question. I think it could never have been intended that there was to be read into the statute of 27 Eliz. c. 4 what in substance would be this: "voluntary conveyances shall be deemed to be fraudulent unless the contrary is proved." The intention was, I think, to get rid of an inequitable rule with regard to voluntary conveyances, leaving them to be destroyed by evidence of fraudulent intent; and, ordinarily, I should have thought that the person on whom the onus of proof would lie under 27 Eliz. c. 4, once the irrebuttable presumption to which I have referred was swept away, was the person alleging fraud, just as under 13 Eliz. c. 5 where an actual intent to defraud the grantor's creditors is alleged, the burden of proving such intent falls on the person alleging it. The two classes of deeds appear to me to be placed on the same footing in this respect; and the Act of 1893 might, in many cases, wholly fail to get rid of the evil it was intended to remove if it was held to have set up a new rule quite as artificial, if not more artificial, than that which it was designed to destroy.

The same method of reasoning induces me, without hesitation, to decide against the appellants' contention with regard to the second question argued by them, namely, that "without any fraudulent intent" did not mean a fraudulent intent to defeat purchasers. The expression "if in fact made bona fide and without any fraudulent intent" must, to my mind, be read as referring to 27 Eliz. c. 4. Of course, there may have been cases where a voluntary deed could have been avoided under 13 Eliz. c. 5 as well as under 27 Eliz. c. 4, where it was found simpler to apply the irrebuttable legal presumption which got rid of it under 27 Eliz. c. 4. But if the latter Act and that of 1893 are read together, as they must be, I cannot read into 27 Eliz.

words which would extend the operation of that statute in a direction, to my mind, never contemplated. Gifts intended to defeat purchasers are the transactions that are avoided. The fraudulent intent in 27 Eliz. is a fraudulent intent to defeat purchasers. Why should I read a fraudulent intent in the Act of 1893 in a different sense from what it bears in the statute 27 Eliz. c. 4?

If sect. 2 of the Act of 1893 was to be taken as a perfectly independent enactment affirmatively avoiding all voluntary conveyance unless any kind of fraudulent intent was negatived, then the contention of the appellants on both grounds might be right; but once I treat it as a statute to get rid of certain effects of judge-made law, and to be read with the Act of 27 Eliz. c. 4, and not as an independent enactment, the construction put upon it by the appellants, to my mind, is not sustainable.

Ronan L.J.:

1. A man with an estate of £50,000 a year charges it with an annuity of £100 for the life of one of his sons. Twenty years after he sells the estate to *X*. 2. A man grants a piece of land to his son. The next day he sells it to *X*. In both cases the first deed is a voluntary deed. In case 1 it was clearly bona fide, and not made with any fraudulent intent. In case 2 it was plainly made with intent to defraud the purchaser. Judicial construction of the Act made the first deed in both cases equally fraudulent and void as against *X*.

In *Doe d., Olley* v. *Manning* 9 East, 59, a case where there was no fraud in fact, Lord Ellenborough said the question was "whether in such case the law do not presume fraud without admitting such presumption to be contradicted" (p.63). That case finally settled the law, and it was held that here was a conclusive presumption that every voluntary deed which had the effect of depriving a subsequent purchase from the grantor of what the purchaser deed purported to give him was made with intent to defraud the purchaser within the Act. This principle plainly treated as fraudulent perfectly honest transactions, and was found, particularly in the case of settlements making provision for families, to operate very harshly and unjustly. However, once the deed was a voluntary deed the law was inexorable. In order to mitigate this evil the Courts adopted the view that a very slight consideration should be taken as sufficient to prevent the deed being a voluntary deed.

I shall now refer to some of the cases on the subject. It will be seen that the result of the cases is that if there is an honest family transaction a slight legal consideration is sufficient to take the case out of the category of voluntary deeds, and the honesty of the transaction rebuts any presumption of fraud. (See judgment of Palles C.B. in *Mullins* v. *Guilfoyle* 2 L.R. Ir., at p.109.)

In *Townend* v. *Toker* L.R. 1 Ch. App. 446 the plaintiff claimed specific performance of an agreement for the sale to him of an estate which at the date of the agreement was the subject of a settlement alleged by the plaintiff to have been voluntary, and void as against him. The vendor and settlor, who was entitled in fee to the estate subject to mortgages, proposed to her nephew that she should come and live with him, and that he should remove into a larger house for the purpose, she contributing a yearly sum towards the housekeeping. The nephew agreed to this, provided she would settle the estate limiting it to him after her death. She agreed to this, and a settlement was accordingly executed, by which the nephew convenanted to indemnify her from all liability in respect of the mortgages, except the payment of the interest during her life. He removed to a larger house at considerable expense, and they lived together for some time. The aunt afterwards ceased to live with the nephew, and subsequently agreed to sell the estate to the plaintiff. Lord Romilly, Master of the Rolls, made a decree declaring the plaintiff entitled to specific performance, but this decree was reversed by Turner and Knight Bruce L.JJ., who held not only that there was sufficient consideration upon the face of the deed itself, namely, the covenant of indemnity, to take the case out of the operation of the statute, but also that evidence was admissible to show consideration for the deed not appearing on the face of it, and that there was sufficient evidence of such consideration, namely, the expenses incurred by the settlor's nephew upon the faith of the settlement being executed. "The question," Lord Justice Turner said, at p.

458, "as I apprehend, in cases of this description is whether there was consideration for the settlement. The Court not entering into the quantum of consideration, in effect the question is, whether the transaction was one of bargain or of gift merely."

In *Bayspoole* v. *Collins* L.R. 6 Ch. App. 228 the bill was filed by a puisne incumbrancer, who sought a declaration that a certain post-nuptial settlement was a voluntary settlement of the premises comprised therein, and was accordingly superseded by the plaintiff's mortgage, executed subsequent thereto, so far as was required to give the plaintiff the full benefit of his security. The exeuction of the settlement was induced by the promise of an advance of £150, secured by promissory note, to pay the interest due on an existing mortgage. Lord Hatherley C., there said (at p. 232):–"I do not think anything could be more unsatisfactory than what we find to be the state of the law under which a person, with full and distinct knowledge of a voluntary settlement, is able at any time to overthrow it. It is quite established that, although a settlor cannot get rid of such a settlement directly, he can do so indirectly by making a mortgage of the property to somebody else for the purpose of being able to destroy the settlement." And he continues:–"It is not for me to say whether the mode by which the Court has attempted to remedy some of the evils of this state of the law, namely, by holding that a small and inadequate consideration is sufficient to support such a settlement under the statute of Elizabeth, has diminsished the extent of the mischief. But so it is, that a very small consideration is admitted to be sufficient." And Lord Hatherley accordingly held that the advance of the £150 was sufficient consideration to support the settlement. In *Rosher* v. *Williams* L.R. 20 Eq. 210 the decision was the other way, the Court there holding that the particular covenant which was relied upon as raising a consideration was valueless; but Malins V.-C. fully recognizes what he describes as the qualification of the old rule of the Court. He says (at p.218):–"I quite agree that *Townend* v. *Toker* L.R. 1 Ch. App. 446 is a very material authority; and I think the fair result of them all [the modern decisions] may be thus stated: that if upon the occasion of executing that which is called a voluntary settlement, that is, a deed which is not induced by marriage or any marriage considerations, or the actual sale of property; if between a father and son, husband and wife, or parent and child, in any way whatever, an instrument is executed which ordinarily is called a voluntary settlement, and it turns out that, instead of being purely voluntary, any consideration whatever was paid or given, or any benefit rendered to the grantor, even such as an agreement to relieve the grantor from the immediate payment of a debt, as in *Bayspoole* v. *Collins* L.R. 6 Ch. App. 228, the Court will anxiously lay hold of any circumstances constituting a consideration moving from the grantee to the grantor, to take a case out of the category of voluntary settlements." In *Mullins* v. *Guilfoyle* 2 L.R. Ir. 95 Palles C.B. (at p. 108) points out that the decision in *Rosher* v. *Williams* L.R. 20 Eq. 210 only amounted to this, "that a nominal consideration is insufficient to support a deed under" the 27th Eliz.

On these authorities, having regard to the general character of the deed, I am of opinion that the covenant by Christopher to pay the sums charged in favour of the daughters is sufficient consideration to take this deed out of the class of voluntary deeds.

The question whether or not there was actual fraud is a question of fact, to be determined from a consideration of the circumstances in which the deed was executed. "That question" – whether the impeached deed was or was not void under the statute of Elizabeth – "depends upon the bona fides of the transaction, to be judged of on all the circumstances of the case. It is a question to be decided by us as a jury would decide it:" per Turner L.J. in *Lloyd* v. *Attwood; Attwood* v. *Lloyd* 3 De G. & J. 614, at p. 654.

In this case I am of opinion that there was no fraud. In *Mullins* v. *Guilfoyle* 2 L.R. Ir. 95, at p. 109, Palles C.B. says: "I can understand cases in which the relation of the parties as husband and wife or parent and child or the nature of the transaction such, for instance, as a family arrangements, will be sufficient to uphold a transaction based upon a consideration which, although valuable, is so inadequate that it might, under other circumstances, have raised an inference of fraud." I think this is a case to which this statement applies. This would dispose of the case, even if the Act of 1893 had never been passed.

Even if the deed were a voluntary deed, I am of opinion that it was "in fact made bona fide and without any fraudulent intent" within the meaning of the Act of 1893, and that therefore it should not "be deemed fraudulent or covinous within the meaning of the 27 Eliz. by reason of any subsequent purchase for value." The purchaser's remedy is either under that Act or at common law. A purchaser has no right to set aside a previous conveyance by the vendor on the ground that it was made with intent to defeat the vendor's creditors. He is not a creditor; he only claims throught the vendor, and the previous conveyance is good against the vendor. I do not think that the result of the Act of 1893 is to giye a subsequent purchaser a right to set aside a deed under the provisions of the 13th Eliz. c. 5. A deed can only be set aside under that Act so far as it defeats the creditors and for their benefit. Save to that extent the deed is good, and the grantee retains the property, save so far as is necessary to give effect to the claim of the grantor's creditors.

A subsequent purchaser gets no benefit where a deed is declared void as against creditors. The purchaser's remedy must, therefore, be at common law or under the statute of 27 Eliz. Mr. Henry really contends that the effect of the legislation is that a subsequent purchaser can set aside a voluntary deed on the ground that it was made with the intent to defeat creditors, and that the deed is set aside, not only so far as it defeats or delays creditors, but for all purposes. The Act of 1893 never intended such a fantastic result as to give a purchaser the right to set aside a deed as a fraud on creditors, and at the same time to allow him to retain the property and give the creditors nothing.

Lastly, even assuming that a deed made with intent to defeat creditors would not be within the protection of the Act of 1893, I am of opinion that the Carson matter does not bring this deed within the 13th of Eliz, c5. In my opinion the deed in this case was "in fact made bona fide and without any fraudulent intent" to defeat either purchasers or creditors. Even if it was within that Act as judicially interpreted it would be "in fact made without any fraudulent intent" within the meaning of the Act of 1893, and therefore within the protection of the latter Act.

Molony L.J.:

This action was brought by the plaintiffs to raise a sum of £750, which, by an indenture of settlement, dated the 11th day of October, 1888, and made between John Moore of the first part, Joseph Kelly and Christopher Moore of the second part, and the said Christopher Moore of the third part, was charged upon certain lands known as Finnea in the Co. Westmeath. The original defendants, Joseph Kelly and Christopher Moore, were sued as trustees of the said indenture of settlement, and subsequently Julia Moore and Rose Moore were joined as defendants, because they claimed to be interested in the lands under an indenture of settlement, date the 14th day of September, 1901; and James Lavallin was also joined as a defendant, to represent the unborn issue (if any) of the said Christopher Moore and Julia Moore.

By the said indenture of the 11th October, 1888, the said John Moore charged the premises with the sum of £150 for his eldest daughter, and with the sum of £100 for each of six other children, said sums amounting in all to £750. There is some evidence that at the time of the execution of this deed John Moore was indebted to a man named Carson in a considerable sum, and it was suggested that the deed was simply intended as a cover against Carson's debt. On the other hand, Rose Moore, the widow of John Moore, states that it was she who told him to get the deed, or to make a will, as he was delicate, and that he then brought the deed in question back from Dublin, and same was subsequently registered. I am not satisfied on the evidence that the deed in question was made for the purpose of preventing Carson from recovering his debt, and there is no evidence of any other debt. Carson, although he took a bond for payment of his debt by instalments several years later, never impeached the deed, and even if the deed could have been set aside as against him, it is not open to the defendants to rely on the protection given to a creditor under the statute 10 Chas. 1, Sess. 2, c. 3.

Christopher Moore, in 1902, married Julia White, who had a fortune of £300, and on the occasion of the marriage a settlement was executed, dated 14th September, 1901, under which John Moore assigned the lands to Christopher Moore and Julia White, subject (inter alia) to the payment of an annuity of £12 to the said John Moore and Rose Moore, and to certain covenants in reference to their support. At the time of the execution of the settlement all the children of John Moore – ten in number – were of age. They had been well educated, and had either entered the Church or been otherwise provided for, and, with the exception of Mary Moore and Anne Moore, had ceased to live on the lands. The plaintiffs in the present action seek to have their charges raised, and the defendants, Christopher Moore and Julia Moore, have both defended, and in particular Julia Moore has pleaded that she is a purchaser for value of the lands comprised in the settlement of the 14th September, 1901, without notice of any of the alleged charges, and that consequently she is entitled to priority over them. She contended that the deed of 11th October, 1888, is fraudulent within the meaning of 27 Eliz. c. 4 (10 Chas. 1, Sess. 2, c. 3, Ireland). It appears clear from the correspondence, however, and from the recitals in the deed of 1901 that all the parties to the settlement were aware of the prior voluntary deed, and that they also believed that no claim would be made under it, as the children had received an equivalent to its benefits in the amounts which had been expended on their maintenance, education, and settlement in life.

The object of the statute of Elizabeth was to make fraudulent conveyances void as against subsequent purchasers, and by a series of judicial decisions voluntary conveyances were deemed fraudulent within the meaning of the statute. As was laid down in *Doe d., Newman* v. *Rusham* 17 Q. B. 723, 724: "The principle on which voluntary conveyances have been held uniformly to be fraudulent and void as against subsequent purchasers appears to be, that, by selling the property for a valuable consideration, the seller so entirely repudiates the former voluntary conveyance, and shows his intention to sell, as that it shall be taken conclusively, against him and the person to whom he conveyed, that such intention existed when he made the conveyance, and that it was made in order to defeat the purchaser. Such deeds have been held fraudulent and void as against such purchasers, even when they have had notice of them: *Doe d., Otley* v. *Manning*" 9 East, 59.

Under this Act when it was once shown that the conveyance was voluntary nothing further was necessary; but a change was made by the Voluntary Conveyances Act, 1893, which enacts (sect. 2) as follows:– "No voluntary conveyance of any lands, tenements, or hereditaments, whether made before or after the passing of this Act, if in fact made bona fide and without any fraudulent intent, shall hereafter be deemed fraudulent or covinous within the meaning of the Act 27 Eliz. c. 4, by reason of any subsequent purchase for value, or be defeated under any of the provisions of the said Act by a conveyance made upon any such purchase, any rule of law notwithstanding."

In the *National Bank* v. *Behan* [1913] 1 I.R. 512 the Master of the Rolls held that the onus of proving that a voluntary conveyance was made bona fide and without fraudulent intent, so as to bring it within the protection of sect. 2 of the Voluntary Conveyances Act, 1893, lies on the party seeking to uphold such voluntary conveyance. This only means, however, that a person seeking to uphold a voluntary conveyance must give some evidence from which a court could prima facie infer that the transaction was bona fide. Assuming in favour of the defendants without formally deciding that the onus is as stated by the Master of the Rolls, I think the evidence given by Rose Moore and the nature of the transaction itself was sufficient to discharge that onus and entitled the Master of the Rolls to find in favour of the plaintiffs.

Notes and Questions

The Court expressly avoided overruling *National Bank Ltd* v. *Behan* [1913] 1 I.R. 512. Do you think they should have overruled O'Connor M.R.? See *Irish Land Law,* para. 9.078.

4. *Settlements by Bankrupts*

RE McCROHAN
(1893) 31 L.R. Ir. 225 (Bankruptcy Court)

The facts are set out in the judgment.

Miller, J.:

This matter has come before me upon charge and discharge, and the charge requires me, in substance, to declare that the bankrupt, who was, previous to and at the time of his marriage, engaged as a trader in carrying on the business of a wine and spirit merchange and general grocer at Killarney, and by a marriage settlement executed upon that occasion so far back as the 25th July, 1883, which reserved to the bankrupt himself (as regarded the facts disclosed in this matter) the full entire and absolute personal control over his whole property and business of every kind which he continued to exercise, under the provision of that settlement, up to the date of the adjunction in this matter, so late as the 10th May, 1892, effectually charged not only the premises in which he had thus carried on his trading business and any chattels thereon at the date of such settlement which were thereby assigned, but also his after acquired property of every kind whatsoever, to which he was in any manner entitled at the date of his adjudication, with the payment of a principal sum of £600 advanced to the bankrupt as the marriage portion of his wife, so far back as that year 1883, notwithstanding the provisions of the 52nd section of the Bankruptcy (Ireland) Amendment Act, 1872, as against the assignees under the adjudication in this matter.

That charge was filed on the 6th July, 1892, by the surviving trustee under that marriage settlement of the 25th July, 1883, above referred to (alone), which after setting forth the title under which the premises in Main-street, Killarney, in which the bankrupt had carried on his business up to the time of his marriage were held, put forward in very full detail the terms and provisions of the marriage settlement of 1883, as the foundation of his claim as set forth by it; and the relief, as sought by that charge which followed is, that the sum of £600 might be declared well charged on the house and premises, and on the licence thereof, and on all the stock-in-trade, fixtures, furniture, goods, chattels, and effects, and all other the personal property of or belonging to the bankrupt at the time of his bankruptcy, and on debts due and owing to him at said date; and that charge then went on to apply for directions as therein set forth, which were consequential upon the relief as thus sought.

The discharge to that charge was filed by the assignees in this matter, on the 8th July, 1892, and they do not appear to have therein seriously disputed the claim as put forward by the charge in respect of the house and premises in Main-street, Killarney, in which the bankrupt had carried on his business, or to the licence attached thereto, or to such fixtures as properly belonged thereto as the bankrupt's fixtures, which have been already very laudably diposed of and realized under a consent order for that purpose, as duly sanctioned by this Court for the benefit of the parties who might thereafter be declared to be entitled thereto; but the assignees by that discharge repudiate altogether the claim as put forward by that charge, so far as it seeks that any residue of that sum of £600, purporting or alleged to be charged thereon which might remain after the application of the proceeds of the premises, &c., in Main-street, Killarney, as already mentioned, and properly applicable towards the payment of that sum of £600 (which are admitteldy insufficient for that purpose), so far as the same would extend, formed any charge upon, or was payable out of the after-acquired personal property (or money) of which the bankrupt was possessed at the time of his bankruptcy, in the manner as set forth in their said discharge, as against them as such assignees, and thus the issue is substantially raised between the parties. It must here be observed at the outset that scarcely any questions have engaged more attention or have been the subject-matter of more legislation as well as of judicial investigation and decision in comparatively modern times than the relative rights or claims as between holders of bills of sale, in which character the said settlement of the year 1883, purported (apparently by the copy of it sent to me) to have been registered, and assigneees in bankruptcy in respect of the personal property of their respective debtors from the period (as I may state) of the earliest Act relating to bills of sale, and as a natural consequence very numerous authorities, including even some lengthened utterances of my own, have been quoted and referred to during the argument in this case, all of which I have again carefully read over; but as many of those cases contain careful reviews of all the previous authorities and Acts of Parliament up to their respective dates, and the question as presented to me upon the facts of this case is, in my opinion, for the most part very different, and much more narrow in its nature, I will not enter upon any such detailed review of the authorities referred to, but will keep within them.

It must further be observed in reference to the facts of this case that it would be a very startling and alarming statement to make that the bankrupt in this matter, as a trader, had been enabled for a period closely bordering upon nine years (which might as likely have been twenty years) by means of any instrument, whether settlement or otherwise, known to or within the compass of the law, to exhibit and hold himself out to the general public as the absolute owner, who apparently carried on an extensive trading business in the house in which he resided, and had in the course, as well as by means of, such trading during a period of nine years obtained on credit those very goods which had been found upon the premises of the bankrupt at the date of his bankruptcy, then remaining unpaid for, or had constituted the very foundation of and consideration for the very debts which were owing to that bankrupt at the date of his bankruptcy, and yet that the sole surviving trustee under that settlement by the bankrupt trader, executed nine years previously, through whose aid or co-operation such a state of things had been thus brought about, should, notwithstanding, sweep away even from merchants, who had supplied to such an apparently trustworthy trader such their goods on credit, not only the entire proceeds of those merchants' goods that remained (at that time), but also the very debts which had arisen from and been created by means of the disposal by the bankrupt of portions of those merchants' goods to the debtors to the bankrupt, as his (the bankrupt's) customers who had not paid the bankrupt for such their goods at the date of his bankruptcy.

It will now be seen how far any of the preliminary observations as above set forth are justifiec or supported by the facts of the case now before this Court, which, if sustainable in the present state of the law would seem calculated to bring about results inconsistent with and repugnant to all the principles of sound bankruptcy legislation which has been rightly designed for the general protection of fair dealing as well as the due administration of debtor's estate, and would necessarily exhibit a very grave injustice loudly calling for a speedy remedy. The bankrupt in this matter was adjudged a bankrupt in manner as hereinafter stated, on the 10th May, 1892, and thereupon, by the 267th section of the 20 & 21 Vict. c. 60 (*i.e.,* in the year 1857), being the earliest Act under which this Court was constituted, all his, the bankrupt's personal estate and effects, present and future, wheresoever the same might be, and all property which he might purchase, and all debts due or to be due to him, became absolutely vested in the assignees for the time being, for the benefit of his creditors, and the assignees had thereby absolute power to recover the same in their own names.

In antagonism to the powers and rights of assignees in bankruptcy, as thus declared, Acts of Parliament were from time to time, subsequently to that year 1857, passed in relation to bills of sale which were properly conversant with and applicable to personal estate alone; and during the same period various decisions were from time to time pronounced by different Courts, and in various directions, relating to the manner and extent of, and as regarded, charges as they properly afected such personal estate; and it thus became necessary as regarded assignees in bankruptcy, in protection of their proper powers and rights as well as of the rights of the creditors whom they represented under that Act of 1857, to pass an Amended Act known as "the Bankruptcy (Ireland) Amendment Act, 1872, which followed an enactment in that behalf in England, similar in substance, and these respective Acts would plainly appear to have been thus severally passed in the true and better interests of fair dealing and of trade, and accordingly it was enacted by the 52nd section of that Act of 1872, that any settlement of property made by a trader not being a settlement of three kinds – 1st, before and in consideration of marriage; 2nd, in favour of a purchaser or incumbrancer in good faith and for valuable consideration; and 3rd, on or for the wife or children of the settlor of property which had accrued to the settlor after marriage in right of his wife; should, if the settlor become bankrupt within two years after the date of such settlement, be void as against the assignees of such bankrupt under the said Act or this Act, and should, if the settlor became bankrupt at any subsequent time within ten years after the date of such settlement, unless the parties claiming under such settlement could prove that the settlor was, at the time of making such settlement, able to pay all his debts without the aid of the property comprised in such settlement, be void.

Thus far that 52nd section recognized the validity as against assignees in bankruptcy of settlements made before and in consideration of marriage, as well as when such settlements were made in good faith, and for valuable consideration, and also as regarded a class of settlement in respect of any property which might accrue to the settlor in right of his wife (as to the existence of which last mentioned property there has not been any proof whatever given in this matter): and then that same 52nd section contains the most specific and conclusive provision in terms as follows:– Any covenant or contract made by a trader in consideration of marriage for the future settlement upon or for his wife or children of any money or property wherein he had not at the date of his marriage any estate or interest, whether vested or contingent, in possession or remainder, and not being property of or in right of his wife, shall, upon his becoming bankrupt before such property or money has been actually transferred or paid pursuant to such contract or covenant, be void against his assignees under the said Act or that Act.

The wisdom of man, with all the aid of previous experience up to that time, could scarcely have better covered all the grounds for complaint, regarded the just claims of rights on the part of assignees in bankruptcy, or have produced a better defined and at the same time comprehensive statement than is contained in that concluding portion of that 52nd section in that behalf, while the earlier portion of that section indicated in the clearest manner what settlements by a trader of property would prevail against his assignees in the event of such a settlor becoming bankrupt, and, on the other hand, what settlements by a trader of such could not stand or be maintained against such his assignees in bankruptcy, and I would especially direct attention to the fact that in that concluding provision as lastly set forth in that section it is expressly declared to be an indispensible requisite for the maintenance of any such settlements as might fall within that section that the property or money of such a trader should have been actually transferred to the claimants thereof, and the debts due to such a trader paid, before he became bankrupt, and that no stronger expression could have been used for the purpose of conveying that meaning than the words "actually transferred or paid" such as have been used therein.

Several years subsequently to the passing of that Act of 1872, the marriage settlement of the bankrupt, to which brief reference has been already made, and upon which alone the claim of the chargeant as the surviving trustee thereunder is based, was executed, which contains as the only recitals some particulars of the lease under which the said premises of the bankrupt, situated in Main-street, Killarney, were held, and that in consideration of the then intended marriage, and of the sum of £600 as the marriage portion paid to the bankrupt, he agreed to assign, and thereby afterwards purported to have assigned, over to the trustees thereof those same premises in Main-street, together with all other the property of the bankrupt of every description that might have been acquired after the date of such settlement until the sum of £600 thereinafter mentioned should have been raised, and the very first trust thereby declared in respect of all the property purported to be comprised in or assigned by that settlement was for the said bankrupt himself until he should die or commit an act of bankruptcy, or be adjudged a bankrupt, or as an insolvent debtor should obtain the benefit of some Act or Acts of Paliament for the relief of insolvent debtors. That settlement then purports thereby to authorize the trustees thereunder upon the happening of any of the said events as thus particularized, without any notice to the bankrupt, by sale or mortgage or any other of the ways and means of realizing properties or securities, to raise, levy, and realize out of the said property, chattels, and premises thereby assigned the said sum of £600; and it was thereby declared that upon the happening of any of those events it should be lawful for the trustees to enter upon the premises and chattels thereby assigned, and to seize the same in manner as therein until they should have received the said sum of £600 in manner as therein.

I must here observe that it is not necessary for me to discuss any such question as what would have been the effect of that settlement if the bankrupt had died instead of being adjudged a bankrupt, as in the former event of the death of the bankrupt different considerations would have been presented, and the bankrupt is still alive. That settlement then concludes with a declaration as follows:– "That all the future property hereinbefore expressed to be assigned shall be subject to the trusts of these presents, and to the powers, covenants, and provisions, hereinbefore contained, although the same or any part thereof may not be capable of passing at law by the assignment hereinbefore contained; and the expression the chattels hereby assigned or expressed so to be' used in these presents shall in all cases extend to such future property." I have set forth at length that concluding paragraph of that settlement of 1883, inasmuch as it has been strongly relied upon as adding force to the previous provision in that settlement as regarded the future acquired property of the bankrupt, solely for the purpose of stating explicitly that I cannot attach or give any such effect to that concluding paragraph in respect of the question and consideration as presented to me for decision in this matter.

This is the proper time for stating plainly that no such settlement as that executed in 1883 by the bankrupt as a trader could have conferred any title at law or (as may be better termed) legal title upon the trustees thereunder to the after-acquired property or money as purported to be comprized therein and assigned thereby, and still further that no such settlement could have conferred any other or higher title upon such trustees in respect of any such after-acquired property or money than a contract in equity, or it might be a covenant by and on the part of the bankrupt, that upon the happening of any of the events as stated in that settlement in that behalf (which was in this matter the adjudication of the bankrupt), he, the bankrupt in the character of and purporting to be the owner and assignor thereof, would transfer to the trustees, as the assignees thereof under such settlement, the interest of the bankrupt, such as it then might be, in and to the possession of such after-acquired property, including (as it must) property of merchants as received by the bankrupt in the course of his trading still unpaid for, or money arising from or produced by debts (at that time) payable or accruing to the bankrupt in the course of his trading, to go in satisfaction to that extent of such contract or covenant under that settlement.

This brings me to the evidence which has been offered in support of that charge by the surviving trustee under that settlement which consists in the first instance of the production of that settlement of 1883, such as I have briefly described it and next an affidavit by the chargeant himself, made no so lately as the 16th July, 1892, being eight days after the filing of the discharge by the assignees, by which he the chargeant neither, on the one hand, alleged that he had himself taken, or had authorized any other person on his behalf to take, possession of such the after-acquired property or debts of the bankrupt, or of any portion thereof, at any time and it further appears from that same affidavit that he, the chargeant, does not thereby deny that he, the chargeant, had left all such after-acquired property and debts in the order and disposition of the bankrupt, subsequently as well as previously to his adjudication, although the assignees had then previously by their discharge so plainly challenged and denied any such alleged title of, or as existing in, the chargeant to any such after-acquired property or debts, as against them as such assignees, and that such affidavit of the chargeant is altogether silent in those respects.

On the other hand, affidavits have been severally filed by the assignees and by the bankrupt himself, by which they have severally testified to the fact that the bankrupt had remained in the absolute ownership and possession of all such after-acquired property and debts apparently up to the time of the adjudication, and subsequently up to the time when he, the bankrupt, was dispossessed by the assignees in this matter.

It must have been under circumstances and upon facts such as I shall show to be presented in this matter that the Legislature rightly, and with a true spirit of equity (in order to guard to some extent at least against a glaring injustice being effected), declared in substance by that 52nd section already mentioned so far as it is here necessary to refer to it in general terms:– That unless there had been not alone an actual transfer of the after-acquired property referred to in that section, which under the circumstances of this matter must have been obtained by the bankrupt under the delusive appearance of being a solvent trader, but also in like manner that all such debts as had been thus subsequently become payable to the bankrupt, had been actually paid at the time of the adjudication of the bankrupt, the assignees in bankruptcy alone in that behalf, as trustees for the general creditors of the bankrupt, had the proper title to such after-acquired property, which under the circumstances of this case, as I shall also presently show, must have been for the most part supplied by such general creditors, and with whom also, for the most part, the debts also thus subsequently becoming similarly payable had been incurred and then remained unpaid, for the benefit of such general creditors, amongst whom may eventually be included in this matter those deriving under such prior settlement if they established any proof of debt therein, who would in that event become entitled to an equal distributive share of such after-acquired property with the other creditors whom the assingees represent.

The bankrupt had originally filed a petition for arrangement in this Court on the 9th April, 1892, and filed his statement of affairs therein on the 25th April, 1892 (which he duly verified on the 19th May, 1892), and in that statement he returned his unsecured creditors at no less a sum than about £2400, exclusive of the sum as claimed by the chargeant in respect of the £600, the marriage portion of the wife of the bankrupt, and to meet those entire liabilities, amounting to £3107 7*s.* 2*d.*; he, the bankrupt, thereby only estimated his stock-in-trade and chattels at £63 1*s.* 10*d,* while he thereby returned the debts owing to him at the date of his adjudication as amounting to £1011 3*s.* 3*d.,* estimating that they would produce no more than £410, and he thereby estimated his freehold and leasehold estates as being altogether of no greater value than £50, as per Schedule H annexed to or embodied in that statement, and when that Schedule H is referred to, he therein estimated the very same licensed house and premises in Main-street, Killarney, which was the only real property of the bankrupt purported to have been expressly transferred by the settlement of 1883, and thereby vested in the trustees thereunder by way of the consideration for the marriage portion of £600 by the wife of the bankrupt in that respect, as being of no value whatever; and he thereby introduced for the first time his shop in New-street, Killarney, and estimated it as not being of any value, and he the bankrupt then further introduced and estimated in Schedule H certain stores and two cottages situated in Well Lane, Killarney, as being held by him under a promise of a lease for sixty-two years as being of the value of £50, but he does not state therein any further particulars in relation to either of such last mentioned premises, except that it was to be at a rent of £8 10*s.* annually, or return any other assets.

On the other hand, a still further inspection of that statement of affairs such as had been thus verified by the bankrupt, exhibits at once (as might have been expected) the fact that by far the largest proportion of the debts due by the bankrupt to his creditors (exclusive of the marriage portion of £600 already referred to), as well as of the debts due and owing to the bankrupt by his debtors to him at the date of his adjudication, had been for the most part contracted very recently, and even so lately as the years 1891 and 1892; and when the bankrupt, relying upon such a statement in substance of his affairs made an offer of but 1*s.* in the £, as a composition for his unsecured creditors upon the amount of such their respective debts, that arrangement-matter was forthwith turned into bankruptcy, and thenceforth formed this present matter in bankruptcy.

If the facts which next follow alone should be looked at and taken into consideration, namely, that the bankrupt himself ony estimated in such his statement of affairs, his place of business, and premises in Main-street, Killarney (which was the only real property actually assigned by the settlement of 1883) as being of no value whatever in the year 1892, and that the same property when sold afterwards in the same year 1892, in this matter only produced the gross sum of £50, while the only means available for estimating the value of the stock-in-trade and furniture actually assigned by the settlement of 1883 are that the stock-in-trade and furniture of the bankrupt found at the date of his adjudication were sold in this matter, for the sum of only £60, being severally coupled with the elaborate nature of the settlement of 1883, no other conclusion could be arrived at under the circumstances disclosed in this matter, than that a case which bore a close resemblance to an attempt at a fraud throughout, against all subsequent creditors who might be induced to give credit to the bankrupt owing to or upon his trading reputation cloaked (as it must here be deemed to be) by the settlement of 1883, had been thereby presented to this Court, which can only at this late period be frustrated to some partial extent by means of that very salutary provision in that 52nd section as already referred to.

At the same time it must be observed that if such contrivances as are indicated by the settlement of 1883 could have led to the full accomplishment of the apparent object of the parties to it, such a result, under the circumstances of this case, could only be fairly regarded as being antagonistic to all proper bankruptcy administration, inasmuch as by that settlement of 1883 the bankrupt was enabled to retain the full possession and control of that property (of which he had by the same settlement previously purported to have altogether divested himself) in the most ample manner; and he, the bankrupt, was thereby armed with a power of effecting widespread mischief, as appears by the results, in holding himself out and exhibiting himself to the community as an apparently absolute owner of such property and as a solvent trader, by means of which he acquired a ready opportunity for preying upon the public for a full period of nine years, at the end of which period the whole proceeds of all such property as purported to have been embraced by that settlement of 1883 would not, according to the valuation of the bankrupt himself, have amounted to more in the whole than a gross sum of £528 1*s.* 6*d.*, which sum, if realized and applicable to such a purpose, would not be sufficient even for the payment of the sum as claimed by the chargeant alone under such settlement of 1883.

In order the better to understand with what matters and figures this Court has in reality to deal, it may be well here to state that it appears from a report of the official assignee of so late a date as the 16th December, 1892, that the stock-in-trade and furniture of the bankrupt at the date of his adjudication, which was then forthcoming, was sold by auction subsequently to that adjudication for a gross sum of £60 7*s.* 7*d*; also that the dwelling-house, shop, and premises in Main-street, Killarney, as already referred to, were likewise sold since that adjudication for a gross sum of £50.

It will thus be seen that the 52nd section of the Bankruptcy Amendment Act of 1872 is in perfect harmony in its spirit and intention with the 313th section of the Bankruptcy (Ireland) Act of 1857, commonly known as "the order and disposition clause"; and extends in a very essential particular the protection for general creditors such as had been designed by that 313th section against any injury being done to them by the apparent reputation of ownership, which might be acquired by persons claiming or deriving through instruments of which such creditors had no previous notice whatever; and also in direct confirmation of the 267th section of that same Act of 1857, conferring such an absolute and complete title as it does upon asssignees in bankruptcy as already stated, even to the extent of suing for debts in their own names. And as regards the assignment of debts as purported to have been made by that settlement of 1883, which would appear to have been separately referred to in the charge, this special observation must be made apart from the operation of the 52nd section as referred to, namely, that all such debts as were due at the time of the adjudication appear also to have been incurred subsequent to the date of the settlement of 1883; and that it does not appear that any power was thereby (in terms) conferred upon the trustees thereunder enabling them to sue in the name of the bankrupt for the recovery of any of such debts such as was possessed by the assignees in this matter under the 267th section of the Act of 1857; and further, that no such stamp as would have been required for such a purpose was ever placed upon that settlement of 1883, and therefore it would be difficult to discover upon what possible ground the trustees under that settlement could rest or seek to establish their pretension or claim as against the assignees to any of such debts as were due and owing to the bankrupt and remained still unpaid at the date of the adjudication of the bankrupt, when it does not anywhere appear in evidence that any notice whatever was given even of the existence of such settlement of 1883 on the part of the trustees thereunder to any of those specific debtors, by whom any of such debts were owing to the bankrupt, either prior or subsequent to the date of the adjudication of the bankrupt.

It is only necessary now to mention that this Court has been placed under some difficulty as to pronouncing a complete judgment in this matter, from the fact that there does not appear from the copy of the settlement of 1883 placed before it, as purporting to have been a bill of sale, that there ever had been any schedule of the stock-in-trade or furniture purporting to have been directly assigned to the trustees thereunder, at any time annexed to that settlement of 1883, and that there is therefore at this time no means of ascertaining with precision whether or not stock-in-trade or furniture as lately sold in this matter, as above stated, consisted of any portion of the stock-in-trade or furniture which belonged to the bankrupt at the date of the settlement of 1883, and had been included in it; and also, further, by reason of no evidence whatever having been offered, and not even any mention made either in respect of the shop in New-street or as to the stores and two cottages of the bankrupt severally situated in Killarney, and described in Schedule H in the statement of affairs as filed as aforesaid by the bankrupt on the 25th April, 1892, other than is set forth in that Schedule H. However, I will for the purpose of disposing of this case, as it is now before this Court, by reason of the insignificant amount of the sum realized by the sale of the furniture and stock-in-trade in this matter, as far as it is in my power, assume without further inquiry, save as hereinafter mentioned, on the one hand, that the furniture as seized under the adjudication and subsequently sold in this matter, as already stated, was the same furniture which had belonged to the bankrupt at the date of the settlement of 1883, and had been asssigned by it; and, on the other hand, I will for the same reason assume that the stock-in-trade, as a whole, as likewise seized under the adjudication, and similarly sold along with the furniture, had been so acquired by the bankrupt after the date of the settlement of 1883, and I will leave any question as to those specific articles of furniture and stock-in-trade open for further direction (if any), giving liberty to either party to take such steps as they may be advised for obtaining further inquiry on their behalf in those respects or either of them before or up to the final audit in this matter.

I shall therefore declare that the chargeant is entitled to the proceeds of the premises in Main-street, Killarney, with the fixtures therein, such as properly belonged to the bankrupt, as the tenant thereof, and also to the proceeds of any chattels belonging to the bankrupt which had been on the premises in Main-street at the date of the settlement of 1883, and were subsequently sold in this matter; but I will declare my opinion that the 52nd section of the Act of 1872 was designed and framed for the very purpose of affording protection to creditors against the injustice which would otherwise be caused by such a state of facts as have been presented to this Court in this matter, to the extent as specific in that 52nd section; and that, accordingly, the chargeant has not any claim whatever against the assignees in this matter to any portion of the property or money of the bankrupt which had been acquired by him after the date of the settlement of 1883, and belonging to the bankrupt at the date of his adjudication, and which had not been at the date of the adjudication actually transferred or paid; and, further, that the chargeant had not any claim as against the assignees to any such debts which had accrued due and became payable to the bankrupt after the date of the settlement of 1883, and which were due and owing to the bankrupt, and had not been paid at the date of the adjudication, save such claims (if any) as the chargeant may be able to establish against the proceeds of any such after-acquired property, money, or debts, under or by means of the reservation hereinafter contained in respect of any claim by way of proof of debt that may be put forward on the part of the chargeant.

I will reserve to the chargeant liberty, if necessary, to put forward in this matter a claim by way of proof of debt in the usual manner, without any declaration of right in that respect here, for any balance that may remain unpaid to him after the application of the funds to which he is hereby declared entitled, if so advised, against the general funds in this matter. I direct the proper officer to take all necessary accounts, and reserve all further directions. The chargeant must have his costs incurred in his charge and discharge, along with his demand, out of the trust funds to which he is hereby declared entitled, when taxed; and the assignees must have their costs out of the funds in this matter; and I may mention here the ground for my direction as to costs, namely, that although the chargeant might have been entitled if he had confined his charge to his claim for the premises and chattels actually assigned by the settlement of 1883 to the costs of an undefended charge out of the bankrupt's estate, as one of the incidents occasioned by the bankruptcy; and it must be assumed from the nature of the discharge, as filed by the assignees, that there would not have been in such case any discharge at all filed; yet when the chargeant put forward the still larger claim as against the assignees, extending in fact to all the after-acquired property, which he had failed to sustain, the estate has been put to costs fully equivalent to the costs of an undefended charge; and I will, in order to stop expense where the assets are so small, set off such costs against each other as the most expedient course which I can adopt, in preference to giving specific declaration and direction in respect of each class of costs. I have pronounced the above judgment as between the parties on the record before me, reserving all questions that may arise upon any application hereafter for payment from time to time of any moneys then standing to the credit of this matter.

Note

See further, *Irish Land Law,* paras. 9.079–80.

Chapter 14

DISCRETIONARY AND REVOCABLE TRUSTS

These are special kinds of trusts which are not as commonly used in Ireland as they are in other jurisdictions, see *Irish Land Law*, para. 9.081 *et seq.*

GRAY V. GRAY

(1862) 13 Ir. Ch. R. 404 (Rolls Court)

A testator bequeathed to his two sons all his property, real and personal, to have and to hold the same in the most absolute manner, and he declared it to be his will and intention that his sons should, at their discretion, and according to their own judgment, allocate to the other members of his family, being his lawfully begotten children, such portions of the said property and goods, be the same more or less, as to them should seem fit and suitable; and he appointed his said sons his executors.

Smith M.R.:

A motion has been made in this case, on the part of George Gray, and William Rutledge and Elizabeth his wife, by way of appeal from the order of W. Brooke, Esq., the Master in this case, dated the 18th of February, and filed the 2nd of May 1862.

The principal facts are stated in my judgment on a former appeal in this cause – *Gray* v. *Gray* 11 Ir. Chan. Rep. 218. The suit is for the administration of the estate of John Gray deceased. The former appeal was from the portion of the decretal order of Master Brooke, of the 27th of April 1860, which was in these words:- "Having regard to the statements in the petition in this matter set forth, respecting the said testator's (John Gray's) intentions, and also by the expressions of the will itself, declare that a trust has been created, of which the trustees are the petitioner John Gray, and his brother Moses Wilson Gray; and the objects of the trust are, the other children of the testator, both real and personal." I affirmed the decision of the Master, for the reasons stated in my judgment 11 *Irish Chancery Reports,* p. 219. The trust so vested in the petitioner and Moses Wilson Gray was a discretionary trust.

In the case of *Hart* v. *Tribe* 18 Beav. 217, Sir John Romilly stated:- "There is no question but that this Court sometimes will execute a trust, where a fund is originally given to a trustee to be disposed of in favour of certain objects, according to his judgment and discretion; but as this Court cannot exercise any discretion in the matter, it performs the trust by dividing the fund equally amongst all the objects of the trust. Where however a discretion is reposed in a person by the testator, the Court does not interfere with that discretion, but allows it to be exercised by that person, although it will prevent a capricious and improper exercise of the discretion." *In re Coe's Trusts* 4 K. & J. 199 is also an authority on the subject.

A suit being instituted by trustees does not prevent their exercising their discretion, with the sanction of the Court: *Sillibourne* v. *Newport* 1 K. & J. 602. There are other cases, establishing the law to be as laid down by Sir J. Romilly, in *Hart* v. *Tribe*; *Lord St. Leonards on Powers*, ed. 1861, pp. 256 and 258; *Lewin on Trustees*, 3rd ed., pp. 538 to 544.

Moses Wilson Gray is resident in Australia, and this has created a difficulty in the exercise of the discretion vested in the petitioner and the said Moses Wilson Gray, under the will of John Gray. On the 18th of February 1862, the Master made a ruling as follows:- "Declare that the trustees are entitled to exercise their discretion with regard to the distribution of the fund; and let the trustees, on or before the 20th, lodge in my office a scheme, unverified, and signed by the solicitors for both trustees, and thereupon prepare final order in a week; and let it incorporate said scheme; and on the summons to settle, I will hear the same." Of course, as the Master directed the scheme to be lodged in his office in two days after the ruling, it was impossible to communicate with Moses Wilson Gray in Australia; and a scheme was accordingly prepared, entitled in the cause and headed thus:- "Copy draft scheme proposed by Moses Wilson Gray and petitioner John Gray, in exercise of the power and discretion vested in them, by the will of testator, for the distribution of the real and personal properties of the testator, in pursuance of the Master's rulings, dated 18th February

1862." The scheme of distribution, with a schedule annexed, then follows, and it is indorsed thus:- "The within is the document suggested in the Master's rulings of 18th of February 1862, and which, upon consultation, was agreed to between us. Dated this 20th day of February 1862." And this indorsement is signed "J.M. Cantwell, petitioner's solicitor; D. Coffey & Co., solicitors for M. Wilson Gray, co-trustees." This scheme was not authorised by Moses Wilson Gray, and is, in fact, contrary to the plan proposed by him in his letters from Australia; and it was an irregular proceeding for the solicitor for Mr. Moses Wilson Gray to sign a scheme exercising a discretionary power vested in his client, and which he had no authority whatever to sign (See Lord St. Leonards on Powers, ed. 1861, pp. 256 to 258.) The solicitor however, I suppose, considered himself bound by the ruling of the Master.

The order of the Master bears date the 18th of February 1862, and one of the documents entered upon the order is entered in these words:– "Scheme of distribution proposed by the petitioner, and the respondent Moses Wilson Gray, of the testator's properties amongst the several persons declared by the order of the 7th April 1860, to be entitled to participate therein." That was not an accurate mode of describing the scheme which was signed by the solicitor for Mr. Moses Wilson Gray, without any authority from him, and in contravention of his views.

The Master's order then declares, amongst other matters, "that the petitioner, and the respondent Moses Wilson Gray, were authorised by the testator's will to distribute the clear residue of the real and personal estate of said testator, to and amongst all or any of the other children of the testator John Gray, and the administrator of Joseph Richard Gray deceased, as they the said petitioner and respondent Moses Wilson Gray should, in their discretion, think fit; and it is further ordered that the scheme of disribution brought in by the petitioner and the respondent Moses Wilson Gray, on the 20th of February 1862, and indorsed by the Registrar, is hereby approved of by the Master:" and then follow declarations in the order, founded in part on the said scheme.

Moses Wilson Gray not having approved of or sanctioned the scheme signed by his solicitors, the order of the Master cannot be sustained, so far at least as it is founded on such scheme. Moses Wilson Gray has not deputed to his solicitor the exercise of the discretion vested in him, nor could he do so in point of law.

If the petitioner and Moses Wilson Gray cannot agree upon the mode in which the discretionary trust vested in them shall be exercised, the Master's order must be set aside, so far as is founded on such scheme.

The proper course of proceeding in such event is pointed out by the cases to which I have referred; and as the Court cannot exercise the discretion, if the petitioner and Moses Wilson Gray differ, the property will have to be divided as pointed out by Sir J. Romilly in the case of *Hart* v. *Tribe*.

It is greatly to be lamented that the small property left by the testator should have been wasted in the manner in which it has.

I sent in an order shortly after the Court rose last Sittings, but I have thought it right to state the grounds of that order for the information of the parties.

The order was as follows:-

> It is ordered by the Right Hon. the MASTER OF THE ROLLS, that the order of William Brooke Esq., the Master in this matter, be set aside and varied, so far as it recites upon the order that a scheme of distribution of the testator's properties was proposed by the petitioner John Gray, and the respondent Moses Wilson Gray; the said respondent Moses Wilson Gray, who is out of jurisdiction of the Court, not having proposed or agreed to the scheme of distribution laid before the Master, the said scheme having been signed by Messrs. D. Coffey and Company, as solicitors for the said Moses Wilson Gray, without any authority from the said Moses Wilson Gray, and the said Messrs. D. Coffey and Company having had no right to join with the petitioner in exercising the discretionary trust vested in the petitioner and the said Moses Wilson Gray. And it is further ordered, that the said order be set aside so far as it declares that the said scheme is thereby approved of by the Master, the Master having no authority of jurisdiction to exercise the discretionary trust vested in the petitioner and Moses Wilson Gray, and the said

Moses Wilson Gray not having approved of or sanctioned said scheme. And it is further ordered that the said order of the Master to be set aside, so far as it contains directions founded on the said scheme, and so far as it distributes the trust funds in accordance with the said scheme. And it is further ordered, that the rest of the motion do stand over to enable the petitioner to hold communication with the respondent Moses Wilson Gray, and to ascertain whether the petitioner and the said Moses Wilson Gray can concur in the exercise of the discretion vested in them; as in case of their not concurring, the Court should distribute the trust fund equally between the objects of the trust. And the Court doth reserve further order and the question of costs. And it is further ordered, that the sum of £10 deposited with the Registrar of this Court be returned, &c.

Note
See further, *Irish Land Law*, paras. 9.081-2.

SIMMONDS V. PALLAS
(1845) 8 Ir. Eq. R. 335; 2 Jo. & Lat. 489 (Chancery)

The plaintiff was attorney for T. and H. in two actions, brought by them against Sir H. G. and his son. P. owned £3000 to another son of Sir. H.G. The actions were comprised on the terms mentioned in the following deed. The deed recited that, for P.'s accommodation, it was agreed that T. and H. should accept £1000 in full for their demand, with the costs of the actions, and that P. should set off the £1000 against so much of the £3000 debt; and that T. and H. should accept a security for the £1000 on estates in Tipperary of another member of the G. family, who was indebted to P., and a collateral security by mortgage of P.'s own property; and that it was agreed that P. should pay T. and H.'s costs of the actions, amounting to about £400, and that the same should be secured by his bills, and collaterally by the last-mentioned mortgage: and recited mortgages of the Tipperary property for £1000 to X. in trust for T. and H., and of P.'s property for £1400 to H., and that the £1400 secured by the latter was intended as a further security for the sum secured by the mortgage to X., and for the costs of T. and H., and of getting X.'s mortgage executed; and it was declared that H. should be possessed of the £1400 on trust – first, to better secure the £1000 to X.; secondly, to secure to the plaintiff, described as "E.S., gentleman, attorney for the plaintiffs in said actions," the costs of them, £100 to be paid in three months, and the rest after taxation; and thirdly, the expense of executing X.'s mortgage. The plaintiff was not a party, and did not execute the deed. P. gave a promissory note to T. and H. for £100, which they indorsed to the plaintiff, and P. paid. The rest of the costs not being paid the plaintiff filed the bill to recover them by enforcing the trusts of the deed.

Sugden L.C.:

This case has taken an extraordinary turn, which arises partly from the character which Mr. Scully's client fills, and partly from the circumstance that Pallas has allowed the bill to be taken as confessed against him and has not appeared now. But the effect of the bill being taken as confessed is simply to admit the facts stated in the bill; and the question, therefore, still remains on the point of law, whether the plaintiff is or is not a *cestui que trust* under this deed, so as to entitle him to file this bill. The taking of the bill as confessed is an admission of the facts set out in the bill, but not that the plaintiff may sustain the bill under the state of facts.

As to the cases cited, there were two which the learned Counsel for the plaintiff avoided entering into, and which are decisive if they apply. Those cases have gone a long way, and I am not disposed to carry the principle a step further than I am compelled by the authorities. They establish, that if parties make an arrangement behind the back of a third person, declaring a trust which might be beneficial to that third person, if it be not in the nature of a settlement which is to be made available by that third person but an arrangement between the parties themselves, that third person cannot, in that naked state of circumstances, file a bill to enforce that arrangement. *Garrard* v. *Lord Lauderdale* 3 Sim.1; S.C. 2 Russ. & M. 451 went a long way, for there the deed purported to be with the scheduled creditors as parties, and there was a schedule containing the creditor's names, and the arrangement was expressly communicated to the plaintiff, and yet it was held that the Duke of York had not bound himself so as to enable the plaintiff to file the bill. The case before Lord Eldon, *Worrall* v. *Harford* 8 Ves. 4, was different in that respect; there there was a mere general provision for the payment of costs and expenses, without stating any particular attorney to whom they were to be paid, but an attorney having a claim for costs conceived himself a *cestui que trust* and filed a bill, which Lord Eldon dismissed.

The last case *Gibbs* v. *Glamis,* 11 Sim. 584 is one in which the Lord Chancellor decided one way and the Vice-Chancellor another. I am speaking from recollection, but I think the facts were these:– Several persons were interested in a fund in respect of which costs had been incurred, and were due to the plaintiff. An arrangement was made by which they assigned the funds in dispute to a trustee. One of the trusts of the deed expressly was to pay the plaintiff – an attorney – his costs. The money being realised and actually in the hands of the trustee, he did not pay them, and the bill was filed to recover them, the plaintiff being the person in whose favour the trust was absolutely declared. The plaintiff's Counsel relied on that circumstance, and distinguished the case from *Garrard* v. *Lord Lauderdale.* It was put as a case not of one person making an arrangement behind the back of the person for whom it was intended to make the provision, but of several persons liable to a demand, who agreed that the particular fund should be the means of discharging their obligation. The Vice-Chancellor gave a decree, but the Lord Chancellor reversed it, and decided that one of the parties to the deed only could enforce the trusts of it, and that it did not signify from whom the objection came, provided it was maintainable. I confess that in such a case I should have felt considerable doubt, but he held that even in that case the attorney could not maintain the suit for his costs.

The present case is not so strong a case as that; for here, Pallas having agreed to satisfy one demand, which he was not liable to, is to have the amount of it allowed against a demand to which he was liable, and he agreed also to pay the costs in question. Those costs were, in point of fact, due to Triston and Hardy; Simmonds was their attorney. The principal sum was £1000, the costs were £370; the latter were due ultimately to Simmonds, their attorney, but they were claimed by Triston and Hardy. They agreed to the arrangement only on the terms of their being paid. The arrangement was that the £1000 should be raised out of the estate of Henry Michael Francis Goold; and accordingly a mortgage was made to Foster of these estates. Then Pallas, who was to have the benefit of the arrangement and for whom the £1000 was paid, gave a mortgage to Hardy alone for £1400, and signed the deed before me now. It is executed by himself alone, and states what had taken place. It states Triston and Hardy's demand, and the suit against Pallas, and the arrangement made at Pallas' request, and the security from Goold's trustees, Pallas' debtors, for the £1000, and that it was also agreed that the said £1000 and the interest thereof should be collaterally secured by a mortgage of certain property belonging to him, and that it was likewise agreed that Pallas should pay the full costs between attorney and client of Triston and Hardy, the plaintiffs in the said two actions, and that the same should be secured by the said Pallas by his bills and promissory notes, and should be collaterally secured by a mortgage of his property, as aforesaid; and that the costs of the said two several actions had been estimated to amount to the sum of £400, or thereabouts. It then recites the mortgages, and proceeds: "Whereas the sum of £1400 so secured by the said last mentioned mortgage was intended to be a further security for the payment of the said sum of £1000 and interest so secured to Foster as aforesaid, and to be a security for the costs between attorney and client" of Triston and Hardy, the plaintiffs in the two actions, and so on. There is not a word of Simmonds in any part of the recited agreement. He is not alluded to in any manner directly or indirectly. Then it is said that Hardy is to stand possessed of the £1400 and interest, secured to him by the mortgage, in trust in the first place for better securing to Foster the payment of the £1000 secured by the other mortgage to him; and secondly, "to secure to Edward Simmonds, gentlemen, the attorney of the plaintiffs in the said two actions, the costs of the plaintiffs in the said two actions; such costs to be allowed as between attorney and client, and to be paid as follows, that is to say, the sum of £100 part thereof to be paid on or before the 15th of December 1842, and the balance of the said costs to be paid within two calendar months after the same shall be ascertained;" and thirdly, in trust to secure the expenses of procuring the deeds to be executed. It is clear that the latter costs could not be recovered except by the person to whom they were payable. The question is, did this direction to secure to Simmonds the costs of the plaintiffs in the two actions constitute him a *cestui que trust* under this deed?

Now, in the last case to which I referred, the attorney was named, as he is here, and the parties themselves were responsible to him for the costs; but it was held, that he was not entitled to recover them under the deed though they were secured for his benefit. It is quite clear on the authorities, that the mere fact of securing a fund to pay a man, unless the dealing is with him, does not entitle him to file a bill to enforce the trust; and, therefore, as at present advised, I think Simmonds cannot maintain the bill to carry into execution the trusts of this deed, under which, according to these authorities, he is not a *cestui que trust*. Mr. Sergeant Warren in fact admits that, I conceive, by not referring to the cases, and attempting to support the bill on other grounds.

The other grounds relied on are these:– "It is said, that in the present state of the suit it is not possible to dispute the right; but that cannot be maintained merely on the ground that Pallas has allowed the bill to be taken as confessed; for as I have before observed, that only admits the facts and leaves the question of law still open, whether Simmonds is a *cestui que trust* or not. A letter too is relied on, but it does not vary the case; it was written after the deed, and merely shows that Pallas meant to pay Simmonds.

The circumstances in favour of the defendant are very strong against Simmonds' claim, under the authorities referred to. It appears that the bills to secure the costs were to be given to Triston and Hardy, and not to Simmonds. The contract was made with Triston and Hardy, not Simmonds. Simmonds says that Triston and Hardy were indebted to him, but he made no stipulation not to go against them, the principal debtors, if he was included in the deed. There is nothing to show that Simmonds ever was intended to be a *cestui que trust* under this deed. The fact that the bills were given to Triston and Hardy and endorsed by them to Simmonds, shows conclusively that the dealing was to be confined to the parties immediately concerned in it, viz., Pallas on the one side, and Triston and Hardy on the other, and that Simmonds was to have the same remedy as before against his own clients, Triston and Hardy, with the additional security of the bills, beside the security afforded by the knowledge and the fact that this property had been assigned on trusts by which these costs might be paid, though he could not enforce these trusts. My view is, therefore, not that this deed cannot be enforced, for it clearly may, but that, according to the authorities, Simmonds is not a *cestui que trust*, and that he cannot enforce it. As I have already said, I consider that the learned Counsel, who is so conversant with the cases and so competent to maintain the position, if it was tenable, admitted the force of these authorities by putting the case on other grounds.

It is said that the case is within the principle of *Ellison* v. *Ellison* 6 Ves. 656, *Ex parte Pye* 18 Ves. 149, and *Pulvertoft* v. *Pulvertoft* 18 Ves. 100, which nobody can dispute are clear law and binding in this Court. They would decide the case if Mr. Simmonds has a right as a *cestui que trust* under this deed. But that would be to alter the entire transaction, because this is not a voluntary settlement in which, without reference to the claim of Simmonds, the parties thought right to make him a *cestui que trust* as a volunteer by a deed, with an actual transfer of the fund, under which the relation of trustee and *cestui que trust* would subsist. This is not that case, but it is a transaction between A and B, the benefit of which, to a certain extent, C is to have, but not as a *cestui que trust*. I think it clear that the authorities binding this case are *Garrard* v. *Lord Lauderdale* and that class of cases, and not *Ellison* v. *Ellison* and *Pulvertoft* v. *Pulvertoft*.

I have already had occasion (see *Browne* v. *Cavendish*, 7 Ir. Eq. Rep. 388-9) to state my opinion as to this doctrine, which I do not much approve of, though it is my duty to enforce it, and I do not wish to carry the principle further than it has been carried. It is most important to keep the line marked and distinct between the two classes of authorities. It appears to me, that the class relied on by the plaintiff does not apply to this case; but as the point is one of great importance I will consider it again, and will look into the authorities before I finally decide.

I have looked through the pleadings in this case and the facts stand thus:– The mortgage, which was the foundation of the arrangement, was made by Pallas to Hardy, and the deed of trust on which the plaintiff Simmonds founds his claim, was executed by Pallas alone. It recites the facts, which appear to be, that two actions had been brought against two of the Goolds, and were depending at the suit of Triston and Hardy. Simmonds was the attorney of Messrs. Triston and Hardy, in these actions. Pallas was indebted to another member of the Goold family, and proceedings were pending against him for recovery of this demand, and it was proposed that Pallas should secure or pay £1000 to Triston and Hardy, and that they should take that in liquidation of their demand; and that that £1000 should be set off against G.I. Goold's demand against Pallas. The arrangement was, that the £1000 should be received out of the estate of Mr. Goold, as Pallas claimed £1000 out of that estate, which claim was the subject of another suit in this Court; accordingly the mortgage was made to Foster, for that £1000, which was to be paid to Triston and Hardy. The payment, therefore, was a payment on account of Pallas. Another mortgage was made for £1400, to Hardy as a trustee, which was in effect to Triston and Hardy. The dealing, therefore, was betwen Triston and Hardy and Pallas, and this deed only shows what the contract really was.

The deed recites what I have stated, and that "at the solicitation and request, and for the accommodation of Pallas, it was agreed between the parties aforesaid" (the parties were those whom I have mentioned), "that Triston and Hardy were to accept the £1000, in full for the amount of their claim in the said two actions, together with their full costs between attorney and client in the two actions;" so that the contract was, that Triston and Hardy should, beside the £1000, take *their* full costs; "and that it was also agreed between the parties aforesaid, at the request and for the accommodation of Pallas," that he should be allowed to set off the sum to be paid to Triston and Hardy, in the way I have stated, and that Triston and Hardy should accept the security on Goold's property to which Pallas was entitled, and the £1000 should be collaterally secured by the mortgage of Pallas's own property; and that it was agreed that Pallas should pay the full costs "of the said Triston and Hardy, the plaintiffs in the said two actions, and that the same should be secured by his bills and promissory notes, and should be collaterally secured by the mortgage of his property." So that Pallas was to pay the costs and collaterally secure the sum secured by the mortgage already given on the Goold estate. The costs were also to be secured by bills. The agreement must have been, therefore, to give the bills to Triston and Hardy. They alone were liable for the costs to their own solicitor, but Pallas was liable to them, and therefore the contract is that the bills should be given by Pallas to Triston and Hardy. The deed states the contract, that the deeds had been executed, and that the £1400 secured by mortgage was intended to be a further security for the payment of the £1000 secured by the mortgage to Foster, "and to be a security for the costs between attorney and client of the said J.H. Triston and S.C. Hardy, in the said two actions, and the costs and expenses of getting the first-mentioned deed executed, and also the payment of the several bills thereinafter mentioned." That is inaccurately stated, for the bills are not again mentioned. In all the recitals there is not a word of the person who was the attorney for Triston and Hardy: but the whole contract and the whole arrangement recited is confined to Triston and Hardy and Pallas. Then follows what the plaintiff contends is in effect a declaration that Hardy is a trustee for Simmonds, "secondly, to secure to Edward Simmonds, gentleman, the attorney of the plaintiffs in the said two actions, the costs of the plaintiffs in the said two actions, as between attorney and client," to be paid at the times mentioned; and thirdly, to secure expenses to be incurred by Hardy, in procuring the mortgage on the Goold property to be executed by the Messrs. Goold, at their respective residences. In regard to these last costs, nobody but Hardy could recover them.

The question arising on this view is merely a question of law, viz. – whether

Simmonds, being introduced by name into the operative part of the deed, is entitled to file a bill as a *cestui que trust* to have the trusts of it carried into execution? That depends first, on the intention of the parties; and secondly, on the authorities.

There is no intention to make Simmonds a *cestui que trust*. There is clearly no contract to make him a *cestui que trust* on the ground on which it was argued, viz. – that this is a voluntary settlement within the principle of *Ellison* v. *Ellison* 6 Ves. 656, and *Pulvertoft* v. *Pulvertoft* 18 Ves. 100, and that class of authorities. For in all those cases there is an intention on the part of the donor to confer a *bounty* on the donee, and it is on the bounty that the matter stands. It may be for a good consideration – namely, connection or relationship; or it may be for other motives less pure; but still it is only *bounty*, and it is impossible without danger to confound those with other cases. I am clearly of opinion this case does not fall within that class of authorities. The distinction is perfectly settled. The property being actually transferred to a trustee, if the relation of trustee and *cestui que trust* were created, Simmonds might sustain this suit; but he is not a *cestui que trust*, for this is within the principle of those other cases where a party provides for payment of an obligation which presses on himself, without dealing with the person to whom he is bound by that obligation for whom the provision is made, and without any new consideration moving from that person for the arrangement. Here Simmonds was the attorney of Triston and Hardy, and had a right to maintain an action against them for these costs. He never lost that remedy – he never relinquished it, or gave further time. He entered into no obligation to come in under this deed. There is no contract made with him; it is merely between Triston and Hardy and Pallas for their own convenience. Pallas agreed to pay them their costs; but Simmonds could have asserted his claim against them the next moment, without waiting for payment till the time mentioned in the deed should expire.

As to the authorities, I am not reconciled to them, and never shall be, but there they are, and I must follow them. I shall certainly not extend them, but I am bound to take the law as I find it. In *Garrard* v. *Lord Lauderdale* I was Counsel; my client succeeded, but I was not satisfied with the case. It established a principle of which there is no doubt. Whether the facts there warranted the decision is another matter, but the principle no one can dispute. It was settled before that case that if a man, without communication with his creditors, behind their backs, makes a provision for them which they are not entitled to require and for which they have not bargained, he may, if he pleases, before the execution of the trusts so created, put an end to them; as he created them, so he may destroy them; they remain within his own power. The questions in that case were, whether, under the circumstances, the grantor had exercised that power or not, or whether, after what had taken place, it could be exercised? There the deed was a mere disposition by the debtor without communication with the creditors, made between him and the grantees, and there was no third party. If the authorities stood there, it might be said that the present case was distinguishable; but there are much stronger cases; for example, *Gibbs* v. *Glamis* 11 Sim. 584, which I before referred to. That was a remarkable case, and very learned Judges differed upon it. The judgment of the Vice-Chancellor was reversed by the Lord Chancellor. I may say of that case, as I did of the other, I am not satisfied with it, and many learned persons would agree with the decision of the Judge below in opposition to the judgment of reversal.

The facts in the latter case were:– Mr. Hele had instituted a suit of *Hele* v. *Fernie*, respecting a sum of £4000, in which Lady Glamis claimed an interest. Her claim being disputed, she and the several other claimants came to a compromise among themselves, the terms of which were that they would divide the money in certain proportions and provide for the payment of all costs, and particularly the costs due to Gibbs; and without any communication with him they executed a deed of trust by which, after stating the compromise, they assigned £4000 in trust – in the first place to defray the costs, charges and expenses of all the parties to the deed in or about the suit of *Hele* v. *Fernie and others* or of the deed or otherwise relating to the claims to the £4000, as between solicitor and client; and also the costs of Gibbs, who was a defendant in that suit; and also the costs to which the trustees might be put in recovering the £4000; and in the next place to pay certain sums to the claimants Hibbert and Hele, and the residue of the £4000 to Lady Glamis, in satisfaction of their respective claims on that sum; so that Lady Glamis had no right whatever until after the costs were paid. There was just as express a trust for Gibbs as there is here for Simmonds. In all those cases the trust is declared in express words. But what was the decision in that case? The costs were not paid, and the trustees had the money in their hands and were willing to pay Gibbs, if Lady Glamis would allow them to do so; but Lady Glamis, who was only entitled to the residue after payment of those costs, said – no, you shall not pay them, he is not a *cestui que trust* and he has no right to file a bill. The Vice-Chancellor held that all claimed a common interest in the performance of the trust; that the compromise was only on the grounds of the payment of the costs of *Hele* v. *Fernie*, and that Hele's executors, who would be liable to pay Gibbs's costs, had a direct interest in having them paid under the deed, and that Lady Glamis was to receive nothing but the residue after payment of the costs; he therefore sustained the bill. That was the opinion of the Vice-Chancellor – the same Judge who had decided *Garrard* v. *Lord Lauderdale*. The Lord Chancellor reversed that decision, and the reversal has been submitted to. The Chancellor says, in his judgment, that the suit having been compromised, Hele was, of course, liable to pay Gibbs the costs of it; and in order to protect him against the consequences of that liability, the parties who were interested in the fund in dispute provided incidentally that the plaintiff's (Gibbs) costs should be paid; and the question then was, whether that provision gave the party, whose costs were so provided for, a right to institute a suit as *cestui que trust*, he having no interest in the fund, not having been a party to the arrangement, and the arrangement having been made between the parties interested in the fund for their own benefit or convenience; and that the case was not distinguishable from *Garrard* v. *Lord Lauderdale* and the other cases cited. He then added that the objection was open to all the defendants in the suit, and it was immaterial what interest the party who made the objection had.

That case was much stronger than this; for there there were several persons agreeing to vest in a trustee a fund on an express trust to meet an obligation which he had against one of them; and yet the Lord Chancellor held that the person for whom that trust was created could not maintain the suit. Lady Glamis could not have recovered the residue until that trust was fulfilled and the costs paid. Therefore, that case proves this, that it is not sufficient that the two circumstances – the declaration of a trust and its partial execution – should concur, to give a right to a person standing in the situation of Gibbs or Simmonds to file a bill. It shows that it is solely a party to the agreement who has a right to do so. The person to be benefited has a right to be paid, but it is a mistake for him to assert a remedy on the deed; he must wait until the party liable to him chooses to call for the execution of the trusts. Hele there could, it is quite clear, have filed the bill the hour after the deed was executed, and have insisted on the trustees paying those costs to Gibbs, or to him for Gibbs, to whom he was liable, before a shilling was paid to Lady Glamis; and if the trustee had paid Lady Glamis, he would have been answerable to Hele for a breach of trust.

In the case before me now, Triston and Hardy contracted for this right. They who employed the attorney contracted that his costs should be paid, and the person with whom that contract was made said that the costs should be paid to the attorney; but that cannot be so as to enable the attorney to file a bill as a *cestui que trust*, and he must be content to pursue his remedy against his own clients, and they theirs against the property provided by the deed. This is a stronger case than those I have referred to, for this reason. Here Hardy is the trustee, and he was one of the persons bound to pay the costs, and being trustee he has the fund himself and can pay the plaintiff out of it: or he may pay the plaintiff – his own attorney – whenever he pleases, out of his own funds, and then repay himself when he executes the trust. This case, therefore, is clearly within the doctrine; for the party who is subject to the obligation in the first instance has the means of paying it.

I was desirous to see the pleadings, because it was said that they distinguish the case from the authorities. I have read them carefully, and I do not think they do. On the contrary, I think they make against Mr. Simmonds, for this reason:– The bill states that, in pursuance of the contract, Pallas gave the first instalment of the costs by his promissory note to Triston and Hardy, and that they indorsed it over to Simmonds. That proves conclusively that there was to be no direct communication between Simmonds and Pallas, but that Pallas was to perform his obligation to Triston and Hardy, and they were to perform their obligation to Simmonds.

It is then said that Hardy admits he is a trustee. That is true; but he is not a trustee in such a sense that Simmonds would be entitled to file a bill to enforce this trust. In the case I have referred to Gibbs was in the same position as Simmonds here, and yet Gibbs' bill was dismissed. The fact that Hardy is a trustee, does not vary the case in this respect.

As to the order to take the bill as confessed against Pallas. There is no decree against Pallas; there never is as decree where there is more than the one defendant who does not answer. There is only an order, and it remains for me to make a decree such as the facts warrant. On these facts, as confessed, I am of opinion that Simmonds has no right to file the present bill, for the contract was with Triston and Hardy, to whom the note was given, and they are the persons to pay their own attorney.

The bill, therefore, must be dismissed with costs.

Note
See further *Irish Land Law*, paras. 9.085-7. See also *Browne* v. *Cavendish*, *infra*.

BROWNE V. CAVENDISH

(1844) 7 Ir. Eq. R. 369; 1 Jo. & Lat. 606 (Chancery)

The facts are set out in the judgment.

Sugden L.C.:

In this case a judgment creditor has filed his bill to obtain the benefit of a trust for the payment of debts created by a deed of 1810. There was some embarrassment for a time as to the deed under which the plaintiff was to claim; but since it has been decided that the deed of the 6th of July 1810 was revoked by the deed of September 1810, the question may be considered without reference to the former deed. Although some of the subsequent deeds referred to the first deed, that does not, I think, vary the rights of the parties. Originally the father was made tenant for life, and the son tenant in tail of all the estates. The judgments were against the father, and would, of course, affect only his life estate at law. By the deed of September 1810, the estates were vested in trustees. The trusts were to sell a particular estate called the Newtown estate, and out of the produce, first to pay the judgment debts and incumbrances affecting the lands of which the recovery had been suffered, and then to discharge the principal, interest and costs of the several debts and incumbrances affecting the estate or person of the father John Browne, and subject to that they are limited to the father in fee. That is an equitable fee. The other estates are limited in strict settlement, charged with a sum not exceeding £4000 in case part of the Newtown estate could not be sold, or, if sold, should not produce sufficient to pay off the debts then contracted or affecting the person or property of John Browne, the father. There is then a power of revocation and new appointment over the settled estate, except as to the jointure to Elizabeth Browne, and the trusts of the five hundred years' term for younger children. I have not now to consider whether that extended to the trusts under the deed for sale to pay debts. Now that was followed by the deed of the 16th of November 1811. That deed recites that a contract had been made by the trustees, with the consent of the father, the elder Browne, for the sale to Cavendish of the estate in question for a sum between £9000 and £10,000, and that sum was to be paid in discharge of the scheduled debts; and accordingly, in consideration of that sum to be applied in payment of those debts, the trustees conveyed to Mr. Cavendish in fee. That deed was not executed by Denis Browne, one of the trustees, but it was executed by the other, and by the father and the son. There is a schedule to it containing the different judgment debts, and headed thus, "a schedule being for the application of the purchase-money," by which it appears that after payment of the judgments and allowance agreed to be made for quit-rent, but a few shillings would remain in hand of the amount of the purchase-money. On the same day, a deed of indemnity was executed vesting the other lands, the settled estate, in trustees to indemnify the purchaser of Newtown from all judgments, mortgages, debts, incumbrances, chief-rents, quit-rents or charges then affecting the lands of Newtown, or thereafter to affect the same by reason of any recognizance, &c., by John Browne or Arthur Browne, or either of them, &c. Thus things continued until the 28th of May 1812. Another deed of that date was executed. This recited that the deeds of the 16th of November had not been executed by Denis Browne, and referred to the judgment debts now in question, and recited that £1000 had been retained by Mr. Cavendish to pay them off, out of the purchase-money; and then recited that the elder Browne had agreed, himself, to pay off the judgments and to procure a release of the estates, and had applied to Mr. Cavendish to advance the greater part of the £1000. The deed then states that the settled account showed a balance in the hands of Mr. Cavendish of £500 after payment of £800 or £900 to the elder Browne, and that certain judgments were to be assigned to Cavendish as an indemnity to protect the estate. Then both the father and son covenanted with Cavendish to cause satisfaction to be entered on the judgments or to procure the estate to be discharged, and to procure an assignment to be executed to him of the other judgments; and if the conveyance was not executed by Denis Browne, Cavendish was to have liberty to resort to the other lands for his indemnity. That was the deed of the 28th of May 1812. The next, and last deed, is that of the 11th of December 1812, which recited the deed of July 1810, the contract to sell, and that the purchase-money should be applied according to that deed. It then recited the conveyance of the 16th of November 1811, and that Denis and Henry Browne had agreed to convey the legal estate to Mr. Cavendish, and they do convey for a nominal consideration; and then it is declared that the trustees shall not be answerable for the title or the application of the purchase-money.

In this state of facts, which I think I perfectly understand, having looked over the documents with great care, it results that in point of law the father's estate was clearly liable to these judgments, and the judgments did not affect, independently of the deeds, any other interest than that estate for life. The judgment creditor was not bound by these deeds; she might have gone against the life estate the next moment if she thought proper, notwithstanding the execution of one or all of these deeds; and as on the one hand she was not bound by them, so on the other hand, I apprehend, she is not entitled to enforce them. She is not a party to them in any manner. No arrangement was made with her in regard to them, and her interest is not bound by them, nor was any new right created by them vested in her. Suppose she had a right in this particular case, that right must be carried much further; for the trusts of the deeds are to pay any debts affecting the person or estate of John Browne, the father; and therefore, a simple contract creditor could have filed a bill to enforce the execution of these trusts and the application of these funds to his demand, if this judgment creditor is entitled to do so. The trusts were created by the father and son; they had power to create them, and did so, without the concurrence of the judgment creditor, and as they so created them, I apprehend, they have power in law to defeat them. A question might have arisen, the force of which I need not consider, in relation to the rights of persons claiming the settled portion of the estates to have this part applied in discharge of incumbrances; but I am relieved from considering that point of law, because the father and the son had a power of revocation over the settled estates. The whole estate, in my opinion, was entirely under their dominion either under the power of revocation and new appointment, or by force of the inherent right which they had to impeach the deed and to set aside and revoke that which they themselves had created, and which was only an arrangment for themselves.

Then the question is, what became of the trusts? I think it exceedingly difficult to ascertain on the face of these deeds exactly the form in which the parties meant to carry them into execution. But the substance of what they intended is plain enough. I think in substance they intended a sale, – which was clearly carried into execution at the date of these deeds – and payment of the purchase-money, by the application of it to judgments. Except as regards these particular judgments before the Court, that was, therefore, an execution of the trusts. As to these two judgments, it would seem as if the parties intended to compromise them, for a larger amount was due than the £1000 which was retained by Mr. Cavendish to answer this demand. One question would be, whether after the £1000 was retained, Mrs. Browne could have filed a bill against anybody to enforce the application of that £1000 to her demand? I think it is clear she could not, because she was not bound to take less than the whole; and the £1000, which would cover only a portion of her demand, was the fund for its payment only as betwen the seller and the purchaser. Those who created the trust defeated it as to this £1000; and I think they had a right to do so, as both assented and gave an indemnity to the purchaser. They were in fact, making a new appropriation of the £1000. The indemnity was necessary, because the life estate still existed, and the judgment creditor might take if it he thought proper. I am of opinion, therefore, that the creditor had no right under this trust against the purchaser, or the produce of the purchase.

Then it is said, that the elder Browne, against whom the judgments were obtained, had the equitable fee. That is true – but that was subject to the legal fee in the trustees, with a trust for sale, and that equitable fee could never take effect in derogation of the trust. That trust had been executed and the sale confirmed by the two Brownes, and a new appropriation was made of a portion of that purchase-money, with the assent of both. That could not let in the right of the elder Browne to the equitable fee, but would, in my opinion, defeat that right; because the trustees had parted with the fee in execution of the trust, and for the purpose of vesting the legal estate in the purchaser, discharged of the equitable fee.

No authority is wanted to prove this; but the same point arose in *Foster* v. *Blackstone* 1 Myl. & K. 297. In that case it was insisted, as it is here, that the judgment creditors had a right to go against the equitable fee vested in the Marquis of Blandford; but the Master of the Rolls, Sir John Leach, there said:- "The scheduled judgment creditors had no legal lien upon the trust estates, but they had a possible equitable lien depending upon a contingency. The trustees had, under the deed of 1812, a full authority to sell and to convert the realty into personalty. If any part had ben unsold by the trustees it would have remained land, and the judgment would have attached upon it; but it was all sold by the trustees and converted into personalty, and the contingency which would have entitled the judgment creditors never took effect." I do not know whether it could be properly called a contingency, but in the result I entirely agree. That is precisely this case. These trusts having in fact been executed, the equitable fee was defeated, and consequently the judgment creditor cannot claim the benefit of it. In the case in the House of Lords, 9 Bli. N.R. 332, nom. *Foster* v. *Cockerell,* that question does not seem to have been agitated.

Supposing that I was wrong in this view of the point, then the question would arise as to the right of the judgment creditor, before the late statute, to attach an equitable fee in this Court where the legal fee-simple has been conveyed by the trustee before execution executed. *Hunt* v. *Coles* 1 Comyn, 222 and *Harris* v. *Pugh* 4 Bingh 335 clearly established that the Statute of Frauds gave no relief unless the judgment creditor proceeded to execution while the legal estate remained vested in the trustees for the benefit of the *cestui que trust*, the debtor. I am not prepared to carry that doctrine further than these precedents. I have several times in the course of my professional life looked with great diligence for any authority to establish the proposition, that before the Statute of Frauds equity had ever given relief in a similar case, or had given a judgment creditor the benefit of the trust estate; but I never could find such a case. Whatever analogy may be supposed to exist between an equitable estate and an equity of redemption, I am not prepared to go further on that point than this statute has done. Therefore, on that ground no relief can be given.

This creditor is in another difficulty also. He had not sued out an *elegit*, and according to *Neate* v. *The Duke of Marlborough* 3 M. & Cr. 407, cited at the bar, the judgment creditor must do so before he can obtain relief in this Court. I give no opinion on that decision, because I do not decide the case on that ground; but I must say that until that case I considered it settled, that it was not necessary to sue out execution. The point was said to have been decided in *Townsend* v. *Askew* (see 3 M. & Cr. 410, 412, 418); but it would appear that the note of that case was not a correct representation of what passed. I remember it made an impression on me, and I always acted on that authority. It is hardly worth while talking about it now, for the recent statute has altered the law, and the point may never arise again.

In reference to the authorities; the most of them, if not all, were cited at the bar. *Walwyn* v. *Couts* 3 Sim. 14; S.C. 3 Mer. 707 and *Garrard* v. *Lord Lauderdale* 3 Sim. 1; S.C. 2 Russ. & M. 451 are authorities that a conveyance by a debtor to trustees for payment of scheduled creditors, who do not execute the deed or conform to its terms, cannot be enforced by the creditors. In *Acton* v. *Woodgate* 2 Myl. & K. 492, which is also an authority on which I am about to decide this case, the Master of the Rolls observes, of *Garrard* v. *Lord Lauderdale*, that it seems to have been considered that a communication by the trustees to the creditors of the fact of such a trust would not defeat the power of revocation by the debtors; but that it appeared to him that this doctrine was questionable, because the creditors being aware of such a trust, might be thereby induced to a forbearance in respect of their claims which they would not otherwise have exercised; and when I first read the case I made an observation in the margin, 'that has also been my opinion.' I do not mean to say that in every case a representation to a creditor would give him the benefit of the trust. That must depend on the character of the representation, and that representation must be acted on. But I should be sorry that it should be understood that a man can create a trust for the benefit of his creditors, and communicate to them the intention of the trust, and obtain from them all the benefit of their lying by and not enforcing their legal right until that legal right is lost, and then insist that the trust is still within his own power. I mention this only to guard any one from imagining that could turn out to be the law; for there was no manner of communication in this case.

The case of *Gibbs* v. *Glamis* 11 Sim. 584, 994 is also an authority for the decree I am about to make. There the person whose costs were provided for must have had a right to recover those costs from one of the parties to the deed, the money had been secured to answer the trust and was in the hands of the trustee, and one of the assignors had an interest against the other to have the trust carried into execution, and yet it was held that they did not give a creditor the right to enforce it. The Vice-Chancellor thought it did, but the Lord Chancellor thought otherwise, and reversed the decision. Now the Vice-Chancellor should have doubted his own decision, for in *Ravenshaw* v. *Hollier* 7 Sim. 3, which was a similar case, he said that it was quite competent for the parties themselves to have defeated the trust. Those who created the trust defeated it, and they had power to do so. In *Gibbs* v. *Glamis* the trust was never defeated; it was an existing trust, and finding that it was for the interest of the assignee that the trust should be carried into execution, and the person who created the trust not having defeated it, he was of opinion that the creditor might enforce it against the trustee who had the money in his hands: but even in that case relief was denied.

It is difficult, but important, to keep in view the distinction between a voluntary settlement and a settlement of this nature. It is difficult to draw the line. The ground of my decision is that here the judgment creditor never was, properly speaking, a *cestui que trust*, and was never intended to be one. The trusts were created by the father and son for their own purposes and their own benefit, and they retained a complete dominion over them. This is not a case where a voluntary trust is created for individuals; for then if there is a fund actually vested in a trustee, though there was no consideration for the creation of the trusts, and though the fund gets back by accident into the hands of the person who created the trust, yet the trust continues and may be enforced for the benefit of the volunteers, because the relation of trustee and *cestui que trust* was created and is not at an end. Now, *Colyear* v. *Lord Mulgrave* 2 Kee. 81, which was relied on, went on this, that the contract was not executed but still remained *in fieri*. In *Bill* v. *Cureton* 2 M. & K. 503, the distinction to which I have adverted is drawn, and was enforced in favour of a voluntary settlement. I refer to it, that nothing falling from me may trench on the validity of settlements for a voluntary consideration.

The doctrine of *Garrard* v. *Lord Lauderdale* and *Walwyn* v. *Couts*, has been carried to the whole extent to which it should have been carried. I am not disposed, and it would not be just, to carry it further. I shall not outstep the authorities, but I think they embrace this case. I shall, therefore, dismiss this bill; but considering the nature of the deeds and the very complicated nature of the transaction (all the circumstances of which, taken together, have introduced so much difficulty into the case as to what the right of this creditor really was); I do not think that I should be justified in dismissing the bill with costs. I shall therefore dismiss it without costs.

As to the cross-suit, the question appears to be a very plain one. The Newtown estate was conveyed to trustees in trust to sell and pay the judgments affecting the lands or John Browne. John and Arthur were entitled to other estates, and those estates were put into settlement reserving a power of revocation and new appointment; and those estates were made an express indemnity fund to the purchaser against all incumbrances. I mention the words "all incumbrances," for the indemnity deed acted as a drag net, and included incumbrances as well against the son as against the father. The purchaser anticipating that the suit against him might succeed, files a bill in order to have relief against both the father and the son, who were bound as the parties selling and creating the trust of indemnity. The son has been since fortunate enough to escape the costs of the suit occasioned by his own conduct; for the judgment creditor was provided for, and he allowed the money to go into a different channel. The bill must be dismissed, and the costs of the plaintiff be paid by Arthur Browne.

Chapter 15

CHARITABLE TRUSTS

Charitable trusts form a most important area of the law of trusts, a recognition of the significance attributed to them by both equity an the State (in the shape of tax advantages), see *Irish Land Law*, para. 9.088 *et seq*.

I. DEFINITION

RE HOWLEY'S ESTATE

[1940] I.R. 109; 74 I.L.T.R. 197 (High Court)

The facts are set out in the judgments.

Gavan Duffy J.:

The late Very Rev. Patrick Canon Howley P.P., died on the 6th of April, 1937; by his will, dated the 22nd of June, 1930, he left all his property to the Bishop and Chapter of Killala for the time being; he directed them to dispose of the yearly income from his "shares," which I hold to include certain stock, at the annual meeting of the Chapter, to giving specified yearly sums (paragraphs (a) to (e)) to certain persons for life, and by giving (f) "£2 each to the members of the Chapter at their annual meeting each year to say eight masses for the repose of my soul and that of my friends and benefactors," and by disposing (g) of "the balance of the income each year at the annual meeting of the Chapter on what in their united wisdom they consider the best interests of religion." I understand that the testator left pure personalty only.

The Most Rev. Dr. James Naughton, the Bishop of the Diocese of Killala, has alone proved the will, on the true construction of which I hold that the Bishop and his successors and the Chapter of the Diocese as a corporate body were appointed trustees as well as executors. I shall return to the legal effect of this appointment of trustees.

The principal question is whether the gift of residue is void for uncertainty and for remoteness.

I hold the gift to be charitable and valid.

The two chief authorities cited against this view are the decisions of O'Connor M.R. and the Court of Appeal in Ireland in *MacLaughlin* v. *Campbell* [1906] 1 I.R. 588, and the opinion of the Judicial Committee of the Privy Council in England in *Dunne* v. *Byrne* [1912] A.C. 407.

In the Irish case a gift "for such Roman Catholic purposes" as trustees deemed fit and proper was held not to be charitable, because the gift was not in terms made for religious purposes and because the purposes thus authorised by the will were much wider than the religious purposes of the Catholic Church; but it was recognised in the Court of Appeal, particularly by Holmes L.J., that a gift for the purposes of the Catholic Church is charitable.

Dunne v. *Byrne* [1912] A.C. 407 is much nearer the present case; there was a residuary gift by Father Byrne, a Catholic priest, "to the Roman Catholic Archbishop of Brisbane and his successors, to be used and expended wholly or in part as such Archbishop may judge most conducive to the good of religion in this diocese"; the Supreme Court of Queensland had held unanimously that the gift was charitable, upon the "overwhelming authorities in support of the rule laid down in *In re White* [1893] 2 Ch. 41 to which I shall recur; the High Court of Austrialia, by a majority of three to two, reversed this decision, mainly on the ground, rejected in the Privy Council, that the Archbishop might spend part of the money on non-charitable objects. The Judicial Committee held the established rule for construing gifts for religious purposes as *prima facie* charitable not to apply to a gift which, instead of being made for "religious purposes," was to be spent as the Archbishop might judge most conducive to the good of religion in the diocese, since a non-charitable purpose might in Catholic eyes be most conducive to the good of religion; the Committee referred, as an instance, to *Cocks* v. *Manners* 12 Eq. 574, where a gift to a community of nuns, established to work out the salvation of the sisters by religious exercises and self-denial, was held not to be a charitable gift in English law, on the ground that private piety in a convent does not tend, directly or indirectly, to edify the public; this dictum (for the bequest was held good as a personal gift for the members of the community) has come to represent established law in England and has sometimes been tacitly accepted here under similar jurisprudence, which constantly resorts for precedent to the vast field of English Judge-made law. I apprehend that the point ought not be taken as having been finally settled for us in England, where the law was determined by the English outlook upon societies for self-sanctification. The assumption that the Irish public finds no edification in cloistered lives, devoted to purely spiritual ends, postulates a close assimilation of the Irish outlook to the English, not obviously warranted by the traditions and *mores* of the Irish people. I need say no more on the matter here, for it is easy to cite instances (though this was selected as the conspicuous example) of non-charitable expenditure, which may be conducive to the good of religion.

"Charity" is in law an artificial conception, which during some 300 years, under the guidance of pedantic technicians, seems to have strayed rather far from the intelligent realm of plain common sense; thus, the textbooks tell us that charity in the eyes of the law includes a bequest for a "Home for Lost Dogs," as an institution for domestic animals must benefit the human race which they serve, and a legacy to further "Conservative principles," if combined with zeal for mental and moral improvement – so catholic is juristic charity – though it must draw the line at the spiritual exercises of a convent or the plans of an Archbishop conducing to the good of religion in his own diocese; such are the vagaries of Judge-made law. There are decisions extant in the charitable domain which suggest that in Ireland, so far as we still have a comparatively free hand, we must proceed with great circumspection where "charity" is concerned.

In my opinion, the final decision in *Dunne* v. *Byrne* [1912] A.C. 407 was a deliberate attempt to curb a growing tendency in English law to benignity, perhaps excessive benignity, where gifts of a religious character were concerned.

The wording of the gift here must be carefully noted; it is to be applied every year in the best interests of religion, as determined by the united wisdom of a Bishop and Chapter of the Catholic Church; the testator thus calls for a solemn decision, year by year for ever, by an official body, eminently qualified to make it, as my examination will show presently.

Since the time of Lord Eldon gifts in the most general terms for the promotion of religion have been recognised as charitable in law; the principle, as it was put by a strong Court (Lindley, Bowen and A.L. Smith, L.JJ.) in *In re White* [1893] 2 Ch. 41 at p. 52, is that "a bequest to a religious institution, or for a religious purpose, is *prima facie* a bequest for a 'charitable' purpose, and that the law applicable to 'charitable' bequests, as distinguished from the law applicable to ordinary bequests, ought to be applied to a bequest to a religious institution, or for a religious purpose"; this passage is adopted by Lord Hanworth M.R. in *In re Bain, Public Trustee* v. *Ross* [1930] 1 Ch. 224, at p. 231.

In this country the principle was applied more than a century ago by Lord Manners in *Powerscourt* v. *Powerscourt* 1 Moll. 616, and it is recognised in recent times by O'Connor M.R., Barton J., and Ross J. in *Arnott* v. *Arnott* [1906] 1 I.R. 127, at p. 134, *In re Salter* [1911] 1 I.R. 289, at p. 296, and *Rickerby* v. *Nicholson* [1912] 1 I.R. 343, at p. 347, respectively.

If Canon Howley had left his residue to be applied in the best interests of religion, I doubt if any one would have had the hardihood to contend that the bequest was not charitable, because the words, "religious purposes" did not appear; but, if his phraseology be taken to have the same meaning as Father Byrne's, I recognise that the reasoning in *Dunne* v. *Byrne* [1912] A.C. 407, applied in *In re Jackson* [1930] 2 Ch. 389, concludes that he contrived to take his bounty out of the charitable category by the malign effect of his confidence in his trustees; and, further, that it makes so effective a distinction between this way of helping the Church and a gift for "religious purposes" that a Court must presume charity in the latter case and reject it in the former. I should be sorry to have to decide the issue on so narrow a dividing line, if any there be here, though I am by no means disposed to minimise the importance of scrupulous attention to the precise words in which a will is expressed. There are no *cestuis que trustent* here, and the residuary gift of income, if not charitable, is clearly too indefinite to stand, since a man may not ask his trustees to make his will for him after he is dead.

I prefer another approach, with the high authority behind it of O'Connor J. (unreported) in the High Court of Australia, in *Dunne* v. *Byrne* [1912] A.C. 407. Here the mandate to perpetual trustees points the way; see the older case law examined by Powell J. in *Moore* v. *The Pope Benedict XV* [1919] 1 I.R. 316. In *In re Davidson* [1909] 1 Ch. 567 where a power to give to objects non-charitable defeated a bequest to the Archbishop of Westminster, Cozens-Hardy M.R. (at p. 569) says that, while a Court cannot hold a trust charitable merely because the trustee has a religious office, he does not doubt that "if you find in a will words indicating that a distribution is to be made by persons in succession as holders of a particular religious or charitable office, that goes far to establish – and, it maybe, goes sufficiently far to establish – the fact that the whole gift is charitable." In my opinion, that is this case and the charitable gift is established by the nature of the perpetual office or offices attributed by the testator to the trustees who are "in their united wisdom" to allot the yearly balance of income in "what they consider the best interests of religion." The precise destination of the balance is left to them and we have here, in my opinion, an excellent example of a case "where," to quote Greene M.R. in *In re Ashton* [1938] 1 Ch. 482, at p. 495, "the purpose named takes its colour from the character of the trustee." I am satisfied that the testator had religious purposes in view and that these trustees would rightly regard any other as a breach of a sacred trust.

The next question concerns the validity of the gift of £2 each to the members of the Chapter at their annual meeting for masses. This bequest for the repose of my soul and that of my friends and benefactors" is, in the language of other days, "a gift to God"; it is a gift of which the paramount intention is beyond all doubt the celebration of mass for the souls and not the *honoraria* to priests, unknown indeed (after a few years) to the testator and not closely connected with him. The character of the Most Holy Sacrifice in the conviction of a Catholic and a dignitary of the Church, like the testator, puts the celebration of mass on a plane so far above the alms to be celebrant that no comparison of their relative importance in the eyes of the testator is thinkable; I have no evidence on this head, nor do I think I need any, because the Catholic teaching on the mass is known to the Common Law; see *O'Hanlon* v. *Logue* [1906] 1 I.R. 247, at pp. 265, 274 *per* Palles C.B. A lawyer can ascertain the Catholic position readily from the evidence of the Bishop of Cork in *Attorney-General* v. *Delaney* I.R. 10 C.L. 104, and there is, I think, a practice of assuming the acquiescence of all parties in that authoritative exposition, where a Catholic testator has left money for masses, because it is felt that to ask for explicit acceptance, when there is no hint of any contest on the matter, would be mere formalism. I see no objection to this assumption, to facilitate that ascertainment of facts familiar to the Common Law, which we are all supposed to know.

But the gift (or gifts) for masses, though charitable, may nevertheless fail, if too remote; see *In re Stratheden* [1894] 3 Ch. 265. And it is well settled that gift of income may offend the rule against perpetuities, although the capital be vested in trustees. If the testator made separate gifts for masses for every year, those gifts may be valid for twenty-one years from his death and void thereafter; I am prepared to hold the mass gifts on that hypothesis to be good for twenty-one years, since each gift in the series is quite independent of the other gifts and each of the gifts thus held valid must take effect within twenty-one years; see Gray, 3rd edn., ch. xi and Appendix H, for a convincing exposition of the logic of this view, sometimes overlooked in the past, when a whole series of gifts has been held void.

I do however, find a difficulty in ascertaining whether the will makes one gift for masses, and one gift of the balance of income every year, or several. The *tot homines* argument for a number of mass gifts is obvious. On the other hand, the scheme of the will is to give the whole property outright to the executor-trustees, whose first duty is to keep it intact; it is to be kept intact for ever and they are not intended ever to distribute anything but its yearly produce; as to that, the disposal of the income every year is introduced by a single governing clause:– "They will dispose of the yearly income accruing from the shares at the annual meeting of the Chapter as follows"; they are to dispose of one thing, the yearly income, by providing first for five distinct life annuities, then for masses, and finally for the application of the residue to religious ends. Of course the residue will grow, as the annuitants die, but, large or small, it remains the residue dedicated to religion. The life annuities are given in five paragraphs, in these words (all but one):- "They will give a yearly income of £—— to A.B. during his (her) lifetime"; but only a highly technical construction would hold the annuitants to get each a separate gift every year; each of them gets, I think, an annuity for life as a single gift. If so, it is perhaps a little more difficult to treat the provision for masses in the next paragraph of the will, though the celebrants vary from time to time, or the provision in the final paragraph for applying the residue of the income yearly in divers ways to religion, as really constituting so many separate gifts; each of the seven disposing paragraphs, or rather sub-paragraphs, is governed by the same single introductory direction for the disposal of the yearly income. On the whole, I think that I adopt a construction more consistent with the governing direction and more in harmony with the five separate single gifts of an annuity by reading the bestowal of money for masses in a number of £2 units as being intended really to make one general gift for masses for souls, a single gift of eighty masses a year for ever, that is, eight masses to be said by each member of the Chapter, which on the evidence numbers ten; since this is a charitable gift, the trustees must, in my judgment, if at any annual meeting the number be short of ten, have the missing masses said, with the appropriate *honorarium*, by a priest or priests chosen by themselves, other than the missing recipient or recipients no longer on the Chapter. Similarly, much in the same way as the modalities of the annual disposal of the annual income are set out under seven heads, in seven sub-paragraphs, to wit, five several annuities, masses, religion, I construe the direction for disposing of the residue of income as being intended to fill in the modalities of a general residuary gift of income, a single gift, for religion. I observe that a similar position arose in *Hearn* v. *Donellan* [1901] 1 I.R. 402n, but the report does not tell us whether the question now under consideration was raised. There are a number of cases in the old Exchequer Reports in England as to death duties, where the question was whether a testator's bounty to the poor, expressed in annual payments of income, was to be regarded as one collective gift or several gifts, but these cases turned on Revenue Acts and on the wording of particular wills.

The trusteeship contemplated by the testator raises further questions; he identifies his trustees with the Bishop and Chapter; he sees the Chapter as a body that will never die; hence the Bishop for the time being as co-trustee must have been intended to include the successors of the present Bishop.

If the Bishop and Chapter are a corporation or corporations recognised as such by our law, no difficulty need arise; if not, a regular trusteeship must be established, since no charity can fail for lack of trustees.

The evidence of the Very Rev. Denis O'Connor, a Bachelor of Canon Law, shows that the Chapter is a Cathedral Chapter of ten Canons for the Diocese of Killala, constituted under a decree of the Sacred Consistorial Congregation in Rome, dated the 14th July, 1913, for the purposes of celebrating the Divine Service with greater solemnity, assisting the Bishop as his senate or council, and, during a vacancy in the episcopal See, administering the Diocese. The witness explains the method of appointment to the Chapter. Under Canon Law the Chapter must meet at least once a year. In practice its annual general meeting is held on Holy Thursday. The deponent, who is official secretary to the Bishop, shows the Chapter to be a very responsible body.

Under Canon Law the Chapter is a corporation with perpetual succession, a common seal, and the right to hold and administer property; its annual decision under the will would be a capitular act, a conclusion reached by a majority of the

Chapter. I am not told whether the Bishop is himself a corporation, nor whether Bishop and Chapter together make another corporation, nor whether the Bishop has the right to attend and vote at meetings; if not, a Scheme may be required to modify the plan of the will; but the affidavits before me do not seem quite consistent as to his position.

The issue here may be put as a claim for recognition of an ecclesiastical corporation, because that species of corporation was recognised at Common Law by virtue of the absorption by the Common Law of portion of the Canon Law, or as a claim for recognition of a foreign corporation; the success of either claim would secure perpetual trustees for Canon Howley's will.

The first alternative raises an important constitutional question, upon which the Attorney-General ought probably to be heard for the State; the answer to the question, if the old Common Law sustains the applicants, must depend upon the proposition that the great stream of the Common Law rolls on from generation to generation, remaining through all vicissitudes (subject to statute law) the same stream so that the interruptions to its normal flow during three centuries must be regarded as temporary pollutions, the removal of which leaves the Canon Law under our Constitution to-day the same vigorous current.

The alternative thesis may also need elaborate argument, though it does not involve the same historical research. Foreign corporations, recognised for commerical reasons in the early eighteenth century, are now recognised under our law for the most varied purposes; the recognition is sometimes based on the comity of nations, whatever its true origin may have been, and the Treaty of the Lateran of 11th February, 1929, coupled with our diplomatic representation, at the Vatican and its diplomatic representation in Ireland, may strengthen the argument for recognition in our Courts of corporations established by the Church, whose special position, as the guardian of the Faith professed by the great majority of the citizens, is formally recognised by the State under the Constitution. On the other hand, these corporations have (apart from their corporate character) little in common with the ordinary foreign company; and the Cathedral Chapter of Killala was organised as a corporation for the express purpose of carrying on its work in Ireland and nowhere else; its claim to recognition here as a corporation, if based on foreign law as distinct from the Common law, must therefore meet the objection that the claim involves the admission by our municipal law of an external jurisdiction to incorporate our citizens in Ireland and have the incorporation acknowledged by the state, though made regardless of our own laws as to incorporation.

A decision on the claim under either of its alternative forms may be far-reaching and would, I fear, involve expense disproportionate to its importance to Canon Howley's estate. If the Legislature sees no objection to recognition of the incorporation of Bishops and Chapters under Canon Law, a statute *ad hoc* would be a most convenient solution. I am not in a position, without further argument and on the material now before me, to attempt to decide the issue; nor is there any immediate need to decide it; if the matter has to be decided, I think further evidence will be necessary as to the precise position occupied by His Lordship the Bishop of Killala in Canon Law with regard to the Chapter and as to the precise corporation or corporations which I am invited to recognise as trustees of Canon Howley's will.

The testator could have avoided the administrative difficulty by resorting to the expedient provided by s. 15 of the Charitable Donations and Bequests Act, 1844, and I trust that means may be devised for making the administration of the trust effective, without asking the Court to decide questions arising out of the Canon Law.

The execution of the trusts of the will may present some difficulty during the time that must elapse before either the lawful trustees of the will are ascertained by the Court or an effective plan for dealing with an anomalous situation is elaborated and carried out, without the decision of this legal question; such a plan, whether in the form of a Scheme or not, may need the sanction of the Court.

I understand that all the property now stands solely in the name of the Bishop of Killala, the only executor who has proved the will, and I think that he should continue to hold the property until the position is clarified.

But, should His Lordship desire my aid in the interim, I shall be very willing to consider a plan for facilitating the execution of the trusts by giving express authority to named persons, being the existing members of the Chapter at the date of my suggested order, to act in the trusts of the will, in their individual capacities, in conjunction with the Bishop, until a date to be fixed, for the purpose of paying the annuities, distributing the money for masses, and deciding upon the application of the residue of income, so far as these duties may not have been performed since the death of the testator; I see no difficulty in making an interim order of that kind under the same jurisdiction as an order for a Scheme.

I have only to add that, if the income for any year be insufficient to meet in full all the payments directed by the will, the annuities and the money for masses must abate rateably and there can be no resort to capital for a deficiency; and that, though the testator expressly directed the Bishop and Chapter not to sell his "shares" and to transfer them into their own names, apparently as a permanent investment, it is, in my opinion, the duty of prudent trustees to place the whole property in trustee investments; I must, however, have regard to the fact that war conditions may have unduly devalued all or some of the securities; I have no evidence on this point; and my general opinion, given in response to a question in the summons and without expert evidence upon the particular securities held by the testator, is meant to be no more than general guidance to the trustees; at the present time a sale may be most undesirable and, in that case, my general opinion is not intended as a direction for sale at this time; upon this question the Bishop of Killala, whom I take to be the only executor acting as such, will, no doubt, take advice; he may then be justified in deciding to defer the sale and he can, of course, if necessary, apply to the Court for an express order in the matter.

Notes and Questions

1. Do you agree with Gavan Duffy J.'s description of "charity" in law being an "artificial conception"? See further, *Irish Land Law*, para. 9.091.
2. See further on gifts for religious purposes, *O'Hanlon* v. *Logue*, p.473, *infra*.

BANK OF IRELAND TRUSTEE CO. LTD V. ATTORNEY-GENERAL

[1957] I.R. 257 (High Court)

The facts are set out in the judgment.

Dixon J.:

The bequest in this case was as follows:-

"£2,000 to Sister Therese of the Carmelite Convent, Blackrock, County Dublin, or should she predecease me then to the Prioress for the time being of the said Convent to be applied in either case for the repair and/or improvement of the Convent." The only question raised is whether this is a valid charitable bequest in law. On the terms of the bequest it is clear that no question of a perpetuity could arise and the bequest is capable of being upheld as a valid non-charitable gift. The matter would, therefore, be academic were it not for the exemption from legacy duty given by the Stamp Duties Assimilation Act, 1842, s. 38, in the case of any legacy which is to be applied "in support of any charitable institution in Ireland, or for any purpose merely charitable." To determine the question of exemption or non-exemption, the Revenue Commissioners were served with the proceedings and have appeared, and been heard, by counsel. As has been pointed out, the word, "merely," does not really add anything to the force of the words, "merely charitable," in the Statute of 1842: see *Attorney-General* v. *Bagot* 13 Ir. C.L.R. 48; and the net question, therefore, is whether the bequest is charitable. The testatrix, herself, so described it in her will, as the bequest is the first of a number which she introduced by the words, "I make the following charitable bequests"; but this does not conclude the matter.

The expressed purpose of the gift is the repair and/or improvement of the Convent, which was taken in the argument to refer, and does in my view refer, to the buildings which house the nuns who form the notional entity of the Convent. Money spent on the repair or improvement of such buildings would contribute to the maintenance and continued existence of that entity and should, therefore, in my view, be regarded as being for the benefit of the Convent, considered as such an entity, although the actual mode of application is specified and limited. It is true that, in *Stewart* v. *Green* 5 Ir. R. Eq. 471, at p. 477, Lord O'Hagan L.C. said:– "In this case, on the contrary, whatever may be our supposition as to the testator's object, his bounty is bestowed only 'for the use and benefit' of the community, and there is not a word in the will to cast upon them the obligation of using it in charity, or for the advantage of any but themselves." In the view, however, which he and his fellow-member of the Court of Chancery Appeals took in that case, the community in question was not itself a valid object of charity. I do not think he intended to suggest that a gift to an institution or organisation, which was itself an object of charity, would not be a charitable gift if it could be applied to the material advantage of the institution or organisation. The question in this case is whether the community of nuns constituting the convent at Blackrock, Co. Dublin, is a charitable organisation.

This community consists of Roman Catholic nuns and belongs to what is known as the Order of Discalced Carmelite nuns. While there are a number of convents of the Order in Ireland, each convent is independent of and unattached to any other convent. Each convent, however, is subject to the rule of the Father-General of the Discalced Carmelite friars or, in certain cases, to that of the local Ordinary or Bishop. Each convent is limited in numbers to 20 or 21 members. The existence of the ladies thus associated together is, by the rule of the Order, a strictly cloistered or secluded one. They are engaged solely in a life of contemplation and prayer, living in strict enclosure in the convent, having contact with outside persons only when strictly necessary as prescribed by the relevant constitutions, and engaging in no outside activities of any kind. Each convent must have a church attached which is not accessible by the nuns but is accessible by the priest, his assistants and such people from the locality as wish to assist. In this church, Mass is celebrated every day at which the public can assist. There is also a daily choral service at which the public can assist. The members of the community assist at the Mass or recite the choral service in a choir which communicates with the church by means of a grating but to which non-members of the convent have not access. The members and the number of members of the community will, of course, vary from time to time.

The purpose of the life of these Carmelite nuns is summarised by the following statement taken from the Prologue to the Constitutions of the Discalced Friars of the Order:– "Two vocations in their due order have been divinely ordained. The more important aim of our life shall be the love and contemplation of divine things and the secondary aim the apostolate, particularly all that pertains to our neighbour's salvation."

For the purposes of this case, there was exhibited, and admitted in evidence, an affidavit sworn for the purposes of the case of *Gilmour* v. *Coats* [1948] 1 Ch. 340 in England (referred to later) by His Eminence Cardinal Griffin, Roman Catholic Archbishop of Westminster.

In that affidavit, the Cardinal Archbishop dealt fully with the life of the Carmelite nuns and with the teaching of the Roman Catholic Church as to their activities. He distinguished first between the active and the contemplative orders and deposed that, as to the active orders, it is the teaching of the Church that the fruitfulness of their exterior works for their neighbour – at any rate so far as his eternal interests are concerned – depends on the degree to which they devote themselves to the contemplative life and its penances. He stated the purpose of a Catholic woman in joining a contemplative order – as indeed any other religious order – as being to promote in herself more fully and pefectly the love of God, expressed in as perfect a submission to His will as she can achieve with the aid of His grace, to promote that love in her neighbour and to make reparation to God for the sins of mankind; and she joins a contemplative order for that purpose because it is the teaching of the Church that the religious life is, as it is called, the state of perfection.

He then referred to the passage from the Prologue to the Constitutions of the Discalced Friars, already quoted, and continued:- "It is evident from this and from what I have previously stated that though the discalced nuns do not engage in exterior works for the benefit of their neighbour, it would be an incomplete statement of their purpose to say that it is merely the working out of their own salvation by religious exercises and self-denial."

There then follow three paragraphs in the affidavit of the Cardinal Archbishop which I think it would be improper to attempt to paraphrase or curtail. They are paras. 5, 6 and 7 which read as follows:-

"5. This becomes the more apparent when one considers the teaching of the Church on the effect of the fulfilment of their purpose on the advancement of religion among those outside their convents and the benefit which they thereby confer on their neighbour. It is the teaching of the Church that none of its members leads a life which is isolated from the lives of his fellow members, except in so far as they associate for the purpose of corporate worship, but that on the contrary all Christians as members and cells of Christ's mystical body are one with Christ and one with another. The present Pope applying the words of St. Paul – 'As in one body we have many members, but all members have not the same office; so we being many are one body in Christ; and every one members of another,' reiterates in his Encyclical Letter 'Mystici Corporis Christi' the teaching of the Church that the ministries of Christ's body, the Church, include not only persons in sacred orders but also all those who have embraced the evangelical counsels and lead either an active life among men, or a hidden life in the cloister, or else contrive to combine the two, according to the institution to which they belong – thus portraying the poverty, obedience and virginity of the Redeemer; that though Christ bestowed upon His Church the boundless treasures of the redemption without any co-operation on her part yet in the distribution of that treasure. He not only shares the work of sanctification with the Church but wills it to arise in a certain manner out of her labour; that the salvation of many souls depends on the prayers and voluntary mortifications offered for that intention by the members of the mystical body of Jesus Christ; and that though public prayer excels any other, nevertheless all prayers, even those said in a most private way, have their dignity and their efficacy and are also of great benefit to the whole mystical body, for in that body there can be no good and virtuous deed performed by individual members which does not through the Communion of Saints redound also to the welfare of all.

"6. Further it is the teaching of the Church that no person can enter into eternal life in heaven unless when he dies he possesses that life which is additional to and above his natural life, and is for this reason called supernatural life, and which raises his natural powers of mind and will and enables him to know, love and serve God in this life and to know and love Him in heaven. It is also the teaching of the Church that this life and the (supernatural) assistance or graces, which enable a person to obtain and preserve and develop it and to recover it if it is lost by the rejection of God, are His free gifts which he can give without the intervention of any man, but which – as the present Pope points out in the passage in his Encyclical Letter to which I have referred – He has ordained that He will give in response to the prayers and mortifications of the members of the Church for their neighbours both inside and outside the Church. It is in view of these truths that the daily prayers and mortifications, which the Carmelite nuns, like other religious, offer for their neighbour both inside and outside the Church, advance religion and are an inestimable spiritual benefit to their neighbour, bringing to those who are ignorant of them or have rejected them the gifts of God and the graces to obtain them and bringing to those who possess His gifts the graces of perseverance and progress in the supernatural life – in a word supplying for those who through ignorance or lack of zeal or the preoccupations of life in the world cannot or will not help themselves. Moreover, it is the teaching of the Church that the prayers and mortifications of the contemplative and practising religious and especially efficacious in view of the high degree of union with God which results from the following of their vocation.

"7. Lastly, it is an undoubted fact that the practice of the religious life of the Carmelite nuns and other religious is a source of great edification to other Catholics – and indeed in innumerable cases to non-Catholics – leading them to a higher estimation of spiritual things and to a greater striving after their own spiritual perfection, and that the knowledge that there are men and women who are prepared to sacrifice all that the worldly in man holds dear in order to attain a great love of God and union with Him inculcates in them a greater estimation of the value and importance of the things which are eternal than they would have if they had not these examples before them."

The question whether a contemplative order could be a charitable institution was decided in 1871 in the well-known case of *Cocks* v. *Manners* L.R. 12 Eq. 574 by Sir John Wickens V.-C. and this case was long taken to have settled the law. That case was concerned with bequests to two religious institutions, one of them a Dominican Convent, the other a Convent of Sisters of Charity. The former belonged to a contemplative order, the latter to an active order; and the decision was that the former was not a charitable institution, while the latter was. The Vice-Chancellor's view of the latter institution was (p.584) that it was "in point of law, a voluntary association for the purposes of teaching the ignorant and nursing the sick"; and, he went on to say, that he could not distinguish it in this respect from any of the numerous voluntary associations established for the purpose of performing charitable functions. As to the former institution – the Dominican Convent – he said (at p.585):- "A voluntary association of women for the purpose of working out their own salvation by religious exercises and self-denial seems to me to have none of the requisites of a charitable institution, whether the word 'charitable' is used in its popular sense or in its legal sense. It is said, in some of the cases, that religious purposes are charitable, but that can only be true as to religious services tending directly or indirectly towards the instruction or edification of the public; an annuity to an individual, so long as he spent his time in retirement and constant devotion, would not be charitable, nor would a gift to ten persons, so long as they lived together in retirement and performed acts of devotion, be charitable." This is an often-quoted passage. It has usually been taken, and I take it, that the Vice-Chancellor used the expression, "religious services," in a wide sense rather than in a narrow liturgical one – if, indeed, he did not merely mean to repeat the expression, "religious purposes."

In *Maguire* v. *Attorney-General* [1943] I.R. 238, Gavan Duffy J., as he then was, took the view that the decision of Sir John Wickens was (p. 248) "a judgment on fact, and the essential fact determined was the fact that the England of 1871 was not edified by sequestered piety, unaccompanied by civic works of mercy." This might, perhaps, be criticised as too narrow a view of *Cocks* v. *Manners* L.R. 12 Eq. 574; but, whatever the evidenciary defects of that case, these were remedied in the later and recent case of *Gilmour* v. *Coats* [1949] A.C. 426 in which the House of Lords affirmed the judgment of the Court of Appeal [1948] Ch. 340, and approved of *Cocks* v. *Manners* L.R. 12 Eq. 574, notwithstanding the evidence of His Eminence Cardinal Griffin, already referred to. The authority, accuracy or sincerity of this evidence was not questioned in any way. The case concerned a settlement made for the benefit of a convent belonging to the same Order as is in question here. The main grounds for rejecting the claim of the convent to be a charitable institution seem to have been that the element of public benefit is essential to render a purpose charitable in law and this applies equally to religious as to other charities; that the benefit of intercessory prayer to the public is not susceptible of legal proof and the Court can only act on such proof; and that, further, the element of edification by example is too vague and intangible to satisfy the test of public benefit.

The proposition that proof of public benefit in any objective sense is necessary to render a religious purpose charitable may be doubted as having been the law in this country, if it ever was, since *O'Hanlon* v. *Logue* [1906] 1 I.R. 247. It is, perhaps, also a little inconsistent with the statement of Lord Reid in *Gilmour* v. *Coats* [1949] A.C. 426, at p. 458 that "the law of England has always shown favour to gifts for religious purposes. It does not now in this matter prefer one religion to another. It assumes that it is good for man to have and to practise a religion . . ." Assuming, however, the validity of the proposition, it is difficult to see why the public benefit inherent in the private celebration of the Roman Catholic Sacrifice of the Mass (as in *O'Hanlon* v. *Logue* [1906] 1 I.R. 247) should be susceptible of legal proof while the public benefit of private prayer is not. *O'Hanlon* v. *Logue* [1906] 1 I.R. 247 of course, was an Irish decision and the decision of Luxmoore J. in *In re Caus* [1934] 1 Ch. 162, which, in effect, applied the reasoning of *O'Hanlon* v. *Logue* [1906] 1 I.R. 247 to an English bequest, was, logically enough, not approved in *Gilmour* v. *Coats* [1949] A.C. 426, at p. 458. Lord Simonds in the latter case (at p. 447) having referred to *In re Caus* [1934] 1 Ch. 162 and to *O'Hanlon* v. *Logue* [1906] 1 I.R. 247 and also to *Attorney-General* v. *Hall* [1897] 1 I.R. 246, went on to say:- "I am unable to accept the view, which at least in the Irish cases is clearly expressed, that in intercessory prayer and edification that public benefit which is the condition of legal charity is to be found." The learned Law Lord here recognised, as did the other members of the House of Lords, and also the members of the Court of Appeal, a divergence between the law of the two countries. In this country, the provisions of Article 44 of the Constitution now deal with religion and it is implicit in the terms of the Article that adherence to and practice of any of the religions there recognised may be assumed to be of public benefit.

In *Gilmour* v. *Coats* [1949] A.C. 426 Lord Reid said (at p. 461) "there must be some limit to the kind of indirect instruction or edification which will constitute a public benefit." Somewhat the same idea was earlier expressed in this country by Mr. Justice Black in *Munster and Leinster Bank* v. *Attorney-General* [1940] I.R. 19, at p. 30, where he said:– "There are perhaps few forms of human activity, good in themselves, but solely designed to benefit individuals associated for the purpose of securing that benefit, which may not have some repercussions or consequential effects beneficial to some section of the general community; and unless a further and sweeping inroad is to be made on the rule against perpetutities, the line must be drawn somewhere. *Cocks* v. *Manners* L.R. 12 Eq. 574 has drawn it." The difficulty I feel about this view is on what basis or criterion, unless a purely arbitrary one, the line can be drawn at any particular point. The evidence must be accepted, if indeed evidence is needed, that, while the members of both types of orders are concerned with their own personal sanctification they are also concerned with that of others. It is only in the means adopted to achieve their purposes that there is any difference, the active orders adding to their other activities the external work of mercy. Yet, Mr. Justice Black can hardly have meant to confine the scope of the beneficial effects to which he referred to merely material benefits to others and not to include what may be termed spiritual or religious benefits.

The question with which I am concerned was decided by Gavan Duffy P. in *Maguire* v. *Attorney-General* [1943] I.R. 238, already referred to. The order with which he was there concerned – the Order of Marie Reparatrice, generally called the Order of Perpetual Adoration – was an enclosed, contemplative order similar in constitution and rule of life to the order in the present case. The ground on which the learned President upheld the gift as a good charitable one was that it was a gift for a pious use which was a good charitable gift at common law in pre-Reformation days in England, and, therefore, also in Ireland from the time that all statutory bars against the application of the common law to gifts for pious uses had disappeared, that is, from at least the date of the Irish Toleration Act of 1793. In this view, he was expressly following one of what he called "the dual grounds" on which Palles C.B. and FitzGibbon L.J. had justified their decision in *O'Hanlon* v. *Logue* [1906] 1 I.R. 247. He stated that he rested his judgment upon the common law and that he had no occasion to look beyond it for the resultant good to the common weal. This observation referred to the second ground in *O'Hanlon* v. *Logue* [1906] 1 I.R. 247, viz., that the gift imported the element of public benefit. Earlier, however, in the same judgment he had said (at p. 248):- "I shall waste no time in establishing the proposition of fact that the cloister is a powerful source of general edification in this country." From this, it may be inferred that, if he had thought it necessary to decide the point, he would have found no difficulty in holding that this element of edification, so far from being incapable of proof, could and should be assumed to exist in this country.

This decision is not binding on me; but, of course, I should follow it unless there were reasons which I regarded as compelling for not doing so. One suggested reason, which on examination proves to be groundless, is the circumstance alluded to in

Gilmour v. *Coats* [1949] A.C. 426 that there is an apparent conflict of opinion on the point in the Irish decisions. The conflict is only apparent. The other decisions are that of Black J. in *Munster and Leinster Bank* v. *Attorney-General* [1940] I.R. 19, already mentioned, and that of Overend J. in *McNamee* v. *Mansfield* [1945] I.R. 13. The former case was concerned with an entirely different point and the observation of Mr. Justice Black already quoted, as to *Cocks* v. *Manners* L.R. 12 Eq. 574, was *obiter*. The latter case was concerned with two gifts, one to a monastery of Carmelite friars, the other to a convent of Carmelite nuns. It was clear that the friars engaged in activities some of which were not strictly charitable or religious in character. The learned Judge said:- "It may well be that many, and probably the majority, of the purposes of the Order are religious in character, but I have also no doubt that there are several purposes which are not charitable in the legal sense and that it would, therefore, be possible for the donee, without breach of trust, to apply the gift for such non-charitable purposes. Accordingly, the gift to the Prior cannot be upheld as a charitable gift, and the same applies to the gift to the Superioress." The judgment was not a reserved one and Mr. Justice Overend did not, apparently, advert to the circumstance that the Convent of Carmelite nuns was an enclosed one, not engaging in any activities of a non-religious character, and, therefore, in a different position from that of the friars. He founded his decision on that of the Supreme Court in *In re Byrne, Deceased; Shaw* v. *Attorney-General and Others* [1935] I.R. 782, as to a gift to the Jesuit Order, and the correctness of his decision, so far as it applied to the Carmelite friars, could hardly be questioned. Inasmuch as he did not consider the position of the Carmelite nuns independently of that of the friars or as one to which any different considerations might apply, I do not think the case should be considered as authoritative on the point with which I am concerned. *Maguire* v. *Attorney-General* [1943] I.R. 238, therefore, stands as the only clear-cut decision here on the point.

While, as I have said, I am not bound by it, I prefer the reasoning, in it to that of *Gilmour* v. *Coats* [1949] A.C. 426 and, therefore, propose to follow and apply it. That decision itself was based on the earlier decisions of the former Court of Appeal in this country. These decisions are binding on me and, while the exact point was not decided, the reasoning in them is compelling and the result of them sufficiently close to the present case to make them coercive. These cases are *Attorney-General* v. *Hall* [1897] 2 I.R. 426 and *O'Hanlon* v. *Logue* [1906] 1 I.R. 247 the former concerned with the celebration of Mass in public, the latter with the celebration of Mass whether in public or private. *O'Hanlon* v. *Logue* [1906] 1 I.R. 247 overruled the earlier decision of the Court of Exchequer in *Attorney-General* v. *Delaney* I.R. 10 C.L. 104 as to the celebration of Mass in private not being a charitable purpose. In both the cases mentioned, the Court of Appeal adopted and applied the subjective test which seems to have been rejected in *Gilmour* v. *Coats* [1949] A.C. 426 so far as a gift for a religious purpose is concerned. Thus, in the former case, FitzGibbon L.J. said (at p. 449):– "It is enough to say that where, according to the religious belief of a body of persons recognised as part of the public, an act of religion done by a public minister of their Church, is for the spiritual advantage of them all, a bequest for the benefit of a minister of religion to perform that act must be deemed charitable."

This subjective approach was carried further and elaborated in *O'Hanlon* v. *Logue* [1906] 1 I.R. 247. It constituted the second of the "dual grounds" to which Gavan Duffy P. referred. The effect of *Attorney-General* v. *Hall* [1897] 2 I.R. 426 and *O'Hanlon* v. *Logue* [1906] 1 I.R. 247 on this aspect of the matter could not be better expressed than in the summary by Lord O'Brien L.C.J. in *Attorney-General* v. *Becher* [1910] 2 I.R. 251, at p. 260. Having first referred to the judgment of Palles C.B. in *O'Hanlon* v. *Logue* [1906] 1 I.R. 247 he continued:– "Lord Justice FitzGibbon, who took a very great interest in the question under deliberation, also delivered an attractive judgment, but his view may be made the more clear by reference to the judgment of Lord Justice Holmes, who, by placing in apposition – in juxtaposition – the view of the Lord Chief Baron, in *Delaney's Case* I.R. 10 C.L. 104, which, with his own concurrence, was overruled, and the view of the Lord Justice FitzGibbon in *Hall's Case* [1897] 2 I.R. 426, brought out the test, the guiding principle of the decision, with great distinctness. Lord Justice Holmes in his judgment (see p. 284 of the report) pursues the test, the guiding principle, from the words. "On what ground is it argued that the bequest in *The Attorney-General* v. *Hall* [1897] 2 I.R. 426 is charitable, while that in *The Attorney General* v. *Delaney* I.R. 10 C.L. 104, is not," down to the end of his judgment. All this is very relevant, but I will content myself with giving one excerpt from it. After, as I said, placing in apposition the view of the Lord Chief Baron in *The Attorney-General* v. *Delaney* I.R. 10 C.L. 104, and that of Lord Justice FitzGibbon in *The Attorney-General* v. *Hall* [1897] 2 I.R. 426, the Lord Justice proceeds as follows;- "It will be observed that the difference in the propositions laid down in the two passages I have quoted is, that in one it is stated that the Court cannot derive the element of public benefit from the efficacy, spritual or temporal, which, according to the faith of the testator, the religious act may possess, but must ascertain the existence of such benefit by independent investigation; while in the second passage the belief of the testator and of the Church to which he belongs is made the only test." Lord O'Brien then went on:- "This last test in the so-called second passage is that which the Lord Justice, in common with the other members of the Court, ultimately adopted as the true test, and which I believe to be and adopt as the true test."

He had earlier quoted the following passage from Walker L.C. in *O'Hanlon* v. *Logue* [1906] 1 I.R. 247 (at pp. 259, 260):–

"There are some legal propositions germane to the case for which it would be mere pedantry to cite authority . . . (c) that a gift for the advancement of 'religion' is a charitable gift; and that in applying this principle, the Court does not enter into an inquiry as to the truth or soundness of any religious doctrine, provided it be not contrary to morals, or contain nothing contrary to law . . . . Whether the subject of the gift be religious or for an educational purpose, the Court does not set up its own opinion. It is enough that it is not illegal, or contrary to public policy, or opposed to the settled principles of morality.

The approach to the matter, and these qualifications on the full acceptance of any belief of a testator, were both combined and expressed in the following words by Gibson J. in *Attorney-General* v. *Becher* [1910] 2 I.R. 251, at p. 265, and which, I think, represent the correct view:– "The decision in *O'Hanlon* v. *Logue* [1906] 1 I.R. 247, where the question related solely to Christian worship, is based on the position that religious charities, like ordinary charities, depend for their validity solely on the subjective creed and intention of the donor, subject to conditions that the objects contemplated are not immoral or contrary to law, and are intended to be for the benefit of others; such conditions being of an objective character."

While *Cocks* v. *Manners* L.R. 12 Eq. 574 is referred to once in argument in both *Attorney-General* v. *Hall* [1897] 2 I.R. 426 and *O'Hanlon* v. *Logue* [1906] 1 I.R. 247, once in the judgments in *Attorney-General* v. *Hall* [1897] 2 I.R. 426, and not at all in the judgments in *O'Hanlon* v. *Logue* [1906] 1 I.R. 247, the result of that case is clearly inconsistent with the principles established in these two Irish cases.

If formal proof were necessary, the affidavit of the Cardinal Archbishop, already referred to, makes it abundantly clear that the religious activities and way of life of the Carmelite nuns are believed to have a special efficacy, to be a strong force in the advancement of religion, and to be of spiritual benefit to a large section of the public.

On the "dual grounds," therefore, I hold the bequest in question to be a good charitable gift. I only think it necessary to make two further observations.

On reading the judgments in *Gilmour* v. *Coats* [1949] A.C. 426, one gets the impression that many of the judges who considered the question in that case were unduly preoccupied with what I might call the problem of the hermit. Their approach was that, unless a gift to a hermit could be charitable, a gift to a voluntary association of hermits could not be charitable. This was an echo of the similar proposition already quoted from Wickens V.-C. in *Cocks* v. *Manners* L.R. 12 Eq. 574. If it is a sound argument, it should equally exclude the numerous associations, engaged in charitable but non-religious works, which have been held to be proper objects of charity. No conclusive answer may be capable of being given to the problem, but there may be elements of distinction in the considerations of the reasonable likelihood of continuity of activities, of the great efficacy of cooperative activity, of the scope of the benefit intended by the testator, and of the circumstances that, as Lord Simonds himself pointed out in *Gilmour* v. *Coats* [1949] A.C. 426, "the law of charity . . . . has been built up not logically but empirically." If a line must be drawn, wherever it should be drawn, the Convent of the Discalced Carmelite nuns will, in my view, be on the charitable side of it.

The other observation concerns the often-expressed idea that the legal conception of charity does not coincide with the popular one. While this is, of course, true, it is at the same time comparatively rare that an institution generally regarded as charitable by the public is not so regarded in law. In the present case, I have no doubt of the emphatic and unhesitating affirmative answer that would be given by any reasonable layman, of whatever persuasion, to the question whether this convent was a charitable institution. A close examination of a rather formidable series of judicial pronouncements has led to the same conclusion.

Notes and Questions

1. What exactly is the difference between the so-called "subjective" and "objective" tests for public benefit? This case involved a gift for religious purposes, was that significant? *Cf.* the *O hUadhaigh* case, *infra*.
2. What is the precise significance in this context of s.45 of the Charities Act, 1961? This reads:

"45. – (1) In determining whether or not a gift for the purpose of the advancement of religion is a valid charitable gift it shall be conclusively presumed that the purpose includes and will occasion public benefit.

(2) For the avoidance of the difficulties which arise in giving effect to the intentions of donors of certain gifts for the purpose of the advancement of religion and in order not to frustrate those intentions and notwithstanding that certain gifts for the purpose aforesaid, including gifts for the celebration of Masses, whether in public or in private, are valid charitable gifts, it is hereby enacted that a valid charitable gift for the purpose of the advancement of religion shall have effect and, as respects its having effect, shall be construed in accordance with the laws, canons, ordinances and tenets of the religion concerned.

(3) The foregoing subsections shall not apply in the case of gift which takes effect before the 1st day of January, 1960."

See *Irish Land Law*, para 9.092.

O hUADHAIGH V. ATTORNEY GENERAL

Unreported (High Court) (1976 No. 93 Sp) (Judgment delivered 5th February 1979)

The facts are set out in the judgment

Gannon J.:

When Gobnait Ni Bhruadair died on the 16th of January 1955, she was over ninety years of age living in Ireland having come from England to live here in or about the year 1906. She took up residence at Castlecove in Co. Kerry where she established a hospital, a co-operative store and shop and she became actively concerned and involved in the social, cultural and political activities of the people. She was a daughter of the Earl of Midleton and was born in England on the 17th of December 1861 and was given the name Albinia Lucy Brodrick. When she came to Ireland she adopted, and was know by, the name of Gobnait Ni Bhruadair. She was unmarried and at the time of her death her domicile was Irish.

By her will dated the 17th of October 1940 she appointed three executors whom she constituted the trustees of the trusts created in her will, and by a codicil dated the 15th February 1947 she reduced the number of trustees to two. Both of these have since died and the plaintiffs are presently her executors and trustees in whom her entire property is now vested in accordance with law. The plaintiffs now come before the Court on the true construction of the terms of the will in relation to the trusts imposed by the will on the residuary estate. They feel in doubt as to whether the terms of the will create more than one trust fund, and whether charitable or not. They find difficulty in understanding the directions of the will in relation to times of payments and persons for whose benefit payments are to be made. The first defendant is sued as protector of charities and in his capacity to represent this State. The second defendant, the present Earl of Midleton is a party appointed by Court Order dated the 24th of May 1978 to represent the interests of the next of kin of the testatrix who would be interested in the distribution of her residuary estate in the event of the failure of the dispositions thereof in her will. The third defendant, by the same Order of the Court dated the 24th of May 1978 is added as a defendant to

represent all persons who might expect to benefit in the event that, and are competent to argue that, the residuary estate is vested by way of a valid charitable gift.

The will and one codicil are made in the Irish language and Probate thereof was granted to the executors named therein on the 7th of October 1955. On the 2nd of December 1955 Probate of the will and codicil in the terms of an English translation were granted to the executors forth of the Principal Probate Registry of the High Court of Justice in England. The terms of the codicil are not of significance to the matters now before the Court.

The following extract is the portion of the will in relation to which all the parties, and in particular the plaintiffs as trustees, require as to its true construction the ruling of the Court.

> "AGUS ORDUIGHIM agus do-bheirim de chomhacht dom' sheiceadóiribh agus dom' fheithmheóiribh nó dá bhfurmhór fuighleach m'eastáit do chur chun tairbhe na Polbachta ar an gcaoi is fearr dár leó AGUS ORDUIGHIM fós dom' sheiceadóiribh agus dom' fheithmeóiribh nó dá bhfurmhór éantráth is dóigh leó gur gábhadh é "The Trust Fund" i, fuighleach m'eastáit do dhíol agus toradh an reaca d'úsáid i néanchuid amháin nó ina gcodaibh ar an gcaoi is fearr dár leó a raghaidh sé chun tairbhe do lucht na Poblachta le linn na huaire de réir cospóirí lucht na Poblachta de réir mar do bhíodh i mbliadhnaibh 1919 go 1921..."

The property invested in the trustees upon which such trusts are imposed is set out by the testatrix in the manner appearing from the following extract from the English translation adopted by the Probate Office in England and concludes with the translation of the Irish extract quoted above.

> "I order my trustees or trustee to put the residue of such money in their or his own name in such securities as are lawful for trustees and I empower them to change or alter if they wish those securities and to buy others that are herein authorised and I declare that the securities authorised herein to be bought or retained which shall come into possession of my trustees or trustee which are called hereafter "The Trust Fund" and the annual income coming thereout shall come to my trustees to pay an annuity of forty pounds (£40) to Cáit wife of Pádraig Ó Breanndáin as long as she lives commencing from the day of my death and to be paid in equal instalments namely a month after my death and every month thereafter free from income tax on her own personal receipt and I Direct and empower my executors and trustees or the majority of them to apply 'the residue of my estate for the benefit of the Republic' in the best way in their opinion And I also Direct and Empower my executors and trustees or the majority of them at any time they think it is necessary to sell The Trust Fund namely the residue of my estate and to use the proceeds of the sale in one share or in shares for 'the benefit of the Republicans of the time according to the objects of the Republicans as they were in the years 1919 to 1921...'"

The function of this Court is to declare what are the testamentary intentions of the testatrix as expressed by her in her will. It is not the function of the court to extract from the will by supposed construction such intentions of the testatrix as might reasonably be expected of a person of her character interests and experiences. In stating, by way of construction, the expressed intentions of the testatrix as stated in the will it may be necessary to explain in different terminology the meanings ascribed to such expressions as are used in the will. For the purposes of construing the will the Court is bound by the Order of the Probate Court as to what comprises the will. But in this instance where the will is given in a language different from that being used by the Court of construction, this Court must express in its own terms what meaning it attributes to the actual language used in the will to express the intentions of the testatrix. In this respect it is not necessary that this Court follows precisely the wording of the translation of the will adopted in England for the Grant of Probate there. Fortunately that translation was made by the member of the Irish Bar best qualified both as a lawyer and an Irish linguist at that time to do so.

Mr. Gaffney, in submitting the case for the trustees summarised briefly and conveniently the matters upon which questions have been posed in the Special

Summons by which these proceedings were initiated. He indicated a doubt as to whether or not the entire estate of the testatrix is affected by the trust directions, and suggested there might be an inconsistency between the gift to the Republic and the gift to the republicans in one or more shares. He drew attention to the difficulties also of identifying with sufficient certainty the objects of the bounty designated as "the Republic" and the class indicated as "Republicans of the time according to the objects of the Republicans as they were in the years 1919 to 1921" and the question of whether these are charitable objects in favour of which a cy près scheme might be settled in the event of uncertainty of the class or purpose of the gifts. He referred to evidence offered in the affidavits and exhibits in relation to the testatrix which might be indicative of her intentions, but referred also to the judgment of Mr. Justice Kingsmill Moore in *Re Julian Deceased* [1950] I.R. 57. I did not have regard to any such evidence other than that contained in the official copy Minutes of the first session of Dail Eireann on the 21st of January 1919 containing a declaration of the objects of the First Dail of the Republic State as it was prior to 1922 and also to the statement of the facts relevant to domicile. Mr. Gaffney adverted also to the possibility of failure of the disposition in trust either for uncertainty of objects or infringement of the rule against perpetuities and the consequent requirement of directions for administration of the estate as on intestacy. Apart from the extract from the Minutes at pages 21 to 23 of proceedings on the 21st of January 1919, and first day of the first Parliament of the Republic of Ireland 1919 to 1921, published as the official record by the Stationery Office at Dublin, the statement relative to domicile, and some matters of historical fact of which I must take judicial notice I have not had regard to any extrinsic evidence purporting to indicate the probable or supposed intentions of the testatrix. The following are the matters of historical fact to which I refer namely:

1. The first Parliament, to the proceedings of which these Minutes relate, was a Parliament convened of deputies from the thirty-two counties of Ireland; 2. from 1922 to 1937 the Republic of Ireland was an independent State comprised of twenty-six counties established under a Constitution adopted in 1922 and was known in the Irish language as Saorstat Eireann; 3. in 1937 the people of these twenty-six countries adopted a Constitution for the Republic of Ireland under the name Eire in the Irish language; 4. the final Declaration of the independent republican status of this twenty-six county State and of dissociation from Great Britain and the British Commonwealth was made in 1948. These are facts which, unless the contrary should appear from the will, I assume were known to the testatrix who made her will on the 17th of October 1940 and died on the 16th of January 1955 without having altered it, otherwise than by codicil of the 15th of February 1947.

In the portion of the will with which I am primarily concerned, there are a few matters of grammatical analysis which I have observed which may be of some significance in helping to extract the stated intentions of the testatrix. In the first place, she commences her directions to her executors and trustees with the words "Agus orduighim & do bheirim chomhacht" but in the next instruction she omitted the words "agus do bheirim chomhacht" although the contrary might be inferred from the translation used in the English Probate. In this context I think there is sound reason for the suggestion that the word "fós" as used in the second direction has a conjunctive force and might be translated as "further" rather than as "also". The submission is that the evident intention of the testatrix is that the second direction is an extension or development of the first and not simply an additional seemingly independent one. Secondly, her direction to her trustees in relation to the residue of her estate where first given is as follows: "Do chur chun tairbhe na Poblachta ar an gcaoi is fearr dár leó". The second direction in relation to the residue is expressed thus: "D'úsáid . . . ar an gcaoi is fearr leó a raghaidh sé chun tairbhe etc.". In the latter direction, there appears to be an element of choice given to the trustees which is not evident from the translation used for the English Grant and there appears also to be a variation in the terms used to signify the nature of the choice. In relation to the choice of time for selling (sic) the residue of her estate she uses the expression "éantráth is dóigh leó gur gábhadh é." Where the testatrix selects different forms of terminology to convey the same idea it may be helpful in the search for clarity of intention to recognise distinctions of meaning where distinctions of language are selected by the testatrix. In the first of these choices, the idea is clearly "in the best way in their opinion" or alternatively "in the manner which is best according to them." In relation to the choice of time "as they think" or "in their opinion" both convey the same idea as the Irish expressions. But in the last phrase "an gcaoi is fearr leó a raghaidh sé" seems significantly different from the two previous expressions of choice. The literal translation would seem to be "in the manner they prefer it should go to the benefit" etc.

In relation to the final phrase used in this particular portion of the will namely: "de réir cuspóirí lucht na Poblachta de réir mar do bhíodh i mhliadhnaibh 1919 go 1921", it is agreed by all parties that the authentic and only proper source of information as to such matters is in Clar Oibre Poblacanaighe, or, as given in English, the "Democratic Programme", declared at the meeting of the first Dail of the thirty-two county Republic and that this is and must be what the testatrix intended. I accept this submission as being correct in the circumstances and well founded in law. But this declaration of "the objects of the Republicans as they were in the years 1919 to 1921" or their aims, aspirations or objectives as in those years is expressed in the Irish language and given in the Minutes with an English translation. If I were to have recourse to such correspondence of Irish and English terminology as a guide to the terms used by the testatrix in her will I would find that the word "Phobalacht" in the only instance where used in these Minutes is there translated in English as "Commonwealth". I would find also that the word "Republic" is consistently used in the English translation as the equivalent of "Saorstat" in the seven places where that word is used in the Irish text.

It has been submitted by Mr. Connolly in the course of his persuasive arguments that the expression "lucht na Poblachta" should be construed as meaning "the people of Ireland". Had this been the meaning intended by the testatrix I think she would more probably have used the word "muintear" for its more general or wider meaning intended than the word "lucht". I consider the correct interpretation of the word "lucht" as indicating a designation or selection of a group, class or body or persons from among or apart from others rather than a generality of persons. The translation used for the English Grant of Probate clearly conveys the correct meaning by the use of the word "Republicans". This final phrase "according to the objects of the Republicans as they were in the year 1919 to 1921" is a key phrase by which, to use an expression adopted from Mr. Connolly's argument, the testatrix provides her own dictionary. It has a qualifying effect but, to the trustees, it is not clear whether it provides a definition of the republicans of the time for whose benefit the proceeds of sale are to be used or determines the manner in which such proceeds of sale are to be used. Mr. Lynch for the Attorney General argues that this phrase qualifies only the manner in which the proceeds of sale are to be used and that the phrase is referable in the adverbial sense to the use only. Both Mr. Connolly, and Miss Carroll in her clearly stated cogent arguments, submit that the clause serves both purposes and is, as Miss Carroll put it "both adjectival and adverbial in its effect". These submissions accord with my interpretation of the true expressed intention of the testatrix. But. Mr. Connolly goes further that I can accept as demonstrable or logical in submitting that this final clause qualifies the word "Republic" in the first part of the residuary gift so that it might be construed as making the people of the thirty-two counties of Ireland the objects of the trusts of the residuary estate. On the contrary, it seems to me more logical and probable that if that significant interpretation of the words "tairbhe na Poblachta" was intended by the testatrix she would have been as careful in her method of expression at that point as she was in the later clause. Mr. Lynch for the Attorney General in his thoroughly prepared argument disclaims any benefit to the State which now is, and in 1955 was, the only "Republic" and supports Mr. Connolly's contention that the testatrix intended to denote the thirty-two counties in using the phrase "tairbhe na Poblachta". But it seems to me the testatrix was conscious of and affected by the distinction between factual circumstances as she knew them to be at the time of making her will (and consequently the time it later became effective) and the circumstances as they had been to her knowledge in the years 1919 to 1921. From the terms of the will and the choice of expression by the testatrix I have no doubt that the clause "fuighleach n'eastáit do chur chun tairbhe na Poblachta ar an gcaoi is fearr dár léo" means to apply the residue of her estate in the best way in the opinion of her trustees for the benefit of the Republic of Ireland as it was at the time of her death. But she proceeded to qualify this vague general direction by the immediately following direction by confining the range of benefit only to those who, at the time of distribution by the trustees, are republicans according to the aims and objects as they were in 1919 to 1921 of republicans. The phrase "le linn na huaire" in the context can only mean at the time when the trustees make their determination to distribute and cannot be construed as the time when the will takes effect namely 16th of January 1955 nor when it was made on the 17th of October 1940. I accept as correct the submissions of all defendants that there is but a single gift of the residue of the estate entrusted to the trustees for the benefit of the objects and in the manner directed. The manner in which the testatrix introduced her directions with the words firstly "agus orduighim & do bheirim chomacht . . .dom fheithmheóiribh", and secondly "agus orduighim fós ... dom fheithmheóiribh", using the word "fós" with the meaning and effect I suggested earlier bear out this construction, and the translation used for the English Grant of Probate is also consistent with this construction.

The directions as to the objects and manner of benefit are as set out in the portion of the will commencing "agus orduighim fós" and concluding "1919 to 1921". This portion contains the directions that the determination by the trustees in the choice given to them for the benefit to the Republic of Ireland is limited to conferring benefit only on those who being within the Republic are republicans having the same aims or objects as had those republicans who subscribed to or adopted the declaration of the Democratic Programme for a thirty-two county independent State. If the concluding phrase "according to the objects of the Republicans as they were in 1919 to 1921" has an adjectival qualification, as I understand to be the expressed intention of the testatrix, not all inhabitants or citizens of the Republic can share the benefit of the gift. If this phrase has an adverbial effect, as I think is the intention expressed by the testatrix, the use to which the fund is to be put must also be determined in accordance with the aims or objects set out in the declaration of the Democratic Programme in the first session of the first Dail of the thirty-two county Republic on the 21st of January 1919. The directions of the testatrix confer on her trustees a choice as to when to distri)ute the fund, qualified only in respect of a necessity apparent to them, with an absolute discretion as to whether by a single payment or by a number of different payments. These directions also confer on the trustees an absolute discretion as to the manner, in accordance with the aims or objects set out in the Democratic Programme of the first Dail, in which the payment or payments in distribution of the residuary estate is or are to be made to the designated republicans.

The questions which now present themselves for determination are whether or not the distribution by the testatrix of her residuary estate to such objects of her bounty and in such manner and at such time or times is valid and effective. For the Attorney General it has been argued by Mr. Lynch and Miss Laffoy that unless the gift be a valid charitable trust it must fail for want of certainty or the objects to benefit, and because it is not charitable, as they contend, it must fail as a gift which may not vest within the time prescribed under the rule against perpetuities. In addition to adopting the arguments advanced for the Attorney General, Miss Carroll for the next of kin contends that whether the gift be charitable or not, the gift cannot become vested until the exercise by the trustees of the discretionary powers conferred on them and that, as the exercise of such powers may be deferred beyond the time limited by the rule against perpetuities, the gift is void and the residuary estate must devolve as on an intestacy. Mr. Connolly proferred the decision of the Court of Appeal in England *In re Smith: Public Trustee* v. *Smith* [1932] 1 Ch. 153 as the most helpful authority in support of his contention that the gift is charitable within the legal meaning of that word, and submitted that the gift vested immediately on the death of the annuitant in the survivor of those republicans of 1919 to 1921 then living subject to such selection as the trustees might make.

Mr. Connolly chose to rely on the authority of *Re Smith* as it conveniently refers to and examines a number of earlier authorities from which guidance may be obtained as to when and of what nature a gift may be charitable in the legal sense. He relied on it to support his submission that the testatrix created a trust of her residuary estate for the benefit of the people of the Republic and that such a gift in such general terms is impliedly for public purposes for a particular class and is charitable in the legal sense because in the performance of the trust the funds can and should be distributed or applied to charitable purposes in such sense.

The following is an extract from the opinion of Lord Macnaghten in the House of Lords decision in *Commissioners for Income Tax* v. *Pensel* [1891] A.C. 531 at page 583:

> "'Charity' in its legal sense comprises four principal divisions: trusts for relief of poverty; trusts for the advancement of education; trusts for the advancement of religion; and trusts for other purposes beneficial to the community not falling under any of the preceding heads. The trusts last referred to are not any the less charitable in the eye of the law, because incidentally they benefit the rich as well as the poor, as indeed, every charity that deserves the name must do either directly or indirectly".

This is an abbreviated summary of the charitable uses referred to in the preamble to the English statute of 1601 entitled "An Act to redress the Mis-employment of Lands, Goods, and Stocks of Money heretofore given to Charitable Uses" 43 Eliz. c. 4, and of those referred to in the corresponding Irish Statute of Charitable Uses (Ireland) Act 1634 10 Car. I Sess. 3 c. 1. A correspondence of these two statutes is given by Lord St. Leonards the Lord Chancellor of Ireland in *Incorporated Society* v. *Richards* 1 D. & War. 298 at 324. Many examples of charities falling within this fourth category given by Lord Macnaghten's summary are discussed in *Smith's case* with helpful extracts in the judgments therein from the opinions of Lord Shelbourne and Lord Cairns in *Goodman* v. *Mayor of Saltash* 7 App. Cas. 633 and of Lord Cave in *Attorney General* v. *National Provincial and Union Bank of England* [1924] A.C. 262. But it seems to me that in their judgments in *Smith's case* the Master of the Rolls and Lords Justices appear to direct a great deal of their attention to questions of how and by whom the trusts should be carried out in their endeavour to construe the intentions of the testator. I note that the House of Lords in *Williams* v. *Inland Revenue Commissioners* [1947] A.C. 447 and the English Court of Appeal in *Strakosch deceased, Temperly* v. *The Attorney General* [1949] 1 Ch. 529 took pains to try to explain the decision in *Smith's case* without expressly approving or disapproving of that decision. In *William's case* [1947] A.C. 447 the House of Lords held that a trust established with the objects of promoting Welsh interests in London by social intercourse; discussing all questions affecting Welsh interests; fostering the study of the Welsh language by lectures on Welsh history, literature, music and art; maintaining a library of literature in the Welsh language or relating to Wales; providing a meeting place for the benefit of Welsh people in London as a centre to promote the moral, social, spiritual and educational welfare of Welsh people was not a charitable trust. In the course of his opinion with which all the Lords present concurred, Lord Simonds said at page 455 of the Report:

> "My Lords, there are, I think, two propositions which must ever be borne in mind in any case in which the question is whether a trust is charitable. The first is that it is still the general law that a trust is not charitable and entitled to the privileges which charity confers, uless it is within the spirit and intendment of the preamble to the statute of Elizabeth 43 Eliz. C. 4, which is expressly preserved by S. 13 s. 3 of the Mortmain and Charitable Uses Act 1888".

In Ireland, the relevant statute is 10 Car. I Sess. 3 c. 1 and the 1888 Act referred to does not apply. Lord Simonds goes on:

> "The second is that the classification of charity in its legal sense into four principal divisions by Lord Macnaghten in *Income Tax Commissioners* v. *Pemsel* must always be read subject to the qualifications appearing in the judgment of Lindley

L.J. in *Re Macduff* [1896] 2 Ch. 451 at 466: Now Sir Samuel Romilly did not mean, and I am certain Lord Macnaghten did not mean, to say that every object of public general utility must necessarily be a charity. Some may be, and some may not be."

Lord Simonds proceeds to quote from the opinion of Lord Cave L.C. in *Attorney General* v. *National Provincial and Union Bank of England* [1924] A.C. 262 at 265. One further quotation from the opinion of Lord Simonds in *William's case* is apposite. At page 457 of the report in [1947] A.C. he says:

"It is not expressly stated in the preamble to the statute, but it was established in the Court of Chancery, and, so far as I am aware, the principle has been consistently maintained, that a trust, in order to be charitable, must be of a public character. It must not be merely for the benefit of particular private individuals: if it is, it will not be in law a charity though the benefit taken by those individuals is of the very character stated in the preamble."

Lord Simonds then goes on to quote the following passage from the opinion of Lord Wrenbury in *Verge* v. *somerville* [1924] A.C. 496 at 499:

"To ascertain whether a gift constitutes a valid charitable trust so as to escape being void on the ground of perpetuity, a first inquiry must be whether it is public – whether it is for the benefit of the community or of an appreciably important class of the community. The inhabitants of a parish or town, or any particular class of such inhabitants, may for instance, be the objects of such a gift, but private individuals, or a fluctuating body of private individuals cannot."

In his judgment in *Munster & Leinster Bank* v. *Attorney General* [1940] I.R. 19 Mr. Justice Black upon reviewing a number of English authorities seems to consider that a limitation of place is acceptable to define a class of the public, but that voluntary association is not. Like the judgments in *Smith's case*, the judgment of Mr. Justice Black in the *Munster & Leinster Bank case* provides an extensive collection of earlier authorities most of which are English. But I do not think that voluntary association would necessarily be unacceptable as a definition of a class of the public in Ireland. Neither do I think a distinction between the intention of the testatrix and the motives of the testatrix pertinent, as Mr. Justice Black seems to think.

The primary and fundamental inquiry is to ascertain what are the intentions of the testatrix as expressed by her, and whether or not they are to invest the ownership of her property after her death in a charity which is recognised as such in the legal sense. It is this inquiry which explains the use of the expression "the subjective test" as adopted in Irish Courts as against "the objective test" seemingly applied in England. In significant respects the law on charities in England and Ireland has diverged and *Cocks* v. *Manners* L.R. 12 Eq. 574 is no longer an acceptable authority in Ireland. (See *Re Cranston: Webb* v. *Oldfield* [1898]1 I.R. 431; *O'Hanlon* v. *Logue* [1906] 1 I.R. 260; *Attorney General* v. *Becher* [1910] I.R. 260; *Maguire deceased: Maguire* v. *Attorney General* [1943] I.R. 238; *Sheridan deceased: Bank of Ireland* v. *Attorney General & Ors.* [1957] I.R. 257). Notwithstanding such divergence in relation to the law of charity in Ireland and England the opinions expressed in the House of Lords in *Inland Revenue Commissioners* v. *Baddeley* [1955] A.C. 572 and the advice of the Judicial Committee of the Privy Council in *Davies* v. *Perpetual Trustee* [1959] A.C. 439 are of considerable assistance on the aspect of identification of a class of the public.

In case of doubt the evidence of the expressed intention of the testatrix may be tested by consideration of the nature of the object of her bounty and her belief in regard to it. It may be tested also by the certainty or otherwise of her means, as expressed by her, of identifying the object of her bounty. If her specification of the object be by classification the vagueness of her definition may leave it impossible to discern an intention within the spirit and intendment required for a "legal Charity". If such intention be discerned the vagueness of identification of the class, provided it be a class, will not defeat the intention. (See *Miley* v. *Attorney General & Ors.* [1918] 1 I.R. 455; *Byrne deceased: Shaw* v. *Attorney General & Ors.* [1935] I.R. 782; *Munster & Leinster Bank* v. *Attorney General & Ors.* [1940] I.R. 19; *Keogh deceased: McNamee* v. *Mansfield* [1945] I.R. 13; *Scott Bayley deceased: Brown* v. *Gregg* [1945] I.R. 224; *Re Meehan deceased: Tobin* v. *Cohalan* [1960] I.R. 82.) The facts that the purposes of a gift may be expressed compositely or alternatively, by words which are conjunctive or disjunctive, may be taken as evidence from which the expressed intention of the testatrix may be ascertained, but do not of themselves determine the nature, whether charitable or not, of the gift. Likewise, whether the choice of objects or of purposes be made by the testatrix or delegated to another are significant only as matters of evidence of the intention expressed of the testatrix and not as evidence of the charitable or non-charitable nature of the gift.

A further test as to the intentions of the testatrix may be found in the consideration of the time for distribution or vesting in possession of the residuary estate. A vesting which may be deferred by and for the purpose of perpetual regular continuous payments may be consistent with and indicative of a charitable gift in the legal sense. Bt a vagueness in her express directions for vesting or payment pursuant to a power of sale which could permit a period too remote to intervene might indicate such indifference as would negative a charitable intention. The difficulties of selection of persons to benefit and the ascertainment of the class from which the selection is to be made when conferred by the testatrix on her trustees, should be present to the mind of the testatrix when creating a trust, even though such difficulties could be overcome if the trust be a good charity in law. (See *Parker deceased: Kilroy* v. *Parker* [1966] I.R. 309). But the fact of such difficulties arising on the construction of the will may be a significant aspect of the evidence of the expressed intentions of the testatrix as to whether or not the trust is a charitable trust.

Bearing in mind these tests I turn again to the will of the testatrix to consider again what she has said in the portion under examination but in the context of the provisions preceding it which I have quoted from the translation used for the English Grant of Probate. My summary of her expressed intentions as I construe what she has said in her will and leading up to this part of the will is as follows. After providing that legacies be paid free of estate duty and legacy duty and that the annuity be paid free of estate duty, legacy duty and income tax she invested all her property not previously disposed of by will or codicil in her trustees. She gave them an absolute discretion as to whether or not to sell and to convert into cash property in specie, and in their absolute discretion to postpone sale, save, however, that the power of sale of reversionary interests before coming into possession may be exercised only for a reason which the trustees think special; and she declared "any real estate I have is to be accounted as personalty". Out of the cash realised on the sale of real and personal estate she directed her trustees to pay her funeral and testamentary expenses and debts, with special provision for mortgage debts, and payment of legacies and the annuity out of her personal estate and then to create a fund invested in securities which she called "The Trust Fund". Having provided for payment of the annuity of £40 by monthly payments out of this fund she directed her trustees to apply the rest of her property including this fund for the benefit of the Republic of Ireland in the way they think best and to sell her invested securities whenever they think necessary, and then to use all in one or more payments in the manner her trustees would prefer it to be applied for the benefit of the republicans at that time who have the aims or objectives of republicans of 1919 to 1921, and the payments to be applied in a manner consistent with such aims or objectives of the republicans from 1919 to 1921.

It seems significant to me that the testatrix gives no indication to her trustees as to what might be the occasion for, or standard of, necessity for the realisation of the securities, some of which at least must be retained to provide income for payment of the annuity for the life of the annuitant. Had she been more specific in her definition of the persons or class of persons she intended her trustees should benefit and as to the manner of conferring benefit on them she might have been able to give some indication of what kind of necessity she had in mind. It seems to me she had no clear idea of how the republicans she considered her trustees would wish to benefit could be recognised, because there appears to be no binding factor or limitation by organisation, by conduct or activity, by location, by regulation or by any unifying factor as a class of the public other than adoption of political thoughts and ideas. Even if she presented her trustees with the Democratic Programme of the Dail of January 1919 as their directions for the spending of her money she would not thereby demonstrate to her trustees any charitable trust or purpose within the spirit or intendment of the legal standards of charity. It is unnecessary to set out here the terms of the Democratic Programme which is essentially a statement of political objectives. I have no reason to believe that these are any different from those of this State save in respect of the area of jurisdiction. In so far as any of them correspond with charitable objects the testatrix gives no indication to her trustees that she wishes charitable purposes only to be chosen by them.

Taking an overall view of the expressed directions of the testatrix with such varied and vague discretions and latitude of apparent duty imposed on her trustees I am satisfied there is no charitable intention nor charitable gift in the legal sense in her will. The fact that her trustees for the time being themselves might have the means and opportunity of satisfying their own charitable purposes or intentions does not assist in construing the expressed intentions of the testatrix. The trustees are entitled under the will to defer beyond the time limited as lawful under the rule against perpetuities exercising their power of sale, selection and distribution and consequently the gift of the residuary estate is void for remoteness. (*Re Kingham* [1897] 1 I.R. 170; *Re Fossitt's Estate* [1934] I.R. 504).

The questions posed in the Special Summons therefore will be answered in accordance with the foregoing ruling on the construction of the will on the basis that there is no gift to charity and the disposition of the residuary estate is void for remoteness.

RE McENERY's ESTATE

[1941] I.R. 323; 75 I.L.T.R. 237 (High Court)

A testator by his will gave the following bequest: "After the death of my said wife I direct that the moneys then invested, stocks, and so forth, shall be regarded as a trust fund for enabling the sons and daughters and male descendants of my brothers to obtain professions, each suitable student to receive one hundred pounds yearly, for a reasonable time, from the dividends arising from said trust fund; and if a sufficient number of students shall not be forthcoming in any one year to exhaust the dividends the unexpended balance shall be invested and added to the trust fund . . . the trustees are to decide who are to be the beneficiaries when more suitable students offer than the dividends can meet."

Gavan Duffy J.:

This is an interesting will, and I am called upon to decide whether or not the testator's bountiful provisions for the sons and daughters and male descendants of his brothers are valid, and, if not valid generally, whether or not they can be supported to a limited extent.

On the general question I shall assume, for the purposes of this case, that charitable purposes in law comprise those described, and those analogous to the purposes described, in the English Act of Elizabeth and the Act passed in the reign of Charles I for this country; both of those Acts have been repealed, though the Elizabethan classification has been kept alive by statute in England; I shall also assume, for the purposes of educational charity here, that there is, apart from certain religious questions, no substantial difference between the intent of the old English Act and that of the unintelligible Irish Act. The English Act speaks of the maintenance of schools of learning, free schools, and scholars in universities, and the Irish Act speaks of the erection, maintenance or support of any college, school, lecturer in divinity or in any of the liberal arts or sciences, and any other like lawful and charitable uses.

Observe the public character of all these purposes. No doubt the scope of statutes passed in another era has been expanded by judicial decisions, and the process has been marked by some inevitable inconsistencies, but Courts of Equity generally have been consistently insistent on the public character of legal charity, importing a benefit to the community, or a section of the community, in the eyes of the common law of the two countries, reproduced, we are told, in the statutes. The vagaries of the supposedly uniform law of charities may be illustrated by one extract from Serjeant Moor's "Learned Reading," appended to the edition of Duke's "Charitable Uses" published in London in 1676:– as to "Scholars in Universities," he says: "These general words must be restrained to the particular Universities of Oxford and Cambridge; and to such students that study divinity, physick or law, not students in arts only, nor to any students of divinity in popery, etc.," and he explains that "Schools of Learning" do not include schools for catechising, because religion is variable and not within the statute. I was not surprised that counsel, insisting that the law of charities for Ireland and England, as explained by the two statutes, is identical refrained from drawing upon such authentic sources as Sir Francis Moor, who must have known more about the true purposes of the Act of Elizabeth than any of his contemporaries, if, as we are assured, he penned it. The fact is that we sadly need a modern, home-made statute for charitable trusts.

While some of the purposes associated with poverty in the Elizabethan Act seem to have a personal touch, perhaps the nearest approach to anything like an individual purpose in connection simply with education in either Act is in the maintenance of scholars in universities; I take that to have in view the foundation of scholarships, as "if one devise £10 a year for ever, out of his land, to maintain two scholars in Oxford and Cambridge," though by nuncupative will, this shall be good (Duke, cap. VI, case 29); but there is a wide gap between such an endowment at some university college and, for instance, a trust for the personal educational benefit, between the ages of 18 and 22, of the heir for the time being of a testator for ever, committed by the testator to his trustees; there is nothing public about that purpose and it would, in my view, be too narrow to be charitable; those prospective heirs would not constitute a section of the community for whom a charitable trust could be established.

In a search for precedent upon which, by Judge-made law, to establish the testator's bounty here as an educational charity, reliance was placed in particular upon such cases as *Spencer* v. *All Souls' College* Wilm 163, *Attorney-General* v. *Sidney Sussex College* 4 Ch. 722, and *In re Lavelle* [1914] 1 I.R. 194, decisions showing that the founder of a charity or a benefactor may lawfully associate his descendants with his bequest to a charitable institution and thus enable them to participate in his liberality; those cases find their prototype in *Griffith Flood's Case* Hob. 136; Duke, cap VI, case 40, where it was laid down that the Act of Elizabeth, overriding the law of mortmain, allowed a man to make a devise to a college at Oxford, to find a scholar of his blood from time to time. But they do nothing to validate the very different provisions of our testator's will.

The trust here is, in my opinion, too narrow to be charitable; the motive may have been charitable, but the intention was to benefit specific individuals, and the fact, though not conclusive, is worthy of note that, if the trust were good, each suitable beneficiary would appear to have an enforceable claim upon the trust, unless the number of suitable beneficiaries were so great a tax on the income as to give the trustees the special discretion allowed to them in that event. I mean that each male descendant of a brother, as he grows to manhood, if he rejects trade as a career for the moment and makes up his mind to qualify himself for an eventual archbishopric or chief justiceship or presidency of the College of Surgeons, will be entitled, on signifying his election, to call for £100 a year during a reasonable time to enable him to become a priest or barrister or surgeon, provided he be a suitable student and that his competitors be not too many.

It is just 200 years since Lord Hardwicke L.C. in *Attorney-General* v. *Pearce* 2 Atk. 87 declared that it is its extensiveness that constitutes a public charity:– "a devise to the poor of a parish is charitable. Where testators have not any particular person in their contemplation, but leave it to the discretion of a trustee to chuse out the objects, though such person is private, and each particular object may be said to be private, yet in the extensiveness of the benefit accruing from them they may very properly be called publick charities. A sum to be disposed of by A. B. and his executors, among poor housekeepers, is of this kind."

And a further difficulty in the present case is that touched upon by Mr. Justice Barton in *Laverty* v. *Laverty* [1907] 1 I.R. 9, that the trust would allow the trustees to pay £100 a year to a delicate descendant, at least if he needed this pecuniary help, to enable him to have a private "coach" in his father's private house to steer him through the examinations for some specialised profession. I do not see my way to adopting Mr. Sweeney's ingenious suggestion that I should validate an invalid trust by reading it as requiring the trustees to establish a number of scholarships, either in some university or elsewhere; that would mean resorting to the *cy-près* doctrine in order to convert a non-charitable into a charitable trust, at the expense of the persons lawfully entitled. You cannot, under cover of *cy-près*, rob Peter to pay Paul.

As to *In re Rayner* 89 L.J. Ch. 369, also relied upon by Mr. Connolly, the gift to educate the children of Maple's numerous employees took in, no doubt, a field wide enough to cover a section of the community, who were, moreover, people "comparatively poor" within Lord Bramwell's definition of a charity in *Pemsel's Case* [1891] A.C. 531, at p. 564.

I pass now to the argument in favour of a limited validity for the trust. It is urged that at least those sons and daughters and male descendants of brothers who were alive at the death of the testator are entitled to benefit. Unhappily the gifts to these beneficiaries, if severable, are suject to multiple contingencies; any beneficiary to enjoy the gift must:-

(a) survive the testator's widow and tenant for life;

(b) by reason of the codicil, survive the time, at testator's death necessarily uncertain, when, after her death, the income of the trust fund shall have proved sufficient to pay legacies amounting to £620;

(c) and, at or after that time when the income has become available, be about to enter, as a suitable student, upon a profession and ask for the testator's annuity to enable him to obtain his profession – incidentally I do not think he will be qualified, if at that time in affluent circumstances, but my decision is given quite independently of this view, which turns on the word "enable"; and he must

(d) take his chance of selection by the trustees in case the legitimate competitors for an annuity shall be more numerous than the number of £100 units produced for the time being by the income of the fund, the single trust fund intended to produce all the annuities.

It is very difficult on the language of the will to discern more than one class here, the single, though composite, class for whom, as ascertained from time to time, the single trust fund is established. It is impossible to say with certainty in advance how many years may elapse before a potential beneficiary may wish to enter a profession, unless one has regard to the actual state of the families concerned at testator's death and that I cannot do – indeed, I could only find probabilities, if I did; the first beneficiary entitled to claim and receive an annuity may be a person unborn at the death of the testator; and participation by any beneficiary depends upon the amount of available income and the number of competitors and his selection, if they are too many, by the trustees, and that may first happen at too remote a time. On principle the case seems indistinguishable from *Moore* v. *Moore* 6 Jones, Eq. 132, as summarised in par. 396 of Gray on Perpetuities (3rd Edn.), except that that case appears to have been concerned with payments out of capital; for a case of annuities out of income void under the rule against perpetuities, see *In re Gassiot* 70 L.J. Ch. 242; see also *In re Whiteford* [1915] 1 Ch. 347, where the limit was cut down by a special power, but the same principle as to uncertainty applied.

The fifth rule in *Cattlin* v. *Brown* 11 Hare 372, at p. 377, relied upon by Mr. McCarthy, has no application, because the annuity desired by a particular beneficiary may be, not merely diminished, but withheld in case of a deficiency of income to meet all the demands of the competing students; nor is the time fixed when distribution depending on a personal penchant for a profession of a suitable student, is to begin. And, as Mr. Ryan pointed out, the difficulty of escaping from the general rule under any exceptional sub-rule is greatly increased by the testator's restriction of his bounty to suitable students.

Accordingly, much as I should have liked to hold for a limited validity of the testator's gift, I cannot see my way to upholding it at all. (*Pearks* v. *Moseley* 5 A.C. 714.)

Note

See further, *Irish Land Law*, para 9.093.

II. CATEGORIES

1. *Advancement of Religion*

O'HANLON V. LOGUE

[1906] 1 I.R. 247; 40 I.L.T.R. 78 (Court of Appeal)

The facts are set out in the judgments.

Walker, C.:

In this case Felix O'Hanlon, the trustee of the will of Ellen McLaughlin, applied by summons to the Master of the Rolls to have the important question involved in the appeal decided, whether a gift for the celebration of Masses for the repose of the souls of her named relatives and herself was a valid charitable gift, though the will contains no direction that such Masses should be celebrated in public.

The gift is contained in a direction by the testatrix to her trustees to sell, in the events that happened, the leasehold mentioned in the will, "and to pay over the income of the proceeds from time to time to the Roman Catholic Primate of all Ireland for the time being, to be applied for the celebration of Masses for the repose of the souls of her late husband, her children, and herself."

The Master of the Rolls by his order, dated 13th July, 1905, has decided that this gift is void, and His Eminence Cardinal Logue has appealed.

It would have been impossible, I think, for the Master of the Rolls, having regard to the existing decisions, to have made any different order than he did. But we have been asked, and are compelled, to reconsider the principle upon which the decisions in *The Attorney-General* v. *Delaney* I.R. 10 C.L. 104 and *The Attorney-General* v. *Hall* [1896] 2 I.R. 291; [1897] 2 I.R. 426 rest; and assuming it to have been now determined in this Court that a gift for Masses for the repose of the souls of the dead to be celebrated in public is a valid charitable gift, to consider further whether such a gift is valid though there be no direction for celebration in public – in other words, whether its validity as a charitable gift does not rest upon far higher grounds than the existence of a direction for public celebration.

I have had the advantage of reading the elaborate judgment which will be delivered by the Lord Chief Baron. The Court of Exchequer, presided over by the Lord Chief Baron, decided in *The Attorney-General* v. *Delaney* I.R. 10 C.L. 104 that a gift simply for the celebration of Masses was not a valid charitable gift; but the Chief Baron expressed the opinion that such a gift would be valid if there were a direction that the Masses should be celebrated in public. That opinion of the Chief Baron passed into decision in the case of *The Attorney-General* v. *Hall* [1897] 2 I.R. 426, and in this Court it did not become necessary for our decision to go beyond that. I was satisfied myself that the point before us would arise later, and I then thought there was no valid reason for differentiating between the two classes of case. Lord Justice FitzGibbon, however, did not shrink from considering the larger question on principle. He says- "I find it necessary to look more deeply for the real foundation of the law, which the Attorney-General has expressly declined to challenge, viz. that bequests for Masses are valid, in order to see whether it is possible to base their validity upon any principle which will not also establish their charitable character, irrespectively of the mode of celebration." Further consideration has satisfied the Chief Baron that the validity of the gift as a charitable one does depend upon a principle which is irrespective of the mode of celebration, and I concur with him in that result.

There are some legal propositions germane to the case for which it would be mere pedantry to cite authority:- *(a)* That in speaking of what is "charitable" we use the word in the artificial sense, which is derived from the statute 43 Eliz. c. 4 (Eng.), and 10 Car. 1, sess. 3, c. 1 (Ir.); *(b)* That included amongst charitable objects is one which, according to the ideas of the giver, is for the public benefit; *(c)* That a gift for the advancement of "religion" is a charitable gift; and that in applying this principle, the Court does not enter into an inquiry as to the truth or soundness of any religious doctrine, provided it be not contrary to morals, or contain nothing contrary to law. All religions are equal in the eye of the law, and this especially applies since the abolition in this country of a State Church. Whether the subject of the gift be religious or for an educational purpose, the Court does not set up its own opinion. It is enough that it is not illegal, or contrary to public policy, or opposed to the settled principles of morality. A remarkable illustration is furnished by the decision in *Webb* v. *Oldfield* [1898] 1 I.R. 431, a gift for the spread of vegetarian principles – ideas that might be in the view of many erroneous and visionary.

It may also be treated as settled law that in Ireland a gift for Masses is not illegal as a superstitious use. On that point *Read* v. *Hodgens* 7 Ir. Eq. R. 34 is a binding and accepted authority; and the case of *The Commissioners of Charitable Donations* v. *Walsh Ibid*. 34, note, has been treated as a decision to the same effect, though it may well be that a careful examination of the gifts there might show, as pointed out by the Lord Chief Baron, that one gift involved a public celebration, and the other an endowment of religion. In pre-Reformation times a gift for Masses would be valid at Common Law and charitable, as that word must be interpreted.

In *The Attorney-General* v. *Delaney* I.R. 10 C.L. 104 evidence was given by Dr. Delaney as to the exact nature of a Mass. He states that, according to the doctrine of the Roman Catholic Church, the Mass is a true and real sacrifice offered to God by the priest, not in his own person only, but in the name of the Church whose minister he is. Every Mass, on whatever occasion used, is offered to God in the name of the Church, to propitiate His anger, to return thanks for His benefits, and to bring down His blessings upon the whole world. Some portions of the Mass are invariable, and some are variable. Amongst those invariable are an offering of the Host for his own sins, and for all present, and also for all faithful Christians both living and dead; and the sacrifice is offered for the Church, and the granting to it of peace, and its preservation and union. It includes commemoration of the living and of the dead and he states it is impossible, according to the doctrine of the Church, that a Mass can be offered for the benefit of one or more individuals living or dead, to the exclusion of the general objects included by the Church. When a *honorarium* is given for the purpose of saying a Mass for a departed soul, the priest is bound to say it with that intention; but that obligation may be discharged by a mental act of the priest, but it cannot be discharged by the ordinary parochial Mass which he says on Sundays and holidays. Such *honoraria* for Masses form portion of the ordinary income and means of livelihood of priests, and are generally in Ireland distributed, by those to whom the distribution is entrusted, amongst priests whose circumstances are such that they stand in need of the assistance offered.

Such is the evidence as to the exact nature of the Mass, both generally, and where a commemoration of named dead is included. It is settled by authority which binds us that where there is a direction to celebrate the Mass in public, the gift is a valid charitable one; but what makes it charitable is the performance of an act of the Church of the most solemn kind, which results in benefit to the whole body of the faithful, and the results of that benefit cannot depend upon the presence or absence of a congregation. Furthermore, adopting the evidence of Dr. Delaney, it seems to me that the bequest of a sum of money for the saying of Masses, which cannot be satisfied by the ordinary parochial Mass, and the conferring of *honoraria* upon the priests who celebrate the Masses, are an endowment of the priest who celebrates this solemn sacrifice, and therefore an advancement of religion just as much in principle as the erection of a Church in which they might be said, or the endowment of an additional priest to celebrate them.

Authority is not needed for the proposition that a gift for such a purpose would be a good charitable one. I may mention *Powerscourt* v. *Powerscourt* 1 Moll. 616 and *Lea* v. *Cooke* 34 Ch. D. 528.

I think the appeal should be allowed, and the question answered according to the result of our decision.

Palles, C.B.:

I concur with the Lord Chancellor in the opinion that this appeal should be allowed; but as doing so involves the disaffirmance of the judgment in *The Attorney-General* v. *Delaney* I.R. 10 C.L. 104, to which I was a party, I desire to consider in some detail the question involved.

The decision of this Court in *The Attorney-General* v. *Hall* [1897] 2 I.R. 426

overruled all the objections to the charitable nature of the bequest there under consideration; a bequest which differs from that as to which the question here arises by a single circumstance only, the absence here of a direction that the Masses shall be celebrated in public.

Thus the question is: Is it an essential condition to the celebration of Mass being charitable that it should be in public?

In my view, *The Attorney-General* v. *Delaney* I.R. 10 C.L. 104 is the earliest decision in this country on the subject. The subsequent decisions were based upon it as the decree of a Court of co-ordinate jursidiction. They therefore will not require separate examination, as if the former be overruled, the others must necessarily share the same fate.

It is true that the nature of a bequest for Masses was considered in two earlier cases – in *The Commissioners of Charitable Donations and Bequests* v. *Walsh* 7 Ir. Eq. R. 34, note, in 1823, and in *Read* v. *Hodgens Ibid.* 17, in 1844 – but the effect of the absence of a direction for public celebration does not appear to have been relied upon in either. It is not, however, for this reason alone that neither of these prior cases can, in my opinion, be relied upon as a decision that a celebration otherwise than in public is charitable. In neither of them was there any evidence that the terms of the bequest could be complied with otherwise than by public celebration.

In the principal bequest in the first of these cases – *The Commissioners of Charitable Donations and Bequests* v. *Walsh* 7 Ir. Eq. R. 34, note – the services specified in the bequest were "*solemn* Masses," at each of which thirteen clergymen were, if possible, to be present, "to perform the *rites accustomed* on these occasions." It was, and is, the common knowledge of every Roman Catholic that the services there pointed at are what are known as "Offices for the Dead," which are necessarily celebrated in public, so that the terms of that bequest were inconsistent with private celebration.

The only other material bequest there was of £20 yearly "to a third clergyman for the *attendance of this parish,* for which I hope he will offer a weekly Mass for the repose of my soul and the benefit of my son." Such a bequest for an additional clergyman for the parish would have been charitable, even had there not been a request for the celebration of Masses: *Thornber* v. *Wilson* 3 Drew. 245.

In the second case – *Read* v. *Hodgens* 7 Ir. Eq. R. 17 – the only question argued was whether the bequest was superstitious, and therefore void: in other words, whether the law, or policy of the law, which in *West* v. *Shuttleworth* 2 Myl. & K. 684 was held to underlie the English statute 1 Edw. 6, c. 14, applied to this country, in which there was no analogous statute. It was decided "in deference to the decree" in the earlier case which, in the opinion of the Master of the Rolls, "closed all further discussion on the point"; and that learned Judge stated that he had not formed any opinion of his own. That case, therefore, did not decide anything which had not been ruled by the earlier decision.

Whilst these two cases were most important on the question afterwards decided in *The Attorney-General* v. *Hall* [1897] 2 I.R. 426, viz. the charitable nature of a Mass celebrated in public, they do not determine the controversy here, further than by showing two very important matters – (*a*) that the Mass was not in this country deemed to be superstitious, and (*b*) that its charitable character was not affected by a request for a particular memorial. They are express authorities that the words of Lord Cottenham, when Master of the Rolls 2 Myl. & K. 684, that in such a case "the intention was not to benefit the priests or to support the chapels, but to secure a supposed benefit to the testatrix herself," are not law in this country. Incidentally, I may remark that the English statute 23 & 24 Vict. c. 134, "The Roman Catholic Charities Act," which was passed in 1860 to modify the effect of the law laid down in *West* v. *Shuttleworth* 2 Myl, & K. 684, affords an argument, almost conclusive in my mind, to show that this difference did exist between the laws on this subject in England and in Ireland; as it is impossible to believe that the relief conferred by that statute would have been confined to England and Wales, if the mischief intended to be remedied extended to Ireland also. The Legislature, by that Act, legislated upon the basis that the law in each country was that which it had been judicially declared in each to be; and consequently that statute is almost a statutable recognition of the decisions in *The Commissioners of Charitable Donations and Bequests* v. *Walsh* 7 Ir. Eq. R. 34, note and *Read* v. *Hogens* Ibid. 17.

Thus stood the law in this country prior to the decision in *The Attorney-General* v. *Delaney* I.R. 10 C.L. 104. To arrive at the *ratio decidendi* there of the question now before us, I must eliminate so much of it as relates to the many questions that had to be decided there, but which do not arise here: questions as to the force of the word "merely" preceding "charitable," in section 38 of 5 & 6 Vict. c. 82 (on the construction of which the liability to the duty there claimed arose); as to the bequest there, being a "legacy" within the meaning of that Act; as to the person who was to be deemed to be the legatee; and as to the mode in which the amount of the benefit conferred was to be ascertained. All these matters had to be considered and determined there, as preliminary to the existence of the question here.

Coming, then, to the actual *ratio decidendi* there, after long and serious consideration which has been forced upon me by the various subsequent decisions of the question, including *The Attorney-General* v. *Hall* [1897] 2 I.R. 426 (in the judgment in which, in the Exchenquer Division, I took part) – a consideration which now, for the first time since the decision in *The Attorney-General* v. *Delaney* I.R. 10 C.L. 104, I am obliged to bring to a judicial test – I feel that the decision cannot be supported. I further feel that had I pressed to its legitimate conclusion the difference of opinion which existed there between me and my learned brothers, I should have found that the opinion I expressed there, that the public celebration of a Mass was charitable, necessarily led to the conclusion that its celebration, although not in public, was of the same character, and that, too, upon the basis upon which the judgment proceeded – that the public benefit necessary to charity must be one which the Court itself could ascertain and declare.

To show the exact point in the reasoning in which, in my opinion, the error lies, renders necessary a rather lengthened examination of the judgment.

I commence with the position the argument had arrived at, after the cases of *The Commissioners of Charitable Donations and Bequests* v. *Walsh* 7 Ir. Eq. R. 34, note and *Read* v. *Hodgens* 7 Ir. Eq. R. 17 had been considered, and *West* v. *Shuttleworth* 2 Myl. & K. 684 distinguished. The judgment then proceeded, in some sentences which I may be excused for repeating, as to do so is necessary to enable my present view to be understood.

The position is stated thus: "Assuming the bequests not to be illegal, and considering them in a country in which there is now no established church, the acts directed to be procured are, *according to the faith which the testatrix professed*, sacrifices to God in the most proper sense and of the most solemn kind, on behalf of all the faithful, living and dead, including a particular memorial of the deceased person specified. On the other hand, they are not necessarily to be offered in the public congregation of the faithful, or in public at all."

To this I should now add, that as the nature and character of a Mass was known to the Common Law in pre-Reformation times, so after the Reformation, and to the present, the nature, and the Roman Catholic belief in reference to it, continue to be known to that law.

The judgment then proceeds to make it clear that in pre-Reformation times the purpose would have been held charitable, in the sense in which that word was used prior to the statutes of 43 Elizabeth, c. 4 (Eng.), and 10 Charles 1, sess. 3, c. 1 (Ir): "The element of charity, in its most extensive, indeed in its truest sense, which they (the bequests) contain, is piety to God. There is no doubt that, *according to the Roman Catholic faith*, each celebration of the Mass involves the most perfect act of charity. But further than this, it appears to me plain that, before the Reformation, bequests for these very purposes were not only legal, but were enforceable by the Ordinary as other charitable bequests."

In support of this, reference is made to the provision in the Statute of Westminster the 1st, that in case one dies intestate, the Ordinary shall depute his nearest and most lawful friends to administer his goods "*and dispend for the soul of the dead*"; and to the opinion expressed by Lord Eldon in *Moggridge* v. *Thackwell* 7 Ves. 69, that the favour with which bequests for charitable purposes (not coming within the Mortmain Acts) have been treated in Courts of Equity, may have had its origin in the practice recognized in that statute. The judgment then adds:- "It seems unnecessary to pursue this subject. The history of the country, and the Statute Law subsequent to the Reformation, appear to me to render the question free from doubt. I concur in the argument of the defendant's counsel that, prior to the Reformation, these bequests would have been deemed pious."

To all this I still adhere. Then the judgment proceeds:- "The next proposition urged by the defendant's counsel is, that assuming the bequests could, prior to the Reformation, have been deemed pious, as every objection arising from illegality and from the existence of an established church has been removed, the bequests are now to be viewed as they would have been before the Reformation; and as they would have been then deemed pious, they must now be deemed charitable." To this an answer is given which I still think is correct: "This is not the real question which we have to decide. We are bound down within much more narrow limits. Our province is confined to determining whether the purpose in question is one 'merely charitable,' within the 5 & 6 Vict. c. 82, section 38" – words which the judgment proceeds to show mean, in reference to the bequests there, "charitable" within the meaning of the Acts 43 Eliz., c. 4 (Eng.) and 10 Charles I., sess. 3, c. 1 (Ir.), or analogous to the purposes therein mentioned.

It was at this point that, in my opinion, the judgment erred. Having ascertained the character which the purpose should answer in order to be charitable, it should have proceeded to ascertain the effect, upon bequests for the celebration of Masses, of the Reformation statutes, and from that effect, ascertained what it could of its nature and character, as recognized and acknowledged by law, at and after the Reformation. Instead of doing this, the judgment, after rightly stating that a purpose, to be within the statutes of Elizabeth and Charles, must, to some extent at least, "be in the nature of a general public use . . . of such a nature that the Court can determine that it can confer a benefit upon the public, or upon some section of the public," proceeds, without, as I now think, sufficient consideration of the nature which the law attributed to the Mass in post-Reformation times, to hold that the bequests "could not derive the element of public benefit from the efficacy, spritual or temporal, which, *according to the faith of the testatrix,* the religious act may possess," that the *only* public benefit the law could recognize as flowing from its celebration was the edification of the congregation, and that, as the presence of a congregation was not essential, the gift was not charitable.

Going back now to the effect of the Reformation Statutes on gifts for Masses, the nearest analogies which I can find to such gifts, with a particular memorial, but without any direction that the celebration shall be in public, are the old common law spiritual tenures to which we have been referred by Mr. Browne and Mr. Pigot during their able and interesting arguments – tenure by "frankalmoyne" and tenure by "divine service." These two tenures differed from each other mainly in this: that in frankalmoyne a certain service could not be reserved; in tenure by divine service the service should be certain, and this distinction had a result not unimportant – that in default of performance, if the tenure were that firstly mentioned, the lord could not distrain, whilst if it were the second he could. The legality of the distress should necessarily be determined, if disputed, in a temporal, as distinguished from an ecclesiastical, Court; and Lord Coke says Co. Lit. 95 (b): "If issue be taken upon the performance of the divine service, it shall be tried by a jury of twelve men." Thus the Common Law had to determine, and consequently was able to determine, whether a particular Mass had been offered up with the specified intention. This disposes of one objection much pressed here and in *The Attorney-General* v. *Hall* [1897] 2 I.R. 426, the strenuous denial that a temporal Court had either the power or the means of determining such a matter.

I come now to the description of these tenures. The former is thus described by Littleton S. 133; Co. Litt., 93 (b):- "Tenant in frankalmoigne is where an abbot, or prior, or another man of religion or of Holy Church, holdeth of his lord in frakalmoigne, that is to say in Latin, *in liberam eleemosinam*, that is, in free almes;

and such tenure beganne first in old time," meaning of course before the statute *Quia Emptores*. "Where a man in old time was seised of certain lands or tenements in his demesne as of fee, and of the same lands infeoffed an abbot and his covent, or prior and his covent, to have and to hold to them and their successours in pure and perpetual almes or in frankalmoigne . . . In such case the tenements were holden in frankalmoigne."

The services which those who held under this tenure were to render to their feudal lord are stated in section 135 (*b*):- "And they which hold in frankalmoigne are bound of right *before God* to make orisons, prayers, masses, and other divine services for the soules of their grantor or feoffor, and for the soules of their heires which are dead, and for the prosperity and good life and good health of their heires which are alive. And therefore they shall do no fealty to their lord, because that this divine service is better for them before God than any doing of fealty; and also because that these words (frankalmoigne) exclude the lord to have any earthly or temporal service, but to have only divine and spirituall service to be done for him." In case of non-performance under this tenure, the complaint (differing in this respect from that in tenure by divine service) should, according to Littleton, be "to their Ordinary or Visitour" S. 136.

In section 137, Littleton describes tenure by divine service thus Co. Litt., 96 (b):- "But if an abbot or prior holds of his lord by a certain divine service in certaine to be done, as to sing a masse everie Friday in the weeke for the soules, *ut supra*, or everie year at such a day to sing a *placebo et dirige*, &c., or to find a chaplain to sing a masse, &c., or to distribute in almes to an hundred poore men an hundred pence at such a day; in this case, if such divine service be not done, the lord may distreyne . . . and such tenure shall not be said to be tenure in frankalmoigne, but is called tenure by divine service . . . for none can hold in frankalmoigne if there be expressed any manner of certain service that he ought to doe."

It is not stated in the above passages, or in any of the old books treating of the tenure of frankalmoigne that I have examined, that the divine service here referred to should be in public. The mode of its celebration under the tenure was that prescribed by the Church, and it is certain that the Church did not prescribe public celebration.

Before coming to the Reformation statutes, it is necessary to form a clear conception of the mode in which the Common Law regarded these gifts. Bracton says that "they were made, in a primary sense and principally, to God and to the Church, and in a secondary sense to the canons or monks or persons." His words are- "*Et ita quod primo et principaliter fit donatio Deo et ecclesiae, et secundario canonicis vel monachis vel personis*"; and so firmly was this principle established, that gifts took the form of gifts to God and a particular abbey and church. Sir Frederick Pollock and Mr. Maitland, in their learned and interesting "History of English Law before the time of Edward the First" Vol I., page 222, say:– "A gift, for example, to Ramsey Abbey would take the form of a gift 'to God and St. Benet of Ramsey Abbey, and the Abbot Walter and the monks of St. Benet,' or 'to God and the Church of St. Benet of Ramsey, and the Abbot and his monks,' or simply, 'to God and the Church of St. Benet of Ramsey,' or yet more briefly, 'to God and St. Benet'"; and they refer to particular charters which contain these words, and later on, in a note to a passage in Bracton, stating, "We do not make gifts to a parson and his successours, we make them to the Church, *e.g.* ' to God and the Church of St. Mary of Dale,'" they add this: "This remark seems fairly well supported by the practice of conveyancers in Bracton's time." So that the instances referred to are not isolated ones. They evidence the usual practice.

All this shows the true reason why the Common Law held the gifts pious. It was because they were gifts to God: gifts which provided for the worship of God. Even had the Common Law acknowledged more religions than one, it would have held pious any gift making provision for the worship of God, irrespective of the particular acknowledged religion according to which the worship was to be offered, provided only such religion were recognised as lawful. The gift here, as it is not illegal, is pious, according to the doctrines of all theistic religions, as all are based on a belief in the existence of the Deity, a belief that service and worship are due to Him, and a belief that the ministers of religion are the persons by whom the worship of the Church in its corporate unity is to be offered to Him. Thus, these gifts were not only pious before the Reformation, but, had they not been made illegal by statute, they would have been charitable within the meaning of the subsequent statutes of Elizabeth and Charles. As to this, *Powerscourt* v. *Powerscourt* 1 Molloy, 616 and *In re Darling* [1896] 1 Ch. 50 are in point. In the first of these cases a devise to trustees to lay out at their discretion £2000 per annum till the testator's son became of age, "in the *service* of my Lord and Master, and, I trust, Redeemer"; and in the second, a gift "to the poor and the *service* of God," were held charitable, the first by Lord Manners, L.C., and the second by Lord Justice Stirling.

The religious act specified is, however, not to be disregarded. It was the divine service of one particular Church. The particular mode in which the general pious intention was to be carried out was by acts of worship of that Church in its corporate unity. The acts of worship of a church are admitted, by all theistic religions, to tend to discharge, to some extent, the debt due to God by the general body of the faithful, and to bring down upon them temporal and spiritual benefits. But these acts must be performed by ministers of that Church; and thus the gifts are in a two-fold manner charitable – first, and principally, by reason of the piety which is the essence of the gift to God, the gift which is to be applied to His divine worship; and, secondly, by the mode in which it is to be so applied, viz. in the maintenance and support of the ministers by whom the acts of worship are to be performed. I have to add that, although Mass *may* be celebrated in private, its liturgy shows that it contemplates the presence of a congregation, although not as an essential part. The response of the clerk are those of the congregation, who, by the "*Orate fratres*," is in words invited to participate in the worship; for whose reception of the Blessed Eucharist provision is made in the ritual; and who is, or possibly in Apostolic times a particular section of whom was, at the conclusion dismissed, by the words from which the name of the service is derived: "*Ite*; *Missa Est*."

Having ascertained the character of these gifts, I come to consider the effect, upon these tenures by frankalmoyne and divine service, of the Reformation statutes, as this effect, to my mind, demonstrates that my last position is correct. These statutes are 2 & 3 Edw. 6, c. 1; 5 & 6 Edw. 6, c. 1; and 1 Eliz. c. 2, in England; and their Irish equivalent, 2 Eliz., c. 2 (Ir.). The English statutes prescribe the altered liturgies of divine service contained in the two Prayer Books, and the Irish statute prescribes that in the second Prayer Book of Edward 6. The effect of the English statutes is thus stated by Lord Coke, as a note upon the words of sect. 135, "to make orisons, prayers, Masses, and other divine services."

"Since Littleton wrote, the lyturgye or Book of Common Praier, and of celebrating divine service, is altered. This alteration notwithstanding, yet the tenure in frankalmoyne remaineth, and such prayers and divine service shall be said and celebrated as now is authorised; yea, though the tenure in particular, as Littleton hereafter saith, viz. to sing a masse, &c., or to sing a *placebo et dirige*, yet if the tenant saith the praires now authorised, it sufficeth . . . And albeit the tenure in frankalmoyne is now reduced to a certainty contained in the Book of Common Praire, yet seeing the original tenure was in frankalmoyne, and the change is by general consent by authority of Parliament, whereunto every man is party, the tenure remaineth as it was before."

Of these statues, the 2 & 3 Edw. 6, c. 1 (Eng.), dealt with "the celebration of the Lorde's Supper, commonlye called the Masse," as a divine service to continue in use. Neither it nor the 5 & 6 Edw. 6, cl. 1 (Eng.), which substituted the second for the first Prayer Book of Edward 6, altered more than its order and form. Indeed, the second Act recites that doubts, the existence of which is stated to be the reason of the Act, arose in the use and exercise of the common service, "for the fashion and manner of the ministration of the same, rather by the curiosity of the mynistre and mistakers than of any other worthy cause."

These statutes did not in terms declare that the performance of the new service should be accepted as a performance of the old. The view of Parliament was that the

Reformed church was the old Church, with a change in certain of its doctrines, and consequent changes in its liturgy and divine service; that the Communion Service was the Divine Service of pre-Reformation times, altered in such a mode as was incident to the change of doctrine; and Lord Coke's opinion involved this, that the Common Law held that the celebration of the altered service, in the mode prescribed by the altered liturgy, was a performance of a condition which prescribed "making orisons, prayers, Masses, and other divine services for the soules of their grantor," &c. Underlying this doctrine is matter of much moment, for we know as matter of history that the secular clergy of the Reformed Church did not, either in England or in Ireland, lose at the Reformation the lands they held by these tenures. Much land is still held under them by various ecclesiastical foundations in England. Some land was, at and after passing of the Irish Church Act, held by them in Ireland; and during some of the earlier years of my judicial career, the choir-master and choristers of Christ Church Cathedral were in the habit of coming into the Court of Exchequer once a year, in Hilary Term, and performing there an act of service, under one of these spiritual tenures, by singing a hymn in open Court.

It being then certain that the lands held under these tenures were not forfeited, it is to be asked, How did this happen in England, when each service involved the performance of an act (prayers for the dead) which in that country was declared to be superstitious by 1 Edw. 6, c. 14, and which by that Act forfeited the lands into the hands of the King? *Adams and Lambert's Case* 4 Rep. 104 (b). How was it that neither the lands held under such a condition were forfeited, nor the condition itself discharged? The only answer that can be given to that question, and I am satisfied that it is the true one, is that the Common Law, after the Reformation, continued to hold, as I have shown it held in pre-Reformation times, that these tenures involved a general principle of piety which, after the Reformation as well as before, rendered the purposes charitable, and that nothing was affected by the so-called superstition, except the particular mode of performance, for which, either by the statute or by the Common Law (it is immaterial which), the altered service was substituted. This was, to my mind, undoubtedly right, and was analogous to the *cypres* doctrine, shortly afterwards established in Courts of Equity in relation to charities. But if it is right, it establishes that, after the Reformation, the gifts would have remained charitable, were it not that they were illegal. When then, in 1793, all laws prohibiting or discouraging the practice of the Roman Catholic religion were repealed, the illegality determined, and they resumed the character they enjoyed in pre-Reformation times, and once more became charitable – (1) because of their piety; (2) because they were devoted to the support and maintenance of the clergymen, the celebrants.

In the present case, the motive and purpose of the gift are similar to those in frankalmoyne, and are consequently charitable.

To prevent misunderstanding, as to my view of the nature of these gifts, I desire to state that I do not consider that the money is the price of the celebration. In no period of the Christian Church would such a bargain be other than simoniacal. The true nature of the bequest is that of an alms to the clergyman, just as in frankalmoyne the gift was in the nature of alms; but the gift of alms is accompanied by a request for the celebration, and according to our equitable doctrines the clergyman, by accepting that gift, binds himself to fulfil the request. He cannot accept the benefit, and disappoint the exception. The *honorarium* then is an alms, and a recognized mode of supplementing the income of the clergyman, and is applicable to his support and maintenance; and for this reason alone would be within the very words of the statute of Charles 1.

For all these reasons, I am of opinion that the narrow view taken in *The Attorney-General* v. *Delaney* I.R. 10 C.L. 104, that the *only* element of public benefit in the celebration of the Mass is the instruction and edification of the congregation present, fails to appreciate it as a gift to God, as a gift made in the expectation that, because of it, the divine service of a Christian Church, a supreme act of divine worship, would be offered in the name of and by the authority of the whole Church, by ministers specially consecrated to represent her, as an act from which the Common Law knew previous to the Reformation, and therefore knows now, that benefits spiritual and temporal flow to the general body of the faithful – benefits which, even were they spiritual only, would render the service charitable within 10 Car. 1, sess. 3, c. 1. In my mind, if the object of the gift could be separated from its effect (which is impossible), either would render the gift charitable. This certainly is the effect of both combined.

This, then, is my first reason for holding that the decision in *The Attorney-General* v. *Delaney* I.R. 10 C.L. 104 was wrong, and that the present appeal should be allowed.

I now revert to the effects of the Reformation. It, as I have already said, altered the service; and without entering upon a consideration of the difference between the old and new services, the latter is identified, by the Act of Edw. 6, as being in law the divine service of the Mass, as altered. Each, the old and the new, is an act of divine worship of the Church, an offering of praise, adoration, and thanksgiving, involving a petition for benefits, temporal and spiritual, for all the faithful alive, whether present or absent. All will admit that the divine service of the Reformed Church was, by virtue of its spiritual efficacy, a charitable act, so long as it remained the established church; and if so, having regard to section 20 of the Church Act, which, subject to a power of change, continues all the "doctrines, rites, and ceremonies," notwithstanding disestablishment, so must it have continued thereafter.

Now knowing, as does the Common Law, that the old service contains in substance all of that which renders that new service charitable, together with something else, that old service, at least since 1869 (when the Roman Catholic and the Reformed Church became equal in the sight of the law), must, too, be charitable, unless those elements which it contains, and which are absent in the new service, prevent the legal result which otherwise would flow from that which is common to both. But such prevention could result only from illegality; and there is now no illegality in the essential differences between the two services. Therefore, because the new service is charitable, so also must be the old. This is my second reason for holding the gift charitable.

There is, however, a third reason, which is of wider application, and which it is therefore right that I should state. The existence of a divine service is essential to all religions; and equally essential is the existence of a privileged class, a priesthood or a class of ministers, by whom that divine service shall be celebrated, on behalf of the Church. The divine service of the particular religion must be defined by the doctrines of its own religion. Without those doctrines it cannot exist as a divine service. Without a knowledge of those doctrines, the spiritual effect of the service cannot be understood. Consequently, the effect of the divine service cannot be known, otherwise than from the doctrines of its religion, coupled with a hypothetical admission of their truth. But the advancement of *any* theistic religion is charitable, and such advancement may result from an increased number of the celebrations of its divine services. Therefore the charitable nature of a divine service must (when the religion is not an established one) depend upon the character of the act, not objectively, but according to the doctrines of the religion in question. The same proposition may be stated in different words. When, in a country like ours at present, where there is no established church, it is alleged that a religion (whose doctrines are not known to the law) is advanced by the peformance of an act of divine service, the law, from the fact that it is a divine service, admits that which is involved in its being such an act, viz. that its celebration tends to the advancement of the religion, and, consequenlty, a gift to procure the performance of the act is charitable. Further, the knowledge that it is a divine service necessarily involves a knowledge of those doctrines but for which it would not exist as a divine service, and therefore renders admissable evidence of these doctrines. But when it knows those doctrines, although it knows that, according to them, such an act has the spiritual efficacy alleged, it cannot know it objectively and as a fact, unless it also knows that the doctrines in question are true. But it never can know that they are objectively true, unless it first determines that the religion in question is a true religion. This it cannot do. It not only has no means of doing so, but it is contrary to the principle that all religions are now equal in the law. It follows that there must be one of two results: either – (1) the law must cease to admit that *any* divine worship can have spiritual efficacy to produce a public benefit; or (2) it must admit the sufficiency of spiritual efficacy, but ascertain it according to the doctrines of the religion whose act of worship it is.

The first alternative is an impossible one. The law, by rendering all religions equal in its sight, did not intend to deny that which is the basis of, at least, all Christian religions, that acts of divine worship have a spiritual efficacy. To do so would, virtually, be to refuse to recognize the essence of all religion: The other result must, therefore, necessarily ensue. It must ascertain the spiritual efficacy according to those doctrines, that divine service does result in public benefit, either temporal or spiritual, the act must, in law, be deemed charitable.

These considerations have satisfied me that, in this respect also, the decision in *The Attorney-General* v. *Delaney* I.R. 10 C.L. 104 was erroneous, and that the celebration of the Mass, whether in private or in public, is charitable; and for this third reason, also, I am of opinion that this appeal should be allowed.

FitzGibbon, L.J.:

The length of time which it has taken to bring the present question to a decision here, and the course of authority upon it, are equally remarkable.

Lord Manners, in 1823, in *Walsh's Case* 7 Ir. Eq. R. 34n, held a bequest for Masses for the repose of a testator's soul to be valid. But the case was not reported.

Blackburne, M.R., in 1844, in *Read* v. *Hodgens* 7 Ir. Eq. R. 31, was put in possession of Lord Manner's decree: holding it to be a decision on the very question, he said that it was his duty to declare a similar bequest to be valid. In his opinion, having given all the time and attention to *Walsh's Case* Ibid. 34 n which it was in his power to command, that case closed all further discussion on that point.

Whether the terms of the bequests in those cases would have raised the present question or not may be doubtful; but certainly no indication was given that the decisions depended in any way upon the presence or absence of a specific direction as to the mode of celebration.

For thirty-two years afterwards we do not know whether such bequests were, for the purpose of taxation, treated as charitable; and their liability to legacy duty was first discussed in 1875 in *Delaney's Case* I.R. 10 C.L. 104, which decided that a bequest for Masses, which did not contain a direction that the celebration should take place in public, was not "charitable," apparently on the ground that, though the bequest was valid in Ireland, where we never had any Statute of Superstitious Uses, it did not import any "benefit of the public," in the absence of affirmative direction that the Masses should be publicly celebrated.

For brevity, I throughout use "charitable" as importing that element of public benefit which is necessary to bring a gift within the Statute of Pious Uses, 10 Car. 1, sess. 3, cap. 1.

The decision in *Delaney's Case* I.R. 10 C.L. 104 seems to me to have followed *West* v. *Shuttleworth* 2 My. & K. 698, in so far as Lord Cottenham put the construction upon the legacies to priests and chapels, that "there was nothing of charity in their object; the intention was not to benefit the priests or to support the chapels, but to secure a supposed benefit to the testatrix herself."

Twenty years have now passed during which *Delaney's Case* I.R. 10 C.L. 104 has been followed by co-ordinate Courts; but it is now, for the first time, challenged on appeal.

In 1897, in *Hall's Case* [1897] 2 I.R. 426, the validity and the charitable character of a bequest for Masses expressly directed to be celebrated publicly in a specified Roman Catholic Church for the the repose of the testator's soul were affirmed by this Court, and were finally established so far as Irish judicial opinion can go.

In *Hall's Case* [1897] 2 I.R. 433, 448, 449 the direction for public celebration prevented the present question from arising; but I ventured to say that if a Mass was *in itself* necessarily an act of public benefit, I could not see how it became less so because it was directed to be said for the soul of the testator, and I suggested that whether a bequest for Masses was "charitable," as tending to the promotion of religion, must depend, not upon positive law, nor upon the testator's intention, but upon Roman Catholic doctrine, and that if the benefit and edification resulting from the celebration were not, in Roman Catholic belief, confined to the testator, but if the Mass was an official act of public worship, or what Protestants call a "means of grace," believed by the testator and by his Church to carry religious benefit to all the faithful, it could not lose its charitable character, if it was celebrated in any manner authorised by the Church, even though the motive which dictated the gift was primarily, or even exclusively, that of securing a share of that benefit for the testator himself in the next world.

I think myself happy now in following the Lord Chief Baron in his judgment – I do not say in his conversion, for since *Hall's Case* [1897] 2 I.R. 433, 448, 449 I have needed no conversion.

My excuse for adding anything to such a judgment is that I believe a principle vital to religious liberty and equality, beyond any denominated interest, to be involved in our decision.

What is the essence of a bequest which is held *charitable* because it is *pious* or *religious*? The Statute of Pious Uses specifies gifts–

> "for the erection, maintenance, or support of any college, school, *lecture in divinity*, or in any of the liberal arts or sciences, or for the building, re-edifying, or maintaining in repair of *any Church*, or for the maintenance of *any minister or preacher of the Holy Word of God*"–

which, however differently used, is certainly not denominational–

> *"or* for *any other like lawful and charitable use and uses warranted by the laws of this realm."*

We have Bacon's authority (Bac. Abr. Charitable Uses, C. 36) that money given for the maintenance of a preaching minister, though not a charitable use mentioned in the statute, yet comes within the equity of it for "summa est ratio quae *pro religione* facit."

What is "religion" here? It can not be abstract religion, for no human being can hold that, or even conceive an "abstract idea" of religion. I suppose Pantheism is the nearest approach to it. Religion for the purposes of the Statute of Pious Uses, must be the aggregate of all the lawful forms of religion conscientiously held by the King's subjects, with the practical limitation that each of them must be held by a number of persons sufficient to make that particular form of religion an appreciable component of the religion of the State, and so to entitle those who hold it to take a benefit for themselves as a benefit to *the public*.

Tridentine Dogma, Anglican Doctrine, and the Non-Conformist Conscience, are all phases of the religion of The Holy Catholic Church to which every one who professes the Apostles Creed claims to belong. Not only all these, but also non-Christian religions, and possibly the religion of some Christian sects also, being "warranted by the laws of this realm," must stand equal before the secular Courts in a country like Ireland, where no particular religion is established by law, and no particular faith has ever been declared superstitious by statute. In determining whether the performance of any particular rite promotes any particular religion, and benefits the members of the Church or denomination, or body, who profess it, the secular Court must act upon evidence of the belief of the members of the community concerned. It can have no other guide upon that subject.

The exclusiveness, the vagueness, or the self-sufficiency of principles religiously held by particular creeds, whether they rest on dogma, on doctrine, or on conscience, cannot exclude those who profess any lawful creed from the benefits of charitable gifts.

It would be strange, indeed, if bequests for the promotion of total abstinence, or even vegetarianism; for the maintenance of a place of worship, or of a minister, for a small congregation of peculiar people; for the dissemination of the works of Joanna Southcote; or for the prevention of cruelty to animals, should be held, as they have been, to be charitable objects, if a provision by a Roman Catholic, for Roman Catholics, for the celebration of the Mass, more especially in Ireland, where "Superstitious Uses" are not *mala prohibita*, were to be excluded from the category.

Upon the broad principle that the Mass is the most solemn official act of worship in the Roman Catholic Church; that it can be celebrated by the ordained priests of that Church, and by none others; that ever since 1793 that Church has been legalised as a religious institution in this country; and that it has been proved by legal evidence in this case that, according to the creed of every member of that Church, the Mass, whenever and wherever regularly celebrated in accordance with the law of the Church, results in benefit and edification to all the faithful, I hold that the promotion of that celebration is "charitable" under our Law.

Speaking with all reverence of a faith which I do not hold, touching the very "Mystery of Godliness," I could not impute to any individual professing the Roman Catholic religion that he regarded a gift of money for Masses as a means of securing from such a Sacrifice a private and exclusive benefit for himself alone, as being much less than blasphemy; and, as I understand the proved doctrine of the Church, it would certainly be heresy. But the hope or belief that, in some shape or form, here or hereafter, a man's good works will follow him – an ingredient of selfishness in that sense – enters into almost every act of charity; and if the act is done in the belief that it will benefit others; for example, in the belief that he that gives to the poor lends to the Lord, it can be none the less charitable because the giver looks for his reward in heaven.

The Lord Chief Baron has shown that the characteristic of charity – in the legal sense – has been attributed to acts of piety to God; his argument from the tenures by Divine Service is most persuasive upon this point; he has shown the recognition of the Mass in pre-Reformation Law, and the effect of the repeal of the Penal Laws in reviving this recognition; he has also endeavoured to identify the Reformed Service with the Mass, so far as their charitable character is concerned. I do not presume to say more on these points than that they all go in aid of the same conclusion which I wish to keep "in the open," and upon grounds even broader that the treatment of these bequests as an additional endowment for particular clergymen. But it is not immaterial to quote the Irish Toleration Act of 1793. Section 5 repealed the penal laws against the Popish clergy, and section 8 excluded from the benefits of the Act any Popish Ecclesiastic who should exercise any of the rites and ceremonies of the Popish religion, *save within their usual places of worship or in private houses*, thereby legalizing those rites and ceremonies when exercised within those limits. Section 11 expressly mentions the Mass, and repeals so much of the Act 8 Anne, c. 3, as subjects any Papist to fine and imprisonment on his refusal to appear and testify on oath before two Justices of the Peace, "*where and when he heard the Popish Mass celebrated as the same is usual in the Church of Rome*." This provision seems to me to reduce the question of the lawful and charitable character of any celebration of the Mass to the single question whether it is to be "celebrated as the same is usual in the Church of Rome"? The answer to that question can be obtained only from legal evidence of the laws and usages of the Church of Rome. Here this is supplied by the evidence given in *Delaney's Case* I.R. 10 C.L. 104, which has been made available in this case, as it was in *Hall's Case* [1897] 2 I.R. 426.

Taking this evidence, as I did in *Hall's case* [1897] 2 I.R. 462, as a paraphrase of the decrees of the Council of Trent, I refer again to the passages in which "*Sacrificium istud ver propitiatorium*" is described as offered "*non solum pro fidelium vivorum peccatis, poenis, satisfactionibus, et aliis necessitatibus, sed et pro defunctis in Christo, nondum ad plenum purgatis, rite juxta Apostolorum traditionem*" – (*Anglice*), "as the same is usual in the Church of Rome" – the very words of the Act of 1793. The same decree commends:- "*Missas illas in quibus solus sacerdos sacramentaliter communicat, partim quod in eis populus spiritualiter communicat, partim vero quod a publico ecclesiœ ministro non pro se tantum, sed pro omnibus fidelibus qui ad corpus Christi pertinent, celebrantur*" *Ibid.* C. VI.

But in the "Catechismus ex decreto Concilii Tridentini ad Parochos" of Pius V., I find an even more conclusive passage – "*Nulla Missa ex communi usu ecclesiœ celebrata dicenda est privata. Ex quo facile perspicitur, omnes Missas communes censendos esse, ut quœ ad communem omnium fidelium utilitatem et salutem pertineant.*"

The fruition of faith, "the evidence of things not seen," is hidden from humanity. It is not within the power of any earthly tribunal to entertain the question whether these propositions are true. But it is for us to decide that belief in their truth is part of the faith of the members of the Church which has laid them down; that the Church of

Rome is, in Ireland, a lawful religious institution; and that providing the celebration of the Mass for its members promotes their religion by supplying them with what they believe to be a benefit common to them all.

Therefore, a bequest for that object is a charitable gift within the Statute of Pious Uses, as interpreted by nearly a century of judicial decisions.

Holmes, L.J.:

The question for decision in this case arises on a bequest in the will of Ellen McLoughlin, by which she directs trustees therein named to pay over the income of certain moneys in their hands, "from time to time, to the Roman Catholic Primate of all Ireland for the time being, to be applied for the celebration of Masses for the repose of the souls of my late husband, my children, and myself."

If this be a bequest for purposes merely charitable, it would not violate the rule against the creation of perpetuities, and would, therefore, be valid; but if the purpose is not charitable, the rule would apply, and the gift must be held bad.

In *The Attorney-General* v. *Hall* [1897] 2 I.R. 436 it was decided by this Court that a bequest to a Roman Catholic priest to be applied for Masses to be celebrated publicly in a specified Roman Catholic Church in Ireland, for the repose of the testator's soul, is a valid charitable bequest, and exempt from legacy duty under 5 & 6 Vict. c. 82, sect. 38. The only substantial difference between the gift in that case and the gift now under consideration is, that there the Masses were to be celebrated publicly in a specified Roman Catholic Church; and I am thus relieved, by a decision which I am bound to follow, from the consideration of all other questions save the one – whether the omission of a similar or equivalent direction in Ellen McLoughlin's will deprives the bequest to the Roman Catholic Primate of the charitable character which would otherwise belong to it. All previous reported cases bearing on the subject were fully considered by Fitz Gibbon, L.J., in *The Attorney-General* v. *Hall* [1897] 2 I.R. 426, 442, and having carefully read his judgment, I agree in his comments thereon, and the proposition he deduces from them.

Although the conclusion announced by him was confined to gifts for the public celebration of Mass, his reasoning seems to me to be equally applicable to cases where the clebration might be, or is directed to be, in private, and that he was conscious of this himself is shown by his final declaration that he is not willing to limit the foundation of his judgment by accepting the decision in *The Attorney-General* v. *Delaney* I.R. 10 C.L. 104. Still, whatever may be the view entertained by individual Judges, *Delaney's Case* I.R. 10 C.L. 104 has hitherto been accepted as an authority, that a bequest for the celebration of Masses for a departed soul given in general terms, and without specifying whether such celebration was to be in public or in private, is not for a charitable purpose. Fitz Gibbon, L.J., says, in *Hall's Case* [1897] 2 I.R. 426, 442, that previous to *The Attorney-General* v. *Delaney* I.R. 10 C.L. 104 there is no reason to suppose that any difference was made between public and private celebrations.

Now, there is one point to which little attention seems to have been paid in *Delaney's Case* I.R. 10 C.L. 104. The evidence is that Mass for a departed soul may be said in private, but in practice generally, and in Ireland almost universally, it is said in a public church.

The Lord Chief Baron deals with this in *Delaney's Case* I.R. 10 C.L. 104 in the following words:– "In the present case there is not, on the face of the will – nor, indeed, at all – an obligation that the Masses shall be celebrated in any specified public congregation in Ireland, or in public at all. The practice is that Masses said in pursuance of obligations imposed by such bequests are usually celebrated in public. The question is not whether the money may be applied to purposes strictly charitable, but whether the legatee is *bound* so to apply it: *Morice* v. *Bishop of Durham* 9 Ves. 399; 10 Ves. 541. This cannot be effected by a usual or even by a universal practice."

The case of *Morice* v. *Bishop of Durham* 9 Ves. 399; 10 Ves. 541, where the language was so vague and general as to cover any benevolent or generous application of the bequest, does not touch my difficulty. Speaking with great deference, I am disposed to think that the passages read during the argument from the Missal or Mass-book show that the Mass is primarily, if not essentially, a public rite, although it may also be said in private; and I am satisfied by the evidence of Dr. Delaney that the normal mode in Ireland of celebrating Masses for departed souls is in a church open to the public. If this be so, there is no reason satisfactory to my mind against holding that such a bequest as we are now considering refers to Masses celebrated in the usual way.

I am unwilling, however, to make this the only ground of my judgment; and I now propose to deal with the gift on the assumption that it directs in express terms that the Masses may be said either in public or in private.

On what ground is it argued that the bequest in *The Attorney-General* v. *Hall* [1897] 2 I.R. 448 is charitable, while that in *The Attorney-General* v. *Delaney* I.R. 10 C.L. 104 is not? In the last-named case the Lord Chief Baron, in answering the argument that as the Mass, even where celebrated in private, is, according to the Roman Catholic doctrine, for the benefit of all the faithful, and therefore charitable, says– "In my opinion this is not so. To constitute a charitable use in analogy to the Statute of Elizabeth the purpose must be one which the Court itself can ascertain, and declare to be public or beneficial to the public. It cannot, in my opinion, derive the element of public benefit from the efficacy, spiritual or temporal, which, according to the faith of the testator, the religious act may possess." This puts very neatly the argument on one side. I shall now read in connexion with it the words of Fitz Gibbon, L.J., in *Hall's case* [1897] 2 I.R. 448:- "I cannot conceive it to be the proper exercise of the jurisdiction of a temporal Court in a country professing to be governed upon principles of absolute religious equality to discuss religious doctrines. Nor can I conceive it possible that the liability to duty of a legacy for the benefit of a public minister of religion can in law depend upon considering the efficacy of his ministrations, or whether or how far benefits, which are conscientiously believed by the members of his own denomination to flow from prescribed ceremonies, are really attainable . . . It is enough to say that where, according to the religious belief of a body of persons recognized as part of the public, an act of religion done by a public minister of their Church is for the spiritual advantage of them all, a bequest for the benefit of a minister of religion to perform that act, must be deemed charitable."

It will be observed that the difference in the propositions laid down in the two passages I have quoted is, that in one it is stated that the Court cannot derive the element of public benefit from the efficacy, spiritual or temporal, which, according to the faith of the testator, the religious act may possess, but must ascertain the existence of such benefit by independent investigation; while in the second passage the belief of the testator and of the Church to which he belongs is made the only test. This difference may be further illustrated by reference to the judgment of Andrews, J., in *Hall's Case* [1897] 2 I.R. 426. He says that "the Court cannot determine that the celebration of the Mass in private confers a public benefit, although according to the faith of the Roman Catholic Church it may, and according to the belief of that Church it does, confer such benefit."

But in the sentence immediately preceding he says– "A Court can, and according to the authorities ought, in my opinion, to determine that the public celebration of the Mass confers a public benefit by the religious edification of those members of the Roman Catholic Church who attend it." I am wholly at a loss to know now, if the Court cannot determine whether the celebration of a private Mass carries with it public benefits, by what means it can determine that a Mass said in public confers such benefits. The reason it cannot determine the first-mentioned point is, because it is not a proper exercise of the jurisdiction of the temporal courts of a country where all religions are in law on an equality to discuss and determine the truth of religious doctrine. But the determination of the second point would equally involve the consideration by the Court of the truth of a religious doctrine. If I were obliged to arrive at a judicial conclusion as to whether the public celebration of the Mass confers a public benefit on those who hear it, I must consider the doctrine that is embodied in this rite. I might adopt the declarations of the Council of Trent regarding the sacrifice of the Mass, or I might adopt the strong language of the 31st Article of Religion in the English Book of Common Prayer. In the one case it would necessarily follow that the celebration, whether in public or private, would confer a public benefit; in the other case it would just as necessarily follow that no such benefit is possible. No Court of

Justice in this country can be called on to decide such a question as this. What we can determine with certainty is, that it is part of the creed of the most ancient Church in western Christendom, of which the testatrix was a member, that the Mass is a true sacrifice offered to God by the priest in the name of the Church whose minister he is; that every Mass, whether public or private, is believed to bring Divine blessings to the world; and that all the faithful, present or absent, alive or dead, participate in those blessings. Now, if this be true, there can, I think, be no doubt that a bequest for the purpose of having private Masses celebrated would be charitable, and a temporal Court in Ireland, having no authority to decide for itself whether it is true or not, must take as its guide the belief of the Church of which the testatrix is a member. I understand this to be the law, and on this ground I concur in holding that the appeal ought to be allowed.

Note

See further, *Irish Land Law*, paras 9.096-8. See also *Re Howley's Estate*, p.450, *ante*.

2. *Advancement of Education*

THE INCORPORATED SOCIETY V. RICHARDS

(1841) 4 Ir. Eq. R. 177; 1 Dr. & War. 258 (Chancery)

The facts are set out in the judgments.

Sugden L.C.:

I am now prepared to decide the only remaining question in this case, namely, the validity of the devise to the plaintiffs contained in the will of Topham Mitchell. That was a gift of all his unsettled estate, after the death of his wife, to "The Incorporated Society in Dublin for the promotion of English Protestant Schools in Ireland." It was contended on the part of the defendant, although but faintly, that those words do not mean that the devise was for the purpose for which this Society was incorporated, but constituted an absolute gift to them, unfettered by any trust. I cannot say that I feel any difficulty upon that ground, because the nature of the trust is expressed in the very description of the Society contained in the gift; and giving it to them in that character, the testator gives it charged with an obligation to devote it to those purposes, and the plaintiffs must take it, if at all, subject to that obligation. As I put it in the course of the argument, it is just as if the testator said "I give to the Governors of the Deaf and Dumb Schools," or to the Governors of any other Charitable Institution – when, although he does not say in express terms that the gift is in trust for the charity; yet it must clearly be taken to be so.

Upon the other question, namely, the validity of the gift itself, the case has been elaborately argued; and in coming to a decision upon it, I have had the advantage of every aid which learning, and talent, and research on the part of the Counsel engaged could afford. The case is one of considerable importance, and the principal subject involved in it has long been matter of consideration and doubt, so that it is desirable that it should be settled, if possible, on some firm basis. The early statutes relating to gifts in mortmain to religious houses have been much referred to in the course of the argument. Those statutes undoubtedly included gifts to other bodies corporate as well as religious houses, although the latter were the principal objects of gifts in mortmain at the time they were passed. They were English statutes, and derived their force in this country from Poyning's Law. I do not think, however, that any difficulty arises from them in the present case, because the plaintiffs here have a licence from the Crown to take in mortmain; and I do not think the time at which that licence was given is material. It was contended by Mr. Brooke, that a writ of "*ad quod damnum*" should have issued; but I think the power given to the plaintiffs to take lands to a certain value, which, it is admitted, they have not exceeded, constitutes a sufficient answer to that.

As to the main question – the validity of this devise – the Statute of Wills in this country, which embodies the provisions of the two statutes in England, contains the same exception as to devises to Corporations which is contained in the second English statute. It has been strongly contended that it is, therefore, impossible to give validity to this devise, because it is a devise to a Corporation for its own purposes, although those are charitable; and the case of *The Attorney-General* v.

Flood has been relied on as a decisive authority for that purpose. It is not unimportant, with reference to this question, to keep in view the object and intention of the Legislature upon the subject. When all the early statutes for restraining gifts in mortmain, to which I have before referred, had failed in effecting the purpose for which they had been enacted, chiefly through the medium of uses, it was thought that all the mischiefs could be remedied by the Statute of Uses. That statute is erroneously called in conveyances "the statute for transferring uses into *possession*;" its more appropriate title would be, "the statute for transferring uses into *possessions*," for it transfers the land itself, and not merely the beneficial interest in it. The Master of the Rolls, in his judgment on this case, when before him at 1 S. & Sc. 603 said, it was extraordinary that the Statute of Uses should save devises previously made. I cannot concur in that remark, for devises had then become common, and it was thought right not to interfere with existing interests. As to the operation of that statute in Ireland, we have very scanty means of information, and must refer to the law of England to shew, by analogy, from what the law there would be but for the 43rd of *Eliz.*, what it is here, where there is no such act. On one side, it is contended that there is an inherent jurisdiction in the Courts of Equity in both countries which enables them to enforce trusts, although the conveyances by which those trusts are declared contravene the rules of law: a jurisdiction which is independent both of the Statute of Wills and of the 43rd of *Eliz*. Now, let us first see what is the true construction of the 43rd of *Eliz.*, and what the view which it gives of the law of England at the time it was passed. It begins by reciting, "Whereas divers lands, tenements, &c., have been heretofore given, limited and appointed," &c., Then it mentions all the different species of charitable uses, and after naming them all, proceeds, "Nevertheless they have not been employed according to the charitable intent of the givers and founders, by reason of fraud, breaches of trust, &c.; for remedy whereof, be it enacted, that it shall be lawful for the Lord Chancellor or Lord Keeper to issue a Commission," &c. Then comes an important proviso, "That neither this act nor any thing therein contained shall in anywise extend to any lands, tenements, &c., given or which shall be given to any college, hall, or house of learning within the two Universities of Oxford or Cambridge, or to the Colleges of Westminster, Eton, or Winchester, or any of them, or to any Cathedral or Collegiate Church within this realm."

In the case of *The Attorney-General* v. *The Skinners' Company* 2 Russ. 407 Lord Eldon is reported to have expressed some wonder at the retrospective effect given to this act; but I think that it must be an inaccuracy in the report, and that such an observation could never have proceeded from so great a master of Equity; for the words of the act are, "any lands, &c. *heretofore* given, or which shall hereafter be given." The construction given to the act in many cases was, no doubt, forced and unnatural; but I do not see how it could be complained of that a retrospective operation has been attributed to it. Let us see, however, whether, on the face of this act, we cannot ascertain what the law of England was before it was passed. It appears, I think, as clearly as possible from the object of the statute, and from its provisions, that the charitable uses mentioned in it were good before it passed, and would have remained good if it had never passed. Its object was not to give any additional power of alienation for charitable uses, which was extensive enough, if not too much so, before it passed; but to create a new jurisdiction, which was to discover and remedy the abuses then existing, and to give to the charities the property that really belonged to them. There is not a word in it to show that those gifts were bad before it passed, but, on the contrary, it appears to me that there is a great deal in it to shew that they were good; it recites:- "Whereas lands, tenements, hereditaments, &c., have been heretofore limited, appointed, and assigned," enumerating the particular charitable uses to which they had been devoted, and then it proceeds, "which lands, tenements, &c., have not been employed according to the charitable intent of the givers and founders thereof, by reason of frauds, breaches of trust, and negligence in those who should pay, deliver, and employ the same." Now, how could the parties interested in the property be guilty of fraud, if the dispositions of that property had been illegal? Then the Commissioners, whom the act authorises the

Chancellor to appoint, are to inquire "of all and singular such gifts, assignments and appointments, and of the abuses, breaches of trust, negligences, misemployments, not employing, concealing, defrauding, misconverting or misgovernment of any lands, tenements, &c., heretofore given, limited, appointed or assigned, or which shall hereafter be given, limited, appointed or assigned for any the charitable and goodly uses before rehearsed."

There is not a word in the act to render any gift valid that was invalid before, but it enforces what was valid before it passed; so that if I were to decide on what was the law of England before the passing of that act, I should say, that the act itself proves to demonstrate that those charitable trusts were binding, although it was necessary to adopt additional means of guarding against the breaches of trust mentioned in the preamble, and that it meant to enlarge the means of carrying into effect charitable uses, but not to affect the validity of the disposition of property to those uses. The proviso in the act, "That neither this act, nor anything herein contained, shall extend to any college," &c., cannot fail to strike us as most important with reference to this part of the subject, when we consider what the law respecting them was before the act passed. In *Flood's Case* Hobart, 136 the Court said:– "We agree that the devise was void at law, because the Statute of Wills does not allow devises to corporations; but yet we hold that it is clearly within the relief of the statute of *Elizabeth* under the words 'limited and appointed;' and it was likewise held by us that the proviso in the statute which exempts colleges, is only intended to exempt them from being reformed by commission, but not to restrain gifts to them." If there are any words which would exempt colleges from the provisions of the act, I think the words in the proviso that I have referred to have the operation; but notwithstanding that it is declared by the Judges that gifts to colleges are good, manifestly because such gifts were good before the act passed: they were good before the act, and the act left them as it found them. I consider, therefore, that the object of the statute of *Elizabeth* was to remedy the abuses that then existed in the management of charitable property and to give new jurisdiction for that purpose, and more extended remedies.

I have dwelt thus upon the construction of this act, because I think the right understanding of it will remove a great many of the difficulties in this case. With respect to the decisions subsequent to the act, I would observe as to one of them, *Bennett College* v. *The Bishop of London* 2 Black. 1132, that it is a decision that I have never known followed: three of the Judges held that a devise to a college for a charitable trust, was good, not only in Equity as an appointment, but that it was good even at Law; because they considered that the 43rd *Eliz.* was *pro tanto* a repeal of the exception in the Statute of Wills relating to devises to corporations. That is a decision which I must say I do not see any ground to support. The statute of *Elizabeth* does not turn an equitable estate into a legal one; nothing can be more simple than the machinery of the statute, it directs that the Chancellor or Lord Keeper shall issue a commission to inquire into the alleged abuses: and it became a question afterwards whether in consequence of its provisions, the Attorney-General had not lost his power of proceeding by information. How is it possible then to say, that legal validity is given to such devises by that act?

Before I refer to the other English authorities that have been relied on, there is one authority which I would wish to call particular attention to – a case which has frequently been cited and never disapproved of, and which I consider a very high authority – that is *Sonley* v. *The Clockmakers' Company* 1 B.C.C. 81. There a testator devised freehold estates to his wife for life, with remainder to his brother in tail male, with the ultimate remainder to the Clockmakers' Company, upon trust to sell and divide the produce of the sale among his nephews and nieces. The testator's widow and brother died in his lifetime, and the devise to the corporation being void at law, the question was, whether the heir took beneficially or subject to the trust. Baron Eyre, sitting for the Chancellor, decreed that although the devise was void at law, yet that the trust was sufficiently created to fasten itself upon the legal estate which descended to the heir, and that the heir was a trustee for the uses of the will. It is perfectly manifest, that the decision in that case must have proceeded on the ground of there being an original inherent jurisdiction in the Court to sustain such a devise, and upon nothing else – for the English Statute of Wills 34 *Henry* 8, c.5 had expressly excepted devises to corporations out of its operation. A gift to a person or a body not capable of taking, is the same in effect as any other case where there happens to be no trustee; the Court fastens on the person who takes the property, as in that case of *Sonley* v. *The Clockmakers' Company*, and makes him carry into effect the trust intended by the testator. That case of *Sonley* v. *The Clockmakers' Company*, shews that although the Statute of Wills does not allow a devise to a corporation, yet that such a devise upon trust for a family or an individual is good in the view of this Court, which, disregarding the legal effect of the devise, will fasten the trust upon the person who takes the property, and compel him to perform it.

With respect, however, to the cases which have been decided before the statute of *Elizabeth*, I must say there does not appear to be any case in which the decision itself is an authority directly bearing on this case: *Simmoms' case* Duke, 163 has been relied on for that purpose; but it is perfectly clear on looking into that case, that the word "sold" which is used in the report, does not refer to a sale for money, but means "bargained and sold," and that the bargain and sale was not enrolled in due time: and the remarks made by Serjeant Warren are perfectly correct, viz., that this case was decided on the general jurisdiction of equity to relieve against accident, and that the same relief would be given in any similar case of a trust for a private family. That case proves what *Sonley* v. *The Clockmakers' Company* proves, that a gift to a person or body incapable of taking, for the benefit of a third person, will be established by a Court of Equity, and the defective conveyance will be made good. It is no answer to say, that relief is given to a purchaser or to the family of the testator, because there exists a valuable or a good consideration which Equity favours, and for which alone it will aid a defective conveyance. That is assuming the very question in dispute, because the argument on the other side is, that charity is in the view of a Court of Equity a good consideration, and that, therefore, a defective conveyance to a charitable use will be aided in equity, and that the Court will support the charity, although the legal title be defective. There was another case cited from *Duke* s. 154, and relied on a good deal. It was this:- "In the 11 *Hen*. 6, a gift was made to the intent to find a Chaplain '*ad divinia celebranda*,' until the feoffor or his heirs should procure a foundation, &c.; there was no employment until the reign of King *Edward the Sixth*; and, therefore, in the Queen's time, one Payne purchased the land as a concealment: after a commission being awarded upon this statute, the Commissioners inquired and found the gift, and thereupon decreed the property to another from Payne; but afterwards this decree was made void by the Lord Chancellor, because the use limited to find a Chaplain '*ad divina celebranda*' was no use within the statute inquirable; but the Chancellor, by his Chancery authority, may decree the lands to the first use." It is evident, however, that the statute there referred to is the statute against superstitious uses, 1 *Edw*. 6, c.14, and that it has nothing to do with the statute of *Elizabeth*.

The cases in *Duke* pp. 360, 361, if we look at the dates, bear exactly on this case; but I am not disposed to place much reliance upon the dates ascribed to them; they appear to me so very uncertain, and the resolution at page 361 only proves that Equity would relieve where there was a defective conveyance or gift in favour of a charity *after* the statute, which is beyond all doubt.

The Mayor of Reading's case was, I think, decided after the statute, and may, therefore, be disregarded as not being an authority on either side. There was an *Anonymous case* cited by Mr. Moore, from 1 *Ch. Cases* p. 267, which struck me at first as a strong case in favour of his client. The case was this.– After the statute of *Elizabeth* a man devised his house in London to a charitable use, which was a void devise, because of his misnaming the Corporation, but the Lord Keeper decreed in favour of the charity, "though," it is added, "before the statute no such decree could have been made." On looking, however, more closely into the case, it appears to have nothing to do with the subject at present before the Court, because something intervened between the two passages that were cited, and that was a discussion whether after the act of *Elizabeth* it was necessary to issue a Commission, or whether relief might be had by means of an Information. Properly the case stands thus:- "The Lord Keeper, notwithstanding, decreed it to be a good appointment for charitable use. But then it was objected that the process appointed by the statute ought to be adopted, and that a Commission ought to issue and an inquisition be taken under it, and that the plaintiffs had no right to sue by original bill;" – then comes the concluding observations cited by Mr. Moore:– "But the Lord Keeper decreed the charity, though before the statute no such decree could have been made." That observation does not mean that before the statute no such right existed, but that there were not the same means of enforcing it. In the case of *The Attorney-General* v. *Newman* 1 Ch. Cas. 157, the same point arose, and no positive opinion was pronounced by the Court; but we know at the present day that in such cases a Commission never issues: relief is invariably obtained upon an information: and that circumstance, of itself, goes a good way to prove that the Court possesses a jurisdiction, independently of the statute, to sustain such proceedings. The machinery provided by the statute has entirely ceased to operate, but the equity is still constantly enforced; and that equity must, it appears to me, be sustained by some jurisdiction not derived from, or dependent upon, the statute of *Elizabeth*.

The principal authorities in support of this position are, certainly, no more than *dicta*, but they are numerous and come from high authorities, and I shall now refer to them in order. In *Eyre* v. *The Countess of Shaftesbury* 2 P. Wms. 118, the following passage occurs in the judgment of Sir Joseph Jekyl, one of the Lords Commissioners:- "In like manner in the case of charity, the King *pro bono publico*, has an original right to superintend the care thereof, so that abstracted from the statute of *Elizabeth* relating to charitable uses, and antecedent to it, as well as since, it has been every day's practice to file informations in Chancery in the Attorney-General's name, for the establishment of charities." Nothing can be stronger, to shew that the law upon this subject was the same before, as after the passing of the statute. I do not, however, look upon this as an authority declaring what the law is, but as an indication of what the learned Judge then considered, from his knowledge and experience of the law of England, that law to be.

There is an important observation of Lord Northington, on this subject, in the case of *The Attorney-General* v. *Tancred* 1 Eden, 14.– "The only doubt is, whether the Court should supply this defect for the charity under the statute of *Elizabeth*; and I take the uniform rule of this Court before, at, and after the statute of *Elizabeth*, to have been, that where the uses are charitable and the person has in himself full power to convey, the Court will aid a defective conveyance to such uses. Thus, though devises to Corporations were void under the statute of *Henry* 8th, yet they were always considered good in equity if given to charitable uses." In the same book the following passage occurs in a judgment of the same Judge, in the case of *The Attorney-General* v. *Bradley* 1 Eden, 487:- "It is true, and I am sorry for it, that there are old precendents in this Court where, by a perverse and mistaken construction of the statute of *Elizabeth*, this Court has enabled persons to give to charities, who had no power to do so; and it is as true, that these precedents not only injured private families, but became a public nuisance, which called upon the Legislature to interpose and stop them. But I found the equity of this Court liberal and impartial, and no respecter of persons, and please God, I will leave it so." In that I do not see that there is any thing to impeach the former observation; he is only stating what is an undoubted fact, that such a construction had been given to the statute; but there is nothing in it to rebut the existence of a jurisdiction in this Court independently of that statute. It is said that the authority of that case of *The Attorney-General* v. *Tancred* was shaken by the observations respecting it, made by Lord Brougham in the case of *The Attorney-General* v. *Sibthorpe* 2 Russ. & My. 116; but I cannot concur in that. The observations which have been referred to, appear to me to leave its authority quite unaffected. Lord Brougham only shews that there was an error in the report as to a particular matter of fact, which does not affect the general opinions expressed by Lord Northington, as to the inherent jurisdiction of the Court before the statute.

The next observation upon this point is by C.J. Wilmot Wil. Cas. & Op. 24:- "The King, as *parens patriœ*, has the superintending power over all charities, abstracted from the 43 *Elizabeth*, and antecedent to it (2 *P. Wms*. 119), and that paternal care and protection is delegated to this Court."

Lord Manners, in *The Attorney-General* v. *Flood* Hayes, 630, entirely adopts what fell from Lord Macclesfield in *Eyre* v. *The Countess of Shaftesbury*. "The Court of Chancery," he says, "having always exercised jurisdiction in matters of charity, derived from the Crown as *parent patriæ*, has proceeded as I have done."

There is, however, another observation of Lord Manners, which may be set off against the observation by the same Judge, just cited. In the same case he says:- "By this mode of proceeding, every devise to a Corporation for charity, though void at Law, would be good in a Court of Equity. But has this ever been done? In England, indeed, it has been done, but not by any original inherent authority of this Court, but under the sanction of the 43rd of *Elizabeth*."

In the case of *The Attorney-General* v. *The Skinners' Company* 2 Russ. 420, Lord Eldon makes the observations which have been so much relied on in the argument, and certainty he speaks with considerable caution. "It may not be quite clear," he says, "that these instruments, originally void, were held to be valid merely by the effect of the statute of *Elizabeth*. It might have been supposed that there was in the Court a jurisdiction to render effective an imperfect conveyance for charitable purposes; and the statute has, perhaps, been construed with reference to such the supposed jurisdiction of this Court, so that it was not by the effect of the 43rd of *Elizabeth* alone, but by the operation of that statute on a supposed antecedent jurisdiction in the Court, that void devises to charitable purposes were sustained. Out of that supposed jurisdiction this construction of the statute may have arisen." I think, however, it is impossible to read those observations without coming to the conclusion, that Lord Eldon had formed a very clear opinion in favour of the inherent jurisdiction of this Court. That view of the subject had evidently been pressed upon him in the argument; and when he comes to deliver his judgment, he does not find any fault with it, he does not condemn it at all, he leaves the question exactly where it was: and from his not expressing any disapprobation of the doctrine in question when thus brought under his notice, it must, I think, be taken, that the opinion of that eminent Judge was in favour of it.

In *The Attorney-General* v. *the Master of Brentwood School* 1 My. & Kee. 376, the following passage occurs in the judgment of Sir J. Leach p. 390:- "It has been argued that the title of the possessions of the school, and the poor people, depends upon this decree, and that the decree is to be considered as the voluntary act of Wystan Browne, and that he was substantially the founder of those charities. In the view which I take of this case, if it were so considered, the decree to be made in this case would not be thereby affected. But I am of opinion that, although at this time no lands so devised, were in Equity bound by a trust for the charity, which a Court of Equity would execute." As the period referred to in that passage was antecedent to the statute of *Elizabeth*, it shews clearly what Sir J. Leach's opinion was upon the subject now in controversy; and there is not any thing, I think, in the case of *The Attorney-General* v. *The Skinner's Company*, which at all diminishes the weight of those observations. In that case of *The Attorney-General* v. *The Skinners' Company* 5 Mad. 200, the same learned Judge says:- "It is very singular, but certainly true, that a devise to a Corporation for a charitable use before the 43rd *Elizabeth*, has been established as a good appointment under that statute. It is a very extraordinary doctrine. The Legislature cannot have meant that: it must have meant by the use of the word 'appointment' in that statute, a legal appointment." That is perfectly correct, but it is perfectly consistent with the observations made by him in *Attorney-General* v. *The Brentwood School*. Neither do I see that there is any weight in the objection that his statement of the law in the latter case is incorrect, because of his overlooking the statute of *Philip & Mary,* which was passed before the will in that case had been made. At most, those observations would only shew that he had made a mistake upon that particular point, and would not detract from the weight of his general observations. But, in point of fact, he was quite correct in those observations. He said that the law did not authorise such gifts to charity as those in that case; and in that he was pefectly well founded, because the statute of *Philip & Mary* did not include such gifts as that to the Grammar School there. *Porters' case* 1 Co. Rep. 22 decided that a Grammar School was not within the 23 *Henry* 8th, c.10, and it shews by analogy, therefore, that such a School was not within the statute of

Philip and Mary, so that when carefully considered, there is nothing in the observations of Sir J. Leach, in the latter case, to weaken his observations in *The Attorney-General* v. *Brentwood School.*

The last authority of this description which I shall refer to, is the case of *The Attorney-General* v. *The Corporation of Dublin* 1 Bligh, N.S. 347. I agree with Sergeant Warren in the observations which he made upon the general import of this case. It was decided, certainly, in part upon the existence of a right to an account against the defendants; and Lord Eldon was particularly anxious to shew that the case had not been decided upon the ground of charity merely. In order to see, therefore, whether I am to give any weight to the observations used in that case, I am bound to look at it carefully with reference to the objections which have been made to it, and see whether they were intended to be general observations applying to charity generally, or merely used by the learned Judge for the purpose of shewing that the court had the power of investigating the accounts in charity cases. The observations of Lord Redesdale are:- "We have been referred to the statute of *Elizabeth* with respect to charitable uses, as creating a new law upon the subject. That statute only created a new jurisdiction; it created no new law – it created a new and ancillary jurisdiction – a jurisdiction borrowed from the elements I have mentioned – a jurisdiction created by a Commission to be issued out of the Court of Chancery, to inquire whether the funds given for charitable purposes had not been misapplied, and to see to their proper application; but the proceedings of those Commissions were subject to appeal to the Lord Chancellor, and he might reverse or affirm what they had done, or make such order as he might think fit for reserving the controlling jurisdiction of the Court of Chancery as it existed before the passing of the statute; and there can be no doubt, by information by the Attorney-General, the same thing might be done." Giving all due weight to the observations made by Sergeant Warren upon that case, I think it impossible to say that Lord Redesdale did not mean that there existed an original jurisdiction in this Court in such cases before the statute, which might have been exercised; and that the statute only introduced new machinery, but gave no new law.

This case concludes the authorities in support of the doctrine contended for. The case of *The Attorney-General* v. *Bowyer* 3 Ves. 714, certainly, as far as it goes, is an authority on the other side; for in that case Lord Loughborough says at p. 726:- "It does not appear that this Court at that period had any cognizance upon informations for the establishment of charities prior to the time of Lord Ellesmere: as far as the tradition in times immediately following goes, there were no such information as this upon which I am now sitting, but they made out the case as well as they could by law." It is certainly true, looking at the earliest cases upon this subject, that they were a great deal mixed with law; in almost every case the Judges of the Common Law were called in to assist. The cases, however, to which I have referred before, prove that charity was an object favoured by Courts of Equity before the statute of *Elizabeth*; and I apprehend, therefore, that a devise to a Corporation for a charitable use is a perfectly good devise. The case of *Jenner* v. *Harper* 1 P. Wms. 247 has been referred to as an authority against the jurisdiction of the Court; but I do not see anything in it in the way of my decision – for the doctrine in that case, is merely that a devise to a charity after the Statute of Frauds must be attested in the manner required by that statute, and it depends upon the effect of the Statute of Wills and the subsequent Statute of Frauds.

If I had, therefore, after considering all those cases, to decide the present case, judging by analogy to the law of England, and putting out of consideration the statute of *Elizabeth*, which does not exist in this country, I should say that an inherent jurisdiction existed in this Court to sustain the devise in question, and I should enforce the Equity accordingly. The case, however, does not depend entirely upon that; there is a statute in this country which is not often referred to, but which is, I think, entitled to more consideration than is usually given to it; the statute I refer to is the 10 *Car.* 1, *Sess.* 3 c.1, commonly called "The statute of Pious Uses." The first section enacts "that all archbishops and bishops of this kingdom and their successors, shall and may from the time of any grant or estate to them or any of them, made or to be made either by our late Sovereign King *James the First*, of happy memory, or by the King that now is, or by any other person or persons, bodies politic or corporate whatsoever, of any manors, lands, tenements, &c., unto the use or upon trust and confidence unto, or for, the erection, maintenance or support of any college, school, lecture in divinity, or in any of the liberal arts or sciences, or for the relief or maintenance of any manner of poor, succourless, distressed or impotent persons, &c." After having enumerated the different gifts, it proceeds to enact:- "That they shall be taken and construed to be good and effectual in law, according to the purport and true intent and meaning thereof; and that the said Archbishops, Bishops, and their successors, &c., shall and may be compelled by subpœna out of the High Court of Chancery, or by petition before the Lord Deputy and the Privy Council, to execute and perform all and every the said trusts and uses, according to the true intent and meaning of the charters, deeds, and conveyances to them in that behalf made, or hereafter to be made."

It is said, and with truth, that this statute is confined to gifts to Archbishops and Bishops; and, therefore, it is contended that it has no operation in a case like this; but would it not be extraordinary that the Legislature should pass an act relative to Bishops and Archbishops, providing for their applying to the proper objects property vested in them upon trust; but that if such gifts were made to archdeacons or any other churchmen, they should be allowed to appropriate them as they pleased? It occurred to me on reading the statute, that there must have been some particular abuse existing at the time, which required correction, and at which it was particularly pointed. I found, accordingly, in *Bishop Mant's History of the Church of Ireland* an explanation of the history of the act. There is a letter given there Vol. 1, p. 474 from the Lord Deputy (Wentworth) to Archbishop Laud, in the year 1634, a short time before the act was passed, in which he says:- "The Bishops aliening their very principal houses and demesnes to their children, to strangers, farming out their jurisdiction to mean and unworthy persons; the schools which might be a means to season the youth in virtue and religion, either ill-provided, ill-governed for the most part, or – which is worse – applied sometimes to the maintenance of popish schoolmasters; lands given to those charitable uses, and that in a bountiful proportion, especially by King *James* of ever blessed memory, dissipated, leased forth for little or nothing, concealed contrary to all conscience and the excellent purposes of the founders; all the monies raised for charitable uses converted to private benefits."

The Archbishop, in his reply Vol. 1, p. 476, says that some of the evils may be easily corrected by keeping the Clergy, "especially the Bishops, from their sacrilegious alienations. For the schools – if your Lordship will remedy anything, you must take the same way of restoring their temporalities. For the third thing your Lordship mentions, I conceive the remedy is more easy; for there you have nothing to do but to turn the money given to charitable uses, to the use intended by the donor."

This it was which led to the passing of the act; and accordingly, it begins by stating what the Lord Deputy wrote to Laud, that it is "for the maintenance and execution of pious uses."

This explains why it was that the Archbishops and Bishops were mentioned in the act. They had a great deal of property in their hands intended for charitable purposes which they applied to their own use. The act was intended to remedy this gross evil, and to prevent for the future the misapplication of charity property by the heads of the Church. The act, however, gives no new jurisdiction to this Court, although it introduced the proceeding by petition before the Lord Deputy and the Privy Council. The Lord Deputy, seeing the want of power in the Privy Council to remedy the evil, wrote, as we have seen, to Laud, and this act was passed early in the next session of Parliament. So far, however, from its affecting in any way the jurisdiction of this Court, I think it is a clear parliamentary recognition of the jurisdiction which existed at the time. It recognises the authority residing in this Court, which could have compelled any man to perform a trust; but as against those particular classes of persons who were possessed of great power that might enable them to disregard its decrees, it establishes a new jurisdiction. I have carefully compared the charitable uses mentioned in this act, with those enumerated in the 43 *Eliz*. and I find there is very little difference between them, although the order in which they are put is different in both. There is scarcely one in the act of *Elizabeth* which is not to be found in the Irish act; but the latter goes farther than the former, with respect to the liberal arts, and it also includes trusts "for the maintenance of any Minister or Preacher of the holy Word of God," which are not included in the former.

This statute proves that all the uses mentioned in it were legal at the time it was passed, independently of its operation. A particular mode of enforcing them is given in certain cases, but their legality is not created by it; it is treated as pre-existing, and it is open to all the observations upon that point which I made already upon the statute of *Elizabeth*. But we come now to a more important part of the statute. After describing the uses which it was intended should be within the remedies given by the act, and adding to that these words, "And for any other like lawful and charitable use and uses warranted by the laws of this realm," it enacts thus, "they are and shall be taken and construed to be good and effectual in law, according to the purport and true intent and meaning thereof." Now, can any man doubt for a moment that the statute, when it speaks of other like lawful uses, means to declare lawful those uses which were enumerated in the early part of the section? These concluding words, therefore, in my opinion, prove, beyond the possibility of doubt or cavil, that the Legislature treated all those uses as lawful. I consider the act of *Charles* as moulded on the 43rd *Elizabeth*, and that whatever the latter gives in England is given by the former in this country. The Irish act gives a powerful remedy for breaches of such trusts, in certain cases, without coming into this Court upon information, namely, by enabling the party complaining of them, by a petition to take the heads of the Church before the Council Board, there to answer for the misapplication of the funds: and is left every other person to the ordinary course of law, to compel them to perform those trusts which they were subject to.

I have been very careful in forming any opinion upon this act, because there have been several opinions expressed upon it, and I am not very fond of new discoveries in such matters. I have, therefore, read the act over several times, to see whether I was right, and have only been confirmed in the view I originally took of it. The opinions to which I have just referred are certainly open to some observations, although they are expressed by high authorities. In *The Attorney-General* v. *Flood* Ha. & Jones Ap. 30, the late Master of the Rolls says- "In discussing the validity of this devise, it becomes first essential to consider whether the 10 *Car*. 1, sess. 3, c. 1, is in any manner analogous in its extent or provisions to the 43rd of *Eliz*. c. 4; for if it be, the case of the relators is, in my opinion, clear – and they would have both the legal and equitable interest in the same manner as either of the universities of England clearly would. I am not aware of any Irish statute material to consider, except the *Car*. 1, sess. 3, c. 1; and that cannot, I conceive, by any possible construction be extended beyond the grantees, the Archbishops and Bishops named in it, although a beneficial remedial law." Now, as the Master of the Rolls does not refer to the other provisions of the statute, but rests his opinion solely on the literal expressions appearing on the face of the act, I cannot consider that as an authority of much weight. In the report of the same case when before the Lord Chancellor, assisted by Lord Downes, C.J. Hayes, 624, the latter is represented to have said:- "It is then contended, on the part of the college, that supposing the statute of *Elizabeth* not to be declaratory, or to shew that the law was the same before as after its enactment, and although that statute does not exist in terms in Ireland, yet that the 10 *Car*. 1, *Sess*. 3, c.1, is in substance the same as that statute; and that, of course, the law of Ireland is the same as that of England with respect to devises to Corporations, after the passing of the 43rd *Elizabeth*. The college must, according to that, take to their own use. Now, what words are there in the statute of *Charles*, which can lay any foundation for allowing devises to eleemosynary Corporations and others; – there is not a word about Colleges and Corporations in it. So that the statute of *Charles*, not saying a word upon the subject would repeal the whole exception in the Statute of Wills, without a single expression ocurring in the act capable of being tortured into such a meaning." Lord Downes is there represented to say, that there is not a word in the statute about Colleges or Corporations. It is strange how such a mistake could have arisen in his Lordship's mind, because the first thing enumerated in the act is a provision for assisting "the erection, maintenance and support of any College, School, Lecture in Divinity," &c. There is a mistake, therefore, on the part of the learned Judge, as to the contents of the statute; and, therefore, I cannot consider his opinion entitled to all the weight ascribed to it. It must have arisen either from some mistake of his own, or from some misapprehension of the Reporter. In the same case Hayes, 634, Lord Manners says, "In the same year with the Statute of Wills in Ireland, was passed another statute, the 10 *Car.* 1, sess. 3, c. 1. – As far as I understand that statute, it does not apply to the present case at all; it seems applicable only to other conveyances than wills. It is enough, however, to say, that Archbishops and Bishops alone are the persons mentioned in it, and grants to them only are protected by it. It is certainly a very imperfect statute. It makes those persons who are specified in it liable to a subpœna from Chancery, to account for such charitable donations as should be given to them in trust. Surely, no act of Parliament could ever be necessary to give such a jurisdiction as that to the Court. If a Corporation be a trustee, it is accountable to this Court just as much as an individual. What the statute meant, I am really at a loss to know, and I am utterly ignorant what jurisdiction which the Privy Council could have had over the matter comprised in it; but it is enough to say, that it does not apply to this case." The answer to that is – not that the learned Judge was ignorant of any jurisdiction the Privy Council possessed when the statute was passed but that he overlooked the fact, that by that statute the Legislature gave the Council a jurisdiction which it had not before. I am compelled, therefore, by the nature of the opinions which have been just mentioned, not to give them the weight which, from the high authority of the Judges who expressed them, they would otherwise be entitled to. The present Master of the Rolls, in his judgment on this case, when before him on the demurrer, says 1 Sa. & Sc. 609, "In Ireland, the statute 10 *Car.* 1, sess, 3, c. 1, is entitled 'An act for the maintenance and execution of pious uses.' It is very imperfect as it appears in the Statute Book, and evidently some portion of the statute was by mistake omitted." I do not quite understand the force of this observation, nor do I think that, even if well founded, it touches the question.

As I said before, however, I am not enamoured of my own construction of that statute; and, if shewn to be incorrect, I will immediately retract my opinion upon it: but even, independently of that statute altogether, there is, I think, abundant ground for the decision I am about to pronounce. The law of Ireland stands now, I think, upon the same footing in this respect as the law of England. In England, the machinery of the statute of *Elizabeth*, is no longer used, and relief is always given upon an information. If I be right, therefore, in considering that the statute of *Charles* in this country is a parliamentary recognition of such devises, the law of the two countries will be precisely parallel. Such, I think, will be the result of an examination of the authorities; and, if so, I should be glad that the law upon this subject in the two countries was still further assimilated, by extending to this country the provisions of the 9 G. 2, c. 36, to which there is no corresponding statute in this country. This is, in my view of the matter, the only difference now existing between the laws of the two counties upon this subject.

I was very much pressed by the case of *The Attorney-General* v. *Flood*; and certainly, if the view of the subject there taken be correct, it may be questioned whether this case would not require the consideration of a higher tribunal. That case was decided by very learned persons, who had much greater opportunity of knowing the law of this country than I possess; but it is my duty to decide according to my own judgment, and, after a most careful consideration of the authorities, I cannot consider that decision as a binding authority.

An objection has been taken to the terms of the devise here, and it has been contended that there cannot be a devise to this Corporation for the charitable purpose mentioned, because the Society is incorporated solely for this charitable purpose – that it is, therefore, a gift to a Corporation for its corporate purposes, which is not allowed by the Statute of Wills. If, however, we look to the cases, it will be seen that a gift may be made by devise to a Corporation for a charitable purpose, precisely as it might to a private person; and, therefore, I cannot see why this devise is void. Let us, however, try the question by putting hypothetical cases. Suppose a devise was made to this Corporation in trust for me, it could not be disputed that that would be a good devise. For that, *Sonley* v. *The Clockmakers' Company* Ante is a clear authority. If, therefore, a devise to a Corporation upon trust for an individual is good, a devise to them upon trust for a charity must be equally good, because the law favours charities. Both devises are void at law, but this Court fastens the trust upon the land into whatever hands it comes. Suppose, again, a devise to a third person, upon trust for this Corporation – that is admittedly good; or even a devise to another Corporation upon trust for this is good – if my decision in the present case be right. Let us put this Corporation aside, and suppose a devise was made to any individual or any other Corporation for maintaining the Protestant Schools of Ireland, that would undoubtedly be good. But, then, it is said this devise is void, because the Corporation to whom it is made is to employ it for its corporate purposes – which are admittedly charitable. But I cannot see how the union of an estate which is void at law, and of an equitable estate which can be made available in this Court, in the same party, will defeat what would otherwise be a good devise. The gift for charitable uses is the subject upon which the trust attaches – the charitable use is the trust to be performed, which this Court will enforce without reference to the medium by which the estate was sought to be conveyed. I feel, therefore, with very great confidence, that I have formed a correct opinion in this case, and I have come to a conclusion as clear as any I ever arrived at in my life, that this is a perfectly good devise – not at Law, I admit – but perfectly good in this Court; and I must, therefore, give a decree for the plaintiffs according to the prayer of the bill.

With respect to costs, the defence which has been set up is certainly not one that is ever favoured in that respect. Any one setting up such a defence must be prepared to pay the costs of it, if unsuccessful; and, certainly, if the bill had been filed within a reasonable time, if there had not been so much *laches* on the part of the plaintiffs, I might have made a different arrangement of the costs from what I am now disposed to do. The manner in which I purpose disposing of the costs at present is this: I will make the defendant Richards pay all the costs occasioned by his setting up the Statute of Limitations. Then, as to the other points set up in defence – although it does not lie well in his mouth to set them up, yet, as there were difficult points of law arising on this will which it was necessary to decide – I think it right to give no other costs up to the hearing. The subsequent costs will depend on the results of the accounts. The accounts I shall direct to be taken on this footing:- the late J.N. Richards representing the life interest of Mrs. Mitchell, and being also an encumbrancer, was bound to keep down the interest on his own encumbrance, out of the rents, and to apply the surplus rents in liquidation of the principal; the sum received on the sale of part of the lands must be brought into the account at the time it was received, and applied in reduction of the debts. If there be any difficulty in drawing up the decree, I should be glad if the case were mentioned while it is fresh in my memory. The parties will see that I have decided the legal questions upon their request, and have not taken it upon myself to decide them.

Note
See further, *Irish Land Law*, para. 9.100.

3. *Relief of Poverty*

BROWNE V. KING
[1885] 17 L.R. Ir. 448 (Chancery Division)

The Trust in a deed was that the trustees should pay the annual rents, issues, and profits of lands to such Roman Catholic clergyman as should for the time being, according to the rules of the Roman Catholic Church, he entrusted with the spiritual care and superintendence of the Roman Catholic inhabitants of the parish of R., for the purpose of having the said rents, issues, and profits applied by the said clergyman for the benefit of the children under the age of twelve years of the tenantry of the grantor, in such manner as to such clergyman should appear most advisable.

Porter M.R.:

The question in this case arises on the validity of a limitation in a deed of the 27th April, 1853. [His Lordship referred to the deed.]

The plaintiff claims to be entitled to this property as heir-at-law of Matilda

Browne, asserting that the ultimate limitation in the deed is invalid as an attempt to create a perpetuity. Two views are suggested against that contention: First, that it is a gift to the persons who should be under the age of twelve years, and children of the tenantry of this property in Mayo, at the death of the tenant for life. Whatever may be the meaning of the word "tenantry," whether it means the tenants in the lifetime of Matilda Browne or the tenantry at any other time, there was plainly no intention to vest an estate in fee in infants under the age of twelve years. The limitation is that the trustees of the deed should pay the rent, issues, and profits to the Roman Catholic clergyman entrusted with the spiritual care and superintendence of the Roman Catholic inhabitants of the parish of Robin, in the county of Mayo, for the purpose of having the said rents, issues, and profits applied by the said clergyman for the benefit of the children under the age of twelve years of the tenantry of Matilda Browne. The intention plainly was to constitute, out of the rents, issues and profits, a fund in the hands of the Roman Catholic clergyman for the benefit of such children *in perpetuum*, not for the purpose of a sale of the lands, and dividing the proceeds of the sale among the children, whatever their number might be. That would be contrary to the plainly expressed intention. Secondly, it is contended that the limitation in the deed can be sustained as a gift for a charitable purpose. I wish I could adopt that view, because it seems to me that it would carry out the intention of the settlor, which was a benevolent and kind one. Is this, then, a valid charitable gift for the children of the tenantry of this estate under the age of twelve years? An affidavit has been put in evidence to show the state of this property. It appears that there are a number of families on this estate, and that some of the children are necessarily objects of charity. *Morice* v. *The Bishop of Durham* 7 Ves. 399; 10 Ves. 522 decides, that a bequest in trust for such objects of benevolence and liberality, as the trustee in his own discretion shall most approve, cannot be supported as a charitable legacy if some of the objects are charitable and some not. Where the principal part fails the whole fails *See* 10 Ves. 538.

A number of cases were relied on by the defendants to show that this is a charitable gift. In *Rogers* v. *Thomas* 2 Keen, 8, a testatrix bequeathed to the inhabitants of Tawleaven-row all that might remain of her money after her lawful debts and legacies were paid, and Lord Langdale held that the persons found to be inhabitants of Tawleaven-row were entitled to the residue of the personal estate, but not on the ground that the bequest was a charitable one. That case therefore is not an authority in the present case.

In the *Attorney-General* v. *Comber* 2 Sim. & St. 93, a bequest to the widows and orphans of a parish was held to be a good charitable bequest. Sir John Leach said that the gift could not in its nature have proceeded from general benevolence to particular individuals; it must have proceeded from general benevolence towards two classes of persons who were suffering under a common circumstance of destitution or privation, and is necessarily to be confined to such of those two classes as are within the scope of general benevolence, and he acted upon this bequest as if the expression had been to the poor widows and orphans of Lindfield, and declared this to be a charitable use.

Those observations show the grounds on which the case was decided. The bequest was to the "widows and orphans of the parish of L—." The word "parish" has had weight attached to it in more than one case in England in determining charitable bequests. It has a peculiar force in an English will by reason of the parochial organization by which the poor-law is administered in England. That organization does not exist in Ireland. The word "parish" is not coupled in this deed with the children for whose benefit the bequest is given; the parish of Robin is used only to describe the residence of the clergyman who is to apply the fund. It was stated at the bar, and not denied, that the parish of Robin is eighteen miles from this property. In *The Attorney-General* v. *Comber* 2 Sim. & St. 93 the gift was "to the widows and orphans." They were, as Sir John Leach says, "two classes of persons who were suffering under a common circumstance of destitution or privation." The "education and preferment of orphans" is one of the charitable purposes enumerated in the statute, 43 Eliz. c. 4.

In *Thompson* v. *Corby* 27 Beav. 649 the gift was to "twenty aged widows and spinsters in the parish of Peterborough," and it was held to be a good charitable gift. Widows or spinsters as such are not enumerated in the statute of 43 Eliz. c. 4; but the Master of the Rolls says: "If the matter had depended on the statute alone, I should have thought the word 'aged' would have been sufficient to create a good charitable bequest for the relief of the poor on the estate – not because they were tenants, for the testatrix had settled the estate, and had only a rentcharge on it, but because they were poor.

Powell v. *The Attorney-General* 3 Mer. 48 was a peculiar case. There was a bequest of residue to the widows of children of seamen belonging to the town of Liverpool. The bill which was filed against the Attorney-General and the testator's next-of-kin for the directions of the Court as to the application of the residue charged that there was no existing charitable institution for the relief of widows and children of seamen belonging to the town of Liverpool, but that there were alms-houses in the town for widows of seamen, erected by virtue of different charitable bequests, and a hospital, under an Act of 20 Geo. 2, c.38, for the relief of maimed and disabled seamen, and the widow and children of such as should be killed, &c., in the merchants' service. The decree made at the hearing is not mentioned, further than that it was thereby referred to the Master to inquire whether there was any and what charitable institution for the benefit of the widows and children of seamen belonging to the town of Liverpool. The Master, by his report, stated several charities for poor seamen's widows, and others for the poor of Liverpool generally, besides the hospital mentioned in the bill; and one under the will of Elizabeth Cain, whereby she directed the residue of her estate to be continued at interest or placed out on securities at the discretion of her executors, and after their death, of the rectors of Liverpool for the time being: the interest to be paid and distributed unto and among such poor sailors' widows and orphans (inhabitants of Liverpool), as should in their judgment be deserving objects of charity. The question on the hearing for further directions was, whether there was a good charitable bequest, and if so, whether it was general, or to go in aid of any of the specified charities. Sir W. Grant held that it was a valid bequest, and that the words were sufficiently descriptive of the last of the charities mentioned in the Master's report. Careful consideration of that case has satisfied me that the decision was that the gift was a valid gift to the institution for the support of poor sailors' widows and orphans. It must have been rejected as a gift to individuals. But the gift to the widows and children of seamen could be supported as a charitable gift, and brought them within the term poor sailors' widows and orphans, for whose benefit the institution was established.

Isaac v. *Defriez* 17 Ves. 373n was a gift to poor relations. In *Gillam* v. *Taylor* L.R. 16 Eq. 581, the gift was of the interest of a fund from time to time for such of the lineal descendants of Richard Wilson, my dearest mother's brother, as they may severally need it. On the authority of *Lily* v. *Hey* 1 Hare, 580, and *The Attorney-General* v. *Price* 17 Ves. 371, it was held that the gift was a charitable one. That case is explained in *The Attorney-General* v. *The Duke of Northumberland* 7 Ch. Div. 745, where it was held that to constitute a gift to the poorest of a stipulated class charitable, it must be construed as a gift to those who are actually poor and not the least wealthy of a wealthy class. There the gift was for the benefit of the poorest of his kindred, such as could not maintain their own charges.

In *The Attorney-General* v. *Gladstone* 13 Sim. 7 the gift was to T.R., to be applied by him to the use of the Roman Catholic priests in and near London at his absolute discretion. T.R. died in the testator's lifetime, and it was held that the legacy was not void for uncertainty, and did not lapse by T.R.'s death in the testator's lifetime, but was good as a charitable legacy; and that it must be applied for the benefit of persons filling the character of Roman Catholic priests in and near London. No objection arises from the indefinite word 'near,' because if the fund is given for a charitable purpose, the Court can solve the difficulty with regard to its application by directing a scheme to be approved by the Master." The Vice-Chancellor then referred to the will, and says:- "Upon the whole, I think that the fair construction of the bequest in question is, that it was intended for the benefit of persons filling the character of Roman Catholic priests in and near London, both at the testator's death and afterwards."

The gift there was a gift for a public religious purpose, and the case is not applicable to the case before me. There is nothing to guide me in deciding that the gift is for children of poor persons, or persons in great need. The law imposes on parents the duty of supporting their children, and there is nothing to satisfy me that the tenantry of Matilda Browne are not able to fulfil that obligation.

For the reasons I have with considerable regret come to the conclusion that the gift is not charitable. I shall make a decree for the plaintiff.

Note

See further, *Irish Land Law*, para. 9.101.

4. *Other Charitable Purposes*

RE CRANSTON

[1898] 1 I.R. 431. (Court of Appeal)

The facts are set out in the judgments.

Lord Ashbourne, C.:

This is an appeal from the Master of the Rolls, and it turns upon the question whether certain gifts in a will can be regarded as charitable under the Irish Statute 10 Charles 1, which is analogous to the English Statute 43 Elizabeth. The gifts are to the officials of the London Vegetarian Society, and the English Vegetarian Society in Manchester. These societies have been formed to induce abstinence from all forms of the flesh of animals, and to encourage instead the use of all kinds of vegetarian produce. They hold out not only that their teachings will improve health, but encourage humaneness by tending to diminish the destruction of animal life.

Are these gifts charitable? They are certainly not so in the ordinary meaning of the word – in its popular sense. But the word "charity" under the statute has acquired a wide, elastic, meaning, which has been laid down or developed in numerous cases. Mr. Justice Chitty in the case of *Cross* v. *The London Anti-vivisection Society* [1895] 2 Ch. 501, 504 has truly said:- "Charity in law is a highly technical term. The method employed by the Court is to consider the enumeration of charities in the statute, bearing in mind that the enumeration is not exhaustive. Institutions whose objects are analogous to those mentioned in the statute are admitted to be charities; and again, institutions which are analogous to those already admitted by reported decisions are held to be charities. The pursuit of these analogies obviously requires caution and circumspection. After all the best that can be done is to consider each case as it arises, upon its own special circumstances. To be a charity there must be some public purpose – something tending to the benefit of the community."

In seeking our analogies it is essential to note that the Irish Statute 10 Charles 1, after mentioning a variety of objects (even including the erection and maintaining of bridges), adds "or for any other like lawful or charitable use or uses warranted by the laws of this realm."

Therefore the question really is – having regard to the authorities, can these gifts to these two vegetarian societies be excluded from the very wide class, deemed to be charitable, according to the broad and gradually widening interpretation of Courts of law?

The gifts here are for rich and for poor, for general public use, not for any particular class or religion. They are for a public purpose – deemed by the testatrix beneficial to the community. Are they charitable within the meaning of the statute and the decided cases? The analogies provided by decided cases are very numerous and very various. Gifts to the British Museum, the Royal Society, for founding a Botanical Society for supporting lectures against cruelty to animals; to the Chancellor of the Exchequer for the benefit of Great Britain, for the repair of sea banks; for the relief of houses of correction; for keeping chimes in repair; for assisting a school for sons of the clergy, and many others, entirely outside the scope of the ordinary popular meaning of the word, have been held to be charitable.

Mr. Justice Romer in the case of *In re Lord Stratheden and Campbell* [1894] 3 Ch.

265 was of opinion that a gift for the benefit of a volunteer corps was a charity.

The case of *Thornton* v. *Howe* 31 Beav. 14 has naturally been keenly relied on because it decided that gifts to encourage the teachings of Joanna Southcote were charitable.

The case of the *Commissioners for Special Purposes of Income Tax* v. *Pemsel* [1891] A.C. 531 has been also much discussed before us. It was not suggested there by any of the noble and learned lords that cases coming under the statutes of Elizabeth or Charles should receive a less broad construction than had been theretofore usual: and Lord Macnaghten took the opportunity of laying down with precision that trusts for purposes beneficial to the community, not falling under the other heads of relief of poverty education or religion might equally be held to be charitable.

In *Armstrong* v. *Reeves* 25 L.R. Ir. 325 the Vice-Chancellor held that gifts to an Antivivisection Society were charitable – a decision not now questioned and followed in England in a case I have already referred to.

The case of *In re Nottage* [1895] 2 Ch. 649 is interesting as showing that a Court plainly felt some regret and hesitation in deciding that a gift for the sport of yacht racing was not a charity – holding that it was not for a public purpose, but for the amusement of individuals.

The cases to my mind all show a desire on the part of the Court to include every reasonable case in a liberal interpretation of the word charity. Can the gift in the present case be excluded? Here there is nothing private, individual or circumscribed in the gift. It is given freely in the hope that it would be widely availed of by all, earnestly aspiring to be a general public benefit. The advantage of all mankind is the object, the elevation of the world is sought by teaching, which the testatrix believed would improve the general health, and foster, a general spirit of humaneness. It may be that this idea of vegetarianism has not as yet made its way in the world. It may be showing no growth. The vast majority may be opposed to it. It may be disapproved of by medical men. Possibly no member of the Bench may believe in it. But these considerations cannot be regarded as decisive to exclude it from the wide class of gifts regarded by the law as charitable. The gifts are given to societies which rightly or wrongly set a public purpose before them, and which have been founded and maintained in the belief that their teaching is for the benefit of the community. I do not feel at liberty to sit in judgment upon objects or purposes, or to measure the success they now have, or hereafter may attain to. In my opinion the judgment of the Master of the Rolls was right, and this appeal should be dismissed with costs.

FitzGibbon, L.J.:

I concur. We must define the sense in which the law uses the word "charity." In its popular sense, charity involves the idea of *misericordia*, or pity, and of aiding those who are in distress. Though the legal sense includes the popular one, it is far wider, and includes many objects to which the popular idea does not extend. The reason of the extension is material; it is because the legal notion is founded upon the analogy of the statute. When we find that the statute includes a number of objects to which the idea of *misericordia* or pity is wholly foreign, it allows that the idea which the law recognizes as essential to "charity" is something different.

Lord Macnaghten's attempt to divide charitable purposes into four categories fails to satisfy the requirements of a logical division, because, if adequate, it is not distinct. He has defined three classes, but he has put everything else, without any definition, into the fourth class. He has, in fact, divided charitable objects into – I., Relief of the poor; II., Religion; III., Education; IV., Et cetera. Such a division gives no help to determine the question which we have here, viz. whether a particular gift, not for poor-relief, religion, or education, is one which the law recognizes as charitable. The first category rests on the good old popular idea of charity. The second and third rest on the statute, because the advancement of religion and education are expressly mentioned therein. But "analogy" has immensely enlarged their application. For example, disseminating the works, and thereby propagating the opinions, of Joanna Southcote, has been charitable, and under the heads of "religion" and "education," cases of gifts to further the tenets, or to advance the teaching, of very small and very peculiar classes in the community, have been established as charitable, even though, if at all beneficial, they were restricted to a very few, and even though the "benefits" conferred on these few were opposed in the strongest manner to the creeds, or to the judgments, or to the prejudices, of the vast majority, and were even regarded as heretical, or even mischievous, by that majority. The essential attributes of a legal charity are, in my opinion, that it shall be *unselfish* – *i.e.* for the benefit of other persons than the donor – that it shall be *public*, *i.e.* that those to be benefited shall form a class worthy, in numbers of importance, of consideration as a public object of generosity, and that it shall be *philanthropic* or *benevolent* – *i.e.* dictated by a desire to do good. We must remember, in cases of the fourth category, that these conditions have been held to be satisfied, in cases of the second and third, by gifts for the benefit of very small sects and sections. Under those circumstances, being bound to clear our minds of the idea of *misericordia*, I can not reconcile the cases by anything short of adopting the principle that any gift which proceeds from a philanthropic or benevolent motive, and which is intended to benefit an appreciably important class of our fellow-creatures (including, under decided cases, animals), and which will confer the supposed benefit without contravening law or morals, will be "charitable." Chitty, L.J., righly points out that benevolence or philanthropy alone will not suffice, because there charity, like faith, is dead, being "without works," and there are plenty of philanthropic and benevolent people who stop at words, or at ideas, and to be "charitable" they must *do* something or *give* something for the benefit of others.

Having got thus far – What is the tribunal which is to decide whether the object is a beneficent one? It cannot be the individual mind of a Judge, for he may disagree, *toto cœlo*, from the testator as to what is or is not beneficial. On the other hand, it cannot be the *vox populi*, for charities have been upheld for the benefit of significant sects, and of peculiar people. It occurs to me that the answer must be – that the benefit must be one which *the founder* believes to be of public advantage, and his belief must be at least rational, and not contrary either to the general law of the land, or to the principles of morality. A gift of such a character, dictated by benevolence, believed to be beneficent, devoted to an appreciably important object, and neither *contra bonos mores* nor *contra legem*, will, in my opinion, be charitable in the eye of the law, as settled by decisions which bind us. It is not for us to say that these have gone too far.

Addressing myself to the question of fact in the present case – whether we call it a fad or not, "Vegetarianism" is a fact. In various forms it has existed from ancient times; it has been the practice, and it is the creed of many, including the most numerous sect under the Queen's sway. The Vegetarian Society has existed for half a century, and its adherents are numerous and widespread. Its principles appeal to humanity, and tend to mercy and to morality, whether they are practical or visionary. Comfort and economy would be promoted by a vegetable diet, even though it might be in some respects injurious. It is hard to see why the promotion of total abstinence from flesh should not be a "charitable" object in the legal sense, if we are at liberty to recognize the promotion of total abstinence from intoxicants as charitable; moderation and temperance may be carried to excess, and though the benefits and the drawbacks may differ in degree, they seem to be the same in kind. The motives of the promoters of teetotalism and of vegetarianism are equally unselfish, and equally benevolent, and the efforts of vegetarians, so far as I can form a judgment, seem less likely to do mischief than those of the anti-vivisectionists, or even than those of the promulgators of the works of Joanna Southcote.

For the reasons which I have summarized, I think that the case falls within the decisions which have established gifts to be charitable.

Walker L.J.:

The gifts in this will which have been challenged are, "to the trustees, treasurer, or other proper officers from time to time of the London Vegetarian Society and the English Vegetarian Society established in Manchester, in 1847." There is another legacy to "The London Society for the total abolition of vivisection" which the residuary legatees do not question.

As the will contains no description of the character or objects of the Vegetarian Societies we have to look to their constitution as defined by their charters. I think they may be described as voluntary associations of individuals and affiliated Societies for the promotion of Vegetarianism, defined as abstinence from the flesh of animals, fish, flesh, and fowl, as food, and the encouragement of the use of seeds, pulses, grains, fruits, nuts, and other wholesome products of the vegetable kingdom. In another place Vegetarianism is described as "the total abstinence from food which has been procured through the destruction of life," which is pronounced to be contrary to humanity. Various methods are pointed out by which the objects may be and have been aided, and results indicated alleged to be useful to the cause of humanity and instruction of the poorer classes, but the objects are what I have stated. The question which we have to consider is whether the gifts are "charitable" in the legal sense which that word has acquired by reason of the wide language used in the statute of 43 Elizabeth and the analogous statute in Ireland of 10 Car. 1. This latter statute after dealing with the subjects of education, relief of the poor, and religious purposes, proceeds, "or for the erection, building, maintenance, or repaire of any bridges, causeyes cashes, paces, and highways within this realme or for any other like lawfull and charitable use and uses, warranted by the laws of this realme now established and in force." As early as 1767 the Lord Chancellor gave a definition of charity under the statute as "a gift to a general public use which extends to the poor as well as the rich": *Jones* v. *Williams* 2 Ambl. 652.

It has long been settled that for the present case, the test is not whether the gift is "charitable" within its ordinary and popular sense, but within its technical, acquired, and legal sense. The difficulty in *Commissioners of Income Tax* v. *Pemsel* [1891] A.C. 531, was in determining which sense it would bear. Lord Cairns, in *Dolan* v. *McDermot* L.R. 3 Ch. 678, says: "There is perhaps not one person in a thousand who knows what is the technical and legal meaning of the word 'charity.'" Lord Halsbury in *Pemsel's Case* [1891] App. Cas. 531, at p. 544, after referring to numerous cases on the statute of Elizabeth says:- "In these and many like cases it appears to me that the distinction between what is charitable in any reasonable sense, and that to which trustees for any lawful and public purpose may be compelled to apply funds committed to their care has been – I will not say confused – but so mixed that where it becomes necessary to define what is in its ordinary and natural sense 'charitable,' what is merely public or useful, is lost sight of." Lord Macnaghten, at p. 583, after giving his division of charitable objects in the legal sense, winding up with as a fourth division, "trusts for other purposes beneficial to the community not falling under any of the preceding heads," says, that a person of education would exclude from endowed charities the fourth division. In the same case in the Court of Appeal, at p. 307 of 22 Q.B. Div., Lord Esher says:- "If you give to the word the larger sense given to similar words in the Court of Chancery, it would include almost anything given for a public purpose, and would include many things which would be beyond the interpretation of the words among ordinary educated people, such as a grant of money to supply waterworks to such towns as Manchester or Liverpool."

A striking illustration of the same doctrine is to be found in the case of *Goodman* v. *Mayor of Saltash* 7 App. Cas. 633. There it was held that a condition that the free inhabitants of ancient tenements in the borough of Saltash should have a right of dredging for oysters in the estuary, could be sustained as a charitable gift, Lord Cairns saying, "Such a condition would create that which, in the very wide language of our Courts, is called a charitable, that is to say, a public trust or interest."

In order to bring any gift within this description the giver must contemplate a public benefit, and not some other immediate purpose from which public benefits may indirectly, and in result follow. It was this consideration which defeated the gift in *Re Nottage* [1895] 2 Ch. 649, where it was held that the immediate object was to encourage the sport of yacht racing. It is that to which Rigby, L.J., refers, when he says, "We must always go back to the analogy of the statute, which furnishes the only test that can be applied to see whether a gift is charitable or not. If the present gift is to be supported as charitable, it must be on the ground that it is for a general public purpose. It is, however, plain from the words of the testator himself that he was not contemplating any such purpose – his object in founding the prize is to encourage the sport of yacht racing.

In the present case I think the object must be attributed to the testatrix of intending to benefit all mankind by helping to spread the doctrines of vegetarianism. Most people will consider that such benefit would not be in fact advanced, but the gift is not illegal or contrary to public policy or opposed to the settled principles of morality. It involves a question of opinion upon which the majority of people will differ from the giver.

There may be cases in which the Court would feel itself at liberty to set up its own view against that of the giver, even though the purpose offended against none of the doctrines I have mentioned. I do not think it can in such a gift as the present. We know from our general reading that there are a large class who believe as the testatrix did, and that there are societies for the spread of vegetarianism in England and other countries.

Take some of the specific objects mentioned in the statute of Elizabeth religion and education. On those subjects which so vitally concern the interests of mankind, the Court, subject to the limitations I have mentioned, does not set up its own opinion: *Thornton* v. *Howe* 31 Beav. 14, is an instance as regards religion, and *Farrer* v. *St. Catharine's College* L.R. 16 Eq. 24, as regards education. It was on this point I referred during the argument to the observations of Lord Selborne, in L.R. 16 Eq. 24:- "One cannot help thinking it is a strong example of the inconvenience of the state of the law which forces upon the public gifts of very doubtful public utility. However, such is the state of the law."

Lord Herschell, in *Pemsel's Case* [1891] App. Cas. p. 573, refers to the same subject, and seems to consider that it makes no difference that opinion should differ widely as to the expediency or utility of the object.

It seems to me these considerations ought to apply much more strongly when we are dealing with the head of what is, or may be, or is supposed by the giver to be, useful for mankind, especially when we are considering the debateable question of what is healthy for the human race, or what is cruel. We know that some of the most valuable discoveries in medical science were for a long time disbelieved in and ridiculed. Again, most people will admit that vivisection should be allowed when it is practised, in the words of the Act of 1876, "for the advancement by new discovery of knowledge which will be useful for saving or prolonging life or alleviating suffering," but a number of persons honestly believe the contrary, and gifts for the total abolition of vivisection have been supported as charitable. I think the principle of those decisions applies to the present.

The principle is summed up in the concluding words of Lord Justice Chitty in *Re Foveaux* [1895] 2 Ch. 501. "It may be truly said that the infliction of justifiable pain is not cruelty. The question of what is and what is not justifiable is a question of morals, on which men's minds may reasonably differ and do in fact differ. The purpose of these societies, whether they are right or wrong in the opinions they hold, is charitable in the legal sense of the term. The intention is to benefit the community; whether if they achieved their object, the community would in fact be benefited, is a question on which I think the Court is not required to express an opinion."

The object of vegetarians is to induce manking to live on vegetables – a more wholesome and cheaper diet than animal flesh, and induce them to abstain from killing animals, which if man does not need them for food, is cruel because needless, and demoralizing because cruel.

The idea may be erroneous and may be visionary, but it was entertained honestly by the giver, and her gift was designed for the benefit of mankind, and I think it is charitable according to the legal sense of that term.

Holmes L.J.:

The question involved in this case is of first impression; and I have found little to assist in its solution in reported decisions.

The term "charitable," as applied to donations and trusts, has received in our law an artificial meaning, which does not lend itself readily to definition or classification. The legal conception of the term is to be traced to the enumeration in the preamble of the statute 43 Elizabeth, c. 4, of a list of charities of a very varied and heterogeneous character. Where the object of a gift clearly comes within one of the classes therein specified, it is held to be charitable, however difficult it may be to reconcile such a conclusion with popular ideas; and the result, although often surprising to a layman, is arrived at without difficulty by a lawyer. But, unfortunately for the latter, this list, comprehensive as it is, does not exhaust the objects of legal charity. It only supplies instances, and where a purpose can be brought by analogy within the spirit and intendment of the statute it is also held to be charitable. It is these analogous cases that cause perplexity. It is difficult to reconcile them with each other or to extract from them any guiding principle. Lord Macnaghten in his judgment in *The Commissioners of Income Tax* v. *Pemsel* [1891] A.C. 531 says:- "Charity in its legal sense comprises four principal divisions – Trusts for the relief of poverty; trusts for the advancement of education; trusts for the advancement of religion; and trusts for other purposes beneficial to the community, not falling under any of the preceding heads." I don't know a better classification, and yet it is obvious that the fourth head is altogether vague and indeterminate. If the gentleman of education without legal training, to whom Lord Macnaghten afterwards refers, were asked whether a legacy for the promotion of vegetarianism is a charitable gift, I doubt if his reply would be "You had better ask a lawyer." He would think that there could only be one answer; and yet, he would be wrong, for it he were to put the question to two lawyers, he would almost certainly receive two different opinions. At all events there are two opinions on the subject in this Court; and there are few cases in which judicial disagreement would be less surprising.

The part of Mrs. Cranston's will, which relates to the matter to be decided, has been already read. It is a devise of the yearly sum of £100, portion of a larger perpetual annual rent to the trustees, treasurer, or other proper officer from time to time of the London Vegetarian Society and the English Vegetarian Society, established in Manchester in 1847, to be paid to them for ever, by equal half-yearly payments in equal moieties, for the use of the said respective societies. There is nothing in the will to indicate that the testatrix considered that the institutions that she intended to benefit were of a charitable nature; but it may be assumed that she would not have made them the objects of her bounty if she did not believe that they would apply her gift to a benevolent and useful purpose.

The aims of the two societies, as set forth in the constitution of the one and in the rules of the other, are practically identical. They are the advocacy of abstinence from the flesh of animals as human food and the promotion amongst mankind of a purely vegetable diet. In considering whether these associations are charities, we ought, I think, to look rather to their objects than to the means by which those objects are sought to be attained. The persons who control them for the time being are given a large discretion in selecting the modes of working. Some of the means employed can hardly be considered charitable, even in the most extended application of that word, such, for example, as the promotion of fraternal intercourse between London vegetarians, whether as individuals or as members of societies, and dinners given to the Press of London. On the other hand, the lectures in Board Schools might be regarded as tending to the advancement of education, and, therefore, charitable. It is a rule of law that a fund which, at the discretion of trustees, may be applied for charitable or other purposes is not a legal charity; but where means varying in character all tend to the same charitable end, the undertaking does not cease to be charitable by reason of the fact that some of its methods, if looked at separately, could not be so regarded.

I have occasionally met with persons who from taste or convenience abstained either temporarily or permanently from animal food; but I have only known one vegetarian on principle. I assume, however, that strict and conscientious vegetarians are more numerous than my own experience would have led me to believe. I gather, moreover, from the report of the London Society, as well as from the references to the subject to be found in current literature, that the foundation of vegetarianism, in the opinion of its promoters, is moral rather than material. The slaughter of animals to provide food for man is considered cruelty; and it is argued that the exercise by him for merely selfish purposes of that dominion which he possesses over the lower creatures tends to blunt his feelings of mercy and humanity, to make him callous to pain and suffering, and generally to degrade his higher nature. I have no doubt that vegetarians at the same time believe that the change of diet which they advocate would improve the general health, introduce a more economical mode of living, and in other ways increase the sum of human comfort.

There is nothing illegal or contrary to public policy in the propagation of these doctrines; and it is not to be supposed that in dissenting from the conclusion of my colleagues I am of opinion that the law regards vegetarian societies with hostility or jealousy. Money may be given or bequeathed to add to their resources or to further their objects without stint or limit. Had Mrs. Cranston desired to increase their funds by a testamentary gift, a lawyer could have suggested to her various ways of effecting her object that could not have been questioned. It happens that the mode she selected creates a perpetuity, with the consequence that the gift fails if the object be not charitable. Hence the necessity for considering the question to which I am now about to apply myself very briefly.

It is, I think, clear that a gift of this kind is not included in the instances of charities contained in the statute of Elizabeth. It is equally clear that it cannot be brought within any of the first three classes enumerated by Lord Macnaghten. It is not given for the relief of poverty, for the promotion of education, or for the advancement of religion. There remains the fourth class. Is it a gift for other purposes beneficial to the community not falling under any of the preceding heads?

The object must be one by which the public, or a section of the public, benefits. So much is admitted; but what is the test or standard by which a particular gift is to be tried with a view of ascertaining whether it is beneficial in this sense? I am of opinion that it does not depend upon the view entertained by any individual – either by the Judge who is to decide the question, or by the person who makes the gift.

There is probably no purpose that all men would agree is beneficial to the community; but there are surely many purposes which everyone would admit are generally so regarded, although individuals differ as to their expediency or utility. The test or standard is, I believe, to be found in this common understanding. The first three heads of Lord Macnaghten's classification are based on it. There is the widest difference of opinion as to the best way to relieve the poor, as to religious dogma, as to the subjects and methods of education; but there is a general concurrence that the lot of the needy ought to be ameliorated in some way, that man should be under the guidance of some religion, and that he should receive some kind of intellectual training. Moreover the idea is widely entertained that a religious or educational system, which, when compared with other systems, would be considered by most men to be defective or objectionable, may have a powerful influence for good on those who accept it, and in any case is to be preferred to atheism or ignorance. In my judgment Lord Macnaghten's fourth class rests on the same foundation of a common understanding. I do not intend to go through the authorities that have been cited during the argument, or others that I have looked at since. It is enough to say that I can find in them nothing inconsistent with my proposition, and that when they are taken as a whole they completely bear it out. The cases which were most strongly relied on for the respondents, and which seem at first sight to extend most widely the legal conception of a charity, will be found on examination to come either within the terms of the statute of Elizabeth such as *Nightingale* v. *Goulbourn* 5 Hare, 484;2 Ph. 594 for within one of Lord Macnaghten's first three classes, such as *Thornton* v. *Howe* 31 Beav. 14, the *Attorney-General* v. *Lawes* 8 Hare, 32, and *Farrar* v. *St Catharine's College* L.R. 16 Eq. 24. We were strongly pressed with *Thompson* v. *Thompson* 1 Collier, 381; and I admit that if the charitable object in that case was to extend the knowledge of those doctrines in the various branches of literature to which the testator had turned his attention and pen, it would be difficult to reconcile it with my view; but the report is an indifferent one, and there is every reason to believe that the true ground of the decision was that the legacy was given for the purpose of providing a pension for a poor and unsuccesful man of letters.

Let me now apply the standard I have suggested to Mrs. Cranston's bounty. From the earliest period of which we have any record, and in every part of the world –

especially in the most refined and civilized countries – a substantial portion of man's diet has consisted of animal food, to supply which it has been customary to kill certain kinds of beasts, birds, and fish. By no code of morality in this practice condemned as immoral. By no school of medicine is it deemed unwholesome. In no scheme of domestic economy is it regarded extravagant. There have been, probably, always a few who have protested against it on conscientious grounds; and latterly several societies have been formed to carry on what is called, in one of their reports, a crusade against this practically universal habit. It is possible they may succeed. Missionaries as few, and apparently as feeble have, from time to time, altered the current of human thought and action; although I doubt whether any change hitherto made in the world was quite so unlikely as what these societies propose. At the present time, however, the enterprise has no kind of countenance from public opinion. Beyond a few eccentrics, no one thinks of connecting it with public utility, or with the moral or material improvement of mankind. We cannot regard it as we might regard an obscure and novel religious sect, as a doubtful branch of a great beneficial and elevating movement. In its most favourable aspect it is a harmless attempt to substitute one kind of food for another. Its promoters, no doubt, believe in its utility. The social missionary thinks that there is no message so useful as his own, although, like Lord Bramwell, I believe in all cases of propagandism there is mixed up a wish for the prevalencee of the opinions entertained by the propagandist, simply because they are his own. But can this belief make a project of this kind a charity in any sense which the law attaches to that term? If it can, it seems to me that every project not actually immoral or illegal must be held a charity. Schemes to promote what is called a rational dress for women, or a more aesthetic costume for men, to substitute canvas tents for the present kind of habitation, to limit our food to a single meal a-day, to make night the time for labour, and day the time for sleep and rest, would each be deemed beneficent agencies by a few human "cranks," but it will require a new definition of legal charities to bring them within that category.

I find that the instructive judgment of the Master of the Rolls in this case mainly rests on the decisions relating to animals. *The University of London* v. *Yarrow* 1 De G. & J. 72, *Marsh* v. *Means* 3 Jur. (N.S.) 790, and *Tatham v. Drummond* 4 De G.J. & Sm. 484 established the proposition that gifts the object of which is to prevent cruelty to animals and to ameliorate the position of the brute creation are charitable. No metaphysical reasoning is required to support these decisions. The Divine Teacher from whom Christendom has learned its lessons of charity and mercy treated the healing of the sick and the relief of a suffering ox or ass as cognate acts, differing, no doubt, in degree, but the same in kind. There is really no difference amongst thoughtful and civilized men on this subject. If it is beneficial to the community to promote virtue and to discourage vice, it must be beneficial to teach the duty of justice and fair treatment to the brute creation, and to repress one of the most revolting kinds of cruelty.

After the cases I have mentioned came the vivisection cases which, in my opinion, are governed by precisely the same principle. Vivisection is a practice confined to a small body of scientific men. It is, or was, before the Act of 1876, undoubtedly attended with great and often excruciating pain to a living animal; and although this may be justified by the object aimed at, it readily degenerates into wanton cruelty when employed recklessly or for the purpose of mere experiment. So strong was public feeling on the subject that more than twenty years ago a statute was passed subjecting the practice to rigid restriction and supervision, and even in its present modified condition, it stands on the border line of cruelty; and there is a great body of well-informed opinion, holding that it would be for the true interests of mankind to put an end to it altogether. I think that there is no analogy between a practice such as this pursued by only a few individuals, attended with the severest suffering, and productive of very doubtful benefit, and the universal habit of killing animals for human food in a manner that causes at the most but momentary pain. There are practices to which animals are subjected for the purpose of preparing them for the table which closely approach – it may be, overstep – the border line of cruelty, just as there may be cruelty in some of the modes in which horses are trained, prepared, and harnessed, with a view to their being driven or ridden. But by no standard now recognized in the world is the mere slaughter of an animal for the purpose of cookery held to be more cruel than using the horse as a beast of burden. It would be easy to amplify by further comment and illustration my reasons for differing from the judgment of the Court; but I have said enough to indicate my opinion, and as it cannot affect future decisions it would be unprofitable for me to occupy further time.

Note
See further, *Irish Land Law*, para. 9.102.

SWIFTE V. ATTORNEY-GENERAL
[1912] 1 I.R. 133 (Chancery Division)

The facts are set out in the judgment.

Barton, J.:-

The question for decision is, whether this bequest of £4000 Consols to the Commissioners of Charitable Donations and Bequests, upon trust to pay the income and dividends for the exclusive benefit of the Dublin Home for Starving and Forsaken Cats, is a valid charitable bequest. [His Lordship referred to the object of the institution and the circumstances connected with it, and proceeded]:-

The law applicable to this class of charitable gifts is tolerably well settled. The prevention of cruelty to animals is an object which the law recognizes as legally charitable. This is especially so in the case of animals useful to man. In *In re Douglas*; *Obert* v. *Barrow* 35 Ch. D. 472, 479 the principle was applied to a bequest to a "Home for Lost Dogs." The late Master of the Rolls has applied the principle to this very institution. In *Swifte* v. *Colam* Unreported, Feb. 16, 1909 he ordered the balance of a sum of £450, after payment of costs, "to be held by the Commissioners of Charitable Donations and Bequests, upon trust to invest the *corpus*, and to pay the interest as it accrues due, to the said Miss Alice May Swifte, or other the Hon. Treasurer for the time being of the institution known as the Home for Starving and Forsaken Cats." The bequest in that case was a simpler one than the present case; and the only question in the present case seems to be whether there is anything to distinguish it from *Swifte* v. *Colam* Unreported, Feb. 16, 1909.

I now turn to the will. We have, in the first place, a bequest of £4000 Consols "to the Commissioners of Charitable Donations and Bequests, . . . upon trust to apply the income and dividends thereof for the exclusive maintenance of the Dublin Home for Starving and Forsaken Cats." That is a good charitable bequest, unless there is something in what follows to invalidate it. The next material sentence is as follows:- "Including the maintenance of the chloroform chamber now existing, or any other painless method of putting an end to cases of hopeless pain, and the maintenance of the boarding department." This sentence commences with the word "including," which in its ordinary and natural meaning means "comprehending *inter alia*." The mention of the chloroform chamber, the use of which is limited to cases of hopeless pain, does not, in my opinion, affect the charitable character of the gift. The boarding department has been criticized because it appears to be self-supporting. That does not, in my opinion, affect the charitable character of the bequest. It appears to be a subordinate adjunct of the Home, and is intended to provide shelter and food for cats who otherwise would be forsaken by their owners when they leave town. The testatrix then uses the words "but for no other purpose." These words refer back, in my opinion, to the word *exclusive*, and mean "for the exclusive maintenance of the 'Cats'' Home, and for no other purpose." She then proceeds to explain why she gives this bequest for the exclusive maintenance of the "Cats'" Home, and for no other purpose. The explanation is given in the sentence of the will commencing with the word "as." [His Lordship then referred to the deed of Feb. 27, 1888, and to the lease of Nov. 28th. 1884, and proceeded]:

The contents of the deed and lease explain why the testatrix insisted that her bequest was to be for the exclusive maintenance of the Cats' Home, and for no other purpose. The reason was that the general maintenance charges which were common to the Dogs' Home and to the Cats' Home were defrayed by the Society under the deed to which she refers, and by the lease of the common site of the Dogs' and Cats' Home. I need not refer to the gift over.

It seems to me that the construction which I have just put upon the language of the testatrix is the natural one, and that there is nothing to cut down or invalidate the original bequest, which in itself is merely a valid charitable gift.

I turn to the arguments which have been adduced *contra*. It was argued that the sentence commencing "as" is a condition precedent to the bequest, and that unless the Dublin Society for Prevention of Cruelty to Animals is under an enforceable legal obligation to pay the rent, taxes, repairs, and caretaker's wages, &c., of these premises, the gift fails. I assume, for the purpose of argument, that the Society is under no such obligation, but I can find no condition precedent. The word "as" is not conditional but explanatory.

It was argued, in the next place, that the word "including" is equivalent to "meaning," and was to be taken as introducing an exhaustive definition of the object of the gift; that the words "but for no other purpose" refer only to the two preceding departments of the Home, and that the bequest was, in fact, a bequest for the exclusive purpose of maintaining the chloroform chamber and the boarding department of the Home, which, by themselves, it is contended, could not constitute a legal charity.

I need not discuss the latter question, because I am of opinion that this would be a strained construction of the bequest. It would be cutting down the clear bequest to the Home by giving to the word "including" a secondary meaning, which it would require a strong context to support.

On the whole, I am of opinion that this is a good charitable gift. The parties are agreed that, in view of these and the other provisions of the will, the order should direct the settlement of a scheme for the regulation and management of the charity, and for the application of its present and future income. (Affirmed by Court of Appeal, 3rd June, 1910).

III. CY-PRES DOCTRINE

RE FFRENCH

[1941] I.R. 49 (High Court)

The facts are set out in the judgment.

Gavan Duffy J.:

Kathleen Emily Sophy Alexandra ffrench died, a spinster, in Manchukuo, on the 1st of January, 1938. By her will, made there on the 5th of September, 1937, she devised Monivea Castle, in Co. Galway, to the Irish Nation for a charitable object – a home for a particular class of aged and infirm beneficiaries.

But the Executive Council is satisfied that the scheme which she had in view is impracticable for lack of funds – a conclusion reached as the result of a careful examination of the place.

The Attorney-General now applies for an order to give effect to the donation *cy près* and all parties assent to the matter being decided on summary summons under Or.III, r. 2, of the Rules of 1926.

The law of *cy près* requires the Court to substitute a practical plan for a charity, as near as may be to the donor's own wishes, where those wishes, as formulated by the donor, cannot be carried out, provided that the will discloses a "general charitable intention"; that time-honoured phrase is not always a happy one, for it has to do duty in widely different circumstances; it may suggest that, in order to save a gift for charity, the Court must find in the will some general words declaring the giver's wish to dedicate the property in question to charity, whereas the tenor of the will or even the nature of the gift may be such as to prove that charity, and not the abortive plan expressed in the will, was uppermost in the donor's mind; and the word "general" seems to me to obscure the duty of the Court to save for charity a gift made in terms for some very narrow and particular charitable purpose, provided that the wish behind the gift appears to be to give to charity; the older cases of this type are reviewed by Brady L.C. in *Daly* v. *Attorney-General* 11 Ir. Ch. R. 41.

Miss ffrench did not declare any general charitable intention in her will, but I have to consider whether such an intention is to be inferred from the language that she used and the dispositions that she made. It is urged that such an intention must be implied from the fact that the gift is made to the Nation, but I must look into the matter much more closely than the argument would suggest.

One way to ascertain whether the will discloses the charitable intention for which I have to look is to inquire whether the whole gift in the mind of the donor depended upon the feasibility of giving effect to her directions: *In re Wilson*, *Twentyman* v. *Simpson* [1913] 1 Ch. 314, at p. 324: in other words, whether the dedication of the residence to the specified charity was a condition precedent: *In re Monk*, *Giffen* v. *Wedd* [1927] 2 Ch. 197; but I think I shall reach the same result if I direct my mind to the rather broader attack made here, the allegation that the will, far from showing charity as the paramount object of the gift, actually reveals the preservation of the Castle of Monivea and its extensive demesne and plantations, a non-charitable object, as the purpose on which Miss ffrench had set her heart, and the plan for the charity in the Castle as quite subsidiary. If that contention be borne out, the charitable gift fails and there is an intestacy. The fact is worth noting that, on the evidence adduced before me, Miss ffrench had no dependants to whom she was morally bound to leave an adequate competence, so that there was nothing to prevent her from devoting any part of her considerable fortune to charity, if she was minded to do so.

I cannot accede to the argument that, once I find a gift of a character recognised by law as charitable, I need go no further, but should at once declare that no difficulty presented by the particular plan outlined in the will can stand in the way of the gift, and that it must be made effective as nearly as possible in the way that the donor would have wished. In my opinion, the fact that poor persons were to benefit does not by itself prove that charity necessarily loomed in the donor's mind, when she was penning the gift. This was the problem presented to Sir Richard Arden, M.R., nearly a century and a half ago in *Attorney-General* v. *Whitechurch* 3 Ves. 141. There, a testator made a number of charitable gifts and devised four houses in London in trust for four poor men of a certain parish, to be chosen by the trustees, and gave a sum of £2,000 to provide a weekly allowance for each man and his wife and the survivor; the gift of the houses was illegal under the law of that time in England, but it was urged that the substantial purpose of providing for four poor men should be established by saving the £2,000 for charity; Sir Richard Arden, however, held, on the wording and conditions of that particular will, that the intention of the testator was to endow alms-houses and that there was no further general intention, so that the gift of the money failed with the gift of the houses. Yet the poor men were within a recognised category of charity. It is true that the claims of charity were not always approached in a benevolent spirit by the Attorney-General, making a claim for charity, is sure of a sympathetic hearing to-day, but the fundamental principles remain, and a similar decision was given in *In re Packe*, *Sanders* v. *Attorney-General* [1918] 1 Ch. 437.

Analysing the will, in the search for the paramount intention which it may discover in regard to the gift in question, I find first, a gift to the Nation of the demesne of Monivea, and I find that the gift of the demesne is to carry the Castle, the bogs, the reclaimed lands and the plantations; so far there is no mention of charity, but the words of gift are coupled with the express condition subsequent, made by the testatrix, that no parcel of these remains of her former estate shall ever be sold, and the testatrix emphasises the condition by recording a "solemn promise" from all her tenants, to whom she had sold their holdings 37 years before, that the demesne should remain inviolate for at least a century; so its preservation was not an old woman's fantasy, but a long-cherished dream; and the old trees must not be felled, so long as they can stand.

In the second place, after the larger and principal gift and after the condition, I find a direction ("I wish") that the Castle of Monivea – that is the residence – shall be made a "home" for aged and indigent teachers or persons engaged in literature, painting, sculpture or music, ten in number and no more, so that they may find peace and comfort in their declining years – clearly a charitable gift. Certain objects of art are to be sent to Monivea. And there is a bequest for the upkeep of the mausoleum at Monivea, where the testatrix and her father are buried, and its surroundings, and special care is to be taken of the chapel there and of the old trees; 16 Masses are to be said every year in the chapel for her father's soul and her own.

Now, a highly significant feature of the gift of Monivea is the language selected by the donor to describe the trustees at three successive points at which she wants to mention them. First, the selection of the ten beneficiaries is to be "left to the trustees appointed by the Irish Free State Government to administer the estate of Monivea"; then the legacy for the mausoleum (£1,000) is to be handed over in trust "to those who shall have been chosen to look after Monivea"; and the only funds which can be drawn upon at all for the charity are left "in trust to those appointed by the Irish Free State Government to look after the estate of Monivea"; the testatrix, as it seems to me, leaves the Government in no doubt whatever as to the duty she is imposing upon the State of appointing a body of trustees to take care of her ancestral property.

Another curious feature is the inadequacy of the financial provision for the ten beneficiaries, a limit obviously ordained to ensure that the Castle should maintain its character and not become an institution. In fact the need of supplying money for the support of the ten residents is almost overlooked and that omission is strange, if the welfare of these worthy old people was the purpose, or a purpose, predominant in Miss ffrench's mind; she leaves the residue of her funds at a London bank to the trustees who are to look after the estate of Monivea, in trust to use the income "for repairs at the Castle also of demesne walls and roads within the demesne and generally for the upkeep of the home" and to pay £16 a year for the Masses. The evidence is that these funds will not exceed £2,000, a very inadequate provision, if I construe "the upkeep of the home" liberally to include the maintenance of the old people, for whom no other fund is left by the testatrix, who probably overestimated the moneys at the bank. The Attorney-General has satisfied me that the condition of the residence is such that it cannot be used for the home without the expenditure of large sums on renovation and repair, and no such sums are available.

As to the testatrix herself, the evidence is that she was born in Brussels of Irish lineage, that she had Russian interests on her mother's side, as some of her legacies show, that she spent nearly all her life abroad and died at the age of 73 at Harbin. It is agreed on all sides that she died domiciled in this State. Monivea had been the family seat for many generations and she inherited the place on her father's death in 1896, afterwards receiving considerable sums on the sale of the agricultural portions of Monivea to the tenants. Her actual, personal contact with Monivea seems to have been slight, and I surmise that the intense interest she evinces in the place was due to family tradition, received from her father, who built the mausoleum. She signs the will "Kathleen ffrench of Monivea."

On the intrinsic evidence from the will, to which the external data add little of relevance to my inquriy, there is really no doubt as to the paramount intention of the testatrix. For the Attorney-General it is urged that the selection of the Nation as donee suggests a charity of national importance in the eyes of the donor: Farwell J. in *In re Ashton*, *Westminster Bank* v. *Farley* [1938] 1 Ch. 482, at p. 503 suggests that it is only in a case where the trust itself is not specified that the office of the trustees may be considered in order to ascertain the purpose of the trust; I need not go so far as that *dictum* in seeking the paramount intention; for the selection of the Nation as donee is open to the alternative, and in the circumstances more likely, explanation that the donor thought that the State would be the surest and most permanent repository of the trust to preserve Monivea. The whole demesne was given to the Nation to preserve, and only the Castle was destined for the charity; the charity is given no prominence in the will; it is put in the second place, introduced by a "wish" and very poorly endowed. On the other side, I have the record of the solemn promise for the inviolability of the demesne for 100 years, the devise of the old family estate on condition that it is retained for ever, the retention made as secure as an old lady's foresight could make it by confiding the duty to the State, the special solicitude extended even to the ancestral timber, and the illuminating and repeated description of the trustees in terms showing that the donor regarded them as the guardians of her property. All these features and the striking contrast between the emphasis on the care and preservation of Monivea on the one hand, and, on the other, the small attention paid in the will to the charity, with little of that particularity which betrays the enthusiasm of a founder, create in my mind a strong impression, that the state of mind behind the will was this:- "If only the Government will perpetuate Monivea, I may as well have the Castle used for a suitable charity."

I do not overlook the distinction, so clearly made by Mr. Justice Meredith in *Governors of Erasmus Smith's Schools* v. *Attorney-General* 66 I.L.T.R. 57, between motive and intention; I disregard the motive, which was very probably a natural family pride; I am concerning myself with the two purposes disclosed by the will and the preponderating importance of the one over the other.

I have no doubt, and I must hold, that the particular charity was a subordinate adjunct to the great object in view, and that the conservation of Monivea was the paramount intention of the testatrix, to which the conversion of the Castle into a home for ten deserving objects was ancillary.

There is, therefore, no case for *cy près* and the charitable gift fails.

The bequest of the art objects fails with the charity and the next of kin take the bank residue, except the £16 a year for Masses.

Note

See further, *Irish Land Law*, para. 9.104 *et seq*.

CHARITIES ACT, 1961

47. (1) Subject to subsection (2), the circumstances in which the original purposes of a charitable gift may be altered to allow the property given or part of it to be applied *cy près* shall be as follows:-

(*a*) where the original purposes, in whole or in part–
  (i) have been as far as may be fulfilled; or
  (ii) cannot be carried out, or cannot be carried out according to the directions given and to the spirit of the gift; or

(*b*) where the original purposes provide a use for part only of the property available by virtue of the gift; or

(*c*) where the property available by virtue of the gift and other property applicable for similar purposes can be more effectively used in conjunction, and to that end can suitably, regard being had to the spirit of the gift, be made applicable to common purposes; or

(*d*) where the original purposes were laid down by reference to an area which then was but has since ceased to be a unit for some other purpose, or by reference to a class of persons or to an area which has for any reason since ceased, either to be suitable, regard being had to the spirit of the gift, or to be practical in administering the gift; or

(*e*) where the original purposes, in whole or in part, have, since they were laid down –
  (i) been adequately provided for by other means; or
  (ii) ceased, as being useless or harmful to the community or for other reasons, to be in law charitable; or
  (iii) ceased in any other way to provide a suitable and effective method of using the property available by virtue of the gift, regard being had to the spirit of the gift.

(2) Subsection (1) shall not affect the conditions which must be satisfied in order that property given for charitable purposes may be applied *cy près*, except in so far as those conditions require a failure of the original purposes.

(3) References in the foregoing subsections to the original purposes of a gift shall be construed, where the application of the property given has been altered or

regulated by a scheme or otherwise, as referring to the purposes for which the property is for the time being applicable.

(4) It is hereby declared that a trust for charitable purposes places a trustee under a duty, where the case permits and requires the property or some part of it to be applied *cy près*, to secure its effective use for charity by taking steps to enable it to be so applied.

(5) This section shall apply to property given for charitable purposes, notwithstanding that it was so given before the commencement of this Act.

48. (1) Property given for specific charitable or non-charitable purposes which fail shall be applicable *cy-près* by a Court of competent jurisdiction as if given for charitable purposes generally, where it belongs-

(*a*) to a donor who, after such advertisements and inquiries as are reasonable, cannot be identified or cannot be found; or

(*b*) to a donor who has executed a written disclaimer of his right to have the property returned.

but in applying *cy-près* property given for specific non-charitable purposes regard shall be had to the wishes of the trustees or other persons in charge of the property.

(2) For the purposes of this section property shall be conclusively presumed (without any advertisement or inquiry) to belong to donors who cannot be identified, in so far as it consists-

(*a*) of the proceeds of cash collections made by means of collecting boxes or by other means not adapted for distinguishing one gift from another; or

(*b*) of the proceeds of any lottery, competition, entertainment, sale or similar money-raising activity, after allowing for property given to provide prizes or articles for sale or otherwise to enable the activity to be undertaken.

(3) A Court of competent jurisdiction may by order direct that property not falling within subsection (2) shall for the purposes of this section be treated (without any advertisements or inquiry) as belonging to donors who cannot be identified, where it appears to the Court either-

(*a*) that it would be unreasonable, having regard to the amounts likely to be returned to the donors, to incur expense with a view to returning the property; or

(*b*) that it would be unreasonable, having regard to the nature, circumstances and amounts of the gifts, and to the lapse of time since the gifts were made, for the donors to expect the property to be returned.

(4) Where property is applied *cy-près* by virtue of this section, the donor shall be deemed to have parted with all his interest at the time when the gift was made; but where property is so applied as belonging to donors who cannot be identified or cannot be found, and is not so applied by virtue of subsection (2) or (3)–

(*a*) the scheme shall specify the total amount of that property; and

(*b*) the donor of any part of that amount shall be entitled, if he makes a claim not later than twelve months after the date on which the scheme is made, to recover from the charity for which the property is applied a sum equal to that part, less any expenses properly incurred by the charity trustees after that date in connection with claims relating to his gift; and

(*c*) the scheme may include directions as to the provision to be made for meeting any such claim

(5) For the purposes of this section, purposes shall be deemed to fail where any difficulty in applying property to those purposes makes that property, or, in the case of property to be applied for charitable purposes, the part not applicable *cy-près* under section 47, available to be returned to the donors.

(6) In this section, except in so far as the context otherwise requires, references to a donor include references to persons claiming through or under the original donor, and references to property given include references to the property originally given or property derived from it.

(7) (*a*) The powers conferred by this section on a Court of competent jurisdiction

in relation to property given for specific charitable purposes may, where the property does not exceed one thousand pounds in value, be exercised by the Board, and, for the purposes of such exercise, references in the preceding subsections of this section to a Court of competent jurisdiction shall be construed as including references to the Board.

(*b*) For the purposes of paragraph (*a*)-

(i) the value of land shall be taken to be fifty times the rateable valuation thereof,

(ii) the value of any periodical payment to which land is subject shall be taken to be fifteen times the annual amount thereof, and

(iii) the value of any other periodical payment shall be taken to be twenty times the annual amount thereof.

(8) This section shall apply to property given for charitable or non-charitable purposes, notwithstanding that it was so given before the commencement of this Act.

RE ROYAL KILMAINHAM HOSPITAL

[1966] I.R. 451 (High Court)

The facts are set out in the judgment.

Budd J.:

The Royal Hospital, Kilmainham (hereinafter generally referred to as "the Hospital"), was formed by Charles II in 1684 for the support and maintenance of old soldiers of his army and that of his successors who, by reason of wounds or infirmity, had become unserviceable. The foundation was made by Royal Charter and the Hospital was endowned by the King with a grant of part of the Royal demesne lands in the Phoenix Park. Part of these lands were acquired in the middle of the last century for railway construction purposes and the compensation monies in respect thereof were lodged in Court. The Hospital during its existence provided a home and support and maintenance for old soldiers of the Crown Forces in Ireland. After the setting up of the Irish Free State the Hospital gradually ceased to function, the remaining pensioners were removed to the Royal Hospital, Chelsea, and the Irish Government took over control of the lands and buildings. The Corporation of the Hospital was later dissolved. The Royal Hospital Kilmainham Act was enacted in 1962. It provided, first, for the vesting of the lands and chattel property of the Hospital in the Minister for Finance. The Act further provided that, on the application of the Attorney General, the High Court "may" order that certain payments be made to the Commissioners of the Royal Hospital, Chelsea, out of the interest accrued on the funds in Court, and also settle a scheme for some specified charitable purposes or purpose for the benefit of some classes of members or former members of the Defence Forces. A question arose during the hearing, however, as to whether the provisions of the Act in this respect were of a mandatory or of enabling nature. With this matter I deal later.

The application was duly brought by the Attorney General. The British Legion applied during the hearing to be added as respondents. It was claimed that some classes of its members had an interest in the funds as the proper beneficiaries of a valid charitable trust created by the endowment of the Hospital and still subsisting with regard to these funds. Alternatively, if the trust had failed, the same classes had a valid claim to benefit under a *cy-près* application of the funds. It was submitted that these claims were not affected by the said Act on its true construction. The British Legion was added as respondent in a representative capacity and I shall deal with the reasons for this and the nature of the claim in more detail later. Counsel for the Attorney General, while not asserting that the Act of 1962 had mandatory force, contested this claim and sought primarily for an order in accordance with the provisions of the Act, and alternatively, for an order that the trust funds be applied *cy-près*. In order to understand the nature of the submissions made to me relative to these contentions and the reasons for my decisions thereon it is necessary to deal first with the nature and history of the foundation.

The Charter of the Hospital was preceded by a Royal Letter of Charles II under the sign manual, dated the 19th April, 1681, addressed from the Court at Whitehall to the Duke of Ormonde, Lord Lieutenant and General Governor of Ireland. It recited that the King had directed the building of a hospital for the maintenance of such aged and maimed soldiers of "Our army in Ireland" as are or should during their continuance in the said army become unserviceable and that the said hospital had already begun to be erected upon part of "Our land now enclosed in Our Park called the Phoenix Park." The King's will and pleasure was that the said land on which the hospital was then built, together with such quantity of land adjoining not exceeding 64 acres plantation measure as the Duke should think fit, should be set apart and for ever after continued for the use of the hospital. The Duke was then authorised to cause effectual letters patent to be passed under the great seal of "Our said Kingdom of Ireland" to such trustees as he should nominate and their heirs to the use of the said hospital, without rent, to the intent that when the said hospital should be finished and incorporated the lands might be conveyed by the said trustees to the said corporation and their successors for ever.

The Duke of Ormonde, following upon receipt of this letter, by warrant, dated the 23rd December, 1681, addressed to the Surveyor General, directed him to survey and set out such quantity of His Majesty's lands in the Phoenix Park as should not exceed the stipulated area to be applied for the use of the said hospital.

The Charter itself is dated the 19th February, 1684. The recitals are of importance because they are relied upon as indicating the motives for, and the nature of, the grant. The first recital shows that the King, judging it fit and necessary that "some provision should be made for such officers and soldiers of Our Army in Ireland, as by reason of their age, wounds, or other infirmities contracted in Our Service, are or shall become unfit to be any longer continued therein, and also are unable otherwise to maintain themselves", had directed a hospital to be erected near Dublin for the reception of such "ancient, maimed, and infirm officers and soldiers, to the end, that such of the said army as have faithfully served, or hereafter shall faithfully serve, Us, Our heirs and successors in the strength and vigour of their youth, may, in the weakness and disaster that their old age, wounds, or other misfortunes may bring them into, find a comfortable retreat, and a competent maintenance therein." The second recital significantly commences with the following words:- "And whereas We, of our pious and charitable inclination to so good a work, have set apart and given sixty four acres of land, plantation measure, of Our demesne lands, formerly inclosed in Our park, called the Phoenix Park . . . for erecting the said hospital therein . . . and for and towards the support of the said hospital . . ." After stating the bounds of the lands, the recital continues:- ". . . and We have also caused the sum of sixpence in the pound for several years last past to be deducted out of the pay of all officers and soldiers of Our said army and other persons placed upon the military list of Our establishment in Our said kingdom towards the charge of building the said hospital, which hath hitherto been wholly employed therein." The recital terminates with the expression of the King's view that it is fit to have the deduction continued towards finishing the building and providing for the purposes of the hospital until the said hospital shall "by the charity of well disposed persons, or by some other ways" be endowed with a sufficient revenue in lands for its support.

Following the recitals comes the operative portion of the Charter, establishing the hospital, stating its name and title, naming and constituting the governors and incorporating them as a body corporate. The words of the Charter establishing the hospital are as follows:- "We do by these presents, for Us, Our heirs and successors, ordain, declare and establish, that the building lately erected and now standing upon the lands of Kilmainham on the south side of the river Liffey" [there follows a description of the lands and buildings] "shall be from henceforth, and shall for ever after continue and be an hospital, in deed and in name, for the receipt, abiding and dwelling of such a number of poor aged, maimed and infirm officers and soldiers of the army of Us, Our heirs and successors in Our Kingdom of Ireland as shall by the governors thereof hereafter mentioned, and their successors, be named, limited or appointed to be lodged, harboured, abide, and be received therein." It is then declared that the hospital shall "for ever hereafter be named and called, the Hospital of King Charles the Second, for antient and maimed officers and soldiers of the Army of Ireland." The appointment and constitution of the Governors of the Hospital, and of the members, goods, lands, revenues and hereditaments thereof follows next. The persons appointed were certain great officers of State in the kingdom, such as the Lord Lieutenant and the Lord Chancellor, the Chief Justices of the several Courts and certain high-ranking military officers holding particular offices in the army and all their respective successors in office. Some of these military officers are designated as holding particular positions in "Our army in our said Kingdom of Ireland" or "Our army there." Others are described by such titles as "Colonel of Our regiment of Guards there" or "Captain of Our troop of Guards there." The Governors and their successors were then incorporated as a body politic and corporate to have continuance for ever with perpetual succession. There follows a grant to the Governors and their successors of the site of the Hospital and the sixty-four acres of land to have and to hold the same for ever to be held from the King, his heirs and successors in frankalmoign without performing any rent duty or service chattel property as should belong to the hospital.

The Governors were also given other powers usual in charters of this kind, such as holding other lands, leasing, sealing and executing deeds with a common seal and of suing and being sued. Provision is made for the staffing of the Hospital. Full power is given to the Governors to do all things necessary and profitable for the Hospital and the persons placed therein in as full a manner as any other body corporate. Power to nominate inmates of the Hospital is given to the Governors in these words:- "The said Governors . . . shall and may have full power and authority to nominate and appoint, when and as often as they shall think good, such a number of officers and soldiers of the said army who, during their continuance therein, have been, or shall be maimed, or who, having served seven years at least in the said army, have been, or shall become aged, infirm, or unserviceable, to be placed, lodged, and maintained in the said Hospital, as the lodging and revenue of the said Hospital shall hold out to maintain and provide for."

With particular regard to the site, precinct and lands of the Hospital it was ordained by the Charter that the Governors and their successors were wholly and utterly disabled in law from doing anything whereby the precinct of the Hospital, the lands or buildings or any part thereof, might be alienated or conveyed to the possession of the King, his heirs or successors, or any other person of body corporate or to any other use than those intended by the Charter, and it was further provided that all such alienations should be utterly void.

Other ancillary provisions are made for such matters as the continuance in operation of the Corporation notwithstanding the death of Governors or the cesser of offices to which the places of Governors are annexed, for the meetings of the Governors or the major part of them and the business to be transacted thereat. The continuance of the deduction of the sixpence in the pound out of the pay of the army and persons upon the military establishment for the use of the Hospital was also ordained. This deduction came to an end in 1794. Thereafter, monies for the support of the Hospital were voted from public funds.

A further charter was granted to the Governors of the Hospital by King George II, dated the 24th April, 1758. Apart from confirming the former charter, it dealt with the necessary quorum of Governors to transact the business of the Hospital. The original charter had provided that a major part of the Governors might transact the business and the new charter in effect reduced the necessary quorum to seven Governors. One of the recitals in this charter is of some importance in connection with the status or nature of the army from which the class of beneficiaries under the charter was to be drawn, variously referred to as "Our army of Ireland" or "in Ireland" or "Our army there." This recital, dealing with the necessity for reducing the quorum, states that many of the Governors "being of high rank in Our army, who from their stations therein are often obliged to be resident in Our kingdom of Great Britain, and others of the said Governors to be absent from Dublin upon Our necessary service, a major part of the Governors of the said Hospital can seldom be brought together . . ."

Some other documents relating to the Hospital, such as a Royal Warrant of Queen

Victoria, dated the 16th December, 1848, regulating the establishment and duties of officers of the Hospital, were adduced in evidence, but the matters in issue do not call for their examination in any detail.

With regard to the objects of the royal benevolence as indicated in the Charter, a minute of the Governors' meeting of the 18th February, 1698, may be mentioned conveniently at this stage, leaving its effect to be dealt with later. It is as follows:-

"That any Soldier, who has served his Majesty in *England*, *Ireland*, *Flanders*, or other foreign parts, for seven years, and belongs to any Regiment now on the *Irish* establishment, or who served in any Regiment formerly on the said establishment, is qualified for the Hospital."

The Hospital continued to serve its purposes as a home for old soldiers during the 18th century. The Union came in 1801 and with it the disappearance of Ireland as a separate kingdom. The *de facto* administration of the Hospital continued, however, during the 19th century despite two unsuccessful attempts to do away with the in-pension establishment at Kilmainham in 1834 and 1853. Questions have been raised, however, as to the legal effect of the disappearance of the separate kingdom of Ireland on the operation of the Charter, having regard to the fact that the object class of the Royal bounty qualfied by reason of their service in "Our Army of Ireland."

The political results of the setting up of the Irish Free State in 1922, followed later by the coming into operation of the present Constitution, had their effects upon the present situation regarding the Hospital. Immediately before 1922 some seventeen Governors of the Hospital held office *ex officio*, their offices being political, judicial, ecclesiastical, or military. In most cases their respective offices ceased to exist in 1922, so that no quorum of Governors was available to govern and transact the business of the Hospital. There were some 126 in-pensioners in 1922. They had decreased to 51 by 1929. The British Government gave these the option of being transferred to the Royal Hospital at Chelsea or becoming out-pensioners. Forty-two of the surviving pensioners were then transferred to Chelsea, the remaining nine becoming out-pensioners. The Hospital ceased to function as such with the departure of the last pensioners on the 31st May, 1929. The costs of maintenance of the forty-two pensioners transferred and the nine out-pensioners were met from the provision in the British votes for the Chelsea Hospital until the last pensioner died on the 17th September, 1952. As the number of the pensioners decreased after 1922, the Irish Government, by arrangement with the British Government, at various dates took over the surplus accommodation in the Hospital until, by the 30th June, 1933, the whole of the Hospital property had been handed over to the Irish authorities.

Following these events the Government, by the Royal Hospital, Kilmainham (Dissolution of Governors and Revocation of Charters) Order, 1955 (S.I., No. 260 of 1955), in exercise of the powers conferred on them by s. 9 of the Ministers and Secretaries Act, 1924, as amended by s. 3 of the Adaptation of Charters Act, 1926, and every and any other power in that behalf enabling ordered the dissolution of the Governors of the Hospital and revoked the charters of the 19th February, 1684, and the 24th April, 1758.

On the establishment of Saorstát Eireann in 1922 the compensation monies in respect of the lands acquired from the Hospital still remained in Court. Owing to the uncertainty of the legal position regarding these funds the income thereof was allowed to accumulate. An agreement was come to later between the Irish and British ' overnments that portion of the accumulated income thereof would be made availabl. to the Commissioners of the Royal Hospital at Chelsea in respect of the support and maintenance of the pensioners transferred as aforesaid to the Royal Hospital, Chelsea.

It is understandable, as stated in the affidavit of the Chief State Solicitor, that following the establishment of Saorstát Eireann, the withdrawal of the British Army and the lapsing of the functions of the Governors of the Hospital, it was not possible to determine with certainty who, if anyone, was legally entitled to receive the income from the investments mentioned in the Schedule to the Act of 1962. The dissolution of the Governors and the revocation of the charters had not lessened the legal complexities.

The Royal Hospital Kilmainham Act, 1962, is stated in the title to be an Act to make provisions consequential on the dissolution of the Governors of the Royal Hospital, Kilmainham. The dissolution date is stated in s. 1 as being the 31st day of December, 1955, on which day the Governors became dissolved by virtue of the Royal Hospital Kilmainham (Dissolution of Governors and Revocation of Charters) Order, 1955. It provided by ss. 2 and 3 thereof for the vesting in the Minister for Finance of the lands and buildings which were comprised in and constituted the Hospital and all other lands and buildings vested in or held in trust for the Governors before the dissolution date freed from all trust and for the transfer to the Minister of the chattel property held in trust for the Governors before that date. With this portion of the Act I am not concerned on this application. Sect. 4 of the Act provided for an application in the form at present before me and is as follows:-

"4 – The High Court, on application made to it by the Attorney General, may:-

"(*a*) order the payment to the Commissioners of the Royal Hospital, Chelsea, of–

"(i) the sum of £2,440 7s. 4d. out of the interest accrued on the portion of the trust funds mentioned in Part I of the Schedule to this Act,

"(ii) such sum as may be realised on the sale of all investments representing accrued interest on the said portion, and

"(iii) all interest accrued on the investments referred to in the foregoing sub-paragraph up to the time of their sale,

(*b*) prepare and settle a scheme for the management and application of the trust funds (including any balance of interest accured thereon) for some specified charitable purposes or purpose for the benefit of all or any classes or class of members or former members of the Defence Forces."

The "trust funds" are defined in the Act as meaning the sums of stock specified in the Schedule to the Act, including all investments which may be substituted for and represent the same. These funds are described in the Schedule as follows:-

"PART 1.

"A. £6,078 6s. 7d. (six thousand and seventy-eight pounds, six shillings and seven pence) 2½ per cent Consolidated Stock of the United Kingdom of Great Britain and Northern Ireland lodged with the Accountant of the Courts of Justice to the credit of a ledger account entitled–

"Ex parte the Great Southern and Western Railway Company and to the credit of the Governors of the Hospital of King Charles II and all other persons interested in respect of all those pieces of land situate in the Parish of St. James County of Dublin, containing 7a. 3r. and 18½p. and Nos. 16, 21, 28, 29 and 31 on the map of said Railway."

"B. £4,027 6s. 11d (four thousand and twenty-seven pounds, six shillings and eleven pence) 2½ per cent Consolidated Stock of the United Kindom of Great Britain and Northern Ireland lodged with the Accountant of the Courts of Justice to the credit of a ledger account entitled–

"Ex parte the Great Southern and Western Railway Coy. to the credit of the Governors of the Hospital of King Charles II and all persons interested in part of the lands of the said Hospital situate in the Parish of St. James, County of Dublin, containing 13a. 3r. and 38½p. plantation measure."

"PART II.

"£369 4s. 0d. (three hundred and sixty-nine pounds, four shillings) 2½ per cent Consolidated Stock of the United Kingdom of Great Britain and Northern Ireland standing in the books of the Bank of Ireland and inscribed in the name of–

"The Governors of the Royal Hospital of King Charles II, Dublin, for relief and maintenance of ancient and maimed officers and soldiers of the Army in Ireland."

From the evidence adduced it appears that the funds referred to in Part I of the Schedule represent the purchase monies originally paid to the Governors of the Hospital on the acquisition of portion of the lands of the Hospital by the Great Southern and Western Railway Company about the middle of the last century. These funds stand in the books of the Acountant of the Courts to the credit of the Governors of the Hospital of King Charles II and all other persons interested and are thus under the control of the Court. The funds mentioned in Part II of the Schedule would appear to represent certain other funds belonging to the Hospital formerly in the hands of the Paymaster which were ordered by the Governors to be lodged to the credit of the Hospital in the Bank of Ireland in 1806.

The Act of 1962 also provides by s. 5 that the Attorney General shall be the sole trustee of the trust funds until the coming into operation of a scheme under s. 4 of the Act.

These proceedings come before the Court by way of an originating summary summons on the application of the Attorney General in the matter of the Royal Kilmainham Hospital and the Royal Hospital Kilmainham Act, 1962, and the Charities Act, 1961. Having regard to certain submissions made to me as to the construction of the Act of 1962, and the possible application of the *cy-près* doctrine to the funds in Court, the summons was amended to enable the issues arising on these matters to be determined. The Attorney General, as the sole trustee of the trust funds of the Royal Hospital, Kilmainham, set out in the Schedule to the Act, now seeks in the amended summons, in the first place, an order directing payment to the Commissioners of the Royal Hospital, Chelsea, of certain sums out of the interest accrued or to accrue on the trust funds as specified in s. 4 of the Act and that a scheme be prepared and settled for the management and application of the trust funds and any balance of interest accrued thereon for the benefit of all or any class of the members or former members of the Defence Forces. In the alternative to the relief first claimed, the Attorney General, as the person in whom is vested by law the administration and control of the business powers, authorities, duties and functions of charities in the State, seeks an order directing that the said trust funds be applied *cy-près*.

The Act of 1962, it will be noted, purports to deal with "trust funds," thereby impliedly recognising the existence of a trust of some sort but without specifying the particular trust or its nature. The Act on the face of it is enabling and not mandatory in form in that s. 4 provides that the High Court, on the application made to it by the Attorney General, *may* make the orders therein specified. It may well be that the decision in *Buckley and Others* (*Sinn Féin*) v. *Attorney General and Another* [1950] I.R. 67, dealing with the constitutional limitations of the effect and operation of legislation purporting to deal with matters purely within the domain of the Courts, overshadowed this particular legislation. The nature of the foundation, as appearing from those parts of the Charter which I have already set out, indicates that the trust recognised by the Act of 1962 might well prove to be a charitable trust. The fact that the foundation might in fact be found to be charitable and the trust still subsisting with regard to the trust funds, so that it would ordinarily according to law be enforceable by the Courts, might well, it was suggested, provide a reason why the Act should take an enabling form.

At an early stage of the hearing it became evident that the point as to whether or not the endowment of the Hospital did create a foundation of a charitable nature in the legal sense with the result that the trust funds to be dealt with were already impressed with a valid charitable trust, would have to be decided. If it was found that the funds were already impressed with a subsisting charitable trust that trust would in the ordinary way be carried into execution by the Court, or, if its purposes had failed, the *cy-près* doctrine of applying the funds to the nearest purposes of the trust would in the ordinary course be applied. In either event the effect and operation of the Act of 1962 relative to any limitation of the application of the doctrine to these particular funds by the Court would arise for consideration and determination.

A situation of some practical difficulty arose during the hearing relative to these matters. The Attorney General is named in the Act of 1962 as trustee of the trust funds and as the person empowered to bring the proceedings for the application of the funds in the specified fashion, whereas he would in the ordinary course, as the protector of charities, be the proper person to contend that the funds were impressed with a valid and subsisting trust where there were reasonable grounds to support such a contention, leaving it, of course, to the Court to determine the issue. There was, thus, at the commencement of the proceedings no *legitimus contradictor* to the contentions which counsel for the Attorney General indicated that they would put forward in support of the application to have the funds applied as first sought in the originating summons as distinct from a general *cy-près* application. This difficulty created by the absence of a *legitimus contradictor* was solved, however, by the appearance of counsel on behalf of the British Legion, a body incorporated by Royal Charter in England but in active operation in this country. Its objects, as is well known, include the promotion of the welfare by charitable means of persons in need who have served in the British Forces. It was stated that this body wished to contend that certain of its members in straitened circumstances constituted a class of persons entitled, notwithstanding the provisions of the Act of 1962, to be held to be beneficiaries under a valid and subsisting charitable trust affecting the trust funds referred to in the Act of 1962; or alternatively, to be entitled to participate in any *cy-près* application of these funds. I was satisfied that a statable case to this effect could be made. The necessity in the interests of justice of having a *legitimus contradictor* was obvious. I decided that this body could properly act in that capacity and I accordingly added the British Legion as respondents in these proceedings to represent the class of all persons who are, or may claim to be, entitled to the benefit of the funds mentioned in the schedule to the said Act other than members or former members of the Defence Forces.

The first question to be decided is whether the Act of 1962 is mandatory or enabling in character. If its force is found to be mandatory, questions as to its constitutionality might well arise, but this would not be so if it be found to be of an enabling nature. Counsel for the Attorney General took the view that the statute was on its true construction of an enabling nature and not mandatory; hence that it did not trammel the Court as to the exercise of its *cy-près* jurisdication, assuming that it was a case for a *cy-près* application of the funds apart from the Act. I must, however, form my own view of the Act.

To determine this question I must have regard to such internal evidence as the Act affords as to the intendment of the Legislature, viewed against the background of the surrounding circumstances at the time of its enactment. The funds are not treated in the Act of 1962 as State property but are treated as trust funds and the Attorney General is made the temporary trustee of these funds. The form of words used in s. 4 is that the Court "may" make such order as stated therein. The word is in itself potential in nature and not significant of any obligation. Is there then to be found any indication that the word was used in a mandatory sense? Since the funds to be dealt with are referred to in the Act as trust funds and no trust is created by the Act, the only assumption that can be made is that the existence of some unspecified, but previously existing, trust is impliedly recognised. But the object for which the power is given is to enforce any already existing right under such a trust or otherwise of members or ex-members of the Defence Forces or of the Royal Hospital, Chelsea. Nor does the Act take the form of conferring any property rights on the proposed beneficiaries. The enjoyment of any benefit is made dependent upon an order being made which gives but a potential nature to the benefit. The uncertainty of the situation at the time of its enactment, particularly the possibility of there being in existence some class of persons who might have rights, or inchoate rights, as *cestuis que trustent* under the impliedly recognised trust, affords an excellent reason for the Act taking an enabling form, whereas words directory in form might well be regarded as being unsuitable to the circumstances of the case as being an encroachment on the proper domain of the Courts in regard to funds under the Court's control and possibly impressed with a charitable trust which is still operative. The background of the legislation and the internal evidence in the Act leads me to the conclusion that the word, "may," should be construed according to its *prima facie* meaning, with the result that I find the Act on its true construction to be enabling and not mandatory in nature. *In re Shrewsbury Grammar School* (1849) 1 Mac. & G. 324, at p. 332, shows that where a statute affecting a charity does not completely regulate the charity there is nothing to oust the jurisdiction of the Court in respect of matters not dealt with by the statute. *A fortiori* the powers of the Court will not be excluded where the Act is merely an enabling Act. Should it be found that the trust funds are impressed with a valid and subsisting charitable trust the provisions of the Act of 1962 do not therefore prohibit the exercise by the Court of its jurisdiction and duty to enforce such a trust or, alternatively, to direct that the trust funds should be applied *cy-près*. I have thus to consider next what is the true nature of the foundation according to the proper construction of the Charter and the results that flow in law therefrom before I can decide whether I can properly accede to the application before me contained in para. 1 of the summons in whole or in part.

A number of questions of no little difficulty arose on the contentions put forward by the parties, which I will only outline at the moment. The first was whether the foundation of the Hospital in the sense of the granting of lands to it by Charles II constituted a valid charitable trust in favour of a class of persons who may be briefly described as maimed and infirm officers and soldiers of the Army in Ireland of King Charles II and his successors. Mr. Matheson, for the respondents, submitted that it did. Consequently, he said, the funds in question remained impressed with a valid subsisting trust and that some members of the classes he represented answered the description of beneficiaries and should be held entitled as such to the benefit of the funds in that they are ex-members of the Army of Charles the Second's royal successor. If they were not entitled as *cestuis que trustent* owing to the failure of the charitable trust for any reason, then, he contended, they were the proper persons to designate as beneficiaries under a *cy-près* application of the funds. Counsel for the Attorney General submitted that the foundation of the Hospital was an executive act of the Crown in its executive capacity and that no valid charitable trust ensued. Such trust as was created had come to an end on the dissolution of the Corporation so that the trust funds had reverted to the State as successors of the Crown, and were now at the disposal of the Legislature, which had under the Act of 1962 designated objects for whose benefit the funds should be applied under a scheme to be settled by the Court. Alternatively, it was submitted, that even if a valid charitable trust was created by the endowment of the Hospital it was so created by virtue of a Crown grant and that by reason thereof the trust property would, on the dissolution of the Corporation, likewise revert to the State as the successor of the Crown and was again capable of disposal by the Legislature. In the further alternative, assuming a valid charitable trust to have been created and that there was no reverter, it was submitted that it had not failed as to objects since some classes of members or former members of the Defence Forces answered literally the description of the object class in the changed political circumstances as being soldiers of the Army of Ireland, and, if otherwise qualified as charitable objects, were entitled to benefit. If, on the other hand, the charitable trust had wholly failed then it was contended that the same classes ought to be the proper objects of any *cy-près* application of the funds. It is thus necessary to determine whether or not a valid charitable trust was constituted on the foundation of the Hospital by virtue of the gift of the lands to it and then, if so, whether the charitable trust was constituted on the foundation of the Hospital by virtue of the gift of the lands to it and then, if so, whether the charitable trust has failed and, if it has, should the funds be applied *cy-près*.

The law requires that if a charity can be administered according to the directions of the founder it should be so administered. When it is established that a gift has been made with a general intention of charity and a failure of purposes ensues it is not allowed to fail but will be carried out *cy-près*. Likewise, where there is an absolute perpetual gift to a charity, even though the trusts be only for the accomplishment of a particular charitable purpose, the same results ensue. The principle is applied where the method indicated by the donor of carrying out his charitable intention becomes impracticable, or his intentions cannot be executed literally, most frequently owing to altered circumstances.

Trusts for charitable purposes in the legal sense include trusts for the relief of aged, impotent and poor persons and such objects as are analogous thereto, and there can be little doubt that a trust for the relief of poor, aged, maimed and infirm officers and soldiers would ordinarily be regarded as a valid charitable gift. The *cy-près* principle is confined, however, to cases where property is given with a general intention to charity with this exception, that where property is given absolutely and perpetually to the charity the fund can be applied *cy-près* irrespective of the donor's particular intention. As to what is to be regarded as a general charitable intention, no hard and fast rule can be laid down. Courts have differed much as to what is sufficient to indicates such an intention. The test suggested by Kay J. in *Re Taylor*; *Martin* v. *Freeman* (1888) 58 L.T. (N.S.) 538, at p. 543, is one that carries great weight: ". . . if upon the whole scope and intent of the will you discern the paramount intention of the testator was to benefit not a particular institution, but to effect a particular form of charity independently of any special institution or mode, then . . . . if the particular mode for any reason fails, the Court, if it sees a sufficient expression of a general intention of charity, will, to use the phrase familiar to us, execute that *cy-près* . . . ." The question as to whether the form of a gift indicates a general intention of charity depends upon the construction of the document by which the gift is given.

It was first submitted by Mr. Garland, on behalf of the Attorney General, that the foundation and endowment of the Hospital by Charles II did not create a valid charitable trust of any sort, being but an executive act of the Crown as part of its government functions whereby the Hospital and lands, as Crown property, were devoted to State uses like any other building used for governmental purposes. On ceasing to be used for the designated purposes the lands would thus become at the disposal of the Crown, now the State. His argument ran thus: Charles II at the time of the foundation was the Sovereign of the separate kingdom of Ireland. He maintained as such sovereign authority an army in Ireland for the welfare and morale of which he was responsible. What was done by the Charter was one way of looking after its welfare. The building of the Hospital was financed by the deduction of sixpence in the pound from the pay of officers and soldiers of that army and the expenses of the Hospital provided for by the same source to begin with, as well as by the endowment by way of the gift of the demesne lands. Even these demesne lands were, he contended, held by the Crown in its political capacity so that the gift was not in the nature of an act of royal bounty involving a charitable benefaction by the sovereign out of his private property. Assuming these submissions were correct, it was further contended that, as there was no charitable gift, any consideration of a *cy-près* application became irrelevant and the lands should be regarded as having been held for public purposes and accordingly vested in the Irish Free State in the same way as any other State lands, such as Government buildings or military barracks, pursuant to the provisions of Article 11 of that Constitution. Such property remained the property of the State pursuant to Article 49, 3, of the Constitution, becoming vested in the Minister for Finance by the State Property Act, 1954. If this result ensued in law the lands and funds now representing them were at the disposal of the State and the Act of 1962 indicated the Legislature's view of the proper method of dealing with the funds and no question of a *cy-près* application arises.

Twentieth-century conceptions of the constitutional position of the Crown in England, the parliamentary control of public funds and the constitutional position of the Oireachtas and Government in our own country should not be allowed to cloud the issue. In the time of Charles II the executive authority lay with the Crown in a real sense. If the King as the Executive wished to provide hospital accommodation for his soldiers or ex-soldiers he could direct the building of a hospital and provide funds to maintain it in the same way that he would provide for an ordinary barracks for his soldiers out of the revenue of the Crown. It would not be done by charter. The fact that the grant to the Hospital was of the royal demesne lands does not make that grant a public executive act. Such lands could be granted to individuals up to the reign of Queen Anne. Such a grant, moreover, deprived the King of rents and profits which he would otherwise have enjoyed. Foundation by charter was the usual method of founding a charity. The wording of the Charter provides the best indication of its nature. Its object was to provide an abiding place for "poor, aged, maimed and infirm officers and soldiers," so that the objects fell within the well-established classes of charitable objects such as the relief of aged, poor, impotent and sick persons. It created a trust in that the Corporation was to hold the lands granted by Charles II for the benefit of the class of persons designated. The Charter recites the necessity to make provision for those of the above class unable to maintain themselves and mentions "Our pious and Charitable inclinations to so good a work." If a purely executive act was intended there would be no need to use such words. The provision of funds for the maintenance of the Hospital by way of the sixpence deduction from pay was only to continue until further revenue should be provided "by the charity of well disposed persons." In any event it is the gift of the lands that we are concerned with, as the funds represent the lands. The gift was perpetual and out-and-out. There is provision against alienation, even against a reversion to the Crown. The intention to devote the lands for charitable purposes for ever is manifest and in my view a valid charitable trust was created by the foundation and endowment of the Hospital.

It was, however, further contended that where the original donor of a charitable gift is the Crown and there ensues a failure of the charitable purposes of the gift and a dissolution of the corporation there then takes place, even where the gift takes the form of a perpetual and out-and-out gift, a reverter of the gift to the Crown free of any trust in favour of charity. The doctrine of *cy-près* is therefore not applicable on the failure of a charity founded by the Crown and on reverter the gift is then at the disposal of the Crown, or, in this particular instance, for historical and political reasons, at the disposal of the State.

This contention appears to me to be founded upon a misapprehension of the true nature of the grant and the foundation thereby created. It may be that in the case of a grant made to a Corporation to hold whatever be granted for itself beneficially there may be a reverter to the donor of the grant if the Corporation is later dissolved. But that is because the body entitled beneficially no longer exists and there is no other person who can have the benefit of the property by *cy-près* or otherwise. That is not the position here. The Corporation – that is, the Governors, – did not hold the property beneficially but in trust. They were trustees to hold the property for charitable purposes. The position in law is the same as if an individual trustee of charitable property had died, which would not affect the nature of the trust. A charitable trust never fails for want of a trustee. The principle is recognised in the State Property Act, 1954, which, in providing for the vesting of the property of dissolved corporations in the State, excepts the case of property held in trust for another person. Furthermore, the Act of 1962 shows that the Legislature itself did not regard the lands and buildings of the Hospital as being already vested in the State for any reason because the Act provided for the vesting of the lands and buildings of the Hospital in the Minister for Finance freed from all trusts and despite the dissolution of the Corporation and revocation of the Charter recognises the existence of a trust in respect of the funds in question.

Regard must also be had to the intention of the donor and the nature of the gift. In this particular Charter of Charles II the very nature of the grant itself makes it clear that the intention is that there should be no reverter to the Crown. The grant is out-and-out and forever. The property is given free of rent and there is an explicit restriction on the alienation of the lands to the King or his successors or anyone else.

Questions as to reverter in the case of a Crown charity are so bound up with the matter of the *cy-près* application of the property of such a charity on failure of the purposes that I turn to examine the *cy-près* aspect. There was no controversy as to the general principles applicable when charitable gifts, which have taken effect, subsequently fail for want of objects. If there is an absolute perpetual gift to a charity, even though the trusts declared are only for the accomplishment of a particular charitable purpose, the subject-matter is applicable *cy-près* upon failure of the trusts. (Tudor on Charities, 5th ed., 1929, at p. 157). *Re Peel's Release* [1921] 2 Ch. 218 supports this proposition. But Mr. Kenny submitted that the general principle does not apply to Crown grants.

In Halsbury's Laws of England (3rd ed., vol. 4, at p. 396), it is stated that on failure of objects in the case of a Crown charter the Court may dispose of the funds *cy-près*. It is, further, stated, at p. 148 of Tudor on Charities (5th ed., 1929) that the doctrine of *cy-près* applies to trusts created by the Crown, citing as authority for this proposition the case of *Wallis* v. *Solicitor-General for New Zealand* (1903] A.C. 173. In that case the view of the trial judge was that there was no reverter to the Crown of lands granted to charitable purposes by what was at that stage treated as a Crown grant and he held that the general purpose of the foundation was charitable and the doctrine of *cy-près* applied. The Court of Appeal in New Zealand allowed an appeal against the decision holding the grant void. The Privy Council discharged the order of the Court of Appeal in New Zealand. It was argued on behalf of the Solicitor-General for New Zealand that the property had reverted to the Crown and that the doctrine of *cy-près* did not apply to Crown grants. The submissions do not appear to have prevailed in that a scheme was directed, but there is no positive statement in the judgment of Lord Macnaghten supporting the proposition in Tudor, and the case has the unsatisfactory feature that the land in question had never been Crown property, the Crown only having a right of pre-emption.

There are, however, several other cases where the funds of a charity founded by charter have been applied *cy-près*, *Attorney-General* v. *Hicks* [1909] 3 Bro. C.C. 166n being an example where the purposes had failed. I deduce from the short note of the case that the charity was founded by charter. Kay J. in *Re Slevin* [1891] 2 Ch. 236, at p. 239, states that there is no reported case of a resulting trust arising upon the failure of a charitable gift which has once taken effect. That the doctrine of *cy-près* is applicable on the failure of a charity founded by a Crown grant appears clearly from the decision of the Court of Appeal in England in *Wilson* v. *Barnes* 38 Ch. D. 507. Elizabeth I as lord of a manor in Cumberland in effect granted to the tenants thereof the woods on the manor in consideration of their undertaking the repair of a sea dyke up to that time chargeable to the lord of the manor. The surplus proceeds of wood cut by them was invested by the tenants. The sea receded from the part of the manor protected by the sea dyke. The tenants brought proceedings for a declaration that, subject to the reparation of the sea wall, they were absolutely entitled to the investments. It was held that the grant of the woods was a gift for charitable purposes and a scheme was directed for the application of the property *cy-près*.

Finally, I refer to the case of *In re Whitworth Art Gallery Trusts* [1958] Ch. 461, where Mr. Justice Vaisey had to consider the very question whether a charity founded by Royal Charter was one to which the *cy-près* application might be directed. He found that the question was answered in the affirmative by the text-books. Having considered some of the authorities in point, he came to the conclusion that the true principle emerging was that while a charitable corporation founded by Royal Charter cannot be re-founded or re-established by the Court it can be regulated and controlled by the Court, which may have regard to altered circumstances and direct a scheme. He approved a somewhat far-reaching scheme.

In the light of these decisions, and for the reasons hereinbefore indicated. I have come to the conclusion that in the case of a charitable foundation of the Crown, reverter to the Crown does not take place either on the dissolution of the corporation or the failure of the purposes of the trust, and, further, that the Court has jurisdiction to order the application of the trust funds of the charity *cy-près*. The trust funds, therefore, remain impressed with the same charitable trust as operated on the lands which they represent. That charitable trust should be administered either by carrying into execution the intentions of the founder in so far as now possible or by ordering the application of the funds *cy-près*. I have already determined that the provisions of the Act of 1962 do not trammel the jurisdiction of the Court to perform its duty to administer the trust according to law. Accordingly, an appropriate order enforcing the trust or providing for the application of the trust funds *cy-près* must be made.

Before I can decide what particular form of order is required in the circumstances of the case it is necessary to consider how far the purposes of the charitable trust have failed. It has been submitted that the charitable purposes of the trust have not altogether failed because there are, it is said, in existence certain classes of persons who literally answer the description of the beneficiaries designated originally in the Charter, and that the trust in so far as it created a benefit in their favour must continue to operate, so that such persons should now, in any order made, be found entitled to receive the benefits of the income of the trust funds, in which event it would only be necessary to provide a scheme dealing with administrative matters. I have thus next to deal with the argument put forward on behalf of the Attorney General that such class of members or former members of the Defence Forces of the state, who otherwise qualified as charitable objects by reason of wounds or infirmity after seven years' service, answers the description of the object class of the Charter, and, on the other hand, Mr. Matheson's contention that certain ex-members of the British Crown Forces, likewise qualified, also answer to the express terms of the Charter.

Those intended in the terms of the Charter to benefit from the Royal benevolence were, it will be remembered, such number as should be nominated by the Governors of "poor aged, maimed and infirm officers and soldiers of the army of Us, Our heirs and successors in Our Kingdom of Ireland." The class later in the Charter was stated in more detail in connection with the power of nomination as "such a number of officers and soldiers of the said army who, during their continuance therein, have been, or shall be maimed, or who, having served seven years at least in the said army, have been, or shall become aged, infirm or unserviceable . . . . ."

In connection with the class of persons who might properly be held to be entitled to benefit as objects of the class it was also submitted that in the case of an ancient charitable foundation usage in the administration thereof may be taken into account in the construction of the charter therof where the precise ambit of the class to be benefited is ambiguously expressed. As to that, reliance was placed upon the resolution appearing in the minute of the Governors' meeting of the 18th February, 1698, "That any soldier who has served his Majesty in *England*, *Ireland*, *Flanders* or other foreign parts, for seven years, and belongs to any regiment now on the *Irish* establishment, is qualfied for the Hospital," as indicating a construction placed on the instrument some fourteen years after the date of the Charter.

The arguments in favour of regarding the Defence Forces of the State as now answering to the designation of the object class in the Charter were these: at the date of the Charter Ireland was a separate kingdom and although the Crown of Ireland was linked with the Crown of England, Ireland was a separate entity and the sovereign power in Ireland resided in the Crown of Ireland. The executive power is a function of sovereignty and an army is an arm of the Executive. Accordingly, the expressions, "Our army in Ireland" or "Our army of Ireland," in the Charter should be construed as a reference to the separate Irish army of the sovereign power in the realm of Ireland. The Defence Forces of the Republic are the army of the sovereign power in Ireland and thus answer, it is said, the description of the army of the Charter described as the Army of Ireland, thus qualifying members and former members of the Defence Forces as proper objects provided that they qualify otherwise as charitable objects.

The internal indications in the Charter relative to the true character of the army are themselves ambiguous. True, such phrases as "Our army of Ireland" and "the army of Ireland" might seem to indicate the separate existence of such an army as distinct from the armed forces of the Crown in England at the same period, save only for the link of the Crown. It is, however, evident that this descriptive wording might equally well apply to such part of the sovereign's army which was geographically situated in Ireland from time to time. One calls to mind possible analogies such as "the British Army of the Rhine" and Napoleon's "Army of Italy." Further expressions used, such as "the army of Us, our heirs and successors in Our kingdom of Ireland," and various references to "Our army there," somewhat increase the ambiguity. The evidence however of Mr. Geoffrey Joseph Hand, Lecturer in Legal and Constitutional History at University College, Dublin, which is uncontradicted, shows that the main basis of the argument in favour of the Defence Forces answering the description of the object class is founded on a fallacy.

Mr. Hand states that the constitutional question of the control of the armed forces was, upon the Restoration of Charles II, settled by statute "firstly by 13 Car. 2, stat. 1, c. 6, and further by 13 & 14 Car. 2., c. 3, which recited: 'Forasmuch as within all his majesty's Realms and Dominions, the sole supreme Power, Government, Command and Disposition of the Militia and of all Forces by Sea and Land, and of all Forts and Places of strength, is, and by the Laws of England ever was the undoubted Right of his Majesty, and his Royal Predecessors, Kings and Queens of England; and that both or either of the Houses of Parliament cannot nor ought to pretend to the same . . .'" He also points out that by the statute, 33 Hen. 8, c. 1. (Ir.), it was provided that "The Kings highnesse, his heyres and successours, Kings of England, be alwayes Kings of this land of Ireland to have, hold and enjoy the said style, title, and honours of King of Ireland . . . as united and knit to the imperial crown of the realm of England." He adds:- "The Royal prerogative was to be the same in both countries.

That this was the case in the matter of control of the armed forces is further implied by the statute, 13 & 14 Car. 2, c. 3, quoted above."

Having referred to the various descriptions of the forces then in Ireland contained in the royal letters and charters concerning the Hospital, he stated that there does not appear to have been any distinction of substance between them. His further evidence relevant to the true character of the army is as follows:- "The troops formed a separate establishment for financial and purely administrative purposes, as did those in Scotland, which was then united to England in the person of the Sovereign"; and further:– "Notwithstanding the separate establishments, all the troops in England. Scotland and Ireland under Charles II were equally soldiers of the King, subject to his sole control, in accordance with the then law of the constitution as set out in the statute, 13 & 14 Car. 2. c. 3."

It appears further from what Mr. Hand says that in the time of Charles II the upkeep of the army on the Irish establishment was met out of the hereditary revenues of the King in Ireland, later receiving subventions from the English and Irish parliaments. He points out also that during the period prior to the Act of Union troops on the Irish establishment did not form specifically Irish regiments and might at any time be transferred to another establishment, or, while remaining on the Irish establishment, might be sent abroad. This is recognised in the minute of the Governors of the 18th February, 1698, already quoted. The existence of a separate Irish establishment was brought to an end following upon the Act of Union.

It would appear then that there was not a separate army of or in Ireland. The army in the time of Charles II was the King's army by virtue of his executive authority as the sovereign of three countries. The soldiers of the army were the King's soldiers maintained out of the royal revenue. The charitable intent of the Charter was to benefit those who suffered "wounds or other infirmities contracted in Our service" or by reason of service in the army of the King's successors in Ireland.

The Defence Forces owe their origin and maintenance not to any Royal prerogative but to the provisions of the Constitution and the legislation of the Oireachtas relevant to their establishment. They are a statutory creation. These forces have their establishment within the territory of the Republic, depend for their maintenance upon the revenues of the Republic and are subject to the laws of the Republic. The fact that part of the King's army in the time of Charles had an Irish establishment does not alter the fundamental distinctions between the King's army of the time of Charles II and the Defence Forces, in that the territorial entities of each establishment are not the same. The Irish establishment at the time of Charles II extended over the whole of Ireland while the establishment of the Defence Forces is confined to the Republic. The members of the Defence Forces do not serve in any army of the successors of Charles II. They cannot therefore be said to come within the charitable intentions of the Charter which were to benefit those suffering from wounds or infirmities by reason of their service in the army of Charles the Second's successors. I am unable to hold, therefore, that the Defence Forces answer the description of the object class in the Charter. That is not to say, however, that members thereof who suffer from wounds or infirmity may not qualify as nearest objects of *cy-près* application of the funds.

It was suggested that during the period from 1922 to the coming into force of the Constitution the position might be different so that the soldiers of the Defence Forces during that period might answer the object class in the Charter. The Constitution of the Irish Free State in Article 46 thereof provided that the Oireachtas had the exclusive right of raising and maintaining the armed forces of the State and that every such force should be under the control of the Oireachtas. Under the provisions of the Defence Forces (Temporary Provisions) Act, 1923, the power to raise and maintain an armed force and the command-in-chief was vested in the Executive Council. The form of the oath to be taken by a soldier is provided for in the Act and is one of allegiance to our country. I find nothing in the Constitution of the Irish Free State or the above Act which would warrant the submission that the army raised in pursuance thereof could properly be described as the army of the successors of Charles II or that its members answer the object class of the Charter.

Mr. Matheson on behalf of the class of persons who are or may claim to be entitled to the benefit of the funds mentioned in the schedule to the Act of 1962, other than members or former members of the Defence Forces, in his turn also contended that there were persons in existence who answered the description of the object class in the Charter. His submission was that ex-members of the Crown Forces who had served prior to 1922 in the British Army in Ireland and had been wounded or had served seven years in that army in Ireland, or elsewhere in a regiment stationed in Ireland, and otherwise qualified as charitable objects, answered the description of the express terms of the Charter provided they were discharged in Ireland and lived in Ireland. He also contended that men living in the Republic or the North who had served since 1922 or were serving or might hereafter serve in the same army were also actual or potential objects.

In making his submission on behalf of what I shall refer to as "the pre-1922" class Mr. Matheson accepted that the benefits of the Charter were confined to an object class of aged, maimed or infirm soldiers who had served in the King's Army in Ireland or in the King's Army elsewhere for seven years, provided that in the latter case they belonged to a regiment stationed or formerly stationed in Ireland. He was however faced with the contention that service in the King's Army in Ireland or elsewhere in a regiment stationed or formerly stationed in Ireland could only mean service in that part of the King's Army on or formerly on the Irish establishment and since that Irish establishment, according to Mr. Hand's evidence, came to an end with the Act of Union, a necessary qualifying factor had disappeared since 1800. He contended, however, that the true spirit and intent of the Charter was that the soldiers of the King's Army who served in Ireland or in regiments stationed in Ireland, and otherwise qualified in their plight, should have the benefits of the Hospital. An administrative change such as was involved in the separate establishment coming to an end and its being replaced administratively by an Irish command did not make such an alteration in substance as would have the result that the class of beneficiaries suddenly ceased to exist in 1800 and the Charter thus became virtually inoperative. The true criterion of eligibility on any reasonable construction of the Charter was service in the King's Army in Ireland or service in a regiment stationed therein. After 1800 there continued to be persons answering this test and there were now in existence persons who had been soldiers of the King's Army stationed in Ireland under the Irish command prior to 1922 who, if they qualified by reason of their physical circumstances, answered the description of the object class.

This submission certainly derives very considerable support from the fact that the Governors of the Hospital, who included in their number many highly-placed members of the Irish judiciary, must have taken this view of the proper construction of the Charter since for more than a hundred years they administered the Hospital and the funds thereof for the benefit of a class of objects qualifying by reason of *inter alia* serving in the Crown Forces in Ireland, or a part thereof at some time stationed in Ireland. Unless the construction they must have placed on the words of the Charter was correct they would seemingly have acted in breach of trust for a very lengthy period and with no intervention on the part of the Attorney-General. In this connection I have to observe that the Attorney-General of the day advised the Governors on matters relative to the Charter in 1806 and stated in the course of his opinion that he had read the Charter. This was shortly after the Union, when changes consequent thereon would be much in the minds of lawyers, and had he considered that any breach of trust was being committed in the administration of the Hospital he would assuredly have drawn attention to the matter.

In further support of his argument Mr. Matheson relied upon the contention that in the construction of an ancient instrument creating a charitable trust matters of construction as regards the ascertainment of the object class may be aided by having regard to long usage. Usage cannot be relied upon to sanction a clear breach of trust. I agree, however, that it is well established that the true construction of such instruments may be aided by long usage and in the case of an ambiguous document the Court will lean towards a construction supported by long usage rather than assume that a breach of trust has been committed. The usage in this case since 1698 has been to include within the object class those mentioned in the minute of the 18th February, 1698. It has also been shown that the usage since 1800 has been to apply the trust funds for the benefit of those soldiers serving under the Irish command of the British Army or in regiments assigned to that command. In my view the construction of the Charter, as exemplified in these usages, is well within the spirit and intent of the Charter and one which it is right in all the surrounding circumstances to accept as properly aiding the construction. I agree with Mr. Matheson's main contentions on this aspect of the case, supported as they are by long usage.

In my view the true intent and spirit of the Charter was to benefit soldiers of the King's Army and that of his successors who served in Ireland or elsewhere in a regiment having its station here. The method of the organisation of that army by way of a separate establishment or a separate command is a purely administrative matter having in my view no material bearing on the determination of this object class. In all the circumstances, historical and otherwise, I am not prepared to hold, on my view of the proper construction of the Charter, that the charitable trust created by it came to an end with the Union in 1801, resulting in a breach of trust having been committed by the manner of its administration after that date. I take the view that during the period from 1801 to 1922 the class of British ex-servicemen above described sufficiently answered the description of the object class in the Charter so as to come within the spirit and intent of the Charter, provided that their circumstances of age, infirmity or unserviceability otherwise qualified them so as to become eligible for nomination. The qualifications of discharge in Ireland and living in Ireland are not expressly mentioned in the Charter but are, I think, implicit. At the time of Charles II, when a separate establishment existed, discharge of a soldier on that establishment must in the ordinary way have been in Ireland where he would then be living so that the intent ought properly be presumed to provide for such soldiers. This is borne out by the fact that the minutes of the Governors' meeting of the 2nd February, 1802, states that the accidental circumstances whether a soldier was discharged in England or Ireland determined his admission to the benefits of the Hospital or those of the Royal Hospital, Chelsea.

It would, however, seem than an entirely new set of circumstances came into existence with the establishment of the Irish Free State in the southern part of Ireland, leaving the other part of the country in the United Kingdom of Great Britain and Northern Ireland, followed as regards the southern part of the country by the establishment of the Republic. After 1922, there did not exist a Royal Army of Ireland or in Ireland in the sense of being on an Irish establishment or command for the whole of Ireland or as being part of the Royal Army stationed throughout the whole of the country. The southern part of the country had its own Defence Forces in lieu of such part of the Royal Army as might previously have been stationed there and such Royal Forces as still remained in Ireland were confined to the smaller part of the country comprised in Northern Ireland. In my view the changed political circumstances created the position that there was as from 1922 no Royal Army of, or in, any political entity comprised of all Ireland, which could supply the object class contemplated by the Charter, so that the object class is closed since 1922. That does not mean that those who had the part qualifications of service and discharge, already mentioned, before 1922 should not fully qualify for the charitable benefits of the trust by becoming aged and infirm subsequent to 1922 and after their discharge in Ireland. The practical position is, however, that while there may be in existence some legitimate claimants to the benefit of the trust funds, the charity cannot function as intended by the continuous filling up of the class.

The application of the *cy-près* doctrine in the present state of affairs and in the light of my findings must be further examined. The practical circumstances are that the Hospital, its buildings, lands and chattel property, have, under the terms of the Royal Hospital Kilmainham Act, 1962, so far as I am concerned in these particular proceedings, become vested in the Minister for Finance. The Hospital had by then long ceased to function as such. The corporation created by the Charter had been dissolved. The Charter has been revoked. The validity of its revocation has been challenged, it is true, but, whether validity revoked or not, the undeniable position is that the sub-stratum of the charity as regards the lands and buildings and the corporation is gone. The mode of carrying out the charitable intent provided in the charter is entirely impracticable. There remain, however, these funds impressed, as I have found, with a charitable trust.

It is clear that administration *cy-près* of some sort is called for, in that at present there exists no means of administering the trust. The only matter requiring particular attention is the existence of this ever-decreasing class whose members appear to be in the position of establishing that they sufficiently answer the description of the object class, so that there has not been a complete failure of the original purposes of the charitable gift. Whatever difficulty there might have been in ordering the application of the funds *cy-près* owing to the existence of this pre-1922 class has however been removed by the provisions of s. 47 of the Charities Act, 1961. As pointed out, in Delany's law relating to Charities in Ireland," that section specified certain circumstances, short of an absolute failure of the trust, which are required to exist before the purposes of a charity can be altered and an order made directing a *cy-près* application. In as much of sub-s. 2 provides that the provisions of sub-s. 1 shall not affect the conditions which must be satisfied in order that property given for charitable purposes may be applied *cy-près* except in so far as those conditions require a failure of the original purposes, I have only to point out that I have already found that the conditions which must be satisfied exist, in that the gift was made in pursuance of a general charitable intention and was made out-and-out.

The relevant provisions of the section are contained in sub-s. 1, paras. (*a*) (ii) and (*e*) (iii):-

"(1) Subject to sub-section (2), the circumstances in which the original purposes of a charitable gift may be altered to allow the property given or part of it to be altered to allow the property given or part of it to be applied *cy-près* shall be as follows:-

"(*a*) where the original purposes, in whole or in part . . .

"(ii) cannot be carried out, or cannot be carried out according to the directions given and to the spirit of the gift";

"(*e*) Where the original purposes, in whole or in part, have, since they were laid down . . .

"(iii) ceased in any other way to provide a suitable and effective method of using the property available by virtue of the gift, regard being had to the spirit of the gift."

The sub-section applies to the circumstances of this case. In the first place the original purposes of the gift cannot be carried out according to the directions given and the spirit of the gift in that the mode of carrying out the purposes through the Hospital and its corporate organisation is gone. Furthermore, the original purposes have in part at least ceased to provide a suitable and effective method of using the property now available by virtue of the fact that there is now no royal army pertaining to the whole of Ireland from whom the object class can derive now or in the future.

The fact that a vanishing remnant still survives of those that could be said to form the object class does not in my view lead to a conclusion that the original purposes provide in whole a suitable and effective method of using the property in that the continuous admission of qualified persons to the benefits of the Hospital was part of the original purposes according to the spirit of the gift. The whole matter is moreover thrown open when an application *cy-près* is directed and the position of this class can be adequately provided for in the scheme by according some particular and appropriate consideration to it. It would be quite possible to frame the scheme in favour of what I have termed the pre-1922 class alone and then to have a further scheme later when it had died out. But it would be quite illusory to have a scheme operating for so short a time and quite unnecessary to throw the expense of a further hearing and a resettlement of the scheme on a comparatively small fund.

Having regard to my findings, therefore, the application, in so far as contained in para. 1(b) of the originating summary summons, must be refused and the proper course to follow in my view is to grant the alternative relief sought in para. 2 thereof, by ordering that the funds in question should be applied *cy-près* and for that purpose that a scheme for the management and application of the trust funds be prepared by the Examiner to be settled by the Court.

During the hearing it was urged on me that if the evidence before the Court justified it the party or parties to benefit under the *cy-près* scheme might be found now. Mr. Kenny advanced the claims of appropriately qualified members of the Defence Forces and Mr. Matheson those of similar classes of British ex-servicemen. Both submitted that there were not to be found any other classes of persons who could put forward a better claim to benefit as nearest objects of a *cy-près* application of the funds.

In examining the claim of members and former members of the Defence Forces I find myself influenced by the following factors: the paramount intention of the donor was the charitable one of aiding the old and infirm, the particular class chosen to benefit being the old soldiers of the Royal Army serving on the Irish establishment. In the course of well over 250 years since the Charter great political changes have come about. The Kingdom of Ireland and the United Kingdom which later included it have their turn gone and with them the armies of the Crown spoken of as the Army of Ireland and later the British Army of the United Kingdom. But there are now other armies appertaining to the present political divisions of the country and the Defence Forces are the army of the greater part of Ireland comprised in the Republic. They are the army of the political successors of the founder in this part of the country and serve in Ireland. Allowing for changed circumstances, the Defence Forces approximate closely now to the former source of objects so far as this part of Ireland is concerned. Thus, members or former members who are proper charitable objects by reason of wounds, age or infirmity can properly be said to form one obvious class of nearest objects who should be included in the scheme.

It is right in dealing with the claims of members and former members of the Defence Forces to refer again to the Act of 1962. It has been urged on me that it enabled the Court to include the class therein designated of members and former members of the Defence Forces in any *cy-près* schemes I should consider proper to direct, whether or not such class otherwise qualified for inclusion. That raises a difficult question. While I am inclined to the view that this is so, I do not find it necessary to determine the point since I have arrived, *dehors* the Act, at the conclusion that this class is entitled to partake in the benefits of the scheme directed.

The claims advanced by Mr. Matheson on behalf of the class broadly describable as those catered for by the British Legion to benefit from the *cy-près* application of the funds have next to be considered. They would appear to fall into two sub-classes. First, we have the sub-class which had served in the British Army stationed in Ireland before 1922, and had been wounded; and those who had served for seven years in that army in Ireland or elsewhere in a regiment stationed or formerly stationed in Ireland and had become old and infirm. This class falls within the object class of the Charter provided they were discharged in Ireland and live in Ireland. The survivors of that pre-1922 class would now be well in their eighties, but during the continued existence of the class its members should be entitled to benefit under the scheme and appropriate provisions made to that end. The second sub-class which it is said should benefit as nearest objects are men living in the Republic or Northern Ireland who have served or may serve in the British Army in Northern Ireland or abroad after 1922 and qualify otherwise as regards wounds received during service or age and infirmity thereafter and are in need. The main basis of the claim made on their behalf is that the charity was a Royal foundation for the benefit of the King's soldiers serving in the King's Army and that of his successors. Many Irishmen residing in Ireland have since 1922 served in the British Army which is the army of the founder's royal successors and no doubt that may well continue. Some, of course, have served and some still no doubt serve in Northern Ireland. The charity, moreover, had Irish characteristics in that it was here in Ireland that provision was made in the Hospital at Kilmainham for the old soldiers who had become unserviceable or infirm and it provided for those then living here in that discharge in Ireland qualfied them. British ex-soldiers return to Ireland on their discharge and thus come to live in the area where the charity provided the relief and benefit afforded by the Hospital. This second class can thus claim to come within so much of the intent of the founder of the charity as was to benefit soldiers of the army of his successors. They also have the additional claim of living in the country where the charity used to operate and which was intended to benefit persons residing in Ireland if and when they otherwise became proper objects of charity. In my view, therefore, British ex-servicemen of the post-1922 class who reside in Ireland and fulfil the other qualifications that would make them proper objects of the charitable intentions of the trust have a good and valid claim to be included in any application of the funds as nearly as possible to the original purposes.

I am unable to envisage any other classes which could have a better claim than former members of the Defence Forces and British ex-servicemen but I consider that it should be left open to other persons or classes of persons to establish a claim to benefit along with them if they can properly do so.

It is not my intention to interfere unduly with the Examiner's discretion on matters of detail but in formulating the scheme he will have general regard to the views I have expressed as to the proper beneficiaries of the *cy-près* application of the funds. Payment of the income to appropriate organisations of former members of the Defence Forces and the British Army catering for the needs of the suggested beneficiaries, to be distributed amongst them, would appear to be the best practical method of distribution. The Examiner will no doubt get in touch with such organisations and obtain relevant facts and figures in preparing the scheme. Sufficient information must be obtained to enable a decision to be made as to appropriate allocation of the income. While it would appear that it is unlikely that any class with a valid claim will emerge outside the classes catered for by the above organisations, steps should be taken by advertisement or otherwise to ascertain if any such class exists and the representatives made on behalf of any *bona fide* claimants should be duly considered.

There are two other matters to which I should refer for the general guidance of the Examiner. The members of what I have described as the pre-1922 class of British ex-servicemen have a particular and paramount claim to benefit, but only for the temporary period of the existence of the class and by means of relief reasonably equivalent to the benefits provided by the Charter, and effect should be given to their claim in appropriate fashion when facts and figures are available regarding them. The second matter arises out of the decision of Mr. Justice Johnston in *Attorney General* v. *Royal Hibernian Military Hospital* 63 I.L.T.R. 86 wherein he expressed his grave doubts as to whether the Court in applying the *cy-près* principle for the disposal of the property of a charity situate in this country would have jurisdiction to endow any charitable organisation resident abroad and he felt that he had no alternative but to apply the property of the Royal Hibernian Military School *cy-près* to the carrying on of some charitable work in this country. I agree with the learned Judge's reasoning and conclusions. In this case the benevolent gift of Charles II was of Irish lands, now in part represented by the trust funds. The Corporation was Irish and its charitable work and administration were carried out in Ireland, the local habitation of the charity being in what was formerly part of the Phoenix Park. The same results should therefore apply in this case. No question arises relative to Defence Forces organisations and, in so far as any difficulty might confront the Examiner with regard to the British Legion by reason of its being incorporated abroad, I am informed that it has a local organisation operating in the State, so that provision can be made in the scheme for distribution by such local organisation. Mr. Justice Johnston remarked with regard to the organisations he was dealing with that there was no reason to suppose that they confined their benevolence to persons within the then Free State. Former members of the Defence Forces may well be living in Northern Ireland as well as British ex-servicemen and provided the operating body carries on its work here there should be no bar, in so far as funds permit, to their aiding proper objects elsewhere. Questions of detail arising on this aspect of the matter can more properly be dealt with on the settlement of the scheme.

The contentions made with regard to the *cy-près* application of the trust funds have necessitated my dealing with that matter first, but the relief sought in para. 1 (*a*) of the originating summary summons relative to directing the payments therein specified to the Chelsea Hospital, pursuant to the provisions of s.4 (*a*) of the Act of 1962, remains to be dealt with. It will be recollected that between 1926 and 1929 forty-two of the remaining pensioners in the Hospital exercised the option given to them by the British Government of being transferred to the Royal Hospital, Chelsea, and the remaining nine pensioners became out-pensioners. The cost of the maintenance of the pensioners transferred between 1926 and 1929 and the remaining out-pensioners was met from the provision made in the British votes for the Royal Hospital, Chelsea. It was later agreed between the Irish Government and the British Government that portion of the income arising from the trust funds should be made available to the Commissioners of the Royal Hospital, Chelsea, in respect of the support and maintenance of the transferred pensioners. It is stated by the Chief State Solicitor in his final affidavit that, in the negotiations between the respective Governments, it was conceded and accepted that the cost of maintaining the transferred pensioners in the Royal Hospital, Chelsea, during the period from 1923 to 1951 exceeded all monies, investments and income mentioned in para. (*a*) of sub-s. 4 of the Act of 1962 and thereby provided to be paid to the Royal Hospital, Chelsea. When dealing, in the ordinary course, with an application brought in a charity matter to sanction payments to meet the obligations of a charity such payments need to be vouched in appropriate fashion. In this case, however, the Chief State Solicitor's affidavit states how the amounts agreed to be paid were arrived at and from what he says it is clear that, assuming an obligation to exist, the amount arrived at involved a compromise in favour of the Kilmainham Hospital. I see no reason whatever to question the propriety of the compromise so that in so far as the quantum of the claim is concerned no question arises and accordingly I have only to consider whether or not an order should be made implementing the agreement in principle.

The provisions in the Act of 1962 with regard to the making of an order for the payments to the Royal Hospital, Chelsea, also fall within that part of the Act which is in enabling form, leaving it to the Court to decide whether the payment should be made.

In the ordinary way when the Court has the trust funds of a charity under its control, and is in the course of regulating the affairs of the charity, the Court has jurisdiction to permit payments to be made out of the funds of the charity to meet outstanding obligations, even of an unusual character, properly incurred in the administration of the charity. This was done, for example, in the Richmond Asylum case in this Court. The circumstances under which the Royal Hospital, Chelsea, incurred the expense in respect of which reimbursement is sought were undoubtedly unusual. Since 1922 there were insufficient Governors of the Kilmainham Hospital in existence to form a quorum, so that there was no means of administering the affairs of the Hospital. No further pensioners could be admitted to the Hospital and its days as a hospital were coming to an end. In these circumstances the remaining pensioners accepted the offer of the British Government. It would have been well within the trust on which the funds of the Hospital were held for the Corporation, had it been able to function, to have used the income of the trust funds for the benefit of the pensioners in the way of providing for their maintenance. Had the Governors for some reason been unable to provide for the maintenance of the remaining pensioners in the Hospital, the Governors would have had to make alternative arrangements for them. In the ordinary course some appropriate application would be brought before the Court to approve of alternative proposals. If, however, owing to some quite unusual occurrence – say, for example, the burning of the Hospital – emergency arrangements had to be made, it is scarcely to be doubted that obligations reasonably incurred by the Governors to provide for the maintenance of the pensioners would be sanctioned by the Court and provision made to meet such obligations out of the income of the trust funds of the charity. A temporary *cy-près* application of the funds would properly have been called for. As it was, the situation was dealt with by way of the British Government's intervention through the arrangement with the Royal Hospital, Chelsea.

The analogy taken above may not be quite complete, but in principle no great extension of the jurisdiction of the Court is involved in its being exercised to allow the payments in question to be made. If the jurisdiction does fall short in any way, then any question that could arise as to the powers of the Court is met by the provisions of the Act of 1962, enabling the Court to make these payments if considered proper as a matter of judicial discretion.

The circumstances which I have to consider on this aspect of the matter are of a quite unprecedented nature but I view them in this fashion: the maintenance and support of these pensioners could normally, but for the intervening circumstances, have been paid out of the income of the funds. It is not sought to touch capital. The Royal Hospital, Chelsea, has borne an expense that would normally have been met *inter alia* out of the income of the trust funds. There was no impropriety involved in the transaction arising out of altogether unusual circumstances and the income of the Hospital has been relieved of a burden that should properly have fallen on it. Had the aid of the Court been sought in appropriate proceedings to enable the funds to be used in the fashion in which it is now sought to apply them there is little reason to doubt that it would have been forthcoming. I have only to add that those appointed to represent the interests of persons other than members or former members of the Defence Forces who might claim to be entitled to the benefit of the funds do not oppose the payments sought. In all the circumstances my view is that the payment is a proper one to be made out of the income of the charity funds and I shall accordingly make the order sought at para. 1 (*a*) in the originating summary summons.

Note

See further *Irish Land Law*, paras. 9.108-9.

Chapter 16

PURPOSE TRUSTS

This is a controversial area of the law, where the courts in many parts of the world have had some difficulties. It is now clear that some non-charitable trusts will be recognised as valid and this has been reiterated by legislation, see *Irish Land Law*, para. 9.114 *et seq.*

RE KEOGH'S ESTATE
[1945] I.R. 13 (High Court)

The facts are set out in the judgment.

Overend J.:

I have given a great deal of consideration to this case. I will not reserve my judgment because I cannot find that there is any real doubt in my mind that would be removed by further consideration.

The testator made his will on the 6th April, 1940, and he subsequently made a codicil thereto on the 17th November 1941. He died on the 24th January, 1942, at the Hospice for the Dying, Harold's Cross, Dublin.

By his will he gave a large number of pecuniary legacies to various people, which would suggest that he had a clear appreciation of his obligation to his relatives and friends. He gave a sum of £300 to the Prior of the Carmelite Fathers, Loughrea, for the repose of his soul and the souls of his deceased relations, and also a sum of £200 to the Prior for the improvement of the Abbey Church, Loughrea.

Then he makes the following disposition:– "To the Superioress for the time being of the Carmelite Convent, Loughrea, the sum of £300 for the purposes of the Order in the Irish Free State." And finally he makes the following disposition of his residue:– "As to all the rest, residue and remainder of my property I give, devise and bequeath the same to the Prior for the time being at my decease, of the Carmelite Fathers, Loughrea, to be applied by him for the purposes of the Carmelite Order in the Irish Free State." It is these two gifts to the Superioress of the Carmelite Convent and to the Prior of the Carmelite Fathers that are in question in this case.

I think that so far as the first branch of the case is concerned, namely, whether the gifts can be supported as charitable gifts, there is no doubt that they cannot. I am quite satisfied that the purposes of the Carmelite Order as envisaged by the testator were not confined to the spiritual purposes of the Order, as set forth by Father Moylan in his affidavit, which he defines as:– *(a)* "Primarily love and service of God, *(b)* The love and service of the neighbour for God's sake." I cannot find any room for doubt that the testator was not thinking only of these purposes when he made the gift of residue to the Reverend Prior. It may well be that many, and probably the majority, of the Order are religious in character, but I have also no doubt that there are several purposes which are not charitable in the legal sense and that it would, therefore, be possible for the donee, without breach of trust, to apply the gift for such non-charitable purposes. Accordingly, the gift to the Prior cannot be upheld as a charitable gift, and the same applies to the gift to the Superioress. I am bound to arrive at that conclusion by the decision of the Supreme Court in *In re Byrne, Deceased; Shaw* v. *Attorney-General and Others* [1935] I.R. 782.

That conclusion brings me to a further branch of the case. If the gift to the Prior is void as a charitable gift, can it be held valid as a non-charitable gift to the Prior for the purposes of the Order? It has been argued that it cannot take effect as a non-charitable gift, on three grounds, really two main grounds – the second one being sub-divided into two parts.

In the first place, it is contended that becaue the gift is for the benefit of an Order which contemplates its own perpetuity and provides for succession for an indefinite period, it is void as offending the rule against perpetuities. But there is nothing in the testator's will to indicate that he contemplated that the money would be applied for a perpetual endowment, or that he had any idea that the whole of it would not be spent within a short period, and, indeed, as the Vice-Chancellor pointed out in *Cocks* v. *Manners* L.R. 12 Eq. 574, the gift might have been expended forthwith and as the donees pleased. Accordingly, I hold that the gift is not void on this ground.

Secondly, the validity of the gift is challenged on the ground of uncertainty – under two heads. 1, Because it is said that there are, in fact, three Carmelite Orders in Ireland, two Orders of Friars and one Order of Nuns. Now, I have no evidence that the testator had any knowledge of any existence of all these three Orders. But he certainly knew of one of them, namely, the Order to which the Camelite Fathers of Loughrea belonged. The evidence before me indicates that the testator, who was a devout man, was in constant attendance at daily worship at Loughrea, and was an intimate friend of some of the Fathers, and I must assume that he had a certain knowledge of the Convent of the Carmelite Friars at Loughrea. The gift of £300 for the repose of souls is to the Prior of the "Carmelite Fathers, Loughrea"; the gift of £200 to the Prior is for the improvement of the "Abbey Church, Loughrea," and, again, in the gift of the residue it is to the Prior of the "Carmelite Fathers, Loughrea," to be applied for the purposes of the "Carmelite Order in Irish Free State." I cannot doubt that the testator thought solely of the Carmelite Order in Loughrea for which he had such a respect and with the members of which he was so closely connected. I do not think it possible to introduce the fact of the existence of other Orders as a ground for uncertainty as to the provision in the will without some evidence of uncertainty in the mind of the testator.

The same applies to the gift to the Superioress of the Convent. In that case he does not specifically mention the Carmelite Order, but he makes the gift to the Superioress of the "Carmelite Convent, Loughrea . . . for the purposes of the Order in the Irish Free State." "The Order" can only mean her Order, *i.e.,* the Order to which the Loughrea Convent belonged.

The final ground of uncertainty relied upon was as to the members who were to benefit by the gift. I do not regard the testator's beneficence as intended for individual members; it was intended for the purposes of the Order. But even if I am to regard the gift as intended to benefit individual members, I am bound by the decision of the Supreme Court in *In re Byrne, Deceased; Shaw* v. *Attorney-General* [1935] I.R. 782 to hold that whatever uncertainty I may have as to the classes of members included in the gift, the uncertainty is not such as to render the gift invalid. That is how I read the decision of the Supreme Court, and I can see no ground on which the present case can be efffectively distinguished. In my opinion the testator intended the money to go the the Prior and to be applied by him for the purposes of the Carmelite Order and I hold that in the context it means the Order of which he was Prior.

Mr. Wilson has also suggested a number of subsidiary grounds for challenging the gift. He says that the use of the words "in the Irish Free State" leaves uncertainty as to whether these words refer to the Order in the Irish Free State, or whether they refer to the application of the money in the Irish Free State. If the former, he says that the money can be used as well for the Order in Los Angeles, which is a branch of the Order in Éire, because such a use of the money would be within the purposes of the Order in the Irish Free State; but if the words indicate that the money has to be applied in the Irish Free State, it could not be applied outside that territorial area. I feel that here is no uncertainty as to what the testator meant. I think he was perfectly content that the money should be applied in the Irish Free State by the Prior for the general purposes of the Order.

Mr. Wilson further contends that the gift must be void for the following reasons. He says that, if it is applicable for the purpposes of the Order generally, the testator's intention becomes defeated, because the Prior, by the Constitution of the Order, is precluded from spending the money except for the purposes of the particular convent of which he is a member. In my opinion that is not a sound argument. I think Father Moylan's affidavit must be read to mean that money which is received in the ordinary course by the Prior of any convent is to be applied by him for the purposes of the

Order in his own particular convent, but I cannot read it as meaning that the Prior is incapable of being a trustee for purposes outside his own convent. Accordingly, I hold that the gift is a good gift to the Prior for the purposes of the Discalced Carmelite order in the Irish Free State.

I may add that I consider that I am bound to arrive at that conclusion by the decision in *In re Wilkinson's Trusts* 19 L.R. Ir. 531.

I have been dealing so far with the gift to the Prior, but for the same reasons I hold that the gift to the Superioress is likewise valid. Accordingly I will answer the question as follows:– The gifts are invalid as charitable gifts, but are valid as non-charitable gifts to the Prior and the Superioress, respectively, to be applied by them in the Irish Free State for the respective purposes of their respective Orders.

Notes and Questions

1. Would the gift have been invalid if construed as being for the individual members of the Order?
2. See further, *Irish Land Law,* para. 9.118.

RE CONNOR

[1960] I.R. 67; 93 I.L.T.R. 86 (High Court)

The facts are set out in the judgment.

Haugh J.:

The textatrix, Mary Leonora Connor, who died on the 2nd August, 1956, by her will, dated the 15th March, 1945, made the following bequest, among others:–"One thousand pounds to the General Cemetery Company of Dublin to be applied for the maintenance and care of the family vault at Mount Jerome."

She appointed the plaintiffs her executors. Mr. Moloney appeared for the residuary legatee, Susan Bridget Lucas, and Mr. O'Shaughnessy for the Dublin Cemetery Company. The deceased's gross assets amounted to some £44,000.

Because of this bequest the plaintiffs have issued a summons in which two questions are asked and which in short are 1, whether this legacy of £1,000 is a valid charitable gift? and 2, if it is not a charitable gift, is it a valid non-charitable gift, or is it invalid or void as infringing the rule against perpetuities?

Counsel for all parties have agreed that the first question must be answered. "No."

Mr. Matheson, for the plaintiffs, did not seek any particular answer, but awaited the direction of the Court. He did, however, draw my attention to the fact that this particular bequest differed from the bequests in all the leading cases on the subject, in that no reference was made by the testatrix to investment or income.

Mr. Moloney, for the residuary legatee, contended that this bequest infringed the rule against perpetuities, in that £1,000 properly invested should yield an income of about £60 per annum and, in ordinary circumstances, the capital sum would not be required to be touched within twenty-one years. In support, he cited three Irish cases – *Toole* v. *Hamilton* [1901] 1 I. R. 383, *Roche* v. *McDermott* [1901] 1 I. R. 394, *Morris* v. *Larkin* [1902] 1 I. R. 103 – and a number of English cases.

One English case, referred to by counsel for both defendants, was *In re Chardon; Johnston* v. *Davies* [1928] 1 Ch. 464, in which a testator gave £200 to his trustees upon trust to invest it and to pay the income thereof to a cemetery company "during such period as they shall continue to maintain and keep" two specified graves "in good order and condition with flowers and plants thereon as the same have hitherto been kept by me."

The decision of Romer J. was criticised in a later edition of Jarman on Wills, but, later again, was viewed with approval by the House of Lords.

At this stage I wish to make a brief digression. I can almost take judicial notice of the fact that the income on the sum of £1,000 would purchase about the same amount of flowers and plants in 1958 as the income on £500 would purchase in the year 1927. Yet the bequest in *Chardon's Case* [1928] 1 Ch. 464, with its investment and income clause and with the restrictive use of the income to be spent on flowers and plants only, was held to be a valid bequest. In the case before me there is no restriction as to how the money is to be spent, provided it is devoted to the care and maintenance of this family grave.

It seems plain to me that care and maintenance can well include, not only flowers and plants, but painting, repairing and works of major or minor reconstruction. It may well happen that a sum of £60 (a year's income) might not be sufficient to meet a demand for work of necessary repair or reconstruction, having regard to present-day prices.

Mr. O'Shaughnessy, on behalf of the Cemetery Company, began by stating that while he was instructed to seek only the order of the Court, he felt justified in making certain legal submissions, which can be summarised as follows:–

That this was an outright bequest of the £1,000 to the defendants; there was no time limit and the sum vested on death. Therefore, the capital sum is not inalienable and if it can be resorted to, at any time, the bequest does not infringe the rule.

Mr. O'Shaughnessy pointed out that it was significant that, unlike all the authorities quoted, this clause in the testatrix's will makes no reference whatever to capital investments, dividends, or income. He has submitted that I am being asked to read into the plain terms of the will words that do not appear therein – words that she could have had written in, but did not: that if it was her intention that the £1,000 should be tied, and only income utilised, why did she not say so? Counsel further suggested that if his clients, during the next two years or twenty years, decided that some reconstruction was necessary to the vault and that an expenditure of £200 was thereby necessary, they would be entitled at any time to resort to the capital to discharge their obligations should the amount of accumulated income be below £200.

He asked that the will should be construed in the manner laid down in vol. 2 of Jarman on Wills, 6th ed., 1910, articles 8 and 16, at pp. 2209 and 2210 – words should be read in their ordinary sense, and the implication was that the testatrix and her legal advisers knew the law and appreciated that an express gift of income only might well be void and accordingly the bequest deliberately avoided any reference to income, inalienability or perpetuity, so as to ensure the validity of the bequest. That is a brief summary of Mr. O'Shaughnessy's submissions.

I was strongly impressed by Mr. O'Shaughnessy's submissions. I do not have to follow *Chardon's Case* [1928] 1 Ch. 464 – or any case opened to me – though I would follow *Chardon's Case* [1928] 1 Ch. 464 if necessary. They are all quite different. They all deal with investment and the application of income. The clause in this will clearly and expressly avoids any such reference. I have no doubt whatever as to the way this question should be answered. The testatrix clearly, and in the plainest possible terms, bequeathed this sum of £1,000 to the defendant Company with one limitation only, that is, that it, the sum of £1,000, should be spent by them in the care and maintenance of this family vault at Mount Jerome, and I can see nothing whatever in law, in equity, or in fact, that prevents them from resorting to the capital if, and when, they think it proper in their discretion to do so for the purposes mentioned in the will.

Accordingly, I answer the second question (which cannot be answered by a mere "Yes" or "No" by reason of the way it is framed) as follows:–

"The gift is a valid non-charitable gift which does not offend against the rule against perpetuities or any other rule."

Notes and Questions

1. What would be the effect on such a case of s. 50 of the Charities Act, 1961, see *infra*.
2. See further, *Irish Land Law*, para. 5.038 *et seq*.

RE KELLY

[1932] I.R. 255; L.J.Ir. 93 (High Court)

The facts are set out in the judgment.

Meredith J.:

The first clause in the testator's will that the Court is asked to construe does not present any great difficulty that I can see. The testator says: "I devise and bequeath all my stock (except those hereinbefore bequeathed to the said Catherine Duggan) and all my property in America, and the residue of my estate of every nature and kind wheresoever situated to my executors and trustees to be sold by them and converted into money." The testator had given a number of pecuniary legacies, and he had specifically devised and bequeathed his several farms in Ireland to several persons, and had also bequeathed the stock on these farms to Catherine Duggan. Accordingly, as he expressly mentions all his stock, he excepts the stock which he had specifically dealt with. Hence the expression "the residue of my estate of every nature and kind wherever situated" obviously includes what remained over and above what had just been mentioned in the same sentence and the stock specifically bequeathed to Catherine Duggan and the farms that had been specifically devised and bequeathed. Here "the residue of my estate" describes the rest of the property that is to come into the hands of the executors and trustees, to be converted by them into money. So coming into their hands, the proceeds of the conversion, which comprise the said residue, all stock not previously bequeathed to Catherine Duggan, and all the property in America, are clearly applicable to the payment of the pecuniary legacies. The testator then adds "with the directions that my said executors and trustees shall divide the residue of my estate in equal shares between my first cousin Mary Cleary (Mamie) and my first cousins James Cleary and Catherine Cleary of Urard aforesaid Doctor Thomas Cleary and Laurence Cleary and Patrick Dunne." Here the testator is dealing with the beneficial interest, and "the residue of my estate" means the residue of what is converted into money remaining over after the payment of the debts, funeral and testamentary expenses and pecuniary legacies. As the testator is dealing with what has all been converted into money he appropriately leaves out the previous words "of every nature and kind." The testator then adds, "and I appoint my said first cousins residuary legatees and devisees of this my will as tenants in common." This addition is quite proper, and indicates the careful manner in which the will was drawn. The residue of what was contemplated as being converted into money might not be thought to include any of the farms specifically devised and bequeathed should any such devise or bequest fail. Consequently, to prevent any uncertainty, the cousins named are made residuary legatees and devisees. The expression, "the residue of my estate," is not used in two different senses in a will simply because in two different connections it may denote different residues. In each case the expression naturally means "that which remains after what has previously been given is withdrawn," *Greville* v. *Browne* 7 H. L. C. 689, at p. 705. But in the case of the residue devised and bequeathed to the executors and trustees for the purposes of the will, the residue denotes what remains after the specific devises or bequests, whereas in the case of the residue given to the residuary legatees it means what remains after what the will had expressly or impliedly provided the executors and trustees should do with the residue of the estate coming into their hands. The present case is *a fortiori* to that of *Thorman* v. *Hilhouse* 5 Jur. (N. S.) 562, which was cited to the Court. Question 1 *(d)* must, therefore, be answered in the affirmative, and questions 1 *(a), (b)* and *(c)* and question 2 need not be answered as 1 *(d)* covers the only point that arises.

The remaining question concerns the validity of the following bequest: "I leave one hundred pounds sterling to my executors and trustees for the purpose of expending four pounds sterling on the support of each of my dogs per year, and I direct that my dogs be kept in the old house at Upper Tullaroan aforesaid. Should any balance remain in the hands of my trustees on the death of the last of my dogs I leave same to the Parish Priest for the time being of the Parish of Tullaroan for masses for the repose of my soul and the souls of my parents, brothers and stepfather."

Mr. Michael Comyn, for the plaintiff, contended that both the gift for the support of the dogs and the gift over, which is to take effect on the death of the last of the of dogs, are void.

It will be more convenient to deal first with the gift of any possible surplus remaining over on the death of the last of the dogs. Here the question, so far as there can be any question, is strictly one of remoteness. If the lives of the dogs or other animals could be taken into account in reckoning the maximum period of "lives in being and twenty-one years afterwards" any contingent or executory interest might be properly limited, so as only to vest within the lives of specified carp, or tortoises, or other animals that might live for over a hundred years, and for twenty-one yeas afterwards, which of course, is absurd. "Lives" means human lives. It was suggested that the last of the dogs could in fact not outlive the testator by more than twenty-one years. I know nothing of that. The Court does not enter into the question of a dog's expectation of life. In point of fact neighbour's dogs and cats are unpleasantly long-lived; but I have no knowledge of their precise expectation of life. Anyway the maxiumum period is exceeded by the lives even of specified butterflies and twenty-one years afterwards. And even, according to my decision – and, I confess, it displays this weakness on being pressed to a logical conclusion – the expiration of the life of a single butterfly, even without the twenty-one years, would be too remote, despite all the world of poetry that may be thereby destroyed. In *Robinson* v. *Hardcastle* 2 Bro. C. C. 22, at p. 30, Lord Thurlow defined a perpetuity in these words: "What is a perpetuity, but the extending the estate beyond a life in being, and twenty-one years after ?" Of course by "a life" he means lives; and there can be no doubt that "lives" means lives of human beings, not of animals or trees in California.

Mr. McGuckin, for the Attorney-General, contended that the rule does not apply in the case of charities, but *Chamberlayne* v. *Brockett* L.R. 8 Ch. 206, at p. 211, cited by Mr. Price, and *Kingham* v. *Kingham* [1897] 1 I. R. 170 , dispose of that contention. For these reasons, I am clearly of opinion that the gift over of the unascertained surplus on the death of the last of the dogs is void for remoteness.

I come now to the question of the validity of the trust in favour of the testator's dogs. The point that in this case there is no *cestui que trust* – for certainly the Court cannot recognise a dog as a *cestiu que trust* was treated as disposed of by *In re Dean; Cooper-Dean* v. *Stevens* 41 Ch. D. 552, and was not relied on. The trustees are ready and willing to apply the £100 for the support of the dogs, as provided by the will, and counsel expressly confined themselves to the question as to whether or not the legacy is void as tending to a perpetuity. I have had the advantage of reading the learned discussions in Mr. Gray's valuable work on "Perpetuities" and in Jarman on "Wills," but it is quite competent to counsel to refrain from raising a point on which eminent authorities differ – and I think they are well advised in so doing where the amount in dispute is so small – and, consequently, I shall deal with the question solely in connection with the perpetuity point.

Now, to begin with, I must refuse to read into the will an implied limitation to a period of twenty-one years or "for so long as the law permits." It is well established that I must first construe the will independently of the rule, and, having so construed it, then determine if any of its provisions offend. But that does not prevent me, when I have impartially construed the terms of the will, from analysing a provision which is manifestly not good in its entirety, for the purpose of determining whether the entire provision does not include a severable part which does not offend. The provision may be for a single, entire and indivisible purpose, and be *ab initio* a provision for a perpetuity and nothing less. Or the provision may in essence be constituted by what, fully and explicitly stated, is a series of provision each for a limited period, say a week, or a month, or a year, and the whole provision may only come to offend by reason of the series being carried on indefinitely or beyond the prescribed period, and not because the provision is *ab initio* a provision for the series as a whole and nothing less. The question is clearly one of construction of the precise terms of the will. No doubt the distinction may be a fine one, but it clearly exists and is a well recognised logical distinction, and, if the adoption of the distinction saves a provision for what is in itself quite lawful from total failure, it seems to me that the intentions of the testator are entitled to the benefit of the subtletly, and certainly the object of the rule is abundantly secure by the invalidation simply of so much of the total provision as offends. So far as a provision for expenditure in a particular way for a term of years is simply provision for expenditure in a particular way for a mere sum of years, I cannot see any reason why that sum should not be treated as a mere mathematical sum divisible in any required manner. Mathematically 50 years can be dealt with as

21 + 29 years, and a provision for 50 years as a series of provisions for 21 years with an additional provision for 29 years. Hence a provision for a term of years may always be split up into provisions for lesser terms, which are comprised in one sum total, unless the provision is qualitatively of such an integral character as to present a mere quantitative division. In the present case the trustees are given £100 for the purpose of expending the sum of £4 "per year" on the support of each of the testator's dogs. As he would appear to have had four dogs the £100 would be exhausted in a very few years by the annual expenditure of the £16 per annum. Consequently, if I am not to speculate on a dog's expectation of life, I am actually definitely precluded from regarding the provision as one for the support of the dogs for life, though I have no doubt the testator hoped that the £100 would be sufficient to make such a provision. But the dogs might all die before the £100 was fully expended, and accordingly the testator made provision for the application of the contingent residue. It was only in that connection that there was any reference to the lives of the dogs, and there was no reference to any definite term. The provision is simply one for an amount, depending upon the number of dogs continuing to live, per year. The provision seems to me to be essentially one for successive annual expenditures, to be accounted for by the trustees at the end of each year. Each of these successive expenditures is what it is, independently of whether sufficient of the capital sum of £100 remains to provide for the future, and independently of whether I hold that any provision for expenditure in the twenty-second and succeeding years is void. The dogs have to take their chance of expenditure year by year without the benefit of any policy of insurance. Accordingly, unless coerced by authority, I shall hold that the provision for the expenditure on the support of the dogs per year is good for the twenty-one years succeeding the death of the testator, but that the possible provision for the twenty-second and succeeding years is void for remoteness. On this view the question of perpetuity in the primary sum does not arise. It is only certain possible future expenditures that are regarded as contravening the rule against perpetuity on the ground of remoteness.

In the majority of the cases of immediate interests which have been held void as tending to create a perpetuity the trust was for an integral purpose involving a perpetuity and for nothing less, and was therefore, *ab initio* for a perpetuity. The only authority in which the possibility of there being a complete trust for a limited period was considered is *Small* v. *Torley* 25 L. R. Ir. 388. Referring to *Dillon* v. *Reilly* I. R. 10 Eq. 152, Porter M.R. said: "It cannot be treated as a decision that in a case where words are used which purport to tie up property beyond legal limits the Court will from thence carve out a life estate, hold it good to that extent, and reject the rest. But in that case what it was suggested to carve out was a life estate, for which severance there was no justification on the words of the will. The learned Master of the Rolls makes it clear in his judgment that the possibity of a severance must turn on the precise words of the will. The trust provided for an annual sum for saying masses for a mere term of years, and the suggestion that there was a complete and severable trust for each succeeding year, and therefore for the first twenty-one years of the term was not raised. The invalidation of the trust for the residue of the term would have in no way affected the trust for any of the preceding years. Some reason has yet to be suggested why what is compendiously described as a mere aggregate is not as divisible in law as it is in mathematics, Suppose the trust had been worded "for twenty-one years and for one additional year," could the words "and for one additional year" have made the trust void? The suggestion seems to me absurd. For these reasons I adhere to the view that in the present case there is a valid severable trust for twenty-one years succeeding the death of the testator, provided any of the dogs live so long.

Notes and Questions

1. What is the policy behind upholding such a gift. Why did the legislators not cover animals in s.50 of the Charities Act, 1961? *Cf.* the views of the English court of Appeal in *Re Endacott* [1960] Ch. 232. See further *Irish Land Law*, paras. 9.119–20.
2. As regards use of animals' lives in calculating the perpetuity period, *cf. Re Dean* (1889) 41 Ch. D. 552. See further, *Irish Land Law*, para. 5.038.

CHARITIES ACT, 1961

49. – (1) Where any of the purposes of a gift includes or could be deemed to include both charitable and non-charitable objects, its terms shall be so construed and given effect to as to exclude the non-charitable objects and the purpose shall, accordingly, be treated as charitable.

(2) Subsection (1) shall not apply where –

(a) the gift takes effect before the 1st day of January, 1960, or

(b) (i) the terms of the gift make, or provide for the making of, an apportionment between the charitable and the non-charitable objects, and

(c) (ii) the non-charitable objects are identifiable from an express or implied description.

(3) This section shall not, by its operation on any gift as respects the period from the 1st day of Janaury, 1960, to the 24th day of September, 1960, entitle any person to reclaim any tax or duty paid or borne during that period, nor (save as respects tax or duty) require the objects declared by the gift to be treated as having been charitable so as to invalidate anything done or any determination given during that period.

50.– (1) Every gift made after the commencement of this Act for the provision, maintenance or improvement of a tomb, vault or grave or of a tombstone or any other memorial to a deceased person or deceased persons which would not otherwise be charitable shall, to the extent provided by this section, be a charitable gift.

(2) Such a gift shall be charitable so far as it does not exceed –

(a) in the case of a gift of income only, sixty pounds a year,

(b) in any other case, one thousand pounds in amount or value.

Note

See further, *Irish Land Law*, para. 9.122 *et seq*.

Chapter 17

POWERS OF TRUSTEES

Trustees have a wide range of powers to enable them to carry out the day-to-day administration of the trust, though in the Republic the statutory powers are not as comprehensive as in England and Northern Ireland as they are still largely contained in the Trustee Act, 1893.

TRUSTEE ACT, 1893

PART II.

VARIOUS POWERS AND DUTIES OF TRUSTEES

Appointment of New Trustees.

10.– (1) Where a trustee, either original or substituted, and whether appointed by a court or otherwise, is dead, or remains out of the United Kingdom for more than twelve months, or desires to be discharged from all or any of the trusts or powers reposed in or conferred on him, or refuses or is unfit to act therein, or is incapable of acting therein, then the person or persons nominated for the purpose of appointing new trustees by the instrument, if any, creating the trust, or if there is no such person, or no such person able and willing to act, then the surviving or continuing trustees or trustee for the time being, or the personal representatives of the last surviving or continuing trustee, may, by writing, appoint another person or other persons to be a trustee or trustees in the place of the trustee dead, remaining out of the United Kingdom, desiring to be discharged, refusing, or being unfit or being incapable, as aforesaid.

(2) On the appointment of a new trustee for the whole or any part of trust property–

(a) the number of trustees may be increased; and

(b) a separate set of trustees may be appointed for any part of the trust property held on trusts distinct from those relating to any other part or parts of the trust property, notwithstanding that no new trustees or trustee are or is to be appointed for other parts of the trust property, and any existing trustee may be appointed or remain one of such separate set of trustees; or, if only one trustee was originally appointed, then one separate trustee may be so appointed for the first-mentioned part; and

(c) it shall not be obligatory to appoint more than one new trustee where only one trustee was originally appointed, or to fill up the original number of trustees where more than two trustees were originally appointed; but, except where only one trustee was originally appointed, a trustee shall not be discharged under this section from his trust unless there will be at least two trustees to perform the trust; and

(d) any assurance or thing requisite for vesting the trust property, or any part thereof, jointly in the persons who are the trustees, shall be executed or done.

(3) Every new trustee so appointed, as well before as after all the trust property becomes by law, or by assurance, or otherwise, vested in him, shall have the same powers, authorities, and discretions, and may in all respects act, as if he had been originally appointed a trustee by the instrument, if any, creating the trust.

(4) The provisions of this section relative to a trustee who is dead include the case of a person nominated trustee in a will but dying before the testator, and those relative to a continuing trustee include a refusing or retiring trustee, if willing to act in the execution of the provisions of this section.

(5) This section applies only if and as far as a contrary intention is not expressed in the instrument, if any, creating the trust, and shall have effect subject to the terms of that instrument and to any provisions therein contained.

(6) This section applies to trusts created either before or after the commencement of this Act.

11.– (1) Where there are more than two trustees, if one of them by deed declares that he is desirous of being discharged from the trust, and if his co-trustees and such other person, if any, as is empowered to appoint trustees, by deed consent to the discharge of the trustee, and to the vesting in the co-trustees alone of the trust property, then the trustee desirous of being discharged shall be deemed to have retired from the trust, and shall, by the deed, be discharged therefrom under this Act, without any new trustee being appointed in his place.

(2) Any assurance or thing requisite for vesting the trust property in the continuing trustees alone shall be excecuted or done.

(3) This section applies only if and as far as a contrary intention is not expressed in the instrument, if any, creating the trust, and shall have effect subject to the terms of that instrument and to any provisions therein contained.

(4) This section applies to trusts created either before or after the commencement of this Act.

12.– (1) Where a deed by which a new trustee is appointed to perform any trust contains a declaration by the appointor to the effect that any estate or interest in any land subject to the trust, or in any chattel so subject, or the right to recover and receive any debt or other thing in action so subject, shall vest in the persons who by virtue of the deed become and are the trustees for performing the trust, that declaration shall, without any conveyance or assignment, operate to vest in those persons, as joint tenants, and for the purposes of the trust, that estate, interest, or right.

(2) Where a deed by which a retiring trustee is discharged under this Act contains such a declaration as is in this section mentioned by the retiring and continuing trustees, that declaration shall, without any conveyance or assignment, operate to vest in the continuing trustees alone, as joint tenants, and for the purposes of the trust, the estate, interest, or right to which the declaration relates.

(3) This section does not extend to any legal estate or interest in copyhold or customary land, or to land conveyed by way of mortgage for securing money subject to the trust, or to any such share, stock, annuity, or property as is only transferable in books kept by a company or other body, or in manner directed by or under Act of Parliament.

(4) For purposes of registration of the deed in any registry, the person or persons making the declaration shall be deemed the conveying party or parties, and the conveyance shall be deemed to be made by him or them under a power conferred by this Act.

(5) This section applies only to deeds executed after the thirty-first of December one thousand eight hundred and eighty-one.

Purchase and Sale.

13.– (1) Where a trust for sale or a power of sale of property is vested in a trustee, he may sell or concur with any other person in selling all or any part of the property, either subject to prior charges or not, and either together or in lots, by public auction or by private contract, subject to any such conditions respecting title or evidence of title or other matter as the trustee thinks fit, with power to vary any contract for sale, and to buy in at any auction, or to rescind any contract for sale and to re-sell, without being answerable for any loss.

(2) This section applies only if and so far as a contrary intention is not expressed in the instrument creating the trust or power, and shall have effect subject to the terms of that instrument and to the provisions therein contained.

(3) This section applies only to a trust or power created by an instrument coming into operation after the thirty-first of December one thousand eight hundred and eighty-one.

14. – (1) No sale made by a trustee shall be impeached by any beneficiary upon the ground that any of the conditions subject to which the sale was made may have been unnecessarily depreciatory, unless it also appears that the consideration for the sale was thereby rendered inadequate.

(2) No sale made by a trustee shall, after the execution of the conveyance, be impeached as against the purchaser upon the ground that any of the conditions subject to which the sale was made may have been unnecessarily depreciatory, unless it appears that the purchaser was acting in collusion with the trustee at the time when the contract for sale was made.

(3) No purchaser, upon any sale made by a trustee, shall be at liberty to make any objection against the title upon the ground aforesaid.

(4) This section, applies only to sales made after the twenty-fourth day of December one thousand eight hundred and eighty-eight.

15. A trustee who is either a vendor or a purchaser may sell or buy without excluding the application of section two of the Vendor and Purchaser Act, 1874.

. . .

Various Powers and Liabilities

17. – (1) A trustee may appoint a solicitor to be his agent to receive and give a discharge for any money or valuable consideration or property receiveable by the trustee under the trust, by permitting the solicitor to have the custody of, and to produce, a deed containing any such receipt as is referred in section fifty-six of the Conveyancing and Law of Property Act, 1881; and a trustee shall not be chargeable with breach of trust by reason only of his having made or concurred in making any such appointment; and the producing of any such deed by the solicitor shall have the same validity and effect under the said section as if the person appointing the solicitor had not been a trustee.

(2) A trustee may appoint a banker or solicitor to be his agent to receive and give a discharge for any money payable to the trustee under or by virtue of a policy of assurance, by permitting the banker or solicitor to have the custody of and to produce the policy of assurance with a receipt signed by the trustee, and a trustee shall not be chargeable with a breach of trust by reason only of his having made or concurred in making any such appointment.

(3) Nothing in this section shall exempt a trustee from any liability which he would have incurred if this Act had not been passed, in case he permits any such money, valuable consideration, or property to remain in the hands or under the control of the banker or solicitor for a period longer than is reasonably necessary to enable the banker or solicitor (as the case may be) to pay or transfer the same to the trustee.

(4) This section applies only where the money or valuable consideration or property is received after the twenty-fourth day of December one thousand eight hundred and eighty-eight.

(5) Nothing in this section shall authorise a trustee to do anything which he is in express terms forbidden to do, or to omit anything which he is in express terms directed to do, by the instrument creating the trust.

18.– (1) A trustee may insure against loss or damage by fire any building or other insurable property to any amount (including the amount of any insurance already on foot) not exceeding three equal fourth parts of the full value of such building or property, and pay the premiums for such insurance out of the income thereof or out of the income of any other property subject to the same trusts, without obtaining the consent of any person who may be entitled wholly or partly to such income.

(2) This section does not apply to any building or property which a trustee is bound forthwith to convey absolutely to any beneficiary upon being requested to do so.

(3) This section applies to trusts created either before or after the commencement of this Act, but nothing in this section shall authorise any trustee to do anything which he is in express terms forbidden to do, or to omit to do anything which he is in express terms directed to do, by the instrument creating the trust.

19.– (1) A trustee of any leaseholds for lives or years which are renewable from time to time, either under any covenant or contract, or by custom or usual practice, may, if he thinks fit, and shall, if thereto required by any person having any beneficial interest, present or future, or contingent, in the leaseholds, use his best endeavours to obtain from time to time a renewed lease of the same hereditaments on the accustomed and reasonable terms, and for that purpose may from time to time make or concur in making a surrender of the lease for the time being subsisting, and do all such other acts as are requisite: Provided that, where by the terms of the settlement or will the person in possession for his life or other limited interest is entitled to enjoy the same without any obligation to renew or to contribute to the expense of renewal, this section shall not apply unless the consent in writing of that person is obtained to the renewal on the part of the trustee.

(2) If money is required to pay for the renewal, the trustee effecting the renewal may pay the same out of any money then in his hands in trust for the persons beneficially interested in the lands to be comprised in the renewed lease, and if he had not in his hands sufficient money for the purpose, he may raise the money required by mortgage of the hereditaments to be comprised in the renewed lease, or of any other hereditaments for the time being subject to the uses or trust to which those hereditaments are subject, and no person advancing money upon a mortgage purporting to be under this power shall be bound to see that the money is wanted, or that no more is raised than is wanted for the purpose.

(3) This section applies to trusts created either before or after the commencement of this Act, but nothing in this section shall authorise any trustee to do anything which he is in express terms forbidden to do, or to omit to do anything which he is in express terms directed to do, by the instrument creating the trust.

20.– (1) The receipt in writing of any trustee for any money, securities, or other personal property or effects payable, transferable, or deliverable to him under any trust or power shall be a sufficient discharge for the same, and shall effectually exonerate the person paying, transferring, or delivering the same from seeing to the application or being answerable for any loss or misapplication thereof.

(2) This section applies to trusts created either before or after the commencement of this Act.

21.–(1)...

(2)... two, or more trustees, acting together, or a sole acting trustee where by the instrument, if any, creating the trust a sole trustee is authorised to execute the trusts and powers thereof, may, if and as he or they may think fit, accept any composition or any security, real or personal, for any debt or for any property, real or personal, claimed, and may allow any time for payment for any debt, and may compromise, compound, abandon, submit to arbitration, or otherwise settle any debt, account, claim, or thing whatever relating to the testator's or intestate's estate or to the trust, and for any of those purposes may enter into, give, execute, and do such agreements, instruments of composition or arrangement, releases, and other things as to him or them seem expedient, without being responsible for any loss occasioned by any act or thing so done by him or them in good faith.

(3) This section applies only if and so far as a contrary intention is not expressed in the instrument, if any, creating the trust, and shall have efffect subject to the terms of that instrument and to the provisions therein contained.

(4) This section applies to ... trusts constituted or created either before or after the

commencement of this Act. [This section was repealed in so far as it applied to personal representatives by s. 8 and Sched. 2, Pt. 3, of the Succession Act, 1965 – Ed.]

22.– (1) Where a power or trust is given to or vested in two or more trustees jointly, then, unless the contrary is expressed in the instrument, if any, creating the power or trust, the same may be exercised or performed by the survivor or survivors of them for the time being.

(2) This section applies only to trusts constitued after or created by instruments coming into operation after the thirty-first day of December one thousand eight hundred and eighty-one.

23. A trustee acting or paying money in good faith under or in pursuance of any power of attorney shall not be liable for any such act or payment by reason of the fact that at the time of the payment or act the person who gave the power of attorney was dead or had done some act to avoid the power, if this fact was not known to the trustee at the time of his so acting or paying.

Provided that nothing in this section shall affect the right of any person entitled to the money against the person to whom the payment is made, and that the person so entitled shall have the same remedy against the person to whom the payment is made as he would have had against the trustee.

24. A trustee shall, without prejudice to the provisions of the instrument, if any, creating the trust, be chargeable only for money and securities actually received by him notwithstanding his signing any receipt for the sake of conformity, and shall be answerable and accountable only for his own acts, receipts, neglects, or defaults, and not for those of any other trustee, nor for any banker, broker, or other person with whom any trust moneys, or securities may be deposited, nor for the insufficiency or deficiency of any securities, nor for any other loss, unless the same happens through his own wilful default; and may reimburse himself, or pay or discharge out of the trust premises, all expenses incurred in or about the execution of his trusts or powers.

I. SALE

RE MURPHY

[1957] N. I. 156 (High Court)

Trustees for sale of property comprising many houses let on periodic tenancies subject to the Rent Acts were advised that when the houses became vacant they should be sold rather than relet. They were further advised that the sales should be carried out by long lease or sub-fee farm grant. A summons was taken out to determine whether they could so sell under powers conferred by the Trustee Act, 1893, or expressly by the will establishing the trust.

Lord MacDermott L.C.J. stated the facts substantially as set out above and continued: This question raises a matter of general importance in this jurisdiction where land is commonly held on long lease or fee-farm grant, and where alienation by way of sublease or sub-fee-farm grant is a matter of everyday practice. I have no hesitation in accepting the evidence given by Mr. Murdoch to the effect that it would be in the interests of the beneficiaries to have the vacant dwellings disposed of by the method which he has described, namely, by giving purchasers a long sub-lease or sub-fee-farm grant, as the case may be, in consideration of any appropriate ground rent and the payment of a fine. The question is whether the trustees have power in law to follow that method.

At this point it must be emphasised that if the trustees have such power they propose to exercise it as and when houses become vacant and opportunity arises to act on the advice they have received. There is no question here of dividing a specific parcel of property into suitable smaller parcels and disposing of each of the latter by way of sub-grant or sub-lease as a conveyancing expedient for disposing of the entirety. Here, we are dealing with the odd house which falls vacant on a large estate, and what the trustees want to do cannot fairly be described as a means of disposing of the entirety. Conditions may change. The entirety may never be disposed of by methods which are now profitable. The question posed must therefore be considered in relation to the odd house that has become vacant and available for sale, and not in relation to the whole estate or to such parts thereof, as are held under different titles.

Moreover, it is also to be remarked that the rent to be reserved by the trustees in the form of transaction which they now propose is not fixed as a proportionate part of the head rent to which the house for disposal is, with other premises, subject. The intention is that as the proposed sales proceed the rents reserved thereon will, in the aggregate, exceed the head rent payable in respect of the grant or lease under which the houses sold are held. It may, therefore, be taken that there is a profit element in the rents proposed to be charged, but the general design of disposal has not, so far, provided for the realisation of these rents.

I must now return to the express powers conferred upon the trustees. Of these (1) is in wide terms, but it remains a trust for sale and does not afford a plain answer to the question under consideration. (2) contains a comprehensive power of investment and all I need say of it now is that, in my opinion, it authorises investment in rents reserved by long leases and fee-farm grants, whether sub-leases or sub-grants or not: see *In re Peyton's Settlement Trust* (1869) L.R. 7 Eq. 463. (3) is a power of management. Read literally, it empowers the trustees to act as absolute owners, but I do not think this should be construed as authorising any form of alienation open to an absolute owner. I think this power must be confined to matters of management and, so read, it does not give the trustees the power they now seek. (4) is also in very wide terms, but in my view it does not help the trustees on this occasion. It provides for the making of grants or leases, with the option of taking a fine, but the power seems clearly restricted to cases in which the trustees put the grantees or lessees under an obligation to improve the land, as by building thereon or rebuilding, enlarging or repairing existing buildings.

So far, then, as the express powers are concerned we are left with – (1) the trust for sale and (2) the power of investment, to the extent to which it may affect the matter in hand. To these should be added a reference to the power conferred upon the trustees by section 13(1) of the Trustee Act, 1893, which, omitting what is not material, says:

> "Where a trust for sale or a power of sale of property is vested in a trustee, he may sell or concur with any other person in selling all or any part of the property ... either together or in lots, by public auction or by private contract, subject to any such conditions respecting title or evidence of title or other matter as the trustee thinks fit . . ."

Before going further it will be convenient to note several points that may be taken as settled and that will help to narrow the issue if mentioned now.

In the first place it is clear, beyond question, that the trustees can sell in parcels or lots, such as single houses. There is no obligation on them to sell together all that is comprised in one title. This is plain from the terms of the trust for sale and section 13(1) of the Act of 1893.

Secondly, a mere power of sale will not normally import a power to alienate the property in question for some lesser interest than that held. For example, if A holds Blackacre in fee simple upon trust for sale, this does not empower A to lease for a long term of years.

But thirdly, what is essentially a sale, that is to say, what is substantially an alienation of the interest held, may be carried out by vesting in the purchaser an interest which is technically less if that is a proper conveyancing expedient for completing the transaction. The limits of this proposition have not been very precisely defined and I must now turn to the principal decisions on which it is founded.

In *In re Webb* [1897] 1 Ch. 14, 149, part of the property held under a lease was sold by auction subject to a condition that the purchase should accept an underlease for the unexpired term less three days at an apportioned ground rent. The question for decision was whether the vendor's solicitor was entitled to a further scale charge in respect of the rent. Stirling J. held that he was not on the ground that the transaction, though in the form of an underlease, was in fact a sale, and in the course of his judgment he said this: "Then, is it a lease? In a sense, no doubt, it is a lease, but in truth it is a sale. It is described as a sale in the conditions of sale, and it is so described in the plaintiffs' bill of costs. It is a sale carried out by an underlease, which is a well-known conveyancer's expedient, where the property sold is held with other property under one lease, to avoid an apportionment of the rent, about which there might be a difficulty with the superior landlord."

Then in *In re Judd and Poland and Skelcher's Contract* [1906] 1 Ch. 684, the Court of Appeal in England held, overruling the decision of Kekewich J. in *In re Walker and Oakshott's Contract* [1901] 2 Ch. 383, that trustees for sale who had sold some but not all of the houses held under a single lease could validly exercise their trust for sale by granting sub-leases of the houses sold at apportioned rents. Romer L.J. said [1906] 1 Ch. at 690: "I may take it that an underlease in substance is not justified, but where an underlease is a pure matter of a conveyancer's expedient, a method of conveyancing for carrying out a sale, then I cannot see that there is any valid objection to it, especially as I have pointed out that this conveyancer's expedient is the best known method of carrying out such a sale, and the best for the trust estate." Then Cozens-Hardy L.J. said Ibid. 691: ". . . .I think it is a fallacy to say, because trustees for sale are not authorised to grant a lease, that they have not power in a case like this to carry out the sale by means of that which is a mere piece of machinery, viz., the grant of an underlease with a nominal reversion, which is something wholly distinct from what I have, in the course of the argument, ventured to call a real underlease."

In *Alexander* v. *Clarke* [1920] 1 I.R. 47, the matter was considered in this country by O'Connor M.R. In that case the trustees were trustees for sale with a power of leasing for any term of years at such rent and subject to such covenants as they should think fit. It appears that much of the trust estate was held, as here, under fee farm grants and long leases and the question submitted to the court on behalf of the plaintiff, the surviving trustee, was in very similar terms to that which I have to consider in these proceedings. In the course of his argument for the plaintiff Mr. Charles Murphy conceded that a trustee for sale had no implied power of leasing but that the trustee in that case had an unlimited power of leasing, and he submitted that "the plaintiff can combine these two powers, and do what is asked for in the summons." As here, what was proposed was to carry out the sale of certain houses by granting the purchasers sub-grants or sub-leases for long terms in consideration of fines and rents which would in aggregate, exceed the head rent payable under the grant or lease by which the property was held and thus create a profit rent, which could also be sold. The Master of the Rolls was satisfied that this mode of sale was the most advantageous for the trust estate and he then addressed himself to the question whether it was authorised by the trust. He said Ibid. 49: "It has been decided that the ordinary trust for sale does not authorise a mere lease, and so it may be said that the making of a sub-fee-farm grant or lease is in itself not a sale; but the substance of the contemplated transaction must be considered rather than the form." Then, after a reference to section 13 of the Act of 1893, he considered the judgment of Kekewich J. in *In re Walker and Oakshott's Contract* [1901] 2 Ch. 383 and passed from that to the judgments of the Court of Appeal in *In re Judd and Poland and Skelcher's Contract* [1906] 1 Ch. 684. These, he thought covered the case before him. "The object of the trustee," he said [1920] 1 I.R. at 51, "is to dispose absolutely of the entire estate of the testator. He does not propose to make sub-fee-farm grants or sub-leases for the purpose of retaining rents for the trust estate. No doubt, he will carve out sub-interests, but so far as the trust estate is concerned, these will have only a momentary existence, because the rents reserved will also be disposed of. Further, there will not be any liability cast on the trust estate."

The facts of *Alexander* v. *Clarke* [1920] 1 I.R. 47, take the Master of the Rolls' decision somewhat further than the decision in *In re Judd and Poland and Skelcher's*

Contract [1906] 1 Ch. 684. In the latter case no question of a profit rent arose as the rents reserved were apportioned parts of the head rent. In the case before the Master of the Rolls the proposal, as here, was to reserve rents exceeding in the aggregate the head rent. But then – and here so far as I can gather from the report of *Alexander* v. *Clarke* [1920] 1 I.R. 47 is where the similarity between the case and the present ends – the profit rents were to be sold. The Master of the Rolls concludes his description of the proposal before him in the first paragraph of his judgment by saying ". . . .and thus create a profit rent, which could also be sold." That seems vague, but later, when he is applying the decision of the Court of Appeal in England, he apparently takes it for granted that the profit rents will only be held by the trustees for the purposes of realisation because he says ". . . . so far as the trust estate is concerned, these will only have a momentary existence, because the rents reserved will also be disposed of." I therefore think it must be assumed that the Master of the Rolls proceeded on the basis that the scheme which was before him was a scheme for the complete realisation of the estate with any profit rent arising out of the disposal of the houses being sold as well as the houses. It may be observed that the head-note of this case refers to the trustee for sale having an unlimited power of leasing, but I would not gather from the terms of the judgment that this circumstance was one of its foundations. In the present case there is no suggestion as to when the profit rents which it is proposed to create will be sold, and I think I must proceed on the assumption that no immediate realisation is intended and that, until some occasion arises to indicate a different course, the trustees will be content to hold such profit rents as part of the estate and to apply them as income thereof.

In *In re Braithwaite's Settled Estate* [1922] 1 I. R. 71, Wilson J. held that a tenant for life, selling lands held under a fee-farm grant in exercise of the powers conferred by the Settled Land Acts, could sell in lots and carry out the sales by making sub-fee-farm grants or long leases to the respective purchasers. The decision only is reported, but it is clear from the argument of Mr. Megaw, for the tenants for life, that it was an application of the principle enunciated in *In re Judd and Poland and Skelcher's Contract* [1906] 1 Ch. 684, and it is to be noted that the proposal before the court was different from that in *Alexander* v. *Clarke* [1920] 1 I.R. 47, and in the present case, as the rents to be reserved on the sales of the lots were to be such as would amount to the rents reserved by the respective head fee-farm grants.

In the High Court of Eire, in *Sims-Clarke* v. *Ilet Ltd.* [1953] I.R. 39, Dixon J. had to consider the nature of a transaction for the purchase of a portion of leasehold premises, to be carried out by an underlease for the residue of the term save the last day thereof. The question arose on a dispute as to costs and was resolved by a finding that the transaction was really a sale carried out by way of underlease. The learned judge thought the decision in *In re Webb* [1897] 1 Ch. 144 ruled the matter and pointed out that the only possible distinction between that case and the case he was considering was that in the latter the rent reserved was such that, having regard to the other property contained in the head lease, there was a profit rent. Though this decision was as between vendor and purchaser, the point arose, as I have said, on a question of costs and not on a question of title. The vendors seem to have been under no restriction such as might affect trustees for sale, and for that reason the case has not a direct bearing on the matter I have to determine.

Now that it seem to me that the current of authority comes near the present case without quite reaching it, I do not think the power of the trustees can be tested merely by asking what people would call the type of transaction they propose. What they propose may well be spoken of, in common parlance, as a sale, for the testator's interest, under that proposal, would pass substantially to the purchaser. But none of the cases raising a question of title regards that as conclusive in itself. They all rely, in addition, on being able to describe the vehicle of completion, the sub-grant or the sub-lease, as a conveyancing expedient for carrying out the sale. They show that this description will apply where what is sold is part of what is held at a head rent and completion is by a sub-grant or sub-lease at an apportioned rent. And *Alexander* v. *Clarke* [1920] 1 I. R. 47, as I understand it, goes on to say that this description of a conveyancing expedient will still apply where the sub-rents exceed the head rent so as to create a profit rent, *if the scheme of realisation provides, not for the keeping of the profit rent, but for its sale as well.*

The facts of the present case are different in an important respect. The intention, no doubt, includes the eventual covering of the head rents, but it goes beyond that. The proposed transactions are provident and in the interests of the trust because they will each produce a profit in the rent as well as a price that will not suffer on account of that profit element. The reality of that sort of transaction seems to me to be that the trustees will get, and get to keep at their discretion, two things for every house sold – (1) the price, and (2) an investment in the shape of a long-term or perpetuity rent. Now I am unable to see how a power or trust for sale, without more, can authorise the acquisition or holding of such an investment. Take the case of trustees with a trust for sale of five houses held under one title, and with a power of investment limited to government stock. If they hold in fee simple it is difficult to see how they could sell each house by fee-farm grant or long lease for a fine and a rent. Not only would such a course not be called for as a conveyancing expedient, but the trustees would have no power to invest in land. If, however, they themselves held in fee-farm or for a long term at a rent of, say, £10 there is no doubt that they could sell, at any rate four of the houses, for a fine and a sub-rent of £2 each. That would be a proper and recognised way of proceeding to realise the entirety. But suppose the houses can only be sold as they fall vacant and there can be no settled scheme of selling the entirety, how could the trustees sell for a fine and, say a £5 rent? Ex hypothesi, they have not the power to change from one form of landed property into another.

And so, if the trustees here had no power to put the proceeds of realisation into anything but stocks and shares. I would conclude that they had not power to do what they propose. But in fact they have power to invest in rents. Does this justify a different answer to the question posed? In my opinion it does. What they propose is (a) to use a method of alienation that is justified by the title under which they hold, (b) to dispose, not of the entirety of the testator's interest, but of such a substantial part thereof as to warrant describing the transaction as a sale, and (c) to retain what remains of that interest for the time being as an authorised investment.

I see no sound reason why the trustees should not do that. It is a sensible way of realising what can be realised, it is beneficial to the trust estate and, as I read this will, it is authorised by the joint effect of the trust for sale and the power of investment. In short, what they propose is to carry out what is, in substance, a sale by what, in view of the title and their powers of investment, can fairly be regarded as a proper conveyancing expedient.

I would therefore answer the question submitted in the affirmative, the term sub-fee farm grant being, of course, related to property held under grant and the trustees remaining under an obligation to consider each sale on its merits and in the light of prevailing conditions.

Notes and Questions

Would it have made any difference if there had been no express powers in the will? Was the fact that the trustees were trustees *for sale* significant ?

See further *Irish Land Law,* para. 10.015 *et seq.*

II. INSURANCE

RE KINAHAN'S TRUSTS

[1921] 1 I.R. 210 (Chancery Division)

This was an application by trustees for the purposes of the Settled Land Act, 1882, to the Court that they be authorized pay out of capital moneys the premium on an insurance of a mansion house against a damage or fire arising out of riot or civil commotion, the subject-matter of the trust, situated in a disturbed district.

Powell J. :

I have no doubt whatever that I have jurisdiction to make the order, having regard to the emergency that has arisen Romer L.J., in *In re New* [1901] 2 Ch. 534, at p.544, says : "In the management of a trust estate, it not infrequently happens that some peculiar state of circumstances arises for which provision is not expressly made by the trust instrument, and which renders it most desirable, and it may be even essential, for the benefit of the estate and in the interest of all the cestuis que trust, that certain acts should be done by the trustees which in ordinary circumstances they would have no power to do. In a case of this kind, which may reasonably be supposed to be one not foreseen or anticipated by the author of the trust, where the trustees are embarrassed by the emergency that has arisen, and the duty cast upon them to do what is best for the estate, and the consent of all the beneficiaries cannot be obtained by reason of some of them not being sui juris or in existence, then it may be right for the Court, and the Court in a proper case would have jurisdiction to sanction on behalf of all concerned such acts on behalf of the trustees." In the present case, I am satisfied that an emergency has arisen. A duty is cast on the trustees, and it is right for the Court "to sanction on behalf of all concerned" the acts proposed to be done. In ordinary circumstances the trustees would not be justified in doing what is supposed in this case, but in the circumstances I am satisfied that I have jurisdiction to make the order, and I therefore sanction the payment of this insurance premium out of capital, that is to say, out of the proceeds of the sale of the lands.

Notes

1. As regards the usual method of payment, *i.e.* out of income, see s.18 of the 1893 Act, p.000, *ante* ; also *Irish Land Law,,* para. 10.019.
2. As regards "emergency" or "salvage" jurisdiction, see further, p.633, *post.*

III. COMPOUNDING LIABILITIES

RE BOYLE

[1947] I. R. 61 ; 82 I. L.T.R. 115 (High Court)

The facts are set out in the judgment.

Overend J. :

The testator, Thomas Boyle, of "Clevedon," Terenure Road, Rathgar, was an old man, aged about 88 years, at the date of his will, 22nd March, 1941. His second wife had died some two years before and he had long retired from business. He had no family, but several nephews and nieces, and after his wife's death a maid, Elizabeth Hayden, kept house for him and looked after him.

By his will he revoked previous wills and appointed Mr. Alfred McCullagh and the defendant Charles B.W. Boyle, executors and trustees, and bequeathed to the former £100 for his trouble in acting as executor.

He directed his executors to sell "Clevedon" and his investments and to pay his debts, funeral and testamentary expenses.

He bequeathed the following legcies :– To Elizabeth Hayden £40 free of duty. £200 each, to his nieces Jean Boyle, Alice K. Wallace, the plaintiff, and Caroline Slack. £200 each, to his nephews Frederick William Sloane, Thomas Boyle Carson and James Boyle ; and £100 each, to his nieces Edith Byrne and Rebecca Crick, and he appointed the plaintiff, Alice Wallace, his residuary legatee. The defendant, George A. Sothern, is not referred to anywhere in the will.

Ten months later, on the 27th January, 1942, the testator made a codicil whereby he revoked the appointment of Mr. McCullagh as executor and also the bequest to him, and appointed the defendant, George A. Sothern, in his place and bequeathed to him the sum of £50 for his trouble in acting as executor.

The testator died upon the 6th May, 1943, and upon the 27th September, 1943, probate was granted to the defendants, the executors named in the codicil, and duty was paid on the assets on a valuation of £4,419 odd.

The solicitor on record for the defendants is Mr. Cyril A. Boyle, a son of the defendant, C.B.W. Boyle. After the son was admitted to the profession some years before the war he was employed by his father, with permission to carry on, for his own benefit, any business given to him personally, and to have the free use of his father's office and staff for such purpose. After the outbreak of war Mr. Cyril A. Boyle joined the R.A.F. and before leaving, his father agreed to act gratuitously on his behalf, as his agent, and to transact any business given him without any fee or reward of any kind.

The defendants agreed that Mr. Cyril A. Boyle should be employed as solicitor and the administration of the estate conducted by his father as such agent, until he should be demobilised.

The probate was extracted in Mr. Cyril Boyle's name and all subsequent correspondence and proceedings were conducted in his name though in fact carried on by his father. The plaintiff's solicitors were all along well aware of Mr. Cyril Boyle's absence "on active service" and that the defendant, C. B. W. Boyle, was "carrying on this matter in his son's name and on his behalf." (See letter 4th July, 1945.) However, they raised no point or objection prior to receiving the bill of costs on the 6th July, 1945, and to the end addressed their letters to Cyril A. Boyle. They do not appear to have been fully apprised of the precise business arrangements between father and son and assumed they were partners until the true position was stated by the defendant in his affidavit, which is uncontroverted.

In this case the arrangement has proved inconvenient and has led to an unfortunate unreality in the correspondence and entries, in the effort to give it full effect, e.g. "my father tells me that," "I have advised my father," etc., etc., when in fact no communication had been made one way or other. Fortunately this created no misapprehension on the part of the plaintiff's solicitors.

Having thus made the true position clear, I can refer to the "defendants' solicitor," which means Mr. Cyril Boyle acting by his father, the defendant, as his agent.

About five weeks after the testator's death the defendant, Sothern, furnished to the defendant's solicitor a claim, dated 14th June, 1943, for £337 10s. 0d., for work and labour done, and services rendered to the testator, by his instructions, between the 5th January, 1939, and 5th May, 1943. [His Lordship read the claim.]

It is to be noted that there is no suggestion that the testator ever did make any payment to this defendant for his services, or every promised to pay a reasonable, or indeed any sum, beyond the statement that the work was done "on the testator's instructions." It is clear no figure was agreed, for the claimant says "I would consider 30s. per week a reasonable sum . . . "

It is not suggested that the defendant ever asked the testator himself for any payment during this protracted period of almost four and a half years and it is to be noted that in January, 1942, after three of those years had expired, the testator bequeathed to Mr. Sothern a legacy of £50 free of duty "for his trouble in acting as executor," but no other sum.

On the 11th August, 1943, the defendants' solicitor wrote to the plaintiff saying "Amongst the debts is a sum of £337 10s. 0d., due to Mr. Sothern for services rendered to the deceased from the 5th January, 1939, to the 6th May, 1943." Then follows a *resumé* of the claim and the letter concludes "My father, who is one of the executors, tells me that he knows Mr. Sothern gave all his time and attention, and sacrificed his evenings, summer and winter, looking after the deceased and shortly before the deceaseed died he assisted the maid and got outside help. I will be glad to hear from you that you approve of this debt being paid as I have advised my father that it is honestly due."

This letter indicates Mr. Charles Boyle's attitude of mind at that time, viz., that he was aware of services rendered so extensive as to create an obligation to reward them. It does not appear that the testator considered Mr. Sothern's name either as a beneficiary or creditor when making his will, in 1941, and the legacy given him by the codicil is expressly given for his trouble in acting as executor. It is clear, therefore, that so far as the testator was concerned, these protracted services remained still unremunerated.

The plaintiff replied to the letter of 11th August, 1943, on the 16th August. She asks did Mr. Sothern make an agreement with the testator; a matter she thought unlikely? She also said she did not consent to Mr. Sothern's "debt being admitted for payment." Mr. Boyle in his letter of 19th August, 1943, emphasises the personal attendance by Mr. Sothern on the deceased and adds that, as he is instructed, the deceased should have had a male nurse for two years prior to his death. To this the plaintiff replied on the 28th "that the position now adopted by Mr. Sothern in no way resembles the position previously mentioned" and that her question (i.e. whether there was any agreement) remained unanswered. On the 31st August, Mr. Boyle replied stating there was no written agreement between the deceased and Mr. Sothern.

On the 16th September, 1943, the plaintiff's solicitors wrote to Mr. Cyril Boyle stating that as there was no agreement, the plaintiff instructed them to dispute Mr. Sothern's claim, unless he was able to satisfy them that the amount claimed was properly due, and giving formal notice that the plaintiff reserved the right to take action if it was paid.

It is unnecessary to review the voluminous correspondence further, in regard to this matter; it is sufficient to say that the plaintiff never receded from the position she had taken up.

The plaintiff had also required "Clevedon," which the deceased directed to be sold, to be handed over *in specie,* and the executors, when sending a case to counsel in October, 1943, on this point, also asked counsel to advise whether Mr. Sothern was entitled, not only to claim, but to retain, his own debt out of the assets, leaving it to the plaintiff to take whatever proceedings she might be advised. To which counsel replied that if the co-executor considered the claim honest and fair this course could be adopted. (This case was put in without objection.)

Accordingly on the 7th March, 1944, a cheque for £337 10s. 0d., was drawn in Mr. Sothern's favour, signed by him and his co-executor.

Before parting with it, however, a further case on this point only, was sent to senior counsel, who after referring to s. 21 of the Trustee Act, 1893, and the decision in *In re Houghton* [1904] 1 Ch. 622, suggested (as I read the opinion) that if further and better details were furnished the defendant, Boyle, might serve the estate well by effecting a compromise, although not satisfied byond all doubt as to the validity of the claim. I assume that counsel meant compromise as an alternative to litigation. (This case was also entered without objection.)

There is no question that an executor has power to compromise even a doubtful claim, if he *bona fide* believes it to be in the interest of the estate. This is clear from the use in the statute of the words "debt or claim" and again "settle any debt, account, claim, or thing whatever . . . " in the section itself (and see *In re Warren ; Weedon* v. *Reading* 32 W.R. 916).

Whatever the reason, the cheque was not handed to Mr. Sothern until the 3rd July, 1945, fifteen months later.

The plaintiff's solicitors in March, 1945, and subsequently, were pressing to have the estate wound up and on the 5th July, 1945, the defendants' solicitor furnished his costs, on the 9th the executors' account (showing the cheque to Mr. Sothern), and on the 25th July, a copy of the residuary account.

No exception seems to have been taken to the payment to Mr. Sothern from the date of the receipt of the executors' account until the issue of the summary summons on the 29th November, 1945, claiming administration, and an enquiry what sums (if any) were due by the testator at the date of his death to the defendant, Sothern, and that the defendants be ordered to account for all sums paid to, or retained by, him.

The plaintiff's counsel say that the alleged compromise is invalid because:– 1. The executors had no sufficient proof of any debt legally recoverable, and they rely on the decision in *Cleary* v. *Sibley* 46 I. L. T. R. 25 – that was not a case of a claim by an executor, nor of compromise or payment by an executor under the Trustee Act. 2. Want of corroboration – which they contend is essential unless the claimant's case is supported by evidence other than the claimant's. This is not the law if the Court is satisfied that the claimant's evidence may be accepted as trustworthy. (See *Minister of Stamps* v. *Townend* [1909] A. C. 633.) 3. The compromise was improper – payment in full cannot be regarded as a compromise if there is room for doubt, – Kekewich J. refused to accept this view in *Houghton's Case* [1904] 1 Ch. 622.

The defendants' counsel rely on s. 21 of the Trustee Act, 1893, the decision in *In re Houghton ; Hawley* v. *Blake* [1904] 1 Ch. 622, and the affidavit of the defendant, C. B. W. Boyle. He deposed that from investigations he made, coupled with his own personal knowledge, he was satisfied that the services were rendered and at the request of the deceased; that the amount claimed was less than the deceased would othewise have had to pay for the like services, and was reasonable, and having so satified himself that the claim was fair, honest and sustainable, he came to the conclusion that it ought to be paid, and did so in all good faith.

This the defendants contend ends the matter. The section says:– "An executor . . . may pay or allow any debt or claim on any evidence that he thinks sufficient." Mr. Boyle has done so and his affidavit is uncontradicted, and there is no suggestion that he did not act in good faith.

This appears to have been the contention put forward by Lord Warrington as counsel in *Houghton's Case* [1904] 1 Ch. 622, and this possible view of the Act was adumbrated by Sir George Jessel M.R. in *Re Owens; Jones* v. *Owens* 47 L. T. 61 at p. 64, but in my opinion it is not supported by the decision in *Houghton's Case* [1904] 1 Ch. 622. In that case the widow, Mrs. Blake, had possession of securities to the value of £1,180 which she claimed as hers. She had produced evidence showing that she was entitled to the amount claimed, from her father's estate or her mother's, and receipts which showed that of this amount £820 was clearly her separate estate; as to the balance there was no evidence, apart from her own testimony, that she was entitled for her separate use. The co-executor was entitled to treat the reciepts for £820 as corroboration of her entire claim. (See *Minister for Stamps* v. *Townend* [1909] A. C. 633.)

The co-executor had admitted the widow's claim to £1,180 and Kekewich J. refused to hold he was wrong in so doing. He says he would be infringing the rule that each executor represents the estate for all purposes, if he held that one executor could not compromise the claim of his co-executor, and he concludes:– "Whether I take the case simply on his executorial power, or whether I take only the last statute to which I have referred [The Judicial Trustees Act, 1896], it seems to me that I must uphold this executor as having done what is right."

I think that I may possibly be differing to some extent from the opinion of that very experienced judge, but I cannot help the feeling that he was affected by the fact that 70 per cent. of the claim had been conclusively established by documents.

Co-executors are regarded in law as one individual: Bac. Abr. Vol. 3, Tit. "Executors and administrators," D. 1, p. 30; Lord Eldon in *Chapman* v. *Turner* 2 Eq. Cas. Abr. 450; Vin. Abr. Vol. 2, Tit. "Executors," D. 2, p. 72; Halsbury: Laws of England, Vol. 14, p. 235 ; Williams on Executors, 11th Ed., Vol. 1, p. 708. That is the reason one can bind all executors and can give a good discharge for a debt: *Smith* v. *Everett* 27 Beav. 446 or assign a term: *Simpson and Others* v. *Gutteridge* 1 Madd. 609. One executor therefore cannot exercise a right of retainer to the prejudice of the other, and a retainer by one can be claimed by all: *Chapman* v. *Turner* 2 Eq. Cas. Abr. 450, (and see *In re Gilbert* [1898] 1 Q. B. 282; Halsbury: Laws of England, Vol. 14, p. 256).

Could a sole executor when called on to account by the residuary legatee justify a retainer of the amount he claimed by saying "I allowed my claim on evidence that I thought sufficient and I rely on the Trustee Act, s. 21"? If so the Act would make him judge on his own cause. If there are two executors A and B can one allow the claim of the other, the two being but one individual? If so A can allow or compromise B's claim, and B allow or compromise A's, and the residuary legatee could not have either scrutinised or investigated. The proposition put in this way, appears to me only to require to be stated to prove its unsoundness, and I think this is the explanation of the passage quoted from the opinion of the Privy Council delivered by Sir Barnes Peacock in *de Cordova* v. *de Cordova* 4 App. Cas. 692, at p. 703, which says:– "It is unnecessary to consider whether the doctrine [i.e. that executors and trustees cannot deal with themselves] is applicable to a case in which several executors compromise a debt due from one of them, or how far such a compromise if beneficial to the estate will be excused and upheld by the Court ..." This was nineteen years after the passing of Lord Cranworth's Act.

But in *Houghton's Case* [1904] 1 Ch. 622 the claim was against the executor of the testator who had compromised with his co-executor, the testator's widow. He was also executor of the widow. The case was fought on the grounds that one executor cannot compromise with another, and that payment in full is not a compromise.

In my opinion the true position is clearly stated by Sir Page Wood V.C. in *Hill* v. *Curtis* L. R. 1 Eq. 90, at p. 98 dissenting from a *dictum* of Lord Cottenham's in *Carmichael* v. *Carmichael* 2 Ph. 101, at p. 103. The Vice-Chancellor says "It is plain that an executor cannot discharge himself by accounting to his co-executor, because he is himself authorised, and it is his duty, to see how the assets are applied. When he has paid over the assets he is not discharged. . . ."

An executor cannot divest himself of his office, or his duties and responsibilities, he cannot absolve himself from liability to account, except by accounting to beneficiaries entitled to call for an account. How can Mr. Sothern refuse to account for the £337 10s. 0d., of the assets retained by him and in his own hands? Is it enough to say "I satisfied Mr. Boyle, my co-executor"? In my opinion it is not enough; it is a *devastavit* on the part of an executor to pay a debt which is not legally enforceable: *In re Rownson; Field* v. *White* 29 Ch. D. 358, – subject to an exception in favour of payment of a statute-barred debt. See Halsbury: Laws of England, vol. 14, pp. 251, 258. In my opinion it cannot be held to be a *devastavit* for an executor, acting *bona fide,* to pay a claim on evidence which he thinks sufficient, because he is protected by s. 21, sub-s. 1 of the Trustee Act, 1893. Suppose for instance that an executor acting *bona fide* pays a claim made by his co-executor, apparently vouched by documents under the testator's hand, will the section not protect him though the documents afterwards turn out to have been forged by the co-executor? But will it also protect the forger? I find nothing in the statute to relieve an executor from the duty of justifying a retainer made by him – though it may, and I think it does, absolve a co-executor who assents to it *bona fide.* It is a remarkable feature of this case that the defendant, Mr. Sothern, has not himself attempted to justify the payment of £337 10s. 0d. to him by his own testimony. He has not deposed that he undertook to do any work for the deceased, on the basis that he would be remunerated, or that the deceased asked him to do any of the work on the understanding, express or implied, that he would be paid for it, he has not even stated on oath what work he did. He has merely made a claim and left it to his co-executor to justify his action in allowing it. It was contended that if Mr. Boyle was justified in paying Mr. Sothern's claim, as I think he was, if followed necessarily that Mr. Sothern was justified in retaining the money without accounting. As I have indicated I cannot share this view. If there was any debt legally payable it arose from a contract, express or implied, between the deceased and Mr. Sothern. The deceased is dead, and the other party to the contract has refrained from giving any evidence. In the circumstances I can see no answer to the claim of the residuary legatee for "an enquiry as to what sum (if any) was due by the deceased at the date of his death to the defendant, George A. Sothern," and I shall direct such enquiry accordingly. This will afford Mr. Sothern an opportunity of supporting his claim by his own testimony and stating the facts as to what passed between him and the testator.

This brings me to the second point raised, the objection as to costs.

As Mr. Harris pointed out, the plaintiff's solicitors at the date of the summary summons were not clear as to the business relationship between Mr. C. B. W. Boyle and his son and were under the impression that a partnership existed. This is not surprising for the names of father and son both appear on the notepaper though when looked at carefully there is nothing which would indicate partnership. Further the father annually renewed his son's licence and did so as "Dublin Agent," but in one year, 1944, the printed alternative description was entirely struck out and the word

"Partner" inserted in writing, which is not Mr. Boyle's and which he cannot identify, though "Dublin Agent" was always the prior and subsequent description.

Mr. Boyle's affidavit has now explained the true relationship and his statement has not been questioned. It seems to me a most natural thing that a father should endeavour to preserve the post-war interests of a son who, as a volunteer, was serving in that branch of the British Forces which bore the highest percentage of casualties in the last war.

That, however, has nothing to do with the case. It is fair to the plaintiff to say that some months after the copy of the bill of costs was furnished to her solicitors, and shortly before the issue of the summons, an offer was made, and on its refusal she relied on her strict rights, whatever they might be, and that is the question I have to decide, a question which it appears is entirely novel, for no similar case has been cited, nor have I been able to find one.

Mr. Cyril Boyle, the solicitor on record for the defendants, may not, and probably did not, know more of the case than its name, and that his father was conducting it for his benefit. His father has done the entire work personally at his own expense. He had told his son he would do all work personal to him gratuitously, as his agent, and he had done so with his son's acquiescence and no doubt grateful consent.

If Mr. Cyril Boyle had been here and had done the work himself no question could arise; he would be clearly entitled to the costs, subject to taxation, for his father does not participate directly or indirectly in the profits of his personal work. This is clear from the decision of Wood V.C. in *Clack* v. *Carlon* 30 L.J. Ch. 639. This is an even stronger case. On the other hand, if Mr. C. B. W. Boyle had acted as solicitor for the executors it is plain he could get no profit costs, for as executor he would be subject to the rule and he could make no profit from his position.

What is the law when a principal, who can lawfully make a profit, employs an agent, who could not be allowed to make a profit, to do all the work?

In my opinion a principal who acts by an agent, who is under a disability, cannot claim to be in any better situation than his agent. So far as I know this is a new proposition and I propound it with some diffidence.

I think, however, that it is involved in the statement of the law as laid down by Lord Cranworth in *Broughton* v. *Broughton* 5 De G. M & G. 160.

He says (at p. 164):–"The rule applicable to the subject has been treated as the bar as if it were sufficiently enunciated by saying, that a trustee shall not be able to make a profit of his trust, but that is not stating it so widely as it ought to be stated. The rule really is, that no one who has a duty to perform shall place himself in a situation to have his interests conflicting with that duty and a case for the application of the rule is that of a trustee himself doing acts which he might employ others to perform, and taking payment in some way for doing them. As the trustee might make the payment to others, this Court says he shall not make it to himself; and it says the same in the case of agents, where they may employ others under them. The good sense of the rule is obvious, because it is one of the duties of a trustee to take care than no improper charges are made by persons employed for the estate. It has been often argued that a sufficient check is afforded by the power of taxing the charges, but the answer to this is, that that check is not enough, and the creator of the trust has a right to have that, and also the check of the trustee. The result, therefore is, that no person in whom fiduciary duties are vested shall make a profit of them by employing himself, because in doing this he cannot perform one part of his trust, namely, that of seeing that no improper charges are made. The general rule applies to a solicitor acting a a trustee, and the only question is how far the circumstances of the present case take it out of this rule."

Now in the present case the will, which I assume was drafted by the defendant, Mr. C. B. W. Boyle, refrains from authorising the executor to act as solicitor and charge the usual professional charges, a clause frequently inserted, and while both will and codicil give legacies to the person to him for his trouble in acting. Yet he has proved the will and he has undertaken the burden of acting as executor without any benefit to himself, directly or indirectly. The case is not one in which there is a conflict of duty and interest such as Lord Cranworth referred to, but in my opinion it is a case where there is a conflict of duty and duty.

His duty as agent to his son was to do all the work in connection with administration, which his son might have done if here to do the work personally; while his duty as executor was, as Lord Cranworth pointed out, to keep an additional check on professional charges. The correspondence and the bill of costs, as drawn, contain a number of illustrations of the difficulty created by Mr. Boyle's dual capacities. Mr. Boyle, as executor, could not also act as solicitor and be entitled to profit costs, and I do not see that his son can be in any better position. In my opinion when Mr. Boyle became executor and proved the will he created in himself an inherent incapacity to earn profit costs in this administration either for himself or anyone else; therefore, when Mr. Cyril Boyle agreed that his father should act for him as agent, he was employing a person who, in this particular case, was under a disability peculiar to this case, viz., that he could earn no profit costs.

It seems to me unfortunate that the plaintiff's solicitors, who appear to have been under the impression that the father and son were in partnership, did not raise this point at an earlier stage when it would have been possible for Mr. Cyril Boyle to appoint another agent to act for him in this case and to participate to some extent in the legitimate profit costs of administration when taxed. However, that point may not have occurred to them although they were aware from the first of Mr. Cyril Boyle's absence and that his father was doing the entire work, as they then assumed, as partner. That this does not amount to such acquiescence as would disentitle the plaintiff to raise the point is clear from *Broughton's Case* 5 De G. M & G. 160 in which the solicitor executor was originally employed to do the work by the testator himself, and continued to do it at the express request of the sole beneficiary, yet Lord Cranworth dismissed his appeal, but without costs – a precedent I am much disposed to follow. However, I shall reserve the question pending the enquiry directed.

Notes

1. See further *Irish Land Law*, para. 10.021.
2. This case involved an executor and note the extension of personal representatives? Powers contained in s. 60 (8) of the Succession Act, 1965, *ibid.* para. 10.022.

IV. LEASING

FITZPATRICK V. WARING

(1882) 11 L.R. Ir. 35 (Chancery Division)

The facts are set out in the judgments.

Law, C.:

This is an appeal from a decree of the Master of the Rolls, and involves the determination of an important though narrow question, viz. whether a trustee of lands, in receipt of their rents and profits, can make an effectual letting of them from year to year. The question arises in this way:–

James Waring, being owner of an estate in the county of Cavan, by his will, dated the 24th May, 1836, devised it to his nephew Richard Waring, in fee, upon trust out of the rents and profits thereof, or by mortgage, to raise a sum of £5000, to be paid to the trustees of the settlement executed on the marriage of the testator's daughter Marion with the Rev. Charles Waring; and subject thereto, upon trust out of the rents and profits, to raise and pay an annuity of £300 to testator's widow for her life; and subject thereto, to hold the lands upon trust for the sole and separate use of the testator's said daughter Marion, for her life, and after her death, if she should have issue her surviving, upon trust for all and any of her children, as she should by deed or will appoint; and in default of appointment, for such children equally as tenants in common in fee, &c. The testator died some time in the year 1842, and thereupon Richard Waring, the trustee, entered into the receipt of the rents and general management of the estate. The testator's widow died many years ago, and so the trust for payment of her annuity ceased to be operative; but the £5000 remained still to be raised, and the trust for that purpose, as well as for the separate use of Mrs. Marion Waring, continued in force until the death of that lady in 1877, soon after which the £5000 was paid off by her son, the Defendant James Waring, to whom she had, in the year 1870, duly appointed these lands in fee, subject to her own life estate, and who accordingly succeeded thereto at her death. Richard Waring, the trustee, seems to have died about the same time as Mrs. Marion Waring, so that it may be assumed that in the year 1877 all the active trusts came practically to an end. Up to the death, however, of Mrs. Marion Waring, in 1877, and the payment by James Waring of the £5000, the duties of the trustee remained subsisting. Now it appears to us that in and prior to 1872, *i.e.* whilst Mrs. Marion Waring, the tenant for life, was living, James Waring held the lands here in question, with others, as tenant from year to year, under Richard Waring, the trustee; but whether at any or what rent is not shown. Being such yearly tenant, and having also the equitable fee-simple in remainder, expectant on his mother's death, he, by lease dated the 31st January, 1872, demised part of the lands to one Michael Shields, to hold for thirty-five years, from the next 1st May, at a rent of £33. In 1875, however, a notice to quit having been served on James Waring by Richard, the trustee, an ejectment was brought by him and Mr. and Mrs. Waring against James Waring and Shields, and judgment having been obtained, an *habere* issued under which James and his subtenant were both evicted, and possession of the lands delivered to Richard Waring. The farm being then vacant, and in the hands of the trustee, he, by deed dated the 17th July, 1875, demised it to the Defendant James Smith, as yearly tenant, at a rent of £43, and Smith accordingly entered and held possession until January, 1878, when Shield brought an ejectment to recover possession of the farm, serving James Waring and a caretaker of Smith's, who alone resided there, but taking no notice of Smith; and the caretaker omitting to take defence, whilst James Waring gave Shields a consent for judgment, Smith was turned out of possession, and the farm re-delivered to Shields, who wisely made haste and sold it to the present Plaintiff, the assignment being dated the 8th February, 1879. In the following month of June, however, Smith brought another action to recover the land; and though the Plaintiff filed his defence, relying on many of the points which he now raises here, Smith got a verdict and judgment in April, 1880, and again obtained possession of the farm. Under these circumstances, the present proceedings were instituted by the Plaintiff in the Chancery Division against Smith and James Waring, making certain charges of fraud and collusion between the Defendants and Richard Waring, which were ultimately abandoned, but insisting that Richard Waring, the trustee, had no power to make an effectual letting of the lands in 1875, as he purported to do, and claiming that the lease of the 31st January, 1872, should be declared valid and subsisting as against the estate of the Defendant James Waring, in priority to the letting of the 17th July 1875, to the Defendant Smith, and that Smith should be declared a trustee for the Plaintiff of any legal estate vested in him by that letting, and for an account of the rents received by the Defendants since the assignment to the Plaintiff, and payment of what might be found due.

The Defendant James Waring did not dispute the Plaintiff's claim. He, in fact, as I gather from his defence, is indifferent as to which of the lettings is to prevail, being willing as far as he is concerned that the Plaintiff should have possession under the lease of 1872 if thought so entitled; and, on the other hand, being equally willing, if Smith's tenancy under the letting of 1875 be established, to let the Plaintiff have the benefit of the £10 additional rent during the remainder of his thirty-five years. Mr. Waring's defence seems to be that the Plaintiff never asked him for either one or the other measure of relief, but commenced his action without making any such application, though, had such been made, he (Mr. Waring) would at once have acceded to it.

The case is thus reduced to a simple dispute between the Plaintiff and the Defendant Smith as to the possession of the farm, and this ultimately depends, as the Master of the Rolls clearly shows, on the question whether Richard Waring, the trustee, had power to make the letting of July, 1875, to the Defendant Smith as tenant from year to year. The Master of the Rolls having considered the question, decided that the trustee had not such power, and has therefore made a decree in the Plaintiff's favour with costs as against the Defendant Smith, and ordered him within a specified time to deliver up possession of the lands to the Plaintiff. From this decree the Defendant Smith has now appealed.

There is one part of the case which I own appears to me not to have been satisfactorily explained, and that is how this controversy which was raised, or at all events might have been raised, in the action of 1879-80 in the Exchequer Division came to be re-opened forthwith by another action in this Division. However, as the Appellant did not press this strongly either here or (according to the Master of the Rolls) in the Court below, I pass it by, and deal with the case on the simple issue – can a trustee of lands holding them upon trust for raising money out of rents and profits, or for paying the rents and profits over to a married woman for her separate use, let the lands from year to year, when from any cause they become vacant and so unproductive of income? But for the respect I have for the learning and sound judgment of the Master of the Rolls, who entertains a contrary opinion, I own I should have no hesitation in answering this question in the affirmative; and having read the report of His Honour's judgment, which has been furnished to us, and carefully considered his reasoning, I still feel unable to concur in his views on this narrow but very important point. What, it may be asked, is a trustee to whom the management of an estate has been committed to do with premises which become tenantless from time to time? If he cannot let them even to yearly tenants, as they probably were let before, must he undertake to farm them himself, and that at no little risk in many ways? Well, the answer given is; – no, he need not assume such labour and responsibility. His proper course is to seek the aid of the Court of Chancery, by which I presume is meant that he should institute an action here for administration and execution of the trusts imposed upon him. Well, putting aside the expense and inconvenience of having to take this course merely to let a farm, I would still venture to ask if a trustee, as such, could not make any letting of even from year to year, however desirable, and for the benefit of the trust, how is it supposed that the Court of Chancery could help him? In the exercise of its jurisdiction for the administration of trusts this Court, I apprehend, has no power to make or authorize any leases or other dispositions of the trust property which the trustee could not have made himself. The Court, in such a case, whether it assumes the place of the trustee, or guides him in the discharge of his duties, is still confined within the limits of the trust as constituted by its author, and has no authority to go beyond those limits. Its business is to *execute* the trusts, not to *alter* them; and if the committing the management of an estate to a trustee did not involve giving him authority to make reasonable lettings (as I believe it does), I do not see what right the Court of Chancery would have to enlarge the conditions of the trust in that respect. That, where property is thus under the control of the Court, it constantly *does* make or authorize such lettings is well known, but this is simply because such a power is inherent in the trust which the Court in such case is carrying into execution. The admitted practice of the Court of Chancery, therefore, in that case, in itself making, or in authorizing the trustee to make, reasonable lettings, instead of showing that the trustee could not make such lettings without the aid of the Court, seems to me to prove the contrary proposition, the only use of the Court being to preclude all future questions as to whether the letting was *in fact* a *reasonable* one or not. We find, accordingly, in all the text books statements to the effect that a trustee, or at least a trustee who, in the discharge of his duties as such, is bound to receive the rents and profits of the property committed to his care, *may* make any reasonable demises of it. The only difficulty of the position is that he or the person taking from him must always be prepared to show, if challenged, that the demise in question *was* reasonable.

In the *Attorney-General* v. *Owen* 10 Ves. 560 Lord Eldon states the matter thus:–"Upon a devise in fee to A in trust for his infant son, to be conveyed to him at the age of twenty-one, and without imposing terms upon the trustees as to the rent, the terms, or the length of the lease, this Court would say the trustee was to do what was reasonable. The Court would [simply] put it upon the trustee and the lessee taking under him to show that the act was reasonable and done in the fair management of the estate." And this, be it remembered, is Lord Eldon's language when discussing, not lettings from year to year, but leases for substantial terms. I am, therefore, not prepared to subscribe to Lord Langdale's or Sir John Wickens' condemnation of the decision in *Naylor* v. *Arnitt* 1 Russ. & M. 501, where Sir John Leach had refused to set aside a trustee's lease for ten years, which, for all that appears in the meagre report of the case, may have been under the circumstances a very reasonable letting. It is also to be observed that, in *Naylor* v. *Arnitt* 1 Russ. & M. 501, the trusts were to receive the rents and pay thereout certain annuities – trusts which therefore involved the active management of the estate – whereas in the cases of *Wood* v. *Patteson* 10 Beav. 541 and *Shaw's Trust* L.R. 12 Eq. 124, before Lord Langdale and Wickens, V.C., there were practically no duties to be discharged by the trustees. They were interposed merely as so much conveyancing machinery, and, besides, their immediate *cestui que trusts* were *sui juris,* and apparently themselves in possession. Under such circumstances it was quite right to decline to sanction the trustee making a sixty years' mining lease in the one case, or even a ten years' lease in the other, especially as in the latter the application was made, not in any properly constituted suit, but merely by way of a special case, and some of the *cestuis que trust* presently entitled were out of the jurisdiction.

But after all the question here is not as to the validity of a lease for ten, twenty, or any other number of years, but as to whether a managing trustee can let at all. For if he has any authority to let it, it must be competent for him to let from year to year, that being the shortest term for which any letting can be made. Now that a trustee, entrusted with the active management of an estate, may so let has, as far as I know, never before been denied. On the contrary the argument of Mr. Pemberton, seeking to set aside the ten years' lease in *Naylor* v. *Arnitt* 1 Russ. & M. 501, was based on the assumption that it was the duty of the trustees there to let the lands from year to year. No case indeed, has been cited by counsel in which the precise point has been decided; but considering how prevalent has been the practice of trustees to make yearly lettings, the absence of any instance in which such a letting has been questioned, may not unfairly be regarded as telling strongly in favour of their validity. There is, too, one reported case in which a letting of this character would certainly have been challenged if it had been thought possible to do so with any success, that is the case of *Ferraby* v. *Hobson* 2 Phil. 255; 16 L. J Ch. 499 before Lord Cottenham. There a testator had died in 1832, having devised his estate to trustees for certain purposes. In 1835 the tenant of one of the farms threw it up, and the trustees, after offering it at £408 to a Mr. West, who refused to take it on these terms, let it at that rent to a Mrs. Rawlins, the sister of one of the trustees, as tenant from year to year. She so held it till Lady Day, 1839, when the trustees having previously served her with notice to quit, and thus determined her tenancy, re-let it to her at an increased rent of £450. A bill was then filed against the trustees by a person beneficially interested in the property, charging collusion between them and the tenant, alleging that the farm had been let at a gross undervalue, and seeking to make the trustees answerable for the higher rent which they might and ought to have obtained. Sir Knight Bruce, V. C., made a decree charging the trustees with £42 a-year more than they had actually got for the three years ending Lady, Day, 1839; and from this there was an appeal. Now, throughout the case, it was assumed and admitted by all concerned, Lord Cottenham included, that when after the testator's death the tenant threw up the farm in question, it was the duty of the trustees to re-let it on a yearly tenancy as before, and the only question was whether in so re-letting it they had got the highest rent which could then reasonably be obtained. Again it was admitted that the moment they had reason to believe that the rent at which they had thus first re-let the farm was too low, it became their duty to serve a notice to quit, and again re-let it from year to year at an increased rent. I venture to think that Lord Cottenham or Sir Knight Bruce, V.C., when so holding that it was the duty of the trustees to let and re-let from time to time, so as to get the best rent obtainable for the trust property, would have been greatly surprised if it had been suggested that the trustees had in fact no power to let at all. It is, however, right to say that Mr. Walker in his able argument took much lower ground than this. He frankly admitted that trustees in receipt of rent and profits could make any reasonable letting; and that this of course might be from year to year. But his contention was that the letting by Richard Waring to Smith in 1875 was not a reasonable one, because the yearly tenancy was not made determinable on the death of Mrs. Marion Waring, the tenant for life. I believe, however, we are all of opinion that such a letting would have been most unreasonable, as it would have been plainly unjust to the tenant for life, for obviously no tenant would pay the full value of a farm for a tenure so absolutely uncertain. Nor can we, I think, regard the Land Act of 1870 as having any bearing on the present question, for if trustees could make yearly lettings before 1870, as I think they clearly might, they can do so still.

On the whole then, both on principle and authority, I am of opinion that the yearly letting made by Richard Waring to the Defendant Smith in 1875 was valid; that the decree appealed from should be reversed so far as regards the Defendant Smith, and the Plaintiff's action be dismissed as against him with costs. If, as would appear to be the case, Mr Waring is willing to secure to the Plaintiff the additional £10 a-year, this may perhaps be sufficiently provided for by the decree; but having regard to the action having been commenced without any previous application to Mr. Waring, and to the unfounded charges of collusion and fraud, I agree with the Master of the Rolls that the Plaintiff should pay his costs in the Court below.

May, C.J.:

The testator James Waring the elder devised the lands in question to Richard Waring and his heirs in fee-simple, upon certain trusts, viz. on trust to raise a principal sum of £5000 by sale or mortgage of the lands, and subject thereto on trust out of the rents and profits to levy an annual sum of £300, and subject thereto on trust to the separate use of Marion Waring for her life, with remainder to such of her children as she should appoint, with a further limitation over in default of such appointment. In 1870 Mrs. Marion Waring made an absolute appointment of the lands to James Waring the younger, one of her sons.

It appears that Richard Waring, the trustee, demised a portion of these lands to the said James Waring the younger, as tenant from year to year; in 1872 James Waring, who was then entitled to this tenancy from year to year in possession, and was also entitled to the estate in remainder, subject to the trusts above expressed, including the estate for life of his mother, demised the lands, with which this suit is conversant, to Michael Shields to hold for a term of thirty-five years, subject to the annual rent of £33. Subsequently Richard Waring determined the tenancy from year to year of James Waring by notice to quit, and recovered possession of the lands demised; and on the 17th of July, 1875, demised the same lands to James Smith, as tenant from year to year, subject to the annual rent of £43. In 1877 Mrs Marion Waring died, and James Waring the younger entered into possession of the estates, and received the rent of £43, payable by the Defenant James Smith. Subsequently, in January 1878, the said Michael Shields brought an ejectment on the title against James Waring and one William Mee, who was then in occupation of the premises in question, as the agent of James Smith. James Smith was not made a party to these proceedings. James Waring and William Mee let judgment go by default, and Shields recovered the possession of the lands. Afterwards, in June, 1879, James Smith brought a counter-ejectment against Shields and the present Plaintiff Fitzpatrick, who claimed as assignee of the interest of Shields. Shields and Fitzpatrick appeared, and filed a defence in which they relied on the equitable title as derived from James Waring the younger. The Defendant James Smith recovered judgment in that ejectment; and this suit was then instituted, in which the Plaintiff, as purchaser from Shields, claims to recover possession of the lands, James Waring and James Smith being made Defendants. Charges of collusion between the Defendants James Smith and James

Waring, contained in the statement of claim, were withdrawn.

The only point apparently relied on in the Court below, as entitling the Plaintiff to relief, was that the creation of the tenancy from year to year in favour of the Defendant James Smith, in 1875, had no legal validity, Richard Waring, the trustee, being incompetent to make any demise of the lands binding on those beneficially entitled to the estate. The Master of the Rolls decided that such tenancy was invalid in equity, and his judgment in favour of the Plaintiff rests entirely on that proposition. And this Court has to consider whether that decision can be maintained.

The question is whether it was competent for Richard Waring to demise the lands, of which he was trustee, to a tenant from year to year. This question is, I think, to be determined, having regard to the true construction, intent, and meaning of the will of 1836. It is certainly true that no express power of leasing was given to the trustee Richard Waring by that instrument. The lands were devised to him upon the trusts above referred to, and it is material to consider the nature of those trusts. In the execution of the trust to raise the sum of £5000 by mortgage it would be absolutely necessary that the trustee should be enabled, after the execution of such a mortgage, to raise the annual interest on the sum borrowed out of the annual rents and profits of the lands; and so the annuity of £300 would be *primâ facie* receivable out of the same rents and profits, and be payable by the trustee to the annuitant; and so also the residue of the rents and profits would be collectable by the trustee for the benefit of Mrs. Marion Waring entitled to her separate use. I think it may be assumed that the estates were in the hands of the tenants. Supposing any of these tenancies to determine, whether by ejectment for non-payment of rent, by efflux of time, or by surrender, and thus the possession of parcels of these lands to become vacant, how was the trustee to receive the annual rents and profits of the lands so vacated? It seems to me that the maxim, that the grant of any subject-matter includes by implication a grant of all powers necesary for the enjoyment of such grant, applies to a case such as the present, and that the will of 1836 should be held impliedly to confer on the trustee such power as was necessarily required in order to enable him to discharge the active duties imposed upon him, including, in the present case, a power to demise vacant and untenanted lands, so as to make them produce an income; and it is, I think, all important to consider the character of the trusts reposed in the trustee.

The case was in the present instance treated in the Court below as one almost closed by authority. I have examined the authorities to which the Court has been referred, and consulted other cases and the text books, and I will shortly refer to those principally relied upon as supporting the decision of the Master of the Rolls.

In the case of *Naylor* v. *Arnitt* 1 Russ. & M. 501 Sir John Leach supported a lease for ten years, made by the trustee, as a reasonable lease. In that case the lands in question were devised to the trustee, upon trust out of the yearly rents and profits to raise two annuities of £60 and £10, and subject thereto, upon trust to permit and suffer William Naylor and his wife to receive the rents for their lives, with remainder in favour of their children. The case was argued by Mr. Pemberton on the one side, and Mr. Bickersteth on the other, counsel of the very highest eminence; and it apparently was assumed by the counsel on both sides that it was quite competent to a trustee under such circumstances to demise the lands from year to year. The only question was whether it was within the power of the trustee to bind the inheritance by an absolute term of ten years. It is to be observed that in that case the trustee was directed to raise the annuities out of the annual rents and profits.

In the case of *Wood* v. *Patteson* 10 Beav. 541 a testator devised some mining property of which he was seised in fee, subject to a term of ninety-nine years, to a trustee, on trust to divide the rents among his four daughters for life, with remainder to their children. The term of years expired, and the tenants for life found they could not work the mines with a profit. Some of the children entitled in remainder were infants. Application was made to the Court to authorize the trustee to grant a mining lease of sixty years. Lord Langdale declined to make such an order. In that case authority was asked from the Court to make the lease as being for the benefit of the minors, and the decision did not turn upon the powers of the trustee, but upon the jurisdiction of the Court to order such a lease to be made. It does not appear to me that that case bears upon the point argued before the Court.

In *Re Shaw's Trusts* L.R. 12 Eq. 124 the testator, after giving legacies and annuities, gave the residue of his estate and the annual produce thereof to trustees on trust, as to one-third, to pay the income to a nephew for his life, and after his death to his children, and the other two-thirds to two other nephews and their children in the like manner. The case came before the Court on a special case one of the questions being, whether the trustees were entitled to lease the real estate for any and what term. Vice-Chancellor Wickens doubted the decision in *Naylor* v. *Arnitt* 1 R. & M. 501, and declined to answer this question. The Vice-Chancellor expressed no opinion as to the power of the trustees to demise the lands from year to year, and it can hardly be contended that this case can be relied on as an authority in support of the decision of the Master of the Rolls.

I can find no authority, not even a *dictum,* that a trustee in whom an estate is vested upon such trusts as exist in this case, cannot make valid demises of the trust property for tenancies from year to year. Such a doctrine would, I think, lead to most inconvenient consequences. I think the decision of the Master of the Rolls on this point cannot be supported.

A good deal was said in argument as to the extensive rights and interests which, under the Land Acts of 1870 and 1881, had become vested in tenants from year to year. It is, I think, enough to say that this question must be determined as if the case had arisen shortly after the date of the will. If that instrument gave by implication a power to demise the lands from year to year, the trustee had such a power under it when it came into operation, and could not afterwards be deprived of it because the legislature subsequently conferred rights and privileges on tenants from year to year.

On the whole, I think that upon this point, which was the only point argued before us, the decision of the Master of the Rolls must be reversed.

Deasy, L.J.:

Assuming that the case set up by the Plaintiff is open to him after the adverse decision of the Exchequer Division in the action in which it was distinctly raised – a decision to which the Plaintiff was a party, and from which he never appealed to this Court – I think it is not well founded in law. There is no authority for the proposition on which the Plaintiff relies, that a trustee of a landed estate occupied by tenants cannot in any case let a part of that estate to a yearly tenant during the life of the tenant for life, so as to make that tenancy binding on the remainderman. Sir J. Wickens enunciated no such proposition in *Re Shaw's Trusts* L.R. 12 Eq. 124; he simply declined to follow Sir J. Leach's order in *Naylor* v. *Arnitt* 1 R. & My. 501, directing trustees to grant a lease for ten years. In *Wood* v. *Patteson* 10 Beav. 541 the application was for an order sanctioning a mining lease which Lord Langdale declined to make.

In *The Attorney-General* v. *Owen* 10 Ves. 560 Lord Eldon says that trustees are bound to at lease as provident management as a provident owner. This Court would say that the trustee was to do what was reasonable. The Court would put it both upon the trustee and the tenant taking under him to show that the act was reasonable and done in the fair management of the estate.

Applying that test, is not the act reasonable and done in the fair management of the estate? This estate was in the occupation of tenants holding at yearly rents, the trustee had it vested in him upon trust to receive the rents and pay them to a married woman for her separate use. He was in the actual receipt of the rents through his agent, and he appears to have made lettings of other parts of the estate. He had recovered the possession of this part in an ejectment founded on a notice to quit, and was put into the actual possession of it by the sheriff. What was he, then, to do with it? He could not allow it to remain unproductive. He could not be expected to farm it himself. That might involve a loss both to himself and to the trust estate. He could not make a demise of it for less than a yearly tenancy, for that is provided against by the 69th section of the Land Act of 1870. It may be said that he might have made the yearly letting determinable at the death of the tenant for life, but that would be a very improvident arrangement to make. It could not be expected that as high a rent could be got for it as upon an ordinary tenancy from year to year, and the tenant holding by that uncertain tenure would have an interest in getting as much as possible out of the land, and putting as little as possible into it in return. It would, I think, be dangerous to hold that a trustee of an estate held by occupying tenants can never make a yearly letting of any part of it which will be binding upon the parties beneficially entitled.

I concur with the Lord Chancellor and the Lord Chief Justice that the decision of the Master of the Rolls should be reversed.

FitzGibbon L.J.:

I fully concur in the opinion that the authority of an acting trustee of the legal fee must include the power to make reasonable lettings of lands which at the inception of his trust he finds in the hands of tenants, and which during the trust come into his possession. If empowered to let at all, his power must at least extend to the creation of a tenancy from year to year in an agricultural holding, at all events where the holding had been previously so held. There is no authority to the contrary. The cases cited seem to recognize such a power, and without it I do not see how the trusts of landed estates could in many cases be executed. Is the trustee to leave the land unproductive, or to embark upon farming at the risk of his trust fund? The Master of the Rolls says he may come to the Court "for a receiver." If "receiver" is here strictly used, it implies that rents are to be received, and so that lettings are to be made; if it means "manager," it implies that the Court would sanction a trustee's undertaking the actual management of lands previously let to tenants, which I do not think it ought; if it means that the trustee should bring the administration of his trust into Chancery, it leaves the matter where it was, for a trustee may at least do out of Court what the Court would sanction if administering the trusts. The Court ought to sanction only what a trustee could do out of Court. It cannot be laid down that lands can be let only through the machinery of the Settled Estates Acts or of statutory leasing powers, and it remains as the only and, I think, as the necessary conclusion, that an acting trustee of the legal fee may make reasonable lettings of vacant tenantable lands.

It remains to apply this power to the present case, and here I confess I am not altogether satisfied that the Defendant's case has been made out. A *reasonable* letting must be one reasonably necessary for the due execution of the trust on behalf and in the interest, not of one, but of *all* the *cestuis que trust.* It further rests upon the person alleging a tenancy under such a letting to show its reasonableness, having regard to the whole scope of the trusts. Here the lands were let by the remainderman from year to year, and he had bound himself by a lease which would operate, not only on his legal tenancy from year to year, but also on his equitable estate in remainder. The trustee's duty and authority were to act reasonably for all the *cestuis que trust,* and did not enable him to make a letting even from year to year, which would unreasonably involve the remainderman in liability, and which his previous lease forbade the remainderman to make for himself, unless it was reasonably necessary in the interests of the other *cestuis que trust* to disregard the special interest of the remainderman. I am not satisfied that the Defendant has given sufficient proof that, having regard to James Waring's position, it was reasonable to determine his tenancy from year to year, and, when re-letting the lands, to omit a provision that the new tenancy from year to year should determine on the death of the tenant for life so as to leave James Waring's estate in remainder free to meet the lease by which he had bound it. Still I am not so confident upon this as to warrant me in dissenting from the other members of the Court, especially as the letting to the Defendant certainly brought in an increased rent, and was of the same character as that for which it was substituted, as a provision for determination must to some extent have diminished the value of the tenancy, and so *pro tanto* diminished the rent receivable by the tenant for life, and lastly as the great importance of the tenancy from year to year now, as against the Plaintiff and the remainderman, has arisen from legislation subsequent to its creation, and not from any unreasonableness in the letting itself.

I wish to add that I am entirely unable to understand why the point at issue in this suit were not fully discussed and finally decided in the action brought in 1879.

Notes and Questions

1. Would it have made any difference if the trust property had never previously been leased?
2. *Cf.* the power to *renew* leaseholds conferred by s.19 of the 1893 Act, p.545, *ante*. See *Irish Land Law*, para. 10.028.

V. DELEGATION

RE O'FLANAGAN AND RYAN'S CONTRACT

[1905] 1 I.R. 280; 39 I.L.T.R. 87 (Chancery Division)

The facts are set out in the judgment.

Porter M.R.:

This is a summons under the Vendor and Purchaser Act brought by the vendors, asking that it may be declared that a good title has been shown, in accordance with the particulars and conditions of sale, to the premises mentioned in the summons, a licensed house and premises, at Thurles, in the county Tipperary. I shall take the will and deed under which the premises are held as read.

The gift to the widow of the testator is "in trust for herself and the children of our marriage, to be applied by her as she shall deem most expedient." Whatever may be the exact effect of these words, it is clear that some trust is imposed upon the widow, and that she is thus a trustee for herself and the children of the marriage, though with wide discretionary powers. The case is not like *Lambe* v. *Eames* L.R. 6 Ch. 597, for there is a trust; nor *Haley's Trusts* 23 L.R. Ir. 130, for the widow takes some beneficial interest. (In that case the majority of the Court of Appeal held that the legatee took none, though it was not necessary to decide that point, as she died before the testator.) Perhaps it most closely resembles *Crockett* v. *Crockett* 2 Ph. 461. At any rate it is clear that there is a trust; and that the *cestuis que trustent* are the widow and the children of the marriage, and no one else. It is possible, too, that, as the shares (when settled on) could only be worked out by a sale of the property and distribution of the proceeds, the widow, who is also executrix, may have an implied power of sale. I think that this is so. Obviously, however, any such sale ought to be made in perfect good faith for the benefit of the class interested, and no one else. What took place in 1891, on the occasion of the second marriage of Mrs. Maher, was not a sale; nor was it authorised by anything in the will. Mrs Maher had no right to convey away the assets to any delegated trustee. Had she died soon after the execution of the deed of 23rd January, 1891, all the assets would have vested in a stranger, subject only to £1000 charged on them for the children, and to £200 left to the son of the testator's first marriage. The transaction was apparently entered into not for the benefit of the entire class, but for her own benefit mainly if not exclusively by securing for her a second husband. It is not necessary, nor would it be proper, to decide this, but it is needful to refer to it as, at least, an extremely serious difficulty in the way of upholding the transaction, even if it were not plain, as it is, that Mrs. Maher had no right whatever to assign away her trust and the trust estate. Indeed her doing so was in fact a complete breach of trust, independently altogether of the question whether a provision of £1000 for the children was under the circumstances a *bona fide* discharge of her duty to exercise, as trustee, an impartial discretion. The vendors claiming under the deed could not give no valid discharge for the property of the minors; and the offer made subsequent to the sale to procure Mrs. Maher's, or rather Mrs. Rahill's, concurrence in the conveyance to the purchaser was no more than a proposal to obtain her ratification of her own improper dealings with the property. The purchaser would have to pay Patrick O'Flanagan and Martin Rahill for property which did not belong to them, and for which they could give no valid receipt. All this is plain, and in great part, admitted.

But Mr. Wilson's argument is that the purchaser is bound by the conditions of sale, so as to be precluded from raising the question, relying on *Scott* v. *Alvarez* [1899] 2 Ch. 611 and cases of that character. But in *Scott* v. *Alvarez* [1899] 2 Ch. 611, and all the decisions of similar import, the question has arisen upon the effect of positive restrictive conditions,in terms binding the purchaser to admit certain facts or to forgo inquiry or investigation of title before a particular period or the like; whereas no such condition forms part of this contract. The only colour for this contention in the present case is the sixth condition, which is as follows:–"By his will the said William Maher bequeathed (*inter alia*) the said premises to his wife in trust for herself and her children to be applied as she should deem most expedient. To give effect to the trust contained in the said will, Mrs. Maher, on the occasion of her re-marriage, vested (*inter alia*) the said premises to trust to raise by sale or mortgage the sum of £1000 for the benefit of the said children, and in pursuance of this trust for sale the vendors are now selling the said premises, and shall convey the same to the purchaser in their character as trustees and not otherwise, and shall not be bound to obtain the concurrence of any other parties to such conveyance as conveying parties."

This, it is said, fully states the facts, and informs the purchaser of what he is to buy; and as it discloses the title which the vendors are prepared to give, no objection founded upon those facts can be admitted. It states correctly enough the sentence of the will, in reference to the matter in hand, and it shows that title is to be made under the deed of 1891. If that title is bad, it is, at least, the title which alone the vendors are prepared to give, and thus the purchaser is precluded from raising the question.

In my opinion this argument is founded on a fallacy. A purchaser under such a condition is entitled to assume that he is getting a good title if it be possible consistently with what is stated that the title may be a good one; and it is plain that, consistently with what is stated, the title here might be a perfectly good one. He is told that the deed of 1891 was made "to give effect to the trust contained in said will," and that by it Mrs. Maher "vested the premises in the vendors in trust," &c. Anyone reading that condition would be entitled to assume, and would assume, that there was some provision in the will, or in some other instrument of title, enabling Mrs. Maher to make a settlement on the occasion of a future marriage in the way stated; that the transaction in short was (as it is affirmed to be) a giving effect to the trusts of the will, and not a breach of them. When the will came to be examined, the purchaser would expect to find at least some power enabling Mrs. Maher to appoint subsidiary trustees, with authority to give receipts for purchase-money. Had this been the case, the difficulty would not have arisen. As it is, if the title were forced upon the purchaser, he would raise the question against him at some future time, when, being fixed with notice of a breach of trust, he would or might be practically defenceless, being constructively a trustee for the persons entitled under the will, and bound to justify a transaction of the merits of which he would know nothing personally, and which is illegal on the face of it. The will contains no other provision, and no other authority is shown, enabling this thing to be done.

If, then, on the conditions of sale, he was entitled to assume that a power to do what was done would be shown, the meaning of that is that he was entitled to have this by the contract, and as he has not got it, a good title has not been shown pursuant to the conditions of sale.

There must be a declaration accordingly, and the vendors must pay the costs of the purchaser. If it is desired, I shall state on the face of the order that the deed of 1891 was a breach of trust. This will enable Mrs. Maher to call upon the trustees of that deed to re-convey the property to her, and place her in the same position as she was before.

The order, which was made on January 20th, 1905, was as follows:–

"THE JUDGE, being of opinion that the execution of the said indenture of settlement constituted a breach of trust on the part of he said Kate Maher, the settlor, who was a trustee under the said will of William Maher, doth delcare that a good title has not been shown by the said vendors, in accordance with the said particulars and conditions of sale; and doth order that the said purchaser's costs of this application and order be paid to him by the said vendors, when taxed and ascertained."

Notes
See the statutory powers of delegation in s.17 of the 1893 Act, p.544, *ante*. See also *Irish Land Law,* para. 10.030 *et seq*.

VI. MAINTENANCE

RE O'CONNELL'S ESTATE
[1932] I.R. 298 (High Court)

The facts are set out in the judgment.

Kennedy C.J.:
The above-named testator, Timothy Jeremiah O'Connell, died on the 25th of February, 1927, leaving his widow, Hanora O'Connell, and his five children, Jeremiah, then aged eight and a half years, Peter, then aged seven and a half years, Dinah, then aged six and a half years, Eileen, then aged about five years, and Tess, then aged about three and a half years, surviving. He was possesed of a farm of registered land containing 60 acreas 2 roods and 15 perches in County Limerick, bought out under the Land Purchase Act of 1903, subject to a purchase annuity of £23 19s. 6d. He had also on the farm live and dead stock and in Bank a sum of money on deposit receipt in the joint names of his wife and himself. His gross personal estate was sworn for probate at £365. The testator made his will, dated the 1st of February, 1927, which was duly proved on the 30th of June, 1927, by the plaintiffs, Denis O'Connell, David O'Connell and John Leahy, the executors therein named. This summons has been taken out for the construction of the will, which is a very defective piece of drafting, though a reference to the Settled Land Acts suggests that the draftsman may have had some contact with law. I will go through the document clause by clause.

After a direction for payment of debts, funeral and testamentary expenses, the testator appointed the three plaintiffs to be his executors and trustees of his will. He then gave to his trustees all his "moneys, stocks, chattels, securities and farm, including the £200 on deposit receipt in the Munster and Leinster Bank" (which receipt he declared to be his own sole property, though in the joint names of him and his wife) to hold upon trust for his wife until she should re-marry or until his son Jeremiah should reach the age of 30 years, whichever should first occur. The will continued:– "When my son Jeremiah reaches the age of 30 years I give him my farm, stock, household furniture and everything on the lands, for his own use and benefit, but charged with the sum of £100 each in favour of my four remaining children, which sum shall not be payable until they reach the age of 21 years respectively."

The testator's widow, on the 17th of March, 1928, married one, Richard Sheehy, and is now the defendant Hanora Sheehy.

After certain provisions, depending on his wife not remarrying, the testator made the following provisions to take effect in the event of her re-marriage. In the first place, he directed that she should leave the lands, and that she should get from his trustees or from his son, as the case might be, the sum of £100, payable by annual instalments of twenty pounds, the first instalment to be paid on the expiration of six months from the date of her leaving the lands, but he directed the trustees to make good any discrepancy in the amount of the stock on the lands out of the £100 (except for loss by death or disease). The testator then directed that in the event of his wife re-marrying or dying before his son should attain the age of 30 years, his trustees should, if his son should have attained 21 years, hand the bequeathed property over to him, subject to the said charges thereinbefore created, as if 21 years had first been stated, but in case his son Jeremiah should be under the age of 21 years on the happening of either of such events, then he directed his trustees "to manage the place generally until he should attain 21 years."

The testator then directed that in the event of Jeremiah dying before attaining 30 years, the will should be read as if the name of his son Peter had been substituted for Jeremiah throughout, and in the like event of Peter's death the name of his eldest daughter, and so on.

He appointed his trustees to be trustees for the purpose of the Settled Land Acts, and he gave them a discretion to withhold payment of legacies of children requiring payment before Jeremiah should reach 30 years.

Finally, the will contained the following residuary gift:– "I direct all of my moneys to go to Jeremiah on reaching 30 years, but my trustees shall have power to utilise same for payment of the charges in this my will if they think fit."

The first and most important question submitted for determination is as to the disposal of the income of the testator's farm during the period from the end of the widow's beneficial interest to the happening of the event upon which the son Jeremiah will become entitled, a gap left uncovered by the draftsman except as regards management.

Now, it is important to observe that, subject to payment of his debts, funeral and testamentary expenses, the testator begins with a universal residuary gift to his trustees on trust for his wife until she re-marries or their son Jeremiah attains the age of 30 years, but the gift to Jeremiah which follows, to take effect on the happening of either of the events mentioned, is not a residuary gift, but a gift of the farm and stock and everything on the lands, and at the end of the will he makes a separate residuary gift to his son, but on different lines, of all his "moneys."

The rule stated in *Genery* v. *Fitzgerald* Jac. 468 (Lord Eldon) and *In re Dumble; Williams* v. *Murrell* 23 Ch. D. 360 (Pearson J.), is not, in my opinion, applicable to the present case in precisely the way in which it was in argument assumed to apply.

To return to the will, reading it as in the events which have happened, let us see the exact position. On the re-marriage of the testator's widow the general residuary trust in her favour came to an end and the residuary property was severed. The farm with the stock, furniture, and everything on the lands, are taken out of general residue and, subject to five charges of £100 each in favour of the widow and the four other children of the testator, are given specifically to the son Jeremiah contingently on his reaching the age of 21 years, to be managed in the meantime by the trustees, but with no direction as to the disposal of the interim income. The way in which the gift itself is made, the provision for management by the trustees during minority, and the provision for replacement of stock out of the £100 given to the widow on her re-marriage, go to show that the testator made a specific gift of his farm and farming business, "as a going concern" as the phrase is, to his son Jeremiah, contingently on his reaching the age of 21 years, in the events which have happend. Though not a *residuary* gift of real and personal estate "mixed up in one mass," as Pearson J. put it in *In re Dumble; Williams* v. *Murrell* 23 Ch. D. 360, yet (assuming for the moment that a farm bought out and registered is to be considered real estate in this connection) it is a very similar thing, an analogous mixture, for we have real property along with personalty severed from the rest of the estate given to the same person on the same contingency; and a like principle as regards the intention to be inferred would appear to be applicable to the income of the gift as a whole, with the result that the income of the whole should be accumulated until Jeremiah reaches the age of 21 years and should then follow the corpus of the gift as an addition to it.

A question was raised in the course of the argument as to whether registered land was within the rule of *Genery* v. *Fitzgerald* Jac. 468, and it was suggested that there is not authority on the point, which may be so, but one case certainly deserved mention, viz.: *In re John Ferguson, deceased, Curry* v. *Bell* 49 I.L.T.R. 110. There, a testator gave his farm to a nephew (to whom he stood in *loco parentis*), when the nephew should be of age, making no other provision for him. The farm was the subject of an agreement for purchase under the Land Purchase Acts made by the testator and was vested after his death during the nephew's minority. It was argued that the farm should be treated as real estate and *In re Longworth* [1910] 1 I.R. 23 was cited. The late Master of the Rolls, however, dealt with the farm throughout his judgment (as reported) as a chattel real, and, having discussed the question whether the specific bequest of the farm was a sufficient segregation of the subject matter of a contingent bequest to carry the income with the corpus of the gift to the donee under the well-established exception to the rule as to pecuniary legacies, he left the question unanswered and decided the case on the point that it was a bequest by a person *in loco parentis* to the donee, for whose maintenance he made no other provision: *In re Bowlby, Bowlby* v. *Bowlby* [1904] 2 Ch. 685. I do not find it necessary for the purposes of the present case to decide whether a registered purchased holding is to be regarded as realty or as a chattel real, because, however the matter is regarded, and especially having regard to the always paramount intention of the testator so far as it can be ascertained from the will itself, whether the gift is one of realty and personalty (the personalty being clearly segregated from the rest of the testator's property) mixed in a mass to which, in my opinion, a principle analogous to the principle of *Genery* v. *Fitzgerald* Jac. 468 and *in re Dumble; Williams* v. *Murrell* 23 Ch. D. 360 ought to be applied; or is a gift of a specific chattel real and specific personalty so segregated; I am of opinion that the income from the widow's death to the son's majority is carried with the gift not only on principle supplementing or taking the place of express evidence of intention but also by the intention of the testator in so far as I can see actual evidence of that intention in the will itself. If the income were not carried with the gift of the corpus, the question would then arise as to whether such income was not carried by the residuary gift to Jeremiah in the words "all of my moneys." In the view I take, however, it is not necessary to pursue this question.

It follows from the view I have taken of the gift of the farm stock, furniture and property on the lands that the son Jeremiah is entitled during his minority to have the income of that property, or so much of it as may be necessary, applied to his maintenance, education or benefit; any surplus of such income being accumulated to pass with the corpus of the property: Conveyancing Act, 1881, sect. 43; *In re Bowlby, Bowlby* v. *Bowlby* [1904] 2 Ch. 685.

On the other hand, Jeremiah is not entitled to have any provision made for his maintenance out of the property comprised in the gift of "all of my moneys" which is contingent on reaching the age of 30 years and has no reference to his infancy: *In re Abrahams, Abrahams* v. *Brendon* [1911] 1 Ch. 108.

The next question which arises on this will is as to whether the son Jeremiah is to become absolutely entitled to the farm on reaching the age of 21 years or, if not, what estate or interest does he take. It is to be observed that the acceleration of the gift to him by substituting the age of 21 for the age of 30 is in express tems applied only to the first statement of age in the will referring, I think, to the contingency upon which he is to take the benefit of the gift. It has not been made applicable to what follows. Accordingly the provision stands unaltered which says:– "In case Jeremiah shall die before attaining 30 years then I direct that this my will shall read as if my son Peter's name had been substituted for Jeremiah throughout and in the like event of Peter's death then my eldest daughter's name, and so on." The effect of this is that Jeremiah if he reaches the age of 21 years is entitled to go into beneficial possession and enjoyment of the farm and farming stock and business and of the income of the fund constituted by accumulations of the interim income left after providing for his maintenance and education, but that the whole gift is subject to an executory gift over to Peter if Jeremiah should die under the age of 30 years, the gift to Peter being subject to similar contingent limitations. Jeremiah, therefore, will not become absolutely entitled to the property unless and until he reaches the age of 30 years, up to which event the property will continue subject to the trusts of the will which may be applicable in the events that shall have happened.

I now come to the questions which arise as to the four sums of £100 for the testator's other children. The first point to be observed about these gifts is that they are not generally pecuniary legacies but charges, and, secondly, that they are charged both on the farm and on the stock, household furniture, and property on the lands. In the third place, these several charges do not arise until the contingent gift to Jeremiah (or Peter, or as the case may be) takes effect. Fourthly, the several sums are not to be payable until the donees respectively reach the age of 21 years. Fifthly, none of the donees may require and insist on payment before Jeremiah reaches the age of 30 years, an absolute discretion being given to the trustees up to that time, if payment be called for, either to withhold payment or to raise the amount. The trustees are, however, empowered to apply the residuary gift of "moneys" in payment off of these charges, not of course before they become payable, *i.e.*, at the respective donees' ages of 21 years. No other provision was made by the testator for the maintenance of these four children. The questions to be decided upon these charges are two, namely, first whether they are given absolutely or contingently on the respective donees reaching the age of 21 years, and, secondly, whether the donees are respectively entitled to have their maintenance provided for out of the interim interest on the several sums.

In my opinion as a matter of construction of the terms of the will itself, each of these gifts of £100 is a legacy to the donee contingent on his or her attainment of the age of 21 years, charged upon the property given to Jeremiah, payment whereof may be postponed by the trustees until Jeremiah reaches the age of 30 years. If the donees were not children of the testator or persons in whose regard the testator stood *in loco parentis,* the donees would not be entitled to have either interest or maintenance during minority, but upon reaching the age of 21 years would become entitled to interest from the time of reaching that age until payment of the principal sum of the legacy. But inasmuch as the legatees are children of the testator, for whose maintenance he has made no other provision, and to whom the legacies are given respectively on the contingency of attaining the age of 21 years, I am of opinion that these legacies fall within the old rule of practice in the Court of Chancery and that they respectively carry interest during the minority of their several donees, and that the donees are entitled to maintenance out of such interest on their respective legacies, in this case indeed to have the whole of the wretchedly small sums of interest so applied.

The declarations which I must make in answer to the questions in the originating summons will therefore be as follows:–

1. Upon the true construction of the said will and in the events that have happened, the defendant Jeremiah O'Connell is entitled to the testator's farm, stock, household furniture, and everything on the lands, for his own use and benefit, but subject to the several charges of one hundred pounds each if and when he reaches the age of 21 years, subject, however, to an executory gift over to his brother Peter in the event of his (Jeremiah's) dying before he attains the age of 30 years.

2. The said Jeremiah O'Connell is entitled to have the income of the said farm, stock, furniture and other property (after payment of all proper outgoings), or so much of such income as may be required for the purpose, applied for his maintenance, education and benefit, from the date of the re-marriage of the testator's widow until he (Jeremiah) shall attain the age of 21 years; so much of such income as shall not be required for that purpose to be accumulated by the trustees and held upon the same trusts as the said farm and other property.

3. The defendants, Peter O'Connell, Dinah O'Connell, Eileen O'Connell and Tessie O'Connell, are not, nor is any of them, entitled to any part of the rents and profits of the said lands during the minority of the said Jeremiah O'Connell.

4. On the true construction of the said will, there is not an intestacy as to the rents and profits of the said lands.

5. Upon the true construction of the said will each of the sums of £100 bequeathed contingently to the defendants, Peter O'Connell, Dinah O'Connell, Eileen O'Connell and Tessie O'Connell respectively, carries interest as from the date of the re-marriage of the testator's widow until the legatee reaches the age of 21 years, and the legatee is entitled to have such interest applied for his or her maintenance.

6. The defendant Jeremiah O'Connell is not entitled to any part of the income arising from the bequest of the property described in the will as "all of my moneys"

unless and until he reaches the age of 30 years, but all such income must be in the meantime accumulated by the trustees and held upon the same trust as the principle moneys.

7. The defendants Peter, Dinah, Eileen and Tessie O'Connell are not nor is any of them entitled to any part of the said last mentioned income, either now or at any time, if the defendant Jeremiah O'Connell attains the age of 30 years.

8. If the defendant Jeremiah O'Connell attains the age of 30 years, there will not have been an intestacy as to the said income.

The questions submitted were raised by the will on the face of it and this construction summons was unfortunately inevitable. I must give the several parties their costs, to be paid primarily out of the general residuary personal estate. I will reserve liberty to apply, in order to avoid the expense of a new summons, if the happening of any other contingency should raise any further question on the will.

Note

See further, *Irish Land Law,* para. 10.042. See also *Re Lynch's Trusts,* p.589, *post.*

JOHNSTON V. O'NEILL

(1879) 3 L.R.Ir. 476 (Chancery Division)

A testator directed his trustees and executors to invest out of the produce of his personal estate a sum of £4000, and to hold the said sum and the securities upon which it should be invested, in trust for the younger children of the testator's nephew, who being sons should attain twenty-one, or being daughters should attain that age or marry; and if there should be no child of his said nephew who, under the said trusts, should become entitled to the said sum of £4000, the testtor directed the same to sink into and form part of his residuary estate. The will contained no express disposition of the interim income of the fund, and the only provision for maintenance of the legatees was given out of the testator's real estate. There was a complete disposition of the testator's residuary property.

Chatterton V.-C.:

The question remaining for decision is, what are the rights of the parties in the interest of the sum of £4000 directed to be invested, and held in trust for the younger children of Edward O'Neill. These children contend that it follows the principal, while the eldest son of Edward O'Neill contends that it forms part of the testator's residuary estate, and is to be invested, with the other residuary estate, in the purchase of real estate, to be settled for the benefit of him and the other devisees of the testator. The trustees of the will were directed to set apart, out of the general personal estate, this sum of £4000, and it was their duty to do so not later than a year from the testator's death. The will requires that it should be invested by the trustees in the manner therein provided for the investment of the rents and profits of the testator's real estate; that is to say, in the public stocks or funds, or Government securities, the interest, dividends, and annual produce of which the trustees were directed to receive. It is therefore a fund which, by the express terms of the will, is to bear interest from the time of its investment. The trustees were to hold this sum, when so invested, in trust for all the children or any the child of Edward O'Neill other than an eldest or only son entitled to the testator's real estate, who, being a son or sons should attain twenty-one, or, being a daughter or daughters, should attain that age, or marry, and if more than one in equal shares. There was, therefore, a complete segregation of this sum from the residue of the testator's personal estate, to be held from its segregation and investment upon the special trusts declared concerning it by the will. The testator further declared that, if there should be no child of Edward O'Neill who, under the trust declared by his will, should become entitled to this sum, it should sink into and form part of his residuary estate, and be applied in the manner thereinafter provided; that is to say, in the purchase of real estate. There is no express disposition of the income of this sum, and thus the present question arises.

It has been contended on the one hand that this legacy, being made payable at a future time, carries to the legatees the interest only from the time of payment, and that the interim interest is undisposed of, and falls into the residue. It is, no doubt, the general rule that general legacies payable at a future day, even though vested, do not carry interest before the day of payment, except legacies given to a child by a parent, or a person *in loco parentis*. But to this general rule there are exceptions, one of which is, that where a fund is directed to be presently separated from the general personal estate for the purpose of providing for the future payment of certain legacies, it carries the interest accruing up to the time of payment, to the legatees, with the capital sum. In such cases, the rule that the interest follows the capital prevails, and the legatee gets his legacy with its interim accretions. The effect of a direction to set apart the special fund at once, or at some time prior to the day of payment, is to dedicate that fund, with its increase, from the time appointed for setting it apart, to the particular purpose, and to take it out of the general personal estate, without waiting for the arrival of the time of payment. In the case of *Boddy* v. *Dawes* 1 Keen, 362, where there was a gift to trustees of a sum of stock for grandchildren of the testator on their attaining twenty-one, and a gift over in case they all should die under that age, Lord Langdale held that the intermediate dividends belonged to the grandchildren. The case was argued for them chiefly on the ground that the fund was separated from the residue of the testator's estate; and this was plainly the main ground of Lord Langdale's decision, though there were expressions in the context of the will aiding the argument. In *Saunders* v. *Vautier* CR. & Ph. 240, the separation of a fund to be held by trustees till the legatee should attain the age of twenty-five, and then to pay over to him the principal and accumulation, was held to make the legacy vested, though there was no gift but in the direction to pay the legatee on attaining twenty-five. I refer to this case only to show the efficacy of a direction to set apart the fund, for it differed from the present in other material respects. In the case of *Dundas* v. *Wolfe-Murray* 1 H. & M. 425, a similar decision was made by Sir W. P. Wood, V. C., and on the same ground. There the testatrix directed her trustees immediately after her death to raise a sum of money and pay it to her nephews and nieces, the shares of sons to be payable at twenty-one, and those of daughters at twenty-one or marriage, with benefit of survivorship among them. There was no gift over in case all should die before the prescribed periods. The Vice-Chancellor held that the legacy was vested, and that the legatees were entitled to the intermediate income. It was, however, contended here on the part of the eldest son that the present case differs from those cited, or at least from *Saunders* v. *Vautier* Cr. & Ph. 240, and *Dundas* v. *Wolfe-Murray* 1 H. & M. 425, on the ground that the younger children only take contingent interests in this sum of £4000, while in those cases the legacies were vested on the death of the testator. It was urged that here there are no words of gift except in the trust to pay; that the only children capable of taking are those who in the case of sons should attain the age of twenty-one years, or of daughters should attain that age or marry; that there is no clause of accruer or survivorship between the children, nor any gift of the interest in the interim for maintenance or otherwise, and that the provision for maintenance out of the rents of the real estate shows that the interest of this fund was not intended for that purpose. The gift over, or rather the direction that this sum should fall into the residuary estate, was also strongly relied on to show that the gift was contingent. I agree with this argument so far as regards the vesting of the gift, and I am of opinion that it cannot be deemed vested. The futurity here is attached to the substance of the gift; no child could take who did not become a member of the class to whom the legacy was given, which could only be by living to attain the prescribed age, or if a daughter, by sooner marrying. There are none of the circumstances which the Court has seized upon in other cases to enable it to hold that the gift was vested, and the gift over here is dependent merely on the failure of all these children to become entitled, and is not coupled with any words imparting any other contingency to which it could be referred. But it appears to me that in consequence of the severance of this legacy from the general personal estate, whether it be vested or contingent, the interest up to the time of payment did not fall into the residue. If vested there is no question; if contingent it must be accumulative, subject to any order for maintenance that may be made under Lord Cranworth's Act, till the time of payment, and then these accumulations, or the portion of them not paid for maintenance, will with the capital belong to the children or child becoming entitled to payment. If no child becomes entitled, they will fall with the capital into the residue. The case of *Kidman* v. *Kidman* 40 L.J.Ch. 359 is an express authority on this point. The fund there was to be set apart on the testator's death, and invested and held in trust for Elizabeth Kidman for life, and from her decease for her children, when and as they should respectively attain the age of twenty-one, but if Elizabeth should die without issue, over. It was there contended, on the language of the gift over, that the legacies were vested, as that gift was not confined to dying without issue who should live to attain twenty-one. Sir R. Malins, V.C., held that the legacy was contingent upon the children attaining that age; but he held that the interest from the death of the tenant for life up to the time of payment was to be accumulated and to go with the capital, each child on attaining twenty-one taking his or her share of the fund as it should then exist. He based his decision on the severance of the legacy from the residue, for a purpose connected with the legacy, namely, to provide the interest for the tenant for life.

The case of *Gotch* v. *Foster* L.R. 5 Eq. 311 was relied on for the eldest son, as showing that even in the case of a severed fund, where the interests of the legatees are future, they are not entitled to the interim interest. But, on looking to the terms of the appointment there, it will be seen that it was not a case of severance of the shares as to which the question arose. The severance there was of a larger fund out of which the appointments in question were made, but those appointed sums were not to be at once severed from that fund, but were to be raised out of it only on the happening of the events on which they were to become payable. It was contended that the words of the clause directing the residue to be invested by the trustees in the purchase of real estate must be held to include the interim interest on the £4000, as being "interest, dividends, and annual produce not otherwise applied under the trusts hereinbefore mentioned." I think that this argument is met by the complete severance of the £4000 from the general personal estate, carrying with it, in my opinion, all the intermediate interest. By the terms of the will the fund was to sink into the residue only in the event of there being no child who should become entitled to it. Unless and until that event should happen, it was not to become a part of that residue which was to be invested in the purchase of real estate.

I shall, therefore, declare that the income of this sum of £4000 does not fall into the residue unless it shall happen that none of the younger children shall become entitled to the capital sum of £4000, and that in the meantime it shall be invested, but subject to any orders that may be made for maintenance thereout of the younger children. The £4000 must be placed to a separate credit and the dividends invested from time to time to the same credit until further order.

Note

See further, *Irish Land Law,* para. 10.044.

VII. ADVANCEMENT

RE O'NEILL
[1943] I.R. 562 (High Court)

Income from a trust fund for minors, who had been made wards of Court, was insufficient to meet their school fees and maintenance charges. An application was made for payment out of the capital.

Maguire P.:

I have previously granted at least two applications of this nature. In one case the facts were very similar to those now presented to me, and I allowed an advance out of the capital of a trust fund which was not sanctioned by the will of the settlor, but which was clearly for the benefit of the minors. In the other case I also allowed an advance out of capital but I required that an assurance policy upon the life of the minor concerned should be taken out to cover the extent of the advance.

Neither of these cases appears to have been reported. In both cases I took the view that in applications of this kind something more is required than evidence that an advance would be of benefit to the minors. I must be satisfied that such a course is not only beneficial but necessary to the welfare of the minors. As to this I accept the view expressed by Kekewich J. in *In re Tollemache* [1903] 1 Ch. 457. at p.459. He says:–"The most common application going beyond the administration of a trust according to the instrument creating it is one for advances for the benefit of an infant out of capital not sanctioned by the instrument creating the trust. I have never hesitated to do this where satisfied that the advancement is certainly beneficial, and where the infant is contingently interested, as, for instance, entitled only on attaining majority. I have included in the advance the sum necessary to effect a policy of insurance to cover the contingency. This is an illustration of the maxim that necessity has no law."

The jurisdiction to make an advance out of capital is not to be exercised lightly. Where a minor is actually destitute the way is clear, but where the minors, as here, are not destitute, the question of the existence of a sufficient element of necessity becomes a difficult problem.

In the present case there is a considerable capital fund subject to the trust of the will of the minors' father. The terms of the will require that the trustees shall pay to the minors' mother the entire income of the estate during widowhood for her own support and maintenance, and the support, maintenance and education of the four minors, and that on her death the capital of the estate shall pass to the minors equally as tenants in common. The evidence before me shows that the minors have reached an age when, if they are to take the position in life for which their upbringing has been preparing them, the expenditure upon their education and maintenance must be increased to a sum greater than the income available. Their mother strongly supports the application. It clearly may be to the advantage of a child to expend capital moneys to which he is absolutely entitled upon his education. Where, however, as here, the interest of the child in the fund is merely an interest in remainder, I have to ask myself, not only would such an expenditure be to the child's advantage, but is it necessary.

Taking all the circumstances into consideration, I hold that the expenditure which I am asked to sanction is necessary. Accordingly I allow the application, and direct the payment out of capital of the sum of £301 8s. 4d., being the amount of the past expenses already incurred on foot of the maintenance and education of the minors, together with the sum of £146, being the amount certified by the Registrar to be required for their maintenance and education for the coming year.

Note

As regards infants, see now s.11 of the Guardianship of Infants Act, 1964, see *Irish Land Law,* para. 10.048.

L'ESTRANGE V. L'ESTRANGE

[1902] 1 I.R. 467 (Court of Appeal)

A testator devised the residue of his property to trustees for the benefit of six of his children, with power to his said trustees to advance such sum or sums as they might think fit, for the education and advancement in life of his said children.

Lord Ashbourne, C.:

Notwithstanding the very clear and able arguments of Mr. Molony and Mr. Wilson, we are all of opinion that the decision appealed from is correct. It is a case turning on the construction of a will, and, like all cases of that class, its decision depends upon the intention of the testator, to be gathered from all the language he has used.

There is no doubt that at the commencement of this residuary bequest the testator used words which would, standing alone, make the children joint tenants, but then they are followed by this clause– "With power to my said trustees to advance such sum or sums of money as they may think fit for the education and advancement in life of my said daughters and my son Patrick." The questions is – Does the use of these words indicate an intention on the part of the testator to cut down the joint tenancy to a tenancy in common? It is one of those clauses of which, when read for the first time, one may not see the full effect, or ascertain how far the words will go; but when read more closely it is clear that the words confer a power, not of maintenance, but of advancement. If a sum, perhaps of a considerable amount, were advanced for one child, it would be right to debit that sum against his or hei share, and that debit could not be worked out if these children were joint tenants, and could not be done unless they were tenants in common.

We find abundant authority to support this view. In *Taggart* v. *Taggart* 1 Sch. & Lef. 88 Lord Redesdale said:–"Joint tenancy as a provision for the children of a marriage is an inconvenient mode of settlement, because during their minorities no use can be made of their portions for their advancement, as the joint tenancy cannot be severed." These words express this view of the question in a clear and pointed manner, and that decision was referred to in *Mayn* v. *Mayn* L.R. 5 Eq. 150. In the course of the argument counsel said:– "Amongst powers usually inserted in marriage settlements is certainly a power of advancement which, according to Lord Redesdale's judgment in *Taggart* v. *Taggart* 1 Sch. & Lef. 88, is in itself a presumption against a joint tenancy having been intended." In giving judgment Lord Hatherley approved of the decision in *Taggart* v. *Taggart* 1 Sch. & Lef. 88. He read the passage from Lord Redesdale's judgment to which I have referred, and he adopted the principle of that decision.

In the present case the testator has used words which show that the governing idea in his mind could only be satisfied by holding that these legatees took the property as tenants in common.

In my opinion the decision of the Vice-Chancellor is right, and should be affirmed, and the appeal dismissed, with costs.

Fitzgibbon, L.J.:

The incompatibility of a discretionary power of advancement with a joint tenancy is absolute, because the exercise of such a power implies the reduction of several parts of the property into possession. Mr. Molony tried to get out of it by contending that if an advancement was made, it was to be made out of cash, and cash might be produced by savings of income. But the words of the will, which describe the subject of the power, are not confined to cash. There was no obligation to save income, and advancement is usually made out of capital. The words of the testator are – "The rest, residue, and remainder of my property, real, freehold, and chattel." He did not confine the power to his cash, though cash must be provided before an advancement could be made. Before any advancement could be made the share of each child would have to be segregated, so that each advancement might be made, not out of the property as a whole, but only out of the share of the child who was to receive the advance. This negatives joint tenancy.

In my opinion the appeal is wholly unsustainable.

Holmes L.J.:

The only ground upon which it would be possible to support this appeal would be by showing that the advancement to the children, which, by the terms of the will, the trustees are given power to make, is an advancement out of the whole of the property, and not out of the share of it devised and bequeathed to the child to whom the advancement is made. But this is opposed to the idea of advancement, which is a term of legal art. It implies that it is to be made out of the property to which the person advanced is actually or contingently entitled. It is now well settled that where a devise or bequest is made to children, followed by a power of advancement, such a power is inconsistent with a joint tenancy in the children, and upon this principle we hold that they took as tenants in common.

Note

See further, *Irish Land Law*, paras. 10.048-9.

Chapter 18

DUTIES OF TRUSTEES

This chapter deals with the many, often onerous, duties of trustees, see *Irish Land Law,* para. 10.050 *et seq*.

I. COLLECTION AND DISTRIBUTION OF ASSETS

MACNAMARA V. CAREY
(1867) I.R. 1 Eq. 9 (Chancery Appeal)

The facts are set out in the judgments.

Blackburne C.: This is an appeal from an order of the late Lord Chancellor, by which he dismissed the petition of the Appellant, Richard Francis Macnamara, against the Respondent, Henry Carey. The Petitioner and Appellant is the son of Connell W. Macnamara and Esther Jane Carey, the sister of the Respondent, Henry Carey, who were married in the year 1839. On that occasion a settlement was executed, whereby various landed properties of the husband were conveyed to Francis P. Smith and Henry Carey, the Respondent, for various uses.

Francis P. Smith died, insolvent, a great many years since; and Connell W. Macnamara, the husband, being also dead, and the title of the Petititioner as issue of the marriage to the property settled having accrued, the object of this suit is to make Henry Carey – the uncle of the Petitioner, and the surviving trustee in the settlement – answerable for the value of certain portions of the settled estate, to which, as the issue of the marriage, the Petitioner is entitled.

Two questions arose in the case. The first is one of the construction of the settlement of the 9th of May, 1839. The trustees of this settlement were, as I have said, the Respondent, Henry Carey, the brother of Esther Jane Carey, and Francis Pratt Smith. This deed, after reciting that Connell W. Macnamara was possessed of different properties, and amongst these of the lands of Quilty, in the county of Clare, and of certain premises in Gardiner's-place, in this city, and that it had been agreed to settle the property recited on the trusts therein declared, in pursuance of this agreement, and in consideration of Esther Jane Carey's fortune paid to her husband, he and she severally convey all the premises thereinafter mentioned to the trustees. It is the fact, however, that in this enumeration Quilty and the lands in Gardiner's-place are omitted. The settlement was not registered until 1843, before which time – in the year 1842 – Connell W. Macnamara mortgaged several of the denominations to Hedges E. Chatterton, who had no notice of the settlement, and amongst them the premises in Gardiner's-place.

The first question that arises is, whether the parcels enumerated in the recitals of this deed, but not mentioned in the words of grant, passed or not. This is a question of construction; and it seems to me plain on authority, that, as the operative part of the deed conveying the parcels omits them, they did not pass to the trustees. If they had been omitted from accident, or other cause, when they were agreed or intended to be included, the deed could be reformed on satisfactory proof of the contract to include them; but, as matter of construction, the deed remaining as it was when executed, the denominations omitted did not pass to the trustees.

The second question is caused by the non-registration of the deed of settlement. This is the ground of relief sought as to certain other parcels of the lands conveyed. These, in consequence of the omission to register the settlement, remained in the disposition and name of the husband, and were by him mortgaged to Hedges E. Chatterton, who had not notice of the settlement. The liability of the trustees, of whom Henry Carey is the survivor, by reason of this omission, has been the principal matter of controversy. Considering the vast variety of circumstances under which questions of this kind may and must arise, it is, I conceive, not possible to lay down any rule of general application: each case must depend on its own peculiar facts. But assuming, as I think we must do, that there are possible facts and circumstances under which this duty may arise, the question is, did such a duty devolve on Henry Carey and his co-trustee, and is he responsible for the omission to perform it? The order appealed from exonerates Henry Carey from this liability; but, assuming, as I have said we must do, that there are possible cases in which it may be the duty of a trustee to see that the deed vesting the trust estate in him be registered, the question is, whether in this case, having regard to its special circumstances, such a duty was imposed on him, and is he responsible for the neglect to discharge it? It is plain that he must have been a party to the negociation for the settlement, and became a trustee of it with full notice of its provisions. It is also matter of reasonable presumption that he knew that registration was essential to the security of the title, for which, as his sister's trustee, he must have been in treaty on behalf of her and her children. How, then, can it be said that he was not responsible for the consequences of an omission by which the property was left under the absolute dominion of the husband? The preparation of the settlement was left to the husband; but, although this was not objectionable in itself, surely it was in the last degree culpable to leave him in possession of power to alienate or incumber the very property which the trustees were appointed to protect and secure. Indeed, his own act in registering the deed, when he found that advantage had been taken of his neglect and the confidence he reposed in the Petitioner's father had been abused, is evidence that he knew his duty, and the consequences of the omission to discharge it. I think, therefore, that, without laying down a rule which would involve all trustees in an obligation to cause the trust deed to be registered, the extreme imprudence and neglect which mark this transaction oblige us to hold Mr. Carey responsible for these consequences.

The case of *Lester* v. *Lester,* decided by the late Lord Chancellor, appears to me to be an authority bearing directly on the question before us. The registration of the deed was as essential to make the assurance and title safe and indefeasible as was the registration of the judgment in *Lester* v. *Lester.* But there is a further ground on which, as it strikes me, Mr. Carey has rendered himself responsible for the value of the trust property, which, in fraud of the settlement, the Petitioner's father alienated or incumbered – I mean the covenant for further assurance contained in the settlement by Connell W. Macnamara to the trustees. This has not been relied on, as far as I recollect, in the course of the argument; but yet it is obvious that, when the trustees discovered (as they did in 1843) that a portion of the settled lands had been alienated, they had a right, and as trustees a duty cast on them, to call on Connell W. Macnamara either to procure a reconveyance of the premises, or to pay to them, for the benefit of their *cestui que trusts,* a full equivalent for the settled property fraudulently sold or incumbered by him. It is not possible to argue that this was not a remedy available to the trustees, or that it was not one which they were bound to resort to for the protection of their *cestui que trusts.* On the whole, I am most reluctantly compelled to hold Mr. Carey liable for the omission to have the settlement of 1839 registered, and for having omitted to sue Mr. Macnamara for the breach of his covenant. I need not add, that the reluctance has been increased by the consideration that at the instance of a son we are inflicting a severe penalty on his uncle for the fraud which was practised by his father.

I have only to add, that the premises in Gardiner's-place, which did not pass by the settlement, and are parcel of those mortgaged to Mr. Chatterton, will be applicable in the first place to pay the mortgage debt, and the deficit must be made good by Mr. Carey.

Christian, J. I have the honour to be of the same opinion as my Lord Chancellor on both the points in this case. With respect to the first – namely, the omission of two of the recited denominations from the granting part of the settlement – as I have the good fortune to be upon that in accord with the late Lord Chancellor also, I do not think it necessary to read the portion of my judgment which has relation to it. The reasons which have ben just assigned by the Lord Chancellor, with those given by his learned predecessor are, I think, abundantly satisfactory.

It should be observed, that the materiality in the case of that first question consists mainly in its bearing upon the other and more important question which remains. The decision we are now making on that first point ascertains that the Gardiner's-place premises are a primary fund for relief of the Respondent from any liabilities which our decision on the second question may throw upon him. Except in that view, the first question could scarcely be raised in a suit constituted like the present. The Petitioner, being heir at law of his father, could not maintain a suit *merely* for the purpose of bringing into the settlement omitted denominations; for that would be to increase the settled estate at the expense of his own unsettled estate. In such a suit his proper place would obviously be that of a Respondent. *His* only equity, therefore (whatever might be the case with his sister, if she were Petitioner), can only be to have the settled estate, whatever it is, relieved from his father's incumbrances, or rather from so much of them as any unsettled estate upon which they are also charged shall not suffice to satisfy. Our decision on the first point places Gardiner's-place precisely in that position with reference to Mr. Chatterton's mortgage, to which only, the Petitioner's counsel admit, their case on the second question must be confined. Thus we are brought to the consideration of the second (the real) question in the case, with this as one of its conditions. Macnamara, after the execution of the settlement, had two estates, and an unsettled estate; but the settled estate was, unfortunately, by the neglect to register it, left as absolutely subject to his control and disposition as the unsettled one; and parcels of both were included in the mortgage to Mr. Chatterton. And the question which thereupon arises is one of those painful questions, so frequent in courts of equity, which of two innocent parties must bear the loss occasioned by the fraud of a third? Shall it be the children of the marriage, who came of age only a few years ago; or the trustee, of whom, probably, the worst that can be said is, that he trusted too much to the honour of his sister's husband.

I confess, this appears to me to be a question of no common importance; and, as the opinion I entertain upon it is at variance with that which appears to have been very deliberately arrived at by the Late Lord Chancellor, and furthermore, as it so happens that, by means of the present Lord Chancellor differing from his predecessor, my voice (though but an accidental adjunct for a few hours to the Court) will in fact decide the fate of the appeal, I fell that I could not with propriety withhold the reasons which have weighed with me, conscious though I am that they can be little more than a dilution of what has been so well condensed by my Lord Chancellor. I have given the case very anxious consideration, and I have studied with all the care which was due to it the judgment of the late Lord Chancellor; and I think the key to the decision will be found in a sentence or two, which I shall now read. After some remarks on the action taken by Mr. Carey, as soon he heard of Macnamara's malpractice, his Lordship defines the question which he considers he has to decide in these terms: "Of intentional negligence I hold him entirely absolved; and *there is nothing more in the case than the single abstract question of the duty of a trustee to see to the registration of the deed of settlement.*" And he then proceeds: "The Registry Act has been in force about 160 years. Settlements without number have been executed since it came into operation, and doubtless very many of them have been affected by want of registration, yet this is the first attempt which has been made to hold a mere trustee of the lands liable for neglect in such a case." And the judgment concludes with these words: "No case, in my apprehension, has gone the length which I am asked to sanction in this case, and I shrink from making the precedent."

With the utmost deference, I feel constrained to think that these passages show that the case has been misconceived. There is surely a great deal more in this case than the single abstract question "of the duty of a trustee to see to the registration of the deed of settlement." Nay, further, I venture to think that that question, *in the abstract,* does not exist in the case at all. And, as to shrinking from making a precedent, it seems to me that immeasurably a more formidable, more dangerous precedent would be made by dismissing this petition, than by granting the limited relief to which the case is now reduced.

To grant that relief would be merely to say that, under the highly special and exceptional circumstances of this case, the trustee did not act with the caution and foresight which the Court expects from a trustee placed in such circumstances. But to dismiss the petition generally would be to say, that in almost no conceivable state of circumstances need a trustee of real estate trouble himself at all about either the custody of the title deeds or the registry of the title, vital though that be to the safety of the trust, until at last he hears that there is danger actually on foot; that is to say, in most cases, until more or less irreparable mischief has been done.

I shall now state the facts which, in my opinion, make of this a highly special and exceptional case. In doing so, it will be necessary to go a little behind the settlement. It is, no doubt, true that in the present suit Mr. Carey cannot be made responsible for anything but some breach of the duty which attached upon him by reason of his having executed this settlement. But, in judging whether what he did under it amounted to due and reasonable diligence, it is legitimate and necessary to look at his antecedent position. Conduct which would be due diligence in one, might be negligence in another.

The first peculiarity in the case is this – before the settlement was made at all, Mr. Carey stood already in a fiduciary position towards his sister. He was his father's executor; and, in that capacity, her fortune of £1700 was standing in his name, or was under his control and management, and it was by his hands that it was paid over to Macnamara on the marriage. These facts are stated in an affidavit of Mrs. Macnamara, filed the 15th of February, 1866, which was specially replied to by Mr. Carey on the 1st of March, but without any denial of those statements. They were stated and commented on by counsel, and there is no doubt of their truth. Plainly, therefore, he had been a trustee of this money for his sister. No blame can be imputed to him for paying over the money. His sister was of age, and mistress of her own actions, and such was her marriage treaty. But the equivalent she was to get was the settlement of her intended husband's estate upon herself and her children: her brother was her selected trustee for this. The settlement was, therefore, in effect a shifting of Mr. Carey's fiduciary obligations from the money to the land; but with this important difference, that, whereas he had been trustee of the money for self-competent *cestui que trust,* he became trustee for the land for one disabled by coverture, and for those still more helpless beings whose existence lay in the future; accordingly, the trusts declared by the setttlement were active, operative trusts. This was no case of mere releasees to uses, whose only duty would be to refrain from joining in any act to destroy the contingent remainders. The whole legal estate in all these leasehold interests remainded in the trustees. The first trust was, "out of the rents and profits to pay head rents and outgoings" (thereby throwing expressly on the trustees the duty of caring for the preservation of the interests). The next trust was, "to reimburse themselves the expenses of the said trusts" (an unequivocal indication that their part was to be no passive one); and lastly came the trust, "to pay" (not to "permit and suffer to receive") "the residue of the rents" to the husband, wife, and children, in the order prescribed. Active care and intervention by the trustees were, therefore, contemplated and prescribed. Surely it is not too much to say, that Mr. Carey was bound to take at least as much care of the land as he had been of the money which was given for the purchase of it. And, if it had been the money that had been put in settlement, can any one doubt that he would be held responsible, if he let it fall under the power of the husband?

The second specialty to be noted is this – the settlor was a solicitor, and he was the only solicitor employed in the transaction. The usual course of business, when the gentleman makes a settlement in consideration of the lady's fortune, is, that the preparation and perfecting of the deed belong to her solicitor. Here the duty was committed wholly to the settlor himself. For this unfortunate peculiarity I do not hold Mr. Carey responsible *as its origin.* The lady and her mother were presumably capable of choosing for themselves; unhappily, they left all to Mr. Macnamara. But the moment the settlement was executed, Mr. Carey's position and duties were altered; new rights sprang into existence, of which he was a constituted guardian; the time for independent action by the trustees had arrived.

Thirdly – Mr. Carey was himself a skilled professional man – a practising barrister, and he executed the deed. Perfect knowledge of its contents – of the rights and duties which it created – of the proper depository for it, as well as for the title deeds, and of the consequences of non-registration – all this knowledge must clearly be imputed to the trustee in this case, even while we give full credit to what he has sworn, that he did not act as his sister's counsel.

But the matter does not rest on presumption. There is ample evidence that Mr. Carey's attention was, in fact, awake to the necessities of the occasion. Trustees have often, perhaps most frequently, suffered for the neglect of things unknown or forgotten: not so here. A most important passage was read from Mr. Carey's affidavit, to this effect:–" The said Connell Wilkins Macnamara *expressly undertook* to have the settlement registered; and I *bonâ fide* believed that same had been duly registered." That is to say, his thoughts dwelt on the subject at the time; and the result was, that , instead of employing an impartial and competent solicitor of his own to register the settlement, he concluded to repose on Macnamara's assurance that he would himself take care of it – Macnamara, the very person on whom the settlement was a fetter – a fetter to be riveted by registering, but shaken off at pleasure so long as that remained undone. And, that no facility or temptation for foul play might be wanting, he left with him all the title deeds, the head leases of the settled denominations, as well as any others there may have been. In a word, he, not ignorantly or inadvertently, but knowingly and advisedly, permitted the settlor to remain as absolutely master of the settled estate as of his own unsettled estate.

Lastly, having left in this position of deadly peril the provision for his sister and her children which he had just purchased with her fortune, he dismissed the subject from his thoughts; never made an inquiry whether his confidence had been justified or abused, whether Macnamara had kept his undertaking or broken it – never asked even to see the settlement, a glance at which would show whether he had or not remained simply supine for close on four years; and then, hearing what was going on, which common foresight would have anticipated, after two irreparable invasions had been already made on the trust estates, he at last awakes, and without trouble or difficulty does the simple act which, if done when it ought to have been done, would have preserved the estates intact.

Is this, then, let me now ask, a case of which it can truly be said, that "there is nothing more in the case than the single abstract question of the duty of a trustee to see to the registration of the deed of settlement?" Is there here nothing special, nothing exceptional, nothing peculiar? A brother, with his sister's fortune in his hands, investing it in the purchase of a settlement on her and on her children of her intended husband's estate, of which he (the brother) is made the trustee on active and operative trusts, leaving that settlement in circumstances which, as a practising barrister, he knew, put it absolutely at the mercy of the settlor, that settlor an attorney, and the only other professional person concerned; and never for four years, nor until he hears that mischief has been actually done, making so much as one solitary inquiry.

But it was strongly argued that the registering of a settlement is no part of a trustee's duty at all. The title, it is said, is complete, the constitution of the trust complete, on the execution of the deed; and all the trustees need do is to perform the things set down for them in the declaration of the trusts. Registering is a matter which the settling parties, as they were called, must look to. I answer, that the title is *not* complete, notwithstanding the estate has passed, so long as it is left in thê settlor's power to destroy it at his pleasure; and that the very first duty of the trustees is to place the trust property, whether it be real or personal, in a state of security. I do not say that trustees are to hunt back into the title in search of flaws (as the case of *Lester* v. *Lester* would seem to warrant); but, if there be in the very framework of the machinery by which the trust is constitued, and to which they are parties, a patent defect, which the trustees (either by being themselves possesed of the technical knowledge, or by being told of it by those who are) know makes the trust insecure, but which it is in their powers to remove, I do say, it is their duty to do the act which will remove that defect. And just as a mortgage, or an ordinary purchaser, owes a duty to himself to register his conveyance, and take up his title deeds, so I hold that a trustee of real estate, upon operative trust for persons under disability, owes a like duty to them.

The Respondent's counsel admit that, when the trustee became aware that the settlor was tampering with the estate, it became his duty to interfere, and to get the settlement registered; and, that if he had neglected to do so, he would have been responsible. But the moment that is admitted, if follows that the act of registering is one not in its nature alien to the office of trustee, and appertaining to the settling parties; for if it were the trustee could not be responsible for danger proceeding from such a source, and the utmost he could be called on to do would be to give notice to the settling parties. But if the act *be* one germane to his office, which therefore he must do as soon as he hears of danger, it seems to me to be repugnant to the principles of this Court to say that he may postpone the action until then. I have always understood it to be the law of this Court, that, if there be an act which it is in the province of a trustee to do, the not doing of which carries in it the seeds of future danger, that it is at the trustee's own peril if he leave that act undone; and if evil ultimately come of it, however unthought of, he must make it good.

Again, it was said, the danger was only a contingency, and that contingency one of fraud; and are trustees, it was asked, bound to presume fraud? No; they need not presume fraud, but they should take ordinary precautions against the possibility of it. The duty of trustees is not to (as has been said of the law itself) trust to what men *will* do, but to guard against what they *may* do. If men were always honest, and provident, and faithful to their engagements, we need not have settlements or trustees at all. But it is because those qualities sometimes fail under temptation that restrictions are necessary.

Extreme cases were put in argument; and it was asked, would trustees be liable for bad registry, as well as for non-registry; or for non-registry of some deed occurring in the anterior state of the title? My answer is, that, when such cases arise, they will be dealt with according to their circumstances. The fallacy of all that class of reasoning lies in the assumption that we are dealing here with an abstract question, instead of with a highly special case. I should myself say, as present advised (special circumstances apart), that if the trustees employ a disinterested and presumably competent solicitor to register the trust deed, and ascertain by inquiry that he has done so, they fulfil the obligation of reasonable diligence, and ought not to be held responsible for the solicitor's want of skill, or mistake. And, as to older deeds, I should have thought (at least, unless the case of *Lester* v. *Lester* be law) that trustees could not be held responsible for defects of which they had no notice in the title anterior to the creation of the trust.

There is one conclusive test by which to try cases of this kind. It is now the settled doctrine (notwithstanding a dictum of Lord Northington, in 1 Eden, 148) that a trustee must exert precisely the same care and solicitude in behalf of his *cestui que trust* as he would do for himself. This is nowhere more clearly laid down than by Lord Nottingham, in the case cited by one of Mr. Carey's counsel, *Morley* v. *Morley* 2 Chan. Ca. 2. Suppose, then, that the £1700 had been Mr. Carey's own money, instead of his sister's, and that the deed of May, 1839, instead of being her marriage settlement, had been a mortgage for that money; would Mr. Carey – would any prudent mortgagee – have left, not only all the title deeds, but the mortgage deed itself, unregistered, in the hands of the mortgagee, trusting in his promise to register it, and never making one inquiry as to whether his confidence had been justified or abused? Does any one doubt that he would have had his own solicitor, that his deed would have been promptly registered, if not the title deeds taken up; and if he would have so done for himself, so much, and not less, he was bound to do for his *cestui que trusts*.

I ought not to close without some reference to the authorities by which, if the case be not touched, it is certainly very closely encompassed. Much stress was laid on the absence of any case in point. No doubt that class of argument is entitled to certain weight; though the worst of it is, that it is not often easy to say on which side it tells – whether it shows complaint to be desperate, or resistance hopeless. The truth is, as we all know, that new points are constantly springing up; and, when they present themselves, all we can do is to bring to bear on them the light afforded by decisions in analogous cases, taking care to extract essential principles, and to disregard immaterial accidents.

We have been referred to the familiar cases in Beavan's Reports, *Fenwick* v. *Greenwell, McGachan* v. *Dew, Dix* v. *Burford,* and others; to which may be added, *Clough* v. *Bond* 3 M. & Cr. 490. The principle which stands out distinct and clear upon those authorities is this: that it is not enough for a trustee to keep within the four corners of the deed, and perform literally what is there set down. The very first point to which he must direct his thoughts is the placing of the trust property in security; and, above all, the making it impossible that it shall ever fall under the control of unauthorized persons. If he, even by mere inaction, suffer a state of things to exist or to continue, which, however apparently at the time natural and harmless, results, in the course of future events, in the fund getting under unauthorized control, even though it be that of a co-trustee only – still more that of the settlor himself – and loss follows, the trustee must make it good. Look, for example, at the force of that case of *Dix* v. *Burford.* A testator, possessed of a mortgage on a copyhold, bequeathed the money specifically to his executors on certain trusts. The executors assented to the bequest, whereby the money became vested in them in the capacity of trustees. Now, there is held to be this very subtle distinction between executors and trustees, viz., one executor may receive and give a discharge for money, but trustees must all join. The benefit of this distinction would have been secured for the *cestui que trusts* in this case if the executors had, after assent, got themselves formally admitted on the court roll joint-tenants of the copyhold. This, naturally enough, they never thought of. The legal estate, therefore, still remained in them *qua* executors; and one of them took advantage of the circumstance, received the money, and discharged the estate. The other was decreed to make it good, merely for having neglected to assimilate the condition of the legal estate in the land to that in which the money had been placed by the assent. Lord Langdale says:– "It is obvious that the moment Yells accepted the trust, it became his duty to take proper stops to prevent his co-trustee alone receiving the money ... The moment he was constituted a trustee, it became his duty, by notice or otherwise, *to make it impossible* for his co-trustee to receive and misapply the trust fund" – and surely, *a fortiori,* in our case – to make it impossible for the settlor himself to alien and make away with the trust estate. Again, in *Fenwick* v. *Greeenwell* 10 Beav. 412, there was a covenant in a marriage settlement with the trustees that £5000 Consols, described as part of the intended wife's estate, should be transferred to the trustees on the trusts of the settlement. There was then in the lady's name a sum of £4946 Three per Cents.; the trustees took no steps to compel a transfer; and the Stock was sold out and misapplied by the husband, who became bankrupt. Lord Langdale was of opinion that that sum of Three per Cents. was not specially bound by the settlement; but he though that the trustees might, by proper measures, have procured a transfer of it, and he held them responsible for having neglected to take such measures. "Though," he says, "they had recognised the trust by executing the deed, and had become liable for their non-performance, they did nothing; they performed no trust whatever, but omitted to pay any attention to the duty which they had undertaken to perform." In *Ghost* v. *Waller* 9 Beav. 497, trustees for sale were held liable for having left the deed of conveyance to a purchaser in the hands of a solicitor, with their receipt for the purchase money indorsed, by means of which the solicitor was enabled to obtain and misapply the money. But there is a case which, I think, was not cited, which seems to me in some respects to touch this case more nearly. It is *Mathews* v. *Brise* 6 Beav. 239:–An executor and trustee, having £5600 in his hands, which he was in treaty to invest in a mortgage, in order to make it profitable in the mean time, directed it to be invested in Exchequer Bills. He gave it for that purpose to certain brokers, and brokers who had been in the testator's confidence, and they made the investment. Now, down to this the Court held that the trustees were fully justified, i.e. in the temporary investment in Exchequer Bills, and in the employment of the brokers. But they never inquired how the brokers had done their duty; and it was found afterwards that they had kept the bills undistinguished from others of their own. The brokers afterwards, before the mortgage was completed, became bankrupts; and it was held that the trustees were liable. The language of the Master of the Rolls seems singularly applicable, *mutatis mutandis,* to this case. [His Lordship read the judgment in that case.]

Another strong case, not cited, was *Challen* v. *Shippam* 4 Hare. 555. The Defendant, the trustee, there, having £300, part of the trust estate, paid to him, was told by the *cestui que trusts* to invest it in the funds. He deposited it with an old-established banking firm, with directions in writing to invest it in his name for the trusts. So far all was correct, and in the ordinary way of business. But the trustee made no inquiry as to how the bankers fulfilled his directions; and it proved, when too late, that the bankers had by mistake, instead of investing the money, opened an account with themselves to the credit of the trustee. Five months afterwards they became bankrupt, and the money was lost. The Plaintiff's counsel rested their case on the delay of five months without inquiry. The Vice-Chancellor said, that "the period of months, all but a few days, having elapsed after the deposit of the money without investment, and without inquiry by the Defendant, he was answerable for the loss which was sustained." Now, the especial bearing of the two last cases is this: that, even supposing Mr. Carey were justified originally in leaving the duty of registering the settlement to Macnamara, the subsequent neglect for four years to inquire whether he had done so would constitute of itself a distinct breach of trust, which would make him responsible. The case of *Jacob* v. *Lucas* 1 Beav. 436 contains a clear intimation of Lord Langdale's opinion, that when the subject of settlement is a fund standing in the names of other trustees for the settlor, the trustees of the settlement must give notice of it to the former trustees; and that, if they neglect to do so, and the settlor is thereby enabled to deal with the fund in favour of third parties, who gain priority by giving the first notice, the trustees of the settlement must make good the loss – a case extremely analogous to the neglect to register a deed of real estate.

I cannot at all appreciate the way in which these cases were dealt with in the Court below. It seems to have been supposed that they proceeded on something peculiar to trusts of money and stock. It was said, the acts to be done in those cases were necessary to vest the trust fund in the trustees, and that steps were necessary to be taken by the trustees which they alone could take. But in *Mathews* v. *Brise,* or in *Challen* v. *Shippam,* or in *Ghost* v. *Waller,* the vesting of the funds in the trustees was complete; and in the cases on the non-transfer of stock agreed to be settled, the step necessary was not only *not* one which the trustees alone could take, but was one which could be done *only* by the settlor. But the judges who decided those cases did not base them on any fanciful niceties of this kind, but upon the broad and irrefragable principle that the trustee was above all things bound to care for the stability of the trust, and to keep the fund out of wrong hands. He must, in Lord Langdale's emphatic words, "*make it impossible*" for any unauthorized person to receive and misapply the fund. And if we will look at realities, and not at delusive forms of speech, what is the difference between leaving stock or money in the hands of the settlor, or of a co-trustee, or of a banker or a broker, and deliberately leaving a settled estate mixed up and confounded with the settlor's unsettled estate, by leaving him in possession of all outward *indicia* of absolute ownership, and placing it at his simple discretion whether the settlement shall ever see the light? Is there sense, or substance, or reality, in telling us gravely, in such a case, the conveyance is complete – the estate has passed? If this deed had been a deed of purchase by Mr. Carey for himself, and with his own money, whose business would the registration of it have been – who would have looked sharply and carefully after it? And is it to be laid down in the Court of Chancery that a trustee owes a less duty to the *feme covert* and the infants whom he has undertaken to protect than he would owe to himself? But there still remains the case, which goes so far beyond the requirements of the present as at once to show that the question here is not whether we shall make a precedent, but whether we shall overrule one. I am to the present moment utterly unable to discern how the dismiss in this case and the decree in *Lester* v. *Lester* 6 Ir. Chan. Rep. 513 can both be law. The difficulty I feel about that case is, I must confess, that I think it a little too strong. If the case made against Mr. Carey had been that he had neglected to find out that some former old lease or deed was unregistered, it would be necessary to rest on *Lester* v. *Lester,* and it might perhaps suffice for the purpose; for what the trustee there was held responsible for was, not leaving undone anything that was necessary to vest the fund in himself – not for neglecting to keep the security such as he found it – but for a thing omitted years before this judgment had been assigned to him, of the necessity for which, or of its non-existence, he, an unprofessional person, was in utter ignorance, and could only discern by a retrospective scrutiny into the security. The conusee of the judgment, one of the subjects of the settlement, had thought proper, whether inadvertently or advisedly, to keep the judgment in its primary condition of a merely personal security, and had assigned it to the trustee in that condition; and the trustee merely kept it so, without the faintest notion that it was in his power to make it better. The only distinction suggested here in argument between that case and the present was this:–After the passing of the Judgment Mortgage Act (1850) (many years after the marriage), the Petitioner and her husband got the trustee to make an affidavit for registry as a mortgage under that Statute; and it was said the trustee's attention was thereby called to the position of the judgment, and that it was considered insecure. But the question is, was there anything in that transaction calculated to awaken a suspiciion that there was any defect in the judgment *qua judgment?* To my mind, I confess, it seems quite the other way. No complaint whatever of the judgment – no suggestion that it was not as good as any judgment could be; but, "we want, in addition, something better than any judgment can be, namely, a mortgage; and this new Act gives us the means of getting it." How can it reasonably be said that there was anything in this to awaken a thought that there was *something else* which might be done to make the judgment better *as a judgment?* Can it seriously be said that, if the trustee would not otherwise be liable for the non-registry under the Act of 1844, this transaction would fix him with that liability? But the Chancellor in that case bases his judgment on broader grounds:–"It does not seem," he says (p.516), "that the Petitioner or her husband was aware that the judgment was unregistered, and it was rather the trustee's duty than theirs to make the inquiry; they were ignorant, and he was ignorant; no moral blame attaches to either; but it was the trustee's business to have made the inquiry, and it was not theirs."

The trustee there was an unprofessional person; the wife there (the Petitioner) was a *quasi feme sole,* for her life estate was to her separate use; her husband had no adverse interest; yet there it was said the duty of inquiry was on the trustee, not on her or her husband. Here the trustee was a practising barrister; the wife was a pure *feme covert;* the Petitioner now is one of the children then unborn; the thing to be inquired about was an essential to the perfecting of the transaction in which the trustee was himself an actor; the person from whom danger impended was the husband; and yet we are told, in the same Court in which the former case was decided, that this trustee was absolved from the duty of inquiry which the other was held subject to; and the obligation of vigilance was held imposed on the *feme covert* (for there was no one else to exert it), and against her own husband. Beyond all comparison, the strongest case in the books in support of the relief which was refused in this case, is that case of *Lester* v. *Lester.* But I do not rest my own judgment upon it; I feel safer with the English cases, though not so much in point; but I must add, that I consider it wholly impossible that we could affirm this dismiss, unless we were prepared at the same time to affirm that *Lester* v. *Lester* is not law.

I will now ask, in conclusion, if this decree were to stand, what would be its range as an authority hereafter? There are other things besides registry necessary to the perfecting of a settlement. Suppose the settlor is a tenant in tail; would it be a perfectly innocent thing for a trustee knowingly and advisedly to leave the business of enrolling the deed in Chancery under the Statute to the settlor himself, and never make an inquiry whether it was done or not? Strong cases were put in argument; let me put this case:– A tenant in tail, who has two sons, settles the estate, on the marriage of his second son, upon trust, after his own decease, for the uses of that marriage. The lady's fortune is paid to the settlor by her trustee, who executes the settlement. The eldest son happens to be an attorney; he is the only attorney employed in the matter; and the trustee (say, himself a practising barrister) intrusts to him the duty of enrolling the deed under the Statute, and troubles himself no more about the matter. The eldest son does not enrol the deed; and, years after, the father dies; the unbarred estate tail descends on the attorney, the eldest son, who at once himself executes and enrols a disentailing deed, sells the estate to innocent purchasers, and absconds, or dies insolvent. Must the wife and children of the second son lose all? Would not the decree now under appeal by an express authority that there would be no redress against the trustees? Is there, then, no mode whatever of protecting the helpless and unborn against such wrongs as these? I can see none, if their specially constituted protectors, who have accepted that position, may with impunity, though with knowledge, neglect the most simple and ordinary precautions. Therefore it is that it has appeared to me that the fear of making a dangerous precedent which swayed the Court below was misapplied; and that, in truth, it has had the effect of landing the Court in the very danger which it apprehended.

In expressing my concurrence with my Lord Chancellor that this dismiss should be reversed, I disclaim all notion of dealing with any abstract proposition; I found my opinion on the special circumstances of the case. I simply hold that a trustee, who is fixed with such antecedents and such knowledge as attach of this trustee, does less than his duty when he commits the registering of such a settlement as this to the settlor himelf, and puts him at the same time under temptation to blink that duty, by leaving him master of the title deeds, and by letting years pass by without inquiry into his conduct.

It is but just, however, that the Petitioner should be obliged to take measures (say, by proceeding in the Landed Estates Court) for realizing the proceeds of the Gardiner's-place premise, before he ever comes upon the trustee; and that the decree against the latter shall be only for the deficiency, if any. The decree will be drawn up on that principle.

The Lord Chancellor concurs with me in thinking that, as the Petitioner has failed in a considerable part of the case made by his petition, the parties should abide their own costs both here and in the Court below.

Note

See further, *Irish Land Law*, para. 10.050.

II. ACCOUNTS AND INFORMATION

CHAINE-NICKSON V. BANK OF IRELAND
[1946] I.R. 393 (High Court)

The fact are set out in the judgment.

Kenny J.: 24th April, 1975

By a settlement made on the 2nd March, 1956, beween Augustus Alexander Chaine-Nickson (the settlor) of the one part and Rachel Chaine-Nickson, Charles Anthony Brett and Robert Cornwall Lewis-Crosby (therein called the Trustees) of the other part of the settlor, who had paid £40,000 to the trustees, declared that they were to hold that sum upon trust to invest it in their unrestrained discretion as if they were the beneficial owners of it and "upon trust to pay, divide or apply the whole or such part (if any) of the income and capital respectively thereof as they shall from time to time in their absolute and uncontrolled discretion think fit between or for the support, benefit, maintenance or education or otherwise of all or any one or more to the exclusion of the other or others of the members of the Family and any future husband and any other child or children of Denys Sophia Pain [*a daughter of the settlor*] and any wife and child or children of Augustus Terence Chaine-Nickson [*the plaintiff*]." The members of the Family were defined as the settlor's wife, Rachel Halley Chaine-Nickson, his daughter, Denys Sophia Pain, his son, the plaintiff, his son-in-law, Horace Pain, and his grand-daughters, Audrey Kate Pain and Jennifer Jaye Pain.

Clause 8 of the settlement read:– "8. The Settlor expressly declares that the Trustees of this settlement shall, in addition to and not in substitution for any monies hereinbefore declared to be payable to the trustees or any one or more of them, be entitled to pay to and to receive for themselves as annual remuneration to be divided equally between them the sum of £300 or 10% of the gross annual income of the trust fund whichever shall be the greater provided always that any fees paid to the Trustees or any of them as directors or as a director of any comapny in which the trust fund or any part thereof is invested shall be given credit for against the aforesaid annual remuneration."

Clause 10 declared that the settlement was to be an Irish settlement and to be interpreted in accordance with the law in the Republic of Ireland.

The draftsman of the settlement had overlooked the application of the rule against perpetuities to it and so, by a supplemental deed made on the 25th April, 1961, between the settlor and the trustees, it was declared that the trusts created by the settlement were to be exercisable only during the life or lives of the members of the Family, as defined in the settlement, and the settlor and a period of 21 years after the death of the survivor of them.

In 1963 Mrs. Rachel Chaine-Nickson retired as a trustee and the Bank of Ireland were appointed trustees of the settlement. The defendants have made payments under the settlement to the plaintiff, to Mrs. Denys Pain and to other members of the Family.

In March, 1973, the plaintiff's solicitor asked the bank for copies of the accounts of the trust for three years. The reply was that it was not the bank's practice to submit a copy of the trust accounts to all or any of the persons or institutions named as being entitled to benefit under a discretionary settlement. They subsequently provided details of the disbursements made by the trustees from 1959 to the 5th of April, 1973, but refused to give any further information. The correspondence shows that the trust fund is invested in a private unlimited company called Muckmore Investments, which does not distribute any of its surplus income by way of dividends, and that the defendants get the money to make distributions to the persons they decide to benefit by the redemption of shares in the private company. The company has also purchased a house and lands worth about £81,000 and now holds marketable securities with an approximate value of £176,000. The trustees have certainly managed the trust fund with considerable acumen.

The plaintiff's solicitors persisted in their demand for trust accounts since 1959 and, when this was refused, they issued these proceedings in which they claim accounts of the real and personal property now vested in the defendants as trustees, of the dealings of the defendants with the capital and income of the property and of the payments of capital and income made by the defendants to the beneficiaries. The parties do not want accounts taken by the Court but have sought a decision as to what documents and information the plaintiff as a potential beneficiary under the settlement should be given.

Counsel for the plaintiff contended that his client, as one of the class entitled to benefit under the discretionary trust, was entitled to information as to what investments were held by Muckmore Investments, as to the persons who were living in the landed property which had been purchased with part of the trust funds, and as to the amounts which had been paid as remuneration to the trustees. For the trustees it was said that the plaintiff was not a person who is entitled to enforce any obligation under the settlement as the trustees had a complete discretion as to the persons to whom they would make payments of capital and income and that, unless there was an allegation of misconduct, the plaintiff had no right to any information or accounts.

When a beneficiary has a vested interest in a trust fund so that he has a right to payment of the income, the trustees must at all reasonable times at his request give him full and accurate information as to the amount and state of the trust property and permit him, or his solicitor, to inspect the accounts and vouchers and other documents relating to the trust: see Underhill on the Law relating to Trusts and Trustees – 11th ed. (1959) at p. 401. When a beneficiary asks for copies of accounts or trust documents, he is bound to pay the copying charges for these. However, in the case of a discretionary trust, none of the potential beneficiaries have any right to be paid capital or income. All the trust fund is held by the trustees in this case on discretionary trusts and, if the plaintiff is not entitled to the trust accounts and particulars of the investments, it follows that none of the potential beneficiaries have a valid claim to any information from the trustees. The result is that the trustees are not under an obligation to account to anyone in connection with their management of the trust fund. This logical conclusion from the defendants' argument leads to remarkable consequences.

The amount of remuneration to which the trustees are entitled is specified in the settlement and the potential beneficiaries have an interest in seeing that the amount is not exceeded, for they are the persons who will ultimately benefit by payments of capital and income. The defendants' contention, however, has the result that they do not have to account for or disclose the amount of their remuneration. This seems to me to be contrary to the basic concept of a trustee being accountable for his management of the trust fund. In a case where the investment powers of trustees under a discretionary trust are limited, the beneficiaries have a clear interest in getting information as to how the trust fund has been invested but again, if the defendants' contention is correct, the potential beneficiaries can never get the details to ascertain whether the trust fund has been invested in accordance with the terms of the settlement. Indeed, the trustees might make loans out of the trust fund to themselves, and the potential beneficiaries would have no means of ascertaining this. These remarkable results of the defendants' argument convince me that the proposition advanced by their counsel is not the law and that a potential beneficiary under a discretionary trust is entitled to copies of the trust accounts and to information as to the investments which represent the trust fund. The obligation of the trustees is not satisfied by giving particulars of the payments made by them.

This conclusion in principle gets some support from one of the cases which were cited. In *Moore* v. *McGlynn* [1894] 1 I.R. 74 the testator left all his property to his brother and his son to be held by them in trust and to be managed by them for the benefit of his wife and children and he gave them power "to arrange for the settlement of my children as they may determine; and in case they disagree, I will that the parish priest, Reverend M. Gaffney, have full and absolute power to determine both as to amount payable and times of payment." The trustees managed the business owned by the testator for some years, then made a valuation of the property available for distribution and divided the sum at which it was valued in 10 equal shares. The testator had been survived by a widow and nine children. When they offered this sum to one of the children, she declined to accept it and brought proceedings for the administration of the estate. The trustees had refused to give any account of the property which was subject to the trust or of their administration of it.

Vice-Chancellor Chatterton said that while the division of the estate into equal shares was free from objection it was going too far to contend that the ascertainment of the assets to be divided was not subject to investigation by the Court. At p.86 of the report he said:–

"The trustes may have had full and absolute authority to arrange and settle the shares to be given to each child of the sum to be divided; but it would be dangerous to hold that there is no control over their ascertainment of the total amount. They would in such case be judges in their own cause. They had from the death of the testator the entire administration of the assets entrusted to them, including the management of the trading carried on by them. The amount distributable among the children of course depended on the due discharge of those duties, so that if their decision on that amount was to be conclusive, it would be in their power to protect themselves against liability for any default. It is not necessary for the *cestuis que trust* to prove any breach of duty by the trustees for the purpose of having accounts taken of the trust property, as their right to this results from the mere relation between them . . . There must, therefore, be the usual accounts of the real and personal estate."

Counsel for the plaintiff has argued that the trust in *Moore* v. *McGlynn* [1894] 1 I.R. 74 was a discretionary one only and that if one of the potential beneficiaries was entitled to an account of the estate subject to the trust, it must follow that each potential beneficiary under a discretionary trust is entitled to information as to the way in which the trust fund has been invested and of the dealings by the trustee with it. I think that this conclusion is correct and is in accordance with principle.

The other case, *Londonderry's Settlement; Peat* v. *Walsh* [1965] Ch. 918, seems to me to have no relevance to the matters in issue in this case. The Seventh Marquess of Londonderry had made a settlement under which the trustees could divide the capital among the members of a specified class in such shares and proportions as they thought fit. Until the capital had been distributed, the trustees were to hold the income of the trust fund upon trust for such member or members of the specified class as the trustees might determine and, in default of any such determination, upon trust to pay an annuity to the wife of the Seventh Marquess and, subject thereto, to pay the income to his eldest son during his life and, after his death, to the child or children of the Seventh Marquess for the time being living and, if more than one, in equal shares until the death of the last survivor of them. The widow of the Seventh Marquess and the Eighth Marquess had died and a daughter of the Seventh Marquess sought details of the administration of the trust fund. Before the proceedings were brought, she had been given copies of the trust accounts and so her right to these was not discussed. The trustees had decided on a division of the capital, and the information sought by the daughter related to the reasons which the trustees had for their decision. The trustees then brought proceedings for a decision as to what information they were bound to disclose to the daughter. She had a vested interest in the income which had not been distributed under the discretionary trust and was, therefore, not a potential beneficiary but one who had an enforceable right against the trustees.

In *Peat's Case* [1965] Ch. 918 the High Court (Plowman J.), missled by a grossly inaccurate report of an earlier decision, ordered the trustees to furnish information as to their meetings and as to the correspondence which they had received from the beneficiaries. The Court of Appeal decided that the trustees were not bound to disclose the agenda of the meetings of the trustees, correspondence passing between the individuals who were trustees and the persons who consent to the exercise of the trustees and beneficiaries, and minutes of meetings of the trustees. The case is not a decision that a potential beneficiary is entitled to copies of the trust accounts or as to the information to which he is entitled. It decides only what trustees under a discretionary trust are not obliged to disclose.

It seems to me that legal principle and the one relevant authority establish that a potential beneficiary under a discretionary trust is entitled to copies of the trust accounts and to details of the investments representing the trust fund. I do not propose to order any accounts to be taken by the Court, but I will declare that the plaintiff, as a potential beneficiary under the settlement of the 2nd March, 1956, is entitled at his expense to be furnished by the defendant with copies of the trust accounts relating to that settlement since 1956 and to the balance sheet and profit and loss accounts of Muckmore Investments since the incorporation of that company. I shall also declare that the plaintiff is entitled to be informed by the defendants of the names of the persons residing in any landed property purchased by the trustees and of the outgoings in connection with it paid out of the trust funds.

As there was no decision by the Courts on this matter, and as the trustees were acting on the advice of counsel, the plaintiff and the defendants will be awarded their costs of these proceedings to be paid out of the capital funds settled by the settlement of 1956.

Notes and Questions

1. What precisely is the point of distinction between this decision and *Re Londonderry's Settlement?* Is any information or document held by the trustees likely to be held to be confidential – in a discretionary trust or any other kind of trust? See further *Irish Land Law*, paras. 10.051–2
2. For *Moore* v. *McGlynn*, see p.374, *ante*.

III. INVESTMENTS

RE LYNCH'S TRUSTS
[1931] I.R. 517 (High Court)

The facts are set out in the judgment.

Johnston J.:

This matter comes before me on a summons taken out by the executors and trustees of the will of one, Cornelius Lynch, deceased, for the determination of certain questions arising upon the construction of the will of the deceased, and affecting the rights of the defendants as legatees and devisees under the will. The defendants are the infant children of Cornelius Lynch, and are wards of Court, under the care of the Chief Justice, who, on July 11th, 1930, made an order giving liberty to the plaintiffs to take the present proceedings, and suggesting the questions which are set out in the summons. I do not know of any rule of law or practice which precludes me under such circumstances from giving the plaintiffs the assistance that they require.

The testator, who died in 1927, left five children, four daughters and one son, of whom the eldest, a daughter, is now thirteen years of age, and the youngest, also a daughter, is now four and a half. He left to his daughter, Annie, a legacy of £1,000, in these terms: "I bequeath to my daughter, Annie, the sum of one thousand pounds if and when she shall attain the age of twenty-one years, and in the meantime I direct that said legacy shall be lodged on deposit receipt in any bank my trustees may choose in the joint names of my trustees and my said daughter, and shall so remain during the minority of my said daughter; and on her attaining the age of twenty-one years the amount thereof, with the accrued interest, shall be paid to her; and it is my will that my trustees shall not otherwise invest said moneys." Legacies of £1,000 are given to the other three daughters, Cornelia, Betty, and Mary, in identical terms. Then there is a provision for the disposal of each legacy, "with the accumulation of income," in the event of any one or more of the daughters dying before attaining the age of twenty-one – an event which has not happened – and all the residue of the testator's property of every kind is devised and bequeathed to Cornelius, the son, if and when he shall attain twenty-one years. There is then a provision that the net income from the testator's lands shall be paid by the trustees to the widow, and used for the support and maintenance of herself and such of her children as may be minors, and the whole family is given the right of residence in the testator's dwelling-house.

The testator directed that the whole of his residuary estate, "other than my said lands, house property and the furniture in my said dwelling-house," should be realized, "and the proceeds thereof placed on deposit receipt in any bank my trustees may choose in their joint names and not otherwise invested, the interest thereon to accumulate, and the accumulation thereof with the principal to be paid to my said son on his attaining the age of twenty-one years." There are also very precise directions as to the disposal of Cornelius's share of the estate in the event of his not attaining twenty-one years of age.

This will might be described as a very tidy will. The provisions which I have set out, and others to which I have not alluded, have been framed and phrased with the most extreme care and orderliness, and the whole document displays great solicitude on the part of the testator for his family, and an earnest desire to make things as easy for them after his death as possible. Each girl is to get £1,000, and the boy is to get all that remains. Whilst the family is growing up, they are to reside in the dwelling-house – Eagle Lodge – with their mother, who is to have the net income arising from the whole of the lands for the support of herself and her children. Everything would have been all right if things had turned out as the testator had planned; but, unfortunately, they did not. The executors have placed upon deposit receipt four sums of £1,000, representing each of the legacies left to the four daughters, and a further sum of £1,000 on account of and in respect of, the son's share in the realized residue. These sums are now represented by five deposit receipts, whose total face value is at present £5,202 7s. 4d. The interest payable in respect of these deposit receipts is at the rate of £1 10s. per cent, per annum, and the executors, after most exhaustive efforts, have been unable to get better terms from any bank. The net income arising from the whole of the lands available for the support of the whole family (the widow being entitled to her support equally with the minors) is only a sum of about £220. It is obvious that the sum is quite inadequate for the purpose, and if it is not supplemented from other sources must leave the family in an extremely miserable, not to say squalid, state of existence. It has been ascertained in Chambers in the Minor Matter that a sum of £365 per annum will be necessary for the proper support and maintenance of the five children, and in an affidavit by one of the trustees – a brother of the widow – it is stated that an additional sum of £100 per annum will be necessary in respect of the widow's maintenance. I accept these figures as being both reasonable and proper. Mr. McCullen, the trustee in question, states further in his affidavit that he was on very friendly terms with the testator, who had in his lifetime carried on a successful business as a cattle-dealer, and that he had maintained his family in a generous and comfortable manner, but that he had made a grave miscalculation as to the income that would be available from the letting of the lands for support of the family.

The first question that I am asked to decide is this : "Is there jurisdiction in the Court to apply the income from the money representing the legacies bequeathed by the said will to each of the said defendants towards the maintenance, support, and education of each such defendant during his or her minority if the Court be of opinion that the moneys otherwise available for such maintenance, support, and education are insufficient!" My unhesitating answer to that question is in the affirmative. There is, apart from statute law, a number of cases in which Courts of Equity have exercised such jurisdiction in circumstances such as the present; but sect. 43 of the Conveyancing Act, 1881, which is an express statutory provision for the proposition that is before me, obviates the necessity for any consideration of the former principles of the Courts of Equity in regard to such a matter. Sub-sect. 3 of that section provides that the section is to apply only if, and so far as, a contrary intention is not expressed in the instrument under which the interest of the infant arises. No such contrary intention is expressed in the will of the testator, unless the direction for the accumulation of the income until the legatee attains the age of twenty-one is to be regarded as such; but it was definitely decided by Pearson J., in *In re Thatcher's Trusts* 26 Ch. D. 426, that such a direction is not an expression of a contrary intention. That decision is in accordance with the old equity cases, and was referred to with approval by O'Connor M.R. in *In re Ramadge's Settlement* [1919] 1 I.R. 205.

The second question in the summons is of a different character. It is this: if the Court be of opinion that it is necessary or desirable in the interest of the said defendants in the circumstances of this estate to direct the investment during their respective minorities of the legacy of each such minor in manner other than by placing same upon deposit receipt, as directed by the said will, is there jurisdiction in the Court to direct such investment? The situation that has given rise to this question is ludicrously pathetic. This family – the mother and her five young children – have a comfortable country house, suitably furnished, in which to reside. They have a net annual income from the lands amounting to £220, and they have a capital sum of £5,000 (not to speak of any further residue that may be realized on behalf of Cornelius), which, if invested in suitable trustee securities, would bring in a sum of nearly £250 a year, the whole being sufficient to enable the family to live comfortably, if not luxuriously. Owing, however, to the testator's strange direction that the capital should be lodged in a bank on deposit receipt, earning interest at the rate of one and a half per cent., and that the executors should not "otherwise invest" it, the available cash, as Mr. McCullen says, "is sufficient for the maintenance, support, and education of the said minors, even if no provision is made for the maintenance and support of the widow. Must the minors wait for years before they can get the full benefit of the provision that has been made for them? Supposing that the testator had directed (as other testators have done in the past) that all the income of the estate should be accumulated until the children had attained twenty-one years, would a Court of Equity be obliged to sit by and see the children starve? There is apt authority to the effect that this would not be done. The illustration that I have put differs from the present case in degree, but not, I think, in principle.

During the course of the argument some references were incidentally made to the famous *bon mot* concerning "judicious breaches of trust" ; but a breach of trust is out of the question. Nothing can be done by the Court except in accordance with the settled principles of equity. As recently as 1913, in *Badger* v. *Badger* [1913] 1 Ch. 385, where there was a question as to the maintenance of an infant who was interested in a reversionary interest in real estate expectant upon the death of a lady aged 85 years, Hamilton L.J. laid down this guiding principle : "I think it would be right to be ingenious in devising any form of order for the benefit of the infant, but we must confine ourselves within the limits of our jurisdiction."

In the present case, what is the predominating trust which the will of this testator has constituted ? It is, primarily, a trust for the distribution, in accordance with the expressed wishes of the testator, of his property, real and personal, amongst his widow and his five infant children when they come of age, and, pending that period, for the suitable support and maintenance of his family, and for the proper education of his children. That is the trust that is expressed in the will in plain and unambiguous language, and it represents the first and predominating object of the testator. All the minor and subsidiary directions in the will must, of course, be scrupulously observed by the trustees and the Court; but in so far as they conflict or are inconsistent with what I have described as the predominating purpose of the testator, they, of course, must give way. It does not require the exercise of much common sense to see that when the main purpose of a testator, as expressed in plain language, cannot be carried out by reason of a subsidiary direction, which renders the carrying out of the main purpose impossible, it is the subsidiary direction which must be disregarded, and not the main purpose. By the application of that principle in the present case I think that, under the circumstances that have arisen, the Court has undoubted jurisdiction to disregard the direction as to the lodgment of the legacies on deposit receipt, and to direct them to be in suitable trustee securities.

This principle has been well established by a long line of authority in Courts of Equity. The most recent of those cases is a decision of that great equity lawyer, Mr. Justice Farwell, who, in a judgment of the utmost lucidity and persuasiveness, has placed this question, to my mind, beyond all doubt. In *Walker* v. *Duncombe* [1901] 1 Ch. 879, it appeared that a testator, who had left a very large settled estate, expressly directed that an infant tenant-in-tail should receive out of it a sum "not exceeding in the whole" £500 a year for his maintenance and education, and that the rest should be accumulated. The net income of the settled property exceeded £14,000 yearly. Farwell J. considered that he had power, notwithstanding the restrictive direction in the will as to the limited amount to be expended upon the infant, to sanction a scheme whereby £4,000 a year should be spent in keeping up the family mansion and maintaining the infant in a state suitable to his means and condition. Farwell J. said: "I decline to accept any suggestion that the Court has an inherent jurisdiction to alter a man's will because it thinks it beneficial. It seems to me that is quite impossible. But in considering what is the true construction of the will, it is open to the Court to ascertain if there be a paramount intention expressed in the will, and if so, to consider whether particular directions are properly to be read as subordinate to such paramount intention, or are to be treated as independent positive provisions." The case of *Havelock* v. *Havelock* 17 Ch. D. 807 is another case illustrating how far a Court of Equity is entitled to go, where the interests of minors are involved, for the purpose of carrying out the main purpose of a trust, even to the extent of disregarding subsidiary directions which are inconsistent with the main purpose, and I think that the same principle was at the root of the decision of Shadwell V.C. in *Bridge* v. *Brown* 2 Y. & C. Ch. Cas. 181. I have been very kindly referred by counsel since the argument to the case of *Minch* v. *Minch* 57 Ir. L. T. R. 135, which seems to have been decided by O'Connor M.R. upon the principle that was enunciated by Farwell J.

In the present case it is not proposed to interfere with the disposal of either the capital or income of the trust estate. The sole desire of the executors and trustees and of the Court is to carry out the trust for the support and maintenance of the widow, "and the support, maintenance and education of all my said children who may be under the age of twenty-one years." Everyone – the widow and her co-executors and trustees, as well as the legal advisers of the parties, including the solicitor and counsel who represent the children – is not only willing, but anxious, that the proposal should be carried out as being necessary from the point of view of the trust, and as a method of considerably enhancing the value of the assets. As Mr. Overend very forcibly points out, a contingency has arisen in regard to the income derivable from the landed property, which was very evidently unforeseen by the testator. It is necessary tht the minors should continue to have what Lord Halsbury, in *Barnes* v. *Ross* [1896] A.C. 625, calls "the inestimable advantage" of their mother's care and help, and it is clear that that was contemplated by the testator. I am satisfied that, in the words of Farwell J., there is "a paramount intention expressed in the will," and that it would be impossible to carry out that intention if the "particular direction" were adhered to. Hard cases may make bad law but sometimes they make good equity. Accordingly, I shall answer the second question in the affirmative.

Notes and Questions

1. What limits are there to the Court's jurisdiction to disregard an express direction as to investment of the trust fund?
2. See further as to investment of trust funds, *Irish Land Law,* para. 10.053 *et seq.*

RE O'CONNOR

[1913] 1 I.R. 69 (Chancery Division)

A will contained the following investment clause :–"My trustees being at liberty to sell all my ships, houses, and other property of mine, and invest same as they think most desirable, but not in the British funds, my trustees to be free from all liability in investing any of the money received for sale of any of my property."

Meredith M.R.:

The clause in the will is as follows:–[The Master of the Rolls read the clause.] The principal question for determination is whether the trustees of the will had power to invest the testator's residuary estate in the purchase of freehold or leasehold property as well as on loan or in the purchase of such stocks, shares, or other property as they should think fit. One thing is certain, however unlimited the power of investment may be, the trustee remains subject to the jurisdiction of the Court. The trustee has no power to act dishonestly, negligently, or in breach of trust to invest on insufficient security, but, subject to the power of the Court to compel a dishonest, grossly negligent, or grossly incompetent trustee to account for money he has so invested, it is in the power of a testator or settlor to place in the hands of his trustee money to be invested in the fullest sense of the word, and I need no further or better authority for the proposition that a power to invest *simpliciter* enables a trustee to invest in the purchase of real estate, provided he does so honestly and as a reasonable man, than the Trustee Act, 1893, section 6 of which is a sufficient justification for the conclusion at which I have arrived on that point. The section runs as follows:–"A trustee having power to invest in the purchase of land or on mortgage of land may invest in the purchase or on mortgage of any land, notwithstanding the same is charged with a rent, under the powers of the Public Main Drainage Act, 1846 to 1856, or the Landed Property Improvement (Ireland) Act, 1847, or by an absolute order made under the Improvement of Land Act, 1864, unless the terms of the trust expressly provide that the land to be purchased or taken in mortgage shall not be subject to any such prior charge." The word "invest" is there used as equivalent to purchase. A reference to Murray's New English Dictionary shows that the term "invest" is used in the sense of to purchase, as well as placing out money on loan or other security.

In my opinion, the dictionaries, lay and legal, support the view of Mr. Brown that the term "invest", unless cut down or minimized by the testator or settlor, embraces purchase of land with moneys, as well as placing money on loan. But Mr. Wilson's argument was a very cogent one, that the liberty given by the testator to the trustees to invest the proceeds of the sale of his property as they thought most desirable, except in British funds, did not authorize them to purchase land, and that a power to invest was not regarded as a power to purchase, and that all the provisions of the Trustee Act assumed or begged the question that there was on the face of the instrument a power to purchase land.

In my opinion there is the clearest and most express power in this will to invest in land, the only investment that is barred by the testator being that which is always regarded as most secure, the British funds. He empowers his trustees to sell all his property, and to invest the proceeds "as they think most desirable, but not in the British funds." There are no restrictions here except one, investment in British funds. If I may misuse the maxim *expressio unius est exclusio alterius,* it comes to this that the negation of the power to invest in British funds is an expression of a power and liberty to invest in any kind of investment known to the law, but the testator was well aware that the Court of Chancery would hold the trustees responsible for moneys that came to their hands, for the benefit of minors and others, if they did not act in the way in which a reasonable man acting with reasonable prudence and not grossly negligent would act, and that when trustees came to make up their accounts with their *cestui que trusts,* it could not be said that they had authority to purchase, *e.g.*, a number of houses in a street in such a state of disrepair that the local authority would order them to be pulled down.

My construction of the will is supported overwhelmingly by the decision of Sir Andrew Porter in this very case: indeed, Mr. Wilson directed my attention to the report of *Blount* v. *O'Connor* 17 L.R. Ir. 620. That case is a clear decision that the investments, one of which is quarrelled with here, were investments by which the parties were bound.

No doubt there is a passage in the judgment of Sir Andrew Porter, at p.631 of the report, as follows:– "These advances were made at the express request of the several persons entitled to the respective shares, and are, so far as I can see, good payments to them on account of their shares." This statement is not accurate, because though the advances were made at the request of the several persons entitled, they were made at the request of tenants for life, not of those that came after. But still I think that the Master of the Rolls came to the conclusion that the investments in land were within the powers of investment conferred by the will.

Then there is the order of July 8th, 1890. It answers in the affirmative the questions referred by the Master of the Rolls to the Chief Clerk. It declares that the division and appropriation of the assets and trust funds made by the executors and trustees of the will which the Chief Clerk found to be for the benefit of the minors were properly made and binding on all persons claiming under the settlement and will. Mr. Brown goes further than is necessary in asking me to hold that the property was rightly converted from that time. I only rely on it as a sanction by the Master of the Rolls of investments as good investments within the power, and not capable of being objected to, or of being set aside, even by persons acting on behalf of minors. I do not think that the Master of the Rolls had the question of conversion before him at all, but I hold that the purchase of land and house property was a lawful investment, and that no on in connexion with the suit objected to the investments on the ground of negligence, extravagance of price, or for other similar reasons, and that the net result is, as regards the Mulhussey property and No. 1 Glendower Place, that the investments being authorized investments, the *cestui que trusts,* not having dissented or elected to take the property one way or another, must be held to have taken the property as they found it, as real estate, subject to this, that the general power to invest for the benefit of a number of persons necessarily implied a power to transpose and re-invest, and therefore that Mr. Brown's contention is well founded, that the £2000, portion of the £5000, proceeds of the sale of No. 1 Glendower Place, is divisible amongst the next-of-kin, and that the heir-at-law takes the rest, which was invested in the real estate, namely, No.5 Glendower Place.

I only refer to two cases; the first is *Legg* v. *Mordan* [1905] 1 Ch. 515, in which the word "invest" received the widest meaning, and though Mr. Wilson pointed out that that was a decision on the words of a particular will, and that reliance was placed in the judgment of Vaughan Williams, L.J., on the word "rents" in the clause of dealing with the distribution of the income, yet I think that his judgment may be divided into two, and that in the first part of it he held that the power to invest upon freehold and leasehold ground rents authorized the purchase of leasehold ground rents. The judgment of Stirling L.J., is free from doubt. He says:–"It appears to me that if the authority to invest on Government securites would justify a purchase of Consols or other Governemnt security, the authority to invest on freehold or leasehold ground rents must equally justify a purchase of freehold or leasehold ground rent." Sir Gorell Barnes agreed. The second case, *In re Gent & Eason's Contract* [1905] 1 Ch. 386, in the same volume, shows that the word "investment" may have a wider meaning than it is supposed to possess, and it is also an authority that trustees may transpose and vary securities.

I shall not refer to other cases which have not been discussed, but I have not been able to find any case which would compel me to give a restricted meaning to the words of this will.

The Court made the following order:–

As to question No. 1 in said summons this Court doth declare that the trustees of the will of the testator in the title hereof mentioned had power under the said will to invest the residuary estate of the said testator, or any part thereof, in the purchase of the properties known as No. 1 Glendower Place, London, and the Mulhussey property in the county of Roscommon. The Court doth not deem it necessary to answer question No.2, and as to question No. 3 the Court doth declare that the said trustees had power to sell the said property, No.1 Glendower Place, and invest portion of the proceeds thereof in the purchase of No. 5 Glendower Place; and, in answer to question No.4, this court doth declare that the estate and interest of Walter Patrick Hussey Walsh in such investments, so far as same consisted of real estate, at the death of the said Walter Patrick Hussey Walsh passed to his heir-at-law, and, so far as same consisted of personal estate, to his personal representative, and the Court doth not deem it necesssary to answer question No.5; and as to question No.6 this Court doth declare that the balance of the proceeds of the sale of No.1 Glendower Place, over and above the portion thereof allocated to the purchase of No.5 Glendower Place, should be deemed to be personal estate; and this Court doth declare the plaintiff and the said defendants entitled to their respective costs of the said application and this order thereon when taxed and ascertained, said costs to be paid rateably out of the portion coming to the said heir-at-law as real estate, and the portion coming to the said personal representative as personal estate.

Notes and Questions

Could the trustees have invested in land if there had been no express power in the will ? See *Irish Land Law,* para. 10.055.

SMITHWICK V. SMITHWICK

(1861) 12 Ir. Ch. R. 181; 6 Ir. Jur. (N.S.) 282 (Rolls Court)

The facts are set out in the judgment.

Smith M.R.:

The petition in this case has been filed by the petitioner to make the respondent William Smithwick, who was one of the trustees in her marriage settlement, dated the 13th of July 1825, liable for a breach of trust.

That settlement was made between Maria Theresa Waller, the petitioner's mother, of the first part, the petitioner, then Maria Waller, of the second part, Michael Smithwick of the third part, Lord Bloomfield and Samuel Waller of the fourth part, and the respondent William Smithwick and John Duke of the fifth part. It recited the intended marriage between the petititioner and Michael Smithwick, since deceased, and that, for the considerations in the settlement mentioned, the estate of the said Michael Smithwick in the lands of Mount Catherine and Emly, and the sums of £4000 and £2000, late currency, should be respecitively settled on certain trusts. It appears from a further recital that the sum of £4000 consisted of £1500, late currency, the marriage portion of the petitioner, which was charged on the Waller estates, and of £2500, late currency, the property of the said Michael Smithwick, and which sums, with the further sum of £2000, like currency, were to be settled on the trust therein mentioned. The deed then contains recitals showing the instruments under which the portion of the petitioner of £1500 was charged on the Waller estates, and said charge of £1500 was vested in the respondent and his co-trustee, on the trusts in the settlement mentioned. Michael Smithwick then assigned to the trustees said lands of Mount Catherine and Emly; and the trustees were to hold said lands and said sums of £4000 and £2000, on trust, to pay the rents and interest to Michael Smithwick for life; and as to the said lands, they were settled in strict settlement after his decease. The settlement then provided that, as to the £4000 the petitioner was to receive thereout, for her life, in case she survived her husband, the sum of £200 a-year, late currency, in full or her jointure, subject to the proviso therein contained; that is, that if she should reside at Mount Catherine, the annuity was to be reduced to £100 a-year.

The settlement then contains a provision that, if the lands of Emly, after the decease of the petitioner, should become of less value, by the amount of £100 a-year, than what they produced at the date of the settlement, the trustees should pay £2000, part of the £4000, to the person entitled to the inheritance of Emly, under the limitations in the settlement, and the remaining £2000 to be at the disposal of the said Michael Smithwick; and if the lands of Emly should not decrease in value, then, after the death of the petitioner, the whole of the £4000 should be assigned by the trustees to the executors of Michael Smithwick, in such manner as he should by deed or will appoint. In the event of Michael Smithwick surviving the petitioner, there are some limitations as to the £4000, which are not material, as that event did not happen.

The settlement then contains a proviso authorising Michael Smithwick, with the consent of the trustees, to call in the £4000 and £2000, or any part thereof, and to lay out and dispose of the same in the purchase of an estate of inheritance or freehold, for a term of at lease three lives, or of a lease for a term of years, whereof ninety-years shall be unexpired, "or otherwise advantageously; which purchase or disposal, when so made, shall be settled and vested to the several uses, intents and purposes hereinbefore mentioned, in respect to said sums." It is strange, where one of the questions in this case is, whether the respondent was guilty of a breach of trust in consenting, at the instance of the petitioner and her husband, that the trust fund should be lent, that the petition should have omitted to state that clause.

There was one child of the marriage between the petitioner and Michael Smithwick, William Henry Smithwick, who attained his age in May 1847. Michael Smithwick died in April 1857, and the petitioner not having exercised the option of residing at Mount Catherine, the petition alleges that she became entitled to the £200 a-year, to be paid out of the interest of the said sum of £4000. The petition then states that the £4000, which was late currency, consisted of £1500, late currency, the portion of the petitioner, and of the following securities – viz., three judgments against Lord Gort, conditioned to secure the respective sums of £1288 6s. 3d., £400 and £800, and which three judgments were assigned to William Smithwick and John Bourke as trustees in the said settlement. A sum of £2000 was due to Michael Smithwick at the date of the settlement, by a person of the name of Bleasby.

John Burke died in 1826, before any of the trust funds were realised, leaving his co-trustee, the respondent William Smithwick, him surviving.

The petition alleges that a sum of £410. 5s. 1d., present currency, part of the petitioner's portion of £1500, having been received by the respondent, he lent same to the late Michael Smithwick, in 1849; and a deed was executed in that year, by and between the said Michael Smithwick and the petitioner of the first part, the said William Henry Smithwick, their son, of the second part, and the respondent William Smithwick, of the third part, whereby the said Michael Smithwick, and the petitioner, and their said son, in consideration of the payment of the said sum of £410. 5s. 1d. to them, released the said William Smithwick from said sum and from all sums due on the £1500, and from the trusts in the settlement regarding the same. The petition omits to state, what it ought to have stated, that the said indenture was acknowledged by the petitioner before Commissioners under the statute. One of the questions which arises is, whether the acknowledgment was of any avail, as, although the £410. 5s. 1d. might, under the trusts of the settlement, be invested in land, it was not necessary that it should be laid out in the purchase of land, under the trusts of the settlement. The petition alleges that the sum of £410.5s. 1d. was paid to Michael Smithwick, and no part to the petitioner or her son; and the petitioner submits that, having been a *feme covert,* she is not bound by the said deed, and that the respondent was guilty of a breach of trust, in respect of said sum.

The petition then proceeds to state, but not correctly, the facts connected with the alleged second breach of trust. The following is, I believe, a correct statement of the facts connected with this part of the case. The sum of £1288. 6s. 3d., late currency, being the amount of one of the judgments against Lord Gort, was paid to the respondent in 1836, as surviving trustee in the settlement. The statements in the petition as to Bleasby's judgment are not material, the petitioner's annuity of £200 a-year not having been payable thereout, as I understand the deed. A sum of £3000 was lent in 1843, on mortgage, to William Henry Brazier Waller, the petitioner's brother. The petition describes him as one W.H.B. Waller – a singular mode for the petitioner to describe her brother. The mortgage, which bears date the 29th of July 1843, was executed to the responent by Mr. Waller, of certain lands in the counties of Tipperary and Limerick, to secure the said sum of £3000, with £6 per cent. interest. The sum paid on foot of the said judgment against Lord Gort formed part of the said sum of £3000; the residue was advanced by Michael Smithwick, out of his own funds, and formed no part of the trust funds on which the £200 a-year was charged. The security on which the £3000 was lent has proved insufficient, and the £3000 has been lost; and the petitioner submits that, although the said loan was made with the knowledge and without the dissent of the petitioner, yet that it was a breach of trust; and that the respondent is bound to make good so much of said sum of £3000 as was chargeable with the petitioner's annuity of £200 a-year; and that she is not, in any manner, affected by her acquiescence in said loan.

The petition states that the residue of the trust funds, secured by the two other judgments against Lord Gort, was realised in the cause of *Gort* v. *Vereker,* and has been invested in the purchase of £1193. 4s. 8d Government New £3 per cent. stock; and the petitioner has received the dividends thereof in part payment of the £200 a-year. The petition then alleges that there is an arrear of £538. 14s. 8d, due to the petitioner on foot of the said annuity of £200 a-year; and it prays that the respondent may be ordered to lodge in Court such sums, portion of the trust funds, as are liable to the payment of her annuity. The prayer should have been more precise; but what is, I believe, meant is, that the respondent should bring into Court the £410. 5s. 1d., paid to Michael Smithwick and his son; and should also lodge in Court so much of the £3000, lent to the petitioner's brother, as consisted of the £1288. 6s. 3d., late currency, paid to the respondent on foot of one of the judgments against Lord Gort. The sum received from Bleasby does not, as I have already stated, appear to have been received by the respondent, or to have been subject to the petitioner's annuity. Thus this is a petition to make the respondent answerable for two sums; the one paid to the petitioner's husband; the second sum lent to her brother, at her special instance and request.

The respondent's affidavit was filed on the 8th of Decemer 1860, and he states therein that the only portion of the trust funds received by him was, first, the said sum of £410. 5s. 1d., being part of the said portion of £1500, late currency, together with £283.1s. 10d., for interest up to May 1833; secondly, the sum of £746. 0s. 5d., old £3½ per cent. stock, and £361. 8s. 5d., old £3 per cent. stock, being the sums paid on foot of the judgments against Lord Gort, conditioned to pay the said sum of £1288. 6s. 3d., late currency; thirdly, a sum of £1193. 14s. 8d., Government stock, received by the respondent in *Gort* v. *Vereker,* on foot of the two other judgments against Lord Gort, and which stock has been transferred into the name of the petitioner and her son. The respondent denies ever having received the sum due by Bleasby, and states that it never was assigned to him: but this is not material, as that sum was not, I apprehend, a security for the petitioner's annuity. The respondent then states the payment of the said sum of £283. 1s. 10d. interest, to Michael Smithwick, which he was entitled to receive under the settlement. The respondent then states the application to him, by Michael Smithwick and the petitioner and their son, for said sum of £410. 5s. 1d., and their offer to release him from said sum; and the affidavit then states the deed of release of the 10th of December 1849.

It is not sought to charge the respondent with the residue of £1500, late currency, of which the £410. 5s. 1d. formed a part, as it was never received by the respondent.

The affidavit of the respondent then states the acknowledgment of the said deed, by the petitioner, before Commissioners, and refers to their certificate; and that, on the due execution of the release, the respondent caused said sum of £410. 5s. 1d. to be paid to Michael Smithwick and William Henry Smithwick, and not to Michael Smithwick alone. The affidavit then states that the said deed was enrolled, and relies on the deed as binding on the petitioner.

The affidavit then proceeds to detail the circumstances connected with the second branch of the case. In the year 1842, William H. B. Waller, brother of the petitioner, having occasion to borrow a sum of £3000, applied to Michael Smithwick for a loan of the said sum. Michael Smithwick applied to the respondent to lend the said two sums of stock, viz., the £746. 0s. 5d. and £361. 8s. 5d., to the petitioner's said brother, and said he would lend the remainder, up to £3000; and, at the same time, he enclosed to the respondent a power of attorney to transfer the said two sums, which respondent then refused to do, for the reasons thereinafter stated. The affidavit of respondent then states a letter from Mr. Worrall, solicitor to the respondent, dated the 23rd of October 1843, in which the circumstances connected with the proposed loan to the petitioner's brother are referred to, and the fact that Mr. Christian, now Judge Christian, had been consulted, and given an opinion that the loan might be safely made by the trustees for the petitioner's marriage settlement; and Mr. Worrall states that the mortgage would be to the respondent for the entire sum of £3000, although the respondent was only required to advance the Government's stock before stated. The letter states that the lands to be mortgaged would be free from all incumbrances except a debt due to Mr. Bessonett; and that, out of the sum to be lent by the respondent and Michael Smithwick, the interest due to Mr. Bessonett would be paid; and that if the interest was not paid, Mr. Bessonett would proceed to have the lands sold. Mr. Worrall's letter concluded thus, "I trust, under the circumstances, you will no longer hesitate executing the power of attorney." The affidavit then states, paragraph 15, that the respondent refused to lend said two sums of Government stock to the said W.H.B. Waller, the petitioner's brother, notwithstanding the urgent requests and entreaties of the said Michael Smithwick, and of the petitioner, who pressed respondent to do so, until he had made inquiry as to the value of the proposed security, and, amongst others, from the said James Worrall, and satisfied himself that the security was, as he the respondent believed, sufficient. The affidavit then states that Mr. Worrall was the solicitor for Michael Smithwick and the petitioner, in whom they reposed great confidence, and that he was well acquainted with the value of the property of the petitioner's brother; and the affidavit then sets out a letter from Mr. Worrall to the respondent, dated the 27th of October 1843, in which Mr. Worrall states that, in executing a power for the transfer of the said two sums of Government stock "and which are part of the sum of £3000 mentioned in the mortgage deed of Mr. Waller to you, I pledge myself that, in thus acting as the surviving trustee of your brother's marriage settlement, you are perfectly safe, and that Mr. Waller's property is ample security, and that you do not incur any responsibility." The affidavit then states that the respondent, believing the statement of the said James Worrall to be true, and that the estate upon which the said money was to be lent was worth between £700 and £800 a-year, and good security therefor, and that the only charge thereon was one vested in Mr. J. Bessonett, for about £6000, consented to lend the said Government stock thereon. The affidavit then states, paragraph 17, that the respondent admits that the security upon which said sum was lent has proved insufficient, and that no portion of the sum so lent has been realised, but the affidavit states, "that the loss thereof arose from the said estate having been forced to a sale in the Incumbered Estates Court, at a time when property was greatly depreciated, whereby said estate sold for half its value; and respondent honestly believed, and still believes, same to have been good security at the time of said loan, at the rate that landed property would then have brought, inasmuch as same was, when said money was lent, worth £16,000." And the affidavit afterwards states that the purchaser in the Incumbered Estates Court has re-sold the lands for more than sufficient to have paid off the said mortgage by the petitioner's brother, and all prior incumbrances.

The affidavit then states that, of the sum of £3000 so lent, only about £1154 was trust money, the rest being the money of Michael Smithwick (the petitioner's husband) himself, which shows the opinion Michael Smithwick then had of the sufficiency of the security. The affidavit then states that the title to the lands mortgaged was perfectly good, and that the loss arose from the property having been sacrificed. The respondent refers to the rental in the Incumbered Estates Court, under which the property was sold, which was £695 a-year, and that the title to the lands mortgaged was perfectly good, and that the timber thereon was valued at £2437. 10s. 6d. The respondent also refers to the valuation of the Incumbered Estates Court of the said lands. The respondent then submits that, having acted with perfect good faith, and due caution, he is not responsible.

An affidavit in reply has been made by the petitioner, which insists, first, that the acknowledgment of the deed of 1849 is not binding on the petitioner, for the reasons I have already adverted to, and to which I shall more particularly refer just now. Secondly; she alleges that the debt due by Bleasby did, in fact, form a part of the trust fund, in the marriage settlement, and that it was the amount of the second and third judgments against Lord Gort which were lent to her brother, together with the sum received from Bleasby; and on which matters the petitioner seeks a reference to the Master. This does not appear to be consistent with the petition. Thirdly; she insists that the loan to her brother was an improper application of the trust fund. Fourthly; she says that there should have been a judgment collateral with the mortgage, her brother having had lands on which the judgment would have attached. Fifthly; that, in addition to Bessonett's mortgage, there were two indemnity deeds affecting her brother's estate at the time of the mortgage of 1843 – one for £164. 13s. 6d., and the other for £155. 1s. 0d.; and that there was also a right of dower affecting the property. The latter objection was decided to be unfounded, by the Incumbered Estates Court. The petitioner then submits that she is entitled to a reference as to the value of the lands at the time of the loan; which reference I shall make, in pursuance of her requisition.

A further affidavit was made by the respondent, stating that the £410. 5s. 1d. was paid to petitioner as well as her husband and son. The affidavit also states that the lands in the mortgage of 1843 were, at the time of the loan, worth more than double the charge thereon; and the acreage and rental, and other matters, are stated to show the value.

The petition in this case is a very unjust proceeding; but I must of course decide the case in accordance with the principles on which Courts of Equity act. I shall first consider the question whether the loan to the petitioner's brother was a breach of trust. With respect to the lands included in the mortgage by the petitioner's brother to the respondent, I believe, on the evidence before the Court, that the value of the lands was, at the date of the mortgage, and the prior incumbrance vested in Mr. Bessonett. It is my intention, however, to direct a reference in such terms as will fully ascertain that fact. Assuming that the value of the lands was far more than sufficient, at the date of the mortgage, to have secured not only the trust fund, but the whole of the £3000, and that the entire of the said sum of £3000, with the amount due on the prior incumbrances, would not have amounted to two-thirds of the then value of the lands, the question then arises, whether a trustee can lend the trust fund on a second mortgage? It is insisted, on the part of the petitioner, as laid down in *Lewin on Trustees,* 3rd ed., p.350, that trusteees should not lend on a second mortgage; "not only because they have neither the legal estate, nor the possession of the title-deeds. but also because they may be placed under serious difficulty by the acts of the first mortgagee. If he file a bill of foreclosure, the trustees will forfeit their interest, unless they redeem, which they have no means of doing; and, if the first mortgage contain a power of sale, the mortgagee may seal the property at a great disadvantage; and the trustees cannot present it unless by redemption, which the state of the trust fund may very probably not permit." The principal cases relied on by the petitioner are *Norris* v. *Wright* 14 Beav. 308, and *Waring* v. *Waring* 3 Ir. Chan. Rep. 337. The effect of the Acts for the Registration of Deeds in Ireland makes the want of the legal estate, or of the title-deeds, of much less importance in Ireland than in England: *Hill* v. *Mill* 3 H. of L. Cas. 854, 855; *Drew* v. *Lord Norbury* 3 J. & L. 302: and I do not concur in the argument that in Ireland, whatever the law in England may be, a loan on a second mortgage is necessarily a breach of trust. It may be that a trustee lending on a second mortgage should exercise greater caution than if there was no prior incumbrance; but I am of opinion that a loan on a second mortgage is not, in Ireland, of itself, and in the absence of other circumstances, a breach of trust.

That question arose before Lord Chancellor Blackburne, in *Waring* v. *Waring;* and, although his Lordship held, in that case, on grounds which cannot be questioned, that there was a breach of trust, his Lordship distinctly stated that he "did not mean to lay down that trustees may not lend money on a puisne security." His Lordship then proceeded as follows, which portion of the judgment is strongly relied on by the petitioner's Counsel:–"But I am decidely of opinion that, where an estate of this value was so incumbered with head-rent and interest on prior incumbrances, to so large an amount compared with its rental, it was in highest degree improvident, and pregnant with the most injurious consequences to the parties beneficially interested, to invest a trust fund in an estate already so exhausted. No prudent man would or could have done such an act; and, in holding the trustee responsible, I expect no more care or caution than, I think, any prudent man might be expected to exercise in similar circumstances." It appears from the report of the case of *Waring* v. *Waring,* that the existing incumbrances at the time of the loan amounted to £27,000 or £28,000. It was stated by an affidavit in that case, made by the trustee and his solicitor, that the value of the property was between £60,000 and £70,000 and that the additional loan of £4500 was, in their opinion, at the time, a perfectly safe and eligible investment. The property was sold in the Incumbered Estates Court, and did not produce any sum to pay the £4500 lent by the trustee, after payment of the prior incumbrances. As the reporter did not state the facts of the case of *Waring* v. *Waring* fully, I have obtained a copy of the printed rental in the Incumbered Estates Court, under which the lands (which are in the county of Waterford, and not in the county of Wexford, as stated in the report) were sold. It appears, from that rental, that the acreage of the estate was 2207a. 1r. 18p., Irish plantation measure. The gross yearly rent was £2100. 6s. 8d. The fee-farm rent and tithe rentcharge payable thereout was the very large annual sum of £440. 12s. 9d The net profit-rent was £1659. 13s. 11d. The incumbrances prior to the loan were £27,000 or £28,000. The observations of Lord Chancellor Blackburne had reference to that state of facts; and no one can dissent from or doubt that decision.

The facts in the present case are wholly different. The lands in the counties of Tipperary and Limerick were held in fee. The value, according to the valuation made by the Commissioners of the Incumbered Estates Court, was between £700 and £800 a-year. The rental, at the time of the sale, was nearly £700 a-year; and the timber appears, from the printed rental, to have been valuable. It was stated, but the fact was not proved, that the sale in the Incumbered Estates Court took place in June 1851, a period when lands were selling for half their value, and that the purchase-money was between £8000 and £9000. There can be little doubt that the property was worth very much more, at the time of the mortgage of 1843, when the average rate of purchase-money in sales before the Masters was, I believe, twenty-five years' purchase. It will, therefore, I apprehend, be necessary, as the petitioner suggests in her replying affidavit, to have a reference so framed as to place the matter beyond any reasonable doubt. If the value of the property was, at the time of the mortgage of 1843, double, or nearly double, the amount due on Bessonett's security, and on the two indemnity deeds, referred to in the replying affidavit, and on so much of the £3000 as consisted of the trust funds liable to the petitioner's annuity, I do not think that a trustee, acting *bona fide,* and at the instance of the *cestui que trust,* ought to be made responsible for the fall in the value of lands, by reason of the public calamity which occurred in 1845, and in the subsequent years. Courts of Equity have recognised the principle that parties may be released from responsibility arising out of a public calamity: *Hackett* v. *Pattle* 6 Mad. 4; *Basil* v. *Atcheson* 4 Br. Par. Cas. 502; *Kirby* v. *Ormsby* Colles, P.C. 134. I shall, therefore, not decide on the question as to whether the loan of 1843 was or was not a breach of trust, until a report shall be made under the order of reference which I have drawn up, and which the petitioner, by her replying affidavit, calls for. The respondent, as I understand, is perfectly satisfied that there should be such a reference.

The next question which arises is one of more difficulty; and that is, whether the respondent is liable in respect of the £410. 5s. 1d.? That sum was applied in contravention of the trusts of the settlement; and, therefore, unless the acknowledgement of the petitioner before Commissioners appointed under the statute 4 & 5 *W.* 4, c. 92, binds the petitioner, the respondent is answerable. The 4 & 5 *W.* 4, c. 92, s. 68, which corresponds with the 3 & 4 *W.* 4, c.74, s. 77, enacts that it shall be lawful for every married woman, in every case, except that of being tenant in tail (which is provided for by other provisions in the Act), by deed, to dispose of lands of any tenure, "and money subject to be invested in the purchase of land; and also to dispose of, release, disclaim, surrender or extinguish any estate which she alone, or she and her husband in her right, may have in any lands of any tenure, or in any such money as aforesaid; and also to release or extinguish any power which may be vested in or limited or reserved to her, in regard to any lands of any tenure, or in any such money as aforesaid, as fully and effectually as she could do if she were a *feme sole,"* save that no such disposition, &c., shall be valid and effectual unless her husband concur in the deed, nor unless the deed be acknowledged by the married woman, as thereinafter directed. The interpretation clause (which is more full than in the statute in force in England) provides that the word "estate" shall extend to an estate in Equity as well as at Law, and shall also extend to any interest, charge, lien or incumbrance in or upon or affecting lands, either at Law or in Equity, whether present, or vested or future or contingent; and shall also extend to any interest, charge, lien or incumbrance in, upon or affecting money subject to be invested in the purchase of lands. . . . And the expression "money subject to be invested in the purchase of lands" shall include money, whether raised or to be raised, and whether the amount thereof be or be not ascertained; and shall extend to stocks and funds, and real and other securities, the produce of which is directed to be invested in the purchase of lands. The word "directed," in this part of the interpretation clause, appears to me to be important. In the clause in the settlement which I have read, relating to the calling in and disposal of the trust funds, it will be observed that it was not imperative that they should be invested in the purchase of land. The trust funds might be invested "otherwise advantageously," on the trusts in the settlement. Under the words "otherwise advantageously," I apprehend that the trust funds might have been invested in such securities, *e.g.*, as Bank of England or Bank of Ireland stock, or Government stock.

Now in considering the construction to be put on the words in the 68th section of the 4 & 5 *W*. 4, c. 92, "money subject to be invested in the purchase of lands," it is clear, in my opinion, that they should receive the same construction as the same words in the 63rd section of the 4 & 5 *W*. 4, c. 92, and 71st section of the 3 & 4 *W*. 4, c. 74. By those sections, which relate to money to be invested in the purchase of lands to be entailed, it is enacted, that where the money arising from the sale of lands *shall be subject to be invested* in the purchase of lands to be settled, so that any person, if the lands were purchased, would have an estate tail therein, and also money *subject to be invested in the purchase of lands* to be settled, so that any person, if the lands were purchased, would have an estate tail therein, shall, for all the purposes of this Act, be treated as the lands to be purchased, and be considered subject to the same estates as the lands to be purchased would, if purchased, have been actually subject to; that is, there must be a disentailing deed of the money: and the section provides that all the previous clauses shall "apply to such money in the same manner as if such money were *directed* to be laid out in the purchase of freehold lands, and such lands were actually purchased and settled." Now those sections and the interpretation clause would appear to show that "money subject to be invested in the purchase of lands" means money *directed* to be invested, and does not apply to money which may or may not be invested in the purchase of lands.

The principle is thus stated in *Cruise's Digest,* 4th ed., vol. 1, p. 46, "Money agreed or directed to be laid out in the purchase of lands is considered in Equity as land; because there, whatever is agreed to be done is considered as actually done;" and in page 73, "It has been stated that money *directed* to be laid out in the purchase of land is considered in Equity as land. In such case, if the land to be purchased is directed to be conveyed to a person in tail, he will be considered in Equity as tenant in tail of the money until the purchase is made." Upon the same principle, "it has been held that a man may be tenant by the courtesy of money agreed or directed to be laid out in the purchase of land."

If money, however, may or may not be invested in the purchase of land, it cannot be considered in Equity that that is done which is not agreed or directed to be done; and it would be difficult in such case to hold that money which is not agreed or directed to be laid out in land is land, so as to make a husband tenant by the courtesy, or to render it necessary to bar the *quasi* entail of the money by a deed enrolled under the statute. If not, the section in relation to an alienation by a married woman should not be held to apply to a case where a Court cannot consider money to be land, by reason of the trust leaving it optional whether it is or is not to be invested in such purchase.

The following cases appear to recognise this distinction: *Curling* v. *May* (cited 3 *Atkyns,* p.225), where £500 was, by will, given to B, on trust that he should lay out the same "upon a purchase of lands, or put out the same on good securities," on the trust in the gift mentioned. It was decided by Lord Talbot "that it was originally personal estate, and yet remained so; and nothing could be collected from the will as to what was the testator's principal intention." In *Walker* v. *Deane* 2 Ves. jun. 183, it was held that the rule that money directed so to be laid out in lands shall be considered as land holds only where the quality of land is imperatively fixed on the money. Lord Loughborough said:–"It is a necessary circumstance that where it is by will, the will, and where by contract, the deed, must decisively and definitely fix upon the money the quality of land." In *Vann* v. *Barnett* 19 Ves. 102, lands were devised to trustees to be sold, and the produce, with the consent of certain persons, was directed to be laid out in the purchase of "land or in Government securities." The latter trust was held not to operate as a re-conversion. *Davies* v. *Goodhew* 6 Sim. 585 appears to have been decided on the same principle. The cases on the subject are collected in *Lewin on Trustees,* 3rd ed., p.806, in which it is laid down:–"In the preceding observations it has, of course, been assumed that the direction or agreement for conversion is by the terms of the instrument made absolute and imperative; for where a mere option is given, the original character of the property continues until the discretion has been exercised, and the conversion actually effected; as if the direction or agreement to lay out money in 'lands or securities,' in 'freehold or leasehold,' or if by any other mode of expression an intention be manifested of not converting the property at all events."

In the present case, the words "or otherwise advantageously," in the clause in the settlement which I have read, would, I think, have authorised an investment of the trust fund, for example, in Bank stock or Government stock. If so, the £410. 5s. 1d. was personal estate until converted; and, in my opinion, the statute only applies where the direction or agreement for conversion is in such terms as to impress upon the money the character of land.

If so, there was a breach of trust as to the £410. 5s. 1d., because a married woman could not in 1849 asssign her reversionary interest in personal estate not settled to her separate use, and the acknowledgment before Commissioners is inoperative unless the £410. 5s. 1d. was to be considered in Equity as land.

I have not referred to the case of *Hoby* v. *Allen* 15 Jur. 835; S. C., 20 Law Jour. 199; first, because there is a doubt whether it is correctly reported: *Briggs* v. *Chamberlain* 11 Hare, 73 *note a.*; secondly, because the case has been doubted by *Lord St. Leonards,* in his *Essay on the Real Property Statutes,* pp. 240-1; and also in the said case of *Briggs* v. *Chamberlain,* and in *Turner* v. *Turner* 20 Beav. 563.

It is not easy to understand *Hoby* v. *Allen,* as the produce of the sale of the land was to be re-invested in the purchase of other estates, and the case was within the words of the statute. I do not think that *Briggs* v. *Chamberlain* or *Tuer* v. *Turner* apply to the present case. I decide the present case, as to the £410. 5s. 1d., on the grounds I have already stated, that the said sum might, under the settlement, have been invested in personal estate, such as Bank of Ireland or Bank of England stock, or Government stock; and that the statute does not apply to such a case.

A question arises as to whether this suit is defective for want of parties, but I offer no opinion upon the point, as it has not been argued before me.

It might be argued, on the principles referred to in *Montgomery* v. *Waring* 6 Ir. Chan. Rep. 533 and *Jesse* v. *Bennett* 6 D., M. & G. 609, there referred to, that if the £410. 5s. 1d. was received by the late Michael Smithwick and his son, or by the former, the assets of Michael Smithwick are liable to contribute to the loss, as well as the son. It was alleged that Michael Smithwick left no assets; but the sum of £1193. 14s. 8d., Government stock, transferred to the petitioner and her son, and the £495. 5s. 1d., form part of the asssets of Michael Smithwick, subject to the annuity of £200 a-year, late currency, claimed by the petitioner, provided the lands of Emly have not fallen in value, under the clause in the settlement to which I have referred. I, however, offer no opinion as to whether this suit is defective for want of parties, or whether a petition might be filed by the respondent, to obtain contribution, the question not having been raised or argued.

I shall make the following decree:–

It is ordered and declared by the Right Hon. The MASTER OF THE ROLLS, that the respondent, William Smithwick, has been guilty of a breach of trust in not having invested the sum of £410. 5s. 1d., in the petition mentioned, being part of the trust funds in the settlement of the 13th of July 1825, executed on the marriage of the petitioner, as directed by the said settlement. It is further ordered, that the said respondent, William Smithwick, do, within two months, invest in new £3 per cent. stock the said sum of £410. 5s. 1d., together with interest at the rate of £5 per cent. per annum, from the 9th day of April 1857 (being the date of the death of the petitioner's husband, Michael Smithwick) to the time of such investment. And it is further ordered, that the said William Smithwick do transfer the said sums, when so invested, and within said time, to the credit of this matter, with the privity of the Accountant-General of the Court. And it is further ordered, that it be referred to the Master in rotation of the Court to inquire and report what part of the sum of £3000 lent to the petitioner's brother, William Henry Brazier Waller (and to secure which the mortgage of the 29th of July 1843 was executed to the respondent), consisted of part of the trust funds in the said marriage settlement mentioned, which was, by the said settlement, applicable to the payment of the petitioner's annuity of £200 a-year, late currency. And it is further ordered, that the Master do also inquire and report what was the annual rental of the lands conveyed to the respondent by the said mortgage; and if any part of the lands were, at the date of the mortgage, unlet, and in the hands of the said William H.B. Waller, what was the annual value of the said part at such time, and what was the value at that time of the timber on said lands, and what was at that time the annual rental of the said lands so mortgaged; and if the said lands, included in the said mortgage, had been sold, what was the value of the said lands, according to the average rate at which lands were then sold in sales in the Court of Chancery. And it is further ordered, that the Master do inquire and report when the said lands were first sold in the Incumbered Estates Court after said mortgage, and for what sum, and at what time the lands were afterwards sold in the Incumbered or Landed Estates Court, and for what sum. And it is further ordered that the printed rentals upon all the sales in the Incumbered Estates or Landed Estates Court be proved and given in evidence before the Master. And it is further ordered that the Master do inquire and report what were the incumbrances affecting the said lands, at the date of the said mortgage, and the actual interest then due on the said incumbrances, and whether the said interest, or any or what part thereof, and when, was paid out of the sum of £3000 so lent to the said W.H.B. Waller, on the said mortgage, or out of any other and what funds. And the Court doth reserve further order, and the question of costs, until the Master shall have made his report; with liberty to the parties to apply as they may be advised. And it is further ordered, that this order be without prejudice to the proceedings (if any) which the respondent may be advised to take, to obtain contribution in respect of any payments or investments which respondent has been by this order, or may be, ordered to make. But the Court does offer no opinion whatever as to whether such proceedings, if taken, would be sustainable.

Notes and Questions

Do you agree that investment on the security of a second mortgage may be a proper investment in Ireland? See *Irish Land Law,* para. 10.066.

IV. IMPARTIALITY

1. *Duty of Loyalty*

RE SMITH'S ESTATE

[1894] 1 I.R. 60 (Chancery Division)

The facts are set out in the judgment.

Monroe, J.:

The petition for sale in this case was filed by John Thomas Hinds and John O'Reilly, for the purpose of realizing the sum of £1000, money lent by the petitioners to the owner, on the security of a mortgage of the lands for sale. John Thomas Hinds, who was a solicitor, acted for the petitioners down to the date of his death in 1887. The property has realized only the sum of £700, and the surviving trustee, as well as the persons beneficially entitled to the incumbrance, deny the right of John Thomas Hinds to recover the costs of the proceedings, inasmuch as he was solicitor and trustee while the proceedings were being carried on, or they contend, in the alternative, and that he should not be allowed any profit costs.

The ordinary rule of equity on this matter is perfectly clear and distinct. A solicitor who is a trustee is not allowed to charge for his services in carrying out the trust, the obligation of which he has accepted. He may, if it be necessary to have a solicitor's services, retain another. If he carry out the work himself, he must do it gratuitously, else his interest and his duty would be in conflict. To this general rule one exception was made in the case of *Cradock* v. *Piper* 1 Mac N. & G. 664, which came before Lord Cottonham as Lord Chancellor. The exception amounts to this, that where a solicitor trustee carries on business in Court connected with the trust estate, and acts not merely for himself as a party to the proceedings, but also for some other party or parties, whether it be for a co-trustee, a *cestui que trust* or any other person interested, he will be allowed his full costs, provided these are not increased in any way by the fact of the solicitor acting also for himself.

This limitation of the general principle has been often questioned, but it has never been overruled. It was spoken of with disapproval by Lord Brougham in *Mansion* v. *Baillie* 2 Macq. H.L. Cas.; and by Lord Carnworth in *Broughton* v. *Broughton* 5 De G. M. & G. 160; but it has been recognized as still a valid and existing authority by Mr. Justice Chitty : *In re Barber* 34 Ch. Div. 77; and by the Court of Appeal: *In re Corsellis Ibid.* 675. Mr. Todd sought to narrow the exception made in *Cradock* v. *Piper* 1 Mac N. & G. 664 to the cases in which a trustee solicitor and his co-trustee were made co-defendants in a suit, and where the solicitor represented both, and he contended that it did not include those cases where a trustee solicitor instituted proceedings on behalf of himself and his co-trustee as plaintiff. For this he relied on some observations of Lord Justice Turner in *Lincoln* v. *Windsor* 9 Hare, 158, and of Lord Cranworth in *Broughton* v. *Broughton* 5 De G. M. & G. 160. There is, however, no decision to this effect, and the distinction is not taken by the Court of Appeal in *Re Corsellis Ibid.* 675. Indeed I find that part of the cost given to the solicitor in *Craddock* v. *Piper* Mac N. & G. 664 were the profit costs, which he claimed as solicitor for himself and his co-trustee in instituting proceedings for the administration of the trust estate.

In my opinion, therefore, Mr. Hinds is entitled to have his cost of these proceedings taxed in the ordinary way, and paid in priority to the claim of those beneficially entitled to the purchase-money, under the deed of mortgage. It was sought to show that the representatives of Mr. Hinds should be debarred from all claim as to costs, as he had made an improper investment of the trust funds in a security which has proved deficient. No proof of this was laid before me, and a claim of a similar character made in a suit for the administration of Mr. Hinds' assets has been already rejected by the Court of Chancery.

Note
See further, *Irish Land Law,* para 10.070.

COURTNEY V. RUMLEY
(1871) I.R. 6 Eq. 99 (Vice-Chancellor's Court)

The facts are set out in the judgment.

Chatterton V.-C.:

The bill in this cause has been filed for the purpose of raising out of the Defendants' shares of the lands there mentioned their proportionate part of certain sums paid by the Plaintiff for the purpose of obtaining grants in perpetuity of these lands, and of certain costs paid by the Plaintiff in connexion with the obtaining of such grants. The lands were portion of the estate of the archiepiscopal see of Dublin, and were held by leases for years customarily renewable. A person named William Peck was, in his lifetime, entitled to sub-interests, carved, but not directly, out of the head lease, in three separate lots of these lands, under three distinct sub-leases, each having a *toties quoties* covenant for renewal. These lots have been called by the names of the persons under whom he so held them – Byrne's lot, Rossiter's lot, and Smyth's lot. Peck, by his will, and a codicil thereto, both made in 1842, in which year he also died, appointed James Duggan and Mary Maguire his executor and executrix both of whom proved the will. Peck thereby bequeathed his interests in these premises with others, to his executor, Duggan, upon certain trusts under which, in the events that happened, three-fifths of the rents became payable to the Defendants, and two-fifths to persons named O'Connor. Duggan survived Mary Maguire, and by his will appointed the Plaintiff and Mary Anne Duggan, and John Classon, his executors. Duggan died in 1849, and his will was proved by the Plaintiff and Classon. The Plaintiff has survived his co-executors, and is the sole personal representative of Duggan, and therefore of the first testator, Peck, and as such he became possessed of the legal estate of Peck in these premises, and the person to obtain renewals of the leases, in trust for the Defendants and the O'Connors. Irregularities had taken place in the lifetime of Peck, and also after his death, in taking out renewals of his sub-leases. No question now arises as to the lot called Byrne's lot, of which a grant in perpetuity was obtained without litigation, the sum paid for this grant being £48 16s. 8d. The plot called Rossiter's plot was, in the year 1864, held by minors of that name, who were wards of this Court, and were the immediate reversioners upon Peck's sublease, and the parties to renew or grant a perpetuity to his representatives. A sum of £79 5*s.* 3*d.* was paid to them for the purchase of the perpetuity fines, and interest on fines, to three-fifths of which the Defendants do not dispute the liability of their shares of these premises. The sum of £11 2*s.* 11*d.* was paid by the Plaintiff to the solicitor of these minors, for the costs of proceedings in the minor matter connected with the obtaining of a grant of the perpetuity, three-fifths of which, and also of the sum of £13 6*s.* 7*d.*, being the Plaintiff's own costs of these proceedings, the Plaintiff claims to charge against the Defendants' shares, but the Defendants dispute their liability to these sums. The principal contention is as to the third lot, called Smyth's lot, in reference to which much litigation ensued, and the costs claimed are large.

It appears that the Plaintiff had become an incumbrancer on the O'Connor's two-fifths of these three lots, and instituted proceedings as such in the Landed Estates Court for a sale of them in the year 1859. Their shares were subsequently sold by that Court, and the Plaintiff purchased them, and obtained a conveyance.

These three lots had been leased many years before by Peck, or the persons under whom he devised, to a person named Ennis, with a *toties quoties* convenant for renewal; and his representatives, in the year 1851, asigned this sub-interest to Parker. But Ennis had also, in the year 1812, acquired the interest in Smyth's plot immediately above the interest of Peck, and thus was both landlord and tenant to Peck. The last renewal of this lot was granted by Smyth to Peck in the year 1806, at a rent of £5. Ennis's representative assigned this superior interest to Parker at the same time as the sub-interest in all three lots – namely, by deed of the 12th September, 1851. The title of these parties thus became very complicated, and, to add to the complication, the boundaries of these lots became so confused that it was almost, if not altogether, impossible to ascertain them. From some unexplained cause, no rent was, so far as has been ascertained, paid on foot of the lease from Smyth to Peck since its date in 1806, nor was any renewal of it ever granted to Peck or his representatives, who held it for over fifty years without any payment of rent or acknowledgment of title. This is the more remarkable from the fact that Ennis and his assignee, Parker, during so long a period paid to Peck and his representatives the full rent payable by the under lease, without making a deduction for the rent payable by Peck to Ennis under the lease or renewal of 1806. In the Plaintiff's petition in the Landed Estates Court for the sale of the O'Connors' interest he erroneously described their tenure as fee-simple. This evidently proceeded from a mistaken notion that Peck and his representatives could have acquired the fee by possession without payment of rent under the circumstances I have stated. It appears that Parker, who was theretofore ignorant of his right to the rent reserved by the lease of 1806, became aware of it during the progress of some inquiries directed by the Landed Estates Court as to the boundaries, and he served a notice on the Plaintiff, dated the 28th March, 1861, to take out a renewal or grant in perpetuity. This led to proceedings in the matter of *O'Connor's Estate,* which brought out the real title to this interest, and the mistake made as to the tenure was corrected, the Plaintiff, on the 16th of August, 1861, serving a notice on Parker, admitting his title, and assenting to take a grant in perpetuity from him, under the Church Temporalities Act. A negotiation then ensued as to the amount to be paid for rent, fines, and interest, and for the purchase of the perpetuity, in the course of which Parker, by a letter of 15th October, 1861, claimed a sum of £180 Irish, for thirty-six years' arrears of rent, and £40 19s. (late currency) for fines, with £39 1*s.* 3*d.* interest thereon. This claim was disputed by the Plaintiff, who insisted that Parker was not entitled to claim any arrears of rent which accrued prior to the conveyance of the lands from Ennis to him in 1851, and also that only one renewal fine, being one guinea, with interest, was due. The Plaintiff, it appears, was ignorant at this time that Parker had, pending these negotiations obtained an assignment from Ennis of all arrears of rent due to him prior to the assignment of 1851. The assignment of the arrears bears date the 15th October, 1861, but it was concealed by Parker from the Plaintiff, and not disclosed till the 19th January, 1863, when it was mentioned as if casually in a letter from Parker's solicitor to the Plaintiff's solicitor. According to the opinion of the Master of the Rolls, in the case of *Courtney* v. *Parker,* this assignment made no difference in the liability of the parties seeking a renewal, as they were bound to pay all rent due, no matter to whom, as a condition for obtaining it. However, if the facts had been disclosed, it would have prevented any such objection being raised.

The draft of a grant in perpetuity was furnished by Plaintiff's solicitor to Parker's solicitor in October, 1861, and retained by the latter, though he was frequently applied to to return it approved of or amended.

In the letter of Parker's solicitor, of the 19th January, 1863, already referred to, he states that Parker was advised he was entitled to be paid all rent due before granting a renewal, and that the Plaintiff's solicitor had been furnished with the amount claimed. This must refer to the last preceding letter of Mr. Dodd, Mr. Parker's solicitor, dated the 18th December, 1862, in which he claims, in default of proof of payment, all rent which had accrued from the grant of the last renewal – namely, the year 1806. But in the letter of the 19th January, 1863, Mr. Dodd asks that if Plaintiff were dissatisfied with this amount he should either show some evidence of the period to which rent had been paid, or make a reasonable offer. A case had been submitted to counsel in December, 1862, on behalf of the Plaintiff, to advise as to Parker's rights in respect of rent and renewal fines, stating that an offer had been made to pay all that had accrued since the assignment to Parker in 1851, on which counsel gave his opinion approving of the terms so offered. After Plaintiff's solicitors had been informed of the assignment to Parker, in 1861, of the arrears due prior to the assignment of 1851, this case was again laid before the same gentleman, who advised, upon grounds unnecessary to be stated, that no further concession should be made to Parker. On the 14th April, 1864, Parker served a formal notice on the Plaintiff, with particulars of his claim for rent, fines, and purchase money, the rent being again claimed from the 16th May, 1806, and the fines and interest as before, and he demanded payment within a month, and stated that otherwise he would hold the Plaintiff debarred from all right to a grant in perpetuity. A reply was given on the 27th of April, 1864, offering £150 in full for all Parker's demands; but this offer was not accepted. The Plaintiff then presented a petition against Parker, under the Church Temporalities Acts, for a grant in perpetuity, in reply to which Parker filed an affidavit, in which he submits that the Plaintiff had absolutely forfeited his right to a renewal or grant in perpetuity, but offers to waive it on payment of all arrears of rent from 1812, and renewal fines and interest since 1824, and of the costs he had been put to in the Landed Estates Court. The date of 1812 appears to have been mentioned as being the time at which Ennis acquired Smyth's interest in the premises, since which time the Plaintiff had admitted that no rent had been paid. The case came on for hearing before the Master of the Rolls in June, 1864, and the questions of forfeiture, and the waiver of it, and of the terms on which the Plaintiff was entitled to a grant, were fully argued. His Honour seemed to be of opinion that the proceedings in the Landed Estates Court did cause a forfeiture, but it was not necessary for him to decide the point, as he held that if there had been a forfeiture it had been waived by the Respondent. He also held that the Respondent's right to require payment of the rent claimed was not limited by the Statute of Limitations, or by any presumption of payment. As to the latter point he expressed some doubt, but he seems to have decided it on the ground of the statements made by the Plaintiff, that no rent had ever been paid since either 1806 or 1812, it does not seem very clear which. An account was accordingly directed, and the Master found that fifty-three years rent, from 1812, was due, amounting to £245 9*s*. 11*d*., and one renewal fine, which, with interest, amounted to £1 6*s*. 3*d*. The proportion of purchase money was found to be £68 10*s*. 3*d*. There were also costs in the Landed Estates Court in *O'Connor's Estate* awarded to Parker, amounting to £31 0*s*. 4*d*., which Plaintiff was held liable to pay as a condition of obtaining the grant, and he was also ordered to pay Parker's costs of the petition matter in this Court; the whole amount, including further rent which had accrued, being £574 19*s*. 9*d*. Parker had withheld the rent under his sub-lease during this controversy, and the amount of it, being £296 17*s*. 10*d*., was deducted from the sum due to him, and left a balance of £278 1*s*. 11*d*., which was paid him by the Plaintiff, and thereupon a grant in perpetuity was executed by him to the Plaintiff. The Plaintiff seeks in this suit to establish a lien for three-fifths of this sum, and of his own costs incurred in these proceedings, and of the costs of the grants of the perpetuity of the three lots, upon the Defendants' three-fifths shares of the trust premises, and to raise the same, with interest, by sale.

The Defendants admit the Plaintiff's right so far as regards the sums paid for obtaining the grants of Byrne's and Rossiter's lots, and also a portion of the sum paid for that of Smyth's lot; but they dispute their liability to a sum of £11 2*s*. 11*d*. paid to the solicitor for the minors in *Rossiters, minors,* and a sum of £13 6*s*. 7*d*. claimed by Plaintiff for his own costs in that matter. They also dispute their liability to payment of any costs in respect of Smyth's lot, and to a portion of the arrears of rent paid to Parker, being the difference between the amount so paid and twenty years' arrears, to which they admit their liability. They ground their defence upon the alleged misconduct of the Plaintiff, which, they contend, occasioned the liability to these disputed sums.

The Plaintiff's position was originally that of executor of the surviving executor of William Peck, under whose will the Defendants derive their interest in this property. The legal estate therein was vested in him as such executor in trust for the several legatees beneficially entitled. He subsequently purchased the interests of the person entitled to the other two-fifths, and became a co-owner with the Defendants of the beneficial interest. This has been relied upon by the Defendants as a circumstance prejudicial to the Plaintiff's case; for they allege that he, in order to advance his own interest, embarked in the litigation which they complain of, and that he sacrificed their interests to his own. I look upon this as affording an argument in the opposite direction, as I think it unlikely that a person who must himself in any event bear a share of any losses that may be occasioned by a particular course of proceeding will recklessly or negligently adopt it. The evidence here satisfies me that the acts of the Plaintiff were done *bona fide* for the common interest of himself and the other persons entitled to this property, and that though he may have been unsuccessful, badly advised, or mistaken, he did not act less cautiously for the Defendants than for himself.

It is not necessary for me in this case to consider whether the Plaintiff was under any obligation to renew these leases. That he was justified in doing so the Defendants concede by their admission of the liability to contribute to the sums paid for obtaining the grants in perpetuity. They derived considerable advantage by the obtaining of these grants, and as to that most in controversy – namely, the grant of Smyth's lot – the last renewal had expired very many years before. It was held but by a yearly tenancy at law, and they not only might have been, but, as is apparent, would have been, evicted from it and lost it altogether, if a renewal or grant in perpetuity had not been obtained. The Plaintiff here does not seek to attach any personal liability upon the Defendants, but only requires that they shall not take the benefit of the grants which he procured for them, without contributing their shares of what he paid for them. I should be warranted in sending this case into Chambers at once to take the accounts prayed by the bill, leaving the matters in dispute to be there adjusted; but as they have been fully discussed on the hearing, and as no further light can be thrown upon them by inquiry, I think it will save delay and expense if I now give my opinion as to the several heads of claim in controversy.

The principle upon which this Court acts in reference to the allowance of expenses to trustees is, that the trust property shall reimburse them all the charges and expenses incurred in the execution of the trust, and in this the Court will always deal liberally with a trustee acting *bonâ fide*. But when the costs or expenses claimed have been incurred through the misconduct or negligence of the trustee, he will not be allowed them. The fact of his having been unsuccessful in litigation, either as Plaintiff or Defendants, will not, in the absence of misconduct, disentitle him to be reimbursed his costs.

The first item in dispute is that of the costs in the matter of *Rossiters, minors,* which consists of two parts – namely, the costs paid the minors' solicitor, amounting to £11 2*s.* 11*d.*, and the costs incurred by the Plaintiff. As these minors, who were entitled to the reversion expectant on Peck's lease, the wards of Court, it of course was necessary that the sanction of this Court should be obtained to the execution of any renewal or grant in perpetuity. Accordingly, by a report of the Master in that matter, made under an order of the 3rd December, 1862, and bearing date the 15th of March, 1864, it was found that the Plaintiff and his then co-executrix were entitled to a grant in perpetuity of their portion of the minors' lands, on payment of the sum of £79 5*s.* 3*d.* Of this sum the Plaintiff, as beneficial owner of two-fifths, was bound to contribute two-fifths, and the Defendants the other three-fifths. It appears that the Plaintiff had not at the time any money of the Defendants in his hands available for payment of their share. The solicitor for the minors wrote to Plaintiff's solicitor in May, 1864, requiring immediate payment, and this not having been made, he served notice of a motion on the 26th of May, 1864, that the Plaintiff and his co-executrix should forthwith proceed to complete the grant, and pay the said sum of £79 5*s.* 3*d.*, with interest, and the costs of the motion. Plaintiff's solicitors served a notice in reply, dated the 28th of May, stating that it was not the intention of the Plaintiff to oppose the motion, but that, as the Defendants had failed to contribute their three-fifth shares of the sum due, Plaintiff's affidavit would be used on the motion, but not for the purpose of opposing same. Although there is not any direct evidence of there having been any prior application to the Defendants for payment of their shares, which probably may be accounted for by the Plaintiff's not being capable of giving evidence, I think there is sufficient in the case to warrant the inference that these ladies had been so applied to before the notice of motion was served. On the 30th of May they were served with a formal notice by the Plaintiff's solicitors, sending them a copy of the notice of motion, and stating that, as the Plaintiff had not in his hands any money of theirs, and as he had made application to them to pay their proportion of the sum required, Plaintiff had made an affidavit which would be used on the motion. That affidavit was offered in evidence by the Plaintiff, but was withdrawn on the objection of the Defendants, to which I thought myself bound to yield. The motion was moved on the 31st of May, and an order made in the terms of the notice, and the guardian of the minors was declared entitled to her costs of the motion, and the order was made without prejudice to any question between the Plaintiff and the persons who, it was alleged by him, were bound to contribute to the purchase of the perpetuity. The Defendants admit that they never paid their share of the purchase-money, and the entire was subsequently paid by Plaintiff out of his own funds. Under these circumstances, I cannot hold that the Plaintiff is disentitled to claim against the trust estate at lease three-fifths of the costs so paid and incurred by him. They were, in my opinion, occasioned not by his misconduct, but partly, if not wholly, by the default of the Defendants in not providing funds for payment of their share of the purchase-money. I think there is sufficient to show that the delay in payment which occasioned the motion was caused by their not having paid their contribution. The Defendants have relied on a letter written by one of them to the

Plaintiff, in reference to a small sum of costs charged by him in one of his accounts as paid to Parker in the matter of *O'Connors' Estate*, and on letters of the same Defendant to Plaintiff's solicitors, guarding against assenting to or undertaking to pay costs or expenses in reference to obtaining the grant of Byrne's lot. In my opinion, these letters do not affect the question, except so far as they go to negative any presumption of assent on their part. They could not suppose that the grants which they desired to have could be obtained without costs of some kind, and, whether they assented or objected, they could not claim to enjoy the benefits so procured for them without bearing their share of all proper costs and expenses incurred in procuring those benefits. The sole question is, whether the costs claimed were occasioned by the misconduct of their trustee.

The next and the most important question is, as to the amount of rent paid, and the costs paid and incurred, in relation to Smyth's lot. These costs consist of two portions – one, the costs paid Parker in the matter of *O'Connor's Estate,* and the other the costs of both parties in the matter of *Courtney* v. *Parker.* The former I do not think the Plaintiff is entitled to. His proceedings in the Landed Estates Court were not in the character of trustee or executor, but as an incumbrancer in his own right upon shares of the O'Connors, in which the Defendants here had no interest. It is true that inquiries were then directed and prosecuted which concerned the owners of all the shares; but these form but a small portion, if any, of the costs in question, the main portion, if not the whole, of which, were incurred in reference to the Plaintiff's unfounded claim to sell the fee. The Plaintiff relied on its having been part of the terms upon which the grant was ordered to be made to him by Parker that these costs should be paid, but that does not in itself give him any right to claim contribution to them from the Defendants. It was equitable to make the payment a condition as against the Plaintiff, who was the only person with whom Parker was dealing, but he must go further in order to claim this sum against the Defendants, and show that it was incurred by him as their trustee, in respect of their interests, and this he has failed to do.

In reference to the costs in *Courtney* v. *Parker,* which are the largest item in dispute, I may observe that the objection to them is not to their amount, as it is not alleged that there was any impropriety in the conduct of that proceeding, or any unnecessary expense incurred in the progress of it. The objection is to the whole amount, on the ground that the proceeding was rendered necessary by the default of the Plaintiff, and that it was never authorized or sanctioned by the Defendants. The dispute between the Plaintiff and Parker, which led to the institution of that matter, was certainly one of terms only, for Parker was willing to execute a grant of the perpetuity on his demands being complied with. There were two subjects of dispute – one being the very large arrear of rent demanded by Parker, and the other the amount of renewal fines and interest claimed, which, though at first much beyond the sum properly payable, had, by Parker's notice of the 14th of April, 1864, been reduced to £6 *9s. 2d.* This latter sum, though still exceeding the amount due, which was only one guinea, was small in comparison of the claim for rent. Parker succeeded in maintaining his claim to the arrears of rent for fifty-three years, and it must, therefore, be taken that the Plaintiff was not warranted in his refusal to pay that amount. If he had assented to the claim, in all probability Parker would have granted the perpetuity without suit. Was, then, the Plaintiff guilty of such misconduct in not yielding to this claim as to disentitle him to the costs thereby occasioned? His position must be considered. He was the executor of Peck's executor, and first became connected with the property in 1849. He was ignorant of the previous dealings with it, and was then, and for many years afterwards, unacquainted with the title. For at least thirty years Peck, his testator, had paid no rent; and during all that time, and down to 1861, neither Ennis, nor Parker, his assignee, had ever claimed payment, and they had paid the rent due by them under the sublease without making or seeking any deduction for the superior rent. The Plaintiff acted on the opinion of counsel selected as being the friend and confidential adviser of the Defendants. The Defendants allege that, but for the Plaintiff's misconduct in claiming the fee, Parker would not have been entitled to claim all these arrears. They submit by their answer that, by reason of the forfeiture incurred by the Plaintiff, and his subsequent application for a grant in perpetuity, Parker was enabled to insist on payment of the arrears of rent for fifty years or thereabouts, instead of for twenty years only, which, as they are advised and submit, is all that Parker would have been entitled to were it not for the Plaintiff's disclaimer of his title and disregard of his notice. One of the matters now in dispute and which I have to decide is, whether the Defendants' shares of the premises are liable for rent which accrued more than twenty years before the notice of 1861. The Defendants contend that they are not, and it may be fairly assumed that if the Plaintiff had applied to them for their opinion as to the course to be taken by him before commencing his proceedings against Parker, they would have taken the same position then which they do now. The Plaintiff did, in *Courtney* v. *Parker,* insist upon this limit of twenty years. He was unsuccessful, but not on the ground of a forfeiture having given any right to Parker to claim more. It is not necessary now to consider whether the Plaintiff's conduct did work a forfeiture. The Master of the Rolls seems to have come to the conclusion that it did, and I express no opinion upon the subject. But he also came to the conclusion, and so held, that if any such forfeiture had been worked, it had been waived by Parker long before that proceeding had been instituted, and his judgment as to the amount of the arrears claimable did not proceed on the ground of any such forfeiture then existing, or of any right in Parker to claim a larger amount by reason of it. I am of opinion that the conduct of the Plaintiff, which is relied on as having worked a forfeiture, did not give Parker any advantage in this respect that he would not have possessed as being the party to grant a renewal on the perpetuity. The ground expressed by his Honour for his judgment on this point was, that as the Plaintiff had all through contended that no rent had been paid from 1812, at latest, he could not be held to insist that a presumption existed of payment up to twenty years before 1861, and on this point his Honour states that he entertained some doubt. A claim for so very large an amount of rent as fifty-three years, and especially under such circumstances, is certainly calculated to raise some doubt, and whether well or ill founded in the result, I cannot blame either the Plaintiff or the Defendants for not readily yielding to it. It was also urged for the Defendants that the admission or contention by the Plaintiff, that no rent had been paid since 1812, deprived him and the Defendants of the benefit of that presumption. But it is not alleged that the statement was untrue, and the Plaintiff was not in my opinion guilty of any misconduct in having made it. I am of opinion that the amount of rent which the Plaintiff was held liable to pay was not incurred by reason of the alleged forfeiture of the right to renewal. I shall, therefore, hold the Defendants' shares bound to contribute to payment of the entire amount of rent so paid by the Plaintiff. I have also come to the conclusion that the Plaintiff was not guilty of misconduct, under the circumstances, in not yielding to Parker's demand, and in submitting it for a judicial decision.

But the conduct of the Defendants is also of importance. It is alleged by the Plaintiff that they were kept informed all through these transactions of what was going on by the friend and adviser I have already referred to as being consulted as counsel upon these questions, and, from the qualified denial of this by the answer, I think there is some ground for the allegation. But, however that may be, I find that within a short time after the petition had been presented, and several days before it came on for hearing, the Defendants' solicitors placed themselves in communication with the Plaintiff's solicitors as to this property generally, and obtained very full information to the then position of the matter. In the letter of Messrs. Dillon to Messrs. Fitzgerald of the 31st May, 1864, the filing of the petition is distinctly stated. On the 4th June a copy of the affidavit verifying the petition in full was sent to them, and any further information required was offered them. The Defendants were thus put in possession of the nature and particulars of the proceeding, and as they do not appear to have asked for further information they must be taken not to have needed it. Surely, if they disapproved of the litigation and preferred to yield to Parker's demands, they should have so informed the Plaintiff at that time. But, instead of doing so, they allow the matter to proceed, and lead the Plaintiff to suppose that they did not disapprove of what he was doing. They cannot in justice now turn round upon their trustee, who, I have no doubt, was acting *bonâ fide* and to the best of his judgment for the interest of both himself and his *cestuis que trustent,* and repudiate all liability to these costs. It is not sought to make them personally liable for them, but only to recover them out of the trust premises; and this, I think, the Plaintiff is entitled to do. It is not to be forgotten that the Plaintiff was bound by the covenant in the renewal to Parker to use his best exertions to procure renewals from his own landlord, and to grant renewals *toties quoties* to Parker.

I shall, therefore, declare the Plaintiff entitled to three-fifths of the sums paid for rent and fines, and interest on fines, and the costs paid in *Rossiters, minors,* and *Courtney* v. *Parker,* with interest on the sums so paid from the dates of payment, and to the costs properly and necessarily incurred by him to his own solicitors in these matters, but without interest. I shall declare that he is not entitled to any costs paid by him in reference to the proceedings in *O'Cònnor's Estate.* The accounts must be taken on the basis of these declarations.

Note
See further, *Irish Land Law,* para. 10.071 *et seq.*

KING V. ANDERSON
(1874) I.R. 8 Eq. 625 (Chancery Appeal)

The facts are set out in the judgments.

Sir J. Napier, C.S.:

The Appeal in this case has been brought against a decision of the Vice-Chancellor, by which he ordered the dismissal, with costs, of a bill that was filed on the 26th February, 1872, for the purpose of setting aside a contract of purchase made on the 19th September, 1859, and a deed of conveyance of the 11th November following, executed in pursuance of the contract. The property that is the subject-matter of the contract and the conveyance formerly belonged to the late Samuel Benjamin King, the husband of the Plaintiff, and an officer in the naval service of the East India Company. It was hereditary property; part of it in the town of Baltinglass, held under renewable leases in perpetuity, partly under the Earl of Aldborough, and another part under a Mr. Darcy.

In 1843 Mr. King conveyed the property to his mother (Mrs. Field), then a widow, upon trust, out of the rents and profits, to pay all rents and other outgoings, and to retain for her sole use and benefit during her life an annuity of £100 per annum, and then upon trust for the said Samuel Benjamin King, his heirs, executors, administrators, and assigns.

Under Mrs. Field, the Defendant, who resided at Baltinglass, was appointed in 1851 to be agent to collect the rents and manage the property. The Plaintiff was married to Mr. King in the year 1849; they came to Ireland early in 1853, and Mr. King had to return to India early in the year 1855, and he died in September in that year. On the 24th January, 1855, he executed a power of attorney to the Plaintiff to act in his name during his absence, and on the 27th January he executed his will, in which he made the following devise of his property:–

"I give, devise, and bequeath any interest I may have at the time of my death in and to certain houses and premises in and near the town of Baltinglass, in the county of Wicklow, in Ireland, to which I am entitled either as heir-at-law of my father, the late Thomas King, or otherwise, unto my wife, Alicia Hobart King, otherwise Malone, for the term of her natural life, free from the control of any future husband she may intermarry with, and for her sole use and benefit; and from and after her death I give, devise, and bequeath my said interest in said houses and premises in and near Baltinglass aforesaid to my son, Thomas Frazer King, and to his heirs and assigns for ever; and if it shall happen that my said son, Thomas Frazer King, shall die during the lifetime of his mother, the said Alicia Hobart King, or before he attains his age of twenty-one years, then and in either of said events I give, devise, and bequeath (subject, however, to the life estate of my said wife) the said interest I may have in said houses and premises in and near the town of Baltinglass to my sister, Anne Saunders King, for life, free from the control of any husband she may have, and after her decease to her children now living, or such of said children as may be then living, share and share alike, and to their heirs and assigns for ever; and if but one then living, the whole to that one. Provided always that in case after my death my said wife, Alicia Hobart King, otherwise Malone, at any time during her life think fit so to do, it may be lawful for her, and my will in such case is that she may be at liberty, to sell or otherwise absolutely dispose of the whole or any portion of the said houses and premises in and near Baltinglass aforesaid for the best price that can be had for the same, and that the proceeds, after such sale or sales (deducting all expenses), be invested by the said Alicia Hobart King in Government or landed security, and that the proceeds, or profits, or dividends, or annual interest arising therefrom shall follow and be applied in the same way as the several devises I have hereinbefore made with respect to said Baltinglass property." And the testator thereby appointed Samuel Benjamin King, Mrs. Mary Taylor, and Alicia Hobart King, the Plaintiff, the executors of his said will.

The Defendant continued in his position of agent of the property, and also was appointed in 1854 to be the agent of the Earl of Aldborough. It is unncessary to refer in detail to the letters that are as evidence to show the intimacy and the confidence between him and the Plaintiff, and the position which he accepted and assumed with reference to the management of this property, with the professed object of acting for the benefit and in the interest of the Plaintiff. I do not think that it is expedient or that it would be relevant to go into further detail at this stage, because not only is the case before the Vice-Chancellor fully reported in I.R. 8 Eq., 147, but we all concur with the Vice-Chancellor in the conclusion at which he has arrived as to the effect of the evidence in showing that, before and at the time of the transaction that is sought to be set aside, the Defendant was the agent of the Plaintiff for the purpose of collecting the rents, and for the general management of the property, and that in this position an influence had been acquired by him, and a confidence obtained, that was sufficient to bring the case within the rule of a Court of Equity that applies to a purchase or other dealing for his own benefit by a trustee. "The principle of this rule," says Lord Kingsdown in *Smith* v. *Kay* 7 H.L. Cas 779, "applies to every case where influence is acquired and abused, where confidence is reposed and betrayed. The relations with which the Court of Equity most ordinarily deals are those of trustee and *cestui que trust,* and such like. It applies specially to those cases, for this reason – and this reason only – that from those relations the Court presumes confidence put and influence exerted. Whereas in all other cases, where those relations do not subsist, the confidence and the influence must be proved extrinsically; but where they are proved extrinsically, the rules of reason and of common sense, and the technical rules of a Court of Equity, are just as applicable in the one case as in the other." Taking this to be clearly established, and that it governs the case of the Defendant in relation to the purchase in question, the onus was thrown on him to prove to the satisfaction of the Court that he acted according to what the rule of the Court requires to be shown beyond question in such transactions, when they are impeached by a suit in Equity. "It is asked," says Lord Eldon, in his instructive judgment in the case of *Gibson* v. *Jeyes* 6 Ves. 278, "Where is that rule to be found?" "I answer" (he replies), "in that great rule of the Court, that he who bargains in matter of advantage with a person placing confidence in him is bound to show that a reasonable use has been made of that confidence – a rule applying to trustees, attorneys, or any one else."

The confidence that was placed in the Defendant is very distinctly shown by several letters of the Plaintiff. In her letter of 12th April, 1859, to the Defendant, she expresses her desire that he would get Lord Aldborough for a purchaser of part of the property, for the reasons she assigns; one of which is that, in her opinion, "he would be more likely to give a better and fairer price than any indifferent purchaser;" and she adds: "from your and his perfect knowledge of the title, &c., much time and law expenses would be saved me in disposing of the *debris* of the Baltinglass property."

In the letters of Mr. Willans to the Defendant in 1855, the value and capabilities of the property were treated as peculiarly within the knowledge of the Defendant – as, for instance, in that of 27th August, 1855, in which Mr. Willans says: "I understand Mr. King will give the whole to his lordship as it now is – viz., £54 19*s.* 10*d.* profit rent, capable of being increased one-half at least, as I need not tell you, for £500." At that time it was an object to Mrs. King (who was then acting under a power of attorney) to get the money for the purpose of enabling her to join her husband in India; but after his death, at the close of that year, her position was altogether changed. Her title then accrued under her husband's will; she became tenant for life of the property, with a power of sale at the best price that could be had, the proceeds to be invested in Government or landed security, for the benefit of those who were the devisees of the property, especially for her son, then an infant of tender years, who was to take in remainder after his mother's death. It was her bounden duty under this power to sell to the best advantage (if at all), and to have the proceeds of such sale invested in the securities and on the trusts pointed out in the will of her husband.

In the reply of the Defendant to her letter of the 12th April, 1859, he says –"Lord Aldborough is away from Paris at the present, but I hope soon to be able to communicate with him respecting the Infirmary, &c., when I shall do all in my power for your interest." This is dated from Baltinglass, "April 19, 1859."

In his letter, dated "Saturday Evening, July 8, 1859," he informs her that he was going to France, and would speak to Lord Aldborough about her matters. "I told you lately" (he says) "I had written to him about the purchase of the houses; but he has not replied directly, futher than to say he would enter more fully into various matters I had brought before him when we should meet. I purpose leaving the nine o'clock packet from Kingstown on Monday morning, and trust at least to see you on my return."

It would seem, from these letters, that at that time no intimation had come from either party as to a purchase by the Defendant. What took place at the meeting in France as to a purchase of the property by Lord Aldborough is not disclosed in the evidence. In his answer to the original Bill, the Defendant says, as to this, "I do not recollect the result of this application, but I communicated the result, whatever it was, truly to the Plaintiff." We are left without further evidence, either from the Defendant himself or Lord Aldborough, as to what the Defendant stated to his lordship with reference to this property, or what arrangement was then made between them. Whatever took place, the Defendant has given no explanation as to the circumstances that led to the making of the proposal on his own behalf, on the 18th September, 1859, to become the purchaser for himself.

At this time he certainly was "master of the situation." He was agent of Lord Aldborough, and bound by his duty to enforce payment of the rents and fines; he was agent for the annuitant, who was to be paid out of the surplus profits after rent and fines were paid; he had undertaken to the Plaintiff to do all in his power to get Lord Aldborough to purchase the interest she had power to sell; and, in his new capacity of proposed purchaser for himself, he was interested in magnifying the claims of Lord Aldborough against the property, and other circumstances whereby its value to Mrs. King and her son would be depreciated. In addition, he was agent and owner in expectancy of the part held under Mr. Darcy. The circumstances in the case were therefore such that the Defendant was specially bound to show that in dealing with his principal for this benefit to himself, he had taken care to provide that, as against such a combination of interested and adverse influences, she had the full protection of some competent and disinterested adviser in the transaction. The Plaintiff, moreover, was not absolute owner, but merely tenant for life, with a power of sale, limited and guarded in its terms; she was a trustee for her infant son, and therefore in a peculiar degree required the protection of adequate independent advice, which a Court of Equity inexorably requires in all this class of transactions between parties in a relation of confidence, and when one of them is exposed to influence capable of being exerted by the other.

On the 18th September, 1859, the Defendant writes his letter of proposal in the following terms:–

"BALTINGLASS,
"September 18, 1859.

"DEAR MRS. KING, – I hereby propose to purchase all right, title, and interest possessed by you and Mrs. Field, as representatives of the late Captain King, in the several holdings you have in the town of Baltinglass, subject to the renewal fines due thereon, and for which I agree to pay, on their being properly conveyed to me, the sum of £300, in manner as follows – that is to say, £50 in cash on the completion of the conveyance, and £50 on the 1st of August following, and an insurance for £200 on life of Mrs. Field, with security for the amount of premium payable on same, together with a rent-charge of £20 a-year to Mrs. Field for her own life, the cost of the deed of conveyance to be paid by me, and also the cost of releasing the deeds and leases connected with the property from the custody of William Russell as far as the sum of £25; any more charges for this purpose to be borne by Mrs. King.

"I am, dear Madam, yours truly,
"ROBERT HENRY ANDERSON."

On the following day the acceptance of this by the Plaintiff was written, at his direction, at the residence of the Plaintiff:–

"19*th September,* 1859.

"R.H. ANDERSON, ESQ.

"DEAR SIR, – I accept your offer dated 18th September, 1859, of £300 payable as proposed, and a rent-charge of £20 a-year to Mrs. Field for her life, for all my interest in and several holdings I own as representative of the late Samuel B. King, situate in the town of Baltinglass.

"A.H. KING."

No adviser intervened for her guidance and protection.

I cannot but observe that in the deed of 11th of November, 1859, which the Defendant got some one in the office of Mr. Scott (Lord Aldborough's solicitor) to prepare, the recital of the alleged power of sale in the will of the late Mr. King is a paraphrase that omits the two material restrictions – that the sale should be for the best price that could be had; and that the purchase money should be invested in Government or landed security for the benefit of the devisees of the property. The execution of the deed by the Plaintiff is attested by two of the clerks in Mr. Scott's office. Mr. Scott does not appear to have been present on the occasion, or to have taken any ostensible part in the transaction at any stage of it. As to the constructive or imaginary receipt of the £300, £100 was to be paid afterwards by two instalments; and the remaining £200 was to be secured by a policy of insurance for that amount on the life of Mrs. Field, the annuitant on the property. The £100 was obviously designed for the present use of the Plaintiff herself, as appears from the letters of 9th November, 1859, and the 24th January following. It is not clear that the whole of it was paid. The transaction in all its parts is so glaring a violation of those obligations which it is emphatically the duty of a Court of Equity to uphold and enforce, and it may be said *"res ipsa loquitur."*

In the case of *Rhodes* v. *Bate* L.R. 1 Ch. App. 252, which was cited by Mr. Holmes in his very able and convincing argument, Lord Justice Turner states in emphatic and authoritative terms the great established principle of a Court of Equity, that "persons standing in a confidential relation towards others cannot entitle themselves to hold benefits, which those others may have conferred upon them, unless they can show to the satisfaction of the Court, that the persons by whom the benefits have been conferred had competent and independent advice in conferring them. This, in my opinion" (he says), "is a settled general principle of the Court, and I do not think that either the age or capacity of the person conferring the benefit, or the nature of the benefit conferred, affects this principle."

In that case there was nothing to induce the Court to hold that the Defendant had not acted with honesty of purpose, and Lord Justice Knight Bruce stated that at the conclusion of the argument his impression was altogether against the Plaintiff, but he acknowledged that he ultimately came round to the view of Lord Justice Turner, and both agreed that the case was to be governed by the great principle and rule of the Court, that the person conferring the benefit on one standing in the relation of confidence and influence should have competent and independent advice, without which the transaction could not stand in a Court of Equity. This seems to me to be altogether conclusive, and makes it unnecessary, because it is irrelevant, to go into the consideration of what was the measure of the Plaintiff's intelligence, the extent of her knowledge as to the property, the intrinsic prudence of the bargain itself as to value, capability, or otherwise. A general rule of a court of equity is said by Lord Hardwicke to be part of the general law of the realm.

I observe that, in a letter of September 27th, 1859, to Mrs. Fraser, who was made a party to the conveyance of November, 1859, for the purpose of releasing certain claims she was supposed to have had against the premises, the Defendant seeks to explain and defend his then recent dealing with the Plaintiff, and concludes by saying: "I don't think Mrs. King has proceeded so far in this matter *solely* on her own judgment; I believe she acts under the advice of her solicitor and guardian, Mr. Burroughs." Mrs. Frazer's letter is not in evidence.

In his answer to the original bill (par. 18), the Defendant says: "I do not recollect, and cannot say, that I had any communication with any professional man acting on behalf of the Plaintiff previously to the acceptance of the proposal; but in the course of its negotiation I asked the Plaintiff what solicitor she would employ, and she asked me who was mine or Lord Aldborough's solicitor, and I told her Mr. Ralph Scott, of Gloucester-street, Dublin, and she replied that she would not desire any body better than Mr. Scott. I submitted to said Ralph Scott all the particulars within my power relative to the proposed arrangement, and desired him to carry it out by the proper and necessary conveyance."

In her affidavit, filed on the 13th of May, 1873, the Plaintiff says, in paragraph 10: "When the said contract was made, I had consulted no one as to the advisability of the said sale except the said Robert Henry Anderson; I had no adviser except him, and I had no knowledge of the state of the said premises, except what was derived from him."

In paragraph 13 she says: "I never knew, or to the best of my knowledge saw, Mr. Ralph Scott. I executed the deed of conveyance in the bill mentioned, in what I was informed was his office, but I did not know that he was then present, and I understood at the time he was not present. Two clerks or assistants of his were there. I had never any communication with any solicitor about the said conveyance, and no solicitor advised me, was instructed by me, or acted on my behalf, in reference thereto."

In the affidavit of the Defendant, filed on the 15th of December, 1873, he says, in paragraph 3, that although he had heard of the fact of Mr. King having made a will, he knew nothing of it or of its contents till the contract of sale to him of September, 1859, was about being carried out by a regular conveyance; when (he says) "my impression and recollection is, I saw a copy of it in the hands of Mr. Scott, the solicitor fixed upon by both parties for completing the sale." How Mr. Scott got this copy we may at least conjecture by referring to the letter of the Defendant to the Plaintiff, of the 27th of September, 1859, in which he says: "I enclose the will, having taken a copy of it."

In his letter to Mrs. Frazer of the same date, in which he explains the terms of the contract in all its particulars, he shows that he was fully aware of the interest that the son of Mrs. King had in the purchase-money to be paid on sale of the property under the power. It is in this letter he states his belief that Mrs. King had not acted in the transaction *solely (sic)* on her own judgment, but that she acted under the advice of her solicitor and guardian, Mr. Burroughs. No reference is here made to Mr. Scott, as the adviser of Mrs. King, in the acceptance of the Defendant's proposal, which had taken place before the date of this letter.

Doubtless, Mr. Scott, or whoever acted in his office in the preparation of the deed in the following month of November, was furnished by the Defendant with a copy of the will, which he had taken, as stated in his letter of the 27th September, when he returned the original to Mrs. King. His memory is certainly not tenacious, as is manifest from the several instances in which it has proved to have been at fault. The plaintiff may have been perfectly willing that Mr. Scott should be employed to prepare the conveyance; especially as, under the terms of the contract, it was to be at the cost of the Defendant. I can find nothing to show more than this, that after the agreement with the Defendant had been concluded between them, the Plaintiff assented to the suggestion of the Defendant that Mr. Scott would be a proper person to prepare the instrument of conveyance. The evidence is decisive to show that, in negotiating and concluding the agreement, she had not the independent advice required by the law of the Court, and it was for the Defendant to prove satisfactorily, as an essential part of his case, that she had the protection of a competent and independent adviser.

The correspondence in the time of Mr. Willans may show that her husband had the opportunity of becoming acquainted with the condition and capabilities of the property in his life-time. When he made his will, he could scarcely have believed that the devise of this property was but that of a *damnosa hoereditas*. Whatever may be the value of this part of the correspondence, it is, in my view of the case, altogether irrelevant to the material issue on which we have to decide, otherwise than as it shows the position of confidence and influence which the Defendant was supposed to occupy, and which continued to exist. Taking it then as beyond doubt or question that the *onus* was on him to prove to the satisfaction of the Court that in the transaction of the purchase he had made a reasonable use of this confidence, especially as to having had the Plaintiff protected in the manner required by law, I have no hesitation in saying that he has wholly failed in making out this, his only available defence. Some reliance was placed, in argument, upon alleged laches; and on the circumstance of an outlay upon the property by the Defendant, and other dealings with it since the date of the deed of sale to him. I do not find the defence of laches expressly relied on in the pleadings, and I cannot admit that it is of any weight in the case. In the case of *Murphy* v. *O'Shea* 2 Jo. & Lat. 422, Sir Edward Sugden decided that, although eleven years had elapsed before the filing of the bill to set aside a deed between principle and agent in that case, the Plaintiffs were not barred of relief by laches, if otherwise entitled to it. Where there is no statutory enactment to govern by its authority, or to guide by analogy, the Court must consider the nature and circumstances of the case. In *Napier* v. *Staples* 1 Moll. R. 231-2, Sir Anthony Hart says:–"Lapse of time and neglect do not form of themselves a rule, but give to the Judge a power and discretion to be used according to circumstances, and whenever a case arises where the inconvenience to the public administration of justice, or the prejudice to the individual overbalances the allowance of a just claim irregularly brought forward, it must be dealt with accordingly." The peculiar circumstances of the present case explain and (reasonably) excuse the forbearance of the Plaintiff during the minority of her son; she had never suspected the Defendant, in whom she had full confidence; but he must be taken to have known that no acquiescence on her part could bind the rights of her son; and that the property which he (the Defendant) had acquired under the deed was bound by a trust, which made his expenditure a matter of risk and speculation. The Court has to consider the equities on both sides, and in upholding and enforcing the beneficial and protective law by which the transaction must be dealt with, care will be taken to avoid injustice.

In the decree provision will be made for repayment of so much of the advances and outlay *bonâ fide* made in beneficial expenditure on the property as shall be found to be fairly and justly claimable by the Defendant, and also for preventing the disturbance of sub-tenancies created since the purchase.

The Vice-Chancellor has fallen into a mistake somewhat alike to that from which Lord Justice Knight Bruce was saved by conference with Lord Justice Turner, in *Rhodes* v. *Bate* L.R. 1 Ch. App. 252, an authority which I willingly follow. The policy of the law is preventive, and, therefore, prohibits at the source the opportunity for the action of influences which it is sometimes difficult to estimate. It is the wisdom of the law to act upon the maxim, *praestat cautela quam medela,* and thus to secure protection for those who otherwise might be exposed to imposition and injustice.

The law of the Court for their protection exhibits the expansive power of our system of equity in the application of great fundamental principles to new combinations of fact, and varying circumstances. I am, therefore, of opinion, in which we all concur, that the decision of the Vice-Chancellor must be reversed, and a decree made in favour of the Plaintiff, the terms of which will be stated by the Lord Justice of Appeal.

Lawson C.S.:

The facts of this case have been so fully stated by Lord Commissioner Napier, that it is quite unnecessary for me to recapitulate them, but I wish to state my reasons for differing from the view of the Vice-Chancellor. The first question is as to the existence of a fiduciary relation between the Plaintiff and Defendant. The Vice-Chancellor's judgment upon that point is very clear, and I entirely concur in what he has said upon it. Anderson was, in the language of the letter of the 27th December, 1854, "agent for all parties." As agent for Lord Aldborough he was bound to secure the payment of the renewal fines, and he was in the same position as regards Mr. Darcy. He was also agent for Mrs. Dorothea Field whose interest it was to see that she got her annuity without thinking about the fines. The Kings on the other hand were interested in keeping down the fines, and the Defendant was, in his character of intending purchaser, the man whose interest it was that the fines should be allowed to accumulate in order to depreciate the selling value of the property; he was, finally, the person who was to negotiate with Lord Aldborough for the Kings, and he thus acquired a knowledge of what they would be willing to take for their interest. Standing then in this position he buys from Mrs. King and I may say from Mrs. Dorothea Field also. The *onus* is thrown on him of proving that all was right and honest in the transaction. In the language so often used, "If persons engage in such transactions, they must not complain if they are called upon to show that they are righteous." In my judgment, the Defendant Anderson has entirely failed to sustain the burden of proof. It has been laid down that a person occupying his position must preserve the evidence to shew that in a transaction of this nature all was right. If there were nothing else, the absence of an independent adviser to guide the Plaintiff would be fatal to the Defendant's case on the authority of *Rhodes* v. *Bate* L.R. 1 Ch. App. 252. The lady was kept in ignorance of the fact that she was committing a breach of trust. Would not an independent solicitor have told her that the very thing she could not do was to sell the property for her own benefit, and if she had been possessed of that information, would not the whole motive that was urging her to sell have been destroyed? The Defendant was aware of this, for he stated in one of his letters that the son was alone interested in the £300 purchase money. This case then stands on higher ground than mere inadequacy of consideration, though the consideration was wholly inadequate. For what was it? That Anderson should pay £480 for renewal fines. What would any person who had not a personal interest in securing the payment of those fines, as Anderson had, have advised her to do? Why surely not to lower the value of those lots which were worth something by throwing in those portions of the property on which an enormous sum had accrued due for renewal fines. There is nothing to show that Anderson ever let this lady know that he was entitled to Mr. D'Arcy's property in the premises. He should moreover have communicated to Lord Aldborough Mrs. King's offers to sell her interest, and I am not satisfied that he ever made any such communication. There is no documentary evidence as to his having done so, and if the communication was made verbally, Lord Aldborough might have proved it. All these considerations are important as showing the Appellant's helpless position, consequent on her not having had an independent adviser. It is plain that if she had enjoyed that advantage she never would have entered into this contract. Upon these grounds, and having regard to the fact that the *onus probandi* is thrown upon the Respondent, and that not only has he failed to sustain it, but that on the contrary the case is covered with the gravest suspicion as regards him, I think the decision of the Vice-Chancellor should be reversed.

Christian L.J concurred

The following is the curial portion of their Lordships' order:–

"This Court doth order that the decretal order of the Right Hon. The Vice-Chancellor, bearing date the 16th day of February, 1874, be and the same is hereby reversed. And this Court doth order that the deed of the 11th day of Nov., 1859, and the agreement proposed in the letter of the 18th Sept., 1859, and accepted by the Plaintiff, as in the pleadings mentioned, be, and the same are hereby, set aside. And it is further ordered that the same be forthwith respectively given up to the Registrar of this Court to be cancelled. And let the following accounts and inquiries be taken and made at the Vice-Chancellor's Chambers, viz.: No. 1. An account of the sums paid by the Defendant Robert Henry Anderson to the Plaintiff on foot of the purchase money in said deed and agreement mentioned, with interest from the time of such payments respectively at the rate of five pounds per cent. per annum. No. 2. An account of the sums expended by the said Defendant, since the date of said agreement, in permanent and unexhausted improvements on the premises of the bill mentioned. No.3. An account of the sums paid by the said Defendant, on account of the annuity of £20, to the Defendant Mrs. Dorothea Ellen Field, or for head rents or renewal fines (if any), or of sums necessarily and properly incurred in procuring fee-farm grants or grants of any portion of said premises. No. 4. An account of the sums (if any) which were in said Defendant's hands at the date of the said agreement, and which were properly applicable to any of the aforesaid purposes; also of the rents and profits of the said premises received by the said Defendant since the date of the said agreement. And it is further ordered that the sums which shall be found payable by and to the parties respectively upon foot of the said accounts and inquiries be set off against each other, and a balance struck; and in case such balance shall be found due from the Plaintiff, it is ordered that the Plaintiff be at liberty to retain the same in liquidation of the costs hereinafter directed. And it is further ordered that the Defendant Robert Henry Anderson do execute a re-conveyance of the said premises to the Defendant Dorothea Ellen Field upon the trusts of the deed of the 23rd of August, 1843, such re-conveyance to be settled by the Judge in Chamber, in case the parties differ with respect thereto, the Plaintiff returning to the said Robert Henry Anderson, and, if necessary, reassigning, the policy of insurance of the life of the Defendant Dorothea Ellen Field, in the pleadings mentioned, and giving up to the Registrar of this Court, to be cancelled, the bond bearing the date the 22nd day of Nov., 1859, passed by the said Defendant for securing payment of the premiums on said policy. This decree, and the re-conveyance hereby directed, to be without prejudice to any leases or lettings *bonâ fide* made by the said Defendant Robert Henry Anderson, since the execution of the said deed of the 11th Nov., 1859, at fair letting value, and which the said Plaintiff, by her Counsel in open Court, undertakes not to disturb. And it is further ordered that the Defendant Robert Henry Anderson do pay to the Plaintiff, Alicia Hobart King, otherwise Field, her costs down to and including the hearing in the Court of the Vice-Chancellor, when taxed and ascertained; and that the said Plaintiff and Defendant to abide their own costs of this appeal matter; and that the deposit of £10, lodged with the Registrar, to be handed back to the said Plaintiff, Alicia Hobart King, otherwise Field, or to Messrs. Hugh and William Stanley, or either of them, her Solicitors. And this Court doth remit this cause to the Court of the Vice-Chancellor; and doth reserve the further consideration of said cause to said last-mentioned Court, with liberty to the parties to apply therein as occasion may require."

Notes

Cf. Smyth v. *Smyth,* p.410, *ante.* See further, *Irish Land Law,* paras. 10.075-6.

2. Apportionments

RE HARRIS' ESTATE

[1907] 1 I.R. 32; 41 I.L.T.R. 18 (Court of Appeal)

A testatrix, after certain specific legacies, left the rest and remainder of her property of every kind, both real and personal (which included leaseholds), to her trustees, upon trust to pay A an annuity of £250, and directed the remainder of the income to be derived from her said property, or the investments representing the same, to be paid to her husband during his life, and after his decease to B, C, and D, in certain shares. She directed that, in the event of A dying without issue, the incomes so provided for should be increased by the amount of his annuity; but that, if A died leaving issue, the said annuity should be paid for the benefit of his child or children, until he or they attained the age of twenty-one years, when, out of all her said property, a sum of £4000 was to be raised, and distributed as directed in the said will. Subject thereto, the testatrix gave all her property to B, C, and D, in certain shares.

Sir Samuel Walker, C.:

The question in this case is whether the well-known rule established in *Howe* v. *Lord Dartmouth* 7 Vest. 137 applies to the bequest in this will, or whether the case is taken out of the rule by an intention to enjoy the property *in specie* being shown by the language of the will. The general rule is, that where there is a general residuary bequest of personal estate, including chattels real, to be enjoyed by persons in succession, the Court puts upon the bequest the interpretation that the persons indicated are to enjoy the same thing in succession, and converts the property as the only means of giving effect to that intention.

It is said, in at least one case, that a slight indication of intention to the contrary will be sufficient, but I adopt the rule laid down by James, L.J., in *Macdonald* v. *Irvine* 8 Ch. D. 101, that the rule in *Howe* v. *Lord Dartmouth* 7 Ves. 137 must be applied unless, upon the fair construction of the will, you find a sufficient indication of intention that it is not to be applied, and that the burden in every case is upon the person who says the rule of the Court ought not to be applied in the particular case.

There are numerous cases in which the burden was held to be discharged by the language of the particular will in question, and two especially were referred to by Mr. Matheson: *Collins* v. *Collins Ibid.* 703 and *Pickering* v. *Pickering* 2 Myl. & K. 699, which he said were undistinguishable from the present.

The first consideration is the language of the will we have to construe:– [His Lordship referred to the terms of the will]. The leading subject dealt with all through is "the rest and remainder of my property of every kind." It is out of that the annuity is given, and what is given to the husband for life in the first instance is "the remainder of the income to be derived from my said property or the investments representing the same"; this clause is more consistent with the interpretation "investments for the time being," but the meaning is not very clear, and the same remaining income, after his decease, is given to the two nieces. It is out of the same property the £4,000 is to be raised if it becomes payable; and, subject to the annuity and the husband's life estate, the appellant gets "one-half of my said property" absolutely, and the other two nieces the remaining half absolutely. Each of the devisees gets the same subject described in the same words, one getting it for life and the others in succession

Prima facie, a clearer case for the application of the rule in *Howe* v. *Lord Dartmouth* 7 Ves. 137 cannot be stated.

Let us now see what were the bequests in the two cases mainly relied on. In *Collins* v. *Collins* 2 Myl. & K. 703 the bequest was: "I give to my wife, Sarah Collins, all and every part of my property in every shape, and without any reserve, and in whatsoever manner it is situated, for her natural life; and at her death the property is left to be divided in the following manner." The Master of the Rolls gives no reasons for his conclusions, but the argument shows that the points relied on were the words, in the wife's case, "without any reserve," and the language of the direction for the division as showing there was to be no conversion till after the decease of the wife.

In *Pickering* v. *Pickering* 2 Beav. 31; 4 Myl. & Cr. 289 the bequest was as follows:– "I give and bequeath to my said wife all the interest, rents, dividends, annual produce and profits, use and enjoyment of all my estate and effects whatsoever, real and personal, for and during the term of her natural life." It appears the executors paid the income to the wife as if she was entitled in specie for thirty years, which influenced Lord Cottenham in his decision, but he relies on – (1) *Collins* v. *Collins* 2 Myl. & K. 703 in the direction to divide after the death; (2) the gift of the rents, dividends, annual produce and profits, during her life; (3) the language of the specific gift of the chattels; and, lastly, the gift, after her life, of "the rest and residue of the estate," which was not the rest and residue at the testator's death. The judgment of Lord Langdale proceeded mainly upon the language of the gift to the wife herself.

On the other hand, the case of *Macdonald* v. *Irvine* 8 Ch.D. 101 seems a very strong authority in favour of the appellant:–[His Lordship referred to the terms of the will there in question, and continued]. Thesiger, L.J., there said: "I come to the consideration whether there can be gathered from the will and codicil in the present case any expression of intention that the property in question is to be enjoyed *in specie.* In almost all, if not all, the cases which have been cited in argument, where such an intention was found to exist, we find either words, in their natural and literal sense, importing use and enjoyment of the property in the state in which the testator left it at his death, or directions contained in the will as to the conversion of the property which were inconsistent with a conversion by the Court taking place upon the death of the testator." On those grounds he distinguished *Collins* v. *Collins* 2 Myl. & K. 703 and *Pickering* v. *Pickering* 2 Beav. 34; 4 Myl. & Cr. 289. Baggallay, L.J., who dissented, rested his judgment upon the language of the codicil, upon which, no doubt, there was much to be said.

The case of *In re Game* [1897] 1 Ch. 881 is very like the present. There the testator, after certain specific bequests, directed that the rents and profits of his residuary real and personal estate which he might be possessed of or entitled to at the time of his decease, should be paid to his wife for life, for her own use and benefit, and after her death, he gave his residuary estate to others in succession, subject to certain annuities, and conferred upon the annuitants a power of distress. Stirling, L.J., there held that neither the use of the word "rents," nor the power of distress conferred on the annuitants, was enough to exclude the rule in *Howe* v. *Lord Dartmouth* 7 Ves. 137.

There may be a difficulty in reconciling all the cases cited, and an element of diference may be noted in some of them, as in *Morgan* v. *Morgan* 14 Beav. 72, by the direction as to varying investments.

But the case before the Court appears to me a typical one for applying the rule in *Howe* v. *Lord Dartmouth* 7 Ves. 137. What is dealt with, in the first instance, is "the rest and remainder of my property of every kind." It is all through, both as regards the tenant for life and those taking in remainder, spoken of as "my said property." There is no postponing of conversion beyond what is implied in every gift to a tenant for life and remaindermen. According to the argument, if three-fourths of the property consisted of wasting securities, there could be no conversion. Further, the £4,000 could clearly be raised out of the house property as well as the other.

Upon the whole, I see no sufficient indication of intention to prevent the application of the rule of law in *Howe* v. *Lord Dartmouth* 7 Ves. 137, and the order of Mr. Justice Barton must be discharged.

FitzGibbon, L.J.:

Not alone on its facts, but also on the language of Lord Cottenham, *Pickering* v. *Pickering* 2 Beav. 31; 4 Myl. & Cr. 289 is a good illustration of the difficulty that arises in cases such as this; and it goes far to show that the present is a typical case for acting on *Howe* v. *Lord Dartmouth* 7 Ves. 137, and holding that there is no evidence of an intention of the part of the testatrix that the property should be enjoyed *in specie* by the life-tenant, sufficient to prevent the duty, and the normal course, of realising and investing capital of a wasting nature.

In *Pickering's Case* 3 Beav. 31; 4 Myl. & Cr. 289 a son and mother had for thirty years acted on the principle that the mother was entitled to enjoy the property *in specie,* and, subsequently, in consequence of the failure of other property, it occurred to the son to get her to state an account on the opposite basis. After the mother's death, proceedings were commenced to set aside this account, and Lord Cottenham held that the son was not entitled to maintain it as a settled account. The question as to conversion then arose upon the will, and the learned Judge held that, to avoid conversion, an affirmative intention must be found on the face of the will, or from the circumstances, that the testator's property should be enjoyed by those to whom he gave limited interests in it, in the same condition in which he left it. It seems to be the fashion to go into small considerations in arriving at a conclusion. In *Pickering's Case* 2 Beav. 31; 4 Myl. & Cr. 289 the enumeration of the classes or property, and the different terms employed to describe the way in which it was to be enjoyed, would have gone far to lead me to the conclusion that the testator looked forward to the wife's enjoying what he left behind him, by using it in the same way in which he would himself have used it if he were alive. He speaks of "interest, rents, dividends, annual produce and profits, *use and enjoyment,* of all my estate *and effects* whatsoever, real and personal, for and during the term of her natural life." The will here, on the contrary, speaks of "the remainder of *the income* to be derived from *all my said property, or the investments representing the same."* This actually contemplates conversion and reinvestment, and amalgamation of all the assets into one cash-producing fund. Again, the direction that, in certain events, the annuity should cease, and that the large sum of £4000 should be raised "out of all my said property," although contingent, shows that a state of facts was contemplated in which money would have to be raised out of the leaseholds as well as out of the rest of the property; but I can see no indication of any desire that a tenant for life, or other limited beneficiary, should keep wasting property *in specie,* so as to give him a more profitable enjoyment of it than those coming after him should have. The fact that the terms of years had only thirty and forty years to run, and that the ultimate devise of the capital might, in certain events, not come into full operation until the youngest child of Espine Ward attained the age of twenty-one years, shows that certain objects of the testatrix's bounty would be placed at grave disadvantage from the wasting of the leasehold property, if conversion did not take place.

I regard this as a case not so much of the presumption of law as of the burden of proof, and I cannot find sufficient indication of intention that the property shall be enjoyed *in specie,* as distinct from its being all turned into permanent capital and enjoyed *en masse,* and, therefore, I am of opinion that *Howe* v. *Lord Dartmouth* 7 Ves. 137 applies, and that the appeal must be allowed.

Holmes, L.J.:

In a case of this nature it must be a matter of guess-work what the testator or testatrix would have directed if the particular question under discussion before the Court had been brought to his or her attention at the time the will was made.

I see certain reasons in this case for thinking that in all probability, if the matter had been before the testatrix, she would have directed an immediate conversion. On the other hand, reasons might be suggested why she would have directed a postponement of the conversion until the death of the tenant for life. I have no right to form any opinion as between these two probabilities. It is important therefore to follow a rule of law if we have one; and the rule of law in *Howe* v. *Earl of Dartmouth* 7 Ves. 137 is one which is clear and definite. *Prima facie,* in cases of this nature there ought to be a conversion; but if any intention can be gathered from the will (and in many cases a slight indication of intention is sufficient) that conversion is to be postponed, and that the property is to be enjoyed *in specie* during the lifetime of the tenant for life, that intention will prevail. I have carefully considered the provisions of this will, and I can find not the smallest evidence of such intention; in fact, the words used are the most general words that could be used in a gift of residue. [His Lordship referred to the will.]

If the rule be not applied in this case, I can hardly conceive any case in which it ought to be applied. It might as well be struck out as a rule of law altogether in favour of a rule that in every case, save where there is an actual direction for conversion, the property should be enjoyed *in specie.*

Notes and Questions

As a matter of policy, does the rule in *Howe* v. *Lord Dartmouth* continue to make sense nowadays? See *Irish Land Law,* para. 10.078 *et seq.*; also *Re Abbott, infra.*

RE ABBOTT
[1934] I.R. 189 (High Court)

Subject to the provision of an annuity for his wife, a testator gave and bequeathed all the remainder of his property (and also, after his wife's death, the fund set aside for the payment of her annuity) to the trustees of his will in trust to pay the income arising therefrom equally among his daughter and his grandchildren for the term of their respective lives, and on the death of his daughter he directed that her share of the income and interest arising from his estate and the investments of same should be payable among his grandchildren in equal shares; and, in the event of the death of any of his grandchildren without issue surviving, their share of the income and interest should be equally divided between the surviving grandchildren and his daughter if she was then living, but if any of his grandchildren died leaving issue, the shares of such grandchildren so dying were to be equally divided among their children. The testator then declared that his trustees should have full power to sell any portion of his property at their discretion and invest the proceeds in any securities authorised by law for investment of trust moneys. And in case of the death of all his grandchildren without issue the testator directed that his estate should be sold, and after payment of all expenses in relation thereto the residue should be equally divided between his nieces and certain charitable organisations. By a codicil he directed that his daughter's share of the income should, in the event of her death, be paid to his son-in-law for his life and after his death be payable to his (testator's) said grandchildren in equal shares. And he further directed that his son-in-law should have the collection of the rents, dividends and other income of his said property.

Meredith J.:

The case has been very well opened by Mr. Matheson and very ably argued by the other counsel, who have given me the greatest assistance.

After the fullest consideration I have come back to my first impression. The testator provides for the payment of an annuity to his wife and provides for his daughter and for his grandchildren. He directs the income of his property to be divided between his daughter and his granchildren for their lives, and then makes further provision as to what is to happen in the event of any of his grandchildren dying without leaving issue, or in the event of any of the beneficiaries doing certain acts. There is then a direction under which the property is to go, under what amounts to a general residuary devise and bequest, to be enjoyed by different persons in succession, and therefore the rule in *Howe* v. *Earl of Dartmouth* 7 Ves. 137 has to be considered.

That case was decided by Lord Eldon, and from circumstances, such as are present in this case, he inferred that the idea of the testator was that a fund should be enjoyed by the tenant for life, and subsequent to that life interest, the remainderman should enjoy the same fund, and that the only way of ensuring that was to invest the fund in securities of a permanent and non-wasting nature. The rule applies in many cases, but there are a number of exceptions where it does not apply, for example, where there is an intention indicated by the testator himself that the property shall be, or may be, enjoyed by the tenant for life, in the exact condition in which he left it.

I was referred to two very useful cases: *In re Pitcairn* [1896] 2 Ch. 199 and *Alcock* v. *Sloper* 2 My. & K. 699. The present case involves both the considerations involved in those cases. The testator gives his trustees power to sell and dispose of any portion of his property at their discretion. That phrase in the will would be meaningless unless the trustees had power to retain the property if they thought it advisable to do so. It is made still more clear when the words are contrasted with the words further down in the will where the testator directs "that all my said estate shall be sold." That is a subsequent event and shows that the testator contemplates the possibility of there being no realisation unless and until the contingency referred to arises on the happening of which the entire property is to be sold. I therefore consider that the trustees had power to retain the property in its original state and to pay the income of the property in that state to the tenants for life. This view is reinforced by the words in the codicil which, to borrow the phrase of Sir John Leach, leaves the trustees "in a passive condition." The testator contemplated the trustees retaining the bulk of the property and must be presumed to have intended the tenants for life to enjoy the property *in specie.*

For those reasons I consider that the rule in *Howe* v. *Earl of Dartmouth* 7 Ves. 137 as to conversion is excluded by the language of the testator himself.

Notes and Question

Does this decision indicate a judicial reluctance to apply the rule in *Howe* v. *Lord Dartmouth?* See *Irish Land law,* para 10.079.

STEWART V. KINGSALE
[1902] 1 I.R. 196 (Chancery Division)

Funds held under a will in trust for A for life, remainder for B for life, with remainder over for certain persons, were invested in 1875 on the security of a mortgage of real estate then of sufficient value. The interest due on the mortgage fell into arrear, and in 1880 a petition for sale and the appointment of a receiver was presented by the trustees of the will, and a receiver was appointed in the same year. In 1898 A (the first tenant for life) died. At her death considerable arrears of income were due to her, a portion of which was afterwards paid to her executors. In 1901 the lands subject to the mortgage were sold under the Land Purchase Acts, and did not realise the amount of the mortgage security. Prior to the sale nothing had been paid to B (the present tenant for life) in respect of interest.

Porter M.R.:

The recognised principle is that laid down by Vice-Chancellor James in *Cox* v. *Cox* L.R. 8 Eq. 343. He says, at p.344 of the report: "The true principle in all these cases is, that neither the tenant for life nor the remainderman is to gain an advantage over the other – neither is to suffer more damage in proportion to his estate and interest than the other suffers – from the default of the obligor. The two must share the loss in the same way as they would have shared it had it occurred when they first became entitled in possession to the fund."

In that case the tenant for life had received nothing out of the investment, so that the question arose in its simplest form, uncomplicated by what I have to determine here, viz. how are the rights to be adjusted when the tenant for life has received interest for a part of the period during which it was payable ?

Turner v. *Newport* 2 Ph. 14, a decision of Lord Cottenham, was not cited to Lord Romilly in *Re Grabowski* L.R. 6 Eq. 12; and, though the facts are different and somewhat more complicated, entirely supports the principle of Vice-Chancellor James' conclusion in *Cox* v. *Cox* L.R. 8 Eq. 343. Lord Cottenham says:–"This case, though certainly peculiar in its circumstances, appears to me to be governed by one of the most ordinary principles in the administration of assets. A portion of the testatrix's estate consisted of a debt. The debtor's estate was insolvent, and, for several years after the death of the testatrix, nothing was recovered, either in the shape of principal or interest. At length a sum is realized; and then, when the question arises what part of it is, as between the parties, to be considered as principal, the tenant for life is told, that, because the gross sum recovered is less than the amount of the original debt, she is to have nothing. Such a proposition is contrary to the plainest principles of justice, particularly when it is considered that the Court itself has restrained her from getting in the debt sooner, in the hope that more might be ultimately recovered. But the other proposition is equally untenable – that she is entitled to the whole of what has been recovered in respect of interest since the testatrix's death. For, besides that there is nothing in the will to entitle the tenant for life to the interest of the residue in its actual state of investment at the death of the testatrix, the circumstances of the estate out of which this debt was to be paid may have been such as to make such a proposition doubly unfair towards the parties interested in the capital. Suppose, for instance, that if, while interest was accruing upon the debts, the fund for payment of them was producing no interest at all, or a lower rate of interest, it is obvious that the longer the recovery of the debts was protracted, the more those parties would be prejudiced; for the proportion of the fund which would be ultimately attributable to the capital of the debts would be continually diminishing. I think, therefore, that the proper course is that suggested by Mr. Parry, viz. to ascertain what the bond would have realized if the debtor's had been administered at the expiration of a year after the testatrix's death, and to allow the tenant for life interest at 4 per cent. on that amount."

Innes v. *Mitchell* 1 Ph. 710, decided by Lord Lyndhurst, and in substance afterwards adopted with variation by Lord Cottenham, appears to have been argued before, and decided some time after *Turner* v. *Newport* 2 Ph. 14, although reported in the preceding volume of Phillips. In some respects it bears a close resemblance to that now before me.

In that case William Innes, by his will, gave to his three natural daughters, Ann, Sophia, and Heriot, the yearly sum of £300 among them, and to the longest liver; and he directed that "a sufficient sum should be invested in the public funds in the names of his executors as trustees for the three sisters, who were to divide the £300 equally between them while all of them were alive, and to the longest liver of them the whole." By a codicil the testator gave and bequeathed "the £300 a year to be equally divided between the sisters during their lives, and to the longest liver, when the stock which produces that sum may then be sold for the use of such longest liver and her heirs." He appointed his three daughters residuary legatees. After the death of the testator a sum of stock was set apart by the executors to answer the annuity of £300. The annuity was regularly paid to the three daughters until 1800, when Sophia died, after which it was regularly paid in equal moieties to the two survivors until 1816, when the surviving executor of the will died insolvent, having sold out the stock which had been set apart to answer the annuities, in consequence of which, there being then no other part of the testator's estate available for the payment of the annuities, they ceased to be paid. After the deaths of the other two daughters of the testator, a sum of money, forming part of his residuary estate, but of less amount than the original fund set apart, became availabe. It was held that this sum was to be apportioned rateable between the arrears due to the two surviving daughters respectively at the time of the death of that one of them who died first, and the sum originally set apart, and which belonged to the last survivor. Thus, the estate of the first of the three sisters who died is left out of account, because she was paid all she was entitled to up to her death in 1800.

The second to die was Heriot (Stewart). She lived till 1837; but her annuity was not paid after 1816, so that £3150 for twenty-one years arrears was then due to her estate. She had, however, received £150 each year from 1800 till 1816, making, I suppose, £2400 or thereabouts.

The last to die was Mrs. Mitchell (Ann), and the arrears due to her were stated to be upwards of £5000; but this must have included a claim to arrears after Mrs. Stewart's death, a claim which was not in the first instance allowed, because on Mrs. Stewart's death Ann Mitchell became entitled under the will to the principal fund, though in another view she might have claimed the whole annuity instead. It was in this latter particular that Lord Cottenham varied the decree of his predecessor.

The point to be observed is that it never occurred to Lord Lyndhurst, or apparently to Lord Cottenham, to take into account the payments of the annuities regularly made down to 1816. The arrears only are dealt with.

So much for the older cases.

More recently the same question has been considered several times, notably in *Re Grabowki* L.R. 6 Eq. 12; *Cox* v. *Cox* L.R. 8 Eq. 343; *Re Moore* 54 L.J. Ch. 432; *Re Foster* 45 Ch. D. 629, and some later cases.

Re Grabowski (1866) L.R. 6 Eq. 12 may be briefly dismissed, as it has been overruled, or at least has never been followed or applied, and is inconsistent with all the other cases on the subject. Lord Romilly, M.R., there held that the whole of the fund recovered should go to replace capital, regardless of the arrears of interest; but this view was manifestly wrong.

Cox v. *Cox* (1869) L.R. 8 Eq. 343 in effect overruled *Re Grabowski* L.R. 6 Eq. 12. In *Cox* v. *Cox* L.R. 8 Eq. 343 by marriage settlement George Cox covenanted to pay to trustees, three months after his death, the sum of £6000, with interest from date of death till payment at 5 per cent. He also executed his bond conditioned to be void on payment of like amount with interest. The trusts of the money by the settlement were declared to be for the widow for life, with remainder (in the events that happened) for the benefit of the children of the marriage. Some years after Mr. Cox's death assets were recovered which were insufficient to fulfil the covenant and bond. It was held that a calculation must be made of what principal, if invested at the date of the obligor's death at 4 per cent. interest, would amount, with interest to the fund recovered. Interest at 4 per cent. on this principal was to go to the tenant for life, and the rest was to be treated as capital. In that case the tenant for life had not received anything, so that no question of giving credits arose, save as far as it may be involved in the statement of the prinicple on which Sir W.M. James proceeded, as embodied in the language I have already quoted; and that language is, on this point, ambiguous, since the rights of the tenant for life under the settlement may mean either his rights as far as from the date of the settlement, or his rights as existing when the loss of capital occurred.

In *Re Moore* (1885) 54 L.J. Ch. 432, decided by Pearson, J., it was held that the fund realized was divisible between tenant for life and remainderman in the proportions in which the arrears of interest bore to the entire original principal money, without allowing interest on either. This in effect follows *Cox* v. *Cox* L.R. 8 Eq. 343 unless the words used in the latter case are construed to apply to the whole original interest under the settlement.

Then comes *Re Foster* (1890) 45 Ch.D. 629, in which Mr. Justice Kay referred to *Maclaren* v. *Stainton* L.R. 11 Eq. 382 and *Re Tinkler's Estate* L.R. 20 Eq. 456, neither of which greatly affects the present question, and then proceeded to enunciate a new rule or formula, materially different from anything to be discovered in the earlier decisions. In that case Thomas Foster, by will, gave his residuary estate to trustees upon trust for sale and to pay the income of the proceeds to his widow for life, with remainder to certain persons absolutely. After Mr. Foster's death, the trustees invested £7535, part of the residuary estate, on mortgage or freehold property at 5 per cent. The trustees afterwards entered into possession of the mortgaged property and paid the rents to the widow, as tenant for life until her death, but such rents were insufficient to keep down the interest; the total deficiency of interest at the date of the widow's death amounting to £3400. Shortly after her death the trustees sold the mortgaged property. The sale realized £7005 only, being less than the principal mortgage money. In giving judgment Kay, J., said:–"I am of opinion that the available fund should be apportioned between the tenant for life and the remaindermen, upon the basis of the following calculation. Treat the capital moneys which have been produced by the sale and all the moneys received by the tenant for life as the fund recovered from the mortgagees. Add them together. Then divide the total sum in this way: Estimate how much the tenant for life would have received if the mortgage interest had been regularly paid, deducting income tax. Then take the capital sum which the remaindermen would be entitled to on the supposition that the capital of the mortgage debt had been fully paid. Then divide the total between the tenant for life and the remaindermen in the proportion of these two amounts which each ought to have received; and in making that division the tenant for life should give credit for what she has actually received. If the sale did not take place until a little while after her death, then the remainderman ought to be credited with interest during that time. For the purpose of calculation they are entitled to receive the whole amount, together with interest at 5 per cent. per annum from the death of the tenant for life. This would be a little addition to the sum which the remaindermen ought to receive. Then it will be the sum actually recovered by the tenant for life and the remaindermen. The total will be divisible betwen them – the remaindermen and the tenant for life – each taking that proportion. The tenant for life must give credit for what she has actually received." It will be observed that the learned Judge does not profess to give any authority for adopting this basis of calculation, nor any reason why it should be adopted in lieu of that previously existing, but leaves it to stand or fall on its own inherent merits. *Cox* v. *Cox* L.R. 8 Eq. 434 and *Re Moore* 54 L.J. Ch. 432 were however both cited in argument. *Re Foster* 45 Ch.D. 629 was followed with possibly a modification by Farwell, J., in *Re Bird* [1901] 1 Ch. 916. In that case Farwell, J., says:–"The question I have to answer is, how the loss caused by the breach of trust is to be borne. The authorities are in a perplexing condition, and I am unable to reconcile the decision of Pearson, J., in *In re Moore* 54 L.J. Ch. 432 with that of Kay, J., in *In re Foster* 45 Ch. D. 629. The present case is distinguishable from both those authorities, as in neither of them was the loss caused by a breach of trust." He then quotes the principle stated by James, V.-C., in *Cox* v. *Cox* L.R. 8 Eq. 343, and says "Applying this principle, I have first to ascertain what the fund for division ought to be on the assumption that the sale and wrongful investment never took place. In that case there would have been £10,021 Consols for division, and the tenant for life would have received the interest on those Consols down to her death. As a matter of fact, she received altogether the sum of £4066 in respect of the income of the wrongful investment. She was in no way responsible for, or indeed cognizant of, the breach of trust, and I could not order her executor to refund any portion of this income. But I am dealing with a case of adjustment of a loss as between tenant for life and remainderman, and so long as any funds are available for that purpose I must so apportion them as to throw the loss on income and capital rateably. The proper method of doing this is to ascertain the total amount of the dividends on £10,021 Consols that the tenant for life would have received if the sale and wrongful investment had not been made, and also to ascertain the value of £10,021 Consols at her death, the proper time for distributing the fund. This will show the amounts that ought to have been available for income and capital respectively. On the other hand, the fund in Court, *plus* the £4066 income actually received, *minus* accretions since the death of the tenant for life, which accretions belong to the remainderman, gives the aggregate amount actually produced by the wrongful investment up to the death of the tenant for life.

"In order to throw the loss on income and capital rateably, this aggregate must be divided between the estate of the tenant for life and the remainderman, according to the rule in *In re Foster* 45 Ch.D. 629, *i.e.* in the proportion which the total amount of dividends that the tenant for life would have received on the £10,021 Consols from the date of the wrongful investment to her death, bears to the value of £10,021

Consols at her death, her executor giving credit for the £4066 actually received, but not being liable to refund any over payment for the reason above stated.

"Whether this is the proper mode of apportionment in a case where the loss has not arisen from a breach of trust is not for me to determine. There was a breach of trust in the present case, and I must restore the *status quo* as far as the funds available will permit."

When the learned Judge explains that the actual decision does not extend beyond cases of breach of trust, he does not suggest any reason why it should not, if correct, apply to all cases of loss of trust funds, and I confess I do not see any reason founded upon principle why it should be so restricted. In *In re Foster* 45 Ch.D. 629 there was no breach of trust; at least, none is mentioned or suggested in the report.

In two other cases, of which only brief notices are to be found in the *Weekly Notes,* and there only, *Re Barker* W.N. 1897, 154 and *Lyon* v. *Mitchell* W.N. 1899, 27, Stirling, J., and North, J., respectively followed *Re Moore* 54 L.J. Ch. 432, and not *Re Foster* 45 Ch.D. 629; and in the last case on the subject, *Re Alston* [1901] 2 Ch. 584, Kekewich J., in a reasoned judgment followed *Re Moore* 54 L.J. Ch. 432. He says (p.589 of the report):–"A sum has been realized which is not sufficient to pay the principal and arrears of interest. The result is that it must be ascertained in some way what is the fair division between those who are entitled to interest and have not received it in full, and those who are entitled to the capital and will not receive it in full. It seems to me that the simplest and most logical way of dealing with that is to apportion the amount which you have actually got between the two estates which are beneficially interested in that amount – the estate of the tenant for life, or successive tenants for life, as in this case, on the one hand, and the estate of the remainderman on the other hand. The real question is what is due to each at the time of the realization. Of course, if a tenant for life has received money he must give credit for that; but what you have to ascertain is what is due at the date you recover the money. That view, as I understand it, agrees with the decision of Pearson J., in *In re Moore* 54 L.J. Ch. 432. It does depart from the decision of Kay, J., in *In re Foster* 45 Ch.D. 629, but the explanation of that decision may be that it is one only to be applied to the peculiar circumstances, and in the case of *In re Barker* W.N. 1897, 154, Stirling, J., appears to have intimated an opinion that the apportionment in *In re Foster* 45 Ch. D. 629 was intended to be confined to the case of a mortgagee in possession. That distinction does not altogether commend itself to my mind. In the present case the amount which has been recovered must be apportioned between capital and income in proportion to the amounts due at the date when it was recovered in respect of arrears of interest and in respect of principal. As between the successive tenants for life, and the amount attributed to interest will be apportioned in proportion to the arrears due to them respectively."

The authorites are therefore, it must be confessed, in a somewhat confused state. I should, perhaps, also mentioned *Ancketill's Estate* 27 L.R.Ir. 331 in this country, in which Monroe, J., followed *Re Moore* 54 L.J.Ch. 432; but *Re Foster* 45 Ch.D. 629 was not cited, and, perhaps, from the dates may not have been reported at the time, not was the precise question here involved discussed.

Conceiving myself, therefore, to be at liberty to act as may seem most just in the matter, I have to decide between *Re Moore* 54 L. J. Ch. 432, and *Re Foster* 45 Ch.D. 629; and I unhesitatingly prefer the former.

A tenant for life of a fund which becomes diminished by means of a breach of trust (to which he is not a party), or by the bankruptcy of a debtor, or by fall in value of the securities on which the trust money is invested, may have received the income of the fund before any such calamity for a long series of years. The amount of income so enjoyed may equal or largely exceed any sum which would be coming to him, on any equitable calculation, out of the remnant of the fund. In either case he will, under the decision of *Re Foster* 45 Ch.D. 629, receive nothing. Yet the payment of the income which has been received by him has in no way caused the loss or diminished the fund to which the remainderman is entitled. The diminution is caused by an act which wrongs both remainderman and tenant for life as from its date. Before its occurrence the income received was rightfully received. Each payment of income or interest belonged to the tenant for life. If withheld, he could have enforced each and every payment by regular process of law; and in no conceivable event could it be recovered back from him in the absence of fraud or the like. .

Further, the calculation adopted in *Re Foster* 45 Ch.D. 629 is incapable of being applied in all cases so as always to carry out the principle it was designed to effectuate. Admittedly, payments of income regularly made before the loss cannot be recalled. Some of the cases state this in terms, and it is clear that it must be so, once it is shown that the payments were at the time in accordance with the trust.

Take, then, the case in which the tenant for life has received more than would be his on the principle of bringing past payments into the account. The remainderman then will receive less, it may be much less, than the calculation would give him, while the life tenant has had more, it may be much more, than his share.

In truth, the equity alleged is a halting and uncertain one, and in my opinion there is no solid basis for it. Even if in the case last put the excess of receipts by the tenant in life could be charged upon his interest in the future income of the diminished fund, that would be a precarious expedient, and would not ensure equality in the way equality is sought to be produced. But indeed I can find no sufficient reason for the practice. The rule in *Re Moore* 54 L.J.Ch.432 ensures to those interested in the trust fund equality of treatment in respect of the rights and interests injuriously affected by the loss which diminishes the fund. But the loss of the fund ought only to affect injuriously the interests of those entitled to it as from the date of the loss. This must be the case where the loss is total. Why then should there be a difference when the loss is partial only I fail to see. Thus the date of the breach of trust, bankruptcy, or decline of securities, or the time at which it becomes apparent that there must be a loss *(Ancketill's Estate* 27 L.R.Ir. 331) is, in my opinion, the time at which persons entitled in succession are injured; and the adjustment as between them should commence and take effect as of that date; and this is, I conceive, the correct interpretation of what was said in *Cox* v. *Cox* L.R. Eq. 343.

In the present case I cannot see any other date to which this consequence is to be attached than the date of the sale. For all that appears, although the interest had partly fallen into arrear, the trust fund and interest on it might have been adequately secured all along till the sale.

Part of the proceeds of sale consists of guaranteed deposit of land stock retained to meet possible defaults of the purchasers. Till that is set free it cannot be dealt with in possession, so far as *corpus* is concerned, at present, for it may never be realized, though there is little doubt that it will. When it is set free it will be subject to the same principle; but the dividends of the stock in the meantime will belong to those persons interested in the capital and arrears, including, of course, the tenant for life.

Note
See further, *Irish Land Law,* paras. 10.022-3.

O'BRIEN V. FITZGERALD
(1851) 1 Ir.Ch.R. 290 (Chancery Division)

A fund secured by mortgage was a marriage settlement, made in 1827, transferred to trustees upon trust to permit the husband to receive the interest of the sum, whether it should continue invested and secured as it was then, or should be invested in any other security, for life, and after his decease upon other trusts, with a power to invest the fund in the public funds or real securities so that the same, with the interest, dividends, &c., should continue and be applied to the same uses, trusts and purposes. The mortgage was paid off and the money vested in £3¼ per cent. stock.

Smith M.R.:

After stating the application, said:–

Margaret H.Comyn claims the dividends under a settlement of the 21st of November 1827, executed on her marriage. Thomas F. Comyn died on the 14th of Augsut 1850, and it is contended on the part of the plaintiff that Margaret Helen

Comyn is only entitled to an apportionment of the dividends, from the 14th of August to the 10th of October 1850. The right to the future dividends is not disputed.

It is admitted that in general there is no apportionment of the dividends of stock. The rule is stated in 1 *Swanst.* p.349, *note* :–"The rule of law which refuses apportionments of rent in respect of time is applicable to all periodical payments becoming due at fixed intervals, not to sums accruing *de die in diem;* annuities therefore and dividends on money in the funds are not apportionable." Several authorities are referred to. But it is contended that, by reason of the provisions of the settlement, and the contract then entered into, the general rule is not applicable to this case, and that the dividends are apportionable – [His Honour read the provisions of the settlement.]

It is contended that, as by the express provision of the deed, the interest on the sum secured by the mortgage was apportionable, when the mortgage was paid off and invested in stock, the trusts being the same, the dividends should also be apportionable. I do not concur in that argument. In the case of *Pearly* v. *Smith* 3 Atk. 260 "a purchaser from a husband of an interest in South Sea annuities during his life, remainder to other persons (which had been originally secured upon a mortgage, but by order of this Court had been transferred to Government securities), insisted that, notwithstanding the husband died before the Christmas half year became due, yet that he was entitled to be paid proportionably, at the rate of £4 per cent. for the time the husband lived, from Midsummer to the day of his death." Lord Hardwicke said:–"If it had continued a mortgage, the purchaser would have been entitled to the demand he now makes, because there interest accrues every day for forbearance of the principal, though notwithstanding it is usual in mortgages to make it payable half-yearly. But South Sea annuities are by Act of Parliament considered merely as annuities, and therefore the purchaser here is not more entitled to receive the half-year's dividends, which did not become due until after the husband's death, than he would in the case of a common annuity payable half-yearly, where the annuitant (in whose place he stands) dies before the half-year is completed."

There is another case to the same effect in the same volume of *Atkyn's Reports* – *Sherrard* v. *Sherrard* 3 Atk. 502. It was decided in that case that where money is directed to be laid out in lands, and in the meantime invested in Government securities, though a tenant for life dies in the middle of a half-year, it should not be apportioned, but be paid to the reversioner. The Master of the Rolls said:–"The constant usage has been, where money is to be laid out on lands upon any settlement, and in the meantime invested in Government securities, that the entire half-year's dividends should be paid to him in reversion, nowithstanding the tenant for life died in the middle of the half-year, and shall not be apportioned; otherwise indeed in the case of a mortgage."

In the case of *Rashleigh* v. *Master* 3 Br.C.C. 99, a fund, which had been secured by a mortgage, was invested in £3½ per cent. stock. A question arose as to apportioning the dividends. The Lord Chancellor said:–"The Court would not apportion dividends; parties consenting to lay out money in stock must abide the consequences."

I have therefore come to the conclusion, that I am bound by the authorities to make the order in the terms of the notice.

Note

See further, *Irish Land Law,* para 10.085.

BRERETON V. DAY

[1895] 1 I.R. 518 (Chancery Division)

The facts are set out iin the judgment.

Porter M.R.:

The only question remaining for decision at present is as to the cost of putting the leasehold house in Merrion-square into repair, pursuant to the covenants contained in the lease of 30th March, 1839.

Does the devisee for life take the house as she finds it *cum onere?* or is the cost of repairing to be borne by the tenant for life and the remainderman in proportion to their respective interests? or is the cost of effecting the needful repairs to be defrayed out of the testatrix's residuary personal estate, so as to give the tenant for life possession of the dwelling in that condition in which it would have been if the testatrix had maintained it conformably to her covenant ?

The first case on the point to which it is necessary to refer is *Harris* v. *Poyner* 1 Dr. 174, which was a decision of Kindersley, V.C. The case has some facts which closely resemble the present, and the decision has the authority of an eminent Judge. At page 181 he says:–"The testator, at the time when he died, having been in the possession, or the holder of this leasehold property, had, in violation of the covenants in the leases under which he held, suffered the property to fall into dilapidation; and it appears by the Master's report, that the amount of the dilapidation which had occurred at the time when the testator died was £900. He had violated his covenants; and I must assume that the testator would have been liable to the landlord in an action for damages for breach of covenant. Shortly after the testator's death, the landlord seems to have made application to the widow, and to have given formal notices to her, and to have called upon the parties to make good the dilapidations; upon which the widow and the son together took measures, the effect of which is that the widow, as I understand, paid the amount of the dilapidations – not all in one sum, but paid them by degrees, so as to satisfy the landlord's demand. Then comes the question, Is the widow to bear that expense out of her own pocket, or is it to be borne by the testator's residuary estate? Now the cases which have been cited, I confess do not appear to me to govern the present case. Whether in the case of a dry specific legacy of a separate leasehold, where the testator was liable for dilapidations at the time of his death – whether as between that specific legatee and the person entitled to the general residue of the personal estate, the specific legatee should discharge that amount of dilapidation out of the general estate or not – the principle of such a case does not appear to me to govern the present case at all. In the case before Lord Truro, *Hickling* v. *Boyer* 3 MacN. & G. 635, his Lordship decided against the specific legatee, principally upon the terms used in the will, though he certainly goes on to say that, irrespective of those terms, and upon general principle, he should still have decided the same way; and I must assume that to be right. But, asssuming it to be right (although, I confess, if it had been *res integra,* I should have questioned it very much – not upon the terms of the will in that case, but upon the general principle), that was a question as between the specific legatee of a separate leasehold, and the residuary legatee of general personal estate. Here it is a question as between the tenant for life and the remainderman or the reversioner, of an aggregate mass of property, all consisting the residuary real and personal estate, of which the leaseholds in question form only a component part"; and he accordingly decided that the repairs were to be borne by the residue and not by the tenant for life.

Hickling v. *Boyer* 3 MacN. & G. 35 was a devise of leaseholds – "subject to the performance of the covenants," &c. The residue was subject to payment of debts. The legatee took *cum onere,* including liability for repairs. Lord Truro decided the case not only on the terms of the gift, "subject," &c., but on general principles. But the case was not one of tenant for life and remainderman, or tenant for life and residuary legatee; but merely as between a specific gift of leaseholds and the general residuary estate. And it is noticeable that a fund was set apart to protect the executors in case the specific legatee did not perform the obligation.

Re Courtier; Coles v. *Courtier* 34 Ch. Div. 136 (distinguishing *Re Fowler* 16 Ch.Div. 723) decided there was no liability on the tenant for life to put in repair. Cotton, L.J., says –"With respect to that question, it is admitted that the words of the will are such that it cannot be contended that there is a trust for immediate conversion; but it is said that if the widow is to have the right to possess the leaseholds in specie, during her lifetime, she is bound to spend her money in putting them into sufficient repair, to satisfy the covenants of the leases. I think that there is no such obligation on her. She is not bound to the landlords under the covenants; the trustees are bound, and it is their duty to repair the houses, in accordance with the covenants in the leases, out of the *corpus* of the estate. There is no rule of law that the tenant for life is bound to do these repairs out of the rents and profits. She is to enjoy these leaseholds in specie, but she is under no covenants to repair, and there is nothing in the will to show that the testator intended her only to have the net rents, after making provisions for the liabilities that arose in the testator's lifetime. It cannot be fairly left to the widow to make good the deficiencies of the testator. The appellants relied on *In re Fowler* 16 Ch.D. 723. But that was a very different case, and the question which arose there does not arise here. Here is is not a question whether the trustees are bound to keep up the houses, but whether the tenant for life is bound. In that case the question was whether trustees ought, out of rents and profits in their hands, to provide for the repairs, and Lord Justice Fry decided that, as under the terms of the will they were to receive the rents, and to preserve the property for the remaindermen, it was their duty to apply the rents in their hands towards the repairs. No question was decided there between the tenant for life and the remaindermen, only that the trustees, having the property in their hands, and having the duty to keep that part of the estate in repair, and, having nothing but rents and profits in their hands, they must apply them for this purpose. If it had been a decision between tenant for life and remaindermen, I should have had some difficulty in following it. But I consider it is no authority in the present case." And Bowen L.J., says:–"I am of the same opinion. The first question on this appeal is whether the tenant for life is bound to keep the leaseholds in such a state of repair as to prevent forfeiture. These houses are given to the widow during her life. What obligation is there on her ? Is she to take on herself the entire burden and repair them out of her own money, or only expend the income which she derives from the rents and profits of the property? Whichever way the point is put, the obligation is quite imaginary; it can arise nowhere unless it is to be found in the will. It is admitted that it is not to be found in the will, therefore it does not exist. The Lord Justice Cotton has explained the distinction between this case and *In re Fowler* 16 Ch.D. 723 and I agree with him. That case did not decide the rights, as between the tenant for life and the remaindermen." To the same effect are the observations of Fry, L.J.

In *Re Fowler; Fowler* v. *O'Dell* 16 Ch.D. 723 there was no other fund for repairs *except* the rents (see judgment, p. 725), and the case is perhaps capable of being explained on that ground. But the case must be considered as at least of very doubtful authority (*Re Courtier* 34 Ch.D. 136), and one which affords no guidance, when the very peculiar circumstances alluded to does not exist.

I think it therefore plain, upon the authorities, that as between tenant for life of a leasehold, specifically bequeathed, and the general assets of the testator, there is no equity in favour of the latter to throw on the former the obligation of putting the leaseholds, which were dilapidated at the time of his death, in repair, and that *Harris* v. *Poyner* 1 Dr. 174 is an authority that the repairs ought to be defrayed out of the general estate.

But Serjeant Campion contended that if this be so, or at least if the entire cost cannot be thrown upon the tenant for life, the equitable doctrine of this Court which generally distributes the burden between tenant for life and remaindermen in proportion to their respective interests, calls for some adjustment of the payment in this case: and he suggested that if the trustees are called upon to pay the cost of putting in repair, interest upon the amount so expended ought to be charged against the tenant for life, during her enjoyment of the leasehold estate. And there is much good sense and apparent justice in this contention. In support of it, he relied on passages found in the judgments in *Freke* v. *Calmady; Re Hotchkys* 32 Ch. D. 408.

In that case the facts were dissimilar to those before me. There was a devise to trustees of "all my freehold, leasehold, and copyhold lands and hereditaments, and all my real and personal estate, of what nature or kind soever, and wherever situate," unto and to the use of Vincent Calmady, and two other persons therein named, their heirs, executors, administrators, and assigns, "upon trust at their discretion to sell and dispose of all such parts thereof as shall not consist of money, and out of the produce of such sale shall first pay all my just debts and my funeral and testamentary expenses, and shall then invest the residue of such moneys in, etc., and shall stand possessed of such real and personal estate, money, and securities upon trust to pay the rents, interest, and dividends, and annual produce thereof unto my dear friend Emily Tuson for and during their term of her natural life as and for her separate estate, and so that the same shall not be subject to the debts or control of any husband of hers, and that her receipts alone be a sufficient discharge for the same, and I direct that if the said Emily Tuson shall alien or dispose of the same, or charge the same or any part thereof by anticipation, whether by her own act or by act of the law, the same shall be thenceforth forfeited to the use of the said Vincent Calmady, his heirs, executors, administrators, or assigns." Then after providing that the trustees might effect the sales of all or any part of her estate, either by public auction or private contract, and empowering them to give receipts to purchasers, she proceeded:–"And from and after the decease of the said Emily Tuson, I give, devise, and bequeath my said real and personal estate, and the securities on which the same may be invested, unto and to the use of the said Vincent Calmady, his heirs, executors, administrators, and assigns for ever, according to the nature and quality thereof respectively." Pancraswick estate was held in fee, in possession, unincumbered. Blatchborough estate was a reversion (subject to heavy mortgages), and was held in fee. The reversion fell in six years after the death of the testatrix. Besides being incumbered, the Blatchborough estate was in need of repairs, which ought to be effected in course of proper management. But the estate was one in fee simple, and not a leasehold. No obligation whatever attached to the testatrix to repair or put in repair. No such liability attached to the estate of the testatrix in any shape. So far as repairs were concerned, it was only a question of prudent management, the determination of which rested with the trustees, whether in the interests of all parties the repairs ought to be effected, and if so, how they should be borne – whether out of the income of the tenant for life or out of the *corpus* of the property. It is in reference to that question that Cotton, L.J. says (page 416): "What then, in that state of facts, is the right as between the tenant for life and the remainderman? The estate was to be vested in the trustees during the tenancy for life. In my opinion, in a case where trustees have property vested in them under circumstances like these, there is an obligation upon them, for the purpose of properly carrying out and performing their trust with regard to the property, to see that the property does not fall into decay from want of proper repair. But when the property has fallen into bad repair, the question will of course arise whether it is worth while to do the repairs. It may be that where there is a devise of two estates, one subject to an incumbrance not made by the testator, and the other not incumbered, it may not be worth while to expend any money out of the unincumbered estate for the repairs of the incumbered one, for it would be throwing away money to repair the property if the circumstances were such that no one but the incumbrancer would be benefited by the expenditure. Then of course the trustees would be wrong in applying anything not in mortgage to repair a property which, when repaired, would not be worth anything to the estate. No doubt, if it was clearly for the benefit of the whole residue to repair the mortgaged property, the Court would say that the trustees must do it, and that the money must be raised in such a way as not to throw the burthen unfairly either upon the tenant for life or upon the remainderman"; and again, "according to my view, the burden of repairing, if it is necessary and proper, ought to be thrown upon the estate in such a way as not to throw it entirely upon the tenant for life or upon the remainderman."

And it is in reference to the same question that the observations of Lindley, L.J., are directed. He says:– "As regards the substantial question, that of the repairs, it appears to me there is no avoiding the application to this case of the rule laid down by Lord Hatterley in *Powys* v. *Blagrave* Kay, 495. The tenant for life is equitable tenant for life, and the remainderman is not entitled to throw upon her the burthen of keeping the property in repair. I think that it is perfectly plain. Whether the property is to be regarded as one property or as two appears to my mind to be for this purpose immaterial. The remainderman cannot be entitled to throw upon the tenant for life the burthen of the repairs by paying for them out of the rents. I quite agree with what

Lord Justice Cotton has said that if it is shown that it is judicious to make repairs, and the trustees come to the Court for authority to make them, that authority will be given, but it will be given on equitable terms as to the mode of paying expenses. If such an application is made it will have to be considered whether the repairs are beneficial, and whether they ought to be made, and if so, how the trustees would be authorised to raise the money, whether by sale or mortgage, or in some other way, but it must be done in a mode which is equitable as between the tenant for life and the remainderman, and not so as to throw the whole burthen upon either." The other questions in that case, viz. – the incidence of the interest on the mortgages on the Blatchborough estate in reference to the rents of the Pancraswick estate, and the claim of the tenant for life to repudiate the devise of the former while accepting that of the latter, do not arise here at all. As regards the repairs, however, I should willingly do what was suggested there and urged by Serjeant Campion if I had any authority for it. But in my opinion there is none. *Re Hotchkys* 32 Ch.D. 408 has no application. Here there is a liability to the landlord for repairs – a liability for which the trustees and executors are liable and primarily liable. The liability was a debt of the testatrix. If the repairs be not made, the interest in the lease will be forfeited and may be evicted. Miss O'Grady is to have the house in Merrion-square as a place of personal residence, subject to her paying the rent and other outgoings. This she cannot do unless the testatrix's covenant is satisfied so as to avoid the forfeiture. She is under no legal or equitable obligation whatever to put in repair (*Powys* v. *Blagrave*) 4 D.M. & G. 418. In cases where it is sought to apply the maxim "*qui sentit commodum idem sentire debet et onus*" there is always a preliminary question, what is the *commodum?* and the case I have quoted shows that in this case the *commodum* was meant to be the house in that state in which the testatrix was as between herself and the head landlord legally bound to leave it. If so, the legatee does not receive the *commodum* till the repairs are effected, and the *onus* which attaches to it is that which is expressed, namely, the payment of the rent and other outgoings, including (no doubt) the maintenance of the place in tenantable order when once repaired.

In *Re Baring: Jeune* v. *Baring* [1893] 1 Ch. 61 Kekewich, J., followed *Re Courtier* 34 Ch.D. 136 so far as was necessary for the case before him: but there was not there any question of putting in repair as distinguished from keeping in repair. There is no indication that there had been any breach of covenant in the lifetime of the testator or afterwards. The case has therefore no bearing on the question here.

For these reasons I am of opinion that the cost of necessary repairs must be borne by the trustees out of the general residuary estate.

Note

See further, *Irish Land Law*, para. 10.086.

Chapter 19

VARIATION OF TRUSTS

The scope for variation of trusts is limited in the Republic of Ireland because of the lack of statutory provisions such as exist in England and Northern Ireland, see *Irish Land Law,* para. 10.087 *et seq.*

RE MILLER
[1897] 1 I.R. 290 (Chancery Division)

The facts are set out in the judgment.

Porter M.R.:
I think that the executors in this case have not acted capriciously, but at the same time that they have misconceived their duties as to this legacy to Timothy Clancy. Timothy Clancy is entitled under the will to a legacy of £1000 and to half the residue. The legacy of £1000 is given in these words: "I give to my executors the sum of £1000 in trust, for my brother, Timothy Clancy of Ballyoran." If the will had stopped there, there would be no doubt; but it goes on:– "in such share or shares and at such time and manner as they think fit and proper." The testatrix then gives to her executors £500 in trust for her brother, John Clancy of Ballyoran, to be paid in such share or shares and at such time or times as they think proper. After giving certain pecuniary legacies she disposes of the residue as follows:– "I leave the net residue and remainder of my property of every kind whatever, of which I may die seised or possessed of or entitled to unto my executors, in trust for my two brothers equally, share and share alike, and to be paid to them at such time or times and in such manner as they" (i.e. the executors) "think proper."

No doubt the testatrix had something in her mind as to her two brothers, and their probable conduct in dealing with the legacies, and that was why she wished that her executors should have some control over the money; but her will does not say that anyone else is to have the legacies in any defined event; there is no gift over: nor is anyone else given a share of the residue. There is a clear gift of the whole £1000 to Timothy; there is no discretion given to the executors to give him a portion only of the money, and to withhold the rest; the whole £1000 is for Timothy and there is no gift over. On principle, if there were no cases on the subject, it is perfectly clear the money belongs to Timothy, and to no one else, and that the executors have no power to retain any part of it. Even if they had such power, the result as to the money legacies would be the same, as the sum retained would fall into the residue. It is inconsistent with the nature of personal property (save in some well-known exceptional instances, such as coverture and infancy) that one person should be absolute owner of it, and that another person should have power to retain it against him. If the money was withheld for a time, the interest on it would belong to the legatee, who is thus sole owner of both principal and interest. Suppose the legatee sold his legacy, or became bankrupt, the purchaser, or the assignees in bankruptcy, would have a clear right to legacy. It is not the case of a life interest being given defeasible in a certain event, nor is it the case of a legacy to a person under disability, *e.g.* an infant or a lunatic. The legatee here is *sui juris*, and no one else has any interest. The testatrix has expressed an intention to superadd to the absolute gift incidents which the law does not allow. The case of *Snowdon* v. *Dales* 6 Sim. 524 is in point, and the case of *Mills* v. *Johnston* [1894] 3 Ch. 204 is particularly so; but, if there were no authority on the subject whatever, I am perfectly clear that the right to the property carries with it the right to the possession. The case resembles the class of cases where money is given to a person for a particular object – the gift does not fail because the particular object cannot be carried out; for example, money given to buy a commission in the army, or to provide a university education; again, a gift of money to a person for the purpose of enabling him to publish a manuscript work of the testator, does not fail because the purpose cannot be carried out. There is not such thing known to the law as an absolute gift of a fund, coupled with a fetter or restriction on its enjoyment, in the case of an object *sui juris*. In the case of the legacy to the other brother, John Clancy, it was not attempted to be argued that on his death any discretion was left to the executors as to the disposition of his legacy. The same considerations which apply to the legacy to Timothy apply to his share of the residue. The law of the case is clear, but no blame can be attached to the executors in coming to the Court for directions; and the costs of all parties will come out of the estate.

Note

See further on the rule in *Sanders* v. *Vautier*, *Irish Land Law*, para. 10.088.

RE JOHNSON'S SETTLEMENT

[1944] I.R. 529 (High Court)

Trustees of a settlement applied to the Court for an order directing that £954, 10s., or such sum as the Court might direct, be raised out of the settled property by sale or mortgage or otherwise, to enable them to carry out alterations, improvements and repairs to the property. The tenant for life was not financially in a position to do the necessary repairs.

Gavan Duffy J.:

In my opinion the jurisdiction given by s. 13 of the Settled Land Act, 1890, to authorise the application of capital money in making additions or alterations to buildings "reasonably necessary or proper to enable the same to be let" is not confined to property unlet at the date of the application to the Court. If the property be habitually let the section applies, although the particular house to be repaired happen to be let at the time of the application. I refer to the judgment of Buckley J. in *Stanford* v. *Roberts* [1901] 1 Ch. 440, which I prefer to the opinion of Farwell J. in *In re Calverley's Settled Estate* [1904] 1 Ch. 150, at p. 154.

Accordingly, but for one difficulty, this application could have been brought under the Settled Land Acts by the tenant for life, who has for more than forty years been drawing a large income out of the property and doing, I understand, virtually nothing by way of even ordinary repairs. The difficulty is that the trustees of the settlement have no capital in hand, so that the improvement provisions of the Settled Land Acts are not available for the existing emergency.

This equitable tenant for life is in a peculiarly advantageous position, and the trustees in the present case appear to be bare trustees with no powers of management. In these circumstances the trustees themselves come into Court and rely on the principle of salvage to justify this application, outside the Settled Lands Acts, having, as they say, no other means of saving the situation. Where trustees are not trustees for sale and have no power of sale or management, and where the limitations are equitable, I hold that the Court can, as a last resort if no other way is open, apply the principle of salvage in order to sanction the expenditure out of capital of the money necessary for doing such repairs, constituting permanent improvements, as are essential to the preservation of the settled property. I need refer only, in support of this view, to *In re Hotchkys* 32 Ch. D. 408, *In re Freman* [1898] 1 Ch. 28, (decided by the same learned Judge who decided the case of *In re Lord de Tabley*; *Leighton* v. *Leighton* 75 L.T.R. 328), and to *In re Smith's Settled Estates* [1904] 1 Ch. 689, to which I may add *Neill* v. *Neill* [1904] 1 I.R. 513.

I am satisfied that the items marked *a* (1) to *a* (10) (inclusive) and *a* (12) to *a* (15) (inclusive) in the estimate referred to in the architect's affidavit represent essential work within this principle and I shall sanction accordingly the raising of a sum of money not exceeding the estimated cost, according to Mr. Miller's affidavit, of those items, together with an addition of 15 per cent. upon that sum, the addition being due to possible fluctuation of prices as a result of the present emergency conditions; to this sum may be added a reasonable sum not exceeding one hundred guineas for the architect's fees.

I authorise the trustees to mortgage or concur in a mortgage of the settled lands for the purposes of raising this money, and the income of the tenant for life will, of course, be reduced accordingly.

Notes

1. See further, *Irish Land Law*, para. 10.091 *et seq*.
2. See also *Re Kinahan's Trusts*, p.550, *ante*.

Chapter 20

BREACH OF TRUST

This is a difficult subject, particularly the law governing beneficiaries' remedies for breach of trust, *e.g.*, the law of tracing misappropriated trust property, see *Irish Land Law*, para. 10.097 *et seq*.

BROWNE V. MAUNSELL

(1856) 5 Ir. Ch. R. 351; 1 Ir. Jur. (n.s.) 197 (Chancery)

The facts are set out in the judgment

Brady LC.:

In this case the petitioner propounds a proposition, respecting the administration of trust estates, which is not countenanced by any case reported since the decision of *Trafford* v. *Boehm* 3 Atk. 440. It is alleged that it is there decided that whenever a *cestui que trust* requests his trustee to lay out the fund on another security, the trustee (whatever shape the transaction may assume on his part) has at all events, and under all circumstances, a right to say that the *cestui que trust* is not only barred from himself proceeding against the trustee, but is absolutely bound to indemnify the trustee from the consequence of any loss which may occur from these changes of investment.

The petitioner pushes the proposition to that extent, and he must go so far to entitle him to succeed in this case. The consequence of holding that doctrine would certainly be convenient to trustees, but the result would be, that facile as trustees have been in adopting improper investments, they would be much more so if sure of having indemnity. I would hesitate, therefore, before making such a decision, if I am not coerced by the authorities, though there might be no great difficulty if I could see that the trustee had not been the active party in selecting the investment.

In respect, however, to this particular loan, there can be no doubt that it was originally suggested by Mr. Browne the petitioner, or perhaps rather by his solicitor. He does not appear to have been influenced by any personal motive, but he seems to have had knowledge and a very high opinion of the position of Mr. Leyne the borrower, and it appears that in fact Mr. Browne recommended Mr. Leyne as a person in whom Mr. Maunsell might have confidence.

I do not think that there was anything like an actual contract on which the petitioner can rely; that allegation is altogether displaced by the documents; the case then rests on the general proposition which is nowhere to be found since the case of *Trafford* v. *Boehm*. All the subsequent cases go on the principle of the *cestui que trust* being liable to the extent of the particular interest which he took under the deed creating the trust, holding that such an interest, and such an interest alone, was liable to make good the loss. That doctrine is founded, however, on a different principle, viz., that the *cestui que trust* who has concurred in the misapplication would have no right to institute proceedings against the trustee, and that the Court would therefore not enforce against the trustee any equity in his favour, though at the suit of other persons.

In *Montford* v. *Cadogan* 17 Ves. 485, and *Greenwood* v. *Wakeford* 1 Beav. 576, the decision amounted to nothing more than the proposition I have just stated. In *Raby* v. *Ridehalgh* 1 Jur., N.S., 363 the case was very plain, for the tenant for life had got the whole fund into his hand, and the only question was, whether the proper remedy was an action at Law or a suit in Equity?

With respect to the case of *Trafford* v. *Boehm* 3 Atk. 440, on examination of the whole report, it seems very uncertain whether the proposition for which the petitioner contends was there laid down. What was the nature of the bill in which the decree was made? It is called a cross-bill, and it is stated that the end of that suit was to have certain sums therein specified applied to make good the trusts of the settlements. Sigismond Behom, or Trafford, the husband of the plaintiff in the first suit, and her father, had directed Charles Behom, the surviving trustee of Sigismond's settlement, to invest a portion of the settled fund upon an invalid speculation, the purchase of South Sea stock, which was then current. The consequence of this investment was, that much of the property was lost. Sigismond then died without issue, and, as I collect from the report, he would take a reversion in fee in the lands which were to be purchased with the trust funds. It is stated that by his will he charged the lands purchased or to be purchased with the plaintiff's portion (expectant on the deceases of himself and the plaintiff Mrs. Trafford and failure of their issue) with his debts, so it seems that in point of fact he took a valuable reversionary interest in those lands, and had this interest in the trust funds, which was liable to make good the loss he had occasioned. Again, he had taken an interest in a sum of money which was to be laid out in land to be settled in the same way as the Hackney lands, and this interest he had covenanted to convey to the trustees of his settlements, to be laid out along with the plaintiff's fortune in the purchase of lands. Sigismond afterwards devised all his real estate to the plaintiff Mrs. Trafford for life. The cross-bill sought indemnity out of the money which was to be laid out in the same uses as the Hackney lands; and it seems hard to say that Mrs. Trafford, taking under his will all the real estate for life, the same interest to which she was entitled under her settlements, was to bear any portion of the loss. I would read the decision as limited to the estate which Sigismond took in the very subject of the settlement, the lands that were purchased with the plaintiff's fortune. That is the only way in which I can understand that case, taken in connection with all those which have since occurred until this present suit. I think that the proposition that a *cestui que trust* is bound to make good to the trustee every loss occasioned by an investment made with his privity has not been sustained; there is not any express contract by Mr. Maunsell to indemnify Mr. Browne, and therefore the petitioner's case has failed.

It is said, however, that the respondent had profited by this investment, to the extent of £12.10s., but the petition does not pray that that sum should be brought into court; that is not the scope of the petition. The petition is founded on allegations of the general proposition of law and of express contract; these are not sustained, and I must therefore dismiss the petition. There is no reason why I should not give costs.

Note

See further, *Irish Land Law*, para. 10.103.

SHANAHAN'S STAMP AUCTIONS LTD. V. FARRELLY

[1962] I.R 368; 98 I.L.T.R. 4 (High Court)

The facts are set out in the judgment.

Budd J.:

Prior to the 12th October, 1954, Jerome Shanahan, A. Desmond Shanahan and Paul Singer carried on the business of dealers in, and auctioneers and agents for the sale of, collectors' stamps and publishers of a magazine relating to philately, under the style of "Shanahans Stamp Auctions Limited" at 38 Corrig Avenue, Dun Laoghaire.

On the 12th October, 1954, Shanahans Stamp Auctions Limited (which I hereafter refer to as "the Company") was incorporated in Ireland as a private company limited by shares, having a nominal share capital of £1,000 divided into 1,000 shares of £1 each. On the 12th November, 1954, the said 1,000 shares were held as to 250 thereof by Jerome Shanahan, a further 250 thereof by Desmond Shanahan, a further 250 thereof by Dr. Paul Singer and the remaining 250 thereof by Irma Singer, the wife of the said Paul Singer. The said shares were allotted as fully paid up for a consideration other than cash and the appropriate agreement in respect thereof pursuant to s. 88 of the Companies (Consolidation) Act, 1908, was duly filed in the Companies Office in Dublin Castle. This agreement took the form of an indenture of the 12th day of November, 1954, made between Jerome Shanahan, A. Desmond Shanahan and Paul Singer (thereinafter called "the vendors"), of the one part, and the Company, of the other part, whereby, after reciting that the vendors had agreed to sell the

Company the whole of the assets of the business carried on by them for the price of £1,000 and that the said purchase price should be satisfied by the allotment of shares in manner above set out to the vendors and Irma Singer, the vendors, in consideration of the said allotment of shares, assigned to the Company all the goodwill of the vendors in the said business and also all the book debts of, and the benefit of all contracts entered into by, the vendors in respect of the said business.

On the 16th September, 1958, the capital of the Company was increased to £50,000 by the creation of 9,000 new preference shares of £1 each and 40,000 new ordinary shares of £1 each. The original 1,000 shares in the Company were converted into founder shares. On the 7th October, 1958, 4,000 of the new preference shares and 10,000 of the new ordinary shares were allotted by way of bonus issues equally between the said Jerome Shanahan, Arthur Desmond Shanahan, Paul Singer and Irma Singer. No money was ever subscribed for shares; therefore the Company never had any capital with which to finance its business save the book debts and the value, if any, of any contracts subsisting.

By article 16 of the articles of association of the Company it was provided that the said Jerome Shanahan should be the first and life chairman of the board of directors of the Company and by article 30 that the said Arthur Desmond Shanahan should be the first secretary thereof. The said Arthur Desmond Shanahan, the said Paul Singer and the said Irma Singer were directors of the Company.

The memorandum and articles of association of the Company stated the objects for which the Company was established *inter alia* to be:-

"3 (*a*) To acquire by purchase or otherwise and to take over as a going concern and carry on the business of dealers in and auctioneers and agents for the sale of collectors' stamps and proprietors and publishers of the magazine-periodical 'Green I.S.L.E. Philately' dealing with philatelic matters at present carried on at 38 Corrig Avenue Dun Laoghaire in the County of Dublin under the name and style of Shanahan's Stamp Auction and all or any of the assets and liabilities of the said business."

"3 (*g*) To receive money on deposit or otherwise from customers and employees upon such terms as the Company may approve, and to guarantee the debts and contracts of customers and others."

The operations of the Company were exceedingly complex. It was of a nature quite unique in this country and therefore outside our ordinary legal and business experience. The official liquidator has been faced with an immense task in unravelling the affairs of the Company. Owing to the lack or incompleteness of records and the difficulties which the official liquidator has had in obtaining information with regard to many of the operations in which the Company and its directors were involved, it has been exceedingly difficult, in some cases impossible, to discover the true or precise nature of many of these dealings and operations.

On the 24th May, 1959, a special resolution was passed for the voluntary winding up of the Company. Mr. Gerard O'Brien was appointed liquidator. On the 8th June, 1959, an order was made for the winding up of the Company by the Court. Mr. O'Brien was then appointed official liquidator.

The nett cash assets of the Company in the hands of the official liquidator at the time of swearing of his affidavit in this matter was £113,566 16s. 6d. In addition the official liquidator holds stamps, which have been valued between July and September, 1959, at £282,787. He has been advised that they have since appreciated in value to the extent of approximately ten per cent.

It appears that some 6,700 persons have made claims against the Company for sums totalling approximately £1,840,000. A number of these persons claim to be entitled to stamps *in specie*, as distinct from being creditors. The claim by ordinary creditors amounts to the sum £34,300 13s 3d.

Stated very briefly the underlying idea of the Company's scheme as stated by it was that it would buy stamps with money subscribed by the public, re-sell them at a profit and then return the capital to the subscribers with any profits earned. It was provided that the Company would charge commission on the sales and guarantee the return of the capital invested. The method by which the Company operated or purported to operate was as follows: first, it procured large sums of money from the public on the representation that they would be used in the above fashion. Large quantities of stamps were then to be purchased by the Company. The stamps purchased were then to be brought to Dun Laoghaire and divided up into lots which were to be allotted to various groups of investors formed into syndicates. The stamps thus allotted to a group of syndicates were then to be auctioned. After the auction each investor was to receive out of the proceeds of sale a sum in respect of the money he had invested calculated by reference to each £1 subscribed by him, which included a dividend on the purported profits of the sales made. The above statement merely outlines the ostensible mode of procedure and it will be necessary to state it in more detail in order to deal with the questions now arising.

It would appear that there were various departures from the scheme as outlined. For example, investors would sometimes receive substantial dividends although the stamps allotted to the syndicates they were interested in were sold at a loss or some not sold at all. Further, there is a huge deficit between the money invested and the cash and stamps now in the hands of the official liquidator. The liquidator is still pursuing inquiries relating to the monies unaccounted for, but I should point out that in these present proceedings I am dealing with questions relative to claims made against the stamps in hands and to what are the rights of interested parties therein.

The Company is insolvent and I have at present to deal with the rights of three classes of claimants. First, the general creditors of the Company, such as those who sold goods to it. These are represented in effect by the official liquidator, suing as plaintiff in the name of the Company, whose duty is to claim what he is advised are assets of the Company in the interest of all the ordinary creditors. Secondly, the class of investors to whom no stamps were allotted. Thirdly, those investors who were formed into syndicates and to whom lots of stamps had been allotted. The first-named defendant is one of the last-named class of what may be described as "syndicated investors" and claims that the stamps allotted to the syndicate which she was formed into with other investors are held in trust by the plaintiffs for the members of the syndicate. Representing the class of syndicated investors, the claim has been made by counsel on her and their behalf that such syndicated investors are entitled to the allotted stamps *in specie* or alternatively that they are held by the plaintiffs upon trust to sell the same and divide the proceeds amongst the members of the respective syndicates to whom such stamps were allotted. They also claim that the difference in sale price and the amount invested, should a sale be directed and a sum less than the amount invested be obtained, should be paid to them. The second-named defendant, who is representative of the second class, or what may be called "unsyndicated investors," claims that the stamps purchased and still held by the plaintiffs are held by them in trust for, or are subject to a charge in favour of, all or some of the investors, and that, if subject to a charge, they should be sold for their benefit. They also claim any difference between the proceeds of sale and monies invested. The plaintiffs through the official liquidator contend that the members of both these classes are mere creditors of the Company to the extent of their respective investments and rank with the ordinary creditors in respect of any dividend to be paid.

So that the position and claims of the parties interested may be properly understood it is necessary to consider in some detail the operations of the Company with regard to the investors.

The Company held an auction of stamps approximately twice a month every month during the period from the 5th May, 1955, to the 9th May, 1959. These sales were conducted by reference to catalogues which were prepared by the Company and circulated to potential buyers throughout the world approximately three weeks before the date fixed for the auction. The catalogue contained a detailed description of the stamps to be included in the auction and in many cases included photographs of the stamps. They also contained the conditions of sale of the stamps. The conditions of sale, as taken from the catalogue of the 7th March, 1959, are as follows:-

"1. The highest bidder shall be the purchaser. Any dispute shall be decided by the auctioneer, who will also regulate the bidding. His decision will be accepted as final by purchaser and vendor alike, not only in this matter but in all other matters affecting this auction. He should also be entitled to reject bids.

"2. All lots are sold subject to purchaser's satisfaction. Postal bidders who have not seen the lots they are buying, either directly or through a representative, are at liberty to reject any lot within 48 hours of receipt, without the necessity of stating a reason, provided the stamps are returned in the same condition as received, postage, packing and insurance both ways at buyer's expense.

"3. Commission is payable by both the vendor and the purchaser at the rate of 10%. Lots once accepted by us cannot be withdrawn before the sale. In case any lot remains unsold, we shall charge to the vendor at the rate of 3/6 per line catalogue space in ordinary type, 5/- per line in heavy type, 15/- in addition if the lot was boxed, and a further £1 1s. 0d. for every illustration. No reserves can be accepted.

"4. All postage and insurance charges are to be paid by the purchaser.

"5. Payment must be made in every case before delivery. In the case of overseas buyers, lots can be sent to a local bank in customer's vicinity, who will hand them over against payment. All bank charges thus incurred must be borne by the purchaser.

"6. Barter transactions are always gladly considered. Mint stamps (at a discount to be arranged) are also acceptable in lieu of cash payment.

"7. Valuations printed in the catalogue are merely the auctioneers' opinion and don't constitute part of any contract. Prices actually realised may be higher or lower. Our valuations, however, are sometimes an indication of the finer points of condition.

"8. Any contract is only between the vendor and purchaser and not between either and the auctioneers.

"9. The auctioneers are not responsible for badly mounted stamps sent by vendors.

"10. Ownership of lots bought passes to the purchaser only after full payment of the purchase price, plus all charges. Even in those cases where delivery has been made before payment, the auctioneer is entitled to demand the return of any unpaid or partly paid for lots."

The conditions of sale in other catalogues issued of recent times do not appear to be different in any material respect.

The Company advertised widely through the press, magazines and by means of brochures and circulars, inviting the public to invest money in what was described as the "large capital gains" of philately. From 1955 to February, 1959, the Company operated two distinct schemes which were known as the "Four Months Simple Plan" and the "Twelve Months Compound Plan."

It is stated that it is believed that all investors completed the coupon attached to the brochures above mentioned when sending in their investments and it has been contended that the brochure and coupon contained the essence of the contract between the investors and the Company. It is therefore necessary to set out the terms of the brochure and coupon in full and they are as follows:-

"PROFIT FROM STAMPS – WITHOUT RISK

"(The '4 Months Simple Plan')

"Stamps mean different things to different people. What can they mean to you?

"If your problem is a small capital which you want to invest with absolute security, but with an unusually large return, then stamps are the solution to your problem.

"You can invest any amount you like from £10 ($28) to £1,000 per calendar month and partiticipate without overhead expenses and without any knowledge of stamps at all in the large capital gains of philately.

"The whole transaction takes 4 months only. During this period we buy, with the investor's money, large stamp collections in all parts of the globe, bring them here and sell the stamps in smaller lots in one of our fortnightly auctions.

"The stamps so bought are invoiced to the respective investors, who are being grouped into syndicates, and treated as their property. You will be advised of the lot numbers in our catalogues you are interested in, and after the sale the prices paid for these lots are published in a subsequent catalogue.

"Exactly four months after receipt of your investment we shall post you our cheque for your capital plus gains accrued.

"Our only charge to you is our standard auction selling commission in force at the time of the sale of your stamps, that is all.

"And remember, your capital is absolutely guaranteed and will be returned to you intact, whatever happens.

"The 'Profit From Stamps – Without Risk' Scheme has been running now for a good number of years during which time we have completed many, many thousands of investment transactions, every one with a very satisfactory return to the investor. Turn over the page and see how our investors fared last year.

"This scheme, now well known all over the world, is available to investors of all countries, and repayments will be made in the same currency as originally received by us.

"If you are interested, fill in the coupon below and enclose your remittance.

"Yours sincerely,
"SHANANAN'S STAMP AUCTIONS LTD."

To the brochure was attached a detachable slip to be used by an investor when sending a remittance in accordance with the offer contained in the brochure. It is in the following terms:-

"Date..........

"To: Shanahan's Stamp Auctions, Ltd.,
"39 Upr. Gt. George's Street,
"Dun Loaghaire, Dublin.

"Please find enclosed herewith my remittance for........This amount to be used to purchase stamps for me. These stamps to be suitably lotted and entered into your next available sale. The total proceeds of the sale of these lots (less your standard commission) to be remitted to me not later than 4 months from to-day. But should the nett proceeds be less than my investment, then you will make good any shortage.

"Kindly confirm my return.

"Yours faithfully,
"Name (in block letters)...........
"Address................."

It appears from the brochure prepared by the Company in respect of the "Twelve Months Compound Plan" that this scheme operated in the same manner as the "Four Months Simple Plan" with the difference that instead of repaying the capital and gains accruing thereon at the expiration of the four months period the capital and gains were retained by the Company and used by them for the purchase of further stamps, the intermediate accrued capital being, however, also guaranteed. This process was repeated again at the end of the eight months from the date of the original investment so that the investor under this system participated in three auctions held by the Company. In or about the month of February, 1959, the "Four Months Simple Plan" and the "Twelve Months Compound Plan" were respectively changed to the "Six Months Simple Plan" and the "Eighteen Months Compound Plan." The only effect of the alteration was to postpone the date of repayment of investments, and, subject thereto, the provisions hereinbefore mentioned with regard to the original plans were applied. I have dealt, it will be noted, with the brochures relating to the Four Months Plan and the Twelve Months Plan, but it is right to say that many of the investors whose cases I am dealing with in fact invested their monies in the Six Months Plan and Eighteen Months Plan. Having examined the brochures relating to these latter two plans, however, it seems to me that the same provisions applied, so that contentions based on the two first plans and any determinations made on them apply equally well to the second two plans.

It would appear from the result of the official liquidator's examination of the records and affairs of the Company that in detail the procedure adopted by the Company in the operation of the Four Months Plan was as follows:-

On the receipt of a sum of money for investment in stamps the Company entered the name of the investor and the amount of his investment in the investment book and at the same time forwarded a standard form of letter acknowledging receipt of the money for investment in stamps. The type of such a letter would be as follows:–

"Investment No.

"Dear........

"*Profit from Stamps – Without Risk – 4 Months Simple Plan*"

"Thank you very much for your remittance for to be used in our Investment Scheme entitled 'Profit from Stamps – Without Risk.'

"We are confirming receipt and that we shall try to deal with the money as requested by you.

"We hope to send you, from time to time, an account of what we are doing with it, and on the we should have your complete account and send you a cheque for the proceeds, capital, plus profits (if any).

"We trust that the results will be pleasing to you, and are,

"Yours sincerely,
"SHANAHAN'S STAMP AUCTIONS LTD."

Approximately three months after the receipt of the investment from the investor the Company wrote to the investor, informing him that the money invested by him had been utilised in the purchase of a large quantity of stamps at reasonable prices at a total value stated and that he and various other investors were being formed into syndicates to be known by a particular syndicate numbers. The letter also stated the number of £1 shares in the syndicate and the number of such shares which it was proposed to allot to the addressee. With this letter the Company also enclosed a copy of the catalogue relating to the auction at which the relevant stamps were to be sold, together with a document known as a "Vendor's Pre-Sale Advice Note." The syndicates were formed by grouping together a number of the investors substantially in the order in which their names were entered in the investment book. A specimen of the type of letter sent is as follows:-

"Investment No. 22845 20th May, 1959.

"Miss Anne Farrelly,
1 Copeland Ave.,
Clontarf.
Dublin

"Dear Miss Farrelly,

"*Re Profit From Stamps – Without Risk.*

"We have utilised the £500 which you sent us on the 2.2.59 by the purchase of a large quantity of stamps at reasonable prices for a total value of £12,419 and we are forming a syndicate to be known as syndicate No. 91020 between yourself and various of our investors.

"There will be 12419 shares of £1 each of which we propose allocating to you 500 shares, and the gross proceeds, less our commission, will then be divided into 12419 parts.

"We are enclosing a copy of your Vendors', Pre-Sale Advice Note giving you the lot numbers in which your syndicate has an interest. Corresponding catalogue is also being sent to you. We hope that when we repay you the capital and gains accrued on 2.6.59 you will be very pleased with the results.

"Yours sincerely,
"SHANAHAN'S STAMP AUCTIONS LTD."

The Vendor's Pre-Sale Advice Note set out the syndicate number of which the particular investor was a member, together with a list of the lots allocated to that syndicate. Each pre-sale advice note contained the following statement:- "These lots will be offered for unreserved sale (notwithstanding any previous instructions) unless we hear from you to the contrary at least twenty-four hours before the sale. We also assume that you have read our conditions carefully." As far as can be ascertained no investor at any time gave the Company instructions or directions with regard to the sale or otherwise of any stamps or lots allocated to a syndicate of which that investor was a member. A specimen of the relevant portion of the type of the vendor's pre-sale advice note is as follows:-

"Miss Anne Farrelly,
1 Copeland Avenue,
Clontarf.

"VENDOR'S PRE-SALE ADVICE NOTE NO. 40738

	"Lot No.	
"We beg to enclose catalogue and your lot numbers in our 6th June Sale are:		Your share 500/12419th parts of the total amount these lots realise, less relevant commission.
"SYNDICATE NO. 91020		

"10, 20, 30, 41, 51, 61, 71, 81, 91, 101, 111, 121, 131, 141, 151, 161, 171, 184, 194, 203, 213, 223, 233, 243, 253, 263, 273, 283, 293, 303, 313, 323, 333, 343, 353, 364, 474, 384, 394, 404, 414, 425, 435, 445, 465, 475, 507, 517, 527, 537, 547, 557, 567, 577, 587, 597, 607, 617, 627, 637, 647.

"These lots will be offered for unreserved Sale (notwithstanding any previous instruction) unless we hear from you to the contrary at least 24 hours before the Sale. We also assume that you have read our Conditions carefully. We trust that the results of this Sale will be pleasing to you.

"E. & O.E."

Immediately after an auction was held the Company forwarded to the members of the syndicates whose lots had been included therein a document known as a "Vendor's After-Sale Advice Note." This document stated the share to which the addressee was entitled, the particular syndicate number, the lot numbers included in such syndicate, the total price realised and the amount payable in respect of each £1 share in the syndicate. The vendor's after-sale advice note also contained a statement to the effect that a cheque would be sent as soon as clearance was effected. A specimen of the relevant portion of a vendor's after-sale advice note is in the following terms:-

"Mrs. E. H. Dawson,
C/o Mr. G. Dawson, 7 Trinity College, Dublin.

"VENDOR'S AFTER-SALE ADVICE NOTE NO. 28279

	"Lot No.	Price Realised
"In the 29.11.58 Sale		
"We were able to sell the following lots for you:	Your share 250/10445th parts of the total amount these lots realise, less relevan commission.	
"SYNDICATE NO. 8799		

"8, 18, 28, 38, 48, 58, 68, 78, 88. 98, 109, 120, 130, 140, 150, 160, 170, 180, 190, 200, 210, 220, 226, 236, 246, 256, 267, 277, 287, 297, 307, 317, 327, 337, 347, 354, 364, 374, 384, 394, 404, 414, 424, 434, 444, 454, 464, 474, 484, 494, 503, 514, 524, 534, 544, 554, 564, 574, 582, 592, 602, 612, 622, 632, 642, 652, 675, 689, 699, 709, 719, 729, 739, 749, 759, 769, 779, 789, 799, 809, 819, 829.

"TOTAL REALISED: £13056 5 0
which comes per
£1 share to £1 5 0
10% Commission 2 6
£1 2 6 Net per £1 share
"Prices individual lots realised will be published in our next catalogue.

"Cheque will be send to you as soon as clearance is effected.

"E & O.E."

Finally, four months after the receipt of the investment by the Company, the Company forwarded to each investor a document known as the "Vendor's Statement of Account." With this document the Company sent a cheque for the amount to which the particular investor was entitled in accordance with the calculations set out thereon. A specimen of a vendor's statement of account is in these terms:-

"VENDOR'S STATEMENT OF ACCOUNT NO. 28560
"Mr. G. W. P. Dawson,
7 Trinity College, Dublin.

	Lot No.	Price Realised £	s.	d.	Commission £	s.	d.
"In the 13th Dec. Sale we were able to sell the following lots for you.		Your share 100/1825th parts of the total amount these lots realise, less relevant commission.					
"SYNDICATE NO. 3811							

"11, 21, 42, 33, 52, 62, 72, 82, 92, 102, 112, 122, 132, 142, 152, 162, 172, 182 192, 202, 212, 222, 231, 241, 251, 261, 273, 283, 293, 303, 313, 323, 337, 362, 376, 386, 396, 406, 407, 418, 509, 423, 434, 444, 453, 463, 473, 483, 498, 520

"TOTAL REALISED £2258 8 9
which comes per
£1 share to £1 4 9
10% Commission 2 5
£1 2 4 Net per £1 share
"Prices individual lots realised will be published in our next catalogue.

	Lot No.	£	s.	d.	£	s.	d.
"Cheque herewith					111	13	4
"E. & O.E."							

All of the dealings between particular investors and the Company were recorded on a ledger card kept by the Company for that purpose.

Between the 5th May, 1955, and the 24th May, 1959, the Company held approximately 97 auctions. It appears that it was the practice of the Company, after the year 1955, to divide the lots offered for sale between ten syndicates. The denoting number of each syndicate contained in the middle figures thereof the number of the auction in which it was represented. Thus syndicate number, 91020, indicated that that syndicate had stamps, allocated to it which were included in auction number 102. The number of investors grouped together in any particular syndicate varied widely and the investment represented by each syndicate also varied from syndicate to syndicate.

The Company advertised two auctions (numbers 98 and 99) to be held on the 9th May, 1959. The first of these auctions was described as general and the second as containing the "mystery" collection of Lombardo Venezia. From the records of the Company it appears that the money invested by investors whose syndicates were represented at this auction amounted to approximately £254,000. All of the stamps which were catalogued for these two auctions (with the exemption of the "Everyman's One Liners") were allocated to the syndicates numbered 9990 to 9999 (inclusive) and Pre-sale advice notes were duly despatched to the members of these syndicates. Due to a burglary which it is alleged took place on the Company's premises on the night of the 8th May, 1959, both of these auctions were cancelled by the Company. I should explain that "Everyman's One-Liner" was a description given by the Company to stamps of a relatively small value which were not allotted to syndicates. In many cases it appears that stamps which were sold under this description were not purchased by the Company but were auctioned on behalf of the owners thereof. I was informed – and it appears from extracts taken from the books – that the lots included in auction 98 were allocated to syndicates 9990 to 9999, so that the distinguishing number would be 99, the middle figures thereof.

The Company advertised a further auction (number 100) for the 23rd May, 1959. This auction was described on the Company's catalogue as a general sale, and from the records of the Company it appears that the money invested by investors whose syndicates were represented at this auction amounted to approximately £35,000. The lots comprised in this auction were allocated to the members of the syndicates numbered from 9100 to 91009 (inclusive). This auction was also cancelled by the Company due to the alleged burglary.

Between the 10th and 23rd May, 1959, a circular letter was sent by the Company to most of the members of syndicates, numbers 9990 to 9999, included in auctions 98 and 99, informing them that the auction in which they were interested had been cancelled due to the burglary and that the Company had decided to pay 25s. 6d. for every £1 invested by the investors comprised in these syndicates. A cheque for the appropriate amount was included with some of the circular letters. A proportion of these cheques was duly honoured by the Company's bankers. From information supplied to me during the case it would appear that approximately 200 of these investors were paid 25s. 6d. for each £1 invested.

By a further circular letter which appears to have been despatched by the Company between the 10th and 23rd May, 1959, the Company informed the members of syndicates number 91000 to 91009 (inclusive), that is, those included in sale number 100, that the auction due to be held on the 23rd May, 1959, had been cancelled by the Company due to the burglary and that the Company had decided to pay to each of the members included in these syndicates a sum of 25/6d. for every £1 invested by them respectively. These payments were never in fact made, and the official liquidator believes that no cheque in respect thereof was ever issued by the Company.

From the official liquidator's researches it would appear that the stamps that were allegedly stolen were some that were included in auctions 98, 99 and 100, being those combined in syndicates 9990 to 9999, inclusive, and 91000 to 91009, inclusive, and one lot, 934, included in auction 101, being one of the lots allotted to syndicate 91013. A catalogue was prepared, showing the missing stamps, which was circulated throughout the world with a view to recovering them. It is therefore known what stamps belonging to the above-mentioned syndicates are missing.

Efforts were made to trace the missing stamps which I need not go into in detail. Proceedings were instituted and some success was achieved, compromises being effected in certain cases and cash and stamps recovered, but some of the stamps recovered by way of compromise were apparently not those that had been in the possession of the Company. It was also part of the arrangement made on the compromise that an authority would be given by an interested party, directed to the Italian and French police, authorising them to hand over to the official liquidator certain stamps which had been seized by them. The stamps in the possession of the French police have not yet been forwarded to him and he does not know whether any of these had formerly been in the possession of the Company. In many cases it is extremely difficult, if not impossible, to say whether stamps recovered in this way had previously been included in one of the Company's auctions as the identity of the stamps may have been altered by dividing what were formerly blocks of stamps.

A list was also prepared of the stamps included in auctions 98, 99 and 100, of which the official liquidator did get possession. While it may not be entirely accurate, it is thus possible to show what stamps allotted to syndicates 9990 and 9999 (inclusive) and 91000 and 91009 (inclusive) are available in the hands of the official liquidator.

Prior to the resolution for winding up, the Company had arranged and advertised an auction (number 101) to be held on the 30th May, 1959, and all of the lots (other than the "Everyman's One-Liners") included in this auction had been allocated to the members of syndicates 91010 to 91019. The money invested by investors in these syndicates would amount to approximately £24,000. As all of the lots included in this auction, with the exception of lot 934, were in the possession of the Company, the liquidator decided to proceed with this auction, but as a petition had been presented to the Court, at his instigation, on the 28th May, 1959, for the compulsory winding up of the Company he provided that all bids made at the auction should be subject to the approval of the Court. The auction was duly conducted by Mr. John Mould, an employee of the company, under the official liquidator's direction, but only approximately 150 bids were received in respect of 934 lots offered for sale in the main part of the catalogue. Bids were received in respect of almost all of the "Everyman's One-Liners" included in the auction. As only a very small proportion of the bids made for the stamps other than the "Everyman's One-Liners" even approximated to the value placed on the lots by the Company's catalogue no application was ever made to the Court for liberty to accept any of these bids.

A further auction was advertised to be held by the Company on the 6th June, 1959 (auction number 102), and all of the stamps included therein are now in the liquidator's possession. The lots which were due to be sold at this auction were allocated to syndicates 91020-91029. The amount of investors' money invested in the syndicates represented in this auction would amount to approximately £85,000. This auction was cancelled by the official liquidator.

The stamps now in the official liquidator's possession fall into the following categories:–

(a) Such of the stamps advertised to be included in auctions 98, 99 and 100 as were still in the Company's possession at the date of the official liquidator's appointment and which are set out in exhibit "M" in his affidavit of the 28th June, 1962. All were stolen save about 300 lots; some were recovered. The valuation of the stamps relating to these sales now in the liquidator's hands would not exceed about £7,500.

(b) All of the lots (with the exception of lot 934) which were advertised to be included in auction 101 and which lots were allocated to syndicates 91010 to 91019. The stamps in lot 934 were valued in the Shanahan catalogue at £750 and were allotted to syndicate 91013.

(c) All of the lots which were advertised to be included in auction 102, all of which had been allocated to syndicates 91020 and 91029.

(d) A large quantity of stamps which had not been described in any catalogue or allocated to any syndicate at the date of the official liquidator's appointment.

(e) The stamps recovered as a result of the aforesaid proceedings and negotiations and of which part may have been allocated to syndicates formed in connection with auctions 98, 99 and 100.

(f) Stamps entrusted by the owners for sale.

The official liquidator has caused extracts to be made in respect of auctions 98-99, 100, 101, and 102, showing the number of syndicates, the denoting number of each syndicate, the number of investors in each syndicate, the total of the syndicates as shown on the vendor's advice notes and the total investments as listed. I am informed that it is possible from the records to trace the names of the persons comprising the syndicates included in these auctions and their respective shares in the syndicates and the stamps allocated in lots to each syndicate. All the investors in earlier auctions had been repaid the amounts of their respective investments before the Company went into liquidation save those of them who, having invested under a "Compound" plan, had not been included in the requisite number of auctions before the liquidation.

The liquidator is informed by Messrs. Robson Lowe, who were employed to value the stamps, that approximately one-third in value of the stamps in his possession had been allocated to syndicates and that the remaining two-thirds in value have not been so allocated. The vast majority of the stamps in his possession appear to have been purchased by Dr. Singer on behalf of the Company as hereinafter mentioned. He has, however, a very small quantity of stamps which were entrusted to the Company by the owners thereof for sale but which were never sold or returned.

So far as the official liquidator can ascertain the vast majority of the stamps now in his possession were purchased by Dr. Singer on behalf of the Company with monies provided by the Company. The Company maintained a bank account with the National Bank Limited, originally at the Dun Laoghaire Branch thereof, later at the Westland Row Branch, and finally at the College Green Branch of that Bank. While it is impossible to say this definitely, it is believed that all the monies paid to the Company by the investors were lodged to this account. The Company kept no other bank account. Very substantial sums were transferred from this account to banks abroad (hereinafter called "the foreign accounts") all of which were in the name of Dr. Singer or Dr. Singer and Irma Singer. From the information supplied to him by the National Bank Limited it appears that sums totalling £1,522,994 3s. 6d. were transferred to the foreign accounts between the 1st July, 1957, and the 28th April, 1959. After his appointment sums totalling £82,954 0s. 0d. were transferred from some of the foreign accounts to the liquidator's account. The balance of the money originally transferred to the foreign accounts and amounting to £1,440,040 3s. 6d. was presumably utilised, the official liquidator says, in whole or in part in the purchase of stamps by Dr. Singer. The Company has no record of what stamps were purchased through foreign accounts and the official liquidator had been unable to obtain any information as to what monies were paid for any particular stamps or to whom the same were paid, nor is the date of acquisition of any particular stamps known save as to part of the Burrus collection. In an interview which he had with Dr. Singer in Mountjoy Gaol on the 3rd July, 1959, he was informed that it was not the practice of stamp dealers to keep any written record of their transactions and that all of these transactions were conducted on a cash basis. On the purchase of the Burrus collection, however, a written record was kept and there are records which indicate that a sum of one million American dollars was paid in respect of the first instalment of the stamps purchased out of this collection.

In addition to the purchase made through foreign accounts it appears that sums totalling £397,763 0s. 0d. were paid by the Company out of its said account with the National Bank Limited to Dr. Singer between the 17th January, 1958, and the 22nd April, 1959, in respect of stamps which were supplied by him to the Company. The only record of these transactions consists of invoice slips showing the date thereof, the amount payable to Dr. Singer, and that the monies are due in respect of stamps. The total amount of these invoice slips amounts to £397,763 0s. 0d. approximately.

The first part of the Burrus collection was paid for by the Company and delivered to it in the month of April, 1959. Part of the collection was included in the auction which was due to be held on the 6th June of that year. As the Company usually included in its auctions the stamps allocated to syndicates which were due for repayment within the week after the auction, the official liquidator presumes that the Burrus collection was allocated to syndicates which were due for repayment on or before the 13th June, 1959. It follows that the investors included in these syndicates must have subscribed their investments before the 13th March, 1959. Apart from this transaction he says it is not possible to say whether or not stamps allotted to a syndicate were purchased before or after the date on which the investors included in that syndicate made their investments.

It does not appear from the records of the Company that the monies contributed by the investors were kept separate from the other monies of the Company. In fact, so far as the official liquidator has been able to ascertain, the Company's bank account, into which the investors' monies were paid, was used as a common fund for the purchase of stamps and the payment of the Company's ordinary expenses, including wages, printing and rent. Presumably also any other monies of the Company, such as those earned by way of commission, were lodged to the credit of this account. Out of that account also came the money repaid to the investors.

It appears that the dividends or alleged profits which were paid to the syndicate members were not calculated on the basis of an appropriate fraction of the proceeds of sale of the lots allocated to that particular syndicate. Mr. Noel Gough, A.C.A., says in his affidavit that in some cases which he selected at random he found that investors received dividends of approximately 25 per cent on their investments although the stamps allotted to the syndicates of which they were members had not realised a sufficient sum to repay even the capital invested by them. Furthermore, so far as the official liquidator can ascertain, from the Company's books and other information he has gleaned, dividends of approximately 25 per cent (subject to deduction of 10 per cent commission by the Company) were paid in very many cases to members of the respective syndicates notwithstanding that many of the lots allocated to the respective syndicates were not sold, or were not the subject of a genuine sale, at the auction. The auction books of the Company disclose a vast number of bids which are "ringed" in pencil or in ink. According to the affidavit of Mrs. Noreen J. Cogan, a member of the clerical staff of the Company the "ringing" of a bid meant that the lot to which it related had not been sold at the auction. It appears from her affidavit that the dividend payable to any particular syndicate was determined after considering the amount invested in the particular syndicate, the total of the lots sold and of the unsold lots allocated to each syndicate. It appears from what she says that figures were included in the books in respect of unsold lots which were distinguished by placing a ring around the bid which was entered in respect thereof. She goes on to say that if the totals of the unsold lots would have provided a higher dividend than the already determined on, then the value of the unsold lots was reduced. All this, of course, means that an entirely fictitious method was adopted in arriving at the dividend to be paid and the amount due to investors. Unsold lots should not have been included in any proper calculation of the profits (if any) made, which would provide the dividend. Furthermore, so far as the official liquidator could ascertain, a lot which was unsold at one auction was later re-allocated to another syndicate participating in a subsequent auction; and if sold then the proceeds were applied in payment of a dividend to such last-mentioned syndicate and no part of the proceeds of sale was paid to the members of the syndicate to which that lot had originally been allocated. If any lot were not sold at such subsequent auction the same procedure was adopted in carrying it forward to a further subsequent auction or auctions. It appears also that in some instances lots were by clerical error allotted to more than one syndicate.

Coming now to the particular facts relating to the first-named defendant, there was put in evidence before me the relevant investment book, the coupon covering her investment of £500, the vendor's pre-sale advice note relating thereto and the covering letter sent therewith, dated the 20th May, 1959. These documents show that on the 2nd February, 1959, she invested £500. It appears that it was stated that her investment of £500 was in part utilised in purchasing stamps to the total value of £12,419. It also appears that she was included in syndicate 91020, that is, one of the syndicates comprised in auction 102 advertised to be held on the 6th June, 1959. The stamps allotted to that syndicate are known from the catalogue prepared for the sale and the actual stamps included in the lots are in the hands of the official liquidator. She is therefore representative of that class of investors who were formed into syndicates to which stamps were allotted and she has been appointed to represent that class.

As regards the second-named defendant, the ledger card with reference to her investments and the amounts repaid thereon has been put in evidence and I am informed that the last investment of £1,000 made by her on the 26th March, 1959, still stands to the credit of her account and that no stamps were allocated to her in respect thereof. She is therefore representative of the class of investors who were formed into syndicates to which stamps were allotted and has been appointed to represent them.

In the state of facts existing and broadly outlined above it is clear that the three classes of persons, namely, syndicated investors, unsyndicated investors and ordinary creditors, have conflicting claims and accordingly the Court has been asked to determine the following questions:–

1, Whether such of the said stamps as were allotted to syndicates as aforesaid are held by the plaintiffs in trust for the members of the said respective syndicates and, if so, how are the plaintiffs to dispose of them?

2, (*a*) Whether such of the said stamps as were allotted to syndicates as aforesaid are held by the plaintiffs upon trust to sell the same and divide the proceeds thereof amongst the members of the respective syndicates to which such stamps were allotted?

(*b*) If the answer to (*a*) be in the affirmative, whether the plaintiffs are entitled to deduct from such proceeds (*i*) the expenses of and incidental to the sale, including the remuneration of the official liquidator of the plaintiffs for his services in connection therewith; (*ii*) the commission payable to the plaintiffs in accordance with the schemes aforesaid, and, if so, at what rate?

(*c*) If the answer to (*a*) be in the affirmative, whether the bids made at the auction held by the plaintiffs on the 30th May, 1959, for certain of the said stamps ought to be accepted and the sale thereof confirmed by the Court?

3, Whether the investors who were formed into syndicates to which stamps were allotted as aforesaid are in the circumstances entitled to claim as creditors of the plaintiffs?

4, Whether such of the said stamps as were not allotted to syndicates as aforesaid are held by the plaintiffs in trust for or subject to a trust in favour of (*a*) all investors who were not formed into syndicates to which stamps were allotted as aforesaid and who have not been repaid the monies paid by them respectively to the plaintiffs; (*b*) all the investors whether formed into syndicates to which stamps were allotted or not and who have not been repaid the monies paid by them as aforesaid? And if so, how are the plaintiffs to dispose of them?

5, (*a*) Whether such of the stamps as were not allotted to syndicates as aforesaid are held by the plaintiffs upon trust to sell the same and divide the proceeds amongst the investors mentioned in question 4 and, if so, which investors?

(*b*) If the answer to (*a*) be in the affirmative, whether the plaintiffs are entitled to deduct from such proceeds (*i*) the expenses of and incidental to the sale, including the remuneration of the official liquidator of the plaintiffs for his services in connection therewith; (*ii*) the commission payable to the plaintiffs in accordance with the schemes aforesaid, and, if so, at what rate?

6, Whether the investors who were not formed into syndicates as aforesaid are in the circumstances entitled to claim as creditors of the plaintiffs?

7, Alternatively, whether all the stamps in the possession of the plaintiffs, whether allotted to syndicates or not, are held by the plaintiffs in trust for, or subject to a charge in favour of, all the investors, whether grouped into syndicates or not, and if so, how are the plaintiffs to dispose of them?

The official liquidator, of course, represents the Company now and it is his duty to get in the assets. It follows that it is part of his function to oppose the claim of the defendants because a decision in their favour would mean in effect that the stamps are held in trust for, or on trust for sale for, or subject to a charge in favour of the classes they represent, with certain qualifications, and in the result that the value of such stamps would not be available to meet the claims of ordinary creditors. The official liquidator thus makes the case for all those ultimately found to be ordinary creditors of the Company and contests the claims of the defendants in the interests of, and in effect on behalf of, the creditors. It is right to say that many subsidiary questions arise for determination and many of these that can at present be foreseen have already been formulated. What has to be decided now are a number of major points on which it is necessary to make a determination before the other subsidiary points can be dealt with.

It is obvious from all that I have set out above that a most complicated state of affairs exists. The difficulties arising on the questions for determination will appear from the contentions made on behalf of the parties represented.

The official liquidator through his counsel in opening the case pointed out that the major initial difficulty facing any Court endeavouring to arrive at a conclusion as to the rights of the various parties interested in the present part of the proceedings, in his submission, was that while the Company had what was described as an ostensible way of carrying on its business to all outward appearances in the fashion I have set out above, it had in actual fact carried on its affairs in a different fashion. He contended that for various reasons of a legal and practical nature the Court in determining the rights of the parties would be forced to have regard – and, indeed, properly should have regard – to the way the Company did in fact conduct its affairs. It was his contention that if that was the correct approach the Court should find that persons in the categories represented by the defendants are mere creditors for certain reasons which will be developed later. The defendants, on the other hand, said that if there was a difference between ostensible and actual method of business of the Company that did not alter their legal position – that the contract between the investors and the Company still ruled their legal or equitable rights. They said that that contract, though not worded with the clarity which a lawyer would wish, is nevertheless reasonably clear and was carried out either in fact or in a fashion closely enough in practice to ensure that certain results in law ensue; in so far as the syndicated investors are concerned that certain identifiable stamps have become the property of that class and that they own the stamps allocated to them *in specie* or at least entitled to have them sold for their benefit. Further, that as regards the unsyndicated investors their monies are sufficiently traceable into the unallotted stamps, so as to make them their property or at least to entitle them to a tracing or charging order giving them a charge on these stamps for so much of their investments as are respresented in them and the right to have them sold for their benefit.

Counsel for the official liquidator proceeded to develop his argument by reference to various matters that he claimed supported his contentions. He pointed out that, contrary to the scheme as outlined and supposedly carried out in practice, stamps allotted to a syndicate were frequently sold at a loss but none the less the investors received a substantial dividend; in short, a false result was arrived at and a false return of the result was consequently made. In other cases payments were made though many of the allotted stamps were not sold at all and again no profit made. Stamps unsold would be put into another auction and allotted to another syndicate.

That the whole operation was bogus is illustrated, the official liquidator says, by what occurred after the burglary. Although the stamps allotted for sale in the auctions of the 9th May and 23rd May, 1959, were in the main stolen in the alleged burglary on the 8th May 1959, and the auctions cancelled, some of the persons formed into syndicates for the auction of the 9th May were sent 25s. 6d. in respect of every £1 invested, although no sale had taken place, and those formed into syndicates for the auction to take place on the 23rd May, were promised a payment of 25s. 6d. for every £1 invested although they did not get paid because the Company went into liquidation.

It was stressed that even though stamps were allocated to investors it did not follow that the stamps thus allocated were bought with the money of the members of any particular syndicate. They might be stamps bought previous to their investment and not sold in previous auctions or they might be stamps bought with later investors' money, which was quite possible owing to the time lag; or again the stamps allotted to a syndicate might have been purchased with the Company's money earned by way of commission on previous sales. It has been stressed that the Company only operated one bank account into which all receipts appear to have been paid and out of which all payments were made. Between the 1st July, 1957, and the 28th April, 1959, there was paid out of the Company's bank account to foreign bank accounts in the name of Paul Singer, or in the names of Paul and Irma Singer, some £1,522,994 3s. 6d. for the ostensible purpose of buying stamps. There is thus, counsel for the official liquidator say, no way of ascertaining what money or whose money was used in the large purchases of stamps that were made, so that it could never be said that any particular investor's money was used to buy any particular lots of stamps allocated to any particular syndicate.

The official liquidator contends that those claiming stamps *in specie* as having been allotted to syndicates of which they were members and identifiable by lot numbers are in no case able to prove that the particular stamps allocated to their particular syndicate were purchased with their money. He says that before they can make good title to the stamps as their property the onus is on them to prove that they paid for them. They are in the same position as any other beneficiary in a trust seeking to recover trust property; they must be able to trace and identify it, he says. Indeed, he goes further; he says that even on the ostensible or stated or allegedly contractual method of procedure it cannot be said on the true construction of the contract that the parties ever intended that individual stamps would be owned by any individual investor or group of investors. It is significant in this regard, it is said, that in the brochure it was stated merely that the stamps will be "treated" as the property of investors on allocation. That, he says, is an ambiguous expression and that the real intention as understood by all was that the "treating" of the allocated stamps of an investor as their property was to provide a measure or yardstick by which the amount of dividends could be determined. The conclusion that he suggests should be drawn from all this is that the stamps were in fact the property of the Company at all times. This would, of course, reduce the status of all syndicated investors to whom stamps had been allotted to that of ordinary creditors who could only claim a dividend in the liquidation as opposed to the position of owning the stamps *in specie*.

As regards unsyndicated investors the argument is that they are faced with the difficulty that all that they can hope to show is that stamps were purchased out of the general funds of the Company which included all the monies paid into the bank account, including purchasers' and Company's monies, and thus they too cannot show that even unsyndicated stamps were purchased with their monies. No one knows what proportions of stamps even were purchased with the monies coming from any original fund paid into the Company's general account. Monies paid in by investors might have gone in many different ways, such as the paying of ordinary expenses, repaying capital to earlier investors, or imaginary profits, buying stamps sold at previous auctions or buying stamps still there, or they may have been put in someone's pocket.

Many other reasons were advanced in support of the general contention that no one could show a good title to any stamps. For example, in the case of syndicated investors, if, in truth, they owned the stamps on allocation then any one investor could stop the sale and make the whole scheme unworkable. Also, the position with regard to the investors in the "twelve months plan," as already referred to; by its operation the investor could not, it was submitted, take either his money or stamps for twelve months, which, it was suggested, was inconsistent with any allegation of true ownership of the stamps.

Mr. Matheson claimed that the stamps allocated to the syndicated investors were their property and that they are now the owners thereof *in specie*.

He relied on the brochure and said that with all its apparent inaccuracies and contradictions the real transaction was clear enough. Since £10 would not buy a large collection he said it was obvious that an investor's money would be used with others'. He said that there was no representation that any particular or specified stamps would be purchased with a particular investor's money. In other words, any investor would know that aggregation would take place.

He submitted, as the next point, that the intimation in the brochure that the stamps would be "treated as your property" should be construed as meaning that the stamps allotted to a particular syndicate became the property of that syndicate as tenants in common. Thus he relied on the time of allocation as the moment when, he contended, the property passed. Investors could discover the lot they were interested in by reference to the numbers in the catalogue.

So far as the syndicated investors were concerned, he said that the steps taken were in accordance with what the Company said it would do in the brochure, namely, purchase stamps, form syndicates from investors, allot stamps to them and then re-sell and repay the invested capital with profit.

Although the contract provided admittedly for commission to be earned by the Company, he claimed that that part of the contract guaranteeing the return of capital could not now be carried out and therefore that his right was to the stamps *in specie*. But if that was not a correct view, then the proper course was for the Company to sell and earn commission, but it would have to make good any loss.

As to the point that there is no proof that any particular syndicated stamps were purchased with any particular syndicated investors' money, Mr. Matheson said that the pre-sale advice note and accompanying letter says:- "We have used your money to buy stamps" to a stated value which are identifiable by lot numbers, and there is nothing to show that what was said was not true.

He made the submission as a matter of legal principle that the Company was a fiduciary agent and that a fiduciary agent, any more than any other trustee, cannot be heard to say, where an act of purchase could have been rightly performed in accordance with a contract, that it was wrongly performed or that the beneficiaries' money had been applied wrongly. Another party might make the case that his money was used to purchase the syndicated stamps but the official liquidator, representing the Company, cannot do so. He accepted that it might be a correct statement of his legal position to say that a fractional share in stamps bought passed beneficially on purchase, but that was only to be understood as being put as an alternative possibility.

Applying that principle to this case, he says that the Company, represented now by the official liquidator, cannot be heard to say that it employed syndicated investors' money other than in purchase of the syndicated stamps identifiable by the lot numbers in pursuance of the contract.

While inclined to suggest that the contract or trust could not now be implemented by way of sale under order of the Court because the plaintiffs could not now fulfil the guarantee as to the return of the capital invested, Mr. Matheson frankly stated that he had no immediate solution to the very obvious practical problem as to how the stamps allocated to the various syndicates could be physically handed over to the members of the various syndicates having regard, in most cases, to the numbers of people comprising each syndicate and the extreme practical difficulty of obtaining any agreed direction from them.

An important point to bear in mind is that this line of argument would very possibly involve the investors who were in a similar position to the first-named defendant, but whose stamps had been stolen, in a complete loss; since they have not been heard, any findings with regard to syndicated stamps would not bind them.

Mr. Finlay, for the large class of unsyndicated investors who had not been repaid, put forward several propositions. Some of these were really directed to their position as regards the fund in the bank account at the time of liquidation, but I am not at the moment concerned with it, except indirectly. He claimed that the contract was contained in the brochure and coupon attached, that one of the terms thereof was a general promise that the money invested would be used for the purchase of stamps for the investor and that thus the Company received the money as a fiduciary agent. The Company he also submitted was as a fiduciary agent precluded from setting up a case inconsistent with the obligations of a fiduciary relationship. He submitted that the evidence had established that the Company had created a mixed fund represented by the Irish and foreign banking accounts arising from monies entrusted to them by the investors and the Company's own money. In such circumstances the Company must be presumed to have drawn on its own money first. Since the total now remaining of the mixed funds is less than the total of investors' money received, the entire is the property of the investors. That submission, I think, really related to the monies in the bank accounts with which I am not dealing at present, but it can with equal logic be applied to the property into which the monies in the mixed fund was converted, namely, the stamps. He proceeded, however, to deal with the position as regards the stamps. He said that where it is established that the only purpose for which the Company could properly draw on the investors' money was for the purchase of stamps, that portion of the investors' money had been drawn from the mixed fund and that the Company had purchased stamps still in its possession, it follows in law, as a consequence of the fiduciary relationship, that the Company is prohibited from asserting that the stamps were purchased with its own money. The Court must thus hold that since the stamps were purchased out of the mixed fund, the investors are entitled, in priority to any right of the Company, to a charge upon the stamps to the extent of the deficit in the trust monies. In the result he maintained that they were entitled to have the stamps sold by the Court and the nett proceeds up to the amount of the deficit paid to them. While agreeing that the rule in *Clayton's Case* 1 Mer. 572, that the first sum lodged should be deemed the first sum withdrawn, would ordinarily apply between *cestuis que trustent*, he said it is not possible to establish in this case the sequence of lodgments of investors' money; therefore the rule in *Clayton's Case* 1 Mer. 572 has no application. It had, he said, no application to the stamps still in the liquidator's hands and the investors are entitled to the charge on the stamps and the proceeds of sale thereof rateably. He was not entirely correct in his contention that the order of the lodgment of investors' monies could not be established, but his contention with regard to the rule not applying to the stamps would not necessarily be effected by that. If the Court should hold that the syndicated investors were entitled to the syndicated stamps he says it must follow that their monies were not represented in the unsyndicated stamps. Finally, he submitted that if it is held that the syndicated investors are not entitled to the syndicated stamps, all investors are in the same position.

Mr. O'Neill's reply to these contentions was that on the true construction of the contract it was never intended that the investor should ever become the owner of any stamps. He submitted that on reading the brochure and coupon as a whole it was clear that the intention of the parties was that the subscribing investors' money was to be used in the purchase of lots of stamps and not any particular stamps. Those purchased were only, he says, to be "treated" as their property, and this was not an apt word to use if the stamps were to become the property of the investor. The same deduction should be drawn from that portion of the document referring to the stamps "you are interested in." The wording of the coupon, taken as a whole, he also maintained, was only consistent with the intention that the stamps should be bought and sold for the investor. He showed that many inconsistencies existed in the wording of the documents. He submitted that the relevant documents showed no intention of creating a fiduciary relationship between the investors and the Company. The real intention as manifested, he submitted, was that the parties were to enter into a commercial transaction partaking of the nature of a partnership to speculate in stamps and that it was intended to create the relationship of debtor and creditor. Put in another way, in effect the investor was lending his money to be used by the Company to speculate in stamps on the terms that the capital was to be returned with a dividend measured by reference tot he prices realised for the lots allotted to the various syndicates. He reiterated that the device of having syndicates and lots allotted to them was merely to provide a yardstick to measure the dividends. He urged that a guarantee of the return of the capital was consistent with a creditor and debtor relationship and not with a fiduciary relationship.

If held incorrect on the above contention Mr. O'Neill submitted that no property in stamps passed until they were appropriated to a syndicate and that as far as unsyndicated investors were concerned they could not claim unsyndicated stamps because the time when ownership would pass, i.e., the date of appropriation, had not arrived.

He also submitted that so much of Mr. Finlay's argument as was based on the right to trace could only properly be based on the ownership of property rather than on a fiduciary relationship. The unsyndicated investors, he said, had never reached the stage of having a proprietary interest.

It was further submitted that the principle of tracing was an equitable principle and being equitable would not, and should not, be applied where an inequitable result would follow. He submitted that applying the principle of tracing to this case would work injustice to the ordinary creditors and that it would be inequitable to allow persons who had given their money to the Company to speculate in stamps to take virtually all the assets to the detriment of the ordinary creditors. The principle is only applied to prevent a person holding another's property from acting in an unconscionable manner and there is nothing unconscionable which the liquidator should be prevented from doing, when he seeks to see that the ordinary creditors, who have supplied what was necessary to enable the Company to function, should be paid in full.

I must first decide what was the nature of the contract between the investors and the Company. That being found, the true nature of their legal relationship must be determined and then the results of that particular relationship must be considered in order to determine the rights of the investors.

While the Company advertised its schemes in a broad fashion in the press and elsewhere, it would seem to me that what may be termed its offer to the public was contained in the brochure and coupon attached. That this was its intention is shown, I think, by the fact that the document intended to be sent to the Company with the investor's money is attached to the brochure with the instruction, "If you are interested, fill in the coupon below and enclose your remittance." What the investor was asked "if he was interested" in was the offer contained in the brochure. It is stated that so far as is known all investors sent in the coupon with their subscription, so that the act of sending in the coupon should properly be regarded as an acceptance of the offer. Even if it were the fact that some investors did not send in the coupon it must, I think, properly be assumed that they contracted on the basis of the offer in the brochure since no other basis of the contract is to be found. The brochure and coupon construed together, therefore, in my view constitute the contract between the parties. What happened afterwards, while not to be disregarded, was in fact the Company's method of carrying out the contract.

I take the brochure covering the "Four Months Simple Plan" and the coupon attached first. The two documents are not easy to construe and contain inconsistencies and contradictions to which attention was drawn by counsel; nevertheless, it was the agreement between the parties in a business matter and I have to determine, as best I can, what it meant in essence. The public were invited to invest in what was described as the large capital gains of philately. The procedure, as stated, was that the transaction was to take four months. With the money which the investors sent in the Company was to buy large collections of stamps and bring them to Dun Laoghaire. They were then to be sold in various lots by auction. Investments as small as £10 were invited and it could not have been reasonably supposed by any investor that large collections could be purchased with one investor's money; therefore it seems proper to draw the deduction that it was implicit in what was said and in the contemplation of the parties that the monies of a large number of investors would be used together in the various purchases. The coupon does say that the amount sent is to be used "to purchase stamps for me," but on reading the documents as a whole that must be construed, in my view, in the above sense.

The stamps so bought are then to be invoiced to the respective investors who are to be grouped into syndicates and the stamps "treated" as their property. The investor is to be advised of the lot numbers in the Company's catalogue that he is "interested in." From a practical point of view, having regard to what I said above, this can, I think, only be reasonably construed as meaning that the collections will be broken up and allotted to syndicates as the Company sees fit. The coupon in the third sentence thereof is consistent with this. The statement that stamps "so bought" are invoiced to the "respective" investors must be read with the rest of the sentence and what has gone before and the whole sentence can then, I think, only mean that each investor is informed of the lots allotted to his syndicate. Since the monies of numbers of investors are to be used in buying large collections to be divided into lots it cannot reasonably be suggested that any specific stamps were to be invoiced to any specific investor. All concerned knew that investments as small as £10 were to be accepted. No investor could therefore, it would seem to me, have thought that any of the specific stamps which were to be purchased by way of buying large collections with a number of investors' monies were to be allocated to him.

It is noted that the words used to indicate the rights of investors with regard to the stamps is that they are "treated" as their property and they are to be advised of those they "are interested in." It is not said that the stamps then "belong to you," nor is it said that "you will be advised what stamps are yours." I am not overlooking the fact that the fourth sentence in the coupon reads, literally, as if the entire proceeds of lots allotted to a syndicate would be sent to the individual investor mentioned in the coupon, but taken in conjuction with what has gone before this does not make sense and can only reasonably be construed as meaning that the appropriate share of the investor would be remitted.

Taking the document therefore as a whole I construe it as meaning that the monies of a number of investors will be used to purchase large quantities of stamps which will be allotted to syndicates of groups of investors and then sold and that fractional shares in the proceeds of sale of the lots allotted to a syndicate will be divided amongst its members. There are, then, the super-added conditions that at least the amount of capital invested will be returned i.e., the Company will make good any difference between the fractional share of the price realised and the amount invested, and that the Company only charged its standard auction selling commission in force at the time of sale, which was in all cases 10 per cent. It further seems to me on this construction and on the words used, taken as a whole, that it was not intended that any specific stamp or stamps should at any time become the absolute property of any individual investor in the sense of his being entitled to claim any particular stamps *in specie*.

I have not overlooked the condition of sale, no. 8, in the catalogue which reads:– "Any contract is between vendor and purchaser and not between either and the auctioneers." This is, however, a condition intended to bind purchasers and, presumably, intended to protect the auctioner and I have come to the conclusion that since it only came into operation after the original agreement was made I should not properly regard it as amending the contract. Similarly I have considered the statement in the vendor's pre-sale advice note to the effect that the lots mentioned will be offered for unreserved sale unless "we hear from you to the contrary at least twenty-four hours before the sale." It is inconsistent with the condition in the catalogue that no reserves can be accepted. What its precise significance is in all the circumstances it is difficult to say, but again it is something arising rather on the Company's procedure and cannot be said in my view to amend the terms already agreed on.

I have thus far referred to the "Four Months Simple Plan." There was also in existence the "Twelve Months Compound Plan." Counsel took the view – and, I think, rightly – that the brochure relating to the Twelve Months Compound Plan must be read in conjuction with the brochure I have dealt with because the only reasonable inference was that those investing in the Twelve Months Plan could not have understood it without also reading the other brochure and must therefore be deemed to have been aware of its contents and to have accepted its terms. The Twelve Months Compound Plan in effect provides for the repetition of what is done under the Four Months Simple Plan three times, the capital and capital gains on each investment after the first being reinvested in the next four months period. What I have said therefore with regard to the nature of the agreement contained in the other brochure and the resultant contract applies equally well to the case of investors under the Twelve Months Compound Plan, save in so far as the dates of repayment is postponed. The views I have expressed apply also to the contracts entered into under the "Six Months Plan" and the "Eighteen Months Plan," since the wording is the same, save only in so far as the date of repayment was postponed.

I have therefore come to the conclusion that it was not the essence of the contract that the investor became the full beneficial owner of any specific stamps at any stage of the transaction. The position arising on the contract, as I see it, was that the investor handed his money to the Company on the basis that the Company would buy unspecified stamps for him and others and then sell them for him and other co-investors, returning a fractional part of the proceeds of sale together with profits, if any.

The investors' money should have been kept separate from the Company's money and not mixed with it and each investment should then have been traceable to a particular bulk purchase, at least in part. After that the stamps should have been allocated in lots to syndicates, the lots being allocated to those investors whose joint monies had gone to purchase them so that the investors' money could be said to be invested in the lots purchased but no particular stamps could be said to belong to any particular investor. The entire members of each specific syndicate would thus have in sense a special joint interest in the stamps allotted to each syndicate, the result of which I will discuss later, but their legal right was confined by the contract to receiving the proceeds of sale, subject to the guarantee and right of commission. This involves also, I think, the result that the Company had also a special property in the stamps since it had the right to hold them and sell them pursuant to the terms of the contract.

Having thus stated the contract and construed it to the best of my ability I have next to decide what species of legal relationship it created between the parties.

On the broad question as to whether a fiduciary relationship can be said to have existed in this case between the investors and the Company the first of the relevant cases cited was that of *Taylor* v. *Plumer* 3 M. & S. 562. In that case a draft for money was entrusted to a broker to buy exchequer bills for his principal. The broker misapplied it by buying American stock and bullion, intending to abscond with it. He was taken before he had quitted England and surrendered the American stock and bullion to his principal who sold the whole and received the proceeds. The broker became bankrupt on the date he received and misapplied the money. It was held that the principal was entitled to withhold the proceeds from the assignees of the broker. Lord Ellenborough accepted the proposition that where the property of a principal is entrusted by him to his factor for any special purpose it belongs to the principal notwithstanding any change in form so long as the property is capable of being identified. It is equally recoverable from the assignees of the factor. Upon a view of the authorities, he said, it should seem that if the property in its original state and form was covered with a trust in favour of the principal, no change of state and form can divest it of such trust. It is true that Lord Ellenborough goes on to say that the right ceases when the subject is turned into money and compounded in a general mass of the same description. The difficulty, he said, is rather one of fact than of law. Counsel for the investors submitted that later developments in the principles of equity enabled the Court to trace even into a mixed fund. In any event, it can be said that the principle applies *a fortiori* where the property has not been tortiously transformed but has been used for the purpose for which it has been entrusted. Applying the case in practical fashion to the present case, it was submitted that the investor's money was received by the Company to purchase stamps for the investor.That, it is claimed, created a trust and a fiduciary relationship. The case however seems limited to the instance where the property can be earmarked.

Taylor v. *Plumer* 3 M. & S. 562 was followed a long time after in *Ex parte Cooke. In re Strachan* 4 Ch. D. 123. Whereas in *Taylor* v. *Plumer* 3 M. & S. 562 the principal was seeking to retain what he held and could earmark, the principal in *Ex parte Cooke. In re Strachan* 4 Ch. D. 123 sought to recover what was in the agent's hands. A trustee employed a broker, who had notice of the trust, to sell out consols and invest in railway stock. The broker sold the consols for cash which he paid into his account at his bankers. He bought railway stock for the same amount for the settling day but stopped payment and went into liquidation. It was held that as the price of the consols was known by the broker to be trust money it could be followed. But James L.J. held that apart from any question of trust he would decide in favour of the trustee because he could not distinguish the case from *Taylor* v. *Plumer* 3 M. & S. 562. Bramwell J.A. stated the view that on the point whether the money could have been followed if it was not trust money, the case appeared indistinguishable from *Taylor* v. *Plumer* 3 M. & S. 562. With regard to that decision, he says that it involved the conclusion that if the broker had been caught with the client's money upon him the client could have claimed it, not because the money was paid to the broker as a trustee in the strict sense but because it was handed to him in a fiduciary character, so as not to create the relationship of debtor and creditor between him and his principal. Thus far it appears that trust monies or monies or property into which it has been converted in the hands of a fiduciary agent can be followed if the money or property can be traced and earmarked. Furthermore, in the case of monies being entrusted to a fiduciary agent, the relationship created is not that of a mere creditor and debtor.

I may also at this stage refer to *Harris* v. *Truman* 9 Q. B. D. 264 which has some similarity to the present case. The defendants were brewers. They employed one, Fairman, as their malting agent. He occupied the malting premises. It was his duty to buy barley in his own name for cash and to malt it. The defendants provided the capital for the purchases, Fairman being entitled to draw on the brewers' bank accounts, but the sums to the credit of these accounts were not intended to represent payments for any specific barley. Fairman's business was to act for the defendants exclusively. Fariman fraudulently misapplied the sums in the brewers' accounts for his own purposes and provided malt by purchasing barley or malt on credit. Fairman subsequently absconded and committed an act of bankruptcy, leaving barley and malt on his premises, the value of which was less than the amount drawn from the banks. The defendants seized the barley and malt on his premises and the trustee in Fairman's bankruptcy sued the defendants for its value. It was held, on several grounds, that the plaintiff could not recover, the relevant grounds as far as this case is concerned being that the money advanced was imbued with a trust and that even if the legal property in the barley and malt was not vested in the defendants but in Fairman, nevertheless he was a trustee for the defendants to the extent of the sum advanced and that Fairman could not have set up his own breach of trust or have been heard to allege that the barley was bought otherwise than according to the authority given him by the defendants and that the trustee in bankruptcy could not in this respect stand in a better position than Fairman himself. Lord Coleridge, in the Court of Appeal, said, at p. 268:– "The judgment of the Court below is founded mainly on two grounds. The first ground is of this nature: when large amounts of money are intrusted to a man to buy goods and to carry on a business he becomes a trustee for the person to whom the money belongs, and the proceeds of the money are affected with a trust. This is an old and well established doctrine in equity: it applies where the relation of principal and agent in the ordinary sense of the words does not exist. According to this doctrine, where a confidence is created between two persons, and where the one receives the money on the faith that he will do a certain thing, and leads the other who has given the money to understand that the thing has been done, as between these two persons it is considered in equity to have been done. Therefore the person receiving the money is bound to hold what he gets for the benefit of the person giving the money. I think that this ground is quite right.

"I think that the second ground of the judgment of the Queen's Bench Division is right also. A person placed in a fiduciary relation with another may have dealings of his own, and may mix up his own dealings with the dealings on behalf of his *cestui que trust*; but it has been held in Courts of Equity that when a fiduciary relation has been created in respect of a fund which has been misapplied, and when it cannot be shewn what portion of the proceeds of the fund is really subject to the trust, the trust shall be considered to be attached to the whole of the proceeds, and it shall not lie in the mouth of the trustee to say that any portion of those proceeds is not affected with the trust. The same rule is applied where by a long course of dealing and by constant representation a person entrusted with money is fulfilling for the benefit of his employer the duties which have been cast upon him by his employment. In a case of this description the person employed is estopped from setting up the real state of matters, because his employer has dealt with him on the faith of his representation that another state of things existed."

Brett L.J., in the course of his judgment, at p. 273, rejected the proposition that a person cannot be a trustee unless there is a contract that the relation of *cestui que trust* shall exist. He said that where the facts were that everything with regard to the barley was to paid for by the defendants, and nothing by Fairman, an equity attaches on these facts. This case goes very far because Fairman had in fact used his own monies in purchasing the malt or barley. It was nevertheless held that as regards the brewers who had entrusted the money to Fairman for a certain purpose, he having led them to think that it had been used for the purpose entrusted, it was to be considered in equity that he had used the money for that purpose. On analogy it seems open to say that a like state of affairs applies in the case of the investors' monies and that the Company cannot be heard to say that the stamps purchased with the money entrusted for that purpose were not purchased with the investors' monies. Further, the claim was held good against the trustee in bankruptcy who would represent ordinary creditors.

By way of contrast, the case of *Lister & Co.* v. *Stubbs* 45 Ch. D. 1 was referred to. The plaintiffs, a manufacturing company, employed the defendant, a foreman, to buy materials for them. Under a corrupt bargain he took from one of the selling firms large sums by way of commission, which he invested. The plaintiffs sought to recover the monies, claiming to be entitled to follow them into the investments. The plaintiffs were held not entitled to succeed on the basis that the relationship was that of creditor and debtor and not that of trustee and *cestui que trust*. Stirling J., however, in the course of his judgment, said, at p.4:– "There can be no doubt that if the monies had been paid by the plaintiffs to the defendant, to be applied by him in payment of the goods ordered, then the defendant would have received those monies in a fiduciary capacity, and they would have come to his hands clothed with a trust, to be applied only for a specific purpose, and if he diverted them to any other purpose, or to his own use, the master could follow them."

Counsel for the plaintiffs, as I have said, sought to suggest that on the true construction of the contract between the investor and the Company it was never contemplated that the investor would become the owner of the stamps and that the real relationship was that of creditor and debtor. It was suggested that the real essence of the transaction was that the investor gave his money to the Company for the purpose of a joint speculation in stamps and that all that the investor was entitled to was an ultimate balance on his account with the Company. It was submitted that the case was similar in some respects in principle to that of *King* v. *Hutton* [1899] 2 Q.B. 555; [1900] 2 Q.B. 504.

A broker on the Stock Exchange was declared a defaulter. All his accounts were closed and after payment of his liabilities a surplus remained. He was later adjudicated a bankrupt with large outside liabilities. Part of the above mentioned surplus comprised a sum of money which represented differences, being profits, due on contracts with jobbers by the broker as agent for an outside customer, Hutton, who was running a speculative account on the Stock Exchange through him. Both customer and the trustee in bankruptcy claimed the money and the matter came before the Court on an issue after the money had been paid into Court on an interpleader summons.

Mr. Justice Phillimore said that this was not a case where a broker had been directed to sell a particular parcel of stock and re-invest the proceeds in some other named stock, in which case some of the language in *Ex parte Cooke. In re Strachan* 4 Ch. D. 123 and *Taylor* v. *Plumer* 3 M. & S. 562, to which I have already referred, might apply. The arrangement was not that in respect of each security the value of it when sold came to Hutton, not even that in respect of each security the difference of profit or loss between buying and selling came to or was paid by Hutton; the only thing that Hutton expected to receive was the balance, if there was one, of profit over loss on the various securities dealt with as each account came through. He was unable to hold that Wood, the broker, was a trustee for Hutton or that Hutton had a lien on the balance. There was no stock to receive and no stock to sell, there was merely a balance, which he held to be a debt due and not the specific money of the customer. The remedy was to prove in the bankruptcy. The decision was affirmed on appeal. I only wish to refer to the opening part of the judgment of Vaughan Williams L.J. [1900] 2 Q.B. 504, at p. 507 where he says:– "I assent thus far to the argument on behalf of the appellant: that if we take the case of a stockbroker receiving from his client a sum of money or securities – in the former case for the purchase of stock or shares, and in the latter for the purpose of selling the securities handed over – the broker has only a special property in the monies or securities handed to him for a specific purpose. Such a case would be like that of a factor who has had goods entrusted to him for sale and has sold them for his principal, but has not received the price. The factor would not have a general property in the money to be received by him, but only a special property, and, if he became bankrupt while the price of the goods was unpaid, that price would not go into the general account in the bankruptcy."

That case is, to my view, distinguishable from the case of an investor in this case. In the case of the "Four Months Plan" the investor gave a specific sum of money to the Company to be used for the purchase of stamps – I concede along with other people's monies. These stamps were then to be sold, admittedly, it must be said, with other stamps, and the capital in the shape of a fractional share of the proceeds with profits was to be repaid. There was not to be a series of transactions in which the profits and losses of several sales were to be set off against one another and the ultimate balance paid by one or other of the parties. One transaction was contemplated. The case of the investor is more like that of the client giving his broker money to purchase stocks, as envisaged by Vaughan Williams L.J., or like the case of an agent who is given money to buy some chattels, say cattle, and sell them for his principal to whom he is bound to return the capital and profits. While the Twelve Months Plan is different, I think that it is similar in principle, involving merely a repetition of the transactions, but always envisaging the ultimate return of capital and not a settling of the account between the parties dependent upon the profit or loss on a series of speculations.

Mr. O'Neill also relied on *Piddocke* v *Burt* [1894] 1 Ch. 343 to support the proposition that every agent was not a fiduciary agent. The case was one where a solicitor, who was a partner in a solicitors' firm, received money belonging to the partnership on account of himself and his co-partner. The question at issue was whether he thus received it in a fiduciary capacity. Since the law permits one partner to receive a debt on account of the firm to whom it is due, Chitty J. felt that he would be straining the law if he held that a partner receiving money on behalf of the partnership – that is, on behalf of himself and his co-partners – received it in a fiduciary capacity towards the other partners. The law allows one partner to receive the whole debt on account of the firm to whom it is due. Whether this be right or wrong, I quite accept that every agent is not a fiduciary agent. It was sought to apply the case, however, in this way. It was suggested that the relationship between the investor and the Company was in the nature of a partnership to speculate in stamps and therefore the receipt of an investor's money was not taken in a fiduciary capacity. I cannot, however, see that any of the characteristics of a true partnership in any business existed. The facts are that the investor, without entering into anything that could be described as an agreement of partnership, handed money to the Company to be used for a specific purpose.

On the facts it seems to me that investor's money was entrusted to the Company for a specific purpose, namely, the purchase of stamps and their re-sale, the capital proceeds and profits to be then remitted to the investor. In these circumstances, and following the decisions of *Taylor* v. *Plumer* 3 M. & S. 562, *In re Cooke. In re Strachan* 4 Ch. D. 123 and *Harris* v. *Truman* 9 Q. B. D. 264, I think that the correct view is that a fiduciary relationship was created between the investor and the Company and I reject the argument that the relationship was that of creditor and debtor only. The monies invested were thus imbued with a trust. Even at common law the monies entrusted to an agent could be followed provided they could be identified and earmarked. Here, however, we have a much more complicated state of affairs in that the investors' monies were first mixed in the Company's bank account with the Company's monies and then another step took place by which stamps were purchased out of the monies in that bank account and further questions arise as to the right of the investors to follow or trace their money into the property, viz., stamps, into which it was converted.

Several leading cases were cited to me in connection with the rights of persons in the position of the investors in this case and these I now propose to examine in order to see what are the general principles applicable in cases of this kind and what resultant rights, if any, accrue to the investors, either at law or in equity.

I come first to the well-known case of *In re Hallett's Estate* 13 Ch. D. 696 which I may describe as the mainstay of the defendants' contentions. Several persons brought claims in the administration of the estate of Hallett against monies in his bankers' hands. Hallett was a solicitor. There was a claim by the trustees of his marriage settlement. A sum was settled for the benefit of Hallett, his wife and children. The trustees had allowed the fund to come into Hallett's hands. Several changes were made in the investment of the fund by Hallett. He held a considerable number of Russian bonds and the Court took the view that he had in 1877 allotted these bonds to the nominal amounts of £1554 and £1036 as representing the trust funds under the settlement. The bonds for £1554 were delivered to the trustees after his death. The bonds for £1036 were deposited by Hallett with his bankers. He had also acted for a Mrs. Cottrill, as her solicitor. It was proved that he had bought or appropriated, and in 1877 held for her, Russian bonds of £450 and £2242, nominal amount. In 1877, without authority from the trustees or Mrs. Cottrill, he directed his bankers to sell one of the sets of the bonds representing the trust funds mentioned above and both sets of Mrs. Cottrill's bonds. The amounts received were lodged to his bank account. Before his death he drew out different sums for his own purposes, so that the balance to his credit at the time of his death (if nothing more had been paid in) would have been £1708 16s. He had, however, paid in other sums, so that at the time of his death in 1878 he had a balance of £3029 15s. 1d. Of this, £2600 had been paid into Court in the administration action. The trustees of the settlement applied for the payment of £770 10s. 5d. out of the £2600 and for a declaration that the produce of the sale of the bonds for £1554 belonged to them. Mrs. Cotterill applied for the payment of the £1708 16s., balance.

I need not dwell on the exact manner in which the Court determined the various conflicting claims but I wish to refer to certain statements as to the principles of equity applicable to such a case made in the Court of Appeal in the course of deciding the matter. Jessel M.R. found that Hallett stood in a fiduciary capacity to Mrs. Cotterill. He stated that the modern doctrine of equity with regard to property disposed of by persons standing in a fiduciary capacity was well settled. At page 708 he said:– "You can, if the sale was rightful, take the proceeds of the sale, if you can identify them. If the sale was wrongful, you can still take the proceeds of sale, in a sense adopting the sale for the purpose of taking the proceeds, if you can identify them. There is no distinction, therefore, between a rightful and a wrongful disposition of the property, so far as regards the right of the beneficial owner to follow the proceeds." He then goes on to deal with the case where the proceeds may have been invested, or have been invested along with money belonging to the person in a fiduciary capacity, in a purchase. In a case where the purchase has been made with trust money, he says, at p. 709:– ". . . the beneficial owner has a right to elect either to take the property purchased, or to hold it as a security for the amount of the trust money laid out in the purchase; or," in other words, "to have a charge on the property for the amount of the trust money." In the case, however, where the trustee has mixed the money with his own the *cestui que trust* or beneficial owner cannot elect to take the property, but, he says, "He is, however, still entitled to a charge on the property purchased, for the amount of the trust money laid out in the purchase and that charge is quite independent of the fact of the amount laid out by the trustee." He then makes it clear that what he has said applies to all persons in a fiduciary relationship. At page 710, he says:– "Therefore, the moment you establish the fiduciary relation, the modern rules of equity, as regards following trust money, apply." Later he refers to what Lord Ellenborough said in his reference to the case where money is mixed, and points out that "he was not aware of the rule of equity which gave you a charge." He points out that as regards following the money there is no difference in the position of the factor and the trustee.

He dealt then in another portion of the case on appeal with the point as to whether beneficiaries were entitled to say that the payments drawn out of the account by Hallett after November, 1877, and applied to his own use should be treated as appropriated to the repayment of his own monies or whether the executors were right in their contention that the payments out should be applied to the first item on the credit side in order of date, which would have meant that the trust funds were diminished. Approaching the point on principle, he said, at p. 727:- "Now, first upon principle, nothing can be better settled, either in our own law, or, I suppose, the law of all civilised countries, that this, that where a man does an act which may be rightly performed, he cannot say that that act was intentionally and in fact done wrongly." On that principle counsel for the investors strongly rely. Further on, he says:- "When we come to apply that principle to the case of a trustee who has blended trust monies with his own, it seems to me perfectly plain that he cannot be heard to say that he took away the trust money when he had a right to take away his own money."

Jessell M.R. then proceeds to deal with the rule in *Clayton's Case* 1 Mer. 572 to the broad effect that the first sum drawn out is attributable to the first sum paid in. That is, he says, a very convenient rule which he has nothing to say against unless, *inter alia*, there be evidence of circumstances from which a contrary intention must be presumed when the presumption gives way to other considerations. Dealing with *Pennell* v. *Deffell* 4 D. M. & G. 372, he states his disagreement with portion of the application of the principle in that case with regard to the rights of the *cestui que trust*. He says, at p. 730:- "No human being ever gave credit to a man on the theory that he would misappropriate trust money, and thereby increase his assets. No human being ever gave credit, even beyond that theory, that he should not only misappropriate trust monies so misappropriated to his own banking account with his own monies, and draw out after than a larger sum that the first sums paid in for the trust monies."

Baggallay L.J. construed the judgments in *Pennell* v. *Deffell* 4 D. M. & G. 372 as enunciating as a general principle that the rule in *Clayton's Case* 1 Mer. 572 must be applied to the banking accounts of trustees for the purpose of determining the proportions in which the *cestui que trust* and general creditors, or the several classes of *cestui que trust*, are entitled to the debt due from the bankers on closing the account. "But," he asks (at p. 738), "was it more than the enunciation of a general principle; that is to say, a principle to be applied in the absence of special circumstances, but liable to be modified in its application by reason of the necessity or propriety of applying some other general principle of equal or paramount importance?" He says that he can find no reason assigned why the rule of attributing honest motives to a trustee was treated as having no application. His view was that, in a case such as that which was the subject of the appeal, full effect should be given to the principle of attributing the honest intention where the circumstances of the case permit of such a presumption. He thus agreed with the Master of the Rolls, so far. He said, however, that in the case where the ultimate balance is not sufficient to meet the claims in respect of distinct trusts the strict application of the rule of appropriating in order of date the drawings out to the payments in probably would be correct. In other words, *Clayton's Case* 1 Mer. 572 would in such instance apply as between various *cestuis que trustent*. Fry J. in the Court below held the same view. He then went on to say that where the dealings of the trustee have never reduced the balances below the amount of the trust monies paid in, it was to his mind difficult to attribute to the trustee any other intention than that of appropriating his drawings to his own private monies, so as to leave the trust monies intact.

It would appear therefore that *Hallett's Case* 13 Ch. D. 696 establishes certain principles.

If money held by a person in a fiduciary capacity, though not a trustee, has been paid into his bank account, it can be followed by the beneficiary. Secondly, the beneficiary has a charge for it on the balance in the banker's hands. Thirdly, if the person holding the money in a fiduciary capacity mixed it with his own the rule in *Clayton's Case* 1 Mer. 572 does not apply; such person must be taken to have drawn out his own monies in preference to the trust monies but it would appear to apply between beneficiaries. Fourthly, if the person in a fiduciary capacity makes a purchase with mixed funds of his own and of the beneficiary, the beneficiary is entitled to a charge to the extent of the amount of the trust money laid out in the purchase. Finally, where a man does an act which may be rightly performed he cannot say that the act was intentionally, and in fact, done wrongly.

There is, however, another point to which I must refer which is relevant to the facts of this case. Jessel M.R. refers (13 Ch. D. 696, at p. 718) to part of the judgment of Knight Bruce L.J. in *Pennell* v. *Deffell* 4 D. M. & G. 372. Lord Justice Knight Bruce had referred to the cases both of the trust fund being kept separate and mixed; and Jessel M.R. quotes with apparent approval what was next said, which is as follows:- "But not in either case, as I conceive, would the blending together of the trust monies, however confusedly, be of any moment as between various *cestuis que trustent* on the one hand and the executors, as representing the general creditors, on the other." As I construe the quotation as approved by Jessel M.R., that amounts to saying that the claim of the beneficiaries ranks before the claim of general creditors. The comments of Baggallay L.J., at p. 745, on *Pennell* v. *Deffell* 4 D. M. & G. 372 also seem to me to support that view in so many words.

In re Hallett's Estate 13 Ch. D. 696 was applied in *Sinclair* v. *Brougham* [1914] A.C. 398. The case concerned conflicting claims in the winding up in 1911 of the Birkbeck Permanent Benefit Building Society, formed in 1851. It was empowered by its rules to borrow to an unlimited extent and developed a banking business. Questions of priority arose between the creditors, the unadvanced shareholders and the bank customers, called the depositors. The assets were insufficient to pay all the claimants in full. The creditors were paid by arrangement. The carrying on of the banking business was held *ultra vires* and it was also held that the depositors were not entitled to recover the monies paid by them on an *ultra vires* contract of loan on the footing of monies lent and received to their use. But applying the principle in *In re Hallett's Estate* 13 Ch. D. 696 it was held that the assets remaining after paying off the creditors must be taken to represent in part monies which the depositors could follow, as invalidly borrowed, and in part monies which the society could follow as having been wrongfully employed by its agents in the banking business and which ought to be distributed *pari passu* between the depositors and unadvanced shareholders according to the amounts respectively credited to them in the books of the society at the commencement of the winding up. That was, however, subject to any application by any individual depositor or shareholder with a view to tracing his money into any particular asset and to the costs of the liquidation.

It was, as I understood it, urged on behalf of the plaintiffs that the judgments in *Sinclair* v. *Brougham* [1914] A. C. 398 showed that a proprietary interest must be shown to exist in the investors in specific stamps before they could claim the stamps or have a tracing order made. Certain portions of the judgment of Viscount Haldane L.C., at pp. 420 and 421, were relied on for this contention. Haldane L.C. stated that it is impossible to confine the right at law to follow to cases where there was a fiduciary relationship. "The principle," he said – and this is what is relied on – "appears to me to cover all cases where the property in the money has not passed, and the money itself can be earmarked in the hands of the person who has wrongly obtained it." He goes on to say, in so many words, that he is dealing with the common law position and, as I read his judgment, goes on to show the limitations of the common law remedy, in that it gave no remedy where the money had been paid into the wrongdoer's account with his banker who simply owed him a debt so that no money could in the contemplation of a court of law be earmarked. But having considered these obsservations, it seems to me that they were as to the first part only directed merely to a consideration of the position at common law, and he later indicated that equity gave a further remedy. Dealing with the case of money paid into a wrongdoer's bank account he says, at p. 420:- "The Court of Chancery could and would declare, even as against the general creditors of the wrongdoer, that there was what is called a charge on the banker's debt to the person whose money had been paid into the latter's bank account in favour of the person whose money it really was." He goes on to point out with apparent approval to what Jessell M.R. said in *Hallett's Case* 13 Ch. D. 696, that this equity was not confined to cases of trusts in the strict sense but applied to every case where there was a fiduciary relationship. He thought it merely an additional right which could be enforced whenever money was held in equity to belong to the plaintiff. He further indicates, in my view, by the way he proceeded that in a case where money was held in equity to belong to a plaintff, he regarded the principle of declaring a charge on any mass of money or securities with which the plaintiff's money had been mixed to be applicable. I cannot read his judgment as in any way cutting down the equitable principle enunciated in *In re Hallet's Estate* 13 Ch. D. 696. Indeed, his judgment may be said to carry the principle of following property outside the range of fiduciary relationships. It will be noted particularly that in that part of his judgment to which I have referred he seems to have regarded the right of the person to whom the money belonged in equity to come before the right of creditors, but it is right to say that he later points out that as the creditors had been paid by consent the House had not to consider their position. At pages 422 and 423 he indicates a distinction from*Hallett's Case* 13 Ch. D. 696 in that the investment of the depositors' money was not made in breach of fiduciary duty, but he states that the depositors had the right to follow their money invalidly borrowed into the assets of the society. It is argued that the investors have a similar right where the Company's purchase of stamps was not in breach of fiduciary duty.

On another aspect of the case relevant to the present case Haldane L.C., at p. 423, expresses the view that it makes no difference that the value of the assets has shrunk so that the two sets of claimants cannot be paid in full. The depositors have no right to disaffirm the transaction to the extent of claiming that their money has been applied in breach of trust, but they can adopt the dealings with the money they have handed over, under circumstances in which it never really ceased to be theirs, and he says that the depositors can claim the part of the mass of assets which represents their money as belonging to them in equity. Depreciation and loss, he says, must be borne *pro rata*. Assuming that specific tracing is not possible, he expresses the view that the proper direction to the liquidator is that he should apportion the remaining assets between depositors and shareholders in proportion to the amounts credited to them respectively in the books of the society at the commencement of the winding up. He later makes it clear that the distribution is to be subject to the payment of all proper costs, charges and expenses and to any application that might be made by any individual depositor or shareholder with a view to tracing his own money into any particular asset.

Lord Dunedin, at p. 438, also takes the view that in the absence of direct evidence the only equitable means is to let each party bear the shrinkage proportionately to the amount originally contributed even though not in a fiduciary relationship to one another.

Lord Parker of Waddington, at p. 440, dealt with the position of lenders in an *ultra vires* transaction. Although dealing with the particular facts, he dealt, I think it may be said, with principles of general application, at the end of page 441. Treating of cases where a fiduciary relationship existed, and having dealt with common law remedies, he stated that equity treated the matter from a different standpoint. "Starting," he said, "from a personal equity, based on the consideration that it would be unconscionable for anyone who could not plead purchase for value without notice to retain an advantage derived from the misapplication of trust money, it ended, as was so often the case, in creating what were in effect rights of property, though not recognised as such by the common law." He then referred with approval to what Jessel M.R. had said with regard to following trust money and particular to the case where a purchase had been made partly with trust money and partly with money of the trustee. He takes an illustration relevant, I think, to the matter for decision in this case. "Suppose," he says, at p. 442, "the property is acquired by means of money, part of which belongs to one owner and part to another, the purchaser being in a fiduciary relationship to both. Clearly each owner has an equal equity. Each is entitled to a charge on the property for his own money, and neither can claim priority over the other. It follows that their charges must rank *pari passu* according to their respective amounts." He adds, however, I should say, that he thinks that as against the fiduciary agent they could by agreement claim to take the property itself, in which case they would become tenants in common in shares proportioned to amounts for which either could claim a charge. This latter *dictum* Mr. Matheson would, no doubt, seek to avail of.

Lord Sumner also thought that the principle of rateable division was sound on the facts of the case, i.e., where there are classes of claimants with equal claims, and he approved the application of the principles of *Hallett's Case* 13 Ch. D. 696. I quote the words which he used, at p. 459, on this aspect of the case: he said:- "My Lords, I agree, without recapitulating reasons, that the principle on which *Hallett's Case* 13 Ch. D. 696 is founded justifies an order allowing the appellants to follow the assets, not merely to the verge of actual identification, but even somewhat further in a case like the present, where after a process of exclusion only two classes or groups of persons, having equal claims, are left in and all superior claims have been eliminated. Tracing in a sense it is not, for we know that the money coming from A. went into one security and that coming from B. went into another, and that the two securities did not probably depreciate exactly in the same percentage, and we know further that no one will ever know any more. Still I think this well within the 'tracing' equity, and that among persons making up these two groups the principle of rateable division of the assets is sound."

Whether the decision in *Sinclair* v. *Brougham* [1914] A.C. 398 extends the principles laid down in *Hallett's Case* 13 Ch. D. 696 or illustrates how these principles can be applied it is not necessary to determine. It does, however, seem evident that the decision does not cut down in any way the principles of *Hallett's Case* 13 Ch. D. 696. The decision seems relevant to the facts of this case in that it shows that where money belonging to a person in equity has been first mixed with the monies of another and then used in a further fashion, so that it is traceable to assets in the other's hands, a remedy of recovery by way of charge is open in equity. Furthermore, where the money thus used belongs to a number of people and the ultimate assets into which the money has found its way have shrunk or become depleted the proper remedy is to declare a charge and order a *pro rata* distribution amongst the parties entitled. Actual identification with any particular asset is apparently not essential to the application of the principle so long as by some process it can be shown that the monies of the claimants can be shown to have found their way into the property or assets held by another. Justice is done by allowing them to claim by way of charge in accordance with the amounts contributed by each.

In addition to the portions of the judgments I have referred to, the matter of the position of general creditors was touched on. Unfortunately the question of their rights did not come in issue directly because – possibly because since their claims were small – they were paid by agreement. Lord Haldane, it will have been noted, said that a person whose money had been paid by a wrongdoer into his bank could in equity obtain a charge, even as against the creditors of the wrongdoer, but with the qualification I have noted. However, dealing with the rights of depositors, at p. 424, he pointed out that there had been no breach of fiduciary duty on the part of the society and he says that that circumstance is material in distinguishing the consequences from those followed in *Hallett's Case* 13 Ch. D. 696, on the footing that there the agent could not gain, at the expense of the principal, an advantage for himself or his general creditors by, in effect, setting up a breach of duty. The depositors could in his opinion only claim the depreciated assets which represented their money. I have some uncertainty as to whether this means merely that their claim is only to such depreciated assets as represent their money in the sense that they have no claim to come in before the shareholders or whether it means that they must take what is left after the creditors have been paid. I incline to the view that it means the former since it is not expressly said that the creditors were rightly paid first and having regard to what he had said immediately before which indicates that he is dealing with the state of affairs where both the society and depositors have rival claims.

Lord Dunedin also dealt with the creditors, at page 437. He started by saying their claims were paid because they were inconsiderable. But, although the point was not in issue, he went on to say that they were in his judgment rightly paid under the cirumstances of the actual case as they would rank, after the expenses of liquidation, first in the ranking. He gave his reasons. In a question with the shareholders they were debts of a character which the directors had power to make. In a question with the depositors they were incurred in a business, illegal, no doubt, as for the society, but one which the depositors were willing that the directors should carry on. He seems then to equate them to the position of shareholders. I shall have to return later to what he said in dealing with the position of the creditors.

Lord Parker of Waddington, also, dealt with the position of creditors at pages 443 to 445. He was dealing with the case of *In re Guardian Permanent Benefit Building Society* (*Crace-Calvert's Case*) 23 Ch. D. 440. The Court of Appeal had decided in effect that the society had no power to borrow at all, a decision subsequently reversed by the House of Lords. Jessel M.R. had held as fully established that the assets of the society, which was in liquidation, had been increased by borrowed monies and had held that after the payment of the costs and all debts and everything to which the members were entitled by way of return of capital and bonus the surplus ought to be returned to the people who advanced the monies on the plainest of principles of equity. Lord Parker said he thought that what was meant was that it would be inequitable for the society to take advantage of the misapplication by its agents of money belonging to others and held in a fiduciary capacity. But he criticised the directions given by the Court with the object of working out this equity. He thought that if the monies were advanced when the assets of the society were insufficient to pay the creditors in full or anything to the contributories, but that by means of the *ultra vires* loans the assets at the date of the winding up had been so increased that both creditors and contributories could be paid in full, it would not be in accordance with equity and good conscience that these creditors and contributories should claim to be paid in full. It rather seemed to him that the increase in assets due to the *ultra vires* borrowing ought to be restored to the lenders. The basis of this reasoning was that the monies were in the position of trust monies. He said that neither creditors nor contributories ought, in equity, to be allowed to retain an advantage derived by reason of the misapplication by the society's agents of monies which were in the position of trust monies. Having criticised the manner in which counsel sought to explain the decision he did, however, say that if an inquiry had been directed it might have been shown that the debts due to the ordinary creditors had really been incurred in preserving the bulk of assets in which the shareholders and *ultra vires* lenders alike were interested, in which case it might be equitable that these debts should be paid first out of the fund. If the debts were shown, however, to have been incurred before *ultra vires* borrowings he said he could not at present see how the creditors could claim to be in a better position because of the *ultra vires* borrowing.

I have dwelt upon the reasoning of Lord Parker of Waddington as above stated because it was relied upon to support the case of the creditors in this case. But I do not think that anything which Lord Parker said is really relevant to the facts of the present case in that he was dealing with the claims of contributories or *ulta vires* lenders as against creditors. In the case now before me there is no question of the claim of contributories or *ultra vires* lenders. The claim is made by investors against the Company, who claim that the Company stands in a fiduciary position to them. They are not in the position of *ultra vires* lenders. Theri investments were made in proper legal fashion. They are therefore entitled to follow or trace their money into the stamps purchased with it and on the principle of *Hallett's Case* 13 Ch. D. 696 they urge that their right to the proceeds of sale of the property purchased with trust monies takes priority to the claims of creditors.

The principles laid down in *Hallett's Case* 13 Ch. D. 696 were further considered *in re Diplock, Diplock* v. *Wintle* [1948] 1 Ch. 465. Each side relied on various parts of the judgments in the case as supporting its contentions.

Caleb Diplock, by his will, directed his executors to apply his residuary estate "for such charitable institution or institutions or other charitable or benevolent object or objects in England as my acting executors or executor may in their or his absolute discretion select." The executors distributed a large portion of the residue amongst a large number of charities. The next-of-kin then challenged the validity of the bequest, which was held invalid. The claims of the next-of-kin against the executors were compromised. They then brought actions against institutions which had participated in the distribution. In most cases the cheques sent by the executors had been paid into the institution's general account. Some of these accounts were in credit, some overdrawn. In some cases payment was made to a special account; in a few instances it had been earmarked for a special purpose. In some instances the money was expended in altering or enlarging buildings on lands owned by the charity.

These claims of the next-of-kin were on two main grounds. Claims "*in personam*," based on an alleged equity of a creditor or next-of-kin to recover from an overpaid stranger, and also claims "*in rem*," based on the doctrine of tracing assets which are identifiable either unmixed or as a part of a mixed fund in the hands of a volunteer who has received them. It is with the parts of the judgments that relates to the latter type of claim that I am concerned in that the principles in *Hallett's Case* 13 Ch. D. 696 and *Sinclair* v. *Brougham* [1914] A.C. 398 were considered. It was the view of the Court that one whose money has been mixed with another's may trace his money into the mixed fund or assets acquired therewith though such fund or assets be held, and the mixing done, by an innocent volunteer, provided that there was originally a fiduciary relationship between claimant and recipient of his money to give rise to an equitable proprietary interest in the claimant and the claimant's money is fairly identifiable. The equitable remedy by way of charge on the mixed fund or assets is not available, however, if it works an injustice.

There are some general observations on the nature of equitable remedies in cases of mixed funds to which it will be useful to refer as having some bearing on the present case.

Having referred to the limited nature of the remedies open at common law, the Court stated, at p. 520:- "Equity adopted a more metaphysical approach. It found no difficulty in regarding a composite fund as an amalgam constituted by the mixture of two or more funds each of which could be regarded as having, for certain purposes, a continued separate existence. Putting it in another way, equity regarded the amalgam as capable, in proper circumstances, of being resolved into its component parts." Later, at p. 521, it is stated:- "The equitable remedies pre-suppose the continued existence of the money either as a separate fund or as part of a mixed fund or as latent in property acquired by means of such a fund." Further on it is said:- "It is, therefore, a necessary matter for consideration in each case where it is sought to trace money in equity, whether it has such a continued existence, actual or notional, as will enable equity to grant specific relief." The equitable forms of relief which the Court was considering therefore extend to cases where the money is latent in property acquired by a mixed fund and may be followed where it has a notional existence. These observations seem very relevant to the claims of the investors in this case if their money be held latent in the stamps in the liquidator's hands which were purchased by the Company.

The next relevant point is that in the reference to the judgment of Wynn-Parry J., starting at p. 523, the Court accepts by implication the principle that equity can operate to enable money in a mixed fund to be recovered, not only where the mixing takes place in breach of some fiduciary relationship and in proceedings against a fiduciary agent, but also where the mixing has been done by an innocent volunteer. The extension of the doctrine is implicit in the decision of *Sinclair* v. *Brougham* [1914] A.C. 398. It also accedes, at p. 525, to the proposition that a person in a fiduciary position being a party to the action is precluded from setting up a case inconsistent with the obligations of his fiduciary position.

A further relevant observation is to be found at p. 527, where the Court points out that the submission that *Hallett's Case* 13 Ch. D. 696 was based "not upon trusteeship in the narrow sense, but upon ownership" was not accepted by the House in *Sinclair* v. *Brougham* [1914] A.C. 398. It also pointed out, at p. 528, that the House had rejected the suggestion that there could not be a tracing order in favour of a class. At page 540 it is made clear that the Court accepts the principle that the remedies in equity which I am at present concerned with are brought into existence in the case of fiduciary relationships, such as that of principals and agents. Thus, these observations as cited follow and accept the principles of *Hallett's Case* 13 Ch. D. 696 as explained in *Sinclair* v. *Brougham* [1914] A.C. 398 and tend to support the contentions of the defendants. Indeed, the decision in the case extending the right to a charge to beneficiaries to the case where the monies sought to be traced are found in a mixed fund in the hands of an innocent volunteer goes beyond what it is necessary for the defendants to establish in this case.

Mr. O'Neill, however, sought to rely on certain other passages in the judgment to show that equity would not apply the principle of following or tracing where it was unjust. He said that, at p. 532, the Court had indicated approval of the view that equity intervenes, not to do what might be thought to be absolute justice to a claimant but to prevent a defendant from acting in an unconscionable manner. A defendant will not be restrained from asserting a claim save to the extent that it would be unconscionable for him to do so. Again, it is pointed out at p. 547 that the equitable owner of the trust money must submit to equality of treatment with the innocent volunteer, followed by the statement on p. 548 to the effect that where a declaration of charge does not produce an equitable result it is inapplicable as a remedy.

The effect of the decision in *In re Diplock* [1948] 1 Ch. 465 can, I think, be summarised in this way: the principles of *Hallett's Case* 13 Ch. D. 696 are extended in this way – that where money mixed with that of another can be traced into a mixed fund or assets acquired therewith it can be followed, even though mixed, by an innocent volunteer, provided the equitable remedy does not work an injustice. As to whether the application of the principles in *Hallett's Case* 13 Ch. D. 696 work such in injustice on creditors in this case as should prevent their application in a matter which I will deal with later.

The principles laid down in *Hallett's Case* 13 Ch. D. 696 which it is said are applicable to the facts of this case are first, that when a person in a fiduciary capacity makes a purchase with mixed funds of his own and the beneficiary, the beneficiary is entitled to a charge to the extent of the trust money laid out in the purchase; secondly, that where a person does an act which may be rightly performed he cannot say that the act was intentionally, and in fact, done wrongly; and, finally, that where a person holding money in a fiduciary capacity mixes them with his own, the rule in *Clayton's Case* 1 Mer. 572 does not apply and such person must be taken to have drawn out his own monies in preference to the trust monies.

Thë practical application of these principles, has, then to be considered. This involves a consideration in the first instance of what was done by the Company with the investors' money and the actual financial position. The total claims against the Company amount to approximately £1,840,000. This sum includes a claim on behalf of the ordinary creditors to the extent of £34,300 13s. 3d.; the balance is to be attributed to the claims of the investors. The total monies received by the official liquidator amounts to £139,760 17s. 1d., from which must be deducted certain sums allowed on account of expenses and liquidation costs. The monies collected include cash to the credit of the Company's bank account, £5,930 13s. 9d., and monies collected from foreign banks, £86,364 7s. 3d. In addition, the liquidator holds stamps which have been valued at approximately £282,787. Roughly one-third in value of these had been allocated to various syndicates in the sales which were cancelled. These stamps are said to have since appreciated in value by about 10 per cent. There is thus a large deficit, so that the unfortunate investors can only hope to recover a small proportion of their capital invested. Whatever conclusions he came to, the claim of the investors that their money can properly be traced into the stamps in the liquidator's hands, formerly the possession of the Company, can be substantiated in the following fashion.

Now, the Company kept only one bank account in this country and so far as is known carried on its business through the medium of this account. The sums sent abroad came from it. It is accepted, as I understand it, in the absence of contrary evidence, that the proper inference is that the Company must have mixed its own funds, such as commissions deducted, along with the investors' money and money received from purchasers in this account. It would also appear to be the position that purchases of stamps were made by monies withdrawn from this account which included the investors' money entrusted to the Company. The Company is precluded in a case such as the present from alleging that the rule in *Clayton's Case* 1 Mer. 572 applies in so far as it is concerned. It must be presumed to have drawn its own monies first. Therefore, having regard to the deficit, no suggestion can be made that any of the Company's money is represented by the stamps in hands.

The plaintiff's own evidence is that the withdrawals sent to foreign banks were, presumably, in whole or in part, used in the purchase of stamps. We know that the value of the stamps found in the Company's possession, even if grossly undervalued, and the other monies recovered by the liquidator are far below the amount of the investors' investments. The claims, less those of general creditors, amounts in round figures to something like one and a half million pounds, while the monies collected and the value of the stamps, at the date of valuation, does not exceed half a million. Even allowing for a 100 per cent under-valuation of the stamps, which seems outside the bounds of practical possibility, it is clearly proved, and the only proper inference is, that the overwhelming portion of the investors' monies was withdrawn from the bank account. Now, the only proper purpose for which the Company could withdraw the investors' money from the bank accounts was for the purchase of stamps. Applying the principle of *Hallett's Case* 13 Ch. D. 696 the Company as a fiduciary agent is precluded from setting up a case inconsistent with the obligations of its fiduciary position; it follows that the investors' money, having been drawn on to a far greater extent than the value of the stamps found by the liquidator in the Company's possession and those later recovered by him, which were formerly in the Company's possession, must be presumed to have been used in the purchase of these stamps. It follows from this that the investors can trace their money into the stamps purchased and held by the Company, including those recovered which were originally in the Company's possession, and are *prima facie* entitled to a tracing order or charge, subject to certain matters which I will deal with later. But I do not wish it to be thought that I have overlooked a submission of Mr. O'Neill's with regard to the unsyndicated investors and I will deal with this before coming to these other matters.

Assuming that it was held that a fiduciary relationship was created, then Mr O'Neill contended that in that case it was a term of the contract that no ownership in the stamps passed until appropriated to a syndicate of which the investor was a member. They were only entitled to trace ownership to the stamps because they had been appropriated under the contract. That results, he claimed, in the unsyndicated investors being unable to claim any right of property, equitable or otherwise, in the stamps, since in their case no property was ever appropriated.

He relied on the analogy of the case of *Sealy* v. *Stawell* (1868) I.R. 2 Eq. 326. We are only concerned here with so much of the case as concerned the fourth question dealt with by the Master of the Rolls, at p. 343 of the report. The relevant facts are that a sum of bank stock was transferred to a trustee to sell and invest the produce on lands which were to be held on certain trusts. After his death his administrator paid out £38,650 of his own money in the purchase of lands which were conveyed to him absolutely. The value of the stock at the time was £23,630. By deed reciting the purchase of the lands thereby conveyed and other lands and that a portion of the purchase money of the lands consisted of the bank stock and that the lands were conveyed to the administrator in part performance of the trusts declared of the stock and that he was desirous of fully performing the trusts by conveying the lands to the trusts, the administrator conveyed part of the purchased lands accordingly. It was claimed that the remaining lands purchased and not conveyed were appropriated to the trust on the basis that the lands were purchased with the intention of performing the trust as recited in the deed. No proof, however, was forthcoming that any part of the trust fund exceeding the value of the lands conveyed could be traced into the purchase. On the contrary, the evidence established that the amount which Francis Stawell, the purchaser, contributed out of his own money was more than the value of the unappropriated lands. The mere fact that he had trust monies on hands when he made the purchase was held not sufficient to attach the trusts to lands bought with his own money. As no part of the trust funds was traced as invested in the remaining lands no lien existed over them. The claims of the persons entitled to the trust estate were simply those of creditors on foot of a breach of trust.

The case was decided in 1867 and it may be doubted whether the same decision would have been arrived at to-day having regard to the principles stated in some of the cases cited. However, it seems to me that the case would only support Mr. O'Neill's argument if he could show that the Company had monies of its own on hands which were used for the purchase of stamps. Unless that can be done, any analogy fails. If the facts show, as Mr. Finlay contends, that only the investors' money went into the purchase of the stamps now in the official liquidator's hands or that they must be deemed in equity to have been purchased with the investors' money, then the case has no application.

Since the facts coupled with the application of the equitable principles indicate that the investors' money is properly traceable into the stamps in hands, the decision does not support plaintiffs' contentions based on *Sealy* v. *Stawell* (1868) I.R. 2 Eq. 326.

But there are certain other matters which I stated I would deal with. The investors' funds have been mixed and depleted. There is a large deficit in the shape of the difference between the funds originally invested by the investors and the monies and stamps now to hand. The possibility of the application of the rule in *Clayton's Case* 1 Mer. 572 between the investors *inter se* must be considered. There is also the peculiar position of the syndicated shareholders and the question arises whether they have any special rights, even though they may have no claim to the syndicated stamp *in specie*. There is the matter of the guarantee and what rights that gives to investors and the matter of the plaintiffs' possible right to commission. There is also the position of the general creditors to be considered. Have they any right to be paid in priority to the investors or any equity to rank equally with them?

Having regard to the fact that the stamps represent the depleted money of the investors coming from a mixed fund, and if it be the fact that it is impossible to say whose money purchased any particular lot of stamps or in what order the purchases were made, it would appear that the principle of a *pro rata* distribution of the property amongst the beneficiaries, as was done in *Sinclair* v. *Brougham* [1914] A.C. 398 would be the proper one to apply at least between the unsyndicated investors. The words of Lord Parker of Waddington, where he said in that case that where owners had an equal equity and neither could claim priority over the other it follows that their charges must rank *pari passu*, seem applicable *prima facie*. Therefore the unsyndicated investors would *prima facie* be entitled at least to a charge over the property in the shape of the unsyndicated stamps unless it can be shown that such relief is inequitable or should not for some particular reason on the facts of the case be applied. That relief would normally be implemented by way of ordering a sale and *pro rata* division of the proceeds of the property amongst the unsyndicated investors and that would seem the proper order to make as far as the unsyndicated stamps are concerned, unless the rule in *Clayton's Case* 1 Mer. 572 is applicable between the unsyndicated investors.

In general the rule in *Clayton's Case* 1 Mer. 572 is applicable as between *cestuis que trustent*; that is, that first drawings out are to be attributed to the first payments in. In other words, the trustee is deemed to draw out first the money of the *cestuis que trustent* that he paid first into the blended account. A difficult question arises as to whether this rule is applicable in the complex circumstances of the present case. It may be that the rule in *Clayton's Case* 1 Mer. 572 does not apply beyond tracing in a bank account and the principle may have no application to property acquired by means of a mixed fund. But I prefer to deal with the situation, for safety's sake, as if the principle can properly be applied to the case of property acquired with such a mixed fund. The practical position is that, in fact, the investors' money has been mixed twice; first, in the original banking account, and secondly, in the property in the shape of stamps in which the investors' money lies latent, again in a mixed fashion. It is, I gather, possible to trace to some extent through the Company's books the order in which investors' money was lodged to the bank account. The position is that after this stage it is impossible to say what monies were used for the purchase of any particular lot of stamps or to whom the monies were paid. I have sought further information on this point and in the result it would seem that while the order in which monies were shifted to foreign banks or made payable to Dr. Singer could be discovered, it is not possible to say in what order any particular sets of stamps in the possession of the official liquidator were purchased, so that it would not be possible from the practical point of view to discover the order in which the investors' money was used in purchasing the stamps now held. In other words, there having been a second mixing of the investors' funds into a second mixed amalgam of property, it would not be possible for any particular investor to say that this particular money was used before others in the purchase of the property in the shape of stamps. Tracing, in the exact sense of the term, is therefore not possible or practicable. A somewhat similar state of affairs arose in *Sinclair* v. *Brougham* [1914] A.C. 398 and in that case, as I have indicated, the House of Lords took the view that a *pro rata* distribution was the practical and equitable solution, leaving it to any particular depositor or shareholder to apply with a view to tracing his own money into any particular asset. Therefore, the rule in *Clayton's Case* 1 Mer. 572 does not apply as between the unsyndicated investors and a *pro rata* distribution is the proper form of relief so far as they are concerned. In order to guard against a remote possibility of an investor being able to trace his money into any particular lot of stamps it may be that the final order should preserve the right of any investor who can do so to make his claim.

But then the peculiar position of the syndicated investors has to be dealt with. I have already stated that in my view, on the true construction of the contract, it was not the intention of the parties that the investors should be entitled to the stamps *in specie*. There is this also to be said with regard to their claim to have the syndicated stamps *in specie*: the Court should not make an order which is totally impracticable and virtually impossible to carry out in practice. No one has been able to suggest to me any practical and workable method whereby the official liquidator could carry out an order to deliver the syndicated stamps *in specie*. The insuperable difficulties of obtaining agreement amongst the very many investors in most syndicates as to what the official liquidator is to do physically with the stamps are obvious.

The question still remains as to whether or not the syndicated investors have any special rights in regard to the proceeds of sale of syndicated stamps. I must not lose sight of the fact that the investors' rights are governed by a contract, and, although certain equitable principles may have become applicable, that does not mean that if particular parties have rights under the contract different to other parties, these rights should not be given effect to.

It was part of the contract, as I have found it, that the stamps when purchased should be allotted to syndicates and then "treated" as their property. As regards the syndicated investors the contract with them at the time of liquidation had reached a certain stage. As. Mr. Matheson says, they had been informed that their money had been used in the purchase of particular stamps, and again applying the principle in *Hallett's Case* 13 Ch. D. 696 that a person who does an act which may be rightly performed cannot say that it was done wrongly, it would seem that at least as between the syndicated investors and the Company it should be assumed that the act of purchase and allotment was done rightly and that the syndicated owners therefore have a particular equity as regards the syndicated stamps. If so, they would be entitled again *prima facie* to a charge over these stamps to which their money has been traced in equity and which have been appropriated to them and to a consequent right to have them sold for their benefit. Such *prima facie* right should not, however, be operated in their favour if it works an injustice. I will deal with the claims of creditors later, but for the moment I must pause to consider whether the declaration of a right to a charge and sale in favour of the syndicated investors as regards the syndicated stamps would operate to work an injustice on the general body of unsyndicated investors. This is undoubtedly a very debatable point, but having regard to the nature of the contract which all investors entered into it must have been clear to all that the stamps purchased with their money would in due course be allotted to syndicates and then "treated" as their property, the proceeds of the sale of stamps allotted being divided amongst the members of the syndicates to which they were respectively allotted. It so happened that in the case of some of the syndicated investors the stage of allotment had been reached. That was their good fortune and it does not seem to me that the unsyndicated investors can properly complain that any injustice is done to them if the syndicated investors are allowed to take advantage of the actual state of affairs that existed at the time of liquidation, because all investors knew the procedure that was to be operated under the contract and if it had reached a stage more favourable to some than others that was something that they must all be deemed to know would occur. Therefore it would seem to me that making a declaration of charge in favour of the syndicated investors over the syndicated stamps does not work an injustice on unsyndicated investors. Therefore sale of the syndicated stamps and rateable distribution amongst the syndicated investors would seem the proper relief to grant, subject again, however, to any rights the general body of creditors may have.

Ordinary creditors of a company who are not paid in full, of course, suffer an injustice in the abstract, but that is not the particular type of injustice I have to consider here where the question is as between them and the investors, whom I have found to have *prima facie* certain rights in equity by way of charge and *pro rata* distribution. In some cases, such as in the circumstances arising in respect of certain of the claims in *In re Diplock* [1948] 1 Ch. 465, the equitable remedy of a charge on a mixed fund will not be granted where it will work an injustice. The question then arises as to whether the making of a tracing or charging order in favour of the investors would result in that particular type of injustice to the ordinary creditors that would make it inequitable to make the order to which I have held that the investors are *prima facie* entitled.

I must start, it seems to me, by having regard to what I may call the general principles applicable. Should a person, having trust property in his possession, die or go bankrupt, the beneficiaries under the trust take their property in full in priority to the general body of creditors. The same thing applies in the case a company in liquidation. The blending of trust funds with the monies of the deceased trustee would not – it would appear from what was said in *Hallett's Case* 13 Ch. D. 696 – make any difference to the priority of the beneficiaries, and so it would be in the case of a company in liquidation. The creditor cannot claim to stand as agent a *cestui que trust* in any better position than the deceased trustee would. Likewise, the creditors of a company are in general in no better position as against beneficiaries of trust monies in a company's hands at the time of liquidation that the company before liquidation. The distinction, as I understand, is based on the fact that the beneficiary seeks his own property, or the proceeds thereof, being aided in equity to obtain restitution. The ordinary creditor, however, can only seek payment of his debt to the extent that there are assets, the property of the deceased debtor, bankrupt or company in liquidation which are available to meet his claim

Mr. O'Neill, however, suggested that the investors should not be given any priority over the ordinary creditors. His first ground was, of course, that the money of the investors was lent or given to the Company in such fashion as to create merely the relationship of creditor and debtor. That view I have rejected. But he also went further in order to meet the possible situation of it being held that a fiduciary relationship existed between investors and the Company and that they were entitled to the benefit of a tracing order or charge. The application of such equitable relief would, he said, work an injustice to creditors and it would be inequitable not to allow those whose goods or services had been used or availed of to enable the Company to carry on its business for the benefit of the investors by providing such things as stationery or doing printing, and so on, to stand in priority to the investors. The equitable relief by way of tracing order and charge were, he said, adopted to prevent a person holding the property of another from acting in an unconscionable manner and there was nothing unconscionable in the action of the official liquidator in seeking to see the ordinary creditors paid in full.

He relied on certain passages in *In re Diplock* (1948] 1 Ch. 465 to support his contentions, which I have already cited and need not repeat. But all these statements of principle must be viewed in the light of the circumstances of the case in which they were made. I have to point out that these observations were directed to the state of affairs where the Diplock money had been used by certain of the charities to alter property of their own. In such cases it does not follow that the trust money can be said to be present in the adapted property. For example, the alterations may have lowered the value of the property. In such cases the machinery of a charge would not place the innocent volunteer in a position comparable to the owner of the trust fund and the Court took the view that in such cases the Diplock money could not be traced in the true sense and that is why it was held that the remedy of charge was inapplicable. The contest in that case was, moreover, between the next-of-kin and institutions that had received the money in the capacity of innocent volunteers, who had done nothing wrong, the equitable doctrines in question thus being extended beyond the wrongdoer. The institutions stood in no fiduciary relationship to the next-of-kin. It was, I think, for these reasons that the limitations were placed on the equitable extension of the doctrine. That is not the state of affairs existing in the present case, where the claim of the investors is made against the Company which I have held to have stood in a fiduciary relationship to the investors. The reasons for narrowing the application of the equitable remedies given to a beneficiary of a charge and tracing order following their own money which existed in *Diplock's Case* [1948] 1 Ch. 465 do not exist in the present case where the fiduciary relationship exists. There are no analogous reasons in the present case.

I do not wish to depart from what was said by the Court in *In re Diplock* [1984] I Ch. 465 without this further comment: while I have treated the defendants as asserting claims against the Company for a tracing order or charge as against the Company, I am now dealing with another and different aspect of the matter. The official liquidator, seeking to collect and secure the assets of the Company is *inter alia* in effect asserting the rights of the creditors to come before the investors. Looked at in this fashion, the defendants may properly say in reply that they are in substance in the position of the innocent volunteer in *Diplock's Case* [1948] 1 Ch. 465. They have done nothing wrong. They have not in fact, like the volunteers in *Diplock's Case* [1948] 1 Ch. 465, received anybody's money. They can properly say:- "We are only seeking to obtain as much as we can of our own property and if we can show that it is traceable in the hands of the Company there is nothing unconscionable in our claiming our own property and resisting the claim of anyone else, such as the ordinary creditors, to share in it."

Reliance was further placed on what Lord Dunedin said in *Sinclair* v. *Brougham* [1914] A.C. 398 about the payment of the creditors before the claims of shareholders and depositors were met. First, it is right to point out that what was said was *obiter*, as the question of the creditors' priority was not in question. Further, Lord Dunedin says they were paid because their claims were inconsiderable, which may well have been the reason. As far as the shareholders were concerned, having been properly incurred by the directors the debts of creditors would in any winding up of a company come before shareholders' claims.

What Lord Dunedin said about their priority to *ultra vires* depositors calls, however, for more thought. The debts were incurred, he pointed out, in a business, illegal no doubt, but one which the depositors were willing that the directors should carry on. He seems thus to have equated them with the position of the shareholders and that may be the true explanation as to why he approved of the payment of creditors first. He cannot, I think, have intended to say that where a person gives his money to an agent to use in a certain fashion, which creates a fiduciary relationship, and the purpose incidentally happens to be something which it is the course of the agent's business to do, the principal is to be subordinated to the creditors of the agent in the business, because that would be contrary to the well established principles of equity to which I have referred. To take a concrete example: suppose that a stockbroker goes bankrupt having in his hands in cash the proceeds of sale of a customer's shares, handed to him for the specific purpose of sale. Could it be contended that the stockbroker's creditors for, say, stationery or office furniture supplied for use in his business, would rank before the customer with whom he stood in a fiduciary relationship and whose monies could be clearly traced? I would say not. That Lord Dunedin did not mean anything of the kind is, I think, made clear in the next page of his speech, where he says that this is not a case where one sharing party has the right to say to another:- "It is not in your mouth to say that the assets are not all mine, to the extent of my full claim." That would be just what a principal in a fiduciary relationship with his agent to whom he has given money for a specific purpose could say to an ordinary creditor of the agent. The true explanation of what was said may also be that the *ultra vires* depositors had not valid contract and the business their money was used in was illegal, therefore they should not rank with those whose money was used in the illegal business to their benefit.

Whatever the true explanation of Lord Dunedin's attitude was, it seems to me that there is no true analogy between the rights *inter se* of *ultra vires* depositors and creditors of an illegal business and the position of the investors in this case who handed their monies in a perfectly legal contract to an agent carrying on a business not in itself illegal. I have already dealt with the observations of Lord Parker of Waddington in the same case and I do not think that they assist Mr. O'Neill's argument on the facts of the present case.

The comments of Jessel M.R. in *Hallett's Case* 13 Ch. D. 696 in referring to what Knight Bruce L.J. had said in *Pennell* v. *Deffell* 4 D. M. & G. 372 seem to me also opposed to Mr. O'Neill's contentions. Some of the other cases cited also indicate that the rights of a person in a position similar to that of a *cestui que trust* and able to trace his money or property in the hands of a trustee or other person in a fiduciary capacity come before the rights of general creditors. In *Taylor* v. *Plumer* 3 M. & S. 562 the principal was held entitled as against the assignees who would, in effect, have been asserting the creditors' claims. Likewise, the trustees in bankruptcy in the case of *Harris* v. *Truman* 9 Q. B. D. 264 would be in a like position, but the principles in both cases were in effect held entitled to their property in preference to the claims of the general creditors.

I was not referred to – nor have I been able to discover – any case in which it was expressly laid down that the ordinary creditors of a fiduciary agent, whose goods or money was used for the purposes of the agent's business, were entitled to rank before those whose money or property was held by the agent in a fiduciary capacity. Such a proposition would seem contrary to the view that equity aims in such cases at restitution. Further, it would seem contrary to the principle that as against a *cestui que trust* the creditors of a deceased or bankrupt trustee cannot claim to be in any better position than the trustee himself could be and, as I understand it, a fiduciary agent stands in the same position as a trustee in a case where he holds the property of his principal for specific purpose. In Hanbury on Equity (7th ed., 1957, at p. 33) I find the general proposition that equities bind *inter alia* creditors, which supports this view. The alleged right of the creditors to take priority over the investors has not therefore been sustained.

I have therefore come to the conclusion that certain of the contentions made on behalf of the syndicated and unsyndicated investors are in principle correct and that the syndicated investors are entitled to a declaration of charge over the stamps allotted to their respective syndicates to be implemented by a sale thereof and the unsyndicated investors are in a like position as regards the unsyndicated stamps. They, too, are entitled to a declaration of charge to be implemented by a sale. The proceeds in both cases should be divided *pro rata* between the members of the two respective classes according to the amounts of their investments, subject possibly to the right I have mentioned of any unsyndicated investor to assert a claim to be able to trace his money into any specific lot of stamps.

With regard to the guarantee, again it seems to me that the fact that the parties' rights are governed by the terms of the contract must be given effect to, and therefore both syndicated and unsyndicated investors are entitled to claim against the plaintiffs any deficit that may arise between what they receive in respect of the proceeds of the sale of the stamps and the amount of their respective investments. In that respect they would rank as ordinary creditors.

With regard to the question of the payment of commission, the contract provided for the payment of commission to the Company. In the sale of the stamps the Company, through the liquidator, will be performing the service to the investors that it undertook to perform and it is therefore in my view entitled to charge commission at the standard rate charged, 10 per cent. The amount arising will in fact for the most part go to the investors in all probability in respect of their probable rights to claim as creditors in respect of deficits on the sales that will take place. But the ordinary creditors also have an interest in this fund, and, while it may not increase the amount of anything recoverable by them to any great extent, their rights cannot be ignored.

Unfortunately, however, while deciding the broad question of principle, I find, as was anticipated by all at the hearing, great difficulty in giving clear-cut answers to the questions asked. That is not because of any imperfection in the fashion in which the summary summons was drafted but because of the complexities of this case due to the way in which the Company ran its affairs. I shall therefore for the present state what appear to me to be the correct answers to the questions, having regard to the decisions in principle to which I have come, and I will reserve the right of counsel to address me on the nature of the answers which I have set out in tentative form below. There remain also numerous subsidiary questions to be decided and care must be taken to see that the rights of parties not so far heard are properly safeguarded. Such answers as I give must therefore be so worded that it is clear that on the main issue, at any rate, only the matter of general principle is decided and that such answers are so worded that it is left open to all who have not been heard on a specific point that concerns them to have subsidiary matters affecting them decided later. On this matter, while I have endeavoured to formulate what appear to me appropriate reservations to the answers, I shall have to ask the assistance of counsel. There may, in particular, be matters not as yet brought to my notice which would be known to counsel and in connection with which modification of the proposed answers should be made. I will therefore state my present view as to the proper answers to the questions subject to this reservation also.

The first question in accordance with my views should, it would appear, be answered in the negative, save to the extent that the members of the syndicates are entitled to a charge over allotted stamps to the extent of their respective investments.

Questions 2 (a) and (b) (i) will be answered, as I see it at present, in the affirmative. Question 2 (b) (ii) will also be answered in the affirmative. Since the liquidation proceedings have inured in part to the benefit of the syndicated investors the answers to questions 2 (a) and (b) (i), it seems to me, require qualification to the extent that an alicquot share of the costs, charges and expenses of the liquidation proceedings should be borne by the syndicated investors based on the gross amount to be payable to them, and counsel will have to consider the terms of this qualification bearing in mind precisely what has to be provided for in the final allocation and especially in respect of these costs, charges and expenses of the liquidation. Some of the stamps allocated to certain syndicates have been lost through burglary and the answer should be qualified to the extent that it is without prejudice to the rights of members of these syndicates, such as they may be. There must also be an appropriate qualification as to the cases where stamps were allotted to more than one syndicate.

The precise method of disposition, that is to say, how the sales are to be carried out, I have been asked to leave over pending my decision in principle.

On question 2 (c) all parties are agreed that the answer should be "no" and on the facts before me I see no reason to disagree.

From the above, and having regard to what I have said, the appropriate answer to question 3 would appear to be "no," save in so far as there is a deficit on the ultimate sale price between the amount invested by each syndicated investor and the fractional share of each such investor in the proceeds of sale. In this respect the syndicated investors would rank as ordinary creditors.

Questions 4 (a) and (b) should be answered *prima facie* also in the negative, save again to the extent that the unsyndicated investors have a charge over the unalloted stamps to the extent of their respective investments and the syndicated investors have a charge over the syndicated stamps.

Questions 5 (a) and (b) (i) should, it would appear, be answered in the affirmative, in favour of the class mentioned at 4 (a), but there will have to be some appropriate qualification with regard to those who were sent cheques in respect of cancelled auctions and those whose monies were paid in after the 29th April, 1959, to whom I refer again later. Question 5 (b) (ii) will also be answered in the affirmative. Again, a similar qualification with regard to this class being found to bear an alicquot share of the costs, charges and expenses of the liquidation proceedings would require to be inserted, based again on the gross amount payable to them. Provision for preserving the right of any unsyndicated investor who claims that he can trace his investments into any particular unsyndicated stamps may also have to be made. The precise method of disposition will have to be considered later on in regard to the unallotted stamps.

Question 6 would be answered in the negative, with the qualification that in so far as there is a deficit between the amount of their respective investments and the fractional share of each investor in the proceeds of sale they would rank as ordinary creditors.

The answer to question 7 is accordingly "no," but subject to the qualification that the syndicated investors are entitled to a charge over the stamps allotted to their respective syndicates and the unsyndicated investors are entitled to a charge over the unsyndicated stamps, both answers being subject to the qualifications above stated in respect of each class.

In order to prevent confusion all these answers would appear to require various other qualifications and exceptions and it is a matter of draftsmanship as to how they should be incorporated. This was recognised by counsel at the outset and certain qualifications were discussed, but it was considered that these could be better formulated when the main question of principle had been determined. The qualifications, as I see them at present, are these: the charges in neither case cover stamps the property of individual owners given by them to the Company for sale; nor do the charges cover stamps received by the official liquidator in settlement of claims which cannot be identified as having been previously in the possession of the Company. Claims may lie against persons alleged to have been wrongly paid in one way or another by the Company and any findings made should be without prejudice to such rights as they might otherwise have should they be found to have been wrongly paid. The evidence indicates that the last expenditure on stamps by the

Company was on the 28th April, 1959. Monies were, however, received from some investors after that date up to the 24th May, 1959. These monies could not have been used in the purchase of stamps. These investors whose payments were made between these dates are therefore not entitled to claim any charge over the stamps. It may also be the position that those of the unsyndicated investors who made their investments after the 13th March, 1959, are not entitled to claim any shares in the proceeds of the unallotted portion of the Burrus collection, but as this matter was not touched on in the argument I express no view regarding it. It may be, however, that some further qualification is required on this matter.

There are certain monies in the official liquidator's hands recovered from the banking accounts of the Company. I should make it clear that I am not purporting to deal with these and the rights of all persons with good claims against these monies are preserved. There may be persons who can, for example, trace their monies into these accounts. Nor am I at present dealing with monies received by the offical liquidator in compensation for stolen stamps, although it is very possible that my decision may indicate by implication the parties who can assert a claim to these monies.

There are also, it must be remembered, a number of subsidiary questions which were put before the Court on a previous application to have various persons appointed to represent particular groups of interested persons. For example, questions remain to be determined as to the rights of infant investors and their priority. If there were persons who invested monies in the various alternative plans such as the "Double Barrel Plan," "Collection Picking Plan" and other similar plans, the decision and answers must be without prejudice to such rights as they may have. There is the position of claimants resident abroad and the question whether these are entitled to be paid if permission to make payment to them is not forthcoming under the provisions of the Exchange Control Acts. There may be other rights that should be safeguarded which will only now become apparent having regard to the particular decisions I have made in determining the matters at present before me. It may be that the best solution will be to state in the order such qualifications, rights and exceptions as are specifically known as being likely to affect the rights or liabilities of those concerned in the present proceedings and then to insert a general clause covering those which counsel are not in a position to state specifically at present; but I will await making a final determination as to the form of the answers and order until I have heard counsel's view thereon, having regard to the determinations I have made.

Notes and Questions

Do you follow the various principles governing the tracing of misappropriated funds discussed by Budd J.? See *Irish Land Law*, para 10.108 *et seq*. See also *Re Shannon Travel Ltd.*, Unreported (High Court) (1970 No. 3849 P) (Judgement delivered May 1972).

LEAHY V. DE MOLEYNS

[1896] I.R. 206 (Court of Appeal)

The facts are set out in the judgments.

Walker C.:

The plaintiffs Thomas Leahy and Samuel Henry Butcher sue as existing trustees of a settlement dated November 22, 1847, and having vested in them, as such, a mortgage security for £3109 representing the investment of a trust fund held upon the trusts of that settlement. This settlement was made upon the marriage of the Rev. Samuel Butcher with Mary Leahy and the then trustees were John Leahy and the Rev. Francis Crawford. On December 15, 1855, those trustees, under the powers in the settlement, invested the £3109 upon the security of a mortgage given by Richard Chute of Chute Hall. John Leahy and the Rev. Francis Crawford were parties to that mortgage of the fifth part, and by it Richard Chute of Chute Hall, and Richard Chute of Leebrook, at his request granted to the trustees and their heirs, subject to redemption, the lands of Portduff and Ballynaboul, held under a lease for lives renewable for ever; and also Richard Chute of Chute Hall, and Edward De Moleyns, at his request granted to the trustees and their heirs the lands of Dulaigue and Broughane, subject to the fee-farm rent payable thereout, and the proviso for redemption; and Richard Chute of Chute Hall also granted unto David Mahoney and his heirs his life estate, under a settlement of October 18, 1836, in the lands of Portduff and Ballynaboul, and a fee-farm rent of £105 payable out of Dulaigue and Broughane, to hold to the use of John Leahy and Francis Crawford and their heirs during the life of Richard Chute, subject to redemption. The mortgage contained a proviso for redemption on repayment of £3109 on January 1, 1857, with interest at 6 per cent. in the meantime, and Richard Chute for himself, his heirs, executors, and administrators, convenanted with the trustees to pay the £3109, with interest, at the time appointed for payment thereof. There was also a proviso for the reduction of the interest from 6 per cent. to 4½ per cent., if paid within three months from each January 1st and July 1st, and also that the principal money should not be called in or paid off before January 1, 1865, in case the interest were paid pursuant to the deed on every January 1st and July 1st, or within three months thereafter.

In the year 1860 John Leahy desired to be discharged, and upon June 6, 1860, Henry Leahy was duly appointed a trustee in his place, and the mortgaged lands and mortgage debt and the benefit of all covenants and securities for the same were duly vested in Francis Crawford and Henry Leahy.

Richard Chute the mortgagor died on September 13, 1862, and by his will, after directing payment of his debts and legacies out of his personal estate not specifically bequeathed, he devised the mortgaged lands to his son the defendant Thomas Aremberg Chute for life, with remainder to his first and other sons in tail male, with like remainders to his other sons; and he devised other freehold lands in Kerry to his son Richard Trevor Chute for life with remainder to his first and other sons in tail male, with like remainder to Thomas Aremberg Chute; and he bequeathed to William Harnett and Edward De Moleyns a charge of £1000 vested in him, and a charge of £1384 12s. 3d. also vested in him, and the residue of his real and personal estates upon trust to convert and pay thereout his debts and funeral and testamentary expenses, and invest the surplus in Government or real securities, and stand possessed thereof in trust for all his children by his then wife born or to be born, save Thomas Aremberg Chute and Richard Trevor Chute, who being sons should attain twenty-one, or being daughters should attain twenty-one or marry, with power to apply the income for maintenance; and he appointed William Harnett and Edward De Moleyns trustees and executors of his will, and they both proved the will on December 23, 1862.

Henry Leahy one of the trustees having died, the plaintiff Thomas Leahy was duly appointed a trustee in his place on October 6, 1870, and the mortgage debt of £3100 and the mortgaged lands so far as subsisting were assigned to and vested in Francis Crawford and Thomas Leahy.

In the year 1877 Francis Crawford desired to be discharged from the trusts, and by deed dated January 1, 1877, the plaintiff Samuel Henry Butcher was appointed a trustee in his place, and the mortgage debt of £3109 was assigned to the plaintiffs, and the mortgaged lands were conveyed to them to hold upon the subsisting trusts of the settlement. Considerable argument was addressed to us upon the differences in these latter deeds by which new trustees were appointed, and there was sought to be inferred an abandonment of the claim against the personal assets. It seems to me that this would be an unnatural inference to draw. The differences are, I think unimportant.

Richard Chute left the following children: Thomas Aremberg Chute, Richard Trevor Chute, Francis Blennerhasset Chute, Marion Chute, Rose Chute, Dora Chute, Frances Chute, and Emily Chute. The sons entered into possession of the lands devised to them, but Richard Trevor Chute died in the year 1880, whereupon Thomas Aremberg Chute, under the provisions of Richard Chute's will, became entitled for life to Richard Trevor Chute's lands. The personal estate of Richard Trevor Chute, including the two charges of £1000 and £1384, was according to the schedule of assets sworn to amount to £11,436 9s. 10d., and the residuary account passed on November 14, 1864, stated the net assets constituting residue to be £8707 11s. 2d. which by the accounts the executor retained for the daughters, and Francis Blennerhasset Chute. This also included a debenture on the Kerry Club of £50 and debentures of small value in the Tralee Gas Company, and Tralee Market Company.

Thomas Aremberg Chute the devisee of the mortgaged lands, paid the interest on the mortgage of £3109, to about the year 1886, but it then fell into arrear, and on February 13, 1888, Thomas Aremberg Chute appointed John Townshend Trench receiver over the mortgaged lands for the purpose of paying the interest on the mortgage, and the interest containing in arrear, the plaintiffs filed a petition in the Land Judge's Court on which an absolute order was made on May 12, 1890, and the proceedings are still pending. It may have been found impossible up to this to sell the lands, and (it is alleged) there will be a considerable deficiency to meet the mortgage.

As one of the main questions in the case is whether, or how far the personal estate was paid to, or appropriated for the beneficiaries, it is material to state the dealings with the estate by the executors. The mode in which the estate of Richard Chute was dealt with, appears to be the following:- William Harnett and Edward De Moleyns proved the will on December 23, 1862. Of the five daughters, one Frances died under age on August 10, 1871; Marion attained twenty-one on June 17, 1871; Dora on June, 24 1876; Rose on April 25, 1879; and Emily on December 30, 1882. The executors paid the debts, save the mortgage for £3109, and they passed a residuary account on November 14, 1864. They did not publish notices for debts, but they of course knew of the mortgage. On February 5, 1869, the executors invested £1297 17s. 7d., portion of the residuary assets, on the security of a mortgage from Francis Blennerhasset Chute to Harnett and De Moleyns. The deed contained a declaration that the money belonged to them upon a joint account. The interest was paid by or on behalf of the mortgagor to or for the daughters and not by Mr. De Moleyns. Mr. Harnett died on December 27, 1886. The mortgage was paid off on July 28, 1892, after this action was brought, and was invested by Mr. De Moleyns in £1337 2s. 7d. consols, and he has paid the dividends to the four daughters, and subject to any question of appropriation for these daughters, this sum is in the hands of Mr. De Moleyns still. In the year 1865, Harnett and De Moleyns invested £386 18s., portion of the assets, in the taking over of so much of a charge of £1661 10s. 9d. on the estate of Francis Chute. By deed dated August 5th, 1865, Arthur Denning in whom the charge was vested assigned to Melicent Agnes Chute, William Harnett, and Edward De Moleyns, this charge of £1661 10s. 9d. to hold as to £1274 12s. 9d., for Melicent Agnes Chute, and as to £386 18s. for Harnett and De Moleyns. By deed dated April 29, 1867, Melicent Agnes Chute assigned to Harnett and De Moleyns this £1274 12s. 9d. and the deed contained a declaration that the £1274 12s. 9d. was vested in them on a joint account. The charge of £1661 10s. 9d., is still vested in Mr. De Molyens but the interest has been paid direct to the beneficiaries. It is therefore circumstanced in the same way as the £1337 4s. 7d. The other outstanding assets consist of £50 Debenture County Kerry Club, and £20 Tralee Market Company, the interest of which has been received by the beneficiaries.

In the year 1879, one of the daughters got married to Milhelm Shakoor, and a settlement was executed, dated November 10, in that year, and made between Mr. Shakoor of the first part, Marion Chute of the second part, and trustees Edward J. Saunderson and Francis Blennerhasset Chute of the third part. It recites the will of Richard Chute and bequest of the residue, and that Rose and Emily, two of the daughters, were still under twenty-one, and Marion Chute thereby assigns to the trustees all the estate, right, title, and interest vested or contingent of her the said Marion Chute, under the will of her father in the sum of £2000, and the two charges of £1000 and £1384 12s. 3d. and the residuary estate of Richard Chute (save a small sum paid to her), to hold upon the trusts of the settlement. This appears to have been an assignment merely of her share whatever it might be, and the trustees did not get possession of the property.

Rose Chute, on September 27, 1889, married Henry Dudgeon, and a settlement was executed as of that date, between Henry Dudgeon of the first part, Rose Chute of the second part, the Hon. Mrs. Rose Chute of the third part, and Joseph Hume Dudgeon, and Thomas C. Oliver of the fourth part. It recites the will of Richard Chute and proceeds: "And whereas the said testator left besides the said two sons, five daughters, of whom one Frances died under age and unmarried, and the remaining four have attained twenty-one, and accordingly the said sums and residue became divisible into fourths and the said Rose Chute is entitled to one-fourth thereof. And whereas the portion of the said residuary assets now outstanding is a mortgage for £1297 17s. 7d., dated February 5, 1869, executed by Frances Blennerhasset Chute, to the said William Harnett and Edward De Moleyns:" and in the operative part Rose Chute assigns to the trustees *inter alia*, "All that her one-fourth or other share of, and in the said sums of £1000 and £1384 12s. 3d. now vested in the said William Harnett and Edward De Moleyns, under the said will of her father, and also all that her one-fourth share of the said sum of £1297 17s. 7d. secured by the aforesaid mortgage of February 5, 1869," to hold upon the trusts of the settlement. It is alleged by the trustees of the settlement, and Mr. De Moleyns supports their allegation by his affidavit, that this settlement omitted by mistake from it Rose Chute's share of the £1661 10s. 9d. and the debentures.

The rest of the residuary assets consisted of £2010 12s. 10d. Government stock and £409 Government stock which were sold out in 1879 and in 1883 and were distributed in equal fourth parts amongst the four surviving daughters.

The result is to leave standing in the name of De Moleyns the £1661 10s. 9d. and the £1337 2s. 7d. and the two debentures.

Inasmuch as I am of opinion that in this case the plaintiffs can follow into the hands of the daughters or the trustees the rest of the assets, it is not material to consider whether there is any distinction between the classes of funds; but as regards the funds actually in the executor's hands with debts unpaid and a clear residue not created, I think the beneficiaries are not persons in the position of legatees who have received the fund. I think the frame of the two settlements prevents them being considered purchasers for value of any specific property, and therefore I think married and unmarried daughters stand particularly in the same position.

The writ in the original action was issued on March 25, 1891, and it named as the only defendants Edward De Moleyns the surviving trustee and executor of the will, and the devisees of the lands, viz. Thomas Aremberg Chute the owner of the mortgaged lands, and Francis B. Chute and Richard Chute the tenant for life and tenant in tail in remainder of the other devised lands. The writ merely prayed to have the real and personal estate of Richard Chute, deceased, administered. When the case came before the Master of the Rolls he required the action to be amended by bringing before the Court the persons who had received or were entitled to the residuary estate; accordingly the writ was amended by adding as defendants Edward J. Saunderson and Francis B. Chute the trustees of Mrs. Shakoor's settlement, and Joseph Hume Dudgeon and Thomas Creswick Oliver, the trustees of Mrs. Dudgeon's settlement; also Dora Chute and Emily Chute, the two unmarried daughters. The amended writ adds a prayer that if necessary it may be declared as to any residuary personal assets of the testator which at the commencement of the action remained in the possession of Edward De Moleyns as the surviving executor of Richard Chute, or which had been previously thereto transferred or paid over to the residuary legatees or to any trustee or trustees for them or any of them, that the said personal assets are liable to discharge the claim of the plaintiffs as speciality creditors.

The defences put forward to the action on the part of Mr. De Moleyns and the other defendants are:- "The Statute of Limitations inasmuch as no interest was paid out of the personalty, but only out of the rents of the mortgaged lands which it is contended does not keep alive the claim against the other devised lands or personal estate. Mr. De Moleyns also contends that so far as any claim against him is founded upon a *devastavit* or breach of trust such claim is barred by the statute; and he further submits that he is as executor a trustee within the meaning of the Trustee Act, 1888: and those representing the four daughters contend that they claim through a trustee within the meaning of section 8 of the same statute. Mrs. De Moleyns is not sought to be made liable upon foot of a *devastavit*, and the relief is limited to assets in his hands or which can be followed.

The main defence, however, is that plaintiffs elected to rely upon the security of their mortgage only, and that, knowing of the death of Richard Chute, they allowed his assets to be segregated and distributed without making any claim, even though, by the death of Richard Chute, a portion of their real security was lost; and, on behalf of Mrs. Shakoor's and Mrs. Dudgeon's trustees, the settlements executed upon their marriages are relied upon as settlements for value of their shares, and it is said that Mrs. Dudgeon's settlement of September 27, 1889, by mistake, and contrary to the agreement preceding the marriage, was limited only to her fourth share of £1297 17s. 7d., whereas it should have included her share of the £1661 10s. 9d. and of the two debentures, and that this settlement should be reformed, or treated as reformed; and on behalf, especially, of the beneficiaries, it is contended that the claim to follow the assets is equitable only, and that after the laches which has taken place, and delay in assertion of rights since 1862, it would be inequitable to allow the personal assets to be resorted to when the legatees had been allowed to regulate their modes of living, and undertake obligations in the belief that these legacies would not be resorted to, whereas the mortgaged lands would have been quite sufficient security if a sale had been enforced within a reasonable time after the testator's death.

The passages in Mr. De Moleyns' affidavit, so strongly relied upon, are contained in paragraph seven: "I say that the said Henry Leahy, and, I believe, Francis Crawford, the persons in whom, at the date of the death of the said Richard Chute, the said mortgage debt for £3109, and the securities therefor were vested, were well aware of the death of the said Richard Chute, and of the segregation and distribution of his personal estate. The said Henry Leahy and Dr. Samuel Butcher were both intimately acquainted with the said Richard Chute." And again: "I say that the said Henry Leahy and Francis Crawford were content with the sufficiency of the security of the lands for the said mortgage debt of £3109, and acquiesced in the said segregation and distribution of the residuary estate of the said Richard Chute by the said Richard Harnett and myself, and made no objection thereto, and I say that Thomas Leahy and S.H. Butcher, from the times at which they respectively became the owners of the said mortgage of the 15th December, 1855, must have been well aware that the said Richard Chute and died long previously, and that no part of the said mortgage had been paid out of the assets, and that the said residuary estate had been distributed or segregated amongst, or for the parties entitled to it, and notwithstanding such knowledge, neither the said Henry Leahy, Francis Crawford, nor the plaintiffs Thomas Leahy, nor Samuel Henry Butcher, nor any persons or person on their, or any of their behalf, until immediately before the institution of this action, ever made any claim against the residuary estate or general assets of the said Richard Chute, deceased, for payment of the said mortgage debt of £3109, or the interest thereon, nor made any application to the said William Harnett, or to me, nor were they, or any of them, ever paid by either of us, as executors, out of the said assets of the said Richard Chute, any sums for or on account of principal or interest due on the said mortgage of the 15th December, 1855, save the proportion of the interest due up to the death of the said Richard Chute."

The first material question is whether the right to go against the personsl estate is barred by the statute, inasmuch as no payment of interest was made out of it, nor any acknowledgment given by the executors in respect of it. As to this question, I am entirely in accord with the decision of the Master of the Rolls. The simple case is that a man effects a mortgage, covenants for payment, and by his will bequeaths his personal estate to legatees. The lands in the mortgage are the primary fund to pay the interest, and the mortgagee gets his interest regularly for a period within twelve years. Can it be said that devised lands and the personalty are discharged? What is the mortgagee to do? He gets his interest from the proper hand, the party liable to pay. Is he to sue the executor every year and get an acknowledgment? We are not even driven to rest on *Roddam* v. *Morley* 1 De. G. & J. 1 and *Pears* v. *Laing* L.R. 12 Eq. 52, from which, I think, this case cannot in principle be distinguished. *Dibb* v. *Walker* [1893] 2 Ch. 429 is on all fours with the present. There, on January 22, 1831, in certain indentures of transfer of mortgages then existing on an estate, Henry Walker, as owner of the equity of redemption, covenanted for payment of the mortgage debt. By a settlement, dated August 17, 1833, he settled the equity of redemption on his son's marriage, giving a life estate to the son, H. F. Walker, with remainder to the wife, Ellen Walker, for life, with divers remainders over. Henry Walker by his will, dated May 8, 1858, appointed the defendant and two others, one of whom disclaimed, and the other afterwards died, executors and trustees, and devised to them his real and personal estate upon trust for sale and conversion, and to pay his debts, and to pay the surplus to the defendant. Henry Walker died on January 19, 1860, and H. F. Walker died on November 11, 1866. The mortgages became vested in the plaintiffs by a deed of August 9, 1870, in which Ellen Walker joined and covenanted to pay the interest on the mortgages during her life. Pursuant to her covenant she paid the interest till her death in February, 1889. The estate was subsequently sold in a suit instituted by the plaintiffs as mortgagees, to enforce their security. The sale produced only £70,000, leaving a deficiency of £30,000 by reason of the fall in the value of land. To recover this deficiency the action of *Dibb* v. *Walker* [1893] 2 Ch. 429 was instituted in May, 1891, by which it was sought to have the defendant declared liable to make good the same out of the estate of Henry Walker. The defendant pleaded the Statute of Limitations. It was obvious that if the payment of interest by Ellen Walker was effectual to keep the right of action alive as against the assets of the covenantor, the statute was no bar to the action. Two points were made for the defendant; the first point was special, turning on Ellen Walker's covenant in the transfer of 1870, and need not be considered in this case. But the second point is very material, being in fact one of the points argued before us, viz. whether payment of interest by a tenant for life of the equity of redemption is not sufficient to keep the right of action alive as against the assets of the covenantor. Dealing with this question, Mr. Justice Chitty said (at p.435):– "For the defendant, it is said that payment of interest by the tenant for life of the mortgaged lands is not sufficient to keep the right of action alive against the general assets of the mortgagor debtor by virtue of the covenant in the mortgage deed. This gives rise to the question, what is the relation of such a tenant for life to the debt? Undoubtedly, the hand of the tenant for life in possession of the mortgaged lands is the proper hand to make the payment of interest. That is peculiarly the case where, as here, the covenantor settles the mortgaged lands without reserving any interest to himself except his right to have recourse to the land in the event of his being called upon to pay. It may be admitted that such a tenant for life could not be sued in an action at law by the mortgagee. But in equity it is plain that the tenant for life could be sued by the mortgagee convenantee in a foreclosure suit, and that he is liable in such an action to be deprived the rents and profits by the appointment of a receiver, if the interest be not kept down. He is liable, also, to the remainderman for default in payment of the interest, and also in such a case as the present, to the settlor, who has a right to have recourse to the estate as an indemnity against the interest of all persons liable by virtue of the indentures, whether at law or in equity, to pay the interest. Ellen Walker was primarily liable to make the payment. But this point appears to be covered by the principle of the decision in *Roddam* v. *Morley* 1 De. G. & J. 1, to the effect that such a payment sets free the action generally, and also by the case of *Forsyth* v. *Bristowe* 8 Ex. 716. There, in an assignment of the equity of redemption by the mortgagor, the assignee covenanted to pay interest on the mortgage debt: no distinction for the purpose of the statute under consideration can be drawn between a covenant for payment of interest by an assign of the entire estate in the equity of redemption and a like covenant entered into by an assign taking merely a life estate in possession in the equity of redemption. This observation applies to Ellen Walker's covenant, and I think it is immaterial whether the covenant is entered into on the assignment or by a subsequent deed by way of further security to which the representative of the convenantor is party. The additional reason given by Lord Wensleydale in delivering the judgment of the Court in *Forsyth* v. *Bristow* 8 Ex. 716 is not a mere *dictum*, but a ground of the decision itself. He lays it down that payment of interest by the assignee of the equity of redemption (which plainly includes tenant for life of the equity of redemption) is clearly payment of interest, and that the Statute 3 & 4 Will. 4, c. 42, s. 5, did not expressly require that it should be made by the party liable or his agent: and that if it implied it, the assignee of the equity of redemption who covenanted to pay is sufficiently an agent for that purpose. In regard to this doctrine of agency, it is to be observed that payment of interest by an agent is not expressly mentioned in the fifth section of the statute under consideration, but it appears to be imported from the other part of the section, which speaks of acknowledgment made in writing, by the party liable by virtue of the indenture or specialty, or his agent, and by the general tenor of the section, which treats payment of interest as an acknowledgment. In

Chinnery v. *Evans* 11 H.L. Cas 115, Lord Westbury, speaks of the large import and meaning attributed to the words 'persons by whom the same shall be payable or his agent' which occur in the 40th section of the Statute 3 & 4 Will. 4, c. 27. Many other authorities were cited at the Bar: but I think it is unnecessary to consider them, and that I may rest my decision on the second point in *Forsyth* v. *Bristow* 8 Ex 716 which has not been overruled or questioned." Accordingly the learned Judge held that the payment of interest by Ellen Walker was sufficient to keep the right of action alive against the defendant as the surviving devisee and executor of the covenantor.

Since this case was argued the case of *Stewart* v. *England* [1895] 2 Ch. 100 has been reported in the June number of the Law Reports, Chancery Division. In that case a testator, who had covenanted in a settlement made on the occasion of his son's marriage for payment of a sum of money after his death, to be held upon trusts under which his son was tenant for life and had charged the said sum with interest upon certain land, by his will devised the land, subject to the charge, to his son in fee-simple. The money was never raised, nor any interest actually paid in respect of it, but the son entered into possession of the land, and for more than twelve years received the rents and profits. In this state of facts the question arose as to whether the personal estate of the testator could be held liable to make good the sum charged in the event of the land proving insufficient to enable the trustee of the settlement to realise the same, and it was held by Mr. Justice Kekewich, that the statute was a bar to the claim against the personal estate. In that case it must be observed that no payment was made. The devisee in fee was in receipt of the rents. He owed no duty to the personal estate of which he was tenant for life. No doubt the learned Judge hazards the opinion that if the devisee in fee had *paid* the interest it would not keep the action alive as against the personalty: but there was no payment: it was a case of mere continuance of possession by the devisee in fee and there was no relation to the personalty, duty or agency.

On this question therefore I think the statute affords no protection. We start then with the assumption that no bar under the statute exists. It is settled that delay in a specialty creditor in not suing for a period less than that which creates a bar under the statute does not disentitle him to sue. As Jessel, M.R., says in *Re Baker* 20 Ch. Div. 230: "The debtor can always pay, and I cannot see how there is any negligence in the creditor in not suing, which is not greater negligence in the debtor in not paying." The same principle is to be found in *Re Birch* 27 Ch. Div. 622. There must be something more than mere delay: there must be some conduct, or act done leading to action on the part of the executor. If this were not so, Mr. Justice Chitty observes: "It would be compelling him to do that which would ordinarily be termed, if the case were inverted, a harsh course, a thing which I think ought to be avoided." How much more do these observations apply to a mortgagee who is getting his interest regularly from his mortgagor, the collateral fund being still liable, and the right to resort to it in the hypothesis kept alive! How does the executor suffer? If he lets the fund go to legatees it is his own fault. Turn now to the cases most strongly relied on by the defendants.

In *Ridgway* v. *Newstead* 2 Giff. 492; and on appeal, 3 D.F. & J. 474, the facts were as follows:- On December 8, 1838, Thomas Newstead, in consideration of a loan of £3000 mortgaged certain leasehold premises, with the buildings and machinery thereon, used as a brewery, to Joseph Ridgway, and covenanted in the usual way to pay the principal and interest at £5 per cent., thereby secured. The mortgagee predeceased the mortgagor. By his will which was proved in 1843, the mortgagor devised and bequeathed portion of his estate specifically amongst his children, giving to one son a life annuity and to one daughter a life interest in a sum of £2000, which after here decease was to go to her children, and naming two other children, his executors and residuary legatees and devisees. In 1857 the mortgagee's executors filed their bill against these two children claiming an account of what was then due on foot of the mortgage, asking that the premises comprised therein might be sold, and that if the proceeds of the sale should be insufficient to satisfy the mortgage debt, the deficiency should be made good out of the mortagor's estate. The interest on the debt had been paid to the plaintiffs down to the year 1856, by the beneficial owner of the mortgaged property. It transpired that some portions of the estate had, in the interval between the death of the mortgagor and the institution of the suit, been set apart and appropriated to meet the claims of the annuitant and the persons entitled to the £2000. It was stated that the loss arose from the deterioration of the mortgaged property since the death of the mortgagor, and the Vice-Chancellor (Sir John Stuart), offered an inquiry as to the deterioration, but the inquiry was declined by the plaintiffs. The case recognized the principle that laches cannot be imputed to a mortgagee who receives payment of his interest, but decided that a special exception in favour of the annuitant and legatees of the £2000. It turned largely upon the special character of the mortgaged property, the high rate of interest receivable, and the election of the mortgagee's representatives, to rely on their security, though they were aware of its wasting nature. Their conduct thus altered the rights and position of the legatees, and therefore it was held that, though their legal claim against the unadministered assets remained, their equitable claim against the legatees was gone, and that the latter should not be asked to refund. In my opinion two propositions may be collected from this case, (1) that the mortgagee's right against the unadministered assets always remains good in law, short of the Statute of Limitations; but (2) that if the claim against the legatees be equitable, circumstances, coupled with lapse of time, may afford a bar to the equitable relief. "Although I cannot accede," says Lord Campbell, in giving judgment 3 De G. F. & J. at p. 485, "to the general rule contended for as to the effect of mere lapse of time, all circumstances remaining the same, I am of opinion that, in the present case, there are circumstances which, coupled with lapse of time, are a bar to the equitable relief prayed. I by no means say that, generally speaking, any laches can be imputed to a mortgagee who, during any period, however long, regularly receives payment of the interest of his mortgage money, if he quietly relies upon all the remedies which the law gives in respect of the mortgaged land, and of the personal liability of the mortgagor. But, in the present case, I think that there are circumstances to take it out of the common rule so far as the equitable claim against the legatees of the mortgagor is concerned."

The case of *Blake* v. *Gale* 32 Ch. D. 571, was strongly relied upon by the added defendants. There the testator had executed a mortgage, dated August 30, 1843, by which he charged his equity of redemption in a freehold farm, in his own occupation, with a sum of £2400. He died in 1859, having, by his will, devised the farm to two of his sons upon trust for his children and issue, and directed that his unmarried daughters should be at liberty to carry on his farming business upon it, subject to a rent of £600, payable to the trustees. He gave his residuary personal estate, in the events which happened, equally among his six children, the above two sons (who were executors as well as trustees), and his four daughters. Shortly after the testator's death, the solicitors of the mortgagees made inquiry as to his affairs, and asked to whom they should apply for their interest. Thereupon the solicitor for the executors wrote a letter fully stating the condition of the assets and adding that the two unmarried daughters would probably carry on the farm for a time, and that their shares of the personal estate would afford them sufficient means to do so. This letter was acknowledged by the solicitors for the mortgagees who wrote back to say that they were very glad to hear that the unmarried daughters were able to continue at the farm with comfort as well as advantage. The two daughters carried on the farm till 1863, when on of them married, and the farm was then let by the trustees to her husband. The interest on the mortgage was paid by the unmarried daughters till 1863, and afterwards by the new tenant, who deducted it from the rent which he paid to the trustees. The interest was regularly paid till 1880, when the security which up to that time had been considered sufficient proved to be insufficient. The representative of the survivor of the mortgagees then brought an action against the executors and trustees of the testator alleging a *devastavit* by the executors in distributing the personal estate without providing for the mortgage debt, seeking to have the mortgaged property sold, and the deficiency, if any, made good by the executors personally to the extent of the personal estate distributed among the residuary legatees. Bacon, V.-C., held that the remedy for *devastavit* was barred, but made a decree for sale of the mortgaged property and for administration of the mortgagor's estate. Two of the executors being also residuary legatees, were treated as having in hand their shares of the residue, and a balance was found due from them which they paid into Court, but which was not sufficient to discharge the sum due upon the mortgage. The property included in the mortgage proved worthless, and the plaintiff thereupon commenced a new action against the other four residuary legatees, the daughters of the testator, for the amount of their shares of the residuary personal estate. The second action also came before Vice-Chancellor Bacon who dismissed it with costs. The plaintiff appealed, and in the Court of Appeal, Cotton, L.J., pointed out the remarkable nature of the case. He said (p. 577):- "It was held in the previous action that the executors were not liable as on a *devastavit* for distributing the estate before this debt was paid, on the ground that the claim for *devastavit* was barred by six years, and when that action was commenced it was more than twenty years since the distribution. But the plaintiff contends that though the personal estate had been divided more than twenty years before the commencement of this action, and though he had lost his right as against the executors, he is entitled to recover from the defendants what they received out of the residuary personal estate." Having pointed out the singular nature of the questions raised by this contention, the learned Lord Justice refers to *Ridgway* v. *Newstead* 3 D. F. & J. 474 and says, "The present case is not at all like *Ridgway* v. *Newstead* 3 D. F. & J. 474 in its circumstances; but, in my opinion, that case lays down a principle applicable to the present, viz. that as the right of the creditors to follow assets which have been distributed without providing for their debt is a right only in equity, equitable considerations, if sufficiently weighty, will make it the duty of the Court not to grant that equitable relief to which under ordinary circumstances creditors are entitled. The question here is – are the circumstances sufficient to prevent the plaintiff from obtaining relief? I do not go into the question of delay, because delay alone (as was said by Lord Campbell in *Ridgway* v. *Newstead* 3 D. F. & J. 474) is not sufficient to prevent the creditor from asserting his right. There must be, to produce that effect, changes of position in the legatees during that period, or other circumstances which would make it inequitable to allow him to do so." Lord Justice Cotton then states that he did not base his judgment on any change of position in the legatees, and proceeds to examine the circumstances of the case. He referred to and read the letters which passed between the mortgagees' solicitor and the solicitors for the executors, and he says that the last letter written by the solicitor for the mortgagees "was really an assent on the part of the mortgagees to the division contemplated, and by the letter of the executors shown to be contemplated; and it must be remembered that this division would be to some extent for the benefit of the mortgagees, because the carrying on of the farm would prevent the deterioration of their security. There was an assent to the division, but an assent to the division for the purpose, so far as necessary, of the money being expended in the cultivation of the farm. . . . In my opinion this assent to the division prevents the mortgagees from saying that the personal estate is still liable to them. It is an equitable release of the right, which they would otherwise have had, to fall back on the personal estate, if from any reason and under any circumstances their security became deficient. To allow creditors aftr such an assent to the distribution of the personal estate, to come after this lapse of time to recover the personal estate from the residuary legatees, would, in my opinion, be wrong, and contrary to what, under the circumstances, is just between the parties." And Lord Justice Bowen says (at p. 581), that for the purpose of deciding the question of the liability of the legatees, "we have to look at the delay which has taken place, coupled with the circumstances under which it has taken place, in order to see whether or not the true inference to be drawn from such delay under such circumstances is, that the party claiming the right either agreed to abandon or release his right, or else has so acted as to induce the other parties to alter their position on the reasonable faith that he has done so. If that inference is to be drawn the claim will, for the purpose of quieting possession, be treated as abandoned. . . . Each case must depend on its own circumstances. In this particular case it seems to me, that the rights of the parties are to be decided upon the ground that, as I read the facts, the mortgagees at the date of the distribution of the personal estate both knew what was going to be done in respect of the distribution and assented to it for their own interest. That amounts really to an equitable release or abandonment of their right of recourse against the personal estate, and it seems to me it would be wrong or impossible to allow a mortgagee who has consented to a distribution for his own interest in this way to come afterwards and say that notwithstanding the distribution he should be allowed to follow the assets in the hands of the legatees."

The decisions in *Ridgway* v. *Newstead* 3 D. F. & J. 474, and in *Blake* v. *Gale* 32 Ch. D. 571, turned on the special circumstances of each case; in the former the conduct of the mortgagees altered the rights and position of the legatees, in the latter the conduct of the mortgagees amounted to an equitable release of the personal estate in the hands of the legatees.

But in my opinion, there are here no such special circumstances or action or conduct. It is true a small portion of the security dropped on the death of the testator, but that was never treated as material, and as regards the legatees being permitted to acquire or retain habits of life and expenditure which would be interfered with by the establishment of a claim against the personal assets, that does not follow from any act of the plaintiffs other than not suing, while they were regularly paid by the natural fund. I do not think this can be treated as an alteration in the position of the legatees traceable to any action or inaction of the plaintiffs. Would not it have been strange if the plaintiffs had sued on the covenant while they were regularly paid their interest?

I will assume against the plaintiffs that they knew of the mortgagor's death, and that his life estate included in the security dropped. There is no evidence that the mortgagees knew of the dealing with the personal estate much less of their having assented to it and I cannot see that the mortgagees should have imputed to them a knowledge that the executor would not properly apply and administer the personalty.

As regards the point under the Trustees Act, 1888, it is plain that the legatees are not persons claiming through a trustee within the meaning of section 8. The Master of the Rolls so held, and I agree with him and his reasons.

It was probably a legitimate consequence of the decision of the Master of the Rolls to hold that the devised lands were freed from the plaintiffs' claim, because the personalty could not be followed; but it is even plainer that if the personalty is liable the devised lands are also in their proper priority liable as assets.

The case seems to me to come round to this – There is no act done or representation made by the creditors which creates an equity against them; they took their interest from the natural and proper fund; persons who were their debtors received personalty, and were not asked to pay their demand out of it till now. There is no legal bar of the statute, and the question is, are the creditors or the debtors to suffer?

I should have been well satisfied if I could have found any special circumstances which would have enabled me to apply to this case the doctrine of *Blake* v. *Gale* 32 Ch. D. 571 and *Ridgway* v. *Newstead* 3 D. F. & J. 474, but not finding such I think the plaintiffs are entitled to judgment for administration in the terms of the prayer of the amended claim.

FitzGibbon, and **Barry, L.JJ.**, concurred.

Note
See further, *Irish Land Law*, para. 10.115.

Chapter 21

NATURE AND CREATION OF POWERS OF APPOINTMENT

The courts have come to recognise that powers of appointment may take different forms and that it is not always easy to distinguish certain powers from trusts, *e.g.*, discretionary trusts (see Ch. 14, *ante*).

MOORE V. FFOLLIOT

(1887) 19 L.R. Ir. 499; 21 I.L.T.R. 21 (Chancery Division)

A testator left to his three nieces, M., E., and R., the entire of his property of every kind whatsoever during their joint and several lives, but subject to legacies, and added – "In leaving my property to my three nieces, as co-heirs, it is my wish that if my grand-nephew J.W.C. conducts himself to their satisfaction they shall leave him the property I now leave to them." J.W.C. died in the lifetime of two of the nieces, M. and E., who both died intestate.

Porter M.R.:

[After stating the manner in which the question arose before him, and the will, proceeded:–]

In considering the case, I may discard the question raised by Mr. Jackson that the power is a joint one, and, as he argued, incapable of being exercised by a surviving donee. I express no opinion upon it, and it is satisfactory that the case does not depend on so narrow a point. There is no execution – nothing which purported to be an execution – of the power by all or any of the donees, and it is not necessary to decide who might have done what nobody did in fact.

There are several classes of cases in which the question arises whether a power to appoint is a mere power, so that its non-execution defeats the objects, or whether it is to be regarded as in the nature of a trust to which this Court will give effect, even when the power is not executed.

First, an estate of inheritance, with power of appointment. If the language used in the execution of the power amounts to a precatory trust, the trust will fasten itself on the inheritance: the donee of the power will be bound to execute it, and if he fail to do so the Court will carry it into effect as if he had. This is the case of *Brown* v. *Higgs* 4 Ves. 708; 5 Ves. 495, 499; 8 Ves. 561; 18 Ves. 192 and the like. In *Brown* v. *Higgs* stress is laid on the circumstances that the testator had given the donee of the power "an interest extensive enough to enable him to discharge it."

On the other hand, if the words used indicate a mere power, and do not impose an obligation, or even amount to a request, then the Court will treat the power to appoint as mere surplusage – such a power being involved in the nature of the estate already conferred on the donee. In such a case, if the power be not exercised, the Court will of course not interfere. Thus, in *Brook* v. *Brook* 3 Sm. & Gif. 280, Vice-Chancellor Stuart said:– "A mere power is never imperative. But where the power is given with particular persons indicated who may be the objects of it, the Court has considered any words importing a direction, or desire, or recommendation, or even a wish in their favour, as imposing a duty on the donee of the power as amounting to a trust in favour of the objects." Sir John Stuart then goes on to point out that in the case before him there was no expression of a wish in favour of the objects of the power, but merely a power superadded to the fee.

In *Ahearne* v. *Ahearne* 9 L.R. Ir. 144 a testator devised a farm, with all stock, &c., share and share alike, to his son and his daughter; and, after some bequests to them, he declared that the bequest to his daughter should be for her own sole and separate use, to be held by her for her life, with a power of apportioning same amongst her children. Sir Edward Sullivan held that the power to the daughter was coupled with a trust for her children, and that she took only a life interest in a moiety of his property. After referring to the passage in Lord St. Leonard's book stating the principle established by *Brown* v. *Higgs* 4 Ves. 708; 8 Ves. 574, Sir Edward Sullivan says: "In my opinion, that is the exact case before me. The will gives the donee of the power an estate amply sufficient to discharge the trust, and plainly cuts down her interest to a life interest. He then refers to *Healy* v. *Donnery* 3 Ir. C.L.R. 213 and distinguishes it from the case before him, on the ground that only a life estate was given in the first instance to the donee of the power, the ground on which Lord St. Leonards bases the decision."

There is, however, a distinct class of cases where the donee of the power takes not more than a life estate. In these, however clear the expression of desire on the part of the donor in favour of a particular person or class of persons may be, yet, as the donee has no estate, or none beyond his life, the trust to exercise the power is as such personal, and does not directly attach upon the inheritance, save in so far as the court finds in the language an implication in favour of the objects of the power in default of appointment. In this case, if they take the estate they take it by implication, and thus by way of limitation under the instrument creating the power. In the former class of cases the Court acts by executing the power in lieu of the donee; in the latter by simply giving effect to the estate implied in the words of the deed or will.

That such an implication may arise from the language in which the power to appoint is itself couched, without anything else, is well settled; and in the case now before me it is not disputed that an implication is to be discovered in favour of James W. Chaine. The question in dispute is, what is the estate or interest to be implied, and in what event? I am of opinion that in cases where the implication is to be gathered from the words of the power to appoint, and from them alone, the estate cannot be greater than the greatest estate which the object would have taken under the power, and that no estate can be implied when the exercise of the power by the donee, if living, would have been impossible. Lord St. Leonards Vol. ii, (7th ed.), p. 167 states the rule thus:– "When the right to appoint never arises, the object of the power cannot be held to take by implication from the power."

The case of *Halfhead* v. *Shepherd*, to which he refers on this point, will be found reported in 28 L.J. (N.S.), Q.B., page 248. In that case J.H. devised all his estates, &c., to his wife for life, and ordered that after her death his brother R.H. should "part and share out or divide all and singular, &c., in such manner amongst all my children, sons and daughters, as they shall severally arrive at their ages of twenty-one years," &c. He also ordered that in case his wife should survive R.H. she should make her will, and devise said estates "amongst my children in the best and fairest manner that she can." All the children died in the lifetime of the wife, who died before R.H.; and it was held that no estate of inheritance vested in the younger children of J.H., as there was no devise to them, and as all the children had died before the power of appointment accrued. Lord Campbell said:– "In all these cases the plaintiff claims the rents on the supposition that an estate of inheritance in the lands devised had vested in both or either of the younger children of the testator. We are of opinion that no such interest did vest in them or either of them; for there was no devise to them, and all the children of the testators died before the power to appoint in their favour had accrued. At the death of the testator, his wife taking an estate for life, the reversion vested in James, the testator's son, liable to be divested if the children had survived their mother; but as they all died in the lifetime of the mother, this power to appoint never accrued, and no estate in the lands could have vested in the younger children. In *Casterton* v. *Sutherland* 9 Ves. 445 and *Morgan* v. *Surman* 1 Taunton, 289, you had an implication; for the testator had devised to his wife for life, with a power of appointment to and among her children. This power accrued immediately on the death of the testator, and in each limitation it might well be supposed that by implication the children took the remainder as tenants in common in fee, subject to be divested by the exercise of the power of appointment. But in the cases at bar there was no power of appointment till the death of the wife, and in her lifetime all the children died. The remainder in fee therefore remained in James, the son, and passed under his will; so that although the plaintiff is now the heir-at-law of the testator, he has no right to any part of the lands for which the ejectments are brought."

Now, what is the power to appoint in the present case? "In leaving my property to my three nieces as co-heirs, it is my wish that if my said grand-nephew, James

William Chaine, conducts himself to their satisfaction, they shall leave him the property I now leave to them." In my opinion this is a testamentary power only, and could not have been executed by any instrument other than a will. The word "leave," means to devise or bequeath by will, and in *Doe* v. *Thorley* 10 East. 438, it was decided that a power to leave is confined to a testamentary disposition. This rule is recognised in *Walsh* v. *Wallinger* 2 Russ. & M. 78, and numerous other cases, and is not touched by authorities such as *Grace* v. *Wilson* M.S. cited by Lord St. Leonards, vol. i. (7th ed.), p. 257; vol. i. (8th ed.), p.210, where ambiguous expressions (in that case, "*dispose* of the same to such of her children which he should leave as she should *devise* and think proper") have been held to include other modes of exercise also. And if this be the law in ordinary cases, it is more than usually clear on the face of the will before me; for the word "leave" occurs in it eleven times, including the phrase with which I am now dealing, and in each and every of the other ten there can be no doubt that the testator means devise or bequeath.

It was contended, however, for Mr. Chaine that whatever the power was in terms, it was in substance only a power to exclude, and that as no exclusion had in fact ever been made and concededly no ground for exclusion existed, James W. Chaine took a vested estate in remainder immediately on the death of the testator, liable to be divested by the exercise of the power, but never, in fact, divested; and that therefore the property is now in those who claim under him. In my opinion this contention is groundless. The frame of the gift or power is such, that to execute it strictly and in exact uniformity with the intention of the testator, a positive appointment by will would have been required, and not the negative act of exclusion. In the events which have happened, the words "if he conducts himself to their satisfaction" may be disregarded, save so far as they indicate that the donees of the power are to retain a control, and the clause would then read thus: "In leaving my property to my three nieces, as co-heirs, it is my wish that they shall leave him the property I now leave to them." This is clearly a disposition which the Court will not allow to be disappointed by the non-execution of the power. Whatever the tenants for life would have done the Court will do – not because it will itself execute the power, but because it is manifest, and the Court will imply, that the testator means the estate to go to the object, even in default of appointment. But what estate, and in what event? Plainly, the same estate and in the same event as if the power had been exercised. But it could not be exercised at all, being purely testamentary, unless the object survived the donees, and in this case he predeceased them all.

I am not aware of any case, and believe none can be found, in which the implied estate, in default of appointment, has been held to be greater than that which could have been conferred by an exercise of the power, nor in which the implication has arisen in events which would have excluded the power.

The cases relied on by Mr. Madden on this view of the case were mainly *Cruwys* v. *Colman* 9 Ves. 319; and *Robinson* v. *Smith* 6 Mad. 194.

Cruwys v. *Colman* 9 Ves. 319, when examined, will be found to be an authority the other way. It was the case of a testamentary power to bequeath to the "family" of the donee, and the Court held that, in default of appointment, the property went to the next of kin of the donee to be ascertained at her death, and not at the death of the donor. It is of course the case of a gift, by implication, to a class, and in that respect differs, as do most of the cases on this subject in the books, from the present, where the object of the power is an individual named. I do not, however, think that this circumstance affects the principle. The naming of the individual no doubt strengthens the presumption of an intention to benefit, and thus renders the implication in his favour, in default of appointment, more plain; but when, as here, the implication, undoubtedly arises, the ascertainment of the individual, however clear and definite, cannot aid us in determining what the extent of benefit is that is to be implied in his favour: and I see no solid distinction, on this point, between the present case and those of powers to appoint to a class.

In *Robinson* v. *Smith* 6 Mad. 194, the marginal note of which is succinct ("construction of a will"), the point arose on a power to executors to pay the testator's personal estate to and amongst the testator's two brothers and his sisters, or their children, in such shares and at such times as they, or the major part of them, or the survivors of them, his executors or administrators should in their discretion think proper. The Vice-Chancellor says:– "There is no doubt that the residuary legatee has an absolute discretion to exclude one, and perhaps all, the testator's brothers and sisters from any share in this property. But the words of this will gave to the three brothers and two sisters a vested interest, until divested by exclusion. This case differs nothing from an interest vested in brothers and sisters, subject to be defeated by a power of appointment in the residuary legatee. Unless the power of appointment in the one case, and the power of exclusion in the other, be exercised, the brothers and sisters would take, and the fund must in the meantime be secured."

There was the clearest estate by implication, and no question arose as to the persons to take. The word is "divide," not confined to testamentary appointment; and there could be no doubt that all the specified individuals took vested interests. But on the point before me, viz. whether one of the objects dying in the lifetime of the donee (in that case, Miss Elizabeth Smith) would take, the facts did not raise the question, and the words of the will excluded it. Nor did the point arise in *Burrough* v. *Philcox* 5 M. & Cr. 72.

In *Kennedy* v. *Kingston* 2 Jac. & W. 431, before Sir T. Plumer, the estate by implication was confined to the members of the class who would have taken under an execution of the power. The language of the learned Judge is most precise. In that case the bequest was of £500 to A for her life, and at her decease to divide it in portions, as she shall choose, to her children, and if she died before the testatrix, to be equally divided amongst her children. The learned Judge said:– "This question arises on a very short clause in a will; the sum is given to Ann Rawlins for her life, and at her decease 'to divide it in portions as she shall choose to her children.' It is first to be considered what is the import of these words taken alone, without reference to those which follow. Two of the four children died in the lifetime of the donee of the power – one before, and the other after the execution of the appointment. The question will be whether it is not to be construed as pointing out as the objects of bounty those only who should survive the mother; for the power given is to divide at her decease. Then could it be executed in favour of one who died in her lifetime? The terms 'children' is general, but as the power is to be executed at her decease, it must be for the benefit of those then capable of taking. It is, therefore, necessarily confined to children in existence at the time of her death. Therefore none but the two who have survived can take under the power; they are clearly entitled to the sums appointed to them. The difficulty is with respect to the part as to which there is, in the events that have happened, a non-execution. There is no gift over in default of appointment in express terms; but if the mother had died without making any appointment, would not the children surviving her have been entitled? Would they, though certainly objects of the testatrix's bounty, have taken nothing? Upon that question the case becomes one of that class where the objects of the power are definite, and the power is only to appoint the proportions in which they are to take, without excluding any. For here the mother must have given a share to each; she could not have made an exclusive or illusory appointment. The power, therefore, must be understood as tacitly including a provision for an equal sub-division of the fund amongst the objects, in the event of no appointment being made. The two who survived would therefore be the only persons to take; they only could take under an appointment, and if no appointment were made they would take by necessary implication."

I have therefore come to the conclusion that, in the events which have happened, J.W. Chaine could not have taken under an exercise of the power, and that therefore he took no estate by implication. Therefore there was an intestacy, and the heir-at-law of the testator is entitled.

MINUTES OF DECREE.

"THIS COURT doth declare than in the events which have happened, and on the true construction of the will of the said testator, there is an intestacy as regards his real estate, and accordingly this Court doth declare that the said Isabella Clinton, the heiress-at-law of the said testator, is entitled to such real estate, subject to the sum of, &c., together with the taxed costs of this motion.

Note

See further, *Irish Land Law*, para 11.11.

RE PARKER'S WILL

[1966] I.R. 309

The facts are set out in the judgment.

Budd J.:

In these proceedings the executors of Patrick J. Parker, deceased, seek the determination by the Court of certain questions arising on the construction of the deceased's will, dated the 31st January, 1959, and one codicil thereto, dated the 10th August, 1960. The testator died on the 13th July, 1963, and probate of his said will and codicil was granted to his executors on the 13th October, 1963.

By his said will, after making certain other provisions and bequests not material, the testator made certain provisions for his nephews and nieces and their children in the following terms:-

"Notwithstanding any direction heretofore contained in this my Will I Will Devise and Bequeath to my executors in trust my holding of Land Bonds and all the rest residue and remainder of my property and I Direct them to retain said Land bonds or to reinvest same and any other residue from time to time in such trustee securities as my executors may be advised and out of the income therefrom after paying all legal and necessary expenses to pay to my niece Miss Marie Parker the sum of £3 per week clear for ten years after my death and to divide the balance of such income amongst such of my necessitous nieces and nephews (alive at the date of my death) and such of their children as my executors in their discretion may think fit. I Direct my executors on a date of ten years from my death to realise the residue of my property including my Land Bonds and convert same into cash and to divide same in equal shares amongst all my nephews and nieces then living."

The said codicil to the testator's will contained a clause revoking the bequest to Marie Parker and is as follows:-

"Whereas by my said Will I directed my executors to pay to my niece Miss Marie Parker a sum of £3 per week clear for ten years after my death Now I Hereby Revoke the said direction and bequest in favour of my said niece Miss Marie Parker and in substitution therefor I will devise and bequeath the sum of fifty pounds to my said niece Marie Parker."

After providing for another bequest and dealing with a matter of identification, the testator confirmed his said will in all other respects.

The questions that have been raised in the Special Summons herein are as follows:-

"1 (*a*). Is the devise and bequest and direction contained in the said will in the following terms: I will devise and bequeath to my executors in trust my holding of Land Bonds and all the rest residue and remainder of my property and I direct them . . . to pay to my niece Miss Marie Parker the sum of £3 per week clear for ten years after my death and to divide the balance of such income amongst such of my necessitous nieces and nephews (alive at the date of my death) and such of their children as my executors in their discretion may think fit' as altered by the revocations by the codicil of the direction to pay as to the testator's said niece the sum of £3 a week clear for ten years after the testator's death and the substitution therefor of a legacy of £50 void for uncertainty or for any other reason and if so to what extent?

"1 (*b*). If the answer to the above is in the negative:

"(i) By what method or by what standards are the executors to decide which of the nieces or nephews of the testator and such of their children come within the class, 'necessitous'? or

"(ii) Are the executors entitled both as to person and as to amount to select from amongst the necessitous nephews and nieces of the testator and their children the persons to share in a division?

"(iii) Are the executors entitled to distribute the entire of the income from the Land Bonds and other residue amongst such of the necessitous nephews and nieces and such of their children as they at their discretion may select and if so for what period?

"2 (*a*). If the answer to 1 (*a*) above is in the affirmative or if there are no necessitous nieces or nephews of the testator is the direction and bequest contained in the will in the following terms: 'I direct my executors on a date ten years from my death to realise the residue of my property including my Land Bonds and convert same into cash and to divide the same in equal shares amongst all my nephews and nieces then living' void for uncertainty or for any other reason? or

"(*b*) Are the executors entitled to divide the proceeds of the conversion of the said Land Bonds and residue amongst the nephews and nieces of the testator living (i) at the date of death of the testator; (ii) who shall be alive at a date ten years from the date of the testator's death; (iii) or is there an intestacy as to the testator's Land Bonds and residuary estate?"

The testator's residuary estate has now been ascertained and the nephews and nieces of the testator are known to the executors. A number of their children are likewise known and since the names and addresses of the parents are known there should be no difficulty in ascertaining the others. The testator's brothers and one sister all pre-deceased him with the exception of one brother, the defendant, Joseph E. Parker.

The main matter at issue is as to whether or not the gifts in trust of income and capital contained in the will are void for uncertainty. The contention made on behalf of the defendant, Joseph E. Parker, is that the gift of income is void for uncertainty and that since the whole residuary clause should be read as one the whole gift of residue is void and falls to be dealt with as on intestacy. Alternatively, it is contended that the gift of income is void for uncertainty and that there is an intestacy in respect thereof. The basis of the contention is that the gift by way of trust to the necessitous nieces and nephews of the testator takes the form of an imperative trust and that being so the result, as a matter of law, is that the gift will be void for uncertainty unless the whole class of potential beneficiaries can be ascertained. This, it is submitted, is something which cannot be done because the class of potential beneficiaries is not stated with sufficient certainty to enable it to be determined who are the members of the class. It is not possible, it is said, in the first place to give a sufficiently precise meaning to the word "necessitous" so as to enable the trustees to know who are included in the class amongst whom the income is to be distributed. It cannot be said, for example, whether it means those who are poor in the abstract sense of the word or those who are necessitous because of their particular circumstances in life. Further, that on the wording of the will it is uncertain as to whether the class is confined to nieces and nephews who are alive and "necessitous" at the date of the testator's death or to those who are alive at the date of the testator's death *or* become necessitous at any time during the period of ten years thereafter. Moreover, it is said, it is not clear as to whether or not the intention of the testator was to benefit the children of "necessitous" nephews and nieces whether they themselves were necessitous or not.

The bequest in the testator's will in so far as income is concerned takes the form of a devise and bequest to the executors in trust of his residuary estate with a direction, after dealing with matters of retention of investments and re-investment, out of the income therefrom, after paying all legal and necessary expenses, to pay a sum of £3 per week to a niece, Miss Marie Parker, for a period of ten years after his death and to divide the balance of such income amongst such of his necessitous nieces and nephews alive at the date of his death and such of their children as his executors in their discretion may see fit. Before dealing with the legal nature of a bequest in this form there is a preliminary matter to be considered. The gift in trust to Miss Parker was revoked by the codicil but the will was thereby in all other respects confirmed. It was submitted that, since the testator must manifestly know that the elimination (by the codicil) of the weekly payment to be paid out of the income would involve the result that the balance of the income would then be such balance as remained after the payment of all legal and necessary expenses, the confirmation of the will in all other respects indicated that his true intention was that this larger balance was to be divided in the fashion indicated. I agree with this view as to the proper construction of the clause as affected by the codicil and consequently proceed to deal with the nature of the bequest in trust on that basis.

The clause I am dealing with contains a direction to the executors to divide the balance of the income of the residuary estate – in effect, the whole income, having regard to the result of the operation of the codicil – amongst the class but according to their discretion. By reason of contentions made during the hearing, a question arises as to whether the testator has by virtue of the words he has used created a discretionary power or a power in the nature of a trust. The importance of the distinction as bearing on the question of uncertainty is as stated by Mr. Justice Cross in his judgment in *Re Saxone Shoe Co., Ltd's Trust Deed* [1962] 2 All E.R. 904, at p. 910, is that "a mere power given to trustees to apply income or capital for the benefit of members of a class, all the members of which cannot be ascertained, with a trust in default of the exercise of the power, is valid, whereas an imperative trust for the division of income or capital between such members of a class as the trustees may select is invalid if the whole class of potential beneficiaries cannot be ascertained." He amplified this, at p.911, by a reference to the views of Mr. Justice Harman expressed in *In re Gestetner Settlement, Barnett* v. *Blumka* [1953] 1 Ch. 672 as to the nature of the distinction. "He" (that is, Harman J.) "pointed out that, though trustees could not release any such power given to them and were under a duty to consider from time to time whether they would exercise it, and that even if all the objects of the power were ascertainable and joined together in calling on the trustees to exercise it, they could not compel them to do so. This being the position Harman J. saw no reason why trustees before exercising a power should have to be able to survey the whole field of objects. On the other hand, he considered that if trustees had a duty to distribute the capital or income in question it was essential that they should know before they performed their duty who were the potential beneficiaries among whom they had a right of selection. This, he thought, was implicit in the judgment of Lord Tomlin in *Re Ogden, Brydon* v. *Samuel* [1933] 1 Ch. 678. This view of the position was accepted by the Court of Appeal in the *Broadway Cottages Case* [1955] 1 Ch. 20. Jenkins L.J. pointed out in that case that if the Court had itself to execute a trust of this character because of the failure of the trustees to do so, it could only execute it by way of implying a trust in default of selection among all the beneficiaries equally, and that such a trust must necessarily fail unless all the beneficiaries could be ascertained." Mr. Justice Cross himself proceeded on the basis of accepting this statement of the distinctions stated and the results flowing therefrom as correct.

From a perusal of this case and those referred to therein, I am satisfied they establish in cases of the type under review, on the one hand, that in cases where the trustees have a duty to distribute the income in question it is essential that they should know, before they perform their duty, who are the potential beneficiaries among whom they have the right of selection, and, on the other hand, in the case of a power with a gift over that there is no reason why trustees, before exercising the power, should have to be able to survey the whole field of objects. The practical result is that a mere power to apply income for the benefit of the members of a class, all of whom cannot be ascertained, with a gift over in default, is valid, and an appointment can validly be made to a person who can properly be said to be a member of the class. But an imperative trust for the division of income between such members of the class as the trustees may select is invalid unless the whole class of potential beneficiaries can be ascertained. It was not suggested, nor do I think it could be, that there is any distinction in principle between English and Irish Law on these matters.

Proceeding, then, on an acceptance of this view of the law, the first question that arises is into which of the two categories stated do the provisions of the clause in question fall – discretionary power, or power in the nature of a trust.

The distinction between trusts, mere powers and powers in the nature of a trust and the function of the Court on a failure of execution in each case is dealt with by Lord Eldon in *Brown* v. *Higgs* 8 Ves. 561, at p. 570, as follows:–

"It is perfectly clear, that, where there is a mere power of disposing, and that power is not executed, this Court cannot execute it. It is equally clear, that, wherever a trust is created, and the execution of that trust fails by the death of the trustee, or by accident, this Court will execute the trust . . . But there are not only a mere trust and a mere power, but there is also known to this Court a power, which the party, to whom it is given, is intrusted and required to execute; and with regard to that species of power the Court consider it as partaking so much of the nature and qualities of a trust, that if the person, who has that duty imposed upon him, does not discharge it, the Court will, to a certain extent, discharge the duty in his room and place."

The question then at issue, as I see it, is whether the testator gave to his executors a mere power of a purely discretionary nature to appoint the income of the fund, or is there here that mixture of trust and power of a nature that the trust is imperative while the method or mode of execution is of a discretionary nature. First of all, it is to be noted that the residuary bequest is made expressly in trust. Next, the provision with regard to the disposal of the income is directory in form. The executors are directed to divide the income against such of the class as they in their discretion may think fit. It is not a case of the executors being given a discretion to decide whether or not the income is to be divided at all and if so amongst which members of the class, but rather is it a case of a direction as part of the trust to divide amongst such of the class as the executors may think fit.

Viewing the clause as a whole, I take the view that the power given to the executors is in the nature of a trust which they are required to perform, that is to say, that it is of an imperative nature. That being so, the bequest will be invalid unless the whole class of potential beneficiaries can be ascertained. The next question, then, is whether the class as an entity can be found and, if so, can its members be fully ascertained?

The first question is, what is the class? The relevant portion of the clause is "to divide the balance of such income amongst such of my necessitous nieces and nephews (alive at the date of my death) and such of their children as my executors in their discretion may think fit." The matter to be decided is whether or not the words "amongst such of my necessitous nieces and nephews (alive at the date of my death) and such of their children as my executors in their discretion may think fit" indicate with sufficient clarity the class of potential beneficiaries, or is the description of the class so vague that it is not possible to determine who are the persons of whom the class is composed, so that the bequest is void for uncertainty?

It is contended in the first place that the word "necessitous" is itself vague and uncertain in meaning. Does it mean, for example, a person in dire need or one who is in straitened circumstances only; or is a person to be regarded as necessitous if, because of his station in life, he faces financial stress as distinct from one who is by any standards necessitous? In the event of the failure of the trustees to execute the trust, could the Court, it is asked, find the persons who fell into the category of necessitous nephews and nieces?

It is said, moreover, that in the context there are other elements of uncertainty. For example, are the potential beneficiaries nephews and nieces who are necessitous at the date of the testator's death and their children, or does the class fluctuate during the ten-year period according to whether the nephews and nieces become necessitous or affluent during the ten-year period? Again, is the class confined to necessitous nephews and nieces and such of their children as are necessitous or does it extend to all the children of necessitous nephews and nieces, whether or not some or all of such children are themselves necessitous?

There are obviously difficult problems of construction to be determined, but before considering them it is desirable to consider the principles upon which a Court approaches the problem of deciding whether or not a gift is to be held void for uncertainty. The difficulties in interpreting a disposition which is ambiguously expressed are not enough to render the disposition void for uncertainty. To be void for this reason it must be utterly impossible to put a meaning on it. I quote from Simonds' edition of Halsbury's Laws of England, vol. 39, para. 1514, which concludes with these words:– "The Court is, furthermore, reluctant to hold a gift void for uncertainty, and adopts the benevolent rule that if there is ever so little reason in favour of one construction of an ambiguous gift more than another, the adoption of construction so favoured is at least nearer the intention of the testator than that the whole disposition should be void and the persons entitled on an intestacy let in." The words of Lord Brougham, spoken in *Winter* v. *Perratt* 9 Cl. & F. 606, cited with approval by Mr. Justice Murnaghan in *Brown* v. *Gregg* [1945] I.R.

224, would seem applicable to a bequest of this kind. They are (at p.230):- "Another principle is equally clear: we ought not, without absolute necessity, to let ourselves embrace the alternative of holding a devise void for uncertainty. Where it is possible to give a meaning, we should give it, that the will of the testator may be operative; and where two or more meanings are presented for consideration, we must be well assured that there is no sort of argument in favour of one view rather than another, before we reject the whole."

In the chapter dealing with the doctrine of uncertainty in Jarman on Wills it is pointed out that "in the construction of wills the most unbounded indulgence has been shown to the ignorance, unhelpfulness and negligence of testators" and that "no degree of technical informality or of grammatical or othographical error, nor the most perplexing confusion in the collocation of words or sentences, will deter the judicial expositor from diligently entering upon the task of eliciting from the contents of the instrument the intention of its author." It is only if he is unable after every endeavour to penetrate the obscurity in which the testator has involved his intention that failure of the disposition is the consequence. It is also pointed out that in modern times, owing to the more matured state of the doctrines relating to the construction of wills and the more practised skill in applying them, instances of testamentary gifts being rendered void for uncertainty are now of less frequent occurrence than formerly. The author of the 8th edition (1951), in footnote (*d*) to page 472 of volume 1, says that it may be doubted whether the rule in favour of the heir and next-of-kin (against their being ousted unless by express words or necessary implication) has much, if any, real force at the present day. "The presumption," the note continues, "is rather the other way, namely, that when a man makes his will he does not intend to die intestate as to any part of his property."

On the issue as to the uncertainty of the bequest it was pointed out that in accordance with the principles of construction stated it would have to be found that the ascertainment of the question as to who were "necessitous" nieces and nephews was one incapable of resolution. A number of cases were cited to me as indicating that Courts had from time to time found classes of persons designated in bequests by somewhat similar or analoguos terms sufficiently ascertainable as to enable these Courts to form the view that the class of potential beneficiaries could be found with the ensuing result that the bequests were valid, and it will be useful to refer to some of these cases as helpful guides.

As far back as 1765 in a case of *Brunsden* v. *Woolredge* Amb. 507, a bequest to the testator's mother's poor relations was considered. The Master of the Rolls, Sir Thomas Sewell, took the view that the word "relation" was a vague term but that the meaning of it had been confined to those who would take under the Statute of Distributions. As to the addition of the word "poor" his opinion was that the true construction of the words was "such of my mother's relations as are poor, and proper objects." He apparently did not regard the addition of the word "poor" as making the gift uncertain. In a foot note, appearing at p. 242 of Jarman (8th ed., 1951), it is pointed out that charity was not the basis of the decision.

The case of *Gower* v. *Mainwaring* 2 Ves. Sen. 87 is one where a provision in a deed of trust was considered by which the trustees were to give the residue of the settlor's real and personal estate among his friends and relations, where they should see most necessity, and as they should think most equitable and just. Two of the trustees died and the third refused to act. The Lord Chancellor, Lord Hardwicke, considered how far the court could exercise the discretion of the trustees. In the first instance he took the view that the word "friends" was synonymous to "relations" on the basis that otherwise "it was absurd." The report is not easy to follow and there appears from the rest of the judgment to be an error in the report where in the eighth last line the word "cannot" appears where "can" is meant. In any event, it seems that the Lord Chancellor's final view of the matter, to quote what appears on p. 109, was that the remainder should be divided between two persons "according to their necessities and circumstances which the Master should inquire into, and consider, how it might be most equitably and justly divided." It emerges from the case that it was the view of the Lord Chancellor, that though it was difficult for the Court to do so, it could judge of the necessities of the benficiaries by a reference to the Master, from which I deduce that he did not consider that a trust whereby trustees were to give a residue amongst relations, where they should see most necessity, was too vague or uncertain to be carried out by the Court. If degrees of necessity amongst a class can be found, is there any reason why those in necessity, or "necessitous," cannot likewise be found?

In the more modern case of *Magee* v. *Magee* [1936] 3 All E.R. 15 it would appear implicit in the decision of the Privy Council that a trust to pay the income of residuary real estate "to such of my children from time to time as to my executors shall appear to be most in need, the payments to be at the absolute discretion of my executors," was not void for uncertainty. Lord Russell of Killowen said that, read according to their literal and natural meaning, the words used by the testator seemed free from ambiguity. The observations which I have made with reference to the case of *Gower* v. *Mainwaring* 2 Ves. Sen. 87 seem equally applicable to this case.

The case of *Mahon* v. *Savage* 1 Sch. & Lef. 111 is a case which has some bearing on the matters at issue in this case. The testator bequeathed to his executor one thousand pounds "to be distributed amongst his poor relations, or such other objects of charity as should be mentioned in his private instructions to his executor." No such instructions were in fact left. Admittedly, the bequest was stated by the Lord Chancellor to be meant as a charitable bequest. Further, the executor had a discretionary power of distribution. The Master was however directed to inquire and report who were the poor relations of the testator and did so, so that the Court must have been of opinion that the class of poor relations was susceptible of determination. Moreover, it was found that a person poor at the time of the testator's death who became affluent afterwards should not be entitled to a payment made to him unless found at the time of payment to have been a poor relation within the meaning of the will, which would *prima facie* at any rate seem to indicate that a class of poor relations may be of a fluctuating variety without that of itself creating invalidity because of uncertainty.

The Scottish case of *Mitchell's Trustees* v. *Fraser* 1915 S.C. 350 is one having some features not dissimilar from the present case.

The clause in the testator's trust disposition and settlement which came before the Court for consideration was that whereby he directed his trustees "from time to time, as they think proper, to make such special payments out of the free residue and remainder of my estate to such of my children or children's children as they may think most deserving, with special instructions to relieve any of them who may appear to be in want, provided always that they have not brought themselves into such circumstances by their own misconduct. My great desire is to assist merit and thrift, and not to acknowledge indolence or folly." One of the questions which had to be decided was whether or not the direction was void for uncertainty.

The Court of Session held that "deserving" meant deserving of pecuniary assistance and accordingly the clause committed an intelligible and workable discretion to the trustees and was not void for uncertainty. It will be observed, however, that the directions as to payments to be made out of the residue were of a two-fold nature, that is, "to such of my children or children's children as they may think most deserving, with special instructions," however, "to relieve any of them who may appear to be in want."

Dealing with what had been suggested to be "clashing criteria" in regard to the elements of merit and poverty in the selection of the beneficiaries, Lord Guthrie, having stated that he was unable to see the inconsistency, said that he read the clause thus:– "The payments to the children or children's children are to be special payments, that is to say, they are not to be made en bloc, but are to receive separate consideration. The general criterion is to be that the recipients must be 'deserving,' that is, deserving, as Lord Salvesen put it, of pecuniary assistance, and those are to be preferred who are 'most deserving of assistance,' subject, however, to the proviso that, among those who are most deserving of assistance, relief is to be given to those who are in actual want. The testator evidently contemplated payment to beneficiaries who, without being in actual poverty, might be unable to secure the education, or other advantages, proper to their station in life, such payments in short as, had he survived, he himself would naturally have made, in the shape of gifts, to his children or grandchildren. At the same time, wishing his trustees to act as he himself would have done had he survived, he ordered them specially to relieve those in want, by which language I think he had in view that they should give a preference to any who might be in actual want." From this it is clear that the trustees in order to carry out the testator's directions would have to find out the class of children or children's children in want. Since Lord Guthrie found that the clause was not void for uncertainty, it follows that he cannot have regarded a class or sub-class, described as "who may appear to be in want," as being too uncertain to be ascertained. From what he said later it is clear that he was at that stage of his judgment dealing with the trust as being non-charitable. The analogy is obvious. If those "in want" can be discovered so, I would think, can those in the very similar position of being "necessitous." I have not failed to notice that the provision as to the payments to be made were to such "of my children or children's children as they may think most deserving," thus giving a discretion to the trustees to decide that matter, but it would appear that those in want would have to be found in an abstract fashion.

Lord Salvesen in the course of his judgment said that "The word 'deserving' is, of course, open to interpretation, but I think in the collocation in which it occurs the word must be construed as meaning deserving of pecuniary assistance." Later he points out that "at any time the circumstances of the children or grandchildren might have been or may yet become such as to call for an exercise by the trustees of their discretionary powers." Further on, he says that "their duty is from year to year to consider whether there is any beneficiary in whose favour they ought to exercise the power bestowed on them." I have drawn attention to these portions of the judgment because I consider that they indicate a certain analogy to the present case. The trust was discretionary but nevertheless it would appear that before the discretion is to be exercised, a class had to be found, namely, those deserving of pecuniary assistance: after that the discretion is to be exercised. If a class of children or grandchildren can be found deserving of pecuniary assistance, is there any reason why a class of "necessitous" nephews and nieces cannot be found? Is the one any more uncertain that the other? Moreover, while there is the distinction that in the case under review the direction was to make the payments from time to time, there is no suggestion that the difficulty involved in carrying out a periodical inquiry is anything more than a difficulty to be overcome. It is not a difficulty of such an insuperable nature as to render the gift void as being of an uncertain nature.

Some other cases were referred to as indicating the very wide descriptions of classes of beneficiaries that have been found not so uncertain in meaning as to render the gift void. Cross J. in the *Saxone Shoe Co., Ltd's Trust Deed Case* [1962] 2 All E.R. 904 took the view that the word "dependant" as defined in the deed that he was construing in that case was not too vague to serve as the description of a beneficiary under a trust or of an object of a power. He was dealing with a deed of trust executed by a company with the object of establishing a fund for the benefit of its employees. The fund or the income thereof was in the discretion of the directors to be applicable to certain specified purposes, including the provision of benefits for employees or dependants. The word "dependant" was defined to mean any person "who is or was wholly dependent or in part dependent upon the earnings of an employee or former employee." He said, at p. 911:– "Even if the definition had been simply 'any person who is or was wholly in part dependent on the earnings of an employee or former employee,' I should have thought that the picture which it conjured up was sufficiently distinct to enable the trustee or the court to say whether one man was or was not 'dependent' on another." I respectfully agree. The fact is, however, that a determination of who is a dependant is often fraught with great difficulty, but that is immaterial in considering whether the description is sufficiently certain. In the case of *Brown* v. *Gregg* [1945] I.R. 224 the validity of a power given to the testator's sister to dispose of his estate in remainder amongst such of his Irish relatives as she should see fit was in question. Mr. Justice Overend had found the gift void for uncertainty on the ground that it was impossible to determine what the testator meant by the expression "Irish relatives." The Supreme Court took the view that it was not necessary for the exercise of a power of appointment that the donee of the power should be able to range in his mind every person capable of taking under the power. It was sufficient if the persons chosen came properly within the description of the class amongst which an appointment might be made. It was a case of a power of selection as distinct from an imperative trust; but it is implicit in the decision, I think, that it was at least possible to discover whether or not a particular person fell within the description which would necessitate being able to give some meaning to a word of a very indefinite nature.

It was also submitted that to be valid a trust of this nature must be one which the Court can control and execute and that by reason of the uncertainty as to its objects the Court could not execute this trust, with the result that it is invalid. The attitude of the Court towards the execution by the Court of trusts of this nature must therefore be considered. The principle is stated concisely by Jenkins L.J. in *Inland Revenue Commissioners* v. *Broadway Cottages Trust* [1955] Ch. 20, at pp. 20-30, that in order to be valid a trust must be one which the Court can control and execute. Before stating the principle in concise form he referred to Lord Eldon's statement of the principle in *Morice* v. *Bishop of Durham* [1805] 10 Ves. 522, at pp. 539, 540:– "As it is a maxim, that the execution of a trust shall be under the control of the Court, it must be of such a nature, that it can be under that control; so that the administration of it can be reviewed by the Court; or, if the trustee dies, the Court itself can execute the trust; a trust therefore, which, in case of maladministration could be reformed; and a due administration directed; and then, unless the subject and the objects can be ascertained, upon principle, familiar in other cases, it must be decided, that the Court can neither reform maladministration, nor direct a due administration." The important point, so far as this case is concerned, is that unless the objects can be ascertained upon principles familiar in other cases it must be decided that the Court can neither reform maladministration nor direct a due administration.

In *Brown* v. *Higgs* 9 Ves. 561 Lord Eldon dealt with the cases of fiduciary or imperative powers. "If," he said, "the power is a power which it is the duty of the party to execute, made his duty by the requisition of the will, put upon him as such by the testator, who has given him an interest extensive enough to enable him to discharge it, he is a trustee for the exercise of the power, and not as having a discretion whether he will exercise it, or not; and the Court adopts the principle as to trusts; and will not permit his negligence, accident, or other circumstances, to disappoint the interests of those, for whose benefit he is called upon to execute it." Further, Lloyd Kenyon M.R., in *Pierson* v. *Garnet* 2 Bro. C.C. 38, at p. 46, stated that if the trust can by any possibility be executed by the Court the non-execution by the trustee shall not prejudice the *cestui que trust*. The Court will even execute the trust retrospectively: per Turner L.J., in *Edwards* v. *Graves* 2 De G.F. & J. 210. It is stated in Lewin on Trusts (15th ed., 1950), at p. 696:- "Where the discretion of the trustee is to be governed by some rule, or to be measured by a state of facts, which the Court can inquire into as effectually as a private person, then it can look with the eyes of trustees, and will substitute its own judgment for that of the individual." Reference is made to the case of *Gower* v. *Mainwaring* 2 Ves. Sen. 87, already referred to, and the words of Lord Hardwicke are cited as in point:– "What differs it from the cases mentioned, is this, that here is a rule laid down for the trust. Wherever there is a trust or power – for this is a mixture of both – I do not know the Court can put itself in the place of those trustees to exercise that discretion. Where trustees have power to distribute generally according to their discretion without any object pointed out, or rule laid down, the Court interposes not, unless in case of a charity, which is different, the Court exercising a discretion as having the general government and regulation of charity. But here is a rule laid down. The trustees are to judge on the necessity and occasions of the family; the Court can judge of such necessity of the family. This is a judgment to be made on facts existing; so that the Court can make the judgment as well as the trustees; and, when informed by evidence of the necessity, can judge what is equitable and just on this necessity."

It would thus appear that in a case where it is incumbent on the trustees to judge the necessity and occasions of the family, the Court can likewise judge the necessity of the family, the judgment to be made on facts existing when informed by evidence. If the circumstances are such that the trustees can execute the trust, the Court will execute it on their failure to do so. The question to be determined therefore remains the same, namely, whether the circumstances are such that the trustees can execute the trust?

From this I turn to construction, applying two principles: that the gift should not be found void unless it is impossible to put a meaning on it, and that every endeavour should be made to elicit from the contents of the instrument the intentions of the testator, who, having made a will, has demonstrated that he does not intend to die intestate.

Having accepted the contention that the clause constitutes an imperative trust, I have first to decide whether or not the class of potential beneficiaries can be determined. Assuming for the moment that the purported class is that of "necessitous" nieces and nephews, without any other complications, it is said that the descriptive word "necessitous" is itself so vague in meaning that a class of "necessitous" nieces and nephews is incapable of ascertainment.

It is said in the first instance that it is impossible to say whether the testator by the use of the word "necessitous" in the context meant that the class intended to be benefited were those who were necessitous by any standard or were those who were necessitous because of their particular circumstances in life during the ten-year period.

In my view there are sufficient indications as to which of these categories of persons the testator intended to benefit. The bequest in trust is mandatory in form and there is no gift over. The testator, therefore, must be taken to have contemplated that the income of the trust fund would be distributed during the period. There is a clear intention to benefit some class, which would be frustrated if there was no distribution of the income. It follows that the testator envisaged that there would be amongst his nieces and nephews and their children during the ten-year period a class who would be eligible as the objects of his bounty. The chances of some of these persons being absolutely poverty-stricken during the ten-year period is obviously a much more remote contingency than that some of these persons would be, or become, necessitous because of their partiuclar circumstances of life during the same period. So much more remote is it that it would seem to me that the more rational construction to give to the word "necessitous" is necessitous according to the particular circumstances in life of the individual whose eligibility comes under consideration. Only thus, I think, can proper force be given to the clearly expressed intention that the income was to be distributed during the period.

While the view that I have just expressed narrows the field of selection to a class of persons who are necessitous because of their particular circumstances of life there is next to be considered whether the word "necessitous" construed in that fashion is yet so vague as to void the gift because of the difficulties of ascertaining the whole class to be benefited.

In considering whether the description of the class as "necessitous," construed as above, in so vague as to import that type of uncertainty which will void a bequest, one has to bear in mind that, as stated in Jarman on Wills (8th ed., 1951), at p.898:– "A trust in favour of a class will not fail merely because it is difficult to ascertain the members of the class." This statement finds considerable support in the case of *Re Ogden, Brydon* v. *Samuel* [1933] 1 Ch. 678. A testator bequeathed part of his residuary estate to Sir Herbert Samuel "to be by him distributed amongst such political federations or associations or bodies in the United Kingdom having as their objects or one of their objects the promotion of liberal principles in politics as he shall in his absolute discretion select and in such shares and proportions as he shall in the like discretion think fit."

Sir Herbert Samuel stated in an affidavit that he was able to ascertain all the bodies in the United Kingdom that fell within the bequest. Lord Tomlin stated, at p. 682, that, leaving out another question, all he had to consider was "whether there is such uncertainty in the field of selection that it is impossible for the selector to determine from which institutions he is to select." He continued:- "The question is one of degree in each case, whether having regard to the language of the will, and the circumstances of the case, there is such uncertainty as to justify the Court in coming to the conclusion that the gift is bad." He referred to the evidence of Sir Herbert Samuel, who had stated that he could in fact ascertain by inquiring all the bodies that could come within the description, and said that he took the view that there was certainty in the field of selection. Having found that there was a class capable of ascertainment, he added the words, "and in my view the bequest is not void on the ground that the field was too vague." It is evident that the ascertainment of bodies having as their objects or one of their objects the promotion of liberal principles in politics was something most persons would regard as an exceedingly difficult task. While not overlooking the fact that Lord Tomlin had Sir. Herbert Samuel's affidavit before him when stating that this could be done, it is, I think, implicit in the decision that the mere fact that difficulty in ascertaining the members of the class arises is not a ground for holding that a bequest to such members as may be selected by the person designated to do so is void for uncertainty. It must be impossible for the selector to determine from whom he is to select. It is also to be observed that in that case no question of a charitable bequest arose.

Is it then impossible for the executors of the testator to ascertain the members of the class amongst whom their selection is to be made? In the first place I must point out that this is a family settlement. The wider class of nieces and nephews, be they those who were alive at the time of the testator's death, or those who may be in existence during the ten-year period, are persons ascertained or ascertainable at any point of time and they constitute a comparatively small class in numbers. There is no reason to suppose that their circumstances in life cannot be discovered so that the executors, in whom the testator evidently reposes confidence, cannot exercise their good sense in deciding which amongst them are "necessitous" in the sense I have indicated. In saying this I am not oblivious of the fact that the bequest in trust in the will does not in form give a power of selection amongst such of the nephews and nieces as shall in the opinion of the executors be necessitous. That is, however, I think the practical result with the limitation that the executors as trustees must act on an opinion honestly formed. On this point the views of Jenkins L.J. in *In re Scarisbrick, Cockshott* v. *Public Trustee* [1951] Ch. 622 are very relevant. Before quoting his observations I should say that he was dealing with the question whether or not a trust in favour of such relations as "in the opinion of the survivor of " the testatrix's "son and daughters shall be in needy circumstances and . . . for such interests and in such proportions . . . as the survivor . . . shall by deed or will appoint" was a trust for the relief of poverty. His observations with regard to the qualifying words "in the opinion of the survivor . . ." were directed to a consideration as to whether their effect on the character of the trust might not be such that an appointment could be made to a person not a proper object of charity. His remarks however seem to me to be equally applicable in principle to a non-charitable bequest. He says, at p. 650:- "'Poverty' is necessarily to some extent a relative matter, a matter of opinion, and it is not to be assumed that the person made the judge of 'needy circumstances' in the present case would have acted otherwise than in accordance with an opinion fairly and honestly formed as to the circumstances, needy or otherwise, of anyone coming into consideration as a potential object of the power. Under a similar trust which did not expressly make the appointor's opinion the test of eligibility, the appointor would in practice have to make the selection according to the best of his or her opinion or judgment. The express reference to the appointor's opinion merely serves to reduce the possibility of dispute as to the eligibility or otherwise of any particular individual on the score of needy circumstances. Accordingly, I dismiss the words 'in the opinion of the survivor' as having no material bearing on the character of this trust." With this view I respectfully concur.

It must frequently arise in cases where a trust is created in favour of persons to be selected by the donee of a power out of a class that a person exercising the power of selection must first satisfy himself as to who are the persons constituting the class. He must decide who are the persons eligible to be members of the class. That is a matter on which he must form an opinion, whether or not his opinion is expressly made to be the test of eligibility under the terms of the trust instrument. It has thus no material bearing on the character of the trust, as Jenkins L.J. points out, whether the test of eligibility is expressly made dependent on the opinion of the appointor or not, because the same result must follow in practice in the case of a similar trust where the appointor's opinion is not expressly made the test of eligibility. It follows that cases decided on questions as to uncertainty on the construction of clauses in wills or trust instruments similar to the clauses in the testator's will in this case, but where the opinion of the appointor was made the test of eligibility, are in point. In this light it would appear that the cases of *Gower* v. *Mainwaring* 2 Ves. Sen. 87, *Magee* v. *Magee* [1936] 3 All E.R. 15 and *Mitchell's Trustees* v. *Fraser* 1915 S.C. 350 apply with considerable force to the present case, in that in practice the executors in this case are called upon to form an opinion as to what persons form the class from whom their selection is to be made. It then becomes a question whether the difficulties in determining the class are so different in this case to the difficulties in those cases that they fail to support the contention that the bequest in trust is valid.

The trust in the case of *Magee* v. *Magee* [1936] 3 All E.R. 15 was to pay "to such of my children from time to time as to my executors shall appear to be most in need." *In Mitchell's Trustees* v. *Fraser* 1915 S.C. 350 the direction to the trustees was "from time to time, as they think proper, to make such special payments out of the free residue and remainder of my estate to such of my children or children's children as they may think most deserving, with special instructions to relieve any of them who may appear to be in want." In *Gower* v. *Mainwaring* 2 Ves. Sen. 87 the trust was to give the residue of the settlor's real and personal estate among his friends and relations where they should see most necessity and as they should think most equitable and just.

In all these cases the trustees would have had to obtain all the necessary information as to the financial circumstances of the potential class of beneficiaries in order to enable them to exercise their discretion of selection in each case. Admittedly, it may be more difficult to find what members of a class are necessitous according to their circumstances in life than to say which, as between several persons, are in more necessity than others. However, it would seem to have been accepted in these cases that sufficient data can be collected and adjudicated upon in order to determine whether one of a class is more necessitous than another. Given that such data can and ought to be secured, it would seem to me that very similar material could be found which would enable a proper finding to be made as to which of a comparatively small number of designated persons in a family trust should properly be regarded as being necessitous according to their particular circumstances.

It may be said that the case of *Mitchell's Trustees* v. *Fraser* 1915 S.C. 350 indeed goes beyond the present case in one particular respect in that in that case a class of children or children's children who might appear in want would have to be found to enable the trust to be executed. If those in want amongst a limited class can be found, then, surely, those who are necessitous in their circumstances in life amongst a likewise limited class can also be found. The case of *Brunsden* v. *Woolredge* Amb. 507 is also very much in point in that the distribution of the residue was to be amongst the poor relations of the testator's mother which involved finding a class of poor relations. So far, therefore, I do not consider that a trust to divide amongst a class of the testator's necessitous nephews and nieces according to the discretion of his executors is so uncertain as to be void on the ground that such a class is incapable of ascertainment.

Other problems of construction however arise. Leaving aside for the moment questions on the position of children of nephews and nieces, is the nature of the trust one to divide the income of the residue amongst such nephews and nieces as are alive at the date of the testator's death and are at any time during the stipulated ten-year period "necessitous," or is the gift confined to such nephews and nieces as are both alive and "necessitous" at the time of the testator's death? It is said that here there is an ambiguity in that it is not possible to say which of two possible classes are to take and uncertainty results. This will be so unless the testator has given sufficient indication of the class which he intended to benefit. In my view two things are reasonably clear: the first is that the testator intended, in so far as nephews and nieces were concerned, to benefit only such of them as were "necessitous" and, secondly, that he intended to benefit such as were necessitous over a ten-year period. That persons' financial fortunes vary from time to time is, I think, the type of elementary knowledge that should be imported to an apparently rational and literate testator. Where two constructions of a clause in a will are open that construction should be given to the clause which will produce a rational result consistent with so much of the testator's intentions as are clear rather than to adopt such a construction as would impute an irrational and inconsistent intention to him. To confine the testator's bounty as a matter of construction to nephews and nieces not only alive, but also necessitous, at the point of time of his death, would seem entirely inconsistent with an intention to aid only those in necessity during the ten-year period, in that those necessitous at the date of death might well cease to be so later on during the period, and others, not necessitous at the date of death, might well become so later. In my view the testator, by indicating an intention to benefit those of the class of nephews and nieces that were necessitous over the ten-year period has thereby given a clear indication that he did not intend to confine the gift to such nephews and nieces, who, as well as being alive at the date of his death, were also at the same point of time necessitous. I therefore take the view than no uncertainty arises on this score.

It is next alleged that a further matter of uncertainty is introduceed by the extension of the class of beneficiaries to the children (*simpliciter*) of the necessitous nephews and nieces. Does that, it is asked, mean all children of necessitous nephews and nieces, even though they themselves be affluent, or must they, in order to qualify as members of the class of potential beneficiaries, be necessitous also? The answer is, I think, that the words used by the testator are clear and unambiguous in their ordinary meaning. There is no qualification of being necessitous applied to the children. All children of necessitous nephews and nieces qualify as members of the class amongst whom the executors must exercise their discretion of dividing the income of the residue. There is, I think, no strange anomaly necessarily involved in this in that it seems not unreasonable to suppose that the testator in all probability assumed that the children of necessitous nephews and nieces might themselves very well be in need of aid by reason of their parents' circumstances. No doubt he reposed confidence in his executors to act in a reasonable fashion in the exercise of their discretion so that an inconsistency of attitude has not to be imputed to him.

The result of the determinations I have so far made is that the potential classes of beneficiaries is, on the true construction of the clause, a fluctuating body, varying from time to time during the period of ten years from the testator's death, according as to whether any of the testator's nephews and nieces became necessitous during that period. That, it is said, again introduces an element of fatal uncertainty. How can the executors, it is asked, find who are the class of beneficiaries when it is a fluctuating one?

The fact that the class in the present case may fluctuate does undoubtedly increase the difficulty of ascertaining the class, but difficulties and impracticabilities should not be allowed to stand in the way if by any possibility the trust can be executed. Are there here to be expected so much greater difficulties than were to be encountered in the case of *Mitchell's Trustees* v. *Fraser* 1915 S.C. 350, where a class of children or children's children in want had to be found from time to time, or than in *Magee* v. *Magee* [1936] 3 All E.R. 15, where the class of children from time to time appearing to be most in need had to be found, as to render the finding of the class quite impracticable? I do not think so. The information to be collected is not so vast as to make it virtually impossible to procure it. Since a pecuniary benefit may result from supplying it, it is reasonably probable that it will be forthcoming from any member of the class who may consider that he or she or his or her child has a just claim. While the testator has not expressly stated that the distribution of income is to be made from time to time, that is something necessarily involved as distinct from any process of continuous division, because the executors must select and that can only mean that they must from time to time select who is to benefit. It is a matter of finding the necessary data from time to time instead of at one particular time. No doubt it adds to the difficulties with which the executors are faced, but the difficulty is one of a practical nature, and by no means insuperable in this case any more than it was found to be in the case of *Mitchell's Trustees* v. *Fraser* 1915 S.C. 350 where there arose a similar problem of a fluctuating class. Lord Salvesen thought that the duty of the trustees was to consider the position from year to year to see whether or not there was occasion for the exercise of their duties under the trust. That would seem a good working plan. There would, however, seem to be no reason why the executors should not operate the trust at any other convenient time according to the exigencies of the situation. That a gift is not necessarily to be held uncertain merely because the class of beneficiaries may fluctuate from time to time seems implicit in the decisions of *Mahon* v. *Savage* 1 Sch. & Lef. 111, *Magee* v. *Magee* [1936] 3 All E.R. 15 and *Mitchell's Trustees* v. *Fraser* 1915 S.C. 350. Several of the other cases I have referred to satisfy me that mere practical difficulty in the ascertainment of the class of potential beneficiaries does not of itself make a gift void for uncertainty unless it be that the difficulties are really insurmountable. There is no reason to suppose that this is so in the present case where the nieces and nephews and known and their financial circumstances can be ascertained. There is, furthermore, no reason to suppose that the executors, in whom the testator has reposed his confidence, will not exercise an honest and reasonable approach to the exercise of their discretion. They have, to borrow a phrase from *Mitchell's Trusts* v. *Fraser* 1915 S.C. 350, an intelligible and workable plan to operate.

The executors' proper method of prcedure would seem to be to find out from time to time the financial position of such nieces and nephews as were alive at the date of the testator's death and then decide which in their respective circumstances of life fall within the category of being necessitous nieces and nephews during the ten-year period. The rest of the class, namely, their respective children, follow automatically. They have then to exercise their discretion as to which of them, and in what proportions, will share the annual income. If it is unarguable that their discretion does not extend to selecting the persons to be benefited within the class and considering the manifest intention of the testator to aid those in necessity, it would be absurd to suggest that their discretion did not also extend to deciding the amount to be allotted to each of those selected to benefit.

There remain to be considered the matters arising on the questions asked in 2 (*a*) and 2 (*b*) of the special summons. I take them in reverse order for convenience. It would appear to me that the testator has, as to the residue of his property, indicated quite clearly the class of persons amongst whom it was to be divided. The division is to be made on a date ten years from his death and to be made amongst all his nephews and nieces "then living." The first part of the entire clause under construction concerned the division of income only and I see no reason for qualifying the description of the class amongst whom the division of the ultimate residue is to be made by way of reference back to the class amongst whom the income of the residue was to be divided. The class amongst whom the ultimate residue should be divided is therefore such of the testator's nephews and nieces as shall be alive on the date which is ten years from the date of the testator's death.

The first supposition on which question 2 (*a*) is posed does not arise. The question is secondly posed in the alternative on the basis, "or if there are no necessitous nephews or nieces" of the testator. I do not consider that the existence or non-existence of a class of necessitous nephews and nieces during the ten-year period can in any way affect the validity of the clearly expressed bequest in trust of the capital of the residue. The class may come into existence at any time during the ten-year period so that, incidentally, no question of acceleration arises, as was suggested was possible. It follows that there is no intestacy as to the capital of the residue and that the executors are entitled to divide that capital residue amongst the nephews and nieces of the testator alive at a date ten years from the date of the testator's death. I should add that if in fact it should turn out that there are no nephews and nieces who can be regarded as being necessitous during that period a question will arise as to who is entitled to the undistributed income, but that is a hypothetical question which should be determined if and when the necessity to determine it arises.

It was also, I should add, urged on me in this case that, if not otherwise supportable in law, this gift by way of trust could be sustained as a charitable bequest. The difficulty in so construing the bequest is, on the face of it, that it has not the necessary quality of being for the benefit of the public. There is, however, to be found in *In re Scarisbrick, Cockshott* v. *Public Trustee* [1951] 1 Ch. 622 support for the proposition that trusts for the relief of poverty, even though limited to an aggregate of individuals identified by some personal tie of relationship, may be charitable although not trusts for the benefit of the public or a section thereof. Sect. 49 of the Charities Act, 1961, would also appear to have a bearing on the matter in so far as it may be suggested that the gift in trust has in part non-charitable objects. In the view that I take of the case it is, however, unnecessary to consider this alternative argument.

The questions in the special summons will be answered in accordance with my findings.

Notes and Questions

1. This decision must now be read in the light of more recent decisions in England, *e.g.*, the decision of the House of Lords in *Re Baden's Deed Trusts* [1971] A.C. 424. Does this suggest any change in the law? See *Irish Land Law*, para 11.13.

2. What are your views on the alternative arguments (viz. a charitable trust or non-charitable trust saved by S. 49 of the 1961 Act) referred to in the penultimate paragraph of Budd J.'s judgment? See Chs. 15 and 16, *ante*.

Chapter 22

EXERCISE OF POWERS OF APPOINTMENT

The failure by the donee of a power of appointment to exercise it in the proper manner can cause all sorts of problems and the material in this chapter deals with most of the major ones.

I. DEFECTIVE EXECUTION

PENNEFATHER V. PENNEFATHER

(1873) I.R. 7 Eq. 300 (Chancery Appeal)

The facts are set out in the judgments.

Lord O'Hagan, L.C.:

This case comes before the Court by way of appeal against a decree of the learned Vice-Chancellor, which was pronounced on the 5th of November, 1872.

Some time has elapsed since it was argued before us, and I shall make my judgment more intelligible if I briefly state the circumstances out of which it has arisen.

By an Indenture of Settlement, dated the 15th of November, 1852, and executed on the marriage of William Pennefather and Kate Scott, William Pennefather granted and demised to certain trustees the lands and premises described in it, to hold for the term of 1000 years from the soleminization of the marriage, upon trust, *inter alia*, in case there should be two children of the marriage, to raise the sum of £3000 for their portions; and if there should be three or any greater number, to raise the sum of £4000 for the portions of those children. And the settlement reserved to William Pennefather a power of appointment amongst the children of those sums of £3000 and £4000, and in default of his exercising it, a similar power to Kate Scott, his intended wife, and in default of its exercise by her, then the £3000 or £4000, as the case might be, was to be divided amongst the children equally, at the times and in the manner prescribed by the deed.

There were ten children issue of the marriage – five boys and five girls. William Pennefather, who was the father of the Plaintiffs, the five sons, and of the Defendants, the five daughters, made his will on the 9th of October, 1866; but did not, as is conceded on both sides, exercise by it his power of appointment. He directed the sale of all his landed property, the produce to be divided so as to give three of his daugthers £1000 each, and the residue, after paying off all incumbrances, to go equally amongst his five sons. It is not necessary to state the bequests more fully. To that will he made a codicil, dated 26th May, 1869, on the construction of which the question in this case has been raised, as between the sons and the daughters. That codicil is in these terms: [His Lordship read the codicil.] William Pennefather made a further codicil on the 31st of May, 1869, but did not, by it, execute his power of appointment, or in any way alter or affect the character of the former codicil, so far as it dealt with the trust fund of £4000.

In this state of things, William Pennefather died on the 2nd of June, 1869.

It is conceded, that William Pennefather never executed the power of appointment by any deed or deeds, and that it remained unexecuted, save in so far as the codicil of the 26th May, 1869, unrevoked and unaltered by the subsequent codicil, may be held to have been a valid execution of it.

Mrs. Pennefather survived her husband. The children were made wards of the Court of Chancery. The lands comprised in the term of 1000 years were sold, in accordance with the directions of the will of William Pennefather, and the sum of £4000 was paid into Court. The expectations of the testator as to the produce of the sale were disappointed; and a controversy then took place as to the effect of the first codicil to his will, and its operation as an execution of the power of appointment. Under the advice of counsel, Mrs. Pennefather made a deed-poll of the 18th of June,

1872, by which she purported to execute the power as still existing. She gave £1100 to her son, William Pennefather, and £600 to each of her other four sons; and, thereupon, on application to the Court, it was ordered that a proceeding, by way of special case, should be instituted in order to obtain a decision on the effect of the codicil as an execution of the power. Under this order, two questions were submitted for the Vice-Chancellor's opinion – viz., Whether the codicil of the 26th May, 1869, to the will of William Pennefather, operated as an execution by him of the power of appointment reserved to him by the indenture of marriage settlement over the sum of £4000, raiseable under the trusts of the term of 1000 years thereby created, as and for the portions of the children of William Pennefather and his wife ? And second, who should pay the costs of the special case and of the proceedings incident thereto?

In answer to the first of these questions, the Vice-Chancellor decided that the codicil operated as an execution of his power of appointment by William Pennefather; and, to the second, that the Plaintiffs and the Defendants respectively were entitled to the costs of the incidental proceedings out of the sum of £4000. After much consideration, I have felt myself constrained to differ from the learned Judge as to his answer to one of the queries, whilst I adopt his answer to the other.

The principles which are applicable to cases such as this are well established, and no longer open to contention or cavil. In the latest of the cases to which our attention has been called, *Garth* v. *Townsend* L.R. 7 Eq. 223, "the true test" is suggested by Lord Justice James in the question – "Is there a distinct intention to execute the power?" It is always a question of intention – and of "distinct" intention. Before we can hold that a power has been executed, we must satisfy ourselves that the donee of it intended its execution, and acted distinctly for the purpose of executing it. Lord St. Leonards says (Sugd. Pow.350), "It is the intention that in these cases governs; therefore, where it can be inferred that the power was not meant to be exercised, the Court cannot consider it as executed." And Lord Thurlow put it in strong language, which has been since approved, in numerous cases, that the act which can be deemed an execution by the donee of a power must be of such a character, "that it is impossible to impute to him any other intention than that of executing the power:" *Andrews* v. *Emmot* 2 Bro. C.C. 303. I need cite no other authority to show that the question is of intention, and of intention distinct and unequivocal, which, according to Lord Tenterden *(Denn* v. *Roake* 10 Moo. 142), should be "clearly demonstrated or manifested by the will."

We have next to consider how such an intention can be so demonstrated? And this, according to the cases, may be done either by an express reference to the power, and a specific declaration of the purpose to execute it, or by a reference to the subject-matter on which the power was designed to operate, and a plain indication of design to do such acts in relation to it as can only be accomplished by the execution of the power. It is not necessary, in this second view of the matter, that there should be a recital of the power, or that the donee of it should consciously design to execute it, or even that he should be aware of the possession of it, at the moment. If he intends to convey property or arrange it in such a mode as makes the exercise of the power an essential condition of its validity and effect, the presumption will be, that he did intend to execute it. Lord Romilly states the doctrine thus in *Carver* v. *Richards* 27 Beav. 495: "It is, as I consider, the rule of this Court, that if the intention to pass the property, subject to the power, be *clearly established,* even though the intention to dispose of it under or by virtue of the power is not shown, still that equity will give effect to the disposition, and hold that the property passes under the power."

It is important to observe that in all the cases in which intention to execute the power has been presumed in the absence of specific reference to it, the intention on the part of the donee to "pass the property," or do an act with reference to it opreative under the instrument which he signs, has been clearly indicated. He must intend to make the gift which is to be validated by implication. In *Adams* v. *Adams* 1 Hare, 540, the Vice-Chancellor says:–"Where a testator in one part of his will has recited that he had given a legacy to a certain person, but it has not appeared that any such legacy was given, the Court has taken the recital às conclusive evidence of an intention to give by the will, and, fastening upon it, has given to the erroneous recital the effect of an actual gift. Where, however, the testator says that only which amounts to a declaration that he supposes the party who is referred to has an interest independent of the will, such a recital is no evidence of an intention to give by the will, such a recital is no evidence of an intention to give by the will, and cannot be treated as a gift by implication." The distinction between the two cases is obvious. In the former, the erroneous recital is evidence of an intention to give by the will, inadvertently not expressed. In the latter, as is observed by Mr. Jarman, "such recitals do not in general amount to a devise; for, as the testator evidently conceives that the person referred to possesses a title *independent of his own,* he does not intent to make an actual disposition in favour of such person." And so, I think, it will be found that, in the various cases adopting the doctrine that the execution of a power must be presumed when it is necessary to validate an act, the act has been always the act of the donee – the gift has been the gift of the donee, meant by him to have effect from himself, of his own will and by his own authority, through the instrument which he executes, and not through some other, establishing a title independent of him and not believed by him to derive force or validity from any interest or choice of his. So it was in *Andrews* v. *Emmot* 2 Bro. C.C. 303. So it was in *Innes* v. *Sayer* 3 M. & G. 606. So it was in *Hunloke* v. *Gell* 1 Russ. & M. 525, and in *Maples* v. *Brown* 2 Sim. 326. In all these cases, and many others, the want of a reference to the power involved the necessity of mention of the property which it affected, and of that property as dealt with by the owner of the power and by the instrument held to execute it. If this be absent – if the property be not so dealt with – there can be no presumption of intent that the power has operated. And, further, if there be not only such absence of presumable intention to execute, but proof that the owner meant not to execute it, the presumption becomes still more clearly impossible.

These seem to me the principles deducible from a careful consideration of the authorities; but though they are very intelligble in themselves, they are sometimes difficult of application. It is often, as was said in *Carver* v. *Richards* 27 Beav. 496, "extremely difficult to distinguish or define the limits between an intention not to execute a power, and the case of no knowledge of the existence of the power; in which case, strictly speaking, there is no intention to execute it; while, in the former, there is an intention not to execute it. The facts from which such intention and such absence of intention are to be inferred may very often run very near to each other, and possibly lead in some cases to very nice and perhaps technical distinctions." And I am not sure that, in the cases before the Court, I might not fairly borrow the words of the Vice-Chancellor in *Westcott* v. *Cullingford* 3 Hare, 269, and say that "satisfactory reasons might be stated for a decision in favour of either the Plaintiffs or the Defendants."

But, some things are manifest. There is not in the codicil with which we are dealing any reference to the power created by the settlement, or any declaration of a design to exercise that power. And, therefore, it cannot be considered to be an execution, within the principle affecting the first class of cases to which I have adverted. The question is – does it come within the principle governing the second class? Has the testator done such an act, in relation to the trust fund of £4000, as would require for its validity the execution of the power, and so demonstrated an intention to execute it? Or, having done no act in relation to that fund, and leaving it to be operated upon not by his will, but by the provisions of the settlement, which he believed, erroneously, to have put it beyond his control, has he failed to demonstrate any such intention?

It is, further, plain that the testator acted in error when the codicil was signed. He believed that his daughters were actually "entitled" to the £4000. He did not advert to the estate given to his wife, and the power vested in her after his own decease, and he assumed that, without intervention of his or hers, the trust fund was vested distributively in the children.

Making the assumption and acting upon it, he added to the bequests given by his will to his daugthers, and directed that his sons should not receive any portion of the produce of his estate until those bequests and the £4000 should have been paid off. But, *quoad* the £4000, this provision added nothing to the operation of the will, which only gave the sons the residue "after paying off all incumbrances," including that £4000, which the settlement had charged upon the estate.

Now, in this state of facts, have we any grounds to say that the action of the testator, as to the £4000, was such as to warrant the imputation of intention necessary to the Respondents' case? Did he affect to pass any property in it? Did he purport to make any gift? Did he pretend to do any sort of thing which would have needed the exercise of the power to give effect to it? It appears to me that he did not. He gave legacies to his daughters; he imposed conditions on his sons. In these things he was active – manifesting intention, and giving it force; but, as to the £4000, looking on it as vested in his daughters, he left it as he found it, exerting no volition, and shaping his course in the belief that he could not exert any. There is no indication that, by the will, he meant in the least degree to deal with the interest of his daughters in the £4000. He treats it as a thing disposed of by another instrument, irrespective of any purpose of his, and incapable of being made subservient to any. Mr. Jarman (Wills, I. 490) considers the case of a testator showing by a recital that he incorrectly supposes a third person to have title to property belonging to himself, and he says:– "Such recitals do not amount to a devise, for, as the testator evidently conceives that the person referred to possesses a title independently of any act of his own, he does not intend to make an actual disposition in favour of such person; and though it may be probable, or even apparent, that the testator is influenced in the disposition of his property by the mistake, yet there is no necessary implication that, in the event of the failure of the supposed title, he would give to the person the benefit to which it is assumed he is entitled." And he cites in support of this proposition the case of *Wright* v. *Wyvell* 2 Vent. 56, where it was held that certain expressions, erroneously implying that lands had been settled on a widow, did not amount to a devise, on the ground "that the testator did not mean to devise her anything by his will, for he mentions that she was estated in it before." And so here, the testator can scarcely be held to have intended to exercise a power in disposing of property to which he declares that his daughters are already entitled, and which he does nothing whatever to effect.

If there had been only a reference in the codicil to the £4000, and the interest of the daughters in it, as given by and under the settlement, could it have been considered an execution of the power? Could it then have been said that there was any intent to execute it? And yet that seems to me exactly what is, in substance, set forth in the codicil as it stands. The daughters are said to be "entitled" to the fund. How entitled? Only under the settlement. They had no other title. And is not the implicit reference quite as effectual as if it had been express, to negative the notion that the title, so created and so subsisting under an anterior instrument, could be and was meant to be made better or worse by the exercise of a power unnamed and unthought of?

Or, suppose there had been no reference whatever to the £4000 in the codicil, would not the effect on the daughters have been precisely the same? Would not they have taken, in addition to the several legacies of £1000 each, whatever the settlement secured to them, and nothing more?

The codicil seems to me to have been designed not to alter the disposition of the settlement, but, by reference to it, whether correct or erroneous, to guard against any presumption that the legacies were meant to stand in substitution for the £4000, but not to alter the fixed relations to, and interest in, that fund, whatever they might be.

We have been pressed by an argument, founded on the provision that the sons shall not have the produce of the sale of lands until the legacies shall have been paid to the daughters, over and above the equal distributive share of the £4000. But this ignores the condition of the will that the sons shall only take their share of that produce "after paying off all incumbrances," one of which was the trust fund in question; so that, as I have already said, the codicil made no change in that regard.

The attention of the learned Vice-Chancellor does not appear to have been called in any way to the terms of the will, which in this respect, are material for consideration. The testator only applied the general provision for the discharge of incumbrances to one of them specially, leaving it to be determined from the settlement, under which he believed the daughters to be "entitled," what was its character and effect.

I do not, therefore, see evidence of that clear intention to execute the power which governs in such cases. Whilst, on the other hand, if there be necessity for observing the distinction, it has not unfairly been urged that an intention *not* to execute it is more apparent when we find the testator – in error, it is true, but according to his own conception and belief, – alleging a title in his daughters which could really have accrued to them only by reason not of the execution, but of the non-exeuction, of the power. They were to be "entitled" under the settlement to "equal distributive shares," if that power remained unexecuted by their father and their mother: and when we find the father averring that they *are* entitled to such shares, is there ground for the inference of intent to execute it? Or is it not rather to be inferred that he did not contemplate for himself or his wife any such execution? If, as it seems to me, he dealt with the £4000 as disposed of definitively and beyond his control, by the settlement, it is not easy to reach the conclusion that the title he assumed, erroneously, to exist was helped by any execution of a power which, by its exercise, would have removd the conditions creating the very foundation of that title.

For these reasons, I am of opinion that the codicil ought not to be held an execution of the power. I do not think that any of the authorities cited to support the opposite view do really sustain it, when well-considered. In none of them has intention been presumed, under such circumstances as exist in this case to negative it, or without such proof of purpose to do an act, or make a gift necessitating such a presumption for the purpose of its validity as, in my judgment, is wanting here.

It has been argued that, though an erroneous statement of a person's rights, independently of the will, and a clear intention to do him a service, will not avail to give him those supposed rights, it is otherwise when the testator has made his arrangements relying on the correctness of his own mistaken assumption. But I do not find that, without clear indication of intention, this doctrine has ever been applied; and in *Westcott* v. *Cullingford* 3 Hare, 272, which Mr. Jarman (I. 492) cites to sustain it, I observe that Sir J. Wigram makes the matter clear, distinguishing that case from *Adams* v. *Adams,* also decided by himself, to which I have already had occasion to refer, and which had been pressed on him as warranting the refusal of the relief which was sought. "In that case," he says, "I refused relief to the widow, because I could not find any expression of intention to confer any benefit on her by the will itself." And so, in this case, although there is indication of a clear intention to bestow the legacies by the codicil, there is none of such an intention to bestow by it the £4000, although the accomplished fact of its bestowal by the settlement is asserted and connected with the bequests probably for the purpose I have already suggested.

Then we were very properly pressed by the considerable authority of *Wilson* v. *Piggott* 2 Ves. Jun. 351. But that case is clearly distinguishable upon its special circumstances, as pointed out by Lord St. Leonards (On Powers, 202). There, an erroneous recital in a settlement described the intended wife as entitled to £1000, and to another sum, "both of which would belong to her husband." "In the settlement," says Lord St. Leonards, "he (the father) declares her entitled to this sum, to which she could only be entitled by his appointment, and the husband makes a settlement in consideration of it. He could have compelled the father to execute the appointment. It is a covenant by the father." And again: "As appointments had been made to some of the other children, there was no mode in which Sarah could take a full fourth, except by an appointment, and the recital was treated as a contract with the husband that he should have the £1000, which was treated as a contract to exercise the power." I need not dwell on the manifest points of distinction between that case and this. The contract, the covenant, the consideration, the necessity of appointment – all are absent here. But, on the other hand, we have a wife who brought to her husband a substantial fortune, and, in consideration of it and of marriage, purchased the power which her husband, who was no purchaser, could not take from her but by his own previous exercise of it in favour of his children. She has exercised that power after his decease, and it has been not unreasonably urged, that we ought not lightly to declare her execution of it a nullity, or strain equitable principles, or go beyond decided cases, to deprive her of a right which she claims for the benefit of her family.

And this brings me to the last observation which I shall make. It is said that, if the codicil be not held an execution of the power, we shall defeat the testator's intention in favour of his daughters. I answer, first, that it is not enough for us to find he had a desire to serve them; w must find whether he meant to execute the power. In *Garth* v. *Townsend* L.R. 7 Eq. 221, the mother's purpose to benefit her children and her relations was expressed strongly and with minute details, but it failed of effect, because her power was left unexecuted. Next, I see no reason why we should be astute to maintain the execution by the, at the least, obscure and equivocal codicil of her father, as against the mother's distinct and unmistakeable execution by deed. And, finally, I feel some relief from anxiety as to the consequences of our decision, when I remember that, confessedly, the testator acted in error as to the operation of the settlement, and in worse error as to the state of his property, and that, in sustaining the action of his wife, warranted by accurate knowledge of the law and facts of the case, we not only, in all probability, are doing that which is practically best for his family, but that which he would himself have done, if he had lived to obtain that knowledge.

On the whole, I am of opinion, on the first question differing from the learned Vice-Chancellor and on the second agreeing with him, that the codicil was not an execution of the power, but that the costs of both parties should be borne by the trust estate.

Christian L.J.:

Although the question which this special case has invited the Court to answer is whether a power has been exercised, nevertheless, the case is quite unembarrassed by the specialties of that kind of learning. It is simply a question of construction of a few words of a codicil. If, by construction, we can educe an intent to alter existing rights, the power has been exercised. If we cannot educe that intent, the power has not been exercised. What, as matter of mere construction, is the true meaning of this passing and parenthetic reference, which, while distributing among his children property that was his own, the testator has made to other property which was theirs already, but over which he had a distributing power ? Did he make this allusion to the settled fund with the purpose of putting his will in the place of the settlement, as the distributing instrument, or rather with the purpose of excluding all idea that his will should interfere in any way with the settlement? That is the whole question, and it is purely one of construction.

It sometimes happens that the argument in favour of a particular instrument operating as an exercise of a power is aided conclusively by the nature and occasion of that instrument. A contract for valuable consideration stands in this, as in so many other particulars, on a very different footing from a merely voluntary act. For example, supposing that the clause in question, instead of being in a will, were in the recitals of a settlement on the marriage of one of the children, and the settlement had then gone on (the father being a party to it) to settle to the uses of the marriage the subject matter of the recital, there, although, literally, the recital would be but a reference to an existing right, and not an expression of intent to create a new one; nevertheless, there could be no doubt at all but that the power would be well exercised. For there the thing would speak for itself. The occasion would construe the act. The necessities of the contract, the obligation to keep faith with the parties to the marriage treaty, would make it necessary to hold that the father of the intended wife had *done* what he had the power to do, and what he in effect contracted to do. It would be simply *Wilson* v. *Piggott* 2 Ves. Jun. 351, and *Poulson* v. *Wellington* 2 P. Wms. 533, over again. But such guidance is wholly wanting when the instrument is a will. There the occasion furnishes no aid to the construction. You have nothing to go upon but the words that have been used. There is no bias in favour of the power being exercised. Rather (if anything) the other way, for the burthen of construction is on him who asserts that it has been exercised. It is for him to show that the widow's right to a survivorship of the power, and the other children's chances of a survivorship of the fund, have been taken away or diminished by the will of the husband and father. As Lord Redesdale once expressed it, *Blake* v. *Marnell* 2 B. & B. 38, n *(a)*, "When a person voluntarily executes an instrument which may have effect under a power, *he must demonstrate* that he meant to execute the power; but when a person acts for valuable consideration, he is understood in equity to engage with the person whom he deals with to make the instrument as effectual as he has power to make it."

The degree before us declares that the will operated as an execution of the power, but, strangely enough, it has not told us how. The parties interested are left to find out as best they can what rights this appointment created, and in whom. This is the more unfortunate, as the two learned counsel who appeared in support of the decree were unable for a time to agree as to those matters amongst themselves. In the leader's view, it was an appointment of the whole fund to all the ten children in equal shares; but the junior thought that it operated only to give £400 each to the five daughters, leaving the remaining £2000 unappointed. The leading counsel gave us his idea as to the exact *modus operandi* with which the will did exercise the power. It was, he said, this – it *stereotyped* (I think that was the word) that clause of the settlement which provided for a default of appointment; by which I understood him to mean that the testator took that clause, which was in itself, of course, liable to be defeated at any time by an exercise of the powers, and made it indefeasible by adopting it as his appointment. Well that does seem to be a somewhat whimsical, not to say fantastic, mode of accomplishing a very simple purpose. If the testator wished to divide the whole fund among his ten children, as one counsel thought, or half the fund among his five daughters, as his learned colleague thought, he might have said so in plain words, instead of *stereotyping* a clause in another instrument, which was meant for the case of there being no appointment at all. It scarcely prepossesses one in favour of a contention to find it needing such far-fetched support. But is there no construction which will give to this clause a signification more simple and natural?

One thing is plain. The main purpose, at all events, for which this testator proceeded to make his will was that of disposing of his own property. If it were not for this parenthesis thrown in near the end of the codicil, the conclusion would be inevitable that he had either forgotton his marriage settlement, or intended to ignore it. There is no recital of it, no recognition of the charge it had created, still less any intimation of an intention of exercising his power over that charge. He treats the estate as all his own, measures the amount of the purchase money which he expects the sale of it will bring, and then goes on to distribute the whole of that, as if it were all subject to his will. Each daughter is to have £1000 of it, and the residue is to be divided among the sons. And with the purpose merely of making it clearer that it is residue only that the sons are to have, and that the daughters' legacies are at all events to be secure, he goes on to direct (in the codicil), "that no part of the produce of the sale of my lands shall be paid to any of my sons until the said sums of £1000 each shall have been first paid to each of my said five daughters, or £5000 amongst the survivors of them," – and then there follows the first and only reference to the marriage settlement, which the will contains, being the clause which has given rise to the present question – "over and above and in addition to the equal *distributive* share of the £4000 mentioned in my marriage settlement which each of them *are* entitled to."

It is plain that if we construe that clause strictly within itself, it is no more than a reference to the existing *status quo* under the settlement, and does not aim at being constituent of a new or altered state. That is self-evident, and comment could not make it plainer. Nor was it disputed. The argument in support of the decree was that we must *not* keep within the clause itself, but must carry down into it the word "paid" from the preceding branch of the sentence, and that, thus aided, the clause amounts to a positive direction by the testator that each daugther shall be paid that share of £4000, which she would only presumptively take by way of distribution under the settlement in the event of no appointment being made. I say "each *daughter,*" for I entertain no doubt that if the clause could operate as an appointment at all, it would be according to Mr. O'Brien's view, that is to say, £400 to each daugther, leaving the remaining £2000 unappointed. But can you, in sound construction, so modify the clause? It is clear that to do so is not a grammatical requirement. Grammatically, the word "paid" is applied specifically to the five sums of £1000, part of the proceeds of the sale of the estate, and there is no pretence for carrying it on to the other subject, unless to do so be a necessity of the conjoining of the two subjects. But is there any such neccessity? Cannot these two subjects be conjoined, in the sense of being cumulative the one upon the other, without necessarily importing into the one all the attributes of the other. The one subject is the legacies given by the will, as to which it is directed that they shall be paid, and in certain priority; the other subject is, the "equal distributive shares," which the legatees "*are*" already entitled to, *dehors* the will, and which may or may not ever issue in payment at all, according as the daughters shall or shall not attain the prescribed times of payment. Why are we to import into the description of this latter subject an element which that description does not contain or require? The description has a subject-matter, which in its own unaided language it precisely and accurately fits, namely, the presumptive distributive share of each child under the non-appointment clause in the settlement. Why not allow the clause to be satisfied by that subject-matter, instead of wresting it to a purpose for which its own language is inappropriate? For the argument of the Plaintiff's counsel requires that we shall not only import a foreign term into a clause which, without it, is perfect and satisfied, but that we shall reverse the language of the clause itself. For if it were held to enure as an exercise of the power, then the daughters' shares, instead of being "distributive," would be taken out of distribution, and instead of being interests which they "*are*" entitled to, would be interests which they would be, by the will, for the first time, made to be entitled to. The thing which is to be "over and above and in addition to" the legacies, instead of being, as the clause describes it, an existing right, in shares distributive, is turned into a new-made right, in shares no longer distributive; so that, to use the clause in the way that counsel seek to do, it must be subjected to a double violence – interpolation and rejection – both alike uncalled for and arbitrary.

If no motive could be assigned for the clause save that exercising the power, there would, of course be, so far, a reason for allowing it so to operate. But its presence can be accounted for in a way much more accordant with the general tenor of the will. To pass over the settlement altogether in silence would be sure to give rise to questions which would scarcely fail to issue in litigation. One of them was referred to by Mr. McDermott – satisfaction, upon the equitable doctrine of presuming against double portions. The other would be, election. It will be seen at a glance that if the will had been without this clause, it would contain all the elements for raising, if not a case of actual satisfaction of the portions by the legacies, at all events, a case of election between them. For, until we come to this clause, we find that the testator has been, both in will and codicil, treating the family estate as at his absolute disposal, and making testamentary distribution of the whole proceeds of the intended sale. But we know that the settled fund consisted in a charge upon the same estate, and would therefore come into collision with the will; so that you have at once the inconsistency which would put the children to their election between the settlement and the will. It is true that in the early part of the will he refers to incumbrances: "the residue of the proceeds of the sale of the property, after paying off all incumbrances," which would *primâ facie* include the settled £4000. But these "incumbrances" are afterwards, in the codicil, referred to as "the mortgages," and upon the tenor of both instruments the argument would be strong, if not invincible, that by "incumbances" he meant outside incumbrances; whilst as to so much of the proceeds of the sale as would be available for his own family, he intended that that should be distributed and governed exclusively by his will. Thus you would have distinctly raised, first, a question of actual satisfaction of the portions by the legacies; secondly, failing that, then one of election between them. But the addition of the clause under construction at once puts an end to both those questions, for it contains the testator's explicit declaration that the legacies he is giving to his daughters shall not interfere with their settled portions, but shall leave those simply as they were.

Having, then, a clause couched in language simple and unambiguous, which has a subject to which that language, taken in its own ordinary and natural signification, is most germane and appropriate, and for which, confining it to that subject, a motive and a purpose substantial and sufficient are assignable; why are we, in construing this voluntary instrument, to depart from an interpretation which combines in it all those advantages, for the sake of adopting one which cannot be approached without doing violence to the language? Why are we to force construction in order to take away from the widow that check upon her infant daughters which the survivorship to her of the power under the settlement would afford, and from the sons the chance of being bettered in their condition which the same power would supply?

To test the argument further, let us look a little more closely into the consequences to which it would lead. If the words "shall have been paid" can be carried down so as to be applied not only to the legacies of £1000 each, but to the "distributive share of the £4000" also, the whole sentence will then run so that no part of the produce of the sale of the lands can be paid to any of the sons until not only the £1000 legacies, but the distributive shares of the £4000 also, shall have been paid to the daughters. Now, when was that to be? The will is itself wholly silent as to the times of payment of the distributive shares; it merely refers to the settlement. Now, the effect of that was, according to the argument, to adopt for an appointment by will the non-appointment clause in the settlement. It is to the latter clause therefore that we must look for the times of payment of the shares. Well, when we do so, what we find is this: The shares are not to be paid until after the death of the survivor of the husband and wife. Now, the widow might survive her husband for so many years as that the sons might have passed middle age before the day of her death arrived. Thus, they might be kept absolutely penniless for the best part of their lives. By the settlement (adopted into the will) they could not claim a farthing of the £4000 during their mother's lifetime, at least, without her consent, and by the coupling together the two subjects in the way the Plaintiff's counsel contend for, they would be prevented from claiming a farthing of their father's legacies either, until after the same period.

I do not myself appreciate a difficulty which seems to have been felt below, namely, that confining this clause to its own natural signification of saving existing rights, not creating new ones, would enable the widow, by means of the power thus preserved to her, to convert equality of portions into inequality. To put it in that way is really to beg the question. The very object of such powers in settlements is to enable that very thing to be done. It was in the highest degree desirable that the surviving mother should retain over her five young daughters, made partially independent of her, as they were, by their father's legacies, that amount of control which the survivorship of the power over the other fund would confer; and it should not be presumed that her husband intended to deprive her of it, unless, to borrow Lord Redesdale's language, he has demonstrated that he meant to do so. Nor is the word "equal" in the least opposed to this. It is merely part of the description of the existing *status quo* – "equal distributive shares" which they *are* entitled to. Equality in all conditions is a characteristic of shares, so long as they remain merely distributive – equal in amount, presumptively, but equal also in their common liability to be increased or diminished by an exercise of the power.

Upon the whole, I am of opinion that this testator has not evinced any intention, either by consciously exercising the power, or in any way, to alter the condition of the subject fund. On the contrary, I think he *has* most distinctly conveyed it to be his will that the gifts he was making out of his own estate should be without prejudice to the settlement.

The Vice-Chancellor's declaration must therefore be discharged and a declaration in the contrary sense substituted. The costs of the special case at both sides, both below and here, will come out of the special fund.

Note

See further, *Irish land Law*, para. 11.15.

MOFFETT V. LORD GOUGH
(1878) 1 L.R.Ir. 331 (Court of Appeal)

The facts are set out in the judgments.

Sullivan, M.R.;

The Plaintiff has filed his bill to obtain the aid of this Court, as against Lord Gough, to make good a lease of the 12th July, 1851, executed by a tenant for life under a leasing power, alleging a mere formal defect in the execution of the power, and praying that Lord Gough, the remainderman, should be decreed specifically to perform the terms of the lease as a contract binding upon him. The case which the Rev. Mr. Moffett presents is as follows:– He sets out the will of Benjamin Bunbury, dated the 10th September, 1820, and proved on the 20th November, 1823. Under it the fee of the three denominations of land included in the lease of 1851, viz., Clonken, Cordevin and Trillickatemple, became limited to Thomas Bunbury for life, with remainder to his first and other sons successively in tail male, remainder to Kane Bunbury for life, with remainder to his first and other sons successively in tail male, remainder to Sir Hugh Gough (under whom the Defendant Lord Gough claims) in fee. The will conferred a leasing power on the tenant for life for the time being, in the following terms:–

"I do hereby declare that it shall and may be lawful for each and every of the several persons to whose use the several estates, lands, hereditaments and premises is or are limited as aforesaid, when they shall respectively be in the seisin and possession thereof by virtue of the limitations in this my will contained, to make any lease or leases of all or any part thereof for the term of one, two, or three lives, provided such demise or demises be made by indenture to be duly signed and sealed and delivered in presence of and attested by two or more credible subscribing witnesses, in possession, and not in reversion, or by way of future interest, and so as by every such lease there be reserved and made payable during the term to be thereby granted a fair improved yearly rent for the premises to be therein comprised, without taking any fine or premium for or in respect of the making thereof; and that in every such lease there by contained the usual clauses of entry in default of payment of the rent to be thereby reserved, and that such leases shall not be made dispunishable of waste, and that the lessees therein to be respectively named shall execute counterparts thereof."

In 1851 Kane Bunbury was tenant for life in possession under the will, and had that power vested in him. It appears that of the three denominations of land comprised in the lease of 1851, two, viz., Clonkeen and Cordevin, containing together 168A. 3R. 11P., had been leased by the testator Benjamin Bunbury to a Rev. Robert Moffett, grandfather of the Plaintiff, on the 10th November, 1787, for three lives, at the yearly rent of £138 14*s*. (Irish), and in that lease there was contained a covenant that the lessee, his heirs, executors, administrators and assigns, would during the demise preserve, uphold, support, maintain and keep the demised premises, and all improvements made and to be made thereon, in good and sufficient order, repair and condition; and at the end or other sooner determination of the demise would so leave and yield up the same to Benjamin Bunbury, his heirs and assigns. The lands of Trillickatemple (the third denomination in the lease of 1851), containing 106A. 1R. 0P. together with 39A. 1R. 21P. of bog, had been leased on the 27th July, 1795, by the same Benjamin Bunbury to the same Rev. Robert Moffett, also for three lives, at a rent of £132 16*s*. (Irish), with a covenant substantially the same as that I have already read from the lease of 1787. Jane Moffett, one of the lives named in each of these leases, having survived the other lives named therein respectively, was still living on the 12th July, 1851. There is no evidence in the cause that she is even yet dead; but it was stated at the bar that she died in the year 1863. The lease of 1851 from Kane Bunbury (which the Plaintiff obtained under very peculiar circumstances indeed) demises the three denominations of land comprised in the two old leases for three new lives, one of them being that of the Prince of Wales, and another that of a boy then about thirteen years old. It reserves a rent of £262 10*s*. of the present currency, which, allowing for the difference of Irish currency, is precisely equivalent to the total of the two previous rents fixed in 1787 and 1795, with a sum equal to the tithe rentcharge which the tenant under the old leases was bound to pay. This lease of 1851 purports to be a lease in possession, and is made without any reference to the leasing power, and not in consideration of the surrender of the existing leases. On reading this lease, one is at once struck by the fact that the lands are demised for three lives, of which two were very young, at a rent which is no more than that reserved out of the same lands at the close of the last century. This seems to have struck the present Plaintiff and his advisers, because, by way of accounting for that somewhat startling fact, they put forward the case that the lands had been allowed to become reduced to a wasted and desperate condition when the new lease was made. For this condition of the lands be it observed that, even on the Plaintiff's own evidence, he was himself, to say nothing of his tenants, to a considerable extent directly answerable. This is apparent on reading the 6th and 11th paragraphs of the Plaintiff's affidaviat, filed the 14th February, 1876. The Plaintiff in his bill states his title to get the lease of 1851 in such a way as to avoid the obvious point which arises upon it as an exercise of the power, viz., that it was a lease in reversion, and not in possession, unless the old leases were in fact or in law surrendered. He says that on the 12th July, 1851, he was the owner of the two old leases, and he alleges his title in these words (par. 4 of bill):–

> "The said Rev. Robert Moffett [that is, the lessee in the old leases] died about the year 1819, and his son Andrew Moffett thereupon became entitled to the lessee's interest in the said two leases. The said Andrew Moffett, the Plaintiff's father, afterwards died in the year 1819, and thereupon the Plaintiff became entitled to the lessee's interest in the two said leases."

It is quite plain upon that averment that he is claiming as heir-at-law of his father and grandfather; he mentions no will or other document of title; he asserts a title accruing and consequent upon death, and therefore the natural conclusion suggested – if it were true – is that the lease of 1851, though made without any formal surrender of the other two, was a good lease in possession, the Plaintiff being at the time of its execution entitled to the interest then subsisting under the old leases. If that were true, the point as to the lease being one in possession, and not in reversion, would have a safe and sure foundation.

The lease of 1851 was attested by only one witness, and the Plaintiff states on the face of his bill that that is the only defect, and it being purely formal he comes into equity to have the lease fastened on the remainderman. He suggests that everything else was right and proper, and that therefore he is entitled at the hands of this Court to have the prayer of his bill carried out.

Kane Bunbury having died in November, 1874, and the title in possesion of the Defendant having then accrued, who refused to recognise the lease of 1851, Lord Gough answered the bill, and at once took issue with the Plaintiff upon the case he set out in his bill, and the answer submits that "the Plaintiff has not shown any title by descent, occupancy, devise, conveyance or otherwise, to the lands demised by the said leases, or either of them;" he denies that the rent reserved by the lease of 1851 was a "fair improved rent," and he submits that the fact that the lands were then reduced in condition demonstrates that the rent could not having been "a fair improved rent." He further asserts that the lease of 1851 was a fraud upon the leasing power. On that answer the Plaintiff took a course which it is right to advert to. He filed a replication and proceeded to hear the cause upon replication, which had the effect that he was able to adduce his evidence without Lord Gough, the Defendant, having had the slightest opportunity of meeting or answering any new allegation which the Plaintiff might put forward or introduce therein.

I need scarcely say that when a cause under the old system was heard on replication, each party addressed himself to the issues knit by adducing evidence which his adversary could not see or be informed of till after the time allowed for giving such evidence had closed. Lord Gough's advisers evidently taking the Plaintiff's averment of his title as I have stated it, and having plainly discovered by reason of the will of the Plaintiff's father, made in the year 1819 (to which I shall again advert), having devised the lands comprised in the old leases to his son John, that the Plaintiff's statement in his bill was not correct, actually examined the Plaintiff by taking his deposition on the 10th of February, 1876, in which he had to admit that his brother John had only attained his age of twenty-one in the year 1841, and that he had no reason to believe that he was dead. Now a few days after making that deposition, the Plaintiff filed his affidavit in support of the bill, and then for the first time, behind the back of his adversary, went into an entirely new and remarkable case, utterly at variance with the title he had stated in his bill. In this affidavit, he alleged that on the 31st August 1808, the Rev. Robert Moffett, the original lessee, had made a settlement upon his son Andrew for life, of the lands of Clonkeen and Cordevin, with remainder to his first and other sons in tail male. The Plaintiff then says that Andrew's father died in January, 1819, and that Andrew the Plaintiff's father became entitled to Clonkeen and Cordevin for life; that Andrew died in December, 1819; and that then the Plaintiff became entitled as remainderman to the lands of Clonkeen and Cordevin; that Robert the original lessee, being seised of the lands of Trillickatemple, devised them by his will of 1817 to his son Andrew; that Andrew made a will in 1819, and purported to dispose of the lands of Clonkeen, Cordevin "and other premises therein mentioned" (a designedly vague statement of the will, as will afterwards appear), but that the will was inoperative as to the settled lands, and was not acted on, but an arrangement was entered into by which the rights of himself and the several members of his family were amicably adjusted, and under which they obtained equal shares of his father's personal property, he himself getting Clonkeen, Cordevin and Trillickatemple. He says that this arrangement was acted on, and that about 1836 he went into possession of those lands and paid the rent therefor, and has since continued in possession of the same.

Evidence was gone into on the part of the Plaintiff and Defendant as to the rent reserved in the lease of 1851, and a good deal of the Defendant's evidence went strongly to show that, even apart from the condition of the lands as brought about by the Plaintiff and his undertenants, the rent reserved in the lease of 1851 was not a fair improved rent. In that state the cause came before the Lord Chancellor for hearing, and he pronounced the decree of the 7th of March, 1878, from which this appeal has been brought. By that decree an issue is directed to be tried by a jury of the county of Longford, where the lands are situated, as to whether the rent reserved in the lease of 1851 was at that date the fair improved yearly rent. It is plain, on reading the judgment of the Lord Chancellor, that in directing this issue he decided all the other points in controversy against the Defendant. We are all of opinion that the decree so made cannot stand, and that upon the evidence adduced in this cause the Plaintiff's bill ought to have been dismissed. I think that, entirely apart from the question of the amount of rent reserved in the lease of 1851, and even before that point is reached in the consideration of the case, there are ample grounds for holding that the lease of 1851 was, in truth, a positive fraud upon the leasing power. In the view I take of this case it will be unnecessary to discuss the question of the rent; but I must observe that it appears to me that there were materials, even on that point, for coming to a safe conclusion within the Court of Chancery itself, without having that question tried upon an issue before a jury. I will say no more as to the direction of that issue, save this, that the Defendant, Lord Gough, would, in my opinion, go heavily weighted to the trial of that issue.

I now proceed to state the reasons which have induced me to think that, altogether outside the question of rent, the Plaintiff's bill must be dismissed from this Court. When one reads the statements of the Plaintiff's title set out in his bill, and the statements in reference to the same matter set out in his affidavit made by way of evidence, the first thing which strikes one is, that the very curious matters alleged in the affidavit are not merely suppressed from the bill, but are at variance with the title therein stated; but what is still more remarkable is the fact that the peculiar title sought to be made out on this affidavit was suppressed from Kane Bunbury and his solicitor when the lease of 1851 was obtained; for on that occasion, when on the part of Kane Bunbury it was insisted on that the lease about to be then made should be a lease in possession, and that the old leases should be surrendered, the Plaintiff distinctly represented that there was no necessity for such surrender, as he was then entitled to the lessee's interest therein, as the heir-at-law of his father and grandfather. That, in my opinion, was a positive misrepresentation made in obtaining the lease of 1851, for it was on the faith of that most incorrect statement that Kane Bunbury and his advisers were induced to act, and to dispense with a valid surrender of the old leases by a person competent to make it. It was of essential moment in relation to the exercise of the leasing power that the tenant for life, who was about to execute it in favour of the Plaintiff, Mr. Moffett, should see that, when no actual surrender of the old leases was to be executed, the estate therein was vested in the person to whom the new lease was to be made, so as to effect a surrender in law, so that Kane Bunbury, or at any rate those in remainder, should not be put to the inconvenience and embarrassment of having two leases existing on the estate, one in possession and the other in reversion, the latter being a positive violation of the terms of the power. The misrepresentation of the Plaintiff on this material point does not rest upon oral evidence only. Letters are produced which show that the tenant for life insisted that the lease should be substantially one in possession, and the Plaintiff is found getting over the necessity of executing a surrender by representing that he was heir-at-law of his father and grandfather, and therefore in a position to surrender the old leases by accepting the new one. Now – when the title that he avers for the first time in his affidavit which I have read, and which the Defendant had not the smallest opportunity of meeting or answering, comes to be examined – it first appears that there is no evidence at all of a settlement having been executed. Upon the Lord Chancellor's decree it appears that what purported to be a copy of that settlement was admitted in evidence; and, having regard to the fact that there was no proof whatever of an original settlement, or of proper search made for the same, or any proof of the copy, I think the Lord Chancellor's attention cannot have been directed to the circumstance that he was admitting *a copy* of an alleged settlement, upon the following passage found in the Plaintiff's affidavit:–

> "I beg to refer to an ancient copy of the said indenture which I now produce and mark 'A,' and which I believe to be a genuine copy thereof. I never had the original thereof in my possession. I do not know where it is, and I believe that the same is lost. I have diligently searched for the said settlement, but could not find it."

We think that there is no evidence whatever of the contents of the alleged settlement adduced by such a statement, unless we are prepared to hold that any copy which an interested party throws down as a copy is to be treated as a true copy of an original settlement alleged by such party. There is no evidence as to where this copy came from, how it was made, or where it was got, or that it was ever acted on, there being all this time not the smallest proof of the original deed. But it was said that the memorial of the settlement was evidence of it; unfortunately even if the memorial was properly in evidence, there is no statement in it of any of the trusts or limitations affecting the lands. The memorial was not, however, receivable in evidence, and the proposition put forward at the bar that a memorial of an ancient deed, signed by the grantee, when produced from the Registry Office is evidence without more of the original deed – and for which proposition *Biggs* v. *Sadlier* 10 Ir. Eq. R. 522; 4 Cl. & Fin. 435 was cited – cannot be maintained for one moment. The proper limits within which such a memorial can be admitted in evidence will be seen in the judgments in that case. It will be found that the Chief Baron prefaced his judgment (p.532) there with these words:–

> "The principal question in this case arises upon the evidence tendered by the Plaintiff as secondary proof of the articles of the 5th of January, 1746, for which ineffectual searches appeared to have been made in the quarters in which they would be reasonably expected to be found."

Lord St. Leonards in his judgment lays down the same rule; he says (p.460):–

> "I certainly am of opinion – and I think the authorities will not impeach that opinion – that the memeorial is good secondary evidence of the contents of the deed of 1746, it being proved upon search that the deed has actually been lost."

This settlement then being out of the case, see how the title stands. The grandfather of the present Plaintiff, whose will is entirely suppressed from the bill, and from the tenant for life in 1851, devised the property in these terms:–

"I devise and bequeath to my son Andrew Moffett, his heirs and assigns, my lease of the lands of Trillick . . . and all the rest, residue and remainder of all my property, real and personal, I give, devise, and bequeath to the said Morgan Crofton and John Robinson, their heirs, executors, administrators and assigns, upon trust to pay three parts of the interest, profits and produce thereof to my grandchildren Jemima, Catherine, Jane, Robert, and Samuel Richardson, equally to be divided between them on their attaining their several ages of twenty-one years [with gifts over between them in certain cases.] And my further will is that the remaining fourth part of the said remainder and residue of all my property shall be equally divided between all the children of my son Andrew Moffett [as therein mentioned]."

If there was no settlement, that residuary gift embraced the lands of Clonkeen and Cordevin, and passed then as to three-fourths to the testator's grandchildren, the Richardsons, and as to one-fourth to the children then living of his son Andrew, the devisee of Trillick. Andrew came to make his own will soon after, and he devises to his son John the lands of Clonkeen, Cordevin, and Trillick, and to the present Plaintiff other lands called "Park Place, Liskett, and Aughentemple." That will ignores the alleged settlement; even if it existed, as alleged, a serious question suggests itself, whether a case of election did not arise. But, be that as it may – settlement or no settlement – the lands of Trillick under those wills were the undoubted property of John – a positive and startling fact, directly opposed to the misrepresentation of title made by the Plaintiff, as well when he got the lease of 1851 as in his bill in this cause. The extraordinary statement of the Plaintiff as to some family settlement by which John's rights to these lands were given over to the Plaintiff, made for the first time in his affidavit, under peculiar and most suspicious circumstances, rests on the Plaintiff's loose and uncorroborated averment. At the time this arrangement is supposed to have been entered into, John, as is now proved, was a boy of fifteen years of age; there is not even an assertion that after he came of age he ever did anything to confirm or even sanction such an arrangement. It is not even alleged that he ever was made aware of his rights, nor is it shown what he got for abandoning his property; the Plaintiff's statement that this boy got a share of his father's personalty, which may have been anything at all, cannot have the slightest weight. The Plaintiff says that John would readily have assented to the lease of 1851; if so, he might as well have told the landlord all about this supposed family arrangement, in which case John's readiness to surrender the old leases in favour of the Plaintiff would have been put to the test. In truth, there was a positive suppression from the tenant for life of all the material facts connected with the title; and I cannot conceive a stronger case of misrepresentation than that which the Plaintiff was guilty of in 1851, to induce the then tenant for life to exercise his power.

It has been contended that, as the Plaintiff has been in undisturbed possession under the lease of 1851 since its execution, this Court must, therefore, assume that John's rights were legitimately dealt with; that would be a very convenient doctrine for persons who enter on a minor's estate with the view of making it their own. Is it to be forgotten that the Plaintiff, when he took possession of John's estate during his minority, was nothing but John's bailiff, and that it is quite consistent with all that has been averred, that John was kept in entire ignorance of his rights, and that he, or those claiming under him, may have this moment, in this Court, ample grounds for making the Plaintiff answerable for all his past possession? Indeed there appears to me no reason why John, if he had known his rights, might not have brought an ejectment, at all events for Trillick, within twenty years after he came of age.

I think that the Plaintiff has failed to show any title to get the lease of 1851, and that that lease was obtained by misrepresentation, and I think that this Court ought never to aid such a transaction. The lease of 1851 was clearly a lease in reversion, and not one in possession, and was in plain violation of and a fraud upon the power.

It clearly follows from what I have said, that the Acts of Parliament (12 & 13 Vict. c. 26 and 13 & 14 Vict. c. 17) cannot be relied on as aiding the defective execution of the power; those Acts themselves at once present an answer to the argument put forward, for they are only intended to aid defects where the leases have been *bonâ fide* executed by tenants for life; and in my opinion it would be a total subversion of language to hold that this lease of 1851 was *bonâ fide* executed. It is not necessary to go into the question of the extent of authority which this Court, has under those statutes, to aid the defective execution of powers. Speaking for myself, I believe the construction of these Acts must be very much controlled by the words of the preamble of the first one.

We all agree, as I have said, that the decree must be reversed, and that the bill must be dismissed, and we think that such dismissal must be with costs.

Christian, L.J.:

The bill in this case is based exclusively on the statute 12 & 13 Vict. c. 26. It treats the indenture of the 12th of July, 1851, as being, notwithstanding the defect in the attestation, a good contract in equity under that statute for a lease under the power; and its sole prayer is for the specific performance of that equitable contract. Now I agree with the Lord Chancellor that this case does not fall within that statute, but not for the reasons assigned by his Lordship. His construction of the words in the second section – in case the lessee named in the lease shall "have entered thereunder" – is, I think, too narrow. I cannot doubt that the lessee's continuance in possession after the accepting of a new lease on the giving up of an old one, was tantamount to an entry under a new lease. My own reasons for excluding the statute are, first, that the lease was not made *bonâ fide,* and, secondly, that one at all events of the points of substance in which the invalid lease departed from the terms of the power is now incapable of being supplied.

The Lord Chancellor remarked very truly that in several respects it is difficult to say what is the meaning of this section. It certainly is, and in none is the difficulty greater than in the two particulars I have just indicated. Luckily for himself, the view the Lord Chancellor was able to take of the little point about the lessee entering relieved him from the necessity of forming an opinion on the graver difficulties of the case. I am less fortunate. What is *bona fides* in the making of a lease under this statute? If the donee of the power knowingly, and, if knowingly, wilfully, ignores the two most substantial of the safeguards provided by the donor for the protection of the remainderman – viz., that the lease shall not be in reversion and that the rent shall be fair and improved – can that lease be said to have been made *bonâ fide?* I venture to think not. Again, the statute says that the lessee shall be entitled to a valid lease under power, to the like effect as the invalid lease, "save so far as any variation may be necessary in order to comply with the terms of such power." What is the force of these latter words? Can any lease be within the statute if there be a defect in substance which is incapable of being made good by the variation? Again I think not. Well, one of the defects in this case was of that character. We could not now by any variation to be introduced into the new lease purge the lease of 1851 from the fault of having been a lease in reversion. Its status in that particular was defined once for all at the time of its execution. The insufficiency of the rent you might cure by a variation; but the other defect is indelible. On that ground alone, if there were no more, I should be prepared to hold that this lease derives no aid from the sttatute. But more – I am also of opinion that this lease was so palpable a sacrificing of the interests of the remainderman to those of the tenant and of the lessor that it is idle to claim for it the character of *bona fides* which is the primary condition of the statute. For these reasons, I think with the Lord Chancellor, that the Plaintiff can derive no aid from the statute 12 & 13 Vict. c.26, and that his case must be sustained, if at all, on the old equitable doctrines of relieving purchasers against formal defects in the execution of powers.

Although, as I have said, the statute exclusively is made the groundwork of this bill, I am not going to hold the Plaintiff so strictly to his pleadings as to exclude him from the other equities; but his position in invoking that jurisdiction is in one important particular the same as it would be prior to the statute. He is asking for the special extraordinary interposition of the Court in his favour, to set up and make valid for him a title which as against the remainderman is legally null and void. The Defendant resists this relief on the grounds that, besides the formal defect of the attestation – which is what gives him his advantage at law, but is certainly relievable in equity – neither of the two substantial safeguards of the remainderman was complied with; for the lease was a lease in reversion instead of being one in possession, and the rent reserved was conspicuously the reverse of being either "fair" or "improved". With respect to the first of these two objections to substance, it is undoubtedly true that unless the whole remaining interest under the two old leases of 1787 and 1795 was at the time of the making of the lease of 1851 vested in the Plaintiff, that objection is sustained; and it is equally true that the burden of proof here lay only on the Plaintiff. Whether he has successfully sustained that burden was the question mainly argued at the bar. It has been now fully discussed by the Master of the Rolls; and I concur in his view of it – that it is alone sufficient to decide the case. Nevertheless I prefer myself to rest my whole decision on the other objection; and for this reason that I feel sure of the facts. As regards the title to the old leases, the success of the Defendant is rather a negative than a positive one. It is plain that we have not all the facts before us; but looking even at what we have, there are forty-two years of unbroken possession of this farm by the Plaintiff, and thirty-seven of these since his brother John came of age; and observe, the whole of these thirty-seven years must be counted, because if John had in him at the time of the lease of 1851 the legal estate in the old existing lease, the new lease of 1851 would have been a graft upon the old one for his benefit, and he would have been entitled to that as well as to the old lease. Therefore his title – if title he had – would stand good during those thirty-seven years. Well, of these thirty-seven years from the time of his coming of age, ten had elapsed before the making of the lease of 1851. It does appear difficult not to feel a certain misgiving that in some way or other, either before or at the time of making the lease of 1851, the whole interest under the old leases had, in truth and substance, if not in technical legality, passed into and become the porperty of the Plaintiff. But still the proof is incomplete, and it is of course on the party on whom lay the burden of proof that the consequences of that incompleteness must fall. Therefore I concur in the Master of the Rolls' view; still it is at the utmost but a case of "not proven."

I turn willingly to the other objection, where I find myself upon firmer ground. Before discussing the facts, I will refer to a case containing a very instructive reading by a very great authority, as to the duty which a tenant for life exercising leasing powers owes to the remainderman – I mean the case of *Harnett* v. *Yeilding* 2 Sch. & Lef. 549. In that case the defendant, the tenant for life, made a lease to the plaintiff for a term of twenty-one years. There was contained in it a covenant by the lessor "for and during the term of his life to renew the said lease for the said D.Harnett, his executors, administrators and assigns, by giving unto him or them a lease for twenty-one years of the said demised premises, when applied to by him or them so to do." The lease contained a clause of surrender. The tenant, thinking the rent too high, availed himself of the clause of surrender and put an end to that lease. The parties immediately came to a new agreement which was worded in these terms:– "I promise and agree" the tenant for life says,– "to perfect a fresh lease to Mr. Daniel Harnett at any time he shall demand the same, at £5 a-year less than the within-mentioned rent." This was indorsed on the old lease. The tenant went back into possession. He remained in possession under the original lease until within a very short period of its expiration, and then called for a renewal on the terms of that instrument which I have just read; and the landlord refusing to grant the renewal, the tenant filed his bill to enforce it – the defendant being, observe, not the remainderman, but the tenant for life himself, who had made the lease, and the plaintiff seeking first for a renewal in the terms of the power so as to be binding on the remainderman, and seeking further, if he could not get that, at all events what the tenant for life had power to give him, namely, a lease for twenty-one years if the tenant for life should so long live. Well, the Court refused to give him either the one relief or the other – not even the relief of a lease for twenty-one years if the tenant for life should so long live – because it held that the lease was, under the circumstances under which it was executed – and which I shall mention presently from the judgment – a fraud upon the power; and that being such, the Court would not make it the groundwork of any decree whatever, even as against the tenant for life himself. The first question in the case was whether the agreement was not too uncertain to be performed at all, on the ground that it was not clear whether it was an agreement for one lease for twenty-one years, or an agreement for a lease for twenty-one years with a renewal for a fresh term of twenty-one years afterwards. Lord Redesdale, after discussing that question, came to consider how the case would be upon the assumption that it was sufficiently certain that it was to be a lease for a double term, namely twenty-one years in possession and a right of renewal for a further term when called for; and here is what he says, at page 558 of the report:–

> "Then there is in this case another consideration which appears to me to be a ground for refusing performance of this agreement; and that is, that this is evidently, on the face of the instrument, a contract by a person having a limited interest, with a leasing power, to act in fraud of that power. It is a contract to execute a lease for twenty-one years, and a further lease for twenty-one years at any time during his life; consequently to execute a lease for twenty-one years, whatever may be the increased value of the property at the time of the lease granted."

In other words, it was a contract which would deprive the person, whoever he might be, who should be in possession at the time when the renewal lease was called for – and he might be the remainderman, though it did not happen to be so in that case – of the advantage of a presumptive rise of rents in the interval. That is the ground on which Lord Redesdale holds it to be a fraud on the power, because of its tendency to deprive the remainderman, if he be the person, or the reversioner at the time, of the benefit of the presumptive rise of rents in the interval between the making of the original lease and the time when the renewal is called for. How infinitely stronger does that apply to a case where it is a renewal, at the old rent reserved some fifty or sixty years ago, of a very old existing lease, still existing for one life, that is sought for; so that the remainderman, when his time should come, would not only be deprived of the presumptive rise of rent from the date when the renewal is being executed down to the death of the old existing life, but also of an infinitely greater rise of rent, counting from the time of the original lease some half-century before down to the time of the expiration of the last life? Therefore this case is far stronger in its circumstances than that which was there considered as constituting a fraud on the power. Then Lord Redesdale goes on:–

> "I think Courts of Equity should never enforce such contracts, whether with a view to the party himself or to the person entitled in remainder. In the first place, it is unconscionable in the tenant for life to execute such a lease, because it brings an incumbrance on the estate of the remainderman, and puts him to litigation to get rid of it; and as to the tenant for life himself, it is compelling him to do what is to be the foundation of a future action for damages, if he dies before the twenty-one years. The Court will never do this, but will leave the party at once to bring his action for damages. And I also conceive that this sort of contract, obtained by a person who knew at the time the nature of the title, is unconscionable in him, as he makes himself a party knowingly to that which is a fraud on the remainderman; and under such circumstances he has no claim to the assistance of a Court of Equity."

So we may say here to this gentleman:– "Make the best of your case with a jury; bring an action against the personal representative of your lessor, Colonel Kane Bunbury; if you do so you will be certain to have a more sympathetic jury than Lord Gough would have if he were so ill-advised as even to bring such an issue to a trial."

Bearing in mind these principles, and turning to the case before us, the requirement of the power in it as regards rent is, that there be reserved and payable during the term "a fair improved yearly rent," without taking any fine or premium for or in respect of the making thereof. "Fairness" must be understood relatively to all the interests involved – those of the remainderman as well as those of the tenant for life and of his lessee. "Improvement," in the case of lands which were let on lease at a rent at the time of the creation of the power, and where the new lease is being made to the old tenant, can hardly have any other meaning than "increase." The same or even a lesser rent, if reserved from a new or more solvent tenant, might well be an "improved rent." But to renew an old lease to the same tenant at the old rent, and to make the doing so serve the purpose of procuring the payment by the lessee of arrears otherwise of doubtful solvency, does seem from the point of view of the remainderman to respond to the requirements neither of "fairness" nor of "improvement."

Turning to the facts of the case, the first thing that it startles one to find is, that the fair improved rent reserved by the lease of 1851 is identically the same rent, reduced to English currency, at which the same lands had been demised for terms then unexpired of sixty-four years as to one denomination, and of fifty-six as to the other, before the date of the new lease. Let me here correct a mistake into which the Lord Chancellor fell in his judgment. He speaks of the new lease of 1851 as having been made at an increase in the rent of £12 a-year. The gross total of the rents in the old leases was £271, of the then currency. But at that time, as we all know, the tenant paid the tithes. When the new lease was made in 1851 the £217, reduced to the currency of the day, would be only £250; but adding the tithe-rentcharge, which in the meantime had been thrown on the landlord, the amount is brought up to the exact rent reserved, namely, £262 odd. So that it is the common case of both parties that the rent reserved in the lease of 1851 is the exact equivalent – in figures I mean – of the rent reserved in the two old leases of 1787 and 1795, *plus* the tithe. Well, this ancient and expiring rent – for it was then, that is in 1851, depending on one life, necessarily an extremely old one – the new lease professed to resuscitate and fasten on the inheritance for three new lives; one, that of the lessee himself; another, that of a boy of thirteen; and the third, that of the Prince of Wales, then a boy of ten; in other words, according to the ordinary duration of human life, some fifty or sixty years. If we had been furnished with information to enable us to make a comparison between the purchasing power of £271 10*s*. Irish, *plus* the tithe, in 1787 and 1795, and its numerical equivalent of £262 3*s*. 10*d*. English in 1851, we should be in a better position for estimating the truth of the assertion which, startling as it seems, is an essential of the Plaintiff's case – that the latter was an improvement upon the former; that is to say, a better thing for the remainderman. I should be curious to know what sum would in 1851, or at the present day, most nearly correspond with what £271 was in 1795. But even without such precise information I think we may fairly infer, from what we know historically of the main current of progress in these matters, that it would be something vastly above £262 sterling of the money of the present day. The Solicitor-General said that we were to look not at the general value of money, but at its value in relation to the particular commmodity – land. With great respect, that would be entirely misleading. It is in the light of its value as the general purchasing medium of the kingdom that we must regard it. The number of pounds sterling which at given periods can be got as rent will vary inversely with the purchasing power of the pounds sterling at those periods, that is, with the quantities of the neccesaries and luxuries of life that would be given in exchange for them. If the number of pounds sterling in 1787 and 1795 would have produced double the quantity of those things that it would in 1851, then it follows that there ought to have been £2 reserved in 1851 for every £1 that was reserved at the older dates. We all know how the falling in of old leases has been looked forward to by proprietors as what would often raise the man of straitened means to a position of wealth, and the man of wealth to that of a millionaire – as is witnessed by what has happened in the cases of some of the great English families, the Grosvenors and the Russells. It is really self-evident that, except under some extraordinary and exceptional casualty, a renewal made in 1851 under a limited leasing power, at the same rent as was reserved in 1787, must stand condemned on the face of it as one of monstrous undervalue. And observe, this is not a case of the kind dealt with in the English authorities, or a case of reforming a lease, such as those to which Lord Eldon's language, relied on by the Lord Chancellor, in the *Queensberry Leases Case* 1 Bligh, 339, applies; it is not a case of that kind. It is the renewal to a middleman for a lengthened term of a most valuable interest outstanding to the prejudice of the inheritance – so valuable that, as the Plaintiff himself tells us, it has been dealt with as the fit subject of marriage settlement and of elaborate family arrangements. The Lord Chancellor seems to have viewed this point of rent precisely as if in 1851 there had been no existing lease, and the question was simply what rent could the lands, if then in hand, be reasonably expected to bring, under the circumstances of that time. And assuming, as he must have done, that this, which would undoubtedly be a question purely of fact, was the turning-point of the case, he, as the decree expresses it, "being desirous of ascertaining the truth," dismissed the task of ascertaining it from himself in Chamber to the more discriminating analysis of a county of Longford jury. With the utmost possible deference, I dissent both from the Lord Chancellor's mode of disposing of the question, and from his choice of the tribunal for "ascertaining the truth." There are elements in this case which the Court alone posseses competency to deal with, and which we should be merely escaping from if we allowed the case to go to a jury. If we had the finding of a jury tomorrow in the Plaintiff's favour upon the issue directed by this decree, the question would be still unanswered – Could the Plaintiff have the relief he claims by this bill? Were the circumstances under which this power was professed to be exercised such as to make it equitable, just, and according to the spirit and policy of the power, to make valid this invalid lease against the remainderman who is a stranger to it? What were the circumstances? Five years before, a terrible calamity had fallen upon, I will not say the land, but the masses of pauper tenantry whose existence upon the land had been the insuperable barrier to all agricultural progress and improvement, and the immediate consequences of which not only entailed suffering to the afflicted masses, but the ruinous depression of all selling and letting values. It needed, however, but a very scanty measure of prescience to be able to foresee that the evil was but temporary, and that prices and rents must ere long regain their buoyancy, for that the visitation under which all were passing was in reality a sure, if sharp, remedy for some of the worst influences that had hung over the Irish soil. Before 1851 the tide had turned – a reaction was already imminent. This was the moment selected for the new letting of the 12th of July, 1851. What were the interests of the several parties to be affected? The land was under an existing lease at a rent calculated on the value of money as it was nearly half a century before. That lease must continue at that rent for one surviving life unless it was surrendered by the lessee. Colonel Kane Bunbury, the then tenant for life of the reversion, could not himself have been a very young man; and he was named the devisee in a will made thirty-one years before. What his age then was we do not know. But running his life against that of the *cestui que vie* under the old existing lease, it may fairly enough be inferred that personally he was not likely to lose very much by granting a renewal at the existing rent, which, under any circumstances, in all probability would last during his own time, and he had no sons to succeed him. His presumptive successor was a collateral descendant, not even of his own name, and about whose interests he would probably be not too solicitous. One personal interest he undoubtedly had, namely, to procure payment of arrears of two years' rents his tenant then owed him, and the payment of which the Plaintiff himself tells us was made the express condition of the granting of this renewal. That was the lessor's position. As to the lessee, his interest in getting a renewal at the ancient rent of some half century old is a thing that needs no dwelling on. These were the two parties to the dealing. The one had little or nothing to lose by it, but, on the contrary, a loss to be saved, while the other had an immense advantage to gain. But how about the absent remainderman for whose interest alone this leasing power had its existence? I answer – it was simply sacrificed: for what was done was, out of the fact that in a crisis like that of 1846 to 1851, under the terror of which no one could be found to offer more than the nominal sum that had been reserved half a century earlier, a pretext was made for stereotyping the panic – for that is what it comes to. What was that but to exercise this power in a way which, even if it would not induce a Court of Equity to set aside as a fraud a lease that had been duly consummated according to all the forms, ought certainly to be held sufficient, as Lord Redesdale says in *Harnett* v. *Yielding* 2 Sch. & Lef. 549, to prevent the Court from lending its extraordinary aid to enforce against the remainderman what is no legal exercise of the power at all? This lease is void at law against the Defendant. What the Court is now asked to do is, by an extraordinary effort of its extraordinary jurisdiction, to compel him to validate it, and by so doing to stamp upon the inheritance against himself and his successors, for a generation or two from its date, the panic-bred depression of an unparalleled, but still temporary, emergency, and to do this under colour of a power, the essential term in the exercise of which was, that a fair and improved rent should be reserved. The rents reserved in 1787 and 1795 were to be still in 1851 regarded as "fair" and "improved," and thus projected onwards well into the twentieth century.

Now let me test one extreme case by another which is hardly more extreme. In place of a devastating famine, let me put a devastating war. Suppose the country had been in the occupation of a hostile army, and that districts had been devastated, houses burned down and lands ravaged to a condition in which nothing could be given, and no one would offer anything, for the ground – would it be a fair exercise of such a limited leasing power, suppose, for the tenant for life to take advantage of the existing state of circumstances – obviously but a temporary one, which sooner or later when peace must come to an end – and make a lease to some speculator at a rent of 5*s*. or 10*s*. an acre, – would that be a fair exercise of the power, and would the Court of Chancery afterwards interpose to compel the remainderman, when better times came and when the land had again become valuable, to execute a lease at a nominal rent? Well, I suppose nobody would contend for that; and in truth there is no difference between the cases. The very specialities to which the Plaintiff appeals are in reality destructive in his case. In proof of his *primâ facie* amazing assertion, that the same figures represented in 1851 a better rent that they did in 1787 and 1795, he refers first to the bad and exhausted condition of the land, that is to say, to his own breach of the covenant in the lease to keep it in good order; and secondly to the famine, that is to say, the very thing for which he made the abuse and perversion of his power. This tenant for life, with no prejudice to himself as regards the rent of the future, and with large benefit to himself as regards the arrears of the past, sacrifices to this reverend gentleman, his tenant, the interests of all his successors, for whose benefit as well as his own he had been entrusted with the power. The answer charges that this was a "fraudulent" exercise of the power. Well, as we are dealing with the case of a reverend Plaintiff, we may as well drop that ugly word, but I cannot designate it more mildly than by calling it a mis-use of the power, so gross as to amount to a flagrant abuse of it. Common fairness, and the expressed intentions of the testator, demanded that until the storm had blown over and the country recovered itself, the *status quo* should be maintained and the power held in abeyance. If care had been taken to comply with the formalities of the power, the Plaintiff would have had a legal estate *primâ facie,* and the Defendant must have taken the initiative either by bringing an ejectment or by filing a bill in Equity to set aside the lease as a fraud. But as matters are, it is the tenant who has had to take the initiative and to come before a Court of Equity asking it to pronounce that the contract embodied in this document of the 12th of July, 1851, is in accordance with the spirit and policy of the power, and so well-timed, and just and equitable towards all in the line of succession, that the Court will interpose its extraordinary authority to enforce it, and legally validate it by a decree.

That is the question which confronts us at the threshold of this case, and I ask what light a jury could throw on it? The Judge at the trial would listen to no equities. He would say, and properly say– "The Lord Chancellor must have decided all that in the Plaintiff's favour before he directed this issue; you and I, gentlemen, have nothing to do but to inquire whether the rent is a fair and improved rent according to the standard of the time when it was made, that is to say, the famine years." Is that a true standard by which to rule this case ? Most certainly not; for the very circumstances which supplied that standard, and which alone would make such a verdict possible – exceptional, transitory and fugitive as they were because of the terrible depression of the moment which was but the harbinger of better times than ever came – were precisely the circumstances which gave to the lease of 1851, viewed as an exercise of the power under M. Bunbury's will, its true character of mere perversion and abuse. Therefore assuming, as I have done throughout, that at the date of this lease no better rent could have been got for the farm than that which is reserved in the lease, I hold to the opinion that this bill must be dismissed with costs.

Well, there is yet a view of this decree by which I must confess I am a good deal embarrassed, and which I do not feel ought to be passed over altogether in silence, because the feature which it presents is from a general point of view by much the most important which appears in the case. Supposing I could agree with the Lord Chancellor that the whole controversy was reducible to the one question on which he directed an inquiry, still I should be obliged to differ from him entirely in the selection he has made of the forum to which to refer that inquiry. The decree is somewhat curiously framed – "The Court being desirous of ascertaining the truth by the verdict of a jury, and being of opinion that the question in controversy may be more conveniently and properly tried in the county where the lands are situate" – and then follows the direction of the issue. Well, that is a somewhat peculiar preamble. I do not myself remember to have seen one like it before. It would almost seem as if his Lordship had some little misgiving lest, perchance, it might be imagined that the course he was taking tended rather in an opposite direction to that in which he hastens to say he was desirous of proceeding. I confess I should myself have thought that if further inquiry on this point were desirable, the Lord Chancellor himself in chamber, with the powers he now possesses of seeing and hearing witnesses examined, and examined *vivâ voce,* and, if he pleases, of himself conversing with them, would under the circumstances of this case be an infinitely more promising extractor of the truth than a jury, and most of all, a jury of "the county where the lands are situate." No doubt the issue is in its terms of a very plain and naked one: "Whether the rent of £262 3*s.* 10*d.* reserved by the lease of the 12th day of July, 1851, was at the date thereof the fair improved yearly rent for the lands by the said lease demised, without fine or premium in respect of the making thereof?" A very simple inquiry. Could any tribunal apparently be more suited to enter on such an inquiry than a jury of farmers – and let us say, of gentlemen-farmers, as it appears that the jury is to be one of the kind at present called "special jurors" – could any tribunal be more fitted for the investigation of a question of the kind? I answer certainly not, if one could only be sure that they would confine themselves to the terms of the issue, and to the evidence properly and legitimately, bearing on the issue. But is there no danger that extraneous topics might be managed to be got into the jury-box? Just look at the repertory which would be at the disposal of some eloquent inflamer of the north-west Bar! Three generations of a respectable tenant family, in undisturbed possession of the farm for now close on a century, at an unaltered rent, and under these a body of occupiers, the old landlord family never thinking of disturbing them – on the contrary, the last of these landlords granting a renewal at the old rent, which would have prolonged for another generation or two the ancient and kindly union of tenant and landlord; but suddenly there comes a change. The old landlord family dies out, and a stranger takes its place; and who is that stranger? An artistocrat, a great lord, whose first step is to serve a peremptory, almost offensive, notice on the old clergyman tenant of the last three generations, saying:–"Sir, your lease is void as against me, and I require you forthwith to give up possession of the land." Tenant-right in its most attractive form – landlord oppression at its worst! Well, all this would of course be entirely irrelevant to the issue. The strongest Judge that ever presided at a trial would be unable to keep it out of the jury-box; and there are some Judges who probably would not deem it at all their duty to try to do so. The jury themselves, or some of them, would be pretty sure to be ardent sympathisers.

Now, I ask, why should the Court go out of its way to expose the claims of property to be baffled by more rhetoric practised upon interested prejudices? It is to no purpose to quote cases in England on leases before the late reforms in the Chancery procedure. Those cases were sent to juries, not because of the superior merits of a jury trial, but because in no other way could at that time a *vivâ voce* examination and cross-examination of the witnesses be obtained. The jury was a necessary evil. But now that *vivâ voce* examination before the Judge himself is established as a normal part of the procedure of Courts of Equity, why should rights of property of a kind which class antagonisms are sure to gather round to be consigned to the rude lottery of the jury-box? Look at what has been happening in England ever since the Judicature Act passed. Suitors obtained thereby the option of originating their cases in any Division of Law or Equity that they preferred ; and what has been the consequence? Why, a steady current has set in from the Law side to the Chancery side of cases formerly triable only at Law; and it has so set in by reason of the anxiety of those suitors who thought that they had good cases to have a trial by a single cultivated practised intelligence. Those who distrust their cases still prefer the Common Law Divisions for the sake of the chances of jury trials.

Again let us look at home. Let us for a moment eschew conventionalities and speak what everyone knows to be the truth, though not what everyone would like to avow. To send certain questions to a jury in England may mean something very different indeed from sending them to a jury in Ireland. The average English juror is a prosaic sort of person, unimaginative, unexcitable, docile to the evidence, and amenable to the advice and guidance of the Judge. His Irish counterpart will be a man of another temper; and, not to push invidious distinctions too far, suffice it to say, that in certain classes of cases which need not be particularized, but of which those of an agrarian order are undoubtedly an example, he is – to put it mildly – prone to be a little unreliable. Nor does he now represent at all the same grade of society, or the same order of education and intelligence, as he did in the days when the late Master of the Rolls, Mr. Smith, made an order in some case in which the Lord Chancellor tells us he was counsel, sending an inquiry of this kind to a jury of the county of Carlow. It is not the course of criminal justice only which has been paralyzed by tampering with the jury-box: the course of civil justice has been also enfeebled, and the ordinary rights of property and powers to dispose of the ownership of it shaken and made insecure. Looking back over the last few years, surveying the action of the tribunals, and seeing what verdicts have been given, and, still more, what have not been given in some remarkable cases, civil as well as criminal, I profess myself unable to understand how any Court which can choose, and which has at its own command all the best resources and methods of investigation, can imagine that the surest way of ascertaining the truth, or indeed of ascertaining anything, is to bundle off an inquiry to one of our popularized Irish juries.

It may be said that this is not a matter for the Court of Appeal – that if it were right to direct an inquiry at all, the form of it must be left to the discretion of the primary Judge. I answer that it is in this particular case no matter of form at all, but a matter of the gravest substance; for I not only look upon this issue as one in which, as the Master of the Rolls has just expressed it, Lord Gough would have to go to trial "heavily weighted," but I regard the directing of it as being simply an indirect mode of deciding this case against Lord Gough. It would be far better for Lord Gough to put him out of pain at once by ordering him to reform this lease, and to pay the costs of the suit. No one would ever advise him to take this case down to trial; and if he did, it needs no gift of prophecy to be able to predict the result. There would be either a verdict against him or the jury would disagree. And so they might disagree if it were tried again and again; and the inevitable result of all, after a more or less protracted litigation, would be either total defeat, or – worse far – the forced abandonment and compromise of an undoubted right in pure despair of being ever able to bring the case to any definite end at all. That is the course held out by the issue which has been directed in this case. But it is needless to dwell further on it, because, as I have already stated, I am of opinion that this issue ought never to have been directed at all. I hold it to be wholly beside the case – to be wholly indecisive of the case. If we had a finding upon it in the Plaintiff's favour tomorrow, it would place him in no better position than he is in without it; and so on the common principles of the Court, his bill must be dismissed with costs; and I fear that, according to the rule now established in all the Courts of Appeal both in this country and England, to the costs of the dismiss must be added the costs of this appeal.

Deasy, L.J. concurred.

Note
See further *Irish Land Law*, para. 11.17.

II. EXCESSIVE EXECUTION

RE ENEVER'S TRUSTS

[1912] 1 I.R. 511 (Chancery Division)

The facts are set out in the judgment.

Ross, J.:

By an indenture of 4th June, 1872, which was a deed executed on the occasion of a separation between William Power and his wife, Cleopatra Power, it was declared that all property acquired during the joint lives of the husband and wife should be enjoyed by the wife for life, and that on her death it should go among the children of the marriage as she should by her will appoint. There were three children of the marriage, Susan Amelia, who died in 1884, intestate and unmarried; Frederick Joseph Power; and John Power. Certain property came to Cleopatra Power, which is to be disposed of under the terms of the deed of 1872.

The said Cleopatra Power was subsequently divorced from the said William Power, and lived with a man called Samuel Bennett, by whom she had one child, James Samuel Bennett. She afterwards married Augustus Enever. She made her will on 24th December, 1883, and bequeathed the property in dispute to her son, James Samuel Bennett, for life, and after his death she bequeathed it to her husband, Augustus Enever, in trust for the children of the marriage with him, and in case there should be no children, which event happened, she bequeathed it to her husband absolutely. In case neither her said son nor her said other children, nor her said husband should live to take the said property, then the testatrix gave the same to John Power, one of her children by her first marriage, with remainders over.

The testatrix died in February, 1911, and her husband died shortly after. A number of the questions before me admit of an easy answer. Did James Samuel Bennett take anything? Certainly he took nothing. He is not an object of the power. Who is entitled to the rents and dividends due at the death of testatrix? Her personal representative. Did Augustus Joseph Enever take any, and what, estate? He took nothing whatever, not being an object of the power.

There remains the question – Did John C. Power take the estate under the appointment, or does it go to him, to Frederick Joseph Power, and to the representative of Susan Amelia, as if unappointed.

When an appointor exercises his power partly in favour of objects of the power, and partly in favour of those who are not objects of the power, there are cases in which the law holds good so much of the appointment as confers the benefits on objects of the power. Everything turns on the intention of the appointor. In *Crozier* v. *Crozier* 3 Dr. & W. 353 the testator appointed to his wife for life, who was not an object of the power, and then to his eldest son, who was an object of the power. Lord St. Leonards held that the appointment in favour of the eldest son was good, but that the rents and profits during the lifetime of the mother passed as in default of appointment.

On the other hand, where there are appointments in favour of persons not objects of the power, with an ultimate limitation in favour of somebody who is an object of the power, and this last limitation is dependent on the former void appointments, such last limitation must fail. There is no means of ascertaining the appointor's intention, or rather, to give effect to the last limitation would be to defeat the appointor's expressed intention.

Take the present case. There is, first of all, a life interest given to James Samuel Bennett. Secondly, after his death, there is a trust to Augustus Enever for the benefit of his family; and thirdly, there is a trust for Augustus Enever himself, in the event of there being no children. All these are void. Lastly, there is an appointment in favour of John, an object of the power. It is plain that the last appointment is dependent on those going before, and that when they fail it must fail with them. I must, therefore, answer the last question by declaring that the estate and all the rents and profits accruing since the death of Clepatra Enever go as in default of appointment equally between Frederick Joseph and John Power, and the personal representative of Susan Amelia Power.

Note

See further, *Irish Land law*, para. 11.18.

RE ROBERTSON'S AND CARDEW'S TRUSTS

[1960] I.R. 7 (High Court)

By a marriage settlement, dated the 23rd October, 1909, it was provded that the income of the settled property should be paid to *A.J.R.* for life and after his death to his intended wife, *A.L.C.*, should she survive him, and after the death of both the trustees were to stand possessed of the capital and future income of the fund " . . . in trust for all such one or more exclusively of the others or other of the children or remoter issue of the said intended marriage . . . as the said [*A.J.R.* and *A.L.C.*] shall by any deeds revocable or irrevocable jointly appoint and in default of and subject to such appointment as the survivor of them the said [*A.J.R.* and *A.L.J.*] shall in like manner or by will or codicil appoint." By a second deed of settlement, also dated the 23rd October, 1909, the income of certain other property was settled on *A.L.C.* for life and after her death on her intended husband, *A.J.R.*, for life should he survive her, and thereafter the deed contained exactly similar provisions to the first deed.

There were five children of the marriage. *A.J.R.* died in 1954 without having joined with *A.L.R. (née A.L.C.)* in any deed of appointment under the settlement. *A.L.R.* died in 1956 having made a will, dated the 18th December, 1951, and three codicils thereto, the second which was dated the 9th February, 1954. The will provided, *inter alia,* as follows:– "I give devise bequeath and appoint all the rest residue and remainder of my property estate and effects whatsoever and wheresoever including in this disposition any propery over which I may have any power of disposition or appointment to my trustees . . . upon trust to divide the same equally between such of my five children as shall survive me . . ." By the second codicil to her will *A.L.R.*, after declaring that her husband, *A.J.R.*, had died in her lifetime, provided as follows:– "I direct my trustees not to pay over to my son *[G.C.R.]* the share of my residuary estate bequeathed to him by my said will but my trustees shall retain the said share in their hands upon trust to invest the same in investments authorised by my said will and to pay the income thereof to my said son *[G.C.R.]* for and during his life . . ." There was raised the question whether the power of appointment had been validly exercised.

Dixon J. :

This is not an easy question, but on the whole I am inclined to the view that the power of appointment was not exercised – or, rather, was invalidly exercised. It is clear that at the date of the will the wife had no power of appointment which she could exercise, as the husband was still alive. But even, apart from that, if the will had been made after the husband's death, I do not think it would have been an exercise of the special power. It is well settled that there has to be some sufficient indication of intention to exercise a special power, and I do not think the phraseology used here, which is in the ordinary general form, could be any indication of an intention to exercise a special power. There is, moreover, a reference to a fund over which the testatrix had a general power of appointment at the time. I think, considering the matter quite apart from the date of the will, there is no sufficient reference to the special power of appointment.

The real crux of the matter turns on the codicil. Was there such sufficient indication of intention to exercise the special power of appointment contained in the codicil? I do not think there was. I think it might be possible that the lady thought, or was advised, that, by declaring that her husband had died and by confirming her will, that would have the legal effect of operating as an exercise of this special power of appointment. I consider it as a possibility, but it seems a somewhat subtle approach. All the lady had to do was to put in a provision that the residuary clause in her will was to be taken as an exercise of the special power. On the whole, I think that if there was any intention to exercise the special power there would have been more specific mention of it. There is the difficulty as to what was the object of the declaration in the codicil, but it may be that there were circumstances that gave some point to that declaration other than the exercise of the special power. My view is that there is not evidence in either will or codicil of sufficient intention to exercise the special power. The power was therefore not exercised.

III. FRAUD ON A POWER

DUGGAN V. DUGGAN

(1880) 7 L.R. Ir. 152 (Court of Appeal)

The facts are set out in the judgments.

Lord O'Hagan, C.;

The question is this case is, whether an appointment to the Plaintiffs by their mother, Honoria Duggan, of a fund brought into Court under the Trustee Relief Act, and a deed, of the same date, by which she assigned to them her life interest in that fund, are valid or void? The claim of the Plaintiffs is full and candid, and states all the facts which are necessary to be considered for the fair decision of the point in controversy.

Mary Donohoe, the sister of the Defendant Honoria Duggan, made a will, by which she gave a farm called Borahard and a legacy of £2000 to the latter, for her separate use, without power of anticipation, and to her children according to her appointment, and in default of appointment to her sons at the age of twenty-one, and to her daughters at that age, or marriage.

Honoria Duggan and her husband had four children, the Plaintiffs, and two of the Defendants who are still minors. Mrs. Duggan and her husband took possession of Borahard, after the death of her sister, and he afterwards died. She possessed, also, another farm called Ladytown. After the sister's death, Mr. and Mrs. Duggan borrowed £1000 from the Hibernian Bank, which was secured by a policy of insurance and a mortgage of her interest in the fund in Court.

The Plaintiff Mary, whilst still under age, joined her father and mother in further securing the advance by a promissory note to which she was a party.

The husband having died, the Bank required further security; and the Plaintiff Christopher, who was of age, and his sister Mary, who was then also of age, became parties with their mother to her promissory notes, instead of that which had been executed in her husband's lifetime. The Defendant Honoria Duggan got into great embarrassment, sold off her stock, and allowed a large sum for rent of her farms to grow due.

The claim sets forth what was done thereupon and in that state of facts by the mother and her adult children, in the 12th and 13th paragraphs –

"12. Under the foregoing circumstances, and in order to provide for her children and support her family, the said Defendant Honoria Duggan, by deed poll dated the 13th day of January, 1880, under and by virtue of the power given to her by the said will of Mary Donohoe, appointed irrevocably the said sum of £4234 0*s*. 3*d*. Government Stock to the Plaintiffs, their executors, administrators and assigns, in equal shares, subject however to the life estate and interest of the said Honoria Duggan.

"13. By an indenture of even date with the said deed poll, and made between the said Honoria Duggan of the one part, and the Plaintiffs of the other part, after reciting, as the facts were, that the Plaintiffs were desirous of obtaining possession of the said sum of £4234 0*s*. 3*d*. Government Stock, and for that purpose had proposed to the said Defendant Honoria Duggan to sell to the Plaintiffs her life interest in the said Stock, in consideration of a sum of £2015, the estimated value of the said life interest, to be paid by the Plaintiffs to the said Defendant in the following manner, namely, by transfer to the said Hibernian Bank of so much of the said Stock as should be equivalent to the sum of £997 6*s*. 8*d*., interest and costs, and by a transfer to the said Defendant of so much of the said Stock as should be equivalent to the balance of the said sum of £2015, provided it should seem fit to this Honorable Court to make the necessary order for effectuating the said proposal, and reciting that the said Defendant had accepted the said proposal, it is witnessed that in pursuance of the said agreement, and in consideration of the said sum of £2015, to be paid as aforesaid, the said Defendant granted to the Plaintiffs and their executors, administrators and assigns, all the estate and interest of her the said Defendant in the said sum of £4234 0*s*. 3*d*. Government Stock, in equal shares absolutely."

The final paragraph of this claim states that this transaction was perfectly *bonâ fide,* and for the purpose of getting rid of the debts and difficulties in which the estate derivable under the will of Mary Donohoe was involved; and not for the purpose of giving any advantage exclusively to Honoria Duggan; but, generally, for that of benefiting her family – as well the Plaintiffs as the minor Defendants.

The two deeds must be taken together and dealt with really as one, carrying out one purpose and aiming at a single end. And, so considered, upon the admissions of the claim and the facts established by the evidence, I am clearly of opinion that the agreement between the Plaintiffs and the mother to purchase her life interest and pay for it out of the moneys appointed to them, for the purpose of discharging her debts and saving her property, must be considered, in a Court of Equity, to have been a corrupt agreement made for a corrupt purpose, and, therefore, invalidating the exercise of the power.

The mother was in difficulties. She had induced her children to become her sureties in getting money. She desired to avoid eviction by her landlord, and possible foreclosure of the mortgage by the bank directors; and she sought to effect her purpose by making the appointment, and thus obtaining the sums required to accomplish it. The appointment appears to me to have been made in the interest of the mother, the donee of the power, and not to have originated in a direct and honest purpose to execute it, with a single regard to the intentions of the donor and the interest of the objects of her bounty. Mrs. Duggan was in embarrassment, and the relief of her embarrassment, the discharge of her liabilities, and the preservation of her lands, were plainly the objects which were to be attained by the double deed, to which she induced her children to be parties – possibly for their future and contingent advantage, but actually and presently for her own.

As to the law of the case, I apprehend no doubt can be suggested. A power cannot be executed with a view to the interest of the donee, or with an object really and substantially different from that for which it was conferred.

A great many authorities have been cited, on either side, with much research, and commented upon with much ability, but I do not think it necessary to discuss them in detail, or to suggest, by such a discussion, that any real doubt exists as to the law. The principle they establish is summed up in part of a sentence by the Lord Chancellor in *Topham* v. *The Duke of Portland* 11 H.L.C. 32, in the House of Lords, in which he says, that the donee of a power must act with an entire and single view to the real purpose and object of the power (11 H.L.C. 84). It seems to me clear, as I have said, that the donee of the power in this case acted *alio intuitu,* and with quite another object; and that, therefore, the execution of it ought not to be sustained.

It has been urged, that the power was executed for the benefit of its objects, though the donee derived some profit from the execution; and under certain circumstances, no doubt, the enjoyment of an advantage by the donee would not vitiate the appointment. The principle seems to me very properly stated by the Master of the Rolls in England in *Re Huish's Charity* L.R. 10 Eq. 9:–

> "The meaning and the good sense of the case appears to be that if the appointor, directly or indirectly, obtain any exclusive advantage to himself, and that to obtain this advantage is the object and the reason of its being made, then that the appointment is bad; but that if the whole transaction taken together shows no such object, but only shows an intention to improve the whole subject-matter of the appointment for the benefit of all the objects of the power, then the exercise of the power is not fraudulent or void; although, by the force of circumstances, such improvement cannot be bestowed on the property which is the subject of the appointment without the appointor, to some extent, participating therein."

This seems to me quite right and reasonable, but the doctrine does not apply to the facts before us. If the primary and simple purpose had been to serve the objects of the power, and if, in serving them, in the peculiar position of affairs, the donee necessarily served herself, there would be no good ground for saying that the execution should be invalidated. But here the primary purpose was to serve the mother; to relieve her embarrassment and discharge her debts; and, although the retention of the farms might possibly benefit her children at some distant day, and under circumstances not to be foreseen, the only immediate and certain advantage was to herself, whilst, as to the debt to the bank, they were merely sureties who could recover against her if they were compelled to pay anything, and find their protection in the mortgage and the insurance. In *Re Huish's Charity* L.R. 10 Eq. 5 the suggested benefit of the donee was ancillary and accidental, and did not invalidate the appointment because it was subordinated to and, in a sense, inseparable from that of the appointees. But here we have the donee of the power trafficking for her own advantage. That of her children was only secondary and equivocal, whilst she supplied the real motive for the transaction as that which was certain and primary, and for her present advantage.

On these short grounds, I am of opinion that the decision of the Vice-Chancellor was right, and that the appeal should be disallowed. I do not go into the question raised before him as to the nature of the life estate, the age of the appointor, and the somewhat strange valuations of the actuary. There may be reason for maintaining, upon the evidence, that the price of the life estate was inadequate, whether it be considered with reference to the facts with which the actuary had to deal, or with the principle on which he proceeded; and if this was so, there could be no validity in the execution of the power, as the exclusive advantage given to the donee must, in that case, have been at once considerable and unfair. But I prefer to rest my judgment on facts which are undisputed, and principles, which, I agree with the Vice-Chancellor, it is of the highest importance to maintain untouched, as they are established beyond doubt or question. The appeal must be dismissed with costs.

Deasy, L.J.:

I entirely agree with the Lord Chancellor. The purpose of the whole arrangement was to benefit Mrs. Duggan. She derived an advantage from her age being represented as forty-five instead of fifty-one, which was of itself sufficient to vitiate the transaction as an appointment, though it might be better for the family to adopt it. The children had no interest in the farm of Ladytown, which it was part of the arrangement to preserve. The doctrine established by the cases is that the donee of a power must stand in a position of quasi-judicial impartiality.

FitzGibbon, L.J.:

In one sense, I am sorry that we cannot accede to this appeal, but we should make a dangerous precedent is we did so. It may be conceded that the mere fact that the donee of a power derives a benefit from its exercise would not vitiate the appointment, if the arrangemnt were for the benefit of all the parties concerned, as well the objects as the donee of the power. But here the parents have involved the children in personal liabilities as sureties for themselves; and the transaction is one not for the benefit of the objects of the power as such, nor for the increase or improvement of the fund, but merely for anticipating the time when the property should fall into possession, converting it into cash, and dividing its present proceeds between the prospective owners and those now entitled to the current income. No doubt it is proposed to discharge the debts out of the donee's share of the anticipated fund, ascertained by acturial calculation; but no benefit is conferred upon the objects of the power by giving them now the present value, ascertained by an actuary, of their future interest. If we were to yield to this arrangement as one for the benefit of the objects of the power, we should encourage parents and donees of powers to involve their children, the objects of their powers, in embarrassment, under the belief that they could escape by anticipating the very fund which was settled with the purpose of preventing such liabilities from being incurred.

Notes and Questions

What was done with the money was clearly for the benefit of the children, was it not, so why was it a fraud on the power? See further *Irish Land Law,* para. 11.22.

SKELTON V. FLANAGAN

(1867) I.R. 1 Eq. 362 (Rolls Court)

The facts are set out in the judgment.

Walsh M.R.: By a marriage settlement, dated in 1809, Hamilton Skelton conveyed certain lands to trustees, to the use of himself for life, then to secure an annuity of £165 to his intended wife; and subject thereto to the use of the children of the marriage in such shares, and for such estates, and subject to such restrictions and sums for their benefit, as Hamilton Skelton should by deed or will appoint, and, in default of appointment, to the use of such child or children, issue of the marriage, who should attain the age of twenty-one, and their heirs, share and share alike, as tenants in common.

Of this marriage there was issue, the Petitioner, John Skelton, and six daughters, all of whom, except one, Harriet Victoria, had attained the age of twenty-one prior to the year 1854, and of whom in that year two – Mrs. McFadden and Mrs. Ruckly – were married women.

Hamilton Skelton was indebted to the Respondent Flanagan, on foot of two judgments, recovered subsequently to the settlement, and he had extended a receiver appointed over the lands to pay them. He had been insolvent in 1844. On the 2nd of March, 1853, he entered into an agreement in writing with Flanagan that all accounts between them should be settled thus – that Skelton, his wife, and all his children then of age, should join in mortgaging the settled property for £850, and that the amount should be liquidated in part by some money due by a railway company, and further instalments paid in the manner mentioned; and that this should be taken as settling all accounts between them; and Flanagan agreed to discharge the receiver, and that Hamilton Skelton should be put into possession on the execution of the mortgage.

On the 13th of May, 1854, Hamilton Skelton executed a deed, by which he appointed the lands to the Petitioner, John, charged with £300 each for three of his daughters (one of whom was the then minor, Harriet Victoria), £150 each for two other daughters, and an annuity of £25 yearly for the remaining daughter. Having regard to the value of the property, this would appear to have been a not unreasonable, but on the contrary a natural exercise of his power; and it is not disputed that, so far as anything appears on the face of the deed, it is a good appointment.

A few days after the date of this deed – that is, on the 31st of May, 1854 – a mortgage was executed between Hamilton Skelton of the first part; Eliza, his wife, of the second part; the Petitioner of the third part; the six daughters, and the husbands of the two married daughters, of the fourth part; and the Respondent Flanagan of the fifth part. It recites the settlement of 1809, and various securities then held by Flanagan (including the two judgments, two insurances on Skelton's life, and a trust deed of 1842), and that the receiver was then in posssession: it recites also (though not accurately) the appointment. It then recited that Flanagan had agreed to abate part of his demand, and remove the receiver, on condition of the several parties joining in the mortgage as a collateral security, to secure him £1000 and interest, in full of all his demands; and that Eliza Skelton (the wife) and all the children – naming them – in consideration of the affection which they bear to their father, and in order to enable him to carry into effect this arrangement, had agreed to convey all and each of their estates in the premises to Flanagan as after-mentioned. The deed then witnessess that Hamilton Skelton and John (the Petitioner) convey to Flanagan the lands, with ample general words, subject to redemption on payment of £1000 and interest; and further witnesses, that the wife conveys her annuity of £165; and all the daughters, and the husbands of those that were married, assign the several sums payable to them under the appointment, and all their estates in the annuity, sums, and premises to Flanagan, subject to a similar proviso for redemption. Hamilton Skelton and the Petitioner covenant for payment of the money. This deed was duly acknowledged under the Act for the Abolition of Fines and Recoveries, by Eliza (the wife), and the two married daughters, Mrs. McFadden and Mrs. Ruckly.

Neither the wife nor any of the children received any consideration for the mortgage. It is admittedly a simple security for an amount ascertained by way of compromise, as due on the antecedent debt of Hamilton Skelton; the only new consideration being the agreement to discharge the receiver. The receiver was in fact discharged, as agreed upon. The only benefit that can be suggested as obtained by the children from the transaction is, that their father was thus enabled to support some who were then living with him, and there is some slight evidence that the family desired this.

The petition states that the Petitioner was fraudulently induced to execute this deed, under pressure and misrepresentation as to its real nature; and that his sisters were induced to execute it on a representation by the father that the amount would be entirely discharged out of the money coming from the railway company, and also in ignorance of its real nature. It further impeaches the demand of Flanagan as between him and Hamilton Skelton. But these charges have either failed in proof, or have been wholly displaced by the Respondent's evidence, and it is now admitted by the Petitioner's counsel that they cannot be sustained.

Flanagan presented a petition for sale in the Landed Estates Court, in 1862. Cause was shown against the conditional order for sale, by the Petitioner John, and some of his sister; but in November, 1862, the cause was disallowed, and the order for sale made absolute, with certain directions calculated to facilitate any remedy over against Hamilton Skelton's life estate, and without prejudice to any application which the parties showing cause might make for an assignment of Flanagan's securities against Hamilton Skelton, or to any steps that might be taken in Chancery to set aside the mortgage.

This suit was instituted soon afterwards – that is, in April, 1863 – and came on for hearing before the late Master of the Rolls. As originally framed, the petition prayed relief against the mortgage only; and, the ground of actual fraud being abandoned, the Court held that that relief could not be given; but, as the Petitioner insisted that the appointment was invalid, he was permitted to amend the petition by praying that it might be set aside. The petition was accordingly amended, and is now again brought to a hearing. In the mean time the lands have been sold in the Landed Estates Court. It is stated in the answer to the amendment that the Petitioner's former solicitor agreed that Flanagan should go on and sell. It appears that there was first a sale in Dundalk, in June, 1866, which the Judge, on the application of the present Petitioner, John Skelton, refused to confirm, as the price was inadequate. The property was then set up to be sold in Dublin, in July – a motion by John Skelton to stay the sale having been refused, with costs. The final schedule of incumbrances was settled in November last. It is stated, and not disputed, that the representative of Harriet Victoria, the daughter who was a minor in 1854, made a claim under the deed of appointment, and by the schedule as ruled is declared entitled to the £300 and interest, which she took under that deed.

The amendment of the petition, besides praying the additional relief of setting aside the appointment, puts in issue a letter of Flanagan, and brings before the Court, as additionl parties, the heir-at-law, and personal representative of Mrs. Ruckly, who died since the institution of the suit; and the personal representative of another daughter, Caroline, who had died before the institution of the suit. It appears by the answer to the amendment, that Harriet Victoria, who had married a Mr. Hynes, has died; and it is insisted that the suit is abated and defective for want of parties, her representatives not being before the Court, and the estates of Caroline and Mrs. Ruckly being also not properly represented. No suggestion has been filed, and there has been no revivor.

In answer to these objections, it is insisted that Mrs. Hynes' husband was a party to the original petition, and is in fact her personal representative, in proof of which a copy of the grant of administration to him was offered; and it is said that her father would be her heir-at-law, and Caroline's, and that he is a party to the original petition. Mrs. Ruckly's heir and personal representative and Caroline's personal representative are made parties by the amendment, and so far the objections are untenable; but I do not think that I can assume, in the absence of any allegation in pleading or proof, that the interest which Mrs. Hynes and Caroline would take if the appointment be invalid, and which would be real estate, necessarily descended to their father; nor do I think that the mere fact that he is a party to the original petition, and that another party to the original petition happens to have become the administrator to Mrs. Hynes, dispenses with the necessity of putting this transmission of interest in issue, and reviving the suit. The position and interests of the parties are entirely changed. The personal representative would take nothing in default of appointment, and no appointment could be now made to him. The relief now sought by setting aside the appointment is quite different from that originally prayed. I think, therefore, that there has been an irregularity which the Respondent is entitled to rely on. There has been so much delay and irregularity, that I should have some difficulty in allowing this to be now remedied; but I might do so, if it were the only objection against giving the Petitioner relief.

Upon the merits of the case, in the argument before me, it was admitted that the case alleged, so far as it rests on actual fraud, cannot be sustained, and there is no allegation of any undue exercise of parental influence. The case was rested solely on the proposition that the appointment, being really intended for the father's benefit, was a fraud upon the power in the settlement of 1809. It follows – and I understood the Petitioner's counsel to admit – that the mortgae, *quà* mortgage, cannot be impeached; and I was asked to set aside the appointment merely, leaving the parties afterwards to derive from that what benefit they can. Now, the Respondent resisting this suit, and against whom this relief is asked, is the mortgagee. I do not see how it is possible, if the mortgage stands, that the Petitioner, who is a granting party in it, purporting to convey under this very appointment, can, as against the mortgagee, have this relief. But there is a further singularity in this case; for every one of the objects of the power on whom the fraud was committed have confirmed the appointment. The mortgage not being impeachable on other grounds, they, with full knowledge of the facts, have concurred in it, and thereby made themselves all, with one exception, parties to the transaction, and confirmed the appointment. The married women formally acknowledged the deed. The one exception is Mrs. Hynes, who was a minor in 1854; but she attained age many years ago, never disputed it, and her representatives have confirmed it; her administrator having proved in the Landed Estates Court, and her heir – if the Petitioner's allegation that her father is her heir, be true – being conclusively bound. Indeed, if the appointment fails, her interest must be bound by the mortgage; for, as I have said, no new appointment could be made to her, even supposing that the power could be again exercised; and her interest, in default of appointment, has descended to her father.

A fraud upon a power as pointed out by Sir P. Wood, in *Rowley* v. *Rowley* Kay, 258, is either on the donor of the power, or the objects of it. It is the former when a power to create a burthen on the estate in settlement is used for a purpose not intended. It is the latter – which alone is in question here – when a power to control the devolution of the estate is used to give a benefit to some one not an object of it. When all the objects, on whom only such a fraud could be committed, concur in or confirm the transaction – there being no imposition or undue influence used to procure their concurrence or confirmation – how can any of them complain of it as a fraud? If there had been no appointment at all, and the children had divided the estate in the same proportions as the appointment divides it, it would have been binding, and the subsequent mortgage would not have affected its validity. Had there been no arrangement, and no appointment, the adult children concurring in the mortgage, in the absence of actual fraud or undue influence, would be bound to give effect to it. There is more than their mere concurrence in the deed; for on the faith of this transaction, acquiesceed in and confirmed by all who could ever take any interest in the reversion, the mortgagee discharged the receiver, and lost the benefit he might have had from the life estate. During the delay of this suit, the whole has been sold.

The argument for the Petitioner must be pressed to this extent, that it is impossible for children entitled in remainder, subject to a power of appointment vested in the father, to concur with him in a mortgage, and that in all such cases undue pressure must be presumed. But, in the absence of some other ground for imputing it, I think, as I have said, that such a transaction would be good if there were no appointment at all; and I do not see the distinction where all adopt and confirm the appointment. In the absence of fraud or undue influence, it is in the power of children to contract with each other, as put by Lord Eldon, in *Davies* v. *Uphill* 1 Swanst. 130, to give a parent who has a power of appointment among them an advantage which he otherwise could not have.

I do not think that any argument in favour of the Petitioner can be rested on the circumstance that, though the appointment is now adopted as to Mrs. Hynes' share, the mortgage does not bind it, and a larger burthen is thus thrown on the other children's shares. All the others knew of her minority, and must be assumed to have taken this risk. Indeed, if the appointment be set aside, the curious consequence before mentioned might follow, that her interest passing to her father might be bound, while the Petitioner's would not.

The authority mainly relied on, and I think the only authority cited which bears on the part of the case which I have been considering, is *Palmer* v. *Wheeler* 2 Ball & B. 18. There an estate was settled on a father for life, with an exclusive power to appoint among his children; and, in default of appointment, on his eldest son and his heirs. The father applied to his eldest son for the purpose of getting him to join in securing a debt of the father, subject to which the estate was resettled. The son having died very soon after the father, his heir disputed the appointment. There were two children on whom the appointment was a fraud; to one of whom £1000 was appointed under the settlement, subject to the mortgage. The case is certainly a remarkable one, from the circumstance observed on by Lord St. Leonards Sugd. Pow. p.614, that the son of the appointee, being the only remainderman, was allowed to impeach the appointment, although probably that very appointment prevented one being made in favour of the other objects. But when Lord Manners is dealing with the objection that the plaintiff, claiming through the son, who was a party to the fraud on the power, could not impeach it, he answers it, as I understand his judgment, not by the proposition argued in the present case, that that was immaterial, but by applying to the case another equitable doctrine, not necessarily connected with the rules applicable to powers at all, but applicable to all dealings between father and child. He held that the son's assent had been procured by the exercise of undue influence, and as he calls it oppression; and he held that, as this continued during all the father's life, and the son had survived him but a very short time, laches could not be imputed to him. If this were so, the son in the view of this court was in the same position as if he had not concurred even with the father, as he plainly had not with the other objects of the power, who were not parties to the transaction. I have consulted the Registrar's book for the decree in that case, and I find that it dismissed so much of the bill as sought to set aside the appointment of the £1000, and declared the Plaintiff entitled, as heir of his father, to the estates comprised in the deed of appointment, discharged from the mortgage. It would appear, therefore, that the appointment was not set aside at all, except as to some provisions in the settlement inapplicable to the present case. I would infer from the mortgage alone being set aside, that the ground of relief was undue pressure on the son, which the existence of the power enabled the father more effectually to exercise; and that the decision, so far, did not rest merely on the doctrine of this court applicable to powers. The relief, at all events, is wholly different from what is asked here, and such as the decision of the late Master of the Rolls has already determined cannot be given in the present suit.

In deciding the present case I am not to be understood as stating a general rule, or holding that in no case can one who is a party to a fraud on a power impeach it; or even that, when all the objects of the power concur in the transaction, it may not still in some cases be impeachable. I express no opinion upon any such general proposition. The circumstances under which the transaction here is sought to be set aside as a fraud on the power are very peculiar; and I merely hold that, after what has occurred, and in the absence of any proof of any other ground of impeachment of the mortgage, it is not open to the Petitioner, as against the Respondent Flanagan, on that ground alone to set aside the appointment.

As to the objections which were urged to the frame of the suit, and the inconsistency of the relief now sought with that originally prayed, I express no opinion; but I should perhaps add, that I entirely dissent from the argument urged on behalf of the Responent as to a previous arrangement or understanding being requisite to constitute a fraud upon a power, in cases like the present. I do not think that is so. I disapprove of the letter of the Respondent Flanagan, which is unexplained. I am not satisfied that this is a *bonâ fide* suit on behalf of the Petitioner; and that the father, Hamilton Skelton, is not connected with it. I shall dismiss the petition; and, as to the charges of fraud, and the impeachment of the mortgagee's demand, it must be dismissed with costs.

Note
See further, *Irish Land Law*, para. 11.24.

GREENE V. GREENE

(1845) 8 Ir.Eq.R. 473; 2 Jo. & Lat. 529 (Chancery)

The facts are set out in the judgment.

Sugden L.C.:

In this case a question arose with regard to the rights of the plaintiffs, who are the younger children of a second marriage. The case is one of some difficulty: it arises out of a will by which the property was given to trustees, with a very unusual power to them to settle the estate on the sons of the testator, either in fee, in tail, or for life, with such conditions, and so on, as they might appoint. A dispute having arisen after the death of the testator, as might naturally have been expected, a suit was instituted by one of the sons. That was compromised, and the estate was divided into three portions and was conveyed to certain uses in favour of the three sons and their issue. Those uses were to each son for life, then to trustees to preserve contingent remainders, then with a limitation in case he should marry with the consent of the surviving trustee, but not otherwise, that such woman or women as he should so marry should receive such jointure, in a certain proportion to her fortune, as the son should appoint; and in case he should marry with consent, but not otherwise, then that he should have power to charge £500 for the portions of his younger children; and in case he should marry with such consent (this condition being again and for the last time repeated), to the use of his first and other sons, in *quasi* tail, remainder subject to the appointment of the son to the daughters, as tenants in common in tail, and in default of such issue to the other two sons for their lives, with remainders to their issue, subject to the same condition.

The first marriage of Samuel Greene was had with the consent of Powell, the surviving trustee, and a settlement was entered into by which Samuel Greene exercised his power of jointuring, and covenanted that in case there should be one or more younger children of the intended marriage, the trustees should raise the £500 which he had power to charge, to be divided among such younger children as he should appoint, and in default of appointment to be divided among them equally, in the ordinary way.

The Act of Parliament was afterwards passed, for which I am responsible; it permitted persons having a power of this nature, not to exclude any child, but to give any sum that the donee of the power might think proper. Treating the first execution of the power as a bad one, and having married a second time, necessarily without the consent of the trustee (for he was dead), Samuel by his will again exercised this power substantially in favour of the children of the second marriage, giving but one shilling to the younger children of the first marriage. The children of the second marriage then filed this bill claiming the portions so appointed to them.

The first question is, whether the consent of the trustee to one marriage was sufficient. I am of opinion that it would not have been sufficient if the trustee had been living, particularly as regards the widow, because it is expressly declared, that in case he shall marry with consent, "such woman *or women* as he shall so marry" shall have the jointure. Nobody is to have it except the woman *or women* whom he shall *so* marry; that is, whom he shall marry with consent. In that respect this case is distinguishable from *Hutcheson* v. *Hammond* 3 Br. C.C. 128. If the case turned on that, I should be of opinion that in this case the consent to the first marriage did not render it unnecessary to obtain consent to the second marriage.

But a different question arises in the case. Powell, the trustee, died before the second marriage. The question is, whether his consent to the marriage is a condition so inseparable from the power that it could not be executed after his death. *Mansell* v. *Mansell* Wilm. 36 was referred to as an authority against the execution of the power, but that case is also distinguishable from this. That, in truth, whether rightly or wrongly decided, was a case in which the Court saw an intention that the power should never be exercised without consent, and held that there was continually a person whose consent might have been obtained if he had thought proper to give it. On the true construction of the settlement executed here, my opinion is, that all the trustee was intended to do was himself personally during his life to have control over the marriage, and as he was no longer in existence his consent to the second marriage was not capable of being obtained. As regards the widow, there is a difficulty in giving effect to this meaning, although I think it should prevail against the technical construction of the words; but there is no such difficulty as to the children. The difficulty as regards the widow arises from the words "woman or *women* as he shall *so* marry." But, as I think that the consent was intended to be a condition only during the lifetime of the party whose consent was required, I do not hesitate to struggle with the words and give effect to the intention. The frame of this settlement satisfies me as to that. By the will the sons were to take the estate in fee as tenants in common in default of a settlement by the trustee, and if the preliminary condition imposed by the settlement, viz., the consent of the trustee, was such as might prove impossible to be complied with, from not supplying a new trustee, *ex.gr.*, then the whole settlement would have been defeated, and the sons would fall back on their estate as tenants in common in fee under their father's will. Therefore, on the whole, my opinion is, that the consent of the trustee was not so inseparable as to prevent the execution of the power after his death.

As to the objects of the power, I am bound to follow Lord Eldon's authority in *Burrell* v. *Crutchley* 15 Ves. 544, and hold that the deed of one 20th of September 1786 includes all younger children. By the settlement executed before the first marriage, and therefore for valuable consideration, independently of the marriage portion of the wife, the power was exercised, and the £500 was directed to be raised. That was a good execution of the power to raise the £500. But then it was appropriated exclusively to the children of that marriage, and that now is not a due execution of the power. It might, however, have been a due execution of it, and was not void on the face of it; for *non constabat* that Samuel would ever marry again; he might not have had power to do so, for his wife might have survived him; and if he had not married again, the power would have been properly exercised, because the execution of it would have included all his younger children. Therefore that was not necessarily and on the face of it a bad execution of the power, although liable to become so by the birth of children of another marriage. I quite agree that, if a man executed a power imperfectly, and there is nothing in the way of contract to prevent the re-execution of it, he may afterwards execute it formally. Therefore I think that the mere previous execution was no impediment in the way here, and that Samuel Greene had still the ability to exercise his power in a valid manner. But then, this important question arises – Could he exercise this power as against the younger children of the first marriage so as to defeat the contract to provide for them, made by the settlement on his first marriage? There is no doubt, both on authority and principle, that a man having a power may, in defeazance of that power, impose conditions on the exercise of it. He may release the power. He may enter into a covenant so as to bind the execution of the power, and this Court will execute that; or he may covenant not to execute the power, and that too will be good, provided in these cases there be a sufficient consideration. If he exercises the power, he must execute it properly; but he may bind by contract that which is a benefit to himself, though it operates directly as a benefit to his children. He may deal with it in any manner so as to bind himself within the limits of his authority as to its exercise or non-exercise. Here Samuel Greene bound himself by his marriage settlement to exercise this power by appointing in favour of the children of the first marriage, reserving nothing to appoint to other younger children. The second marriage necessarily put an end to that, and he could no longer apportion the sum among the children of the first marriage exclusively, as the settlement directed; for the children of the second marriage became entitled with them, and therefore the power to appoint among them became incapable of being exercised. But in default of appointment, the younger children of both marriages are to take the fund among them equally. Is this not in effect a contract by him, so that so far as he could bind the power, his younger children of the first marriage should take the sum, or as much as he can give them, equally between them? And was he at liberty by his own voluntary act to defeat that contract? I am of opinion that he was not; that he had bound himself so far as he could to give effect to the first settlement; and that he could not by a voluntary disposition defeat the provision which he had already made.

Then, what am I to do with the case? I consider the first settlement no longer operative as an execution of the power of appointment. I am of opinion that there cannot be an exercise of the power so as to defeat the interest which the children of the first marriage would take as between themselves and the children of the second marriage. The conclusion, therefore, to which I have come, but not without considerable difficulty, is, that the children of the first marriage and the children of the second marriage take the fund equally between them. I am not called on by the frame of the bill to consider whether the power could be exercised over that portion which belongs to the younger children of the second marriage, because they have filed a bill, content to take whatever they are entitled to. Therefore, meaning to act within the authorities, and not to strain the rule of law, but at the same time meaning so far as I can carry the contract of the parties into effect, and to do that justice to the children of the first marriage to which they are entitled, I shall hold that the £500 belongs to all the children of both marriages as a class, and that the father, after the settlement, could no longer deprive any of the younger children of the first marriage of the share he would take as one of a class in default of a fair exercise of the power in the sum directed to be raised, which was no more than would be a valid execution of the power in the first instance.

I shall, therefore, give a decree for the plaintiffs, and declare that they and the two younger children of the first marriage are entitled to share the fund equally between them, as the younger children of their father. The widow is to be at liberty to go before the Master and establish her right if she can, and if she succeeds in establishing it, declare her claim the first in priority. The costs of raising the money must come out of the estate. That has been often questioned, but I think they ought to come out of the estate. I do not mean the costs of the suit, but only the costs of raising the money.

Declare that the younger children of the first marriage, and all the children of the second marriage, take the sum of £500 in the pleadings mentioned, between them as one class; and that the plaintiffs in this cause are entitled in the events that have happened, and under the instruments which have been executed, to their portions of the said sum of £500, accordingly. Let the expense, if any, of raising said monies, be borne out of the estate; and let the costs of all parties to this cause be paid out of the fund.

Declare, that the defendant Frances Greene, otherwise Moffett, having married Samuel Barker Greene, deceased, in the pleadings mentioned, after the death of Caleb Powell, in the pleadings named, his consent to the said marriage was not necessary to enable the said Samuel Barker Greene to charge his portion of the lands in the pleadings mentioned with a jointure for the said Frances Greene; and let the said Frances Greene be at liberty to go before the Master, and establish her right to the jointure in her answer in this cause mentioned; and if she should established it, declare that she is entitled to have the same provided for her out of the lands, &c.

Note
See further, *Irish Land Law,* para. 11.25.

INDEX